D0142139

# BUILDING IN ENGLAND
## DOWN TO 1540

### A DOCUMENTARY HISTORY

THE ART AND CRAFT OF BUILDING *c.* 1450

# Building in England

DOWN TO 1540

A DOCUMENTARY HISTORY

By

## L. F. SALZMAN

C.B.E., D.Litt., F.S.A.

OXFORD

AT THE CLARENDON PRESS

*Oxford University Press, Ely House, London W. I*

GLASGOW  NEW YORK  TORONTO  MELBOURNE  WELLINGTON
CAPE TOWN  SALISBURY  IBADAN  NAIROBI  LUSAKA  ADDIS ABABA
BOMBAY  CALCUTTA  MADRAS  KARACHI  LAHORE  DACCA
KUALA LUMPUR  HONG KONG  TOKYO

FIRST PUBLISHED 1952
REPRINTED LITHOGRAPHICALLY IN GREAT BRITAIN
WITH CORRECTIONS AND ADDITIONS
AT THE UNIVERSITY PRESS, OXFORD
BY VIVIAN RIDLER
PRINTER TO THE UNIVERSITY
1967

# PREFACE

THE subject of English medieval architecture has been dealt with in a multitude of books by architects, artists, and antiquaries, and occasionally by people with no qualifications at all. The majority of these works have dealt with the evolution of 'Gothic' from Romanesque, and its development into the very practical and entirely English style known conveniently as 'Perpendicular'. On this subject there is probably little more of value to be said; and in this book I am concerned not with artistic deductions from existing buildings but with contemporary documentary evidence on the actual processes of building.

The amount of such evidence existing is prodigious: on a conservative estimate, I have examined some fifteen hundred manuscripts, all more or less concerned with the subject, though naturally of very varying importance; I have also consulted some two thousand printed volumes, of which a large proportion proved to contain nothing to my purpose; but a few were full of matter of importance—as will be seen from my references. So far as possible, I have worked on original documents rather than on printed versions, as I prefer to make my own mistakes rather than to take over those of my predecessors—and in dealing with highly technical documents of this kind, often legible with difficulty, mistakes are bound to occur. To take a single cause of confusion: it is impossible to distinguish between *n*, *u*, and *v* in most manuscripts and it is, for instance, only by tracing variant spellings that one can be certain that 'soudelet' (a saddle-bar) and 'vertivel' (a hinge-band) should be so spelt and not 'sondelet' and 'vertinel', as often printed. There is the further point that the clerks who wrote these documents were not only, like all men, liable to make slips of the pen, but often they were putting on parchment purely local technical terms of which they could at best give a phonetic rendering, when they did not complicate matters by attempting to latinize them. I have done my best to get at the meaning of all these obscure words and to make it clear where my interpretation is hazardous; and I venture to claim that merely as a glossary of building terms this book will be of value. The documents quoted will also in many instances be found of considerable interest from the standpoint of philology.

The sources used fall into two main classes, which may be termed—(*a*) historical and (*b*) economic. In the first class are included references to the erection or destruction of particular buildings, ranging from a dry statement of date up to the most detailed descriptions. A representative collection of such entries is given in Appendix A. The value of such sources for the correct dating of individual architectural features, on which the whole evolutionary pedigree of architectural style depends, is obvious. But although it is obvious, it must be emphasized that no attempt should be made to date a building until search has been made for documentary evidence bearing upon it. Broadly speaking, the narrowest 'margin of error' in dating a building merely from its architectural features is twenty years; a mason of the old school did not adopt the new-fangled ideas of his younger contemporaries; and the most we can say, as a rule, is that such a feature is first known to occur in such a year and that therefore a building in which it figures is presumably of later date. Moreover, even documentary evidence requires careful handling. It is first essential to be sure that the building in question is that referred to by the chronicler and has not been rebuilt. (The abbey church at Meaux was built anew three times in forty years: Abbot Philip (1160–82) began a stone church; his successor, Thomas (1182–97), pulled this down and built another; his successor, Alexander, destroyed this and laid the foundations of a new church in 1207. Henry VI gave elaborate instructions for the building of Eton College Chapel and then, when it was nearly complete, had it pulled down and rebuilt on a larger scale.) Next, allowance must be made for the extreme slowness of much medieval building: the cloisters of Norwich Cathedral Priory took 133 years to complete; work was going on, apparently continuously, on the west front of St. Albans for about forty years; John of Wisbech worked for more than twenty-eight years on the Lady Chapel at Ely; the contracting mason at Helmingham was allowed ten years for the building of a church tower only 60 feet high; and even the erection of a spire at Louth took fifteen years. Too much dependence, also, must not be placed on statements that a particular church is 'newly built'. Buildings retained their newness surprisingly; for instance, the memorial chapel on the battlefield of Towton was 'newly built' in 1486 and was still 'newly built' in 1502.[1] (New College, Oxford, has remained New for five centuries, and in any country town 'The New Inn' is pretty sure to be more ancient by centuries than 'Ye Olde Tea Shoppe'.)

However, we are not here concerned with the dating of buildings. More important for our purpose is the attitude of medieval writers towards the buildings that they themselves saw. In revulsion from the earlier

[1] *Y.F.R.* 241–2.

school of antiquaries, who were apt to see symbolism and a conscious striving after effects in what were actually only conveniences of construction, it is sometimes maintained that the early builders did not deliberately aim at beauty but only achieved it more or less accidentally. The Renaissance certainly introduced a new, self-conscious attitude towards Art, but men in the earlier centuries had their own ideas of beauty in building, which they recognized and consciously aimed at. We are definitely told that the fall of the tower at Beverley, about 1200, was due to the masons being more preoccupied with achieving beauty than strength, and the quotations in the Appendix are full of expressions of admiration; in fact the monastic chroniclers may be said to have rather overworked the adjectives *pulchra* and *pulcherrima*. Most of this admiration was lavished on the new and up to date; thus when Henry III's new Abbey of Westminster is said to have 'outshone all other churches in the world for costliness and splendour, so that it would seem to have no rival', we are told that he 'first removed the old church, which was of absolutely no value'—yet this old church, when built by the Confessor, had been equally admired. William of Malmesbury, who wrote about 1125, had a kinder eye for the past and spoke of Wilfrid's work at Hexham as recalling the splendour of Rome. He also proclaimed St. Paul's as 'of such magnificent beauty that it is rightly numbered among famous buildings', and spoke of Ernulf's rebuilding of Canterbury 'so magnificently that nothing of its kind could be seen in England, for its blaze of glass windows, its glitter of marble pavements, and its painting of many hues'. The writer of the Life of St. Hugh waxes dithyrambic over his hero's work in Lincoln Cathedral, where 'the art equals the preciousness of the materials'; he compares the vaulting to a bird soaring with outstretched wings, and the clustered columns of Purbeck marble to 'a bevy of maidens marshalled for a dance'. Altogether, we may safely conclude that the desire to achieve beauty was one of the motives actuating the architect, or craftsman designer, of the Middle Ages. I have added, in Appendix C, a few specimens of agreements made for the employment of masons and other craftsmen. It had been in my mind to compile yet another appendix of 'master masons', tracing their history and activities as far as possible; but reasons of space and time compelled me to abandon, or at least postpone, the compilation of such a list. Now (1951) Mr. John Harvey has undertaken that task on his own initiative.

The printed sources upon which I have drawn are indicated in my footnotes, but I feel that special reference should be made to a few books.

First, *The Architectural History of Cambridge*, by Professor Robert Willis, completed by J. W. Clark—an admirable example of the combination of documentary and architectural research. The same description applies to Sir W. St. John Hope's great work on *Windsor Castle*. The *York Fabric Rolls*, published by the Surtees Society, and Chapman's *Sacrist Rolls of Ely* are also particularly valuable sources. I should also like to call attention to a series of detailed studies of building accounts by Professor D. Knoop and G. P. Jones, appearing in *Ars Quatuor Coronatorum*. Proofs of these came into my hands only after the greater part of my book was written; of which I am rather glad, as it is always more satisfactory to find one's own theories corroborated than anticipated.

Many friends have shown an interest in my work, notably the late Dr. Coulton and Mr. John Harvey, F.S.A.; and many strangers have gone out of their way to assist me. My thanks are due to the Earl of Berkeley for photographs of four important contracts, and to Lord de l'Isle and Dudley for access to his muniments. Also to the authorities of many Colleges— King's, Trinity, Peterhouse, and St. John's at Cambridge, Merton, Magdalen, Corpus Christi, and All Souls at Oxford; the Cathedrals of St. Paul's, Norwich, Salisbury, Peterborough, and Westminster Abbey; the Bodleian, Cambridge University Library, the Guildhall, the British Museum, and, above all, the Public Record Office. To others I have expressed my indebtedness in my notes.

For permission to reproduce contracts and other matter from printed works I am particularly indebted to the Cambridge University Press for leave to use many contracts given in Willis and Clark's *Architectural History*, several of the originals of which could not be found when I sought for them; also to H.M. Stationery Office for contracts given in Reports of the Historical MSS. Commission and of the National Monuments of Wales; to the Surtees Society, the Early English Text Society, the Wiltshire Archaeological Society, the Oxford Historical Society; and to the late Dr. H. E. Salter and others whose works are duly acknowledged as the sources of my material.

I have also to thank Mr. J. W. Bloe, O.B.E., F.S.A., for the constructional drawing of a timber-framed house; and also the authors, publishers, libraries, and societies indicated on pages xii–xv for permission to reproduce illustrations.

The writing of this book was completed in 1934, but as I could find no publisher who would undertake its production without a subsidy, which I could neither afford myself nor persuade anyone else to put up, I eventually presented the manuscript to the Society of Antiquaries of London, in whose library it proved useful to several students and writers, as they fully acknowledged. In 1949 the Society of Authors made a generous grant from the Crompton Fund, which has rendered it possible for the book to be published. The Society of Antiquaries kindly released the manuscript. My friend Mr. Cyril Kenney, F.S.A., generously arranged for the typing of the body of the work; and I should like to put on record my appreciation of the care and skill of the compositors and readers of the Clarendon Press in dealing with the manuscript, often fantastic in its spelling, of the Appendixes. The whole was carefully revised in the light of recent books and articles, but is substantially as originally written, except that a considerable number of Contracts have been added, mainly through the good offices of Mr. John Harvey.

L. F. S.

LEWES, *October* 1951

## PREFACE TO THE CORRECTED IMPRESSION

SEVERAL corrections have been incorporated into the present impression. These, together with an appendix of building contracts which have recently come to light, owe much to the kind interest shown by Mr. John Harvey, F.S.A. My expressed preference for using originals rather than printed copies (p. v) is confirmed with regard to the Windsor contract (no. 106, pp. 562 and 563). Mr. Harvey tells me that Parker's transcript, used by St. John Hope and, from his book, by me, is simply full of silly blunders. Of these the most important are: par. 2, for 'platte designed' read 'platte deuysed'; for 'to beyre fourth on' read 'to beyre fanes or'; par. 6, for 'not xx$^{li}$. more' read 'not xx mrcs wynnyng'; for 'xj$^{li}$. xiij$^s$. iiij$^d$.' read 'vj$^{li}$. xiij$^s$. iiij$^d$.'.

L. F. S.

LEWES, *June* 1966

# CONTENTS

# LIST OF ILLUSTRATIONS

## IN THE TEXT

CARPENTERS BUILDING A TIMBER-FRAMED HOUSE (1531)

p. 196

From Rodler, *Eyn schön nutzlich büchlin.*

# ABBREVIATED REFERENCES USED IN FOOTNOTES

The following abbreviations are used:

E.          Exch. K.R. Accts.; the first number is that of the bundle, the second that of the individual document.

T.R.      Exch. Treasury of Receipt, Misc. Books, vols. 251, 252; two volumes, paged consecutively, of accounts for Westminster in 1532.

H.C.      Exch. Treasury of Receipt, Misc. Books, vols. 237–41, Hampton Court accounts.

K.H.      King's Hall accounts, twenty-four volumes at Trinity College, Cambridge.

P.          Bursars' Rolls of Peterhouse, Cambridge.

Y.F.R.    *Fabric Rolls of the Minster of York* (Surtees Society).

D.H.B.    *Durham Household Books* (Surtees Society).

R.          *Memorials of Ripon* (Surtees Society), vol. iii.

*Sacrist Rolls*. Chapman, *Sacrist Rolls of Ely*.

J.M.G.    *Journal of the British Society of Master Glass-painters*.

# I

## MASONS AND ARCHITECTS

ONE of the first questions that arise when we consider the history of building is, 'Who was responsible for the buildings of the Middle Ages?' How far did the 'architect' exist before the seventeenth century? Earlier, uncritical generations cheerfully attributed everything artistic to 'the monks'. This, as we shall see, was very far from being the truth; but it is not easy, or even possible, to give an exact answer to our question. Even at the present time it is not always possible to say precisely who has 'built' a particular house. Is it the contractor, who has, more or less faithfully, carried out the architect's plans? or the architect? or the employer and owner, who has very likely dictated the main features of the building? When we read that a house 'was built by the third Duke of Omnium', we do not picture His Grace handling bricks and converting his coronet into a mortar-board, but if we figure him as complacently entrusting the whole business to some professional architect and contenting himself with footing the bills we very likely do him an injustice. The duke may very well have discussed every detail with the architect and may have made or marred the design by insisting on certain features. But this we cannot tell unless we happen to have documentary evidence. Even as far back as the thirteenth century Matthew Paris[1] expressly warns us that the attribution of a building to a particular abbot only means that he arranged for it to be built and provided the funds.[2]

In the very early days of the introduction of Christianity into England it is likely enough that the missionary monks did with their own hands set up the wattle-and-daub walls and thatched roofs of their churches and monasteries. Later, when the more difficult craft of masonry arose, the monks no doubt lent their aid to carry the materials and to do some of the simpler work, but lay craftsmen performed most of the work. Benedict Biscop, about 670, built monasteries at Monkwearmouth and Jarrow, 'being the first person who introduced into England builders of stone edifices and makers of glass windows';[3] and Wilfrid 'made many buildings

---

[1] *Gesta Abbatum* (Rolls Ser.), i. 280.

[2] Still earlier Boethius had said: 'Their names are written on buildings by whose orders they were made and not those by whose work they were brought to perfection': Mortet, *Textes relatifs à l'histoire de l'architecture*, 108.

[3] William of Malmesbury, *Gesta Pont.*, quoting Bede.

by his own judgement but also by the advice of the masons whom the hope of liberal reward had drawn hither from Rome'.[1] From which it would seem that Wilfrid had some skill, or at least ideas, in church planning. So, possibly, had King Alfred, who, in performance of a vow to build a monastery at Athelney, 'made a church, small indeed in area owing to the narrowness of the site, but contrived in a new manner of building. For four piers embedded in the ground carry the whole erection (*machinam*), with four chancels of elliptic plan (*quatuor cancellis opere spherico*) placed round the edge.'[2] Alfred, indeed, assigned a definite portion of his income 'to craftsmen whom he constantly employed in the erection of new buildings in a manner surprising and hitherto unknown to the English'.[3] His grandson, Edred, 'took such an interest in the church (of Abingdon) that with his own hands (*per se*) he measured out the sites of the buildings and laid the foundations, intending to erect there a monastery of famous renown'.[4] This, however, amounts to little more than settling the dimensions and general plan of the building, of which the details and actual construction were probably left entirely to the professional masons. When Edred's contemporary, St. Oswald, in 968 sent Ednoth to build a church at Ramsey we hear nothing of any monastic labour: 'The workmen, out of fervour of devotion and love of pay, stuck to their work, while some carried stones others made mortar and others hoisted both these materials with a windlass.'[5] On the other hand, when the tower of this church some twenty years later developed serious cracks and was condemned by the masons, we are told that the brethren helped the hired labourers to take it down.[6]

Of Geoffrey, Abbot of St. Albans (1119–46), we are told that he 'constructed a spacious and noble hall under a double roof for the reception of guests. . . . And he erected another building, exactly like the hall, with a chapel at the east, namely the infirmary. . . . And he also ordered another hall of the same pattern as those already mentioned to be built by the same craftsman (*artifice*) at Westwike, for the use of a friend and relative of his who had been well disposed and useful to the church.'[7] A later abbot, John (1195–1214), pulled down the west front of the church and collected timber and stone for rebuilding it. After which, 'very many picked masons were summoned together, over whom was Master Hugh de Goldclif, a deceitful and unreliable man but a craftsman of great reputation (*praeelectus*)', by

[1] William of Malmesbury, *Gesta Pont.*, 255.  
[2] Ibid. 199.  
[3] Ibid.  
[4] Ibid. 191.  
[5] *Chron. Abb. Ramesiensis*, 39.  
[6] Ibid. 88.  
[7] *Gesta Abbatum*, i. 79, 80.

whose advice an elaborate design with 'carving (*caelaturis*), unnecessary, trifling, and beyond measure costly', was adopted.[1]

In Ednoth, and the anonymous craftsman of St. Albans, and Master Hugh we have early examples of professional masons definitely mentioned as being in charge of building operations, with hired workmen under them. But it would be an exaggeration to say that the monks had literally no hand in the building of their monasteries and churches. In 1039 when Lanfranc, afterwards Archbishop of Canterbury, visited the then insignificant abbey of Bec he found Abbot Herlwin actually engaged in building;[2] and about 1100 Abbot Hugh of Selby 'himself, *devotus architectus*, set out the foundations of the church and of all the claustral buildings, for up to his time all their buildings were of wood. . . . Every day, putting on a workman's smock (*cucullo operario*), he used with the other workmen to carry on his shoulders to the wall stones, lime, and anything else required for the work; and every Saturday he received his wages as one of the workmen and bestowed them upon the poor.'[3] A greater Hugh, the sainted Bishop of Lincoln, 'often bore the hodload of hewn stone or binding lime'[4] when his cathedral was in building. But one feels that this was rather a gesture, like that of Edward I when he wheeled a barrow on the fortifications of Berwick,[5] than a serious contribution to the erection of the fabric. More definite is the instance of the monks of Gloucester Abbey in 1242, when 'the new vaulting in the nave was finished, not with the help of wrights (*fabrorum*) as formerly, but by the spirited courage of the monks there'.[6] Similarly at Evesham in about 1300 the infirmary buildings were 'constructed by the devotion and industry of the monks'.[7] In the first of these instances we may certainly, and in the second probably, attribute the work definitely to the hands of the monks. More frequently, no doubt, the brethren assisted the hired workmen and acted as unskilled labourers in carting and carrying materials. This was not infrequently the case on the Continent, and such assistance was also often given in moments of enthusiasm by the lay inhabitants of the district. For the building of a church on Lindisfarne, in 1093, the men of the district 'many times united their forces

---

[1] Ibid. 219.

[2] Mortet, *Textes relatifs à l'arch.* 46. When the Cathedral of Carlisle intervened, in 1368, to prevent the parishioners of Newcastle rebuilding the quire of St. Nicholas, their proctor found Sir Robert Merlay, chaplain, working on a block of stone: Welford, *Newcastle and Gateshead*, i. 173.    [3] Mortet, op. cit.

[4] Coulton, *Social Life*, 472. Cf. Matth. Paris, *Chron. Maj.* ii. 470.

[5] Rishanger, *Chron.* 475.

[6] *Hist. Mon. Gloucestriae*, i. 29.    [7] *Chron. Abb. de Evesham*, 286.

to drag loads of stones over the wet sands'.[1] So when the men of Totnes decided to build their church tower in 1450, the parishioners were summoned to the quarry to dig stone and every owner of a horse was expected, though not compelled, to use it for carrying small stones from the quay to the churchyard, the larger stones being carried by men.[2] At Bodmin also, in 1470, parishioners who 'fayled here journayes' (i.e. their day's work) at the quarry for the rebuilding of the church were fined 4*d.* each.[3] But in both instances the skilled labour of building was done by professional masons.

Naturally, also, there would sometimes be in a monastery particular brethren with an aptitude for such work. This may have been so at Bicester Priory in 1412, when we find 'two new rochets provided for Brothers Geoffrey Stratton and John Wanetynge on account of their rochets being spoilt over the work of the new roof over the high altar'.[4] This applies still more to the class of lay brethren, many of whom had worked at various trades before they attached themselves to a house of religion. An instance may be taken from St. Albans in about 1430, when we are told that 'opposite the altar of St. Sith lies Brother William Stubbarde, formerly lay brother of this house, a praiseworthy worker in masonry, whose good works—shown in the cloister, the Prior's seat there and the doors, and other laudable works at Radbourne and Beaulieu—have, as we believe, ensured the passage of his soul to heaven'.[5]

Occasionally these expert brethren did not confine their services to their monasteries. The chief carpenter at Corfe Castle in 1280 was 'Brother Henry',[6] probably a lay brother of the neighbouring Cistercian abbey of Bindon. At Chester in 1304 Brother Thomas le Plummer, monk of Combermere, was employed in removing old lead from the roof of the keep and recasting it;[7] and at Knaresburgh in 1335 Brother William, one of the brethren of the house of St. Robert, mason, was hired to carve stone for the royal lodge of Haywra.[8]

Assuming that the bulk of the building was done by hired masons, carpenters, and workmen, there remains the question who was responsible for the design? Was it king, bishop, abbot, or other landowner, or were there architects in the Middle Ages? To answer this question we must decide what we mean by an architect. An architect, then, is a man who is

---

[1] *Reg. Dunelm. Libellus* (Surtees Soc.), 45.
[2] *Hist. MSS. Com. Rep.* iii. 345.  [3] *Camden Miscellany*, vii. 3.
[4] Blomfield, *Deanery of Bicester*, i. 170.  [5] J. de Amundesham, *Annales*, i. 440.
[6] E. 462, 16.  [7] E. 486, 13.  [8] E. 544, 18.

capable of envisaging a building, complete and in detail, before one stone is laid upon another and is also capable of so conveying his vision to the actual builders that they are able to translate it into actual reality. Such a building as the first chapel of the Franciscans at Cambridge—'so extremely unpretending that a carpenter in a single day could make and set up its 14 pairs of rafters'[1]—might grow up almost spontaneously; but anything more elaborate than the very simplest type of country church must have been definitely designed before its erection. No one can look at a great church built entirely in one style, such as Salisbury[2] cathedral, without knowing that it is the vision of one master mind embodied in stone.

The part played in design by the employer naturally varied very much. Henry VIII, that 'only Phoenix of his time for fine and curious masonry', was as ready to dabble in architecture as in music, medicine, or theology. In 1539 a fort or blockhouse at Cowes was to be made 'according to the platte devised by the King';[3] and in 1513 we are told that 'the King signed the platte (i.e. plan) that he will have of his chapel (at Windsor), which is the platte that was made according to his first device';[4] Henry VI drew up minutely detailed instructions for the erection of his colleges of Eton and King's,[5] and then displayed his unbalanced enthusiasm by pulling down the Eton chapel, nearly complete after seven years' labour, in order to build it on a larger scale, also dictated in detail.[6] Henry III gave most elaborate directions for the decoration of his palaces and chapels, but so far as building was concerned was content to leave everything—except occasionally the general dimensions, the number of windows, and the position of the fireplaces—to those in charge of the operations.

Turning to the prelates, we have seen that Wilfrid had apparently his own ideas on design, while on the other hand we have the warning of Matthew Paris that the ascription of a building to an abbot may imply nothing more than his ordering its erection. In the long list of works carried out under John de Brokehampton, Abbot of Evesham from 1282 to 1316,[7] we find that of some it is said that he 'made' or 'erected' them, while of others we are told that they were 'built in his time and with his help'. Unfortunately we cannot be certain whether any real distinction between the two classes was intended or whether this is merely an example of a

---

[1] *Mon. Francisc.* i. 18.
[2] The spire of Salisbury is, of course, due to the brilliant audacity of a later architect.
[3] *L. & P. Henry VIII*, xiv (1), 899.
[4] *Hist. MSS. Com. Rep., Var.* vii, 21.       [5] See App. B.
[6] Willis and Clark, *Arch. Hist. of Univ. of Cambridge*, i. 366, 423.
[7] See App. A.

medieval writer's fondness for varying his phraseology. Of Ethelwold, Abbot of Abingdon in 960 and later Bishop of Winchester, we are told that he was '*magnus aedificator*', which suggests that he did something more than provide funds for building, especially as he was sufficiently a craftsman to make organs and church ornaments with his own hands. Certainly he displayed a personal interest in the construction of his church, as one day he was working on the building when a huge post fell on him, breaking his ribs and knocking him into a pit, but for which he would have been crushed to death.[1] A later instance of a monastic designer is found at Ramsey in 1135, when Abbot Walter entrusted the management of the abbey to Daniel, a monk who had been 'a poor glassworker', who constructed a tower at Broughton (Hunts.), 'arranging in it many hiding-places and passages (*latebras et diverticula*) fit to accomplish his design',[2]—a rather mysterious sentence. I have deliberately called Daniel a designer rather than an architect, as one cannot be certain that he did not call in lay assistance to translate his ideas into a practical form.

This Daniel evidently held the position of 'master of the works', or 'of the fabric', which is found in a large number of monastic and cathedral establishments.[3]

For instance, one section of the chartulary of Lewes Priory deals with the estates assigned to the Department of the 'Master of the Works',[4] and that office was definitely established at St. Albans in 1430.[5] At Winchester the obedientiary in charge of the fabric was called 'warden of the works',[6] and at Norwich the responsibility was divided between four officials, of whom one was the sacrist.[7] In very many houses the sacrist was responsible for building operations, and in monastic chronicles, such as those of Rochester[8] and Bury St. Edmunds,[9] the work is often attributed to the sacrist instead of to the abbot. Another instance of this is Ely,[10] and here we meet with a very famous sacrist whose claims to be ranked as an architect require examination, Alan de Walsingham. After the fall of the central tower at Ely in 1322, Alan the Sacrist

spent great labour and much money in removing from the cathedral the fallen stones and beams. . . . Finally he measured out in eight divisions, with the art of

---

[1] *Hist. Mon. de Abingdon*, ii. 259.                    [2] *Chron. Abb. Rames.*, 225.
[3] The founder of the nunnery of Fontevrault constituted one of the sisters 'mistress of the works': Mortet, op. cit. 311.
[4] Cott. MS. Vesp. F. XV, ff. 307–13.
[5] J. de Amundesham, *Annales*, i. 279.                    [6] Kitchin, *Obedientiary Rolls*, 209.
[7] Saunders, *Rolls of Norwich Cathedral Priory*, 70.        [8] Cott. MS. Nero D. II.
[9] *Mems. of St. Edmunds*, ii. 289–93.                    [10] Chapman, *Sacrists' Rolls of Ely*.

an architect, the place where he thought to build the new tower; and he set the workmen to dig and search for the foundations of the eight stone columns whereupon the whole building should be supported, and beneath which the choir with its stalls might afterwards be built; . . . Then . . . he began those eight columns, with the stonework which they supported. This he completed in six years. . . . Then without delay that cunningly wrought timber structure of the new tower was begun; a structure designed with the utmost and most marvellous subtlety of human thought, to be set upon the aforesaid stonework. . . . The whole cost of this new tower during the twenty years of Alan de Walsingham's time was £2400. 6s. 11d.[1]

It is conceivable that Alan did nothing more than put the services of his department at the disposal of the cathedral mason; but I am inclined to think that the wording of this passage is definitely intended to imply that he had a large share in the designing of the new structure, and that the brilliant idea of the octagon was due to him, even if he had to leave the technical problems of its construction to the master mason. This is rather borne out by another passage in which Alan, at that time subprior of Ely, is referred to as '*vir venerabilis et artificiosus*',[2] which seems to imply artistic, possibly even architectural, ability.

In 1447, when the executors of Cardinal Beaufort offered 500 marks to the University of Oxford for building the schools, a committee of twelve Doctors and Masters was set up to consider ways and means. They appointed two Masters of Arts, *in aedificando providi et experti*, as supervisors to make all arrangements for the provision of materials and the hire of skilled craftsmen and labourers, as cheaply as possible, and to see that they did their work properly. One of these, it may be noted, bore a name associated with art in later times—John Evelyn.[3] Just ten years later the University of Cambridge set up a similar committee to work out a scheme for building their schools and library.[4] Similarly at Lynn in 1472 the Borough appointed a committee 'to confer with a mason for a new chapel in honour of the Holy Trinity, to be built on the north side of the quire of St. Margaret's'.[5] A glimpse of such a body taking a proper interest in work for which they were financially responsible occurs in 1352, when the royal chapel of St. Stephen, at Westminster, was being completed. The carved stalls were being worked by Master William Herland and his men, and six carpenters were employed 'putting up various panels for the reredos of the stalls to show and demonstrate to the Treasurer and others of the King's

---

[1] Translated in Coulton's *Social Life*, from *Hist. Eliensis.*
[2] Wharton, *Anglia Sacra*, i. 651.
[3] *Munimenta Acad.* (Rolls Ser.), ii. 567.
[4] *Grace Book A.* 8.
[5] Beloe, *Our Churches*, 88.

Council the form and fashion of the said stalls'; and later three carpenters taking the reredos down again.[1] For the royal palaces and similar buildings the equivalent of the 'Master of the Works' was the 'Clerk of the Works', an office usually identical with, but possibly sometimes additional to, that of 'Supervisor, or Surveyor, of the Works'.[2] His duties included the payment of wages and the provision of materials and of workmen,[3] but there is never any suggestion that he was responsible for the design of the building, though when once the design had been settled he would no doubt be expected to see that it was carried out. He was, in fact, the head of the clerical staff in charge of operations and was himself necessarily a 'clerk' in the sense of being literate, and often also in being in orders. We find, therefore, among the supervisors at Windsor Geoffrey Chaucer in 1389 and 1390,[4] Richard Beauchamp, Bishop of Salisbury, in 1474,[5] and William of Wykeham from 1356 to 1361.[6] Wykeham has often been acclaimed as an architect, partly on account of works at Windsor Castle which had begun before his appointment and were carried on more actively after his retirement, but mainly because, after he became Bishop of Winchester in 1367, he was responsible for erecting colleges at Oxford and Winchester and carrying out extensive works in the cathedral of Winchester. But that he was in any way the designer of any of these works there is no evidence. In his will[7] (1403) he desires his executors to rebuild the nave of Winchester Cathedral from the west gate of the quire back to the west end of the Church 'in walls windows and vaults conformably and decently, accordingly as the form and manner of the new work of the aisles shall require'. There is no hint that he had drawn up any scheme for the alterations and he ordains that 'the disposal and direction of the new work shall be in the hands of Master William Wynford, and other sufficient and discreet craftsmen'. He also desires that Sir Simon Membury shall continue to act as supervisor and paymaster, with Brother John Wayte, or some other monk of the convent, as comptroller.[8] Master William Wynford was one of the leading masons of the time. He is found associated with Mr. John Sponle,

[1] E. 471, 5.

[2] For a detailed study of this subject see John Harvey, 'The Medieval Office of Works', *Journ. of Brit. Arch. Assoc.* ser. 3, vi, 20–87. Also the 'Notes on the Superintendents of English Buildings in the Middle Ages', by Wyatt Papworth, in *Trans. R.I.B.A.* N.S. iii. 185–236.

[3] As in the instance of the appointment of William of Wykeham: ibid. 191.

[4] Ibid. 198.          [5] Ibid. 193.

[6] Ibid. 204.

[7] Nicolas, *Test. Vetusta*, 766.

[8] The comptroller kept the counter-roll, a duplicate by which the clerk's accounts could be checked if necessary.

chief mason, at Windsor in 1362[1] and again in 1365,[2] and in 1364 was appointed cathedral mason at Wells, as in that year there is a grant to Master William Wyneforde, mason, of a messuage in Byestewall Street, Wells, and a yearly fee of 40s., with an additional 6d. a day when actually working on the fabric of the cathedral; in return for which he undertakes to oversee the fabric and workmen.[3] Then, in 1370, he was employed by Wykeham, as Chancellor, to collect masons from various parts of the country to go on the king's service overseas.[4] In 1377 he was in charge of operations at Corfe[5] and in 1390 certain repairs at Winchester Castle were carried out 'by the order and advice of Henry Yevele and William Wyndford, master masons, and Hugh Herland, master carpenter'.[6] Finally, his portrait with that of Simon Membury and an unnamed master carpenter[7] is still to be seen in the glass of Winchester College Chapel. It is not unreasonable to conclude that he was chief mason and architect of both college and cathedral and most probably also of New College, Oxford.

But if Wykeham cannot be considered an architect, there is one man whose claims to be regarded as an architect outside the ranks of the masons require examination. Elias de Dereham[8] was already a beneficed clerk in 1205, in which year he was acting as one of the custodians of the archbishopric of Canterbury, and executor of Archbishop Hubert Walter. He was also executor to the two following archbishops, Stephen Langton and Richard le Grant, to Richard Poore, Bishop of Durham, and to Peter des Roches, Bishop of Winchester. The first hint of his artistic abilities is in 1220, when we are told that the new shrine to which the body of St. Thomas Becket was translated, at Canterbury, was the work of two incomparable artists, Master Walter of Colchester, sacrist of St. Albans, and Master Elias de Dereham, canon of Salisbury.[9] In June of 1233 the Sheriff of Hants was ordered to have timber and stone cut and carried to Winchester as Master Elias de Dereham should direct, and also to cause windows to be made according to the disposition of Master Elias in the king's painted chamber, which was too dark.[10] During the next year Elias, as

[1] E. 493, 10.　　　　[2] E. 493, 13.　　　　[3] *Hist. MSS. Com.*, *Wells*, 267.
[4] *Trans. R.I.B.A.* N.S. iii. 207.　　　　[5] E. 461, 9.
[6] E. 491, 21; Foreign R. 13 Ric. II, A.
[7] Presumably Hugh Herland: *Journ. of R.I.B.A.* ser. 3, xlv. 733.
[8] See *Arch. J.* xliv. 365–74. A study of 'The many-sided career of Master Elias of Dereham' by J. C. Russell, in *Speculum* (Oct. 1930), is full but very inaccurate. A better account is that in *Arch. J.* xcviii. 1–34, by Prof. Hamilton Thompson, who does not allow that Master Elias had executive ability as an architect.
[9] Matth. Paris, *Hist. Angl.* ii. 242.
[10] *Cal. Liberate R.* 219, 220.

'warden of the work of the King's hall at Winchester', received several grants of timber[1] including one of six tree-trunks (*fusta*) for making the great *verina* (? window-frame)[2] of the castle. In February 1236 the sheriff was ordered to carry out the work at Winchester, 'according to what Master Elias de Dereham, to whom the King has explained his wishes fully, tells him'.[3] Later in the same year the work at Winchester is to be done 'by counsel of Master Elias and by view of Nicholas Kipping', and Elias is requested to give his advice (*consulens esse*) as far as possible.[4] Next year the Sheriff of Wilts. was ordered to cause the court round the house of the anchoress of Britford to be enclosed with a stone wall 'by counsel of Master Elias de Dereham'.[5] In all these instances Elias appears to be the expert adviser rather than a mere official, and in March 1238 an interesting writ to the Sheriff of Wilts. orders him to cause the marble tomb that Master Elias de Dereham is making at Salisbury to be paid for and carried to Tarrant (Keynes) to entomb therein the body of Joan, Queen of Scotland, the king's sister.[6] At Salisbury he built a house, called 'Ledenhall', in the close, and local tradition, preserved by Leland,[7] asserted that he was 'director (*rector*) of the new fabric of the Church of Salisbury from its first foundation for 25 years'—he died in 1245.[8] Although the evidence is not sufficient to enable us to assert definitely that Elias de Dereham designed the cathedral of Salisbury, I think that an unprejudiced examination of what is known of his history makes it reasonably probable that he may have done so.

If we admit that Elias, as a clerk and business man whose innate artistic talents enabled him to design one of the great churches of England, is an isolated and possibly unique figure,[9] we may, on inherent probability, expect to find that 'gifted amateurs' occasionally produced works of less importance. One such we seem to see in Master Thomas de Northwich, a monk of Evesham, famed for his skill as a physician, who about 1200 built the tower of the abbey church. It is true that this might only mean that he provided the funds, but that he was his own architect is suggested by the fact that soon after 1207, when he died, the tower fell down, shat-

---

[1] *Close R.* 242, 254, 433.
[2] Possibly, however, a mistake for *verna*, a windlass.
[3] *Close R.* 242.                              [4] Ibid. 268.
[5] *Cal. Liberate R.* 273.                      [6] Ibid. 316.
[7] *Itinerary* (ed. Toulmin Smith), i. 366.     [8] Matt. Paris, *Chron.* iv. 418.
[9] Bennon, Bishop of Osnabrück (1054–79), was '*architectus praecipuus caementarii operis solertissimus dispositor . . . architectoriae artis valde peritus*', and was entrusted with the fortification of Saxony: Mortet, op. cit. 70.

tering the quire—though it is only fair to add that the chronicler attributes this to the abbot's misappropriation of the fabric funds.[1]

It is hardly necessary to stress the fact that the stone buildings of the Middle Ages were erected by professional workmen, and hundreds of building accounts show that, as we might have assumed, the work was under the control of one chief, or master, mason,[2] though the actual mason in charge might be changed during the course of the work. A large proportion of these chief masons have left their names in only a single surviving account, but many can be traced in a succession of jobs in different parts of the country, and some obtained official positions. It will be interesting to see how far such chief masons can be shown to have been the architects of the Middle Ages, responsible for the design and details of the buildings upon which they worked.

In the last half of the twelfth century we meet an interesting group of military architects.[3] Ailnoth 'the engineer' (*ingeniator*) was surveyor of the king's buildings at Westminster and the Tower in 1157, receiving the substantial salary of £10. 12s. 11d., equivalent to 7d. a day, and supervised the purchase of stone and lead for work at Windsor Castle between 1167 and 1173. After the rebellion of 1174 he was in charge of the dismantling of Framlingham and Walton Castles, and he also supervised work at Westminster Abbey when the frater had been burnt. His name occurs as late as 1182. Richard the engineer was concerned with the building of Bowes Castle in 1170, and about the same time was employed by Bishop Hugh Pudsey at Norham Castle, being described as '*vir artificiosus . . . et prudens architectus*'.[4] Wulfric and Ives, both engineers, supervised work at Carlisle and Berkhamsted respectively in 1172–3; and Maurice the engineer was employed at Newcastle in 1174 and at Dover in 1181–2. All these men were primarily concerned with military engines, mangonels, trebuchets, catapults, and so forth, and therefore with the designing of defences which would enable them to use their own artillery and resist that of besiegers. When the existing west wall of the lower bailey of Windsor Castle with its three towers was built in 1228, 'the master trebucheter' was one of the two persons appointed to supervise the work.[5]

Following this group of military specialists we have, in Henry, 'master of the King's masons', who received a robe at Christmas, 1243,[6] the first

[1] *Chron. Abb. de Evesham*, 108, 224.

[2] With timber constructions the workman in charge would, naturally, be the chief carpenter.

[3] Hope, *Windsor Castle*, 22.

[4] *Trans. R.I.B.A.* N.S. iii. 186.

[5] Hope, *Windsor Castle*, 33.

[6] *Close R.* 141.

of a long line of royal masons. This Master Henry the mason was sent, in March 1245, with Martin Simon the carpenter to view the site for the new castle which the king proposed to build at York, and to arrange how it should be built.[1] The Sheriff of York was to meet them, bringing with him other masters expert in those crafts. In this instance Henry presumably gave at least general instructions as to the plan, but we cannot say how much initiative was left to the master actually in charge of the building operations. Master Henry ('de Reins')[2] himself was at this time, and until about 1253, in control of the rebuilding of the church of Westminster Abbey and is reasonably regarded by Professor Lethaby[3] as responsible for the design of that magnificent work. He was succeeded, as king's mason, by Master John of Gloucester (1254–61)[4] and Master Robert of Beverley (1262–80),[5] who presumably followed the design which he had originated. It is of some interest to note that work begun by a mason probably from Essex was continued by one from the west country and then by one from the north.

A century later we have the office of royal mason filled for more than thirty years by Henry Yevele.[6] He was already in 1356 sufficiently well established to be one of the freemasons concerned in drawing up the regulations for the masons' craft in London. In 1365 he was 'master of the masons, controlling (*ordinant*') their work', at Westminster.[7] Next year he carried out repairs at Baynard's Castle,[8] and then, and on other occasions,[9] we find him supplying plaster, stones, and tiles, apparently combining the craft of mason with the business of a contractor for building materials. Possibly this accounts for his obtaining a grant of the wardship of Langton Manor in Purbeck,[10] a district which yielded marble, stone, and plaster. In 1385 Hugh Kynton is described as master of the masons at Porchester, 'arranging the work of the masons there under the instructions (*per ordinacionem*) of Master Henry Yeveley',[11] who was at this time himself working at Westminster.[12] This same year Yevele obtained confirmation of his

---

[1] *Close R.* 293.

[2] Lethaby, *Westminster Revisited.*

[3] *Westminster Abbey and the Craftsmen*, 151.

[4] Ibid. 161.                                                          [5] Ibid. 166.

[6] *London & Middx. Arch. Soc.* ii. 259–63; Lethaby, *Westminster Abbey*, pp. 212–19; John Harvey, *Henry Yevele* (1947)—a very full account of this great architect and of all the works that can, or might, be assigned to him.

[7] E. 472, 14.                                                         [8] E. 493, 12.

[9] e.g. at Rochester, E. 479, 28; and St. Paul's, E. 473, 1.

[10] *Cal. Close, 1379*, p. 177.

[11] E. 479, 22.                                                        [12] E. 473, 2.

appointment, made originally in 1369, as 'deviser (*dispositor*) of masonry works at Westminster and the Tower', with a salary of 12*d*. a day.[1]

In 1386 the walling of the city of Canterbury was to be carried out by oversight of John de Cobham and Henry Yevele.[2] Lord Cobham had already employed Yevele as consulting architect at his castle of Cowling, and in 1381 an aisle and porch had been built on to St. Dunstan's Church in Tower Street, at Cobham's expense and by Nicholas Typerton, 'according to the design (*devyse*) of Master Henry Ivelezch (i.e. Yevele)'.[3] In 1390, as we have seen,[4] repairs at Winchester were to be done 'by the order and advice of Henry Yevele and William Wyndford, master masons'; and in 1393 work on the 'Dongeon' of Canterbury Castle was to be carried out by the advice of Master Henry Yevele.[5] In 1394 Yevele, in partnership with Stephen Lote, undertook the contract for the masonry portion of the tomb of Richard II and his Queen.[6] Next year he supplied the '*forme et molde*' for the raising of the walls of Westminster Hall;[7] and in 1399 a vault at the entrance to the Hall was made by his advice and counsel.[8] By this time he was a very old man and had probably long ceased to work with his hands on anything more arduous than drawing plans. Next year he died and was buried in the church of St. Magnus, and was succeeded in his office of king's mason by his partner, Stephen Lote,[9] who had been warden of the masons at St. Paul's in 1382.[10]

The career of Henry Yevele is a good example of the way in which a prominent mason was employed in different parts of the country as a consultant, or definitely as an architect to supply the design from which the work was to be carried out. Stephen Lote was called in, in 1410, to give his advice about repairs to Rochester bridge and was paid 6*s*. 8*d*. as his fee. Subsequently, the warden and William Champneys, the bridge mason, went to Rainham to consult another mason, who was too ill to travel—one rather surmises that he may have been the retired bridge mason.[11] Twelve years later, when Champneys was still bridge mason, one William atte Helle was called in as consulting mason, and eventually Thomas Mapylton, the king's mason, undertook the supervision of the work, at the request of William Sevenoke.[12] As another instance of Mapylton's acting as consultant we may quote from Bury St. Edmunds, in 1430, the payment

[1] *Cal. Patent*, 511.
[2] Ibid. 121.
[3] Harl. Ch. 48. E. 43. See App. B.
[4] Above, p. 9.
[5] *Cal. Close*, 46.
[6] E. 473, 7.
[7] E. 473. 21. See App. B.
[8] E. 473, 13.
[9] *Cal. Patent*, 361.
[10] E. 473, 1.
[11] Becker, *Rochester Bridge*, 84.
[12] Ibid. 85–7.

of 26s. 8d. 'to Master Thomas Mapylton, the king's mason, coming from London to look over the great bell tower and give advice about its repair. Also given to another mason coming with him for the same reason, 6s. 8d.'[1] In September 1438 the Mayor and Aldermen of London wrote to the cathedral priory of Canterbury in great distress that some of the arches of London bridge had got into such a bad condition that they dare not touch them without the advice of persons skilled in this kind of work; and as Richard Becke (who had been appointed cathedral mason on 1 January 1435)[2] was in their opinion skilled above all others, they desired most earnestly that the convent would kindly allow him to come and examine the defects and give his advice for their repair.[3]

Becke was one of the regular masons on the London Bridge works as early as 1409; he succeeded John Clyfford as master in September 1417, and continued in that position until he left at the end of March 1435.[4]

The Westminster Abbey accounts for 1479–80 show 5s. spent 'on rewards given, with a dinner (*recreacione*), to three master masons for inspecting the old (part of the) church and the new and their advice on repairs for the next year'.[5] And when Corpus Christi College, Oxford, was being built, in 1517, we find a payment 'to Mr. Vertue for vj dayis beyng here and rydyng to the quarre of Taynton'—presumably to give an opinion on stone.[6] Again, the accounts for 'Cardinal College' (later Christ Church) in Oxford for 1525 show a sum of 22s. 8d. 'payde to Mr. Redman and Mr. Lubyns, m$^r$ masons, for vj days and for iiij days cummyng to Oxford and from Oxford, for every day beying at Oxford xij$^d$ apece and every day rydyng xvj$^d$ apece'.[7] Before this the resident master mason, William Jonson, had gone 'w$^t$ Redman and Lubyns to see the platte w$^t$ the grownde and devysing the beyldyng'.[8] Robert Vertue and John Lobins were two of the masons who gave an estimate for making Henry VII's tomb, in 1509,[9] and Lobins was associated with Henry Redmayne in control of 'Cardinal College' from 1526 onwards.[10]

How far did these master masons, the most skilled men of their craft, deserve the title of architects? Taking as one of the marks of an architect

---

[1] *Hist. MSS. Com. Rep.* xiv (8), 125.

[2] *Literae Cant.* iii. 165.　　　　　　　　　[3] Ibid. 169.

[4] London Bridge Accts.　　　　　　　　　[5] Rackham, *Nave of Westminster*, 38.

[6] Corpus Christi Coll. MS. 435, f. 59$^v$. This was William Vertue, who contracted to make the vaulting of St. George's Chapel at Windsor in 1517: see App. B.

[7] MS. at Corpus Christi Coll., f. 6. This MS. has been shown by J. G. Milne and John Harvey (*Oxoniensia*, viii. 138) to belong to Cardinal College for 1525.

[8] The same MS., f. 3.

[9] *Trans. R.I.B.A.* N.S. iii. 212.　　　　　　[10] *L. & P. Henry VIII*.

the ability to draw ground-plans, we may work backwards, beginning outside our period with a quotation from Shakespeare:[1]

> . . . When we mean to build
> We first survey the plot, then draw the model;
> And when we see the figure of the house,
> Then must we rate the cost of the erection;
> Which if we find outweighs ability,
> What do we then but draw anew the model
> With fewer offices?

Some ten years before this was written, in 1586, Henry Hunt, alias Hobbes, of Arundel, freemason, contracted to build for Giles Garton the kitchen wing of his house at Woolavington, in Sussex, 'accordinge to foure patterns or samples indented drawne for the purpose and annexed' to the contract. These are referred to in the body of the contract as 'the saide plotte', or plan, and by singular good fortune two of the four, representing the ground- and first-floors, have survived.[2] Though roughly drawn, they are quite workmanlike, showing such features as windows, stairs, fireplaces, and flues, and having dimensions indicated by figures. They are probably the earliest surviving examples of such plans. When Bishop Foxe was arranging to build his college of Corpus Christi at Oxford in 1513, he made a contract with William Vertue, freemason, and Humfrey Cooke, carpenter, for it to be built 'after the manner of a double platt made for the over and the nether lodginge of the same buildings and houses',[3] but neither the contract nor the plans are now known to exist.

We have seen[4] that in 1539 certain blockhouses, at Cowes and elsewhere, were to be built 'according to the platte devised by the king', and that in 1513 the king 'signed the platte' of his chapel at Windsor, and in 1522 there is reference to 'the esteemed charges of the building of the plat of Bridewell that is signed by the King's grace'.[5] There is other evidence that it was customary for the employer to sign the plans submitted to him by his builder, as evidence of his agreeing thereto. A Chancery suit[6] of about this same date sets forth that Humfrey Coke and Nicholas Renell, carpenters, agreed to build a house for James Yarford, alderman of London, 'according to a platte thereof made by your said Oratours and delyveryd to the said James Yarford to the entent the same James should have sygned the

---

[1] *Henry IV*, Pt. 2, Act I, scene 3.
[2] Reproduced in *Sussex Arch. Coll.* lxv. 212.
[3] Fowler, *Hist. of Corpus Christi College*, 61.     [4] Above, p. 5.
[5] *L. & P. Henry VIII*, iii (2), 1547.     [6] Early Chanc. Proc., 489, No. 6.

same plate with his owne hande, which to doe he was then contented as he sayd'. They also drew up a rough draft of the contract, which ought to have been engrossed in duplicate on parchment, but Yarford retained it promising them vaguely that they should be 'wynners and no losers'. In the end, 'by reason of sundry alteracons of the seid workes and platte and augmentačons of the same by the said James', it cost them £64 more than the £300 which they received from him.

In 1380 William de Wyntringham of Southwark, carpenter, undertook to build a chapel and other buildings in Hertford Castle 'as set out in a design made in duplicate' (*par un patron endentee*),[1] which presumably included a plan though it may imply something more elaborate as well. A few years later, in 1386, we have a very interesting instance, from the Continent, of a city architect supplying a plan for work to be done in the provinces. At this time a great tower, 92 ft. by 68 ft., three stories high and containing a stair in the thickness of the wall, was built at the castle of Ripaille in Savoy: 'of which tower the form or pattern (*patronum*) set out on paper in colours was brought from Paris and delivered to the Lady Countess'.[2] To the Continent also we have to go for direct evidence of the use of ground-plans in the thirteenth century. Several such are to be found in the famous sketch-book of Villard de Honnecourt. They are jottings for his own use, but are workmanlike little drawings, containing all the essential features of such plans and perfectly comprehensible to any craftsman. That no plans of earlier date, and exceedingly few that fall within our period, have survived is natural. The mason's working copy would be unlikely to outlast the wear and tear of the workshops; the employer's copy, when he had one, would have no value when once the work was completed and would only be kept by accident, and, if on parchment, would very likely be rubbed off so that the parchment might be used again.

Actually, the ground-plan was the least important part of the builder's architectural drawing. It could be dispensed with if the building to be erected was set out on the ground, and such a setting out was the first step in building, whether the plan existed in black and white or not. Therefore the architect in medieval illustrations is often shown holding a large pair of compasses suitable for such work. A curious glimpse of the most primitive method of setting out a small building is afforded us in the record of

---

[1] See App. B. A number of other references to ground-plans, usually styled 'plattes', will be found in the contracts printed in this Appendix.
[2] Bruchet, *Château de Ripaille*, 343.

PLATE 2

TWO GROUND–PLANS 13TH CENTURY

PLATE 3

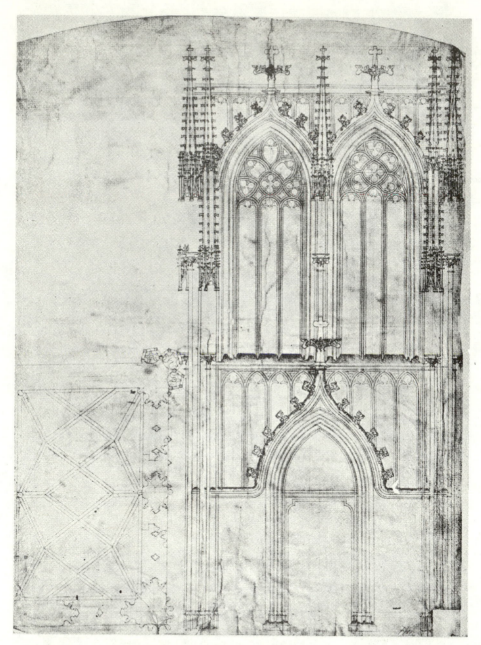

GROUND–PLAN AND ELEVATION *c.* 1440

a vision, or dream, of St. Thomas the Apostle and St. Thomas the Martyr (Becket) ordering a chapel to be built in their honour in the market place of Devizes.[1] The apostle, we are told, 'measured the space of twelve feet with his right foot, but the martyr thirteen with right and left foot, according to the custom of his race (*more gentis suae*)'; it is not quite clear whether the measurements were length and breadth respectively, or whether the right foot was supposed to be considerably longer than the left, but if this method of stepping the lines of buildings was in common use in twelfth-century England it may account for the irregularity noticeable in the plans of many country churches.

For the practical purpose of showing his patron or his workmen what the completed building was to be like, as a whole or in detail, it would be necessary for the architect either to make a model or to make drawings corresponding more or less to the modern elevations and working drawings. Models were certainly used occasionally on the Continent;[2] as for instance for Milan Cathedral in 1390, and for a gate at Ghent in 1416, when the master mason made a model, 3 feet in length, in duplicate; and one such model, for the church of St. Maclou at Rouen, still exists.[3] There seems, however, to be no evidence for the use of models in England. It is also true that this country can show very little in the way of architectural drawings before 1539. The most notable are a design for a tower, said to be one intended to be built at King's College, Cambridge,[4] and a careful sketch of details of the proposed monument of King Henry VI,[5] probably drawn in the last decade of the fifteenth century. An early drawing of the Tower of St. Michael, Cornhill,[6] which was pulled down in 1431, is not a design but a record, possibly made some years later and probably not by an architect. On the Continent, on the other hand, such drawings are fairly numerous and important.[7] Many of the fifteenth century are preserved at Vienna,[8] others, of the fourteenth, at Siena and at Cologne and elsewhere in Germany; two preliminary designs for the façade of Orvieto Cathedral probably date from 1310 and are the work of Lorenzo del Maitano, who

[1] *Mat. for Hist. of Thomas Becket*, i. 531.

[2] *Dict. of Architecture*, s.v. Model. The statement that Glastonbury Abbey was built in 942 'from a model brought from France' appears to be a misunderstanding of the fact that it was modelled on French abbeys of the time.

[3] Perrot et de Lasteyrie, *Mons. et Méms.* xii. 211–24.

[4] Cott. MS. Aug. I, i. 3. Probably drawn *c.* 1520.     [5] Ibid. Aug. II. 1.

[6] It is reproduced, very inexactly, in Wilkinson's *Londinia Illustrata* (1819) and in facsimile in Overall, *Ch. Wardens' Accts. of St. Michael, Cornhill*.

[7] See Briggs, *The Architect in History*, 89–100.

[8] See Grimschitz, *Hanns Puchspaum* (Wolfrumbücher 12).

designed and carried out the existing façade.[1] Somewhat earlier is an elaborate drawing of the west front of Strassburg Cathedral, and a manuscript at Reims was written, not later than 1270, on parchment from which had been almost, but not entirely, obliterated typical architectural elevations and other details of some church not identified.[2] These last drawings must therefore have been approximately contemporary with the sketchbook of Villard de Honnecourt, in which there are a number of fine drawings of such architectural details as struck him during his travels, notably one tower of Laon Cathedral. One of Villard's sketches, of the tracery of a window at Reims, might well have served as the working drawing from which Master Henry de Reins caused some of the windows in Westminster Abbey to be executed.

But if actual architect's drawings of our period are practically nonexistent in England, there is an abundance of evidence that the master masons could and did make such drawings. In 1519, when Horman published his *Vulgaria*,[3] a Latin-English phrase-book, he included one section '*De re aedificatoria*'. The phrases were designed to bring in as many different technical words as possible, but they were useful, sensible phrases, and two of them run, 'He drewe out a platte of the house with a penne', and 'He is not worthy to be called maister of the crafte, that is not cunnyng in drawynge and purturynge'.[4] The rules of the Strassburg masons,[5] which were drawn up in 1459 and probably represent general masonic custom, say: 'If anyone contracts for a work and gives a plan for it, how it shall be; the work shall not be cut short of anything in the design, but he shall execute it according to the plan which he has shown to the lords, cities, or people, so that nothing be altered in the building.' Also: 'No one who has not served his time as a craftsman or been employed in a lodge, and does not know how to execute carved or designed stonework from the ground-plan shall undertake such work; if he does no fellow shall assist him.' And again: 'No craftsman, warden or fellow shall teach anyone that is not of our craft to make extracts from the ground-plan, or other usages of masonry.' From which we see that any qualified mason was expected to be able to draw a ground-plan, and to work a moulding from a sec-

---

[1] *Arch. Review*, 1903, 206.

[2] Burges, 'Architectural Drawing', *Trans. R.I.B.A.*

[3] Republished by the Roxburghe Club.

[4] A classification of craftsmen, for assessment of wages, in 1610 includes 'a freemason which can draw his plot, work and set accordingly, having charge over others': *Trans. R.I.B.A.* N.S. iii. 220.

[5] Gould, *Hist. of Freemasonry*, i. 121–2.

tional drawing. The contracts for the building of the chapel of King's College, Cambridge, in 1512 and 1513 contain a number of references to 'plattes' which are not ground-plans but working drawings:[1] the pinnacles of the buttresses and the corner towers, with their finials, battlements, quatrefoils, &c., are to be 'acordyng to a platt therof made'; so are the vaults of the chapel and of the side chapels and the porches; and certain battlements are to be worked 'acordyng to another platte made for the same remaynyng withal the other plattes afore referred in the kepyng of the said Surveyour signed with the handes of the lordes and kynges executours'.

A few years earlier a carpenter had complained to Henry VII that whereas 'Your Grace had a sight bi picture of the ruffe (roof) of your halle of Woodstoke' and had approved it, the plans had since been altered, by the introduction of certain windows, so that the timber which he had shaped would be wasted.[2] The 'picture' in this case was most probably a drawing in section, or an elevation of one truss, which would serve as a working drawing for the construction of the roof. A group of three such drawings of wooden roof framing occurs in Villard de Honnecourt's sketch-book, and apparently represents not existing work but his own theories, as two of them embody the principle of the hammer-beam, of which no example is known for about a century after Villard's time.

Henry VII in his will (1509) ordered that his tomb at Westminster should be finished according to the design which he had 'in picture delivered' to the Prior of St. Bartholomew,[3] who was master of the works at the time. In 1532 John Russell, a carpenter engaged on work at Westminster, paid 4*d.* for 'one quayre of papire Royalle provided for the drawing of plattes'; and 'iiij skynnes of veelom whereupon plattes were drawen' were also bought.[4] About the same time John Yenggold, a London carpenter, agreed with the churchwardens of 'Seynt Fosters well and workmanly to frame and set up . . . within the steple of the said church of Seynt Foysters a newe bell frame and xvj stalles w[t] iiij parcloses to the same and in the quire of the said church with the same clenly and workmanly according to a patron thereof drawen to maek frame and set upp', for £37.[5] Similarly in 1457 Thomas Kerver of Lichfield agreed to make for the Prioress and Convent of Nuneton forty quire stalls 'after the forme of a

---

[1] See App. B.  [2] *Hist. MSS. Com. Rep.* iii. 318.
[3] *L. & P. Henry VIII*, i. 1.  [4] T.R. 11, 12.
[5] Early Chanc. Proc., 599, 54. The churchwardens refused to advance him money, as agreed, and then sued him for breaking his contract.

pyktur which is remaynyng in the kepyng of the said priores', at 21s. 8d.
apiece.[1] A little earlier, in 1440, we find at Shene 6 skins of parchment used
'in making various *patrons* for portraying various buildings upon',[2] and in
1448 we read of a design (*portratura*) for the completion of the chapel of
Eton College being submitted to the king.[3] When the Merchant Taylors'
Company were going to build a new kitchen, in 1425, they paid 7s. 4d.
to Goldyng Mapylton, a carpenter, '*pur portratur del patron de cuzine*', and
also provided wine and ale for him and other persons '*pur devyse la forme
de cuzin*'.[4]

An interesting example of a mason working from a design supplied by
another occurs in 1442, when John Marys of Stokegursey undertook to
build a tower for the parish church of Dunster. The wording is not quite
clear but apparently the whole design, and certainly that of the windows,
was to be 'according to the patron ymade by the avyce of Richard Pope,
Fremason'.[5] Henry Yevele, as we have seen,[6] supplied working drawings
for others to execute at Westminster Hall in 1395 and for St. Dunstan's
in 1381. In the Westminster instance these, described as '*une forme et molde*',
may have been simply sections of mouldings, or even actual templates.
The provision of such templates was part of the duties of the master mason
from very early times. The actual word occurs for the first time, so far as
I have been able to ascertain, in 1540 in an account of works at Calais,
when white boards were bought for making 'templattes and plumrules'.[7]
Elsewhere in the same accounts 'weynskottes', or oaken boards, were
purchased 'for to make moldes, setting reuelles and squares', and 'moldes'
is the term in constant use during the Middle Ages.

When William of Sens was appointed architect in control of the rebuilding of Canterbury Cathedral after the fire of 1174[8] we are told that 'he
delivered to the carvers who had come together moulds (*formas*) for shaping the stones', and it has been said that the mouldings in his work at
Canterbury are so exactly like those in the church at Sens, of which he had
previously been architect, that the same templates could be used for both,
but Mr. Bilson informed me that this is not the fact. The nature of these
moulds or 'forms' is explained in the account of the building of Rosslyn
Chapel in 1446, when we are told that Sir William Sinclair 'first causd the
draughts to be drawn upon Eastland boords, and made the carpenters to

[1] Add. Ch. 48698.                          [2] E. 503, 9.
[3] Willis and Clark, *Arch. Hist. of Cambridge*, i. 398.    [4] Acct. Bk., f. 149v.
[5] See App. B.                              [6] Above, p. 13; App. B.
[7] *L. & P. Hen. VIII*, xvi. 98.              [8] See App. A.

carve them according to the draughts theron, and then gave them for patterns to the masons that they might thereby cut the like in stone'.[1] So in 1255 at Woodstock 4½d. was paid 'for 3 boards for making moulds';[2] and at the Tower in 1282 Stephen Joignur was paid 'for various planks (*tabulas*) for moulds for the work of the masons'.[3] At Ely in 1323 boards for moulds and iron cramps (*crombis*) for the mason's moulds occur,[4] the cramps corresponding, no doubt, to the 'platis called dusse platis for the joynyng of masons mouldis', bought at 2d. the hundred at Westminster in 1532.[5] In 1350 John Leycestre, chief mason at the Tower, was making moulds for the work on the postern, and 16 masons were 'shaping and working stones according to moulds given to them by John Leycester'.[6] Amongst other similar entries we may note at Corfe in 1376 '4 planks (*tabulis*) called waynescotes for moulds for the mason';[7] at Langley in 1372 '2 sawn ryngoldbord' bought to make *moldes* for the masons',[8] and at York '*j righold pro muldic' faciendis*',[9]—the boards in the last two instances being Riga deals.

The work of making these drawings was carried out in the 'trasour' or 'tracyng house', the drawing office of the master mason.[10] Accordingly we find in the accounts for the building of St. Stephen's Chapel, Westminster, in 1324[11] various charges for erecting a tracing-house (*trasura*) for making the moulds for carved niches (*tabernaculis*); and in 1331 when Master Thomas of Canterbury became chief mason at St. Stephen's he is found 'working on moulds in the tracing-house'.[12] Other items in the account indicate that Master Thomas must have been kept pretty busy: two sawyers were employed all of Friday and on Saturday till noon sawing boards for moulds; an oak board 8 ft. by 3 ft. was bought for moulds, and 300 laths were bought 'to make false moulds[13] for use at the quarry'. The same expres-

---

[1] Britton, *Arch. Antiq.* iii. 51.   [2] E. 497, 12.   [3] E. 467, 9.
[4] *Sacrist Rolls*, 33.   [5] T.R. 556.   [6] E. 471, 3.
[7] E. 461, 6. Cf. at York Place, London, in 1515, 2 wainscots 'to make mooldes for masons': E. 474, 7.   [8] E. 486, 6.   [9] *Y.F.R.* 47.
[10] At Louth in 1500 William Netylton was paid for 'trassyng and makyng molds to the brooch', or spire: Dudding, *Churchwardens' Book of Louth*, 11.
[11] E. 469, 8. Again, in 1343, 7 ells of canvas were used 'for the windows of the tracing house of the master mason' there: E. 470, 13.
[12] E. 469, 11. A 'trasour' is mentioned at Windsor in 1351 (E. 492, 27) and 1397 (E. 495, 23), and at Ely in 1360 (*Sacrist Rolls*, 193), as is the 'trasyng hous' at Exeter in 1374 (Oliver, *Exeter*, p. 385), and the 'tracery house' at Westminster in 1532 (T.R. 106, 416).
[13] The 'false molde' was probably the converse of the 'molde', the one being the actual profile of the moulding, the other the template proper. In the Merton College accounts for 1449 we find—'for laths and nails for facimolde for the masons', and 'for carriage of facemoldys from Oxford to Burford': *Oxford City Docts.* (O.H.S.), 328.

sion is found in the 1324 accounts, when 3 ells of canvas were used 'for false moulds sent to Caen for stones to be worked (*tractandis*) there according to the said moulds'.[1] Among the Westminster Abbey accounts[2] are payments in 1424 to Robert Westerleye going to the quarry 'with faussemoldes', and in 1480 for small nails for making moulds, and for elm boards for making 'falsmolds' for the quarry. This is important as bearing upon the question of how far stones were carved at the quarries, a point with which we shall deal more fully later. That it was an established custom is suggested by an entry in Westminster accounts of 1292: 'for canvas for making models (*exemplaria*) for stones of Caen to be worked (*trahendis*)— 9d.';[3] although not definitely stated, it looks as if these canvas designs were to be sent out to the Norman quarries. At Ely in 1366 both canvas and parchment were provided for moulds,[4] and parchment for 'moldis' is mentioned at Norwich in 1324.[5] In the King's Hall accounts for 1427 and 1429 are entries of the purchase of parchment '*pro skanclyon*',[6] a mysterious word which looks as if it may be connected with 'scantlings' and imply a measured drawing, but elsewhere in these accounts the 'moldys' between 1388 and 1486 are made, as usual, from boards.

From all this evidence we can see that from at least as far back as the twelfth century the architect, or master mason, was accustomed to provide drawings of such details as the mouldings of arches and tracery of windows.[7] It follows that he was responsible not only for the general plan of the building but also for a large proportion of its detail, and that therefore the individual working masons did not have so free a hand or so large a share in the development of the scheme as some writers have imagined. There is the further point that the medieval architect was not so enamoured of originality, or of his own skill, that he would refuse to copy other men's work. Many great churches were deliberately based on earlier buildings. Edward the Confessor's church of Westminster Abbey seems to have followed that of Jumièges fairly closely, and its successor, built by Henry III, was based on Reims, with features borrowed from Amiens and the Sainte Chapelle at Paris.[8] In the western bays of the nave of the abbey we have the very unusual feature of work begun in the later part of the fourteenth century—and not completed till the beginning of the sixteenth

---

[1] E. 469, 8.      [2] Kindly communicated to me by Mr. John Harvey.

[3] 468, 6.      [4] *Sacrist Rolls*, 193.

[5] Communar's Roll.      [6] K.H. 7, ff. 174, 210.

[7] A stone has been found at Byland Abbey on which is set out a section of the great round window in the west front of the church.

[8] Lethaby.

—imitating the existing work of a full century earlier so closely that the casual observer would believe the whole nave to be of one date. Usually the building copied was chosen as a fine, up-to-date example of the style in vogue at the moment. The chief exceptions to this rule were the round churches built, theoretically, on the model of the Holy Sepulchre at Jerusalem, and they had actually little in common with their original beyond rotundity. Similarly, when we are told that Robert of Lorraine, who became Bishop of Hereford in 1079, built his cathedral 'on a well designed plan (*tereti scemate*), imitating the church of Aachen for his model (*pro modo suo*)',[1] we may doubt if he flattered the church of Karl the Great by more than an approximate imitation of its ground-plan.

In 1243 Henry III ordered the work on his chapel at Windsor to be pushed on and gave instructions that a high wooden roof should be made for it 'in the style of the roof of the new work at Lichfield, so that the stonework may be visible (*ita quod appareat opus lapideum*)'.[2] The same year he ordered the Justiciar and Treasurer of Ireland to cause a hall, 120 ft. by 80 ft., to be built in Dublin Castle, 'with windows and casements (*verinis*) in the style of the hall of Canterbury, which they have seen often enough (*quam satis viderunt*)'[3]—or, possibly, 'which they have had a good look at' may give the sense better. In 1373 a block of shops in Southwark was to be built 'in all points as is the longe Rente (i.e. row of houses) of Adam Franceys towards the east end of the church of the Friars Austin'.[4] The kitchen at King's Hall, Cambridge, was to be built, in 1386, 'of the same excellent timber in quality and workmanship as that of the kitchen of the Friars Preachers', with a solar on the west after the fashion of the cloister next the kitchen of the Friars.[5] The contract for the rebuilding of the Dormitory at Durham in 1398 specifies that the masonry of the walls is to be as good as, or better than, the Constable Tower in Brauncepeth Castle, 'which tower, indeed, shall be the model (*exemplar*) for this work'.[6] The roof of the church of Halstead in 1413 was to follow the design of that of Romford;[7] and in 1422 Catterick bridge was to be built 'acordand in substance' to Barnard Castle bridge, with certain slight differences.[8] For

---

[1] Will. Malmesbury, *Gesta Pontif.* 300. No traces of such a plan exist in the cathedral but it is said (Duncumb, *Hist. of Herefordshire*, i. 523) that 'stupendous foundations' were found in 1650 beyond the east end of the cathedral. More probably, however, it refers to the building formerly on the south of the Bishop's Cloister: *Hist. Mons. Com., Hereford*, 90.

[2] *Close R.* 39. Next year the king gave 40 oaks towards the work of the church of Lichfield: ibid. 175.

[3] Ibid. 23.  [4] App. B.  [5] Willis and Clark, *Arch. Hist. of Cambridge*, ii. 438.

[6] App. B.  [7] App. B.  [8] App. B.

the building of Walberswick church tower in 1425 certain features were to be copied from the churches of Tunstall and Halesworth;[1] and in 1448, when the parishioners of Totnes planned to erect a fine new tower to their church, they sent the overseers of the work to inspect the towers of Kelington, Buckland, Tavistock, and Ashburton, to decide which design to follow.[2] Similarly in 1496, when the Pewterers' Company built their new hall in London, they went to examine the halls of the Haberdashers and Carpenters and that of the Pappey Gild, and they also note the expenditure of 10*d.*, 'spent at Hackney with the carpenter to have a view of the Dean's roof there'.[3] When Sir Thomas Lucas was building Little Saxham Hall, in 1505, he arranged for the roof to be 'according to the patron of an hous of Sr. John Cutts in his manor of Thaxstede';[4] and also he records, 'rewarded to Loveday, my carpenter, comyn hidr to London to se Aungil Donnys hows—iii[s]. iiii[d].' Similarly in 1525 Sir Thomas Kitson bargained with John Eastawe to 'macke a house at Hengrave of all manor of mason's worck, bricklaying and all other things concerning ye masondrie and bricklaying . . . according to a frame which the said Jhon has seen at Comby'.[5]

From what has been said we see that the medieval architect was, with negligible exceptions, a master mason, or carpenter, capable of drawing plans and details for others to work from, but not above copying, or at least drawing inspiration from, the work of others. In the majority of instances he superintended the execution of his own designs and took an active part in carrying out the more skilled and artistic portions of the work. But he did not necessarily wield the axe or chisel, or lay hands on a single stone or beam. Nicholas de Biard, preaching in 1261, said: 'The Masters of the Masons, carrying a rod and gloves in their hands, say to others "cut it for me thus", and do no work themselves; and yet they receive the higher wages; and so do many modern prelates.'[6] But if the masters occasionally did no work—for Nicholas, like some modern worshippers of the proletariat, apparently considered design or organization unworthy of the name of work—they were at least capable of doing it, having graduated usually as apprentices and always as working masons, in which capacity they can often be traced before they rise to mastership. In this the medieval architect had a great advantage over his modern representative,

---

[1] App. B.  [2] *Hist. MSS. Com. Rep.* iii. 345.
[3] Welch, *Hist. of the Pewterers' Company*, 82.
[4] Gage, *Thingoe Hundred*, 140–1.
[5] App. B. Possibly 'frame' may have meant a model rather than an actual building.
[6] *Bulletin Monumental*, lxx. 267.

who only too rarely has served as a builder and handled stone and wood and iron in the concrete. On the other hand he lacked the modern architect's training in science and his abstract, but highly practical, knowledge of stresses. The early master had the tradition of generations behind him, but when he departed from the magic circle of that tradition his experiments were fraught with danger and were apt to be made at the expense of his employers.

Medieval architecture was largely empiric. One grows tired of hearing enthusiasts exclaim: 'How splendidly those old monks built!' 'Yes, they built to last!' All this amounts to is that the ancient buildings that we see are those that have survived, and that their survival is often due to a solidity obtained by a most unscientific and uneconomic prodigality of building material. There were, especially after the first quarter of the thirteenth century, master masons who combined tradition, experience, and genius, but they were at all times rare. The average man produced average work, and much medieval architecture that was sufficiently well constructed to last till the present time has nothing but its age and the mellowing accidents of time to commend it. Quicherat says:[1] 'Nothing is more common than to find that churches built in the eleventh century fell soon after their building or by the end of the century', and of the great church towers built in England during the Norman period a considerable proportion collapsed sooner or later and often sooner. There are constant references to the fall of buildings from insufficient foundations, unskilful handling, or bad workmanship—for the medieval craftsman was at least as ready as the much abused modern workman to scamp his work if not carefully watched. The church built by St. Egwin at Evesham collapsed completely in 960,[2] and about 985 the tower of Ramsey Abbey, which had hardly been completed ten years, developed such alarming cracks that it had to be taken down and rebuilt on better foundations.[3] At Abingdon the enlargement of the chancel and the unskilful way in which the new work was joined on to the tower led to the fall of the tower in 1091.[4] That same year there was a tremendous gale and hurricane in London, which shattered more than six hundred houses, unroofed the church of St. Mary at Bow, and reduced other churches to ruin.[5] If it is true that this wind lifted beams 26 feet in length and drove them 20 feet into the ground, the damage done is hardly surprising; but unless such hurricanes were more common in early days it does not speak well for medieval building that in 1210 many of the monas-

---

[1] *Mélanges*, 434, quoted by Mortet, 5.    [2] *Chron. Abb. de Evesham*, 40.
[3] App. A.                [4] App. A.         [5] App. A.

tic buildings at Dunstable fell through the violence of the wind, as did also a tower at Bury St. Edmunds, two at Chichester, and one at Evesham.[1] This last was the one which, as we have seen,[2] was built by the monk, and apparent amateur architect, Master Thomas de Northwich. In 1222 two towers on the west front of Dunstable Church fell in a December storm which also wrecked the tower of Merton Priory and 'many buildings throughout England'.[3] About the middle of the fourteenth century the quire of Norwich seems to have been wrecked by the fall of the spire in a great wind.[4]

At Gloucester the west tower fell, about the end of the eleventh century, 'through default of the foundation',[5] and the central tower of Winchester collapsed in 1107, either because of the wickedness of William Rufus, who had been buried beneath it, or, as William of Malmesbury not unreasonably suggests, through the failure of the foundations,[6] which seems also to have been the cause of the fall of the west tower of Worcester in 1175.[7] As an example of bad workmanship we may take the fall of the fine tower built at Beverley Minster by Archbishop Kinsi in about 1050.[8] Somewhere about 1200 it was decided to crown this tower with a stone 'roof', presumably a short conical spire; the workmen, or, as it would be fairer to say, the architect in charge of the work, paid more attention to its beauty than its strength; the four supporting piers were adorned rather than strengthened with detached shafts, which do not seem to have been properly bonded in. Very soon it was obvious that the piers were overloaded—some of the Purbeck marble shafts split throughout their length— but the work was carried on recklessly, until the whole tower collapsed.

The central tower of Ely, which for some time had been in so threatening a condition that the quire could not be used, fell in 1321[9]—a disaster which proved a blessing to posterity as it made way for the glorious octagonal lantern. Two years later, on 28 June, a large piece of masonry 'on the north side behind the dormitory' at St. Albans fell; but this was due not to bad workmanship but to the carelessness of the monastic officials in allowing the rain to get into the wall until it became 'rotten and unsound to the very foundation'.[10] That same year there occurred at St. Albans a disaster 'so terrible that previous misfortunes might well be considered as little or nothing in comparison'. Two columns on the south side

---

[1] *Ann. Mon.* iii. 32.     [2] Above, p. 10.     [3] *Ann. Mon.* iii. 76.

[4] Wharton, *Anglia Sacra*, i. 415.     [5] *Giraldus Cambr.* vii. 64.

[6] *Gesta Regum*, ii. 379.     [7] *Ann. Mon.* iv. 383.     [8] App. A.

[9] *Anglia Sacra*, i. 643.     [10] App. A.

of the nave suddenly collapsed, bringing down the roof and shattering the south aisle and cloister.[1]

St. Albans also affords us an outstanding example of bad and fraudulent workmanship in the lamentable history of its west front.[2] Abbot John (1195–1214) got together material for this front, with a staff of masons, over whom he put Master Hugh de Goldclif, 'a workman of great reputation, but a deceitful and unreliable man', who ran the Abbey into great expense by persuading the abbot to have a design with quantities of carved panelling and niches, 'unnecessary, trifling, and beyond measure costly'. The abbot grew frightened at the expense; the unfinished walls were not properly covered during the winter and the rain and frosts tumbled the whole into ruin. What exactly happened after this is not clear, but according to the monastic chronicle large funds were applied to the work for thirty years without bringing it two feet higher.

Turning from the sublime of a great abbey church to the comparatively ridiculous, we may note as an example of bad workmanship that when Thomas Burton, Abbot of Meaux, in about 1396 rebuilt a certain horse-mill, 'it afterwards proved useless, because the timber prepared for the mill was so roughly and unsuitably wrought (*carpentatum*) that it caused the building in which it was to become ruinous through its vibration (*motione*)'.[3] Some few years later three parishioners of Little Thornham, in Suffolk, bargained with John Tilley and Richard Cuttyng to build their church tower 'after the patron of the steple of Easthorp in the Counte of Norff' with the amendement of certeyn thynges apperteynyng to the same' for 10½ marks. Half of this was advanced to Tilley and Cuttyng on their promise to find sureties 'for the makyng and continuall abidyng and standyng of the same steple'; but they 'made parcell of the same steple in such forme that it is nowe riven through in too (two) diverse places of the same and the uttermost part of the oon side of the wallis of the same is fallen dowen a fote and more in to the walle the heith of xj fote and so by no menys possible that work may stonde'.[4]

An interesting instance of fraudulent work occurs in 1316,[5] when Masters William de Hoo, John de Hardingham, and John de St. Omer were sued for breach of a contract[6] to build a wall round the manor of Eltham. The jury found that the wall was deficient in thickness by 1½ feet at the base and by 1 foot and more in other parts; the buttresses were similarly defi-

---

[1] App. A.
[2] App. A.
[3] *Chron. Mon. de Melsa*, iii. 241.
[4] Early Chanc. Proc. 76, 30.
[5] Pleas of Exch. 10 Edw. II, m. 15.
[6] Printed in Appendix B, pp. 422–4.

cient and, whereas they ought to have been made of hard stone and good 'cement', they had made them of chalk and soft stone and 'false cement'. The whole would have to be pulled down to make it good. It was 79 perches and 12 feet in length and damages were assessed at 4 marks the perch, and 2½ marks for each of the 56 buttresses—£305. 15s. 7d. in all. The masons were committed to prison, but released on undertaking to carry out the work properly; Mr. Michael of Canterbury,[1] Alexander Le Ymagour, and six other London citizens going surety for them. In 1407 the tower of York Minster was said to be in a state of collapse owing to the carelessness of the local masons, and William Colchester[2] was put in control of the fabric, to the great indignation of the local men, who endeavoured to hinder his work and injure him and his workmen.[3] The tower of Ripon Church was said to be falling 'both through the carelessness, neglect, and ignorance of the craftsmen lately working upon it, and because of thunderstorms, the fury of the winds, and the violence of great tempests', in 1460. It was still in exactly the same condition 22 years later, but in 1512 the whole nave had been blown down.[4]

According to one writer, Cardinal Wolsey's college at Oxford might have been practically finished before his fall if the workmen had not been idle:

> Most cunnynge workemen theare weare prepared,
> Withe spediest ordynaunce for eavery thynge,
> Nothynge expedyent was theare oughtis spared
> That to the purpose myght bee assistynge;
> One thynge (chieflye) this was the hinderynge,
> The woorkefolke for lack of goode overseers
> Loytered the tyme, lyke false tryfelers.
> They weare thus manye, a thousande (at the leaste)
> That thearon weare woorkeynge, still daye by daye
> Their payments contynued, their labours decreaste,
> For welneare one haulfe did noughtis els but playe.
> If they had trulye done that in them laye
> By so long space as they weare tryfelynge
> At hys fall had been lyttle to dooynge.[5]

---

[1] A leading mason, who was entrusted with making the Eleanor Cross in Cheapside in 1292.

[2] He was in charge of the rebuilding of the nave of Westminster Abbey in 1395 (*Cal. Pat.* 643), and was appointed King's mason in 1418 (ibid. 170).

[3] *Cal. Pat.* 383, 482. His appointment was revoked in 1410: ibid. 199.

[4] *R.* 240–2.

[5] Nathaniel Lloyd, *The English House*, 23; quoting Forrest's *History of Grisild the Second*.

From more prosaic records we learn that the Oxford gilds did their best to interfere with the labourers from outside. The carpenters and slaters claimed to be gilds, though there were only two members in each—and those bad workmen. The better carpenter spoilt one house and made a roof 2 feet narrower than the walls and a foot too short; and one of the slaters roofed one side of the college so badly that it all had to be stripped next year.[1] So also at Hampton Court, after it had passed into the king's hands, Cromwell jotted down the comment: 'How proud and false the workmen be.'[2]

From all of which entries, and from others that will be found later in this book, it is refreshingly clear that bad workmanship is not the monopoly of our own generation; that if the medieval craftsman-architect could create masterpieces, he could make as bad blunders as any of his desk-bound successors; and that if the British workman of the present day is not as good as he used to be, he probably never was.

[1] *L. & P. Hen. VIII*, iv. 2735.          [2] Law, *Hampton Court*, i. 161.

# II

## ORGANIZATION

BEFORE dealing with the organization of the building trades it will be well to consider what classes of craftsmen come into that denomination. Primarily they may be divided into the masonry and the carpentry crafts.

The MASONS contain within themselves several subdivisions, more or less clearly marked. For the craft generally the commonest Latin term is *caementarii* (often mistranslated as 'plasterers'—*caementum* is classical Latin for hewn stone); often *lathomi* or *latomi* is used; more rarely, and usually in early documents, *mazones* is found, as for instance on the Pipe Roll of 1165, a payment to a mason (*mazoni*) working at Windsor, and at Woodstock in 1255, 'to a mason (*mazoni*) who is over all the workmen and controls the work'.[1] The superior branch of the craft were those who came to be known as Freemasons. The origin of that term has been much debated, but there seems little question that they were identical with the *sculptores lapidum liberorum*,[2] of 1212. 'Free stone' is the term in constant use for blocks of stone, either carved or faced for ashlar, as opposed to rubble, and it was the freemasons who worked such stone. The term *cementarii libere petre* occurs as early as 1341 at Ludgershall,[3] and the English form 'fre-mason' is used by John Marwe of Norwich in 1432[4] and by William Horwood of Fotheringay in 1434.[5] A variant title, which apparently only occurs on the Westminster Abbey account rolls for 1252–3, is *albi cissores*.[6]

In the Statute of Labourers issued in 1360 the '*mestre mason de franche pere*' is distinguished from ordinary masons, and in 1396 the 'masons called *Fre Maccons*' are contrasted with the 'masons called *ligiers* (i.e. layers)'.[7] Similarly the Woodstock building accounts in 1438 show free masons (*liberi cementarii*) and 'roughleggers' employed,[8] and those of 1494 give both 'Fre' and 'Row masyns'.[9] The masons employed on Cardinal Wolsey's college at Oxford in 1526 include freemasons, setters, roughlayers, and 'hardehewers';[10] and at Westminster in 1532 there are masons 'working upon stone', others 'settyng of stone', 'rougheleyers' and 'hardehewers', as well as 'masons entayllers' or carvers.[11]

---

[1] E. 497, 12.       [2] *Liber Cust.*, p. 86, see below, p. 68.
[3] E. 476, 1.       [4] See App. B.       [5] Ibid.
[6] E. 466, 30.       [7] Gould, *Hist. of Freemasonry*, ii. 308.
[8] E. 499, 3.       [9] E. 499, 19.       [10] E. 479, 11.       [11] T.R. *passim*.

The second class of masons, therefore, consists of the layers, setters, or wallers, who placed in position the stones worked by the (free) masons. They occur as *cubitores* at Westminster in 1252,[1] at Corfe in 1280,[2] and at Carnarvon in 1282;[3] as *positores* at Windsor in 1365,[4] Westminster in 1385,[5] and the Tower in 1440.[6] We find them as 'leggeres' and 'setteres' at Newgate in 1282,[7] as 'leggers' at St. Paul's in 1382,[8] and as 'leyers' in the accounts of King's Hall, Cambridge, from 1412 onwards, while the contemporary term at York is 'setters'. 'Wallers' are found at Middleham in 1533,[9] and a *murator* is mentioned at Dunster in 1417,[10] while at Linlithgow in 1302 there are payments to masons described as *impletoribus muri*.[11] There was no hard and fast line between them and the free-stone masons; the same men are found at different times in the two classes, and on the Tower accounts for 1311 wages are paid to John de Radewell 'mason carver and layer (*entall' et cubatori*)'.[12] In the same way they shade off into the third class of 'rough-layers' and 'hardhewers', who in turn figure as quarriers.

Carvers, of stone, were originally indistinguishable from masons, carving being an essential part of the architecture of the building in which it was employed. Until quite the end of the Romanesque period far the greater part of the sculpture was structurally part of the building, as in carved capitals and corbels, ornate doorways, such as those of Iffley or Malmesbury, pillars, such as are found at Kilpeck, and tympana; only with the coming of Gothic do we get the general use of detached statues. The mason who was capable of executing the one type of work was equally capable of the other, and many statues were fashioned by the masters and other superior masons who also worked the mouldings of arches and window traceries. But there naturally grew up a tendency for the man with a special aptitude for figure work to specialize in this, so that we find a class of 'Imagers' developing quite early. One, Thomas the Imager (*imaginarius*), is referred to casually in a London record of 1226;[13] when Edward I erected the famous series of crosses to commemorate Queen Eleanor, who died in 1290, William de Hibernia '*imaginator*' worked on the crosses of Northampton and Lincoln, while Alexander de Abyndon and Dymenge de Ligeri, '*imaginatores*', were employed on that at Waltham and on the queen's tomb at Lincoln.[14] In 1323 the Exeter Cathedral authorities paid 39s. 'to the

[1] E. 466, 30.  [2] E. 460, 27.  [3] E. 486, 29.

[4] E. 493, 16.  [5] E. 473, 2.  [6] E. 503, 9.

[7] E. 467, 11.  [8] E. 473, 1.

[9] E. 476, 8.  [10] *Arch. J.* xxxviii. 77.  [11] E. 482. 20.

[12] E. 468, 20.  [13] *Liber Albus*, 84.

[14] *Manners and Household Expenses* (Roxburghe Club), 114, 121.

imager of London for cutting images' for the choir screen;[1] and in 1349
Maud, widow of John de Mymmes, a London 'ymaginour' (who had himself died earlier in that fatal year) bequeathed to her apprentice, William,
the best third part of her stock of copies, or patterns, and tools appertaining
to the making of pictures, with a chest to keep them in.[2] Possibly in this last
instance the imager may have been a painter and not a carver; but the other
cases are sufficient to show that from an early date there were men who
might be regarded as sculptors rather than masons. By way of contrast we
may quote a payment entered in the King's Hall accounts for 1435 'to a
chief mason (*lathamo*) for carving and making the King's image standing
at the great gate'.[3] A carver of more than local reputation, evidently, was
John Massingham, of London.  He provided 'ymagerie pro le syne at
Sonne' at Canterbury in 1436;[4] two years later he was employed, as *factor
ymaginum*, at All Souls' College, Oxford, for 15 weeks at 4s. 8d. a week
and his board and lodging, John Massingham the younger, his assistant,
receiving 2s.;[5] and in 1448 he was paid £10 for making an image of the
Blessed Virgin for the high altar at Eton.[6]

There was also a flourishing school of monumental masons in the neighbourhood of Corfe,[7] who carved the Purbeck marble which was in such
great demand throughout England during the thirteenth and fourteenth
centuries. At Westminster in 1385 we find £30. 6s. 8d. paid 'to Thomas
Canon, marbrer (of Corfe) for making 13 stone images in the likeness of
Kings, to stand in the great Hall'.[8] These 'marbrers' or marblers constituted
another subdivision of the masonry crafts and included the 'polishers'.

Of the CARPENTERS there is not so much to be said. Their name, but not
their nature, is occasionally varied by the use of the term 'wrights', or its
Latin equivalent *fabri lignarii*. In woodwork the carver became, on the
whole, more definitely specialized than the sculptor in stone; but, while
stalls at Windsor in 1477 were worked by 'karvers',[9] their predecessors in
1354 are attributed to carpenters—John Lyndesay, carpenter, being paid
3s. 4d. a week 'for making images for the stalls'.[10] Joiners occur occasionally
in connexion with fittings and furniture, but speaking generally, every
type of woodcraft, from felling timber to making tile-pins, was done by
the carpenter. Sawing of large timber was done with the pit-saw, and the
sawyers are therefore usually paid their wages in pairs.

[1] Oliver, *Exeter*, 382.                    [2] *Cal. of Wills in Court of Hustings*, 576.
[3] K.H. 8, 212.                              [4] Bodl. MS., Top. Kent c. 3, f. 149.
[5] *Rationarium*.                    [6] Willis and Clark, *Arch. Hist. of Cambridge*, i. 402.
[7] Salzman, *Engl. Industries*, 92.          [8] E. 473, 2.
[9] E. 496, 17.                              [10] E. 492, 30.

PLATE 4

EMPLOYER AND CHIEF MASON DIRECTING BUILDING OPERATIONS
*c.* 1250

PLATE 5

BUILDING OPERATIONS c. 1180

Connected with, but quite distinct from, the carpenters, were the tilers, slaters, and thatchers, all of whom may be grouped together as 'helyers' or *cooperatores*. We shall have also to consider the plumbers and glaziers, smiths and painters. Lower in the scale come the plasterers and pargetters, and the daubers who make walls of wattle-and-daub but tend to become entangled with the *dealbatores* or whitewashers. The paviour, working in stone, marble, or tiles, makes an occasional appearance; and from the end of the fifteenth century bricklayers occur, figuring at first as 'tile-wallers', as at Beverley in 1461.[1] Finally come the comparatively unskilled labourers, who include the mortarmen, hodmen (*hottarii*), barrowmen, and so forth.

Even if we do not include lime-burners and the makers of tiles and bricks, who manufacture building-material, and the carters, boatmen, and lightermen, who carry it, it is obvious that the building trade is a very complicated organization, with many branches and capable of employing a large amount of labour.

From the beginning of the thirteenth century industry was organized, for the most part, on a system of craft gilds.[2] Such gilds were strictly local; the fact that a man was a member of a craft fraternity in his own town gave him no right to exercise his craft or to expect assistance from the corresponding gild in any other town. This was an unsuitable form of organization for the masons, who were constantly on the move from one part of England to another; and we therefore find that the local, permanent, gild is replaced by temporary associations centring upon the 'lodge' or workshop where they are employed. Before examining in detail the evidence for the fluidity of labour in the building trade and the significance of the masons' lodge it is worth while considering why the masons alone develop this form of fraternity. Carpenters, smiths, tilers, plumbers, glaziers, and painters are all found establishing their gilds in a score of towns, but, with the exception of London, we do not find gilds of masons until late in the fifteenth century, and even then only rarely. On the other hand the carpenters do not exhibit the same phenomenon of lodge fraternities, although they played as large a part in medieval building as the masons, and indeed a larger. It is probably this last fact that accounts for the difference between the two crafts. When practically every building contained, in its roofs and floors, a certain amount of carpentry, and the vast majority of houses were constructed mainly of wood, there was in every town sufficient employ-

---

[1] *Hist. MSS. Com., Beverley MSS.* 47.

[2] The chief exceptions were the free mining communities: see Salzman, *English Industries*, chs. ii–iv.

ment for a fair number of resident carpenters, who would naturally associate themselves in a gild like any other craftsmen. On the other hand, when stone buildings were so rare that many small towns contained none besides the church, and in larger towns stone houses were notable landmarks, the mason who had not the good fortune to obtain a post on the staff of a cathedral or abbey must have been intermittently employed and must have spent a large part of his time travelling from one place to another in search of work.

As the average town would provide insufficient employment for any considerable number of men of the building crafts, so building operations on even a moderate scale would usually exhaust the supply of skilled, and even of unskilled, labour in the immediate vicinity. Both causes tended to the creation of a degree of fluidity of labour rather astonishing to those who imagine that the Middle Ages were a stay-at-home period. When Abbot Baldwin of Bury St. Edmunds prepared, at the Conqueror's command, to build a great church for his abbey, we are told—'*convocat latomos, architectos invitat, cementarios et artis sculptoris peritos viros conducit*'.[1] Similarly, rather over a century later, when Abbot John of St. Albans began his unlucky west front, 'very many chosen masons were summoned together';[2] and in the middle of the fourteenth century, when Edward III started to build the so-called 'Round Table' at Windsor, he 'caused very many workmen to be called together to the castle'.[3] And when he called he saw to it that they came. In 1362, when most of the masons working at Windsor had died of the plague, orders were issued to compel masons to come from various counties.[4] Twenty-nine masons came from Yorkshire in 1362, each receiving a liberal allowance of 6*d*. a day for himself and his horse during the six days of the journey,[5] and the sheriffs' accounts show that others came from Lincolnshire, Lancashire, Shropshire, Hereford, Nottingham, and Derby. A casual list of masons working at Windsor, whose wages were in arrears in 1365, shows four each from London, Norfolk, and Yorkshire, three from Oxford, Northamptonshire, and Gloucester, two from Bedfordshire, Buckinghamshire, Lincolnshire, and Somerset, and one each from Lancashire and Huntingdonshire.[6] For the building of Sandgate Castle in 1539 forty masons were brought from Somerset;[7] and for work at Nonesuch Palace in the previous year two of the staff were sent

---

[1] *Mems. of St. Edmunds*, i. 85.
[2] *Gesta Abbatum*, i. 219.
[3] Walsingham, *Hist. Angl.* i. 263.
[4] *Cal. Pat.* 297.
[5] E. 598, 7.
[6] E. 493, 16.
[7] *L. & P. Henry VIII*, xiv (2), 645.

to Gloucestershire and Northamptonshire to obtain workmen, and 5 free-masons and 33 roughlayers were paid journey money at the rate of 6*d*. for 20 miles, most of them receiving 1*s*. or 1*s*. 6*d*.[1] The names of the workmen employed in 1286 on a comparatively small job at Cambridge Castle show that while many of them came from the immediate neighbourhood, others came from as far off as Ramsey, Castleacre, and Barnack;[2] and those work-ing, a few years earlier, at Vale Royal in Cheshire speak of Caerwent, Pershore, Nottingham, Eynsham, St. Albans, Wymondham, and Ton-bridge.[3] Other building accounts and wage rolls tell the same tale, and this fluidity of labour helps to account for the rapidity with which variations in architectural styles and fashions spread over England.

This fluidity is seen also in the fluctuations in the numbers employed on the same building at various times. Thus the account roll for work at Westminster Abbey in 1253,[4] beginning in May, shows 308 workmen of all classes. This number has risen by the end of the month to 385, and by midsummer to 435, of whom 130 are masons of one kind or another and 220 are labourers. At the end of July this figure has fallen to 335, chiefly owing to the withdrawal of 80 labourers and of 12 out of 28 carpenters. In the last week of August there is a sudden drop to 233, there being now only 93 masons and 91 labourers, possibly owing to the demand for labour in the harvest fields. By Michaelmas the numbers have risen again to nearly 300 and remain about that figure until the winter season sets in, in the third week of November, when there is a drastic reduction of its staff to 100, of whom 47 are masons and 30 labourers. More surprising in rapidity of variation are the figures for the staff at Carnarvon during five successive weeks of June and July 1295:[5]

| | | | | | | | | |
|---|---|---|---|---|---|---|---|---|
| Masons . | . | . | . | 70 | 63 | 92 | 160 | 64 |
| Carpenters | . | . | . | 8 | 13 | 17 | 17 | 12 |
| Quarriers | . | . | . | 20 | 30 | 46 | 54 | 31 |
| Smiths . | . | . | . | 8 | 12 | 22 | 25 | 14 |
| Labourers | . | . | . | 175 | 176 | 247 | 282 | 140 |
| | | | | 281 | 294 | 424 | 538 | 261 |

Although not quite so extreme in the rapidity of their fluctuations the figures for the masons employed at Harlech in 1286 afford a parallel; there

[1] *L. & P. Henry VIII*, xiii (2), 342.      [2] E. 459, 15.
[3] Brownbill, *Ledger-Book of Vale Royal*.
[4] E. 466, 30, printed in Gilbert Scott's *Gleanings from Westminster*.
[5] E. 486, 8.

were 131 on 12 May, 189 by 24 June, rising to 225 on 14 July, and falling again to 163 at the beginning of August.[1] Similarly at Windsor in 1344 the figures for the first six weeks, beginning in the middle of February, are:[2]

| | | | | | | | |
|---|---|---|---|---|---|---|---|
| Cutting Masons | . | . | 15 | 58 | 106 | 128 | 137 | 127 |
| Laying Masons | . | . | — | 18 | 64 | 73 | 73 | 41 |
| Carpenters | . | . | 4 | 8 | 15 | 15 | 14 | 14 |
| Smiths . | . | . | — | 3 | 3 | 5 | 5 | 5 |
| Quarriers | . | . | — | 72 | 121 | 130 | 71 | 63 |
| Labourers | . | . | 17 | 211 | 401 | 193 | 180 | 180 |
| | | | 36 | 370 | 710 | 544 | 480 | 430 |

The seventh week was Holy Week, and immediately afterwards the staff was cut down almost to vanishing-point. The explanation of this is to be found in Thomas of Walsingham, who tells us that 'At first the weekly expenses (of building the "Round Table") were £100, but afterwards, on account of the news which the king received from France, they were cut down to £9, because he thought that a great deal of treasure would have to be applied to other business'.[3] As a final example of fluctuations we may take the rolls of persons employed at Dover on eight successive pay-days, at four-weekly intervals, between 18 July 1535 and the following 15 January:[4] 128, 273, 165, 282, 332, 308, 349, 481.

All these statistics are taken from royal building operations. It is improbable that any private works, even of the wealthiest abbeys, ever employed a staff of anything like such magnitude; their work was carried on in a much more leisurely fashion; the building of a church might be spread over generations, but a castle would be of little use if not completed with the utmost rapidity, and kings did not care to be kept waiting when they chose to build votive abbeys, such as Westminster or Vale Royal, or to enlarge their palaces. Henry III in 1253 wrote to his treasurer and Edward fitzOtho, his clerk of the works: 'We command you, as you wish our love towards you to be continued, that you in no wise fail that the chambers which we ordered to be made at Westminster for the use of the knights be finished on this side of Easter, even though it should be necessary to hire a thousand workmen a day for it'.[5] In the same year Henry ordered the keepers of the works at Windsor to have the upstairs chamber next to his chapel wainscoted 'by day and night', so that it might be ready by the

[1] E. 485, 26.
[2] Hope, *Windsor Castle*, i. 115.
[3] *Hist. Angl.* i. 263.
[4] *L. & P. Hen. VIII*, x. 102.
[5] Liberate R. 28 Hen. III.

day of his arrival,[1] and two years later the Sheriff of Wiltshire is ordered, 'as he loveth his life and chattels', to take diligent care that the Queen's new chamber at Clarendon be finished before Whitsuntide, whenceso-ever moneys for the completion of it may be procured.[2]

To obtain the large numbers of workmen required for their building operations the English kings resorted to pressed labour. From the thir-teenth century onwards the Patent Rolls are full of orders for definite, or indefinite, numbers of masons, carpenters, glaziers, or other workmen to be enrolled, on pain of imprisonment, for the king's works at various places. It must be borne in mind that this does not imply any servile status on the part of the workmen;[3] they were paid for their work, and on the whole the rate of wages tended to be slightly higher than those paid by private employers. The impressment of labour, in fact, was part of the royal prerogative of prise, or purveyance—the right of pre-emption, by which the king's requirements take precedence of those of the general public. Thus labour was commandeered in the same way as building materials or carts and boats for their carriage. For the glazing of St. George's Chapel at Windsor in 1363 Henry de Staverne and John de Brampton were commissioned to take the necessary glass, cause it to be carried to London, where it was to be worked, and to bring 24 glaziers to London.[4] In November of 1414 Henry V appointed certain persons to take masons, carpenters, and other workmen, to the number of 24, and also to take the necessary stone, timber, &c. to complete the collegiate church of St. Mary at Leicester, which Henry of Lancaster, the king's great-grandfather, began.[5] Thirty years later, in 1444, Reynold Ely, chief mason of the college of St. Mary and St. Nicholas (now King's College), Cambridge, William Roskyn, and Henry Beverley were empowered to take both labour and materials for their work.[6] Again, in 1489, a commis-sion was issued for the impressment of masons and the purveyance of carts and crayers, lighters, shouts, and other boats for carrying materials for the repair of Rochester bridge.[7]

The privileged position of the royal works is shown by such an order as that issued in April 1246, by which no stone was to be sold or carried

---

[1] Liberate R. 28 Hen. III.                                    [2] Ibid. 30 Hen. III.

[3] Villeins owing carrying service were sometimes used for the carriage of building materials, but the only instance I have noted of any other use of villein labour was in 1238, when the stone for the great gate of Winchester Castle was to be cut by labour due to the King from men of the Bishopric (then vacant): *Close R.* 176.

[4] *Cal. Pat.* 319.

[5] Ibid. 265.                    [6] Ibid. 269.                    [7] Ibid. 283.

by ship from Kent except for the king's works at Westminster, so that he might have 200 shiploads of stone by Whitsun.[1] Naturally private rights suffered, as is indicated by an order made in 1251 that the stone which the monks of St. Thomas's, Dublin, had collected at Bristol for their abbey church, but which had been seized for the king's castle, should be restored to them.[2] In 1443 we find Sir John Fastolfe, familiar to readers of the *Paston Letters*, obtaining protection by which the materials for the house which he was building, and the ships used for carrying them, were exempted from purveyance;[3] and in 1468 Sir John Crosby had similar protection for the materials required for 'certain edifices' (Crosby Hall) which he was building.[4] Similarly in 1440 the royal officials were forbidden to hinder the carriage of stones from Maidstone by the parishioners of Fulham for the building of their church tower, or to take for the king's service Richard Garold or Peter Chapell, masons engaged on that work.[5] So, also, in 1414, when a parochial chapel was being built on the south side of Hereford Cathedral, orders were given that Thomas Mason and his ten assistant stone-cutters should not be taken away for the king's works until the chapel was finished.[6] In 1396, when building was in progress at New College, Oxford, Mr. John Hulyn had to go up to London about certain masons and carpenters who had been taken for the king's works while engaged on the work of the college;[7] and in 1449 the authorities at Merton gave 20s. 'to the king's servant, so that the masons should not go away from the college on the king's work'.[8] In a suit[9] by Katherine Adams against John Hawkins, carpenter, in 1532, for breach of a contract to erect certain houses in Shoreditch, the defendant alleged that the delay was solely due to the fact that he and all his servants were taken to work on the king's works at York Place and were detained there until the day named in the contract was past. On the other hand we find Bishop Oliver King, in 1503, invoking royal assistance to enable him to keep his workmen. On 25 January he writes to Sir Reynold Bray, then controller of the works at Westminster Abbey and elsewhere, desiring

that ye give no licence to any free mason to absent hym from this buylding [Bath Abbey cathedral church]. Divers masons ther be that wol not comme til after Candelmas trustyng that in the meane saison they wol cause you to be entretyd to write unto me for to suffre theym to work in other mennys busi-

---

1. *Cal. Close*, 413.     2. Ibid. 526.     3. *Cal. Pat.* 206.
4. Ibid. 52.     5. Ibid. 530.
6. Ibid. 226.     7. *Oxford City Docts.* (O.H.S.), 313.
8. Ibid. 329.     9. Early Chanc. Proc. 695, 12; 703, 7.

nesses. One ther ys called Thomas Lynn oone the most necessary mason for me that I can have and oone of theym that ys appointed by Robert Vertu.[1]

When such large numbers of workmen were brought together for building operations the problem of providing accommodation for them must have been considerable. Some of the first entries in the Vale Royal accounts for 1278 are payments to carpenters 'for making the lodges (*logias*) and dwelling houses (*mansiones*) of the masons and other workmen, and the smiths' forges at the quarry of Edisburi and the site of the monastery',[2] and it is said that the town of Rosslyn originated in the houses built for the men working on the famous chapel, begun in 1446.[3] How the 720 men employed, as we have seen, in one week as Windsor were provided for is a problem. When William Cleve was appointed clerk of the works at Westminster in 1444,[4] he was given a piece of vacant land on the west of the hall to make houses for the workers and for stores, such as the 'tymberhawe' and 'trasiers' for the stonecutters; and at Dover in 1536, when there were about 460 men at work, request was made for a couple of old 'hales', or tents, for the men to work in in bad weather and to dine in, instead of going into the town, which wasted time.[5] In the contract for raising the walls of Westminster Hall in 1395, the king undertook 'to find lodging (*herbergage*) for the masons and their mates (*compaignons*) during all the time they shall be occupied about the said work';[6] and in the contract for the tower of Walberswick Church, made in 1425, the parishioners engaged to provide 'an hows to werke inne to ete and drynke and to lygge (lie) in and to make mete inne and that be harde by the place of workyng'.[7]

The 'house' referred to in this last extract is clearly identical with the most important of the workmen's buildings, the 'lodge'. References to such lodges are common in building accounts. As instances we may note that in 1332 oak timber was provided at Westminster 'for the masons' lodge (*loga*) below the Great Hall towards the Thames';[8] at Windsor in 1351 a payment for cleaning the masons' 'logge';[9] and in 1438 for thatching the lodge at Porchester.[10] In the contract for building Catterick bridge in 1422 the employers undertake to 'make a luge of tre (timber) ate ye said brigge in ye quilk ye forsaides masons schall wyrke'.[11] Sometimes the term *astellaria*, or workshop, is used, as at the Tower in 1278,[12] and at Cam-

[1] *Somerset Arch. Soc.*, lx (2), 4.

[2] E. 485, 22.

[3] Britton, *Arch. Antiq.* iii. 51.

[4] *Cal. Pat.* 355.

[5] *L. & P. Hen. VIII*, x. 98.

[6] App. B.

[7] Ibid.

[8] E. 469, 13.

[9] E. 492, 27.

[10] E. 479, 7.

[11] App. B.

[12] E. 467, 7 (4).

bridge in 1286.[1] Stephen Lote, mason, is described in 1382 as 'warden of the new lodge' at St. Paul's.[2] At King's Hall, Cambridge, in 1428 a 'logge' was made for the masons and a key provided for its door;[3] and similarly at Westminster in 1532 a stock-lock and 'shutting plate' were 'set upon a dore belonging to one of the lodgies wherein certein of the masons worke'.[4]

The King's Hall accounts just quoted go on to record the purchase of 3 old 'coverlytes' for the beds of the masons; straw for the same beds; 12 yards of linen for sheets; and 10 'polys de Walyssh (Welsh) blankett' for the workmen's beds. Also the expenditure of 4*d*. on making 3 sheets and 'hemmyng' two coverlytes. Although it is not definitely stated that these beds were in the lodge, it is probable that they were. The lodge was the building on which the life of the temporary community of masons centred. It was primarily the workshop where they shaped and carved stone; but it served also as dining-room and as the place where they took their mid-day nap in the long days of summer, and it is at least likely that it often served as a dormitory. That it was sometimes a substantial building is indicated by the fact that at Windsor in July 1367, when work on St. George's Chapel was practically finished, the masons' lodge was made over to the vicars of the chapel for their residence.[5] In Germany in the fifteenth century, and probably in England also, it was to the lodge that the travelling mason turned his steps when he arrived in a town, and there he was sure of employment when he had made himself known to the master in charge by a particular form of salutation and, apparently, by a special handgrip.[6]

This secret handgrip is the nearest approach to a solid foundation on which later writers erected a vague and fantastic temple, enshrining the mysteries of an occult freemasonry. It may be said at once that, so far as available evidence goes, there is nothing to show that modern philosophical freemasonry has its roots in medieval craft-masonry; it is apparently an independent growth of the seventeenth century, grafted on to the craft and using its technical terms as symbols. There was, no doubt, a certain element of secrecy about the craft; circumstances, as we have seen, made the ordinary organization of a gild, with its ordinances open to the control of the local authorities, unsuitable; the resulting fraternity, with its temporary centres in the lodges, was at once less definite and more

---

[1] E. 459, 15.          [2] E. 473, 2.

[3] K. H. 7, 210: 'the masons loge' was repaired in 1528: ibid. 24, 14.

[4] T.R. 316.

[5] Hope, *Windsor Castle*, i. 203. The masons' lodge of Westminster Abbey was also eventually converted into a private house: Rackham, *Nave of Westminster*, 10.

[6] Gould, *Hist. of Freemasonry*, i. 142.

universal. Over such an organization the authorities, national or local, would find it more difficult to exercise their control. Where there were permanent lodges, as in the case of the cathedrals, the employing body might and, as we shall see, sometimes did, draw up regulations; but there may well have been a body of unwritten tradition, more or less jealously guarded, among the masons. Added to this was the fact that the more skilled men possessed a certain knowledge of geometry at a time when all science, however elementary, savoured of magic, and it is easy to see how the craft was invested with a vague air of mystery. The first hint of 'freemasonry', in its later sense, is often said to be found in a rhymed treatise on the duties and mutual relations of masons, both masters and fellows, or journeymen, dating from the early years of the fifteenth century.[1] Apart from its claim of Euclid as the founder of the craft, through his discovery of geometry, and of Athelstane as its first patron in England, the manuscript contains nothing that suggests mystical peculiarities. Most of its charges would have been applicable to any other craft, and many of them can be paralleled from gild ordinances. The master is to treat his workmen well and pay them their proper wages; he is to act fairly by his employer and not to undertake work that he cannot perform. He is to work brotherly with others of his craft and not try to get any other man's work away from him. Apprentices are to be taken for seven years; they must be free born, legitimate, and sound in body and limb; they are not to tell tales or repeat the gossip of their master and fellows, nor to reveal what is done in 'the logge'. It is worth emphasizing the point that it is only the apprentice who is warned not to reveal the secrets of the lodge; which is pretty clear evidence that there is no reference intended to any masonic ceremonial. Of more particular interest is a section enjoining courteous behaviour when all are dining together 'yn chambur', which we may reasonably interpret as in the lodge.

In many ways the most important, and puzzling, part of this poem is the assertion that there should every year be a general assembly of the craft, apparently at such a place as might be settled by the assembly of the previous year, and

> That every mayster that ys a mason
> Most ben at the generale congregacyon
> Or ellus (unless) sekenes hath hym so stronge
> That he may not come hem amonge.

---

[1] Printed by Halliwell in his *Early Hist. of Freemasonry*; a summary and extracts in Coulton, *Social Life in Britain*, 482–9.

According to the twelfth section, not only shall masters and fellows attend this assembly, but also the sheriff of the county, the mayor of the city, knights, squires, and aldermen, who shall help to enforce the ordinances of the assembly against any disobedient craftsmen. Incidentally this is another disproof of anything in the nature of a secret assembly. Another masonic manuscript, of the latter part of the fifteenth century,[1] similarly says that congregations of the masons are to be held yearly or triennially, as need be, and that the assistance of the sheriff, mayor, or aldermen may be invoked. Yet the only trace of any such general meetings ever having been held is to be found in 1425, when, as a result of a complaint that 'by the yearly congregations and confederacies made by the masons in their general chapters (*chapitres*) assembled', the Statutes of Labourers were broken and made of no effect—in other words, wages were raised above the statutory maximum—an Act was passed by which such chapters and congregations were forbidden, on pain that those holding them should be adjudged felons, and other masons attending them should be liable to imprisonment and fine.[2] If it is hard to believe that any such general assemblies as are described in the two manuscripts quoted, one of which is certainly later than this Statute, were held, it is equally difficult to believe either that they promptly ceased on the issue of this prohibition, or that the law was entirely a dead letter. Yet I have failed to trace a single prosecution under this Act, nor has anyone else, so far as I know, been more fortunate.

That the masons were exceptionally successful in defying the state regulation of wages appears from the references to them in the preambles of various statutes to which we shall refer later. It is also noticeable that Wycliffe,[3] denouncing 'newe fraternytes or gildis' for selfish and antisocial policy, particularly condemns 'men of sutel craft, as fre masons and othere'. His complaint is—in modern English—that 'they conspire together that no man of their craft shall take less for a day than they fix, though he should by good conscience take much less; that none of them shall do good steady work which might interfere with the earnings of other men of the craft, and that none of them shall do anything but cut stone, though he might profit his master twenty pounds by one day's work by laying a wall, without harm to himself'. All of which is delightfully reminiscent of many letters in the present-day press on the subject of Trade Unions, even to the slight exaggeration of the possible value of one day's bricklaying.

Not so many years before Wycliffe wrote, the London masons were by

---

[1] Add. MS. 23198; Gould, *Hist. of Freemasonry*, i. 86
[2] Stat. 3 Henry VI, c. 1.                    [3] Coulton, *Social Life*, 491.

no means at unity, there being many disputes between the 'masons hewers' (or freemasons) and the setters, which are expressly attributed to the fact that their trade had not been regulated by the government of members of their craft in such form as other trades were. Accordingly, in February 1356, the mayor caused each branch of the craft to appoint six representatives: Walter de Sallynge, Richard de Sallynge, Thomas de Bredone, John de Tyryngtone, Thomas de Gloucestre, and Henry de Yevelee (later famous as king's mason) appeared for the hewers; Richard Joye, Simon de Bartone, John de Estone, John Wylor, Thomas Hardegray, and Richard de Cornewaylle for the setters. The first of the rules which they swore to accept would have met one of Wycliffe's objections, as it laid down that every man of the trade might work at any branch of it, provided he had the necessary skill. Anyone undertaking work which he failed to do properly was to be fined; and no one was to undertake work by contract without finding four or six masons of established reputation who would testify to his ability; if he then failed to complete the work properly, they would be bound to do it themselves. Apprentices were to serve at least seven years, and were not to be set to work, except under their master's eye, until they were expert. The masters were to oversee their workmen and to pay them as they deserved and not excessively. If any mason refused to obey the sworn representatives, they were to give his name to the mayor, who would punish him.[1]

The issue of these regulations did not imply the constitution of a gild of masons; but twenty years later, in 1376, when the Common Council was reconstituted by the election of representatives of the crafts, four persons— John Wrek, John Lesnes, John Artelburgh, and Robert Henwyk—were chosen for the masons;[2] and ten years later the 'sworn masters' include John Clifford, Thomas Mallynge, Simon atte Hoke, John Westcote, and Henry Wylor.[3] In neither list, it may be observed, were the carpenters represented. Among the masters of gilds sworn in 1416 William West and John Crokstone are named for *lathami*, or freemasons, and Henry Bostone and William Massam for the *sementarii*, or rough masons:[4] but in 1418 and the following year only the *lathami* are mentioned, and a list of the crafts in London drawn up names only one mason gild, the *cementarii*, who are twenty-ninth in order, followed immediately by the carpenters.[5] The masons were eventually incorporated as a City Company in 1481.[6]

---

[1] Riley, *Mems. of London*, 280–2.
[2] *Letter Book H*, 43.
[3] Ibid. 274.
[4] *Letter Book I*, 172–3.
[5] Unwin, *Gilds and Companies of London*, 167.
[6] Ibid. 171.

One of the masters named above in 1386, Thomas Mallynge, is mentioned with another mason, Richard atte Chirche, and two carpenters in 1375 and 1383 as the official building inspectors, sworn to report nuisances and encroachments and to divide property, when necessary.[1] The City authorities had issued building by-laws, mainly concerned with questions of party-walls and stillicide, in 1189[2] and others, dealing with precautions against fire, in 1212.[3] To see that such laws were carried out, to settle boundary disputes, and to partition land and houses between joint owners, it was the custom to appoint two masons and two carpenters as 'sworn masters'.[4] Thus in 1305 there is a reference to a house, inherited by four sisters as co-heirs, being 'partitioned according to the custom of the city by the sworn carpenters and masons'.[5] Similarly in 1375 the sworn masters were ordered to partition a tenement and deliver half to one of the owner's creditors.[6] In 1373, following a report from the sworn masters that a stone house in St. Lawrence lane was in a dangerous condition, the tenants were ordered to repair it at once;[7] and in the same year a dispute about damage to certain fixtures was determined by the sworn masters, in the presence of Henry Yevele, William Fraunceys, Richard Godchild, William Twyford, and John Simond, acting as arbitrators.[8] In 1419 the Bridgewardens 'paid to the sworn masters masons and carpenters of the City of London for viewing a nuisance of a tenement near the Bridge and giving their verdict thereon, as is customary, 7s.'[9] The same practice held good in York, for which city a number of decisions given by the 'sercheours of the masons and wryghtes' during the fifteenth century are preserved, dealing with boundaries, party walls, gutters, and tenant's fixtures.[10] And at Norwich in 1508 a dispute as to alleged encroachment on a party wall was referred to a jury said to be 'of the maisters of the mister or craft of masons', but actually containing two carpenters as well as three masons;[11] in this instance, however, these seem to have constituted an *ad hoc* jury and not to have been permanent officials.

---

[1] *Letter Book H*, 13, 216.   [2] *Liber Albus*, 321–31.   [3] *Liber Cust.* 86.
[4] For the oaths of the masons and carpenters, see *Liber Cust.* i. 100.
[5] *Cal. of Mayor's Court Rolls*, 178.   [6] *Cal. of Plea & Memo. Rolls*, ii. 229.
[7] Ibid. 163.   [8] Ibid. 150.
[9] London Bridge Accts. ii, f. 368.
[10] Printed in *Engl. Miscellanies* (Surtees Soc.), 11–22.
[11] *Norwich Recs.* ii. 29.

## III

## ORGANIZATION: REGULATIONS, HOURS

THE lodges, as we have seen, were the nuclei round which the organization of the masons crystallized; and such lodges might be either temporary or permanent. In the majority of instances when a castle, church, or house was to be built or enlarged the lodge was set up, became for a few months or years the busy centre of masonic life, and then was removed or converted to other uses. But the cathedrals and some great abbeys maintained something in the nature of permanent lodges, with a small staff of masons and carpenters, and in particular a master mason, who was usually appointed for life and was expected to be continually resident, or at least to put aside all other work when the fabric of the church required attention. Thus at Salisbury, in July 1334, an agreement was made with Richard de Farlegh, mason, that he should have the custody of the fabric, to superintend, direct, and appoint masons, and himself do necessary work. He should make such stay in Salisbury as the needs of the fabric demanded and, notwithstanding prior obligations at Bath and Reading (of which we should like to know more), he should not neglect or delay the work of the cathedral. He was to receive 6d. a day when present, and the salary of 10 marks annexed to the office of guardian of the fabric, if he survive Robert the Mason.[1] Presumably Robert had become incapacitated by age and illness and had retired on a pension. When Master Richard Beke was appointed by the Chapter of Canterbury, in 1435, to have control of all their works of masonry, he was to receive 4s. weekly, a house, clothes, an allowance for fuel, and a pension if he became blind or bedridden.[2] At York in 1351, when William de Hoton was appointed minster mason, in succession to his father, Master William, his salary of £10 was to be paid subject to the condition that if he worked for any others the work of the minster should not be neglected or delayed; and there was a clause that if he became incapacitated by blindness or other disease he should pay half his salary to 'the second master of the masons'.[3] Similarly, when John Bell was engaged, in 1488, as 'speciall mason' by the Prior and Chapter of Durham, to undertake 'all their workes of masonry with ymagre and other, newe and olde', with the aid of an apprentice, it was arranged that

---

[1] Dodsworth, *Salisbury Cathedral*, 151. For similar agreements made in 1394 and 1415 see ibid. 158, 160.　　　　[2] App. C.　　　　[3] App. C.

if he had 'continuall infirmities or great age so that he may not wirke nor labour, nor exercise hys craft and cunnyng', he should receive only 4 marks yearly instead of his full salary of 10 marks.[1] In the agreement made in 1436 by Abbot William Curteys of Bury St. Edmunds, with John Wode, mason—which was for a period of seven years—Wode and his assistant were to be docked of 5*d.* and 3*d.* per day respectively for any days that they were absent through illness, but they might have their food if they came to the hall for it.[2]

We have seen that at Wells William Wyneford was engaged to supervise the works of the cathedral in 1364; in 1490 the Chapter appointed William Attwodde, freemason, to the office that William Smythe had held, with a fee of 26*s.* 8*d.*; he was to reside in Wells and to do any work required on the church before any other work.[3] Here the mason received a small retaining fee and was evidently paid wages when working at the cathedral, but when not required there was allowed to work for other employers. At Beverley in 1304 Oliver de Staynefield, the minster mason, had been given leave of absence, at the request of the Earl of Lincoln and the Lady Alice, his mother, but this having proved detrimental to the church orders were given that he should return at once and that no such leave should be granted in future.[4] As he did not return it was ordered that, so long as he was absent, he should contribute one mark a year to the fabric fund.[5] Another instance of employers having trouble with their workmen occurs in the accounts of King's Hall, Cambridge, in 1415 when we find entries: 'For the expenses of Walton and his horse for two days enquiring for Rayner, our carpenter, and his surety, 16d., for which Rayner shall account. Also for Warin Ingryth, our attorney, for his salary 20d. Also for 2 writs, 20d. Also for a writ called *Capias* against Rayner 10d. And for a writ called *Exigent* against Rayner, 13d.'[6] One rather suspects, also, that the Dean and Chapter of York made William Hyndlee break an existing contract when they secured his services as minster mason, for in 1474 we find them paying £5 'as a present to William Hyndlee in assistance and repayment of his costs, both in bringing his wife, children, and goods from Norwich to York, and in defending the suit brought against him in London by his enemies maliciously and without just cause'.[7]

---

[1] App. C.    [2] App. C.    [3] *Hist. MSS. Com., Wells,* 120.
[4] *Beverley Chapter Act Book* (Surtees Soc.), i. 54.
[5] Ibid., p. 73. In 1391 it was decided that when the office of mason fell vacant it should not be filled up, but the repair of the fabric should be borne by the Chapter: ibid. ii. 275.
[6] K.H. 4, 166.    [7] *Y.F.R.* 80.

It is obvious that these master masons were men of good standing. If attached to the royal household or the staff of a great ecclesiastical foundation they were in the enjoyment of an assured position, with a retiring pension in their old age. Even the masters who were working on their own often undertook contracts running into hundreds of pounds—equivalent to more than as many thousands in modern money; and when they were employed to take charge of building operations they frequently received 7s. a week, equal to just over £18 a year, at a time when the possession of twenty pounds' worth of land entitled, or even compelled, a landed proprietor to become a knight. The great mason, Henry Yevele, in October 1389 received two Kentish manors—Tremworth and Vanne in Crundale —in lieu of his salary of 12d. a day;[1] and his predecessor, Master John of Gloucester, was given the sergeanty of Bletchingdon (Oxon.) in 1256.[2] The same Master John in 1255, in return for his good services at Gloucester, Woodstock, Westminster, and elsewhere, was to receive yearly for the rest of his life two robes with good squirrel fur, such as the knights of the royal household received.[3] His predecessor also, Master Henry, the architect of Westminster Abbey, was given at Christmas 1243 a robe, defined as '*tunica et supertunica*'.[4] John de Middleton, the mason who contracted to build the dormitory at Durham in 1398, was to have yearly 'a robe of the suit of the Prior's esquires'; John Wode at Bury St. Edmunds in 1436 was to 'have hys robe and mete and drynk in the Priourys name, as one of hys gentilmen', and his assistant was to have food and a robe as a yeoman; and John Loose, engaged on the humble task of building a bakehouse for Corpus Christi College, Cambridge, in 1459, stipulated for 'a gowne of yoman's levere'.[5] In 1370 the mason working on the foundations of a row of shops for the Dean and Chapter of St. Paul's was to have '*une cote et une chaperon*' of the Bishop's livery; and the three masons building Catterick bridge in 1422 were promised yearly gowns 'accordande to their degree', as was also John Marwe who contracted to construct a quay at Norwich in 1432.[6] The robes given to the chief mason at King's Hall, Cambridge, at Christmas 1431 were of the substantial value of 16s. 8d.,[7] and the masons at Ely in 1324 received two robes worth 28s., not including the cost of furs,[8] the furs for the master mason and carpenter in the previous year costing 4s. 4d.[9] It may be added that medieval illustrations show the master mason dressed in accordance with the dignity of his office.

[1] *Cal. Pat.* 301.   [2] Ibid. 495.   [3] Ibid. 429.
[4] *Cal. of Close*, 141.   [5] App. B.   [6] Ibid.
[7] K.H. viii. 26.   [8] *Sacrist Rolls*, 44.   [9] Ibid. 27.

In most crafts the term 'master' was applied to one who, having served his apprenticeship, had set up in business; he was a master of his craft but not necessarily an employer of others. With the masons, however, and to some extent with the carpenters, the master was almost always an employer. He was the head of a body of craftsmen, for whose employment and discharge he was usually responsible.

According to the fifteenth-century rules of the craft in force in Germany, applications for work had to be made to the master and any master might discharge a workman on the pay-day;[1] and at York in 1345 orders were given that no one should appoint or remove masons except the master mason.[2] In many cases, when he was acting as contractor, he paid the workmen their wages himself. Thus at Fotheringay in 1434 there was a clause in the contract for building the church, by which if William Horwood, the contracting mason, failed to pay his workmen their wages the clerk of the works should pay them and stop the amount out of the money paid to Horwood.[3] In this contract the employers claimed the right to appoint the setters, or stone-layers, but if Horwood objected to them as inefficient they should be judged by master masons[4] of the district and, if found unsatisfactory, replaced by others. Moreover, when a mason is distinguished as 'Master John', or whatever his name may be, the title has clearly a definite, if not easily defined, significance. As the title, when applied to a clerk, indicated a Master of Arts, so we may say that here it implies a Master of Crafts, one who has not merely graduated but has risen to distinction. Owing to the innate snobbery of the human race it would probably be safer to say that the leading architects, or builders, were habitually called Master than to maintain that every mason styled Master was necessarily in the first rank.

One reason for the rather exceptional position of the master in the building crafts was the unusually large proportion of journeymen—men working by the day—in these crafts, necessitated by the conditions of their employment. In what we may call the resident crafts there were numbers of small masters with their own workshops, employing few, or even no, workmen; in building, as we have seen, labour was fluid and a large body of men had often to work under one master. An army contract for boots or arrows might find work for a score of master bootmakers or smiths; the building of a castle would be in the hands of one master mason, con-

---

[1] Gould, *Hist. of Freemasonry*, i. 141.
[2] See below, p. 55.  [3] App. B.
[4] The term here evidently has the usual craft sense of qualified craftsmen.

PLATE 6

*a.* BUILDING THE ABBEY OF GURK 15TH CENTURY

*b.* BUILDING THE ABBEY OF VÉZELAY 15TH CENTURY

PLATE 7

BUILDING THE TOWER OF BABEL 15TH CENTURY

trolling perhaps fifty masons, of whom a fair proportion would be fully qualified for the rank of master. The main qualification, in fact, for that rank, in masonry as in other crafts, was to have served under a master as an apprentice for at least seven years. The rhyming rules of the masons of the fifteenth century, already referred to,[1] have a good deal to say about apprentices; they figure also, not infrequently, in pay rolls; and in the appointment of John Bell as cathedral mason at Durham in 1488[2] he is specially authorized to have one apprentice, paying him 4 marks yearly for the first three years of his term, 6 marks for the next term, and 7 for his last year. The subject of APPRENTICESHIP[3] in the building trades is involved in considerable obscurity, partly owing to the conflict between theory and practice which is a feature of many medieval institutions. Theoretically an apprentice in any trade was bound to his master for (usually) seven years, during which time he received board, lodging, and instruction, and occasionally a little pocket money, but any profit from his work would go to his master. Accordingly we find in certain instances that payment is made to a mason, or carpenter, for himself and his apprentices. Thus during the building of the chancel of Adderbury Church[4] the master mason, Richard Winchecombe, was paid for himself and his apprentice 5s. 8d. a week in 1412, and 6s. 1d. in 1414—the value of the apprentice's work having risen from 2s. 4d. to 2s. 9d. with his increased experience. At Cambridge, in 1425, John the mason received 7s. 4d. for himself (4s.) and his apprentice (3s. 4d.);[5] and when 'the Bell' was built at Andover, in 1534, we find among the carpenters 'John Bere and hys 4 men for 6 days, takyng for hymselfe and 2 men 4d. a day (each) and 2 other prentyses 2½d. a day'.[6] But sometimes payments seem to be made indiscriminately to the master or his men. In an account of work at Coldharbour Manor in 1485 we have— 'to John Cousin mason for v dayes work, he takyng viijd. a daye,— iiis. iiijd. item payed the same tyme to Willm. Yonge his prentise for v dayes wages vd. a daye beside iijd. yeuen a reward—ijs. iiijd.'; but we also get other payments to 'John Cousin mason and his child'.[7] And more often

---

[1] See above, p. 41.

[2] App. C. In 1536 the master mason of Dundee was to have an apprentice, for 7 years, who should have no fee for his first year, after which a fee of £10 (Scots) should be paid him through his master, whose own fee was £24: Lyon, *Hist. of the Lodge of Edinburgh*, 28.

[3] For a detailed examination of the subject see Knoop and Jones, in *Econ. Hist. Rev.* iii. 346–66.

[4] *Oxford Rec. Soc.* viii.

[5] P. 1424–5.

[6] Magdalen Coll., Oxford, deeds: Enham 255b.

[7] E. 474, 3.

we find the apprentices paid without mention of their masters. In 1331, at Westminster, when the masons were receiving $5\frac{1}{2}d$. a day an apprentice was paid 2d.;[1] and in 1348 two carpenters' apprentices were employed at 4d. a day[2]—which was the rate paid to two others at Eltham in 1479.[3] At Rochester in 1410 an apprentice mason received 4d.;[4] and at Woodstock in 1438, when freemasons had 3s. 6d. a week, 'Thomas Spillesby apprentice to Thomas Spillesby, mason', had 3s.,[5] as did 4 'prentes' at Abingdon in 1538.[6] It would seem, therefore, that some young masons were working practically independently before they were out of their apprenticeship; and the rules of the Torgau masons, in 1462, expressly state that 'if a master has no work for his apprentice and lets him travel he must lend him a banker mark'. At the end of his seven years the apprentice could, in theory, become a master, but in practice he must almost invariably have served for some years longer as a journeyman. If the opportunity arose for him to act as a master by undertaking a contract, he would, according to the London regulations of 1356, produce at least four masons of standing to guarantee his capability.[7] And it is almost certain that for some years such a mason would generally fall back into the position of journeyman between one contract and the next.

Building operations might be carried out, under a clerk of the works or similar official, by a staff of workmen, paid by the day or week or by piecework; alternatively the work might be put out to contract. Frequently both methods were combined. Thus at Windsor in 1360–1 a large part of the building was done by journeymen, collected from all over England, under Master John Sponlay, 'master mason and deviser of the king's works', with Master Robert of Gloucester and Master William de Winford as his foremen; but there are no fewer than 55 contract jobs entered in the accounts.[8] For instance: William Frankeleyn, for building a long chamber, 200 marks; Yvo of Cambridge, for two chambers, £80; Andrew Kylborne, for one chamber, £55, and for two others, £100; five other chambers built by various contractors at £50 a piece; John Martyn and John

---

[1] E. 469, 11.  
[2] E. 470, 18.  
[3] E. 496, 21.  
[4] Becker, *Rochester Bridge*, 84.  
[5] E. 499, 3.  
[6] E. 458, 1.  
[7] Riley, *Mems. of London*, 281. In 1397 Robert Kentbury of Middlesex, Walter Walton of London, mason, John Swalwe of Gloucs., mason, and Reynold Nicole of Henley-on-Thames executed a bond that Thomas Wolveye, mason, should complete the masonry of Henley Church which he had begun, by 1 Aug. following: *Cal. Close*, 239. Kentbury and Swalwe were employed at Westminster Hall in 1395: App. B.  
[8] Hope, *Windsor Castle*, i. 189.

Welot for 389 feet[1] of a wall on the south side of the new work, at
13s. 4d. the 'double' foot, £259. 6s. 8d. A few years later, in 1368, when
Queenborough Castle was being built, Master John Box, Maurice Yonge,
and John Rokesacre (who occurs earlier as chief stone-layer) were paid
£500 for building 55½ perches 1¼ feet of the Barbican wall, each perch
containing 21 feet in length, 20 feet in breadth at the foundation, and 21
feet in depth, at £9 the perch.[2]

As earlier instances we may note that in 1251 Mr. Robert de Waledon
took a contract for building two rooms and certain other masonry at
Havering; and Mr. Richard de Waudon contracted for the carpentry of
these rooms;[3] and the Winchester Castle accounts of 1257 record that—
'the tower over the prison was handed over to Master Henry the mason by
Master John of Gloucester and Master Alexander (the king's carpenter),
to be pulled down and rebuilt . . . for £110'.[4] For late examples we may
take, from the rebuilding of Bodmin Church, 1469–72, 'Richard Richowe
for the taxk work,[5] that is to seye, Receyvd for the pelerys (pillars) yn iij
paymentes. Summa xxij.'[6] Sometimes the English form—'in great'[7] is
used; as at Oxford in 1517: Richard Leyowse 'for the makyng of the
towne wall and the wall abought the closter taskyd in grett by the perch
(of 18 ft.) havyng for every perch xijd. and all maner of stoof found
hym';[8] and at Collyweston in 1500: 'John Wright of Eston a grett for the
squaryng and framyng wᵗ the sawyng of a florth (i.e. a floor) of lxxij long
and xviij fette in brede—47s. 4d.'[9]

In these instances, which might be indefinitely extended, we have
merely the fact of the contract having been made, or at most a few dimensions and particulars, but a considerable number of actual contracts between
the employers and the builders—masons or carpenters—have survived.
These, so far as I have been able to trace them, I have collected in Appendix
B. In general outline these are fairly uniform, though they vary greatly
in the elaboration of their detail. The simplest formula is a mere statement
of the nature of the building, its dimensions and, usually, an enumeration
of such features as doors, windows, and fireplaces; the sum of money to be
paid; and, as a general rule, the penalty for failure to carry out the contract.
Sometimes the building is described in minute detail, the thickness of the

---

[1] Apparently using the long hundred of six score, which would equal 449 feet.

[2] E. 483, 25.  [3] *Close R.* 556.

[4] E. 491, 14.  [5] Latin *tascha*, a job or contract.

[6] *Camden Miscellany*, vii. 13.  [7] Latin, *in grosso*.

[8] Corpus Christi Coll., Oxford, MS. 435, f. 18v.

[9] St. John's Coll., Cambridge, MS. vol. i.

walls, the exact size of all the timbers to be employed, the material to be used in different places. Existing buildings may be referred to as examples to be copied more or less closely, or there may be references to plans and drawings which are to be followed. A date for the completion of the work is usual, but it does not seem possible to make any useful deductions as to the speed of medieval construction. In some contracts the builder is to supply all materials, in others the employer is to do so, the builder providing nothing but the labour and tools: in yet others the responsibility is divided, the employer often undertaking the carriage of the material and, perhaps, the timber required for scaffolding.

In the matter of payment, the general arrangement was a certain sum in advance and the remainder in instalments, either at regular intervals or according to the amount of work done. Thus at Durham in 1398 John de Middelton was to have £40 down and further sums of £40 as he finished each 6 rods of walling, the rod being defined at $6\frac{2}{3}$ ells square. The two carpenters who undertook to make a roof for Hartley Wintney Church in 1415 were to have £10 when they started work, £6 when they framed the timber, and £6 when they set up the roof; and for work on King's College Chapel, on which 60 freemasons were to be employed, money was to be paid out as required for the cost of stone and labour. At Hertford Castle in 1380 the contracting carpenter and his men were to be lodged in the manor of Hertingfordbury; and the mason working at Corpus Christi College, Cambridge, in 1459 was to have in the college 'a chambre j bedstead and a bedde, and his mete to be dyght in the Kechyn at there costes', while Peter Dryng, when completing the dormitory at Durham in 1402, was to have a daily allowance of a white loaf, a gallon of ale, and a dish of food from the monastery kitchen. The two masons at Walberswick stipulated for a cade of herring yearly, in addition to their money payment, and the carpenters at Hartley Wintney for a pig and a wether.

The contractor usually gave a bond of about the value of the contract for its due execution, and often produced sureties who were bound jointly and severally with him for the sum named. In the Fotheringay contract of 1434 the mason, William Horwood, bound himself, exceptionally, to finish the work within reasonable time on pain of imprisonment. As a rule the employer gave no such bond, but a King's College contract was affirmed by mutual bonds of £300.

The master mason, or carpenter, therefore, might be in sole control of building operations or, as at Fotheringay, working to some extent under the supervision of a clerk of the works, or, as in the Windsor instances, he might be executing under contract a portion of extensive operations of which another master was in control. In this last case his exact position is obscure. If there were twenty contracting masons (some of the 55 contracts were for carpentry, paving, quarrying, and so forth) were there twenty lodges? It seems more probable that there was one lodge, in which the various gangs worked under their own masters, and that Master John Sponlay occupied the position of what is called in the German masons' rules the 'building-master' (*baumeister*), supreme over the 'work-masters' but with no power to interfere with their control of their own craftsmen.[1] It seems fairly evident that the general designs of these subcontracts must have been submitted to the chief master, or architect, if they were not actually prepared by him, or a chaos even beyond the toleration of the individualist Middle Ages might have resulted. In this particular instance, at Windsor, Sponlay is definitely described as 'deviser (*ordinator*) of the king's works', which seems to mark him out as the architect, controlling the whole design and probably responsible for assigning the subcontracts. The actual supervision of the work and workmen would have fallen mainly upon Master Robert of Gloucester and Master William de Winford. These assistants I have called 'foremen'; the actual Latin term is *apparillatores* which occurs in French documents as *appareilleurs*,[2] its contemporary English form being usually 'wardens'.

At Vale Royal[3] in 1278, and in North Wales[4] a few years later, the second master is termed *submagister*; an *apparilator operum cement(ariorum)* is found at Windsor[5] in 1351 and at Westminster[6] in 1354, and an *apparitor* at Westminster[7] in 1365. At Havering in 1376 wages were paid to William Love '*apparatori operanti et ordinanti opus carpentarie ibidem*'[8] under Master Hugh Herland, the famous carpenter responsible for the roof of Westminster Hall. John Wynwyk appears as warden (*gardianus*) of the masons, under Thomas Mapledon, at Porchester in 1438.[9] At Eltham in 1479 the warden seems to have had no master mason over him and the carpenters were in charge of a chief warden and two under-wardens.[10] But at Westminster in 1532, when 95 masons were employed, they were under John Moulton, as master, and Thomas Faunte and John Elys as 'wardeyns', while one John Smythe was paid 'at v<sup>s</sup> by the weeke for that he is adioyned with the Maister Mason in devysing and drawing'.[11] Here also there were

---

[1] Gould, op. cit. i. 160.
[2] See an article on 'Maîtres et appareilleurs' in *Bulletin Monumental*, lxx. 263.
[3] E. 485, 22.       [4] E. 486, 1.       [5] E. 492, 27.
[6] E. 471, 11.       [7] E. 472, 14.       [8] E. 464, 30.
[9] E. 479, 7.        [10] E. 496, 21.      [11] T.R. 332–57.

wardens of the 'hardehewers', bricklayers, and carpenters; and in the accounts for Cardinal College, Oxford, for 1526 we find, similarly, wardens of the masons, setters, and roughlayers.[1] Occasionally the unskilled labourers are found working under their own foremen, or gangers—a 'master of the labourers' being paid 5*d*. a day in 1308 at Westminster, when ordinary labourers were receiving only 4*d*.[2] At Sheppey in 1362, although no distinctive title is given, one out of the 601 labourers received 4*d*. and 18 others 3½*d*., while the rest had only 3*d*. or 2*d*.[3] At Vale Royal in 1278,[4] Carnarvon in 1282,[5] and Harlech in 1286[6] the labourers were organized on a semi-military basis under *vintenarii*, though, judging from their numbers, their gangs must have been considerably more than the twenty implied by their title.

In addition to the workmen of the various branches of the building craft, in their varying ranks from master to apprentice, there would be for most operations something in the nature of a clerical staff to make payments for wages and material and to keep accounts. Payments for paper or parchment for the 'journals' or rolls of daily expenses, and for the wages of clerks writing them, are frequently found. Sometimes a single clerk of the works might be sufficient; usually with the more important royal works two account rolls would be drawn up, one being for the comptroller, by which the clerk's account could be checked. At Westminster, in 1532, we find six clerks employed: one to oversee the masons, carpenters, sawyers, &c.; one for the bricklayers and allied crafts; the third and fourth to keep a 'lidger' of all purchases and a 'checke booke of all the artificeres and labourers'; the fifth to draw up accounts for the paymaster's use; and the sixth to engross the ledger.[7] The last two, having the more skilled work to do, were paid 8*d*. a day, whereas the others received only 6*d*.

Having completed our examination of the way in which the medieval building trade was organized in general, we may take one or two particular instances that throw light on the actual working of the organization. The first of these is a very interesting report on the management of the work at York Minster, beginning, on the 9th of January 1344-5, with the evidence of the Master of the Works:[8]

(Dom. W . . .) He says that he believes that the masons have received salaries more than were due and too excessive. Wages used to be paid by the fortnight but payment is now put off for a month or even more. Orders given that in

| | | | |
|---|---|---|---|
| [1] E. 479, 11. | [2] E. 468, 18. | [3] E. 483, 20. | [4] E. 485, 22. |
| [5] E. 486, 29. | [6] E. 485, 26. | [7] T.R. 387. | [8] Y.F.R. 161. |

future payment shall not be delayed beyond a fortnight at most. He says that once he paid Roger de Hirton, mason of the fabric, his wages for almost a fortnight, when he was absent all the time and had done no work. Also concerning money paid for drink. Also there was often removal of timber, stone and lime, and knows not where it went. The roofing of the church and the stonework suffer injury through lack of care. . . . The wardens of the work and also the workmen, though they seemed to be capable, often quarrelled, so that the work was often delayed and is endangered. The outer pilasters (*columpnulae*) which are called 'botraces' have for the most part perished for defect of covering. Also W. the carpenter is an old man and cannot work at high levels (*in altis*). It is ordered that another young man be employed in his place, and that the other old man shall supervise defects. The master of the masons appeared 11 January. He says that there are many of the masons who go against his orders, and also workmen who are not capable or fit for their work, and that some are so disobedient that he cannot restrain or punish them properly. Also that timbers, stone, lime, cement and so forth have frequently been made away with; and that there has been much misappropriation of stone from the quarry, and that almost nothing fit for the work is brought in. For lack of proper care and of roofing there is such a quantity of water that lately a lad (*famulus*) had almost been drowned; and these defects arise from the lack of lead roofing. Also he says that he cannot look after the work, workmen and other things as he ought, because he is interfered with by the Mayor, and he cannot view defects because Sir Thomas de Ludham alone has the keys to the doors of the fabric.

11 January. Will. de Wrsal, under-master of the works, says that the chief defect that he knows is that the cranes (*rotae*) at the west end of the church are rotten and worthless. The master of the carpenters says that he does not know any maladministration by the chamberlain except that he occasionally gives away a stone, and he thinks that he receives money for the gift. Also he thinks that the chamber which Richard de Melton made beside the church is useless and very injurious to the work and ought to be removed.

12 January, orders were given that no one shall interfere with the masons to appoint or remove them, except the master of the masons. Also that the master of the masons shall denounce to the Chapter those who are found disobedient or incorrigible. The said master shall take care that none of his masons receive more than he has earned by diligent work. . . . No mason shall in future claim any right beyond the usual salary due to him.

It is of some interest to notice that the craftsmen were not by any means an ideal 'happy family', but on the contrary were prone to quarrels. Nor did the Yorkshire masons mend their ways; for in July 1408 a commission was issued for an inquiry about conspiracies among the stone-cutters and other evil-doers of Yorkshire to hinder the work on the church of St.

Peter of York and to maim William Colchestre, mason, and other stone-
cutters and labourers taken by him for the work.[1] This followed on the
appointment, in the previous December, of the said William Colchestre,
mason, 'expert in that art and much commended', to rebuild the belfry
of the Minster, which by the carelessness of the stonecutters of the fabric
of that church had partly fallen down, and to supervise all the work on the
church, which was generally in a bad condition, and to take stone-cutters
and labourers for the work, whose wages would be paid by the Chapter.[2]
Colchestre apparently found his position impossible, and his appointment
was revoked in June 1410.[3] That masons were more quarrelsome than
ordinary men is not inherently probable, but that they were more ready
to support a fellow craftsman's quarrel is likely enough, as they certainly
combined on occasion, as we shall see, to enforce standard wages; and we
hear of a free fight, in August 1324, between seven monks of Westminster
and seven of their servants on the one side and a party of the king's masons,
of whom six are named, on the other. In the course of the fight Roger
Alomaly, one of the masons, was killed by Brother Robert de Kertlington,
who was possibly a connexion of the Abbot, William de Kertlington.[4]
The building accounts of Eton College, also, which are exceptional in
recording fines imposed on workmen for various offences, show that they
quarrelled among themselves, interfered with each other's work, and gave
a good deal of trouble in one way and another.[5]

Two important sets of regulations for the craftsmen employed at York
Minster have survived. The earlier of them, compiled in about 1352, is
written in Latin and runs, in translation, as follows:[6]

That the masons, carpenters and other workmen ought to begin to work, on
all working days in the summer, from Easter to Michaelmas, at sunrise and ought
to work from that time until the ringing of the bell of the Blessed Virgin Mary,
and then they should sit down to breakfast in the lodge of the works, if they
have not breakfasted, for the space (of time that it takes to walk) half a league;
and then the masters, or one of them, shall knock upon the door of the lodge,
and all shall at once go to their work; and so they shall diligently carry out their
duties until noon, and then they shall go to their dinner (*prandia*). Also in
winter, from Michaelmas to Easter, they shall come to their work at dawn and
everyone when he comes shall immediately start work, and so continue in the
said way until noon. From the feast of the Invention of the Holy Cross (3 May)
to the feast of St. Peter's Chains (1 August), they ought to sleep in the lodge

---

[1] *Cal. Pat.* 482.               [2] Ibid. 383.                    [3] Ibid. 199.
[4] Coram Rege R. 261, m. Rex 1.
[5] Willis and Clark, *Arch. Hist. of Cambridge*, i. 383.          [6] *Y.F.R.* 171–3.

after dinner; and when the vicars come out from the canons' hall (*mensa*) the master mason, or his deputy, shall cause them to rise from slumber and get to their work; and so they ought to work until the first bell for vespers, and then they shall sit and drink in the lodge, from the said first bell to the third bell, both in summer and winter. Also from the (1 August) to the (3 May), they shall return to their work immediately after their dinner, for which a reasonable time shall be taken, without waiting for the return of the vicars from the canons' hall; and so they shall work until the first bell for vespers and then they shall drink in the lodge until the third bell has rung, and shall return to their work, and so they shall work until the ringing of the bell of St. Mary's Abbey which is called le Langebell, namely, every working day from the feast of St. Peter's Chains to Michaelmas, and from Michaelmas to the said feast of St. Peter, they shall continue to work as long as they can see by daylight. Also each mason shall take less for the week in winter, that is from Michaelmas to Easter, than in summer by one day's wage. Also when two feast days happen in one week, each loses one day's wage (*dietam*) and when three occur, half that week. Also on vigils and on Saturdays, when they rest after noon, out of respect for the next day, then they shall work until noon strikes. Also the said two master masons and the carpenter of the works shall be present at every pay-day (*pacacione*), and there shall inform the warden and controller of the works of any defaults and absence of masons, carpenters, and other workmen, and according to his lateness (*moram*) or absence deductions shall be made from each man's wages, both for a whole day and a half day, as is reasonable. Also the said two master masons and carpenter, for the time being, ought faithfully to observe the said regulations, in virtue of the oath which they take, and they shall see that they are kept by the other masons and workmen working there, on pain of dismissal. And if anyone refuse to work in the said manner, let him be dismissed at once and not taken back again on to the works until he is willing to keep the rules in every detail.

The second set of ordinances was drawn up some twenty years later, about 1370, in English:[1]

Itte es ordayned by ye Chapitre of ye kirk of Saint Petyr of York yat all ye masouns yt sall wyrke till ye werkes of ye same kyrk of Saynte Petyr, sall fra Mighellmesse Day untill ye firste Sonday of Lentyn, be ilka day atte morne atte yare werke, in ye loge, yat es ordayned to the masounes at wyrk in with ye close bysyde ye forsayde kirk, als erly als yai may see skilfully by day lyghte for till wyrke; and yai sall stande yar trewly wyrkande atte yair werke all ye day aftyr, als lang als yai may se skilfully for till wyrke, yft yt be alle werkday; outher, elles, till itte be hegh none smytyn by ye clocke, when haly day falles atte none, sauf yt in with yt forsayde tyme bytwyx Mighelmes and Lentyne; and in all

---

[1] *Y.F.R.* 181.

other tyme of ye yer yai may dyne byfore none, yf yai wille, and alswa ette atte none whar yaim likes, swa yt yai sall noghte dwell fra yair werkes in ye forsayde loge natyme of ye yer in dyner tyme, bote swa schort tyme yat na skilful man sall fynde defaute in yaire dwellynge; and in tyme of mete, atte none, yai sall, na tyme of ye yer, dwell fra the loges, ne fra yaire werke forsayde, ovyr ye space of ye tyme of an houre, and aftyr none yai may drynk in ye loge: ande for yaire drynkyng tyme bytwyn Mighelmes and Lentyn yai sall noghte cese no lefe yare werk passand ye tyme of half a mileway: ande fra ye first Sonday of Lentyn untill Mighelmesse yai sall be in ye forsayde loge atte yaire werke atte ye son risyng, and stande yare trewely ande bysily wyrkande upon ye forsayde werke of ye kyrk all ye day, untill itte be namare space yan tyme of a mileway byfore ye sone sette, if itte be werkday; outher elles untill tyme of none, als itte es sayde byfore, saf yt yai sall, bytwix ye first Sonday of Lentyne and Mighelmes, dyne and ette, als es byfore sayde, ande slepe ande drynke aftyr none in ye forsayde loge; and yai sall noghte cese no lefe yair werk in slepyng tyme passande ye tyme of a mileway, no in drynkyng tyme after none passande ye tyme of a mileway. And yai sall noghte slepe eftyre none na tyme botte bytwene Seynte Elenmes and Lammes; and yf any mane dwell fra ye loge ande fra ye werke forsayde, outher make defaute any tyme of ye yer agayn yis forsayde ordinance, he sall be chastyde with abatyng of his payment, atte ye loking ande devys of ye maistyre masoun; and all yer tymes and houres sall by reweled bi a bell ordayned yare fore. Ande, alswa, it es ordayned yt na masoun sall be receavyde atte wyrke, to ye werk of ye forsayde kyrke bot he be firste provede a weke or mare opon his well wyrkyng; and aftyr yt he is foundyn souffissant of his werke, be receavyde, of ye commune assente of ye mayster and ye kepers of ye werk, and of ye mayster masoun, and swere upon ye boke yt he sall trewly and bysyli at his power, for oute any maner gylyry, fayntys, outher desayte, hald and kepe haly all ye poyntes of yis forsayde ordinance, in all thynges yt hym touches, or may touches, fra tyme yt he be receavyde till ye forsayde werke als lang als he sall dwell masoun hyryd atte wyrk till yt forsayde werke of ye kerk of Sanct Peytr, and noghte ga away fra yt forsayde werke bote ye maystyrs gyf hym lefe atte parte fra yt fersayde werk: and wha sum evyr cum agayne yis ordinance and brekes itte agayn ye will o ye forsayde Chapitre have he Goddys malyson and Saynt Petirs.

These regulations, it will be noticed, deal mainly with the hours of work. First there is the distinction between summer and winter, the dividing date being in each case Michaelmas at the one end, and in 1352 Easter or, in 1370, the First Sunday in Lent. The Statutes of Labourers similarly take Michaelmas and Easter as marking the division; but in actual practice the short days, with their correspondingly diminished wages, are almost always reckoned from All Saints (1 November) to the Purification (2

February). This is definitely stated at Vale Royal in 1278,[1] and at Westminster in 1332,[2] and it is proved in many instances by the wage rolls,
including York in 1327,[3] Exeter throughout the fourteenth century,[4] and
Hampton Court in 1530.[5] Not only were hours shorter about this period
of the year, but very often work practically ceased. On 23 November 1252
orders were given that 'because there are many more workmen in the
Castle of Windsor than is necessary, from whose work by reason of the
shortness of the days at this present time the king derives little profit,
the king wills that the greater part of them be discharged, together with
the painters who are in the same castle, whom the king wills to cease from
their work for a season, since they cannot work properly by reason of the
dampness of winter time'.[6] By way of contrast we may take the orders
issued in August 1243, that work on the king's chapel at Windsor shall go
on 'winter and summer' until it is finished,[7] which in itself implies that
such winter work was unusual. We have seen that the staff of workmen
employed at Westminster Abbey in 1253 was cut down by about 70 per
cent. in the middle of November;[8] and at Dover in 1300 all payments
cease from the middle of December for ten weeks, except to the master
mason, Nicholas de Eynho, who went on cutting stone;[9] and at Tonbridge
in 1325 the carpenters ceased work on 23 October 'on account of the
winter season'.[10]

That building operations should cease in the depth of the winter is
natural, and actually it is surprising to find how much work went on
uninterrupted. This raises the important, but very difficult, question of the
regularity of employment in the building trade. Wages, as we shall see,
were comparatively high; but without forming some estimate of the average
period of employment we cannot get much idea of the economic position
of the builders. The first complication is the astonishing fluidity of labour,
on which we have already commented. A hundred extra hands may suddenly appear on the payroll, only to be discharged at the end of a few weeks,
with nothing to show whence they came or whither they went. When the
names of the workmen are given week by week, if a name drops out there
is nothing to show whether he has gone to another job, possibly pressed
for the king's service in another part of the country, or has been discharged
and remains out of work. An elaborate analysis of existing rolls does not

---

[1] E. 485, 22.  [2] E. 469, 13.  [3] E. 501, 8.
[4] *Ex inf.* Prof. Hamilton Thompson.  [5] H.C. 241.
[6] Hope, *Windsor Castle*, i. 39.  [7] *Cal. Close*, 39.
[8] See above, p. 35.  [9] E. 462, 14.  [10] E. 485, 14.

seem likely to yield any very enlightening statistics.[1] As an example we may take one for work at Carisbrook Castle.[2] This begins in the middle of November 1335, when there were 18 masons, under Master Adam Breton. All of these were employed for 10 weeks; in the twelfth week Adam was succeeded by Master Richard le Taillour, and 8 names disappear and 4 fresh are found; by the beginning of March 1336, one of the new and 5 of the old names have gone and 5 more have come. The final list, in September, shows 4 of the original 18, 1 of the second, and 1 of the third batch, still working under Master Richard. An analysis of a Windsor account for 1365[3] shows that of the masons 20 were employed for 174 days, 5 for 132, 21 for 112, 27 for 102, 1 for 80, 11 for 45, 9 for 31, and 1 for 18 days. Of the layers (*positores*) on the same roll 32 worked for 202 days, 24 for 200, 35 for 122, 10 for 116, 2 for 104, 2 for 94, 14 for 70, 13 for 68, 2 for 57, 60 for 50, and 4 for 27 days. All that can be made of such figures is that employment was distinctly precarious, but that, as Professor Knoop says, 'there was a substantial nucleus of masons who remained more or less continuously in employment on a particular job'.

References to the loss of time through bad weather are less numerous than might be expected. At Walberswick, in 1337, on Monday 4 March 'the tilers could not work on account of the rain and storms';[4] and at Ludgershall in 1341 there was no work between 17 February and 11 March, 'because during this time there was a great storm of snow and ice, on account of which the workmen did no work'.[5] On the last Friday in March 1438 the workmen at All Souls College, Oxford, did not work '*quia pluvia pluebat*';[6] and in one week of 1503 the Lady Margaret's careful clerk of works at Collyweston paid 'wages of layers for v daies except a j$^d$ abbated of the same v dais wherof j day it reigned the space of ij hours'.[7] Generally, no doubt, work could be found in the lodge or under cover, as at Wallingford in 1390, where 12 masons were employed for 60 days on remaking part of the castle wall, 'and also on rainy days mending diverse and various defects in the castle buildings'.[8] At Westminster in 1532 we find 9 sawpits dug under cover[9] and 'a frame made ovir the newe gatehouse covered with canvas for workemen to worke drye under in all wethers'.[10]

---

[1] Since writing this I have had the pleasure of reading the detailed analyses of the accounts for Vale Royal Abbey, Carnarvon and Beaumaris Castles, and Eton College by Prof. Knoop and Mr. G. P. Jones, in *Ars Quatuor Coronatorum*, which, I think, bear out my conclusions.

[2] E. 490, 21.      [3] E. 493, 16.      [4] E. 469, 20.      [5] E. 476, 1.

[6] Rationarium.      [7] St. John's Coll., Cambridge, MS. vol. ii.

[8] E. 490, 4.      [9] T.R. 510.      [10] Ibid. 310.

The working day may be defined as theoretically from dawn to sunset. The intervals for rest and refreshment present some difficulties, particularly in the definition of what is meant by *hora nona*, the hour of 'none'. Originally this was the 'ninth hour' of the monastic day, which was divided into twelve 'hours' between sunrise and sunset. To simplify matters the monastic year was divided into summer and winter at the feasts of Easter and Michaelmas, the service of 'nones' being said about 3 p.m. in the summer and 2 p.m. in winter. For some reason, possibly hunger, from the general association of 'none' with the dinner hour, 'noon' became in popular parlance equivalent to midday, and this would appear to be the significance of 'high noon' in the York ordinances of 1370, by which the masons were to work 'tille itte be hegh none smytyn by ye clocke'. This is borne out by the Calais regulations[1] of a century later, in which the dinner hour is when 'xj [*sic*] of the clocke be stroken at none', work being resumed at 'one of the clocke'. On the face of it, it appears more reasonable to have the principal break and, in the height of summer, a siesta, in the middle and hottest part of the day. The question crops up again over the hour of stopping work on Saturdays and on the vigils, or eves, of feasts. An Act[2] passed in 1402 prohibited members of the building trades from receiving more than half a day's wage when they ceased work, on the eve of a festival, '*al heure de none*'. The Calais regulations show that on the eve of certain great festivals work stopped 'at xj of the clocke at none', but that on other eves and on Saturdays, which always counted as half-days,[3] men left work 'at iij of the clocke at after none'. If we can assume that the rules at Calais were those in general use, it would seem that on Saturdays the craftsmen did three-quarters of a day's work for half a day's pay. And one might suggest that the working day began by being identical with the religious, or monastic, day, perhaps because of the convenience of regulating it by the church bells ringing for the various services, and that when clocks became commoner[4] the more convenient arrangement of a midday meal came in. In fact 'none' was a vague term roughly equivalent to 'dinner time', which eventually identified itself with midday.

It may be noticed that in 1352 the York masons took their times from the minster bells, but in 1370 their hours were to be regulated by 'a bell

---

[1] See below.          [2] Stat. 4 Hen. IV, c. xiv.

[3] At Nottingham in 1357 the working week is reckoned '*usque in die sabbati post horam nonam*': E. 478, 4.

[4] In 1324 Master Thomas de Luda, Treasurer of Lincoln, presented a clock to the Cathedral, which lacked one although 'other cathedral and monastic churches in almost all countries possess one as a matter of course': *Giraldus Cambrensis* (R.S.), vii. 215.

ordayned yare fore'. In 1354 a bell, weighing 58 lb., 'to ring the hours for the workmen' at the Tower was bought,[1] and some two centuries later, in 1533, there is a reference to a bell in the White Tower 'the whiche calleth workemen to worke and fro worke'.[2] At Moor End, in 1365, 7s. 6d. was paid 'to William Belleʒhettere for a bell, weighing 18 lb., to ring at various times to stir up (*exittand'*) the masons, carpenters and other workmen there to hasten their work'.[3] At Carnarvon the place of the bell seems to have been taken by a horn in 1320, as Walter de la Grene was paid a penny a week 'for blowing the horn'.[4] And at Chertsey Abbey in 1538 we find 4d. paid 'for a howre glasse for the workemen to kepe thar howers by';[5] and similarly at Hampton Court in 1529 we read of 'a ronnynge glasse for the artyfycers to kepe ther wourking hours therbie'.[6]

While work normally stopped at dusk, there are instances of its continuing by artificial light. In 1365 three such instances occur: at Moor End 40 lb. of 'parys candel' were bought for the carpenters and others working at night by reason of the king's coming;[7] 370 lb. of Paris candles were bought at Windsor for carpenters and masons working at night by the king's orders;[8] and at Sheppey we find 125 lb. of candles 'to give light for the carpenters, glaziers, plumbers, and other workmen working at night'.[9] At Porchester in 1399 the candles are expressly said to be for the nights between All Saints and the Purification.[10] When a new draw-leaf had to be set up on London Bridge in 1406 the work was done at night, probably to avoid interference with traffic. Five labourers were paid 5½d. the night, and rewards were given—John Brawes, the master carpenter, receiving 10d., and other carpenters and masons smaller sums.[11]

For building operations at Westminster in 1532 tar was bought 'for making cressettes lightes and lynckes for workemen working by nyght'.[12]

At Salisbury Cathedral in 1479 candles were bought 'for men working at night and early morning (*aurora*)';[13] and in 1395 at Westminster Hall 76 lb. of candles were bought 'for men working before day between All Saints and the Purification'.[14]

---

[1] E. 471, 7.

[2] E. 474, 13. Cf. at Westminster in 1532 'the belle wherewith the workemen be ronge to worke': T.R., 11.

[3] E. 544, 31.

[4] E. 487, 3.

[5] E. 459, 22.

[6] H.C. 239, f. 126.

[7] E. 544, 31. 'Paris' candles were a superior variety.

[8] E. 493, 16.

[9] E. 483, 21.

[10] E. 479, 24.

[11] London Bridge Accts., i, f. 95.

[12] T.R. 230 & 312.

[13] Clerk of Works Accts.

[14] B.M. Add. Roll 27018.

The ordinances drawn up in 1474 for the masons and carpenters at Calais,[1] which was then regarded as part of England,[2] serve to illustrate several points that have already been referred to, though they also contain special regulations necessitated by the special circumstance of Calais being a seaport.

(If, by the oversight of the masters and wardens) eny of their felliship be ydell and have none occupation to besye them selfe upon in the Kynges workes That then the sayde masters or wardens and every of them in whom any suche defaute shalbe founde shall forfit for every halfe houre that any of the saide feliship is so founden ydell iiijd. and for every hole houre viijd. of their wages.

Also that every carpenter and mason and every laborer in the kynges workes from hensforthe shall be reddy at his werke dayly where he shall be assigned at suche houre and tyme as hereafter folouthe. That is to wete every workyng daye from the fest of mychaelmas unto our lady daye in Lent as sone and tymely in the mornyng as the daye appereth and as thei may see to werke and labor in the whiche he shall contynue unto xj of the clocke be stroken at none And to departe to his dynner, and by one of the clocke to be at his werke ageyne And so ther to abyde and labor as long as the day light will serve hym. And from our lady daye in Lent aboue saide unto the Fest of mychaelmas then next followyng dayly to be at his werke by halfe hour to v in the mornyng at the fardest And soo to contynye unto viij[th] of the clocke affore none And then to have and (*sic*) hole houre and no more to brekefast and to come ageyne to worke at ix of the clocke and there to abyde unto xj of the clocke and then to departe to his dynner and to be ageyne at his worke by one of the clocke afftre none and there to worke unto iij of the clocke at after none and then to go to drincke yf he wyll and to be ageyne at his werke by iiij of the clocke foloyng and so to contynue unto vij of the clocke at even be stroken.[3] Upon payne of every houre to lose one days wages to the kynges use. . . . And yf any laborer in the kynges workes be not dayly at his werke and kepe his houres affore lymyted he shall forfit and lose in lyke wyse for every di' houre jd. and for every hole houre ijd. to the kynges use.

Also the saide carpenters, masons and laborers shalbe bounde to worke and labor in all water workes as the tydes of the ebbyng water wyll serve theym unto at what tyme of the daye or the night, as any nede shall requyre dayly and

[1] E. 198, 6.

[2] The names of the workmen employed at Calais in 1441 are practically all English: E. 193, 4. In the same way, the masons who repaired the walls of Harfleur after Henry V captured it, in 1415, were brought 'from divers parts' of England: T.R. Misc. Bk. 79, f. 43.

[3] At Edinburgh in 1491, the masons worked from 5 to 8, then had half an hour for their 'disione' (*dejeuner*), going on again 'quhill that xj houris be strikken'. They resumed work at one o'clock, had half an hour's 'recreation in the commoun luge' at 4, and then worked till 7: Lyon, *Hist. of the Lodge of Edinburgh*, 37.

nightly as the case shall fall without any houres of Rest or respyte for that tyme to be taken. And suche tyme as thei may not worke for incresyng and aboundance of the waters to take theyr houres of Rest and Respit betwene the tyme and tyde as it is affore accordyng to the season of the yere that thei labor in.

(Any carpenter or mason disobedient to masters and wardens is to forfeit 2 days' wages and, after three warnings, to be dismissed.)

(No one is to do the work for another of the fellowship without reasonable excuse.)

And for as moche as the saide carpenters and masons must allwey be redye and attendant upon every sodayne casualtie Rage and Chaunce that may happen to fall as well to the water workes by salte water or fresshe water or other wyse what some ever it be as well uppon the holy dais as upon the workyngdais Therefore it is ordeyned that the sayde carpenters and masons shall be lycenced to leve worke every Saturnsdaie in the yere that is no even to any Principall fest at iiij of the clocke. And upon any even of pryncipall fest at none and upon any even that is Vygill at iiij of the clocke at after none accordyng to the rule of the satursdais And upon other sayntes dais hallowed nother even to pryncypall fest, Vygill ne satursdaye, to labor unto v of the clocke in Wynter from Mychaelmas to our lady daye in Lent and till vj of the clocke in somer season from our lady daye in lent at vij of the clocke and so unto mychaelmas folwyng.

Here after folouth the principall festes of the yere

| to leave worke at xj of the clocke at none | Cristmas daye Twelfe day Candelmas day Ester daye Ascention day Wytson day Trenitie Sonday | Corpus Christi day The Assumption day The Natyvitie of our lady Al hallow day The dedication daye of the Church Saynte Nicholas day |

Her'affter folouth the fests that have Vigilles[1]

| to leve worke at iiij of the clocke at after none | Saynt Matheas day Our lady in lent Mydsomer day Saynt Peters day Sante Thoms of Canterburye Saynt James day Saynt Lawrens day Saynt Matheuse day | Saynt Lukes day Saynt Symon & Jude Saynt Catheryne day Saynt Andreas day Conception of our Lady Saynt Thoms Inde Saynt Bartylmewe |

---

[1] At Dundee in 1536 the master mason 'sall werk all festual ewinnis that beis fastyn dais' till 4 pm., except on the eves of Christmas, Easter, Whitsun, and the Assumption, when he stopped work at 12: Lyon, op. cit. 28.

Her'affter folouth the holydais of the
yere which be nother principall festeis
nor Vygyll but meane holydais

| to leve | New Yeres day | ⎤ | ⎡ Saynt Mary Magdalene |
|---------|---------------|----|------------------------|
| worke at | Saynt Georges day | ⎥ | ⎢ Holly Rode day in harvest |
| vij of the | Saynt Markes day | ⎥ | ⎢ Saynt Edwardes daye |
| clocke in | May day | ⎥ | ⎣ Michaelmas daye |
| somer or | Holly Rode day | ⎥ | |
| v in wynter | in May | ⎦ | |

This official list of saints' days, as graded from the point of view of the workmen, is distinctly interesting. It will be noticed that in the first class is included the 'dedication day of the church', that is to say the day of the saint to whose honour the local church was dedicated. So in 1297 the workmen at Windsor did not work on Monday, 7 October, which was 'the feast of the dedication of the church in the township',[1] being St. Mark's day. Both Christmas and Easter were made the occasion of a brief holiday, varying from four days to a week. Thus at York in 1327 work stopped on 24 December and was resumed on the 28th,[2] while at Westminster in 1331 work was suspended from the 23rd to the 30th of December.[3] Occasionally other opportunities for holiday-making were seized, as on the birth of Edward, afterwards Edward III, on 13 November 1312, when the workmen at Westminster took a week's, apparently unauthorized, holiday.[4] On the other hand, as the Calais workmen had to be prepared to work on holidays if urgently required, so we find that in 1324 the smiths and carpenters worked on the feasts of St. Peter's Chair and St. Matthias (22 and 24 February) 'on account of the coming of the Queen';[5] and in 1347 money was given to the Westminster workmen for drinks because they worked throughout a feast day.[6] One of the earliest steps in the Reformation of the Church in England was an attack on the worship of saints, which enabled Henry to seize the treasure of their shrines and the employers to tighten up the hours of labour. Accordingly we find the Bishop of Exeter complaining in 1539 that artificers and labourers, for lack of spiritual instruction, leave their work every Saturday, after the right custom and usage of the Jews, from noon until evensong—the bishop ought to have known that Jews did not work even in the morning on Saturdays—smiths will not shoe a horse on St. Lewis' Day (he meant St. Eloy's), and

---

[1] E. 492, 13.     [2] E. 501, 8.     [3] E. 469, 11.
[4] Salzman, *More Medieval Byways*, 42.
[5] E. 469, 7.     [6] E. 470, 18.

fishermen will not fish on certain saints' days which had been abrogated. The clergy were ordered to point out to their parishioners that these abuses were contrary to the commandment of the sabbath day and to the king's injunctions.[1]

While the comparative frequency of festivals of the Church gave the medieval workman some rest from his labours, it also curtailed his wages rather seriously. Accordingly a custom early grew up by which those employed on royal building operations received wages for one day of every two holidays. This is explicitly stated in 1328:[2]

Note that on the Friday next following the 24th day of February was the feast of St. Matthias the Apostle, for which day the workmen seek and claim to have their wages by a custom of old standing, as they say; which custom is as follows: namely, that when any workmen, of whatever rank or craft they be, have been engaged on the King's works continuously for a fortnight or three weeks, a month, or more, and two or more feast days happen to occur within such time, exclusive of Sundays, the King always has one feast day, beginning with the first, and the workmen the other; so that the workmen shall receive from the King for every alternate feast day their wages full and complete, although they do not work on it, just as they would for a working day. And because the King had the day of the Purification of the Blessed Mary for the first feast day[3] the workmen claim this feast day as the second; and payment was made to them of their wages for that day.

That the workmen were correct in claiming that this was a long-established custom is shown by an order issued in 1251 for the appointment of two men of standing to act as overseers of the king's works at Bristol, in place of two others disqualified by poverty and ill health. Part of their duties was to pay the wages, and it is noted that, 'of festival days (*diebus feriatis*) one shall be reckoned to the King and one to the workmen'.[4] And this was done at Westminster Abbey two years later; e.g. 'The first week after Easter, containing the feast of the Apostles Philip and James on Thursday, which is the King's,' and the feast of the Invention of the Holy Cross on Saturday, which is the masons'.'[5] Nor was it confined to the royal works, as in Easter week of 1381 the Exeter Cathedral workmen were allowed 4½ days' wages, 'as is the habitual custom here and elsewhere, and in accordance with the agreement established between the Chapter

---

[1] *L. & P. Hen. VIII*, xiii (2), 342.
[2] E. 467, 6 (3).
[3] The regnal years of Edward III started on 25 Jan.
[4] *Cal. Close*, 432.     [5] E. 467, 1.

and the same workmen, that feast days ought to be equally divided between them'.[1] By the Statute of Labourers[2] as issued in 1360 no wages were to be taken for festivals, and this was repeated in 1402, with the addition that not more than half a day's wages should be paid when the men worked only up to 'none' on the vigil of a feast.[3]

[1] Oliver, *Exeter*, 385.  [2] Stat. 34 Edw. III, c. x.
[3] Stat. 4 Henry IV, c. xiv.

# IV

## WAGES

THE earliest attempt to regulate wages in the building trade appears to be that made in London in 1212, when the following scheme of maximum daily wages was drawn up:[1]

Carpenters—3*d*. and their food (*conredium*) or 4*d*. without food.
Masons (*caementarii*) and tilers, the same; their assistants, 1½*d*. or 3*d*.
Freemasons (*sculptores lapidum liberorum*), 2½*d*. or 4*d*.
Plasterers, daubers, and puggers (*dealbatores, luti appositores, et torchiatores*), 2*d*. or 3*d*.; their assistants, 1½*d*. or 2*d*.
Ditchers and men working with barrows (*civeriis*), 1½*d*. or 2½*d*.

It will be noticed that there were two scales, according to whether the workmen were fed by the employer or found themselves. As a rule nothing is said on this point in the pay rolls, but it seems to have been more usual to pay the higher rate and let the men find their own food. It will also be noticed that no distinction is made between summer and winter wages,[2] though the latter were, in later times, as a rule actually lower. At Vale Royal, for instance, in 1278, between 1 November and the beginning of February wages were reduced '*pro brevibus diebus*' by from 3*d*. to 5*d*. a week, and at York in 1327 they fell by a halfpenny a day during the same period. In 1332 at Westminster there is a special note that 'the wages of the plasterers and plumbers are not diminished like those of other workmen, which are cut down by 1*d*. a day from All Saints to the Purification'.[3] The reduction was not invariable: for instance, at Somerton Castle in 1335 there was no change in the weekly wages of the masons during the winter[4] and the wages paid to the permanent establishment at London Bridge in the fifteenth century also continued unchanged throughout the year. An apparent reversal of the usual practice is found in a Tower roll.[5] Here the masons were receiving 5½*d*. and labourers 3*d*. in September; then from All Saints to the Purification (just the period of the short days) their wages rose to 6*d*. and 4*d*. respectively, returning to their former level at the beginning of March. The explanation lies in the significant date of the roll—

[1] *Liber Cust.* i. 86.
[2] This may be because of the high purchasing power of money at this date. The deduction of a halfpenny would have been a serious matter for the workman.
[3] E. 469, 13.    [4] E. 484, 11.    [5] E. 471, 3.

1349–50. Wages had been forced up by the Black Death and had then been brought down again by the Statute of Labourers. Turning from the wages fixed to the wages actually paid during the thirteenth century we find carpenters at Dover in 1221 paid 3*d*. and masons from 2*d*. to 4*d*. a day. These *cementarii* were presumably roughmasons and layers, the free-masons (*cissores lapidum*) being paid by piece-work, at from 12*s*. to 13*s*. 4*d*. the hundred (= 120) blocks of stone.[1] In 1227 the Dover masons were receiving 3*d*. and 4*d*., although William Chancellor, 'the master of the masons', only received 3½*d*.; and the rate for cutting stone was 10*s*. the hundred, except that 12*s*. was paid to Gervase and John Long, '*melioribus incisoribus*'.[2] At Marlborough in 1237 Hugh Blouwe, master mason (*mazon*) was paid 5*d*., his help (*conductor*) 2½*d*., and another mason 3½*d*. Two mysterious *chuchatores* received 2½*d*.; and two women who carried stones and mortar were paid only 1*d*. a day.[3] Twenty years later, at Winchester, masons earned 16*d*. to 2*s*. the week, carpenters 4*d*. and 6*d*. a day, and labourers 1½*d*.[4] A fresh scale of wages[5] was drawn up in London about 1280, when Gregory de Rokesle was mayor.[6] In this the year was divided into four seasons and the rates for master (i.e. fully qualified) masons, carpenters, tilers, and plasterers was:

| | | | | |
|---|---|---|---|---|
| Michaelmas–Martinmas | 4*d*. in all, or | 1½*d*. and his food | | |
| Martinmas–Candlemas | 3*d*. ,, | ,, 1*d*. ,, | ,, | |
| Candlemas–Easter | 4*d*. ,, | ,, 1½*d*. ,, | ,, | . |
| Easter–Michaelmas | 5*d*. ,, | ,, 2*d*. ,, | ,, | |

Servants, mortarmen, and so forth, were to have 3*d*. in all between Easter and Michaelmas, and 2*d*. at other times. When the week was a full work-ing week they should have Saturday as a full day. 'At all solemn feasts when men fast', that is to say on the vigils preceding the greater festivals, they should have for a full day if they work till the evening (or vespers), but should take nothing for the feast day, when they do not work. Any-one paying higher wages should be fined. In all probability this ordinance was completely a dead letter. The disproportion between the alternative rates of pay, which were at the discretion of the employer, is gross: if a workman's food was worth 2*d*. to 3*d*. it is a little difficult to see what the unskilled labourer had for dinner on Sunday. Nor have I found any trace of a quadruple wage division of the year.

At Carnarvon in 1282 the master mason, Master Henry de Elreton, was

---

[1] E. 462, 8.      [2] Ibid. 10.      [3] E. 476, 3.
[4] E. 491, 14.      [5] *Liber Cust.* i. 99; ii. 542.
[6] Gregory de Rokesle was mayor in 1274–81, and 1285.

paid 14s. a week, and the same exceptional rate was paid to Master Walter de Hereford at Vale Royal in 1278, though we find Master Walter a few years later receiving only 7s. a week when in charge of works in north Wales. The same rate of 7s. a week was paid to the master in charge at Beaumaris in 1282 and to Thomas de Graham who was master of the masons enrolled, as sappers, for the Welsh campaign in 1277.[1] At Builth, in 1260, the master was paid 4s. 4½d., at Carnarvon in 1295, 3s. 3d., and at Cambridge in 1286 only 2s. 6d. The range of wages paid in the upper ranks of the craft was at this time extraordinarily wide; but one advantage that the master in charge seems always to have had was that his weekly salary was unaffected by holidays and the short days of winter. Master John de Walton, who was chief mason at York in 1327, is expressly said to receive 6d. a day '*tam festivale quam feriale*'. In the lower ranks of the masons also wages varied considerably. For instance, at Exeter during the early years of the fourteenth century there were usually five grades of pay: at 2s. 3d., 2s. 2d., 2s. 0d., 1s. 10d., and 1s. 8d. the week, falling in winter to 1s. 10½d., 1s. 9¾d., 1s. 8d., 1s. 6½d., and 1s. 5½d. respectively.[2] A survey of wages under Edward I may be taken from that king's works at Vale Royal, at Carnarvon, and in north Wales:

| | Vale Royal, 1278 | | Carnarvon, 1282 | | N. Wales, c. 1285 |
| --- | --- | --- | --- | --- | --- |
| | Summer | Winter | Summer | Winter | |
| **MASONS** | | | | | |
| Master . . . | 14s. | 14s. | 14s. | 14s. | 7s. |
| Under-master . | 3s. | 3s. | .. | .. | 4s. |
| Others . . . | 30d.–15d. | 25d.–12d. | 2s. 9d.–2s. 3d. | 2s. 3½d.–15d. | 2s. 6d.–2s. |
| Layers (*cubitores*) . | .. | .. | 2s. 4d.–14d. | 23½d.–15d. | 2s. 2d.–16d. |
| Quarriers . . . | 12d. | .. | 17d.–10d. | 14d.–9d. | 16d.–5d. |
| Quarriers, Master . | 18d. | .. | .. | .. | .. |
| Carpenters . . | 18d. | .. | 18d. | .. | 2s. 6d.–8½d. |
| Sawyers . . . | 12d. | .. | .. | .. | .. |
| Smiths . . . | .. | .. | 2s. 4d.–12d. | 2s.–12d. | 2s. 6d.–18d. |
| Plasterers . . . | .. | 9d. | .. | .. | .. |
| **LABOURERS** . . | 10d. | .. | .. | .. | 12d.–3d. |
| 'Vintenars' . . | 12d. | .. | 18d. | 16d. | .. |
| Barrowmen (*bayard*) . | .. | .. | 12d. | 10d.–9d. | .. |
| Hodmen (*hottarii*) . | .. | .. | 12d. | .. | .. |
| *Faukonarii*[3] . | .. | .. | 6d. | 5d. | .. |

[1] E. 485, 19.  [2] *Ex inf.* Prof. Hamilton Thompson.
[3] A 'falcon' appears to have been a kind of crane or windlass; these were, no doubt, the men who worked it.

These rates of pay remained in fairly general use for the next sixty years or so. The accounts for St. Stephen's Chapel at Westminster in 1331 show a master mason at 6s. a week, working masons at 5½d. a day, and an apprentice at 2d., while John Colyn, 'polysshere', employed on cleaning up marble, was paid only 3d. a day '*quia juvenis*'.[1] In another Westminster account, for 1348, the master mason and carpenter each received 7s., and their foremen 3s. 6d.; of the masons one had 6d. a day, 52 had 5½d., and four 5d.; 16 carpenters were paid at the rate of 6d., and their two apprentices 4d.; labourers received 3d. and 4d., and William Dachett, a lad (*pagettus*) assisting the plumbers, only 6d. a week.[2] He may rank with the *garcio qui vocatur portmater*,[3] paid 1d. a day at Edinburgh in 1338—a title which occurs earlier, in 1302, at Linlithgow, as a '*portemartel*'[4] with the same wage. The form just quoted suggests that he carried hammers, and doubtless other tools, for the workmen. There was at York in 1327 a *pagettus* of the carpenters who, for 'doing small jobs of woodwork and looking after their tools during dinner time', was paid 2½d. a day, while the carpenters themselves received 5d., masons 4½d., tilers, hodmen, and plasterers 4d., labourers 3½d., porters 3d., and night watchmen and women 2d.[5] The usual wage for women was only 1d. and they play but a small part in building operations, being usually employed on odd jobs such as collecting moss for the bedding of tiles or, as at Ludgershall in 1341, 'cleaning the rooms against the King's coming, and collecting bracken for the thatching of a lodge made for the carpenters, masons and other workmen'.[6] At Marlborough, however, in 1237, a workman roughcasting with sand was assisted by his daughter, and two women carried stones and mortar;[7] while at Martinstow in 1295 a woman was employed in throwing stones out of the quarry and helping to load them.[8] It is rather significant of conditions in Scotland that at Linlithgow in 1302, when 103 ditchers (*fossatores*) were employed, at 2d., no fewer than 140 women were working with them, at half their wage.[4] At a much later date we find female labour used to a considerable extent in Durham; in 1532, for instance, 'girls carrying mud for making a wall' were paid 1½d.,[9] and next year there were 'eight girls carrying stones' at 2d. a day.[10] Very exceptionally, women appear to have been put on an economic equality with men at Ripon, if we may judge from the fact that in 1392 a woman helping a dauber was paid 3d., which was the wage paid

[1] E. 469, 11.  [2] E. 470, 18.  [3] E. 482, 25.
[4] Ibid. 20.  [5] E. 501, 8.  [6] E. 476, 1.
[7] Ibid. 3.  [8] Ibid. 5.
[9] D.H.B. 181.  [10] Ibid. 279.

to a thatcher's mate (the dauber and thatcher each received 4*d*.),[1] and that in 1400 women were paid 4*d*. a day, when the wages of masons, carpenters, plumbers, and slaters were only 5*d*.[2]

When the Black Death swept away something like a third of the population of England, the scarcity of labour led to a natural rise in its value as expressed in wages and a further artificial rise due to the endeavour of the workmen to exploit the necessities of the employers. Parliament endeavoured to check this by passing, in 1349, the first Statute of Labourers, ordering that wages and prices should remain at their former levels. This having no effect, the Statute was re-issued in 1351, with a clause specially concerned with the building trade:[3]

Also, that carpenters, masons, and tilers and others that roof houses (*coverours de mesons*) shall not take by the day for their work, but in such manner as they were wont; that is to say, a master carpenter 3*d*. and an other 2*d*.; a master freestone mason (*mestre mason de franche pere*) 4*d*., and other masons 3*d*., and their servants 1½*d*.; tilers 3*d*., and their mates (*garceons*) 1½*d*.; plasterers and other workers of mud walls, and their mates, likewise; without meat or drink, from Easter to Michaelmas, and from that time less, according to the rate and discretion of the justices which be thereto assigned.

These figures correspond pretty well to the rates of wages recorded for 1342–6 by Thorold Rogers[4] and to those which we have quoted. At the same time the City of London issued a lengthy ordinance regulating wages and prices in a great variety of crafts.[5] This ordinance begins with the assertion of 'the damages and grievances which the good folks of the City, rich and poor, have suffered within the past year, by reason of masons, carpenters, plasterers, tilers, and all manner of labourers, who take immeasurably more than they have been wont to take'. It lays down, in the first place, that masons, carpenters, and plasterers shall take no more than 6*d*., without food or drink, for the working day in summer (from Easter to Michaelmas) and 5*d*. in winter. And on feast days, when they do not work, they shall take no wages; nor shall they have any allowance for the making and mending of their tools. Tilers should have 5½*d*. in summer or 4½*d*. in winter, their mates (*garsons*) receiving 3½*d*. and 3*d*. Master daubers should have 5*d*. and 4*d*. and their mates as those of tilers. Sawyers should rank with the masons and carpenters. Any workman taking more should go to prison for 40 days, and anyone paying higher wages should be fined 40*s*. It seems probable that it was owing to the City rate of wages being so

[1] R. 107.　　　　[2] R. 129.　　　　[3] Stat. 25 Edw. III, c. 2.
[4] *Hist. of Agriculture and Prices*, i. 317.　　　　[5] Riley, *Mems. of London*, 253–7.

much higher than the statutory that many workmen employed at West-minster Palace went off to work for other employers; so that in 1353 proclamation was made that they should be brought back and that no one should employ such men on pain of imprisonment.[1]

In 1360 the Statute of Labourers was stiffened up by increasing its penalties, and it was enacted that:[2]

Carpenters and masons are comprised in this ordinance, as well as all other labourers, servants and artificers. Carpenters and masons shall from henceforth take wages by the day and not by the week or in other manner; the chief masters of carpenters and masons shall take 4d. by the day, and the others 3d. or 2d., according as they be worth. And that all alliances and covines of masons and carpenters, and congregations, chapters, ordinances and oaths between them made or to be made shall be from henceforth void and wholly annulled. So that every mason and carpenter, of whatever condition, may be compelled by his master whom he serves to do every work that pertains to him to do, either in free stone or in rough stone; and also every carpenter in his degree. But it shall be lawful for every lord or other to make a bargain or covenant for their work in gross with such labourers or artificers as they please, so that they perform such works well and lawfully according to the bargain so made.

The chief interest in this enactment lies in its reference to the unlawful confederations and 'chapters' of the masons and carpenters, anticipating the special Statute of 1425, to which we have already alluded,[3] suppressing the annual congregations and 'general chapters' of the masons. Such evidence as we have suggests that such confederations were not the official act of the whole craft, but that individuals were active in taking measures to keep up wages. As early as January 1298–9 Walter de Maydenstan, carpenter, was charged with gathering a parliament of carpenters at Mile End, where they bound themselves by oath not to observe an ordinance recently issued by the City authorities touching their craft and wages.[4] And in 1306 John de Offington, mason, was said to have threatened the king's masons and carpenters, who were brought to London by Master Walter de Hereford, mason for the queen's work, that if they accepted less wages than other masons of the city they would be beaten; whereby the queen's work was left unfinished.[5] Again, in 1339 four carpenters were charged with making a confederacy to prevent 'foreign' carpenters coming to the city accepting less than 6d. a day and an after-dinner drink. It was

[1] Ibid. 271.  
[3] See above, p. 42.  
[5] Ibid. 251.  

[2] Stat. 34 Edw. III, c. ix.  
[4] *Cal. of Mayor's Court Rolls*, 25.

found that they had intimidated them, but they were acquitted on the specific charge of having beaten John de Chalfhonte, who had taken service with Richard Denys at a lower rate, and were bound over.[1] Something in the nature of a strike, justified in the circumstances, occurred at Westminster in 1331, when it is noted, on Monday, 13 January, that 'the masons would not work on Monday or Tuesday, because they were in arrear of their wages since Christmas and they thought that they would lose those wages, until the Lord Treasurer promised that they should be fully paid for time past and future, and then they began to work on Wednesday'.[2]

Coming down to a much later period, we read that in August 1535 the men employed on works at Dover had elected a leader and refused to work for less than 6*d.* a day, saying that he that touched one of them should touch all. This strike, however, collapsed with the arrest of four of the ringleaders.[3]

In view of the enactments which have been quoted, it will be of interest to examine some examples of wages actually paid. A series of accounts for work on the royal palace at Woodstock may be given first:

|              | 1346 | 1351 | 1354 | 1357 | 1365 | 1380 |
|--------------|------|------|------|------|------|------|
| Mason .  . | 2*d.* | 2½*d.* | 3*d.* | 3*d.* | 5*d.*–3*d.* | 6*d.*–3½*d.* |
| Carpenter .  . | 3*d.* | 3½*d.* | 4*d.* | 4*d.* | 5*d.*–4*d.* | 5*d.*, 4*d.* |
| Tiler .  . | 2*d.* | 2½*d.* | 3*d.* | 3*d.* | 4*d.* | 6*d.*–3*d.* |
| Plumber .  . | 4*d.* | 6*d.*, 4*d.* | 6*d.* | . . | 5*d.* | 6*d.*–4*d.* |
| Plumber's mate . | . . | . . | . . | . . | 3*d.* | . . |
| Sawyers .  . | . . | 3½*d.* | . . | 4*d.* | 4*d.* | 5½*d.*–4*d.* |
| Labourers .  . | . . | 2*d.* | 2*d.* | 2*d.* | 3*d.* | 3*d.* |

The wages roll for Sheppey Castle in 1362 shows the chief mason as receiving 12*d.* a day, 83 other masons at from 6*d.* to 4*d.*, 185 masons layers at 5*d.* and 4*d.*, with two others, evidently gangers, at 6*d.*, 173 carpenters ranging from 6*d.* to 3*d.*, and 600 labourers at 3*d.* and 2*d.* For 1365 we have accounts at Westminster: master mason 12*d.*, foreman (*apparitor*) 6*d.*, others 6*d.* in summer and 5½*d.* in winter, carpenters at the same rates, and labourers at 3½*d.* and 3*d.*; Wallingford: the master mason at 4*s.* a week, and the master carpenter at 3*s.*, other masons, layers, and carpenters at 5*d.* and 5½*d.* the day; Windsor: master mason at 7*s.* and foremen at 3*s.* 4*d.* the week, other masons—56 at 6*d.*, 32 at 5½*d.*, and 3 (possibly apprentices) at 4½*d.*–3*d.*, layers—8 at 6*d.*, 13 at 5½*d.*, 207 at 5*d.*, and 24 ranging from 4½*d.*

[1] *Cal. of Pleas & Memo. Rolls*, i. 105.　　　　　[2] E. 469, 11.
[3] *L. & P. Hen. VIII*, ix. 110.

to 3*d*. All these figures are presumably exclusive of food; at Ely in 1360 the masons were paid from 2*s*. to 3*s*. a week '*ad mensam propriam*'.[1] The same rates were in force at York for the masons and carpenters in 1371, labourers for the most part receiving 16*d*., with an additional 3*s*. 4*d*. *pro tunica* if they served for a whole year.[2]

Breaches of the Statutes of Labourers were frequent. At Nottingham we have a specific instance in 1395, when Richard Masson, 'leyer', took from John Blyth, butcher, 12*d*. for working two days as a mason, against the assize; and at the same time, we are told that all the carpenters, tilers, and labourers were taking too much daily for their craft.[3] Contemporary evidence at Oxford, covering the period 1390–6, suggests that the members of the building trades habitually took excessive wages and paid a fine of about 8*d*.–12*d*. once a year[4]—just as all brewers of ale seem invariably to have broken the assize. There is a particularly interesting entry among these Oxford records for 1391:

As to John Sampson, for that he is a master freestone mason and extremely knowledgeable and skilful in that art and in carving (*entaille*), and because the takings of such masons cannot be put on a level (*assederi*) with the takings of other masons of another grade and rank in depth of knowledge and judgement of that art, by the discretion of the Justices he was discharged.[5]

On the issue of the Statute of 1425 against the masons the authorities, at least in London, seem to have made a spasmodic effort to enforce the legal scale. The London Bridge accounts show that on 10 February, 'on account of the King's orders for the new execution of the Statute of Labourers', wages were cut down; five of the masons received 3*s*. 4*d*. instead of 3*s*. 9*d*. and one 2*s*. 9*d*. instead of 3*s*., while their servant remained at 2*s*. At Michaelmas, however, the chief masons and carpenter, who were paid at the same rate as their fellows but had a yearly fee of 20*s*., had their fees raised to 26*s*. 8*d*. 'on account of the reduction of their wages'. By the following March wages were back at their old rate, and in the January of next year they had risen to 4*s*., while the chief mason, Richard Becke, was drawing an additional 2*s*. 6*d*. for one '*servo suo cementario*' and 1*s*. 6*d*. for another, presumably apprentices.

The next regulation of importance was the Statute of 1446[6] fixing the wages of a freemason or master carpenter at 4*d*. with food or 5½*d*. without in summer and 3*d*. or 4½*d*. in winter. For a master tiler, slater, roughmason,

[1] *Sacrist Rolls*, 194.   [2] *Y.F.R.* 4, 5.
[3] *Recs. of Nottingham*, i. 275.   [4] *University Archives* (O.H.S.), ii. 1–125.
[5] Ibid. 21.   [6] Stat. 23 Hen. VI, c. xii.

or 'mesne' carpenter 3*d*. or 4*d*. in summer and 2½*d*. or 4*d*. in winter. For labourers 2*d*. or 3½*d*. in summer and 1½*d*. or 3*d*. in winter. It is added that those who desire less shall take less, and that no wages shall be paid for festivals, and on work days only according to the amount of time worked. It is worth noticing that a day's food for a craftsman is reckoned at 1½*d*., which suggests that the unskilled labourer, unless in constant work all the year round, can have had little margin for luxuries, such as a wife and children, or even for necessaries, such as clothes. Some fifty years later, in 1495, another Act[1] was passed, by which the wage for a freemason, master carpenter, roughmason, bricklayer, master tiler, plumber, glazier, carver, or joiner, was set at 4*d*. with meat and drink or 6*d*. without in summer, and in winter, 3*d*. and 5*d*. respectively. This Act also regulates the hours of labour. From mid-March to mid-September work was to begin by 5 o'clock; there was to be half an hour for breakfast, 1½ hours for dinner and sleep, when sleep was permitted, which was from the middle of May to the middle of August, or else one hour for dinner and half an hour for 'nonemete'; and work was not to stop till between 7 and 8 o'clock. From mid-September to mid-March every workman was 'to be at thar werke in the springing of the day and departe not till nyght of the same day'. It is worth noting, in view of what has been said about the tendency of the workmen to violence, that there is a clause that if any workman employed on building or repairs 'make or cause to be made any assemble to assaute harme or hurte any persone assigned to comptroll and oversee theym in their working' he shall be imprisoned for a year. As in the previous Statute, these are maximum wages and where less had been usually paid the lower rate should continue. It will be noticed that the wages are higher than fifty years before, but it is significant that the cost of a day's food is now put at 2*d*., so that the purchasing value of the wages was pretty nearly stationary. This allowance agrees with the practice at Cambridge, where the King's Hall accounts show that the cost of food for the workmen was 2*d*. a day, or 11*d*. for the week of 5½ days—except that the master was allowed double. Thus for a week in 1431 we have:[2]

| | | | | | |
|---|---|---|---|---|---|
| The chief mason for food | | 22*d*., | for salary | 3*s*. | |
| 2 hewers | ,, | 22*d*. | ,, | 4*s*. 8*d*. | |
| 4 'leyers' | ,, | 3*s*. 8*d*. | ,, | 7*s*. 8*d*. | |
| 4 labourers | ,, | 3*s*. 8*d*. | ,, | 5*s*. 0*d*. | |
| 4 carpenters | ,, | 3*s*. 8*d*. | | | |
| 4 slaters | ,, | 3*s*. 8*d*. | ,, | 6*s*. 0*d*. | |

[1] Stat. 11 Hen. VII, c. 22.         [2] K.H. 8, 24.

The rates here given agree pretty well with the rates of wages fixed in 1446; and Thorold Rogers's table of average wages[1] shows that throughout the fifteenth century and down to 1539 the daily wage of a skilled labourer was about 6*d.* and that of an unskilled man about 4*d.*, which agrees with the evidence that I have collected from other sources. At Ripon in 1400 we have carpenters at 6*d.* and 5*d.*, masons, daubers, slaters, and plumbers at 5*d.*, most of them receiving an extra allowance for drinks;[2] and in 1420 carpenters at 6*d.* and 5*d.* and their apprentices at 4*d.*, sawyers at 7*d.*, glaziers at 6*d.*, slaters 5*d.*, daubers and labourers 4*d.*[3] The 43 freemasons at Eltham in 1479 were paid 6*d.* a day, one 'hardehewer' received 7*d.* and two others 6*d.*, and 4 'setters' 4*d.*, all being under a 'warden' who was paid 10*d.*[4] The carpenters had a chief warden at 10*d.*, and two under-wardens at 8*d.*; 43 others received 6*d.*, and two 'prenteyces' 4*d.*; smiths and plumbers were paid 6*d.* and labourers 4*d.* The Westminster accounts for 1532[5] show the master mason receiving 12*d.*, the foreman 8*d.*, the master carpenter 12*d.*, and his foreman 10*d.*; other masons and carpenters received from 8*d.* to 6*d.*, except certain men engaged in carving stone at 10*d.*; plasterers, daubers, tilers, and plumbers were paid 8*d.* and 7*d.*, sawyers 6*d.*, and labourers, of whom there were nearly 500, 5*d.* and 4*d.* Of the workmen employed on Wolsey's College at Oxford in 1526[6] the two masters received the 12*d.* a day which had been the normal rate since the thirteenth century; the wardens or foremen of the masons and setters were paid 3*s.* 8*d.* a week, other freemasons and hardhewers receiving 3*s.* 4*d.*; rough-layers 6*d.* a day, and their foreman 7*d.*; the master carpenter 12*d.* and others 6*d.* It is worth noticing that at Hampton Court in 1530, while the wages of the setters and of the 'lodge men'—defined as 'free masons . . . werkyng in fre stone uppon dores wendowes coynes for butteres and gresses (steps)'—are reduced by 4*d.* a week from the beginning of November to the end of January, the wages of the two apprentices remain constant at 3*d.*[7] In other instances, as at Chester in 1512[8] and at Warblington in 1518,[9] no reductions occur during the winter.

Mention should be made of the fact that sometimes the demand for agricultural labour during the harvest is reflected in the building trade by a temporary rise in wages. Thus at Cambridge in 1286 the masons' weekly wage of 18*d.* rises to 22*d.* during harvest;[10] at Wallingford in 1365 the labourers are paid 3*d.* a day, except during the four weeks of harvest, when

---

[1] *Hist. of Agriculture & Prices*, ii. 514–20.  
[2] R. 129.  
[3] R. 145.  [4] E. 496, 21.  [5] T.R. *passim*.  [6] E. 479, 11.  
[7] H.C. 241.  [8] E. 488, 12.  [9] E. 490, 12.  [10] E. 459, 15.

they receive 4*d*.;[1] and at Bardfield Park in 1344 the labourers, among whom the name of John Schakespere catches one's eye, have 2*d*. before August and 3*d*. during that month, and even the women carrying straw for thatching are paid 2*d*. 'because it was in August'.[2] We also find during the sixteenth century occasional instances of payment for overtime. As work did not end until light failed, such overtime could only be taken from the time which the workmen were entitled to take for rest and refreshment. At Oxford in 1526, when Wolsey's College was in building, 22*s*. 7*d*. was given 'in rewardes to dyverse laborers and playsterers for working in theire howre tymes'.[3] At Chertsey Abbey we find, in 1538, 'fre massons workyng howre tymys and drynkyng tymys for the hasty expedyscyon of certen wydows [*sic*] and dores to Ottlandes, at 1d the howre'.[4] Similarly the Westminster accounts of 1532 show masons, hard-hewers, and carpenters 'working their respite houres after the rate of jd everye houre', while labourers were paid a halfpenny.[5] Details are given of the times worked. Thomas Faunte, warden of the masons, worked 80 extra hours in the month, 18 other masons put in extra time varying from 29 to 10 hours; of the hardhewers the warden put in no less than 112 hours, 5 others 106 hours, and 6 from 50 down to 2; of the carpenters the warden, John Russell, is credited with 60 hours, 6 others working from 15 to 4 hours. It would certainly seem that at Westminster the wardens followed the precept laid down in the ordinances of the Torgau masons in 1462, that 'the warden shall be the first to arrive at the lodge and the last to leave' and shall set an example of industry.[6]

Apart from overtime payments, gifts were often made to encourage industry. At Ely in 1323 Robert the painter was given a shilling 'out of courtesy (*ex curialitate*)',[7] and next year John of St. Ives, carpenter, was paid a yearly fee of 13*s*. 4*d*. and an extra 2*s*. 'out of courtesy because he had done much work'.[8] At Langley in 1368 the workmen were given 3*s*. 4*d*. between them 'of courtesy';[9] and at York in 1371 we find: 'Given to the masons on the *pleghdai* (the day on which they were sworn in), of courtesy, by custom, 20s. And to 6 carpenters on the same day, of courtesy, 2s.'[10]

---

[1] E. 490, 2. The carpenters at Tonbridge received an extra halfpenny *pro tempore autumpnali* in 1325: E. 485, 14.

[2] E. 458, 4.    [3] E. 479, 11.    [4] E. 459, 22.

[5] T.R. 332–57. Next year, at Hampton Court the carpenters were working in their hour times and drinking times 'for the hasty expedicion' of the hall; 9 hours were reckoned as a full day, which was paid for at from 6*d*. to 8*d*.: H.C. 237, f. 125.

[6] Gould, *Hist. of Freemasonry*, i. 139.    [7] *Sacrist Rolls*, 29.

[8] Ibid. 44.    [9] E. 466, 4.    [10] Y.F.R. 5.

At Cambridge in 1475 the sum of 8*d*. 'was bestowed on the masons to drink, so that they may be more willing (*benevoli*) to work on the Schools';[1] and two years later a whole twopence was expended, partly on the purchase of paper and partly 'on labourers that they may be willing';[2] let us hope that they did not spend it all on drink, and that they were duly inspired with benevolence towards the givers! At the sister university in 1509 the authorities of Magdalen College spent 4*s*. 'for drinks (*bibaciis*) given to the carpenters and tilers that they may sweat (*insudarent*) more diligently at their work'.[3] At Ely, where in the first half of the fourteenth century the monks paid low wages but provided food, gifts 'of courtesy' were frequent, and allowances for drink were customary. Thus in 1323 some £71 is entered for 'the wages and fees of various masons . . . with their drinks in summer',[4] and in 1342 the masons were allowed 1*d*. a week for drinks from 23 April to 8 September;[5] while at Canterbury in 1436 Richard Clark, mason, was paid 'for two weeks, including drinks', 6*s*.[6] The Leicester borough accounts record in 1326 the expenditure of 1*s*. 3½*d*. on 'ale given to Master Peter of Bagworth and other masons at various times, and for the ale which is called Closinghale'.[7] It may be suggested that this was drink supplied when the roof of a building was 'closed'— always an occasion for celebrations. Similarly at Bath in 1425 gloves were given to the mason and 2*d*. spent on drink 'at the completion of the two arches' of a new chapel in St. Michael's.[8]

The Statute of 1495, as we have seen, allows the workmen half an hour for their 'none-mete'. This was clearly an auxiliary meal, a snack, and from the context was probably taken in the afternoon; it may, indeed, be equivalent to the vesper pause for refreshment referred to in the York ordinances. In its usual form of 'nuncheon' it occurs frequently and may well have been as vague a term as the modern 'lunch', which can be either a full midday meal or mere 'elevenses'.

The King's Hall accounts for 1342 record 4*d*. spent 'on bread and ale for the *nonsenchis* of the sawyers'; at Oxford in 1372 we have '*pro nonshyns ad eosdem stonemasons*', 3*d*.;[9] and at Wallingford in 1390 ale to the value of 10*d*. was provided for the masons and labourers for 'noensshynches'.[10] A

---

[1] *Grace Book A*, 112.  
[2] Ibid. 131.  
[3] *Magdalen College Reg.* (N.S.), i. 66.  
[4] *Sacrist Rolls*, 34.  
[5] Ibid. 122.  
[6] Bodl. MS. Top. Kent, c. 3, f. 148.  
[7] *Leicester Recs.* i. 351. The community was fined 3*s*. 4*d*., apparently for not having supplied Master Peter with a robe until he sued them for it: ibid.  
[8] *Somerset Arch. Soc.* xxiv. 32.  
[9] *Hist. MSS. Com. Rep.* ii. 140.  
[10] E. 490, 4.

carpenter working on a mill and a latrine at Canterbury in 1398 was given 'nonschenchis';[1] and the account of certain repairs done in London in 1422–3 allows 3 carpenters a halfpenny 'for her noonchyns every day to eche of hem' and gives the wages of a 'hewer of freston' as 8*d*. with a further 2*d*. 'for his noonchyns yn ye forsaide (7) dayes, wt reward'.[2] Probably the 'metesilver' paid to carpenters working on Newgate gaol in 1282[3] was equivalent to nuncheon money. The churchwardens' accounts of St. Mary-at-Hill (London) for 1428 record[4] 'for the none mete on the morwe of iij carpenters and ij plomers, a sholdere and a brist of moton— 4½*d*; on the morwe when they helyd the porche, for a rib of bef—3*d*; also bred and ale—2*d*'. Those of St. Edmund's, Salisbury, for 1483 mention 4*d*. spent 'for the carpenter is none metys and for is drynkyng xviij daysse',[5] and in 1421 the London bridgewardens paid 3*s*. 4*d*. 'to all the masons and carpenters for their Shrovetide feast, as is customary'.[6]

Finally we have miscellaneous gifts and perquisites which helped to eke out the earnings of the builders. As the master builders received furred robes,[7] so their subordinates often were given those articles of clothing which constituted the uniform of their trade. At York in 1423 we find: 'For two skins given to the masons called setters to make *naprons* of, by custom, 12*d*. For 10 pairs of gloves given to the same at the time of setting stones, 18*d*.'[8] In 1499 is a similar payment 'for 2 aprons (*limatibus*) and 2 pairs of gloves for masons for the settyng'.[9] So also the authorities of King's Hall in 1431 provided not only robes for the master mason at Christmas but a striped (*stragulata*) gown for the chief carpenter and hoods (*capuciis*) for two layers; also gloves for the plumber, and 9 belts (*zonis*) for workmen;[10] while next year 3 hoods were bestowed on a carpenter and two layers;[11] and in 1428 they provided, at a cost of 12*d*., 2 'napronys' of leather and 2 pairs of gloves for the chief and second mason.[12] Twelve pairs of 'lether bootis', at 2*s*. 8*d*., were provided in 1532 for labourers working in the water at Westminster.[13] We also find the bridgewardens paying 4*s*. a pair *'pro ocreis vocatis bothes'* for the members of their establishment in

---

[1] *Hist. MSS. Com. Rep.* ix. 137.

[2] *Gent. Mag.* 1830 (2), 592.

[3] E. 459, 27.

[4] *Memorials* (E.E.T.S.), 71.

[5] Swayne, *Churchwardens' Accounts—Sarum*, 33.

[6] Bridge Accts., vol. iii.

[7] A carpenter engaged by Sir John Howard in 1467 was to have not only a gown for himself but also a 'kirtelle cloth' for his wife: *Household Expenses* (Roxburghe Club), p. 400.

[8] *Y.F.R.* 50. For a similar entry in 1404, see ibid. 25.

[9] Ibid. 92.

[10] K.H. viii. 26, 29.

[11] Ibid. 62.

[12] K.H. vii. 210.

[13] T.R., f. 408.

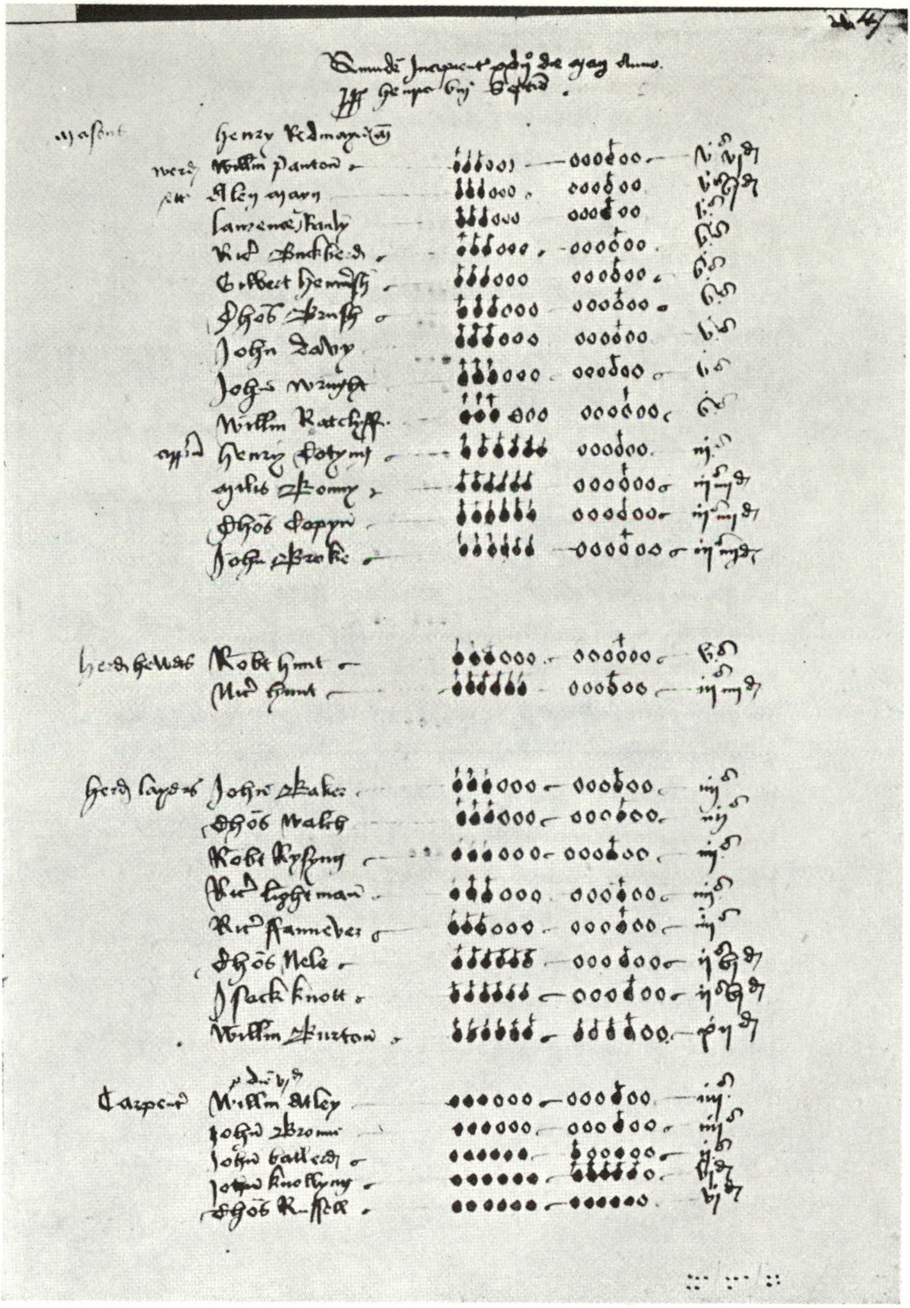

WAGES SHEET: 22 MAY–2 JUNE 1525

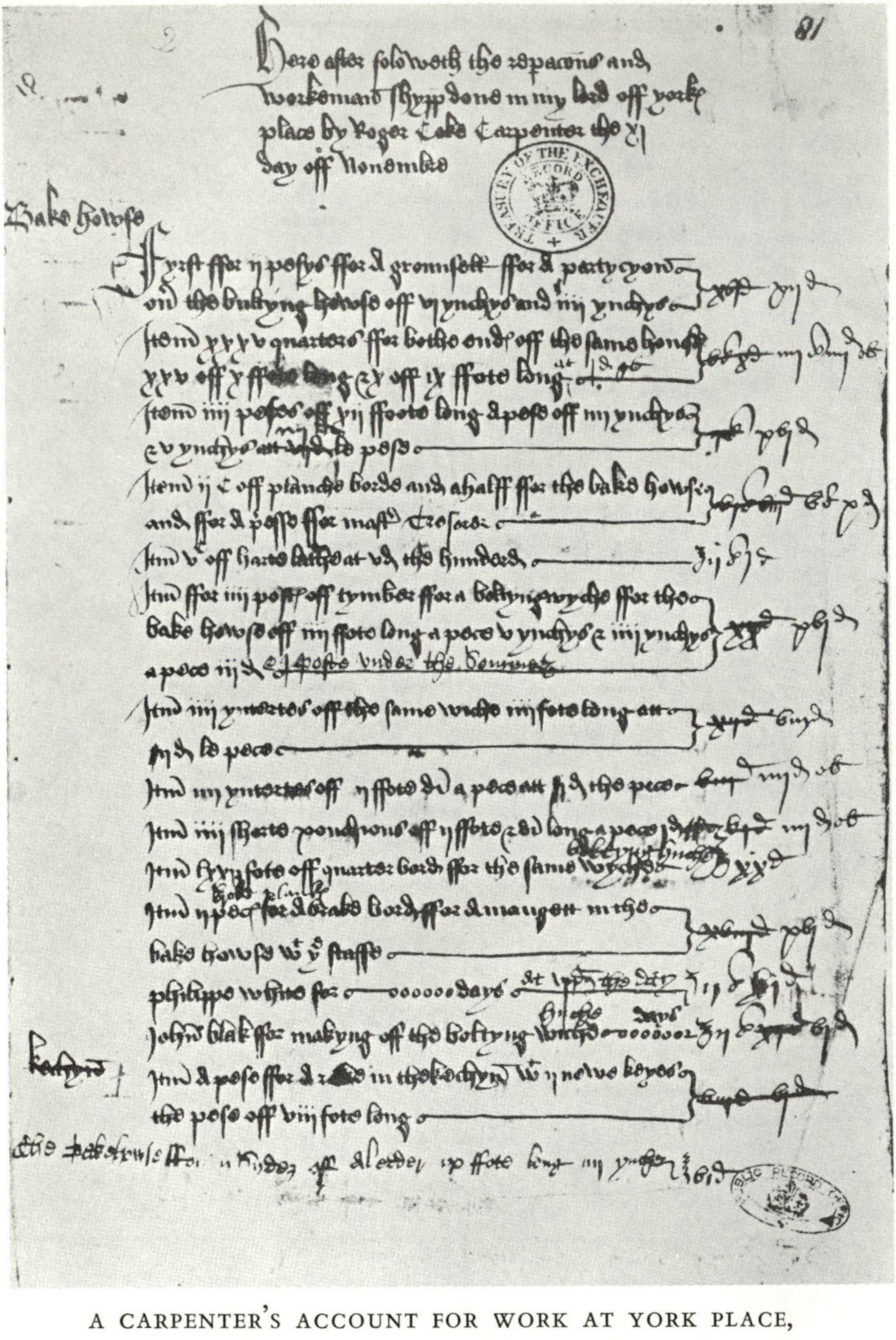

PLATE 9

A CARPENTER'S ACCOUNT FOR WORK AT YORK PLACE,
LONDON, 1515

1382;[1] and in July 1411, possibly during a heat wave, they bought 12 'strawhattes' for their masons.[2] The masons working on All Souls College, Oxford, in the summer of 1439 were also presented with gloves and straw hats (*caleptris strameninis*);[3] and forty years later 2s. 6½d. was expended on hats and gloves given to the masons layers and others engaged in building Tattershall College.[4]

[1] Bridge Accts., Roll 1.

[2] Ibid., vol. i, f. 331.

[3] *Rationarium.*

[4] Penshurst MS. 216.

# V

## FOUNDATIONS, WALLS, WINDOWS, FIREPLACES

WHEN the dimensions and general design of the building had been decided the first business of the mason in charge would be to stake out the main lines and to prepare the foundations. After the fall of the tower at Ely in 1321, we are told that Alan de Walsingham 'measured out in eight divisions the place where he thought to build the new tower; and he set workmen to dig and search for the foundations of the eight stone columns whereupon the whole building should be supported . . . until at last he found solid and secure ground. Then, when these eight places had been carefully dug out and firmly founded with stones and sand, at last he began those eight columns.'[1]

The contract for the making of the bastions (*boccarum*) of the twin towers to the gate of Chester Castle in 1291 stipulates that they are to be '*a profundo rochee infra terram*', up to the level of the bridge, 30 feet.[2] And at Wallingford an agreement was made with David Diker to dig the foundations for a building to be set up in the castle to the depth of 10 feet below the ground and 6 feet in breadth, the measure all round being 81 feet. He was also to dig foundations for the pit, or underground prison for felons, 15 feet below ground and 4 feet broad, this being 24 feet round.[3] Usually, however, we get little more information than is given, for instance, in the Woodstock accounts for 1256, where six workmen are paid 'for searching for and making the foundation'.[4]

An account of the building of Boston Church, with its famous 'stump', written in the eighteenth century but evidently copying an earlier record,[5] says:

The foundation whereof on the Monday after Palm Sunday, anno 1309, in the 3rd year of Edward the 2nd, was begun by many miners, and continued till Midsummer following, when they were deeper than the haven by 5 foot, where they found a bed of stone upon a spring of sand, and that upon a bed of clay whose thickness could not be known. Upon the Monday next after the Feast of St. John Baptist was laid the 1st stone by Dame Margery Tilney, upon wch. she laid £5 sterling, Sr. John Tructdale then Parson of Boston gave £5 more,

---

[1] See above, p. 6.     [2] E. 486, 7.     [3] E. 490, 7.
[4] E. 497, 12.     [5] Britton, *Arch. Antiq.* iv. 90.

and Richd. Stevenson a Mercht. of Boston gave also £5, wch. was all the gifts given at that time.

And William Botoner of Worcester, writing about 1480, gives the depth of the foundations of the tower of St. Stephen's, Bristol, as 31 feet below ground-level;[1] he also says that when houses were built near the cemetery of St. Stephen's the foundations were so bad that they had to dig down to a depth of 47 feet.[2]

Unless the foundations were carried down to actual rock, the trench dug out would be filled to a variable depth with rough stone, &c. to form a footing of somewhat greater breadth than the wall to be raised upon it. At Nottingham we have 24 loads of 'fyllingstones' supplied for foundations in 1367.[3] At Winchester in 1258 we find 80 workmen employed at the chalkpit for a week winning chalk for foundations;[4] and at Shene in 1369 John Robyn of Greenwich was paid 18s. for two freightages of his ship, each time with 18 tuntights (*pond' dol'*) of 'stones called Shalke for the foundation of the walls'.[5] At Westminster three carts were employed to carry gravel (*gravellam*) for foundations in 1292,[6] while in 1532 the foundations of a brick wall were made of 'stone, flynte, chaulk and brick battes'.[7] The orders for the rebuilding of Eton College Chapel, in about 1453, specify that the first course of the 'growndes', or footings, shall be of flat Yorkshire stone, carefully laid; next a course of Yorkshire and Teynton stone mixed, and on this blocks of Teynton stone, 'heath-stone', and flints, set in 'good and myghty morter made with fyne stone lyme and gravell sonde'. No chalk, brick, or Reigate stone was to be used.[8] The footings on the south side were to extend beyond the wall proper by 2 feet more than on the north side, but the extent of the projection on the north is not stated. The foundations of Little Saxham Hall in 1505 were 'to be wrought with calion (i.e. flint) and brick, for foreyns (i.e. offsets) and other necessaries . . . and so to bring it a yard above the ground there to be finished with a tabill of stone, inward and outward'.[9]

In marshy districts and other places where there was neither rock nor reasonably firm ground to build upon, steps had to be taken to improve the conditions. When the first attempt was made to build a tower at Ramsey, in the tenth century, the builders contented themselves with beating the ground as hard as they could 'with frequent blows of rams'; but

---

[1] *Itinerarium*, 282.                [2] Ibid. 268.                [3] E. 478, 7.
[4] E. 491, 14.                [5] E. 494, 7.                [6] E. 468, 6.
[7] T.R. 613.                [8] Willis and Clark, *Arch. Hist. of Cambridge*, i. 367.
[9] Gage, *Thingoe Hundred*, 140.

when this had proved fatally insufficient and they had to start all over again, they dug a deep hole, which they filled with a mass of stones, rammed tight and bound together with a strong mortar.[1] At Bardfield Park in 1344 two men were employed, 'making the place for the new house, and making a bridge over the water, and ramming (*rammand*') the foundations of the said house'.[2] A more usual plan was to drive in piles, and Horman in 1519 says:[3] 'A quavery or maris and unstable foundacion must be holpe with great pylys of alder, rammed downe, and with a frame of tymbre called a crossaundre.'[4] Such a method was known in very early times and was used, for instance, by the Romans when building the walls of Anderida (now Pevensey) on the edge of the marsh.[5] For work on the port at Sandwich in 1463 we find not only 50 elms provided for piles, at 1s. each, but also 'viij gret elmes for planckes for the foundacon', costing 40s.;[6] while at Westminster in 1338, after a great frost had broken the bridge, 31 pieces of great timber of elm were bought for piles and slabbing (*platis*) for the foundation of the bridge,[7] but in this second example the slabs were probably not laid on the soil to give a firmer foundation but were nailed to the piles to form the starlings.

References to piles, apart from planks, are numerous. In 1239 beech trees were given to the Franciscans at Winchester to make piles for the foundation of their buildings.[8] At York in 1327 alders were bought 'to make piles for the foundations (*fundis*) of the cellar underneath the Queen's private chamber and of the cellar below the new chapel and also for the foundation of the latrine'.[9] So also, 9 elms were bought 'for piles for the foundation of the postern' at the Tower in 1348,[10] and 20 elms 'for piles whereof to make the foundation of the King's chamber' at Hadleigh Castle in 1363;[11] while at Sandwich in 1470 a payment of 10s. 8d. is recorded 'to Morice White and his felawys a great (i.e. a contract) to dryve pyles in the fundacon of the Bulwerk'.[12]

Piles were naturally required for the making of such works as wharves and weirs. Thus in 1360 at Gravesend 128 pieces of elm timber were bought

---

[1] *Chron. Abb. Ramesiensis*, 39, 58.                [2] E. 458, 4.

[3] *Vulgaria*, c. xxix.

[4] 'Crosse andrewes' occur at Westminster Abbey about 1475: Rackham, *Nave of West-minster*, 36. Presumably they were balks, notched together, crossing diagonally like a St. Andrew's cross.

[5] See *Sussex Arch. Coll.* li. 101.        [6] E. 481, 26.        [7] E. 470, 5.

[8] *Cal. of Liberate R.* Much of Winchester Cathedral rested until recently on a sort of raft of planks and faggots.

[9] E. 501, 8.                [10] E. 471, 1.

[11] E. 464, 6.                [12] E. 481, 28.

'to make piles thereof for the new wharf'.[1] When a contract was made in 1432 for the construction of a wharf at Norwich the mason was 'to take the ground pile it and plank it with englyssh oke of hert or ebel (i.e. poplar) of a resonable thicknes . . . and therupon begynne the seyd kaye of freston', the part behind the stone facing being filled and rammed with marl and gravel.[2] A similar backing is implied in the accounts for Berkhamstead in 1386, when a man was employed to dig clay 'for ramming the wharf of the new mill at the sides', 8 bundles of moss being at the same time supplied '*pro wharfo stuffando*'.[3] At York in 1365 straw had been used to bind the soil, when men were employed some six weeks repairing the bay (*caput*) of the Fosse stream and 'beating and ramming (*attribant' et tupant'*) the earth and mud, strengthened with straw, with rammers (*tuppis*) and great hammers'.[4] In the accounts for repairing a weir at Nottingham in 1318 we find 8 men driving piles, and '3 carpenters sharpening piles and making howetrys and shorys and setting them upon the weir'.[5] More elaborate details are given in 1400 when a sluice was remade in Windsor Park.[6] William atte Hethe, 'pondemaker', was paid £6. 9s. 10d. for piling and ramming 50 ft. by 40 ft. of the 'netherbay' of the sluice. A list is given of the timbers required for making the said 'sklus' and a great bridge over it; namely, 20 'grundeplatez' each 30 feet long, 65 pieces called 'nedylls', 4 'bembes' (beams); and for the bridge 6 posts, 16 braces, 3 'someres', 4 'entertayes', 120 'gistes', 2 rails; and at the head of the said 'sklus' a grate of 3 postes, 3 braces, 30 'moynells', with a bridge over the same; also a 'flodegate' of 8 postes, 8 braces, 6 flodegates, and a bridge over it; and 7,000 feet of boards, 3 inches in thickness.

In the construction of bridges piles often practically constitute the foundation. Thus when old Rochester bridge, built 1383–93, was removed, it was found that about 10,000 piles had been employed in making its piers. They were of elm, 20 feet in length, the starling[7] being constructed of half-piles driven in close together, filled with chalk, and covered on the sides and top with elm planks; on top of these an 8-inch platform of Kentish ragstone formed a foundation for the masonry of the bridge.[8] Such piles were shod with iron; 2 'pylschoun', weighing between them 100 lb., were supplied for Rochester bridge in 1407, and John Smyth of Chatham supplied another 28, totalling 402 lb., in 1438.[8] These are exceptionally

---

[1] E. 544, 1.   [2] App. B.   [3] E. 458, 21.
[4] E. 501, 11. Tup is a dialect word for a ram, i.e. a male sheep.
[5] E. 478, 1.   [6] E. 502, 15.
[7] 'Starlings' are the protective piling round the piers.
[8] Becker, *Rochester Bridge*, 7.

heavy; 8 shoes of iron used for piles at Calais in 1441 only weighed 27 lb.;[1] and the 110 irons for piles mentioned in the stores of material belonging to London Bridge in 1350 were valued at 4*d*. each,[2] which corresponds to a weight of about 3 lb.

The inventory just quoted also mentions two engines, or machines, with 3 'rammes' for ramming the piles of the bridge. Some contrivance of this kind had been in use from very early times; in fact it would hardly have been possible to drive piles without it. In form the ram, or pile-driver, consisted of an apparatus in the nature of sheer-legs, carrying a pulley by means of which a heavy block of wood or iron, the 'ram' proper, could be hoisted and let fall on the head of the pile. There is reference, in an account of 1256 for Woodstock, to a carpenter making 'sliddreies' and 'rammes',[3] of which the first term can only be guessed at, but may mean the uprights between which the ram slid. The ram occurs in a latinized form of its French equivalent, *mouton*, at Westminster in 1289: '*pro j truncco ad j multonem inde faciendum*', the price paid, 12*d*., showing that it was a very large log.[4] There is a further entry of the provision of a '*haspe cum apparatu*'— some sort of fastening with its fittings—for the *mouton*. In 1324 men were 'driving piles in the foundation with a great engine called "ram"' at the Tower,[5] where also we find 6*d*. spent '*pro iij bideux pro le ram*' in 1348.[6] An inventory of stores at Westminster in 1387 mentions 'a ramme with all fittings'.[7] At Calais 'a gynne called Ram, used for fixing piles' occurs in 1468;[8] 'a machine called a Fallyng Ramme' is found in 1473 at Shene;[9] and 'a gynne with a Rammer of brasse' was borrowed from the Wardens of London Bridge for work at Westminster in 1532.[10]

In the Rochester bridge accounts for 1457–8, we find 18 men employed in working the ram for fixing piles, each working for 58½ tides, at 3*d*. the tide.[11] Probably work would be possible for about 3 hours on each side of low tide, but whether they were all working continuously together or, as seems more probable, in shifts, does not appear. Further entries show 2 lb. of tallow bought for greasing the great 'hauser', and 6*d*. paid for tarring (*terrying*) it. The work was not without occasional incidents to relieve the monotony, if we may judge from an entry in 1409–10. That year 10 'tydemen' were paid at the same rate 'for driving (*pur chacer*) piles during 12 tides, and 2 others for helping during one tide; of which one tide was on

[1] E. 193, 4.                   [2] Riley, *Mems. of London*, 261.         [3] E. 497, 12.
[4] E. 467, 20.                  [5] E. 469, 7.                              [6] E. 470, 18.
[7] E. 473, 2.                   [8] E. 197, 5.                              [9] E. 503, 19.
[10] T.R. 437. For further notices of rams see below, p. 328.
[11] Becker, *Rochester Bridge*, 82.

Sunday after vespers, a great tempest of wind and rain, and 8 men fell into the water and were nearly drowned, wherefor they had extra, as a gift, in firing, bread, verjuice (*veriiose*) and wine, 22d.'[1]

Coming back to dry land—when the footings had been laid and work was to begin on the building of the walls, it was usual in the case of an ecclesiastical building to lay the foundation stone with a certain amount of ceremony.[2] Thus when Bishop William of St. Carilef began the new cathedral of Durham in 1093, on 11 August the bishop himself and Prior Turgot, with other brethren, 'laid the first stones in the foundations', the digging of which had been begun, with religious ceremony, a fortnight before.[3] The founding of Salisbury Cathedral in 1220 was marked by an elaborate ceremony[4] on 28 April, when the bishop laid the first stone in the name of the pope, the second in the archbishop's name, and the third in his own; after which the Earl and Countess of Salisbury and other magnates and dignitaries of the Church laid other stones. So, on 6 April 1291, John Romanus, Archbishop of York, 'most devoutly with his own hands set in position the first stone' of the nave of the Minster.[5] Henry VI, in 1442, laid the first stone of the chapel of his new college of Eton,[6] and on 17 September (? 1445) he wrote to the Abbot of Bury St. Edmunds and other abbots and bishops, asking them to be present at the laying of the first stone of the chapel of his college of St. Mary and St. Nicholas (now King's College) at Cambridge on Michaelmas Day, 'at the whiche, for the grete devocion and desire we have that it should be devoutly and solempnely doon, we had disposed us to have be there in oure owne persone', adding that, owing to the prevalence of the pestilence in Cambridge, he was unable to come but was sending the Marquess of Suffolk to represent him.[7] For some reason, possibly the increasing virulence of the plague, the ceremony seems to have been postponed, as it is pretty certain that Henry did lay the foundation stone himself on 25 July 1446.[8] Finally we may quote from the records of Magdalen College, Oxford, that on 9 August 1492 'the first corner stone for the new bell tower was laid by Master Richard Mayew, the President'.[9]

Alexander Neckam,[10] writing about 1200, after moralizing on the extra-

---

[1] Ibid. 83.
[2] *Archaeologia*, xxvi. 215.  [3] *Symeon of Durham*, 129.
[4] *Reg. of St. Osmund*, 12. See App. A.
[5] *Hist. of Church of York*, ii. 409.
[6] Willis and Clark, *Arch. Hist. of Cambridge*, i. 380.
[7] *Mems. of St. Edmunds*, iii. 246.     [8] Willis and Clark, i. 465.
[9] *Magdalen Coll. Reg.* (N.S.), i. 23.     [10] *De Naturis Rerum*, c. 172.

vagances of contemporary architecture, including sky-scrapers (*turres sideribus minantes*), says:

Now the ground is made even with the rammer (*chelindro*), now the irregularity of the surface is beaten down with frequent ramming (*ariete crebro*), now the solidity of the foundation is tested (*exploratur*) with piles driven into the bowels of the earth. The height of the wall, built of cut stone and rubble (*ex cemento et lapidibus*), rises and soars according to the law of the level and the plumbline (*amussis et perpendiculi*). The flatness of the surface of the wall is due to the smoothing and polishing of the mason's trowel (*trullae*).

He then explains at length that walls must not be exactly parallel but must radiate from the centre of the earth, like spokes from the hub of a wheel, as everything of weight tends to seek the centre. This is, of course, an absurd piece of pedantry, only interesting as reminding us that the roundness of the earth and the general idea of the principle of gravity was known in early times. Three hundred years later Horman puts the matter more briefly:[1] 'All wallis, whether they be of stone or of brycke, or of claye with strawe or mudde, must be made levell and plumme, orels they be redy to fall.' And of mud walls there is little more than that to be said. References to such walls occur from time to time, chiefly in such documents as manorial accounts; for instance, at Southampton in 1312 we find an earthen wall covered with plaster and crested with sods, and other walls finished with a coping of thatch;[2] and at Bridport in 1483 we have payments 'for makynge of the squabbe wallsa bove the stone worke'[3]—'squabbe' being equivalent to cob, a mixture of earth and straw.

Stone walls may be divided into two main classes: those composed entirely of rubble, that is to say, irregular blocks of stone set haphazard in mortar, and those faced with ashlar, that is to say, quadrangular blocks of stone laid in regular courses and worked to present a more or less smooth surface. Only comparatively thin walls, such as those of parapets and quirescreens, were composed entirely of ashlar; often only the outer surface was ashlar, the rest being of rubble. Thus in a contract for building a dormitory at Durham in 1398 the walls are to be 'on the outside of clean stone called achiler, cut flat, and inside of broken stone called roghwalle'.[4] Such rubble walling was practically invariably intended to be plastered over, and the modern practice of stripping the plaster and exposing the rubble in the interior of churches would horrify the original builders. When both faces

---

[1] *Vulgaria*, c. xxix.  
[3] Ibid. 494.  

[2] *Hist. MSS. Com. Rep.* vi. 567.  
[4] App. B.

of the wall were of ashlar the space between would be filled with rubble consisting of mortar and lumps of stone, the chips from the working of the ashlar blocks, flints, pebbles, and so forth. 'Battis and great rubbrysshe serveth to fyl up in the myddell of the wall.'[1] In order to adjust the courses of their ashlar when there were slight variations in the depth of the stones, medieval builders seem to have used oyster shells, as the modern brick-layer uses slate. At Corfe in 1291 we find the large sum of 20s. paid 'for loading oyster shells in boats and carrying them from Poole to Ore';[2] and at London in 1506 'a busshell of oyster shellis' was bought for 3d.[3] In neither of these instances is the purpose stated, but in 1532 the West-minster accounts mention 25 bushels of 'oyster shellis delivered to the masons and by them occupied for the setting of stone'.[4]

While the inner surface of a wall was usually carried up in one flat un-broken plane, the outer surface was generally in two or more planes, divided by courses of thin flat stones known as 'tables' or 'ledgments'. The first of these, where the wall was set back at or near the surface of the ground, to form a plinth, was known as the ground, earth, or grass table and sometimes as the water-table, though this latter term seems sometimes to be applied to string-courses in general.[5] At Langley, in 1366, John Smith, mason-layer of London, was employed to build the house of the Friars, at the rate of 66s. 8d. for the perch of 21 feet, the walls being 26 feet high 'between the Water table and the Corbeltable', the price including battle-ments and other accessories.[6] The corbel-table was the highest of these flat courses and was supported by a row of corbels, those projecting brackets of stone which, with their bold and varied carving, form a striking feature of Norman churches, such as Kilpeck. The finish of the wall above this table would depend upon the nature of the building. It might simply end as a flat surface carrying the timbers of the roof, by whose eaves it would be protected from the weather. If not so protected, it would require some form of coping or crest to throw off rain. So at Launceston in 1464 some 360 feet of 'raggeston' were used on 'le copyng de le courtwalle',[7] and at Hereford Castle in 1404, payment was made 'for cresting (*crestellandis*) the walls of the castle with stone'.[8] And in 1533 at the Tower 'half the White tower and more is new embattalled copyde vented and cressyde wt. Cane stone to themounte of v^c foote'.[9]

[1] Horman, *Vulgaria*, c. xxix.　　　　　　　[2] E. 460, 28.
[3] London Bridge Accts., ser. 2, vol. i.　　　[4] T.R., f. 402.
[5] For further details of the various tables see below, pp. 106–7.　　[6] E. 466, 3.
[7] E. 461, 23.　　　　　[8] E. 544, 14.　　　　　[9] E. 474, 12.

A battlemented parapet was a common method of finishing a wall. Originating as a military device to enable archers to fire from the ramparts without exposing themselves unnecessarily, battlements developed in England into a favourite form of decoration and in the later fifteenth century became an absolute disease, breaking out in all kinds of absurd and unsuitable positions, such as tie-beams and the transoms of windows. They seem still to have been regarded as definitely military in 1321, when the University of Oxford, constantly on bad terms with the townsmen, complained that the parishioners of St. Martin's, Carfax, had newly built an aisle to the church and had caused it to be 'crenellated in the guise of a fortress', to the disturbance of the scholars.[1] Manuscript illustrations show that in many instances the spaces between the upstanding portions of battlements were filled, in military buildings, with hinged wooden shutters, and traces of such fittings can still be seen in places.[2] In 1301, when the castle of Rhuddlan was being put in repair, 500 boards were bought 'for making defences in the battlements around the castle'.[3] In 1313 at the Tower of London[4] John de Lynne, mason carver (*entalliator*), was paid for 'piercing into the battlements for the insertion of hekkes'; and two carpenters were 'working on falling hecks (*heckes cadentes*)[5] to be arranged and set within the battlements of the great tower towards St. Katherine's and the outer tower towards London'. At the same time another mason was working on the turret over the Watergate 'enlarging the battlements for the setting of springalds[6] in the same turret *et pro amsatubus et squach*'[7] *eorundem springald' melius habendis*'. Willis asserts[8] that the upright portions of a battlement were called the 'cops' and the spaces between were called 'crenels'; but I am inclined to think that 'crenel' applied indifferently to the upright and the space. Tenants of the Honor of Mortain in Cornwall were bound to keep in repair one *kernellum* at Launceston Castle for each knight's fee that they held,[9] which presumably means either a riser or the masonry surrounding a space, which would include two risers.

In 1252 repairs to the chapel in the castle of Northampton include an order to 'raise and crenellate the wall round the chapel, to crest the crenelles of the tower there, and to board the alures (*aleas*) round the tower';[10] this again suggests that the crenelles were the risers. The previous

---

[1] *University Archives* (O.H.S.), i. 104.   [2] e.g. at Carnarvon Castle.
[3] Arthur Jones, *Flintshire Mins. Accts.* 16.   [4] E. 469, 16.
[5] The word is probably connected with 'heck' or hatch, a half-door.
[6] Machines for throwing missiles.   [7] The meaning of these words is obscure.
[8] *Nomenclature*, 32.   [9] K.R. Memo. R. 17 Ric. II, Mich.
[10] Liberate R. 36 Hen. III, m. 15.

year the bailiff of Havering had been ordered to complete the alures and
crenelles of the chambers of the king and queen.[1] Although the usual form
of the licence to fortify, without which nothing in the nature of a defen-
sive building might be erected, gave permission *batellare et kirnellare*, the
words seem to have been redundant and not to imply any difference. At
the Tower there is a note in 1317 that 'battlements were made round the
small hall and the two great kitchens this year',[2] while in 1337 money was
spent on 'raising crenellating and cresting the wall between the Watergate
and the common latrine beside the postern'.[3] At Conway Castle in 1286
there is reference to 'the crenelles (*cornell'*) of a breadth (*panni*) of wall on
the north';[4] at Berwick just about a century later 35 crenelles (*kirnell*) of
the wall of the Wyndywarde were made at a cost of 5*d*. each;[5] and at
Hereford in 1404 masons were remaking 'lez batellynges' over the castle
gate.[6]

It will be noticed that in two of these references there is mention of
alures in connexion with battlements, and in 1405 Master Stephen Loot,
or Lote, was paid £33. 6*s*. 8*d*. 'for making the battlement or allier above
the great hall of Westminster at the east end'.[7] The word 'alure', with
variant spellings, was used of any kind of passage but particularly of the
walk behind the parapet on walls.[8] Occasionally it was transferred to the
parapet itself, as for instance in the contract for Catterick Church in 1412,
where the 'aloring' is to be made of one course of ashlar and cresting.[9]
Another word sometimes used for parapets is bretasch or brattise. The
dormitory at Durham was to be finished with '*alours et bretesmontz*'[9] embattled and crenellated. During the repair of the peel tower of Haywra in
Knaresborough Forest in 1335 'Brother William, one of the brethren of
the house of St. Robert of Knaresborough' was hired to cut stones for the
bretasch (*bretag'*).[10]

While walls were in process of erection it was necessary to give them
temporary protection against frost and rain by cresting them with thatch.
So at Vale Royal in November 1278 we find straw bought 'for covering
the walls and foundations of the church against the winter';[11] and in the
same month of 1295 a man was employed at Dover thatching the wall of
the foundation,[12] and at Cambridge Castle the masons spent three days

[1] Ibid. 35 Hen. III, m. 6.
[2] E. 468, 20.     [3] E. 470, 1.     [4] E. 485, 28.
[5] E. 483, 1.     [6] E. 544, 14.     [7] E. 502, 26.
[8] Willis, *Nomenclature*, 33–5.
[9] App. B.     [10] E. 544, 18.
[11] E. 485, 22.     [12] E. 462, 14.

'levelling off (*equandum*) the walls of the new turret before they were thatched with marsh straw' (i.e. reeds).[1] At Windsor in 1362 heather was bought for covering the walls in the winter,[2] and at Gloucester in 1442 the building stone was heaped up and covered with 'pesehalme' against the frosts of winter.[3] When St. Stephen's Chapel at Westminster was being built, in 1333, a wooden penthouse was built over the gable 'to protect it from wind and rain during the winter season'.[4]

Flat roofs being comparatively rare, most end-walls terminated in gables, and naturally building accounts contain many references to gables, either by that name or under some variant of the French *pignon*, as for instance in 1462, when a 'punnion' was built at the east end of Restormel Chapel, with 'a window called Gabilwyndowe'.[5] A few years earlier at Lostwithiel there are payments for 'stone called freston for a wyndbearge over the south ponyon of the great hall', and 'to masons for making le wyndberge, with repairs to all the defects in le poynyon, and le roghcastyng of the same'.[6] The 'wyndbearge' of this entry is presumably the stone coping of the gable, corresponding to the barge-boards of timber gables. In 1243 Henry III ordered four windows in the east gable of the hall at Woodstock to be taken down and replaced by 'one great round and handsome window'.[7] In the same year he gave orders for building a new hall in Dublin Castle, which was to have in the gable over the dais a round window 30 feet across.[8] Other references to round windows occur from time to time, and the term 'rose-window' is found at Westminster Abbey in 1451, when there was a payment 'for Northirnstone for le rose' in the south transept, and during the next ten years, over which the making and fixing of the rose was spread.[9]

Another type of window which appears mainly in the middle of the thirteenth century is the 'upright' (*stantiva*) window. Four such windows were to be put in the hall at Feckenham in 1232; four others in the new hall at Ludgershall in 1243; two in the hall and two in the great wardrobe at Silverston in 1251.[10] The term is puzzling, and I can only suggest that it refers to windows that were taller than the side-walls in which they were placed and were therefore provided with their own gables standing up above the walls. Another entry, in 1231, of the provision of timber for four 'upright' windows to be made in the hall at Clarendon might in that case

---

[1] E. 459, 16.     [2] E. 493, 10.     [3] E. 473, 18.

[4] E. 469, 17.     [5] E. 461, 21.     [6] Ibid. 18.

[7] Liberate R. 28 Hen. III.     [8] *Close R.* 23.

[9] Rackham, *Westminster*, 27.     [10] Liberate R. 35 Hen. III.

refer to the timbering of the roofs of their gables.[1] Possibly the same type may be referred to in the order given in 1251 to block up the 'cowled' (*culiciatas*) windows on the south side of the hall at Nottingham, and to make good 'cowled' windows before the door of the king's chamber over the stairs;[2] but these may have been dormer windows.

When Henry III, in 1243, gave orders for the making of 'two windows with columns, like the other windows',[3] the reference is to the type—a particularly attractive one—very prevalent at that time, in which the scoinson arch is carried on small pillars. Similarly at Winchester in 1222 we find Geoffrey de Hida paid 18*d*. 'for two columns for windows'.[4] So also in 1378 in a list of repairs carried out in the manor house at Apuldram a mason is paid 'for making a new stone pillar in one window of the lord's chamber'.[5] The same list, it may be remarked, includes the glazing of three round windows in the hall.

The ordinary window is described as of so many lights or, usually, 'days'. When composed of more lights than one, the upright dividing mullions are called 'moynels', and the horizontal stone bars 'transoms'. The tracery is called 'forms' or 'form pieces', and occasionally 'molds'. With all these we shall deal more fully in the section on technical terms in masonry.[6] In the contract for the tower of Dunster Church in 1442 the windows are to be of one 'day' with four 'genelas' in the head,[7] and the east window of Wycombe Church in 1509 is to have 'every light gen-losed'.[7] Willis has shown, quoting William of Worcester, 'The west dore ys fretted in the hede with grete genlese and smale', that 'genlese' are cusps, and suggests a derivation from *genouil*, a knee.[8] The frame of a window consists of a sill, or 'soyl', at the bottom, jambs on each side and either an arch or a flat lintel at the top. All the terms are equally applicable whether the construction is in wood or stone. Sometimes the window recess was carried down below the lights and furnished with window-seats, to which references are occasionally found—as for instance at Sheppey in 1365: 'for setting segetables in the windows'.[9]

A few entries may be given as throwing light on the quantity and cost of material and labour involved in the construction of windows. At Langley, in 1367:[10] Walter le Maccon for one *fourme* (i.e. set of tracery) for a window of three lights (*dierum*) on the north side of the fraytour (i.e.

---

[1] *Close R.* 14.    [2] Liberate R. 36 Hen. III, m. 17.    [3] Ibid. 28 Hen. III.

[4] E. 491, 13.    [5] Mins. Accts. 1017, no. 11.

[6] See below, pp. 111–13.    [7] App. B.

[8] *Nomenclature*, 55.    [9] E. 483, 21.    [10] E. 544, 20.

refectory) with the jamb-pieces (*chaumbraunces*)[1]—15s. To the same for 3 *fourmes* for windows of 2 lights on the east side of the freytour with the jamb-pieces, cut by contract at 6s. 8d. the fourme—20s. Next year:[2] Walter atte Forde for 2 *formes* for windows of 3 lights, cut by contract at 15s. the form, and 5 *formes* for windows of 2 lights, at 6s. 8d.—63s. 4d. At Woodstock in 1400:[3] 70 feet of free-stone (*freston*) for making 5 windows within the prince's chamber, each being 6 feet in length and of 4 *daies*, at 2d. the foot. The making of these windows occupied 3 masons for 33 days. At the Tower in 1533:[4] 'in the kynges dynyng chambre iiij wyndowes ij of them wt. iiij lyghtes new made from the transam upward in heyght vj fote and in brede the ij wyndows iiij fot di', and the myddell wyndowe vij fote, the stone amountith unto the same wyndowes unto cx fote'. Two other windows each measuring 3 ft. by 13 in. required 20 feet of Caen stone; and one of 2 lights, measuring 9 ft. by 4 ft., required 56 feet.

From this last account we may also quote: 'made new in the quenes dynyng chambre a great carrall wyndow stondyng on the west syde and lenyng places made new to the same and a halpace[5] under fote new made and new joysted and bourded'. The 'lenyng places' are the flat prolongations of the sill, on which one would lean to look out of the window. A 'carrall' window is presumably one of those windows, so typical of the Tudor period, projecting squarely from the wall. The earlier form of projecting window, the bay window, occurs frequently from the latter part of the fourteenth century onwards. Thus at Easthampstead in 1393 we have mention of '3 windows called Baywyndowes in the oratory of the king and queen within the chapel there',[6] in 1401 of 'a great window called Baywyndowe made with 4 dayes' at Eltham;[7] and of repairs to 'le Baywyndow' in the castle of Berwick in 1444.[8] There remains the much-debated 'oriel', now applied to a projecting bay-window on an upper floor. Willis considered that this 'was a window in every case' and that where it apparently referred to a room it implied a room distinguished by such a window;[9] but this does not seem to be borne out by the evidence. Mr. Hamper, on the other hand, considered, on equally insufficient evidence, that the word had at least five different meanings.[10] The earliest occurrences of the term appear to be in the Liberate Rolls of Henry III: 1232, ordered for the building of a chapel at the end of the oriel (*ad capud oriolli*) of the

[1] Cf. at Dover in 1292, repair of the *chambe* of a door: E. 462, 13.
[2] E. 466, 4.      [3] E. 502, 15.      [4] E. 474, 13.
[5] A dais or raised platform.
[6] E. 495, 17.      [7] E. 502, 23.      [8] E. 483, 11.
[9] *Nomenclature*, 60.        [10] *Archaeologia*, xxiii. 107, 116.

king's castle at Hereford; 1245, order to make an oriel before the door of
the king's chamber at Ludgershall and a covered passage from that door
to the door of the hall; next year an oriel with an upper story (*cum stagio*)
is to be made before the door of the queen's chamber at Brill; 1255, money
had been spent on making a stair with a door and an oriel on the right side
of the king's chapel at Rochester, so that strangers might enter the chapel
without passing through the king's chamber; 1268, an oriel (*auriolum*) to be
built between the new chamber and the queen's chapel in Winchester
Castle, with a fireplace in the oriel to heat the queen's food, and walls
built under the oriel from the chamber to the chapel with a gate for carts
to pass through. The general sense of these entries seems to be something
in the nature of a porch or ante-room; and Halliwell[1] quotes from
Matthew Paris, *in introitu quod porticus vel oriolum appellatur*. In the majority
of instances, if not invariably, the oriel appears to have been on an upper
floor—the word *orell* has survived in Cornwall for the porch at the head
of an outside stairway—and it not unnaturally came to be applied to the
projecting window with which it is now associated.

The porch was a natural accessory to the chief door of an important
building. It served the useful purpose of a shelter from the weather and
also gave a certain dignity to the entrance. In 1244 Henry III gave orders
for making a great porch to Westminster Hall, worthy of such a palace,
between the lavatory (*lotorium*) in front of the king's kitchens and the door
into the lesser hall, 'so that the king may dismount from his palfrey in it
at a handsome façade (*ad honestam frontem*)' and may be able to walk under
it between the door and the lavatory and also from the kitchen to the
knights' chamber.[2] In churches the porch played an important part, as a
large part of the marriage service took place there, and the church porch
was also often specified as the place where debts or other payments were
to be made. Consequently we find many references to the building of
church porches, as for instance in the contracts for Fotheringay Church and
King's College Chapel; but they do not present any features of constructional interest that call for notice. Nor need doors detain us. Their parts
are similar to those of windows—sills, jambs, and lintels—but with certain
variants, the jambs being called doorsteads, as at Westminster in 1532,
'doresteedes' of free-stone,[3] and durns, as in repairs to 'a part of lez durnys
of the cellar' at Lostwithiel in 1445,[4] and 'the durnes and windows of the

---

[1] *Dict. of Archaic Words.*
[2] *Close R.* 273; Liberate R. 29 Hen. III.
[3] T.R. 423.
[4] E. 461, 18.

tower called le Gayle' at Launceston in 1461;[1] and 'for making of a pair of dordarns, with the settyng of them' at Peterborough in 1523.[2]

A long or high wall, unless of exceptional thickness, would usually require the additional support of buttresses. These, in early buildings, take the form of pilasters of slight projection, but with the coming of the pointed, or Gothic, styles become architectural features of importance, until in such a building as King's College Chapel the structure can almost be defined as a stone vault supported on buttresses, the spaces between which are filled with glass. In the thirteenth century they appear still to have been regarded as a variety of pillar. Thus in 1247 two *pileria butericia*[3] were to be made under the king's chamber in Gloucester Castle; in 1251 the chapel at Havering was supplied with *columpnis botericiis*[4] on the outside, and the wall of Guildford Castle was to be 'well mended with columns and supports';[5] and at Winchester in 1256 orders were given to crenellate the buttress column running from the bottom of the ditch to the top of the tower.[6] This last instance may be paralleled by the two corner buttresses to be built at Bamborough Castle in 1384, which were to have above them 'two turrets of good design',[7] and by the two buttresses on the flanks of the gateway at Carlisle Castle in 1378, which were to be 5 feet square at ground-level, 34 feet high and embattled.[7] The contract for the church of Catterick[7] in 1412 stipulates for various buttresses, including, on the wall of the south aisle, 'a botras dyand under the tabil', that is to say, diminishing and coming to an end at the course below the battlements; and similarly 'at the cornere of the southe side of the (east) windowe a franche botras rising unto the tabill that sall bere the aloring'. Other references show that a 'franche botras' was an angle-buttress, either so called because it stood free of the walls, or more probably as being in the French style, which is borne out by the contract for Dunster Church tower, to be built 'with iij french botras and a vice in the fowrth pyler in stede of a botras'.[7] At Fotheringay in 1434 the aisles were each to have 'six mighty botrasse of free stone, clen hewyn, and every botrasse fynisht with a fynial', and just a century later the new aisles of Burnley Church were to have 18 buttresses, each with a finial[8] on the top, according to the fashion of the finials on the new chapel of our Lady at Whalley. So also, in 1448,

[1] E. 461, 20.      [2] Cathl. Accts.
[3] Liberate R. 31 Hen. III, m. 2.      [4] Ibid. 35 Hen. III, m. 4.
[5] Ibid. m. 3.      [6] Liberate R. 40 Hen. III.
[7] App. B.
[8] Printed as 'funnel' in the summary of the contract given in Whitaker's *Hist. of Whalley*, 323.

Henry VI in his instructions for building the chapel of King's College said that it should be 'sufficiently boteraced and every boterace fined with finialx'[1] and in 1513, when the completion of this chapel was undertaken, the finials of the buttresses were 'to be wele and workmanly wrought, made and sett upp after the best handelyng and fourme of good workmanship acordyng to the plattes conceyved and made for the same'. A still more elaborate finish, consisting of carved figures of lions, dragons, greyhounds, and antelopes, holding metal vanes, was provided at Windsor in 1506, when John Hylmer and William Vertue undertook to work the 'archebotens, crestys, corses and the king's bestes stondyng on theym to bere the fanes on the outsides of the said quere'.[1] Arch-buttresses, or flying buttresses, figure in the Westminster Abbey building accounts about 1480, their full description being *le archebottantes et arches ac pynacles*;[2] a century earlier they had appeared under the less elegant form of 'arsbotamis'.[3] Still earlier, in 1320, we find a mason at Westminster Palace 'working upon the *archibuteracium* of Marculf's chamber, which buttress was weak and faulty and on the point of falling owing to the flooding and incursions of the Thames'.[4]

Another structural feature to be found from early times in the more important houses was the fireplace. A well-known passage in William Harrison's *Description of England*, published in 1577, commenting on the increased use of chimneys in his own time and their rarity in the previous generation, is true enough when applied to the smaller houses in the country but is misleading where towns and large buildings are in question. The importance of the fire, the centre of domestic life during a considerable part of the year, is shown by the occasional use of the term 'firehouse' as equivalent to the hall—the one room, unless there was a kitchen, supplied with that luxury. Even as late as 1632 we find reference to 'the Hall or Fierhouse' of a Derbyshire mansion.[5] In 1392, in a lease of property at Nun Stainton, the chief building is that 'called the Fire-house, containing five couples of syles and two gavelforkis'[6]—in other words, two gables and five pair of crucks, making six bays. Similarly, in a Yorkshire lease of 1474 the lessees 'sall uppe halde a fyre house and a crosse chamber' and other buildings.[7] Frequently, one may say normally, the fire was built on an open hearth in the middle of the hall, its smoke escaping through the

[1] App. B.
[2] Rackham, *Westminster*, 39.
[3] Ibid. 7.
[4] E. 469, 1.
[5] Addy, *Evolution of the English House*, 60.
[6] Ibid. 59.
[7] T. W. Hall, *Cat. of Charters of Sheffield and Rotherham*, 61.

windows and through an open louver in the roof. But often, as Harrison says, men made their fire 'against a reredosse in the hall', that is to say, against a wall of earth, stone, or brick, sometimes with the additional protection of an iron fire-back. From this the smoke might be directed upwards by a hood or mantel and carried out through the roof by a flue, terminating in some kind of chimney. The term 'chimney,' with all its variant spellings and French and Latin forms—*cheminee, caminum, cheminum, chemeneya,* &c. was used throughout our period for the whole fireplace, comprising hearth, mantel, flue, and chimney, or for any of its parts. Thus in 1530 Katherine Adams bargained with John Hawkyns of London, carpenter, that he should build two houses in Shoreditch, 'conteyning in lenght and brede xliij fote wt. twoo halles and twoo fayer chymneys in them and . . . twoo kechyns in the backsyde wt. twoo chymneys substancyall for the same'.[1] In 1400, at Eltham, 5,000 'flaunderstile (i.e. bricks) were bought *pro factura soiles jambpeces reredose et tuell' iij caminorum*,[2] that is, for the sills, or hearths, jambs, backs, and flues of three fireplaces. At York Castle in 1364 plaster and 'walteghell'—wall-tiles or bricks—were bought for the *tuellis vulgariter vocatis chymnes* and the reredos in the kitchen, as well as two great stones *pro manteletes pro lez chymnes* and iron bars to insert in the mantels.[3] At Launceston in 1462 we find payments for making 'a great fireplace (*camini*) called mantell and 2 ovens within the said fireplace in the castle kitchen called constabill's kechyn'; and stone called 'mereston' was worked for the 'corbelles clavelles dorestones coynestones and vaultyngstones' for it.[4] Such a fireplace, complete with ovens, constituted a kitchen range; so we find bricklayers paid for making 'in the prevy kechyn a range with a new harthe' at the Tower in 1533,[5] and payments for installing a 'great fireplace of two *raungez* in the new kitchen' at Eltham in 1403.[6] At Old Sarum in 1366 a payment of 22s. was made 'for making a hearth (*astro*) in the hall, with the ironwork for setting up and fixing (*pendendo et affirmando*) the hearth in the recess (*arco*) of the hall';[7] and at Peterhouse, Cambridge, 8d. was paid *pro factura ly harth in aula* in 1502.[8] The hearth was sometimes made of a single large stone, occasionally called an altar-stone—as in 1532 when 'an awterestone' was bought, for 14d., for the oven at the Dolphin in London;[9] or of several stones, as in 1392, when 16 blocks of grit-stone (*petris de grete*) were provided 'to make

[1] Early Chanc. Proc. 695, no. 12.

[2] E. 502, 15.　　　　　[3] E. 501, 11.　　　　　[4] E. 461, 21.

[5] E. 474, 13.　　　　　[6] E. 502, 24.　　　　　[7] E. 593, 32.

[8] Willis and Clark, *Arch. Hist. of Cambridge*, i. 14.　　　　　[9] E. 474, 5.

a new *herthe* in the hall of the prebend of Thorp to replace a *herthe* destroyed there in making the new bells in the hall'.[1] Tiles or bricks were also used for the hearth and still more for the backs of fireplaces. Thus at Porchester in 1397 we find 300 'hurthtigel' (hearth tiles) bought for fireplaces, for 3s., and a thousand 'white tiles of Flanders' bought for their reredoses, for 8s.[2] Two years later 13s. 4d. was paid 'for 400 large pendantigheles used on the reredosses of fireplaces';[3] these were probably flanged tiles set upright with their faces outwards. At Clarendon in 1485 both 'herthtyle' and 'pavyng tyle' were bought for the repair of 'le ovyn'.[4] The use of Flanders tiles for fireplaces is common—as, for instance, at Westminster in 1349[5]—and one of the earliest mentions in England of brick by that name is the purchase of 2,000 '*breke pro chemeneys faciendis*' at Langley in 1427.[6]

At Clipston in 1368 there is mention of 'making in the king's kitchen a wall of stones and chalk to put fire against (*pro igne apponendo*)';[7] and in 1353 masons at Carisbrooke were employed to cut freestone for the reredos in the kitchen, and 'to set the said reredos and to make above it a wall of stone for fear of the fire (*pro dubio foci*) because the wall that used to be there was of wattle-work (*de laticio*)'.[8] By the ordinances of the City of London drawn up early in the fourteenth century it was forbidden to place any reredos where a fire was made for preparing bread or ale or cooking meat near partition walls of laths or boards, or elsewhere where there was danger of fire, and chimneys were no longer to be made of wood but only of stone, tiles, or plaster.[9] When the fire was made against the wall, instead of being set back into it, the flue would be carried up on the inner face of the wall. This seems to have been so in the case of the Earl of Richmond's hall in London in 1317, when a contract was made to plaster the walls 'and also the *tewels* (i.e. flues) to the summit';[10] and probably also at Shene in 1368, when John Lamor, mason, repaired two fireplaces in the king's chambers, and William de Yorke, plasterer, made the four *pipes* of the same fireplaces with plaster of Paris.[11] The presence here of four flues for two fireplaces suggests that these were 'double', that is to say, two fireplaces, back to back, serving adjacent rooms; in this instance each had presumably its own flue constructed on the surface of the wall, but more often both were served by the same flue within the wall. A

[1] R. 109.  [2] E. 479, 23.  [3] Ibid. 24.  [4] E. 460, 16.
[5] E. 470, 18.  [6] E. 466, 11.  [7] E. 460, 20.
[8] E. 490, 30. Laticio might possibly be intended for *latericio*—brickwork, but the sense seems to require some less safe material.
[9] Riley, *Liber Albus*, 288.  [10] App. B.  [11] E. 493, 29.

contract[1] made in 1370 for building 18 shops in London stipulates for 10 fireplaces, 8 of them being double—to be made of brick above the mantel and of stones and tile-shards below, each being $5\frac{1}{2}$ feet between the jambs of the chimney breast and to rise one foot above the roof. At Shene in 1440 three double fireplaces of brick (*breke*) are mentioned and another was made at Langley at the same time.[2] In 1385 William Brown. mason, was paid 'for making a great fireplace of 2 hearths (*focis*) made for the dancing room (*camera tripudiant*') and the King's wardrobe' at Clarendon.[3] As early as 1252 we find Henry III giving orders for the making of a chimney in his wardrobe at Clipston 'through one mantel and through another mantel in the queen's wardrobe by one and the same flue (*tuellum*)'.[4] Six years earlier he had ordered the flue and chimney (*tuellum et caminum*) of the queen's chamber at Oxford to be raised,[5] and in 1239 the flue of his chamber at Woodstock was to be raised 6 feet.[6] In the contract for building the hall at Hamsey in 1321 there were to be two fireplaces—one behind the dais, a position usual in Scotland but rare in England, and the other in the side wall, and their flues were to rise 3 feet above the crest (*summet*) of the hall.[1] From existing examples, of Norman and later dates, we know that chimneys were sometimes of stone, but documentary references are not very numerous, or are disguised by the use of the vague word *caminum*. At Westminster in 1532 we read of 'tonnellis hewen for chymneys' at 26s. 8d., and of the 'hewing setting up and fenysshing of viij tonnellis of chymneys togeders with their heedis and bases',[7] which presumably refers to stone chimneys. In 1368, at Clipston, we find a payment 'for making 2 chimneys (*camenorum*) with plaster of Paris, which had been blown down by the wind'[8]—implying that they were external—and these correspond to the 'chalk whyt chymnees' on a castle roof as described in a contemporary romance.[9] An earthen chimney (*chymenea terr*') was bought from Ralph de Crokerelane in 1278,[10] but the only other suggestion I have found of anything like a modern chimney-pot is at Hadleigh in 1363, when 4 earthen pots (*oll' lut*') were bought for the smoke-vent (*fumerell*') of the barn, and 4 others for the smoke-vent of the King's hall in Rayleigh park, at the high rate of 1s. 2d. each,[11] but the exact significance of these purchases I am not prepared to define. There is also, in the Clarendon accounts for

[1] App. B.                    [2] E. 503, 9.                    [3] E. 473, 2.
[4] Liberate R. 36 Hen. III, m. 17.              [5] Ibid. 30 Hen. III, m. 23.
[6] Ibid. 23 Hen. III.
[7] T.R., ff. 640, 649.                    [8] E. 460, 20.
[9] *Gawayn and the Grene Knight*, quoted in Addy, *Evolution of the English House*, 116.
[10] E. 467, 6.                    [11] E. 464, 6.

1385, a payment of 8s. 3d. 'for 6 gallons of oil called lamp-oil expended on smearing (*limend'*) various stones called lorymers for the said two chimneys (*caminis*) to keep the storms of winter from them'.[1] Lorimers, or lermers, are dripstones, or projecting mouldings to throw off the rain.[2] Similarly at Canterbury College, Oxford, in 1508 a mason was paid for work on *defensorium summitatis caminorum coquine* to keep out the rain which before that used to come down them.[3]

For Hunsdon House in 1528 'parelles of chymneys redy wroght' were supplied, and 'parelles of Fre stone provyded as well for the Chymneys in the Kyng's Watchyng Chambre Palett Chambre and Pryvey Chambre as in the other chambres byneth the same'.[4] And at Westminster in 1532 Gabriel Cauldeham, freemason of London, was paid 5s. 4d. 'for 'viij parellis of chymneys', each containing 5 feet of stone.[5] So, in 1440, 'one enparell of Reigate stone' was used for making a fireplace at Havering, and two similar 'enparells' were sent from Westminster Palace to be used at Langley.[6] That these fittings were concerned not with the chimney-vent but with the fireplace, or chimney breast, is shown by a similar purchase of 'parelles' in 1544, where one is said to be 6½ feet wide and the other two 5½ feet each.[7] They probably consisted simply of the frame of mantel and jambs;[8] but the complete apparelling of a fireplace may be deduced from a list belonging to Leeds Castle in 1361.[9] A *linthel* containing 9 feet, not worked (*non scapulat'*), for the fireplace; 17 feet of hard stone worked for the flues (*tuell'*); 2 *baas* of hard stone for the same work; 34 feet of hard stone for *scheu* and *lermer*, worked for the same, 3 *chapitrelles* of hard stone worked for the same, 11½ feet of worked hard stone called *parpaynassheler*; 2 great *coygnestons* and 6 *corbels*. Here the *linthel* is the mantelstone, over the mouth of the fireplace, probably supported on corbels and on the great *coygnestons*, or angle-stones, each standing on a *baas*; the hood would be composed of the *scheu*, which is stone cut with a bevel, and *larmer*, which we have seen was a projecting moulding, and probably the *parpaynassheler* means stones worked on two parallel faces; the three chapitrelles, or capitals, I should suggest, were placed one in the centre of the mantel and one in each angle between the wall and the hood as brackets to carry lights.[10]

The mantel was often composed of a great beam of wood, as, for instance,

[1] E. 473, 3.
[2] Willis, *Nomenclature*, 10.
[3] *Canterbury Coll. Accts.* (O.H.S.), ii. 249.
[4] E. 465, 20.
[5] T.R., f. 157.
[6] E. 503, 9.
[7] E. 504, 2.
[8] 'For setting 3 geamb' of fireplaces at Baynard's Castle in 1366: E. 493, 12.
[9] E. 466, 19.
[10] Cf. the 'canstycke' in the contract: App. B. p. 561.

in the King's Hall accounts for 1486, when Martin the carpenter was paid for shaping and placing 'lez mantiltrees' in the kitchen.[1] Those mentioned in building accounts, however, are more often of stone; as at Clipston in 1357, when a 'mantelston' and a 'herthston' were provided for a fireplace,[2] or at Windsor in 1480, when 21 brick fireplaces in the vicars' lodging were supplied with 'mantell' jamys and bordurs' of Reigate stone.[3] The form 'le mantelpece' occurs at Kennington in 1400[4] and probably included the hood, as indeed the term 'mantel' frequently does.

The mantel was often a fine architectural feature and was enriched with decoration. Thus Henry III ordered a mantel at Westminster to be painted with 'a figure of Winter, which by its sad countenance and by other miserable contortions of the body may be deservedly likened to Winter itself';[5] another, at Clarendon, to be painted with a wheel of Fortune and a tree of Jesse;[6] and the fireplace in the queen's chamber at Clarendon to be rebuilt with a marble column on each side and the mantel carved with the twelve months of the year.[7]

There remain three mysterious entries connected with fireplaces. First, at Westminster in 1274 is a payment 'for a bushel of salt for the king's hearth(s) (*focar*')';[8] then, in 1353 at Windsor, 'for 1 quarter 3 bushels of salt for rubbing chimneys (*pro caminis fricandis*)',[9] and at Clarendon in 1485, *pro j packe de bayesalt pro dicto camino.*[10] For what purpose was the salt used? I am unable to suggest an answer to the question.

[1] K.H. 18, f. 22.                         [2] E. 460, 17.
[3] E. 496, 24.                             [4] E. 502, 15.
[5] Liberate R. 24 Hen. III.                [6] Ibid. 32 Hen. III, m. 13.
[7] Ibid. 35 Hen. III, m. 6.               [8] E. 467, 6 (2).
[9] Hope, *Windsor Castle*, 171.           [10] E. 460, 16.

# VI

## MASONRY: TECHNICAL TERMS

THE number of trade terms applied in the Middle Ages to worked stones, according to their shapes and purposes, is surprising. Excellent work has been done upon the identifying of a certain number of these by Professor Willis in his *Architectural Nomenclature*, but there are a good many which he does not mention. Unfortunately they usually occur without any illuminating context, being recorded in building accounts simply as varieties of stone bought, without any indication of their purpose.

The simplest form of worked stone was ashlar—rectangular blocks of stone used for building walls and tooled on the one, external, face. These occur at Winchester in 1222 as 'esselers'; at Westminster in 1252 as 'asselers'; and at Ely in 1337 as 'haseler'. The outside face of the walls of the dormitory at Durham were to be '*de puro lapide vocato achiler*' in 1398, and for work at Pittington Manor in 1450 'v$^{xx}$ iij achillars' were bought for 12s. 3d.[1] In 1532 John Orgar of Boughton quarry supplied for Westminster Palace 2,300 feet of 'harde stone of Kente called assheler unparellid', at 24s. the 100 feet, and 106 feet of 'harde assheler redy aparilled', at 33s. 4d.,[2] the difference in cost being the value of the labour of dressing the roughly scappled blocks. At the same quarry in 1365 'rough assheler' was 10s. the 100 feet while 'assheler' was 2d. the foot,[3] and three years earlier 'square assheler' was only 6s. the 100 feet.[4] When the ashlar had to be worked on a curve, for building a round tower, it was naturally more expensive; so that in 1377 we find that '1400 of round esscheler, greater or less, for facing (*cooperiendam*) a tower' at Dover cost £15.[5] Although the actual blocks varied considerably in size, there seems to have been a recognized standard, as about 1465 we have instructions for measuring ashlar: 'First, it is to be understande that every asheler is xij ynche thykke and xviij ynches longe, wiche multiplied to gedere make ij$^c$ xvj ynches; and so every asheler, of what length or brede that he be of, conteyneth ij$^c$ xvj ynches; and that schalbe your devysore ever in meatynge (measuring) of ashelers'.[6] In 1423

---

[1] *Hist. Dunelm. Script. Tres* (Surtees Soc.), cccxxv.
[2] T.R., f. 82.
[3] E. 483, 21.
[4] Ibid. 20.
[5] E. 462, 25.
[6] *Manners & Household Expenses* (Roxburghe Club), 438.

'grand assheler', of which each block was 'of the depth of 11 inches at least', was 37*s*. and 'comyn assheler' 21*s*. the hundred.[1]

Ordinary ashlar was used to form one face of a wall, the other face being formed either of rough stone, plastered, or of other blocks of ashlar, with rubble filling between. But thin walls, such as those of parapets or choir-screens, might be built of ashlar blocks dressed on both faces. Such stones, tooled on two parallel faces and extending right through the wall, were known as 'through-stones'—as at York in 1420 'carriage of 6 stones called *thurghes* from the quarry of Bramham to York'[2]—or, much more commonly, 'parpains' or 'perpins'. In 1252 'parpens' occur among the stone for Westminster Abbey and 89,200 'parpeyns' of Caen stone were bought for the Tower in 1278.[3] Boughton quarry provided 'perpainassheler' at 18*s*. the 100 feet, in 1365, and four years later 66 feet of 'assheler' parpail' was bought, at 12*d*. the foot, for a square cistern at Leeds Castle,[4] while about 1430 'perpoynt' or 'perpendashler' for King's Hall, Cambridge, cost 6*d*. the foot, ordinary ashlar being 4*d*.[5] In 1444, among the stores in the royal stoneyards were '45 ft. of large perpenyassheler, fully worked, for the draught brugge at the chief gate of the manor (of Shene)',[6] and 'parapent achillar' occurs at Pittington in 1450.[7] It is possibly to such stones that allusion is made in the Dover Accounts of 1221, when William de Grimesbi, stone-cutter, and his partners were paid £13. 4*s*. for cutting 2,000 feet of stone, at 12*s*. the 100 feet—'*Et nota quod in cc horum lapidum fuit duplex incisio*'.[8]

When the worked face of the ashlar was cut at an angle, instead of square, it was known as 'skew ashlar'. Thus 'scuassheler' occurs at Rochester in 1369; 'scheuasshlere' at Shene in 1369; and 'skwassheler', also at Shene, in 1444. More often such stones were simply called 'skewes', as at Ely in 1360; 'skyus' at Merton College in 1292; 'scuwes', for buttresses, at Westminster in 1353; 'scu' or 'scues' in many accounts; and 'escus' and 'scutes' in the Westminster Abbey roll of 1252. This last form is probably influenced by a false connexion with *écu*, a shield or scutcheon.

Another form of angled stone was known as 'sconchon', with the usual variety of spellings. Willis says: 'An obtuse external angle was called a scutcheon';[9] but, upon careful consideration, I am inclined to think that the examples which he quotes as 'skouchons' and 'scouchon' ought to be

---

[1] London Bridge Accts., vol. iii.
[2] Y.F.R. 40.
[3] E. 467, 6 (4).
[4] E. 544, 23.
[5] K.H. 7, f. 212; 8, f. 29.
[6] E. 503, 12.
[7] *Hist. Dunelm. Script. Tres* (Surtees Soc.), cccxxvi.
[8] E. 462, 8.
[9] *Nomenclature*, 37.

read 'as 'skonchons' and 'sconchon'. It is impossible to distinguish between *u* and *n* in manuscripts, but the form 'scunchuns', which occurs in the Merton College accounts for 1293,[1] seems decisive. If so, the word should presumably be taken with 'scoinson'. This survives in the 'scoinson' arch, still used to describe the rear arch of a window, and was, as Willis shows,[2] applied in medieval times to the splay of the window opening, between the actual window-frame and the inner surface of the wall. I take it, therefore, that 'sconchon' is used for a splayed stone, which covers and extends Willis's definition. In the Fotheringay Church contract[3] of 1434, the tower is to be taken up square to the height of the nave and then made octagonal, or 'turnyd in viij panes, and at every schonchon a boutrasse fynysht with finial'. Here 'schonchon' is clearly the angle of the octagon. In the agreement with the quarrymen of Kent to supply stone for Eton College in 1442,[3] they are to provide '12 coyns 4 sconchonsanglers and 8 square anglers' for certain ledgements or tablings. Willis interprets this as meaning 12 angle-stones, of which 8 shall be square-cut and 4 'schonchons', probably to carry the tablings round semi-octagonal turrets. At Hadleigh Castle in 1365 'anglers and scunchons' occur together,[4] as do 'coyn and sconchoun' at Sheppey in 1366.[5] The King's Hall accounts for 1430 mention 'sqwynchon aschler' and 'sqwynchoncrest' in connexion with the gate tower and probably for its octagonal flanking turrets; and the stone bought for Louth Steeple in about 1504 included 100 feet of 'achlere and squinches of 18 inches high, and 15 at the least', at 2½*d.* the foot.[6] Finally we may mention the provision of various worked stones for windows at Pittington in 1450, the list of which ends with 'j sol skownsiom';[7] Willis[8] takes this to mean 'a sill and a scoinson arch', but I think it is more probably 'a scoinson, or splayed, sill'.

Of quoins, or corner stones, there is nothing much to be said. They occur at Winchester in 1222 as 'kuinz', and at Ely in 1368 as 'cunes', but usually as 'coynes'. In 1366 the Eglemont quarries provided '956 coignes, whereof 216 whitecoignes', for work at Langley; about the same date 'parpaincoins' occur in several Rochester Castle accounts; and 'pleyncoyns' are mentioned at Westminster in 1444; and 'coyne ascheler' is found in the St. Mary-at-Hill accounts for 1505.

It has already been noted that walls were often marked out horizontally

---

[1] Merton Coll. Roll 4055.
[2] *Nomenclature*, 56.     [3] App. B.
[4] E. 464, 9.          [5] E. 483, 23.     [6] *Archaeologia*, x. 80.
[7] *Hist. Dunelm. Script. Tres* (Surtees Soc.), cccxxv.     [8] *Nomenclature*, 57.

by courses of stone slabs, of which the edges were sometimes carved (as in early string-courses) or moulded. These were known as tables, tablements, or ledgements. Thus at Winchester in 1222 Payn of Christchurch was paid 26s. for 700 feet *de tablamentis* of stone of the Isle (of Wight); in 1286, for Harlech Castle, 200 feet of *tabellamenti* was supplied;[1] at Ely in 1337 we find stone *pro tabulis et leggemens*; 'leggementable' at Westminster in 1444; and at Pittington various parcels *tabularum* in 1450. These terms, however, were applied generally to many varieties of flat stones besides string-courses. So we find at Silverstone in 1279 stone bought *ad tabulamentum fontis*,[2] evidently the coping of the well; *tabul' pro fenestris* at Langley in 1367, which probably means the flat inner sills; and at St. Briavel's in 1375 freestone *pro tablement' porte*, and *pro tablement' faciendo pro le portecolis*,[3] of which the significance is not obvious. 'Scutables' occur at Westminster in 1333 and 1444. They would presumably be a plain variety of the 'skwlery-mer' mentioned in the same 1444 account, the French *larmier*, which occurs as 'lermer' at Rochester in 1379, being a projecting moulding so cut as to throw off the water.[4] Willis opposes to this the 'water-table', which he shows was a term applied to a plain tabling and which he considers implies a moulding that allows the water to trickle down the wall.[5] It is found at Calais in 1468, when 72 feet of '*lystes voc' watertables*' were bought;[6] and at Cambridge, when certain building was to be done at Corpus Christi College in 1459, the water-table was to be made partly of stone and partly of brick.[7] For the London church of St. Mary-at-Hill 'vj^x fote water tabyll' was provided in 1505.[8]

The Merton accounts for 1315 mention 'curstable',[9] and for Windsor Castle 557 feet of 'rengetables' were bought in 1368[10]—both terms signifying a string-course. 'The *renge table* immediately under the bottom of the windows' is mentioned at Lacock in 1315.[7] In 1429 a 'querreour' supplied for work at King's Hall—'leggement', 'joyntable', and 'kyngystáble'.[11] 'Joynttabyl' occurs during the next two years, at 1½d. the foot, a price which shows that it must have been thin and plain. It may be noted that the 'legement table' to be supplied to Eton in 1442 is described as 'beryng ful joyntes at ye lest iij ynches or more'—though whether the 3 inches refers to the thickness of the table or to the joints is left obscure. 'Kynges table', which occurs elsewhere in the King's Hall accounts, and also at Peterhouse

[1] E. 491, 13.   [2] E. 484, 7. Also 4 stones *ad cornar' fontis.*
[3] E. 481, 20.   [4] Willis, *Nomenclature*, 10.   [5] Ibid. 35.
[6] E. 197, 5.   [7] App. B.   [8] *Mems.* (E.E.T.S.), 257.
[9] Merton Coll. Roll 3642.   [10] E. 494, 1.
[11] K.H. 7, f. 212.

in 1462[1] at 3*d.* the foot, appears at Ely in 1334 at 2½*d.* the foot, the same price as plain 'tables and leggemens'. A later entry of 'kyngestables' in the *Ely Sacrist Rolls* is assigned by Professor Willis to 'the upper works of the stone octagon', and he adds: 'Beneath the parapet . . . there is a deep hollow occupied by running leaves, and having small ball-flowers at intervals. The form and arrangement so nearly resembles the ornament beneath the seat of the royal throne in the great seals of Henry III and the first two Edwards, that I conjecture that it derived the name of King's table from this imitation.'[2] This is an ingenious suggestion but not altogether convincing, and I am inclined to think that the price is hardly consistent with work of this elaborate nature. Whatever the significance of the term, it appears to be confined to East Anglia.

At the top of the wall was often a tabling supported, or ornamented, by corbels, and such 'corbeltables' occur with great frequency in accounts. At Westminster in 1333 we have '64 ft of Caen stone worked and carved (*talliat*') for corbeltables' in store—these identical stones being bought, as 'courbletables', four years earlier—and 'corbailtablement' occurs at Sheppey in 1365. In the contract of 1412 for Catterick Church 'the tablyng of the endes' is to be made 'with seueronne tabill'.[3] This, on the analogy of the French *severonde*, meaning eaves, Willis interprets as the common form of gable coping, consisting of flat stones bevelled on the under edge—in which case it is probably the same as the 'gabelston', of which 20 feet was bought for Wallingford Castle in 1376. The Merton College accounts for 1292–4 contain references to 29 feet *de seueronibus*, 'ceuerundchuns' or 'ceuerundcoyn', and 'ceuerundskyus'.[4] For Pittington Manor in 1450 we have '24 ells of severans'; and for Hampton Court in 1535, 720 feet of 'severant tabyll'.[5]

Walls were frequently finished with either a plain or an embattled parapet, with a cresting, and 'crestes' occur with great frequency in building accounts. Sometimes, as at Sheppey in 1366, 'scucrest' is mentioned; at Westminster in 1329 Caen stone was used 'for scuthtables and scucrestes for the new alure (parapet walk)'.[6] The estimate for repairs to the Tower of London in 1532 gives details of the battlements; for instance, on the west side of 'the hye Whyte tower' there were 48 'coppys', or risers, the spaces between being 6 or 7 feet, and each requiring 'xxx fote in skew and crest'.[7] Both 'crestes' and 'spaces' occur together at Rochester in 1367 and

---

[1] P. 1462–3.  [2] *Nomenclature*, 36.  [3] App. B.
[4] Rolls 4055, 4059.  [5] H.C. 238, f. 243.
[6] E. 467, 7.  [7] Bayley, *Hist. of the Tower*, xxix.

1373, and sometimes the form 'vents' is used instead of 'spaces', as at King's Hall in 1430—'*vent pro enbatylment*', and 'venttes crest', and at Hampton Court, about 1530—'420 foote of vent and crest for the haull'.[1] Another item connected with these Hampton Court battlements was—'212 footes of water tabyll for the inner part of the bartyllment of the haull'. It looks as if 'water table' is here used not in the ordinary sense in which we have had it before, but for something in the nature of a gutter.

The rainwater was voided from behind the parapet by gargoyles,[2] on the sculpture of which medieval carvers usually gave free rein to their fancy for the grotesque. For the great gate of Cambridge Castle two 'gargurl' were made in 1286, at a cost of 2s., and 'gargules' at Ely were also a shilling each in 1360, while at Windsor in 1363 Thomas Holford and his partners were paid 13d. apiece for 159 'gargoilles', and at York in 1485 William Busshell, 'entayler', was paid a shilling each for making 32 'gargilles'.

Like gargoyles, corbels—stones projecting from the wall to serve as brackets—were isolated blocks and were often carved. In 1249 King Henry ordered the rebuilding of his chamber in Nottingham Castle 'in such a way that a decent stone tabling be made on the wall and that heads be carved on the heads of the corbels over the said tabling'.[3]

In 1292 repayment was made to Reynold de Gray of money which he had spent on painting and colouring 10 corbels in the king's great new chamber, set in the stone walls under the beams which support the roof, in Chester Castle.[4] That same year, at Corfe Castle, 8s. 8d. was spent on '52 great stones for corbels (*corballos*) to carry the beams called ties (*laquei*) by the walls of the keep'.[5] At Leeds Castle in 1361 we have 2 corbels for the front of the bridge, each 4½ feet in length, and a great *corbell* for the bridge, 5½ feet in length and 2½ feet in breadth.[6] For the Tower there were bought in 1400 two stones of asheler, containing 3½ feet, for making 2 corbels to carry one end of the drawbridge at the Storkestoure;[7] and for London Bridge in 1426 were bought, at 7s. 6d. each, '12 great *corbelstonys* of hardston of Kent, to serve for erecting the new tower at the Drawbregge', each being 6 feet long, 20 inches broad, and 12 inches deep.[8] At Launceston in 1461 'moreston', that is moor-stone, was used for '24 large *corbelles* designed to carry the ends of the timbers of a floor of the tower'.[9]

---

[1] Law, *Hampton Court*, i. 347.
[2] *Gargill voc' gutterston* occurs at Calais in 1468: E. 197, 5.
[3] *Close R.* 145.                          [4] Liberate R. 28 Edw. I, m. 8.
[5] E. 460, 29.              [6] E. 466, 19.              [7] E. 502, 15.
[8] Bridge Accts., vol. iii.                          [9] E. 461, 20.

'Source' is another word that is not infrequently used for the corbels, or brackets, on which images stand, 24 pieces of marble, for instance, being used in St. Stephen's, Westminster, 'for *sources* for images under housings (*tabernaculis*)', in 1347.[1]

Among the many varieties of stones supplied in 1252 for Westminster Abbey are entries of 1,591 feet of *cerch*, and 268 feet of *serches*.[2] In 1365 we find 240 worked stones of Reigate called *skerches* provided for a vice, or winding stair, in Westminster Palace;[3] the King's Hall accounts speak of '*seerch*' in 1417, '*sergez*' in 1430, '*sergh*', at 1½*d*. the foot, and 'greater sergh', at 2*d*., next year, without any indication of their purpose; '*serches* for the well in the widow's house' at Cambridge, occur in 1478;[4] and a London account of 1532 records 4*s*. spent 'for 2 *serchez* bought for the furneys'.[5] Although the term was thus in use over a period of about 300 years it does not seem to have been recorded anywhere, and I am unable to explain its significance.[6] It occurs in company with another uncertain word at Langley in 1368—'*In soillas* (sills) *serches et coperons emptis pro camera regis*'.[7] Similarly, in the King's Hall accounts for 1431 the *sergh*' are followed by 8 *copporons peces* at 6*d*. each, and two years later the smith is paid for clamps *pro caminis jungent' copporons*.[8] The same accounts, for 1394, give 20*d*. spent on 'the coporowne of the fireplace'. The only other occurrence of the word that I have noted is in a list of stores in 1444—'*Et de iiij getons deauratis impos' super les coprons divers' cam'. Et de diversis coronis cupr' cum diversis getons charnellatis et non charnellatis impos' infra ciluracione parlure manerii de Byflete*.'[9] The *getons* are probably metal castings, some of the strips being embattled (*charnellati*), and it looks as if the *coprons* were some form of coping or cornice. Another form of coping is probably implied by the *chapement bowe*, of which 6 feet were bought for Westminster Abbey in 1252.

Coming to the stones that are component parts of windows, we may start with an entry concerned with Pittington Hall in 1450:[10] '*Johanni Knayth et Willelmo Chambre cementariis pro factura ij fenestrarum, ex convencione—C⁵ Et eisdem pro factura ij formpeys chaumeres retournes corbels transoums j sol skownsiom pro ij fenestris, in grosso, —Lxvj⁵ viij*ᵈ.' Here *formpeys*

---

[1] E. 470, 16.  [2] E. 467, 1.  [3] E. 472, 14.
[4] King's Coll. Mundum Bk. vii.  [5] E. 474, 5.
[6] There is a French word *cerche* meaning the brim (of a hat, &c.), so that it may mean a border.
[7] E. 544, 22.  [8] K.H. 8, f. 66.
[9] E. 503, 12. Presumably *cam*' should be expanded *caminorum*.
[10] *Hist. Dunelm. Script. Tres* (Surtees Soc.), cccxxv.

are sets of tracery; *chaumeres* jambs; *retournes*, the angular finish of the hood-molds; the *corbels* would be the bosses at the ends of the *retournes*; *transoums* transoms; and the *sol skownsiom* I have already explained as a splayed sill. As no mullions are mentioned, the windows were presumably of one light. We can now proceed to examine the terms in detail.

Sills present no particular features of interest. They occur most frequently as *soilles*, but with such variants as *suyll* (Sheppey, 1362), and *sewlys* (King's Hall, 1417). The framing of doors and windows being similar, we have at Eltham in 1428 'soilez and jambepeces for hanging the iron door'.[1] Jambs ·usually figure as *iambe or iaumbe*; in the Merton accounts for 1334 is mention of '*yaumbys pro magna porta*'; in those of Peterhouse between 1462 and 1465 they are called *jawmys* and *jamys*; and among stone supplied to Westminster in 1532 from Boughton quarry we have 82½ feet of 'jawme stones wrought for a gate', at 16*d.* the foot.[2] The form *chambraunces* occurs at Ely in 1360 and at Langley in 1368, and *chamberhaunt* at King's Hall in 1466. Among stones supplied to King's Hall in 1428 are *chamerantz pro magna porta*, but the same list also includes *jambes*, which looks as if there were some distinction between the two terms. Later in the same account is a rather puzzling entry—'*pro iiij magnis peciis (petre) pro pomell et pro chosyng de la chamerant.*'[3] Possibly, as is so frequently the case, two entirely distinct items have been lumped together, all four pieces of stone being for the 'pomell'—which is usually some kind of knop on the point of a gable —and the rest of the payment being for selecting jamb-stones.

The stones composing the moulded frame of a window, or door, were also known as 'molds'. For St. Stephen's Chapel at Westminster 231 Caen stones called 'molde peces' were provided in 1324, and nine years later 15 pieces of Reigate stone were used 'for mold pieces for the upper windows'.[4] About the same date *petrae de molde* and 'muldestones for windows' figure in the Ely rolls. In 1400 'mouldestone called skewes skapeled' was sent from Maidstone for use at Sutton Manor,[5] and 'mouldytston'—not, however, specifically stated to be for windows—occurs at Porchester in 1408. These frames, particularly those of doors, were often elaborately worked with a series of varied mouldings, and we are fortunate in having a fifteenth-century plan and description of the series occurring in one of the doors of St. Stephen's, Bristol, and a similar description of the west door of St. Mary's Redcliffe, among the notes of William of Worcester. Professor Willis, who reproduced these in facsimile in his *Architectural*

[1] E. 496, 7.                    [2] T.R., f. 82.                    [3] K.H. 7, f. 247.
[4] E. 469, 8, 11.                [5] E. 502, 15.

*Nomenclature* and analysed them with his usual skill, believed that the descriptions were dictated and the plan actually drawn by a working mason. The mouldings named are: (*a*) the fillet, a flat narrow strip with parallel sides; (*b*) the bowtel, a convex moulding; (*c*) the casement, a concave moulding; (*d*) the ressaunt, an inflected moulding; (*e*) the lorimer, which occurs only as the outermost order and is,[1] as we have seen, a member with a rounded upper surface, undercut. Casements and boutels both occur in the descriptions of wooden cornices and other decorations of the hall at Hampton Court,[2] and in the accounts for making the stalls in St. George's, Windsor, in 1477, one item is 'for rounding the bowtelles of the lyntell'.[3] The contract for Fotheringay Church, in 1434, states that the aisle windows are to be like those in the quire, but they 'shal no bowtels haf at all'. In 1513 the angle towers of King's College Chapel were to have 'rysant', or ogival, gablets. But, generally speaking, details of mouldings did not concern the clerks who kept the accounts, and those who drew up the contracts preferred to rely on patterns rather than verbal descriptions.

Within its frame a window might be divided vertically by mullions, horizontally by transoms, and at the top by tracery. In 1442 the windows in the tower of Dunster Church were to be made 'with a trawnson and a moynell'.[4] At the Tower in 1533 there were 'in the kynges dynyng chambre iiij wyndowes, ij of them wt. iiij lyghtes new made from the transom upward in heyght vj fote'.[5] Two years later at Hampton Court the charge made by William Johnson of 'Baryngton in Cotsolde' for windows of 3 lights with a transom and 3-foot height of jamb was 5s. the light; 4-foot height 5s. 2d., and 5-foot 5s. 10d.; for windows with no transom 4s. 6d.[6] In a Calais account for 1473 there is mention of 'stones called crosse wyndows'[7] which are presumably transoms. The usual term for the upright mullion was some form of the French *moynel*, or *menel*. At Westminster Abbey in 1252 we have 22 feet of *maignauz*; at Merton College in 1293 *moynls*; at Westminster Palace in 1329 *moigneles*; at Dover in 1339 *meinelles*; at Ely in 1360 *monials*. In 1380 there is a payment 'for setting (*esand*') various stone *monyeles* and fixing them with lead in le westgavell' at Ripon.[8] Stones in store at Westminster in 1444 include '14 *moynell* for windows'.

The medieval term for window tracery was *forme* or *forme-piece*. In the contract of 1373 for building the cloisters at Boxley Abbey it is stipulated

---

[1] See above, p. 106.  [2] See p. 217.  [3] E. 496, 17.
[4] App. B.  [5] E. 474, 13.  [6] H.C. 238, f. 243.
[7] E. 198, 4.  [8] R. 101.

that the mason shall put *diversas formas* above the columns of the arcade. At Langley, in 1367, we have: 'To Walter le Masson for a *fourme* for a window of 2 lights (*dierum*) for the north part of the Freytour, with the *chaumbraunces*—15*s*. To the same for 3 *fourmes* for windows of 2 lights for the east part of the Freytour, with the *chambrances*, cut by contract, giving 6*s*. 8*d*. for the forme—20*s*.'[1] Another Langley account, for 1374, mentions '*iiij fourmes iiij fen[estrarum] cum iaumbes et moynels—viij^s. ij^d*.[2]

For Westminster Abbey in 1252, £11 was paid on the contract for tracery for the church (*in tascha formarum ecclesie*), and there are also mentions of the purchase of certain quantities of *formell'*. So at Ely in 1340 both *forma* and the diminutive *formula* occur in a glazing account, and *formalettes* figure in the King's Hall accounts of 1428. For St. Stephen's, Westminster, '10 pieces of Reigate stone to make the tracery (*formis peciis*) at the sides (*costera*) of the chapel' occur in 1333, and there is also an entry of—'various pieces of Reigate stone, completed, containing in all 6 sets of tracery (*formas*) for the chapel.[3] This indicates that 'forme-pieces' are the individual members of the tracery and 'formes' complete sets of tracery. An entry in an account of 1366 for Sheppey Castle introduces an obscure term: '*pro iiij formis et iiij trentis libere petre scapulatis, pro pecia vs.,—xls. Et pro ij trentis . . . ad fenestr' pro gabulo ecclesie dando pro pecia xij^s—xxiiij^s*.'[4] What is meant by *trentis* (or *treutis*?) I cannot say; as they cost the same as the sets of tracery they must have been on the same scale of elaboration, and it is possible that the word, which does not seem to occur elsewhere, may indicate a particular form of tracery.

Professor Willis has pointed out[5] that the contract for glazing the windows in the Beauchamp Chapel at Warwick, in 1458, gives a list of the technical terms applied to the various types of openings in the tracery of a typical window of the Perpendicular style, and is apparently the only document to do so.

The description of the windows on the south run as follows:

In the south side of the chappell be three windowes, every windowe conteineth vj lights. Every light conteineth xxj foote. Item viij smaller batements above; and every batement conteineth ij foote and a halfe. Item iiij angells; every of them halfe a foote and a quarter. Item ij hiest small lights; either of them conteining a foote and a halfe. Item all the katurs; quarrelles; and oylements. So every of the said windowes conteinith clvj (foot). All in tota iiij^c lx foot ix inches.

Here the vertical lights in the head of the window, owing to their start-

---

[1] E. 544, 20.                                      [2] E. 466, 9.
[3] E. 469, 11.                 [4] E. 483, 23.        [5] *Nomenclature*, 51.

PLATE 10

*a.* BUILDING: SHOWING CENTERING OF ARCH
IN POSITION 14TH CENTURY

*b.* MASONS WORKING STONE 13TH CENTURY

PLATE II

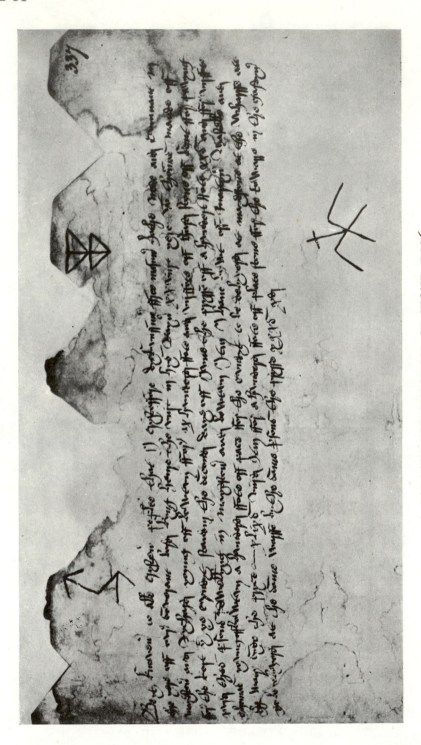

A BARGAIN FOR PURCHASE OF STONE, 1536
ATTESTED WITH THREE MASONS' BANKER-MARKS

ing from the arched heads of the lower lights, have part of their feet cut off, or in technical language 'abated', and are therefore called 'batements'. The 'angells' are simply angular openings. 'Katurs' are quatrefoils. They occur as 'caters' in the accounts for making the stalls of St. George's, Windsor, and the roof of the hall of Hampton Court, and as 'crosse quarters' on the angle towers of King's College Chapel; also, as '2 cater-mysez bought for the king's chamber (at Westminster), containing 8 feet of glays', in 1401.[1] The 'quarrelles' are presumably openings so small that they only use one quarry of glass. 'Oylements' or 'oyletts', as they are called elsewhere in the contract, are small openings which do not fall into any of the preceding categories. The Westminster accounts for 1333 mention '40 pieces of Caen stone for *oyletz*, not worked',[2] and a later account, for 1399, records the purchase of glass for 4 *oylettes* of the louvre, and of other glass, with the arms of the king and St. Edward, for the *oylettes* of 4 windows in the hall.[3] Similarly the glazier's account for Wallingford Castle in 1375 contains several references to *oylettes*.[4]

Purchases of 'fenestrals' occur from time to time on the Merton College rolls from 1292 to 1377, at Sheppey in 1366, and at Langley from 1368 to 1384. At this last date there is an entry of 9s. 9d. paid for 'soill' fenestrals and moynels for 3 windows for the chapter-house'.[5] Taken with a Merton entry of the same date referring to '120 feet in height (*secundum altitudinem*) of fenestrals and sconchons',[6] this suggests that they were equivalent to the 'moldes' mentioned above.

The carved bosses at the end of a hood-mold, on either side of a door, were known as 'beckets'. In the King's Hall accounts '2 bekettes of the great door' cost 20d., and '2 bekettes of smaller size' 12d. in 1417;[7] ten years later there is mention of '2 great bekettes for the door at the entrance to the garden'.[8] In 1444 'bekettes' of Reigate stone, fully worked, were in store at Westminster.[9] For Henry VIII's work at Hampton Court John Whighte of Winchester, freemason, was paid the large sum of £6 'for workyng carryng gravyng and intayllyng yn freston of vj bekketts for iij dores of the new hall', and another mason, John Rogers, was employed 'taylyng the beccattes of the dore yn the kynges great watchyng chambre, wyth the beccattes of the chymney, wyth the kynges badges and the quenys letter'.[10]

[1] E. 502, 23.          [2] E. 469, 11.          [3] E. 470, 17.
[4] E. 490, 3.          [5] E. 466, 9.          [6] Roll 4102 (*b*).
[7] K.H. 6, f. 149.          [8] K.H. 7, f. 248.          [9] E. 503, 12.
[10] H.C. 240, f. 57.

Pillars or columns rarely figure as single items in stone accounts, except Purbeck marble, in which material they were in great demand. For Westminster Palace in 1329, besides 'marble worked for columns', there was bought Caen stone '*pro columpnis et torall' capelle*'[1]—of which I cannot explain *torall'*, though it may mean capitals. Small columns, such as those of the Boxley cloisters,[2] might be made of a single stone, but structural pillars are practically always built up. In the long list of stones provided for Westminster Abbey in 1252, which we have quoted so often, there appear not only hundreds of feet of marble columns, but also, in one parcel, 6 bases, 6 capitals (*chapiters*),[3] and some 17 feet *de grossis rotundis*, which we may take as being stones for pillars. In the Merton roll for 1292–3[4] are a number of entries, such as: 'for 5 *buscell*' for the great column, price of a *buscelle* 7d.'; 'for 20 ft. of small *buscellis*, cut by contract, 20d.'; 'for 21 ft. of great *buscell*' for the great column, price of a foot 7d.'; and 'for 7 ft. of *buscelles* for the great column, cut by contract, and those 7 ft. make 5 *assisas*, 5s. 4d.' The word does not occur in later rolls, nor have I met it elsewhere, but I suggest that it means a complete circular slice of stone, resembling a bushel measure, and that in the last entry the 7 ft. of 'bushels' made 5 courses of the pillar. It may be added that the Abbey list of 1252 mentions purchases of *assises* at 5d. each, which may also be pillar segments. Some time during the fourteenth century the word 'nowel', which has survived in our use of 'newel' for the central pillar of a spiral stair, came into use. We find 552 'nowell', at 10d. each, provided for Sheppey Castle in 1362, and for Hadleigh Castle next year 30 'niewels', at 20d. From this time onwards the term is in constant use, as, for instance, at King's Hall in 1430, at Sandwich in 1463,[5] and in 1505 in London, when 31 'nowelles' were bought for the church of St. Mary-at-Hill.[6] Although I have not yet found direct evidence, I maintain that—considering the frequency with which 'nowels' occur, often in company with other members of arch construction,[7] and the absence of other terms which can be identified as components of pillars—'nowels' applied generally to pillars and not only to the particular variety that supports a winding stair.

The semi-pillar attached to a wall or pier to carry one end of an arch was, and is, known as a respond.[8] 'Respowndez', at 10d. each, occur in the

---

[1] E. 467, 7.     [2] App. B, p. 448.

[3] The forms *chapitrell* and *capitell* occur in the same list: E. 467, 1.

[4] Roll 4059.     [5] E. 481, 26.     [6] *Memorials* (E.E.T.S.), 257.

[7] e.g. at Porchester in 1397: 39 pieces of broad stone, 3 ft. long, called *noweles* mentioned with *rachement* (i.e. responds) and vaulting keys: E. 479, 23.

[8] I suspect that the '*petris voc' rappomis*' in *Ely Sacrist Rolls*, 121, should read '*respouns*'.

King's Hall accounts for 1428, and 'respoundes' were in store at West-minster in 1444. Fotheringay Church, in 1434, was to have 'ten mighty pillars with four responds',[1] and the breadth of the chapel at Eton is given, in 1448, as 'from respond to respond'.[1] At Lacock Abbey in 1315 certain arches are to be made '*entre les deux rachemens*',[1] which, from the context, appears to mean 'between the two responds'; and at Porchester in 1397 we find '20 stones of Bonchurche for *rachement* and keys (or bosses) of the vaulting (*clavibus vousure*) of the cellar of the great tower'.[2]

Arches, whether lying between pillars or over the heads of doors or windows, are constructed with wedge-shaped voussoirs, and that term has been applied to these stones—with the usual vagaries of spelling—from at least the thirteenth century. For Westminster Abbey in 1252 we have chamfered voussoirs (*folsuris chanferitis*), rounded voussoirs (*folsuris rotundis*), and voussoirs worked with a fillet (*folsuris cum filo*).[3] The Merton College rolls mention *vousure*, at 1*d*. the foot, in 1289, and *vousours*, at 1½*d*. in 1293. It is worth noting that the latter account also gives 'parpeyns, bought for the great arch', as voussoirs might quite reasonably be included in the class of perpin ashlar. '*Vousores*' occur at Ely in 1360; *vausure* at Sheppey in 1362; and *vousure* at Langley in 1368. The King's Hall accounts contain several variants; *vowsour* in 1388, *vaucers* in 1412, '*long wousours*' (each 3 ft.) in 1431; '*wowsers* for windows' at 2½*d*. the foot, '*double vowcers*' at 8*d*., and single at 6*d*.—apparently for the great gate—in 1428;[4] and '*vowcerys ryth*' and '*crokyd voucers*', each at 2¾*d*. the foot, in 1432.[5] For the new buildings at Peterhouse in 1463 '*ryght vowsers*' cost 2*d*. the foot at Eversdon quarry, and '*innervowsers*' 1½*d*.[6] These 'crooked' vous-soirs may possibly be the springers of the arches, worked partly on the square with the jamb and then turning at an angle to begin the arch. Twenty 'spryngers', at 1*s*. each, occur at King's Hall in 1435, and '15 pecis of beginners', costing 22*s*. 6*d*., were supplied, with other stones—such as 'moniel', 'soyle' and 'chamberhaunt'—which are components of windows, for new buildings there in 1466.[7] At Peterhouse in 1463 six 'begynners for windows' cost 9*s*. On the whole it is more likely that the voussoirs of an arch were called 'crooked' either as being notched or joggled, or per-haps merely to distinguish them from the 'right' voussoirs which composed a square-headed window-frame. Where such a window was small the top member of the frame would consist of a single stone, the lintel or 'lyntell',

---

[1] App. B.  [2] E. 479, 23.  [3] E. 467, 1.
[4] K.H. 7, ff. 212, 248.  [5] K.H. 8, f. 65.  [6] P. 1462–3.
[7] K.H. 13, f. 294.

which occurs, for instance, at Merton 1315, Ely 1360, Sheppey 1362, Leeds Castle 1382, Hampton Court 1535.

No definite evidence appears to be available as to the terms applied in the Middle Ages to vaulting ribs, but as *ogives* was used in France with that meaning in the seventeenth century[1] it is at least probable that the forms of that word found in early accounts refer to the same objects. The Merton College accounts give us *oguis* in 1290 and *ogeyus* in 1294; at the Tower we have '70 ft. of Reigate stone called *ogeus*' in 1349; at Ely in 1358 *oygifs*; at Windsor, five years later, '486 cartloads of Reigate stone called *ogeux*'; at King's Hall in 1428 *oggez*; and at Tattershall Castle in 1435 *odgyfes*.[2] Neither these nor any other references that I have seen give any indication of the use to which these stones are to be put;[3] but if they are not vaulting ribs, we appear to be left without any medieval term for a distinctive architectural feature.

The stones filling in the vaulting between the ribs were called 'pendants' and were frequently of chalk. At the point of intersection of the ribs, in a simple quadripartite vault, was set a block of stone, now known as a 'boss', but in early times usually called a 'key'; in more elaborate vaulting there might be a number of smaller keys in each bay. The Westminster Abbey accounts for 1252 make a reference to 'keys' (*clavibus*); they also give several purchases of '*bosseus*', which may possibly refer to bosses. In later Abbey accounts for the completion of the nave we have, between 1486 and 1488, three similar entries, each of the purchase of one great stone called *le grete keye* and of five other smaller stones called *lez keyes*, representing three bays.[4] It is worth noticing that in 1491–2 twenty great stones '*qui fuerunt ultra mensuram unius carecte*' were bought, and Mr. Rackham reasonably assumes that these were for the keys of the nave vault,[5] though their purpose is not stated—which is a useful reminder that, although the early clerks of the works had only too many technical terms at their command, they did not always trouble to use them. 'Stones called keyes' are found at Ely in 1358; and in 1431 at King's Hall 5 feet of stone was provided 'for the principal key of the arch of the new great gate' and also '4 keyes or knots (*nodi*) of the great gate'.[6] In the contract for vaulting the quire of St. George's Chapel at Windsor, in 1536, it is stipulated that 'the

---

[1] Félibien, *Principes d'Architecture*, s.v.

[2] *Hist. MSS. Com. Rep.—De L'Isle & Dudley*, i. 213.

[3] Willis considered the Ely *oggifs* identifiable with certain specific window-sills: *Nomenclature*, 11.

[4] Rackham, *Nave of Westminster*, 40.

[5] Ibid. 43.                                                    [6] K.H. 8, f. 62.

principall keyes of the said vawte . . . shall be wrought more pendaunt and holower than the keyes or pendaunts of the body (i.e. the nave)' and shall be carved with the King's arms and badges.[1] The expression 'keyes or pendaunts' is an early instance of the modern application of the term 'pendant' to the prolongation of the boss which is characteristic of these ornate fan-traceried vaults. Such a prolongation appears to have sometimes been known as a 'bullion'—20s. being paid 'for makying and intayling of two bullyns in freston standyng in the vowght of the great bay window' at Hampton Court.[2]

Each bay of vaulting was known as a 'severey'. So in the Windsor contract, quoted above, it is said that the roof 'conteyneth vij savereys', and for the vaulting of King's College Chapel the contractors were to be paid £100 'for every severey'. William of Worcester describing the cloisters at Norwich speaks of 'the civers' and 'civerys',[3] a form which is a link between 'severey' and the Latin *ciborium*, which is used by Gervase in describing the church at Canterbury—or rather, he uses the term 'keys' (*claves*), explaining: 'I put *clavis* for the whole *ciborium* because the *clavis* placed in the middle locks up and binds together the parts which converge to it from every side'[4]. As Willis points out, the *ciborium* is the canopy over the high altar, supported on high pillars and usually vaulted in one compartment, so that the use of this word for a bay of vaulting is natural.

Finally, there are occasional references to stone used for steps, which do not present many features calling for notice. In 1285 we have a payment 'for cutting free stones for the stair (*staeriam*) in front of the chapel of Blessed Mary in the upper Dunjon' at Corfe Castle,[5] and at Winchester Castle, about 1294, there are references to 'the stairway (*gradus*) from Rosamund's chamber to the chapel near the bedroom . . . for making the wooden stairway underneath the stone stairway . . . wages of 12 cutters (*talliatores*) cutting stone for the said stairway'.[6] Such stones were usually called 'paces'—in Latin *passus*. The Westminster Abbey account of 1252 includes 'vij passibus, cissis ad tascham', and at Harlech in 1286 quarriers were paid £4. 4s. 'for hewing and cutting (*tagliand'*) 56 paces (*passibus*) for the stairways of the towers, taking for a pace 18d.'[7] At Windsor 300 feet of *paas* were bought, at 2d. the foot, for the stairs of the gate leading to the canons' cemetery, in 1353,[8] and ten years later more than 3,000 feet

---

[1] App. B.
[2] Law, *Hampton Court*, i. 350.
[3] *Itinerarium*, 302.
[4] Willis, *Arch. Hist. of Canterbury Cath.*, 49.
[5] E. 460, 27.
[6] E. 491, 19.
[7] E. 485, 27.
[8] E. 495, 7.

*passuum* were supplied from the Lincolnshire quarry of 'Heselburgh'.[1] Stones called 'paces' occur at the Tower in 1364, and 'paas' at Rochester in 1369, while at Calais in 1474 we find 40 'steppyngstounes' bought for the stairways of the town.[2] References to vices, or winding stairs, are frequent, in the contracts and elsewhere, and many of the 'nowels'[3] mentioned in accounts undoubtedly refer to their newel pillars. At Odiham Castle in 1401 there is mention of '400 ft. of freston for making a pyler carrying a wyndyngstare to the chamber called Ledyngchamre'.[4] But we need not linger on these steps, as fortunately they do not lead into any haze of obscurities.

[1] E. 493, 11.

[2] E. 198, 7.

[3] See above, p. 114.

[4] E. 502, 27.

# VII

## STONE: QUARRIES

A LARGE part of the cost of masonry lay in the expense of carriage of the stone. Taking the cost of winning stone in the quarry as about 2*d*. a foot, the weight of a cubic foot of stone as averaging 155 lb., and carriage at the rate of 2*d*. per ton per mile, it is obvious that for a distance of 12 miles the cost of carriage would be about equivalent to the cost of the stone itself. For repairs to Tutbury Castle in 1314 the cost of hewing 5,950 free stones in the quarry of Winshill, at 4*s*. the hundred, was £11. 7*s*. 8*d*., that of carrying 4,267 of them from the quarry to the castle, some 5 or 6 miles, at 7*s*. 6*d*. the hundred, was £15. 19*s*. 2*d*.[1] Where water carriage was available the cost was much reduced, but if it was brought from long distances it necessarily mounted up. Thus stone for Norwich Cathedral in 1287 was bought at Caen for £1. 6*s*. 8*d*.; its freight by ship to Yarmouth was £2. 10*s*. 8*d*.; unloading it there into barges cost 2*s*. 2*d*.; carriage in 6 barges to Norwich was 7*s*. 2*d*.; and from the wharf to the cathedral yard was another 2*s*.[2] It is therefore obvious that, wherever possible, it was advisable to use local stone, and in a great many instances houses and village churches were built from quarries opened within a few hundred yards of their site. When the monks of the Conqueror's votive abbey of Battle began to build their church, they imported stone from Normandy, until a woman, through a miraculous, or lucky, dream, pointed out a place close to the site of the abbey where they could find a supply of suitable stone.[3]

In 1232 the Friars Preachers of Exeter were licensed to take stone for their church from the quarry near the castle ditch.[4] Ten years later the Prior of Lenton, near Nottingham, was allowed to dig stone for the re-building of the convent tower outside that town,[5] and in 1357 part of the stone used for the repair of Nottingham Castle came from 'the quarry below the castle'.[6] As later instances, the parishioners of Warfield were allowed in 1429 to dig stone in the adjacent Forest of Windsor during the next two years for repair of their church,[7] and one quarry for Adderbury Church was in the rectory garden and was duly filled up when the build-

---

[1] Mins. Accts. 1, No. 3.
[2] Norwich Communar's Roll.
[3] *Battle Abbey Chronicle* (ed. Lower), 11.
[4] *Close R.* 101.
[5] Ibid. 474.
[6] E. 478, 4.
[7] *Cal. Pat.* 504.

ing of the chancel was completed, in 1418.[1] Cheap water carriage was also obviously desirable, where local stone was not obtainable, and it is not infrequently found in connexion with grants of quarries to monasteries. Towards the end of the twelfth century Osmund de Kent gave to the monks of Meaux a quarry in Brantingham, 120 feet long and 8 perches broad, and all the quarrying rights in a carucate of land, less 24 perches, with a place to store the stone until they could remove it, and free access to the Humber, by which river and up the Hull it could be brought to the abbey.[2]

The abbey of Bury St. Edmunds had from very early times the right of quarrying at Barnack, and the Conqueror forbade the Abbot of Peterborough to prevent their carrying their stone to the water; later Peterborough confirmed their right to carry the stone to the stream and so to the Nene.[3] Similarly, in 1176 Pope Alexander III confirmed to Sawtry Abbey 'the ditch which they had made at their own cost to carry stone (from Barnack) for the building of their church', and in 1192, after a good deal of unpleasantness, Ramsey Abbey agreed that Sawtry should have the use of the one lode leading to their abbey, with the right to build a resthouse for the men working the stone-barges.[4]

A good many monasteries owned quarries, to some of which we shall have occasion to refer later, and, of course, there were many quarries situated on the royal demesnes and on the lands of private persons, which were naturally drawn upon for supplies of stone. When these were not available or were insufficient it was open to the builder either to buy or hire a quarry for his operations, or to buy his stone from quarries that were run as commercial speculations. When there were quarries in the neighbourhood it was simple to acquire one, the same men being employed first as quarriers and then as masons; but if the stone had to be brought from a distance, it was more usual to buy it ready cut. Thus, for the building of Merton College tower, 1448–50, the Headington stone was dug by the college masons, but that from Tainton was bought;[5] though, when the college library was built, *c.* 1375, this procedure had been reversed, as some stones were bought from Wheatley (near Headington) and a quarry (*lapidicinum*) at Tainton was hired, at a rent of 3*s.* and a further payment of 20*d.* for tithes, and was worked by the masons.[6] For Magdalen College,

---

[1] *Oxford Rec. Soc.* viii.   [2] *Chron. Mon. de Melsa*, i. 228. Cf. ibid. 171.
[3] *V.C.H. Northants.* ii. 294.   [4] Ibid. 295.
[5] *Oxford City Docts.* (Oxf. Hist. Soc.), 322, 330.
[6] Merton Coll. Roll 4102 (*b*).

in 1474, one quarry, 38 by 28 ft., was hired from the Prior of St. Frides-wide's, and another, 90 by 46 ft., from Sir Edmund Rede at Headington, but stone was also bought from Wheatley, Tainton, and from the Abbot of Bruerne's quarry at Milton.[1] Another Oxford college, Corpus Christi, was working one quarry in 1514 and also making bargains, with John Warde of Little Barrington (Gloucs.), for 100 tons of stone at 20*d.* the ton, or with his neighbours, Richard Merytt and Robert Taylor of Sherborne, for the same quantity of stone, 'redy scapylde', at 18*d.* the ton.[2]

Quarrying was a regular trade, and in certain districts there must have been a fairly continuous demand for the stone. The greater part of this was in blocks, scappled, or rough-hewn, to convenient sizes. These were often sold by the block, and sometimes the dimensions are given, as in 1397, when a Porchester account contains an item—'for 1,000 pieces of free stone from the quarry of Bonchurch in South Wight, hewn, scappled and carried to the sea, of which each stone—smaller and bigger—comes to 2 feet—giving for the hundred 23s. 4d.'[3] At Harlech in 1286 two quarry-men were paid £25. 10s. for 'quarrying and cutting (*tayliand*') 2,040 stones, each containing 2 ft. in length, 1½ ft. in breadth and 1 ft. in thick-ness, at 25*s.* the hundred'.[4] More often the size is not mentioned, and we have such an entry as that in a Winchester account of 1294—'for the pur-chase of 675 stones at Southampton, at 10s. the hundred'.[5] It seems not improbable that the stone was frequently taken as averaging a cubic foot. It was certainly by the foot that a large proportion of stone was sold. As instances we have at Windsor in 1363–4 purchases of 7,391 ft. of Tainton stone, at 3*d.* the foot, and of 5,718 ft., 3,666 ft., and 2,593 ft. of stone from Wheatley, at 2½*d.*[6] An interesting example of the sale of stone by the foot occurs in the following bargain made in 1536 for stone to be used at Hampton Court:[7]

Be yt knowen to alle Crysten peplee that I Crystoffore Dyckunssun ffree masun hathe made and cumnant in the yere off our Soverant lord Kyng Henre the VIII[t] in hys Rayn xxviij[t] yere w[t] Thomas Maude off Maydston and Rychard Young off Bowton ffor ix Hunderd ffote and vij ffote off hard stone off Kent ffor pavyng ffor the Kort y[t] ye cundyt stand in the second daye off June the prysse off a hundert fote xx[s]. and ffor vij ffote xvj[d] thes psons dwellyng in Maydston and Bowtun. Item I have bowt off Martyn Wastelle and Thomas Young off

[1] *Magd. Coll. Reg.* ii. 228.  [2] Building Accts. H. 10, 19.

[3] E. 479, 23.  [4] E. 485, 27.

[5] E. 491, 18.  [6] E. 493, 11, 16.

[7] H.C. 239, f. 337. The document bears three typical 'mason's marks', instead of seals: see Pl. 11.

Bowtun a hundred ffote off pace for the cundyt to be delyverd at Maydstone at the Wharffe ate the Watr syde the pryce—xlix[s] viij[d]. Item for a hunderd ffote off platee stone ffor the towarre in the gardyn to be delyverd att the same warffe by the same psons the prysse xxx[s] x[d].

Another measure commonly used in dealing in stone was the ton or 'tonne-tite', Latinized as *pondus dolii* or *doliata*; as this was based on the weight of a tun of wine (2,000 lb.) its half was called a pipe. In the contract for building a quay at Norwich in 1432 the topmost layer of stones of the facing were each to be of the weight of a pipe of wine at least.[1] For work at St. Paul's in 1382 Mr. Henry Yevele supplied '30 tunnetyth and 1 pipe of northern stone', at 9s. the ton.[2] In 1385 the freightage of stone from the Isle of Wight to Porchester was at the rate of 8d. the 'tonne-tight',[3] and 'xj tonne of Caen stone' was used at Warblington in 1518.[4] The number of feet to the ton naturally varied somewhat with the type of stone. About 1470 one William Paulden caused to be 'conveyed by aventure of ye sea owt of Yorkshire into ye countie of Norff'' to one Thomas Shakston '2 ton of fre ston by weight', which he entrusted to him to sell to the best advantage. When it reached Salthouse, Shakston sold it to the churchwardens of North Repps and was deputed by them to measure it; but Paulden declared that they bribed him, so that he, 'certeynly knowying yt same tyme yt every xij fote of ye said ston made a ton tyght', delivered to them 'xvj fote for every ton tight'.[5] The Yorkshire stone weighing, on an average, about 160 lb. the cubic foot, would run about 12 ft. to the ton, whereas Caen stone is said in 1532 to run to 16 ft. to the ton.[6]

It is worth noting that about 1400 the stone from the Yorkshire quarries of Huddlestone and Stapleton was reckoned by the 'fother', equivalent to a ton, while that from Thevesdale was reckoned by the ton tight and 'damlade'.[7] This last term is peculiar to Yorkshire and seems to be equal to 10 tons, as shown by the following entry of stone bought for York Castle in 1364:[8] 'In 77 damlades 6 dol' pond' de werkstane rugh—damlade ad 8s. Et 38 damlades 3 dol' pond' werkstane scapeld—damlade inde ad 10s. Et 67 damlades 8 dol' pond' de mayillioum—damlade ad 6s.— empt' apud Tadcastr—£70. 10s. 8¾d.' The vague cartloads and boatloads by which the purchase of freight of stone was often recorded are too indeterminate to justify examination.

| [1] App. B. | [2] E. 473, 1. | [3] E. 479, 22. |
| [4] E. 490, 12. | [5] Early Chancy. Proc. 66, 268. | |
| [6] T.R., f. 48. | [7] *Y.F.R., passim.* | [8] E. 501, 11. |

So far we have been dealing with block stone, suitable for straight-forward walling or for working up in the masons' lodge. But it is impor-tant to realize that a large proportion of the more ornamental stonework—especially such simple members as plinths, string-courses, voussoirs, battle-ments, &c.—was supplied from the quarries ready worked and cut to measure. It was an obvious measure of economy to trim the stone as far as possible before carting it, and as a medieval building of any importance was not the haphazard production of individual masons but was worked out in detail before it was started, it was quite simple to send measure-ments and patterns to the quarriers by which they should cut the stones. Reference to the use of such 'moldes', or templates, has already been made,[1] and when we were dealing with the technical terms of the stone trade it was seen that a great many shaped stones were evidently obtainable direct from the quarries in more or less standardized shapes and sizes. In the con-tract made with five quarrymen of Kent for stone for Eton College, in 1442, it is expressly stated that they shall work the various forms of stones according to the instructions and patterns given them.[2] Thirty years earlier the authorities of King's Hall, Cambridge, made a bargain with a quarrier[3] 'for 100 ft. of tablys and gabylwall, at 4d. the foot, of which the length shall be at least 2 ft., the breadth 16 inches and the thickness $4\frac{1}{2}$ inches; and we shall have the foot of somers and krestys at the same price; and he shall guarantee these stones to last for ever in any kind of weather and shall pay the carriage of them'. When William of Sens rebuilt Canterbury Cathedral, after the fire in 1174, he sent 'moldes' to the quarries at Caen for the work-ing of the stone, and as late as 1532 we find 496 pieces of Caen stone 'redye wrought in dyverse mouldis' being brought over for use at West-minster.[4] One is inclined to surmise that these last were not cut according to patterns supplied but were stock patterns produced for general use. About the same time William Johnson of Barrington, freemason, sup-plied for Hampton Court 5 windows 'of iij fote jame of oon lyght redy made and delyverd at Barenton quarry' at 5s. each, and also 80 lights ready made, at 4s. 6d.,[5] and it is fairly obvious, when one looks at large houses of this period, that windows of stock size and pattern were produced com-mercially at many quarries. It is highly probable that from early in the fifteenth century it was becoming more and more the custom to buy stock mouldings from the quarry for the rebuilding and alteration of churches, in which direction that period was so active. This would help to account

---

[1] See above, pp. 20–21.    [2] App. B.    [3] K.H. 5, f. 360.
[4] T.R., f. 322.    [5] H.C. 236, f. 293.

for the feeling that one has that many, even of the finer, 'Perpendicular' churches lack individuality and give an impression of having been ordered from a firm rather than built for the particular village.

When a quarry was opened the first thing to do was to clear away the superincumbent earth. Moreover, when the top layer of the stone was reached it was almost always of inferior quality, fissured and unsuitable for cutting into blocks, though useful as rubble and filling for walls. The removal of this 'rag' down to the level of the freestone proper was, therefore, the second part of the preliminary operations. So at Rockingham in 1285 William Tappeladel and Baldwin Hunylove were paid 2s. 6d. 'for clearing (*mundand*') a piece of the quarry at Morhawe, 16½ ft. in length and breadth', and 2s. 7d. 'for digging the same piece of the quarry from the rag down to the good stone'.[1] At Moor End in 1365 men were paid a lump sum of 60s. 'for making a new pit (*put*') at the quarry of Conesgrave, containing 24 ft. each way, removing the earth and rag stone in order to get free stone there', with a further £95. 6s. 8d. 'for digging 14,300 ft., by the greater hundred (of six score), and their removal from the pit, at 13s. 4d. the hundred'.[2] For stone for York Minster in 1371 the clerk of the works, the master mason, and others spent a day selecting the quarry (*pro quarera eligenda*); after which 46s. 8d. was spent on clearing (*denudacione*) the new quarry, 3 roods in extent;[3] and in 1434 Thomas Goldesburgh and four others were employed 'ridding, clearing and stripping 15 roods of quarry at Huddlestone for the better getting and winning of stone; and also carrying rubble (*ramell*') to the river bank'.[4] When Magdalen College was being built, in 1474, the accountant records:

First, I paid to Henry Baily and John Chamberlayn his partner, of Hedington, for the digging and removal of the earth lying over the quarry, which earth was 60 ft. square in area (*superficie*) and 8 ft. in depth down to the stones called le freebedde, and also for the digging and removal of stones in the said earth which are called grete pendant and small pendant[5]—3[li]. 6s. 8d. Also I paid to Walter Bladon of Hedingdon for digging and removal of earth, being in length 72 ft. and in depth 7 ft. down to the stones called le cropperagge, and in breadth 22 ft.—40s.[6]

Some letters[7] written in 1549 by his clerk of the works to Sir John Thynne about a house being built for Protector Somerset at Bedwyn

---

[1] E. 480, 28.      [2] E. 544, 31.
[3] Y.F.R. 6.      [4] Ibid. 52.
[5] Pendants were small stones used for the filling of vaults between the ribs.
[6] *Magd. Coll. Reg.* ii. 227.      [7] *Wilts. Arch. Mag.* xv. 180–4.

(Wilts.) are of sufficient interest to be quoted here, although just outside our date limit. The first of these, dated 30 March, runs:

And for that it hath been declared unto my Lord's Grace that neyther chalke nor Wilton stone will abyde the weather, there is in the proof of them here good tokens of them bothe or at the least no cause of despayre in eyther of them. For of the chalke there is iij stones whose nether bed is made the parelment,[1] so that these stones shovers out into brode spalters and thin, but the other that is set with the right bed downwards, or that standyth joint by joint, as they call it, doth remayne sound enough. And in the stone of Wilton considering it was set green and unseasoned and being of the up moste of the quarr which is worste, it spalters out in thick peces and will not abyde; but now they be come to great stones in the quarr that will make ashelour xvj or xvij inches high, and have brought him to a fair bed more workmanlyke that it was before, so that I trust within this fortnight or iij wekes we shall cum to good stone, for it fashioneth in every condition lyke unto the quarr at Mr. Kyngsmille's.

In this letter two points are brought out. First, that the lower layers of the stone are better than the upper;[2] and secondly, that stone should be laid in a wall in the same position as it lay in the quarry. Both these points are of general application, and the second is particularly important. Medieval builders were not so careful of the correct bedding of their stone as might have been expected, and it is not unusual to find a certain number of blocks in a wall set the wrong way of the grain,[3] with disastrous effects. A third point is that stone, like timber, is the better for seasoning.

The second letter is dated 7 June:

The stone of Wylton quar doth make very good lyme . . .; and whereas there is a great heap of dust made by means of the Rubbell which came out of the quar,[4] the same will serve very well to mengle with the lyme in the fylling of the walls; for it is of itself very tough when it is beaten and tempered and much more it wyl be tough when the lyme doth help him to bynd. Thus doth the best of the stone make good ashelour, and the ragged will serve for the foundacions and fylling stuff, and the Rubbell for lyme and the dust for rough work, so that what so ever cost my Lordes grace bestoweth there, it will quit the cost.

---

[1] Facing.

[2] For doors and windows at Peterhouse in 1430 the stone was to be '*de inferiori lecto lapidicini*': App. B.

[3] Instances of this were recently pointed out to me at Shepton Mallet by the master craftsman in charge of the repairs to the church.

[4] Cf. at Huddlestone in 1420: 'for carriage of dust out of the quarry by carts for 23 days—23s.': *Y.F.R.* 40.

Finally, on 14 June he writes:

As touching the old stone . . ., which is urne (ours) but therewith the carriage, the same is well seasoned and wyll abyde all wethers, and I can perceyve none of that quarr that ever fayled which came out of the bottom thereof, where lyeth the best stone in every quar of this stone. In Burbage church, though the grete[1] be sumwhat rougher than Wylton stone, yet as the nature of all these quarrs heare is, the lower the rougher grete, so is it lyk that the same stone which is in Burbage church wall (where is abundance) to come out of the bottom of Shalbourn quarr, or els of Eston, but whence so ever it came it abydeth very well and gathered a great moss and is I am sure of one of these quarrs.

Of the actual working of the quarries there is very little to be said. The preliminary extraction of blocks of stone was effected with heavy malls and wedges of iron, edged with steel, and was regarded, as is shown by the rates of pay, as unskilled, or the lowest type of skilled, labour. The blocks were then reduced by further splitting and sawing, and broached and scappled to the requisite dimensions. The final tooling, as we have said, might be performed at the quarry or in the masons' lodge. For the building of Vale Royal Abbey in 1278 a group of masons (*cementarii*) were paid by contract 100*s*. 'for ten hundreds of stones which they dug from the quarry and cut (*insculpabant*), prepared and worked in full at their own costs'; there were also *quariatores*, of whom the masters were paid 18*d*. the week, the ordinary 'quarriers and strikers with great hammers and men serving the said masters' receiving 12*d*., and 'labourers with spades and hoes (*houwis*) clearing (the earth) in various quarries', 10*d*.[2] As another instance we may quote a notice of '6 masons (*latomi*) called Roughmasons and quarreours working at the digging of stones at the quarry of Purbyk and scappling the stones and preparing them for carriage to Corfe Castle', in 1378.[3] For work at Woodstock in 1256, while the labourers engaged on 'the new quarry of large stone' received 1*s*. a week, 2*s*. was paid 'to a mason (*mazoni*) remaining at the quarry of Tainton to choose and scapple free stone'.[4] With this last we may compare an interesting entry in 1442 in connexion with Gloucester Castle:

Wages of John Hobbys, mason, riding to the quarry of Upton and the quarry of Freme to pick out and prove good stones from the bad stones called cropston, and marking (*signand'*) and scappling and proving the stones so picked out, so that the King should not be deceived therein, at 6d. a day. And to William his servant, working there at the marking, scappling and proving of the said stones, at 4d. a day.[5]

[1] Grit.      [2] E. 485, 22.      [3] E. 461, 9.      [4] E. 497, 12.      [5] E. 473, 18.

This last quotation is the nearest approach that I have found to a documentary reference to those 'masons' marks' about which so much, including some fanciful nonsense, has been written. It is well known that in a great many medieval buildings some of the stones bear on their face a symbol which is the mark of the mason who worked it. These vary from deeply cut devices to mere scratches difficult to discern, and, broadly speaking, the earlier the work the deeper the mark is cut. The custom of so marking stones continues, in a desultory fashion, to the present day,[1] but in post-medieval times the mark has almost always been made on the bed of the stone, so as not to disfigure the face. The latest face mark that I have noticed is on the masonry at Brambletye (Sussex) dating from 1630. This is the 'dumb-bell', or double triangle (⋈),[2] which I have found at all dates from the twelfth century onwards, and on buildings ranging from Aiguesmortes on the Mediterranean to Byland in Yorkshire. These signs are referred to in the regulations of the masons of Torgau, drawn up in 1462.[3] (§ 25) If a master or fellow becomes free of the craft and demands a mark of the workmaster, he shall have it—paying 'to the service of God' what is fixed. (§ 27) At the granting of the mark to an apprentice the master gives him a dinner, to which he may ask ten of his associates. (§ 30) If a master has no work for his apprentice and lets him go on his travels, he must lend him a mark. The Strasburg masons had also a rule that no one should alter his mark, assigned to him by his craft, without the approval of the whole craft.[4] Whether marks were assigned in the same way in England or merely assumed is not known. Their practical purpose must have been to identify the work of the individual mason for the information of the paymaster. It is noticeable that these marks rarely appear on tracery or carved stones, most of which would be worked by the masters and more responsible men and would be easily identified. That they usually appear on only a portion, often quite a small proportion, of the plain stones of a building suggests that they may have applied only to the men who were on piece work, or possibly to the casual labourers who were not known to the master and whose work it was therefore desirable to check. Whether they were put on by the quarry mason or by the building mason, that is to say, at the quarry or in the lodge, is one of several interesting points that might appear if a laborious survey of English

[1] A mason recently told me that he only uses his 'banker mark' on the hafts of his tools. Many banker marks can be seen on the granite sets of pavements in London.

[2] If this has any significance, it is probably a conventional representation of the mason's axe; it has sometimes a vertical line from the centre, suggesting the haft.

[3] Gould, *Hist. of Freemasonry*, i. 137.          [4] Ibid. 128.

medieval buildings were made by skilled geologists who could ascertain the source of origin of their stones.

As the stone from different parts of the same quarry varied in goodness, so to a much greater extent did the stone from different quarries. It was not always an unmixed blessing to have a supply of stone close at hand, and Oxford has suffered from the propinquity of Headington, whose stone has caused her colleges to be smitten with a leprosy hideous to see and costly to remedy. In the last decade of the eleventh century a monk of Durham built on the Isle of Lindisfarne a church in honour of St. Cuthbert,

which he completed with the finest workmanship, of stones laid in courses (*tabulatis*) with wonderful regularity, by his own industrious labour and the generosity of his faithful people. But because on the island an insufficient quantity of stones could be found he obtained from the neighbouring villages waggons and yokes of oxen with carts, and so with much trouble he accumulated a great quantity of stones. The neighbours also, out of devotion to St. Cuthbert, were always ready to lend him the aid of their strength and many times, uniting their forces, to drag loads over the wet sands. The stones indeed which are on the island are reduced to dust (*cinerescunt*) by the vapour of the foam of the surging sea and fall into little bits like sandy pebbles. Wherefore they were not good enough for such a work, except that they could be used to help in small portions of the masonry on the inside.[1]

At the end of our period we have a report made in 1529 on the commencement of the work of Wolsey's projected school at Ipswich: 'It has been found that the stone of Harwich does not last, and we have determined to get ragstone from Kent, which will not cost more than 17d. or 18d. per ton.'[2]

There was, therefore, naturally a demand for those varieties of stone that were known to be satisfactory. London drew largely on Kent and Surrey. The district round Maidstone, with Aylesford to the north and Boughton to the south, supplied great quantities of the hard 'Kentish rag', which had been used by the Romans for the walls of London, the Medway affording cheap carriage for it. Thus in 1317 four barge-loads (*farcostate*) of ragstone of Aylesford, at 7s. the load of 12 tons, was supplied for the Tower,[3] where a barge-load of 'grey stone called ragg' had been supplied at the same price in 1313.[4] Still earlier, in 1278, no less than 304 shiploads of 'grey stone of Aylesford', costing £107. 14s. 10½d., was used at the Tower, together with 3 shiploads, equivalent to 187 cubic yards, of free-

[1] *Regin. Dunelm. Libellus* (Surtees Soc.), 45.      [2] *L. & P. Hen. VIII*, iv. 5458.
[3] E. 468, 20.                                        [4] E. 469, 16.

stone from Folkestone, costing £6. 17s. 4d.[1] Great quantities of worked stone from the Boughton and Folkestone quarries were supplied for the castle at Sheppey between 1362 and 1365;[2] and for a wharf at London in 1389 it was stipulated that the facing should be of ashlar of Kent and the packing of 'ragge'.[3] The Folkestone quarries were supplying stone for Dover Castle as early as 1226, in which year 350 boatloads were provided, at 10d. the load; for the cutting of these stones 10s. the hundred (feet) were paid, and 12s. 6d.—'to Gervase and John Long, superior cutters (*melioribus incisoribus*)'; a further payment of £8 being made 'for the cutting of 1800 ft. of stone of Folkestan against the time when the King wishes work to begin'.[4] As late as 1532 'hard stone of Kent' was still being supplied to Westminster from Boughton quarry.[5]

'Rag', as we have seen, was a generic term applied to the inferior varieties of stone, but it would seem that 'urnel' was a trade term of similar import confined to Kent. In 1338 we find '400 stones of Maydenston called ournal' bought, for 22s., for the water-gate of the Tower,[6] and in 1349 'urnel stone of Kent' for the postern there.[7] Another Tower account, for 1363, has '650 ft. of stone called urnell for mending the walls,—price of a hundred, with freightage from Maidstone, 9s.'[8] At Westminster in 1355[9] and 1385[10] and at the Tower in 1400[11] urnell was used for making gutters, or drains, and at Leeds Castle in 1369[12] and Eltham in 1397,[13] for paving. That it was of inferior quality is shown by the fact that in 1375, while ashlar bought at Maidstone for the new chapel at Havering was 25s. the 100 ft., urnell was only 10s.,[14] and similarly at Sandwich in 1463 ornell was 9s. and ashlar 18s.[15] That it was not mere rubble but was, at least sometimes, roughly worked is indicated by its appearance in a list of varieties of worked stones from Boughton quarry in 1362, when the charge for scappling urnell was $\frac{3}{4}d.$ a foot, against such charges as $2\frac{1}{2}d.$ for 'tables' and 4d. for jamb-stones.[16]

The Kentish stone was useful building material, but for finer work, mouldings and carving, London drew largely upon the Surrey quarries in the neighbourhood of Reigate and Merstham. For the rebuilding of Westminster Abbey in 1252, we find 23,000 of freestone of Reigate bought for £72;[17] and during the whole of the fifteenth century, while the

---

[1] E. 467, 6 (4).　　　　[2] E. 483, 20, 21.　　　　[3] App. B.
[4] E. 462, 10.　　　　　 [5] T.R., f. 82.　　　　　 [6] E. 470, 6.
[7] E. 471, 3.　　　　　　[8] E. 472, 9.　　　　　　[9] E. 502, 17.
[10] E. 473, 2.　　　　　 [11] E. 502, 15.　　　　　[12] E. 544, 23.
[13] E. 495, 23.　　　　　[14] E. 464, 37.　　　　　[15] E. 481, 26.
[16] E. 483, 20.　　　　　[17] E. 466, 30.

nave of the Abbey church was slowly drawing to its completion, 'there flowed every year a stream of stone, of varying volume, from the Reigate hills down to Westminster'.[1] In 1324 Reigate stone was used for slabs in front of the royal bath-tub (*cuve debalniand'*) in Westminster Palace,[2] and also for steps in St. Stephen's Chapel,[3] for which chapel in 1333 'a great piece of Reigate stone, 10 ft. long, for making an image' was bought for 6s., and Thomas Bernak of Reigate, quarrier (*rokar'*), provided two great stones for images.[4] Similar stone was provided in 1329 for window tracery (*formis*) and 'tabernacles', or carved housings for images;[5] and in 1385 a mason was paid 7d. a day 'working at the quarry on the scappling of various Reigate stones hewn (*tract'*) for making 6 housings (*hovell'*) for six images made in the likeness of kings, to be set at the south end of the great hall (at Westminster)'. These housings were carved by Walter Walton, for £4. 13s. 4d.; and he also received £9 for carving two tabernacles for the images of two kings on either side of the door of the hall. The two kings were carved, presumably in Purbeck marble, by Thomas Canon, 'marbrer', at 66s. 8d. each, and he further[6] carved 13 kings to stand in the hall, at 46s. 8d. each, including material. It may be added that Nicholas Tryer received what seems the disproportionate sum of 100s. for painting the two images, and £7. 13s. 4d. for painting six others—no doubt with a lavish expenditure of gold leaf. During the second half of the fourteenth century the Reigate quarries which supplied the royal building yards were managed by the family of Prophete, the first of whom—John— appears about 1351. He and Philip Prophete were appointed masters of quarries at Merstham and Chaldon, for the supply of Windsor Castle, with power to impress labour, in 1359.[7] John Profit provided 142 cart-loads of Reigate stone for fireplaces, doors, and windows at the Tower in 1361, at 3s. the load,[8] and he and William Profyt sent another 120 cart-loads to Havering in 1375,[9] while William Profit and Stephen Prat in 1385 provided 32½ cartloads of the stone, cut for the jambs, bases. and canopies (*typ'*) of tabernacles for images, for Westminster, at 4s. 3d. the load, includ-ing carriage.[10] In this year, 1385, Reigate stone worked as jambs, &c. cost 4s. 3d. the cartload, and unworked (*non tract'*) 3s. 3½d.; in 1533 the same stone, 'squared', was 4s. 2d. the ton, delivered at Hampton Court.[11]

[1] Rackham, *Nave of Westminster* (Brit. Acad. iv), p. 11.
[2] E. 469, 6.                              [3] E. 469, 8.                        [4] E. 469, 12.
[5] E. 467, 7.                              [6] E. 473, 2.
[7] *V.C.H. Surrey*, ii. 277.              [8] E. 472, 9.                        [9] E. 464, 27.
[10] E. 473, 2. Ten years later such stone, supplied for Westminster Hall by William Proffit, cost, respectively, 4s. and 3s. 4d. the ton: Add. Roll 27018.              [11] H.C. 237, f. 20.

For the royal buildings many sources of supply were tapped. Thus Windsor Castle used stone from the Surrey quarries, but also drew largely on the limestones of Totternhoe (Beds.).[1] As early as 1169 'Eglemunt' quarry provided stone for Windsor,[2] and it continued to do so in the second half of the fourteenth century. Twelve cartloads of Egremond stone were also brought from Dunstable to Westminster in 1356,[3] and ten years later 'stone of Egremond from the quarry of Totrenho' was used at Langley.[4] The Oxfordshire quarries of Wheatley, Milton, and Tainton naturally served Windsor—'9755 ft. of Teynton stone, measured by Henry Jenyns, chief mason', being bought for St. George's Chapel in 1477, at 2*d*. the foot[5]—and even the distant quarries of Careby and Holywell, near Stamford, were drawn upon for over a thousand feet of 'crestes' and 'tables'[6] in 1360. These were brought down by water to Surfleet and Lynn and shipped from there.[7]

The importance of the Barnack stone for East Anglia and the Fenland has already been alluded to, but while there is documentary evidence of its use in such places as Norwich, Ely, and Cambridge, it does not seem to have spread farther afield. Certain Yorkshire quarries, on the other hand, were sending their products south on a considerable scale from at least the middle of the fourteenth century. In 1343 there is a record of 92 stones of Pontefract being bought for St. Stephen's Chapel at Westminster;[8] and next year, at Windsor, although the greater part of the stone came from the local quarry at Bisham, there was a small quantity from Stapleton.[9] Freestone of Stapleton occurs also at Rochester in 1368[10] and 1373,[11] and in 1385 Robert Gamulston supplied 40 tons of Stapleton stone for a flying buttress (*archbuttant'*) on the east side of Westminster Hall, at 10*s*. the ton including freight from Yorkshire.[12] The same stone was used for doorjambs at the Tower in 1400,[13] about which time 'northern stone' was being bought for Westminster Abbey.[14] About 1417 ships were being sent to Stapleton, Cawood, and Doncaster and elsewhere in the north, to fetch stone for the building of Sion Abbey.[15] Stone from the Yorkshire quarry of Marr was used for heightening the walls of Westminster Hall in 1395,[16] and is found in store for use on the royal manors in 1444,[17] and stone from

[1] *V.C.H. Beds*. iii. 448.　　　　　　　　[2] Hope, *Windsor Castle*, i. 171.

[3] E. 471, 15.　　　　[4] E. 466, 3.　　　　　　[5] E. 496, 17.

[6] Hope, *Windsor Castle*, i. 189.　　　[7] E. 494, 1.　　　　[8] E. 470, 13.

[9] Hope, *Windsor Castle*, i. 115.　　[10] Foreign R. 42 Edw. III, F.

[11] E. 465, 28.　　　　　[12] E. 473, 2.　　　　　[13] E. 502, 15.

[14] Rackham, *Nave of Westminster*, 11.　　　　[15] *Acts of P.C.* ii. 360.

[16] App. B.　　　　　[17] E. 503, 12.

Huddlestone occurs at Westminster in 1442.[1] When Henry VI was drawing up plans for the building of Eton College Chapel, he specified that the
first course of the foundations should be of 'platt Yorkshire stone', and the
walls of mixed Yorkshire and Tainton, for some reason expressly pro-
hibiting the use of 'Reygate stone otherwyse y-called Mestham stone';[2]
and for the porches of King's College Chapel in 1513 the mason was to
provide 'good sufficient and noble stone of Hampole quarryes in Yorkshier'—most of the other contemporary work in the chapel being carried
out in stone from Weldon (Northants.).[2]

At the opposite end of England the stone of Beer in Devon was not only
used locally, at Exeter Cathedral, but was sent by sea to London. In 1347
William Hamele of Weymouth supplied 68 great stones of Bere for the
king's chapel at Westminster, for £11. At the same time William de
Abbotesburi, mason, was working for three weeks in October, at 12*d*. the
day, 'upon the provision of stone of Bere in the county of Somerset [*sic*]'.[3]
Two years later the Tower accounts include £4. 6*s*. 8*d*. for '100 great
stones of Bere, whereof 50 were worked as voussoirs for the heads (*ad
vosur' pro superclasur'*) of doors and windows . . ., and 50 were in the
rough (*rude*)'.[4] Both these entries lay emphasis on the size of the stones,
and among the stores belonging to the works of London bridge in 1350
there were 18 great stones of Bere weighing 18 tons, valued at 6*s*. 8*d*. the
ton.[5] For the Tower in 1361 Bere stone was bought at 8*s*. 6*d*. the ton 'including freight from the castle of Corfe';[6] this rather suggests that the
stone came from Bere Regis, near Corfe, but on the whole it is more probable that it was either part of the castle stores or else had been brought
there and transhipped. In 1367 Henry Yeveley, the great mason and building contractor, supplied 36 tons of Beer stone for Rochester Castle, for
£18.[7] After this time it appears to have been less in demand, though we
find 'Bereston' used at Porchester for doors, windows, and fireplaces in
1397,[8] and a small quantity used at Winchester in 1428 for the coping of
a wall.[9]

The quality of the stone from the neighbourhood of Bath has long been
recognized, but it was not conveniently situated for carriage and does not
often figure far outside its own district. Two hundred of freestone used at
Marlborough in 1237 cost 'at the quarry beside Bath' 3*s*., but their carriage

---

[1] E. 473, 18.                    [2] App. B.              [3] E. 470, 18.        [4] E. 471, 3.
[5] Riley, *Mems. of London*, 261.              [6] E. 472, 7.
[7] E. 479, 28. Cf. Foreign R. 42 Edw. III, F.
[8] E. 479, 23.                                  [9] E. 492, 3.

came to 22*s*.[1] Stone from Hamdon quarries was used at Exeter in 1301;[2] and these quarries, which belonged to the manor of Stoke, were, in the middle of the fifteenth century, leased out for a payment of about 6*s*. 8*d*. down and a yearly rent of 4*d*. for 24 feet square.[3] Close by was Haslebury (in Box), which became in the seventeenth century 'the eminentest free-stone quarry in the West of England'. Lacock Abbey owned a quarry there in 1241, which they afterwards exchanged with Stanley Abbey.[4] The stone for the columns of the hall of Winchester Castle was obtained from this quarry in 1222,[5] but I have not found it farther afield. This Winchester account also refers to stone from Selborne, and others from 'the Isle (of Wight)'. William Rufus gave Bishop Walkelin of Winchester permission to take stone for his cathedral from the quarries of the island; and in 1243 the Abbot of Beaulieu was permitted to take stone from those quarries at Binstead[6] which gave their name to the adjacent Quarr Abbey. Stone from the Isle of Wight was used for a fireback (*reredos*) in the kitchen of a lodge built in the New Forest in 1360.[7] For Porchester Castle 93 tonne-tight of stone from the quarry of St. Helen's in the Isle of Wight were obtained in 1385;[8] and in 1397 other stone was brought from Bonchurch and also 'ragplatenerston from the quarry of Bynnebrigge (Bembridge) beside St. Helen's',[9] while two years later 200 tons of 'platenerston of Bymbrigge'[10] occurs—the term suggesting some form of flat slabs.

Although the Portland stone achieved its greatest fame in the years after the Fire of London, when the City was practically rebuilt in that material, it had long been appreciated. In 1303 a bargeload (*bargia*) of stone from Portland was used at Exeter Cathedral.[11] It was also employed at Westminster in 1347[12] and for the foundations of a turret at the Tower in 1349,[13] while in 1350 the stores of London Bridge included 690 feet of Portland stone, worked and squared, and 1,044 feet not worked.[14] Other stone from Dorset quarries appears occasionally, as the 'hard freestone of Corfe', of which 9 shiploads, costing £48. 11*s*. 6*d*., were bought for the Tower in 1278;[15] and the stone of Purbeck used at Winchester in 1294,[16] and in the New Forest in 1363.[17] But the important product of Purbeck was its marble.

---

[1] E. 476, 3.  [2] Oliver, *Exeter*, 379.
[3] *V.C.H. Somerset*, ii. 393.  [4] *Somerset Arch. Soc.* lx. 14.
[5] E. 491, 13. The 'Heselbergh' which provided stone for Windsor Castle was in Lincolnshire.
[6] *Close R.* 107.  [7] E. 476, 25.  [8] E. 479, 22.  [9] E. 479, 23.
[10] E. 479, 24.  [11] Oliver, *Exeter*, 380.  [12] E. 470, 18.
[13] E. 471, 3.  [14] Riley, *Mems. of London*, 261.
[15] E. 467, 6 (4).  [16] E. 491, 19.  [17] E. 476, 30.

Purbeck marble, a dark shell conglomerate which is capable of receiving a very high polish, came into fashion about the end of the twelfth century. A marble-quarry near Worth Maltravers is mentioned in about 1190,[1] just at the time when St. Hugh was carrying out in his cathedral at Lincoln the work in which his use of this marble roused his biographer to such enthusiasm.[2] The fashion caught on and there was hardly a great church, from Durham to Exeter, where building went on during the next century and a half, in which slender shafts of Purbeck marble were not introduced; and monumental effigies carved by the Purbeck masons were distributed all over England. In 1229 we hear of a ship loaded with marble for Waltham Abbey,[3] and in 1243 orders were given for a good supply of Purbeck marble to be sent to Windsor for the cloister of the royal chapel.[4] For Westminster Abbey in 1252 three shiploads of marble were bought for £34. 9s. 8d.;[5] and in 1279 the Sheriff of Dorset was repaid £10, which he had spent on 300 columns and 200 capitals of marble, given by King Edward to the Countess of Arundel for her nunnery of Marham.[6] Two marble stones, 'one subtly worked with columns for the slab of the lavatory (*ad tablementum lavor'*), and the other for the threshold (*sullinum*) of the great door of the little hall and for the threshold of the door of the pantry and buttery', are mentioned at Westminster in 1288.[7] When Edward I set up a magnificent series of crosses in honour of Queen Eleanor, after her death in 1290, much of the work was carried out in this material, 41s. being paid 'for the freight of a ship bringing marble from Corfe', and marble being supplied by Robert Blund and William Canon of Corfe.[8] The family of Canon was prominently connected with the industry for several generations. William supplied marble to the value of £26. 13s. 4d. for Exeter Cathedral in 1309,[9] and after his death his son and namesake contracted to supply 11½ great columns of marble, at £10. 16s. each; 60 sets of columns with caps and bases, at 5s., for the nave of the cathedral, and 29 columns for the cloister, at 9d. each.[10] Richard Canon supplied 429 feet of marble for the columns of St. Stephen's, Westminster, at 6d. the foot, in 1333.[11] At Norwich in 1324, when the cloister was being built, 23 columns of marble cost £1. 14s. 6d.; 16 bases, 13s. 4d.; one great base, 6s. 8d.[12] The 500 'pieces of marble stone, each containing 1 foot

[1] *Hist. MSS. Com. Rep. Middleton MSS.*, 30.          [2] Coulton, *Social Life*, 472.

[3] *Close R.* 198.                                      [4] Ibid. 11.

[5] E. 466, 30. Two letters arranging for its dispatch are printed in Scott's *Gleanings*, 9, 10.

[6] Liberate R. 8 Edw. I, m. 5.                          [7] E. 467, 17.

[8] *Manners & Household Expenses* (Roxburghe Club, 1841), pp. 97, 104, 115, 117.

[9] Oliver, *Exeter*, 381.      [10] Ibid. 383.      [11] E. 469, 12.      [12] Communar's Roll.

square', at 6d., bought from the Friars Minor of London for use at Windsor in 1364, are not definitely said to be from Purbeck, but probably were.[1] Between 1387 and 1404 about £500 was spent on the purchase of Purbeck marble for the pillars of the nave of Westminster Abbey, the general price for a pillar being £40.[2] After the beginning of the fifteenth century the material fell out of favour for structural work, though it continued to be used for tombs.

Of other English marbles the only one to which I have found a definite reference is that of Egglestone, on the Tees, where Leland in the sixteenth century said 'very fair marble' was obtained.[3] When a marble lavatory was being made at Durham in 1432, the Abbot of Egglestone was paid 20s. for the hire of his quarries; Thomas Hyndley, mason, had 103s. 10d. for winning marble stones in the quarry there: and 28s. 4d. was paid for their carriage to Durham.[4]

More famous and more widely used than any English stone was the fine white stone of Caen, which from the Norman Conquest until the end of our period was in constant demand. Beyond the fact that Caen stone was used for the rebuilding of Canterbury Cathedral in 1175, references to it seem to be lacking until the middle of the thirteenth century, after which they become numerous. Two shiploads of 'free stone of Came' costing £24. 18s. were obtained for Westminster Abbey in 1252;[5] and at the Tower in 1278 there were used no less than 75 shiploads of this stone, containing 89,200 'parpayns'—stones worked on two parallel faces—costing £332. 2s.[6] Sometimes it seems to have been sent over in rough blocks, such being presumably the meaning of the '250 stones of Caen called gobettes'[7] bought from Robert Vallery at 73s. 4d. the hundred in 1290 for use at Westminster,[8] where in 1320 we read of '50 gobettes of Caen stone and also long gobettes of Aylesford stone, chosen and worked for the flying buttress (*archibuterasio*) which stands in the Thames'.[9] For the belfry at Norwich in 1304 we find 70 gobets, costing £3. 12s. 3d., and 2,675 stones of Caen, costing £23. 12s.[10] Some years earlier, in 1289, we have details of the purchase of 182 stones bought at Caen, viz: '40 large, 25 small pillars

---

[1] E. 493, 16.  
[2] Rackham, *Nave of Westminster*, 10.  
[3] *V.C.H. York*, ii. 378.  
[4] *Hist. Dunelm. Scrip. Tres* (Surtees Soc.), ccccxliii.  
[5] E. 466, 30.  
[6] E. 476, 6 (4).  
[7] In Babraham Church (Cambs.) is cut on the block forming the base of one pillar—'Beverach (?) and Kateryn Sant offyrit this gobyte': *Camb. Ant. Soc.* lxvii. 59.  
[8] E. 468, 3.  
[9] E. 469, 1; cf. '*petre de Came voc' gobets*' at Sheppey in 1365: E. 483, 20.  
[10] Sacrist Rolls.

(*postellis*), 42 ribs (*ogivis*), 75 corner stones (*coyne*) made to measure (*de mensura*),—£1. 6s. 8d.'[1] Caen stone also occurs at Exeter about this time, for instance in 1309 and 1316;[2] at Carisbrooke in 1336, when 100 'stones of Chaam' bought at Newport cost 6s. 8d.;[3] at Windsor in 1344, Sheppey in 1362, and Rochester in 1368.

In 1429 Caen stone for London Bridge was bought at 2s. 6d. the ton at the quarry; its carriage to London cost 5s. the ton—one Norman ship carried 42 tons 7 cwt. 3 qr. 10lb. for £10. 11s. 11d., with another 10s. for 'lothmanage', or pilot's fee, from Caen to the sea, and another 10s. for 'lothmanage' from Sandwich to London.[4] The exactitude with which the weight of the cargo is given is worth noticing. So in 1410 these same accounts enter £4. 11s. 3d. paid for 15 tontight 2 weye 16 clav' of Caen stone; in 1411—£4. 6s. 11d. for 12 tonnetight 3 wayes 14 naill of Stapleton stone; and in 1421—£4. 9s. 11d. for 13 ton 5 wey 16 naill of 'Northerneston', at 6s. 8d. the ton—the 'nail' being presumably the wool 'clove' of 7 lb., and 24 of these constituting a 'wey'. When stone was obtained from Lincolnshire for building Mettingham collegiate church, there is an entry, in 1410, 'for weighing (*tronizando*) the freston' at Yarmouth.[5]

The quality of Caen stone made it particularly suitable for mouldings and carving. It was used for the Eleanor crosses, both for the actual statues of the queen and for other features.[6] So also a single block of 'stone of Cham' was bought, for 8d., at Sandwich in 1347, for making a shield of the king's arms.[7] When the tower of Sandwich Church was being rebuilt, in 1444, the churchwardens spent 25s. on 'v ton tygt of Cane stone', and an additional 5d. 'spendit on the mason of Crystchirche for to have an ynsygt yn the Cane stone for the stepil'.[8] Fifty years later, in June 1494, the Prior and Convent of Canterbury, having decided upon the completion of 'a great tower ("Bell Harry") and other buildings affecting the honour of God and the use and beauty of our church', and therefore requiring stones from the quarries of Caen, 'from which quarries it is well known that our whole church was built of old', appointed William Feraunte of Caen as their agent to procure such stone and ship it to Sandwich. During the next three years some £1,035 were spent on this 'Angel Tower', of which £388. 15s. 6½d. was 'for canestone, with carriage, cranage and

---

[1] Communar's Roll, *ex inf.* H. W. Saunders.        [2] Oliver, *Exeter*, 380, 381.

[3] E. 490, 21. Caen stone for use at Warblington was bought at Newport in 1518: E. 490, 12.

[4] Bridge Accts., vol. ii.        [5] Add. MS. 33985, f. 61v.

[6] *Manners and Household Expenses* (Roxburghe Club), 99, 110, &c.

[7] E. 462, 16.        [8] Boys, *Sandwich*, 363.

customs, 1132 tons at various prices'.[1] In 1531 an elaborate survey of the Tower of London was made and estimates were drawn up of the cost of repairs, which would have involved the use of approximately 3,000 tons of Caen stone, at 5s. the ton.[2] Next year a good deal of work was done there, in which Caen stone was used for the more ornamental features, such as doors and windows—one door being made of Caen outside and Reigate stone inside, and the walls of Kentish rag being provided with 'loppys (loopholes) made wt. Cane asheler ij fote brode and in heygth iiij fote'.[3] This same year, 1532, for work at Westminster £11. 0s. 6d. was paid to 'William Neale of Cotevell in Normandie marchaunte for xlix tonne of Cane stone rough, every tonne cont' xvj fote', at 4s. 6d. the ton.[4]

In 1531 Nicholas Tyrrye or Terry contracted to supply for the royal works 300 tons of Caen stone, at 16 feet to the ton, and 200 tons of 'Luke' (Liége) stone, at 14 ft. to the ton, to be delivered at the Tower wharf, at 4s. 6d. the ton for Caen and 6s. for Luke stone, if approved by John Multon, the king's master mason.[5] Later, in January 1536, complaint was made of the quality of some of the stone which he had supplied. He had contracted to deliver 300 tons of stone of Caen, Luke, and 'Barues' for Wolsey's college at Oxford. Among the stone supplied were some 20 tons of hard stone which belonged to none of these varieties. Stubbes, the clerk of the works, refused to receive any more and a dispute arose, which dragged on for some years. John Aylemer of Southwark, who was mason to the Cardinal, and Thomas Sympson, his purveyor, agreed that the stone was bad—so full of flint that the masons could not work it.[6] Other 'stone of Luk' was bought for Hampton Court in 1533:[7] and in 1491 the churchwardens of St. Mary-at-Hill paid 8d. 'for ij load of Brabant stones'.[8] Three hundred of 'whiteforestoon of Brabant' was bought for London Bridge in 1444:[9] and for the building of a jetty at Calais in 1467 'brode-brabandistone' was brought from Brussels and 'hardasshler' from Mechlin;[10] but there does not seem to have been any large import of stone into England from these parts. Towards the end of the thirteenth century a certain amount of stone from Boulogne appears to have been used in London. Thus in 1274 there are payments to William de Curtines of 62s. 8d. '*pro iiij lineis iiij virgis petr' de Bonon', cont' cccxvj pedes*', at 2d. the foot (316 should presumably be by the long hundred, making 376), and of 42s. 6d.

[1] *Literae Cant.* (Rolls Ser.), iii. 330–2.  [2] Bayley, *Hist. of the Tower*, App.
[3] Ibid. xxix.  [4] T.R., f. 48.  [5] *L. & P. Hen. VIII*, v. 261.
[6] Ibid. x. 194.  [7] H.C. 237, f. 20.  [8] *Memorials* (E.E.T.S.), 177.
[9] Bridge Accts., vol. iv.  [10] E. 197, 5.

'*pro ij lineis xiij virgis ij pedibus dure petre, cont' cciiij pedes*', at 2½*d*. the foot.[1]
Next year 3 shiploads of hard stone of Boulogne, containing 118 yards 2½
feet, cost £9. 1s. 6d.,[2] while three years later 55 shiploads cost £178. 9s. 2d.,
and two shiploads of '*Bleuye petre de Bonon*' were 45s.[3] Finally, in 1292 there
is a payment for cutting 1,400 ft. of stone of Boulogne, at 2*d*. the foot.[4]

It would not be possible or profitable to deal here with all the minor
quarries that supplied stone for local building, but a few miscellaneous
entries may be noticed. At Windsor in 1481 there is mention of '33 tons
of touchstone, both for use in the chapel and for making the king's tomb
there',[5] but its source is not stated. Lias occurs in 1475 in a list of stone in
store—'*j par mouldes petr' de lyes*'.[6] At Corfe in 1285 large quantities *velute
petre* were used;[7] and in 1258, at Westminster, there is a charge for the
carriage *france petre et velute*.[8] At Mere (Wilts.) also *velute petre* are distinguished from *france petre*.[9] What this is I do not know, but presumably the
same type of stone is referred to in the account for building Melbourne
Castle in 1314, where masons are found *sculpantes et cubantes petram liberam
et velosam*.[10]

At Wallingford 228 cartloads of 'stones called *malmeston*' were bought in
1395, and chalk occurs frequently in accounts, though it is not always
possible to tell whether it was for making lime, or for rubble filling, or as
a building stone. About 1190 John de Hessle gave to the abbey of Meaux
a quarry (of chalk) 'both for making the kiln and for building the stone
church and other offices'.[11] It was often used for 'pendants', that is to say,
the filling between the ribs of vaults—as, for instance, at the Tower in
1278—'*pro clij navatis crete ad calcem ardendam et pendantes ad vosuras fac*'[3] and
in 1437 at Shene, when 20 tons of chalk called 'pendandchalke' were used
in making a latrine pit.[12] The 'white stone for filling walls', brought from
Reech to Cambridge Castle in 1295, may have been chalk, but is more
probably clunch—a material frequently mentioned in Cambridge Accounts; as, for instance, at King's Hall in 1415—'*vj$^{xx}$vj de clunche de Bur-
well, pondus dolii pro quinque marcis—iijs. iiijd.*'[13] For the Schools at
Cambridge there were supplied in 1478, amongst other material, 2 barge-

---

[1] E. 467, 6 (2).                                    [2] E. 467, 6 (3).
[3] E. 467, 6 (4).                                    [4] E. 468, 6.
[5] E. 496, 26. For 'towyche stone' at Purbeck in 1549, see *Wilts. Arch. Mag.* xv. 182.
[6] E. 503, 19.            [7] E. 460, 27.            [8] E. 467, 2.
[9] *Earldom of Cornwall Accts. 1296-7* (Camden Soc.), 64.
[10] Mins. Accts. 1, No. 3.            [11] *Chron. Mon. de Melsa*, i. 228.
[12] E. 496, 8.
[13] K.H. 5, f. 167. 'Burvellston' was used at Mettingham in 1413: Add. MS. 33985, f. 79v.

loads of rag (*kelys de rage*), 8 cartloads of 'clunche', and 3 cartloads of 'pebyllis'.[1] Pebbles, for rubble, occur pretty frequently, as 'pubelston' at Chester in 1426,[2] but more often under some form of the French *cailloux*. At Winchester in 1222 we have 26s. paid 'for 400 cartloads *de kaildo*', and 3s. *pro xij mensuris de caildo*,[3] and in 1294, 'for stone which is called *kaylowe* for making the great bridge—16d.'[4] The form at Norwich in 1304 is 'calyou',[5] and this occurs elsewhere, as, for instance, at Ipswich in 1441.[6] The Dover accounts for 1354 include payments for the carriage of 3,464 cartloads of stones from the sea-shore.[7] Similarly, in 1347, there are payments 'to young men (*garcionibus*) collecting flints (*petras de cilice*) in the fields',[8] and at Wallingford 9 men were paid 3d. a day to collect 'stones called flynt'.[9] The earliest occurrence of the English form of the word that I have noted is in 1283, when 96 shiploads of chalk and *flyntis* were provided for a wall at the Tower.[10] Mentions of this material are, naturally, more numerous than enlightening, and there appear to be no references to the skilled craftsmanship involved in the production of the flintwork[11] which is such a feature of many East Anglian churches.

[1] *Cambridge Grace Book*, A. 131.    [2] E. 545, 25.
[3] E. 491, 13.          [4] E. 491, 19.          [5] Sacrist Roll.
[6] E. 575, 28.          [7] E. 462, 18.          [8] E. 462, 16.
[9] E. 490, 2.          [10] E. 467, 10.
[11] Unless the instructions to the mason at Helmingham Church in 1487 to be economical with 'the blacke flint stone' (App. B) may be so regarded.

# VIII

## BRICKS: PAVING

THE Romans used large flat bricks of varying dimensions in their buildings in Britain, but there is no definite evidence that their successors, the Saxons, made either bricks or tiles. They had, however, sufficient appreciation of the utility of such material to make use of Roman bricks in their own buildings. In particular, we are told that Ealdred, eighth Abbot of St. Albans, in about 900 destroyed the ruins of Verulamium, putting aside the whole tiles (or bricks) and stones for the building of his church.[1] Some two centuries later his successor, Abbot Paul (1077–93), followed his example, and 'when he had been abbot for eleven years within those same years had built of brickwork (*opere lateritio*) the whole church of St. Alban'[2]—as anyone may see, now that the plaster with which it was originally covered has disappeared. By the beginning of the thirteenth century the making of roof-tiles was well established, as may be seen from the evidence of the London building by-laws of 1212.[3] A few buildings of about this date may be found in East Anglia, constructed of, or containing, contemporary bricks, probably of local manufacture.[4] Most, however, of the bricks used in England before the second quarter of the fourteenth century seem to have been imported from the Low Countries. Enormous quantities of Flemish bricks were used at the Tower in 1278, one lot of 202,500 *quarellorum de Flandria* being bought from John Bardown of Ypres for £20. 4s., their carriage by sea, by Hugh Bekman of Newport (i.e. Nieuport), costing £32. 5s.[5] Five years later 101,350 such Flemish bricks were bought, for £23. 3s. 5d., for the wall between the Tower and the City.[6]

During the whole of the fourteenth century Flemish tiles figure among the imports of our eastern ports,[7] but it has been claimed by Mr. J. Bilson[8] that the tiles (*tegulae*) being made at Hull from 1303 onwards were bricks rather than roof-tiles. So far as those mentioned in 1303–4 are concerned, the only evidence is the low price—3s. the thousand—which corresponds better with the 5s. which is the normal price for 'wall-tiles' at Hull and

---

[1] *Gesta Abbatum*, i. 24.        [2] Ibid. 54.        [3] See p. 223.

[4] N. Lloyd, *Hist. of Engl. Brickwork*, 3.

[5] E. 467, 7 (4) and (6). As the tiles were bought by the long hundred of six score, 202,500 = 243,000.        [6] E. 467, 10.

[7] Salzman, *English Trade*, 360.        [8] *East Riding Ant. Soc.* iv. 47.

York from 1353 to 1434 than the 10s. which is the average price for roofing tiles during that period. But it should be observed that at York in 1327 roofing tiles and *tylis flandr'*, bought for fireplaces, were alike 10s. the thousand.[1] For some reason roofing tiles were about twice the price in Yorkshire that they were farther south; presumably they were made to a much larger scantling.

The earliest definite reference to the making of wall-tiles in England seems to be in 1335, when 18,000 *tegulae murales* were made, at 12d. the thousand, for use at Ely.[2] Two years later the Ely accounts mention 3,000 'waltyl' bought at Wisbech for 16s. 2d., and another 2,000 bought at Lynn for 7s. 4d., including carriage.[3] 'Waltighel' occur under that name at Hull in 1353,[4] and 37,800 flat tiles (*tegulis planis*) were bought, at 3s. 4d. the thousand, for the walls (*parietibus*) of the chambers of Sheppey Castle in 1365.[5] Just about the same time 'waltill' were bought for the royal manors of Eltham and Shene at prices ranging from 5s. 6d. to 10s. the thousand;[6] and at Windsor plain tiles (presumably for roofing) were 2s. 6d. —'flandrestill' 5s. and 6s. 8d.—large 'squartill' (possibly for paving) 5s. the thousand.[7] At Porchester in 1397 'hurthtighel' for fireplaces cost 10s. the thousand, and 'white tiles of Flaundres bought at London for the *reredosis* of fireplaces', 8s.[8]

In 1400 we find '28,000 Flaundrestyle bought for making the ways called vicez', at 4s. 4d. the thousand, including carriage from London to Sutton Manor;[9] and also 11,500 'waltyll', costing £3. 4s. 10d., bought for King's Hall[10] and very likely imported, as a later batch was obtained for the same college from Lynn.[11] When, however, the tower of Beverley Bar was built, in 1409–10, the bricks used were of local origin, some 125,000 being bought from twenty different persons, mostly at 3s. 8d. the thousand.[12] They are referred to simply as 'tiles' (*tegulae*), but a parcel of roofing tiles bought at the same time—though not for the Bar—is described as 'thaktill'. There is also mention of 'squynchon' (at 4s. the thousand), which were chamfered bricks used for jambs and arches; the term appears again— as 'qwynshontille' and 'squynshontiell'—in a Beverley Minster fabric roll of 1445–6.[13] So, also, the enormous quantities of bricks used for the building of Tattershall Castle, from 1434 onwards, were made in England at Boston and Edlington.[14]

[1] E. 501, 8.  [2] *Sacrist R.* 67.  [3] Ibid. 91.  [4] Bilson, loc. cit.
[5] E. 483, 21.  [6] E. 493, 12, 18.  [7] E. 493, 16.
[8] E. 479, 23.  [9] E. 502, 15.  [10] K.H. 5, f. 76.
[11] K.H. 8, f. 27.  [12] *East Riding Ant. Soc.* iv. 30–45.
[13] Ibid. vii. 54, 60.  [14] Curzon, *Tattershall Castle*, 52–4.

Although these Tattershall bricks are referred to as 'waltyle' their maker is called Baldwin 'brekemaker' and the masons who laid them 'brekemasons'. The term 'brick' had been in use on the Continent at least as early as the thirteenth century, and the stores at Calais in 1390 included 626,000 'brikes'.[1] With the exception of an isolated reference to a stair built in *'petris et brikis'* at Windsor in 1340,[2] the word does not seem to have been used in this country before the fifteenth century.[3] In 1416 John Warefield, as steward of Thomas de Stonor, expended £40 on the making of 200,000 'brykes', and £15 for carting them from Crockernend to Stonor.[4] These were made by 'les Flemynges'. And Flemish, presumably, was 'Henry Sondergyltes, brykeman', employed by the Wardens of London Bridge in 1418 and succeeding years to make 'bryktill' at Deptford. His 'tilkylne for making bryke' was enlarged that year, at a cost of 20s., and 3s. 4d. was spent on 'string and other things for making flekes (i.e. hurdles) for the making of bryketill', and five men were employed for a day unloading *'tegulas de brike'* out of a 'shoute' or barge.[5] Later entries speak of the carriage of fuel, sand, and straw for the bricks, and show that Sondergyltes burnt 345,000 bricks in three 'kylnes'.[6]

Baldwin, the Tattershall brickmaker, is referred to after his death as 'Bawdwin Docheman', when his widow was paid in 1458 'for the making and burning (*anulacione*) of 160 thousand tiles' £11. 13s. 4d.[7] So, also, John Arnold and Hermann Reynold, the 'brekebrennerys' with whom Abbot William Curteys of Bury St. Edmunds made a contract[8] in 1430 for *'lateres vocatos le brike'*, are called *'teutonici'*. It is also more than probable that William Weysy, or Veyse, 'brikemaker' to the king, who was appointed in 1437 to search for earth suitable for making 'brike',[9] and in 1442 was commissioned to impress 'brikeleggers' for the work at Eton,[10] was a 'Dutchman', especially as he was made controller of all the beer-brewers in England in 1441.[11] During the ten years following 1442 he provided some two and a half million bricks for the work at Eton.[12] Even as late as 1483 the brickburner at Kirby Muxloe was 'Antony Docheman',[13] and among the 'brekelayers' we find such names as Turkyn Horwynde

---

[1] Foreign R. 14 Ric. II, m. E.                    [2] Hope, *Windsor Castle*, 230.
[3] At York it apparently occurs for the first time in the Minster accounts, as 'breike', in 1530: *Y.F.R.* 103.                    [4] *Berks., Bucks. & Oxon. Arch. J.* xix. 91.
[5] Bridge Accts., vol. ii, ff. 255, 276, 289, 293.        [6] Ibid., ff. 301, 303, 312, 346.
[7] Curzon, op. cit. 54.                [8] App. B.                [9] *Cal. Patent R.* 145.
[10] Ibid. 93.            [11] Salzman, *Engl. Industries*, 296. 'Dutchman' means German.
[12] Willis and Clark, *Arch. Hist. of Cambridge*, i. 385.
[13] *Leics. Arch. Soc.* xi. 307.

and Charlot Ruddicourt, who were employed on making 'le murther holes', and another group with foreign names—Marc Maligoo, Milhere Wattes, Staner Matlot, &c.—who were 'laying anew le Basse Tours with pict' of the wall', which Professor Hamilton Thompson suggests refers to diaper work in brick.[1] It seems, therefore, fairly clear that the use and the manufacture of bricks was reintroduced into England from the Netherlands, and that they were at first made in the districts, such as East Anglia and round the Humber, where Flemish influence was strong, and often by craftsmen from the Low Countries.

In 1425 licence was given to crenellate Moor Park in Rickmansworth 'with stone, lime and brik';[2] and two years later, 2,000 'breke for making chemeneys' at Langley were bought at Rickmansworth.[3] Other 'breke' used at Langley in 1440 for making fireplaces and ovens in the kitchen were brought from le Frithe near St. Albans,[4] as were the bricks supplied by William Veyse that same year for making the 'creste' of a stone wall at the Tower.[4] For Windsor Castle bricks were made in the immediate neighbourhood in 1430, when we find 2 spades bought for the 'brikemen' and also an entry of 'Money paid to John Gyse working at making brikes, for 80 days; Richard Taylor for 12 days; Peter Preutte for 120 days; and John Whyte for 22 days; each of them taking 6d. a day .... And to John Gyse working at burning the said brikes and watching for 4 nights; Peter Preutte for 4 nights; and John Whyte for 4 nights; each of them taking 4d. a night.'[5]

Medieval bricks were burnt with wood fuel in a kiln or a clamp. For works at Shene in 1440 William Veyse supplied 9,500 'breke', costing 4s. 6d. the thousand 'at the tylekenne'.[4] Next year, at Calais, there is an entry of 'carriage of stones called brekeston from a place called the brek clampe to the Fesaunt Toure'.[6] In the Little Saxham Hall accounts for 1505 Sir Thomas Lucas enters the purchase of faggots 'for my breke kil';[7] and in 1518, for Warblington Manor in Hampshire, £20 was paid for three 'kyll' of bricks, containing 70, 100, and 40 thousand respectively.[8] At Kirby Muxloe, in 1483, we have:[9]

for hyre of 3 men by the space of 8 wikes, every man taking in the wike 8d., for setting of breke in to a newe kylne—16s. Itm. Antony Docheman, every wike for his hyre 10d.—6s. 8d. Item payd for brennyng of the same kylne by the

[1] Ibid. 265, 268.  [2] *Cal. Patent R.* 351.  [3] E. 466, 11.
[4] E. 503, 9.  [5] E. 496, 9.
[6] E. 193, 4.  [7] Gage, *Thingoe Hundred*, 142.
[8] E. 490, 12.  [9] *Leics. Arch. Soc.* xi. 307.

space of a wyke unto the noumbre of breke 100,000—11s. 4d. Item paid for
fellyng and brekyng of 78 loode of wood—9s. 9d. . . . Item payd for a lode of
spyldyng to brene among the grene wood in the kyln—2s. 4d.'

The total cost was 104s. 11d., or slightly over a shilling the thousand.
For Hunsdon House in 1525 we find £199. 10s. paid for burning 'xiiij
clampys of brick', at 20d. and 21d. the thousand;[1] and in 1530 Sir Thomas
Kitson paid 'to my Lorde of Bury for a clamp of brick—vj$^{xx}$iiij$^m$ij$^{cc}$—
xx$^{li}$.x$^s$'.[2]

At Little Saxham Nicholas Kirkeby was engaged in 1505 to make
'vj$^{xx}$ ml. breke—vj$^{xx}$ to the C—taking for every ml. xviij$^d$, and leiying
everything by him, and redy caryed, and he to dig his erth and set it on
tassis (= heaps), and to be in length x inch, in brede v ynche, ij inche and
di' in thiknesse'.[3] These dimensions are rather greater than most surviving
medieval bricks,[4] but correspond pretty nearly to those in Beverley North
Bar, which are 10½ by 5¼ by 2. In a second contract, for 200,000 bricks, it
is stated that they are to be of the same 'scantlen' (10 by 5 by 2½) 'wele and
sufficiently brent and no semel breke nor broken breke to be told but only
ij half brekes for oon breke'.[5] Samel bricks are those on the outside of the
kiln, which are less thoroughly burnt, being pinkish in colour and inferior
in quality. Of a batch of tiles bought from Mr. Laurence Stubbys, vicar of
Kingston (Surrey), in 1532 for Westminster Palace, 65,000 were 'sam-
welle bricke', 24,000 'harde bricke', and 32,000 'in bricke battis'.[6] At York
in 1510 we have purchases of 'hardwaltiel' at 6s., 'basterdwaltiel' at 5s. 3d.,
and 'singlewalltiel' at 5s. the thousand.[7] There is mention at Calais in 1468
of 'brekstones called Whitebrek'.[8] On the other hand we find '*bryk rubei
coloris*' used in London in 1490;[9] in the Hengrave accounts for 1535 there
is a payment 'for makying clene the old red brycke';[10] and at Collyweston
in 1504 a deficiency in the redness of the bricks was helped out with 'stuff
bought for the coleryng of the cheney of Brike: vij lb. of red ocker w$^t$ j
bz. of the offalles of the glovers lether, xijd. Item to John Bradley wiff for
xiiij galons of small Ale for the said cheney of Bryk, vjd.'[11]

Even when the body of a building was made of other material, bricks,

---

[1] E. 465, 20.  [2] Gage, *Hengrave*, 49.  [3] Gage, *Thingoe Hundred*, 140.

[4] Lloyd, *Hist. of Eng. Brickwork*, 96–7. The average is about 9×4½×2. The 400,000
bricks for which the Prior of Westminster contracted in 1496, at 18d. the thousand, were to
be 9½ inches in length 'or more': Westm. Abbey Muniments, no. 16470.

[5] Gage, op. cit. 141.  [6] T.R., f. 48. Bricks at this time ran 500 to the ton: f. 430.

[7] Y.F.R. 95. 'Thaketiell' were now only 2s. 6d.; possibly the statute of 1477 had reduced
the size of York roofing tiles.

[8] E. 197, 5.  [9] Egerton MS. 2358, m. 5.

[10] Gage, *Hengrave*, 50.  [11] St. John's Coll. Camb. MS. vol. ii.

PLATE 12

*a.* BRICK-MAKING 15TH CENTURY

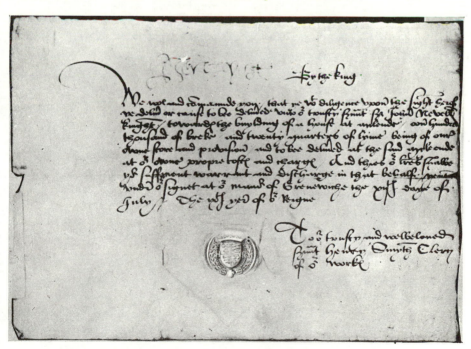

*b.* WRIT FOR DELIVERY OF BRICKS, 1517
UNDER HAND AND SEAL OF HENRY VIII

or Flanders tiles, had been used from the thirteenth century onwards for fireplaces and continued so to be used to the end of our period. Mention may be made of the 'makyng of ij bolsters of bricke in the kichen for to sette pannes on to seath the Kynges brane', at Windsor in 1537.[1] For the chimneys which form such a decorative feature of Tudor architecture the brick had to be skilfully cut. At Collyweston in 1505 William Smyth of Peterborough supplied 4,300 'brike' for the 'tonnelles of the cheymnes', at 10s. the thousand—a price which, even allowing for the fact that it included carriage, suggests that they were either moulded or of picked quality; and a 'brikehewer' was paid 7½d. a day, while bricklayers received only 5d. or 6d.[2] At the same time Sir Thomas Lucas was bargaining with Stephen Gaithorn, bricklayer, 'for leiying and making of all my walles and brek work this yer following to be doon at Saxham, as well walles, splaies, dores, windowes, tabilmentes, gabilendes, batilmentes, and al other, xvj$^d$ for every m! and vj$^{xx}$ to the C., and taking for every ton of hewen brek vj$^s$ viij$^d$ for the chymneys'.[3] About 1530 the large sum of £74. 17s. was paid at Westminster 'for the hewyng of 50 tonells in brycke for chimnes and ventes for jaxys,[4] which hathe byn hewyn thys wynter by taske'.[5] In 1535 bricklayers at Hampton Court were paid 15s. 'for hewyng of iij$^{ml}$ Eyght Canttes servyng for boswelles[6] Towres and squarys for the quenys lodgeyng',[7] and next year John Baldwyn was paid 25s. 'for hewyng of fyve thousande Eyght Canttes Aungulers chamferys skewes and Roundes'.[8] Mention may also be made of 'bricke hewen into turnynge bricke and coynes for cooping of the walle', at the same price of 5s. the thousand, at Westminster in 1532.[9]

Bricks and tiles were also used for paving. In 1368 Henry Yevele provided 1,000 'tiles called valthill' for the pavement of the wardrobe at Eltham.[10] The price, 16s. 6d., makes it clear that, in spite of their name, these were no ordinary 'wall tiles' or bricks, but presumably something fairly ornate. Three years earlier he had supplied '8000 tiles of Flanders for the paving of floors (*arearum*) and other work', at 6s. 8d. the thousand, for Westminster Palace.[11] Thirty-three 'broad pieces of Flemish paving for the pavement of the new vestry' in Exeter Cathedral cost 2s. 9d., being a penny

[1] Hope, *Windsor Castle*, i. 264. 'Brane', I suppose, means 'brawn'.
[2] St. John's Coll. Camb. MS. vol. ii.      [3] Gage, *Thingoe Hundred*, 141.
[4] Jakes, i.e. latrines.      [5] B.M. Roy. MS. 14, B. iv.
[6] Probably the 'bushels' (see above, p. 114) or sections of pillars.
[7] H.C. 238, f. 384. 'Eyght Canttes' = octagons.
[8] H.C. 240, f. 374.      [9] T.R., f. 640.
[10] E. 493, 30.      [11] E. 472, 14.

each, in 1438.[1] The use of tiles for paving was well established by the thirteenth century and Henry III frequently ordered their use in his buildings; for instance, his chamber at Clarendon was to be 'paved with plain tile'[2] in 1250 and 'a pavement of tiles' was to be made on the dais in the hall at Winchester in 1256.[3] In 1237 he ordered the treasurer to use certain marble for the steps before the altar in St. Stephen's Chapel at Westminster, and with the rest of the marble to make the steps before the altar in the queen's chapel, and if there was not sufficient marble for the purpose to make the steps of painted tile; and also to cause the small chapel to be decently paved with painted tile.[4] Ordinary 'paving tiles' were 5s. the thousand at Westminster in 1274[5] and 10s. in 1324;[6] but in 1289 there is mention of 11,500 '*de tegulis subtilibus*' for paving the king's stone chamber and the new chamber with the oriel towards the garden, bought at 5s. the thousand.[7] These certainly suggest ornamental tiles, and may be compared with the 'case (*fraill*) of tiles of Naverne (? Navarre) cunningly painted, called pauyngtyle' bought in 1444.[8] In 1308 Hugh le Peyntour and Peter the Pavier were employed for 28 days 'making and painting the pavement';[9] and the accounts of 1482 for St. George's, Windsor, mention 'various colours for painting (?) locks (*cerur*') and pavyngtile',[10] which suggests that the tiles were sometimes decorated with ordinary paint. More often they were coloured, either in patterns or with a simple glaze, before firing. At Shene we find, in 1385, a thousand 'tiles called pennetyl, painted, used for paving', and 15s. paid 'to Katherine Lyghtfote for 2000 painted tiles for the room set apart for the King's bath'.[11] Yellow tiles occur at Westminster in 1278;[12] black and white 'pavyngtill' were bought, at 4s. 6d. the thousand, by the London Bridge wardens in 1411;[13] 27s. 4d. was paid in 1510 'for a m[1] of pavyng tile to be eneled wt. colours of grene yelowe and black' for Little Saxham Hall;[14] 'paving tyle of yalowe and grene colour', at 5s. the hundred, appear in the Westminster accounts for 1532;[15] and 'Flemyshe pavyng tyll of grene and jowllo (yellow)', also at 5s., figure at Hampton Court in 1535.[16]

Another substance often used for paving was marble. One of the glories of Prior Ernulf's church at Canterbury was the glitter of its marble

---

[1] Oliver, *Exeter*, 391.

[2] Liberate R. 34 Hen. III, m. 12.     [3] Ibid. 41 Hen. III.

[4] *Close R.*     [5] E. 467, 6 (2).     [6] E. 469, 6.

[7] E. 467, 17.     [8] E. 503, 12.     [9] E. 468, 18.

[10] E. 496, 26.     [11] E. 473, 2.     [12] E. 467, 6 (6).

[13] Bridge Accts., vol. i, f. 287.     [14] Gage, *Thingoe Hundred*, 150.

[15] T.R., f. 97.     [16] Law, *Hampton Court*, i. 363.

pavement;[1] and about 1150 Prior Roger of Durham, wishing to adorn his church, asked men who were going on pilgrimage to bring back pieces of foreign marbles for its paving.[1] In 1312 Adam le Marbrer undertook to pave part of St. Paul's with squares of marble;[2] and 1,040 feet of marble was bought, at $3\frac{1}{4}d$. the foot, for the paving of the cloister at Exeter in 1390.[3] In 1355, John Canoun (of Purbeck) and John Mayow supplied 1,200 pieces of marble for the paving of St. Stephen's Chapel at Westminster;[4] and it was presumably this marble with which Athelard le Pavyer laid 285 perches of pavement in St. Stephen's, at 3s. 4d. the perch.[5] That same year, 1355, Athelard—here called 'of Brabant'—made the pavement of two cloisters in front of the canons' chambers at Windsor.[6] In 1459 John Turpyn, mason, paved the east walk of the cloister at Wells, containing 14 bays (*cyuerys*), and one bay of the south walk, each bay containing 150 feet; for which he received payment at the rate of $6\frac{3}{4}d$. a foot, and 10s. 'in reward for his diligent labour'.[7] So, too, in 1420 Richard Carleton, 'paviere', was given 13s. 4d. 'for his great and diligent labour over the paving of 298 *teyses* on the Bridge'.[8] The rate of payment for paving remained curiously stable in London; in the bridge accounts from 1411 to 1507, at least, it was 7d. the 'teys', or toise, of $7\frac{1}{2}$ sq. feet; the same rate was paid for paving 27 'teys' at the king's mews in 1383.[9] This last pavement was of Kentish 'rag', which was also used in 1422 for 'the pavement at le Cheynegate of the Greneyard within the Palace'[10] at Westminster; and 1,100 ft. of the similar stone called 'urnel' was employed in 1393 'for paving the kitchen and a lobby (*interclos*') between the kitchen and the dressour' at Eltham.[10]

Occasionally floors were plastered—as, for instance, the floor of the queen's chamber at Winchester in 1268[11]—but much more often they were covered with beaten earth. In 1260 the Bailiff of Havering was ordered to earth the flooring (*planchicium*) of the chapel.[12] The New College accounts for 1453 give details of the boarding and levelling of a chamber floor, after which comes 'a cartload of red earth for earthing (*terand*') the flore'.[13] Twenty loads of mud (*luti*) were used '*in teryng diversorum florys*' at the manor of Pleasaunce in 1447,[14] and '*a lood of lome to ovircast the flore*' occurs

---

[1] App. A.
[3] Oliver, *Exeter*, 386.
[5] E. 502, 17.
[7] *Hist. MSS. Com. Rep.* x (3), 289.
[9] E. 495, 14.
[11] Liberate R. 53 Hen. III.
[13] Thorold Rogers, *Hist. of Prices*, iii. 717.

[2] App. B.
[4] E. 471, 11.
[6] E. 493, 1.
[8] London Bridge Accts., vol. ii, f. 434.
[10] E. 495, 23.
[12] Ibid. 44 Hen. III.
[14] Dy. of Lanc. Misc. Bks. 1. 11, f. 9.

in the churchwardens' accounts of St. Mary-at-Hill for 1479.[1] Many other instances occur, but these are sufficiently typical. Finally, it may be of interest to note that the floor of the bowling alley at Hampton Court was composed of 'founders yerthe', bought from Houndsditch—probably the earth used for making the core of bells when they were cast—and 'soope asshes', which I suppose is the residue from the manufacture of soap.[2]

---

[1] *Memorials* (E.E.T.S.), 88.          [2] H.C. 239, f. 556.

# IX

## MORTAR: CEMENT

IN order to bind together the stones or bricks composing a wall into
one solid whole it was customary from the earliest times to use mortar,
composed of lime and sand, the common proportion being one part
lime and two or three parts sand. The Romans often mixed pounded
tile with the mortar used on the outer facing of their walls, as this was
supposed to render it less pervious to rain. Roman mortar is popularly supposed to be superior in quality to any that has been produced since, but
this is partly due to the characteristic of well-made mortar that it tends to
harden with the process of time, and in actual fact Roman, like other
mortar, varied considerably in quality and, as a whole, is neither better
nor worse than that produced in later periods.

Naturally, purchases of lime and sand are among the commonest entries
in building accounts. Lime, which is the product of the burning of chalk
or limestone, might be bought ready burnt, or it could be burnt in kilns
specially constructed in the neighbourhood of the building operations. In
a Westminster Palace account for 1258 we find 3s. paid 'for mortar of lime
and sand bought of Sir Hugh of St. Albans, monk', and also purchases of
98 cartloads of sand and 300 of lime.[1] For the most part lime was bought
by the cartload, quarter, or, in smaller quantities, bushel, but a variety
of other measures occur. The 'load' at Hampton Court in 1533 was 4
quarters, and cost 5s. 6d.,[2] while at Nonesuch in 1530 it was defined as 40
bushels, costing 6s.[3] At Salisbury in 1483 lime was 14d. the quarter, 7d. the
'sack', and 3½d. the bushel (*bouchelle*).[4] At Winchester in 1258 'chests (*cistis*)'
of lime cost 8d.,[5] and an earlier account for 1222 speaks of 'a hutch (*arca*)
for measuring lime'.[6] This account also records 75s. paid 'for 100 sesters (*sex-
tariis*) of lime'; the '*cister de lyme*', at 2d., occurs again at Cambridge in 1475
and neighbouring years.[7] The King's Hall accounts also mention 41s. 4d.
paid 'for 15 fother of lime from Reach' in 1400,[8] and lime bought at 3s. the
*fodre* in 1450.[9] At Wallingford in 1390 we have 10s. paid '*pro v doliis de
slekkydlym*'—for 5 casks of slaked lime;[10] at York lime was bought by the

[1] E. 467, 2.     [2] H.C. 237, f. 20.     [3] L. & P. Hen. VIII, xiii (2), 342.
[4] Swayne, *Churchwardens' Accts. . . . Sarum*, 33.
[5] E. 491, 14. Perhaps, however, *cistis* may be meant for 'sesters'.
[6] E. 491, 13.     [7] K.H. 15, f. 21.     [8] K.H. 5, f. 76.
[9] K.H. 11, f. 137.     [10] E. 490, 4.

'mele', or tub, which was defined in 1327 as containing 2 quarters and cost-ing 10*d.*,[1] which was still the price forty years later;[2] and at Chester the local measure was the 'ring'—a small tub or bucket—lime being bought in 1291 at the rate of 100 'ringes' for 5*s.*,[3] while in 1457 ten '*ryngez calcis*' cost 2*s.*[4]

An early instance of the construction of a kiln for the special purposes of building operations occurs at Winchester in 1222, when 50*s.* was paid to Adam de Calce 'for making a kiln (*rogo*)'.[5] Seven years later the Abbot of Abingdon allowed the king to clear the timber from 26 acres of Saghe Wood for fuel for two kilns required for work on the city walls and one for the castle at Oxford; in return the abbot was allowed to assart the land so cleared.[6] In 1242 Master Elias de Derham was granted wood for a kiln for building the chancel of Harrow Church.[7] A kiln (*torale*) was built at the large cost of £14. 8*s.* in 1236, and another, for £20, in 1240, for work at Windsor;[8] and the Hundred Rolls of 1275 complain that the king's two lime-kilns (*rees calcis*) had between them devoured 500 oaks in the forest of Wellington.[9] Such destruction of timber, of which other complaints could be quoted, was lessened by the use of coal, which was common where the presence of coalpits or access to the sea rendered such fuel avail-able. The use of 'sea coal' for burning lime was unavailingly denounced as a nuisance in London at least as early as 1285,[10] and as much as 1,166 quarters of sea coal was bought in 1278 for the kilns (*chauffornia*) in con-nexion with work at the Tower.[11]

It will be noticed that in the entries already quoted four different terms for limekilns are employed, and many others were in use. At Corfe in 1285 there are payments 'for making the pit for a kiln (*rogum*)'; 'for 100 faggots (*astell'*) for lighting the fire under the coal'; and 'for 16 quarters of coal for the kiln'; and also 'to Adam de Crauford, who showed how (*docuit*) to make and set the stones round the kiln'.[12] Six years later, when a kiln was made there for burning lime—for which '80 qrs. of coal of Newcastle on Tyne' were bought at Ore (now Nore) in Purbeck, for £4—the term used is *clibanus*;[13] and in 1377 the English form *le lyme kilne* is used.[14] *Clibanus* occurs also at Langley in 1366, when a kiln, 14 feet square and 14 feet in depth, was made at a cost of 26*s.* 8*d.*[15] Measurements are very rarely given, but for one built in 1400 at York 3,300 bricks and 33 loads of

[1] E. 501, 8.                           [2] E. 501, 12.                          [3] E. 486, 7.
[4] E. 488, 2.                           [5] E. 491, 13.                          [6] *Close R.* 268.
[7] Ibid. 420.                           [8] Hope, *Windsor Castle*, 72.
[9] *Hundred R.* ii. 56.                 [10] Salzman, *Engl. Industries*, 6.
[11] E. 467, 4.                          [12] E. 460, 27.                         [13] E. 460, 28.
[14] E. 461, 9.                          [15] E. 466, 3.

clay were required,[1] and about the end of our period, or possibly rather later, eight kilns erected (apparently at Calais, but the account is defective) were each 20 feet in height, with an average internal breadth of 10 feet and walls 10 feet thick.[2]

At Windsor there is in 1351 an entry '*pro reparacione spelunce supra clibanum*',[3] where *clibanus* seems to be used for the hearth and *spelunca* for the kiln tower, as it is called at Scarborough in 1336, when 10 chalders of sea coal were bought '*pro turriolo calcis infra castrum ardendo*'.[4] Yet another form occurs at [South] Wingfield, Derbyshire, in 1443: 'for carriage of 10 waggon loads (*plaustrat*') of stones for lymeston from Cruchclyff for the burning of lime therefrom—2s. 6d. For 3 baskettes (4d.) and 2 bolles (2d.) for carrying the said stones *usque in ustrinam calcinam*—6d.'[5] From this word *ustrina* may possibly be derived the form found in 1440 at Shene, where 6d. a day was paid 'to Richard Kynge, lymebrenner, working in charge of *le lymoste*'[6]—though the *Oxford Dictionary* derives 'oast', a hop-kiln, from OE. *ast*, cognate with the Latin *aestus*.

Another term, which I have only found in one instance, appears at Wallingford in 1365, when there is mention of 'making an *ode* in the park of Wattyngton for making lime therein';[7] also, £6 paid to John Tyghler of Goring for 'making 2 *ode* for making lime'; also, 3s. 'for 9 empty bariles which had contained tar, for burning lime in the said *ode*'. With this last entry may be compared one at Scarborough in 1423: 'for iij trusses de lyng (i.e. heather) and ij tome (i.e. empty) barell of pikk boght for kyndelyng of ye lyme kyln'.[8] So also at Rockingham we find: '12 Tarrebarelles for the kiln (*thorale*)' in 1355,[9] and '4 tarbarell' used for starting the fire at the 'lyme kilne' in 1383.[10] In this last account payments are made to Robert Mason 'for mending *le brandild del lymekilne*'.

When repairs were done to Pevensey Castle in 1288 we find men 'digging stones and old mortar where the wall had been thrown down', and others 'carrying chalk from the keep to the gate and making old mortar and new'.[11] With this may be compared an entry in the Westminster accounts for 1532: 'for the trying and carting of cciiij$^{xx}$ij of loodis of olde morter, at the paleis aforesaide beaten downe of the olde wallis there, at jd, everye loode'.[12] From this it would seem that old mortar was re-used, either by re-burning, as was certainly sometimes done with plaster,[13] or possibly

---

[1] *Y.F.R.* 15.  [2] E. 504, 4.  [3] E. 492, 27.  [4] E. 482, 4.
[5] Penshurst MS. 57.  [6] E. 503, 9.  [7] E. 490, 2.
[8] E. 482, 8.  [9] E. 481, 2.  [10] E. 481, 9.
[11] E. 479, 15.  [12] T.R., f. 329.  [13] See below, p. 157.

simply by pounding and mixing it with new. This last interpretation seems rather indicated in an entry in the Collyweston accounts for 1504: 'for siftyng of morter erth owt of the old wallis'.[1] The expression 'mortar earth' occurs again in 1367 in the account of some repairs to the lodge of Beaumont in the Forest of Rutland: 'for digging earth for *mortarherthe* for the said lodge'.[2] Apparently when lime was not available ordinary soil was sometimes used instead. So at Clarendon in 1363 we find mention of 'digging and carriage of 2 cartloads of white earth for making mortar';[3] and at Oxford in 1453, 'a cartload of red earth for making mortar'.[4]

The burning of lime was comparatively skilled work and entailed night work, as the furnace had to be kept burning, so that good wages were paid —at Windsor in 1351 *ardatores calcis* received 10*d.* for a day and night[5]— but sand could be dug, sieved, and carried by unskilled labourers.[6] This was done on a very large scale at Dover in 1226, when there is one entry of 11,160 seams of sand, obtained at a cost of £9. 10*s.* 8*d.*, and another of £10. 10*s.*, paid 'for 11,000 (loads) of sand carried for the works, on account of the goodness of the winter season, because it is of better value than in summer'.[7] The probable explanation of this is that the sand was from the sea-shore and that the winter rains washed out a certain amount of the salt which makes sea sand so unsatisfactory for building purposes. Sea sand was evidently used freely at Pevensey Castle, both in 1288, when '4 boatloads of sand from the sea' occurs,[8] and in 1407, when '94 (cart)loads of sand from the sea' were carted at 4*d.* the load;[9] but it may be of interest to note that excavation in the outer bailey showed that, probably in the thirteenth century, a shaft was sunk some 15 ft. to reach a bed of sand underlying the clay.[10] At Winchester, in 1258, 40 *pottes* of red sand cost 10*s.* 1½*d.*, and 50 *pottes* of white sand 3*s.* 4*d.*;[11] the red would have been quarried, the white might have come from the sea-shore, or possibly from the river bed, as in 1428 we find 9 bushels of 'brooksand' bought for 10*d.* —unqualified sand being at the same time 10*d.* le pot,[12] though it is not possible to compare their values without a definition of the 'pot'. The

[1] St. John's Coll. Cambridge MS. vol. ii.                    [2] E. 458, 10.

[3] E. 460, 2.            [4] Thorold Rogers, *Hist. of Prices*, iii. 717.         [5] E. 492, 27.

[6] e.g. at Penshurst in 1466, *pro siftyng zabuli*: Penshurst MS. 121.

[7] E. 462, 10.            [8] E. 479, 15.            [9] Dy. of Lanc. Accts. 32, No. 24.

[10] *Sussex Arch. Coll.* lii. 86. The shaft had fallen in, covering the ladder and some pottery of that date.

[11] E. 491, 14.

[12] E. 492, 1. Sand was bought for Winchester Cathedral in 1409 at 7*d.* the *potte*: *Obedientiary Rolls*, 211.

equivalent of brooksand is found at Westminster in 1532, in the record of the digging and carriage of 332 tons of 'water sande from Chelsey to Lambe Aley', at 3*d*. the ton.[1]

The actual mixing of the mortar was also unskilled—and, too frequently, unskilful—labour, so that 'mortermen' usually received the wages of ordinary labourers, and the work was even sometimes done by women, as at Woodstock in 1271, when 2 women servants (*ancille*) were employed in making mortar;[2] more often the women simply carried water for the mortar-makers. There is a reference in 1399, at Westminster, to 'a sieve in which to sift burnt lime for the making of free (*liberum*) mortar'.[3] Probably this means mortar to be used for plastering exposed surfaces of walls, as opposed to that confined between courses of stones. Another term for it appears in a fourteenth-century account for Leeds Castle, where the daubers had men 'serving them in the tempering of chefmorter'.[4] The Westminster accounts of 1532 mention 'two seevys for the syftyng of lyme and making of fyne morter';[5] and also 'see cole . . . for making of blacke morter nec(essar)ie for the laying of Flynte', and 'xvj busshilles of Smythys Duste provided for blacke morter to be made of, requisite for the leying of Flynte'.[6] I have come across no other reference to such blackening of mortar; presumably it was required for a special piece of knapped flint work, where a uniform dark effect was required.

Where masonry was particularly exposed to the influence of wet it was a common practice to use instead of mortar a cement composed of wax and pitch or resin, applied in a molten condition. The earliest occurrence of this that I have noted is in 1258, when 19 lb. of pitch and 5 lb. of wax for the requirements of the cistern in the King's court at Westminster were bought for 14*s*., and another 7*d*. was paid 'for charcoal for cementing the cistern'.[7] In 1340 certain repairs were done to a buttress of Westminster Palace which projected into the Thames, and the following purchases were made:[8]

For 60 lbs. of pitch for making cement (*symento*) for the buttress—3s. For 100 Flemish tiles for making dust for the same cement—12d. For 3 earthen pans (*patellis*) in which to make cement—6d. For straw bought for the same buttress, to burn upon it and warm it after the Thames floods (*inundaciones*), because the stone could not otherwise have held the cement—7d. For an iron for directing (*addressandum*) and pouring cement between the stones—4d.

---

[1] T.R., f. 323.  [2] E. 497, 16.  [3] E. 473, 11.
[4] E. 466, 24.  [5] T.R., f. 231.  [6] Ibid., ff. 312, 315.
[7] E. 467, 2.  [8] E. 469, 1.

A few years later, in 1349, at the Tower the foundations of 'the turret beside the Thames opposite to the King's Exchange' required repair:

For an iron pan in which to heat cement (*cemento*) for mending the said foundations, holding 2 gallons,—6s. 8d. Also for a cauldron (*cacabo*) bound with iron, in which to make cement, holding 3 gallons,—20d. For an iron *ladel* and an iron *slice*, with a tripod, to serve the masons for making cement—2s. 6d. . . . For straw to warm the stones for the repair and mending of the foundations of the said turret—6d. . . . For *tylpoudre* for making cement for the foundations of the turret—18d. For 75 lbs. of pitch for making cement—6s. 3d. For a bushel of *tyldust* for the same—18d. For straw to warm the stones for the said foundation—8d. . . . For 2 lbs. of *rosyn*, of which to make cement—4d.[1]

For the steyning of a well at Silverston in 1279 we have 6½ lb. of wax, 4 stone of pitch, sulphur to the value of 1½d., and a pennyworth of eggs, all said to be 'for cement', and a payment of 8d. 'for making the said cement'.[2] While this is an unusually elaborate recipe, we find 4 lb. of sulphur, as well as a pound of wax and 4 lb. of resin, used for cement in St. Stephen's Chapel at Westminster in 1324.[3] Wax and pitch were used in 1279 'for making cement for broken stones' at Vale Royal;[4] wax, pitch, and cobbler's wax (*code*) at Westminster in 1355;[5] equal quantities of wax, resin, and pitch 'to make cement for joining stones' at Wallingford in 1365;[6] and a barrel of pitch and 'a stone of resin (*rosyn*) to mix with the pitch to make cement (*cimento*)' at Berwick in 1406.[7] Wax and resin are the ingredients at Leeds Castle in 1362,[8] at Oxford in 1396,[9] and at Sutton Manor in Surrey, in 1400.[10] In London in 1515 we have 'j lb. waxe (at 6d.) and ij lb. rosyn (at 1d.) for the masons to make thereof symon';[11] the same quantities of wax and 'roossen' were used for making 'symonde' at Westminster in 1532;[12] and at Nonesuch wax and rosin were bought 'to make simon for the masons' in 1538.[13] From these entries it is sufficiently clear that the use of such a cement was widely practised through a period of three centuries, but I have been unable to hear of any instance in which traces of it have been found in existing medieval masonry.

[1] E. 471, 3.    [2] E. 484, 7.    [3] E. 469, 9.    [4] E. 485, 22.
[5] E. 502, 17.    [6] E. 490, 2.    [7] E. 483, 7.    [8] E. 466, 19.
[9] *Oxford City Docts.* (O.H.S.), 310.    [10] E. 502, 15.    [11] E. 474, 17.
[12] T.R., f. 96. Also 'waxe made in seamente for masons': ibid., f. 553.
[13] *L. & P. Hen. VIII*, xiii (2), 342.

# X

## PLASTER, WHITEWASH, PAINT

'SOME men wyll have thyr wallys plastered, some pergetted, and whytlymed, some roughe caste, some pricked, some wrought with playster of Paris.' So wrote Horman in 1519.[1] Some ten years earlier Sir Thomas Lucas entered in his accounts for the building of Little Saxham Hall payments

for lathing, row (i.e. rough) and white casting of part of my keechen raunge . . . for prymyng and fynisshing of al my windows . . . and plaisteryng the beystales (i.e spaces between windows) and the splaies above and on the sides . . . for lathing, pargetting, tiryng and white casting of al my roves, walles, particons and staires . . .; and for lathing and leying wt. here (i.e. hair) and morter of iiij chambres, wt. pergettyng and white casting thereof.[2]

Although it is difficult to draw an arbitrary line between daubing, rough-casting, and pargetting on the one hand and white casting or plastering on the other, it is approximately correct to treat the first set of processes as constructional, as we have done,[3] and the second as decorative. When Henry III visited Paris in 1254 'he took note of the elegance of the houses, which are made of gipsum, that is to say plaster'.[4] About two years earlier he had given instructions for work to be done in Nottingham Castle, including the making ('finishing' would be the better word) of the wooden dais in the hall 'with French (*franco*) plaster'.[5] It seems likely, therefore, that it was about this time that the use of this fine type of plaster began to become common in England.

Plaster of Paris is formed by burning gypsum, and owes its name to its production on a large scale from the gypsum beds of Montmartre, outside Paris. It was imported, as is shown by various customs accounts and by such entries as the purchase of 20 cwt. of 'plaster de Parrys' at Southampton in 1532 for use in the vaulting of Winchester Cathedral, at a cost of 3s. 4d., with another 3s. 4d. for its carriage to Winchester.[6] About the same time 7 'mownghtes of playster of Perrys' were bought from John de Payse, merchant of Rouen, for use at Hampton Court, and Harry Nycolas of Antwerp also supplied '38 mountes 20 hundrythwyght of playster', the

---

[1] *Vulgaria*, c. xxix.
[2] Gage, *Thingoe Hundred*, 146.
[3] See p. 189.
[4] Mat. Paris, *Chron.* v. 481.
[5] Liberate R. 36 Hen. III, m. 17.
[6] *Obedientiary Rolls*, 218.

price in each instance being 5s. the mount, delivered in London.[1] From the contemporary Westminster accounts we learn that 'every mounte cont' xxx[c], so that every two mountes amountith to three tonne'.[2]

These Westminster accounts show 'William Denbuke of Roone in Normandie' supplying 'playster of Parysse' at 4s. the mount.[3] Much of it, however, was made in England, and when we find plaster of Paris being carried from Purbeck to Clarendon in 1288,[4] it is almost certainly the 'plastre de Nower' (made from the gypsum deposits at Nore Down, Purbeck) which was already famous about 1300.[5] 'Plaster of Corfe' occurs at Windsor in 1362[6] and 'burnt plaster of Purbyk' at Porchester in 1397.[7] The neighbourhood of Nottingham was famous for its alabaster, of which the waste and inferior deposits were burnt for plaster, and in 1504 we find in the Collyweston accounts payment made to 'William Upton of the Vale of Bever for 62 tonne of plaster of Paris', at 3s. the ton, with carriage—stated to be 22 miles.[8] In Yorkshire also there were deposits of gypsum. At York money was paid '*pro gipso alias dicto litura anglice plaister*' in 1508;[9] and at Ripon in 1394 'plaster' was 1s. the cartload, un-burnt—fuel being bought 'for burning the said plaster'.[10] Similarly, at Knaresborough in 1303 we have 7s. 1½d. paid 'for hewing 53 cartloads of plaster in the quarry';[11] and it was probably the local product that was used in 1284 at Scarborough when 'Richard le Plasterer of York and his mates (*sociis*)' made the partition walls of the porch of the queen's chamber of '*plastre de Parys*'.[12] The term is used still more loosely at Ludgershall in 1342, when we find payment made 'for digging white stone called chalk at Shudebury for making the walls of the chapel and chamber of plaster of Paris'.[13]

Certain varieties of plaster are mentioned in two Westminster accounts. The first is of 1341: 'for 3 bushels of white plaster of Paris, for mending the walls in the chapel of St. Stephen—5s. And for 2 bushels of black plaster for mending the same walls—2s. And for 2 *foliis* of plaster for mending the fireplace in the small chamber beside the Receipt—12d.'[14] The second, of 1386, mentions plaster of Paris at 2s. the bushel and black plaster at 20d., also 'for 1 bushel of powder (*flor'*) of plaster of Paris, used for whitening the walls,—2s. 8d.'[15] Plaster of Paris, bought from Henry

[1] H.C. 238, ff. 156, 267.  [2] T.R., f. 10.  [3] T.R., f. 48.
[4] E. 593, 20.  [5] Salzman, *Engl. Industries*, 100.
[6] Hope, *Windsor Castle*, 186.  [7] E. 479, 23.
[8] St. John's Coll., Cambridge, MS. vol. ii.  [9] Y.F.R. 94.
[10] R. 120.  [11] E. 465, 29.  [12] E. 482, 1.
[13] E. 476, 1.  [14] E. 470, 9.  [15] E. 473, 2.

Yevele, was 16s. the 'mouncell'—which, from the price, must have been about 8 bushels—'plaster of Purbik' 12s. the 'mouncell', and *flor' plastr' anglican'* 20d. the bushel. Sometimes old plaster was burnt and reused, as at York in 1327, when William de Lynton, plasterer, was paid for 'collecting and bringing together (*adunantis*) old plaster coming from the house thrown down in Skeldergate, and making kilns (*toralia*) for burning new and old plaster'.[1]

Plaster of Paris was used not only for the making and finishing of walls but also for fireplaces and chimneys, where it would stand the heat better than mortar plaster. When Adam le Plastrer, in 1317, undertook to make up the walls of the hall of the Earl of Richmond's London house with plaster of Paris, mention was expressly made of the flues (*tuellos*).[2] At Windsor in 1368 William de York, 'plastrer', was paid 40s. 'for making with plaster of Paris the 4 *pipes* of the fireplaces';[3] and in 1370 we have mention of the 'making with plaster of Paris of 2 chimneys (*camenorum*) which were blown down by the wind', at Clipston.[4]

For walls plaster gave a smooth white surface; or if it was not sufficiently white, or had become discoloured, it could be brightened up with a coat of whitewash or paint. The complete construction of a plaster wall is indicated in an entry of 1423, at Brigstock Park, of 'a mason hired by the job (*in grosso*) to do the daubing (*opus terr'*), namely, bemfyllynge, herlynge, pargetyng, plastryng and wasshyng (or whytlymyng)'[5]—in other words the daubing of the wattling between the beams, wattling, rough-casting, plastering, and whitewashing. In the Middle Ages whitewash was fully appreciated and was applied with a lavish hand externally and internally. The Keep of the Tower of London was known as the White Tower from its being resplendent with whitewash, and was provided with downpipes from its gutters to preserve its whiteness from splashes.[6] At Corfe, also, in 1243 orders were given to whitewash the whole of the castle keep externally,[7] and at Guildford in 1255 the hall, the two royal chapels, and other buildings were to be whitewashed, inside and out.[8] The whitening of internal walls is a commonplace of building accounts, but an entry in a Westminster account of 1351 may be mentioned as giving details of the materials used, John Crepelgate supplying 'a bushel of chalk dust and 4 gallons of size (*cole*) for whitening the walls of the downstair (*basse*) chamber'.[9] At Windsor, also, in 1368, 'chalkedust' is found in

[1] E. 501, 8.  [2] App. B.  [3] E. 493, 29.  [4] E. 460, 20.
[5] E. 459, 10.  [6] See p. 266.  [7] Liberate R. 28 Hen. III.
[8] Ibid. 40 Hen. III, m. 10.  [9] E. 471, 6.

company with 'pecches',[1] that is to say, patches or shreds of leather, which were used for making size. Another Windsor account, of 1366, refers to '*diversis patches pro cole inde faciendo pro pictoribus*',[2] and one some twenty years later mentions '*sherdes* used for making cole'.[3] 'Glovers scherdisse' and 'glover shredes for to make syez' occur at Collyweston in 1504,[4] '*sherydes correi pro factione le syze*' in Winchester Priory accounts for 1532,[5] and 4 bushels of pieces of 'glovers lether to make sise' at Hampton Court in 1533.[6] Occasionally the effect was obtained through the more permanent, but much more expensive, medium of paint. At Melbourne Castle in 1314 we have 34s. 9d. paid for 'the wages of a painter whitening the lord's chamber below the lantern, with white lead, varnish (*vernico*), oil and other things bought';[7] and at Windsor in 1356—'for 66 lbs. of white lead for painting the vaulting of the Treasurer's house—22s. And for 12 gallons of oil for the same—24s. And for 4 earthen pots and 2 bottles (*calathis*) for putting the oil in to carry it from London to Windsor—15d.'[8]

A very common form of decoration was to mark out the whitewashed walls, usually with red paint, in blocks to resemble masonry. Traces of such 'masoning' may be found in a great many churches and other medieval buildings, and references to the practice occur. For instance, the great chamber in Guildford Castle was to be 'whitewashed and marked out in squares (*quarellari*)' in 1255.[9] Often the blocks so marked out were decorated with simple devices, such as a rose, which is found in Westminster Abbey.[10] Henry III in 1238 ordered that the walls of the queen's chamber in the Tower should be 'whitewashed and pointed, and within those pointings to be painted with flowers',[11] and at the same time Peter the Painter was employed at Marlborough, 'whitening and lining (*lineand*') the hall behind the chapel', and also 'whitening and lining three windows and round the windows, where the wall was broken, and painting roses (*rosand*')'.[12]

Sometimes a colour wash was employed. This is possibly implied by an entry of the purchase of a pound of 'redying' and three pounds of red lead (*rugeplum*) 'for decorating the walls of the chamber' at Corfe in 1292.[13] A more definite instance occurs at Westminster in 1353, when 16s. 3d. was paid to John Colville 'for 325 lb. of *rodel* for reddening (*rubricand*') the

[1] E. 494, 1.  [2] E. 493, 22.  [3] E. 495, 30.
[4] St. John's Coll., Cambridge, MS. vol. ii.  [5] *Obedientiary Rolls*, 218.
[6] H.C. 237, f. 148.  [7] Mins. Accts. (P.R.O.), 1, No. 3.
[8] E. 493, 1.  [9] Liberate R. 40 Hen. III, m. 10.
[10] Lethaby, *Westminster Abbey Re-examined*, 206.
[11] Liberate R. 23 Hen. III.  [12] E. 476, 3.  [13] E. 460, 29.

buildings of the Staple', another 6s. to Agnes Bury 'for 3 dozen (? pounds) of earth called *mote*, for the same', and 25s. 'for 1,542 lb. of *rodyng* for making the said buildings red'.[1] Here *rodel* is ruddle, or red ochre—chiefly used now for marking sheep—and *mote* is something of a similar nature; it occurs again in 1426, when the churchwardens of St. Mary-at-Hill paid 10d. 'for vj dischis cole and xij lb. moty',[2] and at Cambridge in 1511, when 'moty' figures in a long list of colours bought for use at Christ's College.[3] This same list includes 'red okyr' and 'yelowe oker', and the latter was in common use, often in company with varnish. At Westminster in 1358 we have a payment '*pro dealbacione ocriacione et vernacione camere*';[4] and at Gravesend in 1364 Thomas Shonk was paid £10 'for the painting, ochreing and varnishing of the manor', and there are payments—'for 1800 lb. of *oker*—£6; for 88 lb. of *vernyssh*—51s. 4d.; for 10 gallons of oil—26s. 8d.; for hides bought and *cole* made therefrom for the said work—20s.; to Thomas Jury, potter, for 18 earthen pots for the work of ochreing (*pict' ocrii*)—18d.'[5]

So, at Havering in 1376: 'To Silvester de Herford for half a hundred (weight) of ochre bought in London for the ochreing of the new chapel—3s.; to him for 5 lb. of varnish for the same—22d.; for half a gallon of oil for the same—10d.; for size (*col*) for the same—3s. 8d.'[6] And, as a later instance, at Winchester in 1532: '30 lb. of yolowe oker for the vaulting—5s.'[7]

Not only was the medieval builder blind to the alleged beauty of unadorned rubble walling, but he was not above improving his oak timbers with a coat of ochre and varnish. At the Tower in 1337 Simon Rabos was paid 73s. 4d. 'for the pargetting and whitening of the whole of the great hall, together with the ochreing of the posts and beams, using his own supplies of chalk, size and *okkere*'.[8] There is even, I believe, evidence that he indulged in the Victorian practice of 'graining',[9] and he undoubtedly adopted the parallel practice of 'marbling', as in 1245 Henry III ordered that the posts in his chamber at Ludgershall should be painted the colour of marble,[10] and ten years later that the pillars and arches of the hall in Guildford Castle should be marbled (*marbrari*).[11] That king's favourite form of decoration, however, was green paint with gold stars—possibly some

[1] E. 471, 8.　　[2] *Memorials* (E.E.T.S.), 66.
[3] Willis and Clark, *Arch. Hist. Cambridge*, ii. 199.
[4] E. 472, 4.　　[5] E. 493, 18.　　[6] E. 464, 30.
[7] *Obedientiary Rolls*, 218.　　[8] E. 470, 1.
[9] So the late Sir William Hope told me.
[10] Liberate R. 30 Hen. III, m. 16.　　[11] Ibid. 40 Hen. III.

psychologist will explain the significance of his devotion to this colour. In 1233 his private chapel in Kennington was to be painted with 'histories' or subject pictures, 'so that the field shall be of a green colour spangled with gold stars'; two chapels and the king's chamber at Geddington were to be painted green and spangled with gold in 1252, as were the royal chambers at Windsor ten years later; and the ceiling of the great chamber at Guildford was to be painted green and neatly spangled (*extencellari*) with gold and silver, in 1255. In 1236 Odo the Goldsmith—hereditary Master of the Arts—was ordered to remove the painting, containing panels with figures of lions, birds, and beasts, which had been begun in the king's great chamber at Westminster below 'the great history', and to paint it green in the fashion of a curtain. Next year the panelling of the chamber at Winchester was to be painted green with gold stars, and circles to be made on it containing stories from the Old and New Testaments. At Clarendon, again, in 1245, one chamber was to be painted green, with a border on which were to be the heads of kings and queens; in another the walls were to be painted with the four Evangelists and the story of St. Margaret, and the wainscot green spotted (*deguttari*) with gold, with heads of men and women on it; 'and all these paintings are to be done with good and exquisite colours'.

From the days of the cave-dwellers downwards, men—and small boys —have delighted in drawing and painting on walls. As, moreover, in a predominantly illiterate society pictures were eminently suited both to point a moral and adorn a wall, the Church from early times encouraged the practice in its own buildings. When Benedict Biscop founded his monastery at Wearmouth, in the last quarter of the seventh century, he brought from Rome

pictures of the figures of saints, which he employed for the decoration of the church of St. Peter that he had built; namely, a figure of the Blessed Mother of God, with the twelve Apostles, with which he encircled the middle of the roof (*testudinem*) on panelling carried from wall to wall; figures of the gospel story, with which he decorated the south wall; and figures of the apocalyptic vision of St. John, with which he adorned the north wall, so that all persons entering the church, even if unable to read, whichever way they went, should have before their eyes, at least in image, the ever blessed Christ and his Saints.[1]

The practice of so decorating churches spread, so that when Sir Gilbert, the sheriff, founded Merton Priory in 1114, we are told that he 'most liberally built a church at his own cost, and handsomely decorated it with

[1] Bede, *Opera Hist.* (ed. Plummer), i. 369.

paintings and other images, *as was customary*'.[1] The walls of our churches still bear witness to the prevalence—almost universality—of this form of decoration, ranging from the early twelfth century to the sixteenth, and from the crude efforts of village craftsmen up to such masterpieces as the figure of St. Faith in Westminster Abbey or the medallion of the Virgin and Child in the Bishop's Chapel at Chichester. The *Liberate Rolls of Henry III* contain many references to figures of saints and other religious subjects being painted in the royal chapels and elsewhere. For instance, in 1232, the keeper of the king's houses at Woodstock is ordered to cause to be painted in the king's round chapel, with good colours, the Majesty of the Lord, the four Evangelists, and on one side St. Edmund, and on the other St. Edward; and twenty years later the chapel was to be painted with 'the story of the woman taken in adultery, and how the Lord wrote on the ground, and how the Lord smote St. Paul—and paint something concerning St. Paul, and likewise paint the story of the Evangelists in the upper part of the chapel'. At Winchester in 1247 there was to be painted on the west gable wall of the queen's chapel the image of St. Christopher, 'who, as he is elsewhere depicted, shall bear Christ on his shoulders', and the image of St. Edward the King, 'how he delivered his ring to a stranger, whose figure is likewise to be depicted'. Henry was particularly fond of this legend of Edward the Confessor giving his ring to a poor man, who was afterwards revealed to be St. John, and had it painted many times—as at Guildford, where he ordered the figures of St. Edward and of St. John holding a ring in his hand to be painted both in the hall and beside his seat in the chapel, in 1260. At Winchester Castle, in 1250, the new chapel was to be painted with the history of Joseph, and in 1240 the roof of the state chamber was to be painted with scenes from the Old and New Testaments and its bosses to be gilded.

As a rule the compilers of building accounts do not trouble to state the subjects of the painting for which they enter payments, and often it is not possible to decide whether the painters have been engaged on straightforward application of paint or on pictorial work. So in the accounts for the various monuments erected by Edward I to the memory of Queen Eleanor in 1292 we find various sums of 40s. paid, on account, to Master Walter of Durham 'for painting around the Queen's heart in the Friars Preachers',[2] but are given no hint of the subjects he portrayed. This Master Walter was a great artist and held the position of king's painter from 1260 for about forty years; shadowy traces of his work have survived in West-

---

[1] Heales, *Recs. of Merton Priory*, 2.
[2] *Household Expenses* (Roxburghe Club), 98.

minster Abbey,[1] the most important being the figure of a king on the back of the Coronation Chair, executed for the coronation of Edward I. Some twenty-five years earlier Henry III had given orders for the royal seat at the middle of the table in the hall of Windsor to be adorned with 'the figure of the King, holding a sceptre in his hand—taking care that the seat be cunningly ornamented with gold and paint'.[2] It is probable that in each of these instances a definite portrait was attempted. At Woodstock we certainly find such an attempt in 1265, when the humble sum of 2s. 9d. was paid 'to a painter, with his servant, for painting the figure of the lord King in his chapel, and other heads there'.[3] This is quite definitely distinct from such vague representations as that of 'a king and a queen sitting with their baronage', which was to be painted over the dais in the hall of Dublin Castle in 1243,[4] and is important as evidence that portraiture was attempted in the thirteenth century—an obvious fact that, for some obscure reason, is often denied.

Among the more interesting subjects selected by Henry III we may note his orders in 1248 for a new mantel, or hood, to be made to the fireplace in his chamber at Clarendon, on which was to be painted the Wheel of Fortune and (the Tree of) Jesse;[5] during the rebuilding of the hood, the pictures in the chamber were to be covered with canvas to protect them from injury.[6] Later, in 1265, 'the twelve months of the year'—a favourite medieval subject—were to be painted round a fireplace at Kennington;[7] in 1230 Henry had ordered a new fireplace at Westminster, on which was to be portrayed 'the figure of Winter, which as well by its sad countenance as by other miserable distortions of the body may be deservedly likened to Winter itself'.[8] For a chamber at Clarendon he ordered, in 1250, the painting of 'the story of Antioch and the battle of King Richard';[9] this was the battle in which tradition averred that St. George appeared as the champion of the English crusaders. Still more legendary was 'the history of Alexander', which was to be painted round the queen's chamber at Nottingham in the following year.[10] Four years later we have reference to another legend, of which one would like to have further particulars:

Lately, at Winchester, the King, in the presence of Master William the monk of

[1] Lethaby, *Westminster Abbey*, 261–4.

[2] Liberate R. 34 Hen. III, m. 5.

[3] E. 497, 2.

[4] *Close R.*

[5] A Jesse was painted by 'Master William the painter and his men' on a mantel at Westminster in 1259: E. 467, 2.

[6] Liberate R. 32 Hen. III.

[7] Ibid. 50 Hen. III.

[8] Ibid. 24 Hen. III.

[9] Ibid. 35 Hen. III, m. 6.

[10] Ibid. 36 Hen. III, m. 15.

Westminster, provided for the making, in the wardrobe where the King is wont to wash his head, at Westminster, of a picture of the king who was rescued by his dogs from the sedition plotted against him by his subjects; concerning which the King has sent other letters to Edward (FitzOdo) of Westminster. Philip Luvel, the Treasurer, and the said Edward are to pay Master William the cost of making this picture, at once.[1]

The subject was sufficiently topical, as Henry was at this time in very bad odour with his subjects, owing to his endeavours to squeeze money out of them for his mad Sicilian schemes; one may even suspect that his opponents had stigmatized his supporters as 'dogs' and that this was his artistic retort.

Heraldic bearings were a common form of decoration to which there are occasional references. In 1240 Henry ordered his great chamber in the Tower of London 'to be entirely whitewashed and newly painted, and all the windows (i.e. shutters) of the same to be made anew with new wood and bolts and hinges, and to be painted with our arms';[2] and similarly in 1265 all the doors and shutters of the king's hall and chamber at Winchester were to be painted with his arms.[3] Mention is made at York of the painting of the arms of the archbishop in the south aisle of the Minster in 1432.[4] Much more elaborate was the heraldic decoration executed at Langley in 1292:

To a painter of London who wrought in the hall at Langley, in the summer during my lord's absence, at his own expense in all things, 54 shields and 4 knights seeking feats of arms (*querentes hastilud*')—50s. Also, to the same coming from London to cover with tin the iron columns supporting the fireplace in the lord's chamber, so that they should not be injured by the heat of the fire (*ne possent calefieri igne*)—5s. 4d. And to him for painting in the hall for 47 days, receiving for himself and his assistant (*garcioni*), having their meals in the hall, 8d. a day.[5]

The painter's name was probably Ranulph, as there is a later entry—'for colours bought for painting the hall after the departure of Ranulph the painter, for vermilion and orpiment for the painting by Alexander the painter'; which Alexander was employed on the job for 53 days at 4d. the day. Another, much later, elaborate wall-painting which one would like to have seen was 'the coronacion of our saide sovereigne lorde (Henry VIII), made and sette oute in the low galarye'[6] at Westminster in 1532. It was evidently on a grand scale, great quantities of painting materials being

---

[1] Ibid. 40 Hen. III.      [2] Ibid. 24 Hen. III.
[3] Ibid. 50 Hen. III.      [4] *Y.F.R.* 48.
[5] E. 466, 1.      [6] T.R., f. 33.

provided, and was probably from the designs of 'Lucas the Kinges peyntor'.[1]

So far, with the exception of Benedict Biscop's pictures brought from Rome, we have been dealing with wall-paintings, which may, indeed, be regarded as the only variety strictly appropriate to our subject. But it is worth noting the evidence for panel pictures as a form of decoration. The Windsor accounts for 1244–7 mention 'two decently painted tablets bought and set in the Queen's chapel';[2] in 1252 Henry III gave orders for 'two painted tablets with the figures of two bishops to be set in our great chapel, and a tablet painted with the figure of the Blessed Mary in the chapel of St. Edward', at Woodstock.[3] In 1258 the poor but extravagant king bought, on credit, for the enormous sum of £80, from Master Peter the Spaniard, a prominent artist of the time, two painted tablets, which he gave to Westminster Abbey.[4] An interesting reference to such a panel picture survives in a letter of 1317 from Archbishop Walter Reynolds, in which he protests that he has never forbidden Jordan the Painter to sell his picture; on the contrary, he has constantly endeavoured, on account of its beauty, to secure it for the cathedral.[5] Master Hugh (of St. Albans) Payntour in his will, dated 1361, refers to 'a tablet of Lombardy in seven pieces', which had cost him £20[6]—good evidence of the value attached to such works of art. A less artistic production was presented to Exeter Cathedral in 1438, when 11*d*. was paid 'for the making of a tablet of the descent (*linea*) of England and France, sent to the cathedral by the king's council (*consilium*), and for the fixing of it in the church'.[7] Coming down to the end of our period, we may note in the Hampton Court accounts of 1531 a sum of £20 paid 'to Antony Tote (or Toto, an Italian) paynter, for payntyng iiij great tablys—oon table of oure (Lady) of pytte a nother of the iiij Evangylystes the third of the Mawndythe the forte the sayd antony'.[8] The first of these, Our Lady of Pity—the *Pietà* so common in Italian churches—is the figure of the Virgin with the dead Christ; the third, the Maundy, Christ washing the feet of the disciples; the fourth reads as if it was the artist's own portrait, which seems improbable.

Unfortunately, owing to the custom of painting carved work it is often impossible to tell whether an entry refers to a painting or a painted carv-

[1] T.R., f. 10.

[2] Hope, *Windsor Castle*, 37. Master Thomas the Painter of Chertsey 'who is making the King's images for his chapel' occurs in 1245: ibid. 35.

[3] Liberate R. 36 Hen. III, m. 14.  [4] *Cal. Patent R.*, 613.

[5] *Hist. MSS. Com. Rep., Var.* i. 266.  [6] Sharpe, *Cal. of Wills in Hustings*.

[7] Oliver, *Exeter*, 391.  [8] H.C. 241, f. 16.

ing. Thus at Windsor in 1364, when £4 was paid to William Burdon 'for the painting of a tablet in the King's chapel'[1] at Windsor, one suspects that it was a picture; and it is tempting to read an earlier entry of '2 ells of linen cloth for the new tablet in the great chapel' as referring to his canvas, but this would almost certainly be an anachronism, and the linen was probably for a curtain over it, or some such purpose. On the other hand, in 1369, when William Burdon was paid £40 'for the painting of a tablet in the canons' chapel and of a reredos in the upper chapel'[2] the greater part of this was almost certainly for the painting of the great alabaster reredos, carved at Nottingham at a cost of £166. 13s. 4d., set up in the chapel just at this time. The cost of painting carved work seems disproportionate to the cost of the carving, according to modern standards. For the decoration of Westminster Hall in 1385 Thomas Canon 'marbrer' carved stone figures of kings at 46s. 8d. each, and two larger ones, to stand above the doorway, at 66s. 8d. For painting six of these Nicholas Tryer was paid £7. 13s. 4d., and for the two at the door £5.[3] Similarly, in 1530, Richard Rydge was paid 18s. 4d. apiece for carving two greyhounds and a leopard 'to stande uppon the typpis of the vycys' of the Hall of Hampton Court, and John Hette received 10s. each for painting them.[4] Even the church-wardens of a parish church—St. Edmund's in Salisbury—in 1497 paid the substantial sum of £16 (say £200 in modern value) to John Colcyn 'for the painting of the Rood with Mary and John, and for gilding the figures with gilt stars'.[5]

As an example of the large sums spent on this form of decoration we may quote an item from accounts relating to the manor of Old Windsor in the reign of Richard II:[6] 'To Thomas Prynce for the painting of 5 chambers assigned to the King and 2 small chapels, as well as a great chapel, 70 ft. in length, painted with stags with golden antlers, by contract, including finding colours and gold,—£299. 16s. 6d. So also at Hampton Court in 1535:

For payntyng gyltyng and varnesshyng of the vought in the Kynges New Chappyl:—Payd to John Hethe and Harry Blankeston of London, gylders and paynters, for gyltyng and garnesshyng of the vought in the Chappell with great arches bourd, great pendaunts, wyth angells holdyng schochens wyth the Kynges armes and the Quenes, and wyth great pendantts of boyes pleying wyth instruments, and large battens set wyth antyk of leade gylt, wyth the Kynges

---

[1] E. 493, 16.  
[2] E. 494, 4.  
[3] E. 473, 2.  
[4] Law, *Hampton Court*, 348.  
[5] Swayne, *Churchwardens' Accts.*, 49.  
[6] E. 495, 30.

wordde (or motto) also gylt wyth fyne golde and fyne byse, sett out wyth other fyne collers (i.e. colours) and for castyng of the antyk[1] and letters of lead, and for the pyn nayll, with all other necessaryes belowngyng to the forsayd chappell rowf; wyth two great bay wyndowes of the Kynges and the Quenes holyday closettes, for the sides next unto the Chappell, garnesshyd and guylte wyth the Kynges armes and the Quenys, wyth beests guylte wyth fyne golde and byse, sett owt wythe other fyne collers, in all, by convencion—£457.[2]

It must not be imagined that these large sums were in any way influenced by considerations of artistic merit. As a matter of fact in the Hampton Court instance the work was straightforward application of paint. The high cost of painting was due to the cost of the materials employed. Of these the most expensive was gold leaf; and the best blue was also dear, so that in 1250 we find Henry III in an unusual mood of economy, giving directions for decorations to be done at Guildford, including—'in the chapel of St. Katherine her image and story to be painted behind the altar in a worthy manner without the use of gold and azure'.[3]

Gilding was employed with a lavish hand in great buildings. At Westminster in 1252, when ten painters were engaged, under the direction of Master Peter of Spain, in 'painting behind the table in the great hall', 24s. 11d. was paid 'for 51 dozen (leaves) of gold for the painting',[4] and 29s. 9d. 'for various other colours for the said painting'. The gold was usually of fine quality; for gilding the images of Queen Eleanor on the crosses erected to her memory 203 florins, weighing 3 marks (or two pounds by goldsmith's weight), were bought from merchants of Lucca, in 1292;[5] and an Ely account of 1336 mentions 'making leaves of gold from florins'.[6] Next year we find '800 of goldfyn' bought at 4s. the hundred, '1200 of goldparti' at 3s., and '1300 of silverfoile' at 6d.[7] The 'goldparti' may be equivalent to the 'gilded tin' of which 12 dozen were bought at Westminster in 1275;[8] but it is difficult to say exactly what is meant by the 1,400 *auri beneuoli* bought, at 6s. the hundred, for work at Windsor in 1366.[9] From its price this must have been of good quality; gold leaf was about 4s. the hundred at Exeter in 1320[10] and 4s. and 5s. in London in 1352;[11] at York in 1483 'beaten gold' was 6s. 8d.,[12] and 'fyne gold' for Hampton Court was 5s. 8d. the hundred in 1533.[13] There is also mention

---

[1] 'Antyk' was the term applied to the classical patterns that came in with the Renaissance.
[2] Law, *Hampton Court*, 360.               [3] Liberate R. 35 Hen. III, m. 3.
[4] E. 466, 30.                    [5] *Household Expenses* (Roxburghe Club), 118.
[6] *Sacrist Rolls*, 83.        [7] Ibid. 98.              [8] E. 467, 6 (2).
[9] E. 493, 22.                  [10] Oliver, *Exeter*, 381.       [11] E. 471, 6.
[12] Y.F.R. 77.                  [13] H.C. 237, f. 39.

in the Hampton Court accounts of 'bullyons (i.e. bosses) over gylte with burned gold', which may either mean refined, or more probably burnished gold.[1] In 1420, when elaborate preparations were being made for the decoration of London Bridge for the reception of Henry V and Queen Katherine, John Wytte, painter, was paid 34s. 4d. for painting five banners, and purchases were made of 20 dozen 'goldpaper' for 40s., 2½ 'silverpaper' for 2s. 6d., and 2 'leves de dobeltynfoill', for 6d.[2]

A roll of accounts for the decoration of St. Stephen's chapel at Westminster, covering the period from June 1351 to August 1354, contains a great many items referring to painting.[3] The work was at first under the control of Master Hugh of St. Albans. Then, in 1354, the work was taken in hand by Master John Barneby, senior, who was paid 2s. a day; under him were three 'masters'—John Barneby, junior, Hugh of St. Albans, and John Elham—receiving 1s. a day, and a number of other painters, paid at various rates from 11d. to 9d. Among the large purchases of gold foil— amounting to about 25,000 foils—are 1,500 foils 'for painting of the tabernacles (or carved niches) and of the angels standing on top of the tabernacles', and 1,300 foils '*pro pictura tabulamenti capelle*'. Some 16 dozen foils of tin were also bought, at 1d. the dozen, 'for making borders (*liseras*) for the said tablement', by which is presumably meant a cornice or carved string-course. A pair of scissors for cutting foils of tin (*in j pari forpicum ad reseandum folia de tyn*) was bought for 2d., and half a pound of 'coton'— by which is probably meant unspun cotton, or cotton-wool—'for laying the gold'. There is a later entry of '*coton pro prentes depictis cubandis*', and of hemp (*stupis*) '*pro impressionibus cubandis*'. There are a number of references to these 'prints', such as the purchase of '6 dozen and 8 foils of tin for *pryntes* for the painting of the chapel', and a payment 'for laying gold on the walls and for setting prints (*preyntorum*) on the marble columns'. Print is evidently here used (in a sense cognate with foot-print, &c.) for a stencil. It occurs again in a subsequent account for the same works, in 1355—'*pro xxviij prentis pro ymagine Sancte Marie—viijᵈ*',[4] Master Hugh, the painter, being at the same time paid 15s. '*pro lx doublett' pro ymagine beate Marie*', another 2s. being spent on '*xij doublett' pro dictis ymaginibus*', where 'doublettes' seem to be something of the same kind, but, judging from the price, probably of gold instead of tin. I have not found either term in any other set of accounts.

---

[1] Ibid., f. 406.   [2] London Bridge Accts., vol. ii, f. 460.
[3] E. 471, 6; excellently tabulated by J. T. Smith in *Antiquities of Westminster*.
[4] E. 502, 17.

When the vaulting of the new belfry at Ely was painted, in 1334, we find 2s. 2d. paid for 3 lb. of 'gold coleir'.[1] This is, no doubt, the sulphide of arsenic known as *auripigmentum*[2] or, usually, *'orpiment'*, under which form it occurs three years later at Ely, at 6d. the pound,[3] which was also the price at Westminster in 1275.[4]

For the consideration of the colours employed in medieval decoration it will possibly be best to take a series of representative lists of purchases:

(a) Westminster, 1275:[4] half a pound of tint (*tinctus*)—18d.; flour (*flore*)—1d.; 2 lb. red lead—5d.; 22 lb. green—12s. 10d.; 32 lb. white lead—5s. 4d.; half a pound orpiment—3d.; 1 lb. ocre—1d.; 2 lb. vermell—4s.; ¾ lb. azure—3s.;—brun—3½d.

(b) Exeter, 1320:[5] 1 lb. azure—3s. 6d.; 1 lb. *ynde baudas*—18d.; 4 lb. verdegris—2s. 4d.; 4 lb. vermilion 2s. 8d.; ¾ lb. *cinople*—4s. 9d.; 100 lb. white lead (*blamplum*)—18s.

(c) St. Stephen's, Westminster, 1351–4:[6] ½ lb. *tynt*—2s.; 1½ lb. oker—3d.; 1½ lb. *cynople*—17s. 3d.; 1 lb. *cynople*—30s.; ½ lb. *cynopre*—10s.; 2 lb. *cynopre* of Montpellier (*de Monte Pessulano*)—16s.; 3 lb. azure—30s.; 2 lb. *vermelon*—3s. 4d.; 2 lb. *vert de Grece*—2s. 4d.; white lead, at 2½d. the pound; red lead, at 4d.

(d) Windsor, 1366:[7] 12 lb. *vertegres*, 'for painting the tower called La Rose', at 12d.; 18 lb. red lead, at 18d.; 67 lb. of white lead, at 6d.; 8 lb. *vermelon*, at 2s.; 50 lb. *brown*, at 3d.; 7 lb. *asure de bys*, at 3s.; ¼ lb. *synople*—10s.

(e) York Minster, 1483:[8] 12 lb. *vertgreas*, 2 lb. blew ynde, 2 lb. *vermeyon*, 6 lb. red lead, 2 lb. *ocor*, white lead, *vermyth*, 4 lb. *masticote*.

(f) Christ's College, Cambridge, 1511:[9] 'To Paule Smyth for certen coloures as in whiteled redled generall mastyke vermyssel yellowe moty orpment roch vermylyon vergres bisse oyle coperose white vitriall wex ceruse synoper red okyr yelowe oker Inde fyne gold iij c. di' with other—56s. 4d.'

(g) Westminster, 1532:[10] 'One sack of verdegresse[11]—poz. xij lb.', at 12d. the pound; white lead, at 3d.; red lead, at 2d.; 'generall', at 6d. and 8d.; vermilion, at 14d.; red oker, at 3 lb. a penny; 1 cwt. 3 qr. 12 lb. 'sprewse oker', at 1d. the pound; 376 lb. 'blacke chalke', and other 'chaulke of black colour', at 1d.; 'synapo lake', 'senaperlake', at 13s. 4d.; 'lytmouse', at 6d.; 'mastecote', at 2s. 8d.; bice, at 5s.; 'seeris' at 6d.; 'spaulton', at 4s.; also 3 pecks of 'whete floure', definitely said to be for the painter.

---

[1] *Sacrist Rolls*, 73.  [2] Hendrie, *Theophilus, on the Arts*, 53.
[3] *Sacrist Rolls*, 98.  [4] E. 467, 6 (2).
[5] Oliver, *Exeter*, 381.  [6] E. 471, 6: items selected from a long roll.
[7] E. 493, 2.  [8] *Y.F.R.* 77.
[9] Willis and Clark, *Arch. Hist.* ii. 199.  [10] T.R., ff. 308, 410, 552, 577.
[11] Three sacks of 'verdygrece' contained 23 lb. at Hampton Court in 1535: H.C. 238, f. 136.

The 'tint', which occurs in (a) and (c), was the same thing as the 'general' of (f) and (g)—a neutral colour used for outlines and shading. Four pounds of 'generall', 4 quarts of oil, and other things needed for painting were bought in 1532 from an Austin friar, who was also paid 5s. '*pro pinguendo ly borders*' in the Hall of Queens' College, Cambridge.[1] It is tempting to suggest that the friar was a poor scholar, earning his fees by acting as a painter.[2]

The finest blue was the azure made from a variety of lapis lazuli; but, though this was used for illuminating manuscripts, it was too costly for general use in decoration, and 'bice', a cobalt blue, was generally employed. At Westminster in 1290 an ounce and a half of pure azure cost 2s. 6d., while a quarter (of a pound) of 'asure biz' was only $7\frac{1}{2}d$.[3] 'Blew bysse', at 4s. 8d. the pound occurs in the Hampton Court accounts, from which we may quote two entries relating to the decoration of the roof of the king's chamber: 'First in batons xij$^{xx}$ and three yards, the antyke gylt, the fyld layd wt. fyne beice. Item two casementes (concave mouldings) layd wt. beyce And ij botells (convex mouldings) layde wt. fyne whytt', at 7d. the yard.[4] 'Itm a border of antyk wt. nakyd chyld', wt. a lyst above the boytayle gylt, wt. a casement layd wt. beyce, and a jole pece (cornice, or frieze) under the border, wt. a casement layd wt. beyce. Therin sett the kinges word wt. gilt lettres', of which there were 26 yards, at 6s. 8d. the yard.[5]

Indigo—the 'Inde' of (f)—was also used from quite early times, indigo of Bagdad—the 'ynde baudas' of (b)—being among the imports listed for customs at Marseilles as early as 1228.[6] The 'lytmouse', or litmus, of (g) was used, I think, more as a blue dye than as a paint.

For green verdigris was employed, and its price seems to have been singularly constant from about 1336, when it appears at Ely at a shilling the pound, until 1532, when Henry Veysey was paid 2s. 2d. for two pounds of 'wergresse', and 3s. 8d. for a pound of 'byse', for Queen's hall. Green could also, of course, be made by mixing blue with a yellow paint. Besides orpiment, already referred to, one occasionally gets mention of massicot, a yellow lead paint. This is the 'masticote' of (e) and (g); but the

---

[1] Willis and Clark, *Arch. Hist.* ii. 65.

[2] The Merton College account rolls *c.* 1375 show 'poor scholars' acting as carters and so forth.

[3] E. 468, 2. 'A quarter of azure and a quarter of *biz* for painting the Exchange at the Tower' in 1355: E. 471, 10.

[4] H.C. 237, f. 406.     [5] Ibid., f. 407.

[6] *Theophilus*, 76.

'mastyke' of (*f*) is more likely to be gum mastic, especially as it is put next to varnish in the list. Yellow ochre, as we have seen, was in common use.

The 'Sprewse oker', or Prussian ochre, of (*g*) was probably red ochre, judging from the occurrence of 'sprwce redd'—at the same price of 1*d.* the pound—in the contemporary Hampton Court accounts. Historically, one might say pre-historically, red ochre is the most ancient of paints, and it figures in most medieval church wall paintings. A brighter red, however, could be obtained by the use of red lead, and for work of higher quality vermilion, prepared from cinnabar, a sulphide of mercury, was employed. Another red colouring matter was 'sinoper'. This is properly haematite, but the term seems to have been loosely used for various ochreous earths, and also—owing to resemblances in appearance and in name—it was constantly confused with cinnabar. It was, as will be noticed from the above lists, the most expensive of the paints. Whether the 'synapour lake' was actually a resinous lac or was a variety of sinoper resembling the crimson colour of lac I cannot say.

White lead was always in common use, and it occurs in (*f*) both under that name and as 'ceruse'. 'Spaynyshe white' occurs at Hampton Court in 1535;[1] as does also 'Spaynyshe browne', which was probably umber; it occurs also at York in 1516—'*pro ij lb oker et les brown of spaigne ad pingendum caminum in leid hows*'.[2] Black is not often mentioned; it was usually made from charcoal, lamp-black, or soot: the 'secole blake', which appears among paints used at Hampton Court, may have been made actually from sea coal, i.e. pit coal, or from the soot of such coal. A black earth was also used in the sixteenth century, as we see from (*g*) and from the Hampton Court accounts, which include the purchase of 'iiij barrelles of blak chalk, cont' xij cwt. iij qr. xij lb. . . . to paynt and garnysshe the walles' at a cost of 9*s.* 4*d.* the cwt.—£6 in all.[3]

The 'seeris' and 'spaulton' of (*g*) must remain unexplained, and the use of flour, which occurs also in (*a*), is not obvious. It may have been for cleaning the walls, or, I suppose, it is just possible that it might have been made into a paste for applying gold leaf. According to Theophilus[4] this should be done either with white of egg or with a size, or glue, made from strips of parchment, mixed with gum. Three pennyworth of eggs are among the painting materials at Westminster in 1275,[5] and at Ely 3 bushels of 'scrowes'—probably scrolls or strips of parchment—were bought for making size (*cole*) in 1337.[6]

---

[1] H.C. 238, f. 114.     [2] *Y.F.R.* 97.     [3] H.C. 241, f. 43.
[4] Hendrie, op.cit. 31, 43.     [5] E. 467, 6 (2).     [6] *Sacrist Rolls*, 98.

It is hardly necessary to point out that in the Middle Ages paint was not bought in tins, or even pots, ready mixed. Before use the paint had to be ground and made up, and when extensive operations were in progress it is common to find mention made of this work. As, for instance, at Westminster in 1259, when the 'lad preparing the colours for the painter' was paid 10*d.* a week[1]—the painters themselves receiving about 6*d.* a day. For St. Stephen's Chapel, again, in 1352, the men 'grinding colours' were paid from 4*d.* to 5½*d.* a day, fairly good wages, for the work was not quite unskilled, but only half the rate at which the painters were paid. At Exeter there is mention in 1318 of an iron plate on which to grind colours, but in 1321 we find 'a marble stone for grinding colours' bought for 1*s.* 6*d.*[2] and this was the common practice—so much so that painters were apt to make a convenience of the altar stone if they had not a slab handy. It is rather surprising to find that for the work on the great Coronation scene at Westminster in 1532, the painting of which occupied thirteen weeks, 'iij stones with iij mullers' for grinding the colours were hired instead of being bought;[3] but probably the explanation is that the painters brought their own slabs and charged for their use.

Horace Walpole in his *Anecdotes of Painting in England* (1762) pointed out that at least as early as 1239 oil was being used as a medium for paint. The oil used was a fine quality of linseed oil, specially prepared[4] and rather expensive. 'Half a gallon of oil for the use of the painters for the four Evangelists in the King's green chamber' at Westminster in 1290 cost 10*d.*[5] At Exeter 'a pottle of oil for painting' was 8*d.* in 1302, and '16 gallons of oil for painting' cost 21*s.* 6*d.* in 1320.[6] At Ely 'oil for painting figures on the columns' was 1*s.* the gallon in 1323,[7] and at St. Stephen's, Westminster, it was 4*s.* the gallon in 1352, though only half that price at Windsor in 1366.[8] At Collyweston in 1504 and at Hampton Court in 1533 'a galon of paynters oyle' cost 20*d.*, but as much as 2*s.* 4*d.* was paid for it at Westminster in 1532. Oil was also used for making varnish,[9] by dissolving sandarac in it, and as the 'vernysshe' which appears so frequently in accounts was always bought by the pound, the term was evidently applied to the sandarac, or other similar resinous substance. While varnish occurs constantly in connexion with painting and ochreing, it seems also to have been applied directly to untreated timber, as at Rotherhithe in 1357, when we have entries 'for painting the timber of 7 chambers with *rosine*' and

---

[1] E. 467, 2.  [2] Oliver, *Exeter*, 381, 2.  [3] T.R., f. 590.
[4] *Theophilus*, 33, 97.  [5] E. 468, 2.  [6] Oliver, *Exeter*, 380–1.
[7] *Sacrist Rolls*, 34.  [8] E. 493, 22.  [9] *Theophilus*, 64.

'for painting the new gate with *vernis*'[1] and at King's Hall, Cambridge, in 1434, 'for *vernyssh* and *resyn* for the gate'.[2]

While a great deal of wall-painting was done free-hand, or at most roughly sketched on the wall first, it is obvious that for more elaborate work the artists would make preliminary sketches. So for the work in St. Stephen's Chapel we find purchases made of '*quatern papiri regalis pro patronis pictorum*', at 10*d*. the *quaterna*,[3] 'royal paper' implying exceptionally large sheets. At Westminster in 1532 there are entries such as 'To John Grene stacioner for fyve quayres of papire royalle provided for the peyntours, at viij^d. for the quayre', and 'iij quayres of varye large papire royalle delyvered to the peyntors—ijs.'[4] These accounts also mention 'iij payre of compasses' at 4*s*., and 'xxx irons delyvered to the peyntours to drawe with', at 2*d*. each,[5] and a pound of 'merking stones', which cost 12*d*. and were evidently used for drawing on the walls.[6] There is also mention of 'xliij pounds of heare (i.e. hair) which was made in pensellis for the peyntours', and also 'for ij dussen graye tailes and iiij dussen quyllis wherof were made pensellis, and for threde had for the byndyng of the same'.[7] Here 'pencil' is used in the old sense of a paint-brush, and it is interesting to notice that the hair of badger, or 'graye', was already recognized as particularly suitable for this purpose. In earlier times squirrels' tails were used, *caudis skur*' occuring among materials supplied to the painters at Westminster in 1275.[8] For St. Stephen's Chapel in 1352 we have 2½*d*. paid 'for 30 quills of peacocks and swans and squirrels' tails (*caudis scurell*') for the painters' brushes (*pincellis*)'; 'thread for binding the brushes and pencils (*brussis et pincellis*) of the painters'; and 12*d*. 'for a pound of pig's bristles (*pili*) with which to make brushes for the painters'. A later account of the same work, in 1354, mentions 'pigs' bristles and quills of geese, swans and peacocks'.[9] Pigs' bristles also occur in 1423 at York, 15*d*. being paid '*pro bruscis porcinis pro bruscis faciendis ad dealbaccionem le severyse in le yle ecclesie*',[10] their use for such coarse work as whitewashing being what we might expect.

[1] E. 545, 35.  
[2] K.H. 8, f. 161.  
[3] E. 471, 6.  
[4] T.R., ff. 12, 164.  
[5] Ibid., f. 410.  
[6] Ibid., f. 416.  
[7] Ibid., f. 13. 'Quylles of swanne' were also bought, at 4*d*. the hundred: f. 552.  
[8] E. 467, 6 (2).  
[9] E. 471, 9.  
[10] Y.F.R. 48.

# XI

## GLAZING

A WINDOW is an opening in a wall to admit light and air. In the Middle Ages men were less concerned with ventilation than with lighting. The problem was to admit as much light as possible while excluding an excess of air. Innumerable excavations have shown that in the Roman period this problem was solved in the houses of the wealthy by the employment of glass. But with the coming of the Saxons this, like so many other comforts of civilization, disappeared. We are told that when St. Wilfrid, in the second half of the seventh century, undertook the restoration of King Edwin's church at York—'in the windows light came through linen cloths or a fretted slab (*multiforatilis asser*); he made glass windows'.[1] Assuming the truth of this tradition, he must have obtained his window-glass from the Continent, for shortly afterwards, in about 675, Benedict Biscop, at that time completing his monastic church at Wearmouth, 'sent agents to Gaul to bring over glassworkers, a craft hitherto unknown in Britain, to make the windows of his chancels, chapels and cells. They came; and not only did they carry out the work demanded of them, but also they made the English people understand and learn this craft.'[2] We may, therefore, date the reintroduction of window-glass into England from about 700; but it was the best part of a thousand years before it became a commonplace of house life, even though the usual idea of its rarity in medieval houses is much exaggerated. Horman, writing in 1519, says: 'Paper, or lyn clothe, straked a crosse with losynges, make fenestrals in stede of glasen wyndowes':[3] he might have added that the paper or linen must be greased. References to such window-fillings are not common, partly because most of our more detailed accounts are concerned with houses sufficiently important to use glass, and partly, no doubt, because the purpose for which many purchases of linen or paper were required is not recorded. At Witney in 1217 we find 9*d.* spent on 'linen cloth for the windows of the church',[4] and two years later there is a purchase of 'cloth for the chapel windows'.[5] Interesting details of an

---

[1] Will. Malmesbury, *Gesta Pontif.* 216.  
[2] Bede, *Op. Hist.* (ed. Plummer), 368.  
[3] *Vulgaria*, c. xxix.  
[4] Eccles. Com. Mins. Accts. 159275.  
[5] Ibid. 159277.

unusually elaborate example occur in the accounts of St. George's Chapel, Windsor, in 1426–7:[1]

To John Horstede, joiner, of Windsor for making a fenestral of wood for a window in the chapel called Gaille on the south, 4d. For linen cloth bought of Isabel Northfolke for the said fenestral, 8½d. Paid to Thomas Fletcher for the *seryng* (i.e. waxing) of the said fenestral, 14d. Paid to Thomas Staynour of Windsor for painting the fenestral like a glass window, 4d.

Incidentally, it may be noted that the proportion of the cost of this sham window involved by the artist's fee is, by modern standards, somewhat low. It should be observed that the term 'fenestral' does not necessarily imply this type of glass substitute, but is also used for a small window or a window-frame. At Collyweston, for instance, in 1500 we have 'a fenestral of yren for the wyndowe in my lordes chambre', followed by the purchase of 'iij lb. of fyn sowder to the glassyng of the said fenestrall'.[2]

The device of the 'fretted slab', mentioned in connexion with the first church at York, was chiefly employed in situations where ventilation and the exclusion of birds[3] were more important considerations than light— as in the upper stories of church towers. Sometimes the fretting took the form of a more or less elaborate grille of lead. Apparently the windows of the royal chapel in the castle at Oxford were filled in this way, as in 1243 Henry III ordered that the chancel should be panelled and the leaden windows replaced by glass;[4] and subsequently, in 1246, he gave orders for the two leaden windows in the nave (*corpore*) to be similarly replaced.[5] At Winchester, on the other hand, in 1255 Henry gave instructions to make in the chapel of St. Thomas a glass window with the figure of Christ in Majesty and below this St. Edward holding a ring; and also to make a figure of St. George on the wall in the entry to the hall, with two leaden windows.[6]

Among the items of work to be done at Westminster Palace in 1238, a window of white glass was to be set in the iron-barred window of the end chamber of a garderobe, 'So that chamber may not be so draughty as it has been'.[7] For a similar reason, no doubt, Henry gave orders in 1252 for all the windows in the privy chambers of the king and queen at Clipstone to be glazed.[8] As these would be precisely the places where ventila-

---

[1] Hope, *Windsor Castle*, 396.            [2] St. John's Coll., Cambridge, MS. vol. i.
[3] At Penshurst 'a net for the windows of the hall, to keep out the pigeons' was bought in 1470: Penshurst MS. 129.
[4] Liberate R. 28 Hen. III.
[5] Ibid. 31 Hen. III, m. 8.            [6] Ibid. 40 Hen. III.
[7] *Close R.* 27.            [8] Liberate R. 36 Hen. III, m. 15.

tion would be most emphatically required, it almost necessarily follows that all the windows in the other royal apartments were glazed at this date. But the king was not entirely unmindful of ventilation. For instance, at Sherborne Castle in 1250 the glass windows in the chapel were to be so repaired that they would open and shut;[1] at Guildford a window was to be enlarged and 'closed with glass windows between the columns, with panels which can be opened and shut';[2] and in the hall at Northampton, opposite the dais, a glass window was to be made, with the figures of Lazarus and Dives in it, which could be closed or opened.[3]

By the second quarter of the twelfth century the glazing of church windows was general, and the use of pictorial glass so common that the Statutes of the austere Cistercian Order expressly prohibited such use in their own churches. A century later, in 1240, an interesting agreement was made by the Dean and Chapter of Chichester with John the glazier,[4] by which, in return for a daily allowance of bread and a yearly fee of 13s. 4d., he and his heirs were to keep the windows of the cathedral in repair:

They shall preserve the ancient glass windows (*vitreolas*), and what has to be washed and cleaned they shall wash and clean, and what has to be repaired they shall repair,[5] at the cost of the church, and what has to be added (*augmentanda*) they shall add, likewise at the cost of the church; and there shall be allowed them for each foot of addition one penny. And as often as they repair the glass windows, in whole or in part, they shall be bound, if so ordered by the keeper of the works, to make one roundel (*roellam*) with an image in each. And if they make a new glass window entirely at their own cost, which is without pictorial decoration (*pictura*) and is 53 ft.[6] in total area (*magnitudinis circumquaque*) they shall receive for it and for their expenses, 12s.

This works out at rather under 3d. a square foot, the usual rate payable to glass-workers not on the regular staff of a church being 4d. per foot for white glass.[7] As white glass was 6s. the 'seam', containing 24 'weys' (*pise*, or *pondera*) of 5 lb., and 2½ lb. was reckoned sufficient to make one foot of glazing,[8] the cost of the glass would be 1½d., leaving 2½d. for labour. This is borne out by an account of 1286 for glazing a chapel in the Tower of London: 'For 252 ft. of coloured glass, at 8d. a foot, 8ˡⁱ 8s.; for 227½ ft.

[1] Ibid. 34 Hen. III, m. 5.  [2] Ibid. 30 Hen. III, m. 17.
[3] Ibid. 37 Hen. III.  [4] *Hist. MSS. Com. Rep., Var. Coll.*, i. 193.
[5] A later John Glasiare, in 1472, was paid 1d. each for mending 263 holes in the windows: ibid. 198.
[6] This corresponds to the dimensions of the contemporary clerestory windows.
[7] As at Westminster Abbey in 1253: *J.M.G.* ii. 116.
[8] *Literae Cant.* (Rolls Ser.), iii. 385.

of white glass, at 4d. a foot, 75s. 10d.; for 40 ft. of old glass made up and renewed, at 2½d. a foot, 8s. 4d.; for tin and lead for the same, with laths, nails and cords for carrying the glass, 11s.; for 4 men for 9 days setting and fixing the windows, 9s.'[1] The continuation of this account next year gives us: 'For 2 new glass windows in the great hall, made in colours, being of 66 ft., at 10d. the foot, 55s.; also for 160 ft. of glass for 10 windows in the said hall and in the small hall and the king's chamber, at 4d. the foot, 53s. 4d.; also for 4 windows of coloured glass, containing 40 ft., at 6d. a foot, 20s.'[2]

In the last entry quoted the glass at 4*d.* was obviously white, that at 10*d.* evidently elaborate pictorial work, and that at 6*d.* may well have been grisaille, with conventional patterns, which is typical of the period. The mention, in the Chichester agreement, of roundels containing figures is thoroughly characteristic of the glass of the thirteenth century, as is the description of a window in the hall at Guildford in 1245, 'to be closed with white glass windows, and in one half of the glass window a king sitting on a throne and in the other half a queen, also sitting on a throne'.[3] Next year, two windows in the hall at Rochester were to have the figure of a king in each, and two others the shields of England and Provence respectively;[4] and a little later a window was to be made in the queen's chamber at Clarendon with 'Mary with her Child, and a queen at the feet of the same Mary, with clasped hands, holding in her hands a label *Ave Maria*'.[5] The development of the pictorial subject, covering one or more lights, in the fourteenth century, is suggested by such an entry as that at Ludgershall in 1341: 'For glass bought of John le Glasiere of Calne for glazing all the windows of the chapel, containing in all 180 ft., of which the great window before the high altar is painted with royal shields and with a panel of all the Passion of the Lord,—by contract, 6^li'.[6] About the end of that century we meet the practice of forming the ground of the window of quarrels, ornamented with one or more repeated devices, such glass being usually described as 'flourished'. Glass 'florshyd' with birds, beasts, flowers, or grotesques (*baboueny*) was supplied for windows at Westminster and Eltham by William Burgh about 1400.[7] An entry typical of fifteenth-century glazing may be quoted from an Eltham account for 1402:[8]

For 91 square feet of new glass, diapered and worked with broom flowers,

[1] *J.M.G.* ii. 117.    [2] Ibid.    [3] Liberate R. 30 Hen. III, m. 17.
[4] Ibid. 31 Hen. III, m. 10.    [5] Ibid. 35 Hen. III, m. 15.
[6] *J.M.G.* ii. 119.    [7] Ibid. iii. 25, 26.    [8] Ibid. 27.

eagles (*ernes*), and scrolls inscribed *Soueraigne*, bought of William Burgh, glasier, for 3 bay windows and side lights (*costres*), each of 2 lights, at 3s. 4d. a foot, 15$^{li}$ 3s. 4d. And for 54 square feet of new glass worked with figures and canopies, the field made in the likeness of cloth of gold, bought from the same William for 3 windows, each of 2 lights, in the new oratory, at 3s. 4d. the foot, 9$^{li}$.

Mr. J. A. Knowles has ingeniously reconstructed, from existing examples, an illustrated price-list of the various types of windows supplied by John Prudde, the king's glazier and, one might say, leading firm of glass-workers, between 1445 and 1447.[1] 'Powdered glass with figures of Prophets' cost 8½d. a foot; 'Glass flourished with roses and lilies, and certain arms', 10d.; 'Glass wrought with different figures and borders', 1s.; Subject windows (*vitri historiales*), 1s. 2d.; 'divers pictures', supplied for the west window of Eton chapel, 1s. 4d.; and the very finest figure work, as provided for the Beauchamp chapel at Warwick, 2s. The reiteration of ornament, which is a mark of the later Perpendicular period, comes out in the contract for the glazing of the hall and other buildings at St. John's College, Cambridge, in 1513. The windows of the hall were to be glazed with roses and portcullises (*purcholious*), the only relief being a figure of St. John the Evangelist and the arms of the foundress, the Lady Margaret, in the oriel window.[2] On the other hand, the crowded pictorialism which is another feature of sixteenth-century glass appears in the contract of 1526 for the famous, and happily surviving, windows of King's College Chapel, which were to contain 'imagery of the story of the olde lawe and of newe lawe after the fourme, maner, goodenes, curyousytie, and clene-lynes, in every poynt, of the glasse wyndowes of the kynges newe Chapell at Westmynster'.[3]

In domestic glazing the Tudor period saw the establishment of the diamond lattice which is still a pleasing feature in so many of our older houses. At Little Saxham in 1508 William Duxfold, of London, was paid 'for setting up of white Normandy glas, oon rowe of quarells white, the second rowe powdered or inured wt. bromecoddes';[4] and next year 10s. was paid 'for latys glas to the kechen and bakhous'.[5] And in 1533 we find 21 feet of glass 'in la quarrels', that is to say, ready cut up into quarries, bought at Durham,[6] at 2d. the foot; and a similar price was paid at Croy-don in 1505 'for xvj fote of quarelles'.[7]

[1] Ibid. ii. 85.　　　　　　　　[2] Willis and Clark, *Arch. Hist.* ii. 347.
[3] Ibid. i. 615.　　　　　　　　[4] Gage, *Thingoe Hundred*, 143.
[5] Ibid. 149.　　　　　　　　　[6] *D.H.B.* 267.
[7] St. John's Coll., Cambridge, MS. vol. iv.

The medieval method of composing a window as a mosaic of pot-metal (i.e. glass coloured in the process of manufacture), held together by strips of lead, is unquestionably the most artistically satisfactory; but it was forced upon the craftsmen by the method of manufacture of the raw material.[1] For some obscure reason, the Roman practice of casting glass in comparatively large sheets, rolled out on a flat surface, like pastry, was completely lost sight of throughout the Middle Ages. Consequently the sheets produced were small, and further limited by irregularities of shape and thickness, so that it was difficult to obtain pieces more than a foot in length. The first process in the production of a pictorial window[2] was the drawing of the design. For working purposes this was made on a flat trestle table, which was sometimes sized by washing it over with ale. On this the design was set out full size in outline, with the colours of each portion indicated. At the same time, preliminary designs were often made on paper or parchment, and purchases of these materials for the glaziers occur in various accounts. So, in the inventory of stores at Westminster in 1443 we find[3]— '2 portreyyng tables of waynescote, 2 tables of popeler, and 11 trestles, used for glazing work', and also '25 shields painted on paper with various arms of the King for patterns for the use of glaziers working there, 6 crestis with various arms for the same works . . . and 12 patterns made in the likeness of windows'. Such designs could also be sent to provincial glaziers for their guidance. Thus, when armorial glass was being put in the windows of the Lady Margaret Beaufort's manor of Collyweston, in 1505, by John Delyon of Peterborough, that mysterious heraldic beast the 'yale' was apparently represented wrongly as a common or usual antelope, and 7s. was paid to Delyon—'for the changyng of the Antelope unto an Ivell in the bay wyndowe in the grett chambre, wt xx^d yevyn to William Hollmer for the draght of the said Ivell at London'.[4] And a few years later Sir Thomas Lucas paid to one Wright 10s. 'for purtraying of my chapel windowe and settyng out the coloures of the same unto my glasier'.[5] These cartoons were preserved as part of the stock in trade of the glazier; Sir John Petty, the famous glass-painter of York, in 1508 bequeathed all his tools and 'scrolls' to his brother Robert, and Robert Preston in 1503 left his 'scrowles' to his partner, Thomas Inglish.[6] Mr. Knowles has shown[7]

---

[1] For the manufacture of glass see Salzman, *Engl. Industries*, 183–93, and Knowles, in *J. of Royal Soc. of Arts*, lxii. 567–85.

[2] See the detailed account of 'The Glazing of St. Stephen's Chapel, Westminster, 1351–2', printed in full by the present writer in *J.M.G.*, Nos. 4–6.

[3] E. 503, 12.                                [4] St. John's Coll., Cambridge, MS. vol. i.

[5] Gage, *Thingoe Hundred*, 149.            [6] *J.M.G.* No. 3, 36.            [7] Ibid. 35–44.

that the medieval glassworker had no hesitation in using the same design, with slight variations in colour or detail, many times over, and would even employ a cartoon that had originally been designed some eighty years before.

The design having been drawn on the working table, a piece of glass of the required colour was placed upon it and the outline of that portion was traced on it with chalk ground in water. A hot iron rod, being drawn along the outline, produced a crack, which enabled the outlying portions of the glass to be broken off. The ragged edge so produced was then cleaned up with the grozing-iron. The St. Stephen's accounts of 1351–2 contain a number of purchases of *groisours* or *croysours*, at $1\frac{1}{4}d$. each; 4 *grosers* were among the glazier's tools at Durham in 1404;[1] as were 8 iron *grosyeres* at Westminster in 1443.[2] When the glass had been cut and assembled on the table, the next process was to paint on the details, such as features, folds of draperies, inscriptions, and so forth. For this a paint was formed by grinding up oxide of iron, or copper, with a little water, gum.arabic, to make it adhere to the glass, and urine or vinegar, which has the property of rendering the gum insoluble when once it has dried; in this way it was possible to obtain different depths of shading by giving the surfaces one, two, or three washes of the paint. Often, instead of the metallic oxide, what was known as 'jet' was used; this Mr. Knowles has shown to be the trade name for black beads of an easily fusible lead glass. Usually the glassworker supplied his own paint, but the St. Stephen's accounts show purchases of oxide (*arnement,* or *atramentum*), 'geet', and 'gumme arabik'. The pieces of painted glass were then laid in an iron pan, on a bed of lime, and put into an annealing furnace and subjected to a heat just sufficient to fuse the paint into the surface of the glass. The only reference to this process at St. Stephen's is in the mention of '*talshid*', or fire-wood, bought for the glaziers' work; but in an account of work done at Guildford Castle in 1292 we have 8*d*. paid 'for making a furnace to burn glass';[3] the glazing account for Westminster Abbey in 1469 includes an item 'for *brike* and other necessaries for making the *anelyng herth*';[4] and the glazier's stores at Durham in 1404 include an '*eldyng pan*'.[5] Strictly speaking, this was the only type of painting on glass that was admitted by the good craftsman; but there is some evidence that details, especially such as small heraldic bearings, were occasionally rendered in ordinary paint, not

[1] *Durham Acct. Rolls* (Surtees Soc.), ii. 397.  [2] E. 503, 12.
[3] E. 492, 10.  [4] Rackham, *Nave of Westminster*, 31.
[5] *Durham Acct. Rolls*, ii. 397.

fired in, and therefore very far from permanent.[1] This is suggested by the purchase at Ely in 1326 of 'divers colours for colouring glass',[2] and by such an order as was given by King Henry in 1265 'to make a window of white glass and to cause the nativity of the Blessed Mary to be painted in it'.[3] A more legitimate solution of the problem of producing coloured details too small to be leaded separately was by means of enamel paint, formed from coloured lead glass beads and fired on. This process of enamel painting ultimately displaced the medieval use of pot-metal mosaic, but was used in a small way at least as early as the fifteenth century. In 1471 William Teele of York provided 40 strings of beads of 'yalow glass' for some heraldic glazing in the minster;[4] and the Durham inventory of 1404, already quoted, included '2 strings of beads (*par de bedys*) for gilding in coloured glass'. Mention must also be made of the use of silver to produce the golden stain which is such a feature of fourteenth-century glass. This was applied at the same time as the paint, either in foil or in filings, great quantities of silver filings (*lymail*) being bought for the St. Stephen's windows; the heat of the annealing hearth caused the silver to combine with the glass and produce varying shades of gold and orange.

The glass, having been painted and fired, was reassembled on a glazing-table and held in place with T-headed 'closing'—sometimes called 'cloring' —nails, the pieces being surrounded with strips of lead which were turned down over their edges and soldered at the points of junction. At St. Stephen's '250 *clozyngnaill*, to hold glass while it is being fitted together', cost 18*d*.; and at Westminster in 1443 there were in store '42 *glosyng nayle* used in glazing work'. At Collyweston in 1504 Robert Stone was paid 'for the cloring and settyng in ledd iiij<sup>xx</sup>xv fote of whit glase at jd. the fote', and other glaziers were paid 'for encrossyng and gloryng of xlij fote'.[5] Purchases of lead are naturally a common feature of glazing accounts, and the 1443 inventory mentions 'a leaden *wasschbolle* used to make leads (*calamos*) for glazing windows', while in 1505 '18 lb. of lede redy pared' was bought for glazing at Croydon.[6] Tin, pewter or solder—called 'glas-sawdre' at Canterbury in 1485[7]—had also to be provided, and soldering-irons appear in lists of glaziers' tools—as 'soudours' at Westminster in 1387,[8] 'sowdyngyrns' at Durham in 1404,[9] and 'sowdyng yrons for glass'

[1] *J.M.G.* No. 4, 21.
[2] *Sacrist Rolls*, 60.
[3] Liberate R, 50 Hen. III.
[4] *Y.F.R.*
[5] St. John's Coll. Cambridge MS. vols. i and iii.
[6] Ibid. vol. iv. For a medieval mould for making leads see *J.M.G.* iii. 81.
[7] Bodleian MS. Top. Kent, c. 3, f. 128.
[8] Foreign R. 11 Ric. II, m. C.
[9] *Durham Acct. Rolls*, ii. 397.

at Shene in 1474.[1] (This last inventory includes 'a persyng yron for glass', which may be the iron used at heat for cutting, or rather cracking, the outlines, as we have seen.) In 1333, for work at Westminster, John de Walworth, glazier, was paid 4*d.* a day, and 'John de Southwerke, his mate (*garcio*), for assisting him and heating the *ferrum ad soldandum*', 2½*d.*[2] The St. Stephen's accounts mention purchases of tallow for the glazing, this being used to pack the leading and make the window weatherproof. Towards the end of our period, a cement was used for this purpose. In the works accounts of Salisbury Cathedral for 1531 Luke the glazier was paid 'for settyng 48 ft. of old glass in new lead, the price of a foot with *sement* 2d., and without *sement* 1½d.'; and a contemporary account of glazing at Hunsdon, in Suffolk, mentions 'new glasse maid and bought of Galyon Hone and sett with symond, at vd. the fote'.[3]

With the completion of the leading, the window was finished, and if it had been made in the workshop on the premises it had only to be set up in the window frame and secured to the iron 'soudlets', or saddlebars, by soldered strips of lead. But sometimes windows were bought ready made, or were composed in a distant workshop. Thus at Guildford Castle, in 1292, not only were 13 windows and 8 'rundell', or round windows (possibly plate tracery), made on the spot, but 9 windows—evidently small, as they cost only 11*s.* 9*d.*—were bought in London and sent down.[4] For Westminster Palace, also, in 1322 John de Walworth supplied a number of windows of white glass at 4*d.* the foot, and payments were made, 'for land and water carriage of the said windows and glass from Kandelwekstrete (now Cannon Street) to Westminster'.[5] When some glazing was being done at Carisbrooke Castle in 1353 we find 2*s.* paid 'for 2 figures bought at Winchester to put in the said windows',[6] and at Durham in 1486 four figures for a window were bought from the York firm of Robert Preston.[7] The best example, however, is the series of windows made for the chapel of Windsor Castle in 1351-2 by the same men who were employed on glazing St. Stephen's Chapel, in their Westminster workshop. When these were completed, boards and nails were bought 'to make cases for carrying the glass panels from Westminster to Wyndesore', and 14*d.* was paid 'for hay and straw to put in the said cases for safe keeping of the glass panels', the freightage of which (presumably by water) was cheap at 4*s.*[8]

In small glazing operations, all the processes mentioned could be carried out by a single glazier with, or even without, a mate. But the St. Stephen's

[1] E. 503, 19.    [2] E. 469, 13.    [3] *J.M.G.* iii. 29.    [4] Ibid. ii. 118.
[5] Ibid. 119.    [6] Ibid. 189.    [7] Ibid. 84.    [8] Ibid. 188.

accounts show that for work on a large scale the different processes were assigned to separate individuals or gangs. Here work had begun in 1349, and in March 1350 John de Lincoln, master of the glaziers, was commissioned to obtain glaziers and the necessary workmen—his commission ranging over 27 counties. When the surviving accounts begin, on 20 June 1351, we find Master John de Chestre in control. He with five, and occasionally six, other master glaziers, including John de Lincoln, is employed 'designing various figures', or 'designing and painting on white tables various designs for the windows', at a shilling a day. Some ten to twelve glaziers, 'painters in the same craft', were employed in painting the glass, at 7*d.* a day. Another fifteen or so were 'working on the breaking and fitting together of glass', at 6*d.*, and two or three—probably apprentices—assisted them, or sometimes ground paint for the painters, at 4*d.* or 4½*d.* a day. By November most of the designing had been done and John de Chestre had only three masters with him; in January 1352 the scaffolding for the glaziers was going up; in the second week of February John de Chestre drops out, as do the two remaining masters next week; some 14 painters and glaziers continue for another fortnight, but by the end of the month the windows had been completed. For the period covered by the accounts the cost had been £240; of which just over £195 represents wages, £34 glass, £1. 10*s.* painting materials and tools, and £9. 10*s.* ironwork and miscellaneous purchases.

Before the middle of the fourteenth century the source of origin of the glass supplied is rarely stated in accounts. It is known that from at least as early as 1225 glass was made in the Chiddingfold district, on the borders of Sussex and Surrey, and from 1284 to 1309, and probably later, the abbey of Vale Royal were carrying on its manufacture in Cheshire.[1] That it was made in other places is more than likely, and it would seem that the 'glashous' belonging to Salisbury Cathedral and frequently mentioned in the late fifteenth-century accounts of that church, was a seat not only of glazing but of glassmaking, judging from the quantities of sand that were carried thereto. For the glazing of St. Stephen's Chapel John de Brampton was ordered, in 1349, to buy glass in Shropshire and Staffordshire, and this obviously must have been of local manufacture; but when John Geddyng was sent, in July 1352, on the same errand into Kent and Essex we cannot be certain that he did not obtain foreign glass from the ports. In October 1351 we find payments: 'To John Alemyne for 303 weys of white glass, each hundred of 24 weys (*pondera*) and each wey of 5 lb., for glazing the

---

[1] Salzman, *Engl. Industries*, 186–90.

windows, at 12s. the hundred, 37s. 6d. To William Holmere for carriage of the said glass from Chiddingfold to Westminster, 6s. To John Geddyng, employed in obtaining the said glass for 7 days, going, staying and returning, receiving for himself and his horse 12d. a day, 7s.' Next week the same 'John de Alemaygne' sent up another 36 weys, and in December 60 weys of white glass were bought at Chiddingfold. For the Windsor windows he also supplied 324 weys of white glass, at the same price, in 1351, and another four hundreds, at 13s. 4d., in 1355.[1] English glass was used at Durham in 1397;[2] and for York Minster white glass (presumably local) was bought from John Glasman of Rugeley at 20s. the seam of 24 weys, in 1418,[3] and 16 sheets of English glass from Edmund Bordale of Bramley Buttes in 1471.[4] It is a curious fact that there is absolutely no documentary evidence for coloured glass having been made in England, and this is borne out by the fact that Henry VI in 1449 brought John Utynam over from Flanders to make coloured glass for the windows of Eton and King's College, Cambridge. He was empowered to obtain workmen and materials at the king's expense, and 'because the said art has never been used in England, and the said John is to instruct divers in many other arts never used in the realm', he was not only allowed to make stained glass, at his own cost, for sale, but was granted a monopoly for twenty years.[5] Two years before this, the executors of the Earl of Warwick, contracting with John Prudde for the glazing of the Beauchamp Chapel at Warwick, stipulated that no English glass should be used, but only the best obtainable from overseas.

The chief sources of coloured and the best white glass were the Rhine lands of Burgundy and Lorraine, Flanders, and Normandy.[6] For Exeter 629 pieces of white glass were bought at Rouen, in 1317, for £15. 14s. 9d.[7] The York accounts show glass of various colours bought in 1457 from Peter Faudkent, 'Dochman' (i.e. German), at Hull, 'Rennysshe' glass bought in 1530, Burgundy glass in 1536, and Normandy glass in 1537.[8] For glazing at Westminster Abbey in 1469 purchases were made of '6½ seme of English glass', for £5. 4s., and 'half a wawe of glass of Rene', for 18s. 4d.[9] At Collyweston we find 30s. paid for 'a wahaw of glasse cont' lx sheffes, every sheff cont' vj fote'[10]—though I am inclined to think that 'fote'

[1] *J.M.G.* ii. 188–9.      [2] *Durham Acct. Rolls*, ii. 393.
[3] *Y.F.R.* 37.      [4] Ibid. 83.      [5] *Cal. Patent R.* 255.
[6] See J. A. Knowles, 'The Source of Coloured Glass used in Medieval . . . Windows', in *Glass*, March–June 1926.
[7] Oliver, *Exeter*, 381.      [8] *Y.F.R* 69, 104, 108, 109.
[9] Rackham, *Nave of Westminster*, 31.      [10] St. John's Coll., Cambridge, MS. vol. ii.

is a slip for 'pounds'—a further 2*s*. being paid for its carriage from Lynn to Peterborough, and 3*s*. 4*d*. from Peterborough to Collyweston. From its being bought at Lynn it is probable that this came from Flanders, especially as shortly afterwards we have 'lx sheffes of Flemysh glasse' costing 32*s*.[1] At Hedon, about 1425, we have 2 'walbes' (almost certainly a misreading for 'wawes') of glass bought for 26*s*. 8*d*., and 8*d*. paid 'for colours for making figures in the same glass';[2] and at Shene in 1474 there were in store '3 *wawe* and 2 *bunchis* of coloured glass, azure, purple and red'.[3] In the Durham glaziery there were, in 1404, 'of new coloured glass 2 *scheff*, and of new white glass 76 *scheffe*'.[4] Another term occurs at Westminster in 1395, when John Prest was paid 'for 17 *draghtes* of glass for mending the windows in the white hall and the Exchequer', at 18*d*. the *draghte*.[5] In 1503 we find Oliver King, Bishop of Bath, writing to Sir Reynold Bray, desiring 'that I may have knowledge from my felowe Dawtre of Hampton what bargeyne he hath made for the hundred cases of glasses to be had out of Normandy, with the price of every c. cases bothe of coloured glassys and others'.[6] Just about the same time Sir Thomas Lucas was agreeing to supply Robert Beston of Bury, glazier, with Normandy glass, 'he to make of every caas atte lest iiij$^{xx}$x fete', receiving 'for every skochon of armes garnysshed wt. helmettes, targettes, and scriptures, and for every fote of imagery viij$^d$, and for every fote of white glas, dubled, inured, and garnyshed wt. flowres, poises (i.e. mottoes) wt. luse (?) and colors, ij$^d$'.[7] A few years later, in 1508, Sir John Petty bequeathed to York Minster 'vj tabyls of Normandy white glasse', and to his brother Robert 'a credill of Normandy glasse'.[8] Half a 'credyll' of glass was bought at Durham in 1533 for 8*s*.;[9] and in an account of work done at Sheriff Hutton Castle in 1537 we have—'Payed to Robert Hall, merchant of Yorke, for iiij cradyll of Normandye glasse, at xviij$^s$. a cradyll—lxxij$^s$. Item payed to Robert May of Yorke, merchant, for a chest of wyspe glasse, xvij$^s$. vj$^d$. Item to the said Robert for x wyspes glasse, at ix$^d$. a wyspe—vij$^s$. vj$^d$.'[10] From these various entries it would appear that the case, chest, or cradle of glass was equivalent to the seam of 120 lb. and the wisp to the earlier wey of 5 lb.

[1] St. John's Coll., Cambridge, MS. vol. iii.   [2] Boyle, *Hedon*, cxxii.
[3] E. 503, 19.   [4] *Durham Acct. R.* ii. 397.
[5] Add. R. (B.M.), 27018.
[6] *Somerset, Arch. Soc.* lx (2), 4. According to Randle Holmes's *Academy of Armory* (1688) the 'case' contained 16 'bunches', each of 3 'tables', which were about a foot square.
[7] Gage, *Thingoe Hundred*, 142.   [8] Knowles, loc. cit. 201.
[9] *D.H.B.* 267.   [10] E. 484, 3.

The glass supplied by Herman Glasyer in 1485 for work at Coldharbor (London) included: 'xij pannys of dusche glasse', containing 10 ft., at $4\frac{1}{2}d$.; 'iiij panys of Venys glasse sete in the kytchin wyndowes', containing $26\frac{1}{2}$ ft., at 6*d*.; 'xxvj quayrell of Englyssche glasse set in the said kytchin wyndow', at 1*d*. each; 'xxvij fote of Englysh glasse sette in a baye wyndow in the Steward chambre', at $5\frac{1}{2}d$.; and Normandy glass, at 6*d*. the foot.[1] For the Hall of the Pewterers' Company, in 1497, both Flemish and Normandy glass were supplied;[2] and for Lady Margaret Beaufort's manor of Croydon, in 1505, Barnard Floure provided 16 feet of 'Reynes glas', at 4*d*., 16 feet of 'quarelles', at 2*d*., and 'a pane of Normandy glas for the countinghous', containing 16 feet, at 5*d*. the foot.[3] This Barnard Flower had originally undertaken the glazing of King's College Chapel, Cambridge, and when, after his death, a contract for the work was drawn up with his successor, Galyan Hone, it was stipulated that Normandy glass should be used, but the word 'Normandy' was subsequently struck out.[4] Glass from this source seems always to have been regarded as superior, and, as a final example, in 1532 'Normandie glasse' cost 5*d*. while 'Reynes' (or Rhenish) was $4\frac{1}{2}d$. the foot.[5]

By the fifteenth century glass had so far come into general use that we even find in 1441 that when Peterhouse built a great pigeon-house on their estate at Thriplow they spent 22*d*. on glazing one of its windows.[6] But in ordinary houses glass windows were still regarded as luxuries rather than essentials, and, being set in hung casements, were usually treated as tenant's fixtures. From a Chancery suit of about 1470 we learn that William Smith, a London tailor, felt himself injured because, when he left the house he had rented in St. Gregory's, he was prevented from taking away 'certayn his goodes that is to witte glas wyndowes, latices, dores, lokkes . . . which after the custome of the Citie be removable and be no principals nor fastyned to any principall of the same tenement'.[7] On the other hand, in a later suit of 1535 we find complaint made of a fraudulent sale of 'glasse-wyndows' which the buyer could not obtain, as they were 'fastenyd unto the frehold and parcell of the said tenement'.[8] In 1493 the churchwardens of St. Mary-at-Hill paid 4*s*. 'to Syr James Sannys for hys lattes and hys glase wyndowys that he lefte behynde hym'.[9] It will be noticed that in two of these instances lattices are mentioned in connexion with glass windows.

[1] *J.M.G.* iii. 29.    [2] Welch, *Hist. of Pewterers' Co.*, 87.
[3] St. John's Coll., Cambridge, MS. vol. iv.
[4] Willis and Clark, *Arch. Hist. Cambridge*, i. 615–18.    [5] T.R., f. 582.
[6] P. 1441–2.    [7] Early Chan. Proc. 64, 234.
[8] Ibid. 845, 49.    [9] *Memorials* (E.E.T.S.), 200.

Sometimes these were used to protect the glass: thus at Clarendon in 1445 there is an entry: 'For makyng of iij grete latises set in the kyngges chappelle ther for conservacion of iij glason wyndowys, of wech a pece of latyzys holdytt vj foote in length and j foote and di' in brede, le foote iij^d.—vj^s. x^d.'[1] And Horman in his *Vulgaria* (1519) writes: 'I wyll have a latesse before the glasse for brekyinge.' These were not wire guards—the only instance I have seen of wire used in windows is the 'wyerd wyndows of the tennys play' at Hampton Court[2]— but were composed of thin wooden rods. A distinction is made in the 1447 accounts of the Queen's manor of Pleasaunce between those made with round and square rods: '*j latz de roundstaff voc' a cacelatz de iij panys pos' in fenestris*', and '*j squar latz pos' in alia fenestra*'.[3] They also served the purpose of letting in air and excluding birds when the glass windows were open, or absent. At Canterbury there is mention of 'the *latys* round the windows in the laundry' in 1496;[4] and at St. Mary-at-Hill in 1520 there is a payment of 8*s.* 'for latessing of the iiij wyndowys in the steple next to the belles, for every wyndowe ix yerdis and a halffe of lattes'.[5] With which entry we have come back, full circle, to something very like the 'fretted slab' of primitive days, with which we started.

[1] E. 460, 10.                                      [2] H.C. 237, ff. 117, 170.
[3] Dy. of Lanc. Misc. Bks., I, 11, f. 31.
[4] Bodleian MS. Top. Kent, c. 3, f. 160.           [5] *Memorials* (E.E.T.S.), 309.

# XII

## WATTLE-AND-DAUB

EXCESSIVE preoccupation with the more striking surviving monuments of the Middle Ages tends to produce the impression that the medieval builder was primarily concerned with masonry. This is far from being the fact. Churches, castles, and great houses might be of stone, but even at the end of our period the ordinary dwellings of the vast majority of the population were of humbler construction, and the farther we go back the smaller is the proportion of stone-built edifices. It is at least highly probable that a visitor to England about the time of the Black Death would have found, as did a visitor to Ireland in 1673, that a third of the houses were 'wretched nasty cabbins without chimney, window or dore-shutt, and worse than those of the savage Americans'.[1] The primitive huts of the poorer peasantry, constructed by their owners with walls of sods,[2] trampled earth, or mud-plastered wattles, and roofs of unshaped poles covered with turf, heather, or straw, may seem hardly to come within the category of building. But they contained elements which survived in various forms in more elaborate structures: earth walls and wattle-and-daub continued for centuries to play a part in substantial buildings, and the pole roof framing was the germ from which evolved, by continuous and traceable steps, such masterpieces of wrightcraft as the roof of Westminster Hall.

Documentary references to the making of these early huts are, naturally, scarcely to be found, but manorial accounts contain many unenlightening allusions to mud walls, either as parts of farm buildings or as boundaries. In the latter case they were preserved from the effects of the weather by a coping, usually, as in instances at Southampton in 1326, either of turves or of straw thatch.[3] A glimpse of a building of greater pretensions than a hut, constructed mainly of wattled work, is afforded us by a legend—one can scarcely agree with its author in considering it a miracle—connected with St. Cuthbert and recorded in the twelfth century.

In the furthest limits of the district of Chester is a township, set on the very edge or shore of the sea, called Lixtune, . . . On the borders of which village is

---

[1] *Hist. MSS. Com. Rep.* viii. 90.
[2] For sod huts see *Cumb. & Westm. Arch. Soc.*, N.S., i. 140.
[3] *Hist. MSS. Com. Rep.* vi. 567.

a little church dedicated to the honour of St. Cuthbert. . . . The said little church, constructed of unhewn branches (*virgultis informibus*),[1] was so despised that no one thought it of any importance. . . . By chance it happened that a crow every year built on the roof of the church and there nourished its chicks as they grew up; and their strident voices sounded far and wide and with frequent iteration of hoarse calls tired the ears of the neighbours. Wherefore a certain youth . . . irreverently climbed up and trespassed upon the roof of St. Cuthbert's church to destroy the chicks. And because the wooden wall by reason of its great age had rotted inside, whenever he placed his foot to climb up the weak osier gave way and in many places he broke and pierced the walls . . . When with one hand he had almost reached the inside of the nest and with the other he gripped a wooden bolt of the supporting wall, suddenly his feet and the branches under them flew out and he fell down, breaking nearly all the joints of his bones.[2]

Wattling consists of a row of upright stakes the spaces between which are more or less filled by interweaving small branches, hazel rods, osiers, reeds,[3] thin strips of wood, or other pliant material. On one side, or more usually both sides, of this foundation earth, clay, mortar, or plaster is daubed and thrust well into the interstices, the surfaces being smoothed and usually treated with plaster or at least a coat of whitewash. Walls of this construction, known as 'wattle and daub', 'stud and mud', 'ruddle and dab', and by other terms in different localities, were extremely common at all periods, both as external walls and internal partitions. The accounts of the Bishopric of Winchester in 1223 mention the collection of rods '*ad walduram*', and a payment '*pro pariete bovarii faciendo et waldando*'[4]— which is evidently wattling. The word used at Monmouth in 1370 is *wyndend*'.[5] At Bath we have in 1435 a straw-man (*stipulator*) and his mate making a 'watyll' for a house, and also payment '*pro stodyng et frethyng*',[6] and in 1441 '*pro vrethyng et dawbyng*',[7] while in 1535 'frithyng roddes' occur;[8] in 1349 these wreathing or wattling rods appear as 'watelrys'.[9] At Penshurst in 1470 the term is 'wyndyng':[10] and in Durham in 1472 we have, 'for setting of stakes and ryss and making of the wall',[11] where 'ryss' is the equivalent of the 'watelrys' just mentioned. For repairs to some farm

---

[1] Cf. the temporary resting-place of St. Cuthbert on reaching Durham in 995: '*facta citissime de virgis ecclesiola*': *Symeon of Durham*, i. 79.

[2] *Regin. Dunelm. Libellus* (Surtees Soc.), 139.

[3] For the building of a barn at Uffington in 1454, five score sheaves of reeds called 'thackrede' were supplied for the '*watlyng*' under the plaster: *Lincs. Notes & Queries*, xix. 15.

[4] Eccles. Com. Mins. Accts. 159279.          [5] Dy. of Lanc. Mins. Accts. 9506.

[6] *Somerset Arch. Soc.* xxiv. 45.                                    [7] Ibid. 50.

[8] Ibid. xxvi. 113.                    [9] Ibid. xxiii. 3.              [10] Penshurst MS. 123.

[11] *Durham Acct. Rolls* (Surtees Soc.), iii. 644.

buildings at Grendon in 1500 we have 3s. 4d. paid 'for viij new sparres and for wattelyng of the same housis'.[1] Except for very flimsy structures, such walls required the additional support of stouter upright posts, or 'studs', to which, and to the roof timbers, the wattles were fastened with string or other material. As, for instance, at Cambridge in 1474—'for hemp for binding the *splentes* in the grammar school'.[2] This is possibly referred to in a purchase of twigs and 'byndinge' for a wall at Cambridge in 1348,[3] and again in 1532, when, in addition to a 'bunche' of rods, 3d. was paid for bindings (*ligaminibus*) and 'splentes' (i.e. stakes) for a wall at 'ly Sterre' beside the bridge at Cambridge.[4] On the other hand, at York in 1327, when 4s. was paid for 'one hundred (? weight) of byndes for making the partitions and spaces (*parietibus et intersticiis*) in the cellar where the king's wines are to be put', it is probable that the 'byndes' are the wattling rods: at the same time straw and stubble (*stramine et palea*) were provided for mixing with the earth of the walls and a 'torcher' was employed to prepare the earth.[5]

'Torching' is one of the terms applied to this plastering with mud; as for instance at the Tower in 1278—'*in arcillo* (= *clay*) *empto ad torchiandum*',[6] and in 1337, 'for torching the penthouse beside the smithy, with mud, laths, and nails of the king's finding, 10s.'[7] Sometimes other terms are used, as at Cambridge in 1486—'*pro iiij bigatis de clay xvj^d. item pro claying murorum xiiij^d.*',[8] or at a lodge in the New Forest in 1368, where two men were employed digging red earth *pro parietibus plastrandis*,[9] though 'plastering' is usually applied to the finishing of a wall with plaster. The expression used at Bath in the fifteenth century was 'rudyng'—as, for instance, 'for *rudyng* the old walls of the chancel', and '*pro castyng de terra et rudyng*' of a house for which wattling had been made.[10] At Penshurst in 1470 there is reference to 'radelyng and daubing of the walls of the barn; and carriage of clay called *lombe* for the said work'.[11] More often the word used is, in Latin, *terrand*', which simply means earthing. For walls in Cambridge Castle, in 1267, we find 'splenteware' and 'batthes' (bats, or sticks) bought, and 'wytthes' for binding them, and a payment 'to daubers for making the

---

[1] K.H. 19, f. 396.  [2] King's Coll. Mundum Bk. vi.
[3] *Hist. MSS. Com. Rep.* i. 65. Cf. canvas and nails bought for binding the walls of a house: ibid. 120.
[4] K.H. 24, f. 228.  [5] E. 501, 8.
[6] E. 467, 7 (4).  [7] E. 470, 1.  [8] K.H. 18, f. 21.
[9] E. 477, 2. Two years earlier men were hired *ad terram grubband' et cariand' ac muros plastrand' faciend' et pergettand'*: E. 477, 1.
[10] *Somerset Arch. Soc.* xxiv. 32, 45.  [11] Penshurst MS. 129.

said walls and *terryng* the kitchen'.[1] And in 1454, when a gable was made
to a stable in Stamford, there were payments 'to a man ij daies teryng ye
same govell—x<sup>d</sup>.; for ij lodes of erthe to ye same warke—vj<sup>d</sup>.'[2] The commonest term, however, is 'daubing'. As this is latinized indiscriminately as
*dauband*' and *dealband*', and the workmen as *daubatores* or *dealbatores*, it is
often impossible to be certain whether the process alluded to is daubing or
whitewashing, unless the context gives a clue. At York in 1423 we find 200
'stours' (= stakes) provided for daubing (*dobacione*) over the kilnhouse,
and also rods, 'templis', which are also rods, and withies;[3] and similarly
in 1531 at Durham rods and 'dalbyngstours' were bought for daubing
(*dalbura*) above four fire-places in St. Giles' Street.[4] At Clarendon in 1480
payments are made for collecting rods and for 'shreddyng' them to make
the walls in the new chambers, and for 'bredyng and dawbyng' the same
walls;[5] and four years later we find '*pro bredyng et dabyng vij panys muri*',
and also[6] '*pro le stodyng bredyng and dawbyng pro pariete logie*'. Here 'stodyng'
refers to the studs or upright timbers, 'bredyng' is the braiding or wattling
between these.[7] Often, especially in later times, laths rather than wattles
were employed, as at Sutton in 1402, when Henry Dauber was paid
113*s*. 4*d*. for the lathing and daubing of the walls of certain houses re-
erected there,[8] or at Clare in 1347, when money was paid for the daubing
of the 'countrelatthynge' of a room,[9] possibly implying laths on each side
of the wall. A few years earlier, in 1341, there is a charge for daubing the
king's room, at Clare, on the outside and plastering it, and for stopping
cracks (*pro crauesses stoppand*') round the queen's room.[10]

To make the earth, or mortar, adhere properly it was customary to mix
with it some fibrous material such as hair, straw, or hay. Palsgrave,[11]
writing in 1530, says that 'daubing may be with clay onely, with lime
plaster, or lome that is tempered with heare or strawe'; and two years
later we find 'lxx stone of heare provided for the playsterers' at Westminster,[12] and also 'cowheare to make mortter for dalbyng of walles'.[13] In
1286 'white straw' was bought for plastering the walls of the hall in Cam-

---

[1] E. 553, 2.                     [2] Penshurst MS. 59.                          [3] *Y.F.R.* 48.
  [4] *D.H.B.* 86; cf. ibid. 182. For a mention of 'dobyngstoures' in 1443, see Boyle, *Hist.
of Hedon*, clxxxiii.
  [5] E. 460, 15.                                                         [6] E. 460, 16.
  [7] Cf. *In stodes pro interclauso faciendo* . . . . *In virgis pro dicto interclauso breydando*, at Old
Sarum in 1346: E. 593, 32.
  [8] E. 502, 23.                    [9] E. 459, 26.                    [10] E. 1159, 24.
  [11] Quoted in Innocent, *Building Construction*, 142.
  [12] T.R., f. 406.                                   [13] B.M. Roy. MS. 14 B. iv.

bridge Castle,[1] and in 1375 at Leeds Castle 8 cartloads of straw were bought
for daubing the floors (*aris*) and walls of various buildings.[2] At Ripon in
1454 we have 3 wagon-loads (*plaustrata*) of mud for a room, 2*d.* spent on
litter (*liter*) and water for the same mud, and 20*d.* paid to two men for the
daubing (*doubura*) of the same room and the making of its floor (*floure*).[3]
The churchwardens of St. Michael's, Bath, used hay and straw for daubing
in 1477,[4] and those of St. Mary-at-Hill, London, provided 'strawe to make
mortere with to the dawbere' in 1491.[5]

Closely allied to daubing was pargetting or rough-casting, the chief
difference, so far as any real distinction was made in the technical use of
the terms, being that in pargetting mortar or a coarse form of plaster was
used instead of clay or loam.[6] The surface of the parget might be finished
either smooth, with a coat of whitewash, or as rough-cast with sand or
small stones. For work at Launceston in 1469 'six dozen seams of sand
called roghcastyngsonde and helynsonde (= covering sand)' were supplied;[7] and Thomas Lucas in the accounts for building his house at Little
Saxham in 1507 distinguishes between the two types of finish:[8]'for lathing,
row and white casting of part of my kechen raunge'; 'for lathing, pargetting, tiryng and white casting of al my roves, walles, particons and staires':
'for lathing and leying w^t here (= hair) and morter of iiij chambres, w^t
pargettyng and white castyng thereof'. As early as 1237 we read of the
'pargetting (*pariactand'*) of the wall behind the leaded chamber' at Marlborough;[9] and at Corfe in 1285 there is reference to 'Stephen the Dauber
who pargetted the long chamber';[10] and *pargettatores* occur at Nottingham
in 1314.[11] As the '*dealbatores et luti appositores et torchiatores*' were classed
together in the wage list of 1212,[12] so daubers and pargetters are identified
at Wallingford in 1390: 'For 8 casters of walls and party-walls (*jactatoribus
murorum et parietum*) otherwise called dauberes . . . lathing and daubing a
great gable at the west of the hall and newly lathing, daubing and pargetting (*parietand'*) a party-wall of the Almerhouse—and completely casting
with rowe morter a great portion of the castle wall.'[13] Repairs done to the
royal mews at Charing Cross in 1440 include '*pergettynge et purlymeynge
(= lime-washing) cujusdam hautepace de novo fact' in gardino*',[14]—the 'haute-

<hr />

[1] E. 459, 15.  [2] E. 544, 3.  [3] R. 161.
[4] Innocent, loc. cit.  [5] *Memorials* (E.E.T.S.), 175.
[6] Innocent, op. cit. 148, says that cow-dung was mixed with the plaster, but I have found
no documentary evidence of this.
[7] E. 461, 24.  [8] Gage, *Thingoe Hundred*, 146.
[9] E. 476, 3.  [10] E. 460, 27.  [11] E. 478, 1.
[12] *Liber Cust.* 86.  [13] E. 490, 4.  [14] E. 503, 9.

pace' being elsewhere defined as a 'Spyhouse', or what later generations
would have called a gazebo. A variant form of the word occurs in the
north, as at Finchale in 1488: 'for the pergenyng and weschyng of the
church', for which chalk and lime were bought;[1] and at Durham in 1531:
'*in le pargenynge et emendacione foraminum*'.[2]

Finally we may quote from Winchester in 1532 a payment 'to John
Welles, tiler, working on the parchettyng of the infirmary windows, for
two bushels of hair (*crinibus*) for the tyryng for the windows'.[3]

In the Windsor accounts for 1345 is a payment to Walter le Proute for
making the 'beemfullyng and pariettyngye' in the stable;[4] at Brigstock
Park a mason was employed, in 1423, to do what is called earth work
(*opus terr*'), defined as 'bemfyllynge werlynge (= wattling) pergetyng
plastryng and wasshyng (elsewhere, whytlymyng)';[5] and the churchwardens of St. Mary-at-Hill, London, in 1488 paid James Dawber for
'walling floryng and beame fillyng'.[6] These three entries may serve to
emphasize the fact that in the more substantial houses of the Middle Ages
wattle-and-daub, if fairly ubiquitous, played a secondary part as the filling
between the beams. The typical medieval house was essentially a timber
structure, though, for reasons of economy, its construction was eked out
with cheaper material; and, speaking loosely, the later the house the greater
the proportion of cheap material.[7] Such a building as Greensted Church,
in Essex, which is pre-Conquest in form whatever its date may be, with
solid walls of half-trunks, was out of the reach of the ordinary individual
except when timber was extremely plentiful and labour was either unpaid
or paid at a very low rate.

The importance of wood as a building material has already been alluded
to. Until the eleventh century it was exceptional for even a church to be
built of stone. Finan, in about 655, built a church at Lindisfarne, 'not of
stone, but, in the Scottish fashion, of cleft oak'.[8] St. Aldhelm, towards the
end of the seventh century, did build several churches which were identified in the twelfth century with stone buildings then existing, but the
building at Doulting which witnessed his death, in 709, 'was a wooden
church, into which as he was breathing his last he ordered that he should
be carried'.[9] The church in which the martyred King Edmund was first
buried, about 890, was built *vili opere*, probably like the chapel of St.

---

[1] *F.* ccclxxxii.                                    [2] *D.H.B.* 82.
[3] Kitchin, *Obedientiary Rolls*, 220. 'Tyryng' = dressing.
[4] E. 492, 24.                                        [5] E. 459, 10.
[6] *Memorials* (E.E.T.S.), 88.                        [7] Innocent, *Building Construction*, 112.
[8] Bede, *Opera* (ed. Plummer), i. 181.              [9] Will. Malmesbury, *Gesta Pont.* 382.

Cuthbert referred to above,[1] and even the magnificent church that replaced this a generation later was of wood and was not rebuilt in stone until the time of Cnut.[2] In the same king's reign the other East Anglian abbey church of St. Benet Hulme was rebuilt, having formerly been 'of mud (*lutea*)'.[3] With the advent of the Normans masonry received a great impetus, many churches being rebuilt, as for instance at Lewes, where the Cluniac monks were established in the stone church which William de Warenne had substituted for the wooden chapel of St. Pancras.[4]

When Lanfranc founded hospitals at Canterbury he built 'on the north side stone houses for the poor of all kinds, on the west side wooden houses for those afflicted with scrofula (*regia valetudine*)'.[5] The nucleus from which the priory of Barnwell developed at the beginning of the twelfth century was a *parvulum oratorium ligneum*,[6] and a visitation of Berkshire in 1220 shows that there were still a number of small churches of wood, though they were evidently regarded as survivals, to be replaced as soon as possible: thus the chapel of Hertmere, attached to Godalming, is noted as '*lignea adhuc*';[7] at Knook 'there is a wooden chapel, the chancel roofed with lead and the body of the church with shingles';[8] at Arborfield the old wooden chapel was in ruins,[9] as was the wooden baptistry at Ruscomb;[10] while at Erleigh the chapel was of wood, but 'there are lying there stones piled up in heaps as if for the building of a stone chapel'.[11]

One would have expected fortifications to precede churches in the adoption of masonry, but we are expressly told that the castle of William Fossard near Birdsall, destroyed after the anarchy of Stephen's reign, was *ligneum*,[12] and as a matter of necessity the keeps of Norman castles of the motte-and-bailey type must have been, for the first twenty years or so after their construction, of timber, as a freshly piled mound would not have afforded foundation for masonry. The greater part, therefore, of the multitude of adulterine castles which sprang up in Stephen's time must have been timber-crowned mounds, similar to the castle set up at Hastings by William of Normandy, as shown in the Bayeux tapestry. Even the outer defences of towns long retained their primitive nature of stockades. At

---

[1] See p. 188.   [2] *Mems. of St. Edmunds*, i. 19.
[3] *Chron. J. de Oxenedes*, 292.   [4] *Chartulary of . . . Lewes* (Suss. Rec. Soc.), i. 3.
[5] Will. Malmesbury, *Gesta Pont.* 72.
[6] J. Willis Clark, *Liber Memorandorum*, 42.
[7] *Reg. of St. Osmund* (Rolls Ser.), i. 297.   [8] Ibid. 295.
[9] Ibid. 282.   [10] Ibid. 279.   [11] Ibid. 309.
[12] *Chron. Mon. de Melsa*, i. 105. Its timbers were given to the monks of Meaux, who built therewith their combined dormitory and chapel: ibid. 107.

Bridgnorth the town wall had only recently replaced an oaken stockade in 1235,[1] and about ten years later the bailey round the important castle of Chester was still enclosed with a stockade (*palo*), which the king then ordered should be replaced with a wall of stone and lime.[2] As late as 1301 Edward I, that great builder of castles, wrote to 'Mestre Jakes de Seint George le Machoun', whom he had ordered to build certain gates and towers of stone at Linlithgow, saying: 'The King has taken counsel thereon and has changed his mind and intends that instead of these works good gates and towers shall be made entirely of timber.... And the King also wills that the said Peel be made well and strongly of whole trunks or of great trunks hewn without much reducing them (*de fustz entiers ou de gros fust fenduz saunz les plus ameneuser*).'[3] Even when the castle walls were of masonry many of the buildings behind them were of timber, as at Pevensey, where the hall and chapel were entirely rebuilt in wood, with clay daubing, in 1300.[4] And Henry III, extravagant as he was in building, was not above ordering 'a fair, great, and becoming hall of wood, and a kitchen of wood' for his manor at Clipston in 1254.[5] When, therefore, it took so long for stone to supplant timber in the construction of churches, castles, and royal houses, it is obvious that the typical building of the Middle Ages, lying between the one extreme of lordly masonry and the other of villain mud, is the timber-framed house.

[1] Chanc. Misc. bdle. 11, file 1, No. 23.        [2] *Royal Letters, Hen. III*, ii. 45.
[3] E. 482, 21.        [4] E. 479, 16.        [5] Liberate R. 28 Hen. III.

# XIII

## THE TIMBER-FRAMED HOUSE

IN the most primitive types of timber-framed buildings the framing of walls and roof is continuous. A series of pairs of beams, or stout poles, arranged in line, with their thicker ends embedded in the ground and their thinner ends pegged together, constitutes the frame; smaller poles or branches, being fastened horizontally from one pair to another, serve to support a covering of thatch which extends from the ridge of the roof down to the ground, and the ends of the inverted V thus formed are filled with wattle-and-daub or boarding, leaving an opening for a door and possibly a window. Such a building is obviously deficient in headroom, and the next step in advance was the 'cruck-built' house.[1] To construct such a house it is necessary to select an oak with a branch growing out at an angle of about 45°;[2] the upper part of the tree, above the fork, having been cut off, the trunk and branch are roughly squared and divided in half. If the two halves are then placed opposite one another, with the branch ends pegged together, they constitute what was usually known as a 'cruck' or, more correctly, 'a pair of crucks'. Each pair of crucks was steadied by a horizontal tie-beam pegged into each member, and the series of crucks carried in the forks formed by their overlapping ends the longitudinal ridge-rafter or roof-tree. In such houses the division between wall and roof would be more or less clearly marked according to the sharpness of the angle of curvature of the crucks.

In the accounts for building a bakehouse at Harlech Castle in 1278 there is mention of 'two great twisted beams called *crokkes*, 25 feet in length'.[3] In 1233 six '*postes tortos*' are among the timber supplied for an almonry at Kempton.[4] Two such 'twisted posts' were used for the kitchen at Windsor in 1236,[5] and other similar entries occur about this date, as for instance an order for 'four oaks to make twisted posts' in 1251.[6] This is probably also the meaning of the grant made in 1276 to the Dean and Chapter of Lincoln of fifty oaks from Sherwood Forest, 'whereof six shall be *transversar*'.[7] In a lease of land at Knitton (Staffs.) in 1325 the tenant undertook to build

---

[1] For a study of the cruck-built houses in Yorkshire, see *Yorks. Arch. J.* No. 145.
[2] If a tree could be found with its trunk bent at a convenient angle, so much the better.
[3] E. 485, 29.  [4] *Close R.* 199.  [5] Ibid. 394.
[6] Ibid. 483.  [7] Ibid. 277.

Carpenters constructing a timber-framed building (1531)

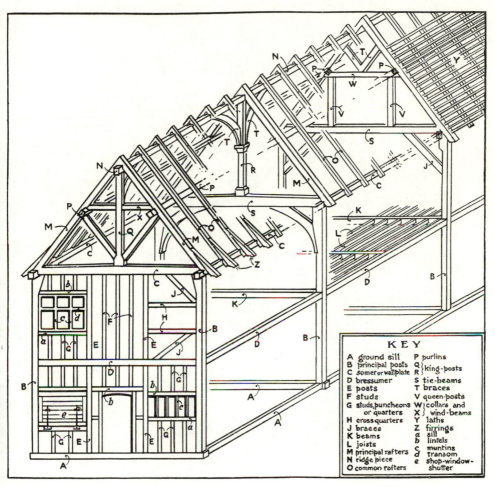

KEY

A ground sill
B principal posts
C somer or wallplate
D bressumer
E posts
F studs
G studs, puncheons
   or quarters
H cross quarters
J braces
K beams
L joists
M principal rafters
N ridge piece
O common rafters

P purlins
Q } king-posts
R }
S tie-beams
T braces
V queen-posts
W } collars and
X } wind-beams
Y laths
Z firrings
a sill
b lintels
c muntins
d transom
e shop-window-
   shutter

DIAGRAM OF THE CONSTRUCTION OF A TIMBER-FRAMED HOUSE

on to the cottage two '*furcas videlicet crockus*',[1] but *furca* seems to be used equally for a straight post, so that it is not always possible to be certain of its significance, as for instance in 1245, when the keeper of the manor of Ludgershall was ordered to make an almonry of five *furcis*, with walls of daub (*torchlicio*) and plaster,[2] though in this instance the probability is that it implies crucks. Crucks were also termed 'syles' in some localities; for instance at Durham in 1458: 'for the carpentry of 7 couple of *sylez* for the new barn', and 'to David Forster for making 2 couple of sylez and the setting of a *fiste* (= ridge-piece) in the said buildings'.[3]

In the fully developed timber house the framing of the roof and walls is separate. Reduced to its essentials, the frame consists of a rectangular base formed of massive balks of timber, the ground-sills (*A*), which are morticed together at the corners. Into the angles of this construction are morticed upright principal posts (*B*) running unbroken to the height of the walls and carrying the horizontal wall-plates (*C*) which in turn support the timbering of the roof. Until the end of the thirteenth century most of these houses, and in later times many of the smaller examples, seem to have consisted simply of the single room thus formed, which served as kitchen, living-room, and bedroom. Later this formed the hall, with annexes at either end, the one for the preparation of food and the other for sleeping-apartments of the women and the privacy of the owner and his family. These annexes were usually built at right angles to the hall and that for the bedrooms was usually of two stories, the upper being known as the 'solar', a name often applied to the whole wing. In towns, where space was limited, it became increasingly usual to build the whole house of two stories, the lower containing the shop and workrooms, the upper hall, kitchen, and chambers. But this seems to have been the limit of building enterprise, even in London, in the middle of the thirteenth century, as we are told that on the occasion of his visit to Paris in 1254 Henry III was much struck with 'the elegance of the houses which were made of plaster, and were three-chambered and even of four or more stories (*stationum*)'.[4]

In a building of more than one story the divisions between the stories were marked by massive wooden girders or 'summers' (*D*), morticed into the principal posts and serving to carry the timbers of the floors. The wall space between the principal posts was framed with upright posts (*E*) and 'studs' or 'quarters' (*F, G*). Sometimes, in place of serried ranks of studs, the wall is divided into panels by transverse quarterings (*H*), often

---

[1] Anct. Deeds C. 6239.
[2] Liberate R. 30 Hen. III.
[3] *Durham Acct. Rolls* (Surtees Soc.), iii. 637–8.
[4] Matt. Paris, *Chron.* v. 481.

strengthened with diagonal braces (*J*). Broadly speaking, the type composed entirely of uprights is earlier than that with panels, but the difference
constitutes at best a very rough and unreliable indication of date.

The frame thus formed was completed by filling in the spaces between
the timbers with a 'beam-filling' of wattle-and-daub or plaster or, in later
times, bricks. The aperture for the door was framed by the ground-sill and
two posts, the summer or an extra quartering forming the lintel. For
windows the usual practice down to the middle of the sixteenth century
was to leave an unglazed space, protected from intruders by square mullions, set diagonally, and closed with a shutter. But in the fourteenth century the more pretentious houses were inserting larger windows, separately
framed and often glazed, which definitely constituted a decorative feature.
For instance, in a contract for shops in London in 1369 there are to be two
bay-windows, and the others are to have '*bone lyntels bels et nettes*'.[1]

In the type of house we are considering the place of the curved portion
of the crucks, carrying the roof, is taken by pairs of straight rafters, pegged
together at the top and having their other ends fastened to the wall-plates.
While it was possible to form the frame of a roof out of a series of such
identical pairs of rafters, it was more usual, and more satisfactory, to employ
a system of trusses. At each end, constituting the gables, two massive principal rafters are set, carrying at their apex the longitudinal ridge-piece (*N*);
and between the gables are set one or more such pairs of principals (*M*),
which are prevented from spreading by a tie-beam (*S*), morticed into the
wall-plates. The truss is further tied together by an upright king-post (*R*)
from the centre of the tie-beam to the ridge, with braces (*T*) from it into
the principals and the ridge-piece. Sometimes, instead of the king-post, the
tie-beam may carry two upright queen-posts (*V*) supporting a wind-
beam, or collar (*W*); and there may be a second collar (*X*). Between the
wall-plate and the ridge-piece, and parallel with them, a purlin (*P*) usually
runs from principal to principal, and this carries the common rafters (*O*).
Across these common rafters are nailed laths (*Y*) to carry the outer covering of thatch, tiles, or lead.

A house thus constructed, with all the timbers morticed and pegged into
one another, formed so complete a unit that it could, at least in theory, be
moved as a whole. Horman speaks of a house which 'may be remoued
with trocles and slyddis',[2] that is to say with pulleys and rollers. There may
possibly be a reference to such a bodily transference in a deed of 1520, the
year after Horman's book appeared, dealing with a house and land in

---

[1] App. B.                                          [2] *Vulgaria*, c. xxix.

Newport, Isle of Wight: 'Mem^d. be yt knoyne . . . that the study and the chemney and soe backe ys no part of thys indentur, as yt may appere by the buyldyng for yt had been sett closse upon Harry Haulys land . . . and that the bourgys of the towne had not bene ther at the settyng up of the same frame and soo made yt be caryd southward as John Hedlye the carpynter doth testyfye who was a workeman abowght the house the same tyme'.[1] This certainly reads as if the building regulations had been enforced by a bodily withdrawal of the offending erection, but other interpretations are possible, and I know of no other reference to such operations. On the other hand it was a comparatively simple matter to take a timber-framed house to pieces, remove it, and re-erect it elsewhere, and this was frequently done. The first buildings of St. Catharine's College, Cambridge, in 1473, were mainly formed out of two 'framed houses' bought at Coton,[2] and in 1401, certain houses were bought at Northall, taken down, and carted to the royal manor of Sutton, where they were set up and duly lathed and plastered.[3] In 1432 a house of 4 bays (*beyes*) was newly built at Allerton in Shirwood at a cost of 8 marks. A carpenter was then paid a mark for taking it to pieces (*dissolvend'*), and 14 carts were employed to carry the timber to Nottingham Castle, where 6 carpenters worked for three weeks 'reryng' the house and making doors and other fittings for it.[4] A hall, with two chambers attached, roofed with tiles, was bought at Wimbledon and removed to Shene, where it was set up and completed with partition walls, &c. in 1377.[5] The previous year a great barn had been bought at Wimbledon for £8, and in the same way removed to Shene and used for storing the king's hay there;[6] and in 1363 a chamber 40 ft. long by 18 ft. wide was taken from the manor of Thundersley and set up as a hall in Rayleigh Park, in Essex, at a total cost of 73*s*. 4*d*.[7] At Boston in 1452 there is reference to 'the taking down of an old house beside the windmill, with carriage thereof from the north end of the town of Boston to Skirbygote by water, and passage of the timber to the place of erection'.[8] In 1470 Thomas Aleyn, carpenter, was paid 'for taking down a building (*domus*)—from the cost it can hardly have been more than a shed—at Penshurst called le Bockherehous,[9] and setting up of the said building at Northpark, by contract,—4s. 4d.'; and carriage, 16*d*.; straw, 5*d*.; laths, 12*d*.; 1,500 sprigge (nails), 16*d*.; 100 fourpenynayle, 4*d*.;

---

[1] Anct. Deeds A. 12443.    [2] Willis and Clark, *Arch. Hist. of Cambridge*, ii. 86.
[3] E. 502, 23.    [4] E. 478, 13.    [5] E. 495, 1.
[6] E. 494, 29.    [7] E. 464, 6.    [8] Penshurst MS. 20.
[9] Perhaps the laundry where clothes were 'bucked'.

thatcher, 5*d*.; for 'wyndyng' (wattling) and daubing, 2*d*.[1] One suspects also that when the Abbot of Evesham, in 1357, bought the great hall of the manor of Feckenham, 'to wit all the timber of the said hall with a pentice for a pantry and buttery and another pentice behind the high table, and all the doors and windows of the hall, with the porches and external posts (*repostallis*) and supports and all boards and shingles',[2] he most likely intended to re-erect it in one of the abbey manors; but, in view of the habit of re-using timber, he may merely have seen a good opportunity of obtaining a supply of well-seasoned building-material.[3] This, also, seems to be implied by an entry in the building accounts of Tattershall Castle in 1435, concerning 'the cost of taking down the houses bought in the Abbey of Revesby and the carriage of 13 cartloads of timber—and of 40,360 tiles, 6 doors, and 10 shutters (*fenestras*) coming from those houses'.[4]

Even when the house was a new construction, the elaborate process of 'framing'—cutting the tenons and mortices and fitting the timbers together, on the ground—was often conducted at a distance from the site upon which it was to be re-erected. The 'framyngplace' at Eltham in 1401 was beside the gate of the manor;[5] but the wonderful roof of Westminster Hall was worked many miles from its ultimate destination, as is shown by the order given in June 1395 for 30 strong wains to go to 'the place called the Frame by Farnham, for carriage of the timber there wrought for the King's great hall at Westminster', each wain to carry five loads during the four weeks after Trinity[6]—a time when the roads might reasonably be expected to be at their best. Similarly, when the Dean and Chapter of St. Paul's made a contract, in 1405, for shops to be built in Bucklersbury, the carpenter was to cut the timber and take it to a convenient place for framing and they would then have it brought to London.[7] In 1460 John Spencer of Hodnell (Warws.) agreed with the nuns of Nuneaton to make a house of two bays. The convent were to 'frame hit w^tin the place of Nun Eton at theyr owne costes and expenses And the seid fermer to cary hit whom (= home) to Hodenhyll and to grouncell hit plaster hit and tyle hit and to make a chymney therin and all other thynges necessary therto longynge'.[8] The list of stores belonging to the Wardens of the works

[1] Penshurst MS. 123.  [2] *Cal. of Patent R.* 545.

[3] Of the constantly alleged use of ship timber in ancient building the only documentary evidence I have found is at Dover in 1227, when 43*s*. was paid 'for an old ship bought for the planking of the turret': E. 462, 10.

[4] Penshurst MS. 236.  [5] E. 502, 23.

[6] *Cal. of Close R.* 352.

[7] App. B.  [8] Add. Chart. 48701.

of London Bridge in 1350 includes timber for 14 shops, fully wrought and framed for immediate building, valued at £36.[1]

When the timbers were assembled for framing they were marked by the carpenter, so that the workmen would know where each of the more important timbers was to go. In most medieval roofs the assembly marks are still visible on the trusses, the tie-beam and its principals bearing the same mark; and these are usually continuous, the timbers of the first truss having one cut, the second two, and so on.[2]

When the timbers had been worked and framed and assembled on the building site, the next step was the actual setting up, or 'rearing', of the frame. For this work, involving the hauling of heavy timbers and their nice adjustment, extra hands would usually be required. So, in a contract for building an annex to the Blue Boar at Salisbury in 1444, we find the employer undertaking to provide two men for seven days at the 'reryng' of the house.[3] In 1307 the authorities at Merton College paid to John the Carpenter 5s. 'for the feeding (*mensa*) of those who set up the new chambers', and another 2s. 'for workmen helping to set up timber during two days and a half'.[4] And in 1420 the churchwardens of St. Michael's, Bath, dispensed the more modest sum of 2d. 'for drink at the reryng of the house at Alford';[5] while in 1437 2s. was spent on 'food and drink for various men helping to set up the chamber' at Takeley rectory, and 9d. 'for gloves for the carpenters at the time of the setting up'.[6]

When the house was small there is some reason to think that all the timbers of the two ends (short of the roof) would be assembled and pegged together and raised as a whole;[7] but in larger houses the timbers would have to be raised separately. First would come the ground-sills. To preserve these from rotting they were often set on a low wall of stone or brick. For instance a wall of 'underpynnyng', 440 feet in total length and 3 feet in height, was made for the houses which were brought, as we have seen, from Northall to Sutton.[8] And in 1357, when a new hall was made for one of the lodges at Clipston, there was a 'groundwall' of stone 5 feet in height, the rest of the building being of timber.[9] Just a century later we find John Loose paid at Cambridge 'for setting stones under the groundsillys'.[10]

[1] Riley, *Mems. of London*, 261.
[2] For an early and apparently unique use of Arabic numerals see *Sussex Arch. Coll.* lxv. 66.
[3] App. B.  [4] Merton Rolls, 3635.
[5] *Somerset Arch. Soc.* xxiii. 27.  [6] Mins. Accts. 917, No. 18.
[7] e.g. at Peterborough in 1541—'to Robert Hackman the wryght for reryng up the govyl end (gable)': *Northants. Rec. Soc.* ix. 151.
[8] See above, p. 199.  [9] E. 460, 17.  [10] Peterhouse Roll, 1456-7.

These Peterhouse Rolls also contain other references to *'pynnyng fact'* sub *grunsole'* (1375), and *'pynnyng de la growncell'* (1442) which probably refer to such stonework, though some of the frequent mentions of 'pinning' and 'underpinning' merely refer to the driving in of wedges under the sill to correct irregularities.[1] When the sills were laid directly on the ground it would first be levelled and beaten down, a process usually included in the term 'groundsilling', found—under a variety of spellings—in many building accounts; at Cambridge in 1375 we have a definite reference to 'two rammeres employed for two days under the grunseles' of a new building.[2] Occasionally this treatment was not sufficient, as for instance at Ashell, where in 1530 payment was made 'for grownsyllyng of the old stable at Canons (Farm) and for prysyng up of yt and settyng stulpys of ock in the ground to bere the grownsylles by cause the grounde was not sure'.[3] The term 'sowlbasyng', equivalent to groundsilling, occurs at Peterborough in 1523.[4]

When the groundsills were in place the tenons of the principal posts were inserted in their mortices; but Moxon,[5] writing in the last quarter of the seventeenth century, notes that, in order to leave plenty of play for the insertion of the summers and other beams, the principals and sills were not at once pegged together but were temporarily held together with 'hook-pins'. These were long tapering wooden pins, shaped rather like a tent-peg, so that they could not be driven in too far and could easily be loosened and withdrawn. At Scarborough in 1423 we find 'j qᵃtron of wood for hokepynnes for carpenters' supplied;[6] and in 1532 ash timber was used 'for hock pynnes for the carpenters' at Westminster.[7] The wooden pins with which the tenons were secured in their mortices when the frame was eventually closed were sometimes called 'trashnails',[8] but more often they figure in the accounts simply as pegs (*caville*) and are indistinguishable from the tile-pins, to which the same term was applied.

The horizontal beams into which the tenons at the upper ends of the posts were morticed were known by a variety of names. One of the commonest terms was 'wall-plates', which applied equally whether these beams, carrying the timbers of the roof, were supported by the posts or by walls

---

[1] Cf. a payment to carpenters for *'suppodia et wegges ad suppodiendum cameram'* at Gloucester Castle in 1280: E. 463, 26. So also at Bath in 1474 'spykenaylles' were provided for the 'undersettyng' of a tenement: *Somerset Arch. Soc.* xxv. 69.

[2] Peterhouse Roll.        [3] E. 458, 3.        [4] Receivers' Acct.

[5] *Mechanick Exercises*, 136.        [6] E. 482, 8.        [7] T.R., f. 159.

[8] e.g. in 1532 'traysshe nayles' were made by a carpenter at Westminster at 20d. the thousand: T.R., f. 313.

of brick or stone. Thus at Drysellan in 1306 a mason was paid 'for breaking the wall of the castle beside the bakehouse—making it exactly level (*equalem per liuellum*) with the new wall of the bakehouse to put walplates on it':[1] and at Westminster in 1346 there is reference to 'a piece of timber called plate, 20 feet long and 3 feet broad, lying in (*infra*) the wall under the roof, on which various beams are set and fixed'.[2] In the contract made in 1445 for roofs to the chapter-house and dorter at Stamford Priory reference is made to 'walplates and syde trees'.[3] Here the term wall-plates is confined to the beams going across the ends of the building; and similarly in the Salisbury contract of the previous year a distinction is made between 'walplates' and 'sideresons'.[3] 'Reson' (A.S. *raesn*, a beam) is another term applied, in various forms, to these beams.[4] Thus at Harlech in 1286 four beams called 'rasewepeces' [*sic*], 20 feet in length, were used for a new bakehouse;[5] a piece of timber was supplied for 'le resen' of the porch of the Constable's hall at the Tower in 1348;[6] in a contract of 1369 for shops in London the 'resnes' are distinguished from the '*plates pour la frount*'.[3] At Boston in 1452 there is mention of 'sydewyvers'[7]—'wiver' being an old word for a beam, which occurs in 1341, in a note of the expenditure of 3 long bars of iron and a piece of Spanish iron, half an ell long, 'for binding the great *wyure* in the Eagle Tower' at Carnarvon Castle.[8] Pan (Fr. *panne*) is also found, apparently in the sense of wall-plate. The Canons of St. Margaret of Marlborough were given, towards the erection of their belfry in 1234, 4 postes 4 *sullivas* (groundsills) 4 *pannas* and 20 *cheverones* (= rafters);[9] and the timber supplied next year for buildings at Kempton and Hereford included in each instance 2 *pannas*.[10] Similarly in 1306, when the chapel in Pevensey Castle was rebuilt, 2 pannes, 4 beams, and 4 posts were provided.[11] The repeated occurrence of pans in pairs[12] suggests that the term was applied to the side-plates, those at the ends being probably included under the description of beams (*trabes*); and this is borne out by a list of timbers bought in 1284 for a bakehouse at Scarborough Castle, in which we find 'one pannepece of oak, 40 ft. long,—4s.; one pannepece of alder (*eller*) of the same length—2s.,' the cross-beams, of which there were five, being 16 feet in length.[13] Even more definite is the evidence from

[1] E. 486, 18.

[2] E. 470, 16. A 'plate' of identical measure was among the stores at Westminster in 1333: E. 469, 11.    [3] App. B.

[4] e.g. 'raysynys' in the Peterhouse Roll 1415–16.    [5] E. 485, 29.

[6] E. 471, 1.    [7] Penshurst MS. 20.    [8] Pipe R. 5 Edw. III.

[9] *Cal. of Close R.* 16.    [10] Ibid. 199, 347.    [11] E. 479, 16.

[12] The exception, the canons' belfry, was presumably square.    [13] E. 482, 1.

Knaresborough in 1303, when four carpenters were employed in making and setting up the feet of the rafters in the great chamber and in placing new *pannes* under them.[1] 'Ele (= elm) pannys' and 'panpesys' both occur at Farnham in 1472,[2] and the form 'pantres' is found at Somerton in 1360,[3] and at Clipston in 1362.[4] A less common term is 'filet', which is explained by an entry in the 1237 account for Marlborough Castle—'for making one filet (*filetto*) and placing it on the wall over the king's private chamber, and for lengthening the rafters, which were perished and rotten, as far as the filet of the same chamber, and for making gutters and corbels'.[5] At Corfe in 1285 there is a purchase of great beams '*ad philettas et ad gistias* (joists)'.[6] As the wall-plate was often formed of two parallel beams, with a space between them, I think the filet may have been the external plate.[7]

When the building was of more than one story the beams between the principal posts, marking the divisions and carrying the floors and other similar cross-beams, were usually called 'summers', or sometimes 'dormants', equivalent to the modern term 'sleepers'. Thus in work at Trinity Hall, Cambridge, in 1374, we have a reference to '*summeres sive dormannes*';[8] at Berwick in 1373, 'three great joists (*gistis*) called dormandes';[9] at Ripon in 1396 John Wryght was paid 9*d.* for a day and a half's work in making a 'dormand' in the stable;[10] and at King's Hall in 1414 'a great beam called a dormaunt, 2 pendauntys and 2 brasys' were bought for 26*s.* 8*d.*[11]—the dormant in this instance being evidently a free-lying beam supported at either end by a bracket formed of a pendant, or short post resting on a corbel, and a brace. 'Bemes that lyen by hemself', as they are called at Queens' College in 1448,[8] are also called 'laces'; as at Harlech in 1286, where 2 beams called 'laz', 14 feet in length, are mentioned,[12] and at Corfe, where 6 pieces of timber were used for 'laces' for a bridge in 1356.[13] At Scarborough in 1284 they appear in the Latin form *laquei*,[14] which we may compare with the *laqueare*, translated in fifteenth-century vocabularies as 'post-band' or 'post bondde'.[15]

In a building of small span the joists of the floors might be carried straight across from wall-plate to wall-plate, but for anything over, say, 15-foot

---

[1] E. 465, 29.  [2] E. 463, 13.  [3] E. 484, 15.
[4] E. 460, 18.  [5] E. 476, 3.  [6] E. 460, 27.
[7] Filets are sometimes merely strips of wood: '*pro fylettis ligneis expenditis in factura de le lateys*': E. 503, 11.  [8] App. B.  [9] E. 483, 2.
[10] R. 125.  [11] K.H. 6, 57.  [12] E. 485, 29.
[13] E. 461, 1.  [14] E. 482, 1.
[15] Wright, *Vocabularies*, 668, 777. The '*lacertos et brachia*', supplied with other timber for work at Hereford in 1233 (*Close R.* 437), were probably laces and braces.

span it was customary to insert one or more summers to carry the joists, which would then run longitudinally. The joists might either be morticed into the summers and endplates or be laid on top of them. Horman says: 'The carpenter or wryght hath layde the summer bemys from wall to wall and the ioystis a crosse';[1] and in 1357 corbels were inserted in a wall at Nottingham Castle '*ad supponendum someras subtus gistas arearum*'.[2] The method of laying the joists over the summers was particularly employed when the upper floor was intended to project beyond the lower. This form of construction was popular in the Middle Ages and still lends an additional touch of picturesqueness, at the expense of sunlight, to the narrow streets of many towns on the Continent, where such houses have survived more frequently than in England. The contract of 1405 for shops in Bucklersbury definitely states that the first floor 'shall jut (*gettabit*)' on the north and south, the second floor only on the north,[3] but usually the jutting seems to have been taken as a matter of course, or else left to the discretion of the builder. It was a feature that did not make for stability, and Horman[4] remarks that 'Buyldynge chargydde with iotyes is parellous when it is very olde'. The ends of the joists projecting beyond the summer carry, in their turn, another summer beam, which seems sometimes to have been called a 'coiffetre'—such a beam being mentioned in a contract of 1369 as lying over the joists and carrying the 'poncheons', or studs, of the upper wall-framing.[3] The only other reference to this term that I have found is at Southwark in 1403, when timber was bought for 'resonpeces and coyfshydes'.[5]

The smaller timbers which constituted the framing of the walls between the posts, sills, and plates were usually called 'studs' and the three processes for completing the walls were studding, wattling, and daubing. Thus the churchwardens of St. Michael's at Bath record a payment in 1478 '*pro stodyng frethyng* (= wattling) *et dawbyng j poynyn* (= gable)'.[6] At Corfe 30 small timbers were bought '*ad studas in muro terre*' in 1285[7] and 'stodes' or 'stothes' occur constantly in building accounts. Amongst the timber bought in 1284 for a bakehouse and brewhouse at Scarborough Castle were '27 stodes, 14 ft. in length, for gables and walls',[8] and the same list includes various 'postelles' of 15, 8, and 4 feet, which were practically the same thing. They also occur as 'punchons' (for instance at the Tower in

---

[1] *Vulgaria*, c. xxix.       [2] E. 478, 4.       [3] App. B.
[4] loc. cit.       [5] E. 502, 24.
[6] *Somerset Arch. Soc.* xxv. 77. Cf. '*pro dicto tenemento studdando et breydando*': ibid, 64.
[7] E. 460, 27.       [8] E. 482, 1.

1348, and at Clarendon in 1400), 'punsuns' or 'pounsouns' (Westminster 1259 and 1324); and as 'stanchons' (Gravesend 1367) or 'stanzons' (York 1434).[1] Since the seventeenth century these terms have been superseded by 'quarters', a term which is occasionally found earlier, as for instance in the churchwardens' accounts of St. Mary-atte-Hill, London, in 1478— 'for vj quarters for the walle',[2]—and ten years later 'for v quarters for traunsones',[3] which are usually the cross-bars of windows but may here mean horizontal framing-pieces. Still earlier, '2 pieces of timber, 8 ft. long, called quarters' were among the stores at Westminster in 1333.[4]

The construction of timber-framed buildings may be illustrated by the complete accounts for the erection of two such buildings. The first was part of the college of King's Hall, afterwards absorbed into Trinity College, Cambridge, in 1338. This seems from the first entries to have been entirely rebuilt on an existing stone foundation:[5]

For stone for repairing the foundation—8s.

4 quarters of lime for the foundation and for repairing all the walls with mortar —at 10d. the quarter.

60 cartloads of mud for the walls and for the floor of the solar, at 2½d.

6 pieces of timber for groundsulles for the length of the building, each piece 24 ft. in length, at 14d. each.

4 pieces for the breadth, each of 16 ft., at 10d.

14 ,, ,, postis, at 17¼d.

104 ,, ,, stothes (= studs), at 2¼d.

36 ,, ,, bendes (? diagonal braces), at 1½d.

12 ,, ,, peytreles,[6] each 12 ft. long, at 4d.

6 pieces for rasens, at 2s. 2d.

110 ,, the rafters (*tignis*), each of 16 ft., at 2d.

7 ,, ,, bemes, at 12d.

— ,, ,, laces,—2s.

3 pieces for a herne,[7]—2s.

3 ,, somers for the solar, at 2s. 2d.

66 ,, gistes (= joists) for the solar, 12 ft. long, at 2½d.

124 pieces of assch for splynttes for the walls, at 2d.

1500 stonlatth (= laths for stone slates), at 10d. the hundred.

2000 sapelatth, at 3s. 4d. the thousand.

140 Estrigesbordes (= Baltic boards) for 6 doors, 10 shutters (*fenestris*), and 6 speres (= screens), at 2d.

---

[1] At Penshurst in 1470 a notice of 'stanchenyng' the end wall of a barn: Penshurst MS. 123.　　[2] *Memorials* (E.E.T.S.), 85.　　[3] Ibid. 137.　　[4] E. 469, 11.
[5] E. 348, 1.　　　　　　　　　　　　　　　　　　　　[6] Possibly bressummers.
[7] Probably the ridge-piece. It may be connected with O.E. hern- or harn-pan.

12 pieces of timber for peytrels, at 4d.[1]
148 bordes of popeler (= poplar) for the solar and for the solar stairs, at 1½d.

|  | li. | s. | d. |
|---|---|---|---|
| Wages of various sawyers, by agreement . . . . . | 4. | 2. | 0 |

Paid to various workmen working on and tiling (*cooperiantibus*) the said building and 2 porches with steps (*greces*), the workmen finding stone, lime and sand therefor, by agreement . . . 4. 10. 0

Wages of various workmen making the walls and the floor of the solar, by a fixed agreement . . . . . . . 16s. 0

12,000 latthnail, at 10d. the thousand.
2,000 spikyng, at 3s. 4d. ,,
4,000 bordenail, at 2s. 1d. ,,
12 henges and 12 hokes for 6 doors at 6¾d. (the set)—6s. 9d.
6 locks, at 4s.
6 thorughdryuell[2] of iron, at 3d.
2 cartloads of straw for making mortar with—2s.
30 pillers (= mullions) for 10 windows, at ½d.
6 crampes of iron for fastening beams to posts, at 4d.
6 iron rings for 6 doors, at 2d.
4 pieces of timber to carry two stairs, at 6d.
3 stothes to carry the rafters (*tigna*) of the porch over the stairs at 2½d.
8 rafters for the same porch, 13 ft. long, at 1½d.
3 pieces of timber for braces (*bras'*) to carry the stairs beyond (*ultra*) the two doors, at 3d.

| | li. | d. | | li. | s. | d. |
|---|---|---|---|---|---|---|
| TOTAL— | 23. | 19½ | Whereof, in timber | 7. | 10. | 2½; |
| | | | in stone, lime, mud and straw | | 25. | 10d; |
| | | | in laths and boards | | 59. | 4d; |
| | | | in nails, fastenings, rings and locks with keys of iron | | 38. | 3d; |
| | | | in wages of carpenters, sawyers and plasterers— | 9. | 8. | – |

It is not easy to get an exact picture of the building from these details. Three groundsills on each side give us a length of 72 feet, with which 'six peytreles' agree, and two sill-pieces at each end give a breadth of 32 feet. From their price the 'somers' and 'rasens' may well have been about 32–35 feet in length, and 55 couple of rafters would agree well enough with a length of 72 feet; but if the rafters were only 16 feet the roof must have

[1] Possibly repeated in error.
[2] Possibly bolts: a 'dryvell' is usually a drill or boring-tool.

been of remarkably low pitch. It is not clear whether the solar ran the whole length of the building, but taking the joists at about 8 inches broad with 8 inches between them—about the average, as shown by various contracts—the 66 joists would cover three bays, their ends resting on a bressumer and the three 'somers of the solar', of which the third presumably supported a partition wall, giving a total length for the solar of a little over 36 feet. Presumably, therefore, half the building was a hall, open from ground-level to roof, and the other half was in two stories.

Our second example is the shire-house[1] which was built at Ipswich in 1442:

| | li. | s. | d. |
|---|---|---|---|
| 13000 waltyll (= bricks), at 4s. the thousand | 52. | – | |
| 13000 tiles for roofing the house, at 4s. 6d. | 58. | 6. | |
| 2 pieces of great timber for dormands of the house, 30 ft. in length | 53. | 4. | |
| 39 pieces of timber for gistes, 13 ft. long, at 12d. | 39. | – | |
| 8 pieces of timber for grounsell | 20. | – | |
| 64 ,, ,, ,, ,, stothes, 10 ft. long, at 12d. | 64. | – | |
| various pieces of timber for sull' | 20. | – | |
| 4 principal beams (*trabibus*), 30 ft. long, at 13s. 4d. | 53. | 4. | |
| 52 pieces for sparres, 24 ft. long, at 3s. 4d. | 8. 13. | 4. | |
| 26 ,, ,, wyndebemes, at 4d. | 8. | 8. | |
| 20 ,, ,, 2 gabul' and the 2 upper windows[2] | 20. | – | |
| timber for stairs | 5. | – | |
| plaunchebord for planking the house | 25. | – | |
| 9 waynscotbord for the door and shutters (*fenestris*) | 3. | – | |
| timber for the seats of the Justices and clerks, and for forms and the bar (*barrura*) and for a pair of stocks in the prison | 30. | – | |
| 1300 laths, both for the roof (*domate*) and for lathing the walls | 13. | – | |
| freston (= freestone) for the door and 2 windows | 9. | – | |
| 60 cartloads of pebbles (*calyon*) for the walls | 50. | – | |
| 1500 splentes for the daubing of the walls | 13. | 4. | |
| 74 cartloads of clay for the same, at 4d. | 24. | 8. | |
| 1 fother of lead for gutters | 6. – | – | |
| 1200 nails | 6. | – | |
| 9000 lathnayl, at 2s. 6d. the thousand | 22. | 6. | |
| 16 hooks (*gumphis*) and 16 doorbands (*vertivellis*) for the door and shutters | 8. | 4. | |
| 3 masons, at 5d. a day, for 40 days | 66. | 8. | |

---

[1] E. 575, 28.

[2] Or, more probably, shutters, as these seem to be the windows for which stone was provided.

PLATE 13

CONSTRUCTION OF A TIMBER–FRAMED BUILDING 15TH CENTURY

PLATE 14

BUILDING AND TILING OPERATIONS 15TH CENTURY

|  | li. | s. | d. |
|---|---|---|---|
| John Tarell, master carpenter, for 83 days . . . . . | 34. | 7. | |
| 8 carpenters at 3d.—one for 83 days, the other for 43 days . . | 96. | – | |
| 5 tilers, for 12 days . . . . . . . . | 15. | – | |
| 5 daubers, for 20 days . . . . . . . . | 25. | – | |
| 7 labourers, at 1½d. . . . . . . . . | 19. | 9 | |
| 1 plumber, by agreement . . . . . . . | 16. | – | |
| TOTAL . . . . . | 63. | 6. | – |

The first point that comes out on a comparison of these two accounts is the enormous rise in the cost of timber during the hundred years. This is borne out by other evidence, and accounts for the progressive reduction in the scantling of timbers employed in buildings and the increasing space between them. The depletion of our timber resources, which so alarmed Tudor economists, was already beginning to be felt and was producing its effect on domestic architecture. Partly as a result of this rise in the cost of materials, it is noticeable that wages account for only about 15 per cent. of the total cost at Ipswich, whereas they had accounted for about 35 per cent. at Cambridge.

## TIMBER ROOFS

THE timber roof may be regarded as a notable feature of English architecture. Although this country can show fine examples of stone vaulting in its cathedrals and great churches, the use of stone for roofing was nothing like so common here as on the Continent. On the other hand, nowhere outside England can be found such a series of magnificent timber roofs as those of which Westminster Hall, Hampton Court, and the angel roofs of East Anglia are examples. In its simplest form the framing of the timber roof consists of a series of pairs of rafters with their feet pegged to the wall-plates and their upper ends halved and pegged together. Each pair of rafters was known as a 'couple', and in the orders for timber, for the royal buildings or as gifts to religious houses, issued by Henry III such couples figure frequently. As an early instance, in 1229 the Prior of Brockley was given timber *'ad xx copulas'* to make a chamber for the reception of the king when he should pass that way.[1] Four years later, the timber ordered for constructing an almonry at Hereford was 6 posts, 2 wall-plates (*pannes*), 20 couples, and laces and braces (*lacertos et brachia*).[2] In 1250 orders were given to lengthen the queen's chamber at Gillingham by 15 couples, and beyond them to make a little chapel of 9 couples for her use.[3] The roofs being open, they also served as a convenient means of indicating distances, or divisions, in a room: so that, for instance, in 1243 King Henry ordered the Sheriff of Oxford to cause his hall at Windsor to be panelled 'to the extent of five couples beyond the king's seat'.[4] In later times they are more often defined as couples of rafters or of spars. Thus at Clarendon in 1400 there is mention of *'xlvj couplez raftres'* among other timber;[5] and in 1472 at Farnham rectory 14s. was 'payed for viij postes of oke iiij bawkys iiij panpesys and banddes langynge therto boght be grete (i.e. as one parcel) for one lath (barn)', and 3s. 9d. 'for xv copyll of sparrys boght at Wynnysley for ye said lath—price of one copyll iij<sup>d</sup>'.[6]

In order to give the couples stability they were usually pegged together by a horizontal beam at about a third of their length from the ridge. Such

---

[1] *Close R.* 269.  [2] Ibid. 347.  [3] *Liberate R.* 34 Hen. III, m. 5.
[4] Ibid. 28 Hen. III.  [5] E. 502, 15.
[6] E. 463, 13. The 'banddes' are presumably braces from the posts to the wall-plates and transverse balks.

a beam, now usually called a collar, was formerly termed a wind-beam. 'Wyndbemes' occur, for instance, at Westminster in 1373[1] and at Cambridge in 1433;[2] at Somerton in 1360 the timber bought included 60 'wyndbalkes' at one penny each,[3] and 'wyndebawes' occur at Clipston in 1362.[4] Further rigidity was given by struts from the lower part of each rafter to the collar-beam; these, when they are not indefinitely termed braces, are presumably the 'sous-laces' which occur, in a variety of spellings, among lists of roof timbers. Moreover, while the feet of the rafters were carried down to the outside edge of the wall-plate, upright studs known as ashlars were set at the inner edge of the wall-plates, their upper ends being morticed into the rafters. It is a roof of this usual type that is implied in the contract made in 1374 for Trinity Hall, Cambridge, the carpenter undertaking to provide the necessary oak timber—'*videlicet copulas sive sparres, wyndbems, suthlaces, aschelers, corbels, jowpes, balkes, summers sive dormannes, giystes et etiam stures pro mediis parietibus in dictis cameris*'.[5] Here the first four items are the constituents of the roof-framing; the 'jowpes' are cornices, the corbels are massive blocks of wood let into the wall to carry the balks, into which the joists of the floor—the building being of two stories—are framed, and the 'stures' are the upright stakes of the wattle-and-daub partition walls. In the 1448 contract for buildings at Queens' College the 'sparres' are to be 7 in. by 6 in. at the foot and 6 in. by 5 in. at the top, and 'all the sowthelases and the asshelers shall accord in brede with the sparres and on the other part thes shall be iiij inches squar; and all the wynbemes shall conteyne in brede squar vj inches and in the other part v inches'.[5] So also, in the Bucklersbury contract of 1405, the 'upright roof' of the hall is to be made 'suitably and handsomely with soulaces, assheler and jowpeces, with an archecouple in the middle of the hall to support the roof'.[5]

In this last instance we have a development of the framed common rafter roof, the central pair of rafters being of larger scantling and supported by curved braces, forming a pointed arch. Such braces are mentioned in 1375 at Gravesend as 'archebras',[6] and at York in 1434 as 'archbandes'.[7] It became a common form of construction to concentrate the support of the roof on a certain number of more massive couples, known as 'principals',[8] connected longitudinally by 'purlins', which in turn carried the common

---

[1] E. 469, 13.  [2] K.H. 8, f. 111.  [3] E. 484, 15.
[4] E. 460, 18.  [5] App. B.
[6] E. 544, 3.  [7] Y.F.R. 53.
[8] Timber sawn 'for principalles and spares (i.e. spars)' at Kirby Muxloe in 1483: *Leics. Arch. Soc.* xi. 322.

rafters, and it was also usual for the rafters to be morticed into a longitudinal 'ridgepiece' instead of being pegged together, as in earlier roofs.
The additional pressure put upon the wall-plates at the points where these
principals were attached was counteracted by inserting massive tie-beams[1]
extending across the building from one wall-plate to the other. These are
referred to by such general terms as beams and balks, and also as 'interties'
—as at Westminster in 1333, 'eleven great pieces of timber called entreteyses', each 37 feet long and 4 feet round,[2] and at Hedon in 1424, 'a beam
called entretasse',[3] and 'liernes'—as at Porchester in 1338, '2 bymes, 2
walplates, 2 liernes, 24 rafters (*cheverons*) 36 ft. in length, 4 laces', &c.[4] and
at Merton College in 1312, 'for setting liernes and beams (*tigna*) in the
chamber'.[5]

While the tie-beam held the walls together pretty effectually, its length
and bulk gave it a tendency to sag. Additional support was afforded by
placing under it at either end a post, resting on a corbel, usually of stone
but sometimes of wood, lower in the wall, with a brace morticed into the
lower end of the post and the under surface of the tie-beam. These posts
were called 'pendants'. Thus at Ely in 1360 oaks were provided to make
'postes pendauntz' and others for long 'brases',[6] and for King's Hall 'a
great beam called dormaunt, 2 pendauntys and 2 brasys' were bought
from Smyth of Braintree for 26s. 8d. in 1414.[7] The whole formed a
'bracket'—as at Peterhouse in 1375, 'for 2 braces and 2 brackets'[8]—and the
spandrels were usually filled with cusping or more elaborate tracery. Frequently a stud, or post, almost always worked as a pillar with base and
capital, was set on the centre of the tie-beam and attached by braces to the
principals and the ridgepiece. Such a stud was called a 'mountant'. Thus
the timber in store at Westminster in 1333 included '10 pieces of timber
called polrenes' (probably a blundered form of 'purlin'), and 6 pieces called
'mountaynes';[9] 'mountauns' occur at Porchester in 1329,[10] and in the contract of 1369 for shops in London the 'lyernes' are to be 6 inches thick and
8 inches broad 'and mountans and braces for the lyernes good and sufficient'. A later development of roof construction, chiefly used in such
buildings as barns, was, instead of the central king-post to set on the tie-
beam two uprights framed into a collar-beam, which was then set lower

---

[1] 'Byndyng bemes' at Gloucester in 1483: App. B; and at Bath in 1464: *Somerset Arch. Soc.* xxv. 62.

[2] E. 469, 11.    [3] Boyle, *Hist. of Hedon*, clviii.    [4] E. 479, 18.

[5] Merton Roll 4071.    [6] *Sacrist Rolls*, 193.    [7] K.H. 6, f. 57.

[8] P. 1375. Cf. in 1410, 'for 2 brakettes': K.H. 8, f. 111.

[9] E. 469, 11.    [10] Pipe R. 3 Edw. III.

than the normal collar. Such uprights are now called queen-posts, but it is improbable that they were distinguished in medieval terminology, and I have found no references definitely assignable to this type.

The normal roof may be taken to be composed of wall-plates, tie-beams, principals, purlins, common rafters, collars, and ridge-pieces. The principals are sometimes called 'couples', which we have seen originally applied to all pairs of rafters, and houses are occasionally defined by the number of couples, or bays, which they contain—as in a lease made at Henley-in-Arden in 1446, when the lessee undertook to build a hall containing two couples.[1] Similarly at Dunster in 1413 Thomas Touker was admitted to a vacant burgage on condition that he should, within the next two years, build a new house with one couple and two 'inschydes' (i.e. gables).[2] At Bury St. Edmunds in 1439 the roof of St. John's Church was to be 'wrought of vj pryncepal couplys archebounden', of which each spar was to be 10 inches broad and 8 thick, and between each two principals a purlin, a jope, and 4 spars, each 7 in. by 3 in., and 'havyng a rof tre (ridge-piece) abovyn', the principals, purlins, and jopes being 'convenably embowyd', that is to say, bevelled to an arch section.[3] Similarly the roof to be made at Queens' College in 1449 was to have 5 tie-beams 'with jopees from beam to beam', principals 11 in. by 10 in., common rafters 8 in. by 7 in. at the foot and 7 in. by 5 in. at the top, purlins from one principal to another, and a 'crown tree' 9 in. by 8 in.[3] Of the two roofs for Stamford Priory contracted for in 1445,[3] that of the chapter-house was to be 63 ft. long by 24 ft. wide and was to be of 'vj bemes vj wyndbemes vj principals xxvj cople sparres, with walplates and side trees, with brases from the principals to the said side trees'. This gives five bays, each containing five spars—probably the number of the spars should have been 25—and would allow of their being set about 10 inches apart. The roof of the dorter was of the same breadth, 24 feet, but 138 feet long, and was to contain 'xij grete bemes xij principals xij wyndbemes lxvj cople sperres', with wallplates and braces. Here we have 11 bays of 6 spars, which would allow a similar spacing, 10 inches being the normal interval at this time.

No difference is made in description or in constitution between the free-standing trusses and those at the end of the buildings, constituting the gables. In a Gloucester contract of 1483 it is stipulated that the 'pynnyons' are to be 'of standard worke',[3] which I take to mean that they are to be constructed of upright studs framed into the summer and the principals.

---

[1] Anct. Deeds (P.R.O.), A. 8362.    [2] Lyte, *Hist. of Dunster*, i. 288.
[3] App. B.

It may be observed that various forms of the French *pignon* occur in the south-western counties for what is almost invariably called a gable else-where.[1] The churchwardens of St. Michael's, Bath, account for 4 planks of elm for the 'punyon' in 1460,[2] and for 'stodyng frethyng and dawbyng j poynyn' in 1478';[3] at Launceston there are payments in 1460 for the 'framyng and joynyng of a ponyon between the hall of the old Receipt and the high chamber'; and at Lostwithiel carpenters were employed setting two 'resteris' on the 'ponyon' of the hall in 1455.[4] Similarly the Bath churchwardens' accounts for 1425 include 6*d*. 'for a couple of resters for the wyndbarge of the new chapel'.[5] This term occurs as early as 1238 at Marlborough, when 4*s*. 6*d*. was paid '*ad winbargias faciendas*' at the two ends of the great hall,[6] while as late as 1532 there is a payment to carpen-ters at Westminster 'for hewing, entaylling (carving), framyng and rearer-ing [*sic*] of one payre of barge cooples, fixed at the ende of the Galorye'.[7] The word 'barge' is connected with 'verge', and the term 'barge-boards' is still applied to the carved and decorated boards which form the trimming of the projecting hood of a gable, such a hood being presumably what is implied by the word 'windbarge'.

So far we have been dealing with open roofs, but there were also roofs of which the constitutional features were not visible from the floor of the building. Those constructed above stone vaults need not delay us, as they were wrought on the same principles as the open roofs with which we have been dealing, as may be gathered from the names of the timbers employed in the roof over the nave of Westminster Abbey.[8] But there were others in which such members as the tie-beams were visible but the rafters, braces, and so forth were hidden by a ceiling of boards or plaster. Such a roof appears to have been called a 'false roof', as in a list of repairs done at the Tower in 1532 we read, 'In the Kynges closet a falce roffe made above hede to batton upon',[9] 'a falce flower (i.e. the ceiling or under-side of the floor) made in the chambre where Kyng Henry the VIIth lay in, for the battons to be framed unto over hed';[10] and in later entries, 'the roffe new playstered, wt. whytyng betwene the battons', and 'in the cownseill chamber in the rownde tower, the whytyng betwene the battons, wt.

---

[1] We do, however, find 'ponyons' in a Tattershall account of 1440: Penshurst MS. 238.
[2] *Somerset Arch. Soc.* xxv. 56.  [3] Ibid. 77.
[4] E. 461, 18. 'Restour', for rafter, is found at Salisbury in 1444: App. B; and 'resters et walplates' at Clarendon in 1477: E. 460, 14.
[5] *Somerset Arch. Soc.* xxiv. 32.  [6] E. 476, 3.  [7] T.R., f. 510.
[8] Rackham, *The Nave of Westminster* (Proc. Brit. Acad. iv), 36.
[9] Bayley, *Tower of London*, App. xx.  [10] Ibid. xxii.

stoppyng betwene the joysts'.[1] In 1508 Sir Thomas Lucas records the making of 'two windows in my fause rofe' at Little Saxham.[2] (On the other hand, the 'false roof of elm' over certain unfinished buildings at Thornbury Castle in 1521[3] may only imply a temporary structure.) A 'bastardrofe' is mentioned at Sutton in 1400,[4] but the fine ceiled roof which still remains in the University Library at Cambridge is called by the less equivocal term 'a double roof' in the contract of 1465 for its construction.[5] In this there are 6 'right bemes', or tie-beams, between which run longitudinally 3 'crosse dormauntes' which, with the 'joppys', or cornice, support the joists, eight inches broad and the same distance apart, and on the joists are laid planks of an inch in thickness. The beams are supported by brackets, with a carved figure of an angel (so called in the contract but more resembling a don in fact) at the foot of each 'pendaunte'. Above the ceiling each beam carries a king-post, here called a 'lierne stud', braced into the spars and the 'crownetree', and on either side of the king-post is a 'punchion' supporting a purlin. As the roof was to be covered with lead the pitch is low, only 3 ft. 6 in. from the beam to the ridge, and the rafters, which are uniform and not distinguished as principals and common rafters, are massive, being 8 in. by 6 in. at the foot and 6 in. by 5 in. at the top. The contract shows that the lower members of this roof—beams, joists, and planks— were practically a duplicate of the ceiling floor separating this room from the one below it. In fact, the division between two stories may be considered as either a floor or a roof, and the medieval builders seem to have felt the confusion. In the King's Hall accounts for 1528 we have: 'Bargaynyd wt. Thomas Loveday for makyng ij floyrs (*altered to* one floyr and a roffe) of the tower, fyndyng tymber bord and warkmanshype—viij[li]'.[6] In the Stamford Priory contract the chapter-house is to have 'a low flore— contenyng vij someres and lx trasons (cross-beams, equivalent to joists)'. Here 'low floor' is evidently to identify it as a floor at ground-level, and by way of contrast we find a carpenter at Woodstock in 1435 making 'le myddelflore',[7] and similarly in 1460 payments 'for shaping and making the timber for le medell flore of the tower called le Gayle' in Launceston Castle.[8] Roofs intended to be covered with lead were usually of low pitch and often almost as flat as floors, particularly on the towers of castles, where they were intended to be used by the garrison. So at Odiham in 1366 we have the upper chamber of the tower remade with a 'platrof

[1] Bayley, *Tower of London*, App. xxvi.    [2] Gage, *Thingoe Hundred*, 144.
[3] *L. & P. Henry VIII*, iii. 1286.    [4] E. 502, 15.    [5] App. B.
[6] K.H. 24, f. 76.    [7] E. 499, 3.    [8] E. 461, 20.

for laying lead upon'.[1] A similar roof is implied in the orders given in 1244 for the building at Westminster of a chamber for the use of the knights 'without couples', to be covered with lead: an additional reason for keeping this roof low being 'that the view of the windows of the great hall be not interfered with'.[2]

During the fifteenth century the boarded or ceiled roof became increasingly popular, and in many instances roofs of this type were elaborately decorated with carvings of foliage or figures at the junctions of the beams and battens by which the ceiling was divided into panels. The larger of these carved blocks were known as bosses or keys, like the carved stones at the intersection of stone vaulting ribs, and were sometimes like them constructional; the smaller were called knots and were merely superficial decorations. For the wooden vault of the lantern at Ely in 1337 we have payments 'to a turner (*tornatori*) for turning the boces for the vault', 'to John Roke for carving (*talliando*) a key (*clave*) for the upper vault', and to John de Burwelle 'for carving a figure on le principale keye of the upper vault—2s. and his food'.[3] At Eltham in 1402 carpenters were making 'cylor bord batentz and keys for cyling the parlour';[4] and next year 40 'bottomholtbord' were bought to make 'keyes' and Peter Davyn, carver, was paid 18*d*. apiece 'for kervyng 68 keys for cylyng the King's chamber, namely, 44 angels with shields (*escuchons*) and 12 archangels with scrolls in their hands, and 24 dimy keys'.[5] There was a further payment for 'coal burnt for the gluing (*conclutinacione*) of the keyes called angels and archangels'. In 1425 another such ceiling was being put up at Eltham, carpenters being again paid for making and putting up 'cilebord and batentz' and for making 10 'keyes' to be fixed onto the 'celor'.[6] Ten years later at Shene wainscots were used 'for making various keys scocheons and batand' for the ceiling (*sillur'*) of various rooms'.[7] A list of materials in store for use in the royal manors in 1473[8] mentions '90 knottes of estrich (i.e. Eastland boards), not yet fully worked, with anteloppes and swannes, hertes, hyndes and various other beasts, 67 di' knottes (i.e. half-knots) of estrich, not yet fully worked, with branches of trees—20 corner knottes of estrich—9 knottes of estrich with roses and suns, greater and less, fully worked',[9] and '*xlii harborowes de estr' pro nodis fiendis*', of which the exact

[1] E. 478, 28.       [2] Liberate R. 28 Hen. III.
[3] *Sacrist Rolls*, 97.       [4] E. 502, 23.       [5] E. 502, 24.
[6] E. 496, 7.       [7] E. 496, 8.       [8] E. 503, 19.
[9] Cf. '*Willelmo Hunte pro factura ij knottes lign' integr', vj knottes lign' voc' di' knottes et iiij knottes lign' voc' corner knottes . . . expend' in factura et silluracione nove turris*', at Charing Cross in 1440: E. 503, 9.

meaning is not obvious. There is also mention of 'crestes'[1]—probably to go on the cornices and beams—worked with lions and armorial bearings and '*lxvij keies de entaile (carving) pro parlura manerii de Shene*'.

For building at Corpus Christi College, Oxford, in 1517 Roger Morwent was 'to seale the flower over the parlour with panys glued and frett with well ynbowyd batons off a yard square',[2] and for the roof of the chapel Thomas Roossell of Westminster was paid 'for the kerfyng of iiij<sup>xx</sup>xviij hoole knottes and xliij halffe knottes—a hoole knotte att xvj<sup>d</sup> the peese'.[3] At Hampton Court the ceiling of the king's chamber is divided into panels by battens, of which 243 yards were bought, at 7d. the yard. When put up these battens were brightly painted—the ground 'layd with fyne beice (blue)' and the 'antyke', or carved decoration in the Classical manner, gilt, the two 'casements' (concave mouldings) also blue, and two 'botells' (convex mouldings) 'layde with fyne whytt'. The 'joll pece', or cornice, was painted red and blue and 'therein sett grete leves gylt'.[4] On the ceiling are a number of bosses, or pendants, which were gilt and painted blue and white. The plaster panels of the ceiling, which contained '131 badges of the Kynges armys and the quenys in garlondes of antyke moldyd worke—gylte with fyne golde and byse, garnesshyde with other fyne colers (colours)', were supplied by Robert Skyngke of London, whose name looks Dutch and who is described as a 'mowlder of antykeworke'.[5] It is a fine and exceptionally early example of a type of ceiling which became very popular in later Tudor times.

Hampton Court also provides us with the only detailed account that I have found of the erection of a hammer-beam roof.[6] This is the very elaborate roof, happily still existing, in the hall. Unfortunately, although the building accounts give us a certain number of technical terms and the names of those who carried out the details, they do not tell us who designed it. The hammer-beams are carried on brackets resting on stone corbels, which are here termed 'refryses' and were carved with the king's badges and initials by John Wryght of South Mimms, at 22s. 6d. each. The posts from the corbels to the beam were let into the wall, bricklayers being employed 'hewyng of romys for the refrece postes'. The term 'pendants', which we have seen was applied to these posts in earlier times, was now given its modern sense of hanging bosses. These, which are most elaborately

---

[1] 'Flourdeliez (fleurs-de-lis) worked for crests to be put in the ceiling (*silur'*) of the chapel' at Shene occur in 1444: E. 503, 12.

[2] C.C.C. MS. 435, f. 3.          [3] Ibid., f. 53.

[4] H.C. 237, f. 406.          [5] H.C. 238, f. 303.

[6] H.C. 237; partly summarized by Law, *Hist. of Hampton Court*, i, App. C.

carved with Renaissance decoration, were the work of Richard Rydge of London; for the lowest, and most ornate, series of 'pendauntes standyng under the hammer beam'[1] he was paid £3. 3s. 4d. each;[2] for the second series, 'stondyng in the crosse mowntyn[3] above the hamer beam', 25s.; and for the third, 'in the upper purloynes (purlins)', the same. Mychell, the joiner, was responsible for the 'spandrelles to stand upon the refryses under the hammerbeames' and the other 'spandrelles standyng in the (?) purlin-basys[4] under the nether purloyns', and also for 'the Kynges and Quenys badges, standyng upon the caters' (i.e. bands of quatrefoils,[5] above the hammer-beams). There are also payments for cutting 'traylles standyng above the hamer beame, every trayle contenyng one lyght'; a 'trail' is usually a strip carved with foliage, but here it evidently refers to the quatre-foil panels just mentioned, of which the lower portion forms a cusped light. A number of entries occur of carpenters making 'lyntells' containing varying numbers of 'lyghtes', and there is one of 'vj great lyntelles for the seconde vought (vault) in the hall conteynyng xxvj lyghtes' which appears to refer to the window-like tracery rising from the collar-beam into the crest of the roof. An entry of 26 'great pyller for the chaptrelles of the bosselles of the hall' at 13d. the foot—28s. in all—I cannot explain. Finally, 2,000 'fine selyng bourddes' were provided for the 'vaught' and the whole was painted and gilded.

For the earlier roof of Westminster Hall we have an account of 1395 which gives certain details.[6] The timber was worked at 'the Frame' near Farnham, and £19. 1s. 4d. was paid 'for carriage of 26 half-beams (*xxvj di' trabes*) and 26 *pendant postes* from the Frame to Hamme on the Thames, 16 leagues, in two carts (*chariett'*) with 16 horses, making 52 journeys, at 7s. 4d. a time'. Also 26 corbels; 263 cartloads of timber at 4s., 76 at 3s. 4d., and 69 at 3s. A large number of carpenters were paid, at 6d. a day, 'for working on the roof (*domate*) of the Hall', and there are payments: to Robert Brusyngdon for the making and carving of 4 angels, each holding a shield of the king's arms, on 4 corbels in the Hall, at 26s. 8d. each—106s. 8d. To William Canon for making 4 similar angels, at 20s.—£4. To Peter Dauyn and Hubert de Villers for making 6 similar angels, at 15s.—£4. 10s. To Robert Brusyngdon for making 2 similar angels 30s. To John Fippard for carving 70 wooden lintels in the roof, at 12d.—70s. To John

---

[1] The earliest quotation for 'hammer-beam' in *O.E.D.* is 1823.

[2] Not '3s. 4d.', as in Law, loc. cit.

[3] The arched mountants rising from the hammer-beams and running at right angles to them.  [4] Law reads 'plum basys', but it appears to be 'p<sup>r</sup>lnbasys'.

[5] Willis, *Nomenclature*, 52.  [6] B.M. Add. Roll 27018.

Wotton for carving 19 wooden lintels, at 6*d*.—9*s*. 6*d*. To William Beigneny for carving 39 similar lintels—19*s*. 6*d*. To John Fippard for carving 96 lintels, at 4*d*.—32*s*. The pendant posts were the wall-posts resting on stone corbels; the wooden corbels are clearly the hammer-beams, which terminate in angels carrying shields, as described. The half-beams (if that is the correct translation) must be the curved principals, of which each pair forms an arch. The 224 lintels can hardly refer to anything except the tracery fillings above the beams, but it is difficult to understand their exact significance, or why they varied from 12*d*. to 4*d*. apiece. But it is still harder to see why the angels, all of which appear, and are stated to be, similar, should have ranged from 26*s*. 8*d*. to 15*s*.; one can only suggest that after the contracts for the first batch had been given out at the higher price, the Clerk of the Works found that he could get them done much cheaper.

An important decorative feature of the Hampton Court roof was the louver, which no longer exists. The normal position of the fire in a medieval hall being the centre of the room, it was usual to make a louver, or smoke-vent, in the roof above it and in later times this developed into an elaborate lantern, which served for decoration, ventilation, and lighting even when the central hearth had been superseded by wall fireplaces with chimneys, as in many college halls. The Hampton Court accounts for 1535 give details of the construction of the louver,[1] or 'femerell', as it is there called, which show that it was in keeping with the roof. It was of three stories, separated by 'courbes', and was hexagonal, with a 'type' or domed top. At its junction with the roof 4 'pendenttes' hung down, and these were carved, at 40*s*. the piece, by Richard Rydge, who also carved the crowned rose in the 'crowne vought of the femerell'. The bays of the first story contained 3 lights—18 in all, of which 12 were glazed—those of the second story 2, and of the third one, the glazing of which is not clearly defined. There were carved 'traylys' and mouldings, and the whole was painted and gilt. The outside was covered with lead; round it stood 4 lions, 4 dragons, and 4 greyhounds, carrying vanes, all painted and gilt, and a great lion, crowned, holding 'the great pryncipall vane baryng the close crowne'.

At the opposite extreme from this gorgeous erection we may set the 'ij smoke holys' made in William Osborne's house in Bath in 1420, at the cost of 3½*d*.'[2] In 1464 another house in Bath was thatched and a board

[1] H.C. 238, ff. 160–2; partly summarized by Law, op. cit. App. C.
[2] *Somerset Arch. Soc.* xxiii. 25.

provided 'pro la lopehole'.[1] This last was an old form, as in 1373 at Westminster '3 loupebord[2] of oak' were provided for 'louvers (*lodiis*) in the chandlery; also 14 pieces of timber called quarters, 7 ft long, for studs (*stothis*) for the windows and louvers', and '6 pieces of oak timber to make corants for the said louvers'.[3] Similarly, in 1292, 4 '*lupebord cum curantis pro coquina*' occur at Westminster,[4] and in 1275 '*iiij bordis ad louer cum viij corantis*'.[5] At the Tower in 1335 we have payments for '*ij lodiis novis et ij corantz*' for the Constable's hall.[6] Some louvers could be revolved, like cowls, according to the position of the wind, as is shown by the entries in building accounts of 1365: the first, at Moor End, being the purchase of 'a block (*massa*) of bronze on which the louver of the hall may be turned round';[7] the other, a payment of 2s. 4d. 'for a morteys of bronze weighing 7 lbs. for the louver of the small hall', at Westminster.[8] It might, therefore, seem that 'corantz' were something on which, or by which, the louvers ran round; but the fact that they were of wood is rather against this, and the word occurs in 1532 in another connexion—'for the corrants of the same frame (of 7 "houses of office" erected at the Tower) alle the hole length'[9]—the exact meaning of which is not clear. It is probably significant that in two of the instances quoted above the 'corantz' are twice the number of the louver-boards; for the boards of a louver were arranged, like the slats of a Venetian blind, so that they could be closed down or opened to the required degree, and I would suggest that the 'corantz' were the upright side-pieces in the grooves of which the horizontal louver-boards ran. References to the strings by which the boards were worked are fairly numerous. For instance, 'cord for the louver' occurs at Marlborough in 1238,[10] at Gloucester in 1280,[11] and at Hadleigh Castle in 1363.[12] The 40 lb. of 'loupcord' bought at Westminster in 1354[13] was probably for this purpose, and at Clipston 9d. was spent on 'belstrynges for the chapel and louerstrynges for the kitchen' in 1370.[14] Clipston also provides us, in 1362, with the record of the making of 'ij louerliddes'[15]—presumably movable tops to louvers—while at Cockermouth Castle in 1322 carpenters were paid 3d. '*pro amp(utatione?) vj louerchames*',[16] which may possibly mean

---

[1] *Somerset Arch. Soc.* xxv. 62.
[2] Cf. at Winchester in 1387—'*In iiij bordis pro lowpys—ijs*': Kitchin, *Obedientiary Rolls*, 414.

| | | |
|---|---|---|
| [3] E. 469, 13. | [4] E. 468, 6. | [5] E. 467, 6 (2). |
| [6] E. 469, 18. | [7] E. 544. 31. | [8] E. 472, 14. |
| [9] Bayley, *Tower of London*, xxiv. | | [10] E. 476, 3. |
| [11] E. 463, 26. | [12] E. 464, 6. | [13] E. 502, 17. |
| [14] E. 460, 20. | [15] E. 460, 18. | [16] E. 460, 25. |

the jambs, or side-pieces, referred to when discussing 'corantz'. At Clarendon in 1288 we find hinges provided for the 'hacchis' of the louver
(*fumbrell*).[1]

In 1425 disputes arose between the tilers and carpenters at York owing
to the tilers' making new 'louvers (*lodia*), called draughtlouers', for sale,
which the carpenters held to be an infringement of their craft. Five representatives of each craft appeared before the Mayor and Council, who
ordered them, literally, to kiss and be friends, and decided that in future
any tiler might make louvers, provided he paid a penny yearly towards
the carpenters' pageant; the louvers were to be inspected by the searchers
of the carpenters and to be sold at 10*d.* for the best and 8*d.* and 6*d.* for
smaller sizes, whoever made them.[2]

The latinization of 'louver' gave the medieval accountants a good deal
of trouble, or perhaps it would be more correct to say that it gave them
opportunities for extemporizing. The correct form was *lodium*,[3] and this
was occasionally used. In 1247 Henry III ordered two great *lovaria* to be
made in the Queen's chamber at Woodstock.[4] More often the word used
is intended for a derivative of *fumus*—smoke. Thus a *fumatorium* was to be
made in the hall at Windsor to carry off the smoke in 1250;[5] a great
*fumerium*, covered with lead, for the hall of Nottingham Castle next year;[6]
and a *fumerillum* at Havering the following year.[7] At Langley, in 1292,
Henry de Bouindon, carpenter, was paid 20*s.* '*pro carpentria ij fumerariorum
in summitate aule*',[8] and the form *fumerale* occurs at Moor End in 1365,[9] in
which year a new *femural* was provided at Dover.[10] Lead of 'Munydep' (the
Mendips) was used in 1397 'for covering the hall and kitchen and the two
new louvers (*femerallorum*) over them' at Porchester;[11] and about 1470 a
'bolster', or iron bolt, was bought 'to carry a lion set over the *femerelle* of
the great kitchen' at Shene.[12] Our list of variants draws to a conclusion with
the form *femorale*, used several times in a Tower account of 1339.[13]

Next to a mere hole in the roof, the simplest way of making a louver
was to use a barrel with the ends knocked out. So we find '*barrell pro
lovers*' bought at Hedon in 1443 and 1481,[14] and 4*d.* paid for a cask (*cado*)
for a louver (*fumerale*) at Cambridge in 1415.[15] At Hadleigh in 1363 there
are two entries of 4*s.* 8*d.* paid 'for 4 earthenware pots (*ollis luteis*) for the

---

[1] E. 593, 20.    [2] *York Memorandum Book* (Surtees Soc.), ii. 173.
[3] Wright, *Vocabularies*, 668.    [4] Liberate R. 32 Hen. III, m. 6.
[5] Ibid. 35 Hen. III, m. 1.    [6] Ibid. 36 Hen. III, m. 7.
[7] Ibid. 37 Hen. III.    [8] E. 466, 1.
[9] E. 544, 31.    [10] E. 462, 23.    [11] E. 479, 23.    [12] E. 503, 15.
[13] E. 470, 6.    [14] Boyle, *Hist. of Hedon*, clxi, clxxxiv.    [15] P. 1415.

louver(s)', in one case of the barn and in the other of the King's hall in the park;[1] as the word *'fumerell'* is not expanded in either instance, it is not possible to be sure whether pots were used separately—though four vents in one roof would be unusual—or fitted one into the other to form a sort of chimney-pot. More often the louver took the form of a lantern, or turret, sometimes called a 'hovel', as at the Tower in 1315, when 'John le Rook began to cover in the louver (*fumerallum*) of the Constable's hall in a round hovel (*houallo*) on the 2nd November and finished it on Saturday the 15th of the same month',[2] after which it was covered with lead. The same account mentions the provision of 3 pieces *'curbi maeremii'* for making 2 hovels for louvers over the great hall; these may be wooden curbings to go round the base of the hovels, or possibly only curved timbers. Such hovels were occasionally used for other purposes, as at Berkhamstead in 1386, when a hovel was made in which to hang the bell of the chapel;[3] and at St. Julian's Hospital, Southampton, in 1301, there was a 'louver placed in the chamber at the west end of the hall for getting out by to clean the gutter between the halls'.[4]

[1] E. 464, 6.
[2] E. 469, 16. Cf. at Westminster in 1399 'carpenters working on making the hovels (*hutellorum*) of the roof of the King's hall': E. 473, 11.
[3] E. 473, 2.                               [4] *Hist. MSS. Com. Rep.* vi. 559.

# XV

## THATCH, TILES, SLATES, VANES

THOUGH the timber-framed roof might be, and often was, a thing of beauty, its real object was simply to act as a support for a layer of some material that would keep out the wind and the rain. It was, therefore, not complete until 'heled' or covered with such weatherproof material. This outer layer was generically known as 'thack', but, owing to the fact that the vast majority of buildings in early times were covered with a thacking of straw or some similar material, 'thatch' gradually acquired its modern restricted significance of straw, or reed, heling. On the occasion of St. German's visit to the tomb of St. Alban, about 450, a fire broke out, and we are expressly told that the houses burnt 'were covered with marsh reeds'.[1] Some two centuries later, while people were feasting in a house near Maserfield, 'a great fire having been kindled (in the middle of the hall) it happened that sparks flew up and the roof of the house, which was wattled (*virgis contextum*) and thatched with hay, was filled with sudden flame'.[2] The prevalence of thatch helps to account for the frequency and devastating nature of fires in the early Middle Ages, of which the more spectacular instances are recorded from time to time in the contemporary chronicles. Thus in 1077 London was burnt 'so terribly as it never was before since it was built', and ten years later the greatest and richest part of the City, including St. Paul's, was completely burnt. In 1161 London, Canterbury, Exeter, and Winchester were all devastated by fire; in 1180 the greater part of Winchester was again destroyed by fire, as was Glastonbury in 1184, Chichester in 1187, and Worcester in 1202. In 1212 building regulations were issued in London,[3] by which no roofs were in future to be covered with reeds, sedge, straw, or stubble, but only with tile, shingles, boards, or lead, or plastered straw (*estra detorchiato*). All existing reed or sedge roofs were at once to be plastered; if this was not done they might be pulled down. Like most medieval legislation this was probably incompletely enforced, and the existence of thatched roofs in London fifty years later is suggested by the allegation that de Montfort had schemed to burn the city by liberating a number of cocks with flaming brands tied to their feet.[4]

---

[1] Bede, *Opera* (ed. Plummer), i. 37.    [2] Ibid. 147.
[3] *Liber Cust.* 86.    [4] *Hundred Rolls.*

The preparation of straw for thatch, which was known as 'yelming', consisted in damping it and 'drawing' it with a thatching-fork, or great comb, so as to get the straws parallel.[1] This was done by the thatcher's assistant, and women were often employed on the job. The thatcher then laid the 'yelms', or bunches of drawn straw, on the laths, beginning at the eaves and working up towards the ridge. The straw was held in place either by short straw ropes passed across it and tied to the rafters, or more often by rods, usually of hazel, known as 'ledgers' and 'temples', which were secured either by tying the ends to the rafters or by pegging them with 'broaches', 'spars' or 'spits' of hazel twisted into the shape of great hairpins and thrust into the straw. The edges, exposed to the action of the wind, were further secured by binding or sewing with string. At the ridge the thatch might be finished either by allowing the yelms from each side to overlap alternately, forming a crest, or by the application of a ridging of clay, or occasionally of turves.

Ignoring a thousand entries that simply tell of the purchase of straw for thatching, we may start with an entry in the Peterhouse accounts of 1504 of 3*d*. for a day's work *pro ly ʒelmyng straminis* and another 3*d*. *pro ly drawynge straminis*.[2] The same accounts for 1495 have payments 'for a man drawing straw and *ly schateynge*'; and for '*ly temperynge luti et ly shakynge straminis*'—the shaking being to rid it of foreign objects and in particular of grain, which would otherwise sprout, preparatory to drawing it ready for '*ly thegsgyng*', as thatching is here spelt, and the tempering of the clay being its preparation for '*le regsgynge*' or ridging. At Ripon in 1380 we find 'a woman helping to draw straw and carry water' in connexion with 'the thatching and drawing of straw and ridging (*ruggand*') it' for certain buildings.[3] And at Hedon in 1443 two thraves of barley straw were bought for 2*d*., Alice Carleton and Katherine Coke were each paid 2½*d*. a day for 'drawing the said thatch (*cooperturam*) and serving the thatchers', and there are also payments 'for tempering mortar for the ridging (*riggacione*) of the said tenements'.[4] Barley straw is mentioned in this instance, but the particular variety is not usually specified. At Ripon, however, in 1392 we have details of the purchase of 160 thraves (*travis*) of barley straw for thatching, at ½*d*.—6*s*. 8*d*.; 20 thraves of rye straw—2*s*.; and 22 thraves of wheat straw—2*s*. 9*d*.;[5] for which it would seem that wheat was regarded as the

---

[1] Innocent, *Building Construction*, 192–202.

[2] Cf. payments at Bicester in 1409 for thatching and 'ʒelmant' pigstyes: Blomfield, *Deanery of Bicester*, i. 136.      [3] R. 102.

[4] Boyle, *Hist. of Hedon*, clxxxiv. In 1477, at Cambridge, 10*d*. was paid 'to Bugge's daughter *pro le drawyng straminis*': King's Coll. Mundum Bk. vii.      [5] R. 107.

best for the purpose. For repairs to Farnham rectory barn in 1472 we have: 'paid for iiij^xx threfe of wynter-corne stra to ye said lath (barn) vj^s. viij^d ... unto John Rote for drawyng of the said stra x^d ... unto William Pepylton for thekyng of ye said stra by v days ij^s. 1^d.'[1] Here 'winter corn straw' presumably means stored straw from which the grain has been thrashed; such straw suffered in the process, its life, as thatch, being reckoned as not much more than half that of unthrashed stubble.[2] The medieval habit of reaping the ears with a sickle left high stubble for the thatcher's use. At Dover in 1283 we find 3s. 4d. paid for '500 sheaves of stubble (*stipulis*) for thatching the well-house in the keep (*dungone*) and the wash-house and the house in which Simon the clerk dwells'.[3] A later Dover account, for 1365, shows 50 sheaves of stubble bought for 9d., and a hundred of 'gloit' for 3s. and six hundreds of 'roskebard' for 11s. 6d., all for the same buildings adjoining the church.[4] 'Gloit' is long straw, usually of oats, and occurs at Rye in 1284, when 18d. was paid to a thatcher for thatching part of a house with 'gloy'.[5] It is also found at Scarborough in the same year, 1284—'for 1400 of gloye for thatching the bakehouse and brewhouse, 7s.';[6] and in 1336—'for 3 thousand of gloy bought from men of the neighbourhood, 22s. 6d.'[7] 'Ruskebard' occurs at Dover as early as 1347,[8] and seven years later there is a purchase of 'four and a half hundreds of thack called ruscum-bard';[9] it is presumably some kind of rush.

It will be noticed from the quotations above that thatch was bought not only by the thrave or sheaf but also by number, in which case the word 'pounds' seems usually implied, so that ' — hundreds of thatch' means so many hundredweight. It was also sometimes bought standing; as at Bath in 1420: 'for an acre of thache at Battwyke, 20d. For baggyng and beryng of the same 8d.'[10] Similarly, for work at Pevensey Castle in 1300: 'For 6 acres of rushes bought at Willingdon for thatching the hall and chambers, 18s. For cutting, spreading and collecting the same, 7s. For carrying the said rushes from Willingdon to the castle in 17 carts, 5s. 8d.'[11] Here the material is rush, which was as much in demand for thatch as straw, parti-cularly in the Fen districts. In the neighbourhood of Cambridge it was sometimes called 'fenstraw'[12] and 'fenthakke';[13] in the Cambridge Castle accounts it is referred to as 'straw namely rush (*in stramine scil' ros*)' in 1286,[14] and in 1295 three hundreds of 'marsh straw' were used on the walls

---

[1] E. 463, 13.
[2] *Dict. of Architecture*, s.v. Thatch.
[3] E. 462, 9.
[4] E. 462, 23.
[5] Mins. Accts. 1028, No. 10.
[6] E. 482, 1.
[7] E. 482, 4.
[8] E. 462, 16.
[9] E. 462, 18.
[10] *Somerset Arch. Soc.* xxiii. 26.
[11] E. 479, 16.
[12] P. 1469–70.
[13] P. 1447–8.
[14] E. 459, 15.

of the new turrets.[1] At Westminster 200 of rush (*ross'*) were bought in
1259 for cresting an earthen wall;[2] and the Ely accounts show frequent
purchases of 'pilled', or peeled, rushes and 'great' rushes, as much as
£5. 9s. 6d. being paid in 1357 for 35,850 *rosci pilate*;[3] in 1326 the rather
unusual term *lesch'* is used instead of *rosci*.[4] At Gravesend in 1367 we find 58
cartloads of rushes (*cirp'*) supplied for thatching buildings, at 12d. the load;[5]
and two years later 140 'wypys' of rushes (*cirporum*), at 10s. the hundred, were used at Rochester to protect stored timber.[6] So, in 1333, the
engines of war, mangonels and so forth, at the Tower were protected from
the weather: 'for 3000 of reeds (*arund'*) for covering the engines, 25s.; for
24 bundles of rods of *withi* for binding the said reed to the timber, 3s.; for
half a hundred of *shotis* of hazel rods for binding the reed, 3s. 1½d.'[7] When
a pigeon-house was built at Thriplow in 1442 John Beer was paid 24s. 'for
reedyng of the pigeon house, taking 2,900 of reed; and 21d. for schredyng
4 cartloads of roddes'.[8] He was also paid for 'ryggyng and stepyng of the
pigeon-house', the roof, no doubt, being made of two or more different
levels, or steps, and for this 2 cartloads of 'halmestrawe' were used. A later
Thriplow entry[9] mentions 5 loads of 'almestrawe', which is stubble, and
19 of white straw. Possibly this last term means thrashed straw, that being
the natural contrast to stubble; it occurs again in 1455 in work done at
Chesterton:[10]—'*pro cc þakke xxijᵈ. Item* (?) *plūme þakke for þakkyng of ye
walle viiijˢ iiijᵈ: item in cariagio cc segetis ijᵈ: item pro stramine albo ad ryggynd'
xijᵈ.*' Here we have plain 'thakke', most likely reed, a mysterious 'plumme
thakke', white straw, and sedge. This last occurs frequently in the fifteenth-
century accounts of King's Hall; as for instance in 1428, '*vjᶜ seggis pro
coopertura logge*'; next year 'For wages of Brown, seggeman, for thatching walls, 7d. Also in reward to 6 boys carrying segge, 6d.'; and in
1439, 'for the dinners of 2 seggethakkers for 4 days, 16d.'

The large part played by reed in thatching is shown by the fact that the
French word for thatch, *chaume*—which appears, semi-latinized, at Marlborough in 1238, '*In xij trussis de caumo ad cooperturam*'[11]—is derived from
the Latin *calamus*, a reed. Although *arundo* is the usual translation of reed in
English building accounts, *calamus* is found, as, for instance, at the Tower in
1278, when we have 6,250 *calami* employed for a temporary thatching of
the workshop (*hasteleria*) and walls against the winter.[12] For such temporary

[1] E. 459, 16.  [2] E. 467, 2.  [3] *Sacrist Rolls*, 3, 7, 18.
[4] Ibid. 60.  [5] E. 464, 2.  [6] E. 545, 8.
[7] E. 469, 15.  [8] P. 1441–2.
[9] P. 1447–8. Cf. at Bath in 1420, *pro stipulacione et helma*': *Somerset Arch. Soc.* xxiii. 26.
[10] K.H. 12, f. 33.  [11] E. 476, 3.  [12] E. 467, 7 (4).

winter thatching heather and similar substances were used; at Windsor 125
cartloads of heath (*bruer'*) were bought for that purpose in 1362,[1] as were
5 thraves of ling at Nottingham in 1369.[2] Bracken was occasionally used,
and at Ludgershall in 1342 three women were employed, at a penny a day,
'cleaning the rooms against the King's coming, and collecting bracken
(*feuger'*) for the thatching of a *loge* made for the carpenters, masons, and
other workmen'.[3] Even hay was sometimes employed for rough thatching,
as on several occasions at Hedon about 1470,[4] though it is not satisfactory,
as it absorbs the wet and soon rots.

The ledgers and spars used for pinning down the thatch appear under
various forms. At Rye in 1284 we have 8*d*. spent '*in virgis et horcis ad tec-
turam*'; and similarly at Pevensey Castle[5] about the same time the same
terms are used, as in the purchase of '28 bundles of rods and 1500 withies
(*hartium*)' for 4*s*. 2*d*., withies (*hart*' or *horc*') being also used to bind the
scaffolding. At Gravesend 1,500 rods and 3,000 'sprendles' were used for
thatching in 1367;[6] at Gloucester 'roddis and brochis' occur in 1406;[7] and
at Porchester '300 rods called sparres, for fixing the straw on the buildings'
were bought in 1438, at 4*d*. the hundred.[8] In the Peterhouse accounts for
1500 'spyttes and roddes' occur, and in 1523 nine 'bonche of roddes' were
bought in connexion with the 'clayng thackyng and rydgyng' of walls;
a century earlier 'bungess', or 'buggess', of rods were bought, at 1*d*. the
bunch.[9] In 1413 the churchwardens of St. Michael's, Bath, paid men for
making 'spykys' and assisting with the thatching of houses,[10] and three years
later there are payments '*pro helme* (stubble) *et spicis*'.[11] In the North, at
Scarborough in 1284, eight hundred of 'templewand' for thatching were
bought for 20*d*.;[12] at Berwick-on-Tweed in 1343 we find 'lathes thak wyker
and temple' for thatching a penthouse,[13] and thirty years later—'*lx trus de
medowthak pro coopertura bracine; item pro iiij ponderibus de wyker et temple
pro ligatura ejusdem*';[14] and at Somerton (Lincs.) 30 bundles of 'templeropes'
were used for thatching in 1360.[15] These last would be ropes used instead
of the ledgers, like the 'thakke rope', of which 4 'bounchis' were bought
for 4*d*. for works at Collyweston in 1493, 'pakke threde' being bought at
the same time for other thatching-work,[16] evidently to tie the ledgers to the
rafters. The King's Hall accounts contain numerous entries of 'byndyng'

---

[1] E. 493, 10.    [2] E. 478, 4.    [3] E. 476, 1.
[4] Boyle, *Hist. of Hedon*, cxciv.    [5] E. 483, 2.    [6] E. 464, 2.
[7] E. 502, 26.    [8] E. 479, 7.    [9] P. 1415–16, 1424–5.
[10] *Somerset Arch. Soc.* xxiii. 21.    [11] Ibid. 24.
[12] E. 482, 1.    [13] E. 482, 26.    [14] E. 483, 2.
[15] E. 484, 15.    [16] St. John's Coll., Camb., Accts., vol. ii.

and 'byndyng threde', and at Peterborough both 'thackroppe' and 'russh rope' occur in 1523.[1]

Finally we may note that thatchers were also known as reeders, an early instance being in 1333 at Westminster—'Robert Gamun *redere* working on the building called the sparrowhawks' mews (*mouta pro houstour'*) and lathing it anew and covering it with reed'.[2] The King's Hall accounts for 1378 mention 'a sclattere with his servant, a theccher with his servant, and 2 reders'.[3] In Latin the usual forms are *cooperator* and *tector*, both of which are also used for tilers. Occasionally the form *architector*[4] is employed, as, for instance, at Peterhouse, Cambridge, in 1375, at Clarendon in 1380,[5] and in the King's Hall accounts for 1415,[6] in which accounts, for 1475, we find *sartitector*, and *sartitectura* for the thatching of a house.[7]

Another form of roof-covering which was common in early times was shingles, which may be defined as oak tiles. References to these are numerous, and on the whole unenlightening, in the thirteenth century. Thus, in 1248 Henry III ordered rooms at Kennington and at Woodstock to be roofed with shingles;[8] and in 1260 he gave orders for the shingles to be taken off the roof of his great kitchen in Marlborough Castle, which was to be covered with stone tiles, while a chamber in the high tower was to be stripped of its thatch and roofed with the shingles from the kitchen.[9] In 1295 men were employed at Woodstock 'sawing blocks of wood (*gobones*) to make therefrom shingles (*cendulas*) for the covering of buildings'.[10] At Clipston 31,500 'chinkell' were made in 1362, at 8*d*. the hundred,[11] and the same price was paid for making 6,200 'chynkill' at Nottingham in 1375.[12] In 1238 shingles cost 2*s*. the thousand to make at Marlborough,[12] and in 1316 at Clarendon 3*s*. 6*d*.,[13] while 1500 'shyngle' bought from Hugh Hattere of Croydon in 1329 for use at Westminster cost 9*s*. 4*d*. the thousand;[14] others, to cover the 'Prynceshall' at Dover in 1365, were 12*d*. the hundred;[15] and shingles (*scindul'*) brought from Croydon to Westminster in 1386 were 13*s*. 4*d*. the thousand,[16] showing the rise in price that we have noticed at this period with other timber articles. It was the cost of this material that led to its use being very much restricted. Even as early as 1314, when various buildings roofed with shingles in the manors held

---

[1] Receiver's acct.      [2] E. 469, 13.      [3] K.H. 3, f. 229.

[4] At the capture of Sault, *c*. 1000, Adémar de Limoges climbed out on the church roof *more architecti*: Mortet, *Textes relatifs à l'hist. de l'architecture*, 7.

[5] E. 499, 1.      [6] K.H. 5, f. 166.      [7] K.H. 15, f. 81.

[8] Liberate R. 23 Hen. III.      [9] Ibid. 44 Hen. III.      [10] E. 497, 21.

[11] E. 460, 18.      [12] E. 478, 9.      [13] E. 459, 27.

[14] E. 467, 7.      [15] E. 462, 23.      [16] E. 473, 2.

by Queen Margaret in dower were in need of repair, it was found that it would be much cheaper to re-roof them with stone slates or earthen tiles than with shingles, and she was therefore allowed to take that course.[1] A local term for shingles in the north was 'spone'; thus in 1357 we find 4s. paid 'for covering the chancel of the church of Abeley with *spone* in various places',[2] and in 1329 'sponail', i.e. shingle-nails, were bought in Durham.[3]

The Romans used tiles for the roofing of their buildings in Britain, but there seems to be no direct evidence that the practice continued under the Saxons. The London building regulations of 1212 mention, as we have seen, tiles as one of the materials that might be used instead of thatch; so from at least the beginning of the thirteenth century tiles must have been available, and the evidence points to their becoming increasingly popular during that, and still more during the following, century. It is rather curious that in all the mass of detailed instructions for the construction and repair of buildings issued by Henry III there appear to be only three or four references to tiled roofs. In 1236 William de Burgh was ordered to cause the roof of the King's chamber at Kennington to be stripped and re-covered with good tile,[4] and three years later he was repaid various sums which he had spent at Kennington, including 3s. 1½d. for tile used to cover the hall.[5] The last entry is an order given in 1260 to remove the gardener's cottage at Windsor to a more suitable position and roof it with tile.[6] The probable deduction to be made from the paucity of these references is not that tile was rarely used on the royal estates, but that it was so generally in use that, unless lead or some other material was definitely named, it might be assumed that the roofs would be tiled; the special mention in the case of the gardener's cottage was probably needed because the existing building was thatched.

It is not always possible to be certain whether an entry of tiles (*tegule*) in a building account refers to roofing, building, or paving tiles, but those used for roofing are sometimes defined as 'thaktyle' or, more often, as 'flat (*plane*)' tiles. In 1237 they cost 3s. the thousand at Marlborough and the same price holds good in London in 1258 and 1278; but at Guildford in 1291 they cost only 2s., with an extra 3d. for carriage. In 1350, when the Black Death was causing a rise in prices, the City Council of London fixed the maximum price of tiles at 5s. the thousand,[7] and in 1362, when a great

[1] *Cal. of Patent R.* 100.     [2] *Durham Acct. Rolls* (Surtees Soc.), ii. 558.
[3] Ibid. 515.     [4] Liberate R. 21 Hen. III.     [5] Ibid. 24 Hen. III.
[6] Ibid. 44 Hen. III.     [7] Riley, *Mems. of London*, 254.

tempest had unroofed numbers of houses and created a great demand for tiles, they ordered that the price should not be raised, and that manufacturers should continue to sell at the usual price and not hold up their stocks for a rise.[1] At the Wye tileries,[2] belonging to Battle Abbey, with an output of about 100,000 tiles, the price was 2s. 6d. the thousand in 1355; but the usual cost in building accounts of the second half of the fourteenth century is from 4s. to 5s. 6d. At Langley in 1366 some were bought from Simon Molder of Ruislip at 3s., and others from Richard Tielere of Botley at 4s. 6d.[3] For work at Wallingford 36,000 tiles were obtained in 1365 from Nettlebed at 4s., and in 1390 the price at that tilery was 3s. 4d., with carriage in addition.[4] Woolwich seems to have been a great centre of the industry: in 1375 John Frost of Woolwich supplied 20,000 flat tiles for covering the chapel at Havering, at 5s. 10d.;[5] ten years later 1,100 flat tiles, used at Westminster, cost 7s. 6d., including carriage from Woolwich;[6] and in 1437 the cost of tiles at Shene was 4s.–4s. 6d. the thousand, or, with carriage from Streatham and Woolwich, 5s.[7] For some reason exceptional prices seem to have ruled in York: the tiles bought in 1327 from Constance Tiler (*tegulatrice*) cost 10s. the thousand;[8] 'thakteghell' were 11s. the thousand in 1364,[9] and 8s. in another account of about the same date;[10] and they were still 10s. in 1421 and 1458;[11] but by 1510 they had fallen to about 2s. 6d., as in that year 42,000 'thaketiell' cost £5. 8s. 5½d.[12] It is possible that the York tiles were of exceptional dimensions.

During the fifteenth century complaints were made of the lack of uniformity in the size,[13] and still more in the quality, of the tiles. It was said[14] that many of the tiles then being produced would last only four or five years instead of forty or fifty, and this is borne out by many series of manorial accounts, which show that a surprising amount of tiling repairs had to be carried out every year on the farm buildings.[15] To remedy these defects, an Act was passed in 1477 regulating the process of manufacture[16] and the size of the products. The standard for flat tiles should be 10½ in. by 6¼ in., with a thickness of at least ⅝ in.; ridge tiles or crests should be 13½ in.

[1] Riley, *Mems. of London*, 309. The monks of Boxley got 10s. the thousand for tiles from their tilery this year: Mins. Accts. 1253, No. 13.

[2] Salzman, *Engl. Industries*, 177.          [3] E. 466, 3.          [4] E. 490, 2 and 4.

[5] E. 464, 27.          [6] E. 473, 2.          [7] E. 496, 8.

[8] E. 501, 8.          [9] E. 501, 11.          [10] E. 501, 12.

[11] *Y.F.R.* 45, 71.          [12] Ibid., 95.

[13] *V.C.H. Essex*, ii. 456.          [14] *London Letter Book L*, 77.

[15] My attention was first called to this by Mr. W. D. Peckham in connexion with the Apuldram accounts.

[16] For an account of medieval tile-making see Salzman, *Engl. Industries*, 173–83.

by 6¼ in., and gutter tiles 10½ in. long. Infringements of this assize entailed fines of 5s. the thousand flat, 6s. 8d. the hundred crest, and 2s. the hundred gutter or corner tiles sold. Thorold Rogers points out that 'the size of the tiles is probably a declaration of the custom, the fine is the price at which each kind was ordinarily sold in the fifteenth century'.[1] In 1488 John Goldray of Caversham agreed to supply 24,000 tiles for Thomas Engle-field's new buildings at Englefield, such tiles to be 'of the best, and that he shall deliver hym no crokyd tyle, crop tyle nor grounde tyle', every tile 'to be at the lest of the leynth of xj inche, of brede vij inche, and of thyk-nesse iij quarter of an inche at the lest', at 4s. the thousand 'at the kylne'. He was to receive another 12d. for packing them in the carts which Thomas would send and to replace any that were broken.[2]

The tiles shaped to cover the ridge or edges of a roof appear under various names. 'Crestes voc' hypetyl' at Clarendon in 1363 were 2s. 6d. the hundred;[3] at Wallingford in 1365 'crestes and hupetill' were 4s.;[4] and about the same time 'riggetyle' or 'rigtighell' ranged from 2s. to 3s. 6d. at York,[5] and London.[6] Sometimes these ridge tiles were ornamented with a more or less elaborate cresting. Such, judging from their prices, were the 52 earthenware crests (*crestis luteis*) bought for 3s. 4d. at Carisbrook in 1353;[7] the 30 *'crestes de figulo'*, at 1½d. each, for covering the ridge of the hall and chamber at Moor End in 1366;[8] and the 36 'krestys of tyyl' for King's Hall, costing 6s. 2d. in 1432.[9] Still greater triumphs of fictile art are recorded at Banstead Manor in 1373, when 2s. were paid 'to John Pottere of Chay-ham for two crests made in the fashion of mounted knights, bought for the hall'.[10]

At Shene 'holtill', i.e. hollow tile, and 'fyneux' are classed together in 1369,[11] as are 'tiles called creste fyneux and hiptyl' in 1385.[12] These 'fyneux' seem to be the same as the 'festeux', made at the Wye tileries,[13] which occur also at Rochester in 1367, when 475 'tiles called fisteux and corners' were bought at 3s. 6d. the hundred.[14] They occur again at Canterbury as 'festewys' in 1408 and as 'festeouse' in 1485,[15] and belong, no doubt, to the class of tiles described at Havering in 1415 as 'holoware',[16] and in 1376 as 'holughtyll',[17] priced at 6d. the hundred. They are found at the Tower in 1357 as 'holghtiell', at a penny each, and are usually latinized as *tegule*

---

[1] *Hist. of . . . Prices*, i. 490.  [2] *Anct. Deeds* (P.R.O.), D. 10316.
[3] E. 460, 3.  [4] E. 490, 2.  [5] E. 501, 11, 12.
[6] E. 544, 3.  [7] E. 490, 29.  [8] E. 544, 33.
[9] K.H. 8, f. 68.  [10] E. 494, 18.  [11] E. 494, 7.  [12] E. 473, 2.
[13] Salzman, *Engl. Industries*, 177.  [14] E. 479, 28.
[15] Bodl. MS. Top. Kent, c. 3, f. 105.  [16] E. 465, 1.  [17] E. 464, 30.

*cave*, or *cavate*, or occasionally *concavate*. At York in 1327 'gotertyles' were six a penny, when 'riggetille' were four a penny,[1] but in 1364 both 'gotertighell' and 'rigtighell' were 2*s*. the hundred,[2] and at Wallingford 'crestes and gotertyl' are classed together at 3*s*. 4*d*. the hundred.[3] At Leeds (Kent) in 1382 'regteghle', at 4*s*., are classed with 'cornerteghle',[4] which occur in various accounts, including one of about 1365 for York Castle, where 8*d*. was paid for '14 cornertil and 20 kointil', though what the difference might be is not obvious.[5]

It should be noted that 'tiles' sometimes are stone slates, which is usually shown by the context. Thus in the Finchale Priory accounts for 1457 is an entry of 'carriage of 24 fothers of tiles from the quarry',[6] and at Woodstock in 1390 there is a purchase of '24,500 tiles called courssebat for roofing the cloister, with the digging of them in the field of Burton', at 2*s*. 8*d*. the thousand.[7] Usually they are defined as stone tiles, as, for instance, in a manorial account of Stanton Lacy in 1390: 'From the sale of stone tiles out of the quarry newly found in the wood, nothing this year. The thousand, however, is usually sold for 6s. 8d., besides 6s. 8d. for the digging of them.'[8] At Clipston they appear in 1368 as 'thakestone', four and a half thousand being bought for 18*s*.[9] An early reference to slates occurs in 1238, in the order to roof with slate (*sclata*) a mill at Woodstock,[10] in which neighbourhood laminated stone suitable for splitting into slates is found. For work at Cambridge Castle in 1286 'sclatestone' of Peterborough was employed.[11] But the most famous quarries were those of Collyweston in Northants. These were used extensively at Rockingham Castle, as, for instance, in 1375, when 9,500 stone slates were bought at 8*s*. the thousand, and in 1390 when 4,500 'sclastones' were bought at 6*s*. 8*d*., carriage to the castle being at the rate of 3*s*. the thousand.[12] For Oakham Castle 5,000 'sklat' were bought, at 6*s*. 8*d*., at Collyweston in 1383.[13] As the manor of Collyweston belonged to the Lady Margaret, mother of Henry VII, her building accounts naturally contain a good many references to slates; as, in 1504, 'sclatt to the hillyng (i.e. heling, or roofing) of the new house'.[14] These accounts also give some of the trade terms applied to the slates;[15]

---

[1] E. 501, 8.      [2] E. 501, 11.      [3] E. 490, 4.      [4] R. 480, 7.
[5] E. 501, 12.      [6] *Finchale* (Surtees Soc.), cclxvii.
[7] E. 499, 1.      [8] Mins. Accts. 967, no. 27.
[9] E. 460, 20.      [10] Liberate R. 23 Hen. III.
[11] E. 459, 15.      [12] *V.C.H. Northants*. ii. 296.
[13] E. 478, 23. 'A sclater of Okeham' was employed at Peterhouse at 4*d*. a day and his food and bed : P. 1463–4.
[14] St. John's College, Cambridge, MS. vol. iii.      [15] Ibid., vol. ii.

an entry of 'broodstones for plasterers', and another of 'the gadring and cariage of xx cartloads of bastards at ijd. the lod', are explained by a third, under the heading—'Bastardes for gutters and particōn of tymber: Item paid to John Fleshman of Colyweston for the [*sic*] of iij cart loddes of broode stons from Eston pyttes for gutters and plastrers to sett particōn wᵗ all—viijᵈ.' In this instance the slates seem to have been used partly instead of laths or wattling as a beam-filling between the studs. Other terms occur in a Woodstock account of 1493:[1] 'for sclattes—a lod of euys ston iijˢ.—a lod of comen largys xvjᵈ.—ij lod of brood stone iijˢ.—iiij lod of small stone iiijˢ'. The 'euys ston', or slates used at the eaves of the roof, were considerably larger than the general run: in 1438 'slattes' were 3s. and 'eueslattes' 3s. 4d. the hundred, and 'crestys' (specially cut out of the stone) 3d. each.[2]

The blue schist slates of Cornwall and Devon were used, probably from very early times, in their own district. For buildings put up for the use of the miners at Martinestowe in 1296 we find 23,000 'sclattes' quarried at Birlond, at 5d. the thousand, and 10,000 at Hassel;[3] 19,500 slates were bought, at 11d. the thousand, 'between Golant and Fowey', and 80,000 were drawn from Bodmalgan quarry, at 6d., for buildings at Restormel in 1343.[4] They were also exported from this district, as 2,000 'sclat de Cornwayll' were bought, for 10s., for a house in the New Forest in 1363;[5] and in 1436 Thomas Wylby of Southampton was given leave to buy in Devon 'a hundred thousands of the tiles called sclat' and take them to the abbey of Mont Saint Michel, in satisfaction of the ransom of William Jacob of Southampton, a prisoner there.[6] It is probably such slates that are referred to at Windsor in 1481 as 'tiles called sklates of blue colour',[7] and at Warblington in 1518 in payments to 'John Hellyer for hewyng off vijᵐˡ. blew ston'.[8]

Earthen tiles and stone slates were hung in the same manner. Wooden pegs were driven into holes near the top edge of the tiles, which were then hung on the laths by means of the projecting pegs. Each layer of tiles overlapped the row below it, and to keep the wind and wet from penetrating between them they were bedded on moss. Moreover, the lowest layers, and sometimes all the layers, were pointed, or rendered, with mortar. The whole process is indicated in brief in an entry in the Woodstock accounts

[1] E. 494, 19.
[2] E. 499, 3. '*Sclatston pro guter et heues*' at Moor End, 1365 : E. 544, 31.
[3] E. 476, 5.  [4] E. 461, 11.  [5] E. 476, 20.
[6] *Cal. of Patent R.* 512.  [7] E. 496, 22.  [8] E. 490, 12.

for 1265:[1] 'For 2 slaters (*sclattatores*) pointing the chambers and hall in the steward's court—2s. 6d. For a thousand slates (*clatorum*)—2s. For a hundred crests for the same—2s. 6d. For collecting moss (*mossa*)—6d. For 2,000 wooden nails—2d.' A tiler was paid 5*d.* a day for 'moseying and poyntynge' at Bath in 1478,[2] and two years earlier 6*d.* was paid at Cambridge 'for poyntyng iiij rodes of sclate'.[3] Tiles were made with holes ready for pegging, but slates had to be pierced. At Woodstock in 1285 is a payment of 3*d.*, '*pro j perforatore sclate per ij dies*';[4] at Merton College a slater who bored slates for 4 days in 1300 was paid 10*d.*,[5] while in 1307 Ralph le Sclattere was paid 18*d.* for boring 3,000 stones,[6] which—assuming that the long hundred of six score was in use—would give 500 as a good day's work. In 1335 the rate was only 4*d.* the thousand,[7] but at Oakham in 1383 'boryng' 2,500 slates cost 4*s.*[8] The work was evidently done with some kind of drill, as in 1313 Simon de Norton, tiler, was paid 1*d.* 'for a hide bought whereof to make a spyndelthoung for boring slates'.[9] Often the slates were bought ready bored; as at Rockingham in 1375, when 76*s.* was paid for 9,500 '*petris tegulis penetratis et batratis*'.[10] The same formula occurs in a New College Roll of 1453—'*dcc sclatston bateratis et penetratis emptis, cum cariagio,—iiij[s] x[d]*'.[11] The term 'battering' I take to apply to the thinning down, or bevelling, of the upper edge of the slate, where the hole was made. The smaller slates were more or less fish-scale in shape and hung by a single peg at the narrower end; the battering enabled them to overlap more closely. At Woodstock in 1365 a man was paid 7*s.* 6*d.* for the making and battering (*batura*) of 5,000 slates;[12] at Finchale in 1450 '*le bateryng ml sklatt*' cost 5*s.*;[13] and at Collyweston in 1504 the 'clevyng batteryng and boryng of xxij[ml]. slatte' was paid at the rate of 22*d.* the thousand.[14]

The wooden tile-pins (*cavillae*) seem to have been of oak, which crafts-men tell me is an unsatisfactory material, a fact that may help to explain the constant need of repairs, already mentioned as a characteristic of medieval tiled roofs. They were sometimes made for the work in hand—as at Merton College in 1335, when 59,000 tile-pins were made from timber in store, at 1*d.* the thousand[15]—and sometimes bought, either by number or by measure—as at King's Hall in 1528, when 3*d.* was paid 'for a peke

[1] E. 497, 2.   [2] *Somerset Arch. Soc.* xxv. 74.   [3] K.H. 15, f. 148.
[4] E. 497, 18.   [5] Merton Coll. Roll 4062.
[6] Ibid. 3635.   [7] Ibid. 4086.   [8] E. 478, 23.
[9] E. 469, 16.   [10] E. 481, 3.
[11] Thorold Rogers, *Hist. of . . . Prices*, iii. 717.   [12] E. 498, 20.
[13] *Finchale* (Surtees Soc.), cclxiii.   [14] St. John's Coll. Accts., vol. ii.
[15] Merton Coll. Roll 4086.

(i.e. peck) of Sklaytt pynne',[1] and at New College in 1453, when 2 bushels of 'sclatpynnys' cost 2s. 8d.[2] Sometimes the tiles, especially crests and corners, were secured with iron nails; as for a house in Cambridge in 1375, when 250 corner tiles were bought, and also 250 'spykyng' for the corner tiles.[3]

Entries of the collection of moss for bedding the tiles are numerous, the work being usually done by women. The quantities are usually stated vaguely, often as so many bundles (*fasciculi*); at Winchester in 1289 two shillings were paid for 24 '*fessis de moos*';[4] and at Ripon in 1454 five '*pond*' *de mosse*' cost 5d.,[5] while in 1493 one '*cercina mussi*', whatever that may be, was 1d.:[6] in fact, whatever the denomination, it seems almost always to have been valued at a penny.

The final crowning touch set upon the roof was, when it attained that dignity, the weathercock, or vane. In the Bayeux Tapestry the Confessor's completion of his abbey of Westminster is signified by the figure of a man planting the weathercock on the roof of the church. When the steeple of Louth Church was at last finished, after dragging on for fifteen years, we have a note:[7]

Md. the 15th Sunday after Holy Trinity of the year (1515) the weathercock was set upon the broach of Holy Rood Eve after, there being William Ayleby parish priest, with many of his brethren priests there present, hallowing the said weathercock and the stone that it stands upon, and so conveyed upon the said broach; and the said priests singing *Te Deum Laudamus*, with organs, and then the kirkwardens garred ring all the bells, and caused all the people there being to have bread and ale; and all to the loving of God, our Lady and all Saints.

There is a further note that Thomas Taylor, draper, gave the weathercock, which was 'bought in Yorke of a gret bassyn and mayde at Lyncoln and the Kyng of Scotts brought the same bassyn in to Ingland with hym'.[8]

At Dover in 1365 a '*vana*' was bought, for 12d., and set up on the great tower 'to show the quarter (*stacionem*) of the wind';[9] and at Eltham in 1369 a weathercock (*ventilogium*), costing 3s. 4d., was fixed on the top of the kitchen 'to know how the wind lies (*ad cognoscendum ubi demonstrat*

---

[1] K.H. 24, f. 15.  [2] Thorold Rogers, op. cit. 718.

[3] P. 1374-5.  [4] E. 491, 17.  [5] R. 161.  [6] R. 164.

[7] *Archaeologia*, x. 85, where the spelling is thus modernized. The exact form of the entry is given in Dudding, *First Churchwardens' Book of Louth* (1941), 181.

[8] Dudding, op. cit. 182. The version in *Archaeologia* converted the basin into 'a great baron' and left readers wondering why he should have carried a weathercock in his baggage.

[9] E. 462, 23.

*ventus)'.*[1] These were cheap vanes, serving a useful purpose; at Dover the wind was of primary importance for shipping, and in a kitchen the opening and closing of the louvre would be regulated by the position of the wind. But they had their decorative value, which accounts for their multiplication, as at Bicester Priory, when 'two vanys de tyn' were bought from a local smith to be set at either end of the dormitory,[2] or the six vanes bought, at about 15*s.* each, from William Latoner to set on six towers of Sheppey Castle in 1365.[3] These, from the name of their maker, were obviously of latten, a kind of bell-metal, as was the *'fane de laton superdeauratum'* on the hall of Hadleigh Castle, which was taken down and repaired in 1363.[4] At York in 1485 'a great basin and 2 other pieces of basins' provided the metal for 'les faydes', or vanes, set on the new west tower of the Minster, and they were gilt with beaten gold.[5] The vane set over the hall at Windsor in 1352[6] was of copper, painted with the King's arms, and other ornate vanes were provided for the Tower in 1532, as is shown by the provision of 'ij little frames of bourdes for to close in the great faynes that cam from Elysys the paynter for hurtyng of the gildyng, to every fayne one'.[7] This was an age of glitter, and such vanities as vanes were much in fashion. The hall of Hampton Court must have flashed and sparkled in the sunlight in a veering wind, for not only was there a cluster of vanes on the louvre, to which we have alluded, but the three stair-turrets had nine vanes apiece, each gilded and painted with the arms and badges of the King and Queen, the battlements carried another 16, and each gable was crowned with a lion or dragon carrying a vane 'oon of the Kynges armys, the other of the Quenys, wrowghte wyth fyne golde and in owyle (oil)'.[8]

---

[1] E. 494, 7.
[2] Blomfield, *Deanery of Bicester*, i. 110.
[3] E. 483, 21.
[4] E. 464, 6.
[5] *Y.F.R.* 88.
[6] Hope, *Windsor Castle*, i. 171.
[7] Bayley, *Tower of London*, xxiii.
[8] Law, *Hampton Court*, i. 346–8.

# XVI

## TIMBER

THE medieval builder had no hesitation about using green timber. When building operations were undertaken the carpenters were sent to the nearest available wood—at Peterhouse in 1438 they had only to step into the garden[1]—to fell suitable trees, lop the branches and rough them up, to be carried, whole or sawn, to the framing-place. So, for instance, at Hedon in 1343 we find 4d. paid for felling an oak to mend the high bridge, and 5s. 10d. for cutting the said oak and sawing it into 15 planks, each 24 feet long;[2] and in 1505 Sir Thomas Lucas enters in his accounts 6s. 8d. paid 'to Loveday, carpenter, for felling and chosing of xxvj okes in the parkes of Wynerston and Badmondisfeld for my werkes at Litil Saxham'.[3] For the extensive building operations at Windsor Castle in the middle of the fourteenth century a whole wood was bought at Cagham,[4] which provided 3,004 oaks, of which the bark, branches, and charcoal were sold for £135. For the same works some ten years later, in 1363, 820 oaks were cut in Combe Park and 120 in Pamber Forest.[5] At Devizes in 1377 we have a payment of 3s. 'for felling 12 oaks called *blatrones*, picked out in the Forest, of the size of 1 foot square; and the carriage of them was paid for with *le loppus*'.[6] A century earlier, in 1275, for work at the Tower 28 beeches and 5 *bletrones* were cut in 'the King's wood of Attewoode', rough hewn, loaded and carried by land to Bray and thence by water.[7] The Nottingham building-accounts of 1358–66 refer to felling and 'brittening' (*britnand'*) of trees,[8] and at York also, in 1393, we find John Baker paid for cutting 20 oaks and '*pro byrtynyng de predictis quercubus*'.[9] This word is connected with the Anglo-Saxon *brytan*, meaning 'to break', a term which is also sometimes used for the cutting up of timber; as, for instance, at Hampton Court in 1523, 'for brekyng of tymber after all scantlons above xviij ynches',[10] and 'for brekyng of ix fote of bechen plankes of iiij fotes iij fotes at the lest ij foote and viij inches depe'.[11] Some allowance must be made for the leisureliness of medieval building

---

[1] P. 1438: 'for 1350 planks (*tabulis*) sawn from trees cut in the garden (*orto*) of the college'.
[2] Boyle, *Hist. of Hedon*, xxii.        [3] Gage, *Thingoe Hundred*, 141.
[4] '*In uno bosco in grosso empto apud Cagham*': Hope, *Windsor Castle*, i. 170.
[5] E. 493, 11.      [6] E. 462, 5.          [7] E. 467, 7 (3).
[8] E. 478, 4–7.     [9] *Y.F.R.* 130.
[10] H.C. 237, f. 142.        [11] H.C. 238, f. 163.

operations, but by modern standards most of the timber was definitely green when set in position.

One result of the use of unseasoned timber was the tendency to warp and twist, which has produced in so many medieval buildings irregularities of line and surface, more delightful to the artist than to the architect or to the unsentimental occupier. This tendency was resisted by the use of massive timbers of most uneconomic scantling. The specifications for the timbers to be used in a range of shops in London in 1369 give the following dimensions of the various pieces, in breadth and thickness, in inches:[1] plates (groundsills) *'pour la frount'* 7 by 12, and *'par dedeins'* 6 by 12; principal posts 14 by 12 at ground level, 12 by 10 at tip; principal puncheons of first story 12 by 9, of second story 10 by 8, of third story 9 by 7; first somer 9 by 13, second 8 by 12; 'entreteys between the posts' (end wall-plates) 10 by 9, 'resnes' (inside wall-plates) 10 by 8; 'lyernes' (tie-beams) 6 by 8; rafters 6 by 5 at foot and 5 by 4 at top; joists over the cellar 12 by 10, of first floor 10 by 8, of second floor 9 by 7, with 6 inches between the joists.

A similar specification for an addition to the Blue Boar at Salisbury in 1444 gives:[2] groundsills 15 by 10; principal posts 13 by 12; somers 16 by 15; wallplates 8 by 9 and 'sideresons' 11 by 6; tie-beams 9 by 15; rafters 5 by 7 at foot and 4 by 5 at top; joists 9 by 8, with 10 inches between them. Finally, two contracts for buildings at Queens' College, Cambridge, give:[3] somers 12 by 14; wall-plates 9 by 7; tie-beams 10 by 15; rafters 8 by 7 (and 7 by 6) at foot and 7 by 5 (and 6 by 5) at top; ridge-piece 9 by 8; studs 8 by 5; joists 8 by 6, with 10 inches between. The greater massiveness of the rafters in the Queens' roofs is probably due to their being intended to carry stone slates instead of tiles.

To illustrate the progressive diminution of scantlings we may note that the average sizes laid down for timbers after the Fire of London in 1666 were: summers 14 by 10; wall-plates 8 by 6; rafters 5 by 4; joists 7 by 3, not more than 12 inches apart.[4]

As regards length, anything much over 30 feet was unusual, especially after the middle of the fourteenth century. The stores at Westminster in 1329 included 11 beams of 37 feet and 16 of 50 feet,[5] but at that very time Alan of Walsingham was seeking far and wide for great beams—actually 50 feet in length—for his lantern at Ely and only obtained them at vast expense.[6]

---

[1] App. B.                          [2] Ibid.                          [3] Ibid.
[4] Moxon, *Mechanickal Exercises*, 143.                          [5] E. 469, 11.
[6] Coulton, *Social Life*, 481.

Although unseasoned timber was in general use, the leisurely progress of medieval building must often have given it time to dry off to some extent, of which the desirability was recognized, as may be seen from this letter addressed to John Thoresby, Archbishop of York, in January 1355/6:[1]

all the timber as yet obtained, which it was supposed would be sufficient for quite a long time, is in the hands of the carpenters, prepared for setting up, if God will, in the near future; and unless new timber is cut during the winter season, so that it may dry off (*exsiccari*) during the summer, the carpenters and our other workmen employed on the building of the said work will, for lack of timber, stand absolutely idle throughout the next winter season. Be so kind, therefore, as to order the delivery of suitable timber, which consists more of bent trees than of those of greater price and value which grow straight up, to be cut during this present winter-time.

Moreover, there was an appreciation of the fact that seasoned wood was preferable, when it could be obtained, and it was occasionally stipulated for in contracts.[2] The gate of the range of shops, built in London in 1369, was to be 'of old heart of oak' (*danxien meryn de coer de keyne*): the roof of Halstead Church, in 1413, was similarly to be of heart of oak, '*bene siccato et indurato*'; the laths to carry the lead over the roof of the Cambridge Schools, in 1466, were to be 'of herty ooke sufficiently dried'; and the rood-loft gallery at Tempsford Church in 1512 was to be of 'clene seson-able hart of oke'. By the sixteenth century the demand seems to have been beginning to create the supply. For work at Croydon in 1507 purchases were made of 750 feet of 'drye bordes', at 2*s.* 4*d.* the hundred, and of 480 feet of 'grene borde' at 20*d.*[3] Similarly at Corpus Christi, Oxford, in 1517, 'drye planchbord' was 3*s.* the hundred, while that 'not seasonyd' was 2*s.* 6*d.*[4] 'Sesoned elmyn borde' was bought at Windsor to make 'hoddis, bossis (mortar hods) and whelebarowes' in 1532,[5] and 'playnche bourddes sesenyd' were used for the doors of the new tennis court at Hampton Court in 1535.[6]

The building-timber of the Middle Ages was emphatically oak. It grew plentifully in many districts and where it did not grow it could usually be brought by water without unreasonable expense. In character it is pro-verbially strong and enduring, so that we are not surprised to find a thirteenth-century abbot of Meaux praised for constructing the manorial buildings of his abbey *de quercu imputrabili*.[7] Henry III, who loved building

---

[1] *Y.F.R.* 171.  [2] App. B.  [3] St. John's, Cambridge, Accts., vol. iv.
[4] C.C.C. MS. 435, f. 2.  [5] Hope, *Windsor Castle*, i. 264.
[6] H.C. 238, f. 94.  [7] *Chron. Mon. de Melsa*, ii. 63.

for its own sake and men of religion for theirs, was lavish in his gifts of oaks from the royal forests.[1] So we find him giving 30 oaks for the building of Hales Abbey in 1248, and the same number for the repair of the central tower of the monastic church at Bury St. Edmunds in 1251; 60 oaks to the abbot of Bindon in 1233, 100 for the abbey of Gloucester in 1234, another hundred for Chichester Cathedral in 1232, with an additional fifty two years later, with innumerable smaller grants of timber, implying, if not actually specifying, oak. Such lavish expenditure of natural resources soon made itself felt. Even as early as 1233 there were complaints of the difficulty of finding really good timber in the Forests of Windsor and Cornbury,[2] and we have seen that a century later Alan of Walsingham was hard put to it to find the great beams that he required for his work at Ely,[3] and that by the middle of the fifteenth century the price of timber had risen enormously.[4]

It is unnecessary to labour the fact that oak was in constant use for building purposes, the contracts printed in the Appendix and many casual references on other pages are sufficient evidence of the fact: and it may be taken for granted that when the nature of the wood is not stated in any particular entry it was oak. This applies not only to timbers but also to boards and laths. Laths are thin strips of wood nailed across the rafters to carry the roofing material, whether thatch, tiles, or lead; they were also used on walls as the support for plastering. They were not sawn but rent or riven from the solid wood, and as they were used in enormous quantities, occurring in almost every building account, their production must have been a minor industry of considerable extent, though productive of labour rather than wealth. Sometimes the accounts record payments for making laths from timber supplied, as at Havering in 1414, when Richard Priour was paid '*pro kleveffyng de lathes*',[5] and at Langley in 1441, when 12 oaks were bought for 15s. and 7,000 laths were made from them, at 20d. the thousand.[6] More often the laths were bought ready made. Their usual length seems to have been 5 feet, and in the time of Edward III they had to be an inch broad and half an inch thick. By an assize issued in 1528 'the lath shall conteyne in length v fote, and in brede ij ynches, and in thyckenes halfe a ynche of assize, upon payne for every c lathe put to sale to the contrarye ij$^d$'.[7] Laths varied in size and quality, the chief distinction being between those made from the inner heart of the oak and those made from the outer,

[1] *Close Rolls.*  [2] Ibid. 41, 85.  [3] See above, p. 238.
[4] See above, p. 209.  [5] E. 465, 5.
[6] E. 466, 11.  [7] *Dict. of Architecture*, s.v. Lath.

sappy, wood. The labour, and therefore cost of making them, was the same, but the price of the finished article was very different. Of the 7,000 laths which we have mentioned as being made at Langley, 4,000 were 'hertlath' and the rest 'bastardlath', an unusual term evidently corresponding to the common 'saplath'. Among the stores of the works of London Bridge in 1350 are mentioned 57,000 hertlatthes, at 4s. the thousand, and 30,000 saplaths, at 2s.[1] At Windsor, in 1295, oak laths were 6d. and sap laths 3d. the hundred;[2] at Westminster in 1386 the long hertlaths were 10d., short hertlaths 7d., and saplaths 5d.,[3] the same varieties being priced at Shene in 1435 at 5s., 4s., and 3s. 4d. the thousand.[4] At Windsor in 1366 the contrast is between saplaths, at 2s. 6d. and 'troulath' or 'trowelatth' at 5s.,[5] and 'troulath' are also found in the Hadleigh Castle accounts for 1363,[6] while at Leeds Castle saplath at 4d. the hundred are contrasted with 'oak laths called lyflath' at 8d. in 1381.[7] On the other hand, at Sheppey in 1366 oak laths at 5s. the thousand occur with '*lath de coua*', which, from their price, 3s. 4d., are almost certainly sap laths.[8] Occasionally laths are reckoned not by their number but by the 'bunch' or bundle; as at Cambridge in 1529, when 'vj bonches of harte lathe' cost 3s. 4d.,[9] which suggests that the bunch contained about a hundred; but at York, where 'xj bonche lattes' cost 22d. in 1508, when sap laths were 8d. the hundred,[10] the bunch can hardly have contained more than 25 or 30 (the hundred in all these instances is probably the long hundred of six score).

While ordinary laths were strong enough to carry thatch or tiles, specially stout ones were required for heavier material, so that we find mention of 'ledlathes', as for instance at Woodstock in 1365 and 1380, for use under lead.[11] Similarly, where heavy stone tiles were used; as, in 1358, for a lodge in the New Forest, 6,000 'stonlathes' were made from 10 oaks;[12] at Ripon 'stanlate' were 12d. the hundred in 1408;[13] and at York 7s. 4d. the thousand was paid, including carriage, for 'stanelattes' in 1421,[14] 'saplattes' being then 4s. When exceptionally broad laths were required, barrel-staves were sometimes employed; thus in 1333 we find in the Tower accounts mention of '50 tonnestavis, coming from the empty casks, for laths'.[15]

Oak boards figure under a great variety of names. The thickest were

[1] Riley, *Mems. of London*, 261.
[2] E. 492, 11.
[3] E. 473, 2.
[4] E. 496, 8.
[5] E. 493, 22.
[6] E. 464, 6.
[7] E. 480, 7.
[8] E. 483, 23.
[9] K.H. 24, f. 93.
[10] Y.F.R. 94.
[11] E. 497, 19; 498, 20.
[12] E. 476, 25.
[13] R. 137.
[14] Y.F.R. 44.
[15] E. 469, 15.

termed 'planks' and were sometimes extremely massive. For instance, in the
bell tower at Durham in the twelfth century a platform was made to
prevent the ringers being injured when the iron clappers fell out of the
bells—a very common form of accident in the Middle Ages. 'On the
beams of this intervening platform is placed a plentiful supply of planks
of great size and immense weight, which are fixed firmly to the beams
with wooden pins. The weight of a single plank exceeds a man's weight,
for it is 12 feet in length and in breadth runs about 3 or 4 feet, the thickness being a little over half a foot.'[1] For work at Merton College in 1488
Thomas Geffrey of Newbury, carpenter, agreed to supply 'xiiij plankys of
ooke clene tymber, off xx ynchys brode, eche of them vj ynchys thykke and
xiij fote longe; also xij plankys of ooke clene tymbyr, eche off them xiij
fote of lenghthe v ynches thykke and xvij ynchys brode'.[2] These were
exceptional, the general run of planks being about that of the '*bord*' *pro
plaunch*' mentioned at the Tower in 1324 as averaging 10 ft. by 1 ft. 6 in.,
and listed at 4*d*. each.[3] Although no thickness is given in this instance,
other entries suggest an average of about 1½ inches. In the Westminster
accounts for 1532 we find that 333 'plaunche boordes of oke' contained
4,413 feet of timber and weighed 9 tons,[4] which—taking the weight of a
cubic foot of oak as about 55 lb.—would agree quite well with planks
10 ft. by 18 in. by 1½ in. The same entry gives 39 'quarter boordes' as
containing 500 feet and weighing 1 ton. From this it would seem that
planks and quarter-boards were approximately equal in content, though
the latter may well have been longer and thinner. A later entry shows
Thomas Marten of Crawley supplying 2,068 feet of 'plaunche okyn
bourde' and 900 feet of 'quarter boorde'.[5] But although quarter-boards
figure frequently from the second half of the fourteenth century onwards,
I have found nothing to indicate the exact significance or origin of this
term. It is possible that they were sawn from trunks that had been quar-
tered, that is to say, divided lengthwise into four by medial cuts at right
angles. If so, it is obvious that even the boards formed from the same tree
would tend to vary in breadth, but the Middle Ages were not meticulous
over standardization. A further complication is introduced in a Windsor
account of 1444: 'for sawing of 500 of slitware, at 16d. the hundred, and
500 of quarter bord, at 14d., and 500 of bastard quarter bord, at 14d.'[6]

[1] *Reginaldi Dunelm. Libellus* (Surtees Soc.), 203.
[2] *Merton Coll. Register* (O.H.S.), 109.          [3] E. 469, 7.
[4] T.R., f. 53.                    [5] T.R., f. 84.
[6] Hope, *Windsor Castle*, i. 396.

When the identity of legitimate quarter boards is unknown, who shall define their bastard brothers?

It is puzzling, in this last entry, to find 'slitware'[1] sawn, as one would imagine that it belonged to the form of boards made by splitting with wedges instead of sawing, but possibly the reference is to the further cutting up of such riven boards. Three 'oak boards called clouenbord', 6 ft. by 2½ ft., were used for covering the king's bath at Westminster in 1345,[2] and 'clife burde' occurs at York in 1516,[3] as do 'revyn burdes' in 1457.[4] At Leeds Castle, also in the time of Edward III, we have a note of the cutting of great trees for 'clofbord' for a brattise, or gallery,[5] and 'rentbord' occurs at Rockingham in 1375.[6] An entry in the Durham accounts for 1531 of payments *pro laceratione asserum*', at 3s. the thousand,[7] must, from the rate of pay, refer to small boards, or even what are now termed battens,[8] and may be compared with one of 1355 at Nottingham—'*in fissura ducentorum bordorum thacgorum—3s.*'[9] Thack boards were small boards nailed over the rafters to carry the 'thacking', whether of straw, tiles, or lead.[10] In 1327 we find 66 'small boards called thackbord' bought for 2s. at York,[11] and in 1355 at Ripon 'thakbord' for roofing the plumbery cost 5s. 4d. the hundred,[12] while five years later 1,000 'thakbord' bought in Sherwood Forest for repairs to Bonby Church in Lincolnshire cost, with carriage, 73s. 1d.[13] Allied to these would seem to be the 'cotbord' bought in 1339 'for roofing the chapel beside the keep' in Dover Castle.[14] This is probably a variant spelling of the boards which appear in Canterbury accounts between 1264 and 1290 as 'scocbord', 'schatbord', and 'schotbord',[15] and at Clipston in 1362 as 'schotebord for roofing the chambers'.[16] 'Schotbord for making baiard' (handbarrows) of' occur at the Tower in 1278 at a price—22s. 2d. for 800—which shows that they were small.[17] 'Shooting' being a medieval term for planing, we may probably identify these shot-boards with the 'planebord

---

[1] Cf. 'for slytting worke att xijd. the c': C.C.C. Oxon. MS. 435, f. 14.

[2] E. 469, 6.   [3] Y.F.R. 96.   [4] Ibid. 69.

[5] E. 466, 24.   [6] E. 481, 3.   [7] D.H.B. 85.

[8] The 'battanz' at Wallingford in 1375 were 'great slabs' costing 11d. each: E. 490, 3.

[9] E. 544, 36.

[10] At Oxford in 1508 a carpenter was paid for setting 'novi fulsimenti ad supportandum onus tegularum quod vulgari sermone ly fester appellatur': *Canterbury College* (O.H.S.), 248. While 'fester' suggests an object to which something is fastened, it may perhaps have been an extra purlin to take the weight.

[11] E. 501, 8.   [12] R. 91.   [13] E. 458, 28.

[14] E. 462, 15.   [15] Lambeth MS. 242, ff. 6v, 29, &c.

[16] E. 460, 18.   [17] E. 467, 7 (4).

for repair of the roof of the leaden-covered chamber' at Westminster in 1402, which cost 3s. 4d. the hundred.[1]

Eaves-boards, which were placed at the edge of the roof to give the slates a tilt for the better throwing off of rainwater, occur frequently, under a variety of spellings, of which the commonest variants—'euesbordes' and 'ouesbordes'—both occur in the same Winchester Castle accounts for 1428.[2] Winchester Cathedral Priory supplies another form in the 'hoveseborde' used in 1382 for the gabled coping of a garden wall,[3] and at Langley in 1446 they appear as 'evyssebordes'.[4] They were cut more or less triangular in section, the upper edge being thinner than the lower. Similar boards were used for weatherboarding[5]—covering the surface of a wall with overlapping boards. At Clarendon boards were provided for 'le wederbordyng de la owt logge' in 1482,[6] and at Winchester two carpenters were employed '*ad wetherbordandum finem coquinae*' in 1515.[7] Boards, at 2s. 8d. the hundred, were bought by the churchwardens of St. Mary-at-Hill 'for to wederborde the south side of Wolston Wynnys howse' in 1536.[8] A similar construction used on water-mills and other buildings beside streams was known as water-boarding. At Forncett in 1378 nails were bought for nailing 'le waterbord' of the farm buildings,[9] and at Cambridge payments were made in 1532 for 'ly waterbordyng' of the walls of a house called 'ly Sterre' beyond the bridge.[10]

Boards are also sometimes distinguished as coming from particular districts. Thus at Woodstock in 1380 we find 81 'bord' de Arderne' bought at Stratford-on-Avon for making doors and window-shutters,[11] and the Merton College accounts for 1291 mention 3s. 2½d. paid for 13 boards of Ardern.[12] Boards of Kendal were used at Ripon in 1391 and 1396.[13] The 'hombre bord' used in considerable quantities at Ely in 1324[14] may possibly have taken their name from the Humber, and the 32 'weldichsbord' bought at Havant, at 4d. apiece, for Porchester Castle in 1321[15] presumably came from the Weald of Sussex. More distant sources were also drawn upon. When Abbot Faritius (1100–35) rebuilt his abbey at Abingdon we

[1] E. 502, 23.   [2] E. 492, 3.

[3] Kitchin, *Obedientiary Rolls*, 281.   [4] E. 466, 11.

[5] What appears to be an exceptionally early, and isolated, use of the term is the 'viderbord' mentioned at Southwark in 1223: Eccles. Commission, Mins. Accts. 159279.

[6] E. 460, 16.   [7] Kitchin, op. cit. 461.

[8] *Memorials* (E.E.T.S.), 372.

[9] Davenport, *The Economic Development of a Norfolk Manor*, lvi.

[10] K.H. 24, f. 227.   [11] E. 499, 1.   [12] Merton Roll 4054.

[13] R. 107, 125.   [14] *Sacrist Rolls*, 40.   [15] E. 479, 17.

are told that: 'For all the buildings which the abbot made he caused beams and rafters to come from the district of Wales with great cost and heavy labour. For he had six wains for this purpose, and 12 oxen to each of them. Six or seven weeks was the journey, coming and going, for it was necessary to go as far as Shrewsbury.'[1] At a later date, in 1370, 'Walschborde' occurs at Bath,[2] and *'walyshborde'* at Lostwithiel in 1455.[3] Irish boards are mentioned at Canterbury in the thirteenth century, 400 being bought in 1236 for 38s. 3d.,[4] and 300 in 1264 for 28s.;[5] they also occur at Dover in 1227,[6] and in 1224 protection was issued for William de Dublin bringing a shipload of timber to England.[7]

In addition to native timber, a large amount was imported, mostly in the form of boards, from the ports of the Baltic and the North Sea. From the later years of the thirteenth century onwards, this trade, which was mainly in the hands of the Hanseatic League,[8] became of increasing importance and its products found their way all over England, appearing in building accounts under a variety of trade terms. As early as 1275 'bord de Alemain' were bought for work at Westminster at 3d. each.[9] The common appellation, however, is Estland or, still more frequently, Estreche boards. They were always reckoned by the long hundred (120); at Corfe, in 1292, a purchase of 200 estrichboard for doors and shutters is expressly said to be 'by the hundred of six score';[10] in 1300 there is an entry of *'v$^{xx}$ tabulis de estrich'* on the Rockingham Castle accounts;[11] when wainscots were bought for Hampton Court, in 1533, from Hermann Shewet of London, merchant of the Steelyard, at a shilling each, the half hundred cost 60s.,[12] and 'one quarter of waynescottis cont' xxx bordis' occurs at Westminster in 1532.[13] (It is probable that the long hundred was frequently, even generally, used for all kinds of boards and laths in early times, but there is less direct evidence, and there are instances which point to the use of the hundred of five score in some places, at any rate in the sixteenth century.) 'Estricheborde' of 10 feet, which was probably the standard length, are mentioned at Westminster as costing 2d. each in 1329,[14] which was about the usual price at that time. But 500 (i.e. 600) 'hesterysbord' bought at Lynn in 1346 cost, with carriage to Ely, only

[1] *Hist. Mon. de Abingdon*, ii. 150.　　[2] *Somerset Arch. Soc.* xxiii. 8.
[3] E. 461, 18.　　[4] Bodl. MS., Top. Kent, c. 3, f. 89.
[5] Lambeth MS. 242, f. 6v.
[6] E. 462, 10.　　[7] *Patent R.* 444.
[8] Salzman, *English Trade in the Middle Ages*, 362–5.
[9] E. 467, 6 (2).　　[10] E. 460, 29.　　[11] E. 481, 2.
[12] H.C. 237, f. 21.　　[13] T.R. 83.　　[14] E. 467, 7.

£2. 10*s*., or 1*d*. apiece,[1] which suggests that they must have been of exceptionally small scantling; especially as 200 (240) 'boards of Estrysch' similarly bought at Lynn and carried to Ely cost £1. 19*s*. 4*d*. in 1357. In the accounts of King's Hall, Cambridge (where the eccentric variant 'esteriggedborde' occurs in 1493),[2] 12 'hestryschbord' of the best quality (*de optimis*) cost 5*s*. 8*d*. in 1432, and at the same time 15 'hestrysbord viz. wanyscot' cost 6*s*. 8*d*.[3] At Wallingford in 1375 there are references to 'Estrichbord called waynescot', at 24*s*.–28*s*. the hundred, and 'Estrichbord de Rygald' at 8*d*. each.[4] These are the two commonest varieties of imported timber, wainscot being Dutch, or rather German, oak probably deriving its name from having originally been used for making wains, or waggons, while Righolts were timber from the neighbourhood of Riga.[5] The latter were presumably of larger scantling, as they are considerably more expensive. Thus for work at Moor End, in 1366, 12 'regalbord' for making a back piece (*dorsario*) at the head of the king's bed cost 9*s*., while 'waynscot' for doors, shutters, and screens cost only 3½*d*. each.[6] It may be noted in passing that this imported timber was favoured for such work as doors and screens, where it was important to avoid warping, as being better seasoned than the local stuff, so that, for instance, in the contract of 1369 for shops in London it is specified that the doors and shutters shall be of '*tables Destland*'.[7] For the stalls of St. George's Chapel at Windsor a hundred 'ringoldbottes' were bought for 48*s*., and half a hundred 'waynscotbord' for 7*s*. 6*d*., in 1351.[8] Another contemporary Windsor account shows 'cv$^{xx}$ Righoltis, m$^l$m$^l$ Estrichebordis' among the timber used.[9] There is mention of 'rigallis' at Scarborough in 1343, 'ryngoldbord' at Westminster in 1348, 'regaud' at York about the same date, and 'rygolt' at Havering in 1376. So far as my evidence goes it would seem that the differentiation of Eastland boards as wainscots and righolts began about the first quarter of the fourteenth century.

The Customs Accounts for all the ports on the East coast, from Newcastle to Dover, show large imports of Baltic timber, and in 1360 we find 60 boards called 'waynshot' bought, for 10*s*., at Barton-on-Humber for

---

[1] *Sacrist Rolls*, 131.      [2] K.H. 18, f. 347.

[3] K.H. 8, f. 63. Cf. '*in vj estreybords viz. waynscots*' bought for 2*s*. 2*d*. at Sturbridge Fair for Burcester Priory in 1425: Kennet, *Parochial Antiquities*, ii. 254.      [4] E. 490, 3.

[5] Riga was later the centre of the export of deal, but on the whole the uses to which 'righoltz' were put, and the general terms in which they are referred to, point to their having been of oak.

[6] E. 476, 11.      [7] App. B.      [8] E. 492, 27.

[9] Hope, *Windsor Castle*, i. 170.

the ceiling over the altar in the chancel of Bonby Church.[1] For work at York in 1482 'waynscottes' were bought at Hull,[2] and for Ripon in 1520 we find a hundred 'wayngscot' bought for 76s. 8d. and two hundred 'clapbordes' for 6s. 8d., with additional charge 'for cranage (*craneagh*) of the waynescot at Hull, 12d., and for cranage of the clapbordes there, 4d.'[3] Clapboards were small, thin boards, primarily intended for barrel staves, but also used for other purposes. They occur frequently as items in the cargoes of Hanseatic ships—as for instance at Newcastle in 1500, where the *Cristofer* of Danzig brought in 2,400 'clapholt' and the *George* of Wismar 1,500 'waynskettes' and 4,400 'clapholt',[4]—but hardly ever appear in building accounts. They may be equivalent to the 'pipe-bordes', of which twelve were used at Eltham in 1397 '*in factura de shelves pro reliquis Regis superponendis*',[5] while in 1386 we find 761 feet of 'pipebord' bought for boarding a bridge at Westminster, at 8s. 4d. the hundred feet[6]—a price which, it must be admitted, suggests something more substantial than barrel staves. 'Knorbordys' were bought for works at Calais in 1473,[7] and 'knarholt' is a not uncommon ingredient in timber cargoes; the name suggests wood full of knots, but the only instance that I have found of its use in buildings in England—the purchase of '82 boards called knorholte for doors, shutters and louver in the kitchen' at Dover in 1365, at 3d. each —is not enlightening.[8] At Langley in 1368 the boards used included '490 waynskot, 20 ryngold, and 30 boards called bottemholt';[9] while at Porchester in 1397 six 'botineholt' (or 'botmeholt') boards were used for doors and shutters, and another six for masons' molds.[10] Three 'bord de lidholt', at 7d. each, were used at Westminster for masons' molds in 1324,[11] and other 'lydholt' boards, 7 ft. by 18 in., costing 6d., were bought in 1333.[12] But that is all that it seems possible to say about them.

While the wainscots were definitely, and the other varieties probably, of oak,[13] there was also a considerable import of fir or deal boards. They are definitely distinguished from Eastland boards in 1260, when 'half a thousand of Eastland (*estrengium*) boards and half a hundred of deal (*sapio*) boards' were bought for Windsor.[14] But in some London accounts of 1490

---

[1] E. 458, 28.   [2] Y.F.R.   [3] R. 206.
[4] Customs Accts. 108, 4. 'Barelholt' occurs in Newcastle cargoes of 1390: ibid. 106, 18.
[5] E. 495, 23.   [6] E. 473, 2.   [7] E. 198, 4.
[8] E. 462, 23.   [9] E. 466, 4.   [10] E. 479, 23.
[11] E. 469, 8.   [12] E. 469, 11.
[13] A partition in the Exchequer at York in 1320 was made of 'Estland boards of oak': Jenkinson and Johnson, *Engl. Court Hand*, pl. xxiii.
[14] Hope, *Windsor Castle*, i. 48.

there is an entry *'pro vj asseribus de Estriche vocatis deales'*—14s.[1] 'Boards called dealis', at 60s. the hundred, occur at Calais in 1468;[2] *'iiij deles de firre'* were used at Shene in 1473;[3] and 'deles' figure among a variety of boards brought into Newcastle in 1390 by a ship from Hamburg.[4] Although the term 'deal' does not appear until comparatively late, the wood itself was in use in England certainly by the early years of the thirteenth century. In 1252 Henry III ordered the bailiffs of Southampton to buy 200 Norway boards of fir (*sapino*) to be used for panelling Prince Edward's room in Winchester Castle. In 1238 he had ordered the construction at Winchester of a house of deal running on six wheels, and roofed with deal (*sappo*), though unfortunately nothing is said of the size or purpose of this rather intriguing construction.[5] Still earlier, in 1232, the sheriff of Oxford was told to provide fir boards to put round the well at Woodstock.[6] Boards of fir (*sapino*) occur at the Tower in 1278,[7] and at Ely in 1292 (at 12s. the hundred) and 1357 (at 15s. 6d. and 22s. the hundred),[8] but they do not appear to have been used as extensively as might have been expected, and I do not remember having seen any reference in modern architectural works to medieval deal still in position. If the three 'bordis de sap' used at Cambridge Castle for making shutters in 1295[9] were of deal, it is possible that some of the entries, occasionally found, of *'lathis de sap'*[10] also refer to deal and are to be distinguished from the 'saplaths' which, as we have seen, were an inferior variety of oak lath. But the general use of fir timber in England was as spars for scaffolding[11] or for ladders. Thus at York in 1371 two hundred 'firspars' were bought for the scaffold and for ladders,[12] and in 1421 three 'fyrsperres' were used for making a ladder for lighting candles in the choir,[13] and at Westminster 8 'mastes of fyrre' were bought for ladders in 1532.[14] Five 'polis de firre' for measuring the building are referred to in the Windsor accounts of 1345,[15] and 10 'great sperris de firre' were used for the parclose, or dividing screen, of a chamber in the castle of Scarborough in 1343.[16] Deal was also used for furniture. A very detailed inventory of the fittings in the Exchequer at York in 1320 mentions 'a great counter (*scaccarium*), 13 ft. long by 12 ft. broad, well boarded with 18 boards of *fur*, with 4 borders (*listis*) of oak, with three great joists of

[1] Egerton MS. 2358, f. 5.   [2] E. 197, 5.
[3] E. 503, 19.   [4] Customs Accounts, 106, 18.
[5] Liberate R. 23 Hen. III.   [6] Ibid. 17 Hen. III.   [7] E. 467, 7 (4).
[8] *Sacrist Rolls*, 8, 18.   [9] E. 459, 16.
[10] e.g. at the Tower in 1348: E. 471, 1.   [11] For scaffolding, see pp. 318–20.
[12] Y.F.R. 8.   [13] Ibid. 44.   [14] T.R., f. 310.
[15] E. 492, 25.   [16] E. 482, 6.

oak to support it'; another counter, 11 ft. by 8 ft., 'well boarded with 11 boards of *fur* well bordered with borders of alder'; and a partition of oak topped by a joist (*gista*) or beam, of *fur*, 22 feet in length.[1]

Of the other varieties of timber, beech occurs most frequently, owing to the great use made of beech laths, which are usually about the same price as saplaths, or slightly cheaper, and were chiefly employed as foundation for plaster walls, where the tendency of the wood to suffer from damp and worm would not matter. Beech boards were also used, but more for fittings and such structures as the centerings of arches than for general purposes. Possibly the earliest reference occurs in 1222 at Winchester, when 5s. 4d. was paid '*pro clxxv bordis de fow*'.[2] At Westminster '*lath de fohn*' occur in 1259[3] and at Canterbury, in 1281, both laths and boards '*de fov*'.[4] Three hundred beech boards for centerings and doorsteads (*bordis de fagina ad cyntros et durnell*') figure in a Dover account of 1227.[5] For works at the Tower in 1324 'bechbordes' for doors and shutters are mentioned, and 'bechlatthes' for daubing (*pro torch*') and 'for mending the walls of the Constable's quarters' cost 3½d. the hundred, oak 'hertlathes for tiles' being 5d.[6] So, also, at Sheppey in 1365 beech laths were 4s. and oak laths 6s. the thousand,[7] and ten years later at Gravesend some 5,000 beech laths were bought at prices ranging from 5s. to 5s. 10d. the thousand, as against twice the number of oak laths at 8s. 4d.;[8] but in 1386 at Westminster 'bechenlaths', at 7d. the hundred, ranked with 'short hertlaths'; and above 'saplaths' at 5d.[9] Finally, as instances of the use of this wood for fittings, we may note that in 1240 orders were given for the delivery of a good beech tree from Windsor Forest to Master Simon the carpenter, wherewith to make tables in the king's kitchen at Westminster against Christmas,[10] while in 1485 two boards of beech, each 10 ft. by 1 ft. 6 in., were used for making shelves in the larder at Coldharbour Manor.[11]

Elm, a timber now in disrepute because of its tendency to warp and also to attract worm, was in pretty constant demand in the Middle Ages. We have already referred to its pre-eminence for piles and in wet situations.[12] It is perhaps significant that it does not appear to have been used for general purposes before the middle of the fourteenth century, when large oak

---

[1] Jenkinson and Johnson, *Engl. Court Hand*, pl. xxiii.  [2] E. 491, 13.
[3] E. 467, 2.     [4] Lambeth MS. 242, f. 67ᵛ.
[5] E. 462, 10.     [6] E. 469, 7.    [7] E. 502, 3.
[8] E. 544, 3.     [9] E. 473, 2.
[10] *Close R.* 259. So in 1255 a great beech tree was ordered for the king's kitchen tables in readiness for Easter: Liberate R. 36 Hen. III.
[11] E. 474, 3.       [12] See above, p. 85.

timber was becoming scarce and expensive. Thirty-eight boards '*de olmo*' occur at Windsor in 1352,[1] and three years later a list of timber there includes 4 holms (*holmis*)—the only mention I have found of this tree—and 4 elms.[2] Five hundred feet of elm boards, at 2s. the hundred feet, were used over 'le storehous' at Eltham in 1397,[3] and elm boards were also used in 1442 in the making of 3 sheds (*shuddorum*) in the king's private garden at Westminster.[4] Both of these are instances where inferior material might well be employed, and a rare example of elm being used for the main timbers of a building—'ele (= elm) postes intaws ele pannys and ele sparrys' being bought—in 1472, refers to farm buildings belonging to the rectory of Farnham.[5] In 1454 we find 1,200 'elmynborde' bought from the Abbot of Lesnes for works at St. Paul's, or more probably to be used in houses belonging to the cathedral, at 2d. each.[6] This price agrees with a standard board length of 10 feet, as 'elmyn bordes' at Devizes in 1460 cost 2s. the 100 feet,[7] and at Windsor in 1462 from 20d. to 2s., oak board being 2s. 8d.[8] The same price, 2s., still held good in 1532 at Westminster, where it was used in large quantities, there being payments for sawing 6,700 feet of 'elmyng borde',[9] and next year 3,800 feet of elm board was bought for Hampton Court.[10] By this time the increasing demands of the iron furnaces for fuel were making such serious inroads on oak timber that supplies for ship-building were threatened: which may account for this large use of elm. Like beech, elm was occasionally used for fittings, as at Coldharbour in 1485, when 'ij newe dressyngbordes of elme', 10 ft. by 2 ft., were supplied for the kitchen, and 'j dressbord of elme in the larder'.[11]

Poplar, a very poor, soft wood, makes its appearance occasionally. At Carisbrooke Castle, in 1353, a poplar (*populo*) and an ash were used for making certain wicket-gates,[12] the poplar, no doubt, providing the boards and the ash the framing. Small quantities of 'popeler' boards occur at Hadleigh in 1363 and 1364;[13] 3 'bordes de pipler' were used for a wardrobe at Dunster in 1405;[14] and 'vj bords of popill . . . for amendyng of the louer of the quyeneschambre' are mentioned at Scarborough in 1423.[15] Its most extensive use appears to have been at King's Hall, Cambridge, where in 1417 long poplar boards cost 7d. and short ones 3d.;[16] in 1431

[1] Hope, *Windsor Castle*, i. 170.                          [2] Ibid. 175.
[3] E. 495, 23.                     [4] E. 473, 18.            [5] E. 463, 13.
[6] St. Paul's, Misc. Roll A. 52.
[7] E. 462, 6. About a thousand foot was bought.
[8] E. 496, 16.              [9] T.R., ff. 8, 510.            [10] H.C. 237, f. 21.
[11] E. 474, 3.              [12] E. 490, 29.                 [13] E. 464, 6 and 8.
[14] *Arch. J.* xxxviii. 74.  [15] E. 482, 8.                [16] K.H. 6, f. 150.

'poppillbord' was bought for roofing the studies;[1] and in 1450 seven hundred feet of 'popyll' cost 15s.[2] It also appears under the name of 'abele' in the Peterhouse accounts for 1461—6s. 3d. for sawing '*v<sup>c</sup> di*' *pedum asserum de abel et fraccino*'.

Willow is even less satisfactory as a timber tree than poplar and it is only found so used in the Fen District. For Cambridge Castle in 1295 four boards of willow (*salice*) were used to make a gate, and 11, costing only 9d., for a manger in the stable.[3] So at Ely between 1334 and 1337 willow boards were used for bridges on the causeway and for making centerings.[4] A certain Roger de Multon brought an action in 1317 against two carpenters, who had undertaken to build a house for him at St. Ives, using only new oak timber, but had put alder and willow timber into the house. Presumably they had used it only for unimportant fittings, as they were fined only 6d. and Roger's damages were assessed at 2s.[5]

The chief virtue of ash is its pliancy and resilience, which makes it admirable for such purposes as the handles of tools but unsuitable for building, especially as it is liable to worm. So at Scarborough in 1284 we find 9 poles of ash (*palis de freno*) used for making shores and levers (*fausetis et leuours*),[6] and at York an ash was supplied for 'haxshaftes' in 1422, and 16d. was paid in 1471 'for 40 shydes of ash for the shafts and handles of the carpenters' and masons' tools'.[7] At Westminster in 1532 'asshen tymber' was used for 'ladder rounds', Nicholas Webbe of Marloo in Sussex supplied 18 'shides of grounde asshe' for helves of mattocks and hammers, and there is mention of 'ij loodes and xx shides of asshyn talwoode, wherof was made handebarroughes', costing 12s., at 5s. the load.[8] An ash was cut for studs at Corfe in 1292,[9] and there are many instances of ash being used for 'splints'—the upright stakes of wattling; and 'xij plankes of asch off xvij foot of lengyth and xx ynchis in breddyth for a knedyng trooffe (trough) pastery bredes (boards) and tables for chambers' were bought, at 18d. each, for Corpus Christi College, Oxford, in 1517.[10]

Lime, or linden, is another timber of rare occurrence. It is a soft white wood and is classed, in a fourteenth-century tract on architecture, with the white poplar as '*in fabrica inutiles, in sculpturis grate inveniuntur*'.[11] Accordingly we find Henry III in 1234 granting lime (*teyl*) timber to the Friars

---

[1] K.H. 8, ff. 29, 63.   [2] K.H. 11, f. 137.
[3] E. 459, 16.   [4] *Sacrist Rolls*, 67, 72, 91.
[5] *Select Cases on Law Merchant* (Selden Soc.), i. 104.
[6] E. 482, 1.   [7] *Y.F.R.* 47, 75.   [8] T.R., ff. 7, 8, 159.
[9] E. 460, 29.   [10] C.C.C. MS. 435, f. 2.
[11] Bodl. MS. Auct. F. 5. 23, f. 160.

Minor of Nottingham for their stalls.[1] At Clipston planks of lime (*tiliarum*) were used for tables and benches in the hall in 1357, and in 1370 there is a payment 'for the felling and sawing of a lynd for dressours in the kitchen'.[2] At Nottingham in 1314 lime boards were sawn for the doors of the mill, and limes were used for scaffolding[3]—for which purpose any available timber was made use of—and at Scarborough 90 'lymebord', costing 2*s.* 3*d.*, were employed to cover the roof of a chamber in 1284.[4] The sycamore, or plane, is not indigenous and does not seem to have established itself in England in the Middle Ages. The only reference to this wood that I have seen is in a list of payments to Stephen 'le joignur', in a Westminster account of 1274—'a coffer *de plana* well bound with iron—and *j tabula cum kernettis* (hinges) *de plana*'.[5] Aspen occurs at Kirby Muxloe in 1481—'sawing two pieces of *le aspes* for shutters'.[6] Walnut has always been a wood for furniture rather than construction and seems to have been little employed in any capacity in the Middle Ages, being probably valued for its fruit. The King's Hall accounts for 1491 include 3*s.* 6*d.* '*pro sawyng unius walnotetre et hewyng*',[7] and those of Windsor Castle for 1536 mention the carriage to the timber-yard of 24 'loodes of walnotry and hasshen tymbre',[8] but in neither instance is there any indication of their purpose.

Chestnut is an excellent timber, closely resembling oak. Gwilt[9] cheerfully asserts: 'We know that it was much used in the buildings of our ancestors, and was, perhaps, even the chief timber employed', and it is constantly asserted that certain roofs are of chestnut. Actually there appears to be no known instance of chestnut existing in a medieval building in England,[10] and the only reference that I have found to its employment is in 1278, when a hundred *robora castanearum* from Milton in Kent were assigned for works at Dover Castle.[11]

[1] *Close R.* 22.    [2] E. 460, 17 and 20.    [3] E. 478, 1.
[4] E. 482, 1.    [5] E. 467, 2.
[6] *Leics. Arch. Soc.* xi. 251.    [7] K.H. 18, f. 263.
[8] Hope, *Windsor Castle*, i. 264.    [9] *Enc. of Architecture*, 483.
[10] *Journal of R.I.B.A.* iv. 192; xv. 231.    [11] *Close R.* 449.

## XVII

## DOORS, SHUTTERS, PANELLING, SCREENS

OF all the fittings that the carpenter was called upon to provide, doors were the most essential. In a stone-built edifice the door-frames were, as we have seen, of stone; in a timber frame they were usually of wood, but constructionally similar. Thus we have, for instance, 'a thresshewolde and 2 dorstedes' provided for a mill at Sken-frith in 1420;[1] '2 dore chykes to the great dore' at Farnham Rectory in 1472;[2] and 'a piece of oak for making a *dorne*' at Bath in 1460, with 1*d.* paid '*pro settynge over de dicto dorne*'.[3] At Collyweston there is a payment in 1500 'for to make a new dorne and a dower leff'[4]—the door proper being usually termed a leaf, or in Latin *folium*; as at Corfe in 1357, when we find '2 leaves (*foliis*) for a door at the entry of le Gloriet'.[5] Occasionally the Latin *valva* is used instead; thus in the second quarter of the twelfth century 'the double door-leaves (*valvas*) at the front of the church [of Bury St. Edmunds] were carved by the hands of Master Hugh, who, as he excelled all men in his other works, in this marvellous piece of work excelled himself'.[6] While doors more or less elaborately carved are still not uncommon in our churches, they do not figure in our records, where as a rule a door is just a door—though in two London contracts for shops, in 1369 and 1410, it is specified that the doors shall be made of good East-land boards.[7] For the great gallery in Westminster Palace in 1532 John Ripley supplied:[8]

Dores of waynscotte lyned and doble battened, at 20s.–30s.
Dores of like stuffe lyned and single battened, at 16s.
Dores of like stuffe lyned on bothe sides with draperye pannelle,[9] at 20s.
Pleyne dores of waynescotte with rabettes and feelettis, at 6s. 8d.
Dores of like stuffe without rabettis and feelettis, at 6s.

Whatever the treatment of their surfaces, all but the lightest doors require something in the nature of a framing. In a contract of 1374 for work at Trinity Hall, Cambridge, it is specified that the carpenter 'shall

[1] Mins. Accts. Duchy of Lancs. 9514.
[2] E. 463, 13.
[3] *Somerset Arch. Soc.* xxv. 55.
[4] St. John's Coll., Camb., MS. vol. i.
[5] E. 461, 6.
[6] *Mems. of St. Edmunds*, ii. 289.
[7] App. B.
[8] T.R., f. 615.
[9] The well-known 'linen panelling'.

work all the doors and shall provide the wooden braces (*ligamina*) sufficient and necessary for them'.[1] The usual form of bracing was by means of
square-sectioned wooden bars, known as 'ledges', crossing either at right
angles or diagonally, on the inside of the door. References to these ledges
are numerous: at Dover in 1283 we find a payment to 'two sawyers
(*sioribus*) sawing *legges* for doors and shutters',[2] and an earlier Dover
account, of 1220, mentions '16 planks for making the new gate, a flail
(*flagello*) and 22 bars'[3]—the latter being evidently equivalent to ledges.
At Clipston 3*s*. 8*d*. was spent in 1357 on '800 large spikyng for 8 great doors
newly made, for each door 100 spikyng, because they were much braced
(*lig'*) with *crosslegges*':[4] and at Westminster in 1373 we have '4 pieces of
sawn timber called *quarteres* for *legges* for the door of the great hall, 8 ft.
in length; and a piece of timber for the *lynia* of the said door, 11 ft. in
length, of squared oak 1 ft. in breadth',[5] where the *lynia* is probably the
main upright of the framing. In 1435 George Carpenter was paid 'for
making smaller the door of the Daunsynghous, and replacing the legges
on the said door' at Woodstock;[6] and repairs to a house in London in 1500
included 'iiij leggs behynd ye dore'.[7] The accounts of the churchwardens
of St. Michael's, Bath, in 1478 mention 'a load of *sclattes* (i.e. slats) of oak
for making the legges of the door', and also payments 'for paryng hewyng
and planeyng of 4 boards and 5 legges of the new door; for half a hundred
of bordenayle for the said door, and for settyng on of 3 locks (*cereis*);
for one new twyste (i.e. hinge-band) and the making of another from
material in store; for hackenayle for the said door; and to Richard Smyth
for nayling hangyng and dressyng of all the fittings (*apparatu*) of the said
door'.[8] The same accounts, ten years later, mention the 'listyng' of the
west door of the church, that is to say, making the wooden frame round
its edge.[9] The almost contemporary accounts of St. Edmund's, Salisbury,
for 1491 recorded the expenditure of 8*d*. 'for makyng of ij wedyr dorys
in the stepulle and legyng (i.e. ledging) of Watkyns dore',[10]—'weather
doors' being a term still applied to doors in a tower opening out onto the
leads.

A large door or gate was often provided with a smaller 'wicket' in, or
beside, it. Thus at the Tower in 1278 timber was provided 'for the gate of
the tower, with two leaves and a wicket (*guigetta*)';[11] and at Corfe, seven

---

[1] App. B.      [2] E. 462, 9.      [3] E. 462, 8.
[4] E. 460, 17.      [5] E. 469, 13.      [6] E. 499, 3.
[7] Jupp, *Hist. of the Carpenters' Company*, 221.
[8] *Somerset Arch. Soc.* xxv. 76, 77.      [9] Ibid. 89.
[10] Swayne, *Ch. Wardens' Accts. Sarum*, 40.      [11] E. 467, 7 (4).

years later, the carpenters made *wykettas* to the conduit house (*cysternam*) and the prison called 'Malemit'.[1] At Clarendon we find a lock and key provided for the *wyket* of the great solar in 1316; and in 1369 two rings (*circul'*), a staple, and a hingehook (*gunph'*) were provided for the *wycat* of the gate of Hadleigh Castle.[2] In an account for repairs to the castle of Monmouth in 1370 mention of '*le wikegate* of the gate'[3] points to a mistaken derivation from 'wike gate'; and this seems to be supported by a reference to '*le wike magne porte*' at Lostwithiel in 1455.[4] Another type of small door is the 'hatch', or half-door. This is now chiefly associated with a buttery, and in 1352 we find mention of '4 hinges for the *hach* of the king's butter' at Westminster,[5] and in 1423 'a *Hache* for the chamberlain's larder (*salario*)' at Carmarthen.[6] At Dunster in 1426 Thomas Pacheboll was employed for two weeks, at 18*d*. a week and his food, 'making the screen (*enterclos*) and *hachys* between the lord's hall and the chapel', and Thomas Smyth was paid 2*s*. 'for 6 pair of hinges (*yemeaux*) for the *hacchys* in the chapel'.[7]

Trap-doors are occasionally referred to; as for instance at Banstead in 1372, when hinges were provided 'for a door called *trappedore*'.[8] At Westminster in 1352 we find 'a platelok for a folding (*plicato*) door'; and sliding doors are mentioned at Windsor in 1311—iron bands and ties being made *pro porta currente* at the entrance to the castle[9]—and in London in 1488, when 'a rynnyng dore' was made between two tenements.[10] Portcullises may be regarded as a type of gate and naturally figure in castle accounts, but very rarely in any detail, the fullest entry that I have noted being in 1374, when there were in store at Leeds Castle—'8 portecolys, to which belong 20 pykes with 20 plates of iron, 14 long iron plates, and transverse iron plates, and 188 nails for re-ironing the same portecolys'.[11]

Closely associated with doors are shutters, which may be regarded as window-doors. Thus in 1364 at Sheppey Castle £16. 19*s*. 3*d*. was paid to Guy Withot and Richard Snowe, carpenters, for 407 doors and shutters in the castle, made by contract at 10*d*. apiece'.[12] At Clarendon in 1316 we have '142 boards of oak for making doors and shutters',[13] and in 1359 a large purchase of 'estrichbordes' for making 23 doors and 43 shutters.[14] Similarly, in the London contracts quoted on p. 253, Eastland boards were

[1] E. 460, 27.     [2] E. 464, 11.
[3] Mins. Accts. Duchy of Lancs. 9506.     [4] E. 461, 18.
[5] E. 471, 6.     [6] E. 487, 17.     [7] *Arch. Journal*, xxxviii. 212.
[8] E. 494, 15.     [9] E. 471, 6.     [10] *Mems.* (E.E.T.S.), 139.
[11] E. 480, 3.     [12] E. 502, 3.     [13] E. 459, 27.
[14] E. 460, 1.

to be used for the doors and shutters, doubtless as being better seasoned. At Hedon, in a fourteenth-century account, is mention of '6 boards called fyve fote burde for repairing the hatch (*le hek*) and shutters'.[1]

In all these entries the word for shutters is *fenestrae* and it is worth stressing the point that this, and not 'windows', is the correct translation, as it explains a passage in Wace's account of the battle of Hastings which has puzzled several writers. Wace, describing the famous shield-wall formation of the English troops, wrote:

> Fet orent devant els escuz
> De fenestres e d'altres fuz;
> Devant els les orent levez.

Mr. Freeman translated the second line as 'of ash and other timber' (incidentally perverting *escuz* into 'barricades'); Mr. Archer rendered *fenestres* as 'windows', and Mr. Round, while scoffing at this, could only suggest that the word was 'either a corruption or quite inexplicable'.[2] Wace evidently pictured the English as improvising shields out of shutters and other bits of wood. That this translation is correct may be seen from orders given in 1245 for making a window, with two marble columns, in the queen's chamber at Guildford: 'the window to be wainscoted (*lambruzcari*) and closed with glass windows between the columns, with panels which can be opened and closed, and wooden shutters in one piece (*fenestras bordeas integras*) inside to close over the glass window.'[3] Here *fenestra* is used first for the stone frame of the window, then for the glazing, and finally for the shutters, and in accounts it is sometimes difficult to be certain which sense is intended. The confusion extended into English. In some London accounts of 1450 we have: 'Adam Carpenter for iij dayys for the turnyng of dyverse wyndowys wych wold nate wele opon nor schot as they hyng aforetyme . . . item . . . for polys and ropeys to the same wyndowys.'[4] The pulleys and ropes at first suggest sash windows—a distinct anachronism. Harman, in 1519, writes:[5] 'I have many pretty wyndowes shette with levys goynge up and downe', which is shown to refer to shutters by another of his sentences: 'Wyndowe leves of tymbre be made of bourdis ioyned to gether, with keys of tree let into them.' The 'ij newe wyndowis of tymbre' at Collyweston in 1500 are also clearly shutters.[6]

Window-frames, for insertion in masonry, were sometimes used. Such

---

[1] Boyle, *Hist. of Hedon*, liv.
[3] Liberate R. 30 Hen. III, m. 17.
[5] *Vulgaria*, c. xxix.

[2] Round, *Feudal England*, 346, 402.
[4] Mins. Accts., 917, No. 23.
[6] St. John's Coll., Camb., MS. vol. i.

possibly was the *magna verina* in Winchester Castle hall (for the making of which Elias de Derham was given 6 balks of timber (*fusta*) in 1233.[1] Usually they seem to have been called 'casements'; as at Leeds Castle in 1369—'for *casemens* made of wood for glass windows in the Gloriet';[2] and at Westminster in 1386—'for a wooden casement (*cas'*) made for a glass window beside the council room'.[3]

A wooden *fenestra*, therefore, may be taken to be a shutter. Such were the '60 *fenestrae* square and round, made of estrychbord' in store at Westminster in 1444;[4] and such was the *fenestra* referred to at York in 1327, when 4*d*. was paid 'for the cost of a man and his boat going to Fulford to seek and bring back a great wooden *fenestra* which had been stolen from the house pulled down in Skeldregate'.[5] In 1232 the king ordered 'shutters of fir (*sabo*), well bound with iron', to be made for his great chamber at Woodstock;[6] and in 1238 'shutters of fir', made for the new stone window made in the gable of the Queen's chamber at Marlborough, cost 20*d*.[7] Among other work to be done at the Tower in 1240, Henry III ordered 'our great chamber to be whitewashed and repainted, and all its shutters to be remade with new wood, new catches and hinges, and painted with our arms'.[8] Similarly, in 1265, he ordered the Constable of Winchester 'to paint all the doors and shutters of the king's hall and chambers with his arms'.[9] At King's Hall, Cambridge, 40*s*. was paid in 1432 'to the painter for painting the King's arms and oiling (*unctione*) other shutters, the great gate, and the great shutter of the warden's chamber'.[10]

Shutters were often braced like doors: '*legges pro ostiis et fenestris*' occur at Peterborough in 1523;[11] and the accounts for work on the manor of Pleasaunce, at Greenwich, in 1448 mention both doors and shutters as '*legyd et batant*',[12] that is to say, ledged and battened. These same accounts show[13] '2 joiners (*junours*) engaged in making shutters for 2 bay wyndows, namely, 4 leaves, with *selyng* and *bordonyng* of them, and also making 5 small leaves for the same standing under the glass; and also making 15 leaves set in 15 lights within 2 (? 3)[14] bay wyndos in the parlour'. The entry is rather obscure, but apparently the upper part of the bay windows was glazed and the lower filled with lattices and closed with shutters; the '*selyng* and *bordonyng*' one would take to refer to the panelling of the

---

[1] *Close R.* 242.  [2] E. 544, 23.  [3] E. 473, 2.
[4] E. 503, 12.  [5] E. 501, 8.  [6] Liberate R. 17 Hen. III.
[7] E. 476, 3.  [8] Liberate R. 24 Hen. III, m. 17.
[9] Ibid. 50 Hen. III.  [10] K.H. 8, f. 62.  [11] Receiver's Acct.
[12] Dy. of Lanc. Misc. Bks., 1, 11, f. 14.  [13] Ibid., f. 10v.
[14] Cf. 'for 15 latez of wayneskot set in 15 lights within 3 baywyndos': ibid., f. 13.

top and bottom of the bays rather than to the shutters. But in a Nottingham Castle account of 1313 is an entry: 'For boards for new shutters in
the great hall, in the gable. Also for 7 blocks (*lignis*) for making *legges
stapplys* and *selys* for the said shutters. Also for iron ties, bands and hinge
hooks for hanging the shutters.'[1] Here *selys* seem to be the 'sills' or bottom
pieces, and *stapplys* are presumably the side pieces of the framing.

It was from early times a common custom to 'seal', or panel, rooms.
The Liberate Rolls of Henry III are full of orders to panel (*lambruscare*)
various apartments in the royal manors and castles, often with further
instructions to paint the panelling green with gold spots, as medieval man
had not the modern reverence for his oak. The panelling was usually
carried out in wainscot. Thus in 1510, when the chapel of Christ's College,
Cambridge, was being panelled, there is an entry of 'costes of Nicholas
Joyner to London to bie waynscott to performe the selyng of the quere . . .
and bowt none by cause of the grett prices then'.[2] Most of the earlier
panelling was plain work, calling for no particular remark, but towards the
end of our period more elaborate work was coming into fashion. For the
gallery at Westminster Palace in 1532, we find John Ripley providing 68
yards of 'pleyne sealing', at 12*d.* the yard, 421 yards of 'sealing of creste
panell', at 19*d.*, and 827 yards of 'sealing of drapery pannell'—the linen-
fold pattern which remained in common use for the next century and
more—at 21*d.*[3] For the same job, which included the ceiling as well as the
walls, he supplied also 195 yards of 'jowepecis with bullions'[4]—cornices
with pendants—at 6*d.*; 950 yards of 'flatte battons', at 2*d.*; 2,057 yards of
'streight battons enbowid', at 3*d.* the yard; and 714 'croked battons
embowid', at 3*d.* each. The precise meaning of 'inbowing' is slightly
obscure; it is generally said to mean bending or cutting wood into the
shape of an arch, but from consideration of a large number of instances in
which the word occurs I am inclined to think that it means cutting timber
to an arch section—trimming the projection of a beam, or similar piece,
more or less to a point, often by a series of mouldings. This sense will, I
think, be found to fit every occurrence of the word, whereas the usual
definition will hardly apply to the 'straight battens' mentioned above, and
in such an entry as occurs at Shene in 1440—'for enbowyng and making
various lyntells and moynells (i.e. mullions) for doors and windows'[5]—

---

[1] E. 478, 1.

[2] Willis and Clark, *Arch. Hist.* ii. 198.        [3] T.R., f. 615.

[4] The 'jowe pecis' were garnished with 'the kinges poisie', or motto, in letters of gilded
lead: ibid. 579.

[5] E. 503, 9.

it is difficult to see how so essentially straight a feature as a mullion could be cut into the shape of an arch.

At the same time as the Westminster Gallery was being panelled, work of a highly ornate character was being carried out in the hall of Queens' College, Cambridge. The necessary wainscots were brought from Lynn, and it is worth noticing that the panels, which still exist, though not in their original place, were carved with linenfolds, a fact which does not appear from the accounts.[1] Five carvers, or joiners, were employed to carve small heads 'de ly Antik' (i.e. in the classical style), at 16*d.*, large heads, at 20*d.*, 'skochyngis', or shields of arms (the designs for which were provided by John Ward, painter, at 2*d.* apiece), at 20*d.*, and 'Antyk' borders and cresting at 8*d.* the yard. There were also 64 small columns down the sides of the hall and 25 columns round the high table. The chief carver was Dyrik Harison, who had been employed on the panelling of Christ's Chapel in 1510, when he and Henry Plowman were paid 3*s.* 4*d.* 'for ther costes and cariage of ther tolys from London to Cambrege, with rewardes for lettyng (i.e. hindrance) of certen daies werke or (i.e. before) ther toles come'.[2] From his name, Dyrik was probably a Fleming, and the names of his companions—Giles Fambeler, Lambert, Arnold, and Peter, suggest that they were also his compatriots. The men of the Low Countries had always been particularly skilled in woodwork. As early as 1251 Master John of Flanders was 'the king's carver',[3] in which capacity he was then working at St. Albans on a great lectern for Westminster Abbey. In 1411 John Van de Nym, 'carpenter de entaill', in other words carver, was employed by the London Bridge wardens for one week at 8*d.* a day,[4] evidently for some special pieces of decoration. And when the ornate woodwork of St. George's Chapel, Windsor, was being prepared, in 1477, Dirick Vangrove and Giles Vancastell were entrusted with the carving of figures of St. George and the dragon, St. Edward, and the Rood with the Virgin and St. John—calculated prosaically at the rate of 5*s.* the foot of length.[5]

When the walls of a room were covered with tapestry hangings, instead of panelling, something in the nature of a picture-rail was sometimes put up. Thus, at Carmarthen in 1428 we have mention of 'making *lez raeles pur lez dosers* (dorsers, or back-cloths) hanging in the hall of justice';[6] and

---

[1] Printed in full in Willis and Clark, *Arch. Hist.* ii. 61–6.
[2] Ibid. ii. 198.   [3] *Close R.* 495.
[4] London Bridge Accts. i, f. 366.
[5] E. 496, 17. The accounts, from 1477 to 1481, are printed in Hope's *Windsor Castle*, and are unusually detailed.   [6] E. 487, 18.

at Queen Margaret's manor of Pleasaunce in 1447 tinned 'dicehedenayles' were used '*in naylyng le rayle de novo fact' pro le aras*', and carpenters worked at 'framyng planyng and making the rayle in the Queen's Ward for the safe keeping of the aras and hangynges'.[1]

A notable feature of the medieval hall was the screen at the lower end. This probably originated in the single-room house as a partition shutting off the part of the room where the food was prepared from the living-room. In later times it became an ornamental feature, but served the useful purpose of keeping out some of the draught from the door. Screens and 'spurs' were often put for that purpose near doors in other rooms than halls. The spur, strictly speaking, is a screen projecting from the wall but not going right across the room, but the terms spur and screen seem to have been used as practically synonymous. In 1237 orders were given to make 'a spur of boards, good and becoming, between the chamber and the chapel in the new turret near the hall', at the Tower.[2] Repairs at Clarendon in 1250 included—2 spurs (*sporas*) in the chamber of Alexander, a screen (*escrenum*) in the chamber of Prince Edward, a spur at the upper end of the King's chamber, and another in the outer chamber of his wardrobe.[3] Next year orders were given to panel a chamber in Nottingham Castle, to put wooden stalls in it on every side, and make a spur (*esporum*) in front of the door, and to fix candlesticks in the walls.[4] A Nottingham account for 1313 mentions the provision of '3 great spurs (*speris*), one opposite the door of the King's wardrobe, another at the door of the chamber, and the third at the King's head'.[5] It also mentions 'boards for a screen (*screna*) hanging over the fireplace between the hearth and the King's bed'. So also, 'a wooden *skrene* for a fireplace' occurs at Dover in 1390,[6] and 16*d*. was paid at Westminster in 1386 'for a screen made for the king to have between him and the fire'.[7] Probably something similar is implied in the 'two t(r)anyngsperez (? or tu(r)nyngsperez)' in the King's chamber at Shene, for which hinges were supplied in 1363;[8] they were evidently adjustable screens of some kind.

Five boards of 'popeller' were supplied for a 'sper' in the King's chamber at Havering in 1376,[9] and 2 (?) lattices (*chancell'*) and an Eastland board for the door of a 'spere' at Westminster in 1289.[10] At Cambridge Castle in 1295 we have an entry: 'for 10 deal (*saap*) boards for making a spere in front

[1] Dy. of Lanc. Misc. Bks., 1, 11, ff. 8, 10v.     [2] Liberate R. 22 Hen. III.
[3] Ibid. 35 Hen. III, m. 17.     [4] Ibid. 36 Hen. III, m. 17.
[5] E. 478, 1.     [6] Foreign R. 13 Ric. II.
[7] E. 473, 2.     [8] E. 493, 18.
[9] E. 464, 30.     [10] E. 467, 20.

of the seat of the latrine (*le setle cloace*) of the wardrobe of the hall, 2s. 6d. Also for hooks and hinges for the door of the said speer, 5s.'[1] In these last two instances the spur, being provided with a door, was evidently a complete partition. When a screen separated off a portion of a room, forming a closet, it was often termed either an 'interclose' or a 'parclose'. In 1260 Henry III ordered Richard Fremantle 'to make an interclose (*interclusum*) of board on each side of the high altar in the King's chapel at Windsor, with proper doors, and to paint the interclose and doors as the King had instructed him'.[2] At Clarendon there is a payment in 1477 'for making the *enterclose* in the chamber beyond le Bolpit';[3] and at Scarborough in 1343 we find mention of '10 great spars of firre for the parclose of the chamber'.[4]

Something in the nature of a matchboard partition seems to be implied in the 'paper walls' made by carpenters in the Tower *c.* 1525: 'iiij particions otherwise callyd paper wallys under the said vij chambres to devyde the houses of office, and in every particion there a dore new made, and w^tin one of these particions a stole made to a jaques'.[5]

Tables, benches, chairs, cupboards, and beds, though they were made by the same carpenters and joiners employed on structural features, can hardly be regarded as pertinent to our subject, and may therefore be passed over. But one may be excused an exclamation of surprise at finding '4 *slyddys de gorst ad implenda lecta*' at Cardigan in 1428.[6] True, nine pennyworth of 'litter' was also provided for the same beds, but anything less restful than gorse for bedding would be hard to find. One wonders if it was intended to discourage visitors?

[1] E. 459, 16.   [2] Liberate R. 45 Hen. III.   [3] E. 460, 14.
[4] E. 482, 6.   [5] E. 474, 13.   [6] E. 487, 18.

# XVIII

## PLUMBING, WATER-SUPPLY, SANITATION

LEAD has been used as a protective roof covering from very early times. In the second half of the seventh century Eadberht removed the thatch from the wooden church which Finan had built at Lindisfarne and 'covered the whole, that is the roof, and the walls themselves, with sheets (*laminibus*) of lead'.[1] St. Wilfrid, also, when he repaired the church built by Paulinus at York, 'raised the roof and protected it from injury by storms with leaden sheets';[2] and the church of the Confessor's Abbey of Westminster had a wooden roof 'carefully covered with lead'.[3] As lead was found in considerable quantity in Derbyshire and elsewhere in England[4] this material was more commonly used in this country than in most parts of the Continent, and it is significant that when Bishop Geoffrey de Mowbray repaired his cathedral of Coutances, after it had been struck by lightning in 1091, 'he sent to England and called to him Brismet the plumber'[5] to see to the leading of the church. The Liberate Rolls of Henry III and later building accounts are full of references to leaden roofs, and lead was even used as a temporary coping for the unfinished walls and pillars of Westminster Abbey nave when work was suspended during the reign of Henry IV.[6] Roofs covered with lead are certainly ugly, but that consideration would not weigh with medieval builders (they would have used corrugated iron if they had possessed it) against the merits of the material. If well laid the whole roof forms one impervious sheet and can therefore be set on a low-pitched or flat roof;[7] unlike tiles, lead did not require constant repairs, and unlike thatch it was not inflammable—though when a fire did occur the molten lead lent an additional terror to it, and more than one fire occurred through the carelessness or forgetfulness of plumbers, as, notably, the burning of the tower of Bury St. Edmunds in 1456.[8]

---

[1] Bede, *Hist. Eccl.* iii, c. xxv.     [2] Will. Malmesbury, *Gesta Pontif.* 216.

[3] *Lives of Edw. the Confessor* (Rolls Ser.), 417.

[4] Salzman, *Engl. Industries*, ch. 3.     [5] Mortet, *Docts. relatifs à al'rchitecture*, 75.

[6] Rackham, *The Nave of Westminster*, 12.

[7] I have heard it suggested that the English fondness for battlemented parapets is attributable to the greater frequency in this country of low-pitched roofs. A point worth examining.

[8] *Mems. of St. Edmunds*, iii. 283.

The chief deterrent factor in the use of lead for roofing was the cost of the material. In 1474 over £187 was spent on leading three bays of the 'stepe roof' of the nave of Westminster Abbey.[1] The char, cartload (*carectata*), or fother—a weight fluctuating between 19 cwt. and a ton, and sufficient to cover about 160 square feet—between 1250 and 1350 cost from £2 to £3;[2] possibly owing to the Black Death the price then leapt up and stood for some 20 years at about £7, subsequently dropping to about £5. Naturally the total cost varied according to the locality, carriage being an important item. Much of the Derbyshire lead was sent by water to Boston and exported from there. Thus for Winchester Castle in 1222 we have—'for 20 chars (*charcatis*) of lead bought by Elyas West-man, mayor of Winchester, at Boston Fair, £27. 6s. For carriage of the same by sea to Southampton, 32s.'[3] For Westminster Palace in 1259 four chars (*chareis*) of lead were bought, for £8. 8s., at Boston Fair.[4] We even find, in 1310, that 3 fothers of lead were bought, for £9. 12s., at the same fair for Exeter Cathedral. Weighing, marking, customs, and carriage to the water cost 5s. 9d.; carriage by sea to Topsham, 18s.; discharging it there, 17d.; and carriage to Exeter, 3s. 5d.[5] One might have expected that Exeter would have been supplied entirely from mines nearer at hand. At Restormel in 1343 two fothers of lead were bought for £4. 4s., and another 4s. 8d. was spent 'on carriage of the said lead from the mine of Devon with 14 horses employed therefor, at 4d. for a horse'.[6] The Mendips, also, were a centre of lead mining, and lead of 'Munydep' was supplied to Porchester, at £5. 6s. 8d. the fother, in 1397.[7] For Corfe Castle in 1367 four 'foudres' of lead were bought in London for £30; another 4s. was paid for their carriage from Candelwykestrete (now Cannon Street) to the river; 13s. 4d. for carriage thence to the castle.[8] At Knaresborough in 1303 we find 6 'wayes' of lead bought at Ripon for 28s. 1½d.—each 'waye' containing 15 stone, which, with a stone of 12 lb., makes the 'waye' equivalent to the wey of wool (182 lb.).[9] In 1363 we have an interesting note on the cost of bringing lead from Yorkshire to London for the use of Windsor Castle: 'For hire of two waggons (*plaustrorum*), each with 10 oxen, carrying 24 fothers of lead from Caldstanes in Nitherdale (Nidderdale) by high and rocky mountains and by miry (*profundis*) roads to Boroughbridge, more or less (*quasi*) 20 leagues, namely for 24 days, each waggon with the men for it taking 3s. a day—£7. 4s. Carriage from Boroughbridge to York by

[1] Rackham, op. cit., 37.  [2] Cf. Thorold Rogers, *Hist. of . . . Prices.*

[3] E. 491, 13.  [4] E. 467, 2  [5] Oliver, *Exeter*, 380.

[6] E. 461, 11.  [7] E. 479, 23.  [8] E. 461, 5.  [9] E. 465, 29.

land and water at 2*s*. 4*d*. the fother. Carriage by water from York to London, of 40 fothers, £26. 13*s*. 8*d*.'[1] Most, however, of the London supply was drawn from Derbyshire. So in 1332 we find £80 paid to the Sheriff of Notts. and Derby for '136 pieces of lead weighing 30 great cartloads (*carrat*')' for use at Westminster,[2] and just two hundred years later, in 1533, Derbyshire lead was bought in London, at £4. 6*s*. 8*d*. the fother, for Hampton Court.[3]

Against the initial expense of lead may be set the fact that when a leaden roof got into disrepair it could be stripped and recast, and there are fairly frequent references to this being done. On the other hand, this fact made it rather tempting for workmen to steal lead off the buildings on which they were working, and one of the ordinances of the London plumbers, drawn up in 1365,[4] was that—'None shall buy stripped lead from the assistants of tilers, bricklayers, masons, or women, who cannot find warranty for it.' Another clause enforced the favourite medieval theory of fair play: 'None shall oust another from the work that he has begun, or take away his customers, by enticement through carpenters, masons or tilers.' The ordinances also laid down the rates of pay for piece-work: for working a clove (7 lb.) of lead for gutters or roofs, ½*d*.; for working a clove for furnaces,[5] 'tappetroghes,'[6] and conduit-pipes, 1*d*. This exact rate is found in one instance, at Salisbury in 1494, when William Plummer was paid '*pro le multyng et leiyng de v*ˣˣ *c de plumbe novo et veteri*' at the rate of 8*d*. the hundredweight;[7] but the payment for piece-work varies very considerably. For instance, in the King's Hall accounts, in 1486, a plumber was paid 7*s*. 9*d*. '*pro leyng et shotyng de ij fudderys*', which is approximately 2½*d*. the hundredweight, while in 1533 the same work was paid at the rate of 5*d*., and in the same year at Durham Simon Blewmynaye was paid 'for melting 62 stone of lead for a cistern in *le fyshouse* for salt salmon', at 1½*d*. the stone, equivalent to 12*d*. the hundredweight.[8]

Sometimes the lead was bought in sheets, when it was, of course, more expensive than the raw material. For instance, for York Castle in 1365 'half a fother and 40 stone of *wroughtlede*—at 10*d*. the stone—was bought for re-roofing the turret beside the chapel and for remaking the gutters and *evesplates* for the kitchen'.[9] And at Collyweston in 1504, while raw

---

[1] E. 598, 9.    [2] E. 469, 13.    [3] H.C. 237, f. 147.

[4] Riley, *Mems. of London*, 322.

[5] The medieval equivalent of our 'copper' was a 'lead (*plumbum*)'.

[6] Presumably troughs supplied with a tap.

[7] Swayne, *Churchwardens' Accts. of St. Edmund's, Sarum*, 43.

[8] D.H.B. 267.    [9] E. 501, 11.

lead cost 3s. 9d. the hundredweight, that 'redy casten in webs' was 5s. 3d.[1]
The form 'web' is one of the English equivalents of the Latin *tela*, generally
used for a sheet of lead. It occurs at Scarborough in 1343—'four plumbers
working lead in webbys for the roofing of the chamber';[2] at Corfe in
1363—'wages of a plumber making webbes, 12d.';[3] and at Cambridge in
1431, when 3 'webbes' of lead cost £3.[4] At Eltham in 1397 we have
30s. 8d. paid *pro j cloth plumbi*, used for roofing a vice, or winding stair,
in the new gate, and weighing 3 cwt. 3 qr. 10 lb., at 8s. the hundredweight.[5]
And at the Tower of London in 1402 half a fother of lead was bought 'to
make therefrom 2 *cloth* for the repair of the round tower called Prisontour
beside the Dongeon and for mending the roofing and *le trapedour* of the
said garettour beside the great tower'.[6] Another word occasionally used
was 'tabbard'. Thus we find a plumber and his mate employed at Winchester Cathedral in 1532, '*circa le settyng unius tabbart plumbi*'.[7] In an earlier
instance the word is apparently applied to stone roofing slabs, as at Cambridge Castle in 1367 we find a payment 'to a mason making and setting
tabbardes over the said chamber, and for putting 2 gargolles there to discharge the water', and it would be contrary to medieval practice for a
mason to handle lead, though I am inclined to think that in this instance
he may have done so.[8]

When lead is laid directly on wood it is liable to be affected by the
vegetable acids contained in the wood, especially when this is unseasoned,
as so much medieval timber was, and the timber is affected by the changes
in temperature of the lead. It was therefore a common practice to put
earth or sand between the wood and the lead. So in 1227 at Dover 4d.
was paid 'for 100 horseloads of earth called arzille (i.e. clay) bought from
the land of a poor old (*paupercule*) woman to put on the towers between
the planks and the sand which lies under the lead to prevent the material
rotting (*pro putredine materiei*)'.[9] At Rhuddlan in 1302 payments were made
'for removing the earth called *roboill* placed between the joists and the lead
of the upper story of the tower; making new joists, putting them in place,
and placing earth afresh between them and the lead'.[10] And the same year,
among the charges for repairing the keep of Pevensey Castle we find—
'For wages of a plumber employed in removing all the lead over the
kitchen in the great tower, where the joists were set, and in repairing

---

[1] St. John's Coll., Camb., MS. vol. ii.    [2] E. 482, 6.
[3] E. 461, 5.    [4] K.H. 8, f. 24.    [5] E. 495, 13.
[6] E. 502, 23.    [7] Kitchin, *Obedientiary Rolls*, 221.
[8] E. 553, 2.    [9] E. 462, 10.
[10] A. Jones, *Flintshire Mins. Accts.* 17.

defects and relaying the said lead, 8s. . . . For 8 barrows (*curtenis*) employed for obtaining sand to lay under the lead there, 8d. For digging the said sand, 2d. For carrying the same up onto the tower, 6d.'[1] Another entry in the same account refers to the digging of sand, partly to form a bed for casting the lead and partly to put under the lead. Sometimes, especially where the pitch of the roof made earth unsuitable, moss was used instead. For instance, at Corfe in 1280 there is mention of 'a woman who brought *mosse* to put under the lead',[2] and in 1292 there is a payment 'for collecting moss (*musso*) to put under the lead', another payment being made 'to 2 masons making channels (*rygollos*) on the wall for the fixing of the lead'.[3] At St. Briavel's in 1375 twelve horse-loads of *musset* were provided for laying the lead,[4] and at Bristol in 1482, also '12 bundles (*sarcin'*) of *mosse* were used in the laying and new leading of the Dongon'.[5]

Apart from its use as a roofing material, lead was in constant demand for gutters, spouts, and pipes. Sometimes the gutters were made of wood and lined with lead, as at Pevensey in 1300, when gutters to go between the hall and the castle wall were cut out of timber, and men were employed casting lead to cover these same gutters. In other instances they were, like modern gutters, composed entirely of metal and supported by iron brackets; as in 1532 at Westminster: 'iij stiroppes of iron made for the assuraunce of a gutter of leade', and 'xij squyres (squares, or angle brackets) of iron for the steying of certeyne gutters of leade'.[6] At Guildford Castle in 1390 there is mention of '2 gutters of lead, containing in length 72 ft. and in breadth 2 ft., and a gutter for the end of the same chamber, 34 ft. in length and 2 ft. in breadth'.[7] It is not worth while multiplying unilluminating references to gutters, but an entry in the Bardfield Park account of 1344—'wages of a *ledder* soldering the gutters over the great gate'[8]—may be quoted for the sake of its rather unusual use of 'ledder' for plumber.

While the majority of gutters discharged their contents by means of spouts, the use of leaden stack pipes was by no means unknown. In 1248 Henry III ordered 'all the leaden gutters of the Keep (of the Tower of London), through which rainwater should fall from the top of the same tower, to be carried down to the ground; so that the wall of the said tower, which has been newly whitewashed, may be in no wise injured by the dropping of rainwater'.[9] At Rockingham Castle in 1276 we find '8 lb.

---

[1] E. 479, 16.       [2] E. 460, 27.       [3] E. 460, 29.
[4] E. 481, 20.       [5] E. 472, 18.       [6] T.R., ff. 315, 320.
[7] Foreign R. 13 Ric. II, m. G.       [8] E. 458, 4.       [9] Liberate R. 25 Hen. III.

of tin bought for joining and mending the gutters over the vaulting (*volticium*) and the *pypes* extending from the vaulting—And 100 lednail for joining *claspes* over the *pypes*'.[1] So also at Dover, in 1283, William Plomer was employed mending faults in the roof, spouts (*stillicidia*), and pipes of the church in the castle: and there is also reference to the *pipam turris*.[2] In 1353 sheets of lead were cast, from which to make pipes (*fistul'*) to be put from the top of the Keep of the Tower of London to the ground;[3] and at Porchester a new pipe of lead was made in 1397 'to convey the water from the great tower to the ground'.[4] In 1440 also, at Pevensey Castle, William Chilwell, plumber, was employed 'melting and casting 3771 lb. alike of new lead (2325 lb.) and of old torn and holey lead sheets (1446 lb.) taken by him from (certain) roofs . . . for roofing and covering rooms with the new sheets so made . . ., also for making a leaden pipe reaching from the top of the tower called the Dungeon down to the ground on the west side of the same tower to carry off the water from its wall'.[5] In the accounts for the rebuilding of Bodmin Church, *c.* 1470, there is a reference to 'hokis to bere the lede pipis';[6] and at Collyweston in 1505 is recorded the purchase of 'xxx clapsis of yren w$^t$ xxx pynnes of yren for pypes of lead otherwise called spowtes of leed'[7]—'spowt' being apparently used, as it often is now, for a rainwater pipe. Finally we may mention the 'square pipes of leade, garnysshid with the kinges armes and badges', made for Westminster Palace in 1532.[8]

When a castle was being built at Queenborough in 1375, Robert Man, cooper, was employed 'mending and binding the water casks appointed to receive the rain water coming down through leaden pipes within the circle (*rotund'*) of the castle'.[9] This was necessary because of the shortage of water there, as is shown by an interesting entry in the same account:

In wages of Jasper Fishkoc and other workmen of Romney Marsh, ejecting salt seawater out of a pond near the castle, called Foxlesgore, overflowed and drowned in November by the unusually high tide . . . for the purchase of *pillogg'* and *barrerlogg'*[10] to fix in the said pond . . . (other expenses incurred) from great and urgent necessity because fresh water is not available either for the use of men or for watering beasts for the castle or the vill of Quenesburgh, within the space of a league from the said castle and vill.

By way of remedying this defect, a further entry records the employment

[1] E. 480, 19.  [2] E. 462, 9.  [3] E. 471, 7.
[4] E. 479, 23.  [5] Mins. Accts., 454, No. 7292.
[6] *Camden Miscellany*, vii. 25.  [7] St. John's Coll., Camb., MS. vol. ii.
[8] T.R., f. 505.  [9] E. 545, 5.  [10] Logs for piles and barriers.

of 'John Colyn with other workmen, digging in a place in the field called Chereshethe and searching for springs (*saltus et erupciones*) of fresh water for a conduit from the said place to the castle'.

Although the ordinary house in the Middle Ages, and long afterwards, depended for its supply of water on natural sources, such as streams and ponds, or on a well, the monasteries frequently, and great houses occasionally, had a more or less elaborate system of water-supply, laid on to various parts of the building and often brought from a considerable distance. About 960 Ethelwold, Abbot of Abingdon, is recorded to have made 'the water-course (*ductum aquae*) which runs under the dormitory to the stream which is called Hokke';[1] but this was probably simply a stream for flushing the convent drains. Just about a century after the Norman Conquest, however, the monks of the Cathedral Priory of Canterbury obtained a grant of land containing springs and, under their energetic Prior Wibert (d. 1167), installed a very elaborate and complete system of supply, of which a most interesting contemporary plan has fortunately survived. This plan has been reproduced and elucidated by Professor Willis.[2] Close to the source was a circular conduit house, from which the water was carried by an underground pipe, of which the end was covered by a pierced plate. Between this point and the city wall the water passed through five oblong reservoirs or settling-tanks. It then went directly to the laver—a raised cistern from which water trickled into a washing-basin below—in the infirmary cloister; and from there another pipe led to the laver in front of the refectory, which, from the drawing, must have resembled that in a similar position at Durham, where—'Within the Cloyster garth, over against the Frater House dour, was a fair Laver or Counditt for the Monncks to washe ther hands and faces at, being maid in forme round, covered with lead, and all of marble, saving the verie uttermost walls; within the which walls you may walke round about the Laver of marble, having many little cunditts or spouts of brasse, with xxiiij cockes of brass, rownd about yt.'[3] From the tank of this laver, carried on a central pillar to give it sufficient head, two pipes ran respectively north and east. That to the north ran under the refectory, scullery, and kitchen, supplying each by means of a standpipe with cock, and across the court to the bake-house, brew-house, and guest-hall, giving off on the way a branch to the bath-house. The eastern pipe ran to a third laver, in front of the

---

[1] *Chron. Abingdon*, 278.
[2] *Hist. of the Mon. of Christ Church, Canterbury*, 159–90.
[3] *Rites of Durham* (Surtees Soc.), quoted by Willis.

infirmary hall, giving off on the way, before reaching the first laver, a branch which ran south, under the church, to a tank in the lay folks' cemetery—probably for the use of the town—where it replaced or supplemented an adjacent well. The waste from both these branches ran into the stone 'fish-pond' east of the church. From there a pipe ran to a tank beside the Prior's chamber, and so to 'the Prior's water-tub (*cupa*)', where it was joined by the waste from the bath-house and flowed into the main drain running through the reredorter, or *necessarium*. This drain also received all the rainwater from the great cloister and from the roofs of the church and other buildings and was carried across the court and under the city wall into the city ditch. In the infirmary court was a well and beside it a hollow column, standing on the main pipe—a note on the plan explaining that 'if the (supply from the) aqueduct fails, water can be drawn from the well and being poured into this column will be supplied to all the offices'. At the angle of every pipe, where it is turned vertically to feed a tank, a short horizontal branch is shown, terminating with a stopcock close to the nearest gutter. These branches are labelled *purgatorium* and were for the purpose of flushing, or purging the pipes from sediment. Similar purge-pipes are shown at the supply end of the settling-tanks. The whole formed a very efficient water system and possibly explains, even more than the holiness of the inmates, the exemption of the convent from the effects of the terrible Black Death of 1349. The only improvements effected before the Dissolution were certain additions to the drains and gutters for disposing of the rain-water, carried out by Priors Chillenden (1390–1411) and Goldston (1495–1517).[1]

The Cistercian abbey of Waverley had a water-supply as early as 1179, but this suddenly gave out, and in 1215 a monk, Simon, found another spring and 'after great difficulty, inquiry and invention, and not without much labour and sweating', brought the water into the monastery by underground pipes, a distance of 570 yards.[2] That some of these early water-supplies involved excavations of considerable depth is shown by one of the miracles of St. Thomas (Becket) of Canterbury. Roger, Archbishop of York (d. 1181), planned to supply Churchdown (Gloucs.) with water from a spring on the hill, 500 paces distant. William of Gloucester, who was in charge of the work, was standing in a cutting 24 feet below the surface, holding a leaden pipe, when the earth fell in on him. The local priest promptly celebrated Mass for his soul, but by the invocation of St.

[1] Willis, op. cit. 170.
[2] Brakspear, *Waverley Abbey*, 89.

Thomas he was saved and was dug out alive next day.[1] Equally significant is an accident that occurred in London in 1256, when certain diggers, while they were pulling up the pipe of the conduit to clear it of mud, as the water had ceased to flow through it, were overcome by foul air.[2]

At Bury St. Edmunds we are told that when Walter de Banham became sacrist (*c.* 1200) 'he enclosed in lead the water-supply (*aqueductum*) from its head and spring for a distance of two miles, and brought it to the cloister through ways hidden in the ground'.[3] A plan of part of the water system at Bury, drawn up in the reign of Elizabeth, is in the British Museum,[4] but whether this is as it was constructed by Walter de Banham it is impossible to say.

The Grey Friars of London obtained from William, tailor to King Henry III, a grant of land and springs for their water-supply, and Brother William de Basynges caused a conduit to be constructed, obtaining the funds from King Henry, Sir Henry de Basynges, and other persons.[5] At some later date an elaborate description of the course of this conduit, from the Friary to the source, was drawn up as a guide when repairs were required.[6] From this it may be noted that the main was carried under Newgate at a depth of 12 feet and was taken under the Holbourne stream 3 feet below the water, close to the bridge. Here, we are told, was the first *spurgellum*, 4 feet below ground, covered with a marble slab; some distance farther on was a second spurgel, nearly 7 feet 'in height' (i.e. depth). Near the mill of Thomas de Basynges the pipe was 18 feet down and in the ditch beside the mill was a third spurgel. Nearly a *stadium* (? a mile) west of this was the chief head of water; there was a secondary supply farther west, marked by a stone conduit house, but this was then leaky and in bad repair. The 'spurgels' seem to be settling-tanks, which combined the purposes of clearing the water and reducing its pressure in the pipes.[7] Reduction of pressure was also often effected by means of a 'suspirail' or 'wind-vent'—an upright pipe soldered into the main and furnished with a stopcock—which acted also as a standpipe for drawing off water. 'Suspirail' is also used as the equivalent of 'spurgel'.

In 1430 the London Charterhouse obtained a grant of springs at Islington, and some 25 years later, when these began to fail, had permission to

---

[1] *Materials for Hist. of Thomas Becket*, i. 253; ii. 261.
[2] Mat. Paris, *Chron.* v. 600.    [3] *Mems. of St. Edmunds*, ii. 292.
[4] Add. MS. 14850, f. 177.
[5] *Mon. Francisc.* (Rolls Ser.), i. 509.    [6] Ibid. 510.
[7] In the Elizabethan drawing of the Bury supply each 'cespirall', or settling-tank, is shown with a 'breathyng pype' and one such pipe is shown by itself.

tap other springs there.[1] A plan of the course of this conduit from its head to the convent, about a mile, was drawn, and subsequently, about 1512, altered and annotated. In its course, this pipe passed over the supply pipes of the Hospitallers of St. John[2] and the nunnery of Clerkenwell. Several settling-tanks are shown, one of which is described as 'a susprall w$^t$ a ta(m)pioun (or, plug) to clense the home pype', while another is referred to as a 'spurgell'. There is also a 'wynde went closid in stone'—shown as a round grating; and a 'receyte'—reservoir, or conduit house. Crossing a ditch the pipe was 'kevered with a creste of oke' and under the road it was 'closid in hard stone'. In the middle of the great cloister is drawn the conduit house with a pyramidal roof, and there is a note: 'Md that thys age ys made viij$^{th}$ square and in that square which ys northwarde dyrectlye from the suspyrell the mayne pype dothe come and rysythe up into the age in the myddes of a fayre square cestron of leade. Wh' yt runnythe downe out of the (*erasure*) in the top of the age into another pype on the weast syde of the same wills (= wells) whych dothe serve the howse.' From the 'age' (French *auge*, a trough) pipes running north-west and east serve the monks' cells; and one to the south runs to a laver in the cloister wall with a row of taps. From the laver cistern two pipes run to serve one or two cells, the laundry, buttery, brewhouse, and 'Egipta the fleyshe kychyn'. From this last a pipe ran to the Windmill tavern, and its over-flow was carried to the White Hart, but there is a note that this overflow was only 'by the sufference of the Charterhouse', and a suit brought by three brewers in 1451 proved that this was so and that the public had no claim to such supply.

Several towns benefited by the enterprise of the religious houses in this way. At Southampton, in 1290, the Friars Minor had licence to enclose with a stone wall the spring of Calwell and take the water underground to their house, and twenty years later the friars allowed the burgesses the use of one pipe from their lavatory cistern, the waste from the town cistern being returned to the friary cloisters. In 1420, when the supply required expensive repairs, the friars made it over to the town, and the burgesses agreed to repair it with two equal pipes, one to the friary and the other to the town conduit opposite Holy Rood Church. Later, in 1515, John Flemynge made over to the town a second head of water, in Lovbery Mead, reserving the right to put a 'sosprey, otherwise called a small pipe

---

[1] Hope, *The London Charterhouse*, ch. iv.

[2] A fifteenth-century description of the course of the hospital conduit is printed by Hope: ibid. 143.

of lead made with a stop', fitted with a brass cock, into the main pipe of the conduit at the south-west corner of All Hallows Church.[1] Thomas Beckington, Bishop of Bath and Wells, in 1451 made an agreement[2] with the burgesses of Wells for a head for a water conduit, with reservoirs, vents, and other engines above and below ground, for taking water from within the palace precinct, where he had built a conduit house, sufficient for lead pipes 12 inches in circumference, with dikes, trenches, ponds, cisterns, &c., within the precinct and the city; with power to break ground and lay pipes to the high cross in the city market or elsewhere. The first head and reservoir, to take all the bishop's water, was to be round, of 10-foot diameter within the walls, built of stone at his cost, with a round cistern of lead, 5 feet in depth and 4 feet in diameter, with a pipe attached at either side of the cistern, at the city's cost, half the water to be led towards the city and half to divers parts of the palace. This head was to have a door with two keys, one with the bishop and one with the burgesses. This reservoir was to be cleaned out every six months; and when the palace moat was scoured, all the water was to be turned into it until it was refilled. In return, the master and burgesses of the city were to visit the bishop's tomb in the cathedral once a year and pray for his soul—for which the bishop promised them 40 days' indulgence.

The water-supply of Exeter in 1346 was brought in lead pipes from St. Sidwell's to the cathedral churchyard, and there divided into three branches, for the Dean and Chapter, St. Nicholas' Priory, and the City.[3] Next year, the Grey Friars, whose house was 'in a dry place to which the water does not have access', were licensed to enclose two springs in the city ditch and to bring the water 'by an underground pipe across the high street into their house'.[4] By an agreement made in 1387 between the mayor and citizens and the priory of St. Nicholas, the monks were allowed to open up and dig the streets and pavements in order to put down pipes for a conduit from their spring in St. Paul's street to the priory, provided such digging was done under supervision of four persons appointed by the city. They might also dig up the streets when necessary to execute repairs, provided that they made them good again within three days of finishing such repairs, and that they covered and guarded such excavations, so that passers-by should not be injured, and if any did suffer injury the priory should compensate them.[5]

---

[1] J. S. Davies, *Southampton*, 114–16.
[2] *Hist. MSS. Com., D. & C. Wells*, i. 433.
[4] Ibid.
[3] *Hist. MSS. Com., Exeter*, 284.
[5] Oliver, *Mon. Exon.* 123.

PLATE 15

DIAGRAMMATIC PLAN OF WATER-SUPPLY, CHRIST CHURCH,
CANTERBURY *c.* 1167

PLATE 16

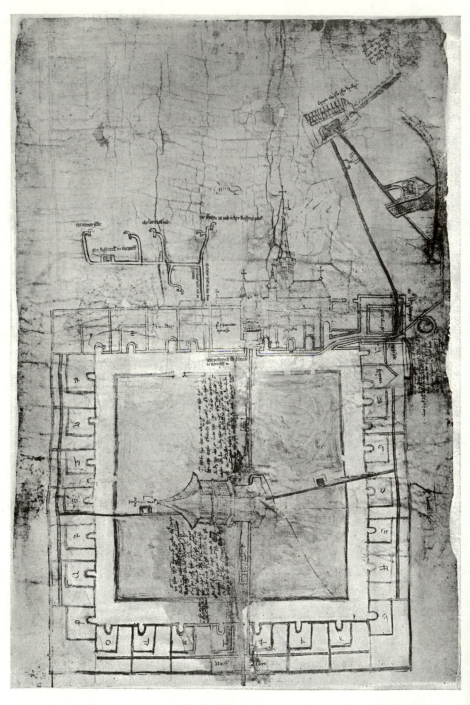

DIAGRAMMATIC PLAN OF WATER-SUPPLY, THE CHARTERHOUSE,
LONDON 15TH CENTURY

London obtained its first supply in 1237, when Gilbert de Sandford, at the request of the king, granted to the City all the springs and waters in his fief of Tyburn, with leave to bring them through his land by a conduit to the City, and the right to repair the pipes and the tower or reservoir where the waters were collected, when necessary.[1] An additional plot of land in the same neighbourhood was obtained for a fountain-head to the conduit in 1354.[2] From the accounts of the Keepers of the Conduit for 1350 it appears that yearly water rates of from 5s. to 6s. 8d. were levied on various houses, and presumably these had water laid on from the main.[3] In 1478 one William Campion unlawfully tapped a conduit pipe and brought water into his house in Fleet Street. His punishment was ingeniously made to fit the crime, as it was ordered that he should be set on a horse and led through the streets 'with a vessell like unto a conduyt full of water uppon his hede, the same water rennyng by smale pipes oute of the same vessell, and that when the water is wasted newe water to be put in the saide vessell again'.[4] As this was in November, it would be an abuse of metaphor to say that he had got himself into hot water through his misdeeds. In addition to these water rates, larger sums were obtained yearly from numerous persons for their 'tankards', which were large wooden cans, and 'tynes' or barrels. The 1350 accounts include payments, at 40d. the time, for cleaning out the fountain-head twice each quarter; for examining the conduit when it was 'slandered for poison'—32s. 2d.; and for mending broken 'spurgails'. In 1378 the executors of Adam Fraunceys gave 500 marks for the extension of the conduit from the Cheap to the cross-ways on Cornhill.[5] Ten years later it is stated that many losses and injuries had befallen the people of Fleet Street through the frequent bursting of the pipes of the conduit, which flooded their houses and cellars. It was thought that this might be remedied by making a vent-pipe (*aventum*, glossed as *pinnaculum*) over the main, so it was agreed that one should be made, at the cost of the people there, near the hostel of the Bishop of Salisbury (now Salisbury Court), provided that if it were found injurious it should be removed.[6]

A movement for a further supply was set on foot in 1440, when the abbey of Westminster allowed the mayor and council to erect a fountain-head with tanks, ages (*augeis*), sesperels, cisterns, &c. in their manor of Paddington;[7] and it was presumably in this connexion that John West,

[1] *Letter Book A*, 14.    [2] *Letter Book G*, 210.    [3] Riley, *Mems. of London*, 264.
[4] *Letter Book L*, 160.    [5] *Letter Book H*, 108.
[6] Ibid. 326; Riley, *Mems.* 503.    [7] *Letter Book K*, 233.

'plummer', was appointed in 1446 to control the work of the new conduit, 'and to leve ther fore all other occupacōns'.[1] But little progress was made with the scheme, and in 1453 it was said that the City had 'a conduyt hede with diverse springes of water gedered and conveyed in to the same' at Paddington, from which leaden pipes ran to Tyburne 'and no farther as yette and there it hath leyn the space of vj yeere and more and yette doth'. The executors of Sir William Estfeld then offered to ʾbring the water to a pipe of lead which had been laid 'beside the grete conduyt hede at Maryburne—and so streccheth from thens unto the sesperalle late made and sett agenst the chapell of Seint Mary of Rouncevale beside Charyng Crosse and no ferther'. They undertook to carry it by lead pipes into the city and there make 'resceites, sespiralles and ventes'.[2] Thirty years later one of these executors, John Midleton, had water conveyed from Highbury to St. Giles', Cripplegate, where the parishioners made a conduit and cistern, the repair of which the City undertook.[3]

In 1442 the Master and Brethren of St. Bartholomew's Hospital allowed Thomas Knolles, grocer, to convey the overflow of their water-supply by pipes to Newgate and Ludgate, for the relief of the poor prisoners there.[4] And in 1447 the inhabitants of Westminster were given the overflow from the king's conduit in the palace, with leave to convey it to a conduit in a convenient place.[5] This last grant seems to have followed a reconstruction of the palace water system, an elaborate conduit house being built during 1443–4, when we read of 'bolts of iron for the support of the buttresses of the conduit; and great nails called broddes used in the fastening and ceiling (*sillurac'*) of the same conduit called the standard', and find carpenters employed on making and 'frameyng' the conduit called the standard and setting it up within the great palace of Westminster, towards the great door of the hall, and framing the battlement of it and 'seleyng and garnessyng' it. Also 600 'estrychbord and waynescottes' were used for making the vault of the new conduit house and 'the bosses (*bouces*) with various badges—Anteloppes skochones and hawthernes'.[6] The palace had long had its own water laid on; in 1260 there is a reference to repairs done to 'the conduit of water which is carried underground to the King's lavatory and to other places there'.[7] Probably its installation dates from 1233,

---

[1] Ibid. 318. In 1443 the mayor had been licensed to buy 200 fothers of lead and to take masons, plumbers, and labourers, at reasonable wages, for the making of new conduits: *Cal. Patent R.* 188.

[2] *Letter Book K*, 356.      [3] *Letter Book L*, 207.

[4] Ibid. 4.      [5] *Cal. Patent R.* 45.

[6] E. 503, 11, 12.      [7] Liberate R. 44 Hen. III.

when Master William the conduit-maker (*conductarius*) was sent 'to bring water to our court of Westminster in accordance with what we have told him'.[1] In 1338 two plumbers and their apprentice (*pagettus*) were employed upon 'the cistern in Pergatesward and on the pipes (*fistulas*) of the conduit', and a certain Brother Silvester and a partner of his were working for 28 days—at 12*d*. each—on the setting in order (*ordinac'*) and repair of the great conduit newly made.[2] Three years later there is mention of the purchase of 5 fathoms of wire (*teys de wyr*) for cleansing the pipe of the conduit at the king's mews.[3] Then, in 1373, we find five workmen employed for a week 'examining the pipes of the conduit, which was broken and it was not known where, and water did not come to Westminster'; and next week they are called in again, 'because the water was lacking in the hall and the kitchens and did not come through'.[4] Mention may also be made of the purchase of 103 lb. of lead in 1490 'for the lengthening of the pipe between the cistern in the courtyard and the Ewery at the screens (*scrinium*) in the hall'.[5] The same accounts refer to 'an instrument of brass called a cok for the cistern'.[6]

As already mentioned, the tanks and lavers were supplied with spouts and taps, stopcocks or 'keys', the fittings of which were often decorative. At Dover in 1227 a mark was spent on 'two bronze heads (*testis*) for two cisterns, without which the cisterns could not well be made safe (*salvari*')'.[7] At Westminster, in 1288, Master Robert the Goldsmith was paid 40*s*. 'for the working of five heads of copper, gilded, for the laver of the small hall', and 25*s*. 'for the images of the said laver, and for whitening the laver (probably by tinning it) and gilding the hoops (*circulis*')';[8] and next year Thomas the plumber made 'a key (*clavi*) of copper for receiving the water in the house of Sir Otto'.[9] In 1348, again, 12 'keyes' of latten were made for the new conduit, at a cost of 24*s*.; and '12 heads of metal for the same keyes' cost 7*s*.; while 2*s*. was paid 'for a quilet (i.e. a small pipe) of latten set in the mouth of a leopard made of stone, on the wall under the hall called Sturmyn, pouring water into the cistern'.[10] At Canterbury there are payments in 1443 for 'ij waterkeyys'[11] and '*pro clavibus aquaticis imponendis in lavatorio*', while in 1485 John Clark, 'tynker', was paid 8*d*. for making a 'grate' for the conduit, and 3*s*. 4*d*. for mending 4 'watercockes'.[12] And at Hampton Court—to which place Cardinal Wolsey brought water from

[1] *Close R.* 530.  [2] E. 470, 18.  [3] E. 471, 6.
[4] E. 469, 13.  [5] Egerton MS. 2358, f. 6.  [6] Ibid., f. 8.
[7] E. 462, 10.  [8] E. 467, 17.  [9] Ibid. 20.
[10] E. 470, 18.  [11] 'Waterkeies' occur at Shene, 1473: E. 503, 19.
[12] Bodl. MS. Top. Kent, c. 3, ff. 128, 151.

Coombe Hill, 3 miles away on the other side of the Thames, with an expenditure of about 250 tons of lead for pipes[1]—there is mention in 1533 of 'a new key to the cokke for the cowndythe'.[2]

Water was also sometimes laid on to the baths. At Westminster in 1275 we have a number of payments made to Robert the Goldsmith:[3] for a key to the laver in the bath room (*domo balnei*) together with purchase of metal for the key—14*s.*; for 4 keys of gilt bronze and 4 heads made in the shape of leopards, for the *baynes*, 26*s.* 8*d.*; for making 4 large keys of *latun* for the *baynes*—20*s.*; for making a waste-pipe (*spurgelli*) and 4 keys to it—10*s.*' Edward III could even boast of a 'bath (h. and c.)', besides the usual offices, at Westminster in 1351, when Robert Foundour was paid 56*s.* 8*d.* 'for 2 large bronze keys for the king's bath-tub (*cuua balnei*) for carrying (*conducend'*) hot and cold water into the baths'.[4] This is the only definite instance that I have found of hot water being laid on to a bath-house, or 'stews'[5]—to use the English term. At Langley, however, in 1368 'a square lead for heating water for the *stues*' is mentioned[6] and this might have been piped direct to the bath; but it seems to have been usual to carry the hot water in jugs. Thus at Bardfield Park in 1344 we find 41 earthen pots (*olla*) bought for the *stues*, costing 18*d.*;[7] and 125 such pots, evidently large, as they cost 8*d.* each, '*pour les stewes*' at Windsor in 1366.[8] At Windsor, also, in 1391 we find 'the furnace of the King's *stywes*' remade, and John Brown, carter, employed 'for 2 days carrying with his carts 229 earthen pots from Farnborough to the Castle for the use of the stywes'.[9] Similarly, at Eltham in 1364, John Jury, potter, supplied 120 *pottes pro styuez*, and Thomas Mason was paid £4 'for making the walls and setting 2 leads called *fournaysez* and 120 pottes for the *stuuy* house'.[10] In this instance it looks as if the pots were heated directly and not merely filled from the leads. Finally we may quote a Westminster account of 1325[11] for the light which it throws on the subject of medieval bathrooms:

William de Wynchelse for 3 boards called righok for crests and filetts of the bathing tub,—18d. For 3 oak boards called clouenbord for making the covering[12] of the said tub, 6 ft. long and 2½ ft. broad,—3s. . . . for 100 fagett for heating and drying the *stuwes*—3s. For a small barrell (*cumelino*), 2 bokettes and a bowl (*boll'*) for carrying water to the stuwes . . . carpenters working on the covering

---

[1] Law, *Hampton Court*, 24.  [2] H.C. 237, f. 217.
[3] E. 467, 6.  [4] E. 471, 6.
[5] 'For 2 great tubs serving for the bath in le styus house' at Windsor, 1393: E. 495, 17.
[6] E. 466, 4.  [7] E. 458, 4.  [8] E. 493, 22.
[9] E. 496, 2.  [10] E. 493, 18.  [11] E. 469, 6.
[12] Medieval illustrations of baths often show them with a kind of canopy.

of the bathing tub and the partition (*interclaus*') in front of the said tub—For 6 pieces of Reigate stone for making a slabbing (*tabliamentum*) in front of the partition of the said tub in the King's ground-floor (*bassa*) chamber . . . . For 2250 pauingtil for the said chamber . . . for 24 mattis, at 2d. each, to put on the flore and pavement of the King's chamber on account of the cold.

A casual allusion is made to baths at Hampton Court in 1529 in a reference to 'empcon (i.e. buying) of canvas being an instrument for burning the knottes of the pipes for the baynes'.[1] The canvas, I presume, was for 'wiping' the joints, that is to say, smoothing over the solder. A later entry mentions 2 ells of canvas 'spent by the plummers in brynnyng of pyppes whiche ware broken and decayd at the cowndyth hedde', for which purpose also 4 lb. of tallow were bought.[2] Similarly the purchase of 'lard (*uncto porcino*) for lead' is mentioned at Corfe in 1292,[3] and on other occasions, especially in connexion with the soldering of window-leads. Another accessory was salt, and accordingly we find 'a bushel of salt for soldering (*consolidand*') the junctions of the pipe' at Leeds Castle in 1381,[4] and at Westminster, five years later, 'half a bushel of salt used on making lead pipes for the stywe and soldering (*soudand*') various gutters'.[5] Purchases of tin in small quantities are constantly found in conjunction with purchases of lead. Thus, at Restormel in 1343, we have '2½ foot of white tin for making *soldura*—at 22d. the foot';[6] next year, at Bardfield Park, '3 lb. of tyn for soldering (*soudant*') gutters—6d.';[7] and 163 lb. of tin, at 3d., *pro souder*, at Dover in 1365.[8] Sometimes pewter was used; as at Wallingford in 1390, when 6 lb. of 'peweder' for soldering faults in the gutters cost 12d.;[9] and at Ripon in 1408, when 41 lb. *de peltro pro soudara* for the plumbers and glaziers cost 6s. 10d.[10] It also appears simply as 'solder': Winchester Castle, 1392, 'for 12 lb. of *saudre* used on the leaden roof of the tower called Manesiestour—3s.';[11] *soudure*, at 2d. the lb., at Porchester in 1397;[12] and *sowder*, at 3d., at Durham in 1531.[13]

Where, as in the vast majority of cases, water was not brought into a building by a conduit, the source of supply would be a well. Casual allusions to wells—as at Corfe in 1377, 'cleaning the bottom of the well in the castle so that water may bubble up (*ebullire*)'[14]—are common, but I have found little more on the subject. At Sheppey in 1365 Robert de West-mallyng was paid 20d. the foot for digging and making up with masonry

[1] H.C. 239, f. 127.  [2] Ibid., f. 618.  [3] E. 260, 29.
[4] E. 480, 7.  [5] E. 473, 2.  [6] E. 461, 11.
[7] E. 458, 4.  [8] E. 462, 23.  [9] E. 490, 4.
[10] R. 138.  [11] E. 491, 23.  [12] E. 479, 23.
[13] D.H.B. 78.  [14] E. 461, 7.

83 feet of a well;[1] and at Queenborough in 1393 Robert Weldyker, possibly the same man, 'master of the making of the new well' was paid £10 for 60 weeks' work—at 3s. 4d. the week.[2] One entry at Clarendon in 1482 is also worth quoting for its unusual amount of detail:

For mending the *hopys chaynys* and *coterels* at the well . . . For 2 *herynropes* (? hair ropes) for cleaning the well . . . To Thomas Warmewell for going down into the same well to clean it—at 2s. a day—8s. For great candles called *talowe perchers* for lighting the said Thomas at the bottom of the well and burning there for 4 days—2d. Paid to 4 labourers running in the great wheel[3] for the said 4 days—6s. 8d. For a great new rope called a *grete gabull* (i.e. cable) for the well, 24 fathoms in length, weighing 117 lbs.—at 1¼d the lb.—12s. 2¼d.[4]

Usually the water was drawn with a bucket and windlass, though the twelfth-century drawing of the Canterbury waterworks shows that the well in the lay folks' cemetery was supplied with a dipping beam and counterweight, of the type common in the East. Towards the end of the fifteenth century pumps were beginning to come into use. William of Worcester in 1480 refers to certain information given him by one Dynt, a 'plump-maker' of Bristol.[5] At Croydon in 1504 Richard Lyncoln was making 3 pumps and the pipes belonging to them, 62 feet in length, and other pipes to convey the water from the well to the 'wasshynghous';[6] and next year leather 'for the soker of the pimp' was bought and Richard Lyncoln was paid 2d. a foot 'for makyng xlvj foot of pymps' and also 'for the making of a newe pompe in the courte, in greate—23s. 8d.'[7] The same Richard Lyncoln, of Lynn, made a 'pompe', containing 43 feet, for King's College in 1500.[8] Later, in 1519, the King's accounts mention 10d. paid 'to one who made a wooden *pompe*', and 4s. 'to another man who made a *pompe* of lead by which water may flow into the kitchen'.[9] There is mention of the 'repayring of a olde Water Pompe in the Kechin Courte' of Cardinal College, Oxford, in 1525;[10] and the Westminster accounts for 1532 contain the following details: 'Three pooles of fyrre redye planed, for the pumpe made for clensyng of the foundacion in the Lambe Aleye';[11] 'William Dalylande and John Strande of Southwark pumpemakers . . . for a staffe with a buckette of lether and flappis to it—16d. For a boxe and a spowte—5s.';[12] 'The newe shotyng of ij long irons for the pumpe,

[1] E. 483, 21.  [2] Ibid. 30.
[3] A tread-wheel of the same type as the donkey-wheels, of which examples still exist.
[4] E. 460, 16.  [5] *Itinerarium*, 268.
[6] St. John's Coll., Camb., MS. vol. i.  [7] Ibid., vol. iv.
[8] King's Coll. Mundum Bk. ix.  [9] Ibid. x.
[10] E. 479, 11.    [11] T.R., f. 159.    [12] Ibid., f. 162.

togeders with more iron leyde upon the same';[1] two 'awgers', 10 feet long, 'for the boaring of two pumpes'.[2] Finally, in 1536, the churchwardens of St. Mary-at-Hill paid 'to Mr. Osborn for a pompe yat lyeth to brynge the water owte of ye diche into ye ponde'—5s. 8d.[3]

We have seen that in the twelfth-century system of waterworks in the Cathedral Priory of Canterbury arrangements were made for the disposal of the rain-water. The same city provides an instance of an underground sewer in 1485, when we have a notice of

the preparation of the high road in High Street on account of the building of a stone arch constructed under the ground there, into which arch all the rainwater running down High Street may be discharged into the high stream (*rivum regium*) beside the church of All Saints. Which arch William Prat of London, mercer, caused to be made at his own expense.[4]

Half the persistent legends of underground passages attached to ancient buildings (and usually said to lead to quite impossible places) are due to the existence of such drainage arrangements, and references to such means of getting rid of rain and other waste water are numerous. At Westminster in 1532 there is mention of 'an Iron Gate sette in the Orcheyarde for conveying of water under the grounde';[5] and at Leeds Castle in 1369 we find 'an iron grate fixed in the pavement to receive water'.[6] Such a drain was sometimes known as a swallow, and at Canterbury there is mention, in 1496, of the scouring of a 'swallowyth';[7] something of the same kind appears to be implied in the payment made in 1478 by the churchwardens of St. Michael's, Bath, '*pro fodio et factura j thrye pro aqua bullente ex opposito de la post tenementi Ricardi Lacy*'.[8] An earlier Canterbury account, for 1372, gives the cost of 'repair of various drains (*gutterarum*) in the courtyard round the Prior's laver, with a new drain made from the new tank (*puteo*) beside the door of the brewhouse into the great drain coming from the third dorter, for emptying the water under the vats (*cacabos*)'.[9] At the Tower 26s. 8d. was paid 'for making a pit with stone walls by way of a swallow (*ad modum voraginis*) beside the Lieutenant's kitchen for the receiving of all water falling there', in 1386;[10] and at the same time three diggers were employed at Westminster on 'making new channels (*rigol*') between the great kitchen and the vicars' garden for a new drain made for the issue

[1] Ibid., f. 236. 'Shotyng' = welding.
[2] Ibid., f. 416.
[3] *Memorials* (E.E.T.S.), 370.
[4] *Hist. MSS. Com. Rep.* ix. 145.
[5] T.R., f. 422.
[6] E. 544, 23.
[7] Bodleian MS. Top. Kent, c. 3, f. 160.
[8] *Somerset Arch. Soc.* xxv. 78.
[9] Bodleian MS. Top. Kent, c. 3, f. 72.
[10] E. 473, 2.

of all the filth (*putredinis*) of the said kitchen'. Such a convenience was commonly provided for kitchens; in 1260 payment was made for 'making a conduit through which the refuse of the King's kitchens at Westminster flows into the Thames, which conduit the King ordered to be made on account of the stink of the dirty water which was carried through his halls, which was wont to affect the health of people frequenting the same halls'.[1] The King's Hall accounts for 1448, under 'expenditure on the conduit (*aqueductum*) to the kitchen, larder and river', enter 3s. 6d. 'for a grate at the stream (*rivulum*) and a plate in the kitchen';[2] at Shene 'a great grate for the kitchen drain' was made in 1372;[3] and at the Tower in 1313 four men were employed for a week 'working on clearing and mending a drain from the great kitchen, which receives all the refuse (*ordur'*) from the kitchen and was stopped up and blocked with the same refuse'.[4] At Canterbury College, Oxford, in 1440 we find payments for cleaning the sink (*gurgitem*) of the kitchen and for setting an iron plate at its opening.[5] This is elaborated in 1506 in payment of 16d. 'for two *emunctoriis* called ly grattes to keep back bones and other things of that kind which if they got into the channel of the evacuation duct would prevent the flow of water to clean the course under the ground'.[6]

We have seen that at Christ Church, Canterbury, the waste from the water-supply, and all the rain water, was carried under the 'Third Dormitory' or *necessarium*, flushing its drain. The provision of such flushing was so usual a feature of monastic economy that it often determined the position of the buildings, and in the majority of instances in which the conventual buildings are on the north side of the church it will be found that this is due to the greater facilities for drainage on that side. The normal position of the latrine, or 'reredorter' as it is usually called, was at the end of the dorter, with which it communicated directly. In the description of Durham Priory, written in Elizabethan times but referring to conditions before the Dissolution, we are told:[7]

Also there was a faire large house and a most decent place adjoyninge to the west syde of the said Dortre, towards ye water, for ye moncks and novices to resort unto called the p(re)vies, w^ch was maide w^th two greate pillars of stone that did beare up the whole floore thereof, and every seate and particion was of wainscott close of either syde verie decent so that one of them could

[1] Liberate R. 44 Hen. III.   [2] K.H. 11, f. 115.
[3] E. 494, 15.   [4] E. 469, 16.
[5] *Canterbury Coll. Oxford* (O.H.S. N.S. vii), 156.   [6] Ibid. 249.
[7] *Rites of Durham* (Surtees Soc.), 85.

not see one another, when they weare in that place. there was as many seates or p(re)vies on either side as there is little windowes in ye walles w^ch wyndowes was to gyve leighte to every one of the saide seates.

At St. Albans we are told of Prior John, who became abbot in 1396, that he made a stone cistern in which to store rain-water 'so as to cleanse the filth of the convent latrine . . . and he built the necessary house, commonly called the privy dormitory, than which none can be found more beautiful or more sumptuous'.[1] He also built a prior's chamber: 'but because the latrine of that chamber seemed to be rather close to the chapel of the guest-house the convent was reported by many to have made a place of retirement at the horns of the altar'. His predecessor, Abbot Thomas, made at the abbey's cell of Redburn Priory 'a new building, that is to say, a privy dormitory or retiring-place for the brethren there, and a latrine for himself, because formerly one building served him and the brethren there, wherefore they were ashamed (*erubescebant*) when they had to go to the necessary in his presence'.[2]

Modesty, or shyness, on this subject is of long standing and is shown by the variety of euphemisms employed for the building itself—four synonyms occurring in our last quotation. This sometimes leads to vagueness, so that, for instance, it is often not clear whether a 'privy chamber' is a private sitting-room or a latrine. The commonest of these terms is 'garderobe'. This is now used in architectural descriptions for a latrine, and it was frequently so used in medieval times. For instance, at Kenilworth in 1314 an entry concerning the remaking of the Earl's *latrinam* is glossed in the margin—'*custus garderobe domini Comitis*',[3] and at York Castle in the time of Edward III, 10s. was paid 'for making the pit of the garderobe of the Exchequer'.[4] The original meaning of the word, however, was the place where clothes were kept, and its exact equivalent in double meaning in modern English is 'cloak-room', a latrine being a common appendage. Thus in 1248 Henry III ordered 'a wardrobe and a privy chamber to the same wardrobe' to be made at Brill, and instructed the Sheriff of Wiltshire to 'cause the fireplace of our wardrobe at Clarendon to be pulled down and a new one to be built, and renovate and enlarge the privy chamber of the same and make a wardrobe of 30 ft. in length in front of the said privy chamber';[5] and at Hadleigh Castle in 1365 is a payment of 2d. 'for mending a latrine within the King's wardrobe'.[6] 'Privy'

---

[1] *Gesta Abbatum*, iii. 442.
[2] Ibid. 399.
[3] Mins. Accts. 1, No. 3.
[4] E. 501, 12.
[5] Liberate R. 23 Hen. III.
[6] E. 464, 9.

we have seen was used in describing the Durham *necessarium*, and at Launceston in 1462 we have '*pro emendacione unius playsterwall de le prevey*', and also a reference to 'the chamber called *withdraghte* over the gate called Southyate'.[1] 'Withdraught', or 'draught', was a term in common use. Thus at Collyweston in 1500 there were payments 'to the gongfermor, for the feyng of xij draghtes'.[2] 'Gong' is the Old English word for a latrine, and 'gongfermor' is applied to a man whose business was to 'fey', or cleanse, cesspits. So at Westminster in 1532 we have mention of 'Philip Longe, gongfermer, for the clensyng of certeyn jakis'[3]—which last term will be familiar to any student of Elizabethan literature. It occurs frequently in the sixteenth century, as for instance at the Tower *c.* 1525— 'Item a particion made in the forebreste of the same jaques $w^t$ a clere storey therin to geve light unto the same jaques'.[4] In the Peterhouse accounts for 1495 there is an entry '*pro mundacione bocardi*', and, more definitely in 1504, '*pro remocione fumi in bocardo*', but the term, probably an allusive use of 'Bocardo', the name of a prison at Oxford[5]—seems to have been purely local or scholastic; it occurs at King's College in 1470— 'for repairing *le bocard* in the little garden'.[6]

Water flushing seems to have been practically confined to monastic houses, except that public latrines[7] were often built over a stream. In 1237 owing to the extension of a private quay, 'the necessary house built at Queenhithe at London by Maud formerly Queen of England for the common use of the citizens' had to be extended also, so that it might have access to the Thames, as before.[8] In 1415 orders were given to shift an offensive common latrine from 'the Moor' (near Moorgate) on to the Walbrook, where the filth could be removed by means of 'a watergate called a scluys or a speye'[9]—something in the nature of a penstock. At the opposite extremity of the sanitary scale from such a system as that in use at Canterbury was the latrine with a shoot leading straight out to the foot

---

[1] E. 461, 21.　　　　　　　[2] St. John's Coll. Camb. Accts., vol. i.
[3] T.R., f. 436.　　　　　　　[4] E. 474. 13.
　[5] This was a subtle allusion to a term in Logic, defined in the *Oxford Dictionary* (where its first occurrence is dated 1509) as 'A mnemonic word, representing a mood of the third syllogistic figure in which a particular negative major premiss and a universal affirmative minor give a particular negative conclusion'—which I hope means more to readers than it does to me. One suspects the Cambridge use to veil a pun on 'bog'.
　[6] Mundum Bk. vi.
　[7] 'A privey both for women and men' at Bristol is mentioned in 1480 by William of Worcester: *Itinerarium*, 194.
　[8] *Close R.* 564.
　[9] Riley, *Mems. of London*, 615.

of the wall, or simply corbelled out.[1] These were common in moated houses and castles,[2] but were also found in towns, and in 1321 complaint was made that a lane called Ebbegate, in London, was blocked by people who had made overhanging latrines, '*quarum putredo cadit super capita hominum transeuntium*'.[3]

The normal form of latrine was the cesspit. Medieval houses were well supplied with these, but it may be doubted if their builders always bore in mind Horman's advice, that 'A wyse buylder wyll set a sege house out of the wey from syght and smellynge'.[4] ('Sege' means a seat; at Eltham in 1400 we have the making of 'a new *seeg* for the King's latrine beside the stews (*stug*')';[5] and in 1479 there is a London entry of 18*d*. paid 'for clensyng of the sege holis'.)[6] Henry III in 1245 wrote to Edward FitzOtho, his Master of the Works: 'Since the privy chamber of our wardrobe at London is situated in an unsuitable place, wherefore it smells badly, we command you, on the faith and love by which you are bound to us, that you in no wise omit to cause another privy chamber to be made in the same wardrobe in such more fitting and proper place as you may select there, even though it should cost a hundred pounds.'[7] William, Abbot of Thorney (1305–22), also, is recorded to have arranged for 'a walk (*deambulatorium*) from the side (of the Dorter) towards the garderobe to purify the air and shut out the smell from the Dorter, so that in future persons staying there or passing through should not be affected by any stench or unclean air'.[8] Henry III was not above dictating the details of such buildings: in 1238 he ordered the Constable of the Tower to 'cause the drain of our privy chamber to be made in the fashion of a hollow column, as John of Ely shall more fully tell thee';[9] before going to York for the marriage of his sister to Alexander of Scotland in 1251 he gave orders for the construction of a privy chamber, 20 feet long, 'with a deep pit', adjoining the room he was to occupy in the Archbishop's palace;[7] and in 1268 he ordered the privy chamber of the Queen's room in Winchester Castle to be made 'in the fashion of a turret with double vaulting'[10]—presumably a vaulted

---

[1] These can be seen in some French villages, but are not, I think, in use.

[2] In 1313 Sir William de Norwico ordered a stone wall to be made to hide the filth issuing from the shoots (*tuell*') of the garderobes of the Keep at the Tower: E. 469, 16.

[3] *Liber Custumarum*, 449.

[4] *Vulgaria*, c. xxix.      [5] E. 502, 15.

[6] *Memorials* (E.E.T.S.), 87. A carpenter was employed at Cambridge Castle in 1295, joisting the garderobe of the hall and making '*le setle cloace dicte garderobe*': E. 459, 16.

[7] *Close R.*      [8] Cambridge Univ. MS. Add. 3021, f. 459.

[9] Liberate R. 23 Hen. III.

[10] Ibid. 53 Hen. III.

roof and a vault under the floor. When a contract was made in 1370 for the building of 18 shops in London, the mason preparing the foundations was to make '10 stone pits for *prevez*, of which pits 8 shall be double (i.e. serve two houses) and each in depth 10 ft., and in length 10 ft., and in breadth 11 ft.'[1] At Eltham in 1425 stone was provided for a new latrine 12 feet in depth below the ground, and masons were employed *circa cavyng latrine*.[2]

The account of some repairs done to houses in London in 1450 is interesting as showing that ventilating shafts were sometimes employed: 'for the makyng a vente for a prevey to voyd y$^e$ heyr (= air) a wey by . . . item to the same vente iiij li. of pyche and ij li. of reson (= resin) . . . to Herman tyler for to tyle agane y$^e$ howse y$^e$ wyche whas broke for to lete y$^e$ vente thorow y$^e$ howse . . . makeyng of a parte of a towel (i.e. shoot) of a privey the wyche was broke for to set in a vente to voyd a wey the eyr.'[3] The same accounts include 5s. 6d. 'for the dygyng of a pyt and takeyng owte of a serteyne of dounge owte of a privey and for to bery y$^e$ dounge in y$^e$ same pyt'; while 'for y$^e$ caryyng a way of vj ton of dounge owte of a privey in the ten' y$^t$ John Boyd armyrer held', no less than 17s. was paid. Both the way in which the contents of the cesspits were allowed to accumulate before clearing and the high wages paid for this unskilled but most unpleasant work are brought out in other entries. The state of the gaol of Newgate in 1282 can be imagined from the fact that thirteen workmen were employed for 5 days cleaning the *cloacam*; their pay, at 6d. a day, was about three times as much as the ordinary unskilled worker earned at that date. Subsequently 'the hole where the filth (*stercora*) of the cesspit was cast out' was walled up again with stone.[4] Similarly at Queenborough in 1375, after William Mokkyng and Nicholas Richeandgood had cleaned the latrines and carried the muck out of the castle to distant places, Robert Webbe, mason, blocked up the outer openings of the latrines with masonry.[5] In 1406, at Westminster, the considerable sum of 40s. was paid to Thomas Watergate, *mundatori latrinarum*,[6] for clearing out and cleaning a latrine under the chamber of the Keeper of the King's Privy Seal, and for clearing out 2 drains (*gutter'*) leading from the King's cellar to the Thames.[7] Finally we may quote certain sums expended by the church-wardens of St. Mary-at-Hill on parish properties: in 1478, 'for voyding

[1] App. B.                [2] E. 496, 7.              [3] Mins. Accts. 917, No. 18.
[4] E. 467, 11.                                   [5] E. 483, 29.
[6] Cf. at Oxford in 1503—*sol' cloachario purgenti latrinam*—14s. 8d.: *Canterbury Coll. Oxford* (O.H.S. N.S. vii), 237.
[7] E. 502, 26.

of ij tonne owte of a pryve in Harry Williamson house'—5s. 4d.;[1] 1500, 'to Donyng, gong fermere, . . . for fermyng of a sege in George Gys-borow the clarkes chamber wherin was v tone, at ij[s]. the tone—x[s]. Item to Rychard, servaunte with John Wolff, for watchyng with theyme to see the tomys (*sic*) wele fylyd—iiij[d].';[2] and similarly in 1536, 'to a man yat watched y[e] gongfarmers ij nyghtes'—8d.[3] Certainly, if any medieval workmen might be excused for scamping their work or overcharging their employers, by undercharging their barrels, those engaged on this work might be.

[1] *Memorials* (E.E.T.S.), 82.
[2] Ibid. 87.      [3] Ibid. 373.

# XIX

## IRONWORK, NAILS

THE amount of iron used in medieval building was considerable, not only for such accessories as the stanchions and glazing bars of windows and door furniture but also for definitely constructional purposes. Professor Lethaby has called attention to the extensive use of iron tie-bars in Westminster Abbey, particularly in the chapter-house, where the central pillar was provided with an umbrella-like arrangement of iron rods from the capital to the vaulting ribs.[1] Various types of rods, clamps, anchors, and so forth, to say nothing of vast quantities of nails, were in demand and the smith was an important figure on the building establishment, even apart from his work in making and repairing the workmen's tools. Consequently the accounts show many purchases of iron, both native and imported, most of the latter coming from Spain. For the works at Westminster Abbey in 1252-3 some 4 tons of 'tough (*tenaci*) iron of Gloucester' was purchased, at 4s. the hundredweight.[2] How early iron reached this country from Spain is uncertain, but it was being brought to Winchelsea in 1266,[3] and it occurs in building accounts at Canterbury in 1275, at 3s. 1d. the cwt.,[4] and again in 1280 at the remarkably low price of 2s. 4d., including carriage from Sandwich.[5] At Corfe Spanish iron for window bars cost 3s. 6d. the cwt. in 1292;[6] and at Dover in 1339 iron, presumably from the Weald, was 6s. and Spanish iron 7s., though another parcel of Spanish iron was at the same time bought at Sandwich at the rate of 4s. 3d.[7] At Hedon in 1343 Spanish iron was bought at 4½d. the stone, equivalent to 3s. the cwt.,[8] and at Ely three years later it was 3s. 6d.[9] For some reason the Ely price in 1358 was 7s. 3d.,[10] although at Westminster in the same year it was only 5s. 11d.[11] At Leeds Castle in 1370, while native iron cost from 5s. 6d. to 7s., Spanish iron was from 9s. 3d. to 10s.,[12] and its use at such a price suggests that its quality was definitely superior to that of the local product. It was carried as far inland as Nottingham, where in 1363 there is mention of its purchase at 6s. 8d. the cwt., and also of '*j gada*

[1] *Westminster Abbey*, 139.     [2] E. 466, 30; 467, 1.
[3] Salzman, *English Trade*, 409.     [4] Lambeth MS. 242, f. 29.
[5] Ibid., f. 63v.     [6] E. 460, 28.     [7] E. 462, 15.
[8] Boyle, *Hedon*, p. xxii.     [9] *Sacrist Rolls*, 131.
[10] Ibid. 176.     [11] E. 472, 4.     [12] E. 466, 19.

*ferri de Spayne'* for hooks and bands, costing 5s. 4½d.[1] Similarly at Tatters-hall in 1438 we find 4 *'gaddi ferri Ispanie'*, weighing 314 lb. (probably = 3 cwt. 14 lb.).[2] This would make the 'gad' of iron roughly three-quarters of a hundredweight, which corresponds more or less with the sixteenth-century 'gad' in Wales or the Wealden 'bloom'.[3] Other terms occur occasionally: for instance, in the Winchester Castle accounts for 1222 we find *'xlii hes de ferro'* costing 13s. 6d.; as '1 seam and 17 *hes'*, bought from the same merchant, also cost 13s. 6d., we may take the seam (*summa*) as equivalent to 25 *hes*.[4] Other items in these accounts show the seam at 9s. 6d. and the *hes* at 5d. At Rockingham in 1278 there is a note of '2 seams of iron, containing 144 (*vii*ˣˣ*iiij*) pieces of iron, bought at the fair of Derby, for 17s. 8d.'[5] This, if the seam is, as usual, 500 lb., gives a weight of 7 lb. for the 'piece' and a price of 1½d. which corresponds to the price of the '112 *esperdites*[6] of iron, for picks and hinges' bought at Dover in 1227 for 15s. 1d.[7] On the other hand, in the catalogue of stores in the castles of North Wales in 1323, which includes 11,729 'pieces of iron', we find '24 seams (*summagia*) of iron, each seam containing 72 pieces', and also '10 byndynges of iron, each byndyng containing 25 pieces'.[8] At Vale Royal in 1278 sixty 'dozens' of iron cost 60s.—'and each dozen (*duodena*) contains six pieces, of which each is worth 2d.';[9] and at Corfe in 1363 we have 15 'dosene' of iron costing 11s. 4½d., a price which indicates that the 'dozen' was, as we might expect, 12 pounds.[10]

We have seen that Gloucestershire iron was used at Westminster in 1252, and 'iron of Gloucester' was bought, at 16d. the 'piece', for use at Moor End in 1365.[11] The Wealden iron-fields of Sussex are mentioned in 1278, when Master Henry of Lewes, the chief smith at the Tower, bought 75 rods (*kivill'*) *in Waldis* for 65s. 7½d., and paid £4. 3s. 4d. 'to a smith *in Waldis* for 100 iron rods'.[12] Weardale iron occurs occasionally in northern accounts, as in 1532 at Durham,[13] where Spanish iron cost 9d. the stone, 'Werdall yron' 5d., and there is also mention of 'wodyron', the meaning of which is obscure. At Finchale in 1473 'Wardell' iron was 5½d. the stone

---

[1] E. 478, 6.  [2] Penshurst MS. 236.
[3] Salzman, *English Industries*, 32, 36. At Dover 19 cwt. of iron called *'blomhisen'* (i.e. iron in blooms) is mentioned in 1330: Pipe R. 4 Edw. III.
[4] E. 491, 13.  [5] E. 480, 19.
[6] Connected with French *espardre*, to cut up. At Bamborough there were 500 *sperdutis* of iron in 1223: Foreign R. 8 Hen. III.
[7] E. 462, 10.  [8] Pipe R. 5 Edw. III.
[9] E. 485, 72.  [10] E. 461, 5.  [11] E. 544, 31.
[12] E. 467, 6 (6).  [13] *D.H.B.* 140.

—Spanish 7½*d*., and 'iron of Lukys' (i.e. Liége) 6*d*.[1] Iron from 'Amias' (i.e. Amiens) occurs at York in 1526 and 1528,[2] and iron of 'Pont Audemar' (Pont-Audemer in Normandy) at Norwich in 1285,[3] at the high price of 15*s*. 6*d*. the cwt., there being also an entry in the Tower accounts for 1278 of a purchase of 'half a hundred of iron *de Pontawmeri* for mending the masons' tools' for 9*s*.[4] This high price suggests that this Norman iron was of the nature of steel, similar to the Swedish 'osmonds'. The Tower accounts just quoted also mention '174 sheaves (*garbis*) of osmond iron', costing £6. 16*s*. 8*d*., and '128 sheaves of steel', costing £4. 5*s*. 4*d*. At Norwich in 1316 we find purchases of '4½ scefh of small Osemund and 1½ scefh of large Osemund', for 8*s*. 7*d*., and '2 scefh of steel' for 20*d*.;[3] and at Tattershall in 1438 an entry of '18 gaddez 1 sheaf (*garba*) of Osmundez, and 5 pieces of foldynyryn and 2 pairs of iron bands called Wyndow-bandez'.[5] (The 'foldynyryn' may be equivalent to the 'welded (*junctum*) iron in gobbets, at 100 to the hundredweight', mentioned, with other varieties of iron, as belonging to Spanish merchants in London in 1338.)[6] The Vale Royal accounts show that the sheaf (*glavett*') contained 30 'pieces',[7] and a Windsor account of 1355[8] gives also 30 'gaddes' (not to be confused with the great iron gad, mentioned above) to the sheaf (*garba*), and 6 sheaves to the *pondus aceris*, equivalent to the 'burgh', mentioned in North Wales in 1332,[9] and the 'burden steill' which occurs at York, at 3*s*., in 1526 and 1528.[10]

Steel was required for the edges of the workmen's tools; it was too costly a material to be wasted and the method, therefore, was to shut, or weld, a piece of steel on to the edge of the iron tool.[11] So at Ely we find '6 sheaves of steel for putting on the iron tools (*ferramentis*) of the masons' in 1323;[12] at Porchester 94 lb. of Spanish steel, at 1½*d*. a pound, were used in 1397 'for the hardening (*duracionem*) of the axes and other tools of the masons';[13] and at Windsor, in 1536, 'vj gaddes of steel spent on stelyng of wegges to cleaffe heth stone, at iiij for a peny'.[14] From its use for the edges of tools it appears at Ely in 1346, and again in 1358, as 'eggestel'.[15] The Ely accounts also, in 1324, contain a reference to 'a sheaf of Garlok Stel',[16] costing 10*d*., which is about the normal price for steel at this time.

[1] *Finchale Priory* (Surtees Society), cccxxvii.  [2] *Y.F.R.* 101, 102.
[3] Camera Roll.  [4] E. 467, 6 (4).
[5] Penshurst MS. 236.  [6] Salzman, *Engl. Trade*, 410.
[7] E. 485, 22.  [8] Hope, *Windsor Castle*, 176.
[9] Pipe R. 5 Edw. III.  [10] *Y.F.R.* 101, 102.  [11] See below, p. 330.
[12] *Sacrist Rolls*, 33.  [13] E. 479, 23.  [14] Hope, op. cit. 264.
[15] *Sacrist Rolls*, 131, 176.  [16] Ibid. 67.

Medieval references to constructional ironwork are for the most part unenlightening, consisting of lists of the purchase or manufacture of bars, clamps, crampons and so forth, without any indication of their exact use. As, for instance, in 1364, when Stephen the smith at Windsor was paid for working '*in diversis anulis plates parvis barris lecch' cacch' cases hokes boltes slotth' stapl' et levours'*.[1] Westminster accounts of 1532 mention 66 'crampettes of iron made for the cramping and joyning of harde stone togethers',[2] and there is also a reference to 'xvj ringes with crampettis provided for the masons', at 3*d*. each,[3] the purpose of which is not clear, though they may have been tackle for hoisting stones. They were, naturally, chiefly required in positions where the stones projected or were set at an angle at which they were liable to slip, as in a spire or gable. For St. Stephen's Chapel, Westminster, in 1334 Walter the smith was paid 'for 18 irons called *tyrauntz*, 2 feet in length and 2 inches in breadth each way (*quadratim*), for the work of the gable towers—for 12 crampons called *tiraunz* of iron for fastening stones of various shapes in the high work of the two towers beside the gables—and for 6 iron instruments called *tyraunz fourches*, 3 ft. in length'.[4] Similarly, in 1399, Master William Smyth was paid 'for 126 crampons, weighing 143 lb., for the great window in the gable of the King's hall' at Westminster.[5] Another entry in the account just quoted is a payment to 'Thomas Lokyere for 3 long iron crampons for repairing the great broken marble table against the King's coronation'. An earlier Westminster account, for 1351, contains a number of items:[6] 'for 8 iron bars for fastening stones on the top of the eastern vice of the chapel'; 'for 2 iron hoops (*circulis*) for the top of the western turret of the chapel'; 'for making 4 gudgeons (*goions*), weighing 33 lb., to hold the upper stones at the top of the great pinnacle of the chapel'; 'for 43 gudgeons, weighing 20 lb., for the finials (*filiolas*) over the chapel'; 'to John del Thele, smith, for filing up (*limacione*) the ironwork supporting the marble columns in the east gable, 4d.'; and 'for setting 2 hoops on two stones covering 2 tanks connected with a drain'. Two years later 8 'pikes' were provided for fixing a 'pomell'[7]—some kind of ornamental sphere—on top of the Staple Hall at Westminster.[8] Iron pins were used for fastening the menagerie of 'king's beasts' that ramped over the roofs at Hampton Court, and also for the stone 'types', or domical caps, at the gable ends of the 'tennis play' and

---

[1] E. 493, 16.      [2] T.R. 314.      [3] Ibid. 416.
[4] E. 470, 15.      [5] E. 473, 11.      [6] E. 471, 6.
[7] Cf. at Westminster in 1275: 'for 24 bands (*bendis*) of iron for the pomel of the hall': E. 467, 6 (2).
[8] E. 471, 8.

elsewhere—two 'ston persers', or tools for piercing stone, being provided 'for the masons to make holys to yowte in the sayd pynnys',[1] the pins being held in place by lead 'yotted', or cast, round them. Similarly, in 1282, the smith at Carnarvon Castle made '3 crampons to hold a stone eagle upon the great tower'. An instance of an opposite use of spikes—for keeping birds away—may be quoted from the Sandwich churchwardens' accounts for 1444: 'for xxiij yryn pykys that were made for to sette up on the poynts of the crossis of the pynacles of the stepyll for ravouns schuld not stond ther on to soyle the stepyll and goterie with bonys and other thyngs'.[2]

At Leeds Castle in 1370 there is an entry of 2 irons and 4 crampons *pro machecoll'*,[3] that is to say for the stone brackets of the machicolations: and at York Castle '4 stays of iron to support the hoarding (*tabul'*) called *le bretesse* within the tower' are mentioned in 1362.[4] In 1259 payments were made at Westminster 'to smiths employed on making the ironwork which supports the shaft (*tuellum*) from the fireplace of the king's chamber against the force of the winds';[5] and in 1532 'viij aunkers for byndyng of chymneys', weighing 106 lb., were provided at Westminster.[6] In this last entry 'chymney' probably means fireplace, as iron constantly entered into the construction of the hood or mantel. At Corfe in 1292 we have 4*d.* paid 'for clamps (*grapis*) for the fireplace';[7] at York Castle in 1364 'iron bars for setting in the mantels of the *chymnes*';[8] and in London in 1490 payment 'for an anchor of iron, 2 bars (*repagulis*) with forelockes, broodes and other large nails, for the construction of a fireplace'.[9] An interesting entry concerning the repair of a fireplace at the Tower occurs in 1335:[10] 'for 4 cwt. of Spanish iron for 2 pillars and a crossbar (*traueseyn*) made thereof, the length of each pillar 8 ft., to support the great fireplace in the Queen's chamber, because it broke and stones fell from it while the King's daughters and their nurses were sitting in the room,—16s. To Walter de Bury, smith, for making the said pillars, taking for their making the value of the iron, namely 4s. the cwt., as none was left over, 16s.' At Cambridge the King's Hall accounts for 1432 mention '32 crawfett and 16 clampes for fireplaces for joining the copporons',[11] which, as we have seen,[12] are

---

[1] H.C. 238, f. 139.　　　　　　　　　　　[2] Boys, *Sandwich*, ii. 363.

[3] E. 466, 19.　　　　[4] E. 598, 6.　　　　[5] E. 467, 2.

[6] T.R., f. 51. Cf. at Peterborough in 1495 carpenters were paid 'for ankeryng of ij bemes' and Thomas Buk received 5s. 'for makyng of ij ankyrs and ij boltys': *Northants. Rec. Soc.* ix. 61.

[7] E. 460, 29.　　　　[8] E. 501, 11.　　　　[9] Egerton MS. 2358, f. 1.

[10] E. 469, 18.　　　　[11] K.H., f. 66.　　　　[12] Above, p. 109.

probably the projecting hoods. 'Crowfoot' was a term used for a trifid clamp, sometimes also called a 'goosefoot', as in 1482 at Clarendon—'for ironwork, namely hokes, gosefett and other things'.[1]

In the Hampton Court accounts of 1539 we find 'a dougge of irne servyng to claspe ij beames together in a mantell of a chymney'.[2] The term 'dog' is frequently used for a bar or band of iron joining, or strengthening, woodwork; as at Cambridge in 1470—'*pro ij dogges ferreis copulantibus latera domus Thome Kemp*';[3] and in London in 1454—'to Stephen Clamparde for 8 *dogges* of iron for mending the rafters on the south of the roof, each *dogge* weighing 15 lb.'[4] With this last entry may be compared one relating to the new hall at Eltham in 1479: 'for x grete clampes of yron for the bynddyng of the princyples weyng ciiij$^{xx}$xvj lb., price the lb. at London ijd.'[5] A reference to 8 'dogges of irne', weighing 164 lb., for the roof at Hampton Court, with 'pynnes and revettes serving for the same', occurs in 1533, when there is also mention of 'ij dukkes for the gynnes' (i.e. machines) and a later entry of 'mendyng of oon of the douckes'.[6] In 1497 the churchwardens of St. Mary-at-Hill record a payment 'to the smythe for iij stays and a litill sterope and a forth right dogge of iryn for the rodelofte'.[7]

The last of our dogs—'2 iron dogges used on the repair of the drawbridge' at Gloucester Castle in 1442[8]—may serve to introduce an entry of some interest giving details of the ironwork made for a drawbridge at the Tower in 1324:[9]

To Walter de Bury, smith, for 2 iron *bolsters* to carry the bridge,—2s. To the same for 2 iron *goiouns* to lie on the said *bolesters*,—2s. For 2 iron hoops (*hopis*) for binding the *axtrou* (i.e. axle-tree) at either end,—2s. For 6 iron bands (*ligaturis*) to bind the weights (*pois*) called *ballokis*,—6s. For 3 great iron pins to fasten the bridge to the *axtrou*,—18d. For 2 rings with staples, 1 *pyn*, 1 *gunph*'[10] for raising the bridge, 2 *haspes* with 4 staples,—21d.

Large quantities of iron were used in windows, serving the three purposes of strengthening the construction, excluding intruders, and supporting the glazing, where present. The strengthening, it may be noted, might be regarded as temporary, and even fallacious, for iron in exposed positions by its rusting tends to dislocate masonry. The ironwork of a

---

[1] E. 460, 16.  [2] H.C. 239, f. 425.  [3] P. 1470–1.
[4] St. Paul's, Misc. Roll A. 52.  [5] E. 496, 21.  [6] H.C. 237, f. 105.
[7] *Memorials* (E.E.T.S.), 224. Cf. 'Two iron instruments called *stiroppys* for binding the wheel of the well', at Clarendon, 1482 : E. 460, 16.
[8] E. 473, 18.  [9] E. 469, 7.
[10] *Gunfus* is part of a hinge. See below, p. 295.

window, consisting of upright and transverse bars, was sometimes known as a 'ferment', from the Latin *ferramentum*. Thus in 1437 the churchwardens of St. Mary-at-Hill paid 'to ye smyth for a ferment of iron to the wyndowe', 6s. 8d.[1] Repairs to houses in Coldharbour (London) in 1485 include —'a ferment to the botery wyndowe', and 'mendyng of ij fermentes to the celar wyndowe';[2] and at Winchester in the same year there is a payment *'pro le fermentyng fenestrarum'*.[3] At Woodstock in 1435 Nicholas Smyth of Abingdon was paid 47s. 8d. *'pro cclxviij lb. de ferro facto fermerywerk pro fenestris nove turris'*.[4] For Salisbury Cathedral[5] in 1479 payments were made 'for mending *le fermente werke* of the windows in the belfry', and this is later defined as *'firment' ferr' fenestrarum ut in standerd transummys sokettes* [sic] *et aliis'*, with an additional 21d. for 21 dozen 'smalle keys' of iron, these being the small iron wedges which are driven in where the uprights pass through the crossbars: they occur, about 1295, at Winchester, where 7s. was paid for 700 *'weggis ferreis ad fenestras'*.[6]

Where a window was of more than one light it was usual to have one horizontal 'stay-bar' running from jamb to jamb through the mullions, and a number of smaller bars, parallel to it, from mullion to mullion, or from jamb to mullion. When these bars were made with eyes to fit round the upright 'standards' they were called 'lockets'. The small bars, to which the glazing was wired and soldered, were called 'soudelets'—a term which is often printed as 'sondelets', but the various forms given below show that this is a mistake. Stay-bars are presumably implied in the 66 'thurtouerbarres for windows' bought at Clarendon in 1288,[7] and the 13 'thurtbarres made for windows' of Rochester Castle in 1377 by Master Stephen the smith of the Tower of London.[8] Similarly, at Westminster in 1288 John de Ledes was paid *'pro j trauersino de ferro'* for the great window of the pantry and buttery,[9] and in 1351 three 'trauersbarres', weighing 34 lb., were supplied for windows;[10] and the King's Hall accounts for 1432 mention '2 trawasones barres', weighing 28 lb.[11] At Rockingham in 1277 we have 'spindlis and trauerseins for the windows in the great cellar',[12] and at Sheppey in 1366 '72 traunceynbarris of iron and 12 standards for the church'.[13] For the Friary buildings at Langley in 1372 we find 24 'staybarres', 48 cross-bars (*ferram' trans'*), and 16 'standardes', weighing in all 16½ cwt., supplied for the cloisters and windows of the cells.[14] Four years

---

[1] *Memorials* (E.E.T.S.), 67.   [2] E. 474, 3.

[3] *Obedientiary Rolls*, 386.   [4] E. 499, 3.   [5] Clerk of Works accts.

[6] E. 491, 19.   [7] E. 593, 20.   [8] E. 544, 20.

[9] E. 467, 17.   [10] E. 471, 6.   [11] K.H. 8, f. 66.

[12] E. 480, 18.   [13] E. 483, 23.   [14] E. 466, 6.

later Master Stephen the smith made '4 great standards 6 traunson and a steybarr', weighing 69 lb., for a window at Havering.[1] At Launceston in 1455 'standardys and crossebarrys', weighing 97 lb., were supplied for the window of the gaol,[2] and it may be noted that five years later 86 lb. of iron was used 'for mending a grill (*gredell*') which lies over *le pitte* in which thieves and felons are put in ward'.[3] For the choir windows at Langley 'stapelbarres and soudelettes' were sent from London in 1368,[4] and thirty years earlier at Ely we find charges 'for working stapolbarris' and '*in sowdelibus faciendis*'.[5] In 1532 the Westminster accounts mention 'iij sowdelette barres tynned sette in a pane by the lanterne in the librarye in the kynges bed chambre',[6] and next year, at Hampton Court, there are references to 'sodelettes for the windows of the new tennys play'[7] and to 'sodlettes for the harnessyng of the great wyndow at the ende of the haull':[8] it is probable that in this form of the word 'soudelet' we see the origin of the term 'saddle-bar' now in use.

Repairs to the west window of the chapel at Windsor in 1295 included 'renewing 5 bars, with 18 lakettcs and takettes'.[9] Here 'takettes' may possibly mean wedges, and 'lakettes' are presumably the eyed bars which were afterwards called 'lockets'. The earliest use of that word that I have noted is at Cambridge in 1432, when 'lokettes and standardes' are mentioned:[10] but at Ely there is reference to 'mending and making eyes in (*oculandis*) bars for the glass windows' in 1350.[11] The Westminster accounts for 1532 contain many entries such as 'lij lockette barres and xxvj uprightes for certeyne windowes',[12] and 'one steybarre of iij lightes with ix lockettis and vj uprightes made for a windowe in the galarye';[13] and from those of Hampton Court we may quote one of '28 lokettes, 4 staybarres and 14 standards for the lower transummes for 2 great windows in the upper end of the new hall'.[14]

When glazed windows were intended to open it was necessary to set the glazing in an iron frame, or casement, usually described as a 'case'. In 1365 no less than 160 'iron cases with their hinges (*gumphis*) for glazing the windows of the castle' were provided, at 5s. each, at Sheppey;[15] 'iron cases tinned (*stann*')', bought for Langley in 1368, also cost 5s. each;[4] while at Wallingford in 1375 the '4 iron cases for 4 glass windows' were 22d.

[1] E. 464, 30.  
[2] E. 461, 18.  
[3] Ibid. 20.  
[4] E. 466, 4.  
[5] *Sacrist Rolls*, 96.  
[6] T.R., f. 14.  
[7] H.C. 237, f. 146.  
[8] H.C. 238, f. 11.  
[9] E. 492, 4.  
[10] K.H. 8, f. 66.  
[11] *Sacrist Rolls*, 143.  
[12] T.R., f. 106.  
[13] Ibid., f. 315.  
[14] H.C. 237, f. 124.  
[15] E. 483, 21.

each, with another 20*d*. for '4 lacches with 4 wrestes';[1] and at Eltham, in
1401, 16 iron cases cost 32*s*.[2] In the accounts of Lady Margaret Beaufort's
buildings at Collyweston 'fenestral' is used instead of 'case'. Thus in 1500—
'for a fenestrall of yren for the wyndowe in my lordes chambre weyng xj lb.
with hokes and cagges (i.e. catches)', and a purchase of 'fyn sowder to the
glassyng of the said fenestrall';[3] and in 1505 there is reference to 'xj duble
fenestralles of yren for a xj lyghtes'.[4] 'Double' probably means that the
glazed frame was hinged into an outer metal frame. At Westminster in
1532 there are mentions of 'a doble case sette in a windowe within a
jakis in the Ladye Wilshires lodgeinge';[5] and 'iij doble casementes everye
of them cont' in bredith ij foote, and in depth iij fote di', sette in certeyn
wyndowes'.[6] There is also an entry of payment 'for fyling of the nether
ends of xxix casis sette in diverse wyndowis, . . . for that the saide cases
wolde spare (spar = fasten) or shitte close'.[7] From the contemporary
accounts of Hampton Court we may quote the provision of hinges for
the 'casis of the wyerd wyndows in the tennys play'.[8]

   When Sir Thomas Lucas was building Little Saxham Hall in 1505 he
bargained with Alexander Boyn, smith, of Bury: 'for making of barres
of iron, lokettes, hookes, henges, cases, nailes and other thinges necessary,
paying for every lb. of the said cases being wele and clenly wrought and
sufficiently rede vernysshed ijd. ob., and for every lb. of naile, blak, ijd. and
for every lb. of henges, white tynned, jd. ob., and for every lb. of the residue
of al his workmanship being rede vernyshed jd. ob.'[9] It is interesting to
notice that the greater part of the ironwork was protected by varnishing.
There is mention of 465 lb. of 'ferment' verneshid' being provided for
windows at Clarendon in 1477,[10] and it is probable that this was the usual
alternative to painting. The nails that were to be black may have been
simply left in their natural colour, but ironwork was sometimes definitely
blackened. Thus at Windsor in 1352 we find 'a barrel of pitch for blackening various ironwork' bought for 5*s*.[11] and at Kirby Muxloe there is mention of 'pyk (i.e. pitch) called stonne pyk for vernysshing le firmentes'.[12]
Much more frequent, as we shall see, was the whitening of iron by dipping it in tin. At Queenborough in 1375 there is an entry of 'half a pound
of fresh fat, with which to grease nails, bolts and other ironwork to keep

[1] E. 490, 3.                                                    [2] E. 502, 23.
[3] St. John's Coll. Camb. Accts., vol. i.                        [4] Ibid., vol. ii.
[5] T.R., f. 419.              [6] Ibid., f. 508.                  [7] Ibid., f. 420.
[8] H.C. 237, f. 170.                   [9] Gage, *Thingoe Hundred*, 142.
[10] E. 460, 14.                        [11] E. 495, 7.
[12] *Leics. Arch. Soc.* xi. 291.

them from rust until they are tinned'.[1] At Moor End in 1365 there are purchases of '9 lb. of pitch for blackening hinges and hooks', and of 'tin bought for whitening hinges';[2] and just about a century later money was paid at Shene 'for working various hokes, hynges, garnettes and jemewes (hinges) of iron, and for tinning and pychyng thereof'.[3]

Iron was also required for the hanging and furniture of doors, shutters, and windows. The earliest and most primitive method of hanging a door was by means of the pin hinge, the back beam of the door having at its end an iron, or iron-shod, spindle which turned in a socket in the threshold. This type was usual in Roman times and may still be found in such buildings as barns. Two fifteenth-century vocabularies[4] give *cardo* as meaning 'a har of a dore' and 'durherre' respectively, and 'har' is still in dialect use for such a socket, the beam which turns in it being the 'har-tree'. But I have not noted either the Latin[5] or the English word in any building record that I have examined and can only point to one, very late, entry which seems to indicate this type of construction. This is in the 1532 accounts of King's Hall, Cambridge: '*pro 2° bz ly plates a huppe et a googen pro magnis portis*'.[6] Here the hoop was probably for binding the spindle, the gudgeon was the socket in which it turned, one of the plates being on the threshold and the other on the under edge of the door. Such plates seem to be implied in the 'underlaghers' of iron supplied for the outer gates of Somerton Castle in 1334.[7] It is very likely that many entries of hoops, spindles, gudgeons, and so forth without any illuminating context may actually refer to 'har' hanging; but the majority of doors seem, from the late thirteenth century at any rate, to have been hung by the hook hinge which is practically universal for church doors. In this type the hook, an iron wedge, from the broader end of which a round iron pin rises vertically to carry an eyed piece of iron attached to the door, is inserted in the door-frame. Normally a pair of hooks is sufficient, but with very heavy doors three or four may be required. The hook is almost invariably,[8] I think, known by that name or the equivalent 'crook', though of course sometimes included with its rider as 'a pair of hinges'—and is latinized as *gunfus* (with variant spellings), connected with the French *gond*. Oddly

[1] E. 483, 29.  [2] E. 544, 31.  [3] E. 503, 15.
[4] Wright, *Vocabularies*, 729, 777.
[5] Except at Oxford in 1505—*pro j cardine ad hostium* and *pro j cardine ad fenestram*: Canterbury Coll. (O.H.S. N.S. vii), 243.
[6] K.H. 24, 227.  [7] E. 484, 11.
[8] At Leverton (Lincs.) in 1530 the term 'thimble' was used—'for yryn thymbulles and vertevailes to ye chirche yaites': *Archaeologia*, xli. 352.

enough the two vocabularies quoted above give, respectively —'*gumfus*, a dorbande'—which is the rider, and '*gumsa* [*sic*], a hengle'—which is usually either the rider or the complete hinge; but the whole evidence is against this interpretation. We have, for instance, at Nottingham in 1313— '*pro ligaminibus et gumfys scilicet henglys et okys*',[1] and, more definitely, at Corfe in 1285: 'to a mason making mortices (*mortasios*) for setting hooks (*guncias*)', and 'to Walter Plogge, who made the mortices in which the hooks (*gunci*) for doors and windows[2] were set with lead'.[3] Being set in the stonework, such hinges are sometimes called 'stone hinges'; as at St. Paul's in 1490: 'stonhengis with iron hooks (*hamis*)';[4] in 1442 at Gloucester: '2 pair of iron stonehingel set on the door and window of the wine cellar';[5] and next year at Westminster: 'a pair of iron stonehokes used for hanging the door at Cheynegate'.[6]

The eyed portion of the hinge is usually latinized as *vertivella*. As this can be read, and has frequently been printed, as *vertinella* it may be as well to point out that it is connected with the French *vertevelle* and *vervelle*, and that the forms in which it occurs in documents place the correct reading beyond all doubt. Thus at Canterbury it appears in 1264 not only as '*guns et verteuel*' but also as '*gunos et vertefles*',[7] and in 1298 as '*vertiwell*';[8] and at Boston in 1452 we have '*vertibales et hengles*'.[9] In English several different terms are found. In Kent and Sussex the term was, and is, 'rides', but it appears to be peculiar to that district.[10] The Canterbury accounts show 6s. 11½d. paid in 1273 '*pro xxx pariis de riden*'; 9d. for 8 pair of 'rides' next year; 18d. '*pro duobus henges de rydes*' in 1275; and '*ryden and hokes*' in 1276.[11] At Penshurst in 1466 payment is made for '*ij hokis and ij rydis*';[12] and the following year the churchwardens' accounts of Arlington in Sussex mention '18d. paid for a ryde and nails for the church door'.[13] Elsewhere they are commonly called 'twists', the eye being formed by twisting the end of the iron band round. At Woodstock in 1265 we find a payment 'for hooks, twists, and a lock (*gunphis thuistis et cerura*) for a gate',[14] and in 1295

---

[1] E. 478, 1.

[2] It is impossible to distinguish between 'windows' and 'shutters', see above, p. 256.

[3] E. 460, 27.      [4] Egerton MS. 2358, f. 2.

[5] E. 473, 18.      [6] E. 403, 11.

[7] Lambeth MS. 242, f. 7.      [8] Ibid., f. 196v.

[9] Penshurst MS. 20.

[10] The exception is at Canterbury College, Oxford, where the accountants were probably from Kent—1396, *pro hokis et rydis*, and 1477, *pro iij paribus de ridis pro ostio: Canterbury Coll. Oxford* (O.H.S. N.S. vii), 143, 202.

[11] Lambeth MS. 242.      [12] Penshurst MS. 121.

[13] *Sussex Arch. Coll.* liv. 23.      [14] E. 497, 3.

'twystes and hokes for a window'.[1] At Winchester in 1294 '*iiij paria twystarum ad fenestras*';[2] at Corfe 'twysten and hokes' in 1363;[3] at Clarendon 'a pair of twystes and hokys for the trapdore of the lodge' in 1483;[4] 'twistes and hockys and hengis' at Carmarthen in 1423;[5] and 'twistes and crokis for the dore' of Bodmin Church in 1470.[6] An alternative, found particularly in the Midlands, is 'hengle'. Thus at Nottingham in 1313 we have 'hokys' and 'henglys' for a window;[7] at Oakham 'a pair of *engles* for the great door' in 1374;[8] and next year at Rockingham 'hokys and hyngles' for doors, at 8½*d*. the pair, and for windows at 3*d*.;[9] at Somerton in 1360— '2 pair of iron hyngles, 3s. And a piece of iron for making crokes for doors, 6d.';[10] and in the 1432 accounts for King's Hall, Cambridge, '13½ lb. of iron for hygylles to the wicket (*portulam*) at the entrance of the great gate'.[11] At Coldharbour (London) there is mention in 1485 of 'a payre henges and hokes to a wyudrawte dore';[12] and at Westminster in 1532 'a peyre henges and hookys to the dore of the masons lodge'.[13]

The ride, being usually prolonged into a band extending across the woodwork, was also termed a door-band. So at Ripon we have in 1380— 'for lengthening a doreband, 1d.'; in 1420—'for 4 pair of dorebandes and 1 wyndoband, 8d.'; and in 1400—'4 small bands (*ligaminibus*) with 4 crokys and 2 bolts (*slechis*) of iron for 2 doors';[14] at Newcastle in 1365 'bandes and crokes' for irons and windows;[15] and in 1531 at Durham—'6 peyr duyrbands with croykks', and 'bands with cruks'.[16] On the other hand, for light work the eyelet might be fastened on to the woodwork without any prolonged band. At Westminster in 1532 we have 'hookis and oylettis for latesse windows',[17] and also 'vj platis and vj hookis with oylettes tynned sette upon a folding laddre ordeyned for the kinges privie lodgeing'.[18] An earlier instance appears to be the '18 iron eyes (*oculis*) for doors and windows' mentioned among the stores at Langley in 1368.[19] At the manor of Pleasaunce '6 ulettes of iron with as many hokis' were used for doors in 1447, and '2 pair of hengis with hokes, called ulethenges' are mentioned.[20]

Another type of hinge was the 'garnet', a T-shaped hinge, of which the short crossbar was fastened to the frame of the door. At Westminster '4

[1] Ibid. 21.  
[2] E. 491, 18.  
[3] E. 459, 27.  
[4] E. 460, 16.  
[5] E. 487, 17.  
[6] *Camden Miscellany*, vii. 15.  
[7] E. 478, 1.  
[8] Ibid. 18.  
[9] E. 481, 3.  
[10] E. 484, 15.  
[11] K.H. 8, f. 63.  
[12] E. 474, 3.  
[13] T.R., f. 99.  
[14] R. 102, 106, 145.  
[15] E. 579, 15.  
[16] *D.H.B.* 70.  
[17] T.R., f. 583.  
[18] Ibid., f. 419.  
[19] E. 466, 4.  
[20] Dy. of Lanc. Misc. Bks. 1, 11, ff. 6, 13.

great *kernettes* for the garden door' occur in 1275,[1] and '3 pair of tinned *gornettes* for hanging the door of the bathroom' in 1325.[2] There is mention in 1348 of 'a pair of gernettes for a trappedore of a prison' at the Tower, and as many as '208 pairs of garnettes', at 2*s.* 6*d.* each, were provided at Windsor in 1364.[3] At Eltham in 1403 we find an entry of '7 pairs of *garnettes removabil*', tinned, for shutters',[4] being presumably so made that the straps, attached to the shutters, could be lifted off their pins. The Westminster accounts for 1532 mention 'x paire side garnettis' used on presses, or cupboards,[5] 'side' being used in its old sense of 'long'; and also 'one payre garnettes doble joynted made for a foolding wyndowe in Mr. Comptrollers chaumbre'.[6] These same accounts mention 'a peyre pawme henges made to the sande pitte gate',[7] and 'a greate paire of paulmed hengies', weighing 48 lb.,[8] of which the meaning is not obvious. They also refer to 'streight joyntis imployed to a breade bynne', at 8*d.* the pair and 'joyntis doble joynted for cupbordes', at 12*d.*[9] These would be garnets of which the portion attached to the frame was of the same breadth as the strap, as opposed to the garnets with crossbars. The two varieties occur in a Westminster account of 1329, in which are payments for '*kernettes ferreis rectis*', 3 feet in length, and '*kernettes ferreis cruciatis*', 2 ft. 6 in. in length.[10] At Eltham in 1425 both 'crosgarnets' and 'potentgarnettes' occur;[11] the latter, which are mentioned also at Westminster in 1386,[12] take their name from their resemblance in shape to a crutch, or 'potent', and would therefore seem to be practically identical with the crossgarnets. At the Tower in 1348 'a pair of potenthenges for a window' cost 1½*d.*,[13] but two years later 'two pairs of potentehenges for the door of the lion house' cost 4*s.* 4*d.*,[14] being, not unnaturally, somewhat more substantial. The crossbar and strap being constructionally similar to the hook-and-eyed bar, we find at Westminster in 1334 a payment of 18*d.* '*pro iij paribus vertivell' et gunf' vocatorum potentes pro fenestris in celario*'.[15]

The type of hinge consisting of an identical pin-plate and hanging-plate, with no strap, was known as 'gemels' or 'gemews'.[16] Mention of these is frequent. As, for instance, at Bardfield Park in 1344: '*in ij paribus iomellorum pro hostio closett* ';[17] at Hadleigh Castle in 1363: 'for 2 pairs of

---

[1] E. 467, 6 (2).          [2] E. 469, 6.          [3] E. 493, 16.
[4] E. 502, 24.            [5] T.R., f. 317.        [6] Ibid., f. 101.
[7] Ibid., f. 99.          [8] Ibid., f. 170.       [9] Ibid., f. 631.
[10] E. 467, 7.            [11] E. 496, 7.          [12] E. 473, 2.
[13] E. 471, 1.            [14] Ibid. 3.            [15] E. 469, 19.
[16] From the French *jumeaux*, twins. They figure as '*chymols*' at Louth in 1500: Dudding, *Churchwardens' Book of Louth*, 11.                    [17] E. 458, 4.

*gemeaux* for the window between the King's chamber and the chapel';[1] at Winchester in 1425: '*gymeaux* for the louvre in the kitchen';[2] for a lodge in the New Forest in 1436: 'for 9 pairs of *iemeux* for windows called iete-wyndowes';[3] 'xxxv peyr of jemywisse' at Collyweston in 1500;[4] and at Ripon about 1520 'a par of gemmers' for a door.[5] Finally, we may note 3 '*henges rotundis*' for a great window at Northampton in 1389,[6] presumably horizontal pins fitting into round sockets, on which the window was pivoted.

The simplest way of closing a door or window is by means of a latch and catch, operated by a 'snatch' or 'sneck'. References to these are therefore numerous. Thus at Clare in 1341 we have 'for 2 lacches and snacches for 2 windows—2d.';[7] and next year at Ely a charge for making '*vertiuell' gumph' lasches snasches et rening barres pro hostio pro les nouises*':[8] the 'running', or sliding, bar here mentioned went right across the door and when not in use was pushed back into a deep socket in the wall; such sockets, sometimes still containing wooden bars, are a common feature of medieval doorways, and a 'rennynge barr' for the door of the masons' lodge is mentioned at Exeter in 1405.[9] At Bardfield Park in 1344 'lacches and snacches' were provided for 'the windows of the wardrobe',[10] and 'fyve laychis with springes, tynned', were 'sette upon the leevis of the pressis in the Juelhous' at Westminster in 1532.[11]

At Hadleigh Castle there is mention in 1363 of '6 rings with lacches and kacches'.[1] These rings, forming the handle by which the latch was raised—as on most church doors at the present time—were known as 'haggadays', a word still in use in northern districts for a thumb-latch. 'Rings with plates, tinned, called hagodayes, for doors', occur in 1383 at Windsor,[12] and 'rynges called hagadays' at Eltham in 1402.[13] At Westminster in 1353 we have 3s. paid 'for 6 pairs of laches and hagondays for the doors of the staple house';[14] and '79 boltes, 38 wrestlacchis, and 12 hauegodaies of iron' were supplied for Sheppey Castle in 1365,[15]—'wrest-latches' being latches lifted by turning the ring. The King's Hall accounts for 1414 include 4s. 3d.

[1] E. 464, 6.  
[2] E. 491, 29.  
[3] E. 477, 9.  
[4] St. John's Coll. Camb. Accts., vol. i.  
[5] R. 206.  
[6] Foreign R. 13 Ric. II, m. E.  
[7] E. 459, 4.  
[8] *Sacrist Rolls*, 118.  
[9] Oliver, *Exeter*, 388.  
[10] E. 458, 4.  
[11] T.R., f. 317.  
[12] E. 495, 14.  
[13] E. 502, 23.  
[14] E. 471, 8.  
[15] E. 483, 21. Cf. at Havering in 1376: 'for 5 rings and 2 wrayst lach': E. 464, 30.

'*pro v ceris¹ x clauibus et v hafgooddays j lacche iij stapyls et v laminis*';² the spelling here, and in the previous entry, suggests that the popular, and possibly correct, derivation of the name of this type of latch was from the words of greeting spoken when the door was opened. For Dunster Castle we have '2 iron hinges (*geminis*)—and a hagodeday with a lacche, for the leaf (*valva*) of the gate', in 1418.³ Although much of all this iron door furniture was ornate and decorated, little indication of the fact comes out in the building accounts. To the accountant a doorband was a doorband, whether it was a plain strap or elaborately scrolled, though the price might differ according to the amount of workmanship involved. An entry at Moor End in 1365 of '24 rings with flowers (*flor'*) and nails for the same, tinned—and 12 lacches and snacches with flowers, tinned, for various doors',⁴ is one of the few hints that we get of decoration, and it is possible that here 'flowers' is merely used for the round plates on which the rings were mounted, which were often termed 'roses'—as at Ripon, about 1520, 'for rygges [*sic*], roses and key plattes'.⁵ The 1532 accounts for Westminster mention 'handellis with oylettis and rooses', 'ringes harte fasshion for dores', 'handilles for dores made after harte fasshion', at 2s. the dozen, and 'rounde handilles for dores', at 2s. 4d.⁶

For fastening doors, bolts and various types of locks were in use. An entry in some Windsor accounts for 1345 gives a list of door furniture: '*In xv boltis ferreis cum xxij auriculis pro dictis boltis ponendis, viij lokstapulis, xix hapsis cum xxxvj stapulis pro eisdem, xx hokes, j vertiuell', iij pikes, xiiij dorehokes.*'⁷ With this may be compared an entry concerning Nottingham Castle in 1348: 'For making a prison under the high tower to keep the Scots safely, namely, for double doors with bands and hasps, locks and iron *shutles*, with wooden bars.'⁸ The 'shutles' of this last entry are either bolts or the sockets into which the lock-bolt shoots, sometimes called 'shutting plates', as at Westminster in 1532—'a plate locke with a plate for the keye hoole and a shytting plate'.⁹ The 'ears' (*auricule*) of the Windsor account are usually called staples, but at Westminster there is an entry of 'two peyre rounde boltes with lowpettis'.¹⁰ An earlier Westminster account, for 1443, mentions 'a bolt with a *clapse* of iron, weighing 3 lb., set on the door of the Jewelhouse', and 'a great lock with a *closestapyll* of iron belonging thereto set on the wyket of the new gate'.¹¹ 'Clapse', it may

---

¹ *Cera, cerura,* and *sera* all occur as forms of *serura*—a lock.
² K.H. 6, f. 57.                                  ³ *Arch. J.* xxxviii. 77.
⁴ E. 544, 31.                 ⁵ R. 206.                 ⁶ T.R., ff. 99, 418, 633.
⁷ E. 492, 24.                 ⁸ E. 544, 35.            ⁹ T.R., f. 17.
¹⁰ Ibid., f. 314.             ¹¹ E. 503, 11.

be observed, is the early form of 'clasp', just as 'hape' is of 'hasp'—so in 1372 we find, at Hadleigh Castle—'for a clapse', and '2 staples with a hapsen for the castle gate'.[1] Bolts are frequently referred to as 'slots'. Thus at Westminster in 1353 we have '12 staples and 2 *slottes* for dores',[2] and about the same time at York—'to Alan the Smith for a *slotte* for the door'.[3] So also at Clare in 1347—'a *sleet* with 3 *stapelles* of iron with fittings (*apparatu*) for a new door by the Lady's chamber', and 'for 6 small *sletes* of iron with fittings for windows'.[4]

Folding doors and entrance gates were often fastened by means of a 'flail' or 'sweep', an iron bar, pivoted in the centre so that when the gates were shut it could be brought horizontally across them, each end fitting into an iron hook or plate, which was often provided with a hasp by which the bar could be locked in position. Such a flail, on an exceptional scale, was provided for the Watergate at the Tower in 1324. For its production Master William de Hurlegh, the chief carpenter, made a pattern (*patron*) in wood, and at its forging several smiths, under Nicholas Lythfoot, worked for seven weeks. John de Thorney was paid 42*s*. 'for a thousandweight of iron for a great bar of iron by way of a *fleyl* for closing and fastening the great gates of the Watergate', but its actual weight was far from being so much, as there is a note that 'two thirds of the same iron was wasted in the fire and the working'. The iron supplied by John de Thorney would seem to have been of poor quality, as another entry is—'for 6 cwt. of iron bought of him for making nails and rivets (*riuett*') for the new great gate of the Watergate—26s.; and of the said iron there was wasted in the fire and the working 2 cwt., namely the third part'.[5] In 1353 there is mention of 'nails for the *flailles* of the water gate' at Westminster,[2] and at York, about the same time, '2 plates for the flail (*flagell*') of the castle gate'[6] were bought. In 1351 'a platelok, with a new key for it', was provided 'for the *sueyp* of the gate by the Roundehous' at the Tower of London.[7] Robert Westwode, smith, in 1485 supplied 'a swepe of a dore, ij hookes and a bowte (= bolt)' and also 'a lok and a key to the same swepe' at Coldharbour Manor;[8] in 1492 'the swaype of the church dore' is mentioned in the churchwardens' accounts of St. Mary-at-Hill; and 'sweepis with staples for dores' occur at Westminster in 1532.[9]

Various types of locks were in use in the Middle Ages, the simplest being the 'clicket lock'. This occurs as early as 1324 at Westminster—'for

[1] E. 544, 7.　　　[2] E. 471, 8.　　　[3] E. 501, 12.
[4] E. 459, 26.　　　[5] E. 469, 7.　　　[6] E. 501, 11.
[7] E. 471, 6.　　　[8] E. 474, 3.　　　[9] T.R., f. 631.

a cliket for the door of the new drawing-office (*trassure*)'.[1] At Ely in 1342 'a cliketloc[2] with 3 keys' cost 5*d.*; at Shene in 1366 'two locks called clikets' cost 2*s.* 4*d.*;[3] and at Windsor in 1383 we find purchases of '2 cliketlok', '4 locks with keys, newly made, and a clyket', and also '4 keys called clikettes for various doors'.[4] It will be remembered that in Chaucer's 'Merchant's Tale' the key of which Damyan took an impression·in wax was a clicket. In 1425 'a klyketlok for the door of a latrine' is mentioned at Eltham.[5] When the action of the lock was assisted by means of a spring it was known as a 'spring lock'. This device was known to the Romans and was probably in use in the early Middle Ages, but the earliest use of the term that I have noted is in 1366, when John Halmarke supplied 'a springloc', costing 16*d.*, for a door at Shene.[3] In 1525 the churchwardens of St. Mary-at-Hill bought 'ij keys for the wykket next to the parsonage and ij keys for the spring of the sowthe dore'.[6] The door between the king's dining-room and bedroom at Westminster was provided with 'a sprynge locke with a staple and a flappe' in 1532[7]—the 'flappe' being the hinged plate to cover the keyhole. These same Westminster accounts mention 'a plate for a key hoole',[8] which may either mean a similar 'flap' or, more probably, a plate surrounding the keyhole on the outside of the door. Of keys there is nothing much to be said, except that a distinction was sometimes made between those with solid and with hollow barrels. 'A key called hollowe key for the lock of the water conduit within the privy palace' at Westminster is mentioned in 1443;[9] 'a holowe key to the upper vestry dore' of St. Mary-at-Hill was bought in 1536;[10] and in 1538 there is reference to 'the makyng of ij pyped keyys' for locks at Abingdon.[11]

Those locks of which the outer plate was visible—and often more or less elaborately decorated—were known as 'plate-locks'; while those which were buried under a block of wood fastened on to the door were called 'stock-locks'. In 1347 '*iij platelockes pro host(iis) de latys juxta le storhous et pro porta novi muri*' occur at Clare;[12] and four years later we find 'a platelok with 3 keys, and a hagoday with all fittings (*apparatu*), set on the wiket of the door of the great hall' at Westminster.[13] At Corfe '4 stoklokkes with keys for setting on doors' were bought in 1357;[14] and at

---

[1] E. 469, 8.  [2] Printed 'clikecloc': *Sacrist Rolls*, 118.
[3] E. 493, 12.  [4] E. 495, 14.  [5] E. 496, 7.
[6] *Memorials* (E.E.T.S.), 327.
[7] T.R., f. 103.  [8] Ibid., f. 583.  [9] E. 503, 11.
[10] *Memorials* (E.E.T.S.), 331.  [11] E. 458, 1.
[12] E. 459, 26.  [13] E. 471, 6.  [14] E. 461, 1.

Windsor '16 large platelokkes with fittings' cost 6s. 8d. each in 1364.[1] At Havering '6 locks called stoklokkis and 2 clyketlokkes' occur in 1374,[2] and 'locks called platelok and stoclok' in 1376.[3] There is an entry at Langley in 1389 of 2s. spent on 'a new platelok with keys bought and set on the door of the Friars' church to shut and keep the said Friars out of the King's household'.[4] For work at St. Paul's 'a new stock lock (*sera truncata*) with an iron called a stonstaple' was provided in 1490;[5] and the Westminster accounts for 1532 mention 'one stocke locke with the apparell, and also a shytting plate set upon a dore belonging to one of the lodgies wherein certein of the masons worke',[6] and also certain 'doble howpid stoclockis'.[7] At Windsor also there is reference in 1534 to 'a doble hoopped stocke-locke sett upon the Colege garden dore to save the Kynges platt locke oon to the begynnyng of somere',[8] which looks as if the plate-lock in question must have been considered too fine a piece of work to run the risk of rusting.

In addition to fixed locks, considerable use was made of padlocks, though that term occurs very rarely, the earliest instance, apparently, being in 1438 at Windsor, when '2 padlockes' cost 16d.[9] The same thing is presumably implied by the 4 'bade lokes' bought, for 4d. each, at Colly-weston in 1500,[10] at which time 'horse lokes for the garden yattes' were also provided. 'Hanging locks' occur occasionally, as at Ripon in 1420, when '3 hynglokes for various doors' were purchased;[11] at Clarendon in 1477—'2 lockes pendent' for 2 gates of the manor;[12] and in London in 1490—'*pro una sera pendente cum una pessula et ij stapulis*'.[13] One variety of the padlock was the 'terret' or 'turret', which seems to have been the same as the fetter-lock, well known in heraldry. Some Westminster accounts of 1275 mention among the ironwork various 'turettes', but these were in some instances, and possibly in all, 'for fastening falcons to their perches'.[14] The same applies to the 32 'turrettes' supplied by 'Stephen Smyt del Toure' for use at Eltham in 1368, as they are said to be 'for haukestokez';[15] but an entry, in a Westminster account of 1289, of '*j turrell ferr' ad hostium geminatum prope dresser*', shows that this type of lock was occasionally used on doors.[16]

An examination of building accounts shows that great quantities of

[1] E. 493, 16.   [2] E. 464, 25.   [3] Ibid. 30.
[4] E. 473, 5.   [5] Egerton MS. 2358, f. 8.   [6] T.R., f. 316.
[7] Ibid., ff. 17, 413.   [8] Hope, *Windsor Castle*, 264.
[9] E. 496, 9.   [10] St. John's Coll. Camb. Accts., vol. i.
[11] R. 146.   [12] E. 460, 14.   [13] Egerton MS. 2358, f. 3.
[14] E. 467, 6 (2).   [15] E. 493, 30.   [16] E. 467, 20.

nails, called by a surprising variety of names, were used in medieval building. Thus the stores at Calais in 1390 included '494,900 nails of various
kinds',[1] which, as nails were often reckoned by the long hundred of six
score,[2] may be actually 593,880. Purchases made at Wye Fair for the needs
of Canterbury Cathedral in 1273 included 30,000 'prig'—a small variety
of nail—and 10,000 of other types,[3] and almost identical quantities were
bought next year; similarly in 1323 the Sacrist of Ely paid £3. 4s. 8½d. 'for
37,500 and a half (hundred) nails bought at Reche and Sterisbrigia (the
fairs of Reach and Sturbridge) and carried to Ely', with a further 1s. 7¾d.
'for a basket (*basketto*)[4] and 4 panniers (*corbellis*), together with canvas,
bought for putting the said nails in and for covering them'.[5] At Hadleigh
Castle in 1363 we find purchases of 2,500 great spikyng, 10,000 planchnail,
4,000 black dorenail, 1,500 dorenail with tinned heads, 7,600 black
wyndownail, 2,000 wyndownail with tinned heads, 42,000 refnail, 21,000
traues, 6,000 shyngelnail, 3,000 lednail, 25,000 sprig', and 200 latisnail.[6]
A list of nails bought for use at York Castle in 1327 may be given as a
sample of the variety of nomenclature:[7]

| | | | |
|---|---|---|---|
| 220 braggenayl, | at 15d | the hundred, | 'by the great hundred'. |
| 100 knopnayl, | ,, 6d | ,, | ,, |
| 3,260 doublenail, | ,, 4d | ,, | ,, |
| 1,200 greater spyking | ,, 4d | ,, | ,, |
| 5,200 spyking, | ,, 3d | ,, | ,, |
| 3,250 thaknail, | ,, 3d | ,, | ,, |
| 1,800 lednail, | ,, 2d | ,, | ,, |
| 300 grapnayl, | ,, 2d | ,, | ,, |
| 7,760 stotnayl, | ,, 2d | ,, | ,, |
| 1,100 smaller stotnayl, | ,, 1½d | ,, | ,, |
| 300 tyngilnayl, | ,, 1d | ,, | ,, |
| 18,600 brodd', | ,, 1d | ,, | ,, |

The largest types of nails were 'bragges', 'gaddes', and 'spikes'—
diminishing through various grades of 'spikings' and 'spikenails'. But all
these terms were vaguely generic and imply no standardization. '*Brags pro*

[1] Foreign R. 14 Ric. II, m. E.

[2] But at Westminster in 1329—*pro j quartron videlicet xxv clavorum voc' spikyngnail pro
facture scaffot*: E. 467, 7. And in North Wales in 1323 nails were bought, apparently indiscriminately, by the long and short hundred: Pipe R. 5 Edw. III.

[3] Lambeth MS. 242, ff. 16v, 24v.

[4] Two 'berebarells' were bought, for 16d., for carriage of 4,000 nails at Windsor in 1400:
E. 502, 15.

[5] *Sacrist Rolls*, 27.          [6] E. 464, 6.          [7] E. 501, 8.

*le schaffald'* occur at York in 1371, at 3s. the hundred,[1] and although in 1504 and 1530 the price of 'bragges' is only 16d.[2] that is still by far the highest price for any kind of nail. So also in 1537 for work at Sheriff Hutton Castle 'gret bragges' cost 3s. 6d. the hundred.[3] In the 1532 Westminster accounts the term 'broddis' is used apparently as equivalent to 'bragges', though usually 'broddes' seem to have been the small headless nails still known as 'brads'. Thus we have—'cc broddis, every of them cont' in length ix ynches, made for the jowepecis of the previe bridge', other 'greate broddis' of 7 inches, and other 'broddis' ranging down to 2 inches.[4] There is also mention of 'c greate spykynges poz. xxvii lb.'[5] In 1441 at Calais 500 'scaffoldnaill' weighed 80 lb., but other entries of similar nails show 300 weighing 61½ lb.[6] The same accounts include '328 nails called spykynges weighing 275½ lb.', and others, of which 5 weighed 5 lb., and 7 weighed 4½ lb., while 150 'spikes' totalled 91 lb., another 40 weighing 26 lb. Certain 'great spykis for fixing the rafters' were bought for St. Paul's in 1454 at a halfpenny apiece,[7] and therefore presumably weighed about a quarter of a pound each; at the same time 20d. was paid *'pro cc spykys pro furryng*[8] *des rafters super le south yle'*. The Windsor accounts of 1297 mention '12 great nails, each of 6 inches', the price of a nail being a halfpenny;[9] and in 1363 at Clarendon '13 great nails called waternail, for mending the great gate of the manor broken by the violence of the wind', cost 4d.[10] 'Waternayll' appear again at Winchester in 1392, when they cost 12d. the hundred,[11] and in 1409, when the price was 10d.,[12] but why they were so called is not obvious. 'Gaddes with tinned heads' were bought for Hadleigh Castle, at 2s. 6d. the hundred, in 1364;[13] and the following year plain 'gaddes' were 15d. the hundred at Moor End, and 'gadnayl' for repairs in Beckley Park were 12d. On the other hand, 'gaddes' bought at Woodstock were only 6d. in 1346, but this is just before the general rise in prices.

There is mention at Shene in 1435 of 'spikeynge used for the making of doors and windows and for punchonyng and plaunchebordyng and for the fixing and nailing together (*conclav'*) of various feet of raftres and evisbord';[14] and other entries show that these were nails for general purposes. 'Great

---

[1] *Y.F.R.* 7.  [2] Ibid. 93, 104.  [3] E. 484, 3.
[4] T.R., f. 101.  [5] Ibid. 10.  [6] E. 193, 4.
[7] St. Paul's MSS., Misc. Roll A. 52.
[8] 'Furring' is nailing on extra pieces of timber, either to extend their length or to make them level.
[9] E. 492, 13.  [10] E. 460, 2.  [11] E. 491, 23.
[12] *Obedientiary Rolls*, 21.  [13] E. 464, 6.  [14] E. 496, 8.

spikyng' occur at Rockingham in 1279, at 3*d*. the hundred; 'spiknayl' at
Winchester Castle in 1283, at 10*d*.; 'grospykyng' at 6*d*. and 'middel-
spykyng' at 3*d*. at Norwich in 1292. At Clarendon 'spyknayl' were 14*d*. in
1316; at Ely 1,400 'spikyngges for steyringg' cost 5*s*. 5*d*. in 1323, and in
1337 large spiking were 7*d*. and small 3*d*.; and at Restormel in 1343 'large
spiknail' were 8*d*. In 1353 'large spikyng for the pipes of the latrine of the
Staple house' at Westminster[1] cost 10*d*. the hundred, and about the same
time at Ripon 'large spykynges for roofing buildings' cost only 5*d*. At
Moor End in 1365 we find large spiking at 16*d*., middle at 6*d*., and small
at 5½*d*., while 'small spykenail' were only 4*d*. Middle spiking cost 6*d*. at
Rockingham in 1375 and at Woodstock in 1380, and 5*d*. at Brigstock Park
in 1423; but at Ripon in 1400 and 1420, and at York in 1406, the price was
only 2½*d*.—the cost of 'dublespykyng' being 4*d*. at Ripon, and 5*d*. at York.
'Dobel spikyng' occurs as early as 1362 at Clipston, at 6*d*.—ordinary
'spikyng for making Bordynwohes' (i.e. wooden partition walls) being
2½*d*.,[2] and it is found as late as 1533 at Middleham, where 'dowbil
spikeynges' were 4*d*. the hundred. Mention may be made of 'a hundred of
bacspikyng for mending windows', costing 3*d*., at Scarborough in 1336;[3]
and of 'nails called *kocspykyng*', at 8*d*., which occur at Chester in 1426[4]
and may have taken their name from a likeness to cock-spurs.

The nomenclature of nails depended upon the purposes for which they
were used, their shape, or their price. Ordinary nails are therefore often
termed board or plank nails. In 1208 we find 3*s*. 5*d*. paid for *clavis plancheret*
for repairs at Farnham,[5] and in 1222 both *clavi plancheiz* and *bordelez* at 12*d*.
the thousand were provided for Winchester Castle. At Westminster 'great
nails for planks' cost 19*d*. the hundred in 1259 and 'bordnail' were 2*s*. the
thousand in 1275. At Winchester 'bordnayl' were 2*d*. the hundred in 1283
and the same price at Nottingham in 1313, when they were used 'for
joining boards and shingles (*cindulis*)';[6] but at Clarendon in 1316 they were
4*d*., while at Ely they were 16*d*. the thousand in 1337, rising to 2*s*. 4*d*. in
1357. 'Nails for fixing planks' were 4*d*. the hundred at Westminster in
1324, as were 'plonchisnaill' at Bardfield Park twenty years later, and also
'bordnayle' at Woodstock in 1346. 'Bordnail' were also 4*d*. at Moor End
in 1365, but those 'with tinned heads' were 6*d*., while at Woodstock in
1380 'tinned bordnaill' were 14*d*., the plain variety being only 5*d*. The
stores for London Bridge works in 1350 included 15,000 'planchenails' at
4*s*. the thousand, and in 1375 'plonchesnayl' were 9*d*. the hundred at

---

[1] E. 471, 8.  [2] E. 460, 18.  [3] E. 482, 4.  [4] E. 545, 25.
[5] *Pipe R. of Bpric. of Winchester*, 35.  [6] E. 478, 1.

Woodstock. During the fifteenth century the average price seems to have been about 5*d.* or 6*d.* the hundred. In an account of repairs to Newgate prison in 1282 there is mention of 'florneyl for planks', and the following year 'flornayl', at 4*d.* the hundred, occur at Winchester, where they are also found in 1392 and 1409, on all three occasions in company with 'bordnayles' and therefore, presumably, distinguished from them.

There is mention at Westminster in 1324 of 'nails for fastening studs (*stotes*)', at 3*d.* the hundred, and 'stodnayl' occur at Clarendon in 1316, at 4*d.*, and in 1477, at 3*d.* For York Castle 'stotnayl' were provided in 1327, and for a lodge in the New Forest 1,100 'stodenaill and ouesebordnail' were bought, in 1368, for 5*s.* Similarly in 1341 at Ludgershall we find both 'stodenail for great laths' and 'nails for heuesbord', at 2½*d.* Equivalent to these stud-nails were the 'staunchounnail used on the work of the barn door and for fastening staunchouns' at Leeds Castle about 1370.[1] 'Staunsonayl' occur at Windsor in 1321, at 3*d.* the hundred; and 'stanchonaill', at 6*d.*, at Gravesend in 1367 and 1375. In the north we have, at Cockermouth in 1322, an expenditure of 2*d.* on '60 spikes for joining *stouris* for the stable',[2] and 'stouryngnayl' appear at Scarborough in 1284, and at Tattershall about 1410.[3] The East Anglian equivalent seems to be 'splentnayl', which figures in the King's Hall accounts for 1431, and as 'spleyntnayle' at Ely in 1346.[4]

A form which seems chiefly, if not entirely, confined to the neighbourhood of London is the 'transom' nail. It occurs among other nails at Westminster in 1357 as 'traunsen', at 12*d.* the thousand. In 1376 there is mention at Havering of 'nails called traunson for making various partitions';[5] and the same year at Shene 'traunessonayll' were bought at 14*d.* the thousand. At Shene, again, in 1435, 'nails called traunson, used for countrelathyng of the buildings', cost only 7*d.* the thousand.[6] 'Transonaill' also occur at Westminster in 1389, and 500 'transum' are mentioned with other varieties of nails bought in 1425 by the churchwardens of St. Mary-at-Hill. Owing to the inability of the medieval scribe to distinguish *n* from *u*, it is not possible to be certain whether the fourth letter of the 'tranesheynnayl' which occur at Westminster in 1324[7] should be *n* or *u* (i.e. *v*), but the latter is rather favoured by the form 'trauiseynail for lathing partitions' in a Latin account of 1337;[8] the more so as we find in 1351 'trauers-

---

[1] E. 466, 24.    [2] E. 460, 25.    [3] Penshurst MS. 55.
[4] *Sacrist Rolls*, 130: cf. 'splettenail' in 1326: ibid. 60.
[5] E. 464, 30.    [6] E. 496, 8.
[7] E. 469, 7.    [8] E. 469, 20.

nail for mending the roof of the porter's house'.[1] The form *traues'* occurs among lists of nails at Hadleigh in 1363, and at Langley in 1367, and from its context appears to be probably an iron nail; otherwise one might hazard a conjecture that it was connected with 'trash' or 'tree' nails of wood. These do not occur as often as might be expected in building accounts; but 'traysshe nayle' were supplied, at 20*d.* the thousand, for work at Westminster in 1532 by John Russell, carpenter:[2] and 'trasshnaill for fixing plaster' were bought at 10*d.* the thousand at Eltham in 1425.[3]

Nails used for ceiling or panelling rooms are occasionally distinguished; in 1367, for instance, 'celingnail' occur at Langley at 19*d.* the thousand; which seems to have been about the normal price, as 'celyngnaill' at Westminster in 1389 and 'cylenaill' at Eltham in 1425 were alike 20*d.* the thousand. In such a position the nails would tend to be unpleasantly visible, so we find at Havering in 1375 'selyngnaill with tinned heads', at 3*d.* the hundred,[4] were employed, and at Clarendon 22*s.* was paid 'for 6,000 tynnayles for celyng' in 1356.[5] We have seen that door furniture was often ornamented with a coat of tin, and nails, for use with it, or in other positions, were also often so treated. 'Tynnayl' occur at Clarendon in 1316, Ely in 1337, and Woodstock in 1346, amongst other places. At Corfe in 1357 'whitnail for the windows of the hall' cost 12*d.* the hundred;[6] 'withehedenayll' occur at Shene in 1376, and 'quytnayles' at Ripon in 1420. Such nails were especially used on doors. Thus at Westminster in 1295 we have 8*d.* paid 'to James the Smith for tinning nails for the door of the Treasury',[7] and at Ludgershall 'white nails called tynnayl for the doors' were bought at 5*s.* the thousand, in 1341.[8] Doornails occur at all periods. For Christ Church, Canterbury, 'durenel' were bought in 1264 and both 'gretdorenayl' and 'smaldurenayl'—2*s. 6d.* and 2*s.* the thousand respectively—ten years later.[9] 'Dorenayl' were 2*d.* the hundred at Westminster in 1275, and 3*d.* at Dover in 1283 and 1292. In 1367 they were 5*d.* at Gravesend and 6*d.* at Langley, where the tinned variety were 10*d.*, and at Leeds in 1374 'dorenayl for the bretasch of the Prynceschambre and for a *schrudweghel* (mill-wheel) in the castle' were also 6*d.*[10] At Westminster in 1389 they were 4*d.*, and at King's Hall, Cambridge, in 1499, 3½*d.* Often they are called 'hatch-nails'. The stores purchased for the castles of north

---

[1] E. 471, 6. Riley (*Mems. of London*, 361) gives 'traversnails' among the stores of the London Bridge works in 1350.

[2] T.R., f. 313.           [3] E. 496, 7.              [4] E. 464, 27.
[5] E. 459, 29.            [6] E. 461, 1.              [7] E. 468, 6.
[8] E. 476, 1.             [9] Lambeth MS. 242, ff. 6v, 24v.
[10] E. 480, 3.

Wales between 1323 and 1326 include 32,000 'hachenail';[1] in 1343 'hach-nail', at 3*d*. the hundred, occur at Restormel, in Cornwall: they also appear under that name in the New Forest in 1436, and at Clarendon in 1477, in both instances at 4*d*. the hundred. The 'gatenail' which appear at Wood-stock in 1350, at 2*s*. the hundred, and at Hadleigh in 1369, at 3*s*., were evidently very much larger than the ordinary doornails.

The proverbial deadness, or immobility, of doornails may be due to the way in which they were secured by clinching or riveting. At the Tower in 1323 'Richard Spark, clincher (*clenchar*'), working on the gates at clinch-ing and riveting great nails', was paid 4½*d*. a day,[2] and 'nails and rivets (*riuett*') for the gates of the Watergate' figure in the purchases. Rather earlier, in 1311, the Tower accounts mention '*clavos de ryvet*' and record payments of 7*s*. to John Michel, shipwright, working for 14 days at 'nail-ing and riveting the gate', and of 4*s*. 8*d*. to 'William Litelwille working at counter-riveting (*contrarivettand*') with John Michel'.[3] At Corfe Castle in 1363 we have 6*s*. 3*d*. paid 'to a smith working 1 cwt. and 1 qr. of iron for nails and *clenches*', and 'a clencher with his mate (*famulo*) for clinching nails, receiving 4*s*. 6*d*. a week', other '*clenchours*' being paid 4½*d*. a day.[4] Similarly at Queenborough in 1375 we find '*clencheres* fixing and fasten-ing large nails in the postern'.[5] 'Pynnes and revettes' for fastening certain 'dogges of irne' used in the roof of the hall of Hampton Court are men-tioned in 1533,[6] and the Westminster accounts of 1532 record 'revette nayles', for hinges, at 25*d*. the hundred.[7] These last accounts also mention 'a newe platte varnysshid, with staples, skrewis, and vices to the same, provided for a dore'.[8] Here we seem to have a reference to bolts and nuts, the 'vices' being evidently the nuts gripping the ends of the screws. I have not found any similar entry and I am inclined to think that the device of bolt and nut for such purposes was not introduced much before this date.

'Rofnaill', or roofing nails, occur at Westminster in 1259, and in the Gloucester Castle accounts for 1280 are payments 'for 300 rofnayl for the cresting (*cresta*) of the Lord Edward's chamber,—9*d*.; and for 200 rofnayl of smallest size for the shingles of the same chamber—5*d*.'[9] In 1324 'rofnail for tiles' cost 10*d*. the thousand at Westminster; 23,000 such nails among the London Bridge stores in 1350 were priced at 12*d*. the thousand; and during the latter half of the fourteenth century they figure in many accounts at from 16*d*. to 18*d*., particularly in the neighbourhood of

---

[1] Pipe R. 5 Edw. III.       [2] E. 469, 7.       [3] E. 468, 20.
[4] E. 461, 5.       [5] E. 483, 29.       [6] H.C. 237, f. 105.
[7] T.R., f. 554.       [8] T.R., f. 106.       [9] E. 463, 26.

London. At Shene 'roffenaile used for latheynge and tiling' were 14*d.* in 1435; at Langley in 1446 they were 12*d.*; and in 1533 '6000 of Inglyshe ruff nayles' were bought for Hampton Court at 8*d.* the thousand.[1] The equivalent 'helyeresnaill' is found at Winchester in 1425,[2] and 'thackprig', or 'tacchprig', at Leeds Castle about 1370.[3] In a Berwick Castle account of about 1530 we get '1,800 nails called dublethaknayl', at 40*d.* the hundred, and '8,200 nails called afalthaknayl', at 2*s.*[4]—prices which show that they were in quite a different category from the other roofing nails already referred to.

Of the various nails connected with roofing, lath-nails were the commonest, occurring in the majority of accounts. As early as 1208 we find 21,000 'nails for laths' bought for repairs at Farnham, for 11*s.* 4½*d.*,[5] and in 1222 from 12*d.* to 14*d.* a thousand was paid for *clavis laterez* at Winchester.[6] At Westminster in 1259 'nails for oak laths' were 12*d.*, and those for beech (*fohn*) laths 11*d.* the thousand.[7] They appear as 'lathenail' at Rockingham in 1279 and at Winchester in 1283. At Clarendon in 1316 'latneyl' were 11*d.*; at Woodstock they were 9*d.* in 1346, rising to 12*d.* in 1351 and 20*d.* in 1357, figures which agree with the general run of prices. Later they fell, being 15*d.* at Brigstock Park in 1423, 11*d.* at Clarendon in 1477, and 10*d.* at King's Hall, Cambridge, in 1499 and 1529.

At Westminster there is mention in 1333 of '*wounail pro lath' firmandis*', at 7*d.* the thousand,[8] and of others 'for mending partition walls'. For work at Gravesend 20,500 'woughprig' were bought, at 14*d.* the thousand, in 1367,[9] and about the same time 'woghprig' appear, at 1½*d.* the hundred, in a Leeds Castle account.[10] This form is connected with the O.E. *wogh*, meaning a wall,[11] and 'walnail' occur at Windsor in 1394.[12]

The 'latneyl' just mentioned are not to be confused with 'latisnails for latticing windows', which occur at Westminster in 1337, at 4*d.* the hundred. 'Tinned latysnail' are mentioned at Clare in 1347 and at Langley in 1367. At Havering we have the purchase of 'latisnayll for making various fenestrals' in 1376,[13] and 'latesnayle' were used in 1447 in connexion with lattices made for the bay windows of Queen Margaret's manor of Pleasaunce near Greenwich.[14] It is not quite clear whether the window-nails which occur with some frequency were used for the framework of

---

[1] H.C. 237, f. 147.  [2] E. 491, 29.  [3] E. 466, 19 and 24.
[4] E. 482, 28.  [5] *Pipe R. of Bpric. of Winchester*, 35.
[6] E. 491, 13.  [7] E. 467, 2.  [8] E. 469, 13.
[9] E. 464, 2.  [10] E. 466, 24.
[11] E.g. 'ly gabilwowes': Norwich Sacrist's Roll for 1403.
[12] E. 495, 19.  [13] E. 464, 30.  [14] Dy. of Lanc. Misc. Bks. 11, f. 13.

windows or for shutters; they were not identical with lattice-nails, as both appear in the Langley accounts for 1367. 'Wyndowenayl' appear at Clare in 1341, at 2*d.* the hundred, and at Westminster in 1357, at 3*d.* Elsewhere in the latter half of that century they are usually 4*d.*, except when tinned, when they ranged from 7*d.* to 10*d.*, and in the King's Hall accounts for 1499 they cost only 16*d.* the thousand. The 'loketnayles' mentioned in connexion with windows at Ripon in 1380 and 1390[1] are presumably the iron wedges used to tighten the locket-bars against the standards.[2]

In 1238 there is mention at Marlborough of 'nails for shingles (*scendul*')' at 15*d.* the thousand, which is also the price of 'scyngnaill' in 1259 and 'shinglenail' in 1329 at Westminster. At Nottingham 'shiggilnail' were 10*d.* in 1313, and three years later at Clarendon 'shingelnayl' were 20*d.* the thousand. For work at Clipston, where shingles appear as 'chinkel', 16,000 'chinkelbroddes' were bought in 1362 at 3*d.* the hundred, and the same price was paid for 'shingilnaill' at Westminster in 1389. Nails for fastening lead, presumably made with broad flat heads, figure constantly in accounts but present no particular features of interest. 'Lednayl' were 1½*d.* the hundred at Canterbury in 1273, at Rockingham in 1279, and at Ely in 1327. During the second half of the fourteenth century they were generally about 3*d.* and in the following century about 2½*d.*

'Teghelenail', or tile-nails, make a rare appearance at Westminster in 1329,[3] as do 'tielprig', or 'tegheleprig', used for the roofing of various buildings at Leeds Castle about 1370.[4] At Woodstock in 1380 there is mention of 'stonenaill for buildings covered with (stone) tiles', at 2*s.* 2*d.* the thousand.[5] Among the nails bought for use in the castles of north Wales about 1325 were 6,000 'stonnail',[6] and 'stonayl', at 13*d.*, occur at Clarendon in 1316. Similarly, 'stanebroddes' appear at Ripon between 1392 and 1420,[7] and at York in 1406, at 16*d.*, and in 1504, at 10*d.* the thousand.[8]

Of other 'purpose' nails the commonest are 'clout-nails'. These were used for nailing on patches of iron and are particularly associated with the repair of carts and ploughs but are also found in use for building purposes. 'Tinned nails for clouts (*cluta*)' occur at Woodstock in 1292.[9] At Rockingham 'clutnail' appear in 1279, at 1½*d.* the hundred, and '14,700 clouthnayl for fastening laths and lead' were bought in 1375 at 2*s.* 6*d.* the thousand,[10] which is also their price in 1367 at Langley and in 1380 at Woodstock,

---

[1] *R.* 101, 125.   [2] See above, p. 292.   [3] E. 467, 7.
[4] E. 466, 19 and 24.   [5] E. 499, 1.
[6] Pipe R. 5 Edw. III.   [7] *R.* 110, 133, 145.
[8] *Y.F.R.* 35, 93.   [9] E. 497, 19.   [10] E. 481, 3.

where 'clutnayl' were 20*d*. in 1346. At King's Hall they were 2*s*. in 1415, and at Brigstock Park in 1423 2*s*. 6*d*. the thousand.

The 'strakenail', of which 160 were bought for 12*s*. 9*d*. at Ely in 1357,[1] are also chiefly associated with carts, being used for fastening the strakes, of which iron tyres were composed. An earlier Ely account, for 1342, mentions 'cleyingnail', at 10*d*. the hundred;[2] if this is not a slip for 'celyngnail' it may mean nails used for hurdles, for which the contemporary term was 'cleyes'. At Shene in 1386 there is an entry of 2*s*. 8*d*. paid 'for 100 great nails called bruggenail (i.e. bridge-nails) for making a stair for the King's passage to the water'.[3] In 1389 Master Stephen the Smith, at the Tower, was paid 2*d*. a pound—the usual rate when nails were forged and not bought ready made—'for great nails called shipnaill for fixing planchbords on the great bridge'.[4] Similarly at Bristol in 1442 Robert Yremonger provided 600 'calfat nayle', at 15*d*. the hundred, which were presumably the type used in connexion with 'calfatting', or caulking, ships, though here they were used 'for the repair and plaunchyng of various buildings and rooms within the keep (*le dungon*) of the castle of Bristowe'.[5] The 'gotenayle for the foundations of the mill' at Nottingham in 1363[6] probably took their name from the 'gut', or water-channel, of the mill; and the 'schrudnail' which occur at Hadleigh in 1372[7] may be connected with the 'schrudweghel', which—judging from accounts of repairs to watermills—seems to be the water-wheel of a mill. 'Gullet nayles' appear at York in 1419[8] and at Ripon about 1520[9] and were, no doubt, used for gutters or pipes. The 'twistenayl' mentioned at Clarendon in 1316[10] were obviously for fixing 'twists', or hingestraps; and possibly the 'hangenayl' which occur at Hadleigh in 1369[11] were for a similar purpose. As there is a mention at Clarendon in 1363 of 'taknail for fixing the hupetiles' (i.e. hip-tiles),[12] it is possible that this was the purpose of the 'hupenayll' and 'huptenail' which occur at Windsor in 1295 and 1394;[13] and the 'cornernayl' mentioned at Clare in 1341 may have been for corner tiles.[14] What the 'howeyg nales', at 7*d*. a thousand, which appear in a Ripon account of about 1520,[15] were, I am unable to say, and the 'countre nayl' and 'siltnayl', bought for repairs at St. Mary-at-Hill in 1426, are also obscure.[16]

---

[1] *Sacrist Rolls*, 176.  
[2] Ibid. 118.  
[3] E. 473, 2.  
[4] E. 473, 5.  
[5] E. 473, 18.  
[6] E. 478, 6.  
[7] E. 544, 7.  
[8] *Y.F.R.* 38.  
[9] R. 206.  
[10] E. 459, 27.  
[11] E. 464, 11.  
[12] E. 460, 2.  
[13] E. 492, 11; 495, 19.  
[14] E. 459, 24.  
[15] R. 206.  
[16] *Memorials* (E.E.T.S.), 66.

Of the smaller nails in common use 'prigs' and 'sprigs' appear to be identical. At Dover in 1288 'prig for buildings broken by the violence of the wind' were 12½*d.* the thousand,[1] and five years earlier 'lath prig' were 9*d.*, while at Windsor in 1295 a thousand '*clavorum de sprig ad lath*'' were 7*d.* 'Prig for partition walls' were 5*d.* at Westminster in 1337, and 20,500 'woughprig', or wall-prigs, were bought at Gravesend in 1367, at 14*d.* the thousand, which was the price of 'spryg' at Moor End in 1365, while 'sprygnayll' were 10*d.* at Shene in 1376. The 1532 Westminster accounts mention 'one bagge of sprigge', costing 9*d.*,[2] and later entries show 'sprigges' bought at 7*s.* 6*d.* the 'bagge' of 20,000,[3] and at the same time both 'Inglysshe sprygges' and 'Flemysshe sprygges' were bought for Hampton Court at 10*d.* the 'bagge'.[4] Closely associated with this type of nail was a variety known as 'hussem', apparently peculiar to Kent and Sussex. Among the purchases for the cathedral priory of Canterbury from 1264 to 1274 are entries of 'hutzeam' and 'oussem', at 10*d.* the thousand—prig being about 7½*d.*[5] At Dover in 1283 '*j millear de hussem et ij millear de schingelprig*' cost 32*d.*,[6] and three years later the two varieties are again mentioned[7] together as used for shingling. For work at Pevensey Castle 25*d.* was spent on 2,000 '*clav' de hussem*' in 1288,[8] and the same in 1300, when 18,000 prignails were also bought for lathing, and next year prignails, at 8*d.*, and 'houssem', at 12*d.* the thousand, again occur together.[9] There is also a mention of *clavis de houssem* at 15*d.*, together with 'stonprigg' at 8½*d.*, in an account of repairs to the manor of Laughton, in Sussex, in 1337.[10] The name may possibly be connected with the Old French *heusse*, meaning a peg, but the termination suggests a connexion with the 'semnails' not infrequently found in accounts.

The *Oxford Dictionary* defines 'seam' as 'a kind of nail or rivet for fastening the overlapping edges of a clinker-built boat, the end of the nail·being clinched on a rove'—which is a small plate of metal, pierced for the nail to pass through. I have found one instance (at Portsmouth in 1430) where this definition certainly applies: *in mcccclxvj lib. seme et nede ferri alias voc' clenche ·et rof.*[11] But generally there is no indication of any association of roves with 'semnails', though it is possible that they were similar to the boat-nails and were simply clenched without the elaboration of roves.

[1] E. 462, 12.  [2] T.R., f. 10.  [3] Ibid., f. 554.
[4] H.C. 237, ff. 124, 147.  [5] Lambeth MS. 242, ff. 6v, 16v, 24v.
[6] E. 462, 9.  [7] E. 462, 11.
[8] E. 479, 16.  [9] E. 479, 16.  [10] Add. Ch. 32134.
[11] E. 479, 25. 'Nails called seeme and neede' were used for making a chest at Mettingham in 1461: Add. MS. 33987, f. 35v.

They occur at Rockingham in 1279, at 1¼d. the hundred, at Woodstock in 1346, at 2d., at Moor End in 1365, at 3d., and at Shene in 1435, at 2s. the thousand. In the north they seem to have been called 'scotsem', which the *Oxford Dictionary* suggests may be connected with Dutch *schot*, a partition. Thus at Nottingham we have *clavi de scotsem* in 1273; at York 'scotsomnail for ceiling' in 1371, and 'scotsem' in 1406 and 1504; at Ripon 'scotsum-nayll' in 1400 and 'scotsemenayll' in 1420; and for work at Sheriff Hutton Castle in 1537 'scotsem nayles otherwise called lathe nayles'.[1]

The Sheriff Hutton accounts, just quoted, also mention 'small takkettes for cases of wyndos', at 2d. the hundred. 'Taketnayle' were 10d. the thousand at Ely in 1346, and 12d. at Westminster in 1347. At Wallingford in 1375 'black tacnail for ceiling' were 3d. the hundred, 'white tacnail' 4d. and 'great taknail for fastening battens' (*batauns*) 12d.[2] These tacks were distinguished by having broad, flat heads, in which they differed from the 'broddes', which were flattened nails with no head, or at most a slight lip on one edge. 'Broddes for fixing hollow tiles' occur at the Tower in 1333, at 6d. the hundred; others, for fastening laths, at Clipston in 1362, at 1½d., which is also their price at Moor End in 1365. At York '1,000 brods for roofing the school house' cost 18d. in 1371,[3] and there is mention in 1406 of both 'stanebrod' and 'strabrod'—the latter being defined in 1434 as '*strebroddes pro strelattis firmandis*',[4] that is to say, for fixing straw-laths for thatching.

One of the smallest types of nail was the 'tingle-nail'. These appear as 'tyngnaill' at Westminster, at 16d. the thousand in 1259, and at 12d. in 1275. At Norwich 'tyngelnayl' were 1½d. the hundred in 1292 and at York in 1327 they were 1d. We find them at Restormel in Cornwall in 1343 at 2d., at Moor End in Northants. in 1365, and at Sheriff Hutton in York-shire in 1537 at the same price. Another variety of small nail occurs in 1327 at York as 'grapnayl', at 2d. the hundred, at Clare in 1341 as 'gropnayl' at 1d., and at Bardfield Park in 1344 as 'gripnaill' at 1¼d.; and to the same group belong 'souwyngnail' 'for joining boards together', which make their appearance in two Nottingham Castle accounts of about 1312 and are priced at 1½d. the hundred.[5]

The heads of large nails used on doors are often shaped and faceted. At the Tower in 1278 we find a payment of 17s. 9d. for '280 large nails with square heads for the gate of the turret;[6] for Newgate gaol 'nails called heuednegl' (i.e. headnails) were provided in 1282,[7] and the 'knopnayl',

[1] E. 484, 3.   [2] E. 490, 3.   [3] *Y.F.R.* 7.   [4] Ibid. 54.
[5] E. 477, 20; 478, 1.   [6] E. 467, 7 (4).   [7] E. 467, 11.

mentioned at York in 1327, presumably had knobbed heads. 'Dicehead' nails figure in the Tower accounts of the mid-fourteenth century: '100 nails called *discenail*, for hinges', in 1348;[1] 'half a hundred of large nails called *dizhednayl* for the bars (*latez*) of the lion house', in 1350;[2] '250 *deyhednail* for the watergate', in 1353;[3] and '500 *dizhednail* for the windows of the Black Hall', in 1355.[4] '*Dyshedenayll*' also appear at Shene in 1376;[5] and '300 tinned nails called *dicehedenayles*, used for naylyng the rayle newly made for the aras (or tapestry hangings)', were supplied for Queen Margaret's manor of Pleasaunce near Greenwich in 1447.[6] A payment 'for nailes with v strok hedes' occurs in the accounts for building Bodmin Church in 1470;[7] and 'stroknaill', which are found at Odiham Castle in 1376,[8] may belong to this class.

During the fifteenth century the classification of nails according to their price per hundred came increasingly into fashion. The earliest instance that I have found seems to be at Ely in 1346, when 'ij ml. de tepenineyl' cost 3s. 4d., which is equivalent to 2d. the hundred.[9] Just fifty years later 'threpenynayl' are found at the Tower.[10] Then, in 1438, the nails supplied for the stores of St. Paul's include '2,000 fourepenynayll bought of William Maunsell of Derby, 5s. 8d.', and '2,500 fyfepenynayll, 9s. 2d.';[11] as these prices work out at $3\frac{1}{2}d$. and $4\frac{1}{2}d$. respectively, there was presumably a discount on taking a quantity. 'Nails called fippenynayle', at 5d., appear at Penshurst in 1471;[12] and at Clarendon '300 xpeny nayle for the newe roffe at the manor' cost 2s. 6d. in 1474,[13] but in 1477 'xpenynayll' were only 8d. the hundred,[14] and in 1494 'sixepenynayle' were 5d.[15] It would seem, in fact, that the nails had become standardized at some earlier date and that prices had fallen. So at Eltham in 1479 we find purchases made in London of 'xpennynayle' at 8d., 'vjpennynayle' at 4d., and 'iiijpennynayle' at 3d.[16] Similar discrepancies occur in other accounts of about this date; for instance, in 1500, for work done on Lady Margaret Beaufort's manor of Collyweston,[17] purchases were made of 8,000 'vjpenynaile', at 3s. the thousand, 9,000 'iiijpenynaile', at 2s. 4d., 5,000 'iijpenynaile', at 1s. 10d., and 5,000 'ijpeny naile', at 1s. 2d. Still lower prices occur at Westminster in 1532, ranging from 'ijd. nayle' at 12d. the thousand up to 'syngle x peny

[1] E. 471, 1.                                            [2] E. 471, 3.
[3] E. 471, 8.                                            [4] E. 471, 10.
[5] E. 494, 29.              [6] Dy. of Lanc., Misc. Bks., 11, f. 8.
[7] *Camden Miscellany*, vii. 18.        [8] E. 479, 1.          [9] *Sacrist Rolls*, 130.
[10] E. 495, 23.      [11] Mins. Accts. 917, No. 18.          [12] Penshurst MS. 129.
[13] E. 460, 13.        [14] E. 460, 14.          [15] E. 460, 16.
[16] E. 496, 21.              [17] St. John's Coll., Camb., Accts., vol. i.

nayle' at 4s. 2d., but 'doble x^d. nayle'[1] are priced at 10s. There is also an entry of 'one thowsande v^d nayle of beyonde see making tynned—vs. 11d. For another thowsande v^d nayle of Englishe making with square heedis tynned—iiijs.'[2] References to imported nails before this date are rare, but in 1495 the churchwardens of St. Mary-at-Hill bought 'ij c Spayneshe nail' for 10d.[3] In the accounts for the building of 'the Bell' at Andover in 1534 'a seam (*sm^a*) of northern lathe nayle', containing 10,000 nails, cost 8s. 4d., 'a sm^a of Normandy lathe nayle' 6s. 8d., and 'ij sm^a of Normandy lathe nayle of ye best and ye cariage from Salisbury', 15s. 4d.[4] On the other hand when we read of 'Forest nayle' being used in 1460 at Devizes,[5] it is probable that they came from the Forest of Dean, and in 1519[6] and 1540[7] we have references to 'homewroughtnaile' being used in Cambridge. Considering that nails were, until a comparatively recent time, a side-line of almost every forge, it seems odd that emphasis should be put on these being a local product; but there seems reason to believe that the Midlands had become a centre of nail-making at an early date—mention has been made above of nails being bought in London from a Derby trader in 1438,[8] and for London Bridge nails were bought from Thomas Bonde of Coventry.[9] As a large proportion of the nails used in Cambridge were bought at the great fair of Stourbridge, it is quite likely that local makers may have been swamped by the mass production of the Midlands —though this is admittedly rather too much to build on the interpretation of two isolated entries.

Finally there are a few varieties of nails which make rare, or isolated, appearances in accounts. In the Canterbury Cathedral accounts for 1276 'scarfneil', costing 12d. the hundred, are mentioned;[10] and next year there are entries of '250 sarpnail', for 3s., and '2,000 smalsarp' for 4s.[11] These may be connected with the 'nails called sharpelynges' which figure at Boston in 1452[12] and at York between 1406 and 1530.[13] 'Pynail', stated to be for roofing a chamber, at Cockermouth Castle in 1322[14] are presumably pin-nails. 'Doublenail' appear at Scarborough in 1284, at 3½d., and at York in 1327, at 4d. the hundred, and 'middelnayl' at Windsor in 1321, at 15d. the

---

[1] These appear again at Abingdon in 1538 at 11s. 4d. the thousand: E. 458, 1.
[2] T.R., f. 506.      [3] *Memorials* (E.E.T.S.), 208.
[4] Magdalen Coll. Deeds, Enham, 2556.      [5] E. 462, 6.
[6] Bought at 4d. the hundred: King's Coll. Mundum Bk. x.
[7] P. 1540–1.      [8] See above, p. 315.
[9] Bridge Accts., vol. i, ff. 282, 288.      [10] Lambeth MS. 242, f. 29.
[11] Ibid., f. 47.      [12] Penshurst MS. 20.      [13] Y.F.R. 35, 93, 104.
[14] E. 460, 25.

hundred, but what they were double of or intermediate between does not appear. This same Windsor account[1] mentions 'standiznail', or 'staundiznayl', at about $2\frac{1}{2}d$.; and 'standysnayll', at 6*d*., occur also at Shene in 1376,[2] but without any indication of their nature. 'Shetnayle' are found at Newcastle in 1365,[3] and 'nayles synck heedid for setting on of plates of iron' at Westminster in 1532.[4]

Readers who have toiled through these pages on nails may feel inclined to quarrel with the infliction of so much tedious detail. But the subject affords a good illustration of a typical feature of medieval business—the contradiction between an apparent exactitude and the really haphazard casualness which that appearance conceals. At first sight it would seem that even such insignificant things as nails were scientifically graded and labelled: but examination shows that twenty different terms were applied to an identical article, while the same name may cover widely different objects. This holds good for a great many sides of medieval life, and many ingenious theories owe their existence to the ignoring of the fact that medieval clerks often liked to vary their wording for the mere sake of variety and did not greatly worry if they used one term in several senses.

[1] E. 492, 20.  
[2] E. 494, 29.  
[3] E. 579, 15.  
[4] T.R., f. 553.

# XX

## SCAFFOLDING, CRANES, AND OTHER MACHINES

FOR the building of anything more than a breast-high wall some kind of scaffolding was necessary. This might take the form of a platform, nothing much more than a kind of substantial trestle table, such as is probably implied in the *alta catasta* of wood 'made for the masons to stand on while they made holes for hooks in the pillars' at St. Paul's in 1490,[1] or the 'trestals for scafullyng' at Kirby Muxloe in 1481.[2] But for higher work scaffolds of the type still employed were constructed, consisting of tall uprights—judging from illustrations the modern[3] custom of planting these in barrels was not often followed—with similar long poles lashed horizontally, carrying one end of the short logs of which the other end rested on the wall; on these short logs lay the platform, composed of hurdles, instead of the planks now used.

The uprights were most commonly of alder, though all kinds of timber were employed. At Westminster in 1324 we find 25 pieces of alder, 20 feet in length, 400 others of 38 feet, and 61 pieces of ash, 42 feet in length, for scaffolding;[4] and in 1333, for the east gable of St. Stephen's Chapel, '12 great beams 30 ft. in length for standards for the scaffot'.[5] The 'skaffolde powles' bought for work at Westminster in 1532 included 24 of alder and 70 of ash,[6] while at Exeter in 1325 we find 15 great poplars and 100 alders used.[7] Three beams of lime (*tilie*) for a *schaffald* occur in 1314 at Nottingham;[8] and at Ely, when particularly long standards were required for building the Lantern, in 1324, the large sum of £2. 8s. was paid 'for 24 fir trees for stagyngg'.[9] Scaffolding naturally formed a large item in the cost of rebuilding the nave of Westminster Abbey, with its vaulting more than 100 feet above the ground, in 1472–92. 'In 1472–3, while preparations are being made for its roofing, we find that there are three scaffolds—the lower, higher, and highest (*inferior, superior,* and *supremus*); elsewhere we read of the great scaffold and the small scaffolds.'[10] From 1482 to 1490 'the carpenters had been occupied chiefly in moving the scaffolding from

---

[1] Egerton MS. 2358, f. 4.       [2] *Leics. Arch. Soc.* xi. 241.

[3] Perhaps I should say 'recent', as the old wooden scaffolding has in the last few years been almost entirely replaced by metal tubing.       [4] E. 469, 8.

[5] E. 469, 11.       [6] T.R., f. 8.       [7] Oliver, *Exeter*, 383.

[8] E. 478, 1.       [9] *Sacrist Rolls*, 47.       [10] Rackham, *Nave of Westminster*, 36.

severy to severy as the work advanced. The scaffolding was elaborate. Each portion of the great scaffold, upon which the centres stood and where the masons worked, was floored and shut off by partitions from wind and weather'.[1]

The particulars of materials bought in 1509 for the 'nether scaffolds of the broach and the middle scaffolds' for the building of the spire of Louth Church are not very enlightening: for eight pieces, 8*d*.; and for middle scaffold two pieces going through, 16*d*.; eight small 'lyggars', 4*d*.; 'weyng wode', 4*d*.; four trees, 12*d*.; nine pieces 'lyggyng aboon trees', 4*d*.; four spars, 2*s*.; two pieces over scaffold, 19*d*.; two pieces going through, 12*d*.; four spars, 12*d*.; eight pieces 'liggars', 12*d*.; 'rassing tree and beyme', 10*d*.; 'weyng wode and liggars', 4*d*.[2] The 'liggars', or ledgers, were logs lying horizontally—now called putlogs—and the spars were probably the uprights, but beyond that nothing very definite emerges. Even the medieval passion for variety in nomenclature did not find much room for display on this subject. At Dover in 1347 we have '4 raftres and 12 staunsones for scaffolds',[3] and 'raftres' for scaffolding occur again at Corfe in 1376;[4] and 'spyres' for the same purpose appear at Ripon in 1393.[5] Usually some quite vague term is used, such as the 'scaffoldlogges', of which Agnes Dissher supplied 300, at 3*d*. apiece, for the Tower in 1361,[6] or the 'stagyngtymber' mentioned in the King's Hall accounts for 1493,[7] or some disguised spelling of poles, of which the 'poowelles', found in the Kirby Muxloe accounts,[8] is an exaggerated instance.

The logs composing the scaffold frame were lashed together with either ropes or withies. The ropes were usually made of bast, or similar fibre. At Calais in 1441 there is mention of 'cords called *bastropps* used for binding the masons' scaffolds at the Develstour', and also of cords called 'double bastroppes'.[9] So, at Westminster in 1443 we find 6*d*. paid '*pro vj fadom de bastenrope pro ligacione scaffald*'.[10] In 1515 'bast roppes for scaffoldyng' occur in London,[11] and 'baston ropes for scarfoldys' in Oxford,[12] and in 1533 'bast ropes for the scaffald makers' at Hampton Court.[13] At York in 1479 we have 'twichyngropes for the scaffolds',[14] and at Collyweston in 1503 'iij grett roppes of emp, iij other for skafoldyng'.[15] More often, and before the

---

[1] Ibid. 42.
[2] *Archaeologia*, x. 83; Dudding, *First Churchwardens' Book of Louth*, 123.
[3] E. 462, 16.     [4] E. 461, 6.     [5] R. 115.
[6] E. 472, 9.     [7] K.H. 18, f. 347.     [8] *Leics. Arch. Soc.* xi. 233.
[9] E. 193, 4.     [10] E. 503, 11.     [11] E. 474, 7.
[12] Corpus Christi Oxon. MS., f. 2.     [13] H.C. 237, f. 22.
[14] *Y.F.R.* 83.     [15] St. John's Coll., Cambridge, Accts.

fifteenth century almost invariably, the binding was done with withies. At Westminster withies (*scort'*) for binding scaffolds cost 3s. 4d. the thousand in 1290[1] and in 1324,[2] but the price had exactly doubled in 1361.[3] For the scaffolding at Windsor in 1368 as many as 185,000 'twists' (*torquibus*), of withies, were bought.[4] Bundles of rods for scaffolds are mentioned in the King's Hall accounts, about 1430, and '*roddes pro ligacione de lez scafoldes*' at Windsor in 1482.[5]

The lashings were tightened, as is still the practice, by driving in wedges. As these could be made out of odds and ends of wood, they do not often figure in accounts, but they appear, as 'warrokes',[6] at Westminster in 1324: 'for 6 pieces of timber for *warrokis* for binding the scaffolds', and 'for half a hundred of *talwode* of ash for *warrokes* for making scaffolds',[7] and in 1333: '*talwode* . . . for *warrokis* for the scaffold'.[8]

Hurdles were a regular constituent of scaffolding. In 1256 at Woodstock 6d. was spent '*in cleys* (i.e. hurdles) *faciendis ad stairuras*',[9] which is explained by an entry that occurs at Westminster in 1290, and again in 1333: 'for 24 hurdles (*crat'*) for making the way onto the scaffold'.[10] At Clarendon in 1316 a man was making '*clates pro steiryng et scaffot, capiens pro herdell q<sup>r</sup>*',[11] and at Dover in 1347 a shilling was paid 'for 6 hurdles (*claiis*) for the masons to stand upon'.[12] 'Hurdels' appear at Corfe in 1376, and 'hirdeles' at Northampton in 1399, for making scaffolds, '*herdyll pro stagys*' in the 1412 King's Hall accounts, and '*stagil herdils*' at Little Saxham in 1506.[13] Hurdles were also called 'flekes', as, for instance, at Clipston in 1362, when 4 'scaffaldeflekes' cost 12d.;[14] and next year at Durham, '*pro flekes et spyrys pro skafaldynges*'.[15]

In several of the building contracts printed in Appendix B it will be noticed that the employers undertake to provide the necessary scaffolding and *centerings* (under a variety of spellings). For any vault or arch constructed out of a number of stones or bricks, some form of centering is required, to support the members of the arch in position until the mortar has solidified them into one whole. It naturally follows that reference to

---

[1] E. 468, 3.  [2] E. 469, 3.  [3] E. 472, 9.

[4] E. 494, 1. Cf. '*In virgis pro clatis et torq' inde faciendis pro scaffot*': E. 466, 4.

[5] St. John's Coll., Cambridge, MS. vol. ii.

[6] Cognate with 'garrock', which means a crossbow bolt (Mins. Accts. 824, 18).

[7] E. 469, 8. 'Talwode' is wood cut into small pieces for firewood.

[8] E. 469, 12.  [9] E. 497, 12.

[10] E. 468, 3; 469, 12.  [11] E. 459, 27.

[12] E. 462, 16  [13] Gage, *Thingoe Hundred*, 142.

[14] E. 460, 18.  [15] *Durham Acct. Rolls* (Surtees Soc.), ii. 386.

PLATE 17

*a.* TREAD–WHEEL CRANE 14TH CENTURY

*b.* TREAD–WHEEL CRANE, AND LEWIS 16TH CENTURY

PLATE 18

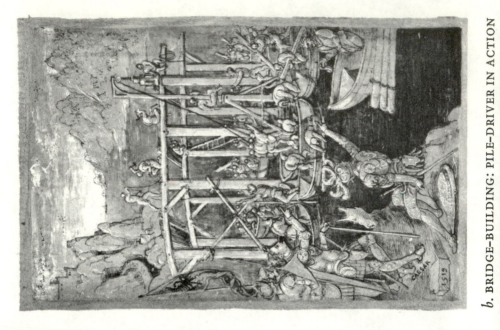

b. BRIDGE-BUILDING: PILE-DRIVER IN ACTION

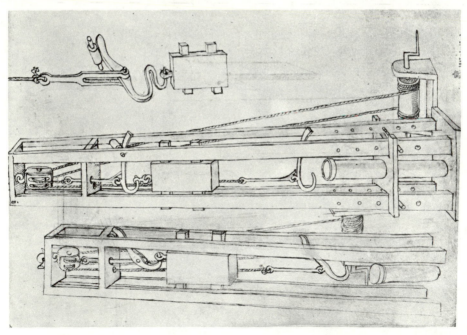

a. PILE-DRIVER 16TH CENTURY

centerings are numerous, but they are chiefly noticeable for vagaries of spelling. In 1227 beech boards for *cyntros* occur at Dover;[1] and the same form occurs at Winchester in 1257[2] and Cambridge in 1295.[3] At Corfe in 1290 boards were bought 'to make *cintrillos* for making two (?) wall-cupboards (*hartas*) under the east room',[4] and at Westminster 'bechbord for *cyntrelis* for making the windows' in 1324.[5] Also at Westminster, in 1399, we have 400 elm boards for making 2 *cyntours* to support the arch of the great window at the north side of the Hall,[6] while at the Abbey in 1486 there are various references to the *centures* of the vaulting.[7] For the building of Norwich Guildhall, in 1410, 'popyl bordys' were used to make *syntrees* for the stair turret;[8] at Salisbury in 1479 'the new syntryns' are mentioned, and at Kirby Muxloe 4*d.* was paid 'for making the *seynters* for the vowte over the 3athous'.[9] An entry in a Yarmouth account for 1470 gives rather more detail:[10] 'a greate elme squared to make bord for sentours' cost 4*s.*, '3 smale elmes for to make legges for sentours' 4*s.*; these 'legges' are the boards, now known as 'laggings', nailed round the arc of the centering to carry the intrados of the arch; they are referred to again in the same account as made of cask-staves—'for 4 pipes bought to naylle upon the sentours'. .

To avoid the trouble and expense of erecting a scaffold for the execution of repairs at a height, use was often made of a platform bracketed out from the wall. Such devices are to be seen in medieval illustrations, and in the Collyweston accounts for 1500 there is mention of a carpenter employed 'for to make brakettes for the skafoldes for the chymnes'.[11] Another plan was to use a cradle, or stage slung on ropes and lowered from above. At Westminster in 1352 there is reference to 'a cable, weighing 49 lb., for hanging the plumbers' *cradel*',[12] and similarly at York in 1434—'3 hemp ropes (*cordis*) for making *hausors*, and 2 ropes for hanging the plumbers' *credell*'.[13] At Hadleigh Castle in 1365 a *cradel* was hired 'for taking down the scaffold round two towers and blocking up the holes'[14]—evidently the 'putlog holes' where the cross-pieces of the scaffolding had rested in the

[1] E. 462, 10.    [2] E. 491, 14.    [3] E. 459, 16.

[4] E. 460, 28.    [5] E. 469, 11.    [6] E. 473, 11.

[7] Rackham, *Nave of Westminster*, 42.    [8] *Norf. Arch.* xv. 170.

[9] *Leics. Arch. Soc.* xi. 298.    [10] E. 481, 28.

[11] St. John's Coll., Cambridge, MS. vol. i.

[12] E. 471, 6.          [13] *Y.F.R.* 54.

[14] E. 464, 9. Cf. at Oxford in 1505 payments 'for blocking the openings called *schafful holes*': *Canterbury Coll.* (O.H.S. N.S. vii), 245. They seem to be referred to in a payment in 1517 at Leverton (Lincs.) to 'ye masyn for myndyng of crakes and *sparsettes*': *Archaeologia*, xli. 346.

walls. 'Two *credill* for the workmen to stand on and make holes in the
town walls for the insertion of corbels' occur in Berwick accounts of 1422;[1]
and at Windsor in 1534 there was 'a great rope for the glasyers to hange
ther cradelles on the outsyde of the wyndowes to make clene the glasse'.[2]

In some accounts of about 1385 for work at Berwick there is mention
of '*j cradill pro petra wyndanda*'[3]—evidently something similar to the '3
chests for raising stones' at Purton in 1449,[4]—and medieval illustrations
show a variety of baskets, barrells, and other receptacles used for the hoisting of stone. Large blocks were lifted separately, usually by means of
'slings'—stout ropes hitched round the stone and over a hook at the end
of the lifting rope. At Westminster in 1348 a rope, weighing 14 lb., was
bought 'for the slyngges',[5] and in 1448 the stores included '*j rope, j tarre
rope, iij par slynges pro petris exaltandis et gubernandis*',[6] and 'slynging ropes'
occur at Cambridge in 1508.[7] 'A horse-hide for making *le slengg*' is mentioned in 1323 at Ely,[8] and at York, about 1400, is a payment '*in baudrikes
factis de telis equorum cum basts pro portagio lapidum*';[9] 'bawdricks' are straps—
the term is often used for the straps by which bell-clappers were hung—
but whether *telis*, properly 'cloths', is here misused for 'hides', or whether
it means 'tails' and the straps were composed of horsehair and bast together
seems uncertain.

Large blocks of stone, particularly keys, or bosses, were often raised by
means of a lewis. To use this, a rectangular hole was cut in the centre of
the upper surface of the block, the two ends of the hole being cut on the
slant so that the base of the hole was considerably longer than its aperture.[10]
The lewis itself, as used from the end of the fifteenth century, consisted of
three iron wedges, side by side, on a bar; the two outer wedges, cut with
an outward bevel, were inserted in the hole and held in place by the centre
wedge, and the bar was then thrust through the eyed upper ends of the
wedges. The two ends of the bar were joined by a semicircular bar with
an eye for the hook of the lifting rope.[11] The earlier form of the lewis, however, seems to have been that of a reversed 'grip' (see below); that is to
say, two crescent-shaped irons hung from a common ring, with their con-
vexities facing inwards. Their lower ends being inserted in holes drilled

[1] Foreign R. 9 Hen. V, m. G.          [2] Hope, *Windsor Castle*, 250.
[3] E. 483, 5.                          [4] *Oxford City Docts.* (O.H.S.), 325.
[5] E. 470, 18.                         [6] E. 503, 12.
[7] King's Coll. Chapel Accts.          [8] *Sacrist Rolls*, 34.          [9] *Y.F.R.* 23.
[10] For drawings of lewis-holes in stone at Whitby Abbey, see *Archaeologia*, x. 126.
[11] A rough sketch of a lewis is used as a mason's mark on one of the Norman pillars in
Gloucester Cathedral; but I could only find one such mark.

obliquely in the stone, the strain on the ring would hold them in position.[1] The great advantage of this method of lifting was that a boss could be swung over the space between the vaulting ribs, accurately adjusted, and dropped into position. The earliest certain references that I have found to this instrument are at Windsor in 1357—'*ij paria lowys*'[2]—and at Langley in 1368—'*j lowys, j hamo pro eodem*',[3] but in 1282 there is mention of 14*d*. spent '*in lussis ad opus cementariorum*', at the Tower,[4] which is probably the same thing. In the 1532 Westminster accounts we find: 'John Moulton of Westminster, mason, for two paire lowettis of iron by him delyverd for the saufe cranage of stone redy wrought from breaking oute of shippes and lighters'; and also: 'To the same for two payre of doble robenettes with their poleys of brasse and other apparelle . . . for the hoysing of wrought stone'.[5] With some hesitation, I suggest that 'robenettes' were 'grips' or 'scissors'—a pair of more or less crescent-shaped irons, bolted together near their upper end so as to act as great pincers; the lower, free, ends of the grip are placed in nicks cut on either side of the block of stone, and the lifting rope, attached to the upper ends of the irons, tightens the pincers on the stone. Unlike the lewis, this device figures frequently in medieval illustration of building operations. An entry referring to work on the hall at Eltham in 1479 records a payment 'for iiij calueskynnes bought for the keweveryng (i.e. covering) of the robynnettes and the Xfoldtaklyng for the rayne (i.e. against rain)'.[6] Here 'crossfold tackle' seems to fit in with the arrangement of the chains or ropes at the upper end of the grip, necessary to produce the pincer-like action. This interpretation would also fit quite well with an entry in the King's College Chapel accounts for 1507, of a payment of 20*d*. 'to Richard Symson for caryage of a cheste wyth gynnes and robynettes for the cranes, weying ij^cweyght, from London to Cambridge'. The London Bridge accounts for 1407[7] mention the purchase of '25 polyftrendeles (i.e. pulley wheels) for instruments called robynett'— which is, at least, perfectly consonant with my suggestion; nor does there appear to be any other medieval word available for these grips, which we know were in use.

While it is possible to carry bricks and small stones up on to the scaffolds, it is obviously a saving of labour and, where large stones are used, a necessity to have some simple kind of machine for hoisting them. As

---

[1] Such pairs of holes occur in the vault at Peterborough: *ex inf.* W. D. Peckham. They can also be seen on top of the centre keystones of the vault in the roof of King's College Chapel, Cambridge.

[2] Hope, *Windsor Castle*, 216.  [3] E. 466, 4.  [4] E. 467, 9.
[5] T.R., f. 307.  [6] E. 496, 21.  [7] Vol. i, f. 148.

Horman says: 'There must be made a trace whele to wynd up stone';[1] or, in the words of the Collyweston accounts, a few years earlier, 'a wyndes for to weyn up the timber'.[2] As early as 1222 we find tallow bought at Winchester 'for greasing the machines (*ingenia*) for lifting timber and water'.[3] Similarly at Westminster in 1333 tallow was used 'for greasing the *polyfs* and beams for lifting up great blocks of marble';[4] and at Hampton Court in 1533, 'blake sope for the berrells and pynnys of the gynnes'.[5] The principle of all the 'gins', or machines, was a rope running over a wheel or pulley fixed above the position to which the stone, or timber, was to be delivered, one end of the rope ending in a hook, or other means of attachment, and the other passing round an axle rotated by a wheel. This type of gin was known as a 'verne'. At the Tower in 1282 we have '2 brass *poleis* for the verne for raising timber';[6] and ten years later a log of alder was provided 'for the machine which is called *verne*' at Corfe Castle, and Hugh the smith was paid 9*d*. for making straps (*bendas*) for it.[7] The Tower accounts for 1316 contain mention of '2 iron loops (*lupis*) made for *sneckis* at the end of the ropes for the verne';[8] and at Ely, when the lantern was being built in 1323, iron bands, a hoop, brass hinges (*vertivellis*), and great iron nails for the brass wheels were provided for the 'ferne', and 6*s*. 8*d*. was paid, 'out of courtesy, to Master Thomas the Carpenter, setting up le ferne'.[9] In 1329 we have details of the making of a 'verne or machine built for lifting or winding up (*guyndando*) timber' at the Tower: 2 iron rings for binding the ends of the axle (*axis*); 2 iron rods for the hawk (*hauka*) of the verne, on which rods the wheels (*trendelli*) have to turn or rotate (*girari*); an iron strap (*benda*) 3 ft. long and 3 in. broad, for binding and strengthening the beam (*virga*) of the verne, broken or cracked (*falsata*), with 18 nails called *spikynges* for fastening the same strap onto the beam.[10] Here the beam is an upright post, carrying on its upper end a short horizontal 'hawk', which projected on either side and had at each end a brass wheel running on an iron pin. The hawk was also sometimes called a 'falcon'—*fauconneau* being the term applied to it in France at least until the end of the seventeenth century[11]—and we have a reference to 'a carpenter making *faucon*' at Winchester in 1257,[12] while the men working these machines were occasionally called *falconarii*, as, for instance, at Vale Royal. Among the stores at Westminster in 1444 were:[13] 'a ferne called

---

[1] *Vulgaria* (1519), c. xxix.  [2] St. John's Coll., Cambridge, MS. vol. ii.
[3] E. 491, 13.  [4] E. 469, 12.  [5] H.C. 237, f. 104.
[6] E. 467, 9.  [7] E. 460, 29.  [8] E. 468, 20.
[9] *Sacrist Rolls*, 33.  [10] E. 467, 6 (1).
[11] Félibien, *Principes d'architecture*, pl. xx.  [12] E. 491, 14.  [13] E. 503, 12.

wyndas, 3 great fernes, a broke, 3 great haukes for the said fernes, a long wooden bekerell[1] with a hauk belonging to it'. A similar list for 1399 includes: 'a machine called *wynde*,—a machine called *brokke*, and 4 vernes'.[2] The 'brokke', or brake, was something in the nature of a capstan; and in France in the seventeenth century[3] the *vindas* was also a horizontal capstan-like device; but it is probable that 'verne' and 'windas' were used indiscriminately for such wheels, whether turned horizontally or—like those which still exist over the north-west gable at Peterborough (? thirteenth-century) and in the tower of Salisbury Cathedral (fifteenth-century)—vertically. In 1367 there is mention at Corfe of 6s. 8d. spent on 'a cable and a rope, with two *poleyues* for the windas to the high tower',[4] and at Beaumont Lodge in the same year, 'a wyndel for conveying stones to the masons'.[5] At Ripon 2d. was bestowed 'in drink given to various persons helping at the wyndas' in 1380;[6] and two 'wyndylles' are mentioned in the King's Hall accounts for 1448;[7] and at Ludgershall in 1342 we find a rather mysterious 'machine called a *garlewynd* made for raising the timber of the chapel'.[8]

Besides these wheels turned by hand, others were made on the treadmill principle, turned by the feet of men standing inside them. One such exists in the great Bell Harry Tower at Canterbury and is presumably contemporary with its erection at the end of the fifteenth century. Another is drawn as standing on the top of the north-west tower of Westminster Abbey in the 'Islip Roll' of 1532,[9] and a similar 'great wheel' is mentioned in the Abbey accounts about 1482–90 as standing above the vaulting of the nave and being shifted, with the scaffolding, from bay to bay.[10] In 1331 the authorities at Merton College spent 2d. on 'drink for the men (*garcionibus*) on the day when the wheel was removed and the ladders were set up';[11] and in 1396 the 'great wheel in the tower' of New College was mended.[12] Although in none of the instances is there any actual reference to their being walk-wheels, I am inclined to think that was implied by the term *magna rota*, especially as we have in 1488 an entry of 6s. 8d. paid at Clarendon 'to four workmen running in the great wheel for 4 days'.[13] This type of wheel figures in several medieval pictures of cranes. The difference between the crane and a gin of the windas type was that whereas in the

[1] Equivalent to the *virga*, above.    [2] E. 473, 11.
[3] Félibien, op. cit., pl. xx.    [4] E. 460, 29.    [5] E. 458, 10.
[6] R. 99.    [7] K.H. 11, f. 19.    [8] E. 476, 1.
[9] Rackham, *Nave of Westminster*, 49.    [10] Ibid. 42.
[11] Merton Coll. Roll 4084.    [12] *Oxford City Docts.* (O.H.S.), 309.
[13] E. 460, 16.

latter the trendel or pulley was fixed either to the scaffolding or to a separate beam, the pulley on a crane was carried at the end of a movable beam, which projected at a variable angle from beside the wheel.

Cranes were largely used for discharging cargoes from vessels, and by the fifteenth century most ports were furnished with them.[1] The earliest use of the term that I have noted is in 1347, at Dover, when grease and tallow were bought 'for the machine called la crane'.[2] At Shene in 1369 two great brass wheels were provided for a crane,[3] and the stores at Westminster in 1444 included '*machina vocata a crane*', for which there was a great hempen rope.[4] In 1474 Magdalen College paid 10*d*. 'to the Abbot of Rewley for a great machine called a crane for conveying stones and cement onto the wall'.[5] At the sister University, fifteen years later, the authorities of King's Hall borrowed, and broke, a crane from 'Gunvyle-halle' (now better known as Caius),[6] and one was employed in 1507 for unloading stone for King's College Chapel from the barges—'a styrrop w$^t$ a bolt and a band w$^t$ iiij chekes for the crane at the watersyde' being among the entries in the chapel accounts of that year. The 1532 Westminster accounts mention[7] 'gable roopis', or cables, and a 'brasen polleye', weighing 23 lb., for a crane, and also—'One great capsteye, and xv boultes with their forelockis[8] and keys, also two doggis of iron with iiij boultis, two rounde hoopis, one square hoope, two greate platis with their keys and forelockis, and one dryfte pynne . . . for the newe crane'.

In the Merton College accounts for 1449 there are several references to an '*antempna* for lifting stones to the belfry'; it was apparently brought from Abingdon, and grease was bought for it, and also 'a rope for binding the *antempna* to other machines'.[9] The strict meaning of *antempna* is a sail-yard, and as such a yard was often fitted with pulleys and tackle for hoisting boats, it was presumably something in the nature of the beam of a crane. Of the other fittings the trendals, or wheels, and the pulleys, or blocks in which trendals were set, occur with some frequency. At Marlborough in 1238 tallow was bought for the pulleys (*polannis*);[10] at Guildford in 1290 a smith was paid for working a piece of iron for a pulley (*puliuam*);[11] and in 1333 William de Algate, 'potter', made 3 pair of *trendell* of brass for the vernes.[12] The Westminster accounts for 1399 contain a pay-

---

[1] Salzman, *English Trade*, 232–4.      [2] E. 462, 16.
[3] E. 494, 7.      [4] E. 503, 12.      [5] *Magdalen Coll. Reg.* ii. 234.
[6] K.H. 18, f. 178.      [7] T.R., ff. 13, 311, 414.
[8] Forelocks were pins inserted in holes through iron bars, like linchpins.
[9] *Oxford City Docts.* (O.H.S.), 326.      [10] E. 476, 3.
[11] E. 492, 10.      [12] E. 469, 12.

ment '*pro iiij trendell de laton pro pulliues*';[1] at Winchester iron 'polypynnes' occur in 1425,[2] and about the same time William Clacyere, 'belleyetere', was paid 12s. 6d. 'for 4 copper *trendel* called *sheverys*, weighing 38 lbs., made for the great machine', at Bristol.[3] And among the stores at Westminster in 1444 were '2 brass *tryndal*, 2 *fotebraces* for the machine newly made for the unloading of *shoutes* (or barges) with stones'.[4]

References to ropes naturally occur with considerable frequency, with or without reference to their use for cranes or other gins. Some Tower accounts for 1282 mention:[5] '6 ropes of twisted string (*cordis de filo filato*), weighing 1200 (pounds), at 18s. the hundred'; '6 great ropes, containing 108 *lucellos*, at 22d. the *lucellus*', and '4 great ropes, containing 26 *lussellos*, at 16d. the *lussellus*'—whatever the *lussel* may have been; and 'a rope containing 60 *teisas*, 16s.' In a Westminster account of 1329 we have '*corda longitudinis xvj teisarum seu brachiat*', *ponderante xviij lb.*'—the toise or brasse being approximately 7 feet. The '*magna corda de vj cluis vocata haucer*', mentioned at Westminster in 1324,[6] is presumably a hawser of 6 strands. 'Hausors' occur at York in 1471 together with 'jolraps' and 'giraps',[7] the latter being our guy-ropes. At Wallingford 2 lb. of *talwe* (tallow) were bought in 1368 'for greasing the cable, so that it should not rot with rain';[8] and at the same date, at Langley, we have 'a cable of hemp bought of Simon le Ropere for lifting stones and timber, containing 12 toises (*taic*') and weighing 64 lb., at 2d. the pound', and also 'an iron hook and ring for the cable'.[9] 'A great rope called a *gable*, weighing 104 lb., for raising stones and timber on the tower' occurs at New College, Oxford, in 1396.[10] At Westminster in 1532 we find payments[11]—'for viij eyse to the said cables; . . . for smalle lyne for the fastenyng of the endis of the saide gables from revyng oute'.[12] The same accounts mention 'one warpe of cable roope', and 'iij webbis of handeroopis'.

Ropes have from early times been made of hemp; so we have at Ripon in 1355—'13 stone of hemp bought at Selby for 3 cables (*cablis*) for the church, 10s. 10d. For wages of Robert Raper making cables from 17 stone of hemp 5s. 8d.';[13] and at Scarborough in 1423—'v stone of femell (i.e.

---

[1] E. 473, 11.     [2] E. 491, 29.     [3] E. 473, 18.
[4] E. 503, 12.     [5] E. 467, 9.     [6] E. 469, 8.
[7] Y.F.R. 8.     [8] E. 490, 2.     [9] E. 466, 4.
[10] *Oxford City Docts.* (O.H.S.), 309.     [11] E. 503, 12.
[12] The mending of ropes by splicing occurs at Louth as 'slyssyng': Dudding, *First Churchwardens' Book of Louth*, 8, 29, 197. At Peterborough in 1540 the term 'shutting' which is usual for welding iron, occurs—'mendyng and shootyng of the Roope we borrowyd': *Northants. Rec. Soc.* ix. 145.     [13] R. 50.

hemp) to make of ropes for wyndyng up and downe of stone, vj$^s$. Item for wynchyng and leiyng of the forseide v stone of femell, xx$^d$.'$^1$ So far as the manufacture of ropes was localized, the chief centre of the industry was Bridport, and purchases of ropes from there are mentioned occasionally, 'a piece of Brydportlyne', for instance, being bought for the London Bridge works in 1440.$^2$

Mention has already been made of the fact that rams were employed for driving piles.$^3$ The detailed accounts of a pile-driver constructed by Master John de Hurland, carpenter, in 1329 are of considerable interest:$^4$

To Roger de Waltham of the Roperie for a rope, 20 brasses (*brachiatarum*) long and weighing 24 lbs., for lifting the beam (*virga*) of the machine carrying the ram employed for fixing piles in the water, 3$s$. To the same for a piece of *selyskyn* (i.e. seal-skin) 3 brasses in length, for hanging the said beam or ram (*rama*), 15$d$. And for 3 gallons of *dregges* (presumably of ale) to put the piece of *selyskyn* in, to temper it, 1$d$. And for half a gallon of *heryngsayme* (i.e. herring oil) for greasing the *selyskyn* after tempering, 6$d$. And for 4 iron hooks (*hamis*) for controlling (*ducendand'*) the said ram after its hanging, 12$d$. And for 4 rods (*roddis*), each of the length of one and a half brasse, for supporting the said hooks, 2$d$. Also, to a man instructing (*informanti*) the Master of the work in the preparation of the ram and of the machine carrying it, 3$d$. Also, for grease, both for the said machine and for the verne employed for winding up (*guyndando*) timber. And for 2 wooden *trendell* for the same verne, as the others bought before were broken, 4$d$. And for a quarter of *spykyng nail* bought of Thomas de Thorneye for making the machine employed for the ram, 1$d$. And for carriage from London to Westminster of the said ram, obtained on loan from Robert Suote, citizen of London, the rope, seliskyn, hooks, grease, roddes, and trendell, 2½$d$.

The leather strap, here made of seal-skin, by which the ram was attached seems to have been known in London as a 'swerd'$^5$—O.E. *sweard*, meaning skin—and figures frequently in the bridge accounts; as, for instance in 1381, 'for 3 horse hides, curried (*corodatis*), for making *swerdis*', and 'for fat to grease the *swerd* for the ram'.$^6$ The later bridge accounts show that there were two rams, the smaller being known as the 'gybbetram',$^7$ from its frame being like a gibbet, while the larger was the 'rennyngeram', or

---

$^1$ E. 482, 8.   $^2$ London Bridge Accts., vol. iv.
$^3$ See above, p. 86.   $^4$ E. 467, 6 (1).
$^5$ An inventory of goods belonging to a house and wharf in Billingsgate in 1330 includes: 'a ram of wood and a *swerd* of leather', and '20 fathom (*toises*) of the skin of the fish which is called sele': Exch. Plea R. 57, m. 20.
$^6$ London Bridge Accts., vol. iv, ff. 7, 9.
$^7$ Cf. 'A *jebet* of iron for the drawbridge' at Shene in 1473: E. 503, 19.

running ram, presumably so called because the ram ran on, or between, two upright beams, being kept in place by the angle-irons, or hooks, referred to above.

In a Calais account of 1468 there is reference to 'a great rope (*funo*) bought and used on a *jynn* called *le reryng jynn*'.[1] This may have been used for raising the frames of wooden houses into position, or for lifting them when underpinning was required, as was done at Odiham in 1400, when we read of 'the hire of various instruments called *gynnes* for the lifting of the said Ledenchambre and the support of it for making its foundations and a *somere* to support the same chamber'.[2] Towards the end of our period the use of some form of screw-jack seems to have been known, judging from a payment to William Wetteresk, carpenter, 'for vj payre of scruse, at v$^s$. ij$^d$. the payre, servyng to rayse the flore of the haull' at Hampton Court in 1535.[3]

[1] E. 197, 5.     [2] E. 502, 15.     [3] H.C. 238, f. 335.

# XXI

## TOOLS

THE tools in use in the building trade varied little between the Roman period and the nineteenth century, and it is chiefly in the matter of nomenclature that the study of them presents any particular difficulty. It is, however, worth while for us, who live in an age when the country is littered with tins, old pails, fragments of bicycles and motor cars, and other scrap that it is not worth anyone's while to collect, to remember that throughout the Middle Ages iron was a valuable material and steel even more so. Consequently such implements as spades and shovels were made, both blade and handle, of wood and provided with an iron shoe. So, at Canterbury in 1277, we find 3 'spadetres' and 9 'soueltrowes' (shovel 'trees') bought for 12d., and at the same time 2 'spadhisenes' and 4 'souelhisene'—the irons with which they were shod—bought for 11½d.[1] At Woodstock we find '4 *sholeirennes* for binding 4 shovels', in 1400,[2] and mention of '4 schoueltre and spadetre' in 1435.[3] At Bardfield Park in 1344 6d. was spent on 'ironing 6 shovels (*tribulis*)' and 8¾d. on 'ironing 6 spades (*vangis*);'[4] at Hadleigh 'iron for 3 shovels' cost 9d. in 1363,[5] and in 1365 at Sheppey 249 wooden shovels were bought, at 1d. each, and 26 shovel irons, at 4d.,[6] a good many of these shovels being evidently used for such purposes as mixing mortar, for which they would not require to be shod. For repairs to York Place, in London, in 1515 two 'shodshovilles' were provided,[7] and the 1532 Westminster accounts mention 26s. paid 'for vj dussen di' shovilles shoid with iron', and also 6s. for 'xij steale spades'.[8] Cutting tools were made of iron with a piece of steel 'shut', or welded, on to the edge. At Porchester we have '94 lb. of Spanish steel expended on the hardening (*duracionem*) of axes and other tools of the masons' in 1397;[9] and at Scarborough, in 1425, 'j shefe of steale for stealyng of the instrumentes'.[10] In 1367 Thomas Cokham was paid 1d. apiece 'for steeling (*asceratione*) of 63 axes and chisels for the masons with steel supplied by the King';[11] and a smith at Woodstock in 1494 received 16d. 'for stelyng of ij pykax and a hewyng ax and mendyng of a crowe'.[12] When

---

[1] Lambeth MS. 242, f. 47.      [2] E. 502, 15.      [3] E. 499, 19.
[4] E. 458, 4.      [5] E. 464, 6.      [6] E. 483, 21.
[7] E. 474, 7.      [8] T.R., f. 11.      [9] E. 479, 23.
[10] E. 482, 8.      [11] E. 479, 28.      [12] E. 499, 19.

Chertsey Abbey was being pulled down, in 1538, the smith was paid 6*d*. 'for new shuttyng poyntyng and stelyng of vj crowes of irne', and 10*d*. 'for new transposyng of x mattockes w^t stelyng of the same';[1] and such entries could be multiplied indefinitely. During the sixteenth century it was not unusual to make the masons a fixed allowance for the re-steeling of their tools. So, in January 1508, we find 69 masons working on King's College Chapel paid 12*d*. each 'for stelyng of ther toles a half yere';[2] and similarly at Warblington (Hants) in 1518—'For stelyng for vij maisons for our Lady Day quarter at vj^d every maison iij^s. vj^d.', and 'for stelyng for ye maisons for mydsomer q^r. p^d. for stelyng of vij maisons axes at vjd a pece—iij^s. vj^d.[3]

Beginning with the simple tools in use for quarrying stone, there were at the Yorkshire quarry of Stapleton in 1399—'10 iron wegges, weighing 100 lb.; a pulyng ax; 2 iron mauls (*mallea*); 3 iron gavelokes; 2 iron kevelles; and 4 brocheax';[4] and at Scarborough in 1425—'for the quarell ij grete hokkes of iren, ij grete malles of iren, ij pule pykkes of iren, ij gauelokes and j crawe of iren, vij wegges of iren'.[5] The 'pulyng' axe, 'pule' pick, or poll-axe was a heavy hammer-axe, and the 'kevel' was very similar, while the 'brocheax' was a smaller tool used for broaching, or rough dressing, the stone blocks. A 'gavelock' (cognate with 'javelin') was a large crow: at Knaresborough in 1334 we find 'an iron gavelok for breaking stones in the quarry'.[6] For the building of Vale Royal Abbey, in 1278,[7] we have 3*s*. paid '*pro ij coruailis (crows) ferreis pro lapidibus levandis de quarrera*', and 5*s*. '*pro xxiiij coynis ferreis videlicet wegges ad quarreram*', and provision was also made of spades and shovels (*bechis et trublis*), and of 'houwis',[8] or hoes, which were practically spades with the blades set at right angles to the hafts. At Porchester 63 lb. of iron were bought in 1385 'for *weggis* and a *crowe* for getting stone in the quarry', and also 'a *stonax*, weighing 10 lb., for scabbling stones at the quarry';[9] and at Launceston 'an iron tool for breaking stones in the quarry, called *polax*, weighing 16½ lb., and 2 new wegges, weighing 10 lb.' were provided.[10] Among the tools used in 1474 for getting stone for Magdalen College were '3 great mauls (*malleis*) of iron and steel, weighing 70 lb.', wedges (*cuneis sive fissoriis*), weighing 16 lb., and 'a tool called a crowe of iron, weighing 72 lb.'[11] An even heavier crow occurs at Oxford in 1514, when 'a crawe of yrne', weighing

---

[1] E. 459, 22.    [2] Chapel Accts.    [3] E. 490, 13.
[4] *Y.F.R.* 19.    [5] E. 482, 8.    [6] E. 544, 18.
[7] E. 485, 22.    [8] Cf. '*in ij houwes emendandis*'; Hadleigh, 1363: E. 464, 6.
[9] E. 479, 22.    [10] E. 461, 13.    [11] *Magdalen Coll. Reg.* ii. 228.

91 lb., appears in company with 'a malle of yryn', weighing 21 lb., and a 'betyll'—a beetle, or wooden mallet—weighing 18 lb.[1] From Cambridge we may quote the provision of 'a crawe, malle and pyke exe' for Hinton quarry in 1449.[2] At Durham 2d. was paid 'for mending the wegges', and 1d. 'for sharpening (*exasperacione*) the pykke', at the quarry, in 1533;[3] and at Ripon in 1425 is an entry '*pro scharpyng et wellyng* (i.e. welding) *of wegges de ferro*[4]—a simplification of Latin prose which a schoolboy might envy.

The tools just mentioned were also in use for heavy work in the actual building operations. Thus at Scarborough in 1425 'gavelokes, mattokes, and wegges' were supplied not only for the 'quarell' but also 'for takyng downe of the Constable Toure . . . whilk was in poynt to fall'.[5] At Winchester, again, in 1222 we find '2 crows (*corvicibus*) for breaking the wall, and 3 wedges (*cuinz*, or *cuniz*)';[6] and to the same family belong the two 'rauenysbylles for breaking stone walls', weighing 12 lb. between them, in use at Mettingham in 1466.[7] In a York Castle account for 1327 are payments for 'mending an iron gavelok, borrowed from the master of the works of St. Peter's (the Minster) and broken in shifting stones in the wall, and for the ironwork of 12 *butours*, borrowed from the same, for lifting timber'.[8] 'Butters' were stout poles, shod with iron, used as shores for such purposes as raising, or holding up, the frame of a house during underpinning. They occur in 1315 at Merton College,[9] 7d. being paid for six 'buturs' and 4d. 'for iron hoops and points (*aculeis*) for them'; at the same time 3d. was paid 'for an iron bar (*clavo*) for lifting timber'. At Westminster in 1289 there is mention of '2 poles of alder for boturs', and 'ironwork for the boturs';[10] and at Bardfield Park '4 iron pikes for 4 botours' were bought in 1344.[11] For the work in Westminster Hall in 1396 purchases were made of '*vj viroll vj pykes pro hastis vocatis botours ad maeremium sublevandum*'[12]—and similarly in the London Bridge accounts for 1413 we find 6d. paid 'for mending, in hooks (*virol'*) and pyles, of 3 poles called *botteres* for the carpenters'.[13] Ten 'spykes to heve tymber with' are mentioned at Tickenhall (in Bewdley) in 1526.[14]

A Tower account for 1333 mentions 'a piece of iron called *crouwe* for lifting timber',[15] and another, twenty years earlier, refers to 'levers (*leuatores*), bars (*cauill'*), *chasatores*, crowes and various other kinds of tools for

---

[1] Corpus Christi Coll. MS., f. 2.          [2] K.H. 11, f. 115.          [3] D.H.B. 280.

[4] R. 152, cf. '*pro viij wellynges malliorum*', 1396: *Oxford City Docts.* (O.H.S.), 308.

[5] E. 482, 8.                    [6] E. 491, 13.                    [7] Add. MS. 33987, f. 88.

[8] E. 501, 8.                    [9] Merton Coll. Roll 3642.          [10] E. 467, 20.

[11] E. 458, 4.          [12] B.M. Add. R. 27018.          [13] Bridge Accts. ii, f. 48.

[14] Exch. T.R. Misc. Bks. 250, f. 57.          [15] E. 469, 15.

taking the machines (or artillery—*ingeniis*) to pieces'.[1] The exact meaning of *chasatores* is uncertain, but the word suggests something in the nature of wedges. Another unusual term is the '*cachepe* for breaking stone', which occurs in a Westminster account of 1351;[2] it appears again in the London Bridge accounts for 1411—'for steeling of 2 *hameres* and a *cacchepee*—10d.'[3] A rather curious tool is the 'crow of yrren w$^t$ a spone at oon end', weighing 28 lb., which turns up at Cambridge in 1507.[4] Similar to the crowbar is the pitching-iron—'a great piece of iron for making a *pyccher* for the wharf' occurs at Gravesend in 1360;[5] and 'a long *picheyngyrne* of iron for the *lymeost* (i.e. lime-kiln)' is mentioned in 1444.[6]

Picks, for digging foundations or breaking down walls, occur with frequency. At Woodstock in 1256 is a charge 'for sharpening and mending *picas*' and *crawes*',[7] but the usual form is *picois*, or *pykoys*. This became corrupted into the modern form, 'pickaxe', so that, for instance, at Westminster in 1532 we have mention of 24 'pykaxis', weighing 1½ cwt., 10 lb., and 'iij pyckaxis with hamber heedis provided for brekyng downe of the greate Toure in the palesse'.[8] Mattocks, also, which are picks with broad adze-like blades, occur, but less frequently. During the pulling down of Abingdon Abbey in 1539 there was 'paied to Richard Smythe for the makyng of viij Ies to viij mattokes at iiij$^d$ the I—ij$^s$. viid$^d$.'[9]

The chief tools of the mason were the axe and the chisel, and the most momentous change in the working of stone was the introduction of the use of the chisel not only for carving[10] but, to a rapidly increasing extent, for dressing stones, which occurred in the second half of the twelfth century. In his account of the rebuilding of Canterbury Cathedral after the great fire of 1172, Gervase[11] calls attention to the fact that the capitals of the new work were carved with the chisel, whereas those of the older work were carved with the axe. It is frequently assumed that all carving before this time was done entirely with the axe, but without depreciating the extraordinary skill with which a craftsman can wield so apparently clumsy a tool as a mason's axe, it may be doubted whether the more elaborate carving, especially figure work, was not finished with a chisel. In the matter of surface dressing, although documentary evidence is absent, we have evidence of the stones themselves, with their unmistakable

---

[1] E. 469, 16.  [2] E. 471, 6.  [3] Bridge Accts. i, f. 324.
[4] King's Coll. Chapel Accts.  [5] E. 544, 1.  [6] E. 503, 12.
[7] E. 497, 12.  [8] T.R., f. 16.
[9] E. 458, 1. The 'Ies' were 'eyes' or sockets for the hafts.
[10] The intricate carving found on Saxon stonework must obviously have been done with chisels.  [11] App. A.

axe-tooling, diagonal on flat surfaces and vertical on the rounded surface of pillars. It must, however, be borne in mind that tooling is only a very approximate basis for dating; for while the presence of chisel dressing—where the stone has not been retooled—may prove that the work is not earlier than, say, 1150, the old masons, and probably their more conservative apprentices, would often have continued to use the axe in preference to the newfangled chisel. Curiously enough, I can find no documentary reference to the toothed dressing tools, introduced in the thirteenth century, which have left their marks in such a multitude of buildings; but they figure in many medieval illustrations. Nor is there any implement named in building accounts which can be identified with the drag, used to give a fine finish to the surface. My own impression, based partly on illustrations, is that the drag of the Middle Ages was simply the blade of the mason's hammer-axe, used with a drawing motion; if this tool was also used for striking, it would leave a mark which, I imagine, would be very difficult to distinguish from the mark of the claw-chisel. There were two main types of axes in use: the mason's axe proper, as still used, had two vertical edges; the hammer-axe was like a small mattock, having one horizontal edge and on the other face a hammer-head. These axes formed the badge of the mason's craft, and both forms—but chiefly the hammer—may be seen, for instance, in scores of inscriptions by Renaissance masons who visited the Pont du Gard and the famous vice of S. Gilles, in Provence, and testified their admiration of those architectural masterpieces by defacing the stones with their signatures.

According to the regulations for the craft, drawn up at Torgau in 1462, a travelling mason on arriving at a lodge and obtaining a job should ask first for an axe, then for a piece of stone, and afterwards for such other tools as he required,[1] which should be lent him. In England, also, it seems to have been the custom for the mason to travel light-handed and to use tools provided by the lodge. This is suggested by the payment, at Vale Royal in 1278, of 10s. 'to Robert de Salisburi, William de Winchecumbe (and nine others), masons, who brought with them their own tools, namely 20 axes (*hachiis*) and 48 iron (tools) for carving stones, because it is the custom that their tools, if they bring any, shall be allowed for (*comparata*)'.[2] It is also borne out by the number of tools bought or made during operations or kept in the lodges. Thus in the masons' lodge in the Minster yard at York in 1399 there were: '69 stanexes, a great kevell, 96 chiselles of iron, and 24 mallietes bound with iron', and in another build-

---

[1] Gould, *Hist. of Freemasonry*, i. 142.   [2] E. 485, 22.

ing '6 stane hamers, great settyng chisiles' and other tools.[1] At Durham in 1404 we find '10 stanaxys, 2 pykkis, 2 hakkis, a kevyll, 3 gavelokis, 3 chysel, a shackle for lifting purposes (*schakyll pro cariacione*), 4 ponchons, 2 mattoks, an iron mell, 6 wedgis, with a grape for daubyng'.[2] At Scarborough in 1425 there were 'iij stone axes, vj irens, ij settyng chisells, j kevell, j hamer ax, and ij trowell in the logge';[3] and five years later at Portsmouth: '12 iron crowes, 12 settyng chesilles, 8 masons' axes, . . . 6 trowell, . . . 24 iron wegges, an iron kiuell for scabbling (*pro scapul'*), 3 slegges, 3 scabbling axes (*securis scapul'*)'.[4] Here the sledges are probably for breaking, rather than working, stone—as at Warblington in 1518, when 4*d.* was 'payd for ye makyng of a scleyg for (to) brek ye grytt stonys'.[5] The 1532 Westminster accounts show an unusual variety in the types of axes, or hammers, employed: 'a greate hamber for the masons whiche is stealid at bothe endis for the brekyng of stone, poz. xvj lb. q[r].';[6] '12 skabelinghambers for the roughleyers', at 8*d.* each,[7] and therefore weighing about 5½ lb.; 'setting hambers with hollowe heedis for the hardehewers';[8] 'a small hachette for the masons', 6*d.*;[9] '6 flatte hambers sharpe at bothe endes, for the hewyng of flynte', and other 'flynte hambers with flatte edges steeled at both endes', at 5*d.*;[10] also 'a greate hamber called a pilcharde', weighing 8 lb.[11] There is mention at Shene in 1444 of '2 stonhamers called bateryngaxes'.[12]

All of these axes were mounted on handles, which were practically always made of ash; for instance at Berwick about 1385 we have 6*d.* spent '*in xvj manubriis de fraxino pro stone axes*',[13] and at Westminster in 1532 'asshe tymber, wherof was made . . . helves for hoddis, hambers, mattockis, malles and suche other like necc(essar)ies', and 'shides of grounde asshe' for the helves of mattocks and hammers.[14] On the other hand, the brick-axe was entirely of iron, with steel cutting edges, being a straight tool like a double-ended cold chisel, or wedge, narrowed in the middle for the grip. In a Westminster account of 1490 we have a charge of 2*d.* '*pro induracione cujusdam securicule le brikaxe ex utraque fine*';[15] with which we may compare the six 'hookis stealed at bothe endes provided for tylars to cutte with bothe weys certeyne stuffes appertaynyng to their occupieng', bought, at 6*d.* each, in 1532.[16] At Warblington in 1518 is a payment to Thomas Smyth for repairing 'viij endes of breyk axys, at iiij endys j[d], ij[d]';[17]

---

[1] *Y.F.R.* 17.      [2] *Durham Acct. Rolls* (Surtees Soc.), 397.      [3] E. 482, 8.
[4] E. 479, 25.          [5] E. 490, 12.          [6] T.R., f. 16.
[7] Ibid., f. 51.      [8] Ibid., f. 103.      [9] Ibid., f. 106.      [10] Ibid., ff. 238, 316.
[11] Ibid., f. 51.          [12] E. 503, 12.          [13] E. 483, 5.
[14] T.R., ff. 159, 310.      [15] Egerton MS. 2358, f. 14.      [16] T.R., f. 317.      [17] E. 490, 12.

and at Windsor in 1533 'a new bryke axe for the bryklayers' cost 8*d*.[1] So, also, at Chertsey Abbey in 1538: 'for new mendyng of hamers chezelles brykeaxes', and also 'for new makyng of iij chezelles and a clensyng irne servyng for the brykelayers'.[2]

Both masons and bricklayers made constant use of trowels, which therefore figure in most accounts. 'For working 3 pieces of iron to make 12 *truell* for the masons' at Cambridge Castle 9*d*. was paid in 1295;[3] and in 1301 we have 3*d*. spent on 'a *trulle* of iron for smoothing the walls' at Southampton.[4] At Carnarvon in 1320 a smith was 'working 2 iron *truels* and an iron for a shovel';[5] and at Westminster 'a *trowell* for the layers' occurs in 1444,[6] and 15 *trowellis*, at 6*d*. each, in 1532.[7] There is an interesting entry in the King's Hall account for 1519, when the new gate tower was being built, of 2*s*. 8*d*. spent 'for a bronze trowel (*pro trulla enea*)';[8] the material and price are so unusual that it is tempting to suppose that it was specially made for the ceremony of laying the foundation stone and was the first recorded ancestor of those engraved silver trowels that embarrass so many public personages of the present day.

Tools were also required for cutting up and piercing blocks of stone, so that saws and borers are often referred to. There were at Westminster in 1329 'a great borer (*terebrum*), $3\frac{1}{2}$ ft. long', and 'a saw for sawing stone, 4 ft. long';[9] and such a saw and borer figure among the stores there in 1444. Three stone 'wimbells' were bought at Cambridge, for 26*d*., in 1488.[10] The Clerk of the Works at Salisbury Cathedral in 1479 paid 'for fylyng of an instrument called stoon sawe' and for the purchase of 'an instrument called a stoon naugor (i.e. auger)'. Similarly, at Westminster, 'stone sawis for masons' were bought at 8*d*., and 'a fyle for the saide sawis' cost 16*d*., in 1532;[11] and next year we have references to purchases of 'ston persers for the masons' at Hampton Court.[12]

These tools naturally lost their edge pretty rapidly, and the smiths were kept busy reworking them—'battering' is the usual term. For instance at Sheppey in 1365 the smith was paid 'for battering (*bateracione*) of 1,594 masons' axes, at $\frac{1}{4}$*d*. each; and for battering of 5,720 masons' tools (*instrumentorum*), at 1*d*. for 20'[13]—the figures obviously implying the reworking of the same tools on a number of occasions. At Ely

[1] Hope, *Windsor Castle*, 263.  [2] E. 459, 22.
[3] E. 459, 16.  [4] *Hist. MSS. Com. Rep.*, vi. 559.  [5] E. 487, 3.
[6] E. 503, 12.  [7] T.R., f. 15.  [8] K.H. 22, f. 131.
[9] E. 467, 7.  [10] King's Coll. Mundum Bk. i, f. 83v.
[11] T.R., f. 607.  [12] H.C. 237, f. 171; 238, f. 139.
[13] E. 483, 21.

PLATE 19

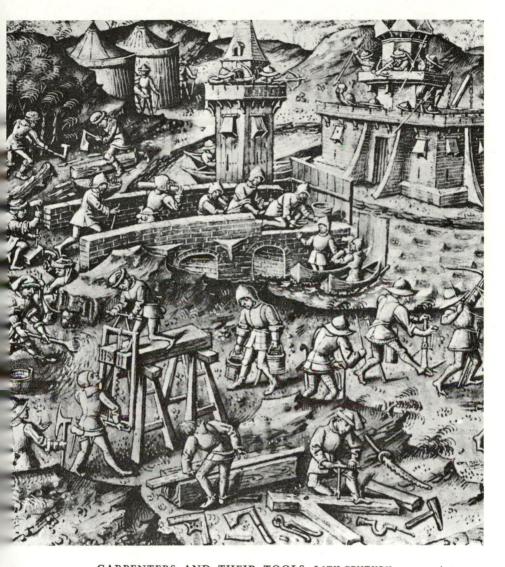

CARPENTERS AND THEIR TOOLS 15TH CENTURY

the form of entry in 1323 is '*in securibus et ferramentis cementariorum ponendis et acuendis*',[1] the interpretation of which in 1342 is '*in le leyingg et bateringg securium cementariorum*'.[2] An entry in the York Castle account of 1327 reads '*in acuicione pennacione et emendacione securium*',[3] where the exact interpretation of *pennacio* is obscure; the literal interpretation should be 'feathering', and it may mean working to a feather edge, or bevel, or conceivably it might refer to putting a toothed edge on the axes, but I do not think this likely. At Westminster in 1348 there are payments 'to Katherine the smith-wife (*fabre*) for steeling and battering of the masons' tools';[4] it would be interesting to know whether she was merely an employer of male labour or actually worked at the smithy herself. In the London Bridge accounts for 1422 we have '*pro bateryng de tool cementariorum*'; and at Scarborough in 1435 a smith is paid '*pro acuacione et layng de lez stoneaxes*'.[5] For work at Warblington in 1518 Thomas Smyth was paid 'for batryng of xxxiij endys for ye fre maisons at iij endes a jd.', and also 'for battryng of iiijˣˣ ix endes of ye maysons towylles at iiij endes jᵈ.'[6] And at the destruction of Chertsey Abbey in 1538 the smith was paid 1½d. apiece 'for batteryng and sharpyng of cxv mattockes at sundry tymes servyng for the bryckelayers'.[7]

Besides reworking, tools were sharpened by grinding, and at York we find Robert Read, smith, paid '*pro les gryndyng les axes et tules*', in 1499.[8] The stone used for the purpose was known as either a grindstone or a 'gressour'. So in two London entries the first, of 1324, records the purchase for 3s. of 'a great round stone for sharpening the masons' tools, called a *gresour*',[9] the other, of 1339, a charge of 6s. for 'a round stone for sharpening iron tools, called a *gryndelston*'.[10] At Westminster we have '*grese ad martella acuenda*' in 1253,[11] and 4 '*ingressur*' *ad utensilia cementariorum*' in 1278;[12] 'gresours' occur at Windsor in 1351 and at Langley in 1365, at 4s. and 3s. respectively; and 'a *grynston* and 2 pieces of a grynston, broken and used up in the sharpening of the masons' tools' at Porchester in 1397.[13] 'A millstone (*molar*') called a *qwetter* (i.e. whetter) for sharpening tools', costing 3s., is mentioned at Westminster in 1444;[14] and 'rubber stones for sharping of the tooles', in 1532.[15]

For the making of mortar it was necessary to sift the sand and lime with sieves or riddles. At Winchester 3½d. was paid for two sieves (*criblis*) in

[1] *Sacrist Rolls*, 33.   [2] Ibid. 118.   [3] E. 501, 8.   [4] E. 470, 18.
[5] E. 482, 10.   [6] E. 490, 12.   [7] E. 459, 22.
[8] Y.F.R. 91.   [9] E. 469, 8.   [10] E. 470, 6.
[11] E. 467, 1.   [12] E. 467, 7 (4).   [13] E. 479, 23.
[14] E. 503, 11.   [15] T.R., f. 312.

1222,[1] and at Woodstock in 1256 there is mention of 'sieves, riddles and rakes (*rastellis*) for sand'.[2] In 1376 '2 *ridles* and a *ceve* for cleansing sand' were bought at Corfe for 6*d*.,[3] and a few years later at Berwick is a purchase of '*ij cribris raris vocatis ridels pro calce et zabulo purgendo*',[4] where the adjective 'rare' probably means wide-meshed. The 'casier', bought for 2*d*. at Bodmin in 1470, is said to mean a sieve,[5] but I have not found the term elsewhere. Six 'bare shofelles for the playsterers to make morter with' occur at Windsor in 1533,[6] and similar entries in earlier accounts are common enough. 'A vessel called *bos* for carrying mortar up onto the chapel' is mentioned in a Westminster account of 1333,[7] and a 'boket called *le bosse*' figures in the Abbey accounts for 1423,[8] and 'vj hookis made and sette upon vj bossis', for tilers—presumably so that they could hang them on the laths while working on the roof—occur in 1532.[9] A bowl (*bollo*) for mortar occurs at Beaumond Lodge (Rutland) in 1367,[10] and 'xv boolles for morter' at Collyweston in 1503.[11] At Sheppey in 1365 we find '179 treies for putting morter in' bought, at 1½*d*. each;[12] '2 *beryngtrowes* for carrying mortar, and a *standard* for putting mortar on' occur at Southwark in 1406,[13] and about the same time the London Bridge wardens bought '2 treys for carrying mortar', for 8*d*., and '2 mortroghes', for 9*d*.[14] '*Haukes* for masons to put lime on' appear at Kirby Muxloe in 1481,[15] and 'hawk-board' is still in use locally as a term for the slab on which mortar is dumped. Many varieties of vessels for carrying the water for making mortar and other purposes occur from time to time; as, for instance, a 'bocat' at Cambridge in 1295;[16] 'a skope and a pail' at Langley in 1365,[17] and 'pailles for setters and layers' at Collyweston in 1503;[11] 'a great tub (*fatula*), *Anglice* a *covell*, for carrying water' at Devizes in 1460,[18] and 'a *covill* for carrying water' at Clarendon in 1477,[19] 'casks, barrels and *soes* for carrying and holding water' at Nottingham in 1375,[20] and 'ij saes for beryng of water and lyme' at Scarborough in 1425,[21] 'scoos' also occurring in the Tattershall College accounts for 1478.[22] According to Halliwell (*Dict. of Archaic . . . Words*) the 'so' was equivalent to the 'coul'

[1] E. 491, 13.　　　　[2] E. 497, 12.　　　　[3] E. 461, 6.　　　　　　　　[4] E. 483, 5.
[5] *Camden Miscellany*, vii. 11.　　　　[6] Hope, *Windsor Castle*, 263.
[7] E. 469, 11.　　　　[8] Rackham, *Nave of Westminster Abbey*, 41.
[9] T.R., f. 316.　　　　[10] E. 458, 10.
[11] St. John's Coll., Cambridge, MS. vol. ii.　　　　[12] E. 483, 21.
[13] E. 502, 26.　　　　[14] Bridge Accts. i, ff. 192, 195.
[15] *Leics. Arch. Soc.* xi. 240.　　　　[16] E. 459, 16.
[17] E. 466, 3.　　　　[18] E. 462, 6.
[19] E. 460, 3.　　　　[20] E. 478, 9.
[21] E. 482, 8.　　　　[22] Penshurst MS. 216.

and was 'a large tub, holding from 20 to 30 gallons, and carried by two men on a stang or pole'.

An implement that might not be expected to appear in the mason's hands was a pair of bellows, but this was the medieval equivalent of the vacuum cleaner, though its converse in action, used for dusting intricate and delicate carving. So, at Westminster in 1351 we find 'a pair of bellows for cleaning the work of the finials (*filiol*) of the niches'.[1] Oddly enough we find bellows in the unusual singular both at Westminster in 1324—'*pro j folli ad petras mundandas*'[2]—and at Porchester in 1397—'*pro uno belw expendito in mundacione petrarum dentaille* (= carving)'.[3]

Certain tools were used alike by masons and carpenters—such as squares, plumb-rules or levels, and measures. One of the regulations of the Torgau masons was that any fellow who left his square hanging on the stone, or allowed the level to lie about and did not hang it up by the hole provided for that purpose, should be fined.[4] Squares were sometimes made of iron; there were, for instance, in the lodge at Westminster in 1387 '2 irons made in the shape of *sqwiers*',[5] and at Porchester in 1430 '3 squaryngirnes'.[6] More often they were of wood, and usually made from cask-staves. At Westminster 10*d.* was paid 'to Dame Joan la Vyntenere for an empty cask for making rules (*regulis*) and *scuyris* for the masons',[2] in 1324; and in 1443 'a wooden pipe', that is to say, a half-cask, was used for making 'swyers and rewlez' for the masons and layers.[7] At York in 1399 we find a 'renyspipe', that is to say, a pipe that had contained Rhine wine, and two 'wadetons', or woad-casks, bought for the masons' 'reulor and sqwyers'.[8] The King's Hall accounts for 1428 mention 7*d.* spent on 'making rewlers, squyres and levell',[9] and in 1508 2*s.* 4*d.* was paid 'for a levell and 2 long rewels' for the work on King's College Chapel, and Peter Joyner was paid 'for a dozen squiers', at 1½*d.* each, and 'for iiij greate leavells', at 10*d.* each.[10] 'A plank (*tabula*) for an instrument called *liuel*', costing 4½*d.*, occurs at Oxford in 1374,[11] and '19 plomettes of lead' are mentioned at Shene in 1444;[12] while at Westminster we have in 1444 'a *rolle lyne* for testing (*reguland*') the walls of towers and chimneys',[12] and in 1532 '24 skeynes of chaulke lyne for the plumbe rewlis of masons and hardhewers'.[13]

For measuring, either wooden rods or strings were employed. 'A long

---

[1] E. 471, 6.    [2] E. 469, 8.    [3] E. 479, 23.
[4] Gould, *Hist. of Freemasonry*, i. 140.
[5] Foreign R. 11 Ric. II, m. C.    [6] E. 479, 25.
[7] E. 503, 11.    [8] *Y.F.R.* 7.
[9] K.H. 7, f. 212.    [10] King's Coll. Chapel Accts.
[11] Merton Coll. Roll 4102 (*b*).    [12] E. 503, 12.    [13] T.R., f. 160.

rod (*virga*) for the carpenters' measure(s)' occurs at Westminster in 1354,[1] and 'metroddes', or measuring-rods, for carpenters, at York in 1485.[2] At Windsor '5 poles of firre for measuring the said building' were bought in 1345;[3] '2 *poeles* for the carpenters' measures' cost 7*d.* in London in 1409;[4] and at Collyweston in 1503 we find 'iij polles to take mesur of the said warkes'.[5] Finally, at Westminster in 1532 'a fyrre pole whereof was made a measuryng pole for the carpenters' cost 4*d.*[6] In a Westminster account of 1490 is a reference to '7 iron spikes (*spinteribus*), perforated, so made that the masons might with them obtain the measurement of the privy kitchen' —a building elsewhere referred to as 'the place where the chief cooks prepared delicious and elaborate dishes (*cibaria deliciosa et subtilia*)'.[7] Presumably this kitchen was irregular in plan and the spikes were pegged into the walls and string passed through the holes in them for measuring. At York in 1327 there is mention of 'string (*philo*) bought for measuring fireplaces';[8] and at Windsor '2 lines for measuring stones' were bought in 1366,[9] and 'string called *pakthrede* for making *lyne* for the masons' in 1462.[10] 'Pakthrede whereof was made rayngyng lynes for the bricklayers' figures at Westminster in 1532,[11] and the same accounts record charges 'for iiij pecis of Sandwiche lyne provided for the setting oute of foundacions—ij[s]. And for iiij poundes of botome packthrede provided for lynes for the brickleyers—ij[s]'.[12] The contemporary accounts for Hampton Court mention 'rayngyng lyne, to meser owth the fundashon of the quenys new lodgyng', costing 1*d.* for 6 fathoms.[13]

For the consideration of the tools used by carpenters in the Middle Ages a good basis is the fifteenth-century poem, *The Debate of the Carpenter's Tools*.[14] In this curious work the various tools discuss their master's character and prospects; some of them content themselves with variations on the theme that he is a drunken fellow who will never thrive, but others say exactly how they will work to make money for him. The tools named are—shype ax, belte, twybylle, wymbylle, compas, groping iren, saw, whetstone, adys, fyle, chesyll, lyne and chalke, prykyng knyfe, persore, skantyllyon, crow, rewle, pleyn, brode ax, twyvete, polyff, wyndas,

---

[1] E. 502, 17.  [2] *Y.F.R.* 88.  [3] E. 492, 25.
[4] Bridge Accts., vol. i, f. 194.
[5] St. John's Coll., Cambridge, MS. vol. ii.  [6] T.R., f. 12.
[7] Egerton MS. 2358, f. 14.  [8] E. 501, 8.
[9] E. 493, 22.  [10] E. 496, 16.  [11] T.R., f. 94.
[12] Ibid., f. 12.  [13] H.C. 237, f. 217.
[14] Largely quoted in Innocent's *Building Construction*. Printed, from the MS. in the Bodleian, by Hazlitt, *Early Popular Poetry*, i. 79–90.

rewle stone, gowge, gabulle rope, squyre, and draught nayle. Some of these we have already dealt with, as the windas, pulley, crow, square, and rule—the 'rewle stone', whose remarks are unilluminating, is probably a plummet; also the whetstone, who says:

> Hys axes schall I make fulle scharpe
> That they may ly3tly do their werke;

and the cable, who promises:

> Hayle and pulle I schalle fulle faste
> To reyse housys, while I may laste.

Pride of place in the ranks of the carpenter's tools, as with the mason's, belongs to the axe. To begin with, the timber must be felled before it can be worked, and we may logically start with the 'merkyngaxe for marking (*signandum*) timber selected for the King's works', bought, for 2*d.*, at Eltham in 1406.[1] This is probably also the significance of the felling-axe '*pro sing' silu''*, mentioned in the Kirby Muxloe accounts of 1483.[2] The felled timber was roughly squared with axes, and frequently it was split into boards by means of axes and wedges. In skilled hands the carpenter's axe, or 'wright ax',[3] was a most efficient tool, capable of almost anything. The 'shype ax' of *The Debate* probably took its name from being used by shipwrights and may be the same as the 'chipax', which occurs in a list of tools in 1408.[4] For the most part an axe is simply an axe, without any distinguishing title, but there is mention at Clarendon in 1477 of 'an axe called a froward',[5] which one is inclined to associate with the 'frow'—'a thick-backed, rigid, dull-bladed steel knife . . . hafted at right angles upward from its blade', used for splitting logs.[6] At Portsmouth in 1430 there is mention of '2 axes for sharpening piles, and 2 *foteaxes* for smoothing (*planand'*) piles';[7] and the London Bridge accounts between 1410 and 1426 contain references to a 'waterax', costing 14*d.*, an 'axe pro le tid' (20*d.*), and a 'tydax' (18*d.*).[8] In what way these differed from ordinary axes does not appear. In *The Debate*

> The brode ax seyde withouten mysse,
> He seyd: the pleyn my brother is;
> We two shall clence and make full pleyne.

---

[1] E. 502, 26.

[2] *Leics. Arch. Soc.* xi. 342. Professor Hamilton Thompson interprets this as 'for thinning timber'.     [3] York, 1399: *Y.F.R.* 18.     [4] *Y.F.R.* 207.

[5] E. 460, 14.     [6] Mercer, *Ancient Carpenters' Tools*, 11.

[7] E. 479, 25. A 'fot ax' is mentioned in 1404 at Durham: *Durham Acct. Rolls* (Surtees Soc.), i. 396.     [8] Bridge Accts. i, f. 281; and vol. iii.

The 'broad axe' was made with a chisel edge, bevelled only on one side, which enabled it to follow a marked line accurately.[1]

Actually, the adze would seem to have an equal claim to brotherhood with the plane, its use being chiefly to smooth the surface of boards. For work at Restormel Castle in 1343 6*d.* was spent on 'an *ades* for smoothing old timber, because the timber was so full of nails (*clavosum*) that the carpenters would not set their own tools to it'.[2] It figures at Winfield as an 'aase' in 1443;[3] and for the London Bridge works in 1382 we have 2*s.* 6*d.* paid 'for a new adze for water work under the Bridge',[4] another 'new adese for the water' costing 13*d.* in 1407, and 8*d.* paid in 1411 'for steeling and mending 2 wateradeses'.[5] A variety of adze known as a 'thyxtyll' occurs at Durham in 1404.[6] Planes themselves figure very rarely in building accounts; they were more a joiner's tools than a house-carpenter's. One of the few entries referring to them is in 1425 at Scarborough, where there were 'in the trasynghous ij peir of compasses of iren, one of the lengthe of a yerd another lesse, and iiij planes'.[7] Oddly enough, compasses are rarely mentioned in the accounts, and I am inclined to think that as a rule they were the private property of the master mason and carpenter. In the Minster lodge at York in 1399 there was 'an iron *compas*';[8] also '2 tracyngbordes', or drawing-tables, and '4 leaden *chargeours* for *moldes*', which I cannot explain, unless they were to be cut up to form templets. There was also 'a small *hachett*'—no doubt equivalent to the 'axe for making *moldes*' mentioned among the tools in the Westminster lodge in 1444,[9] and no less than 400 'iron *fourmers*', or chisels.

The timber, when it was not split with axe and wedge, was sawn up with two-handed pit-saws. The Westminster list just mentioned includes 'an iron saw (*serra*) and a *puttesawe*', which are probably those bought in the previous year, when 'a saw called *kytter*, for sawing various large pieces of wood', cost 3*s.* 5*d.*; 'a saw called *qwypsawe*', 7*s.*; and 'a *fyle* and a *wrestle* for sharpening and settyng the said saws', 16*d.*[10] The 'kytter' is probably a framed pit-saw, in which the narrow blade is strained upon a long rectangular frame, to the ends of which it is fastened.[11] The 'qwypsawe', or whip-saw, was an 'open', or unframed, saw with a broad blade and a

---

[1] Mercer, op. cit. 81–6.                         [2] E. 461, 11.
[3] Penshurst MS. 57.                             [4] Bridge Accts., Roll 1381–2, m. 10.
[5] Ibid., vol. i, ff. 149, 344. Three 'wateraddes', valued at 3*s.*, are mentioned in 1330 in connexion with a wharf in Billingsgate: Exch. Plea R. 57, m. 20.
[6] *Durham Acct. Rolls* (Surtees Soc.), i. 396.
[7] E. 482, 8.                        [8] *Y.F.R.* 17.                        [9] E. 503, 12.
[10] E. 503, 11.                            [11] Mercer, op. cit. 17, 22–4.

handle at each end.[1] In the London Bridge accounts 'a long whippesawe' cost 5s. 8d. in 1411; a 'cuttyngsawe' 2s. in 1421; and 'a tenonsawe' 2s. 6d. in 1423. This last, which appears again in 1532, at Westminster—'2 ten^ante sawis delivered to Rawlins the Maister Carpenter', at 2s. 8d. each[2]—was a hand-saw in which the blade was stiffened by a metal rib along the upper edge.[3] Such was probably the 'handsagh' mentioned in the York Minster inventory of 1399.[4] Two 'handsawes' are found at Durham in 1404, with 3 'twhertsawes', which are probably equivalent to whip-saws.[5] The pit-saw, as its name implies, was used with a pit, or rather a trench, dug in the ground; the balk to be sawn was supported over the pit, in which one sawyer stood, while the top-sawyer stood above, and sometimes on, the baulk. There are, therefore, occasional references to the digging of saw-pits; for instance in 1535, when Hengrave Hall was in building, 10s. 8d. was paid 'for makyng xvj sawye pitts at Sowe wood'.[6] In the same year, after timber had been sawn for use at Hampton Court, 20 sawpits were filled up, and during the operation 'roulles', or rollers, were employed to bring the logs to the sawpits in the wood.[7] Illustrations show that a trestle platform, or something in the nature of a sawing-horse, was sometimes used instead of a pit, but the only documentary evidence of this that I have found is an entry in the account for building 'The Bell' at Andover in 1534: 'for grett naylis to make sawyng trestilles'.[8]

We have mentioned files in connexion with the sharpening of saws, and in 1473 a saw and a *fylyryn* were bought, for 6s. 8d., for work at St. Benet Hulme.[9] In *The Debate* the 'fyle' says:

> I schalle rube with all my myght,
> My mayster tolys for to dyght.

In 1406 we find 8d. paid 'to one Peterkyn for the mending and *fylyng* of various *vyles*';[10] and at Cambridge in 1507 payments 'for setyng of a fyle', and 'for batteryng of vj^xx toles, at x toles a jd., and for betyng a fyle'.[11]

*The Debate* mentions a 'prykyng knyfe', which was probably something in the nature of a 'pricker' or 'scratch-awl',[12] used like a modern pencil for marking on the surface of wood. Two 'markyng irons provided for carpenters for marking of boorde and tymbre' occur at Westminster in

---

[1] Ibid. 21, 27, 28.　　　[2] T.R., f. 94.　　　[3] Mercer, op. cit. 139, 141.
[4] Y.F.R. 17.　　　[5] *Durham Acct. Rolls* (Surtees Soc.), i. 396.
[6] Gage, *Hengrave*, 50.　　　[7] H.C. 238, f. 163.
[8] Magdalen Coll. Deeds, Enham 255 b.　　　[9] Bodleian Roll 71.
[10] London Bridge Accts. i. 95.　　　[11] King's College Chapel Accts.
[12] Mercer, op. cit. 61, 64.

1532.[1] A later entry in these accounts is 'for chaulke lyne for carpenters'.[2] This was cord coated with chalk, which was stretched along the board or balk to be sawn and, when twanged, left a chalk line to guide the sawyer. It was also used for marking stonework, 'chalkelyne for masons' being bought at Woodstock in 1435.[3] The 'skantyllyon' of *The Debate*—evidently, from its name, a kind of gauge—does not appear elsewhere under that name, so far as I am aware.

The 'belte', 'twybylle',[4] and 'twyvete' are all said by the *Oxford English Dictionary* to be types of axes; but it seems to me probable that the last should be a maul or hammer, that type of tool being otherwise unrepresented. The 'twyvete' may be the 'twybitle', defined by Halliwell (*Dict. of . . . Archaic Words*) as 'a very large mallet'—a double, or two-handed, 'beetle'. At Odiham in 1440 we find John Spytfyssh being paid for '4 wooden *betelles* used in the cleaving of timber'.[5] Another equivalent term was 'commander',[6] which occurs at Windsor in 1533, when we have the purchase of 'elme for to make ladders rolles levers and commaunders'.[7]

Hammers present few features of interest. The '*hamer pro aqua*', for the steeling of which 2*d*. was paid in 1419,[8] may have been made with a specially long handle, for working below the water; otherwise it is difficult to see why the bridge wardens took the trouble to distinguish, in their accounts, between land and 'water' tools. A list of tools at Shene in 1473 includes a 'handhamer' and a 'clouehamer', for carpenters.[9] The latter was, no doubt, a claw-hammer, equivalent to the '*hamer furcata*' which appears at Windsor in 1358.[10] The claw-hammer was known to the Romans and figures in early illustrations; it was apparently the normal form of carpenter's hammer, the claw being useful for drawing nails that had gone astray in the driving. For the works at Restormel Castle, in 1343—where, as we have seen, they were reusing old timber full of nails[11]—'an iron bar made in the shape of a pig's foot, for drawing nails out of the old timber' was provided.[12] A Tower account of 1333 mentions 'a pair of *pinsouns* for drawing nails out of beams',[13] and pincers are mentioned from time to time—as at Cambridge in 1462, when 3½*d*. was paid for a '*par de le pynsons*' and 1*d*. for 'small borers (*penetralibus*)'.[14]

---

[1] T.R., f. 13.   [2] Ibid., f. 50.   [3] E. 499, 3.

[4] For the twibil, or mortising axe, see Mercer, op. cit. 174–5.

[5] E. 503, 9.   [6] Mercer, op. cit., 171, 175.

[7] Hope, *Windsor Castle*, 263.   [8] London Bridge Accts. ii. 321.

[9] E. 503, 19.   [10] Hope, *Windsor Castle*, 216.

[11] See above, p. 342.   [12] E. 461, 11.

[13] E. 469, 15.   [14] P. 1462–3.

Of the boring tools the simplest was the awl-like 'persore' of *The Debate*, which says:

> Faste to runne into the wode
> And byte I schall with moth full gode.

Then comes the 'wimble', or gimlet,[1] with a screw-turned point:

> Zis, zis, seyd the wymbylle,
> I ame als rounde as a thymbylle;
> My maysters werke I wylle remembre,
> I schalle crepe fast into the tymbre.

A smith at [South] Wingfield, Derbyshire, was paid 12*d.* 'for making anew a *wymbubytt* for the drilling (*teracione*) of the *spynduls* of the louvre', in 1443;[2] and in 1481 '*le layinge ij womyls*' figures in the accounts of Finchale Priory.[3] A larger variety of the wimble is the auger, with screw-point and cutting edge and a horizontal handle-bar, worked with both hands.[4] Sometimes additional force was given by pressing the chest upon a pad set on top of the shank, but, although I have found the 'breast-auger' in ship-building accounts, it does not seem to figure in ordinary building. 'An iron *augur* for making holes in bemes' cost 5*d.* at Westminster in 1443,[5] and 4*d.* was paid 'for steeling a *nauegore*' in 1382.[6] A 'waternawger' occurs in 1404[7] and a 'wateravger' in 1419[8] in the Bridge accounts, the two forms marking the period when the initial *n* was evidently beginning to lose its hold. A *terebrum grossum* $3\frac{1}{2}$ feet long is mentioned at Westminster in 1333,[9] and might be translated either 'auger' or 'drill'.

The 'draught nayle' of *The Debate* is, no doubt, the same as the 'drift pin', a punch with which nails were driven below the surface of the wood —as is shown by the entry of '4 dryfte pynnys for the carpenters to drive the saide broddes' in a Hampton Court account.[10] 'A long peg (*cavilla*) called *driftpyn*' occurs at Westminster in 1444;[11] 'a dryffe pynne for carpenters' in 1532;[12] and 'ij dryft pynnys servyng for the carpenters' at Chertsey in 1538.[13] In 1350 Master Andrew, the chief smith at the Tower, supplied 'an iron punch (*poncona*) called *drivel* for (?) knocking out (*educend'*) wooden pegs'.[14] This seems to be the early form of the word,

---

[1] A 'gemelot' occurs at Nottingham in 1416 (Add. MS. 33985) but I have not found the word elsewhere.　　[2] Penshurst MS. 57.

[3] *Finchale Priory* (Surtees Soc.), ccclvi.　　[4] Mercer, op. cit. 178–92.

[5] E. 503, 11.　　[6] London Bridge Accts. 1381–2, m. 10.

[7] Ibid., vol. i, f. 25.　　[8] Ibid., vol. ii, f. 357.

[9] E. 469, 11.　　[10] H.C. 240, f. 17.　　[11] E. 503, 12.

[12] T.R., f. 15.　　[13] E. 459, 22.　　[14] E. 471, 3.

which became 'drift-pin' and also 'dribble'[1]—defined by Halliwell (*Dict. of . . . Archaic Words*) as 'an iron pin; a carpenter's term'. Six 'thorough-dryuell' of iron, at 3*d*. each, appear at Cambridge in 1338;[2] 2 iron 'dry-uelles' at York in 1399;[3] and 2 'drewills', again at Cambridge, in 1432.[4]

The two remaining tools of *The Debate*—the 'groping-iron' and the 'gowge'—seem to have been similar tools in the nature of concave-bladed chisels. Richard de Brigges, a carpenter of York, in 1327 bequeathed, among other things, '*j hachet et j wymbell cum meliori meo grophirne*',[5] and in 1363 at Hadleigh we find 'a *gropeire*, a great chisel, a small chisel, a rod (*virga*), a plate with a bolt of iron bought for a great *lathe* for the carpenters'.[6] The 'pole lathe', in which a one-way rotary motion was produced by a cord passed round the spindle and operated alternately by a treadle below and a spring pole above the lathe,[7] was known from very early times. There was 'a great lathe for the carpenters' at Dover in 1320;[8] at Windsor in 1351 we find 2*s*. spent '*in quodam ferro ad quandam rotam ad vertendum chapitreux*',[9] that is to say, for turning the capitals of the wooden pillars for the screens and stalls in St. George's Chapel. Next year, at Westminster, 2*s*. was paid 'for a sharp instrument with 2 great bolts (*clav'*) for the lathe for cutting boards crescent-shape (*lunaliter*) and joining'.[10] 'A lathe for the carpenters' shop' appears in a number of Westminster inventories,[11] while at Shene we have in 1444 'a lathe with fittings (*apparatu*), brought from Sutton, and a long lathe',[12] and thirty years later 'a lathe for the joiners, with fittings'.[13]

For the final smoothing of woodwork the medieval equivalent of sandpaper seems to have been the rough skin of the dog-fish, as 'a skin called *hundysfishskyn* for the carpenters' was bought, for 9*d*., at Westminster in 1355.[14] This also appears at Windsor four years earlier: '*in j pelle piscis canini pro operibus stall'—vjd.*'[9]

Finally, we have the glue-pot, which makes a rare appearance at Westminster in 1386, as '*olla plumbea pro glutine*'.[15] But while references to the pot are very scarce, those to glue are very common. It was usually made from fish-sounds. So in 1348 we have 18*d*. paid 'for 100 soundes for making glue for the carpenters',[16] and four years later 3*s*. 'for 100 greylyngsondes for joining boards'.[10] In 1358 glue (*gluten*) was 4*d*. the pound, but 25 'fisshe-

[1] Not in *O.E.D.*　　　　[2] E. 348, 1.　　　　[3] *Y.F.R.* 18.
[4] K.H. 8, f. 66.　　　　[5] *Y.F.R.* 207.　　　　[6] E. 464, 6.
[7] See a thirteenth-century illustration in Salzman, *Industries*, 172.
[8] Pipe R. 4 Edw. II.　　　[9] E. 492, 27.　　　　[10] E. 471, 6.
[11] e.g. 1387: E. 473, 2.　　[12] E. 503, 12.　　　[13] E. 503, 19.
[14] E. 471, 15.　　　　[15] E. 473, 2.　　　　[16] E. 470, 18.

soundes' cost 2s.,[1] which seems disproportionately expensive. At Moor End payments were made in 1366 'to Brassingbourne, fisherman of Northampton, for 60 sounde of hard fish for making gleu—18d. And to William Glovere for paccheis (i.e. patches of leather) for the same—2d.'[2] 'Soundglue' is mentioned in the Pleasaunce accounts of 1452;[3] but we have also 'hornglu' at Mettingham in 1417,[4] and in London in 1421;[5] and 4 lb. of 'Norwiche glue' was bought for work at Hampton Court in 1529 for 14d.[6]

Smiths' tools are barely within the scope of our inquiry, but the smithy was so much a part of the organization of building works that we can hardly ignore them. Many, in fact most, of the tools were variations of those used by masons and carpenters, the most obviously distinctive being the anvil. This, naturally, varied considerably in size, and therefore in cost. In 1477 John Tresilian, the king's chief smith, was employed for six days, supervising the making of a great *anvile*, which was subsequently sent to Windsor.[7] One bought at Hythe in 1265 for Dover Castle cost £5,[8] but an 'anefelt', bequeathed by a Hackney smith to the works of St. Paul's in 1395, only fetched 20s.[9] The Dover account just quoted also contains an item—'for a wooden block (*trunco*) on which to put an anvil in the smithy', but whether this was the Hythe anvil is not stated. 'A block for the *stythistok*' occurs at Scarborough in 1284,[10] and '2 blocks called *stithstokes* for the smith'—evidently pretty massive, as they cost 9s.—at the Tower in 1355.[11]

A good idea of the tools in use can be obtained from the inventories drawn up when a fresh clerk of the works took charge. One such inventory of the smith's tools at Rochester in 1363[12] contains: an *anuell*, 4 *slegges* (sledgehammers), 2 large hammers, 4 small hammers, 2 *keruyngisnes* (carving, or cutting, irons), 8 *tonges*, 3 *nailtol'* (tools for making nails), a *bicorne* (properly an anvil with two horns, or cones, at its ends, for shaping iron to a curve (later the term was corrupted to 'beak-iron' and applied to the cone)), a *spentonge* (gripping-tongs: O.E. *spenn*, to clasp), 8 *punchonys*, 2 *viles* (files), a *folo^r* (?), a *wassher* (a sprinkler, made of rushes, for throwing water on the fire), a *herthstaf* (poker), a *grindston* with an iron for it, 2 *bolsters* (plates with holes in them, placed under a piece of

[1] E. 472, 4.                                    [2] E. 544, 33.
[3] Dy. of Lanc. Misc. Bk. 11, f. 31.
[4] Add. MS. 33985, f. 103v.                      [5] Bridge Accts., vol. ii, f. 467.
[6] H.C. 239, f. 126.
[7] E. 496, 17.            [8] E. 462, 23.         [9] E. 473, 8.
[10] E. 482, 1.           [11] E. 471, 10.        [12] E. 465, 28.

iron which is to be pierced), a pair of bellows, a *toyer* (the iron vent-plate of the bellows).

With this list may be compared two Shene inventories, for 1444 and 1473. The first of these[1] contains: a *handhamer*, a *naylehamer*, 5 *maundrell* (iron cones round which iron is forged), 6 iron bolsters specially made (*ordinat'*) for 6 *maundrelles*, a *chesell*, . . . 4 maundrells for *garnettes* (hinges), an iron *gouge*, 2 *colde chiselles*, 2 *colde punchons* (i.e. used on cold metal), a *paylerne* (?) for the *lokyers*, 2 *bryttyrons* (cutting tools of some sort) for the same, 2 *dappelyng ponchons*, 4 *ponchons* of another shape, a *clenchyng-hamer*, 4 *fyles* called *querettes*, a great square *fyle*, an iron *bolster* for the *lokyers*.

The later inventory[2] contains: a pair of *smythesbelowes*, 2 iron hammers called *slegges* . . . a pair of *stelyng tonges*, 2 iron *naile tooles*, a *cove yron* (a hollowed tool, possibly a gouge), a round iron *maundrill*, 4 square iron *maundrill* for making *jemewes* (hinges), 4 instruments for the smiths, namely, a *herthstaffe*, 2 iron *aundeuill'* (anvils), and a *wesher*, 2 worn-out files, a worn-out *hote yrons* (?), a *filyng stake* of wood bound with iron (probably a post on which tools were rested for filing).

Almost all the tools mentioned above recur in other building accounts, but as a rule the entries record nothing more than the fact of their purchase or manufacture and no useful purpose would be served by repeating them here.

[1] E. 503, 12.                                    [2] E. 503, 19.

# XXII

## CARRIAGE

IN all building operations, except the construction of the simplest type of buildings from absolutely local materials, the cost of carriage was a considerable item in the accounts. As an example we may quote the expenses of three years' work at Vale Royal Abbey, summarized by Professor Knoop and Mr. G. P. Jones,[1] where, out of a total expenditure of £1,526 nearly £350, was spent on carriage of stone and over £25 on carriage of timber and lime. It is obviously impossible to lay down any even approximately general proportion, as the cost would vary with the distance that the materials had to be carried and with the facilities for carriage, and would be affected by the consideration whether the carts employed belonged to the employer or were hired. Usually the accountant is content to enter the number of cartloads and the rate per cart, rarely mentioning even the distance involved. An exceptional entry was made in connexion with certain lead purchased for Windsor in 1363, in order to explain its high cost: 'For hire of two wagons (*plaustrorum*), each of 10 oxen, carrying the said 24 fothers of lead from Caldstanes in Nitherdale by high and stony hills and by miry (*profundas*) roads to Burghbrigge (Borough Bridge), about 20 leagues, namely, for 24 days, each wagon with the men for it taking 3s. a day—£7. 4s.' Carriage from Borough Bridge to York, by land and water, was at 2s. 4d. the fother; and the carriage of 40 fothers by sea from York to London cost another £26. 13s. 4d.[2] Unfortunately the entry does not state how many journeys were made by the wagons: at a guess, I should hazard a load of 4 fothers, or tons, to each wagon, taking five days to come loaded and three days to return empty, involving three trips. For the carriage to Windsor of the great alabaster reredos made at Nottingham in 1367 ten carts, each with eight horses, were employed for seventeen days.[3] But land carriage involving such long journeys was exceptional.

So far as possible water carriage was employed for the transport of stone and heavy timber. Something has already been said about the importance of water carriage, and the significance of this factor in the development of architectural styles would be brought out by a detailed study of the sources

---

[1] 'The Building of Vale Royal Abbey', in *Ars Quatuor Coronatorum*.
[2] E. 598, 9.  [3] Pipe R. 41 Edw. III.

of the stones employed in surviving medieval buildings. References to the use of various types of vessels, the use of particular waterways, and the purchase of material by the shipload are numerous, but need not be accumulated here. In 1233 we find the monks of Canterbury receiving permission to carry six shiploads of stone—probably Caen stone—down the Thames for the completion of their refectory.[1] For the works of the Guildhall in 1415 the Mayor and Council of London were allowed to have 4 boats and 4 carts to carry 'ragge' stone, lime, and freestone;[2] and in 1444 John Hardy, mason of London, and James Palden, mason of Laughton (Yorks.), were licensed to use their ships for the forwarding of the work of the monastery of Sion,[3] but whether, as contractors, they actually owned ships or only chartered them does not appear. When Sir John Fastolf was building his castle in Norfolk he received, in 1443, a grant— that is to say, protection from seizure—of two ships called 'playtes', a 'cogship', a ship called a 'farecost', and 2 'balingers'.[4] The 'farecost' was a type of cargo-boat which occurs with some frequency in connexion with stone-carrying. For instance, in a Westminster account of 1380 there are payments 'to Simon Cristemasse, mariner and merchant, for a *navata farcostata* of grey stone', and 'to Adam le Pipere of Hoo, *farcostario*, for a *farcostata* of stone.[5] In 1315 a ship of Clays de Donkyrke called a 'farcost', laden with Flemish tiles for sale, was lying off the Tower when a quarrel broke out, in which one of the crew was killed;[6] and in 1350 John Lorkyn was paid 'for a ship called *farcost* bringing timber from the wynwarf to the Tower, for making the lion house'. The Tower account just quoted mentions the carriage of Purbeck stone from Westminster to the Tower in a 'dong bot'; and two years earlier, in 1348, there are payments 'For carriage by water, namely, to Thomas de Slappole for his *shoute*, 2s.; also, to Godwin with his *dungebot*, and to two partners of his with two other *dungebot*, 9d.'[7] The 'shout' was a type of barge constantly employed on the Thames,[8] and the 'dungboat' seems to have been something of the same type—probably the aquatic equivalent of the dung-cart.

For the magnificent roof of Westminster Hall, constructed in 1395, the timber was worked at 'the Frame' near Farnham and then sent by land to the Thames and so down to Westminster. We have, therefore, a payment of £19. 1s. 4d. for the carriage of 26 half-beams (*xxvj di' trabes*) and

---

[1] *Close R.* 205.   [2] *Cal. Patent R.* 296.   [3] Ibid. 312.
[4] Ibid. 206.   [5] E. 468, 18.
[6] Memo. R., K.R. 105, m. 125.   [7] E. 471, 1.
[8] See Salzman, *English Trade*, 211.

26 'pendant posts' to Hamme on the Thames, 16 leagues, in two carts (*chariett*') with 16 horses, making 52 journeys at 7*s*. 4*d*. a time. Also the carriage of 26 corbels, and of 263 cartloads of timber at 4*s*. the load, 76 at 3*s*. 4*d*., and 69 at 3*s*.[1]—prices which were probably governed by the number of horses employed. At about the same time in York the carriage of 34 'damlad' of stone from Thievesdale quarry to Tadcaster by carts cost £6. 6*s*. 8*d*., and the carriage of 43 'damlad' from Tadcaster to York £8. 12*s*., the short land journey and the much longer distance by water coming alike to 4*s*. the load. On arrival at York a further 67*s*. 8*d*. was paid for 'sleddyng' the stone from 'Seint Lenard lendyng' (the wharf of St. Leonard's hospital) to the Minster yard.[2] The use of sleds is mentioned from time to time; thus, at Bristol in 1442, there are references to 'the carriage of 2 fothers of lead on a *slede*',[3] and 'the carriage of timber on *sledys* with oxen and horses'; ten years later at Cambridge 'planks and nails for a *slede*' cost 10*d*.;[4] and in 1533 the smith at Hampton Court was paid 'for 4 strakes, with 54 nayles to the same, servyng the sleddes to carry lyme from the watersyde to the workes'.[5]

When Totnes Church was being rebuilt in 1450 it was agreed that every parishioner who had a horse should use it to carry the smaller stones up from the river, the larger being carried by men[6]—evidently because the streets were not suited for wheeled traffic. At Exeter in 1393 we find 3,417 horseloads of stone bought, for £15. 14*s*. 6*d*., and 10½*d*. spent on 4 pair of 'panyerys' for carrying stone.[7] Similarly at Scarborough in 1435 there is a purchase of '2 *garthwebbes* (girths) for a *lodesadell* for the carriage of stones to the castle walls'.[8] But although pack-horses were occasionally used to carry rubble and small stuff, this was unusual, almost all the material being carried in carts of one kind or another. In the masons' lodge of York Minster in 1399 there was 'a great *kerr* with 4 wheels for carrying stone, timber, and such like, and 2 *kerres* with wheels for carrying other stones out of the lodge'.[9] The carts naturally varied in capacity, a cartload of timber, for instance, being 60 feet at London in 1425,[10] and 40 feet at Cambridge in 1532.[11] At Vale Royal in 1278 carts with one horse were paid 3*d*. a journey from the quarry, and those with two 4*d*.; each made two journeys a day, and this was possibly thought too easy money, as the pay-

[1] Add. Roll (B.M.), 27018.
[2] *Y.F.R.* 20.
[3] E. 473, 18.
[4] K.H. 11, f. 297.
[5] H.C. 238, f. 11.
[6] *Hist. MSS. Com. Rep.* iii. 345.
[7] Oliver, *Exeter*, 387.
[8] E. 482, 10.
[9] *Y.F.R.* 17.
[10] Bridge Accts., vol. iii.
[11] King's College Chapel Bk.

ments were reduced to 2*d.* and 3½*d.* respectively.¹ In the Magdalen College accounts it is noted that the *bigata*, or cartload of stone, from Taynton quarry contained 15½ ft. or more; but from Wheatley *le bigat* contained 23 feet of cut stone;² and at King's College, Cambridge, the load of stone was 20 feet in 1532. The *biga* should be a two-horse cart, but the term seems to have been applied to one with two wheels, as in a Calais account of 1468 the tumbril-men are paid 8*d.* a day, 'each working and carrying stone with one horse or mare and a *tumbrell* or with a *curta biga* called shortcart'.³ The four-wheeled cart is sometimes termed *plaustrum*—a wagon, or wain: so, at Bodmin in 1470—'for carriage of the resteris fro Lestithiell yn wenys'.⁴ For work on Gloucester Castle in 1406⁵ we have 28*s.* 8*d.* spent on

bread, ale and cheese given to various men coming from the park and doing 88 cartings of timber from the park to the castle, with their own horses and with a *brakke*, or cart, of the king's, appointed for the carriage of the said great timber. . . . And for a *brakke*, or cart, bound with iron in the fashion of a wain (*plaustri*), bought for the carriage of great timber, 33*s.* 6*d.* And for grease for the easier running (*leviori versione*) of the said cart, 6*d.*

Something similar was the '*poukwayn*, on which to carry great timber', mentioned at Westminster in 1324.⁶ 'Wheels for the *pukeweyn*' occur at Canterbury in 1276,⁷ and it is possibly the kind of wagon used for carrying 'pooks', or cocks of hay. A timber-tug, a four-wheeled frame without body-works, occurs at Leeds Castle in 1370—'2 pairs of wheels for a *tugge* whereon to carry timber'.⁸ At Guildford in 1293 we have: 'For a pair of wheels for carrying posts and great timber from the park, 5*s.* For 2 pieces of iron for (?) tyring (*luand'*) the said wheels, 5*d.* For an axle (*exa*) for the same, 1*d.*—For carrying 3 posts out of the park, with 21 men helping, and for the expense of John, a (lay) brother of Waverley, and 5 men with him with 24 oxen, for 2 days, 4*s.* 3*d.*'⁹

For lighter work handcarts, sometimes called 'croudwains', were in use. Thus we have a 'handwen' at Canterbury in 1276,⁷ and 'wheels bought for the handwayns' at Dover in 1339,¹⁰ and a 'thruste wayne' at Tickenhall in 1526.¹¹ At Newgate Gaol in 1282 there is mention of 'workmen who cleared out earth and rubbish (*robus*) with *crudweyns*',¹² and 'croudewayns' occur at Westminster in 1333¹³ and 1387.¹⁴ Barrows of various kinds were

¹ E. 484, 22.          ² *Magdalen Coll. Reg.* ii. 228.          ³ E. 197, 5.
⁴ *Camden Misc.* vii. 16.          ⁵ E. 503, 26.          ⁶ E. 469, 8.
⁷ Lambeth MS. 242, f. 29.          ⁸ E. 466, 19.          ⁹ E. 492, 10.
¹⁰ E. 462, 15.
¹¹ Exch. T.R. Misc. Bks. 250, f. 57.          ¹² E. 467, 11.
¹³ E. 469, 11.          ¹⁴ Foreign R. 11 Ric. II, m. C.

in constant use. In the stores at York in 1399 there were '10 beringberwes and 2 whelebarwes'.[1] The former, which occur at Calais in 1441, as 'hande-barwes',[2] were a form of stretcher with projecting handles, carried by two, or more, men. A large type of handbarrow was known as a 'bayard', the 'bayarders', or 'bairdores', being defined in the Vale Royal accounts of 1278 as 'men carrying with barrows (*cenouectoriis*) large stones to be carved, into the workshop and out'.[3] Apparently additional support was given to the carriers by straps from the handles attached to some kind of yoke worn by the men. At Harlech in 1286 we have 'girths (*cingulis*) bought for the bayard(ers)',[4] and at Carnarvon in 1320 '*iij couples de colers pro bayardariis*'.[5] During extensive works carried out in 1314 at Melbourne Castle the wages of 'bayarders carrying stone and mortar' amounted to over £132;[6] and '2 *baiard* for carrying stone' occur at Havering in 1374.[7] Illustrations show that a lighter type of hand-barrow commonly used had its base constructed of bars or rods; and it is presumably to this type that reference is made at Winchester in 1257, when 4*d.* was spent on five '*civeris virgeis*', a wheel-barrow (*civera rotaria*) being bought at the same time for 7*d.*[8] Similarly at Clarendon in 1316 six '*barwes de virgis*' cost 6*d.*, and two '*whelberghs*' 2*s.*[9] Boards for making barrows (*civires*) occur at Winchester in 1222,[10] and laths for '*berghows*' at Norwich in 1325.[11] At Winchester, again, in 1390 there is reference to '*cinivectoriis de virgis factis*';[12] and at Wallingford in the same year a pound of grease was bought 'for greasing the wheelbarrows (*senofactoriis rotalibus*) that they may run more lightly'.[13] At Scarborough 'whelebarowes' were made of wainscot, (i.e. oak), ash, and willow (*wanscote, asshe, sely*) in 1425.[14] Ash was bought in 1531 for making 'le drug' and 'bordebarous' at Salisbury;[15] with which entry we may compare one at Winfield in 1433 'for making the baroes and troges'.[16] The term 'trug' is still used in Sussex for a basket made of split wood: it occurs at Nottingham in 1400: 'for barrels and *truggis* for carrying water and cement'.[17] A Windsor account of 1532 records the purchase of two hundreds of 'sesoned elmyn borde' to make 'hoddis, bossis, and whele barowes'.[18] The 'bosse' has already been referred to,[19] as a receptacle of mortar; the hod was originally a pannier carried on the back. As early as

[1] Y.F.R. 17.  [2] E. 193, 4.  [3] E. 485, 22.
[4] E. 485, 27.  [5] E. 487, 3.  [6] Mins. Accts. (P.R.O.), 1, 3.
[7] E. 464, 27.  [8] E. 491, 14.  [9] E. 459, 27.
[10] E. 491, 13.  [11] Communar's Roll.
[12] Foreign R. 13 Ric. II, m. A.  [13] E. 490, 4.
[14] E. 482, 10.  [15] Clerk of Works Accts.  [16] Penshurst MS. 57.
[17] E. 477. 9.  [18] Hope, *Windsor Castle*, 264.  [19] See above, p. 338.

1208 there is a reference at Taunton to 'workmen carrying earth up out of
the ditch with hods (*hottis*)',[1] and similarly at Dover in 1226 there is mention of 'material for making steps in the ditch for the hod ways (*ad vias
hottorum*)'.[2] A later Dover account, for 1295, includes payments 'to the
hodmen (*hottatoribus*) carrying sand for the making of mortar',[3] and some
ten years earlier hodmen (*hottarii*) appear in accounts for building the
Welsh castles.[4] These hods seem to have been made of wicker; in 1295
at Cambridge we have 2*d*. spent '*in virgis emptis ad hottos*', with a further
payment to Alexander le Panermakere for making the hods,[5] and at Calais
3 '*hottes de wekere*' are mentioned in 1441.[6] That the modern type of
wooden hod, carried on the end of a long staff, was known in the sixteenth
century is suggested by an entry in the Westminster accounts for 1532 of
ash used for 'helves of hoddis'.[7]

Various kinds of baskets make an occasional appearance in building-
accounts: as, for instance, 2 'lepes'—a word which survives in 'seed-lip'—
used for carrying lime at Rockingham in 1300;[6] 8 'mawndes' employed
'for removal of rubbish (*rubell*)' at Calais in 1441;[6] and 4 'skeppis' for
carrying clay at Cambridge in 1448.[8] 'A grete beryng baskette' occurs,
again at Cambridge, in 1532,[9] and in the same year, at Westminster,
'baskettes of grene wykers for the takyng downe of tyles of howsis', at
18*d*. the dozen.[10] But these are practically domestic utensils pressed into
the service of builders rather than definite implements of the building
craft, and need not detain our attention.

[1] *Pipe R. of Bpric. of Winchester*, 68; printed '*hoccis*'.
[2] E. 462, 10.  [3] E. 462, 14.  [4] E. 485, 26; 486, 29.
[5] E. 459, 16.  [6] E. 193, 4.  [7] T.R., f. 310.
[8] King's College Mundum Bk. i, f. 85.
[9] King's College Chapel Accts.  [10] T.R., f. 11.

# APPENDIX A

IN this Appendix I have brought together a selection of passages from medieval writers and from other sources, to show the nature of the material that exists for the study of the documentary history of building. Some of these passages illustrate points dealt with in the body of my book, others show the attitude of men in the Middle Ages towards the work of contemporary craftsmen, describe buildings that have perished, or help to date those that survive. Some of the accounts of building operations carried out under particular abbots or priors may seem too much of the nature of mere catalogues; but they are inserted as a reminder of the immense amount of building activity that was constantly going on, not only in the erection of churches and great houses, but also in the building and repair of manor houses, farms, and barns. The old exaggerated idea of the personal part played by the religious as craftsmen has been exploded (see, for instance, Coulton's *Art and the Reformation*, and Swartwout's *Monastic Craftsmen*), but the importance of the great religious houses as patrons of art, and owing to their wealth and wide estates particularly of architecture, remains. The influence of the royal patron is illustrated by a selection of entries from the Liberate Rolls of Henry III (most of the architectural entries on these rolls were printed, in translation, in Hudson Turner's *Domestic Architecture*). Of bequests for building purposes, which are a common feature of medieval wills, I have only given a few typical examples. They are a source of much value for the dating of existing work in churches, and occasionally other buildings, such as bridges, but require using with considerable care. It must be remembered that, even where the bequests were not conditional on the parish, or other persons, contributing, executors quite frequently failed to carry out the terms of a will, or postponed action for a considerable time. Two well-known passages from poems are included—one from 'Piers Ploughman's Creed' and the other from Lydgate's 'Troy Book'; the first is a description of the Dominican Friary in London, the other an imaginary account of the building of Troy; but on the whole medieval romancers were rather surprisingly vague in their descriptions of such buildings as they introduce into their tales.

*675 Abingdon*

The minster of Abingdon that Heane, the first abbot, built was on this wise:—
It was 120 ft. long and was rounded at both the west and the east end. This
minster was founded in the place where the monks' cellerage is now, so that the
altar stood where now is the lavatory (or laundry?). All round this minster
were 12 cells (*habitacula*) and as many chapels, and in the cells were 12 monks,
who fed, drank, and slept there; nor did they have a cloister (*clausum*) as they
now have, but they were surrounded with a high wall.

*Hist. Mon. de Abingdon*, ii. 272.

*c. 690 York*

The church formerly built at York by King Edwin, by advice of Paulinus,
lacked a roof, and its walls, half-ruined and threatening complete ruin, served
only for the nesting-place of birds. The bishop [St. Wilfrid], moved by grief
at this unworthy state of affairs, strengthened the masonry, raised the roof, and
when it was raised protected it from injury by storms with leaden sheets. In the
windows light came through thin linen cloths or a fretted slab (*multiforatilis
asser*); he made glass windows. Age and variations of weather had destroyed
the neatness (*decorem*) of the masonry; he whitewashed it with shining lime.

Ripon also experienced the industry of the bishop, a new church being built
there from the foundations, with marvellous curve of arches, courses of stones,
and adornment of porches.

Will. Malmesbury, *Gesta Pontif.* 216.

*c. 700 Hexham*

It is marvellous how many buildings [Wilfrid] brought to perfection, with
walls of imposing height and surrounded with divers winding spiral passages
(*diversis anfractibus per cocleas circumducta*); many by his own judgement, but also
by the advice of the masons whom the hope of liberal reward had drawn hither
from Rome. It was then commonly said among the people, and even recorded
in writing, that never had there been such a building on this side of the Alps.
Now those who come from Rome say the same thing, that those who see the
building at Hexham would swear that they could fancy the pride of Rome was
here. So little have the ravages of time and war robbed the buildings of their
beauty.

Ibid. 255.

*c. 700 Malmesbury*

When Aldhelm came to this place quite a small church was to be seen there,
which ancient report doubtfully alleged that Meildulf had built. Aldhelm raised
a nobler church in honour of our Lord and Saviour and of the chief apostles
Peter and Paul.

Ibid. 345.

The seat of the monastery, as I have said, was in the church of St. Peter. But
. . . [Aldhelm] determined to make within the circuit of the same convent a

second church, in honour of Mary the Mother of God. He therefore made the church, and another close to the same in honour of St. Michael, of which we have seen the ruins. For the whole fabric of the greater church has remained to our own age [*c.* 1125], famous and uninjured, surpassing in beauty and size any ecclesiastical building of ancient time to be seen anywhere in England.

*Ibid.* 361.

### *c. 700 Wareham (Dorset)*

There [Aldhelm] made a church in which, when his companions were busy, he might commend to God his journey [to Rome] and his return. Of this build-ing the stone walls (*maceriae*) still remain standing empty and open to the sky above them; save that a piece projects over the altar to keep the consecrated stone from the fouling of birds. [Tradition that, however hard it rains, no drop ever falls within its walls; so shepherds are in the habit of sheltering from storms therein.[1]]

*Ibid.* 363.

### *c. 700 Bruton (Somerset)*

[Aldhelm returned from Rome, bringing] an altar of shining white marble, six feet in thickness, four feet in length and three palms in breadth, with a lip projecting from the stone, and beautifully carved round the edge. A camel, so it is said,—for what animal of our land could carry such a burden?—was its bearer as far as the Alps. [The altar and the camel's back were both broken, and both miraculously restored by the saint, but the break in the marble is still visible.] He gave the altar to Ine, who placed it for the service of the Mother of God in a royal vill called Briwetune, where it stands to this day [*c.* 1125], a liv-ing proof, so to speak, of the sanctity of Aldhelm. There is there also another larger church in honour of St. Peter, which tradition not lightly asserts was built and consecrated by the blessed man. The east front of this has lately been en-larged in accordance with the modern taste in building.

*Ibid.* 374.

### *c. 870 St. Albans*

The churches of St. Peter on the north, St. Stephen on the south, and St. Michael on the west [Abbot Wulsin] piously built in part, both for the adorn-ment and for the use of the neighbourhood, and for the salvation of souls.

*Gesta Abbatum,* i. 22.

### *c. 900*

[Abbot Ealdred destroyed the ancient remains of Verulamium.] The whole tiles and stones fit for building which he found he put aside and reserved for the fabric of the church. He intended, indeed, if circumstances permitted, to pull

---

[1] This tradition suggests that the church had the high walls and narrow span typical of very early work: in a driving storm such a place might well remain dry though unroofed.

down the old church and build a new; for which reason he dug deeply into the ground to find stone buildings. . . . But Ealdred, when he had already collected a great quantity both of stones and tiles and of timber for the fabric of the church, cut off by too early death, went the way of all flesh, leaving the work unfinished.

*Gesta Abbatum,* i. 24.

### c. 935  Exeter

King Ethelstan first brought this city under the power of the English, driving out the Britons, and fortified it with towers and surrounded it with a wall of squared stones.

Will. Malmesbury, *Gesta Pontif.* 201.

### c. 950  Glastonbury

There is there a wooden church with stone ends, of which no lying tradition asserts that King Ine was the founder. This [Dunstan] extended a great space by adding a tower; and that its breadth might square with (*conquadraret*) its length he added what are called aisles or porches. So our hero labours wholeheartedly in order that, so far as the plan of the ancient building permitted, the church might be immense on every side. And if there is a certain lack of lovely beauty, there is no want of needful space. The cemetery of the monks on the south side of the church he enclosed with a wall of masonry stretching many feet. With squared stones he converted this space into a burial-place (*tumulum*), and it seems like a most charming meadow, remote from all noise of passers-by, so that it may justly be said of the holy men who lie there—'Their bodies are buried in peace.'

*Vita Sancti Dunstani,* 271.

### c. 955+  Abingdon

[King Edred] took such an interest in the church that with his own hands (*per se*) he measured out the sites of the buildings and laid the foundations, intending to erect there a monastery of famous renown. And he would have done as he intended if Fate had not snatched him away. However, [Abbot] Athelwold went on with what had been begun, but before he had put the finishing touch to the business he was removed to the see of Winchester by King Edgar. Ordgar, promoted by him to the abbacy, completed the undertaking of his master.

Will. Malmesbury, *Gesta Pontif.* 199.

### c. 968  Ramsey

[St. Oswald of Worcester sends Ednoth to Ramsey]—and there he at once hired craftsmen and rebuilt on a larger scale the [little wooden] chapel that he found, and also erected the necessary monastic offices on a beautiful plan, according to the method and design already shown to him by the saint.

[German is made prior in 968] and all the following winter they prepared whatever it was foreseen that masoncraft would require, both in iron and wooden tools, and all things that seemed needful for building. When at last winter had passed and spring raised her flower-garlanded head, there is an out-pouring of accumulated treasure, picked craftsmen are hired, the length and breadth of the church to be built are measured out, the foundations are laid full deep by reason of the marshy nature of all that district and are beaten with repeated blows of rams into a solid mass strong enough to bear the weight. The workmen therefore, inspired by fervour of devotion and by love of pay, go on with the work; while some carry stones others make mortar and others send up both these materials on high with a windlass (*rotali machina*). . . . Two towers rose above the ridges of the roofs, of which the smaller at the west front of the church offered a beautiful sight from afar off to those who came into the island, while the larger, in the midst of the cruciform (*quadrifidae*) building, leant upon four columns linked together by arches carried from one to the other so that they should not spread and collapse (*ne laxe defluerent*). A building sufficiently remarkable according to the standard of building used in those ancient times.

*Chron. Abb. Rameseiensis,* 39.

### 970 Ely

[Brythnod, the first abbot] then manfully turned his attention to his church, which, formerly ruined by the Danes, he strove with high endeavour to bring to perfection. For what had partly fallen he, not without great labour, set up again as new; and then, when the roofs which had been burnt were repaired, the church rebuilt appeared no less noble and notable than in former times.

Thomas of Ely (*Anglia Sacra*, i. 604).

### c. 985 Ramsey

One day when [the monks] rose in the morning, behold! there was visible to those who looked a crack in the wall of the higher tower, gaping from the top to the bottom, which seemed to threaten utter ruin in its fall to all the rest of the whole church joined onto it. And this disastrous injury, whether it came from the weakness of hurried work or from default of too weak a foundation, had certainly occurred through the lack of foresight of the masons. . . . [The monks appeal to their patron, Duke Aylwin, who comes to see it.] The leaning portion struck the minds of those who considered it with fear. The opinion of masons is asked; they all assert that the default of too soft a foundation was the cause of the injury, and that it is not possible to consolidate the shattered building without taking down the whole of the discredited erection. . . . Leave, therefore, having been given, the brethren, hiring workmen, attack the tower from the roof and, a certain stubborn pride lending strength to their labours, leave not one stone standing upon another on the ground. Examining into the cause of all this disaster, on the removal of the soil to a greater depth, they realize the faultiness of the foundation. Then they fill up the cavity anew with a mass of stones more firmly compact with pounding of rams and with tough mortar, and building upon this rejoice in the outcome of their daily labour.

*Chron. Abb. Ramesiensis*, 87–8.

### —1065 *Westminster Abbey*

> Now [Edward the Confessor] laid the foundations of the church
> With large square blocks of grey stone;
> Its foundations are deep,
> The front towards the east he makes round;
> The stones are very strong and hard;
> In the centre rises a tower,
> And two at the western front,
> And fine and large bells he hangs there.
> The pillars and entablature
> Are rich without and within;
> At the bases and the capitals
> The work rises grand and royal,
> Sculptured are the stones
> And storied the windows;
> All are made with the skill
> Of a good and loyal workmanship.
> And when he finished the work
> With lead the church completely he covers.
> He makes there a cloister, a chapter-house in front,
> Towards the east, vaulted and round,
> Refectory and dormitory,
> And the offices around.

*Lives of Edward the Confessor* (Rolls Ser.), 244.

### c. 1066 *Durham*

There were in the White Church, in which [the body of St. Cuthbert] had originally rested, two stone towers, as those who have seen have told us, projecting high into the air, the one containing the quire, the other standing at the west end of the church. Those were of wonderful size and carried on their summits brazen (*aerea*) pinnacles; which were an exceeding marvel and a cause of great wonder to all; so that they thought that no such building could be made elsewhere, because all the things needful therefor could certainly not be found within the closer bounds of the immediate neighbourhood in one place in like manner.

*Reginaldi Dunelm. Libellus* (Surtees Soc.), 29.

### 1067+ *Canterbury*

The city of Canterbury was set on fire by the carelessness of some persons, and the rising flames caught the mother church thereof . . . and the whole was consumed. . . . This was that very church which had been built by the Romans, as Bede bears witness in his history, and which was duly arranged in some parts in imitation of the church of the blessed Prince of the Apostles, Peter. . . . The venerable Odo had translated the body of St. Wilfrid from Ripon to Canterbury and had worthily placed it . . . in the great altar which was constructed of rough stones and mortar close to the wall at the eastern end of the presbytery. After-wards another altar was placed at a convenient distance before the said altar and dedicated in honour of our Lord Jesus Christ. . . . To reach these altars a crypt which the Romans call the confessionary had to be surmounted by means of several steps from the quire of the singers. This crypt below was fashioned in the likeness of the confessionary of St. Peter's, the vault of which was raised so high that the part above could only be reached by many steps. . . . Thence the quire of the singers extended westwards into the body (*aula*) of the church and was shut off from the multitude by a proper enclosure. In the next place, beyond the middle of the length of the body, there were two towers which projected beyond the aisles of the church. The south tower had an altar in the midst of it, dedicated in honour of blessed Pope Gregory. At the side was the principal door of the church . . . called the 'Suthdure' and often mentioned by this name in the law-books of the ancient kings. . . . The other tower, on the north, was built in honour of St. Martin, and had about it cloisters for the use of the monks.

The [west] end of the church was adorned by the oratory of Mary the blessed Mother of God; which was so constructed that access could only be had to it by steps. At its eastern part there was an altar. . . . When the priest performed the divine mysteries at this altar he had his face turned to the east, towards the people who stood below. Behind him to the west was the pontifical chair constructed with handsome workmanship of large stones and masonry (*cemento*) . . . set against the wall surrounding the building. . . .

When [Lanfranc] came to Canterbury and found that the church of the Saviour, which he had undertaken to rule, was reduced to almost nothing by fire and ruin, he was filled with consternation. . . . He pulled down to the ground all that he found of the burnt monastery, whether of buildings or the wasted remains of buildings, and having dug out their foundations from under the earth, he built in their stead others which greatly excelled them both in beauty and size. He built cloisters, cellarer's offices, refectories, dor-mitories, with all other necessary offices, and all the buildings within the precinct (*curia*) as well as the walls thereof. As for the church, which the said fire, combined with its age, had rendered completely unserviceable, he set about to destroy it utterly and erect a more noble one. And in the space of seven years he raised this new church from the very foundations and nearly completed it.

Eadmer, quoted and translated by Willis, *Archit. Hist. of Canterbury Cathl.* 9–16.

*1076  Canterbury*

A little while before, fire had destroyed the buildings of his cathedral church; piles of fallen walling and fragments of roofs lay in ruinous heaps. [Lanfranc], after clearing away the old foundations, re-erected all on a larger scale; whether with greater speed or beauty it is hard to say. For the speed of his industry increased the splendour of his design. And he housed the monks in buildings, cramped and ill-ordered at first, but afterwards splendid and well designed.

Will. Malmesbury, *Gesta Pontif.* 69.

*1085+  London, St. Paul's*

[Maurice, appointed Bishop in 1085.] Truly a sign of his generosity is the church of the Blessed Paul at London, which he began. It is of such magnificent beauty that it is worthily numbered amongst famous buildings. Such is the breadth (*laxitas*) of the crypt, such is the spaciousness of the upper building, that it would seem to be large enough for any crowd that could be brought together. Therefore, as Maurice was a man of vast ambition, he passed on the burden of this laborious work to his successors. At last, when Richard, who succeeded him, had assigned all the rents of the see to the building of the church, supporting himself and his dependants from other sources, he seemed to effect practically nothing. Wherefore the energy which he had at the start of his episcopate slackened as years went on, in desperation, and little by little died away.

Ibid. 146.

*—1088+  Wells*

[Bishop Giso (1061–1088)] increased the number of the canons in the church of Wells, and made for them a cloister, dormitory, and refectory.

A Canon of Wells (*Anglia Sacra*, i. 559).

[Bishop John of Tours (1088–1122)] destroyed the cloister and other noble buildings made by Bishop Giso for the use of canons, and forced the expelled canons to dwell among the townspeople.

Ibid. 560.

*1089  Gloucester*

On the feast of the Apostles Peter and Paul (29 June) this year the foundation of the church of Gloucester was laid, the venerable Robert, Bishop of Hereford, setting the first stone, by the agency of the Lord Abbot Serlo.

*Hist. Mon. Gloucestriae*, i. 11.

[The church which Serlo built was dedicated 15 July 1110: ibid. 12.]

*1091  Abingdon*

The abbot decided to enlarge the sanctuary (*oratorium*) of the old church. The foundation of the work was laid, and they were preparing, with less care than was necessary, to unite the new work to the old tower on its east side, where the attached chapel had been taken down; its foundations were everywhere shaken and disturbed, and on Friday, 28 March, 1091, while the brethren were attending the nightly service in the place where the chapter was held and had just finished the third lesson, the tower fell in a marvellous manner. For when they had assembled in the church to perform these 'vigils' the prior, moved by divine inspiration, had instructed the convent to withdraw from there and go into the chapter-house near the tower;—collapsing suddenly, it spread abroad so dense a cloud of particles of masonry that the lights burning where the brethren were singing were all extinguished.

*Hist. Mon. de Abingdon*, ii. 23.

### 1091  *Winchcombe and London*

There were thunderstorms and whirlwinds. On 15 October at Winchcombe a bolt (*ictus*) from heaven struck the tower of the church with such force that a hole was opened about the size of a man, entering by which it struck a great beam and scattered its fragments all over the church, and even threw down the head of the Crucifix with the right arm and the image of St. Mary. At this time also winds, blowing from all quarters in a way marvellous to relate, began on 17 October to blow so violently that they shattered more than six hundred houses in London; churches were reduced to heaps (*cumulabantur*) with houses, and stone walls with those of timber (*parietibus*). . . . The fury of the wind lifted up the roof of the church of St. Mary which is called at Bow (*ad Arcus*) and crushed two men there. Rafters and beams were carried through the air, and of these rafters four of 26 ft. in length when they fell in the public street were driven with such force into the ground that they scarcely stood out 4 ft. and, as they could in no way be pulled out, orders were given to cut them off level with the ground.

*Ann. Mon.* i. 5.

### 1093+  *Lindisfarne*

[The monk Edward] built from the foundations a new church within the Island in honour of St. Cuthbert, which he completed with the finest workmanship, of stones laid in courses (*tabulatis*) with wonderful regularity, by his own industrious labour and the generosity of the faithful. But because on the Island an insufficient quantity of stones could be found, he obtained from the neighbouring villages wagons and yokes of oxen with carts, and so with much trouble he accumulated a great quantity of stones. The neighbours also, out of devotion to St. Cuthbert, were always ready to lend him the aid of their strength and many times, uniting their forces, to drag loads over the wet sands. The stones, indeed, which are on the Island are reduced to dust by the vapour of the foam of the surging sea and fall into little bits like sandy pebbles; wherefore they are not good enough for such a work, except that they could be used to help in small portions of the masonry on the inside.

*Reginaldi Dunelm. Libellus* (Surtees Soc.), 45.

*1093 Winchester*

This year, in the presence of almost all the bishops and abbots of England, on 8 April, with great joy and honour, the monks came from the old monastery at Winchester to the new. On the feast of St. Swithin a procession was made from the new monastery to the old and they brought the shrine of St. Swithin and placed it in the new [church]. Next day, by order of Bishop Walkelin, men began to break up the old monastery; and it was all broken up in that year except one chapel (*portico*) and the high altar.

*Ann. Mon.* ii. 37.

[Bishop Walkelin began to rebuild the church in 1079: ibid. 32.]

*—1094 Bury St. Edmunds*

[Abbot Baldwin] with careful consideration orders stones to be brought from the quarries; he calls together stoneworkers (*latomos*); he invites architects (*architectos*); he hires masons and men skilled in the art of sculpture. Then, when the foundations have been laid, the work, noble and delightful to look upon, is happily begun.

*Mems. of St. Edmunds*, i. 155.

By order of the elder King William he laid the foundations and began a more artistic (*artificiorem*) and more beautiful church, wrought with work of columns, vault and marble (*columnari testudinali marmorali opere fabrefacta*), than which many who have seen it declare that they have never seen one more handsome and delightful.

Ibid. 351.

*1094+ Norwich*

[Bishop Herbert Losinga] bought for a great sum a large part of the town of Norwich and, having torn down houses and levelled the ground for a great space, built in an excellent position on the river Yare (*Gerne*) a most beautiful church in honour of the most high Trinity, in memory of that [abbey of Fécamp] of which he had been a monk, adding also spacious offices for the requirements of the monks whom he placed there to serve God in that church, which he constituted the chief and mother seat of the bishopric of Norfolk.

*Chrons. of Stephen, &c.* (Rolls Ser.), iv. 123.

*1099+ Durham*

[Bishop Ranulf Flambard] concerned himself with the work of the church with greater or less energy according as money from the offerings to the altar and burial fees flowed in or was lacking. For with these funds he had built the nave of the church, with its outside walls, up to the roof. But his predecessor, who began the work, had laid it down as a principle that the bishop should build the church out of his own income, and the monks should build their monastic offices out of the church offerings. Which rule died with him. For the monks, neglecting the building of their own offices, pressed on the work of the church, which Ranulph found already built as far as the nave. . . . The cramped precincts (*angustias curiae*) of the monks he enlarged, extending their dimensions in length and breadth. . . . Though nature had made the city a fortress, he made it stronger and more imposing with a wall. He made a wall extending in length from the chancel of the church to the keep of the castle. The space between the church and the castle, which had been occupied with a number of hovels, he reduced to a bare and open field, so that the church should be untouched by the contamination of filth or dangers of fire. He linked the parted banks of the river Wear by building an arched bridge of massive stonework. And he founded a castle [at Norham] on the crest of a precipitous rock overlooking the river Tweed.

Monk of Durham (*Anglia Sacra*, i. 708).

### 1102+ *Old Salisbury* (*i.e. Old Sarum*)

[Bishop Roger] made these buildings, wide spreading in extent, lavish in costliness, most beautiful in appearance. So accurately adjusted is the setting of the stones that the joints confound observation and one would mistakenly assert that the whole was a single rock.[1] He so remade the church of Salisbury and so enriched it with ornaments that it yields to none in England and excels many.

Rudborne (*Anglia Sacra*, i. 275).

### —1109+ *Canterbury*

At Canterbury [Prior Ernulf] rebuilt the fallen west end (*priorem partem*) of the church, which Lanfranc had erected, so magnificently that nothing of the kind could be seen in England for its blaze of glass windows, for its glitter of marble paving, and its painting of many hues.

Will. Malmesbury, *Gesta Pontif.* 138.

[Prior Conrad] magnificently completed the chancel of the church which the venerable Ernulf, his predecessor, had left unfinished, and when finished he adorned it with noteworthy painting, and so adorned he enriched it with precious ornaments.

*Anglia Sacra*, i. 137.

### 1113 *Worcester*

[Bishop Wulstan died 18 Jan. 1095 and was buried in the cathedral.] He lies between two pyramids with a fair stone arch over. A beam projects above, which has fixed in it iron network which they call spiders' webs. This I have mentioned because it is material to the following miracle. Several years after his death fire, coming by misadventure from the town, completely burnt the

---

[1] An interesting reference to the introduction of the fine-jointed masonry which distinguishes later Norman work.

roof of the church. As the fire raged the planks (*asseres*) were charred by the molten lead, and then rafters large as whole trees burnt and fell to the ground. What could escape the fire within the church the downfall of all this mass broke and shattered. Amid this destruction the tomb of the saint was not only hidden safe from the fury of the flames, but not discoloured by either the heat or the ashes. And, to increase the miracle, the matting whereon worshippers were wont to prostrate ·themselves before the tomb was found unharmed. The beam also which I have said projected over it was found whole so far as it stood out from the stonework, but the part which the stone enclosed, the stone itself perishing, was reduced to ashes.

Will. Malmesbury, *Gesta Pontif.* 288.

### 1114+ *Merton Priory (Surrey)*

Gilbert the Sheriff freehandedly built the said church, with the assistance of his household, and diligently engaged in the new building; at one moment with the Prior perambulating the place, now tracing out the site of the church, now measuring the bounds for the cemetery, and now to what point the mill should be removed, and where walls should be built. Thus, with the assistance of neighbours on all sides, the appearance of the place day by day became ameliorated, and many wooden chapels were there at the same time constructed. . . . The Convent was now transferred to the new building [in 1117]. This was two years and almost five months after the time when the Prior had entered the limits of the place; and on 3 May, being the day on which the Lord's Ascension was celebrated, the Brethren, who were now fifteen in number, entered the place of their new habitation.

Heales, *Recs. of Merton*, 6.

### c. 1115 *Yarmouth*

There was at that time on the seashore at Yarmouth a small chapel, in which divine service was celebrated only during the season of the herring fishery; for there were not then more than four or five small houses provided for the reception of fishermen. The Bishop [Herbert] besought King Henry [I] for leave to build a church on the same sands. The desired licence being obtained, he built a church there.

Register, D. & C. Norwich: quoted *Norf. Arch. Soc.* vii. 226–7.

### 1130 *Canterbury*

King Henry caused the church of Christ at Canterbury to be dedicated with splendour: the church blazed with lights, and every altar was assigned to a separate bishop, so that when all together began the chant *Terribilis est locus iste* and the peal of bells sounded forth wonderfully, the noble king, not restraining himself for joy, swore with his royal oath 'by the death of God' that truly it is aweful.

*Ann. Mon.* iv. 19.

*1138 England*

This year Bishop Henry caused to be built a house like a palace, with a very strong tower, in Winchester; also the castles of Merdon, Farnham, Waltham, Dunton, and Taunton; Roger, Bishop of Salisbury, the castles of Salisbury, Sherborne, Devizes, and Malmesbury; the Earl of Gloucester strengthened Gloucester, Bath, Bristol, Dorchester, Exeter, Wimborne, Corfe, and Wareham; Brian [Fitz-Count] Wallingford and Oxford; Bishop Alexander, Lincoln; John Marshal, Marlborough and Ludgershall; Geoffrey de Mandeville, the Tower of London and Rochester. There was no one of any position in England who did not make or strengthen his stronghold.

*Ann. Mon.* ii. 51.

*c. 1140 Durham*

[Roger, the Prior] designed to lay the pavement of the church with marble; for as he had heard that churches visited by pilgrims in lands beyond the seas were glorious with beautiful work of this kind, he decided, for the glory of St. Cuthbert, to adorn his church with a similar scheme of decoration. Wherefore he spoke to various devout persons who were going on pilgrimage and earnestly desired them to bring back with them bits of marble stones for the work.

*Reginaldi Dunelm. Libellus* (Surtees Soc.), 155.

*1150 Meaux Abbey*

The Earl of Albemarle . . . caused to be erected a great building, though of wretched masonry (*ex vili cemate*), where the bakehouse is now situated, so that the convent should come and dwell therein until he should make more convenient arrangements for them. He made also a chapel beside the said building, which is now called the cellarer's chamber, where all the monks afterwards used to sleep (*decubabant*) in the lower solar (*inferiori solario*) and in the upper they devoutly celebrated divine service.

*Chron. Mon. de Melsa*, i. 82.

[*c.* 1155] The chapel of which mention has been made above, which then served as place of worship and dormitory for the monks, was too constricted for so many monks to dwell and chant (*psallerent*) in. Abbot Adam and the monks erected that building, where now our malt is made, out of the planks which came from the wooden castle [of William Fossard at Montferrant, destroyed by the king's orders]; and in the same way they for a long time used the upper part of this for a place of worship and the lower for a dormitory.

*Ibid.* 107.

*1153+ Durham*

[Bishop Hugh de Puiset] began to build a new work at the east end of the church. Columns and bases of marble were brought from overseas. But when many were appointed masters—to their danger, from the misfortunes which befell them,—and the work had as many fresh starts as masters, after great sums had been spent on workmen and the walls had risen to scarcely any height, at last it fell into ruin, and it became clear that it was not acceptable to God and his servant St. Cuthbert. So, leaving that work, he began another at the west, in which there should be admission for women, who, though they had no actual access to the privacy of the holy places, might have some comfort from the sight of them. . . . In the castle of Durham he renewed the buildings which had been burnt at the beginning of his episcopate; and the castle of Norham, which he found weakly fortified, he strengthened with a mighty tower. At Allerton also he founded a fortress (*oppidum*), and obtained leave from the King that it, alone among the adulterine castles which were then ordered to be destroyed throughout England, should be privileged to be untouched. But later the King ordered that it should be thrown down and razed to the ground.

Geoff. of Coldingham (*Anglia Sacra*, i. 722).

### c. 1155 Scarborough

A cliff of stupendous height as well as mass and unapproachable, with precipitous rocks on almost every side, is thrust forward into the sea, by which it is entirely surrounded except for a narrow neck, as it were, which appears on the west; it has on its summit a beautiful grassy plateau, covering something like 60 acres or more, and a little stream of running water flowing out of the rock. On the neck, to which access is gained only with difficulty, the royal keep is set; and under the same neck is the beginning of the town, which stretches out either side to south and north but has its front to the west, and on its front is protected by its own wall, but on the east by the castle cliff, which on each side is washed by the sea. So Earl William, since he had great possessions in Yorkshire, considering this place suitable for building a castle, assisting nature with elaborate workmanship, surrounded the whole plateau of the cliff with a wall and erected a keep on the narrow neck; and when, in course of time, this fell down, the King ordered a great and famous citadel to be built there.

Will. Newburgh, *Chron. of Stephen, &c.* i. 104.

### c. 1170 Gloucester

When Roger, Bishop of Worcester, was celebrating mass at the high altar in the monastery of St. Peter at Gloucester, it happened that the great and high tower of the church, through a defect in the foundations, suddenly crashed (*corruisse*) to the ground at the very moment that mass was completed (*confectionis*) . . . so dense a cloud of dust from the shattered stones and mortar filled the whole church that for some time no one was able to see or even to open their eyes, . . . yet from all this great downfall no one received any injury. For while the tower stood at the extreme west end of the church, at that moment all, both men and women, had drawn near to the high altar for the Bishop's blessing.

Giraldus Cambrensis, *Opera*, vii. 64.

In the year of grace 1174, by the just but occult judgement of God, the church of Christ at Canterbury was consumed by fire, in the forty-fourth year after its dedication, to wit, that glorious quire which had been so magnificently completed by the industry of Prior Conrad.

In the aforesaid year, on the nones (i.e. 5th) of September, at about the ninth hour, and during an extraordinarily strong south wind, a fire broke out before the gate of the church and outside the walls of the monastery, by which three cottages were half destroyed. From thence . . . cinders and sparks carried aloft by the high wind were deposited upon the church and being driven by the fury of the wind between the joints of the lead remained there among the half-rotten planks and . . . set fire to the rotten rafters: from these the fire was communicated to the larger beams and their braces, no one yet perceiving—for the well-painted ceiling below and the sheet-lead covering above concealed between them the fire that had arisen within.

Meantime the three cottages being destroyed, . . . everybody went home again. But, beams and braces burning, the flames rose to the slopes of the roof, and the sheets of lead . . . began to melt . . . and the flames beginning to show themselves, a cry arose in the churchyard:—'See! see! the church is on fire!' Then the people and the monks assemble in haste, they draw water, they brandish their hatchets, they run up the stairs, full of eagerness to save the church, already, alas! beyond their help. But when they reach the roof and perceive the black smoke and scorching flames that pervade it throughout, they abandon the attempt in despair, and thinking only of their own safety make all haste to descend.

And now that the fire had loosened the beams from the pegs that bound them together, the half-burnt timbers fell into the quire below upon the seats of the monks; the seats, consisting of a great mass of woodwork, caught fire, and thus the mischief grew worse and worse. And it was marvellous, though sad, to behold how that glorious quire itself fed the fire that was destroying it. For the flames, multiplied by this mass of timber and extending upwards full 15 cubits, scorched and burnt the walls and more especially injured the columns of the church.

*   *   *   *   *   *   *   *

In this manner the house of God . . . was made a heap of ashes and laid open to all the injuries of the weather. The people were astonished that the Almighty should suffer such things and, maddened with excess of grief and perplexity, they tore their hair and beat the walls and pavement of the church with their heads and hands, blaspheming the Lord and his saints, the patrons of the church.

*   *   *   *   *   *   *   *

So the brethren remained in grief and sorrow for five years in the nave of the church, separated from the people only by a low wall. Meantime the brotherhood sought counsel as to how the burnt church might be repaired, but without success; for the columns of the church, commonly termed the *pillars*, were exceedingly weakened by the heat of the fire and were scaling in pieces and hardly able to stand, so that they frightened even the wisest out of their wits. French and English craftsmen were therefore summoned, but even these differed in opinion. Some undertook to repair the columns without mischief to the walls above. On the other hand there were some who asserted that the whole church must be pulled down if the monks wished to be safe. This opinion, true as it was, tormented the monks with grief. . . . However, among the other workmen there had come a certain William of Sens, a man active and ready and as a craftsman most skilful in both wood and stone. Him therefore they retained, on account of his lively genius and good reputation, and dismissed the others. And to him and to the providence of God was the execution of the work entrusted. And he, . . . carefully surveying the burnt walls in their upper and lower parts, within and without, did yet for some time conceal what he found necessary to be done, lest the truth should kill them in their present state of faint-heartedness. But he went on preparing all things that were needful for the work, either of himself or by the agency of others. And when he found that the monks began to be somewhat comforted, he ventured to confess that the pillars rent with fire and all that they supported must be destroyed if the monks wished to have a safe and excellent building. At length . . . they consented, patiently if not willingly, to the destruction of the quire. And now he addressed himself to the procuring of stone from beyond sea. He constructed ingenious machines for loading and unloading ships, and for lifting masonry and stones. He delivered moulds for shaping the stones to the sculptors who were assembled and diligently prepared other things of the same kind. The quire . . . was pulled down, and nothing else was done in this year.

As the new work is of a different fashion from the old, it may be well to describe the old work first and then the new. . . . I will first describe the work of Lanfranc; beginning from the great tower, not because the whole of this church has been destroyed, but because part of it has been altered. The tower, raised upon great pillars, is placed in the midst of the church, like the centre in the middle of a circle. It had on its apex (*pinna*) a gilt cherub. On the west of the tower is the nave or *aula* of the church, supported on either side upon eight pillars. Two lofty towers with gilded pinnacles terminate this nave. A gilded *corona* (i.e. a circular chandelier) hangs in the midst of the church. A screen with a loft (*pulpitum*) separated the tower from the nave and had in the middle, on the side towards the nave, the altar of the Holy Cross. Above the *pulpitum*, and placed across the church, was the beam which sustained a great cross, two cherubim, and the images of St. Mary and St. John the Apostle. . . . The great tower had a transept (*crucem*) from each side, to wit, a south and a north transept, each of which had in the midst a strong pillar; this sustained a vault which sprang from the walls on three of its sides; the plan of the one transept is exactly the same as that of the other. The south transept carried the organ upon its vault. Above and beneath the vault was an apse (*porticus*) extending towards the east. . . . Between this apse and the quire the space is divided into two, that is, for the few steps by which the crypt is reached, and for the many steps by which the upper parts of the church are reached. . . . [And the same on the north, where was 'the place of martyrdom' of St. Thomas.] The pillar which stood in this (north) transept, as well as the vault which rested on it, was taken down in process of time . . . that the altar on the place of martyrdom might be seen from a greater distance. Around and at the height of the said vault a passage was constructed from which hangings and curtains might be suspended. From the transept to the tower, and from the tower to the quire, many steps ascended. There was a descent from the tower into the south transept by a new entrance. Also a descent from the tower to the nave through a double door. Thus much for the church of Lanfranc. . . .

Now that the quire of Conrad, so gloriously completed, has been in our own days miserably consumed by fire, my pen shall attempt its description. . . . Let us begin therefore with the aforesaid great tower, which, as already explained, is placed in the midst of the whole church, and proceed eastwards. The eastern pillars of the tower projected as a solid wall and were each formed into a round semi-pillar. Hence in line and order were nine pillars on each side of the quire, nearly equidistant from each other; after these, six in a circuit were arranged circularly, that is from the ninth on the south side to the ninth on the north, of which the two extreme ones were united by the same arch. Upon these pillars, both those in the straight line and those in the circuit, arches were turned from pillar to pillar; above these the wall was set with small blank windows. This wall, on either side, bounding the quire, met the corresponding one at the head of the church in that circuit of pillars. Above the wall was the passage which is called *triforium*, and the upper windows. This was the termination upwards of the interior wall. Upon it rested the roof and a ceiling decorated with excellent painting. At the bases of the pillars there was a wall built of marble slabs, which, surrounding the quire and presbytery, divided the body of the church from its sides which are called aisles (*alae*). This wall enclosed the quire of the monks, the presbytery, the high altar dedicated in the name of Jesus Christ, the altar of St. Dunstan, and the altar of St. Elfege. Above the wall, in the circuit behind and opposite to the altar, was the patriarchal seat formed out of a single stone, in which . . . the archbishops were wont to sit during the solemnities of the mass, until the consecration of the Sacrament; they then descended to the altar of Christ by eight steps.

From the quire to the presbytery were three steps; from the pavement of the presbytery to the altar three steps, but to the patriarchal seat eight steps. At the eastern horns of the altar were two wooden columns, gracefully ornamented with gold and silver, sustaining a great beam, the extremities of which rested on two of the pillars. This beam, decorated with gold, sustained the Lord in glory (*majestatem domini*), the images of St. Dunstan and St. Elfege, and seven chests, covered with gold and silver, filled with relics of divers saints. Between the columns stood a gilded cross, surrounded by a row of sixty transparent crystals. In the crypt, under the altar of Christ, stood the altar of the Holy Virgin Mary. . . . This crypt occupied precisely the same space . . . as did the quire above it. In the midst of the quire hung a gilded *corona* carrying four and twenty wax lights.

The exterior wall of the aisles was as follows. Beginning from the *martyrium* of St. Thomas, that is the transept of Lanfranc, and going east as far as the upper crossing, the wall contained three windows. Opposite to the fifth pillar of the quire the wall received an arch from it and turning to the north formed the north transept. The breadth of this transept extended from the fifth to the seventh pillar; for the wall going northwards from the seventh pillar, as from the fifth, and making two apses, completed the transept on the east side. In the southern apse was the altar of St. Stephen, under which in the crypt was the altar of St. Nicholas. In the northern apse was the altar of St. Martin, and under it in the crypt the altar of St. Mary Magdalene. . . . From this apse of St. Stephen, the wall going east had a window opposite the side of the high altar. Next came a lofty tower, placed as it were outside the said wall, which was called St. Andrew's tower, from the altar of St. Andrew therein, below which in the crypt was the altar of the Innocents. From this tower the wall proceeding, slightly curved and opening into a window, reached a chapel which extended eastwards at the end of the church opposite to the high seat of the archbishop. [The similar course of the southern exterior wall is then described, until it] arrived at the aforesaid chapel of the Holy Trinity at the end of the church. An arch, springing from each wall, that is from the south and the north, completed the circuit. . . . In the middle of this chapel there stood a column which sustained arches and a vault that came from all sides. . . .

The master began, as I stated long ago, to prepare all things necessary for the new work and to destroy the old. In this way the first year was taken up. In the following year, after the feast of St. Bertin (Sept. 5, 1175) before the winter, he erected four pillars, that is, two on each side; and after the winter two more were placed, so that on each side were three in order, upon which and upon the exterior walls of the aisles he framed seemly arches and a vault, that is three *claves* on each side. I put *clavis* for the whole *ciborium* because the *clavis* placed in the middle locks up and binds together the parts which converged on it from every side. With these works the second year was occupied.

In the third year he placed two pillars on each side, the two extreme ones of which he adorned with marble columns placed round them, and because at that point the quire and transepts were to meet, he constituted these principal pillars. To which, having added the keystones and vault, he interspersed the lower triforium from the great tower to the said pillars, as far as the crossing, with many marble columns. Over which he adjusted another triforium of other materials and also the upper windows. And in the next place, three *claves* of the great vault, namely, from the tower as far as the crossing. . . .

In the summer of [the fourth year], beginning from the crossing, he erected ten pillars, that is five on each side. Of which the two first were adorned with marble columns to correspond with the other two principal ones. Upon these ten he placed the arches and vaults. And having completed on both sides the triforia and upper windows, he was, at the beginning of the fifth year, in the act of preparing with machines for the turning of the great vault, when suddenly the beams broke under his feet and he fell to the ground, stones and timber accompanying his fall, from the height of the capitals of the upper vault, that is to say fifty feet. Thus sorely bruised by the blows from beams and stones, he was rendered helpless alike to himself and for the work, but no other person than himself was in the least injured.

The master, thus hurt, remained in his bed for some time under medical care . . . but his health amended not. Nevertheless, as the winter approached and it was necessary to finish the upper vault, he gave charge of the work to a certain ingenious and industrious monk, who was the overseer of the masons; an appointment whence much envy and malice arose, as it made this young man appear more skilful than those of higher rank and position. But the master lying in bed commanded all things that should be done in order. And thus was completed the ciborium between the four principal pillars. In the keystone of this ciborium the quire and transepts seem as it were to meet. Two ciboria on each side were formed before the winter, when heavy rains beginning stopped the work. In these operations the fourth year was occupied and the beginning of the fifth.

The master, perceiving that he gained no benefit from the physicians, gave up the work and returned to his home in France. And another succeeded him in charge of the works: William by name, English by nation, small in body, but in workmanship of many kinds acute and honest. He in the summer of the fifth year finished the transept on each side, and turned the ciborium which is above the high altar, which the rains of the previous year had hindered, although all was prepared. Moreover, he laid the foundation for the enlargement of the church at the east end, where a chapel of St. Thomas was to be built. . . . The master William began, on account of these foundations, to dig in the cemetery of the monks, from whence he was compelled to disturb the bones of many holy monks. These were carefully collected and deposited in a large trench, in the corner between the chapel and the south side of the infirmary. Having formed a most substantial foundation for the exterior wall with stone and cement, he erected the wall of the crypt as high as the bases of the windows. Thus was the fifth year employed and the beginning of the sixth,

In the beginning of the sixth year from the fire, when the works were resumed, the monks were seized with a violent longing to prepare the quire, so that they might enter it at the coming Easter. And the master set himself manfully to work to satisfy the wishes of the convent. He constructed with all diligence the wall which encloses the quire and presbytery. He erected three altars in the presbytery. He carefully prepared a resting-place for St. Dunstan and St. Elfege. A wooden wall to keep out the weather was set up transversely between the penultimate pillars at the east and had three glass windows in it. . . . [So the monks, after being in the nave 5 years 7 months and 13 days] returned into the new quire in 1180, on 19 April, at about the ninth hour of Easter Eve. . . . In the same summer, of the sixth year, the outer wall round the chapel of St. Thomas, begun before the winter, was raised as far as the turning of the vault. And the master had begun a tower at the east end, outside the circuit of the wall as it were, the lower vault of which was completed before the winter. The chapel of the Holy Trinity, above mentioned, was then levelled to the ground; this had hitherto remained untouched out of reverence to St. Thomas, who was buried in the crypt. [The bones of various saints and archbishops were removed.] The translation of these Fathers having been thus effected, the chapel with its crypt was destroyed to the very ground; only that the translation of St. Thomas was reserved until the completion of his chapel. . . . In the meantime a wooden chapel . . . was prepared around and above his tomb. Outside of this a foundation was laid of stones and cement, upon which eight pillars of the new crypt, with their capitals, were completed. The master also carefully opened an entrance from the old to the new crypt. Thus the sixth year was employed, and part of the seventh.

The differences between the [old and the new] work may now be enumerated. The pillars of the old and new work are alike in form and thickness but different in length. For the new pillars were lengthened by almost 12 feet. In the old capitals the work was plain, in the new is exquisite sculpture. There the circuit of the choir had 22 pillars, here 28. There the arches and everything else were plain, or sculptured with an axe and not with a chisel; but here almost throughout is appropriate sculpture. No marble columns were there, but here are innumerable. There in the circuit around the choir the vaults were plain, but here they are arch-ribbed and have keystones. There a wall set upon pillars divided the transepts from the quire, but here the transepts are separated from the quire by no such partition and converge together on one keystone, which is placed in the middle of the great vault which rests on the four principal pillars. There, there was a ceiling of wood decorated with excellent painting, but here is a vault beautifully constructed of stone and light tufa. There, there was a single triforium, but here are two in the choir and a third in the aisle of the church. All which will be better understood by inspection than by any description.

The new work is higher than the old by so much as the upper windows of the body of the quire, as well as of its aisles, are raised above the marble tabling. And as in future ages it may be doubtful why the breadth which was given to the quire next the tower should be so much contracted at the end of the church, it may not be useless to explain the causes thereof. One reason is that the two towers of St. Anselm and St. Andrew, placed in the circuit on each side of the old church, would not allow the breadth of the quire to proceed in the direct line. Another reason is that it was agreed and necessary that the chapel of St. Thomas should be built at the end of the church where the chapel of the Holy Trinity stood, and this was much narrower than the quire. The master, therefore, not choosing to pull down the said towers and being unable to move them entire, set out the breadth of the quire in a straight line as far as the beginning of the towers. Then, receding slightly on either side from the towers and preserving as much as he could the breadth of the passage outside the quire, on account of the processions which frequently pass there, he gradually and obliquely drew in his work, so that from opposite the altar it might begin to contract, and from thence, at the third pillar, might be so narrowed as to coincide with the breadth of the chapel of the Holy Trinity. Beyond these, four pillars were set on the sides at the same distance as the last but of a different form; and beyond these, other four were arranged in a circle, and upon these the superimposed work (of each side) was brought together and terminated. This is the arrangement of the pillars. The outer wall, which extends from the said towers, first proceeds in a straight line, is then bent into a curve, and thus in the round tower the wall on each side comes together in one and is there ended. All which may be more clearly and pleasantly seen by the eyes than taught in writing.

Now let us carefully examine what were the works of our mason in the seventh year from the fire; which, in short, included the completion of the new and handsome crypt, and above the crypt the exterior walls of the aisles up to thin marble capitals. The windows, however, the master neither would nor could turn, on account of the approach of the rainy season. Neither did he erect the interior pillars. . . . In this eighth year the master erected eight interior pillars and turned the arches and the vault with the windows in the circuit. He also raised the tower up to the bases of the highest windows under the vault. In the ninth year no work was done, for want of funds. In the tenth year the upper windows of the tower, together with the vault, were finished. Upon the pillars was placed a lower and an upper triforium, with windows and the great vault. Also was made the upper roof, where the cross stands aloft, and the roof of the aisles as far as the laying of the lead. The tower was covered in and many other things done this year (1184).

### GERVASE OF CANTERBURY

[Gervase's account has been translated by Prof. Willis in his *Architectural History of Canterbury Cathedral* (ch. iii), and I have followed this translation, with a few unimportant verbal alterations. In order to condense it, I have omitted passages referring to the position of various tombs and shrines and other matters of not strictly architectural import.]

### 1176 *London Bridge*

This year the stone bridge of London was begun by Peter, chaplain of Cole-church.

*Ann. Mon.* ii. 240.

### 1195+ *St. Albans*

[Abbot John (1195–1214)] threw down to the ground the wall of the front of our church, built of ancient tiles and enduring mortar. . . . He began to bring together beams and to accumulate no few stones, with columns and slabs. Very many chosen masons were summoned together, over whom was Master Hugh de Goldclif—a deceitful and unreliable man, but a craftsman of great reputation (*praeelectus*); the foundations were dug out, and in a very short time a hundred marks, and much more, not counting the daily allowances of food, were spent and yet the foundation wall had not risen to the level of the ground. It came about by the treacherous advice of the said Hugh that carved work (*caelaturis*), unnecessary, trifling, and beyond measure costly, was added; and before the middle of the work had risen as high as the water-table (*tabulatum domitialem*) the abbot was tired of it and began to weary and to be alarmed, and the work languished. And as the walls were left uncovered during the rainy season the stones, which were very soft, broke into little bits, and the wall, like the fallen and ruinous stonework, with its columns, bases and capitals, slipped and fell by its own weight; so that the wreck of images and flowers was a cause of smiles and laughter to those that saw it. So the workmen departed in despair, their wages not paid them for their work. But the abbot, not despairing, placed Brother Gilbert de Eversolt over the work as warden, and assigned to the work one sheaf from every acre of land sown. And this lasted from the time when it was first given, namely the third year of his abbacy, all his life, 17 years, and about 10 years in the life of the following abbot; nor did the unlucky work ever show any visible advance. . . . The years, then, passing uselessly so far as that work was concerned and Brother Gilbert de Eversolt dying, the wardenship of that dead or dying work came to the hands of Brother Gilbert de Sisseverne, who was in charge of it about 30 years; and he applied the above-mentioned funds to the work, but during all his period of office scarcely achieved two feet of increase altogether.

*Gesta Abb.* i. 219.

[The same Abbot John] pulled down the old dark and dilapidated refectory and began a new and very beautiful one, which he had the good fortune to bring to a happy conclusion in his lifetime and to feast joyfully with the brethren therein. He caused the old dormitory, ruinous and tottering from age, to be pulled down, with its annexes, namely the necessary house, and built a new and splendid one in its place and completed it in every detail faultlessly.

*Ibid.* 220.

## —1197+ *Meaux Abbey*

Under Abbot Thomas (1182–97) William son of William de Rule, rector of Cotyngham, began the stone-built refectory of the monks and at his own expense completed it as it appears at the present time. And Abbot Thomas himself built the warming-room and kitchen little by little as he was able.

*Chron. Mon. de Melsa*, i. 217.

Abbot Thomas began a new church, and as much of it as had already been built [by Abbot Philip (1160–82)] he pulled down because it was unsatisfactory in plan and construction. But afterwards his successor Alexander, the fourth abbot (1197–1210), destroyed this same new building and began to rebuild afresh the existing church.

*Ibid.* 234.

Abbot Alexander completed the lay brothers' refectory, begun by Abbot Thomas, and began the upper building, namely their dormitory. He also commenced the stone cloister of the monks and made a new necessary house for them. . . . And when he had completely torn up all the work which his predecessors had done towards building our church, in 1207, on Palm Sunday, which was 15 April, the first stone in the foundations of the new church was laid by Abbot Alexander himself, and so he commenced the church as it appears at the present time.

*Ibid.* 326.

## c. 1200 *Beverley*

There was at that time in the midst of the crossing of the church a very high tower erected [by Archbishop Kinsi, *c.* 1050], of astonishing beauty and size, so that in it were combined the cunning and achievement of mason-craft. The building of this tower had gone so far that the stonework was finished, and it only remained for its completion to set up on it a roof of stonework of proportionate height. The craftsmen who were in charge of the work were not as cautious as was necessary; not as prudent as they were cunning in their craft; they were concerned rather with beauty than with strength, rather with effect than with the need for safety. When they set up the four piers (*columnas cardinales*) as supports to carry the whole mass, they let them into the old work ingeniously but not firmly, in the manner of those who sew new cloth into old. Whence it came about that they made neither the bases nor the shafts of the columns of such strength as would suffice to carry the enormous mass of so wonderful and hazardous a construction; and although their weakness could easily be seen, as the work proceeded, by the gaping cracks of the parts and by the splitting of some marble columns from base to capital, yet they did not consider it necessary to desist from proceeding with the work they had begun, though it is clear enough that that building which is set upon a weak foundation is bound to fall. So the more they piled up an increasing heap of stone, so much the more did they hasten the downfall of the tower, the cracks in the bases and shafts became the more enormous the more they rashly overweighted them. At last it came about that from fear of the threatening ruin a great part of both clergy and people abstained from entering the church. [In October a priest, unable to sleep, rang the bell for matins an hour too soon. When the canons assembled a number of stones fell from the tower; they left their stalls and, after a second fall of stones, went to the west end of the nave and finished the service there. Hardly had they returned to their houses, when the whole tower collapsed.]

*Hist. of the Church of York* (Rolls Ser.), i. 345.

### 1214+ St. Albans

First indeed [William, 22nd Abbot (1214–35)] completed in admirable manner the dormitory, with the privy house (*secretiori domo*) belonging to it, with beds of oaken timber, and assembled the convent therein. Moreover in his time the roofs of both aisles of the church were strengthened with oaken timber excellently tied and joined with rafters; for previously they were so eaten up with rot and decay that they let in much rain. The summit also of the tower, which stretches out like some huge scaffold (*machinae*), was built of the best timber well joined and raised much higher than the old, which was threatening to fall. And all these, at no small cost, were covered with lead. And these things were brought to perfection by the care and diligence of Richard de Thidenhanger, a monk of our convent and Chamberlain, without neglect of his office; but they are to be ascribed to the Abbot, out of respect. For he by whose authority anything is done does it.

But after the death of that same Richard of blessed memory the abbot himself caused the tower to be stripped, because it was improperly covered, and with the addition of no small quantity of lead had it re-covered more properly and thoroughly, adding ornaments on the sides, namely eight raised strips stretching from the cap (*tholo*) to the parapet (*murale*), so that the octagonal shape of the tower might show more clearly; all at his own expense, by the advice of Dom. Matthew of Cambridge, then his personal attendant and seal-bearer. Which was evident from the fact that he was put over the work as agent, superintendent and careful warden. And he changed the covering into that kind which has horizontal conical projections (*quae ex transverso conos protendit*). And the above-mentioned strips, which are commonly called 'herring-bones' (*aristae*) both strengthened the tower wonderfully and when so strengthened adorned it and kept out the rain more completely; for formerly, through the blending of the eight sides (*costis*) it stretched out its smooth graceful and slender shape less properly and less in accord with the parapet.

And the [west] front of the church, after [it had suffered] a most damaging collapse, Abbot William, with sorrow and regret, because it had dragged on with such tedious delay, took upon himself to carry out to completion. And within a short time he had brought it up to the old work, with a roof of seasoned (*praeelecta*) timber, rafters and beams, with tie-beams (*laquearibus*), and with glass windows, complete in every detail, properly covered with lead.

Of the windows also which are in the stretch of wall above the place where the great Ordinal lies and where those who have been bled are wont to sing Mattins and Hours, he prepared the stonework with the glazing; moreover, with the assistance of the warden of the altar of Saint Amphibalus, he completed the stonework and glazing of very many others in the north and south aisles of the church; so that the church, illuminated with the gift of fresh light, seemed almost like new.

In his time also, when Master Walter of Colchester then sacrist—an incomparable painter and sculptor—had completed, out of the funds of the sacristy but by the diligence of his own labour, a quire-screen in the middle of the church, with its great Rood and Mary and John and other carvings and adornments, Abbot William himself solemnly transferred the shrine with the relics of St. Amphibalus and his companions from the place where it had formerly stood, namely behind the high altar near the shrine of St. Alban, on the north side, to a place which is enclosed in the middle of the church with a dividing iron grating (*pariete ferreo et craticulato*), building there an admirable altar with frontal (*tabula*) and super-altar most exquisitely painted.

　　　*　　　*　　　*　　　*　　　*　　　*　　　*　　　*

And because the walls on all sides [of the chapel of the Blessed Virgin] were awry and misshapen from their damaged and ruinous state the Abbot at his own expense restored all that was ruinous; and besides this he completed a piece of chiselled stonework (*opus ex incisa petra*) wherein to set two large glass windows, that, for the completion of his good work, all might be illuminated with fitting light; so that the church seemed in great part renewed. And over the execution of this work he put Dom. Matthew of Cambridge, his attendant, who in a short time carried out the work entrusted to him in a praiseworthy manner.

　　　*　　　*　　　*　　　*　　　*　　　*　　　*　　　*

Abbot William also beautified the church wonderfully by [putting] a roof which is commonly called 'panelling' or 'ceiling' (*labrescura vel caelatura*), with which he covered the row of beams above the said image of Mary [carved by Master Walter of Colchester] so that [the appearance] of the rafters and beams, which age had blackened, should not offend the eyes of beholders. For the same reason also he whitewashed (*dealbavit*) the greater part of the walls of the church, which the dirt and dust of ages had defiled; so that if he had completed what he began he would by a happy and pleasant change have renewed the age-worn church.

    *         *         *         *         *         *         *         *

And so it redounds to the eternal glory of his memory that he pulled down the old chapel of St. Cuthbert, whose worm-eaten roof and bulging stonework threatened to fall, and built a new one most handsomely of chiselled stone, with glass windows and all other fittings. In which he built an altar and caused it and the chapel itself to be dedicated by Bishop John [of Ardfert] in honour of SS. Cuthbert, John the Baptist, and Agnes. . . . This same chapel also, rising high above its undercroft, which is commonly called the vault (*avolta*), makes up for the contraction and deficiency of the dormitory. Moreover, into this room (*domicilium*), which contains about twelve beds, the light is admitted by many glass windows, by which it is well lit; and the roof, wrought of seasoned timber, is strengthened with a leaden covering.

    *         *         *         *         *         *         *         *

Several cloisters also he built, namely one between the Chapter House and the chapel of St. Cuthbert, so that those going by should not be annoyed and be-spattered by dripping; another, three-sided, from the kitchen to the door of the regular cloister; this he assigned to the charge of the Kitchener. This also extends on the other side from the said door of the monastic cloister to the door of the Guest-house, which further is used as the Guest-house of the Black Order; and this he assigned to the charge of the Guest Master. But the third side of the said cloister leads from the said door to the door by which the path goes to the tailory; and this he assigned to the charge of the Chamberlain. Also another cloister, four-sided, through which goes the path to the Infirmary; and this he placed in the charge of the Infirmarian. And all these he built strongly and well of oaken timber, with rafters and tie-beams (*laquearibus*), and covered them with oaken shingles. And the three-sided cloister, which extends from the kitchen to the door towards the tailory, he protected by surrounding it with a wall of wattle-work (*pariete concraticulato*), so that there should not be free access for all persons to the space in the middle, namely the little garden (*virgultum*). And that garden he arranged should belong to the Guest Master.

*Gesta Abb.* i. 280–90.

### 1220 *Salisbury*

On the day of St. Vital the martyr, which was 28 April, was laid the founda-tion of the new church of Salisbury. . . . The Bishop himself laid the first stone on behalf of Pope Honorius, who had given leave for the removal of the church of Salisbury; the second he laid on behalf of Stephen, Archbishop of Canterbury and Cardinal of the Holy Roman Church, who was at that time engaged with

the King on the Welsh border; the third he added to the fabric on his own behalf; the fourth stone William Longsword, Earl of Salisbury, who was present,
laid; the fifth Ela de Viteri, Countess of Salisbury, wife of the said Earl, a woman
worthy of praise as being full of the fear of God. After this certain nobles, but
only a few, each laid their own stones; then A. the Dean, W. the Precentor,
H. the Chancellor, A. the Treasurer; and the archdeacon and canons of the
church of Salisbury who were present. . . . In the course of time, when the nobles
came back from Wales, some of them came to this place and each laid their own
stones, binding themselves to some definite contribution during the next seven
years.

*Reg. of St. Osmund*, ii. 12.

[The new church was so far advanced by 1225 that on 28 September three altars were
dedicated, and next day service was held, the Archbishop preaching: ibid. 37, 39.]

### *c. 1235  St. Albans*

Twice within three years the church of St. Alban was set on fire by lightning,
which no one remembered to have seen before, or to have heard of. And as it is
no use to rely upon the privileges or indulgences of the Saints, so the papal seal,
on which is figured the Agnus Dei, which is placed on the top of our tower, did
not avert the lightning, although it is said to have virtue and power to drive
away such storms.

*Gesta Abb.* i. 313.

### *1235+  St. Albans*

[Abbot John] built a splendid hall for the use of guests, to which adjoin many
bedchambers; a splendid painted one, with closets (*conclavibus*) and fireplace and
porch (*atrio*) and undercroft (*subaula*); and it might be called a Royal Palace,
for it is two-storied and has a crypt. At the entrance a splendid porch adjoins it,
which is called a portico or an oriel: and many bedchambers, very handsome,
with their closets and fireplaces, for lodging guests. For the hall which was
formerly built there was ruinous, dark, and ugly, with walls falling from age.
Moreover it was roofed and covered with shingles and weather-boarding
(*lateribus*), but he caused the new hall, with its chapels and annexes, to be covered
with lead in the best fashion. Moreover, he caused it, with the bedchamber
beside it, to be properly painted and delightfully decorated (*redimiri*) by the
hand of Richard, our monk, an excellent craftsman. Also the said abbot built a
noble house, very long, of stone, covered with tiles, with three fireplaces, opposite the great gate, by the look and appearance of which the whole court is
adorned. This house has two floors (*duplicem aream*) and so it is most conveniently assigned in its upper part to the abbot's superior servants (*ministris liberiori-
bus*), and the lower part to the larderer.

*Gesta Abb.* i. 314.

### 1237 Kennington

Order to make at Kennington, on the spot where our chapel which is roofed with thatch is situated, a chapel with an upper story (*ad stagium*), of plaster, which shall be 30 feet long and 12 feet wide; in such manner that in the upper part there be made a chapel for the use of our queen, so that she may enter that chapel from her chamber; and in the lower part a chapel for the use of our household. Also lengthen the wardrobe of the chamber beneath our chamber with plasterwork (*plastricio*), and wainscot the queen's chamber beyond her bed.

Liberate R. 21 Hen. III.

### 1239 Winchester

Order to make in the castle a drawbridge with a *bretache* above it at the entry of the great tower; to repair the joists of our chamber in that tower, where our wardrobe used to be; to make a fair porch before the chapel of St. Judoc, with a bell-turret for the chapel of St. Thomas in the same castle; to panel the passage from our chamber to that chapel; to roof all the buildings in the castle; to make an enclosure there, and 2 ovens in the greater kitchen, and a fireplace in our room above the porch of the great hall. Also to cause all our stone which is at Stoneham to be carried to the castle.

Liberate R. 23 Hen. III.

### 1239 Windsor

Order to make in the castle a chamber for our use beside the wall of the castle, 60 feet in length and in width 28 feet; and another chamber for the queen's use, 40 feet in length, near our chamber and under the same roof, along the wall; and a chapel, 70 feet in length and in width 28 feet, also along the wall, but leaving a sufficient space between the chambers and the chapel to make a little grass-plot.

Ibid.

### 1240 The Tower of London

The queen's chamber to be panelled and entirely whitewashed inside and newly painted with roses; a partition wall of panelling (*parietem in modo lambruschure*) to be made between that chamber and the garderobe thereof and the same to be tiled outside. Our great chamber to be whitewashed and re-painted and all its shutters (*fenestras*) to be remade with new wood, new catches and hinges, to be painted with our arms and newly barred with iron. Also all the glass windows in the chapel of St. John the Baptist are to be repaired, and also the windows in the great chamber towards the Thames, and in the corner of the same chamber towards the east a great round tower to be made so that the lowest chamber of the tower (*turellus ultime camere*) goes down into the Thames; and a louver (*fumericium*) to be made above the top of the kitchen of the keep.

Liberate R. 24 Hen. III, m. 17.

*1242 Gloucester*

The same year was begun the new tower at the west on the south side of the church by Walter de St. John, then prior.

*Hist. Mon. Gloucestriae*, i. 29.

[This was finished *c.* 1246: ibid. 30.]

*1244 Kennington*

The gateway which the King sent from Westminster to Kennington is to be erected there in the manner in which it was formerly built within the King's court at Westminster.

*Liberate R.* 28 Hen. III.

*1245 Winchcombe*

15 December. Inquiry whether it would be to the injury of the town or of the Abbey of Winchcombe, or of anyone else, if the King should allow Master Henry, rector of the church of St. Peter of the same town, to lengthen the church 12 ft. eastwards, and to enlarge an aisle begun on the south side of the church to the length of 30 ft. and the breadth of 12 ft. [The jury] say that if the chancel were lengthened 12 ft. eastwards it would be to the damage of the Abbot and Abbey, because the Abbot could not have a free way in and out for his carts and for carrying his timber. Also they say that if Master Henry is allowed to enlarge the aisle, as aforesaid, and the wall of the church is set towards the high street, two carts would not be able to pass, and this would be very much to the damage of the town in fair-time.

*Inq. ad quod damnum*, i, no. 8.

*1246*. The King allows the Prior of Winchcombe to lengthen the chancel of his church 12 ft., provided the road to the Abbey remains 30 ft. broad; also to enlarge the aisle 30 ft. by 12 ft., provided the highway remains 18 ft. broad.

*Close R.* 462.

*1246 Kennington*

Orders to make a fireplace of plaster in the queen's chamber; to repair the glass windows in the king's chamber and chapel and in the queen's chapel; to cover the chambers of the king and queen with shingles and to repair their walls. To make a door to the chamber towards the wardrobe; two leaden gutters, and a crest of lead in the salsary; also mud walls (*muros luteos*) round the grange-dairy; and to repair the ruined kitchens, and underpin (*suppodiare*) the almonry.

*Liberate R.* 30 Hen. III.

*1246 Guildford*

Orders to make a chamber for the use of Edward the King's son, with fit windows well barred with iron, to be 50 feet in length and 26 feet in width, extending from the wall towards the field as far as the corner of the wall towards the kitchen, with a privy chamber, and in breadth from the wall towards the field as far as the almonry, so that the said Edward's chamber may be in the upper part and the chamber of the king's gentlemen-in-waiting (*vadlettorum regis nobilium*) below, with fit windows and a privy chamber and a fireplace in each room. Also below the wall towards the east opposite the east end of the king's hall a penthouse of as many bays as the length requires (*quamvis arcum compotent' tam longum*), with a fireplace and a privy chamber to (*ad*) the queen's garderobe; and in the queen's chamber a window, to extend for the breadth of the window which is now there and as much farther as it reasonably can, with two marble columns, the window to be panelled (*lambruscari*) and closed with glass windows between the columns with panels which can be opened and closed and wooden shutters in one piece (*fenestras bordeas integras*) inside to close over the glass windows. And in the king's hall the upper window to the west near the dais to be closed with white glass windows, and in one half of the glass window a king sitting on a throne and in the other half a queen also sitting on a throne.

Liberate R. 30 Hen. III, m. 17.

### 1249 Nottingham

The King to the Sheriff of Nottingham:—As you have signified to us that our chamber in our castle of Nottingham cannot be strengthened with a sound foundation, unless the roof of that chamber be taken down, we command you to remove it and rebuild it; so that a decent stone tablement (*tabulamentum*) be made on the wall, and let heads be carved on the ends of the corbels which will be above it.

Liberate R. 33 Hen. III, m. 7.

### 1249 Woodstock

Orders to crenellate the queen's chamber with freestone, and to raise the chimney of that chamber to the height of 8 feet; to panel the lower chamber, and make the privy chamber in the fashion of that chamber where Bartholomew Pecche used to sleep; to build a chamber at the gateway of Evereswell, 40 feet long and 22 feet wide, with a wardrobe, privy chamber, and fireplace. Also to repair Rosamund's chamber, unroofed by the wind; and to make a door to the queen's chamber, and a door to the old larder. Also to repair the bays of both our fish-stews and the causeway of the lower stew near the (?) enclosure (*closarium*); to put 2 windows of white glass in the gable of the hall, and 2 in the chamber of Edward our son, and 2 windows barred with iron in the old larder. To make leaden spouts round the alures of the same Edward's chamber; to repair all the buildings of each court where necessary; to bar the windows of the porch with iron; to build a house for our napery; and to pull down the rooms of William our chaplain and rebuild them between the hall and the queen's stable, making a garden (*herbarium*) on the site of the said rooms.

Ibid., m. 4.

*1250  Westminster Abbey*

Relaxation of one year's enjoined penance to penitents who assist the fabric of the church of wonderful beauty now being built by the King at Westminster.

*Cal. Papal Reg.* i. 262.

*1250  Clarendon*

Orders to make a baptistery in the chapel of All Saints there, and to put on the chapel a bell-turret with two bells, and to make a crucifix with two images on each side of wood, and an image of Blessed Mary with her Child. And let the queen's chamber be decently paved. And in the queen's hall let there be made a window towards the garden (*herbarium*), well barred with iron; and two windows in the queen's chapel, one on each side of the altar, which are to be divided down the middle so that they may be opened and shut when necessary. . . . And make a bench round our great garden (*herbarium*) beside the wall, and whitewash the wall above it. In Alexander's chamber let there be made a wardrobe with a privy chamber, and roof those buildings well. Make a garden below our chamber on the north; also a window in our wardrobe; and lengthen our chandlery by four or five couples.

*Liberate R.* 34 Hen. III, m. 5.

*1251  Guildford*

The posts of our hall which are deficient are to be mended and underpinned (*sublevari*) with good Reigate stone; the spensary and buttery to be roofed and in each a new window made; the whole roof ridge of our chamber to be remade 5 feet higher and the walls raised so that there can be made 3 glass windows similar to the new window lately made in the same bedroom. The passage between the hall and the said bedroom to be panelled and earthed over (*desuper terrari*) and better windows to be made in the passage, and the panelled bedrooms (*talami lambruscati*) to be painted green. The downstairs wardrobe (*bassa warderoba*) of the bedroom of Edward our son to be panelled and a stone vault (*vouta*) to be made in it, in which our shrines and relics can be put; and the wall between that bedroom and the almonry to be crested; and in the little wardrobe by the gate a window to be made. A new lattice (*laticium*) to be made in front of the chapel of St. Stephen, and in the chapel of St. Katherine her image and story to be painted behind the altar in a worthy manner without the use of gold and azure (*absque auro et azuro*). The wall of the castle to be well mended with columns and supports, and to be whitewashed; the lead on the keep to be mended, and the keep whitewashed. The wall outside our bedroom to be thrown down and moved 15 feet from the bedroom and rebuilt at its present height, and a herb garden made between our bedroom and the wall.

*Liberate R.* 35 Hen. III, m. 3.

### —1252 Ely

[Bishop Hugh de Northwold] built the episcopal hall in Ely, and buildings in Ditton, Shipdam and in almost all the other manors. He also built from the foundations the new work of our church at the east, which is called the presbytery; which work he completed in 17 years, and on the building of this work he spent £5400. 18. 8, besides gowns [given to the craftsmen]. He also built anew the wooden tower by the Galilee, from the masonry to the top. . . . When the new work had been built the whole church of Ely was dedicated, on 17 Sept., 1252, to the honour of Blessed Mary, Blessed Peter and Blessed Etheldreda, in the presence of King Henry III and Sir Edward his son.

Monk of Ely (*Anglia Sacra*, i. 636).

### 1253 Winchester

Orders to cause an image of Blessed Mary with her Child to be made on the front of the chapel of St. Thomas in Winchester castle; to paint the queen's wardrobe with green paint and golden stars; to paint an angel on the other side of the chapel, and the figures of the prophets round the chapel; to paint in the glass window of the chapel St. Edward with the ring; to pave the chamber of Edward the king's son with flat tiles; to put forms round the king's chamber; to put glass windows in the chapel of St. Catherine on the top of the castle; to make mats for the king's chapel; to panel the chapel of St. Catherine; to widen the doorway of the king's hall for the entrance of carts; and to make a house for the use of the chaplains dwelling in the castle in a fitting place. Also to make in the king's upper wardrobe, where his cloths are deposited, two cupboards (*armariola*) one on each side of the fireplace, with two arches (*archeris*) and a partition (*interclusum*) of board across the wardrobe.

Liberate R. 37 Hen. III.

### 1267+ St. Benet's Holme

Abbot Adam de Neteshirde 'in the second year of his rule, on 8 May, laid the foundation of the new quire (*presbyterii*) and with his own hand set the first stone with his blessing'.

Abbot Richard de Bukenham (1268–75) 'was the careful continuer of the work of the new quire, and as much of that work as his predecessor had left incomplete he, supplying what lacked, honourably brought to a perfect finish'.

J. de Oxenedes, *Chron.* 298–9.

### 1268 Clarendon

Orders to pull down the long house beside the great gateway and to make instead a chamber with a fireplace, and an outer chamber for the use of the king's esquires; to build a small gate beside the same gateway; and a good strong prison; and a house for the use of the carpenters working there; and a fireplace in the chamber over the king's cellar in the rock. To put 2 large windows in the chamber of Alexander: and the 4 evangelists in the glass windows of the King's hall. To build a long house for a pantry and buttery for the use of the queen and of Eleanor the consort of Edward the King's eldest son; and a kitchen for the queen's use, with a passage from the kitchen to the queen's chamber.

*Liberate R.* 52 Hen. III.

### 1280 Horton (Leics.)

During the dispute, which has lasted 16 years, over the church of Horton between Sir Thomas de Neville and Mr. Robert de Picheford, the chancel of the said church has fallen completely down. . . . The fruits of the benefice are to be sequestrated and given to two or three parishioners that therewith they may rebuild the chancel.

*Reg. J. Peckham,* i. 129.

### 1283 Leominster

[It being necessary to close the doors of the monastic-parochial church at night, Archbishop Peckham ordered,]—that the said monks shall build and complete within one year, outside their doors in a place suitable therefor, a decent chapel of reasonable size in honour of the glorious martyr St. Thomas, to which there may be free access for fugitives at all hours and in which the body of Christ may be honourably kept for sick parishioners.

*Reg. J. Peckham,* ii. 507.

### 1282+ Evesham

[Abbot John de Brokehampton (1282-1316)] worthily made the chapel of the Blessed Virgin Mary, with windows and handsome vaulting and gilded bosses; in which chapel were magnificently depicted the story of the Saviour and stories of various virgins. . . . He also made the chapter-house, ingeniously designed within and without, with excellent vaulting, without a central pillar (*base*), beautifully adorned with gilded bosses, and surrounded with glass windows. Which building on account of its spaciousness and beauty is held to be one of the chief of the chapter-houses of this realm. Also, that walk (*pagina*) of the cloister opposite the chapter-house, over which the monks' studies are built, was erected in his time and with his aid. Also he made a good broad dormitory, well and strongly supported on vaults from one end to the other; under which various offices are arranged, namely, the chapel master's chamber, the sacrist's chamber, the misericord, and others. The noble infirmary building, also, was erected in his time and with his aid at great expense, where there are now various chambers for the sick, built by the devotion and industry of the monks of this church, as may clearly be seen. He also gave the convent towards building the refectory £100, with all the timber. . . . All these buildings were covered with lead, except the infirmary—and of that the chapel was covered with lead. Also he made the long chamber for those who have been bled, with the vault, over which is built the ambulatory and the privy dormitory. He made also the noteworthy hall of the abbot, of which all the walls are carried out in stone, and he set up over it that roof of remarkable timber construction and covered with lead, and a porch at the door of the hall, with vaulting, and over it a house of receipt, likewise covered with lead. To this hall he attached a kitchen, which he made worthily entirely in stone. He made also a pantry beside the kitchen, and the abbot's chamber painted with the story of Joseph, with a small chapel attached to it; and under this chamber is built a strong vault, where now is the wine-cellar. Likewise he had the brewhouses and bakehouses strongly and finely built. Moreover he made two new chambers on the west of the court, with their vaults, for guests, and the cellarer's chamber, with the other joined to it well built upon an arch of stone. Also he made the long stable for guests, on the same side. The long stable on the north side of the court, assigned to officials [of the abbey], was built in his time and with his aid. The kitchener's pittancery, with a vault, and over it the hall built for guests, was erected in his time and with his aid; and he built and completed the convent kitchen, adjoining the abbot's kitchen. Also he provided eight fine granges in the manors, . . . and built the chancels of Honeybourne, Willersey, and Hampton, and the church of Norton. . . . Also he built sixteen water-mills in various manors.

*Chron. Abb. de Evesham*, 286.

### 1297+ Norwich Cathedral

In the year 1297 was begun the work of the cloister of the church of Norwich in front of the chapter-house, with the chapter-house itself, by Sir Ralph Walpole, then Bishop of Norwich, as appears by an inscription carved on a stone set on the west side of the cloister in front of the chapter-house door, which is:— '*Dominus Radulphus Walpole Norwicensis episcopus me posuit*'; and also by Richard Uppehalle, founder of the said work, as appears by an inscription carved on a stone set on the east side of the same cloister on the north of the same chapter-house door, which is:—'*Ricardus Uppehalle hujus operis inceptor me posuit*'; and there were made by them three 'civers' only, with the chapter-house; the other 5 towards the church, with its door, and towards the door leading to the infirmary and from that door to the 'civerys' in which the towels[1] hang, were made at the cost of Sir John Elys, Bishop of Norwich, and other friends, and by the office of the pittanciary, specially appointed for this; but the north part, as regards the wall by the church and the 'voltyng', was made at the cost of Henry Well, namely 210 marks, and 20$^{li}$ given to the same by Master John Hancock, and also by the said office of the pittanciary. From the towels, with the door of the refectory and the lavers, it was made at the cost of Geoffrey Simonds, rector of Marsh, namely 100$^{li}$, and from the door of the guest-house to the entry into the church, with the door of the same; and as regards the wall by the said hall and the 'voltyng' it was made by the executors of Sir John Wakeryng, formerly Bishop of Norwich. And so the work of this most famous cloister was finished

[1] Printed '*mariatagia*', but presumably it should be '*manutergia*'.

in the year 1430, in the time of Sir William Alnewyck, Bishop of Norwich, and the third year of Sir William Wursted, Prior of the same church; the time from the beginning of the work to the end being 133 years.

Will. de Worcestre, *Itinerarium*, 302.

### 1314 London, St. Paul's

The same year were the cross and ball (*pomellum*), with a great part of the bell tower, of St. Paul's church taken down, because they were weak and dangerous; and a new cross with a well-gilded ball was erected, and many relics of diverse saints were placed in the cross, for the protection of the bell tower and of the whole church lying below it, with a great procession and ceremony, by Bishop Gilbert on 4 October, that Almighty God by the glorious merit of His saints whose relics are contained in that cross may deign to preserve it from all peril of tempest.

The same year was the said church measured. And its length contains 690 feet; breadth 130 feet; height of the western vault (*testudinis*) from the pavement 102 feet. The height of the vault of the new fabric contains 88 feet. The roof-ridge (*cumulus*) of the church contains in height 150 feet. The whole church contains within its bounds 3½ acres 1½ rod 6 yards. The height of the bell tower of the church from the ground level contains 260 feet. The height of the wooden fabric of the same bell tower 274 feet. Altogether, however, it does not exceed 500 feet. The ball of the same bell tower can contain in its hollow 10 bushels of corn. The length of the cross standing above the ball contains 15 feet, and the cross-limb (*transversorium*) of the same cross is 6 feet in length.

Ann. Lond. 276.

### ? 1314 St. Albans

King Edward of Carnarvon, making a journey through St. Albans, carefully examined the old quire of the church at night, in the presence of the convent. And when the abbot mentioned to the said king his predecessor's wish to make a new quire, the king at once declared that he would like to fulfil his father's promise. And for its happy commencement he ordered 100 marks at once to be given in money, and also with gracious liberality assigned to the same work a great quantity of timber from the wood formerly belonging to the Templars of Dynesley. The abbot, therefore, took care to spend the money wisely, hiring various workmen highly skilled in carpentry, in cutting and carving; over whom he placed one Master Geoffrey by name, a cunning man, by whose industry he might bring the work to its desired conclusion. And this Master Geoffrey for many years received from the warden of the shrine and altar 4s. every week for himself and his assistant. Moreover he received a robe yearly of the suit of the abbot's squires, and another for his assistant of the suit of the palfreymen, of the abbot's gift, with many other advantages and perquisites which it would take too long to write.

Gesta Abb. ii. 124.

*1321+ Ely*

In the night before the feast of St. Ermengilde, after matins had been sung in the chapel of St. Catherine, because the convent dared not sing them in the quire on account of the threatened fall [of the tower] . . . behold! suddenly and swiftly the bell-tower crashed down upon the quire with such a thunderous noise that one might think an earthquake had occurred, but without injuring anyone in its fall. . . . [The sacrist, Alan de Walsingham] first, at great labour and expense, had the fallen stones and beams carried out of the church; and as rapidly as possible cleared it of all the dust that had accumulated. And the place where the new tower was to be built he measured out with the skill of an architect into eight divisions, in which eight stone columns supporting the whole edifice should be set up, within which the quire with its stalls should afterwards be built; and he caused it to be dug and searched until he found solid ground on which the foundations of the work could safely be laid. And when these eight places, so carefully examined, had been strongly consolidated with stones and sand, then at last he began the eight columns with the stonework above them; which, in the course of 6 years, was finished up to the highest string-course in the year of our Lord 1328. And immediately, in that year, the ingenious wooden structure of the new tower, designed with great and astonishing subtlety, to be erected on the said stonework, was begun. And at very great and heavy cost—especially for the huge beams required for that structure, which had to be sought far and wide, found with much difficulty, bought at a great price, and carried to Ely by land and water, and then cut and wrought and cunningly framed for the work by subtle craftsmen,—at last, with God's help, it was brought to an honourable and long-hoped-for finish. The cost of the new tower during the twenty years that Alan de Walsingham was sacrist was £400. 6. 11, whereof £206. 1. 0 came from gifts. The cost of the new chamber beside the infirmary, during three years, was £60. 17. 9½. The cost of the new wall by the cemetery, with the booths acquired there, together with the making of new houses, gates and walls all round the sacristy precinct, during twelve years, was £180. 13. 11¼. . . . Note, that nothing is allowed above for food and drink, horses, carts and so forth. . . . The new quire was made in the 12th year of Edward III, A.D. 1338, and the following years by Brother Richard de Saxmundham.

Monk of Ely (*Anglia Sacra*, i. 643).

*1323 St. Albans*

The same year, on the day of St. Paulinus the Bishop, after celebration of the Mass of the Blessed Virgin, occurred an accident so terrible that previous misfortunes might well be considered as little or nothing compared with its magnitude. For when there was a great crowd of men and women in the church to pray or to hear mass, suddenly two great columns of the south side of the church, giving way first from the foundation, fell successively to the ground with a terrible noise and crash. So, laity and brethren running together from all sides, stupefied with terror, to gaze upon this fearful sight, scarcely an hour had passed when, behold! the whole wooden roof, which was built upon the said columns, with beams, rafters and ties, and the aisle on the south side of the church, and almost all that side of the cloister followed in the same way. . . . But when, three days later, a crowd of servants laboured to remove the timbers, stones and lead, which lay all heaped together, one daringly climbed up on top of the walls with a crowbar (*ligone*) and as he tried to dig and throw down part of the wall hanging and on the point of falling, all that portion on which he was standing fell, carrying him with it; but although he broke his thigh and was badly wounded, yet he escaped marvellously from death, receiving no mortal injury.

*Gesta Abb.* ii. 129.

### 1326+ *St. Albans*

The almonry was built by order [of Abbot Richard] by the hands of Richard Hetersete, almoner, from the foundations, with hall, chapel, chambers, kitchen and cellar and other buildings necessary for the scholars and their masters; but this has now been destroyed, to build the new gate; for it was situated in that place where now we see the great gate stand. Also he laid the first stone in the foundation of the new cloister and of the work of the church, from the wall of the abbot's chapel towards the cloister; on which stone was written his name, with the year of Christ; and under the same stone he sprinkled the foundation with fragments of relics of Saints and with earth found with the bodies of St. Amphibalus and his comrades. And the Abbot's payment each week to his workmen was 30s., from his own means; and he did not burden his barony or his rents, as they were but slender for the needs of the house, and indeed seemed insufficient. Also he made a beautiful ceiling for the chapel of his own chamber, most pleasant to the eyes of beholders. And there are other works which he carried out, as the covering of the abbot's chamber with lead, and so forth, which to set forth would take too long.

*Ibid.* 283.

### 1339 *London, St. Paul's*

This year, about the feast of St. Luke, was removed the old screen (*pulpitum*) which stood before the entrance to the quire:—likewise the quire was transferred from the nave of the church of St. Paul, where it had stood for seven years because of the danger of the bell tower, into the new work where it now is; and on All Saints was the first celebration at the high altar and in the quire.

*Ann. Paulini*, 338.

The same year the top of the bell-tower of St. Paul's, with the cross and ball, was newly repaired; for which reason on St. Mary Magdalen's day Bishop Richard and Gilbert the Dean, with all the ministers of the church, made a solemn procession round the church and cemetery, in silk copes and barefooted. The Bishop, unshod and with great reverence and many lights in procession, carrying the relics which were found in the ball and cross, with various other relics, in a precious vessel, as far as the door of the south vaulting (*testudinis*) of the church; and there he handed over the relics to the chamberlain of the church and others of the quire who could more easily climb up to finish the business. And so the said relics were hidden in the top of the cross and its two arms and in the ball, to the honour of God and to the protection of the said bell tower. This was done by Sir Nicholas Housebonde, then overseer of the old work, and John de Clabatone, then chamberlain of the church.

*Ibid. 369.*

### 1339 Southleigh

The Bishop of Exeter to Master Simon de Fareweye, rector of Southleigh:— Whereas a chapel was formerly built adjoining the chancel of your church for the sake of a chantry of St. Catherine, the celebration of which services has long since ceased to be observed; by reason of which chapel rebuilding (*refeccio*) is more difficult, there is excessive darkness and an ugly (*indecens*) narrowness and very many other inconveniences are occasioned in the chancel, and for this reason you are unable to enlarge the chancel as you propose; we, approving your laudable purpose in this matter, give you licence that you may demolish, wholly or in part, the said chapel in order to enlarge the chancel of your church to the adornment of the sacred edifice.

Hingeston-Randolph, *Exeter Episc. Regs., Grandisson*, 908.

### 1341+ Durham

[Prior John Fossor] erected on the north side of the crossing of the church, at the altar of SS. Nicholas and Giles, a great glass window, with three other smaller windows. . . . Also he made a window of 6 lights, tall and magnificent, on the north side of the crossing of the church by the said altar, for which he paid £100 and for its glazing £52. . . . Also for a window at the south end of the prior's hall £40. . . . Also in his time were many new buildings made and old ones restored, both within and outside the abbey, and especially the kiln (*thorale*), granary, and kitchen, the great window of 7 lights at the west end of the nave of the church, and 3 others on the north of the nave, and 2 on the north of the quire, by John de Tickill, and 2 on the south of the choir by [the offerings at] the Shrine.

Will. de Chambre (*Anglia Sacra*, i. 768).

### 1341+ Durham, &c.

[Works done during the time of John Fossor, Prior of Durham (1341–74).]
First the Larder, which is called Sclauterhus; and a house for lead. Also two neat (*proprias*) chambers, upstairs and down (*altam et bassam*), and all the windows with their glass. Also his own chapel. Also a great barn for the hay of the guest-

house (*ostellariae*). Also the great stable and a forge. Also a gable of the chapel over the gate. Also a great roof (*ruf*) over the brewhouse. Also a roof over the bakehouse. Also a chamber which is called Lehum. Also a malthouse (*mallthus*). Also a great granary. Also a mill, entirely rebuilt from the ground. Also the milldam (*meldam*) of 140 feet, entirely new. Also the barn at Estrington. Also the barn at Allerton. Also at Beaurepaire two new dairies (*deyhus*), the whole 'sowtsyd' of the wood and of the wall (*murae*) round the wood, and he discovered a quarry of 'sclatstane'. Also the bridge of Beaurepaire over the Broue and a barn (at) Westflodgat. Also all the manor of Beaurepaire after the Scots had withdrawn, and a great byre (*byr*) and a sheep-cot (*cot pro ovibus*). Also the whole quire of Pittington church, and a porch (*porg'*), and he roofed the hall. Also the barn of Pittington, and a mill and a bakehouse (*bachows*). Also a stable and a dairy at Pittington. Also a great stable for palfreys and a kitchen. Also his own chamber at Pittington and the chamber of his monks there. Also in the manor of Rainton a great barn. Also the mill of Rainton. Also in the manor of Dalton a new barn. Also the hall and chamber at Dalton. Also in the manor of Heworth the hall and barn. Also a water-mill at Heworth. Also in the manor of Wyve-stowe a chapel. Also his own chamber with two latrines. Also a byre and a stable. Also a roof for the great barn. Also the gates and the mill. Also a tithe-barn at Harton. Also a new windmill at Southwike. Also a new windmill at Hesilden. Also in the manor of 'Belu' a great barn. Also a mill at 'Oventon Belu'. Also a granary and a kitchen. Also a porch over the door of his chamber. Also the hall, which had been often on the point of falling down. Also the steward's chamber. Also a granary at Belassis. Also a watermill at Billingham, and a gable of the church and a window. Also a mill at Wolston. Also a mill at Bermpton. Also at Ketton the whole of the manor, because it was in very bad condition. Also a watermill at Ketton. Also the mill at Fery. Also the mill at Merington, and a barn and byre, and a building for mules, and a kiln and a wall. Also the mill at Aclif. Also a gable of the quire at Aclif. Also the whole quire of the church of Heighington. Also the whole dam of Scaltok mills. Also the whole mill. Also a new barn at Hoghall. Also an almshouse, which is called Maysyndu. Also a row (*rau*) in Sowrbalke, by his procurement; rent [*sic*] xxxˢ. Also in the church of Durham, a great window on the north side; also a small window beside it, and a small one over the altar. Also in the street called Crossgat a 'rent' which comes to 1 marc. Also in New Elvet a tenement which now gives 6s. 8d. Also in Old Elvet 2 tenements which now give 6s. 8d.

*Hist. Dunelm. Script. Tres*, cxli.

## —1349 Ely

[Bishop Simon Montague (1337–45)] contributed many large sums towards the building of the new chapel of St. Mary on the north of his cathedral church and heartily desired to bring it to completion. But, cut off by death, he could not complete the building according to his purpose. However, he left its completion to a simple monk of Ely, Brother John de Wysbeche, who, inspired by God, had begun the chapel from the foundations, with the alms of the faithful in Christ. Now this Brother John began the building of this chapel in honour of the Virgin Mary on the feast of her Annunciation at the beginning of 1321. Of which building that venerable and skilful (*artificiosus*) man, Brother Alan de Walsyngham, then subprior of Ely, laid the first stone. . . . Now it happened that on one occasion he called together some of his fellow monks and also some laymen and desired them to come at a time agreed upon, to help him dig the four sides of the place where the foundations were to be. When the agreed time came, one night, they came and began to dig, each by himself in the place assigned to him. [Brother John dug up an urn full of money, which he concealed and used for paying the workmen.] . . . And when he had with the greatest enthusiasm continued the work for 28 years and 13 weeks, and had completed the stonework, with the images within and without the chapel, 147 in number, not counting the small images on the reredos above the altar and the images at the entrance door, and the wooden roof covered with lead, and the east gable with two windows on either side of the chapel beautifully finished with iron and glass, on 16 June, 1349, at the time of the widespread pestilence, he died, and left the control of his work to his successor free of all debt.

Monk of Ely (*Anglia Sacra*, i. 651).

### 1351+ Gloucester

Abbot Thomas de Horton (1351–77)—He built the great hall in the court, where the king afterwards held his parliament; and he built a parlour (*locutorium*) at the vineyard, and brought to completion the surrounding wall of the vineyard, which his predecessor had left unfinished. In his time . . . the high altar, with the quire, as well as the stalls on the abbot's side, was begun and finished. And the aisle of St. Paul in the abbey church of St. Peter, which was begun on the morrow of the Epiphany 41 Edward III (1367) was completed, by the grace of God, on Christmas Eve 47 Edward III (1373), of which work the total expenses came to £781. 0. 2, of which the abbot paid £444. 0. 2, as appears from the rolls of the said work. Also he set up at the entrance to the choir, on the north side, images in niches (*tabernaculis*).

Hist. Mon. Gloucestriae, i. 50.

### 1352 York

[The Chapter of the Cathedral of York . . . give notice, that, whereas Archbishop William le Zouche proposes to build a chapel of SS. Mary Magdalene and Martha on the south side of the quire of the Minster,] We . . . grant that the said venerable father, his heirs or executors, may pierce the wall of the said Cathedral adjoining the same chapel at its west end, making an arch or two arches and set doors there between the enclosures, and have free entrance and egress through the same wall, arches and doors for the masons and other workmen

engaged on building the said chapel, and for the chaplains and ministers serving there in future, . . . and also for those wishing to hear divine service there, at
reasonable times; and may freely build, construct and complete, at their own
expense, the said chapel, already begun. . . . Provided that the said venerable
father, his heirs and executors, in future support and repair at their own expense
the said chapel, when it is built, with its walls, windows, glazing, doors, roof
and roofing; for the support of which we and our successors do not and will not
make ourselves in any way responsible.

*York Fabric Rolls*, 169.

### 1354 *Windsor*

King Edward began a new building in the castle of Wyndeleshore, where he
had been born. For that reason he took trouble to adorn that place with buildings of greater size and splendour than those elsewhere. And of this work he
appointed as surveyor Sir William de Wycham, a man of foresight and judgement.

T. Walsingham, *Hist. Angl.* i. 288.

### 1372 *Durham*

Sir John de Nevill . . . made the new work of marble and alabaster under the
shrine of St. Cuthbert; for which he paid more than £200. And he caused it to
be packed in cases (*in cistulis includi*) at London and sent by sea to Newcastle, and
the Prior (had it carried) to Durham. And again, when this work was finished,
at the suggestion of Prior John and the monks, he gave for the work above the
altar, called La Reredos, five hundred pounds or marks, and the Prior and
obedientiaries 200 marks. And he caused it to be packed in cases at London and
at his own cost sent by sea to Newcastle; and the Prior had it carried to Durham.
[Prior John Fossor, before he could set it up, died at the age of 90, on Martin-
mas 1374. Robert Berrington, his successor, 'provided food for 7 masons for
nearly a year, setting up that work', and it was dedicated 'die quatuor Coronatorum', 1380.]

*Hist. Dunelm. Script. Tres*, 135–6.

### 1381 *Guisborough* (*Yorks.*)

Will of William, Lord Latimer.—To be buried in the priory church. Also I
will that my executors cause to be completed the vaulting over the aisle on the
north side of the said church as I have begun it . . . that the prior and convent of
Gisburn shall have 500 marks to make their belfry (*clocha*), provided that they
do not use it for any other purpose.

*Test. Ebor.* i. 114.

### 1388 *Effingham*

Monition to Merton Priory by Bishop William of Wykeham:—Since at each
of our visitations it was discovered and shown that the chancel of the church of
Effingham, in our diocese, appropriated to your monastery, is well known to be

in a state of great and obvious ruin as to its roof, walls and windows, as also the grave complaint of the parishioners has of late informed us, so that no one for a long time past has been able to, nor can now, celebrate divine service in the said chancel . . . We therefore . . . order and command you that before the feast of St. Michael next coming you cause the said chancel of the church of Effingham to be repaired as it requires in decent fashion; otherwise, when that term has expired, we will cause the said chancel to be repaired at your expense from the issues of the church.

*Surrey Arch. Soc.* ix. 393.

### 1389+ Durham, &c.

[Walter Skirlaw, Bishop (1389–1406).] He built the bridge of Shincliffe and the bridge of Yarum, . . . and the bridge of Auckland; he also set up at his own cost the great stone gates at Auckland, from the foundation to the top of the building. He also built the belfry of Houldon (Yorks.) of great size, which he made so that it might be a refuge for the inhabitants of that place if by chance floods should occur. He lavished great sums on the repair of the said church; and built them a very beautiful chapter-house, joined on to the church. He also built the whole hall of the manor of Houldon. . . . He also built a great part of the belfry, commonly called the 'Lantern' of York Minster, in the midst of which he set his arms. . . . He also caused a great part of the Cloister in the monastery of Durham to be made, at a cost of £600. He moreover gave for the building of the Dormitory 330 marks, and his executors gave, by his direction, for the building of the Cloister £400, and he himself had before given £200. On all of which buildings he set his arms, viz. 6 rods intertwined in the form of a sieve (*cribri*).

*Hist. Dunelm. Script. Tres*, 144–5.

### 1390+ Canterbury

Works of Prior Thomas Chillenden (1390–1411).

The nave (*navis*) of the church of Canterbury with the various parts of the steps and quire screen (*pulpiti*), with the stations of the cross and the chapel of the Blessed Virgin Mary in the same nave. . . . Also the whitewashing of the whole church, with a new chamber for the sacristy of the boys, with a chapel of St. Andrew below. Also a privy chamber, lead-covered, beside the vestry. Also the pavement on the north side of the quire remade. Also the passage (*via*) from the church to the dormitory, with the repair of the lavatory there, and underneath a new leaded shaving-room (*rastura*). Also the enclosure of the passage on either side of the cloister to the prior's chamber; and the passage from the prior's chamber to the court remade and leaded. And the repair of the drain (*gutterii*) from the cloister running by the passage which leads from the cloister to the infirmary, first by the same passage direct to the outer end of the chapter-house, thence direct outside the prior's chapel on the south side to the subprior's chamber, thence transversely through the subprior's chamber and transversely through the great hall of the infirmary, thence lengthwise through the privy chamber of the prior, and so through the chamber below the Gloriet, thence to the head of the third dormitory, and then it turns into the conduit (*aqueductum*) in the third dormitory. This drain was ancient, ruined and forgotten, but was repaired at great expense and piped (*plumbatum*) underground to a great extent. Also the repair of the dormitory with a new leaden roof and new windows and many beds. Also the roof of the privy dormitory with new windows. Also the prior's bed, with a new study and hall above, and a garderobe practically rebuilt and leaded. Also the passage from the prior's chapel to his chamber newly ceiled (*selata*) and repaired with new windows and a new fireplace. Also a new chamber below built entirely, with a new roof covered with lead. Also another chamber downstairs (*inferius*) with a chamber and a decent bath. Also upstairs (*superius*) a new privy chamber with a passage to it, leaded. Also a new place for storage (*deporto*), with a cellar underneath. Also kitchens and other requirements (*honesta*) for the four chambers in the infirmary. Also the repair of Maisteromers for the most part throughout. Also the new work in the cloister which is still not finished. Also the new chapter-house finished. Also the roof of the refectory (made) out of the old lead with the addition of twelve fothers of new lead. Also the new chamber of the cellarer, with the new school of the monks.

. . . At Oxford all the buildings, except the hall and two chambers, were rebuilt, as well as the chapel. . . .

. . . A new roof to the chancel, with glass windows, at Mounketon [          ] and the same at Birchington, and the same at Wode [          ]. . . .

. . . At Eastry a new kitchen, with a new roof to the chancel.

*Literae Cantuarienses*, iii. 114–20.

*c. 1395 London*

The speaker goes to the convent of the Dominican Friars:

| | |
|---|---|
| And whan y cam to that court | y gaped aboute. |
| Swich a bild bold, y-buld | Opon erthe hei3te |
| Say i nou3t in certeine | sithe a longe tyme. |
| Y 3emede upon that house | and 3erne theron loked, |
| Whou3[1] the pileres weren y-peynt | and pulched[2] ful clene, |
| And queynteli i-coruen | with curiouse knottes, |
| With wyndowes well y-wrou3t | wide up o-lofte. |
| And thanne y entrid in | and even-forth went, |
| And all was walled that wone | thou3 it wid were, |
| With posternes in pryuytie | to pasen when hem liste; |
| Orche3ardes and erberes | euesed well clene, |

[1] *Whou3*: how.          [2] *pulched*: polished.

And a curious cros craftly entayled,  
With tabernacles y-ti3t to toten[1] all abouten.  
The pris of a plou3-lond of penyes so rounde  
To aparaile that pyler were pure lytel.  
Thanne y munte me forth the mynstre to knowen,  
And a-waytede a woon wonderlie well y-beld,  
With arches on eueriche half and belliche y-corven,  
With crochetes on corners with knottes of golde,  
Wyde wyndowes y-wrou3t y-written full thikke,  
Schynen with schapen scheldes to schewen aboute,  
With merkes of marchauntes y-medled bytwene,  
Mo than twenty and two twyes y-noumbred.

\*     \*     \*     \*     \*       \*     \*     \*

Thanne kam I to that cloister and gaped abouten  
Whou3 it was pilered and peynt and portred well clene,  
All y-hyled[2] with leed lowe to ye stones,  
And y-paued with peynt til iche poynte after other;[3]  
With kundites[4] of clene tyn closed all aboute,  
With lauoures of latun louelyche y-greithed.  
I trowe the gaynage of the ground in a gret schire  
Nolde aparaile that place oo poynt til other ende.  
Thanne was the chaptire-hous wrou3t as a greet chirche,  
Coruen and couered and queyntliche entayled;  
With samlich selure y-set on lofte;  
As a Parlement-hous y-peynted aboute.  
Thanne ferd y into fraytour and fond there an other,  
An halle for an hey3 kinge an housholde to holden,  
With brode bordes aboute y-benched wel clene,  
With windowes of glas wrou3t as a chirche.  
Thanne walked y ferrer and went all abouten,  
And sei3 halles full hy3e and houses full noble,  
Chambers with chymneyes and chapells gaie;  
And kychens for an hy3e kinge in castells to holden,  
And her dortour y-di3te with dores ful stronge;  
Fermery and fraitur with fele no houses,  
And all strong ston wall sterne upon heithe,  
With gaie garites and grete and iche hole y-glased;  
And othere houses y-nowe to herberwe the queene.

*Pierce the Ploughman's Crede* (E.E.T.S.), 7–9.

---

[1] *to toten*: to look, or gaze.      [2] *y-hyled*: roofed.  
[3] *iche poynte after other*: probably, set diamond-wise.     [4] *kundites*: conduits.

*—1396 St. Albans*

To the making of the cloister lavatory [Abbot Thomas (1349–1396)] contributed £16. 13s. 4d. And afterwards he pulled down the wall of the Refectory adjoining the cloister, which was weak and ruinous, and caused it to be supported (*fulciri*) internally and strengthened with stouter (*grossioribus*) columns cut from large blocks of stone of Egelmounde, as is clear to all who now see it: and he placed on it the very beautiful roof which we now see; £50 and more he spent, besides the timber given for the same work of the church, the belfry and other buildings, both within the monastery and outside, built by the prior and other officials of the convent and valued at over £300.

     ★     ★     ★     ★     ★     ★     ★     ★

The Great Gate, which had been thrown down by a great wind, he built from the foundations with chambers, prisons and vaults and covered its strong roof with lead.

He built the walls also from the Hall called 'Royal' to the Almonry, which also he built from the foundations with its annexes; on the execution of this work Brother William Stubarde, John Bukkedene and John Clifford, deputies of Master Henry Yevele, laboured effectually, his monks and others assisting in praiseworthy fashion in digging stones for the same work. One thousand pounds and upwards were spent on these same works.

The Royal Hall, also, which from weakness was threatening to fall, he strengthened most excellently by adding two great supports (*fulcimentis*) of hard stone, commonly called buttresses (*boteras*); and he took down the roof, which from its dangerous height and the weakness of age seemed to threaten many perils, and set up a new one of reduced height and covered it excellently with lead and lighted it with new windows of stone and glass.

Also he built from the foundations, to the great adornment of the monastery, the chamber adjoining the wall of the church, which is called the New Chamber, near the ancient chamber of the same, for the use of noble visitors, with its appurtenances: and Dom John Mote, then cellarer but afterwards elected prior of the church, assisted with the expenses, which were reckoned at 600 marks and more.

His bakehouse also, weak from its great age, he restored most usefully, spending a great sum of money thereon; and he added for the use of the same, a vessel of bronze holding a thousand gallons.

Also he built the tower of the gate called 'Watergate', William Wyntershulle and Adam Houghton providing expenses and assistance for it; he put on a parapet (*crestavit*) of hard stone and covered the roof excellently with lead; and the cost thereof was reckoned at £157. 18s. 10d.

His kitchen also, with the chambers and other appurtenances, he built from the foundations; spending on the same work £155. 15s. 8¼d. and more.

Also he made a structure or closet (*caelaturam*) of wood within his own chamber, where his chaplains might all lie together and attend upon him better, for they previously used to lie scattered in different places; 20 marks and more were spent on the same.

Also he raised the walls of the chamber called 'the Wardrobe' and rebuilt its solar and closet (*arcam*) and roof, covered it with lead and adorned it with panelling (*coelatura*), Brother John Mote providing funds and assistance. Also he raised the pentice there and panelled (*coelavit*) the walls of the studies there, having first put up walls of stone and earth faced with plaster, and placed windows therein. And this pentice afterwards he painted brightly with the arms of various lords and with golden stars on a green background.

*Gesta Abb.* iii. 386–8.

## 1396+ *St. Albans*

This abbot [John (1396–1401)], while he had charge of the office of cellarer, besides the labours and troubles which for twenty years and more he bore in looking after the rights of the convent in that office, as has been shown to some extent amongst the doings of Abbot Thomas, built within the enclosure of the monastery a very beautiful chamber for the Lord Abbot, adjoining the aisle of the church, spending, as was said, 600 marks and more on the same work.

Also he built a chamber which is called 'the Stewards' chamber' between the Almonry and the gate which leads to the stable. Also he made a building required for storing hay, with an earthen wall extending from it to the gate which leads to the great orchard.

＊　　　＊　　　＊　　　＊　　　＊　　　＊　　　＊　　　＊

But after he undertook the office of Prior, as he had part in nearly all the offices of the convent, so he far excelled others therein. For within the enclosure of the monastery he rebuilt two parts of the cloister, with the studies and library and the chapel of St. Nicholas; and above the vault of the same cloister the library; and under the vault of the chapel of St. Nicholas he intended to make cupboards (*almariola*) in which to put the muniments of the convent, but being prevented by death he left them to be made by others.

The Dormitory and also its undercroft (*suffultoria*) he strengthened with new arches and a cresting of hard Kentish stone. And he also covered its floor with paving and placed at its end a great window of very clear glasswork. Moreover he built from the foundations the kitchen, bakehouse and brewery with chambers to keep their stores in and conveniences for the officers and servants, and provided them amply with all necessary furniture. Also he built a beautiful hall called 'the Oriole of the Convent', praised even by kings; and under it are buildings made very usefully for a larder and for the keeping of fish and storing other things. Also the cloister towards the kitchen and tailory, with the vaults and chambers built above it and in the midst a cistern, of which the bottom is stone and the wall square, crested with hard stone, in which to store the rain-water coming from the neighbouring buildings so as to cleanse the filth of the convent latrine. Also he made underground openings from the convent cemetery and the cloister garth, by which the rain water coming from the neighbouring buildings might run into the said cistern; and he made the receptacles for the water in the cloister of hard stone in the part adjoining the refectory and the wall of the studies; and he built the necessary house, commonly called the privy dormitory, than which none can be found more beautiful or more sumptuous. Also a chamber at the end of the same building, very beautiful and covered with lead, for the Lord Abbot if a great number of guests should come together; and below, a wide place in front of the vents (*foras*) of the said latrine, and under that place double chambers for the needs of the chamberlain and his tools; and under these chambers offices suitable for tailors and cobblers. Also he made for the Prior's use a chamber over the dormitory chapel, ceiled with most beautiful panelling (*tabulatu pulcherrimo seluratam*), useful for his own requirements and beautiful to behold. But because the latrine of the said chamber seemed to be too close to the chapel of the guest-house (*hostriae*) the convent was famed by many to have made a place of retirement at the horns of the altar. In the Prior's dwelling-house he carried out (*extulit*) the chapel with lofty walls, and above and beside this chapel he built very beautiful chambers; and he also greatly adorned the chapel with new windows of stone, excellently glazed, panelling (*coelaturam*) and screens (*interclausas*) excellently painted. Also he made there a cellar suitable for wine, but private. Also he made there a summer parlour or supper-room (*coenaculum*) under another old chamber, illuminated by many lights towards the garden and its floor is covered with a very beautiful pave-ment. Also he rebuilt other chambers at the end of the hall there, adjoining the Infirmary; and did many repairs to the old chambers there. Also he built a great and ingenious (*artificiosum*) pigeon-house in his own garden and excellently repaired the old pigeon-house there. Also he made a wall or walk between the said garden and the Infirmary, most convenient for walking along in rainy weather. Also he removed the Archdeacon's chamber from the place where the said privy dormitory stands into the great orchard and divided it into several chambers.

   ★  ★  ★  ★  ★  ★  ★  ★

The house also of the Infirmarian (? at Estbury) he repaired partly with lead and partly with shingles; in the vault also below the Dormitory there, formerly called 'the chamber of the blooded', he built a new fireplace for the warming of the monks (*claustralium*) and lighted the same with two stone windows, leaving other intended works unfinished. . . . At the rectory of Houghton he built anew an excellent grange, based on a stone wall, with gate and other houses; and its site he walled with a very strong earthern wall of timber well tiled (*muro terreo fortissimo ex materia lignea optime tegulato*).

Moreover he built from the foundations the chancel of Sandridge (Herts.) and Greneburgh (Bucks.). Also he newly repaired the roof of the chancel of Norton. Also he paid from the issues of the chamberlain's office the greatest part of the cost of the chancel of Langley, finished after his death by William Westwyk, chamberlain. In the guest-house of the convent, formerly assigned to White Monks, he built a new fireplace; and he placed a new door, with new windows, in that side of it adjoining the cloister towards the tailory.

   \*   \*   \*   \*   \*   \*   \*   \*

He, when he became abbot, took down the parapet (*crestam*) of the Greater Gate of the monastery, of Eglemounde stone, fragile and broken, and put up a parapet of hard Kentish stone, very lasting; spending on the work forty pounds and more, besides carriage. . . .

Moreover the said Abbot, seeing that the houses of the scholars at Oxford, of very old timber, were quite ruinous; the place also, owing to the neighbourhood of the kitchen, neither pleasant nor large enough to take as many scholars as he intended to send thither; began to build on a place near by, adjoining the monks of Norwich; . . . and before his death he had erected nearly half of the stonework. And he had provided for the same work timber, with planks (*tabulis*) of 'estlondebur' and other materials; but dying he left the rest to be done by his successor.

*Gesta Abb.* iii. 441–7.

1401. [William, 32nd abbot.] By the diligence and at the cost of this abbot was completed the work of the House of Scholars at Oxford, begun, more lavishly than was right, by his immediate predecessor.

Ibid. 496.

### 1396 Kayingham

On the night following Midsummer Day, 1396, a hurricane from the south, accompanied by thunder and lightning, struck the church of Kayngham with astonishing force, so that the small stonework set up over the east end of the nave adjoining the quire, and the top of the stone bell-tower built at the west end of the church, for a space of about 30 ft., and the other lower part of the tower towards the east, were thrown down with such force that some stones of the tower were hurled into the rectory, and other stones in the tower on the east side hung almost unsupported, threatening to fall. The north stone porch of the church, and the doors of that porch and the other doors of the church and tower, strongly wrought of oak planks, were so shattered by the blow that anyone who wished could put his hand through the cracks. And, what seemed astonishing, the beam (*axis*) on which one bell was hanging in the tower was split lengthways, as if by the the blows of the stones falling on it, and the bell itself, cast in fragile metal, remained just hanging on it, unharmed by any blow. In many places, also, in the church the stones of the windows were shattered, as if someone had pounded them with hammers, and the glass in those windows remained entirely unharmed. And the wooden rafters on the north side of the church were broken *quasi in oblongum*, but the thin roof of planks attached to these rafters was preserved intact. In some places, also, in the church carvings appeared on the walls contortedly broken, as if someone in derision had gouged (*exarasset*) them out, and in the south part of the church, near the tomb of Master Philip Yngleberd, formerly rector and professor of theology, one square stone was so removed from the wall that it looked as if there had never been a stone there. In the middle of the nave fire coming from the lightning completely burnt 12 couple of rafters with all the planking with which they were covered. But from this point it failed to spread either eastwards to the quire or westwards towards the tower, where the said Philip while rector had had it lengthened and had put up rafters. And while this was happening, the villagers, aroused from sleep, ran from all sides to the church and, putting up ladders, strove to put out the fire. So when 13 men, with their tools and vessels full of water, were struggling up a ladder to get on the roof, the ladder suddenly broke and all the men fell to the ground together. And with the breaking of the ladder a great stone fell among them, but, by the favour of God, all were preserved without any injury to life or limb.

*Chron. Mon. de Melsa*, iii. 193.

### 1400 *Wensley (Yorks.)*

Will of Sir Richard Scrope of Bolton:—I will that the rest of all my goods be employed in the building and complete partitioning (*plenariam separacionem*) of my house for poor persons to be built at Wensley and, if God grant, to be restored and completed, if it has not been completely built and restored by me in my lifetime; and this is to be done according to the arrangements that I shall make for it.

*Test. Ebor.* (Surtees Soc.), i. 278.

### 1403 *Durham, &c.*

Will of Bishop Skirlawe of Durham:—Also I leave to the building of the dormitory of the priory of Durham 100 marks, if the work is not finished before my death. Also to the building of the church of Howden £40. . . . Also I leave to the building of the church of the Carmelite Friars of York, if it is not finished before my death, £40.

*Ibid.* 310, 313.

### 1406 *Harewood (Yorks.)*

Will of Sir John Scot:—I leave for the erection of a new parish church at Harwood 100 marks, of which I have paid £20 in my lifetime: on this condition, that the patrons (*patroni*) of Harwood begin to rebuild the said church within the next year, and continue continuously to the best of their ability until it has been completely rebuilt; otherwise the 100 marks shall revert to my executors.

*Test. Ebor.* (Surtees Soc.), i. 346.

### 1406 Bishopstone (Wilts.)

Will of Henry Berwyk:—Also I leave 20 marks to the building of a tower over the church of Bishopstone, when the parishioners of the same begin to build it anew.

*The Tropenell Cartulary*, i. 220.

### 1409 London

In this yere also was yᵉ Guylde halle of London began to be newe edyfied, and of an olde and lytell cotage made into a fayre and goodly house as it nowe apperyth.

*Fabyan's Chronicle* (ed. 1811), 576.

### 1409 York

It is agreed that Sir Thomas de Haxey be overseer of the work on the fourth column. Also that the offerings coming to the tomb of Richard [Scrope], late Archbishop, be applied to the work on the fourth column. . . . Also that the lodge to be built for the masons working on this column be between the council chamber (*consistorium*) and the door of the chapter-house. Also that in the same lodge there be at least twelve masons. Also it is agreed that in the old lodge there be at least twenty masons. Also the task of providing stone is put upon Sir Thomas Haxey, with his consent. Also provision shall be made for carrying a great quantity of lime, namely two or four 'kylnes', at least. Also provision shall be made for sand [to be carried] in great quantities, on the river Ouse, with cart and horses, and by boat, and, if it can be done, with the boat of St. Leonard's [Hospital]. Also it is agreed that the corner-stones (*coynes*) at the angles of the belfry on the outside be cut back (*subducantur*) and that the wall go up flat (*pro plano modo*) at the angles of the belfry. Also that a flight of steps from the church to the belfry be made on the north side of the aisle by arrangement of Sir Thomas Haxey, Master Alan, Sir Thomas Garton and Sir Richard Blakburn. Also that Sir Thomas Garton cause 'sperres' and timber to be sent, without delay, from Cawod to the works.

*York Fabric Rolls*, 199.

### 1411 London

Richard Whityngton, citizen and mercer, grants to Sir John White, rector of St. Michael's, called 'Paternosterchirche', in the street called 'la Riole', land in the parish 113 ft. from east to west, by 53 ft. from north to south,—'to the end that upon the same parcel and upon the land upon which the said church now stands, which is now so small, frail and ruinous, a larger church may be built and reconstructed to the honour of God and St. Michael the Archangel, together with a graveyard adjoining thereto'.

Riley, *Mems. of London*, 578.

*1415 London*

The Council order:—That the Little Postern [in Cripplegate ward] built of old in the wall of the City should be pulled down and made larger on the south side thereof . . . by adding a gate thereto, the same to be shut at night and at all other fitting times. And that upon the Moor there should be laid out divers gardens, to be let at a proper rent to such persons as should wish to take them, alleys being made therein lengthwise and across; as more plainly depicted and set forth on a certain sheet of parchment made by way of pattern for the plans aforesaid.

Ibid. 614.

*c. 1415*

[Lydgate relates how Priam built the city of Troy.]

He made seke in euery regioun
For swiche werkemen as were corious,
Of wyt inventyf, of castyng merveilous;
Or swyche as coude crafte of gemetrye,
Or wer sotyle in her fantasye;
And for eueryche that was good devysour,
Mason, hewer, or crafty quareour;
For every wriȝt and passyng carpenter,
That may be founde, owther fer or nere;
For swyche as coude graue, grope, or kerue,
Or swiche as werne able for to serue
With lym or stoon, for to raise a wal,
With batailling and crestis marcial;
Or swiche as had konyng in her hed,
Alabastre, owther white or redde,
Or marbil graye for to pulsche it pleyn,
To make it smothe of veynes and of greyn.
He sent also for euery ymagour,
Bothe in entaille, and euery purtreyour
That coude drawe, or with colour peynt
With hewes fresche, that the werke nat feynt;

    ★    ★    ★    ★

And thus Priam for euery maister sent,
For eche keruer and passynge joignour,
To make knottis with many corious flour,
To sette on crestis withinne and withoute
Upon the wal the cite rounde aboute.

    ★    ★    ★    ★

And first the grounde he made to be souȝt
Ful depe and lowe, that it faille nouȝt
To make sure the foundacioun.

     ★　　　★　　　★　　　★

And euery tour bretexed[1] was so clene
Of chose stoon, that wer not far asondre,
That to behold it was a verray wonder.
Therto this cite compassed enviroun,
Hadde sexe gates to entre into the toun.

     ★　　　★　　　★　　　★

And portecolys stronge at euery gate,
That hem thar nat noon assailyng charge;
And the lowkis thikke, brode and large,
Of the gatys al of ȝoten[2] bras.
And withinne the myȝty schittyng[3] was
Of strong yrne barres square and rounde,
And gret barrerys picched in the grounde,
With huge cheynes forged for diffence,
Whiche nolde brake for no violence,
That hard it was thoruȝ hem for to wynne.
And euery hous that was bilt withinne,
Euery paleys and euery mancioun,
Of marbil werne thoruȝout al the toun.

     ★　　　★　　　★　　　★

And if I schulde rehersen by and by
The korve knottes by crafte of masounry,
The fresche enbowyng, with vergis riȝt as linys,
And the vowsyng[4] ful of babewynes,[5]
The riche koynyng, the lusty tablementis,
Vynnettes[6] rennynge in the casementis—
Thouȝ the termys in englisch wolde ryme,
To rekne him alle I haue as now no tyme,
Ne no langage pyked for the nonys
The sotil joynyng to tellen of the stonys,
Nor how thei putten in stede of morter
In the joynturys copur gilt ful clere,
To make him joyne by leuel and by lyne.

     ★　　　★　　　★　　　★

---

[1] *bretexed*: surrounded with a 'bretasche', or projecting gallery.
[2] *ȝoten*: cast.　　　[3] *schittyng*: shutting, i.e. fastening.　　　[4] *vowsyng*: vaulting.
[5] *babewynes*: grotesques.　　　　　　[6] *vynnettes*: trails of carved vine-leaves.

And euery hous cured was with led;
And many gargoyl and many hidous hed
With spoutis thoru3, and pipes as thei ou3t
From the stonwerke to the canal rau3t,
Voyding filthes low into the grounde
Toru3 gratis percid of yren percid rounde;
The stretis paued bothe in lengthe and brede
In cheker wyse with stonys white and rede.

*Lydgate's Troy Book* (E.E.T.S.), pt. i, 158–66.

## 1429 Durham

Letter, written 27 May 1429, to the Bishop of Durham.

. . . On the night before Corpus Christi, from the tenth hour to the seventh hour after midnight, there was in our neighbourhood thunder and lightning, terrible and unexampled: and especially a little before the first hour after midnight, when we were at matins, there was such a burst of thunder that we feared a great part of the church had fallen. At which time, as seems most probable, the upper part of the great bell-tower, under the cap (*tolus*) which is called in English the 'poll', was set on fire by lightning; but the fire was not suspected or visible until the seventh hour of the day; from which time until the twelfth hour a terrible fire lasted; and the cap of copper or bronze, $2\frac{3}{4}$ yards in circumference, blazing violently, with heavy ironwork and beams blazing like torches, fell upon the church, but, blessed be the Most High!, in the place where it would do least harm. And in this God was gracious unto us: for ten or twelve men who were labouring to put out the fire in the burning timbers, though sprinkled with molten lead and struck by the brands of the cap as it fell, were uninjured. And so, at the prayers of the people, who had crowded to the spot, and by the will of God, soon after the first hour after midday the fire was entirely put out; whereupon the hymn *Te Deum Laudamus* was devoutly sung by us and the crowd; for every one who saw this held it a miracle that the whole tower, and therefore the church and buildings adjoining, had not been burnt by such a blaze,—considering that the upper part of the tower which was burnt is said, by estimation, to be 20 feet in length.

*Hist. Dunelm. Script. Tres* (Surtees Soc.), ccxvii.

[The repair of the tower cost £233. 6s. 8d. : ibid. cclxxiii.]

## 1429+ London

[St. Stephen's, Walbrook, rebuilt; foundation stones laid, 11 May, 1429.]—
Maister Thomas Mapulton the kynge's mason then beyng Maister mason of the saide churche werke, and the forseide Robert Chechile gate and gave to the seyd churche werke c$^{li}$, and also he made all the tymbri werke of the prosescion

plase of his owne coste and also he gave us all the tymbyr and borde for the ij side ylis and paied for the cariage therof.

[The church was consecrated on St. Erkenwald's day, 1439.]

London & Middx. Arch. Soc. v. 331.

## 1435 York

Will of Richard Russell, merchant of York:—I will that the bell-tower of the church of St. John the Baptist in Hundgate in York be completed in the way in which the work has been begun, at my expense, by supervision of John Cotom, mason. And I will that John Bolron, carpenter, work a door, a ladder, and all the timber for hanging the bells in the said bell-tower, and that bells be hung in the tower. Also that the church be adorned within as is fitting for the said church next summer. And that an altar be made of (?) planks (*tabulis*) well and work-manly on the north side of the church before the images of the Blessed Mary and St. Anne, and under the same altar a cupboard (*almarriolum*) for the safe keeping of the books and vestments belonging to the same altar. And that another altar be decently made on the south side of the church before the images of SS. Catherine and Mary Magdalen after the form of the other altar. And that the three new stone windows in the church be glazed and filled during next summer as best they can be according to the discretion of my executors.

Test. Ebor. (Surtees Soc.), ii. 53.

## —1439  Warwick, &c.

Concerning the buildings of Richard Beauchamp, the most noble Earl of Warwick, according to the narration of . . . Brewster, his receiver-general.

Richard Beauchamp, the noble Earl of Warwick, restored the Castle of Warwick on the south side, with a splendid tower, and many houses of office. He caused to be built at Warwick a stable of great size, of 'plaister de Parys', at a cost of 500 marks.

The fortalice of Hanley, 7 miles from Worcester, he had rebuilt. Elmley Castle, 7 miles north of Worcester, he had repaired and rebuilt. Drayton Basset, 14 miles from Stafford, he likewise repaired and rebuilt. Cavysham manor, 1 mile from Redyng, he had rebuilt; and there was born Lady Anne, his daughter by Elizabeth Lady Spencer. Hanslape Castle, a barony, 7 miles from Northampton, he had rebuilt. The lodge of Claverdon, 5 miles from Warwyk, he arranged should be rebuilt. The fortalice of Bathe-kyngton, 2 miles from Coventry, first founded by William Bagot, knight, Earl Richard restored. Sutton manor, with the chace and the park, 14 miles from Colsylle in Ardern, he had rebuilt. The lodge in the park of Berkyswell, 2 miles from Kyllyngworth Castle, he had completely rebuilt at a cost of about £200.

The college and the chapel, where the said Earl Richard lies buried, with a dean and 6 canons, he caused to be increased by 2 priests, and had it restored and enlarged. At Gyb-clyff (i.e. Guy's Cliff), half a mile from Warwick, he newly founded two chantries, for priests called *heremites*, and had a beautiful dwelling-place made for them.

Will. de Worcestre, *Itinerarium*, 352.

### 1449 Stamford

Will of William Bruges, Garter King of Arms:—My body to be brought and buried in the church of Saynt George within Staunford. . . . Item I bequeathe and ordeyne that the gret framd [      ] that I have lying in the gret berne in my place at Kentishton to be sold to the most value, and the mony raised therof to be bestowed upon the complesshyng and endyng of the seyd chirch of Staunford; that is to be understand, in coveryng with lede, glassyng and makyng of pleyn desques, and of a pleyn rodelofte, and in puyng of the seyd chirche, nourt curiously but pleynly; and in pavyng of the hole chirch, body and quere, with broad Holand tyle. . . . Item I ordeyn and bequethe that the ij chapelles of our Lady and Seynt George wythyn the seyd chirch of Seynt George be closid with estrich boarde and clere storied after such quantitie as the closure of pleyn borde there now containeth.

Nicolas, *Test. Vetusta*, 268.

### 1452 Chesham (Bucks.)

Will of William Duffield:—To the fabric of the church of Chesham £6. 13. 4, on condition that the parishioners on their part carry out at their own expense the work, recently begun, of restoring the church, and not otherwise.

*Test. Ebor.* iii. 127.

### 1452 Beverley

Will of Richard Patryngton:—I leave for the building of 'lez crosse yles' of the church of the Blessed Virgin Mary to be built anew, provided that such work be begun or finished within three years after my death, £10.

*Ibid.* ii. 157.

### 1453

Will of Thomas White:—I leave for the building of 'lez crosseylez' of the same church to be built anew, £6.

*Ibid.* 167.

### 1470 Eye (Suff.)

'The steple of Eye was built in aº 1470 as aperith by a book of Accompt.' The churchwardens 'gatheryd that yere partly with the plough, partly in church ales, partly in legacies given that waye, but chiefly of the frank and devoute hartes of the people the some of xl$^{li}$ and litell odde money'. They obtained 25 cwt. of lead from the Prior, to be repaid in kind or else 'to pay for the same at yᵉ Sturbridge fayre folowinge'. They remain 'indebted for all the flynt stone to yᵉ worke or for a gret parte therof bought by Mr. Hynnyngham'.

*Hist. MSS. Com. Rep.* x (4), 531.

*c. 1480 Bristol*

The quantite of the dongeon of the castell of Bristol after the information of
. . . porter of the castell.

The tour called the dongeon ys in thykness at fote 25 pedes, and at the
ledyng place under the leede cuveryng 9 feet and dimid. And yn length este and
west 60 pedes, and north and south 45 pedes, with 4 toures standyng uppon the
fowre corners. And the hyest toure called the mayn, id est myghtyest toure
above all the 4 towres, ys 5 fethym hygh abofe all the 4 toures, and the walles
be in thykness there 6 fote.

Item the length of the castelle wythynne the wallys est and west ys 180 virgae.
Item the brede of the castell from the north to the south wyth the grete gardyn,
that ys from the watergate to the mayng rounde of the castell to the walle
northward toward the blak-frerys 100 yardes. Item a bastyle lyeth southward
beyond the watergate, conteynyth in length 60 virgae. Item the length from
the bullwork at the utter yate by Seynt Phelippes chyrch yerde conteynyth
60 yerdes large.

Item the yerdys called sparres of the halle ryalle conteynyth yn length about
45 fete of hole pece. Item the brede of every sparre at fote conteynyth 12 onch
and 8 onch.

Will. de Worcestre, Itinerarium, 259.

*1480/1 King's Lynn*

It is assented this day [9 March] that the commons shall close and defend the
church of St. Margaret and take down the old roof and the lead of the same
church at the cost of the commons; and the commons shall have the timber of
the same old roof to the church use; and the executors of Walter Cony grant to
make the clerestories of both sides of the same church, finding to the same
church lime and sand, stone and workmanship to the same, and to set up a new
roof, and roof the same with the old lead of the same church, and glass the
windows of the said new stories at the cost of the said executors; and if so be
that the old lead of the church be not sufficient to lead the new roof again, then
Thomas Thoresby, alderman, granted to deliver to the said executors as much
lead as shall perform the leading of the church.

E. M. Beloe, Our Churches, 92.

*1494+ Durham*

Richard Foxe, Bishop (1494–1502). He altered the hall in the castle of Durham;
for there were there two seats of estate (*regalitatis sedes*), one at the upper end
and the other at the lower end of the hall; but now he left that at the upper end,
and in place of the lower made a cellar (*penum*) with a pantry, and over that set
seats for trumpeters or other musicians (to play) at meal times (*tempore servitii*);
and a counting-house (*cubiculum computatorium*), and a spacious kitchen, and all
the offices belonging thereto, with the closets (*cubiculis*) annexed to the offices—

all the new work situated on the west of the hall and kitchen, he set up at his own cost. He also began to build in the high tower of the castle a hall, kitchen and many other buildings; but before they were finished he was translated to Winchester.

*Hist. Dunelm. Script. Tres*, 150.

### 1494+ Durham

Dr. Thomas Castell, Prior (1494–1519). He repaired the east gates of the Abbey, decayed by long lapse of time and fallen to ruin. He levelled the whole building to the ground and at great cost rebuilt them, with the porter's lodge in which he sleeps, and high above them he made a chapel in masonry of worked (*laevigatis*) stones, covered with lead sheets. . . . Moreover in the same building he made a bedroom for the priest, where he might sleep.

Ibid. 153.

### 1526 Oxford, Cardinal College

Letter of Dr. John London to Mr. Larke.

. . . First, all the lodgings in the west side be fully finished, save only battleing of the stonework, and the great tower over the gate is as high erect as the said lodgings. Towards the street the King's grace and my lord Cardinal's arms in three sundry works most curiously be set over the middle of that gate, and my lord's Grace's arms goodly set out with gold and color. All those lodgings be thoroughly covered with lead.

Inwardly the carpenters have done right good diligence to prepare the doors, windows, partitions and other necessaries, so that almost nothing shall let but that my Lord's scholars shall at his Grace's pleasure inhabit the same. At the south end there is a great tower, which within four foot is erect as high as the other lodgings. And so upon the south side the chambers which be towards the hall be almost come to bear the floors of the upper lodging. And the foundation of the hall is in most places five or six foot high. The foundation of the church in the north side is equal with the ground, and in like manner the foundations of lodgings of the east side be upon the outer side erect unto the old church door, and in the inner side nigh as far as is required.

Over this, almost all the foundations of the cloister be as high as the ground. The kitchen is finished, save only the louer; and all this Christmas the Dean and Canons had all their victuals prepared there. Behind the kitchen southward be goodly larder houses, pastry houses, lodgings for common servants, slaughter and fish houses, stables, with such other necessary buildings, substantially and goodly done in such manner as no two of the best colleges in Oxford have rooms so goodly and convenient. And these places be all cleansed with water, as oft as need shall require, currently passing thorough them all, either by the common stream or else by policy. For all the water which shall at rains issue into my lord's Grace college is by a goodly vault conveyed into the sink of the kitchen; and that sink is in every place so large that if any stopping should chance, a man may go in to purge the stoppage, and is as well and substantially wrought as any part of my Lord's college.

And where as the old lodgings of Pekwaters In do stonde, now be made houses for masons to work in. Would God there were so many masons as there is stuff ready carried requiring their work! This last summer stone came in from Burford, Teynton, Barendon and Hedyngton, sufficient to find many mo masons than yet be here until Midsummer. And as good provision is made for lime and all other necessaries. The carpenters in their timber work be as far forward as their work requireth, and every part of their and the masons' work is as clean wrought as ever we saw any done in any place, and every thing in like substantial manner done as my Lord's gracious purpose is to have his meritorious act perpetually to endure.

*L. & P. Hen. VIII*, iv. 2734.

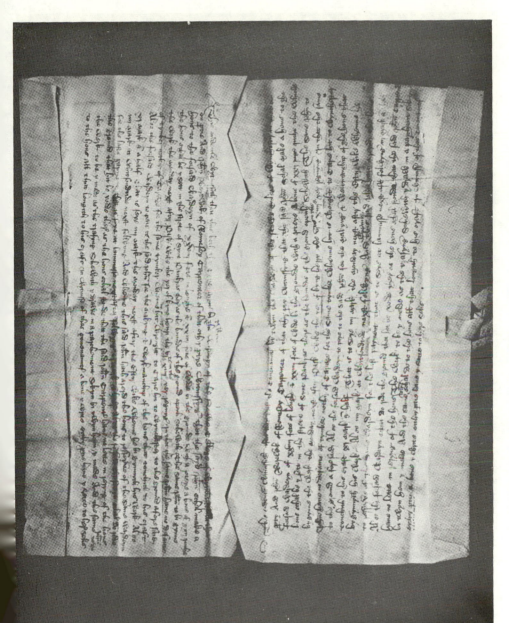

PLATE 20

A CONTRACT, SHOWING BOTH PARTS OF THE INDENTURE 1436

PLATE 21

A TYPICAL CONTRACT WITH A CARPENTER 1491

# APPENDIX B

## BUILDING CONTRACTS

IN the following pages I have collected all the surviving building contracts that I have been able to trace. It is rather curious that, while the second half of the fourteenth century yields 27 examples, the first forty years of the sixteenth century can only produce 19, of which 4 belong to King's College Chapel and two to St. George's, Windsor. While this might suggest a change in the relations between employers and builders, it is possibly simply due to the use of paper instead of the more permanent parchment for the engrossing of such contracts. The contracts printed range from such elaborate work as the ornate vaulting of St. George's, Windsor, to a mud-walled malting-house at Exeter and involve sums between £800 or £900 and £4. 13s. 4d. They include churches, castles, houses, shops, bridges, wharves, and a windmill and concern 23 counties, besides London, and one Welsh instance (No. 43); I have also included two Scottish examples (No. 40, Edinburgh, and No. 44, Arbroath)—or three, if Roxburgh (No. 32) is to be considered Scottish. A few of the documents are not strictly contracts but might be regarded as specifications for such contracts (Nos. 8, 38, 39), with which may be included Henry VI's detailed schemes for his foundations at Cambridge and Eton (Nos. 76, 77). I have also included two groups of summarized contracts, one for a granary at Felmersham (No. 82) and the other for work at Corpus Christi College, Oxford (No. 114).

The importance of this series of documents for the study of the organization and economics of the building industry can hardly be exaggerated and is obvious, but I may call attention to certain particular items. In No. 15 (A and B) we have the contracts with both the mason and the carpenter for building a tavern in Paternoster Row, and in No. 98 (A, B, and C) contracts for the masonry, carpentry, and tiling of Great Chesterford manor. Two specifications for London shops (Nos. 21 and 51), and two others for work at Queens' College, Cambridge (Nos. 78, 79), are noticeable for the details given of the scantlings of all the timbers. Finally, there is a group of contracts in connexion with the castles of Bolton, Carlisle, and Roxburgh (all in 1378) and Dunstanborough (1380) in all of which the contracting mason is John Lewyn. He was mason to the Bishop of Durham about 1370, and had been employed by the king to repair Bamborough Castle in 1368.[1] His contract for Roxburgh Castle amounted to

---

[1] *Patent R. 115.*

£900, but he carried out extra work there, for which the king still owed him nearly £400 in 1388[1]—an interesting proof of the large sums of money which a leading mason could command.

It may also be pointed out that these documents have considerable etymological value; those in English in many instances carry back the use of particular words behind the earliest occurrence known to the *Oxford Dictionary*, and there are many Latin or latinized words which are not in the medieval Latin dictionaries.

A few contracts known to have existed have eluded my search. One for work on the tower of Lincoln Cathedral in 1306, though referred to by a number of writers, does not appear to have been seen since 1775, when John Bradley sent notes from it to Governor T. Pownall (*Archaeologia*, ix. 125). Another, for the building of a tower to the church of Houghton Conquest (Beds.) in 1392, appeared as for sale in the catalogue of a book-seller—H. T. Wake, of Windfield Park, Derby—in 1882, but has not been traced. Two contracts with William Orchard for work at Magdalen College, Oxford, in 1495 and 1497 have also vanished.

The contracts here printed are arranged in chronological sequence, except that the series opens with the undated fifteenth-century formal 'type' contract.

The spelling of the originals is retained, but compendia (e.g. ꝑ for 'per', ꝑ̃ for 'pre', &c.) are expanded, as are many of the obvious contractions in Latin documents. The erratic use of capitals (which are here given to all names) is not usually followed, and some punctuation has been introduced where helpful.

There are a number of interesting contracts for what may be called 'fittings'—such as woodwork, glazing, tombs, &c.—which I have not printed. These include the following:

1394: the tomb of Richard II and Anne of Bohemia, in Westminster Abbey.— Exch. K.R. Accts. 473, no. 7; printed in Rymer, *Foedera*, vii. 795.

1419: the tomb of Ralph and Katherine Greene, in Luffwick church.—Willis, *Nomenclature*, 79.

1449–54: the Beauchamp Chapel, Warwick. Contracts for (*a*) the marble tomb of Richard, Earl of Warwick; (*b*) the effigies and other metal-work; (*c*) painting; (*d*) desks and screens; (*e*) the glazing of the windows.—Dugdale, *Antiqs. of Warwick*, 321–3.

1466: desks and benches for the Divinity School, Oxford.—Legge, *The Divinity School, Oxford*, 19.

---

[1] *Close R.* 544.

1475: rood-loft and stalls, Eton College chapel.—Willis and Clark, *Arch. Hist. of Cambridge*, i. 596.

1486: rood-loft, Merton College.—*Reg. Coll. Merton.* (O.H.S.), 520; *Arch. Journal*, ii. 181.

1492: seating and pulpit, Bodmin Church.—*Camden Miscellany*, vii.

1499: rood-loft, St. James's, Bristol.—*J. of Brit. Arch. Assoc.* xxxii. 350.

1511: the tomb of Lady Margaret, Countess of Richmond, in Westminster Abbey.—*Archaeologia*, lxvi. 366.

1526: the grille round the said tomb.—Ibid. 373.

1513: the glazing of windows in the chapel of St. John's College, Cambridge.— Willis and Clark, op. cit. ii. 347.

1516: the tomb of Henry VII, in Westminster Abbey.—Britton, *Arch. Antiqs.* ii. 27–31.

1526: the glazing of windows in the chapel of King's College, Cambridge.— Willis and Clark, op. cit. i. 615–17.

1531: rood-loft in Stratton Church (Cornw.).—Goulding, *Blaunchminster's Charity*, 91.

1532: rood-loft in St. Mary's Church, Cambridge.—M. R. James, *Hist. of St. Mary's, Cambridge*, 64.

1536: the tombs of Sir William and Margaret Sandes, at Basingstoke.— Baigent, *Hist. of Basingstoke*, 15.


I

*Early Fifteenth Century* [*Oxford*]. A specimen contract.

This contract is found in three manuscripts of a *Formulare*, or book of precedents, compiled by William Kingsmill, who taught letter-writing, conveyancing, &c., at Oxford, *c.* 1420. He had a habit of inserting his own name as one party in most of the deeds which he gives as examples, and it may be doubted whether this contract was actually made by him or concerned a house in Catte Street, Oxford; but it was clearly based on some original, or originals. It was printed by Mr. W. A. Pantin in the *Antiquaries Journal* (July–October 1947) from a manuscript in the Bodleian Library, collated with two others in the British Museum (Add. MS. 17716, f. 70v; Royal MS. 12 B 24, f. 245). The version here printed is taken from Add. MS. 17716. It is followed in the original by a note, in French, to the effect that the carpenter must either be bound by a bond or must find sureties for performance of the contract, which bond may be included in the written contract or endorsed.

Presens convencio facta inter W[illelmum] K[ingesmyll] de Oxonia ex una parte et Robertum W[hiteleg']¹ de eadem carpentarium ex altera parte testatur quod idem Robertus construet et de novo edificabit totam sitam sive vacuam placeam infra mansum predicti Willelmi K. in vico de Cattestrete Oxon', quod

¹ The full names are taken from the Royal manuscript.

quidem edificium sic de novo construendum continebit in longitudine a vico regio de Cattestrete usque ad alterum finem eiusdem siti quaterviginti et unum pedes et in latitudine in fundamento xviij pedes ad caput a[u]str'[1] versus dictum vicum et ad finem borialem[1] xxj pedes; in quo quidem edificio erit unum solarium cum uno gite[2] extendente in longitudine et latitudine eiusdem edificii cum duplici solar' et duplici gitee ad caput australe super vicum predictum de amplitudine et factura prout decet principali camere huiusmodi edificii. Et erunt in dicto edificio viij principales postes quorum quilibet erit in latitudine viij pollicium et in densitate vij pollices, gruncelli iacentes super fundamentum erunt latitudinis viij pollic' et in densitate v pollic'. Item erunt ibidem vj principales someres quorum quodlibet erit in latitudine xj pollic' et in densitate x pollic'. Item ij someres ad fines dicti edificii erunt quilibet eorum in latitudine x pollic' et in densitate viij pollic'. Item erunt viij bemes quorum quilibet erit in latitudine viij pollic' et densitate vj pollic'. Item ij walplates latitudinis vij pollic' et densitatis x pollic'. Item faciet ibidem punchons necessar' quorum quodlibet erit latitudinis vj poll' et densitatis iiij poll'. Item laces faciat ibidem latitudinis vj poll' et densitatis iiij poll'. Item lez gistes erunt latitudinis vij et densitatis v poll' et inter quodlibet giste spacium unius pedis. Item lez reftres necessar' que erunt quodlibet eorum latitudinis vj pollic' in pede et iiij pollic' densitatis in pede et in le tope iiij pollic' latitudinis et in densitate iij pollic' et di', et inter quodlibet reftre erit spacium unius pedis. Item lez syderesenes erunt vij poll' latitudinis et densitatis v poll'. Item ex una parte dicti edificii erit paries de lapidibus factus usque le evese illius solarii iuxta le lane sumptibus ipsius Willelmi, qui supportabit edificium predictum ex parte illa; et erunt in eodem edificio subtus per terram iiij intercloses pro pastura, pincerna, coquina et stabulo; et in predicto solar' post predictam duplicam cameram erunt quinque intercloses pro aula cameris, pincerna, et latrinis, prout oportunum et necessarium est per avisement' dicti Willelmi; et in aula ibidem j femerell', j spere, et j fenestra versus sportum[3] eiusdem loci vocata Baywindowe bene aptata de opere talliato cum iij dayes et j staundys wyndowe versus venellam ibidem. Et predictus carpentarius omnes domos eiusdem edificii bene et competenter ostiabit, bordabit et fenestrabit, cum tot gradibus, ostiis et fenestris prout oportunum et necessarium fuerit ad tale edificium secundum advisamentum dicti Willelmi. Et inveniet predictus carpentarius totum meremium sufficiens et competens, necnon stoddes, bordes, et lathes de corde quercina, ac dictum edificium fideliter construet et perficiet citra festum sancti Michaelis archangeli proxime futurum. Et habebit idem carpentarius de eodem Willemo pro edificio predicto sic construendo xx libras sterlingorum, unde idem

---

[1] The Bodleian manuscript reads 'occidentale' and 'orientalem', which Mr. Pantin points out would be more correct for Catte Street, which runs north and south.

[2] *gite*: a 'jetty', or overhang. For the other timber terms see above, pp. 202–5.

[3] *sportum*: probably, a courtyard.

W. solvet prefato carpentario pre manibus ad confeccionem presencium x marcas et ad levacionem dicti operis x marcas et cum idem opus fuerit completum x marcas. In cuius rei testimonium etc.

## 2

### Englefield (Berks.)

An agreement (undated, but apparently early 14th century) with (? a mason or a carpenter) to build a room, 40 ft. by 24½ ft., with a wardrobe 20 ft. by 14 ft.; there are to be 5 doors, a bay window in 'the vault', and 2 windows on the west side. To be finished in 2 months; for 6 marks, in three instalments, half a quarter of wheat, and a robe.

Anct. Deeds (P.RO.), D. 6548.

Ceste endentur fayt a engelfelde le dymayn procheyn devant la feste seynt barnabe le apoustylle: Entre Phelypp de Engelfelde del un part e Jhon le Rede de lautre part: par couenaunt feyt entre eus que le dyt Jhon fra un chambre de la longur karaunte pes a de lee¹ vynt e katr' pes e demy Owf² la gardrobe de la longure de vynt pes e de le katosse.³ E synk uss⁴ e un vay⁵ wyndou en la vowt e deu fenestr's en la part ocsydental bons e couenables. a payer a dyt Jhon ou a son certeyn atorne sys mars de argent e demy qᵃrter de forment e un robe E a son commencement la moyte de syss mars E la qᵃrte partye quant yll leua la dyte chambr E le remenaunt quant yl est parfet. De ceste chose parfere le dyt Phelyp e Jhon unt myt lour seaus. Ensy qe ceste chose sey parfet entre sy e la feste de la assompsyoun de nostre dame.

## 3

### 1308 London

Agreement by a carpenter to build a hall, chamber, solars, with a stable, kitchens, and other offices. To be completed in about six months. The client, a furrier, to pay partly in money and partly in furs.

Guildhall muniments: Letter Book C, f. 96. Translated in Riley, *Mems. of London*, 66.

Simon de Cantuar' carpentarius venit coram Maiore et Aldermannis die Sabati proxima post festum Sancti Martini episcopi anno regni Regis Edwardi filii Regis Edwardi secundo et cognouit se facturum sumptibus suis propriis usque seruras Willelmo de Hanigtone pellipario circa festum Pasche proxime futurum unam aulam et cameram cum camino, et j dispensam⁶ inter predictas aulam et cameram, et j solarium super predictas cameram et dispensam, et j oriole in capite aule ultra summum scamnum, et j gradum cum oriole a terra usque hostium aule predicte extra illam aulam, et ij clausturas in celario ex

---

¹ *lee*: breadth.  
³ *katosse*: quatorze.  
⁵ *vay*: presumably for 'bay'.  

² *owf*: *avec*, with.  
⁴ *uss*: doors.  
⁶ *dispensam*: a larder.

transuerso sub aula, et j claustura ad cloacam, et ij pipas ad dictam cloacam, et j stabulum longitudinis inter dictam aulam et veterem coquinam latitudinis xij pedum cum solario supra stabulum predictum et unum garectum[1] supra solarium predictum, et in uno capite solarii predicti j coquinam cum camino & j oriole inter predictam aulam et veterem cameram latitudinis viij pedum, et nisi fecerit concedit &c.—Et predictus Wills. de Hanigtone cognouit se teneri predicto Simoni pro opere predicto in nouem libris quinque solidis iiij$^d$. sterling', et dimidio centum cabl'orum[2] orient', una furr' ad capucium mulieris precii v$^s$. et in una furrura pro roba ipsius Simonis &c.

# 4

## 1310 *London, St. Michael in the Cornmarket*

Agreement by a carpenter to build a range of three shops, with two stories above them; on the first, two halls, buttery, pantry, and kitchen; on the second, two large chambers. He is to have such of the timber of the old house on the site as is not fit for re-use, and 33 marks—10 marks in advance, 10 marks when he begins work, 10 marks when he begins to erect the frame on the (stone) foundations, and the rest on completion. To be finished in four months. He finds as sureties the rector of St. Michael's and two other carpenters.

St. Paul's MSS. no. 1497.

Fet a sauer qe cest le couenaunt fet le Lundy prochein apres le iour de Paumes, En lan del regne le Roy Edward fitz le Edward (*sic*) Tierz, entre Sire Johan de Mundene Clerk de une part et Richard de Rothinge Charpenter de autrepart. Cest a sauer qe mesme cely Richard edifiera une place en le Tenement qe le dyt Sire Johan auoyt del doun et del feffement Henri de Gloucestr' en la paroisse de seint Michel as Bleez en Loundres. La quele place gyst entre le Tenement iadys Huwe de Oxenford de vers le West, et la Porche del hus[3] de la sale du tenement le dyt Sir Johan de vers le Est, Et entre le Real chemyn de vers le Suth, et le mur de la Cosine[4] du dyt Sire Johan de vers le North. Le quel edifiement serra de bon meryn et gros, couenable et loable, et nomeement les Gystes des solers et les Postz, de quei le dyst sire Johan se tendra bien a paye. Et serrount en mesme le edifiement treys schopes par aual pres du Real Chemyn, et treys Chaumbres apertenauntz oue double estage par amount, et contendra dys pie de hom mesurez de haut en chescune Schope de la terre iesq's as Gystes du soler. Et en le premer estage sur les schopes serrount deus Sales, oue Chimynees, botelerie, panetrie et Quisine, sulom coe que la place est graunde. Et en le Estage par amount sur les sales serrount deus beles chaumbres, oue chaumbres curteyses.[5] A quel edifiement lauaundyt Richard trouera totes choses qe a coe apartenent a fere en la fourme auaundite a ses custages propres. Hors pris Chauz, Perre,

---

[1] *garectum*: a garret, or loft.  [2] *cabl'orum*: Riley suggests 'marten-skins'.
[3] *hus*: door.  [4] *cosine*: kitchen.
[5] *chaumbres curteyses*: probably a euphemism for privies.

Sabloun, arsyl,[1] Tule[2] (*sic*), Tilepin, plastrure, et loks pur les hus. Et pur ceo durra le dyt Sire Johan alauaundyt Richard Trente et treys mars de bons esterlings. Des queux le dyt Sire Johan payera a lauaundyt Richard dys mars deuaunt la meyn. Et il payera alauaundyt Richard ou a soun certeyn attornee dys mars si tost come mesme cely Richard ou ses gent comencent pleynement de ouerer en le oueraygne de cel edifiement. Et dys mars quaunt lauauntdyt Richard ou ses gent comencent de leuer le edifiement sur le foundement de la dite place. Et quarante souz si tost come lauauntdyt Richard auera pleynement parfourmy lauaundyt oueraygne en la fourme auaundyte. Et voet et graunte le dyt sire Johan qe lauaundyt Richard eyt tut le veil meryn de la veille mesoun de la dite place. Sauue le bon meryn qe profitable seyt al edifiement auaundyt. Et mesmes cely Richard a graunte et promys certeynement, pur ly et pur ses heirs et pur ses executours, qe totes les choses susdites, quanqe en ly peut a fere, serrount prestz et apparaillez deci qe a la Goule de Aust[3] prochein a uenir ou dedeinz les huyt iurs procheyns siwauntz. Et a coe se oblige lauaundyt Richard ly et ses heirs et ses executours et trestuz ses biens moebles et nient moebles presentz et auenirs, ou qil seyent trouez. Et a meillure seurte fere de totes les choses susdites lauaundyt Richard ad trouee au dyt sire Johan plegges suz escritz, Cest a sauer sire Johan de Hatfeld, persone del Eglyse de Seint Michel as blez en Loundres, Adam de Rothingge Charpenter et Oede le Charpenter. Les queux chescun de eaux se obligez principalment pur lauaundyt Richard eux lur heirs et lur executours et trestuz lur biens moebles et nient moebles, presentz et auenirs, a fere lauaundyt oueraygne en la fourme auaundyte. En tesmoignaunce de mesmes les choses susdites a la partie de cest escrit endentee demoraunt vers le dyt sire Johan de Mundene les auaundyz Richard Johan Adam et Oede ount mys lur seals. A lautre partie demoraunt vers lauaundyt Richard le dyt sire Johan de Mundene ad mys soun seal. Ces sunt les tesmoignes, Sire Johan de Breynford, Sire Richard le Reuestiayr' et Sire Wyllem de Derham, chapeleyns del Eglyse de seint Poel, Thomas le Cyrg', Willem le Cyrg', Willem de Claktone et autres.

## 5

*1312 London, St. Paul's*

Agreement by a marbler to pave four severies of the new Lady Chapel, at 5[d], 'or more', the square foot, inclusive, measured by a pattern of agreed size and thickness. He is to be paid 25 marks on beginning each severy, and is to finish the whole four within the year. He produces three sureties.

St. Paul's MSS. no. 843.

In dei nomine amen. Anno domini mccc[mo] duodecimo In festo Conuersionis Sancti Pauli sic conuenit inter venerabilem patrem dominum Radulphum dei

---

[1] *arsyl*: clay.
[2] *tule*: for *tuille*, tile.
[3] *la goule de Aust*: the beginning of August.

gracia episcopum London' ex parte una et Adam dictum le Marbrer ciuem London ex altera videlicet quod ipse Adam fieri faciet pauimentum quatuor spaciorum subtus quatuor nouas voltas medii tecti Noui operis beate Marie Sancti Pauli London, que spacia superuisores per dominum Episcopum ad hoc deputati designare decreuerint, de bono marmore spissitudinis et bonitatis irreprehensibilis, vel saltim tria spacia, iuxta voluntatem domini episcopi, mensurato spacio per pedem certe mensure inter ipsas partes contrahencium diuisim ad modum tallie communi assensu remanentis, mensuram eciam necessarie spissitudinis petre continentis, quemlibet videlicet pedem in quadro usque ad perfectam complecionem totius illius pauimenti, quo ad singula illi necessaria et sine defectu, pro quinque denariis siue pluri, absque vendicacione alia vel exactione qualibet per ipsum Adam ulterius facienda. Et preter hec idem Adam petras ad ipsum pauimentum per ipsum prouidendas quadrabit et ex transuerso angulatim vel directe secundum mensuram conuenientis quantitatis secabit aptabit et cubabit prout melius et decentius requirit fieri huius materia iuxta arbitrium et ordinacionem dictorum superuisorum. Ad quod quidem opus peragendum in inchoacione operacionis primi spacii recipiet dictus Adam a dicto domino Episcopo viginti quinque marcas sterlingorum cuius spacii pauimento per eum ut dictum est peracto, et inchoato ulterius opere de pauando secundum spacium consimiliter ipse Adam iterum percipiet alias viginti quinque marcas pro pauimento et opere eiusdem secundi spacii, et sic deinceps de ceteris duobus spaciis pauandis, conuencione et distinccione eadem premissa. Hoc adiecto quod duorum primorum spaciorum pauimentum congrue et sine defectu peragatur citra festum Sancti Michaelis proxime sequens et aliorum duorum comode compleatur ante festum conversionis Sancti Pauli proxime subsequens. Ad quam conuencionem in singulis articulis fideliter et sine variatione tenendam et complendam dictus Adam omne illud quod habet in cimiterio seu procinctu ecclesie Sancti Pauli obligat voluntati et disposicioni dicti domini Episcopi. Et nichilominus fideiussores et pleggios inuenit videlicet Ricardum Jordan, Paternostrer, Hugonem de Oxon', Cissorem, et Ricardum de Rothingge, Architectorem,[1] quorum quilibet ad iam dictam conuencionem ut conuenit complendam principalem se constituit debitorem et in solidum se et bona sua et catalla ad hoc obligentes. In cuius rei testimonium uni parti huius scripti indentati penes prefatum Adam remanenti sigillum dicti domini Episcopi est appensum et relique parti eiusdem dictus Adam et sui fideiussores prenominati sigilla sua appenderunt. Actum et datum London' die supradicta. Hiis testibus [*sic*—no names].

---

[1] *architectorem*: properly, a helyer, or tiler. If, as is probable, this is the carpenter of the preceding contract, it may be meant for 'house-wright'.

## 6

*1313 Lapworth (Warwickshire)*

A mason and his partner, a quarry-owner, agree to build for Sir John de Byssopesdon a gate-house of stone, 40 ft. by 18 ft.; the outer walls to be 3½ feet thick, exclusive of the plinth, and the inner 2½ feet. The gate to be in the middle, with a room on either side, one with fireplace and privy, the other without, 11 feet in height from the ground to the beams of the first floor. Above these shall be a great room, with two fireplaces and two privies, 9 feet in height, crowned with a parapet 2½ feet high. They shall provide the stone, and Sir John will provide carriage of it, timber, sand, and lime. The whole to be done within a year, for 25 marks, paid in two instalments. They give a bond for 25 marks.

Anct. Deeds (P.R.O.), A. 4375; printed in Parker, Domestic Architecture, ii. 5.

Ceo sount les covenauns fees entre Mouns' Sire Johan de Byssopesdon chivaler de une part e Will' Heose masoun e Joh'n de Pesham de Rouenton de autre p't. Ce est a sav' qe les avaunt dys Will' e Joh' frount au dyt Sir Joh'n a sun Maner de Lapworthe une mesoun p$^r$ porte de pere fraunche bone covenable e byen overe. La quele mesoun contend' en loung deens murs qaraunte pees e en leyse dys e ut pees. E la foreyne mur s'ra ove les gables treys pees e demy epes sauns deus peyres descuys[1] au foundem't de hors. E les denseyns murs serrount deus pes e demy epes dount la porte s'ra en my la mesoun. E de une p't la porte une chambre base ove une chymeneye e garderobe etendue hors de la dyte chaumb$^e$ e ove fenestres e hus covenables e de altre p't la porte chaumb$^e$ saunt chimene e saunt garderobe ove hus e fenestres covenables. E la porte avant dite s'ra de laour[2] solum le devys le avaunt dite Sire Johan. E de amp't le entre de eyns la porte mur de pere ausy haut c' la porte au ques murs ceo jundrount deus coluns de per' sur les ques les foyles[3] de la porte pendrount e s'ra la porte avant dite ensemblem't ove les chamb$^e$s bases avaunt dites unse pees de haut du soyl jekes au trefs p' mereyns. E a de sus la porte e les dytes chaumbres bases s'ra un chamb$^e$ estage de longour e la leysour avaundyt ove deus chimenes deus garderobes etendans hors de la dite chamb$^e$ covenablem't ov hus e fenestres covenables a le ordeynem't de le avant dyt Sir' John' et la chamb$^e$ sovereyne avant dite serra neof pees de haut de gites a de souz jeqes au tref a de sus, e a de sus les sovereyne gites s'rount alures[4] de per' de deus pees e demy haut. E s'ra la dite porte issy fete qe un pount t$^r$nes byen ceo acordera solum le ordeynem't le avant dyt Joh'n; e le dyt Will' Heose e Joh' de Pesham ou un de eus t'veround fraunche per' bon e covenable p$^r$ le dyt overeyne parfer'. E le dyt Syr' Joh' la per' f' carier de la q'rer' Joh' de Pesham de Rouentone jeqes a le overeyne avant dyt ou de ausy p's lu sy le dyt Will' de plus loyns la vod$^a$ quer'. E le dit Sir Joh' t$^o$vera merym charpentrie sabeloun chaus prest saunt deturbaunse (?) de le avaunt dyt overeyne. E les avant dytes Will' e Joh' ou un de eus parfrount tot le

---

[1] *peyres descuys*: skew stones, evidently a plinth of two courses.
[2] *laour*: breadth.       [3] *les foyles*: the leaves, or valves, of the door.
[4] *alures*: here used for the parapet of the roof-walk.

overeyne avant dyt avant Le Touzseyns p'cheyn aven' ap's la confexioun de cet covenaunt avant dyt. e p$^r$ ce covenant fer' e parformer ausi c' avant est dyt. Je Joh' de Byssopesd' moy oblige p$^r$ moy e p$^r$ mes heyrs e p$^r$ mes exeq'tors estre tenuz a les avant dys Will' e Joh' ou a un de eus en Vynt e sinq mars a payer a deus t'mes. ceo est a saver a la purificacioun n're Dame p'cheyn aven' apres la confexioun de cete escryt doze mars e demy. E quant la dyt overeyne s'ra finye solum la forme ava't recorde aut$^e$ doze mars e demy p$^r$ cete overeyne en la forme e au jour avant dyt leaument a fer' nos avant dys Will' e Joh' de Pesham de Rouenton nos oblisouns e grauntoms de estr' tenuz juntem't e severauntm't p$^r$ n' e p$^r$ nos heyres a le dyt Sir' Joh' e a ces heyrs en Vynt lyveres de esterlynges a payer ap's la Qu$^i$seyne de Touzseins p'cheyn aven' ap's la confexioun de cete covenant e n' avaunt dys Will' e Joh' de Pesham voloms e grauntoms p$^r$ n' e p$^r$ nos heyrs q$^e$ le dyt Sir' Joh' e ces heyrs purrount destreyndre touz nos teneme's en Rouenton en qe meyns qe il devyne't e ce destresse garder encontre gaie e plege issynt qe p' tref ne sant bref ne seyt deliver' si la qe les vynt lyvres seyent paye ou le overeyne parfet solum le covenant avant dyt. En teymoynanse de cete chose nos John' Will' e John' aviun mis nos seus. Escreyt a Lapworthe le Lundy p'cheyn ap's la feste Seynt Martyn en le an du regne le Rey Edward fyz le Rey Edward setyme.

## 7

*1315 Eltham*

Agreement between the representatives of Queen Isabel and four masons for building a wall on the edge of the moat round the manor. They are to go down to a good foundation, and, if necessary, to drive in piles. The wall to be 5 feet thick at the base, diminishing by courses to 4 feet at the top, as designed by Master Michael of Canterbury, and 12 feet in height. If, owing to their having to go deeper in places to get a good foundation, it is more than 12 feet they shall be paid accordingly. The foundation course is to be of hard stone, without any chalk or soft stone; on the outer side, towards the water, the wall shall be, for half its thickness, of good stone; on the inner side, below the earth, it shall be of good chalk, and above of good stone. At the end of each perch, of 18 feet, shall be an arch-buttress rising from the base of the wall to support 'the old work' (presumably the buildings of the manor); and at each corner shall be two buttresses to support turrets; the earth on the outside shall be made level with the ground inside. The masons shall have 100s. for each perch, finding materials and labour. If any of them is prevented by illness or other reason from carrying out the work, the others shall be responsible. They shall finish the first half by All Saints (1 Nov.) and, beginning work again the following Easter, shall complete the whole by the next Michaelmas.

[Owing to the masons scamping their work, they were sued and compelled to rebuild the wall: see above, p. 27.]

Pleas of Exchequer, 10 Edw. II, m. 16.[1]

Fait a remembrer q' Lundy lendemeyn de la feste de Pentecouste lan octisme du regne le Roi Edward fitz au roi Edward a Eltham est acouenu par Mons'

---

[1] I am indebted to Mr. J. H. Johnson, F.S.A., for calling my attention to this document.

William Inge, Mons' Johan Fillol, Mons' Johan Launge, chiualers, Johan Vanne marchaunt de Loundres et William de Boudon clerk de part ma Dame la Reyne dune part, et Mastres William de Hoo, Johan de Offynton, Johan de Hardyngges-ham et Johan de Seint Omer, mazons, dautre part, q' les auantditz mazons William Johan Johan et Johan ont empris de faire un mur entour la mote du manoir ma dite dame de Eltham de piere et de chauz en la manere q' sen suyt. Cest assauoir q' les auantditz mazons a lours propres custages front cercher dekes a certeyn et sur fundement, si auant come il couent par la veue Mestre Michel de Cant'bir' ou dautre qui ma dame assignera. Et si par aventure aueigne q' hom ne puisse trover fundement sur terre certeyne par quoi il couient mettre pieus[1] p$^r$ bon fondement faire, ma dite dame la Reyne fra trouer le meryn pur les pieus et les ditz mazons les front ouerer et mettre a lour propres custages, et serra le mur par desouth au fondement v pees espes et paramont au somet de iiij pees espes, et serra du fondement desk au somet xij pees de haut le mur retreant par de hors desq' au somet solonc lespessure auantdit par lauissement le dit Mestre Michel, et si mestier soit de plus haut fere le mur par lieus par defaute de bon fondement ils le front prenantz al afferant ce qe la perche deura amonter par couenant, et troueront les auantditz mazons piere et chauz et totes choses q' au mur busoigne soit a lour propres custages, et serra le fondement du dit mur coche de bone piere dure, un cours permy saunz mettre creye ou piere mole, et puis a leuant contre mont serra tout le coste uers lewe a la montance de la moite del espessour du dit mur coche de bone piere et dure bien et sarreement, et p$^r$ront bien les auanditz mazons mettre deuers la terre en le dit mur si auant come il serra couert de terre bone piere de creye ou bon morter de chauz et la ou le mur se leuera par amont la terre serra coche par my de bone piere et dure, et front les ditz mazons a checune perchee q' serra de xviij pees dedentz deuers la terre une arche boteraz de bone pierre et dure par lauisement le dit Mestre Michel q' serra au fontz de lee[2] et despessour de v pees, et par amount de iiij pees, et sourdra le dit arche del fondement du dit mur et se leuera desk a vyl [=viel] oueraigne par amont la terre a sousteyner le dit fondement du viel oueraigne, et issuit par tut en uiron solonc ceo qe la place se taille front il les boterez en la manere auantdite, sauue a la place entour deux toreles deuers le Est qe fuist nadgaires herberge[3] ou la place nest mye a ore herberge, et front le mur par liuel par tut solonc lauisement Mestre Michel, et serra a chescune des corneres deux boteraz p$^r$ meutz susteyner les toreles, et front les auantditz mazons raser la terre au mur et sarreement mettre au mur destre owel a la terre par dedentz a lour propres custages; et aueront les ditz mazons p$^r$ chescune perchee de xviij pez a faire en la fourme auantdite oue les arches Cent souz desterlingges. Et troueront piere et chauz et cariront a lour propres custages, et ouerours et q$^a$ntqz il couendra p$^r$ loueraigne auantdit. Et sil aueigne q' dieu defende q' aucun des auanditz mazons par maladie ou par acheson renable soit destourbe qil ne

---

[1] *pieus*: piles.      [2] *lee*: breadth.      [3] *herberge*: a lodging.

puisse a la dit oueraigne entendre les autres lenpernent a parfaire, et se obligent a ce faire checun pur le tut. Et comenceront les ditz mazons a ouerer sur le dit oueraigne le Lundi prochein apres ceste quinzayne de la Trinite procheine et oueront delors enauant oue tantz des gentz et tiel espleit qil aueront parfait la moyte del auantdit oueraigne auant la feste de tous sayntz prochein auenir. Et sur le remenant comenceront a la quinzeyne de Pasqz prochein auenir, et plus tost sil pleyse a ma dite dame, et aueront parfait deuant le seint Michel prochein suant. En tesmonance de queu chose est faite ceste endenture, dont lune partye demoert deuers les auantditz mazons enseale p$^r$ ma dite dame des seals les auantditz Mons' Johan Fillol, Johan Vanne et William de Boudon. Et lautre partie demoert deuers ma dite dame en le meyn le dit Johan Vanne enseale des seals les auantditz mazons. Don a Loundr' lan et le iour auantditz.

# 8

## *1315 Lacock Abbey*

This is not strictly a building contract but an agreement between the Abbey and Sir John Bluet, who had presumably given money for the enlargement of the church. The convent undertake to complete a Lady Chapel, 59 ft. by 25½ ft., with four windows, of which two have already been made. The wall between the church and the chapel is to be taken down, two arches being inserted, as broad as is consistent with the safety of the church vault. The roof of the chapel to be covered with lead and panelled and painted inside. Two-thirds of the work to be done within eight years and the remainder within four years after that. The convent give a bond for 200 marks, which is probably the amount advanced by Sir John.

*Wilts. Archaeological Mag.* xvi. 356.

Ceo est le covenaunt feat entre Dame Johanne de Mountfort abbesse de Lacoke e covent de mesme le lyu dune part e monsire sire Johan Bluet seigneur de Lacham dautrepart. Ceo est asavoir qe les avauntdites abbesse e covent o lour successeres ferrount feare e parfeare une chapele de nostre Dame en lour abbeye de lacoke. Quele chapele se joynt a lour haut Eglise de mesme labbeye E si serra la chapele de la longure de cynkaunte e neof pez e de la largesce de vynt e cynke e demi E serront en lavauntdite chapele quatre fenestres. Ceo est asavoir en chescun gable une fenestre si large com la une est feate e chevie e lautre com elle est comencee serra bien feat e finie e en le forein costee de lavaunt-dite chapele la une soit telle com elle est feat e chevie e lautre si large com elle est comencee serra feat e finie de bone overaigne e covenable. E serront les avaunt-dites fenestres covenablement ferrees e verrees. E serra le veul mur abatuz de la poynte des deus fenestres qe furent e parerent le jour de la fesaunce de cest escript en le mur avauntdit taunke a la renge table[1] prochein de soutz les bas de memes les fenestres. E serront deus arches feates la ou le mur issi serra abatuz si large ceo est asavoir com bien e enseurement purra estre soeffers entre les deus rachemenz[2] issi qe la veille voute purra estre sawne[3] sanz peril. E frount les

---

[1] *renge table*: string-course.    [2] *rachemenz*: responds.
[3] *sawne*: evidently an error for *sauue* = safe.

avaunditz abbesse e covent o lour successeres feare le comble de mesme la
chapele de bon merym e covenable overaygne. E de tel manere coumble com-
menz plerra al avauntditz abbesse e covent o lour successeres. E serra lavauntdite
chapele ceo est asavoir le comble covert de plum bien e covenablement. E serra
le coumble de denz lavauntdite chapele tot bien laumbresche[1] e depeynt. E
serront les deus parties de lavauntdite chapele feate e parfeate en totes overaignes
com sus est dit Del jour de seynt michel en lan du regne le roy Edward filz au roy
Edward neofyme de denz les ust[2] aunz procheinz ensuvaunt pleinementz soient
acompliez. E la terce partie de la chapele avauntdite serra enseurement feate e
parfeate de denz les quatre aunz procheinz apres les ust aunz avauntditz pleinementz soient acompliez en chescune manere de overaigne com sus est dit. E si
lavauntdite chapele ne soit feate e parfeate e en totes overaignes chevye e finie
bien e covenablement en touz poynz com sus est dit qe dieux defende aydunqe
serra les avauntditz abbesse e covent o lour successeres tenuz alavauntdit monsire
sire Johan ou a ses excecutours en deus cent marcs dargent. Des queux deus
cent marcs les avauntditz abbesse e covent ount feat e livere a monsire sire Johan
Bluet de ceo un obligacion [etc.]. E pur ceo qe les avauntdites parties voelent
dunepart e dautre qe les avauntditz covenaunz en totes choses susdites soient
fermes e estables A cest escript endente entrechaunjablement ount mys lour
seals par iceaux tesmoignes Sir Wauter de Pavely, Sir Johan de Hales, sire Johan
de la Mare, Chivalers, Johan Tourpyn, Johan de Stodleghe, Johan Percehaye,
Johan de Bourleghe e autres. Done a Lacoke le Jeody procheyn apres la feste
seynt bartolomeu lan du regne le roi Edward filz au roi Edward neofyme.

[*Attached*] Fait assavoir qe le temps qe remeint uncore a parfaire la chapele
nostre dame amounte de la feste seint michel prochein passe Lan de la Incar-
nacion nostre seigneur mil. ccc. xxj taunqe a sys aunz prochein suvauntz e de
mesmes la feste seint michel taunqe la feste de la translacion seint Thomas le
martir apres les sys aunz. Tachez ceste escrouoite al escrit qe touche mesme la
matire.

# 9

*1317 London*

Bond of a plasterer to finish off the walls and flues of the Earl of Richmond's hall with
plaster of Paris, within eight weeks, for £24 paid in advance.

Guildhall muniments, Letter Book E, f. 61;
translated in Riley, *Mems. of London*, 125.

Die Jouis in festo Sancti Dunstani anno regni Regis Edwardi filii Regis
Edwardi decimo venit Ada le Plastrer et cognouit quoddam scriptum esse
factum suum cuius tenor talis est:—Pateat uniuersis me Adam le Plastrer ciuem
London' teneri et obligari domino Johanni de Brittannia Comiti Richemondie
ad inueniendum plastruram paris sumptibus meis propriis sufficientem et bonam

---

[1] *laumbresche*: panelled.  [2] *ust*: eight.

sine defectu prout pertinet ad aulam dicti Comitis faciendam nec non ad dictam aulam sumptibus meis propriis competenter plastrandam et faciendam ac muros dicte aule interius et exterius cum dicta plastrura reparandos bene et decenter, nec non tuellos[1] ad summitatem prout pertinet ad predictam aulam reparandam pro xxiiij libris sterling' quas dictus dominus Comes michi soluit premanibus, ad quod quidem opus in forma predicta fideliter faciendum a die Sancte Trinitatis proxime ventura infra octo septimanas proxime sequentes obligo me et omnia bona mea mobilia et immobilia videlicet terras domos et tenementa mea infra ciuitatem London existencia districtioni cuiuscunque balliui domini Regis &c. ad quorumcunque manus deuenerint ad obseruacionem omnium et singulorum premissorum. In cuius rei testimonium &c. Dat' London die Jouis proxima ante festum Pent' anno regni Regis Edwardi filii Regis Edwardi decimo.

10

### 1321 Hamsey (Sussex)

Agreement by which a mason is to build a hall, 60 ft. by 36 ft., with side walls 24 ft. high, with two fireplaces, five windows and a door; at the east end there are to be three doors, leading into the pantry, buttery, and passage to the kitchen, respectively. This he is to finish within eighteen months, receiving 35 marks and a quarter of wheat, by monthly instalments. He produces two sureties.

Westminster Abbey Muniments, 4063; printed in *Archaeological Journal*, xxiv. 6; translated, with ground-plan, by W. H. Godfrey, in *Sussex Notes & Queries*, iii. 133–6.

Ceste endenture tesmoigne qe le sisme jour de Martz lan du regne nostre Seignur le Roy Edward fuiz au Roy Edward quatorzsime Issi acouint entre Monsieur Geffrei de Say, chivaler, de une part, e Johan Rengwyne de Wogham, mason, de aultre part, ceo est asavoir qe le avauntdit Johan fra en le Manoir le dit Monsieur Geffrei de Hammes quatre murs de pere e de chaux pur une sale, des queux les deux murs de les costeres serrount sessaunte pees de long deins les murs, e vinttequatre pees de haut de la plaine tere; e les deux boutz serrount gables de tele longure qe la sale soit deins les murs de trentesis pees de lee, e de tele hautesse come le comble de la sale voudra suffire. E le dit Johan fra[2] en la gable vers le West, qe serra au deys[3] de la dite sale, une chimenee qe avera de leour deins les ganbes[4] sesse[5] pees, e en la costere de la dite sale devers le suth une aultre chimen[   ] nef pees de lee, e les tuels de ambedeux les chimenees passerount de haut le summet de la sale treis pees. E le dit Johan fra en la costere de la dite sale devers le North treys fenestres croyses, cheskune sis pees de lee e de aultre tele hautesse come les murs porront suffire, e en la costere devers le suth

---

[1] *tuellos*: flues.

[2] On each of the five occasions where the word '*ferra*' occurs it is distinctly written '*fra*' without any compendium for *er*.

[3] *deys*: dais.  [4] *ganbes*: jambs.

[5] *sesse*: this should mean 16 ft., not 6 ft., as given by Mr. Godfrey.

serra le us de la sale de covenable leour e hautesse, e deus fenestres acordauntz as
fenestres de la costere du North. E en la gable devers le Est serrount treis us,[1]
une pour la panetrie, une aultre pour la botelerie, e la ters pur une alee devers la
cuisine. E auxi le dit Johan fra un mur de pere e de chaux a sesse pees du but de
la sale de trentesis [pees] de loung e dis pees de haut pur receivre un pentis qe
serra outre la panetrie e botelerie, e un us en mylu pur lissue devers la cusine, e
les elles acordauntz al costere del comble,[2] e en cheskune ele une fenestre covenable. Estre ceo dit Johan foera, treera e tailiera[3] toute la pere qe covendra pur les
avauntditz murs, us e fenestres e chimenees, en toutes les places ou le dit Monsieur Geffrei voye qe soit a son profit, horspris la pere qe serra pur lastre e le reredos[4]
des avauntditz chimenees countre le feu; e le dit Johan foera sablon pour tutz
les avauntditz overaynes, e trovera chaux a ses custages, auxi ben pour les dites
overaines come pour le coverir de toute la sale ove le pentys. E lavauntdit
Monsieur Geffrei fra car[ier] toute la dite pere chaux e sablon sur la place ou la
sale serra faite; e dorra au dit Johan pour son overayne e tutz aultres custages
susditz trentecink mars e un quarter de furment, e ly paera de moys en moys
solom le espleit de son overayne, commensaunt al myquaremme prochein apres
la date de cest escrit avenir, issi qe tutz les avauntdit murs e les aultres overaynes
soyent parfaitz e lavauntdit Johan de son covenaunt purpae deins un an e
demy prochein suivant le terme susdit. E a tutz cestes choses ben e loialment faire
e acomplir le avauntdit Johan ad trove pleges, ceo est asavoir, Williame atte
Rye e Richard Page, qe ensemblement ovesqe lavauntdit Johan obligent eux
lur heyrs e lur executurs, e tutz lur biens e chateux, ou qil soyent troves, a la
destreese cheskun ministre nostre Seignur le Roy ou aultre bailif qe lavaunt[dit]
Monsieur Geffrei voudra a ceo elire. En tesmoinaunce de queu chose les avauntditz [Johan,] Williame e Richard a la partie de ses escritz [qe] demurt devers
Monsieur Geffrei unt mis lur seaus, e a la partie qe demurt devers lavauntdit
Johan lavauntdit Monsieur Geffrei ad mis son seal. Donne a Hammes, lan e jour
susditz.

## II

*1321 Darley (Derbyshire)*

An eighteenth-century copy of an agreement for the removal and re-erection of a hall
and chamber, of timber on a masonry base, with stone doorways. The mason to receive
8 marks and a robe.

B.M. Add. MS. 6670, f. 122.

Ista indentura testatur quod die sabbati proxima ante festum inventionis
Sancte Crucis anno domini 1321 Ita convenit inter Johannem de Derlegh ex una

[1] *us*: doors.
[2] *les elles* . . . : 'the aisles', or outer walls of pantry and buttery, 'agreeing with the side of
the (*pentis*, or lean-to) roof'.
[3] *foera, treera e tailiera*: shall dig, hew, and cut.
[4] *lastre e le reredos*: the hearth and fireback.

parte et Willelmum de Keylstedis cementarium ex altera vidz. quod dictus Willelmus concessit et fide mediante fideliter manucepit se removendam aulam et cameram Johannis de Derlegh et illas reparandas in quodam loco qui vocatur Robardyerd. Aulam vidz. de eadem mensura sicut steterat in antiquo loco et duas fenestras in aula quaque fenestra de duobus luminaribus et duas gabeles tabulatas[1] super aulam, longitudo camere vidz. quadraginta pedum inter parietes, latitudo vidz. sicut meremium antique camere dicte postulat, cum tribus fenestris [    ] quaque fenestra de duobus luminaribus et una fenestra de uno luminare et uno chimeno[2] de meremio usque le baas cum ij gabelis tabulatis cum uno warderobe et uno oriell predicte [camere] pertinente cum novem[3] hostiis de petris aule et camere pertinente (*sic*) et predictus Willelmus debet ponere [    ] singultum[4] super cameram quod fuit super aulam. Ad quamquidem convencionem fideliter faciendam dictus Willelmus [obligavit] se heredes et executores suos et omnia bona sua ad districtionem cujuscunque Judicis Ecclesiastici vel [    ] Et dictus Johannes concessit pro se et heredibus suis dare dicto Willelmo pro dicta operacione octo marcas [    ] pro vicus (*sic*) sicut opus suum operaverit et unam robam servient' [    ] ipsius usual'. In cujus [    ] datum apud Derl[    ].

# 12

*1322–3 Chester*

Agreement by a mason to build a round tower, 10½ ells in diameter and 24 ells in height; also a wall, 8 ells in height, containing a gate, properly embattled for defence. He is to work continuously and to remain in Chester until it is finished. He shall receive £100, and reasonable payment for any extra work done. He produces four sureties.

Copy in Harl. MS. 2046, f. 26v, printed in R. H. Morris, *Chester*, 244.

Indentura facta 16 Edward II inter majorem et cives Cestrie, Willelmum Clark majorem Ricardum de Lewode et Robertum de Strangwas cives de eadem et Johannem de Helpeston cimentarium testatur quod predictus Johannes de Helpeston pro c libris sterlingorum faciet et fundabit quandam turrim rotundam spissitudinis x ulnarum et dimidie cum concavitate distantem a turri de Benewaldestham usque in fluvium aque de Dee per estimacionem viij ulnas quarum quelibet continet viij ulnas regias (*sic*), quequidem turris erit altitudinis xxiv ulnarum regiarum a sabulone usque ad borialem. Et idem Johannes faciet et fundabit ibi quendam murum solidum altitudinis viij ulnarum regiarum cum quadam porta [    ] cujus quidem muri solidi spissitudo erit iv uln' reg' et qui quidem murus super collocatus [    ] erit sufficienter batillatus ex utraque parte ita quod hii qui ibidem fuerunt (*sic*) sufficienter et secure se defendere possint

---

[1] *tabulatas*: possibly 'weatherboarded'.

[2] There should presumably be a comma after *chimeno*.

[3] *novem*: query, *novis*?

[4] *singultum*: probably a misreading, but for what is not obvious.

ubicunque. Et idem Johannes inveniet omnia et singula que ad predictam operacionem pertineant sumptibus suis propriis calc' et cap' lapid' in quarrera predicti operacion' contigua non sufficiat (*sic*). Et continue in predicta operacione pro posse suo morabitur et residebit [in Cestria usque ad] consummacionem operis supradicti. Et ad hec omnia et singula in forma predicta perficienda prefatus Johannes [obligavit] se et heredes suos et omnia bona sua et catalla et eciam fidejussores invenit subscriptos, vidz. Ranulfum de Daresbury, Willelmum de Dalbye, Willelmum de Sunden et Willelmum le Serjeaunt de Ruthyn qui simul cum predicto Johanne [      ] majori et civibus Hiis scriptis indentatis alternatim sigilla sua posuerunt. Dat' apud Cestriam die et anno supradictis. Et preterea si predictus Johannes aliquid augeat in predicta operacione ultra convencionem supradictam predicti major et cives concedunt allocare eidem Johanni quicquid fuerit et rationis.

# 13

*1324 Westminster*

A plumber undertakes to strip the roof of the small hall in the Palace and re-cover it in the same fashion as the south roof of Westminster Abbey church. The King to provide fuel for melting the lead, and to pay 10s. for each 'carrate', or cart-load, of lead worked. The plumber binds himself to work as speedily as possible, and to have the work done by others if he cannot do it himself.

K.R. Memoranda R. 17 Edw. II, Trin. Rec.[1]

Memo. quod Johannes de Wynton' de London plomer venit coram Baroniis v die Sept' et manucepit sumptibus suis propriis discooperire parvam aulam Regis in Palacio Westm' de plumbo unde eadem aula nunc existit cooperta et eandem aulam de plumbo predicto per ipsum de novo fundendo et de alio plumbo sibi per Regem inveniendo, si necesse fuerit, bene et absque aliquo defectu recooperire, eo videlicet modo quo ecclesia Abbatie Westm' ex parte australi est plumbo cooperta. Ita tamen quod Rex inveniat sibi buscam pro fusione plumbi predicti. Et predictus Johannes percipiet de Rege per manus clerici operacionum palacii predicti qui nunc est vel qui pro tempore fuerit pro qualibet carrata plumbi per ipsum ad dictam cooperturam noviter fundendi, vidz. pro cariagio dicti plumbi ab aula predicta et ab aliis locis infra dictum palacium usque domum plumbar' infra idem palacium, et pro fusione et operacione plumbi predicti et omnibus aliis ad eandem cooperturam pertinentibus x$^s$. Et dictus Johannes omni festinacione qua poterit dictam operacionem incipiet et eam absque aliqua intermissione et dilatione perficiet. Et si per infirmitatem vel per mortem vel aliquo alio casu fuerit impeditus per quod non poterit per se operacionem predictam perfurnire, idem Johannes obligat omnes terras et omnia tenementa et bona et catalla sua ad quorumcumque manus devenerint ad perficiendum eandem operacionem per alios in forma supradicta.

[1] I am indebted to Mr. J. H. Johnson, F.S.A., for calling my attention to this document.

# 14

*1335 York*

A contract between the parishioners of St. Martin in Coney Street, York, and Robert Giles, carpenter, for the building of a row of houses, 100 feet in length and 18 feet at one end and 15 feet at the other in breadth. Details, measurements, and scantlings of timbers are given, but the whole is extremely confusing. He is to complete the work in a little over three months, under pain of excommunication, and to receive 62 marks and a robe of blue cloth.

The original is in the *Registrum Antiquum* of the Dean and Chapter, and I am indebted to Mr. John Harvey for the loan of this transcript, made for him by the Rev. Angelo Raine.

Haec indentura testatur quod die Jovis prox' ante festum Nat. Sci. Johannis Baptistae 1335 convenitur inter Ricardum de Thorp, Nich. de Appleby, Willm. de Shireborn, cives Ebor' ac inter ceteros parochianos ecclesiae Sci. Martini in Coningstret Ebor' ex una parte et Robertum Egidii de Ebor' carpenter ex altera viz. quod dictus Robertus concessit de fide media tactis insuper sacrosanctis Dei evangeliis firmiter se obligavit dictis parochianis quoddam edificium construere continens in se septem domos rentales in venella Sci. Martini predicti scilicet inter dictam ecclesiam Sci. Martini ex parte australi et venellam memoratam ex parte boriali in forma subscripta Videlicet quod dictum edificium continebit centum pedes in suo longitudine, in latitudine vero versus stratam octodecim pedes et inferius circa finem quindecim pedes. Hujus edificii sex domus habitabiles erunt sub una tectura et habebunt jacturas suas ex utraque parte viz. versus venellam continentes duos pedes et unum solarium ostendit se modo [      ] versus regiam stratam, quod quidem solarium continebit viginti duos pedes de balco(?) et erit conformatum per omnia edificio Ricardi de Briggenall in North Stret. Habebit eciam jacturas suas ex utraque parte viz. versus venellam et versus stratam et dicta jactura continebit quatuor pedes versus venellam et versus stratam totidem. Dictum vero solarium habebit fenestras et unum hostium versus stratam, habebit eciam fenestras et unum hostium versus venellam. Tertium vero hostium cum uno gradu ut sic eatur in superiorem cameram. Ceterarum domorum qualibet habebit fenestras et unum hostium per se et fenestram similiter versus dictam venellam cum gradibus competentibus dicto operi. Et unumquodque solarium habebit suam fenestram versus ecclesiam et quelibet camera habebit unum caminum cont' quinque pedes infra mantellum et hoc de emplastro et unum luuarium[1] similiter. Fenestre vero et hostia de Estrichborde cum ligaturis et crokis hespis et stapulis clavis seruris et clavibus et aliis instrumentis de ferro bene competentis (*sic*) et paratis. Planchera eciam erit competens juxta quod dictum opus exigat et requirat. Longitudo eciam postis erit undecim pedes viz. sub subpanno.[2] Ceteri vero postes a parte australi versus ecclesiam habebunt suam longitudinem sufficientem et respondentem et

---

[1] *luuarium*: 'louvre' is here apparently used for the chimney-flue.
[2] *subpanno*: the lower wall-plate.

competentem dicto operi. Latitudo vero postium continebit duodecim enchias spissicas. Uter ipsorum continebit decem. Longitudo vero postium circa finem versus domos Vicarii erit vel sexdecim pedum vel octodecim pedum juxta elevacionem et dimissionem placei ibidem. Et hoc sub subpanno ut dictum est. Postis vero cornerii versus venellam erit sexdecem enchiarum lat' et tredecem enchiarum in spissicata. Stanciones vero erunt novem enchiarum et panni tredecim enchiarum et septem enchiarum et solos ejusdem formae, ita quod bene competent' dicto operi. Gesturae[1] vero erunt septem enchiarum et thurugistes[2] bene ligati cum ty3oun[3] et aliis ligaturis competentibus et predicti postes omnes ad quos haec ligatura pertinet erunt ligati cum ty3oun. Longitudo vero postium camerarum sub panno continebit octo pedes, sperrae eciam continebunt sex enchias in lat' et octo enchias in spissicatione. Wawes[4] eciam habebunt quatuordecim enchias in lat' et octo enchias in spissicatione. Sperrae vero erunt ligatae cum ciner'(?) competent' cum ligaturis pertinentibus ad idem. Ad hoc lignea summaria interlacia ac omnia alia genera meremiorum dicto operi pertinentia se coaequabunt et conformabunt edificio Simonis le Gower situato ex opposito dicti operis per omnia. Grundes eciam erunt pilati cum pilis et lapide et erigent se super terram per unum pedem largum sub solo.[5] Omnes parietes tam extra quam infra interclausi et alii si qui sint cum le bemfillyng tam de subpanno quam de panno superiori cum superjectura fluorii erunt de emplastre paris firmiter constituti et parati. Ad hoc vergablum[6] versus venellam erit sufficiens et competens de estrigbord et in fine versus domos Vicarii erit finis dicti operis de (? tabulamento) emplastri latres insuper broddes tylepinnes cum tegula bene figulata cum calce sabulo decente composito et non aliud dicto operi apponetur [    ] omnia et singula predicta cum operariis cuiuscunque generis et stipendiis operariorum [    ] dicto Roberto corporali sacramento ad haec prestito ut predictum est se fideliter et sine condicione aliquali dicto operi inventurum et inpensurum, et dictum opus ad festum Sci. Michaelis prox' fut' vel infra quindenam post lapsum dicti festi dumtaxat sine ulteriore prolongacione fideliter consummaturum; et ad majorem securitatem super hiis optinendam coram audit' causarum venerabilium virorum dominorum Decani et Capituli Ebor' condemnatur sub pena excommunicationis. Et si continget dictum Robertum in fata decedere dicto opere non consummato, quod absit, obligat se heredes et executores suos ac omnia bona sua mobilia et immobilia ad quorumcunque manus devenerint supplemento consummacioni et [    ] dicti operis modo quo predictum est ad omnia facienda. Preterea parochiani ecclesie Sci. Martini

---

[1] *gesturae*: joists.

[2] *thurugistes*: the significance of 'through-joists' is not clear.

[3] *ty3oun*: ties, or braces.  [4] *wawes*: beams.

[5] The foundations to be made firm with piles and stones and above the ground level to be 1 ft. broad under the sill-beam.

[6] *vergablum*: the barge-board of the gable.

predicti in principio dicti operis memorati solvent dicto Roberto decem marcas argenti ad festum Sci. Petri ad vincula prox' fut', decem marcas arg' ad festum decollacionis Sci. Johannis Bapt' prox' sequentem, decem marcas arg' ad festum exaltationis Sce. Crucis prox' seq', decem libras arg' ad festum Sci. Michaelis prox' seq' et in fine operis septemdecim marcas arg' et unam robam de blueto percipiendam de Vicario dicte ecclesie ad curialitatem. Et sic pro toto opere consummando percipiet sexaginta duas marcas arg' cum una roba solvend' eidem Roberto ad terminos prefatos et sic putat se contentum per omnia. In cujus rei test' partes predicta alterna parti hujus scripti cirograffiti sigilla sua alternative apposuerunt. Hiis testibus: Hen. de Welton tunc Major civitatis Ebor', Joh. de Bristol, Joh. Caperoun tunc ballivis dicte civitatis, John de Barneby, Stephano de Getrington, Gilberto Hothom et aliis.

# 15 (A) and (B)

*1342 London, Paternoster Row*

Two contracts for building a tavern on a site formerly occupied by five shops.

Bridge House deeds (Guildhall), Portf. G, nos. 16, 17.[1]

(A) Agreement by which a mason is to dig and remove the earth to a depth of 17 feet, and in one corner to carry down a pit, 7 feet square, for a privy as deep as the water allows. The groining and arches of the cellar to be of freestone, and the filling of the vault of chalk; the walls to be of ragstone, 3 feet thick, carried up 2 feet above the pavement, with four windows, on the street, and carried up to the first floor on the other side. The stairs, down to the cellar and up to the first floor, to be of ragstone. A fireplace at each end of the cellar, to be carried up in stone to the level of the first floor. He is to have £26, and 1 mark for a robe.

(B) Agreement by which a carpenter is to build (on the foundations mentioned in (A)) a house with two jutting stories and two gables towards the street. In one gable shall be a garret; under the other, on the second floor, a hall, with kitchen and larder. Part of the ground floor shall be partitioned off; in the rest he shall make seats for its use as a tavern, as also on the first floor. The hall and bedroom each to have a bay window, flanked by lintelled windows. He is to have £24, and a robe worth 20s.

## A

Cest le couenaunt fait entre William Marbrer Citein et vineter de Loundres dune part, et Phelip de Cherche masoun dautre part. Cestassauer qe le dit Phelip fra fodier une place qest au dit William en paternosterrewe en la paroche seint Michel ate Corne sur quele place y ount ore v schopes vielz, de profondure de xvij piez et fra amener de illoeques ou qil voudra tote la terre ales coustages le dit Phelip et sera cele profoundure de loungure et de leure de touz les dites

---

[1] For transcripts of these deeds I am indebted to Miss Helen Chew.

v schopes. Et al bout de cele profoundure en la Cornere vers le Northwest desouth la Flore de cele profoundure fra une voute a j Gardrobe de longure de vij piez et de leure de vij piez et auxi profound come il puyt bonement pur ewe et fra estopper le ewe si nul y soit. Et cele voute de la garderobe sera de croye et fra la pipe de cele garderobe tut sus parmy le mur de pere et tut de piere de la hautesse del primer getteye[1] paramount la voute del celer. Et serrount les murs de la dite voute del dit Celer tut de bon piere de Rag parmy tut le dit voute amount de la hautesse de primer getteye vers la place et les tenementz Thomas Leg Citein de Londres qe nule pere ne monstre dehors ne dedeinz mes net Rag. Et la dite voute et les arches serront de Franche pere et le parfurnir de la voute de Croye come apent que soit bien et suffisament fete a la vewe de totes bones gentz come couenant est entre eux. Et le mur de la dite voute vers la Rue sera auxint de net Rag de la hautesse paramount le pauement de ij piez oue iiij fenestres vers la Rue. Et qe touz les paas de les degrez[2] del dit celer soient auxint de bon pere de Rag bien et nettement faites et les Jaumbes del huys del celer serrount auxint de bon Rag. Et fra un autre croyz degrez les paas de Rag auxint bien et nettement faites solounc ceo qils deuiserount tantqe al primer Flore sur la voute del celer et tantqe ala Flore del celer paraual. Et fra les paas del huys de la sale de Rag auxint. Et fra al un et lautre bout del celer une chymeneye bon et suffisant et les mayntendra de pere de hautesse del mur al Getteye. Et touz les ditz murs de la voute paramount tut entour hors vers la Rue serront de espes de iiij piez. Et auera le dit Phelip pur tut ceste ouerayne xxvj[li] et j mark desterlinge pur une robe et trouera a ceo tote manere masonerie pere croye lym et sabloun. Et a touz ceux couenanz bien et loialment peremplir delune et lautre partie chescun de eux se oblige a autre par cestes endentures et touz lour biens ou qils soient trouez. Et desouth les auantditz degrez fra un Cawet[3] voutee nettement oue j huys de pere en le dit celer. En tesmoignance de quele chose les auantdites parties a cestes endentures entrechangeablement ount mys lours seals. Done a Londres lundy proschein apres la feste seint Andre lapostle. En lan du regne le Roy Edward tierz puis le conquest seszime.

## B

Cest le couenant fait entre William Marberer Citeyn et Tauerner de Londres dune part, et Richard de Felstede Citeyn et Carpenter de mesme la Cite dautre part. Cestassauoir qe le dit Richard fra sur la place le dit William en Paternoster-rewe en Londres ou qil y auoyent Cynkes schopes a la fesance de cestes Cestadire entre la Chambre desus la porte de la Tauerne Thomas Legge Citeyn de Londres quele Chambre sire Johan de Okebroke chapeleyn tient a terme de vie vers lorient en longure deuers la Rue tauntqe au Tenement le dit Thomas Legge vers le West, et auxint tauntqe au Tenement le dit Thomas Legge vers le Suthe en

---

[1] *getteye*: jutty, the projecting upper story.
[2] *paas de les degrez*: steps of the stairs.
[3] *cawet*: a cave, or recess.

la longure par la Rue vers le North de xij aunes et un quarter come la place contient. Et en leeure vij aunes et dim' et un quarter. Sur quele place le dit Richard fra une nouele meson ouesqe deux Sometz gableez vers la Rue oue deux estages ambedeux oue gettyes. Et sur les deux estages desouthe lun somet dedeinz fra une garite[1] dount les pouncheons serront de la hautesce de vj piez, et desouth lautre somet vers la Rue de Paternosterrewe fra une sale sur le plus haut estage. Et al bout de cele sale vers le Northe fra une despence[2] et une Cusyne, et cy fra il touz les entreclos qe apendent a tote la nouele meson auantdite. Et sur le plus bas leyr[3] sur la voute fra une chambre entreclosee, et tut le remenant de cele basse Leyr fra tretut seges pur tauerne et un entreclos parmy tut cel bas leyr en lungure. Et auxint en le secounde leyr paramount fra tretut seges pur Tauerne. Et sur ceo paramount en la sale fra une baye Fenestre vers la Rue. Et del une et lautre partie de cele fenestre fra une fenestre lyntelle. Et en la chambre du lyt fra une autre baye Fenestre oue tieux autres fenestres . . . de chescun partie lyntellez. Et par tut ailleurs fra fenestres . . . degreez la ou . . . sount et en la chambre du lyt fra le celure paramount le lyt. Et . . . ouveraigne auera le dit Richard . . . oueraigne de carpenterie(?). Et le dit William Marberer trouera mesmes tote manere de meryn et tote le syer[4] de meryn et totes autres choses qe apendent a ces propres coustages. Et auera le dit Richard pur son oueraigne auantdit vynt et quatres lyures destarlinges et une Robe pris de vynt soudz oue vynt soudz destarlinges. Et de touz ceux covenantz de la une partie et de lautre bien et loialment peremplir chescun de eux se oblige a autre et touz lour biens ou qils soient trouez. En tesmoignance de quele chose les dites parties a cestes endentures entrechaungablement ount mys lour seals. Done a Londres le Jour seint Thomas en la semaigne de Noel. En lan du regne le Roy Edward tierz apres le Conquest seszisme. Et qe tut cest oueraigne soit prest par la feste seint Michel a plus tost proschein auenir. Et sera paie de x li. a le fesance des cestes et del remenant come il oeure.

## 16

### 1347 *London*

Agreement with a carpenter to rebuild a wharf on the Thames, with framework of oak posts, the uprights being 12 feet in length. In the middle there is to be a bridge with steps down to the water, and at each end a shed; there is to be a wooden fence, 10 feet high, all round, and three other fences on the wharf. He is to receive £20, in three instalments, and a robe worth 1 mark, his employers providing for any necessary digging, piling, &c., and retaining the old timber. His two brothers go surety for him.

St. Paul's MSS. nos. 980, 1239.

Hec indentura facta inter Decanum et Capitulum ecclesie Sancti Pauli London' ex parte una et Ricardum Coterel carpentarium ex parte altera testatur quod

---

[1] *garite*: a garret.   [2] *despence*: a larder.
[3] *leyr*: floor.   [4] *syer*: sawing.

talis est conuencio inter predictos Decanum et Capitulum et predictum Ricardum facta, quod predictus Ricardus faciet et construet de nouo meremio suo proprio unum Wharuum juxta le Brokenwharf super quandam placeam terre predictorum Decani et Capituli iacentem inter tenementum Abbatis de Lesnes ex una parte et tenementum Johannis Siward ex altera, sicut predicta placea se extendit contra Thamisiam in longitudine et profunditate constructum modo subscripto, videlicet quod una quaque postis per totam latitudinem predicte placee contra Thamisiam sit firmiter coniuncta cum alia et quod sit longitudinis a fundamento terre usque ad summitatem Wharfi duodecim pedum, que quidam construccio anglice Nedlyng,[1] cum bonis kaiis et sufficientibus ad hoc pertinentibus ad modum Wharfi Johannis de Oxenford, faciet etiam duas Garderobas,[2] unam ex parte una Wharfi, et aliam ex altera, que includi debent cum bordis et meremio competenter cum duobus hostiis ad easdem intrantibus, faciet eciam unum pontem in medio Wharfi de forti et sufficienti meremio cum gradibus descendentibus, faciet eciam super predictum Wharuum unam palliciam de competentibus bordis et meremio, extendentem se in altitudine, a summitate Wharfi usque ad altitudinem pallicie per totam latitudinem Wharfi contra Thamisiam ad decem pedes, construet eciam idem Ricardus tres alias pallicias ejusdem altitudinis de competentibus bordis et meremio super predictam placeam in illis locis in quibus antique pallicie modo sunt constructe. Et predicti Decanus et Capitulum facient expensas pro predicto Wharfo, circa pilyng si necesse fuerit, et circa fossura tocius predicti operis, et inuenient insuper omnia alia necessaria pro predicto Wharfo sumptibus suiis propriis. Et pro isto opere bene et fideliter perficiendo et construendo predictus Ricardus percipiet de predictis Decano et Capitulo viginti libras sterlingorum et unam robam precii unius marce, videlicet in principio operis decem marcas et alias decem marcas quando predictum meremium fuerit integre super predictam placeam paratum ad leuandum et perficiendum, et alias decem marcas cum predictum opus fuerit super predictam placeam in construccione bene leuatum. Et ad istam conuencionem ex parte predicti Ricardi bene et fideliter tenendam & perficiendam predictus Ricardus Willelmum et Simonem Coterel fratres ejusdem Ricardi inuenit fideiussores. Et predicti Decanus et Capitulum totum vetus meremium nunc in predicto Wharfo existens possidebunt. In cuius rei testimonium partes predicte huic indenture sigilla sua alternatim apposuerunt. Dat' London' die Martis proxima post festum Natiuitatis Beate Marie Virginis, Anno regni Regis Edwardi tercii post conquestum viceimo primo.

Et est sciendum quod totum meremium predictum erit de quercu.

---

[1] *nedlyng*: a 'needle' is an upright post with a hole in the upper end to receive a transverse beam.

[2] *garderobas*: probably signifies sheds, or warehouses, for storing goods.

## 17

*1347 Kenilworth Castle*

Contract between the council of Henry, Earl of Lancaster (who was then in France), and Mr. Richard de Felstede, carpenter of London. He is to make a roof for the hall, 89 ft. by 46 ft., with the doors, shutters, and three screens; also roofs for the pantry and buttery, and for the kitchen beyond them. The earl is to provide all timber and carriage, but Mr. Richard shall find carpenters and sawyers and scaffolding, &c. He shall start work as soon as the masonry is ready, and shall be paid 250 marks and shall also have clothing 'of the livery of the gentlemen' so long as he is engaged on the work.

Duchy of Lancaster, Misc. Bks. 11, fol. 52v (repeated on fol. 61v).

Ceste endenture faite parentre le tresreverent piere Johan par la grace de dieu Euesque de Nicole Mons. Piers de la Mare seneschal des Eres le noble homme Mons. Henri Counte de Lancastr' & Sire Piers de Wotton receivour general le dit counte dune part & Mestre Richard de Felstede citeseyn & carpent' de Loundres dautre part tesmoigne qe le dit Meistre Richard ferra une somet a une sale de Kenilworth de la longur de iiii<sup>xx</sup>ix pees de assise & en leoure xlvj pees ensemblement oue toutes les fenestres & huys apartenantz a la dite salle & oue tres espeeres[1] en la sale susdite. Item il ferra au boute de la dite sale une bas somet pur panetr' & butr'. Item il ferra une sumet pur une cusine a boute de la dite sale par dehors la panetr' & botrie. Et pur le dit oueraigne faire le dit Mestre Richard trouera carpentiers & sarrers a toute maner de carpentrie & sarure qapendra a la dite oueraigne del hure qil le merisme soit mys en la place ou lez ditez mesons serront faites. Et lauandit Counte de Lanc' trouera tote manere de merisme & cariage tanqe en la dite place ou le dit oueraigne serra leue. Et le dit Meistre Richard ferra le dit oueraigne bien & couenablement com il est ordeigne & deuise. Et auxint acorde est entre les dites parties qe le dit Meistre Richard pur le dit oueraigne a ses custages demeigne trouera skaffoldes cordes ginnes[2] & toutes autres instrumentz qe apartenent pur lauantdit oueraigne faire & leuer. Mais mons' de Lancastr' susdit trouera merisme pur les dites skaffoldes ginnes & pur toutes les autres instrumentz. Et pur loueraigne susdit auera le dit Mestre Richard deuz cent & sinkaunte marcz desterlinges. De les queux ccl marc desterlings le dit Mestre Richard serra paie en la feste de Saint Martin en yuerne lan du reigne le Roi Edward tiers puis le conquest vintisme primer de xl liures desterlinges, En la feste en la Purificacion notre Dame adonqes proschein auenir xx<sup>li</sup> destr', En la feste de Pask adonkes prochein auenir xxx<sup>li</sup> desterlings, En la feste de la Natiuite de Seint Johan le Bapt' adonkes prochein ensuant xxx<sup>li</sup>, Et en la feste de la decollacion Seint Johan le Bapt' adonkes prochein suant xx<sup>li</sup>. Et ceo qe remandra aderere adonqes de les ccl marcz le dit Mestre Richard serra pleinement paie com le dit oueraigne soit tout parfait. Et auera le dit Mestre Richard de dit Counte robe de la liuere de gentils hommes par tout le temps qe le dit Mestre Richard esterra en le dit oueraigne faire. Et si tout come la masonerie

---

[1] *espeeres*: screens.      [2] *ginnes*: machines, such as windlasses and cranes.

de piere isoit prest le dit Mestre Richard y serra prest de sa partie aperformer les dites besoignes issint qe nulle defaute ne serra en lui troue. En tesmoignaunce de quele chose les auantdits Euesqe, Sire Piers, & Piers, & le dit mestre Richard a ceste endenture entrechaungeablement ount mys lur seals. Escript en le manoir de Sauuoye pres de Loundres le xvjᵉ iour Octobr' lan susdit.

# 18

*1348 Sandon* (*Herts.*)

Agreement with a mason to pull down and rebuild the chancel of the church on the old foundations. The side walls to be 17 feet in height; the east window to be of three lights; each side wall to have two two-light windows of similar design. There are to be angle buttresses, and one buttress on each side wall. He is to have all the material of the old chancel, and 20 marks, paid by instalments. He takes an oath to perform his contract.

St. Paul's MS. no. 1264.

Hec indentura facta inter Magistros Alanum de Hothom et Johannem de Barnet canonicos Sancti Pauli London' nomine dominorum Decani et Capituli ecclesie supradicte conuenientes ex parte una, et Thomam Rikelyng de [Berkweye cem]entarium ex altera testatur quod inter dictas partes sic conuenit videlicet quod dictus Thomas sumptibus suis propriis faciet muros [cancelli] ecclesie de Sandon usque ad fundamentum eorum penitus demoliri et si quem defectum post demolicionem dictorum murorum repererit [      ] huius defectum faciet congrue reparari ac super antiquum fundamentum dicti cancelli nouos muros videlicet duos [    sep]temdecim pedum computando altitudine et fundamento supradicto et unum murum in capite orientali altitudinis conuenientis [      ] muris predictis faciet eciam in dicto capite orientali unam fenestram tria diuersoria que Dayes dicuntur habentem fabrice [      ] in quolibet angulo capitali dicti cancelli faciet unum Botras latitudinis quinque pedum in fundamento spiscitudinis pedis et dimidie [      alt]itudinis conuenientis et faciet scuwes dictorum Botras de lapide lapidicine de Bernaco residuum vero de bona alba p[etra     ]. Item faciet in quolibet muro laterali duas fenestras similes fabrice et forme dicte capitalis fenestre quarum quelibet habebit duo diuersoria que Dayes nuncupantur et in quolibet muro laterali unum Botras latitudinis quatuor pedum et spiscitudinis pedis et dimidie et altitudinis competentis faciet eciam ex parte australi unum hostium competens in altitudine et latitudine. Pro isto autem [opere] sic ut predicitur suis sumptibus adimplendo habebit dictus Thomas totam materiam lapideam dicti cancelli et viginti marcas [sterl]-ing' sibi succesiue per particulas prout circa construccionem dicti cancelli operatus fuerit persoluendas ad quod quidem opus in [      ] bene et fideliter adimplendum dictus Thomas obligat se heredes et executores suos et omnia bona sua et nichilominus ad [      ]cionem in forma predicta quatenus ipsum concernit fideliter obseruandam corporale prestitit iuramentum. In quorum testimonium [partes predicte] sigilla sua huic indenture alternatim apposuerunt.

Data apud Sandon predictam xj die Mensis Julii anno domini millesimo ccc^{mo} quadragesimo octauo.

[*Dorse*] Memorandum quod x die Julii anno domini m[cccxl]viij [hora] prima in Cancello ecclesie de Sandon Thomas Rikelyng de Berkweye cementarius ad infrascript' [　　] sancta dei euangelia corporale prestitit iuramentum presente domino Martino de Hoxton tunc Vicario de Sandon.

## 19

*1348 Stafford Castle*

A sixteenth-century copy, with a number of blunders, headed: 'The copy of the [　　] betwyxt Sir Raufe & the french mason for the buylding of Stafford Castle in this sort as hit now ys.' To which William Hamper has added a note that the mason was not French but took his name from Bicester in Oxfordshire. I am indebted to Miss M. Gollancz, Librarian of the William Salt Library, for a photograph of the document.

This is hardly a contract so much as a vague and jejune note, to the effect that the mason is to build the castle according to the device and orders of Sir Ralph. The towers are to be 10 ft. higher than the other buildings; the walls are to be 7 ft. thick at the base; and he is to be paid at the rate of 5 marks for every perch (of 24 ft.) in length and foot in height, and to have fuel for his lodging and hay for his horse.

> Bagot MSS. in William Salt Library, Stafford.

Cest endenture faicte entre mons' Raufe baron de Stafford dune parte & mestre John de Burcestre mason de autre parte Tesmoigne q' acouenu est entre eux q' le dit mestre John fera un Chastelle sur la moete[1] deinz la maneire[2] de lee & de longe & de haunt oue tours sales chambers chapele gardrobes chemeinees vys fenestre huis & portes ensemblement en voussmes[3] solonc de deuys & lordinaunce le dit mons' Rauf & q' tous les tours soient plus hautes q' la sale & les chambers par dies pies & q' le comencement del miur soit de lee sept pies roialls horspries les escuemenes & leggementz[4] prenant pur chescun perche de pie roiall cynke marcis & de la perche de xxiiij pec' Et q' les vises voutz fenestres chemenees & huis soient mesures par totz lours planes de deinz le miure. Et le dit mons' Rauf fera cariere pere sabiloun & caus tanq a pie de la moet. Et le dit mons' Rauf trouera scaffoldes escheles claies barwes bokettes fernes cables & vessels necessaries pur le oeure, fuall pur son hostell pur lui & pur sez gentes, & feyne pur son chiuall. Et le dit mestre fera cariere pere sabiloun & toutz autres choses necessaries q' partenent al sem^r e[5] del pie de la moete tanq' a somet a ces costages propres, tanq le sem^r e[5] del dit Chastell soit tot parfaite. En temoignance de quele choese a cestes endentures les parties auantditz entrechangeablement ont mys lours soials. Et pour ceoque le soiall mons' Rauf nest pas preste les soials

---

[1] *moete*: motte, or mound.
[2] *maneire*: 'de Stafford' probably omitted.
[3] *en voussmes*: perhaps for 'ove voussures', with vaults.
[4] *escuemenes et leggementz*: splays, or plinths, and string-courses.
[5] *semere*: probably a misreading of 'oeure', work.

mestre Willm. de Colton & John de Pikstoke son mys. Escript' a Chastell de Stafford le iour Seint Hillarie lan due regne le Roy Edward tiers apres le conquest vintisme premiere.

20

### 1359 Vale Royal Abbey (Cheshire)

The Prince of Wales and his Abbey of Vale Royal engage Master William de Helpeston, mason, to build twelve chapels round the east end of the quire of the abbey church. He is to have a free hand over details, and to carry up the walls from the plinth to the level of the crest of the parapet of a chapel beside the quire already built by him. He shall choose such masons, &c., as he needs, the convent procuring them, and shall discharge them if unprofitable, and shall pay them their wages and provide iron and steel for their tools. He shall construct a tracing-house (or drawing-office) in the north transept, for 10 marks paid down. The convent shall provide lodging for the workmen. The Prince shall pay him yearly 200 marks, to the total amount of £860. If these payments stop before a third of the work is finished, Master William may withdraw and work elsewhere; if a third or more has been finished, he may not only go elsewhere, but shall also have a due proportion of the life pension which the convent have agreed to pay him when the work is completed; if the convent cause any delay, they shall pay him the whole pension.

Exch. T.R., Misc. Books, 279, f. 197.

Ceste endenture faite parentre lui nobles homme mons' Edward Prince de Gales ses chapelleins Abbe et Couuent de sa maisoun de Vaureal dune part et Mestre William de Helpeston masoun dautre part, tesmoigne q' le dit William ad empris le oeuereigne de masounerie de dusze chapelles enuyronantes le qoer de la eglise auantdite vers le Est affaire et apperformer oue leide dieu en bone et couenable manere a chaunger et ordiner ses moldes a sa volentee et a cesser le orbe oeuereigne[1] de les chapelles susdites saunz chalaunge de nully, comenceant la dite oeuereigne de les chapelles auntdites al ligement table[2] paramont la terre en hautesse tanq' la crest del alure duce (*sic*) chapelle esteant ioust le dit coer de nouel par le dit William faite. Et auxint le dit William nomera et eslira touz les masouns et autres oeuerours quant il enbusoigne p^r les dites chapelles cestassauer masouns bayardours mortermakeres wyndres des porrez[3] (*sic*), p^r queux les ditz Abbe et Couent p^rchaceront commission de n̄r̄e dit s^r le Prince p^r faire venire les ditz ouerours deinz sa s'ie[4] trouez au dit William, et quant ils ne sont profitables p^r le dit ouereigne ils serrount remuer par le dit William a sa volente. Issuit qil ne soit mye delaie nendamage del dit oeuereigne, et estre ce le dit William trouera fer et assier affaire et damender les instrumentz des masouns susditz, Cestassauer haches et feres saunz estre charge dascunes autres instruments. Et estre ce le dit William paiera a les ditz masouns bayardours mortermakeres et wynderes de pieres lour salarie et a feuere p^r son oeuereigne[5] des ditz haches

---

[1] *orbe oeuereigne*: traceried panelling, in which the tracery is 'blind' and not pierced.

[2] *ligement table*: 'earth table', or plinth: see above, p. 106.

[3] *porrez*: a blunder for *pierres*.  [4] *s'ie: seigneurie*.

[5] Note that the masons, &c., are paid wages, the smith is paid by piecework.

[et] fers lower saunz ascunes autres charges ou autres choses a trouer tochantz le oeuereigne des chapelles auantdites, Forpris louereigne dun traisour deinz mesme leglise en certein lieu entre eux limitez Cestassauer en la partie de la North crose pnant des ditz Abbe et Couent p$^r$ la dite trasour dis marcs dargent deuant la meyn. Et estre ce les ditz Abbe et Couent troueront touz maneres des ouerours et touz autres choses prestz s$^r$ la place touch' louereigne auantdit al garnissement le dit William. Et auxint les ditz Abbe et Couent troueront a les ditz masouns et oeuerours maisouns fowail[1] et liter, et en cas q' la dite ouereigne soit arrerisse ou le dit Will' endamagee par les ditz Abbe et Couent q' adonqes amendes y soit fait au dit Will' par les ditz Abbe et Couent selonc la taxacion de bons gentz du pays et masouns, p$^r$ quele oeuereigne des chapelles auant ditz n$\overline{\text{re}}$ dit s$\overline{\text{re}}$ le Prince paiera par an au dit William en la dite Abbee par les meyns le dit Abbe deux cent marcs dor ou dargent a les festes de Seint Mich' et de Pasqz par oweles porciouns tanqz la somme de dccclx li. dor ou dargent soit pleinement paie, comenceant le prime terme de paiement a la feste de Seint Mich' proch' ensuant la confeccion du cestes. Et en cas q' n$\overline{\text{re}}$ dit s$^r$ le Prince cesse de soun paiement faire au dit William apres q' la tierz partie du dit oeureigne soit fait q' adonqs la tierz partie dun corrodie et dun empension de xl$^s$. grantez au dit William p$^r$ terme de sa vie par les ditz Abbe et Couent solounc le p$^r$port du faite meismes ces Abbe et Couent demoerge au dit William p$^r$ terme de sa vie selonc de meisme le faite et le remenant du dit corrodie et empension cesse en toute en cas q' nulle defaute soit troue en les ditz Abbe et Couent des choses susdites ou ascunes dycelles et outre le dit William soit alarge de faire son profit aillours saunz chalange de n$\overline{\text{re}}$ dit seignour le Prince ou des ditz Abbe et Couent ou nulle autre. Et en cas q' n$\overline{\text{re}}$ dit seignour le Prince cesse de son paiement faire au dit William deuant la tierz partie de dit oeuereigne y soit faite et nulle defaute y soit troue en les ditz Abbe et Couent des choses susdites ou dascuns dycelles q' adonqs le dit William soit a large de faire son profit saunz chalange de nully et les dites corrodie et empension cessent en toutes. Et apres lacomplissement du dit tierz partie du dit ouereigne tanq' a la complissement de les trois parties de mesme louereigne deuise en quatere soient les dites corrodie et enpension encrescez proporcionalement solonc la quantite del trauail le dit William countre la tierz partie dycelle come dessus est dit. Et apres laccomplissement des ditz trois parties du dit ouereigne en cas q' n$\overline{\text{re}}$ dit seignour le Prince cesse de son paiement faire au dit William q' adonqs le dit William soit a large de faire soun profit saunz chalange de nully et les dites corrodie et empension demoergent entierrement au dit William soulounc le p$^r$port du fait susdit. Issuit toutesfoiz q' les ditz Abbe et Couent soient trouez en ascun defaute durant la dite ouereigne par quel la dite ouereigne soit delaie ou destourbe q' adonqs les auantdites corrodie et enpension demoergent entierement au dit William p$^r$ terme de sa vie solounc le p$^r$port du faite susdite. En tesmoign de quele chose les parties

---

[1] *fowail*: fuel.

auantditz a cestes endentures ount mys lour seals. Don &c. a Cestre le xx iour daugst lan &c. Dengl' xxxiij et de Fraunce xx.

Ceste copie examinee par Delues en la presence de Wolmestr'.

# 21

## *1369 London*

Two carpenters agree to build a range of 86 yards in length, containing twenty shops, with a gateway between the first two at the north end. They are to be built of heart of oak, and each shop shall have a gable on the east and west. The windows on the street front shall all be of one design, with well-worked lintels, except at the corner, where there shall be two bay windows. The doors and shutters are to be of Eastland boards; the partitions, stairs, water-pipes, and benches in the halls of oak. Scantlings of all the timbers are given. (For identification of the names of these timbers, see above, pp. 197–205.) The whole is to be finished in a little under 2½ years; for which they shall receive £303, in three instalments. Each party gives a bond of £300 for fulfilment of the terms, the carpenters associating two other carpenters with themselves.

St. Paul's MSS. No. 1796.

Ceste endenture faite en le Chapitre del esglise de seint Paul de Loundres le septisme iour Daprill lan du regne nre. s' le Roi Edward tiercz apres le conqueste quarante tiercz parentre le Dean et Chapitre de mesme le lieu dune part et Roger Fraunkeleyn et Johan Page carpenters dautrepart tesmoigne q' acorde et assentuz est parentre les parties auantditz en manere qensuyt. Cestassauer q' les auantditz Roger et Johan edifieront a lour coustages demesne tout le soil des auantditz Dean et Chapitre de la porte de lour Pistrine en la part boriale taunq' al corner de meisme le pistrine vers le South, et meisme le corner, et auxint de meisme le corner tout lour soyl tanq' a les mesons labbe de Burgh en le West, quele place contient en tout iiij\*\*vj verges de fer dassise, et ferront les auantditz Roger et Johan vynt mansions en le dite place, bones et couenables, et serront edifiez a la manere des shopes par toute la dite place vers le haut chemyn, et owelement les ferront aporcioner en meisme la place, et outre ceo ferront une porte bone, nouele et couenable de bone carpentrie et nette, et en meisme la porte un wyket, et serra toute la porte danxien meryn de coer de keyne[1] bone et nette, et tut le remenant del dit edefis de nouel meryn de coer de keyne bon et gros de double stage par tut, et serra la dite porte faite parentre des deux shopes primers en le Este vers le North, et ferront toutes les fenestres du dit edifis oue bone lyntels, bels et nettes dune seute vers le haute chemyn par tout, forpris q' al dit corner en le Est ils ferront deux fenestres bayes bones et bels. Et auxi ferront le dit corner et tout le edifiz auantdit de bone carpentrie et nette oue vynt gables vers le Est et le West, et ferront auxint tout le dit edifitz de la largesse qest le Celer q'icy est illeoq's oue ses murs, et en chescune mansion ferront un entreclos tout droit de la terre tanq' al summite de meisme les mansions tout en haut oue greses[2]

---

[1] *coer de keyne*: heart of oak.  [2] *greses*: stairs.

bones et couenables par queles lem porra aler esement en toutes chambres des ditz mansions, et ferront auxint pipes des tables de mer' de keyne pur les longaynes de chescun mansion ensemblement oue bankes[1] couenables en les sales dicelles, et troueront auxint les auantditz Roger et Johan latthes de queor de keyne a tout le edefis auantdit a lour coustages demesne, et ferront touz les huys et fenestres de mesme le edefiz de tables Destland bons et couenables, et tout le remenant de tables pur le dit edifitz sibien pur les solers come pur les goters serra planchis-bord de queor de keyne bon et de couenable assise. Item acorde et assentuz est parentre les parties auantditz q' le meryn dont tous les ditz maisons serront faites serra de lassise desouth escrite Cestassauer les plates pur la frount de vij pouces en espessete et xij pouces de laeure. Item les plates q' serront par dedeins serront vj pouces despessete et xij pouces de laeure. Item les principals poncheons del primer stage serront xij pouces en laeure et ix pouces en espessete. Item le primer somer serra del espescete ix pouces del seute des poncheons et en laeure xiij pouces. Item les moynels en mylieu des fenestres pur les shopes serront en espescete vj pouces et ix pouces en laeure, a seruyr lespessete del somer. Item les gistes del primer stage serront chescun de eaux x pouces en laeure et viij pouces en espessete. Item le coiffetre q' gisera sur mesmes les gistes serra en espessete vj pouces et viij pouces et demy pouce en laeure. Item les principals poncheons q' serront desuz le dit coiffetre serra chescun de eaux x pouces en laeure et viij pouces en espescete. Item la seconde somer outre mesmes les poncheons serront de xij pouces en laeure et viij pouces en espessete del seute des poncheons par desouth. Item les gistes q' giseront sur le dit seconde somer serront ix pouces de laeure et vij pouces en espessete. Item le coiffetre outre mesmes les gistes de v ponces et demy en espessete et en laeure vij pouces et demy. Item les princi-pals ponchons sur meisme le coiffetre ix pouces de laeure et vij pouces en espessete. Item wyndow ponchons serront bons et couenables come en espessete et laeure solonc la proporcions de lautre meryn. Item les gistes del Seler xij pouces en laeure et x pouces en espessete. Item les principals postes de mesme la meson xiiij pouces en laeure de la terre et xij pouces en laeure al top et somet et xij pouces en espessete al terre et x pouces en espessete al top et sommet. Item les entreteys parentre les postes x pouces en laeure et ix pouces despessete. Item les resnes de toutz les maisons auantditz x pouces de laeure et viij pouces des-pessete. Item les Raftres pour touz les ditz maisons vj pouces de laeure al pee et v pouces al top en laeure et v pouces despessete al pee et iiij pouces al top despessete. Item les lyernes pur toutz les ditz maisons vj pouces despessete et viij pouces de laeure; et mountans et braces pur les lyernes bons et suffisantz come appent. Et ne serra lespace parentre chescun de gistes du dit edefis quaunt ils serront mys forsq' de vj pouces dassise. Et serra toute la dite place parentre la porte susdite et le dit corner ensemblement oue meisme le corner plenerement edifiee et meisme le edefiz leuee et tout pleynement apparaille des bons meryn

[1] *bankes*: benches.

et carpentrie en manere come desuz est dit parentre le iour de la fesaunce dicestes et la feste de seint Michel proschein venant et tout le remenant de la dite place en meisme la fourme edifiee come desuz est dit parentre la dite feste de Seint Michel et la feste de Seint Michel a deux anns adonqs proschein ensuant saunz outre tarrier celle partie. Et en cas q' lun des ditz Carpenters deuye auant le fournysement des dites ouerages, q' dieu defend, lautre de eaux q' suruyuera parfournera meismes les ouerages en manere come desuz est dit. Et prendront les auantditz Roger et Johan de auantditz Dean et Chapitre pur mesme loue-raigne ccciij$^{li}$ desterling ou door a la value, et prendront meisme la somme par menues parcelles toutdroit come ils oueront Issuit q' la tierce partie de tout le dit ouerage faite ils serront paiez de c$^{li}$ de la dite somme et la seconde tierce partie aussint faite ils serront auxint seruys des autres c$^{li}$ de la dite somme. Et la tierce partie de dite ouerage parfaite serront seruys et pleynement paiez de ciij$^{li}$ en parpaiement de toutes les ccciij$^{li}$ suisdites. Et come les auantditz Dean et Chapitre soient obligez par lour lettres obligatories a les auanditz Roger et Johan en ccc$^{li}$ desterling Et mesme ceaux Roger Johan Page Johan de Glemesford et Johan Godwot Carpenters soient auxint par lour lettres obligatories obligeez as auanditz Dean et Chapitre en ccc$^{li}$ come en les dites lettres est contenu plus a plein vuillent et grauntent sibien les auanditz Dean et Chapitre pur eaux et pur lour successours come les auanditz Roger Johan Page Johan de Glemesford et Johan Godwot pur eaux et lour executours q' si toutes les couenantz contenuz en ceste presente endenture soient bien et loialment tenuz et pourfournez dune part et dautre qadonq' les dites lettres obligatories soient tenuz pur nulles et perdent lour force et autrement estoisent en lour force et vertue. En tes-moigneance de quele chose a ceste endenture les parties auantditz entrechaunge-ablement ont mys lour seals. Dat a Loundres le iour et lan auantditz.

22

*1370 London*

A mason agrees to build the stonework for a range of 18 shops. He is to pull down an existing wall to 1 foot above the ground, and level it to carry the groundsills of the shop-fronts; to build another wall, 2 feet thick, parallel with this at the back, carrying it up to carry the joists of the first floor; to make sleeper walls, 1 foot high, at the ends, and party walls, dividing the cellars and reaching up to the first-floor joists, and foundations for the principal posts. He is also to make ten stone pits for privies, 10 feet deep, eight of them being double (i.e. serving two houses); and ten fireplaces, eight of these also being double, of which the hearths shall be made of stones and tilesherds, and the flues of 'Flanders tiles', or bricks, the chimneys being carried 1 foot above the roof. All materials shall be supplied to him, except the bricks and plaster for the fireplaces, which he shall provide. For this he is to have 50 marks, and a coat and hood; 40s., and 10 marks for a shipload of bricks, being paid in advance, and the rest as the work advances.

St. Paul's MSS. no. 1074.

Ceste endenture faite parentre le Dean et le Chapitele de Seint Pol en Loundres dune part: et Pieres de Webbenham Mason de mesme la Cite dautre part, tesmoigne q' le dit Pieres ad aconuenuz oue les auauntditz Dean et Chapitele et enpris p$^r$ abatre une mur de pere iesqs' a une pe$^1$ desus la terre quele mur estet a Powlesbrewerne sur la place q' serra nouuel edifie. Et pus le dit Peres ferra le dit mur playn p$^r$ mettre sur la dit mur lez plates de xviij nouelz schoppes, queles schoppes chescun continera en longure xj piez et en layeur xxv piez. Et tut le veille roboise$^2$ del auauntditz mur qil abatera il mettera al profit del nouel ouereigne auauntdit. Et le dit Pieres ferra un autre mur del longure dez auauntditz schoppes oue le fundement quele mur leuera en hautesse del terre a lez gystes dez auauntditz schoppes et serra en spissitude ij pez, la quele mur esteera de deins en mesme la place. Et le dit Peres ferra en la Southpartie du dite place fundementz trauerz del une coste al autre p$^r$ lez enterclosez dez ditz schoppes bonz et sufficiauntz p$^r$ porter lez plates dez auauntditz schoppes queux leuerount une pe desus la terre, et en le Estpartie del auauntdit place le dit Peres ferra enterclosez mures p$^r$ departier lez celerez desouth lez ditz schoppes, queux leuerount en hautesse alez gystes auauntditz. Et auxi le dit Pieres ferra en la dite place certeynes fundements p$^r$ porter lez principalez Postes queux esterount enmy lez schoppes auauntditz. Et ferra le dit Peres en la dite place x Puttes de pier p$^r$ Preuez,$^3$ dez quelz Puttez viij serrount dowblez et chescun en profundite x piez, et de longure x piez, et de layeur xj piez. Et auxi le dit Pieres ferra en lez auauntditz schoppes x Chemeneyes dez queux viij serrount dowblez et serrount faitz desus lez Mantles de Flandrisch Tyle, et desouth lez Mantles de perez et Tylescherd, et leuerount lez ditz Chemeneyes une pee desus lez couertours dez auauntditz Schoppes et chescun dez auauntditz Chemeneyes serra en layeur parentre lez Jambes v pies et di'. A quele ouereigne lez auauntditz Dean et Chapitele trouerount toute manere de pier zabulon et Lym, Scaffoldynge, Witthes et hurdles et toute manere choses qapartient a masonrie, forspris lez flaundrysch Tyles et plastre p$^r$ lez Mantel-schides dez auauntditz Chemeneyes queux le dit Peres trouera a ses propres costages. Pur quele ouereigne de parfaire come desus est dit le dit Peres prendra dez auauntditz Den et Chapitele l mars dusuel moneye et une cote et une chapron del leuere del Euesque del iour dez Innocents. Dount il receuera al comencement du dit ouereigne xl$^s$ et auxi x mars p$^r$ payer p$^r$ une Nef pleyn de flandrischtyle quant il vient, et le remenaunt come il enbosoygne et le ouereigne espleite. En tesmoyngnaunce de quele chose syben lez auauntditz Den et Chapitele come le dit Peres a cestes presentz endentures enterchaungeablement ount mys lour seals. Donez a Loundres le iour de Seint Mathie Lan du regne du Roi Edward tierce puis la conq' dengleterre quarantisme quatre.

---

$^1$ *une pe*: one foot.  $^2$ *roboise*: rubble.  $^3$ *preuez*: privies.

## 23

*1372  Arlingham  (Gloucs.)*

The parishioners contract with a mason to complete the bell tower of their church within the next three years, building 12 feet of height each year. He is to set inside the walls corbels to carry the various floors; to make a door on the east side, leading into the roof; a handsome window on the west between the first- and second-floor levels; and a small window in each wall of the uppermost story. At each floor level there shall be stone tabling, and, on the top, battlements, with gutters. He shall also make a spiral stair, with doors at top and bottom. The parishioners shall provide all materials, except tools, and shall bring them to a suitable place within 40 feet of the tower; and he shall bear all costs of workmen's wages, but they will provide board and lodging for him and his men. He shall be paid, by instalments, at the rate of 17s. and a bushel of wheat for each foot of height built round the tower.

Berkeley Castle muniments, no. 547.[1]

Hec indentura facta apud Erlyngham die Veneris in crastino Sancte Katerine virginis anno regni Regis Edwardi tercii post conquestum quadragesimo sexto inter Johannem de Yate, dominum Rogerum vicarium, Willelmum de Erlyngham, Robertum de Middelton, Walterum Hutt'(?), Johannem de Thornhulle, Johannem Heyward, Willelmum Scheef, Walterum Jakemones, Walterum Frer', Johannem Bulgaston, Radulfum Wych, Ricardum Bulgaston, Ricardum Kokkes, Hugonem atte Wode, Walterum Symondeshale, Johannem Forster, Walterum Hykemones & Johannem Cordy et omnes parochianos ecclesie de Erlyngham tam non nominatos quam nominatos ex parte una et Nicholaum Wyshongr' cementarium de Gloucestr' ex parte altera testatur quod predictus Nicholaus edificabit construet & perficiet turrim campanilis ecclesie de Erlyngham ad modum quo incipitur tam murorum quam aliorum membrorum in tribus annis proxime sequentibus post datum presencium, videlicet in quolibet anno trium annorum predictorum duodecim pedes in altitudine computandas de artificio prius facto cum quatuor boteras competenter perficiendas ad modum quo incipiuntur. Item construet ac faciet corbayllas[2] ubi fundi[3] predicti turris competenter poterint poni & unum hostium in parte orientali predicti turris ut homo supra trabes ecclesie vocatas Wyntbeemes[4] intrare et egredere poterit. Item construetur in parte occidentali predicti turris una fenestra artificialiter constructa inter primum fundum & secundum. Et secundus fundus sit positus in loco sibi apto super corbayllas sufficienter interius. Et supra superiorem fundum erunt quatuor fenestre bene et artificialiter constructe videlicet in quolibet muro una que vocantur dreinholes.[5] Et ad primum fundum et secundum et in superiore parte murorum exterius erunt tabule lapidee undique cooperientes

---

[1] I am indebted to the kindness of the Earl of Berkeley for a photograph of this document.

[2] *corbayllas*: corbels.

[3] *fundi*: floors.

[4] *wyntbeemes*: wind-beams, or collar-beams. The roof was evidently ceiled.

[5] *dreinholes*: possibly small round windows (? looking like the ends of drains). I have not found the word elsewhere.

muros predictos supra quas tabulas stabunt alie tabule videlicet batelynges[1] bene
et artificialiter constructe in circuitu murorum sicud decet cum una guttera
circum circa turrim predictum cum aliis minoribus gutteris dicte guttere deser-
vientibus. Item construetur et perficietur via girat[ur]a extendens supra superiorem fundum ita quod homo possit competenter ascendere et descendere et per
illam intrare in fundum predictum sub campanis cum hostio superius et inferius
et fenestris et omnibus aliis pertinenciis suis constructa habens exterius artificium[2]
sicud muri turris predicti. Et predictus Nicholaus edificabit et perficiet omnia
supradicta ac cementarios et operarios conducet sumptibus suis propriis ext'
capiendo de predictis parochianis pro singulis pedibus in altitudine supradicti
turris computando unicuique pedi latitudinem tocius turris in circuitu septemdecim solidos bone et legalis monete et unum bz. frumenti soluenda predicto
Nicholao in quatuor temporibus anni predictorum trium annorum, videlicet in
quolibet anno ad festum Natalis domini xl solidos ex tunc proxime sequens et
ad festum Pentecostes ex tunc proxime sequens iiij li. et sex bz. frumenti et ad
festum Sancti Petri ad Vincula xlij solidos et ad festum Omnium Sanctorum ex
tunc proxime sequens xlij solidos et sex bz. frumenti. Et ad hec facienda implenda
et perficienda et predict' pedum altitudinem construendam infra festum Natalis
domini extunc proxime sequens et festum Omnium Sanctorum eodem anno
predictus Nicholaus predictis parochianis in xl solidos se obligat et sic secundo
anno et tercio. Et iidem parochiani inuenient lapides sablonem et calcem cum
aliis utensilibus ad dictum opus necessariis in loco apto et satis propinquo infra
spacium xl pedum de campanili predicto exceptis malleis latomorum et aliis
instrumentis eorum. Et etiam parochiani inuenient predicto Nicholao et operariis
cum illo venientibus focalia et hospicia pro mora eorum et fenum pro uno equo
suo, nec predictus Nicholaus nec alii operarii skaffold nec aliquid meremium
capiant nec presumant absque licencia dictorum parochianorum. Omnibus et
singulis articulis in supradicto bene faciendis et implendis parochiani predicti tam
non nominati quam nominati se cognoverunt predicto Nicholao in xl solidos
fore obligati per presentes. In cuius rei testimonium hiis indenturis partes predicte sigilla sua apposuerunt. Hiis testibus Domino Roberto rectore de Free-
thorne, Thomas Cadul, Waltero Cl . . . .

## 24

*1373 Southwark*

Agreement by which a carpenter undertakes to build on to the gatehouse of the Prior
of Lewes, behind and at right angles to it, two rows of shops, five on the east and six on
the west, the latter projecting 22 feet. The shops are to be 12 feet from front to back, each
with a jutting upper story, on the lines of Adam Fraunceys's range of shops at the Friars
Austin. Across the farther, south, end of the rows he shall build two stables, each 14 feet
long, for 10 horses, with a loft, separated by a gateway with a chamber over (for which

---

[1] *batelynges*: battlements.        [2] *artificium*: an arrangement, i.e. battlements.

gate and chamber the prior shall find the materials). The whole to be finished before Christmas year. For this he shall have £120, in four instalments. Both parties give mutual bonds of £100 for performance of the contract.

Cotton MS. Vesp. F. xv, f. 183. Translated in<br>a full abstract, in *Surrey Arch. Coll.* xliii.

Ceste endenture faite a Suthwerk le primer iour de Decembr' lan de regne nre. Seigno[r] le Roi Edward tierce puis le conqueste dengleterre quaraunte septisme entre les Religiouses hommes Johan Prio[r] de la mayson de Lewes et le couent de mesme le lieu dune part et William Wyntryngham de Suthwerk carpent' dautre part tesmoygne q' le dit William ad grauntee et se oblige de fayre en lest partie deinz launciene porte qarest de lostel des ditz Priour et couent en Suthwerk cynk Schoppes chescun Schoppe oue une estage oue getteiz estendauntz en longure de la North deuers le South de la mayson de dit William quatrevyntz et quatre peez dassise; et ser[r]a chescun des ditz cynk cent (*sic*) schoppes en layeure quatorze pees dassise. Et auxi le dit William ferra en le West partie de dite porte sys autres schoppes en mesme le maner quels estendrount en longure de le North vers le South de la mayson de dit William cent et sys pees dassise, et serra chescun de mesmes les schoppes en laeyure dousze pees dassise, des queux sys schoppes en la dite West partie ysserount de hors la dite porte vynt et deux pees et de deinz quatrevyntz et quatre pees. Et serrount toutes les dites schoppes faitz en la manere et forme en touz poyntz come est le longe Rente[1] de Adam Fraunceys vers lest fyn del eglise des Freres Austines en Loundres, tout as coustages de dit William, salue chymeneyes et un mur de piere adors le dit Rente de dit Adam. Et outre ceo le dit William ferra al south bout des ditz unze schoppes atrauers deux estables, chescun pour dyz chiuaux et quatorze peez en layeure oue solores desus saunz getteyz pour eyns mettre q'cumq' chose q' pleira as ditz Prio[r] et Couent. Et auxi le dit William ferra entre les auauntditz deux estables une porte bone et sufficeaunt oue une chambre desus. As quels porte et chambre desus les ditz Prio[r] et Couent troueront toute manere de merysme et toute manere de ferrure et couuerture pour ycelles porte et chambre tout as coustages des ditz Prio[r] et Couent. Et serrount tous les auauntditz unze schoppes oue les soleres, estables, porte et chambre paramount, parfaitz en la manere auauntditz entre cy et la feste de Nowel proschein venaunt apres le fesaunce dycestes, et un an adonq' proschein ensuant. Et pour tout lauauntdit ouereigne oue quantq' enbosoygnera a ycelle come desus est specifie lauauntdit William prendra des ditz Prio[r] et Couent ou de lour successores cent et vynt lyueres desterlinges et tout le veille merysme ore illeoq' esteaunt et touz autres choses syaunt come les ditz unze schoppes oue gardynes a ycelles appurtenauntz estendront en lauauntdite place. Cest assauoyr, al feste de Seint Michel proschein venaunt apres le fesaunce dycestes quarante marcz, al feste de Pasq' adonq' proschein ensuaunt sessaunte marcz, al feste de Seint Johan le Baptistre

---

[1] *rente*: a row of houses; cf. 'Chichester Rents', off Chancery Lane.

adonq' proschein ensuaunt quaraunte marcz, et al feste de Seint Michel adonq' proschein ensuant quarante marcz en parpayement.[1] Et a touz cestes couenauntz susditz pour bien et lealment tenir et parformer en touz pointz come desus est dit, les parties auauntditz se obligent et chescun de eux par soy a autre en cent lyures desterlinges.[2]

25

## *1373 Boxley Abbey (Kent)*

Agreement between the convent and a mason for rebuilding their cloister, and making four windows in the south wall of the church, and doors to the church, dorter, and refectory. He is first to remove the old foundations, and to build a wall $2\frac{1}{2}$ feet high and $1\frac{1}{2}$ feet thick, with a stone gutter outside it. For this the convent shall find materials; the rest of the stone he shall provide from a quarry which he rents from the abbey. Detailed measurements of the various piers and columns are given; above these shall be tracery, and on top of the wall a stone tabling under the wood of the roof. He shall finish the whole within five years. The first year he shall hew and prepare the stone for one walk of the cloister and the dorter and refectory doors, so that it can be carried to the abbey in the summer and he can carve it during the winter and set it up in the spring, or, if the weather is unfavourable, in the summer. So each year he shall make one walk; and the third year he shall also make the four windows and door of the church and a reading-desk in the north wall. All the tracery and moulded work shall agree with the patterns and drawings and shall be of good stone. The convent shall provide all carriage, scaffolding, iron, lead, &c., and shall pay him £30 for the first year, and £22. 10s., by eight instalments, for each of the next four years—£120 in all.

Exch. K.R. Accts. 622, no. 46.

Hec indentura testatur quod Ita convenit inter Abbatem et Conventum de Boxele ex una parte et Stephanum Lomherst de Souttune masoun ex altere vid[t] quod predictus Stephanus faciet et fideliter et integraliter perficiet eisdem Abbati et conventui totum opus lapideum quod pertinebit ad unum novum claustrum circumquaque in monasterio [? suo] de Boxele faciendum simul cum quatuor fenestris faciendis et ponendis in australi muro ecclesie sue supra dictum claustrum scil[t] de magnitudine duarum aliarum fenestrarum ibidem nunc positarum unde una erit ejusdem forme et alie tres alterius forme et cum tribus hostiis Ecclesie scil[t] Dormitorii et Refectorii per modum et tempus infra limitatum vid[t] predictus Stephanus fodiet fundamentum veteris claustri et reimplebit illud usque ad solum et leuabit supra dictum fundamentum unum murum duarum pedum et dimidie in altitudine et unius pedis et dimidie in spissitudine et ponet defforis unam gutteram circumquaque de lapide sculpto et predictus Abbas et conventus invenient lapides calcem et sabulum et cariagium ad omnia ista. Deinde predictus Stephanus inveniet lapides ad totum residuum operis perficiendum de

---

[1] If the date of the contract is really 1 December, it is difficult to understand the terms appointed for these payments.

[2] The shops, &c., are leased to the said William Wyntryngham on a repairing lease for the term of his life.

lapide voc' Ston of grece[1] de quarrario ejusdem Abbatis et conventus in Chyn-
gele quod idem Stephanus tenet ad firmam de eisdem, et erunt omnes lapides
sani et integri absque defectu et bene et munde excissi et politi. Et ponet primo
supra dictum murum bases vocatos sulis[2] altitudinis dimidie pedis et latitudinis
unius pedis et dimidie, deinde eriget columpnas majores et minores et erunt
omnes majores columpne spissitudinis basis scil[t] unius pedis et dimidie latitudinis
unius pedis et altitudinis trium pedum, bases vero et columpne angulares erunt
singule duorum pedum latitudinis ex utraque parte, minores columpne erunt
ejusdem altitudinis, latitudinis vero dimidie pedis, spissitudinis dimidie pedis et
quarterie, et erunt omnes columpne minores singuli de uno lapide integro.
Deinde levabit diversas formas[3] secundum diversitates columpnarum latitudinis
spissitudinis et altitudinis ejusdem, et supra dictas formas ponet unam tablementum circumquaque subtus meremium. Et perficiet idem Stephanus omne
istud opus totius claustri fenestrarum et hostiorum una cum porgecturis[4] et
brussuris[5] et omnibus pertinentiis suis tam non nominatis quam nominatis inter
datum presentis indenture et festum Sancti Johannis Baptiste quod erit anno
domini m[l]ccc[mo] septuagesimo octavo per modum infrascriptum vid[t] primo
anno petras fodiet excidet planabit et parabit unam panam[6] scil[t] quartam partem
claustri cum duobus hostiis Dormitorii et Refectorii ita ut Abbas eam cariari
possit eodem anno tempore estivo ante fenacionem[7] et ipse Stephanus eam
formare et sculpere tempore yemali sequenti et erigere et ponere tempore
quadragesimali sequenti cum predictis hostiis si tempus opportunum fuerit
alioquin tempore estivali ita tamen opportune ut carpentarii et coopertores non
impediantur de opere perficiendo per defectus ipsius, et sic de anno in annum
quolibet anno eriget et faciet integraliter unam panam et tercio anno posicionis
sue faciet unam panam et pulpitum collacionis in eadem et predictas quatuor
fenestras cum pertinentiis suis et dictum hostium ecclesie cum gradibus suis, et
erunt omnes bases columpne forme fenestre et ostia excisa sculpta et polita bene
et munde juxta formas et mensuras moldas et portreturas inter eos inde indentatas
et de bono et electo lapide et pro posse uniformis coloris et absque fissuris et
ventis. Et predictus Abbas et conventus invenient ad dictum opus totum
cariagium et cementum ferrum et plumbum et scaphot[8] et crates et solvent
predicto Stephano a principio hujus convencionis usque ad festum Sancti
Michaelis post unum annum revolutum triginta libras bone et legalis monete,
deinde quolibet anno quatuor annorum sequentium viginti duas libras et decem
solidos per octo equales porciones et ad octo eque distantes terminos vid[t] usque
ad persolucionem centum viginti librarum. Et ad hec omnia et singula bene et
fideliter facienda tenenda et implenda tam predictus Stephanus obligat se et

---

[1] *grece*, or *grete*, = grit-stone.
[2] *sulis*: sills.
[3] *formas*: tracery.
[4] *porgecturis*: pargetting, or plastering.
[5] *brussuris*: the meaning is obscure.
[6] *panam*: a pane, or walk, of the cloister.
[7] *fenacionem*: hay harvest.
[8] *scaphot*: scaffolding.

heredes et executores suos terras suas et tenementa et omnia bona sua mobilia et immobilia ad quorumcumque manus devenerint predictis Abbati et conventui et successoribus suis Et predictus Abbas et conventus consimili modo obligant se et monasterium suum et successores suos et omnia bona sua predicto Stephano et executoribus suis. In cujus rei testamentum tam predictus abbas et conventus sigillum suum commune quam predictus Stephanus sigillum suum hiis indenturis alternatim apposuerunt. Data apud Boxele die Sancti Petri ad Vincula anno domini m¹ccc^{mo} septuagesimo tercio et anno regni Regis Edwardi tercii post Conquestum anglie xlvij^{mo}.

*Dorse*] M^d quod licet fiat mencio de quodam Pulpito faciendo in parte boriali Claustri infrascripti, non tamen ad hoc tenetur nisi de nova convencione.

# 26

## *1374 Cambridge, Trinity Hall*

Agreement by a carpenter to supply the necessary timbers, of good oak, for the frame, partition walls, floors, and doors of a range of chambers which he is to erect within the college on the lines of the existing buildings. The whole work to be completed within a year, for £100, payable in instalments.

Willis and Clark, *Arch. Hist. of Cambridge*, i. 238.

Hec indentura tripartita facta Cantabrigg' decimo septimo die Septembris anno regni regis Edwardi tertii post conquestum Angliae quadragesimo octavo inter venerabilem in Christo patrem et dominum Dominum Simonem dei gratia London' Episcopum ex una parte, et Johannem de Mildenhale de Cantabrigg' Carpentarium ex alia parte, testatur quod predictus Johannes concessit et manucepit inuenire maremium quercinum bonum et sufficiens pro omnibus cameris nouiter faciendis in manso habitacionis scolarium Collegii Aule sancte Trinitatis Cantebrigg': videlicet copulas siue sparresWyndbems suchlates¹ Asthelers Corbels jowpes balkes summers siue dormannes giystes et etiam stures² cum pertinenciis pro mediis parietibus in dictis cameris sub et supra, videlicet tam in solariis quam in celariis, ac etiam steires et steyretres.³

Concessit insuper prefatus Johannes et manucepit inuenire huiusmodi maremium quercinum pro domibus construendis a boriali fine Aule dicti Collegii versus boream usque ad venellam communem vocatam Heneylane de materia forma fabrica ac bonitate simili fabrice tecti eiusdem Aule cum sumers et giystes pro solariis, et cum stures et grunsiles⁴ cum pertinentiis pro mediis parietibus sub et supra dicta solaria versus coquinam de nouo facienda. Et etiam idem Johannes inueniet omnimodum maremium pro omnibus et singulis domibus cameris et ceteris supradictis necessarium vel qualitercumque requisitum, et dictum marem-

---

¹ *suchlates*: this should read *suthlaces*; *see* above, p. 211.
² *stures*: the uprights of the wattling.
³ *steyretres*: the timber framing of the stairs.
⁴ *grunsiles*: groundsills.

ium faciet ad dictum mansum adduci, ipsumque maremium operabitur formabit leuabit et perficiet sumptibus suis: et, quantum ad cameras predictas secundum magnitudinem spissitudinem rectitudinem bonitatem et omnimodam formam fabrice camerarum orientalium habitacionis dicti mansi. Et quantum ad domos alias superius memoratas secundum omnimodam bonitatem et formam Aule habitacionis supradicte. Et ista omnia complebit bene et fideliter circa festum Assumpcionis beate Marie proxime futurum. Et dictus Johannes operabitur omnia ostia, tam maiora quam minora, et ad illa inueniet ligamina lignea sufficientia et requisita. Ac etiam fenestras et fenestrellas[1] et plaunchers omnium camerarum coquine et solariorum et hoc circa quatuor menses postquam super hoc fuerit requisitus ex parte dicti Collegii. Et pro dicto maremio et opere prout supra dicitur inueniendo et perficiendo dictus Johannes recipiet de venerabili domino antedicto centum libras, soluendas inde eidem Johanni ad festum sancti Michaelis proxime futurum quinquaginta libras, et ad festum Natalis domini decem libras, et ad festum pasche decem libras, et ad festum Natiuitatis sancti Johannis Baptiste decem libras, et infra quindecim dies post complecionem dicti operis viginti libras: et dictus dominus inueniet tabulas pro plaunchers ostiis et fenestris. In cuius rei testimonium partes predicte presentibus indenturis alternatim sigilla sua apposuerunt. Dat' apud Cantebrigg' die et anno supradicto.

## 27

### *1374 Cambridge, Merton Hall*

Two masons undertake to rebuild parts of the outer walls, with four buttresses, and to repair a broken vault, and certain windows and stairs, finding their own materials. For this they shall have £32. 13s. 4d., payable by instalments.

Merton Coll. Deeds, no. 1639.

Hec indentura facta apud Cantebrigg' testatur de convencione facta inter Thomam Hulman procuratorem custodis et scolarium domus scolarium de Merton in Oxon et ejusdem domus consocium ex una parte et Adam Mathie et Johannem Meppushal lathomos ex altera parte quod illi reparabunt unam domum vulgariter nominatam Mertonhall in Cantebrigg' quo ad omnia que pertinent ad officium lathomorum videlicet unum murum externalem eiusdem domus versus partem occidentalem una cum parte muri australis de longitudine octodecim pedum a fundamento reedificabunt in tantam altitudinem quanta est altitudo antiqui muri eiusdem domus cum quatuor boteras quorum duo erunt boteras fourthes[2] unum in uno angulo dicti externalis muri et aliud in [alio] angulo eiusdem muri et duo alia erunt competentia secundum visum et discrecionem artificium seu peritorum in arte lathomie. Et predicti Adam et

---

[1] *fenestras et fenestrellas*: shutters and (?) lattices or casements.
[2] *boteras fourthes*: presumably 'projecting' buttresses; cf. the application of the term 'franche buttress' to an angle buttress, above, p. 96.

Johannes voltam fractam reedificabunt et alios defectus eiusdem domus vedelt. (*sic*) hostium quod existit sub illa volta fracta fenestras et gradus per quos fit ascensus ad aulam bene et sufficienter reparabunt secundum visum et discrecionem in arte lathomie peritorum. Que omnia predicti Adam et Johannes quo ad omnia edificacionem emendacionem dicte domus complebunt ante festum Nativitatis Sancti Johannis Baptiste proxime sequens datum presentis et predicti Adam et Johannes invenient lapides calcem arenam et omnia que necessaria sunt pro domo emendanda quantum pertinet ad lathomos et capient inferius que capienda sunt propriis sumptibus et expensis. Et pro omnibus predictis habebunt predicti Adam et Johannes de alia parte predicta Triginta duas libras tresdecim solidos et quatuor denarios bone et legalis monete solvendas eisdem per manus Thome Marbelthorp de Cantebrigg' quem predicti Adam et Johannes sufferunt pro debitore ad terminos subscriptos proxime sequentes datum presentis videlicet in festo Omnium Sanctorum quinque marcas Et in festo Nativitatis Xpi. alias quinque marcas Et in festo Purificationis Beate Marie alias quinque marcas Et in festo Pasche decem libras Et in festo Pentecost' decem marcas et novem marcas in festo Nativitatis Sancti Johannis Baptiste. Si contingat predictos Adam et Johannem dictam convencionem in omnibus ut premissum est observare. In cujus rei testimonium presentibus indenturis partes predicte sigilla sua alternatim apposuerunt. Hiis testibus Petro Smyth, Simone Buschell, Henrico Hosteler et aliis. Dat' Cantebrigg' die Martis proxima ante festum Omnium Sanctorum anno regni Regis Edwardi tercii post Conquestum quadragesimo octavo.

28

### 1374 Rye (Sussex)

Agreement for the pulling down of a timber-framed house at Brede and its re-erection at Rye, the vendor undertaking to make good any deficiencies, except laths and the cost of sawing any necessary planks. The whole to be completed, ready for thatching, within about six months, for £10. 13s. 4d. From the wording it looks as if the vendor was a carpenter and was to do the work himself.

B.M. Add. Ch. 20088.

Hec indentura testatur quod Rogerus Cropwode de Brede concessit et vendidit Jacobo Hooker de Ria quandam domum mansionis ejusdem Rogeri stantem super placeam suam apud Brede cum omnibus cameris eidem domui annexis modo et forma subsequentibus. Videlicet quod prefatus Rogerus omnimodis sumptibus suis dictam domum cum cameris prostrabit et totum meremium inde una cum omnibus hostiis fenestris et plaunchys ad eandem domum quoquomodo spectantibus usque Riam cariabit et super placeam dicti Jacobi ibidem levabit et competenter construet. Et si aliqua pecia meremii dicte domus deficerit vel nimia debilis pro eadem fuerit, prefatus Rogerus alias pecias meliores pro eadem ad custus suos providebit et invenerit, exceptis plaunchys si que deficerint, que erunt ad custus dicti Jacobi in sarratura tamen ita quod idem Rogerus inveniet truncos pro eisdem et exceptis ccc latt'. Et predictus Rogerus construet dictam (*sic*) ita quod parata sit ad cooperiendam infra quindena Pentecosten proximam futuram post datum presencium sine ulteriori delacione. Predictus vero Jacobus solvet prefato Rogero pro dicta domo cum cameris et aliis necessariis ad eandem spectantibus et pro prostracione cariagio et levacione ac construccione ejusdem in omnimoda carpentria $x^{li}$.xiij$^s$.iiij$^d$ sterlingorum ad terminos subscriptos, vide-licet ad festum Natalis Domini proximum futurum post datum presencium cvj$^s$. viij$^d$., et cum parata fuerit ad cooperiendam cvj$^s$. viij$^d$. Ad que omnia et singula bene et fideliter tenenda et adimplenda predicti Rogerus et Jacobus obligunt se heredes et executores suos et omnia bona et catalla sua mobilia et immobilia ubicumque fuerint inventa per presentes. In cujus rei testimonium tam sigillum dicti Rogeri quam sigillum supradicti Jacobi presentibus indenturis alternatim sunt appensa die Jovis in festo Sancti Andree apostoli anno regni Regis Edwardi tercii a conquesto Anglie quadragesimo octavo.

## 29

### 1377 York, The Gaol

Two carpenters undertake to repair the gaol and a certain pond-bay. Part of the gaol, which threatens to fall at any moment, they are to pull down and rebuild; the other part they shall repair, including two fireplaces; the roof to be covered with boards (in readiness for thatching). At the mill pond they are to rebuild two bays and strengthen them with a timber frame and a filling of large stones and clay. For this they shall have £39. 6s. 8d.—£11 in advance and the rest in two instalments—and all of the old timber that is fit for nothing but burning. They produce five sureties.

Exch. K.R. Accts. 598, no. 24.

Hec indentura tripartita inter Radulfum de Hastinges vicecomitem Ebor' . . . ex parte una et Ricardum de Thorne unum canonicorum ecclesie beati Petri Ebor' . . . ex parte altera, et Robertum de Donnom et Stephanum de Barneby carpentarios ex parte tercia testatur quod ita conuenit inter eos, quod predicti Robertus et Stephanus concesserunt et manuceperunt ad reparandum et emen-dandum certus defectus Gaole et capitis stagni predictorum magis dampnosos et magis periculosos apparentes scilicet ad deponendum fere dimidiam partem magne domus Gaole predicte versus orientem que tam debilis est et putrida quod stare non potest nec seruire set magis apparet quod subito caderet & prisones subtus existentes occideret, et illam partem domus predicte bene et sufficienter reedificabunt et reparabunt ut in aera superiori et in superficie ac in gutteris plumbeis et in omnibus aliis necessitatibus suis, Alteram vero partem predicte domus similiter reparabunt tam in aera et superficie¹ partis huius quam in duobus caminis de plastre uno scilicet subtus in camera Gaolatoris et alio desuper in parte predicta domus huius, et in omnibus aliis necessitatibus suis ac totam domum

---

¹ *in aera et superficie*: in floors and walls.

predictam de nouo cooperient de unica plita[1] de Thakborde, et eciam ad mun-
dandam quandam fraccionem[2] cuiusdam partis stagni predicti propinquioris
molendinis domini Regis ibidem, et illam partem confractam exaltabunt ante,
cum uno grosso houuetre[3] et retro deponent unum vetus Bay ligneum quod est
nimis debile et ibi reedificabunt unum Bay nouum satis sufficiens, et in medio
fraccionis predicte reedificabunt unum alium Bay nouum que quidem Bayes
retro et in medio simul cum le houuetre predicto ante, fortificabunt et alligabunt
insimul ex transuerso cum longis et fortibus lignis maeremii et eciam fraccionem
predictam sic reparatam cum grossis lapidibus et luto ac alia mixtura congrua
implebunt usque ad summum modo que decet. Ad que quidem opera perficienda
bene et fideliter ad opus et commodum dicti domini Regis iidem Robertus et
Stephanus prouidebunt et inuenient maeremium plauncheour thakborde clauos
ferreos plumbum plastre waltyghel & operarios ac omnia alia predictis operibus
competentia et oportuna. Ac eciam opera illa cum omni festinacione qua poterint
incipient et profecte consummabunt indilate. Et super hiis inuenerunt plegios et
manucaptores scilicet Andream Monemaker de Ebor', Johannem Hunter de
Ebor', Henricum Plummer de Ebor', Simonem Warde de Ebor', & Willelmum
Bernard de Grymston. Pro quibus operibus faciendis ut predictum est idem
Vicecomes per consensum et superuisum eiusdem Ricardi de Thorne dabit
eisdem Roberto et Stephano de denariis dicti domini Regis in toto triginta nouem
libras sex solidos et octo denarios. Primo scilicet et pre manibus undecim libras,
et in dimidio facti quatuordecim libras tres solidos et quatuor denarios, et in fine
totius operis predicti quatuordecim libras tres solidos et quatuor denarios. Et
preterea predicti Robertus et Stephanus habebunt penes se ex propria conuencione totum quod extrahitur et remanet de antiquo putrido siue nimis debili
maeremio thakborde et plauncheour predicti domus, quod quidem non valet
ad aliquod maeremium et solomodo ad ardendum. In cuius rei testimonium tote
tres partes predicte sigilla sua alternatim apposuerunt huic indenture tripartita.
Dat' in Castro Ebor' die dominica proxima post festum Sancti Barnabe apostoli
anno regni Regis Edwardi tercii post Conquestum Anglie quinquagesimo primo.

## 30

### *1378 Bolton Castle (Yorks.)*

John Lewyn agrees to build for Sir Richard Scrope, at Bolton—a kitchen tower, 10 ells
by 8 ells, and 50 feet high, with walls 2 ells thick; between this and the gate, a vaulted room
with three stories over it, 12 ells by 5½ ells, and 40 feet high, the outer walls being 2 ells and
the inner 4 feet thick; a tower, 50 feet high, containing a gateway, with three stories over it;
in this tower, south of the gate, a four-story building; west of the gate a vaulted room, with
another over it and a chamber above, 10 ells by 5½ ells, and 40 feet in height; all the rooms
having doors, windows, fireplaces, privies, &c.; also a vice in the kitchen tower and two in

---

[1] *plita*: ply, or layer.  [2] *fraccionem*: breach.
[3] *houuetre*: sense uncertain.

the gate tower; all inner walls to be 3 feet or 4 feet thick. Sir Richard shall provide carriage for the materials, timber for scaffolding, and wood for the limekiln. For all this work John Lewyn shall have 50 marks, and 100s. for every perch, of 20 feet, of construction.

*Ars Quatuor Coronatorum*, x. 70.[1]

Cest endenture fait parentre mon[s] Richard Lescrop Chivaler et Johan Lewyn mason dautrepart tesmoyne qe le dit Johan ferra les overaynes a Bolton en Wenselawedale en manere quensuit: primerement une Tour pur une cusyne qi serra voute & bataille & serra de hautesse de l pees desouth lembataillement & serra de longure de x alnes & de leoure viii alnes & les mures dehors du dit Tour serront despessure de ii alnes. Item serra fait parentre le dit tour pur le cusyne & la port une meson voute & bataille & amont le vout serront iii chambres chescune sur autre & chescune chambre de longure de xii alnes & de leoure v alnes & di & serra le dit meson de hautesse de xl pees desouth lembataillement & lespessure des mures dehors de ii alnes & dedeins de iiii pees. Item serra une tour bataille qi serra de hautesse de l pees desouth lembataillement, en quele tour serra une port voute & amont le port serront iii chambres chescune sur autre & serront en longure de x alnes & di & de leoure de v alnes & di. Et en mesme le tour al partie de port devers la South serra une chambre voute & sur icelle chambre serront iii chambres chescune sur autre qi serront en longure de xiii alnes & en leoure de vii alnes & les mures dehors des dits chambres serront despessure de vi pees & dedeins de iiii pees. Item serra une chambre enjoynant al dit tour al partie devers la West qi serra voute & bataille & de hautesse de xl pees desouth lembataillement & amont le dite chambre voute une autre meson voute & damont cella une chambre qi serront en longure de x alnes oveske lentre & v alnes & di en leure & les mures dehors des ditz chambres serront despessure de ii alnes & les mures dedeins de iiii pees. Item tous les meson & chambres avantditz averont entrees chymynes huyses fenestres & privees & autres necessaires qembosoynont a lavantdit overeyne. Item serront iii vices un dedeins la cusyne & ii pur le tour del port. Item tous les mures dedeins les chambres avantditz qi serront perclos serront despessure de iii pees ou iiii pees issint come ils embosoynont. Et le dit Johan ferra a ses custages toutes maneres de overeynes qa masonrie appent en service pur ecelles & ferra gayner toutes maneres des peres & trovera calice a ses custages en touz poyntz pur le dit overayne forspris qe le dit Mons[r] Richard luy trovera meresme pur le brandret[2] pur les torailles[3] qant ils serront ardz mais le dit Mons[r] Richard trovera cariage pur touz les peres sabulon & calice a ses custages. Et le dit Mons[r] Richard trovera Richard (*sic*) meresme pur syntres[4] & scaffald mais le dit Johan les ferra a ses custages. Pur le quele overayne le dit Mons[r] Richard paiera le dit Johan pur chescun perche mesure par xx pees par lalne sibien pur voltes come pur mures c s. & autre en tout l marcs. Et prendera le dit Johan en partie du paiement la somme qest ore despendu par laccompt entre

[1] For this contract I am indebted to the Rev. H. Poole, F.S.A.

[2] *brandret*: hearth.     [3] *torailles*: kilns.     [4] *syntres*: centerings.

luy et S^r William Wynterton forspris x li. qi serra rebatu de la dite somme. Et serra la dite overayne mesure selonc la hautesse de la base de la port. En tesmoynance de quele chose a les parties de ceste endenture les parties avantditz entrechangeablement ont mys lour seals. Don a Bolton le quatorzisme jour de Septembre lan du regne nostre Seignour le Roi Richard second puys le Conquest second.

31

### 1378 *Carlisle Castle*

John Lewyn undertakes to build a tower, 55 ft. by 32 ft. and 34 ft. high, containing a gateway, in front of which shall be a barbican; in the turret on the south of the gate shall be a cellar, 28 ft. by 18 ft., and on the north a prison and another chamber, each 14 feet square; the gateway shall be vaulted and flanked by buttresses; there shall be a kitchen in the tower, 32 ft. by 20 ft., with two fireplaces; and over the gateway a hall, 30 ft. by 20 ft., with a wooden screen, and a room, with fireplace and privy, opening out of the upper end of the hall. All the walls are to be 6 feet thick from ground-level up to the vaulting, and above that 5 feet; and partition walls to be of a suitable thickness. He is to dig stone from the king's quarry and to provide all materials, except timber for scaffolding. For all this he shall have 500 marks.

Exch. K.R. Accts. 483, no. 31.

Ceste endenture faite parentre nre. s' le Roy dune part et Johan Lewyn maceon dautre part tesmoigne q' le dit Johan ad empris de faire bien et suffissantment la maceonerie dune port et dune Tour paramont en le Chastel de Kardoill deuers la ville de Kardoill la quele Tour contendra en longure cynquante et cynk pedz et en laeure trente et deux pedz et en hautesse trente et quatre pedz desouz le pee de lembataillement et serra la dite porte de unze pedz de lez et serra devant mesme la porte un Barbycan q' contendra dys pedz en longure droit de la dite porte et se tournera a trauers par une vousure entre lentree vers la dite porte tanq' sur une meindre Tour q' serra une Cusyne et le dit barbycan serra doublement embataillez[1] auant la vousure de la dite porte et serront en la meindre Tour a la porte de lentree vers le suth un celer contenant vynt et oyt pedz en longure et dys et oyt pedz en laeure voutez ouesque un chemyne et un priue et a lautre part de la dite porte deuers le North serra une prisone q' contendra quatorze pedz squarr' et outre celle prisone serra une Chambre ouesq' chemyne et priue de quatorze pedz squarr' et la dite porte serra voutee et auera deux botraces sur les iowes[2] de la hautesse de trente et quatre pedz desouz lembataillement et serront les ditz botraces de lesepessure a la terre de cynk pedz squarr' et serront bataillez et la dite Tour q' serra la Cusyne cestassauoir deuers la fossee contendra dehors trente et deux pedz en longure et vynt pedz en laeure a quele Tour serront deux mesons voutees desouz la basseure[3] ouesq' chemynez et priueez et paramont la

---

[1] *doublement embataillez*: the next contract shows that this means embattled on both sides of its walls.

[2] *iowes*: cheeks, or flanks.

[3] *basseure*: the meaning is not clear.

dite porte serra une sale de trente pedz en longure et vynt pedz en laeure ouesq'
un mur parclos de maerisme[1] et la dite Cusyne auera deux chemynez couenables
de pere et en la chambre estante deriere le dees[2] serront un chemyne et un priue
ouesque huysses fenestres et entrees couenables p^r toutes les dites mesons. Et tous
les murs de les dites Tours dehors serront de lespessure de sys pedz amont la terre
tanq' a les vousures et de lespessure de cynk pedz amont [les dites vousures]. Et
les murs des parclos q' serront de maceonerie serront couenables. Et trouera nre.
dit s' le Roy quarrere maerisme pur scaffaldes et syntres et paiera au dit Johan
p^r son oeueraigne cynk centz marz [      ]enablement et ferra le dit Johan
debruser la dite quarrere & trouera calce et sabulon et ferra faire et carier toutes
les choses appertenantes a la maceonerie de les Tour porte et mesons susdites et
me[sme la maceon]erie ferra bien et conuenablement en touz pointz preignant
comme desus est dit. En tesmoignance de quele chose a la partie de ceste endenture demorante deuers nre. dit s' le Roy le dit Johan [ad mys son seal.] Don
a Westmonst' le xiij jour daurill lan du regne de nre. dit s' le Roy primer.

## 32

*1378 Roxburgh Castle*

John Lewyn undertakes to build one wall of the castle, with three towers, each 50 feet
in height; in the central tower shall be a gateway, with a barbican, of which the walls shall
be 12 feet high; over the gate and its flanking chambers shall be a hall, 40 feet long, and to
the south of this a kitchen, with three fireplaces; each of the angle towers shall contain four
rooms, one above the other; and the curtain wall shall be 30 feet high and 10½ feet thick,
containing vaulted passages 4½ feet wide. He is also to raise the old walls to a height of
30 feet and to make a turret, 6 feet square and rising 10 feet above the battlements, in the
centre of each wall. For the centre tower he shall have 550 marks; for each angle tower
300 marks; and for the walling £20 for each perch, of 20 feet, of wall 7 feet thick, and if
more or less than 7 feet, then at a proportionate rate. If he is prevented by war with the
Scots he shall not be bound by this contract.

Exch. K.R. Accts. 483, no. 32.

John Lewyn sent in his account for raising the south wall of the castle in 1387, this being
probably the last part of the work done. It came to £121. 6s. 8d.—being 9 perches 2 feet
in length—and of this amount he had received £50 on 24 Feb. 1386–7; an order was given
on 14 Nov. 1388 for payment of the remaining £71. 6s. 8d.

Foreign R. 11 Ric. II, m. 3.

Ceste endenture faite entre nre. s' le Roy dune part et Johan Lewyn maceon
dautre part tesmoigne q. le dit Johan ferra au Chastel de Rokesburgh les oeuereignes q. ensuent cestassauoir Un mur de pierre et de calce embatallez au trauers
du dit Chastel du bout de la veille scilz. enuers le suth tanq' a lautre mur du dit
Chastel enuers le North et troys Tours chescun de cynquante pedz en tout en
hautesse paramont la terre et lez murs des ditz tours sys pedz en espesse des queux

---

[1] *un mur parclos de maerisme*: evidently the screens at the kitchen end of the hall.
[2] *le dees*: the dais, or high-table end of the hall.

troys tours un serra en mylieu et les autres deux tours serront lune ioignante sur lancien mur du dit chastel enuers le suth et lautre tour sur lancien mur de mesme le Chastel deuers le North, dont en la tour q. serra en mylieu [serra] une porte et deux chambres voutez chescune chambre de la longure de vynt pedz et de laeure de unze pedz et demy et paramont la dite porte et les dites chambres une sale de la longure de quarante pees et de laeure de [     ] pedz ouesq' trois chemynez en mesme la sale, et paramont la sale une priue et un chemyne pur une chambre, et serra deuant la porte un Barbican de la longure de dis pedz dedein et une arche voutez et les murs du Barbican serront en espasse cynk pedz et de la hautesse paramont la terre de dousie pedz desouz le pee et bataillez dedenz dehors, et en la Tour deuers le suth serra un larder voutez et une cusyne voutee paramont mesme le larder ouesq' [? trois] chemyneez en la dite cusyne et paramont mesme la cusine une priue et une chemyne pur une chambre, et en la Tour deuers le North serront quatre chambres chescune desus autre ches-cune chambre ouesque une priue et une chemyne, des queux quatre chambres des deux serront voutees et serront toutes les dites mesons en ambedeux les Tours chescune meson de vynt et quatre pedz en longure et de dys et oyt pedz en laeure deinz les murs et serra le mur parentre la dite tour en mylieu tanq' a les autres deux tours susdites de la hautesse de trente pees en bataillure et tout de dys pedz et demy espesse ouesq' alees voutees deinz meisme le mur de laeure de quatre pedz et demy pur [aller] de la dite Tour en mylieu tanq' a les autres deux tours susdites. Et le dit Johan enhancera les deux veilles murs du dit chastel lun de lune costee et lautre de lautre costee du dit chastel des dites tours deuers le Suth et le North jusq' au dongeon tanq' a la hautesse de trente pedz en tout paramont la terre et en mylieu de chescun des ditz murs q' serront ensi enhances serra un Tourret de dys pedz en hautesse paramont le mur enhance et serront mesmes les Turretz chescune de sys pedz squarr deinz lembataillement. Et ferra le dit Johan totes les dites oeuereignes bien et suffissament de pierre et de calce ouesq' entrees vices huys fenestres et toutes autres chose appartenauntes a macconerie et ferra debruser le quarrer et faire calce redder les founds et faire scaffaldes et syntres et trouuerra sablon et ferra la carriage de toutes chose appartenauntes a la maceonerie de les oeuereignes susdites. Et trouuera nre. s' le Roy sib'n quarrere come maerisme pur scaffaldes et syntres busoignables pur les dites oeuereignes et ferra paier au dit Johan cestassauoir pur louereigne de la dite Tour en mylieu ouesq' la porte cynk centz et cynquante marcs b'n et en convenable temps paiez et pur louereigne de chescun de les autres deux tours trois cents marcs et pur louereigne sib'n de la nouelle mur affaire ensi come desus come de lenhanceure de les vielle murs et pur la fesure de les deux turretz pur chescune perche de vynt pedz en long' de sept pedz en espesse et de trente pedz en hautesse paramont la terre vynt liures et pur atant de mesmes les ouereignes come passera sept pedz en espesse ou q' soit mains q' sept pedz en espesse ferra nre. dit s' le Roy paier au dit Johan pur la perche selon lafferant de vynt lyures pur la perche paramont declaree. Et toutes les dites ouereignes en qu$^a$q' appartient a la maceonerie dycelles le dit Johan se oblige a faire et accomplier en la manere auantdite sil ne soit destourbez par la guere descoce preignant le dit Johan come desus est dit issuit toutes fois q' en cas de tiel destourbance le dit Johan ne soit plus auant tenuz ne chargez de parfaire les dites oeuereignes par force de ceste presente endenture. En tesmoignance de quele chose a la partie de ceste endenture demorante deuers nre. dit s' le Roy le dit Johan ad mys son seal. Don a Londrez le primier jour daugust lan du regne de nre. dit s' le Roy le second.

# 33

*1380  Hertford Castle*

A carpenter undertakes to build, within the next three years, a chapel and other new buildings within the castle, according to a design drawn by agreement. He is to carry out the whole work, including the stonework of foundations and fireplaces, tiling and plumbing, and to provide labour; he is to. use the material of the old buildings on the site, such extra timber and boards as may be required being supplied. For this he shall have 440$^{li}$—50 marks down, and then 50 marks quarterly: if the payment is a month in arrear he may leave the job; moreover, he shall have the use of certain old buildings in the manor of Hertfordbury.

Duchy of Lanc., Misc. Books, 14, f. 81.

Ceste endent'e faite parentre Johan Roy[1] &c. dune part et William de Wyntringham de Southwerk carpenter dautre part tesmoigne les couenantes faites et tailles par lauys du bone conseille du dit Roy et Duc et le dit William Cestassauoir q' le dit William ad empris p$^r$ faire bien et loialment et conuenablement certeins nouelles mesons, Chapelle et autres cloistures deinz le chastel de Herteford selonc le p$^r$port et come appiert par une patron endentee[2] parentre eux faite des mesons auantdites parentre le io$^r$ de la fesance de cestes et le fin de troys ans procheins ensuantz apres le feste de seint Johan le Baptistre prochain auenir, deinz quel terme les auantdites mesons et ouereignes selonc le p$^r$port del patron auantdite serront en toutes choses bien et entierement faites et parfourmez Cestassauoir en fundementz, chemeneys, huses, fenestres, esteyres, lathyng, tylyng et daubyng, et en certeins lieuz couerez oue plumbe cestassauoir demy loriell et le fin del grant chambre attrauers et de lautre part quinze pees et auxuit le bayes fenestres, as queles mesons et oeuereignes le dit William troeuera toutes maneres des oeuerours et autres costages queux as dites mesons resonablement enbusoigneront, horsprises fermentz Colo$^r$s Glaces ou aucun autre ouereigne de nouelle auys; toute manere de merisme et bordes couenables, les queles toute manere de merisme et bordes le auantdit Roy et Duc trouera as ses costages propres oue le cariage tanqs au manoir ou le dit William oeuera issuit q' le dit William ne soit tarie. Pur queles mesons et ouereignes bien et loialment affaire et a complier en toutes choses come dessus est dit le auantdit Roy et Duc ad grantez q' le dit

[1] John of Gaunt, Duke of Lancaster and titular King of Castile.
[2] *une patron endentee*: a design in duplicate.

William auera quatre centz et quarrante liures desterlinges et toutes les vielles mesons entiers et chemeneyes et pareys[1] a ore esteantz sur la place ou les dites nouelles mesons serront assys. Nep<sup>r</sup>quant acorde est q' le dit William prendra de les dites vielles mesons le mearisme qil semble couenable a loeuereigne des dites nouelles mesons p<sup>r</sup> le profit mons'. Et ensement les peeres illeoqes ordeinz p<sup>r</sup> le dit nouelle ouereigne. De quele somme auantdite le dit William serra paie en manere qensuyt Cestassauoir le io<sup>r</sup> de la fesance de cestes cynquante marcs et a le fest de seint Johan le Baptistre prochein auenir cynquante marcs et issuit de quarter en quarter et dan en an tanqz la somme auantdite duement soit paie a dit William ou a ses assignes. Et en cas q' le dit William ne soit mye paiez en manere susdit par lespace dune moys qadonques bien lise au dit William son dit ouereigne lesser. Et ensement le dit Roy et Duc ad grantez au dit William q' il auera son easement deinz les veilles mesons deinz le manoir de Hertfordbury; et aussint p<sup>r</sup> auoir licence de prendre peers en les quarrers a Herteford et q' ses ministres et officers celles parties serront eidantz a dit William en resonable manere p<sup>r</sup> auoir les oeuerours du pays et cariages come ils on[t] u auant ces heures a ses costages propres p<sup>r</sup> le dite ouereigne acomplier. En tesmoignance de quele chose &c. Don &c. le primer io<sup>r</sup> de May lan &c. tierz.

## 34

*1380 Dunstanborough Castle*

John Lewyn undertakes to build for the Duke of Lancaster a mantlet wall round the keep, 11 rods in length, 20 feet in height with the battlement, and 4 feet thick, within the year, bearing all costs and receiving 10 marks for each rod.

Duchy of Lanc., Misc. Books, 14, f. 81v.

Ceste endent'e faite a Baumburgh le xxv iour doctobre lan &c. quart parentre Johan Roy de Castille &c. dune part et Johan Lewyn mason dautre part tesmoigne les couenances faites parentre le dit Johan Roy et Duc par lauys de son conseil et le dit Johan Lewyn. Cestassauoir q' le dit Johan Lewyn ad empris p<sup>r</sup> faire de nouell bien et couenablement un mantelett[2] de freeston en certein lieu a lui diuise par le dit Johan Roy et Duc et son Conseil ento<sup>r</sup> le grant tourre deinz son Chastel de Donstaneburgh contenant en longure per estimacion unze Rodes et serra le mure de dit Mantellet en haut desus la terre vynt pees dassise oue le bataillement et en laioure quatre pees dassyse parmy partout et ferra le dit Johan Lewyn toutes maneres des coustages p<sup>r</sup> ceste oeure, sibien del myno<sup>r</sup>e[3] des peres de lyme de sabule come de cariage et toutes autres choses busoignables et app<sup>r</sup>tenantes p<sup>r</sup> meisme loeuereigne. Et auxuit le dit Johan Lewyn ad empris de parfaire entierment et bien et couenablement parfournir le dit mantelett a ses coustages propres come desus est dit parentre cy et le fest de seint Michel pro-

---

[1] *pareys*: probably the 'parels' of fireplaces, i.e. hood, jambs, &c.: see above, p. 101.
[2] *mantelett*: a surrounding wall.                    [3] *mynoure*: the digging.

chein venant apres la date de cestes sans plus outre delaye et prendra le dit
Johan Lewyn du dit Roy et Duc p$^r$ la fesure et coustages del oeuereign susdite
p$^r$ chescun Rode del dit mantelett dys marcs p$^r$ toutes maneres de coustages come
desus est dit par les mains del Receiuo$^r$ n̄r̄e dit S' de Dunstaneburgh qore est ou
qi p$^r$ le temps serra. En tesmoignance &c. Don &c. les iour lieu et an susditz.

## 35

*1381  Cowling Castle (Kent)*

Two indentures between Sir John, Lord Cobham, and Thomas Crump, mason, concerning the great gate of the castle.

(A) To the effect that Crump has been overpaid to the extent of 56s. 8d.; that he is to
be paid 40s. for every perch, but he has charged for 2½ perches too much, according to the
measurement made by Mr. Henry Yevele, and must therefore give back 100s.; he also owes
for 366 feet of 'coyn', or quoin-stones, and has not made a postern, as he undertook to do.

(B) Crump undertakes to provide worked stone for loopholes, stairs, door-frames, corbels,
&c., and to set them in the walls, for £20. Significantly endorsed with a note to make sure
that he has delivered as many newel-stones as he undertook to provide.

Harl. Chart. 48 E. 44 and 37; printed by Knoop and Jones in 'Some Building<br>Activities of John, Lord Cobham', Trans. Quatuor Coronati, xlv.

(A)

Ceste endenture tesmoigne qe le xxvi$^{me}$ iour de Septembre lan r' r' Richard
seccounde (*sic*) puis le conq' quinte mons. Johan de Cobeham s$^r$ de Cobeham
ad acompte oue Thomas Crump masoun de Maydestan pur la graunde porte
de Coulyng. Cestassauer solonc son acompte lun tour contient sept perches et
demi et tres quarters dune perche, lautre tour contient sept perches et demi et
un quarter dune perche. Et une perche est par soun acompte parentre les deux
toures. La somme des perches amounte en tout diz et sept perches. Et prendra
le dit Thomas pur le perche xl$^s$ come comps est en sez viels endentures. Et ad
le dit Thomas de ceo resseu deuaunt le iour de fesaunce du (*sic*) cestis qaraunte
siz liueres seze south et sept deniers issint qe le dit Thomas ad deservi oue lez
diz liueres resseu pur fraunche piere qaraunte et qatre liuerez. Et si doit le dit
Thomas alauantdit mons. Johan le iour de fesaunce du cestis par son acompte
propre cinquaunte siz south sept deniers. Et outre ca le dit Thomas paiera pur
tout le coyn qest en la dite porte et tours come apiert par sez endentures auantditz. En tesmoign' de quelle chose a ycestes endentures lez parties auanditz entrechaungeablement ount mys lour seals. Donne a Coulyng le iour et an susditz.

M$^o$ que le dit Crompe deyt al s$^r$ outre les parcelles susdictez ccclxvi pees de
coyn pris le pee v$^d$. Item il deyt al s$^r$ unne posterne par soun primer endenture.

*Endorsed*: Lendenture Thomas Crump masoun dil mesure et acomp$^t$ del graunde
porte a Coulyng.

Fayt a remembrer que Crompe ad acompte plus que il ne doyt ij perches et demi pee et quarter, que amounte cˢ que il est tenuz a restorer al seignur solom la compte mestre Henry Yevele fayt a Coulyng devaunt le assencion Anno regni Regis Ricardi vᵒ.

## (B)

Ceste endenture faite parentre monsieur Johan de Cobeham seignur de Cobeham dune parte et Thomas Crompe mason dautre parte tesmoigne que le dit Thomas ad empris de dit monsieur Johan a faire cestassauer x arketholes[1] de iij peez de longour en tout et saunz croys oue le pareile deinz et de hors, vij petitz huis[2] chescun de ij peez et demi de largesse oue le hautesse de les ditz huis come affiert oue laparaile deinz et dehors, et liiij nowelles[3] chescun de iiij peez et demi de longour et de hautesse vij pous et xxx autres nowelles chescun de iij peez de longour et de vij pous dautesse, et liij corbelx i pee squarr et de bone et couenable longour pur machecolle,[4] et xliij peres pur demi archis les quex archis et corbelx serront nettement chanffreiez.[5] Et auera le dit Thomas pur toutz les peres et pur toute loueraine et cariage tanque a Maidstane et pur asser les ditz peres en la dite oueraine en sesonable prochein sesoune xxˡⁱ les queux luy serront paiez comme il fait son oueraine. As queulx couenantes bien et loialment faire les ditz parties soy obligeont par cestes endentures. En tesmoignance de quele chose entrechangeablement ils ount mys lours sealx. Donne a Loundres le iour de Seinte Luke Levangeliste lan nostre Seignur le Roi Richard second puis la conquest quint.

*Endorsed*: La darreine endenture Thomas Crompe.

Soyt examine sy le dit Thomas ad amene touz ses nowels solom le purport de soun endenture a Coulyng ou nemye.

*Seal*: *A text ʒ, and in the border* C R V M P.

## 36

*1381 London, St. Dunstan's Church*

A mason undertakes to dig and lay the foundations for a south aisle and porch, according to the plans prepared by Master Henry Yevele, during the next four months, for 25 marks.

Harl. Ch. 48 E. 43.

Ceste endenture faite parentre Mons' John de Cobeham s' de Cobeham dune part et Nich' Typerton masoun dautre parte tesmoigne q' le dit Nich' parferra le foundement del southele de Seint Dunston en Tourstrete de Loundres du longeur del esglise bon et suffisaunct ou le foundement dune porche solom la

---

[1] *arketholes*: loopholes, in this instance without a horizontal cross-slit.

[2] *huis*: doorways.

[3] *nowelles*: newel-stones, each forming a step and a section of the central pillar of a spiral stair.

[4] *machecolle*: machicolations.

[5] *chanffreiez*: chamfered.

deuyse Mestre Henry Iuleʒch[1] et taunt de foundement des boteras et oue une watertable[2] bon et suffisaunt de durre pere solom la deuyse le dit Mestre Henry et auera pur fower le dit foundement et trouer pier, craye, lyme et sabloun et tablement, cariage et toutz choses q' apertent al dit ouerayne vintz et cynqz marcz, come il ferra soun ouerayne, cynqz marcz al comensement les queux le dit Nich' ad receuz del auauntdit Mons' John et ensy de temps en temps cynqs marcz; tanq' les ditz xxv marcz serrount parpaiez. Et la dite ouerayne serra parfourmy bien et suffisauntement parentre la fesaunce dycestes et le moys prochein apres le feste de Pasq' solom la deuyse lauauntdit Mestre Henry. A quel chose bien et loialement parfourmer lauauntdit Nich' se oblige per cestes presentz. En tesmoignaunce de quele chose les parties susditz ount entrechaungeablement mys lour sealx a ycestes. Don a Loundres la veille de Nowell anno regni Regis Ricardi secundi post conquestum quinto.

## 37

*1383 Dunstanborough Castle*

A mason undertakes to rebuild the gatehouse, which is to have a portcullis, barbican, postern, and fittings for a bridge. He is to use the materials of the old gatehouse and to provide what else is necessary, receiving 10 marks for each rod of masonry.

Duchy of Lanc., Misc. Books, 14, f. 81v.

Ceste endent'e f'te parentre Johan Roy &c. dune part et Henry Holme mason dautre part tesmoigne q' le dit Henry ad empris de faire une nouelle Gatehouse de Frestone a le Chastel du dit Roy et Duc de Dunstanneburgh et p[r] remuer[3] les Vowsers[4] Jambes et barbicans[5] illeoqes et p[r] prendre le veille Gatehous illeoqes p[r] eyder al oeuereyne del nouelle Gatehouse susdite et meisme le Gatehouse serra vowtez et auera un portculys un barbican et un posterne et une ordenance p[r] un pont affaire en meisme loeuereine. Et ferra le dit Henry toutes maneres des coustages p[r] ceste oeure, sibien del myno[r]e des piers de lyme de sabule come de cariage et toutes autres choses busoignables et app[r]tenantz p[r] meisme loeuereyne. Et prendra le dit Henry du dit Roy et Duc p[r] la fesure et coustage de loeueraigne susdite p[r] chescun Rode dycel dys marcs p[r] toutes maneres des coustages come desus est dit par les mains del Receiuo[r] du dit Roy et Duc de Dunstanneburgh qi po[r] le temps serra. En tesmoignance &c. Don &c. a Duresme le xx iour de Juyl lan septisme.

[1] *Iuleʒch*: Yevele, see above, p. 13.
[2] *watertable*: here evidently used for 'earth-table', or plinth.
[3] *remuer*: to remove; or possibly *rennier*, to re-use(?).
[4] *vowsers*: voussoirs.
[5] *barbicans*: outworks. Apparently the old gateway was flanked by towers, the new one set in a central tower.

## 38

*1384 London, St. Dunstan's*

Although this is a building lease and not a contract, it resembles the contracts in its details sufficiently to be included here. The lessee of a site between Thames Street and the river undertakes to build a house of new oak timber; its front on the street to be of three stories, with a hall, kitchen, buttery, and parlour on an undercroft; also warehouses, with cellars.

Anct. Deeds (P.R.O.), A. 1779; printed in Archaeologia, lxxiv. 155.

M$^d$. that John Chirteseye of the Schyr of Hertford Gentilman made a statt bi dede endented unto Richard Willysdon and to Anneys hys wyf of all hys Wharf callyd Pakemannys Wharf w$^t$ all the land and tenementys and pertin' in the parsch of Seynt Dunstonys in the Este in London And to holde unto the seyd Ric' Wyllysdon and Anneys hys wyf to ther eyrs and ther assynes from the date of seyd Endentur unto the ende of a ʒer the wych dat of the seyd Endentur was in the feste of seynt Archunwolde[1] the ʒer of Kyng Ric' the ij$^d$ the vij$^d$. . . . Also Ric' Wyllysdon shall up on hys owne proper costes wyth yn x ʒer next folowyng affter the date of the seyd Endentur enlarg' strecchyng in the themesward[2] the seyd wharfe iiij fote of a sise and wall all only of maydenston ston'. Also the seyd Ric' Wyllesdon schall w$^t$yn the terme of the seyd x ʒer to take doun all maner of hosyng[3] at the tyme of the seyd lese beryng up on all the seyd soyl and byld all the soyle all only wyth new tymbre puttyng to no thyng to of the olde tymbre. And that to be performyd yn the forme after wrytten. That ys to wytten all the Frounte of the seyd soyle aʒenst the hye Strete and xl fote ynward of iij storyes of heygh' the fyrst story of xij fote of heygh' te ij of x fote te thryd of vij fote propossenyd of sufficient tymbre all only of harte of oke as sufficienttyly longyth to sych maner of Byldyng wyth all maner of dividyng Garnyssyng and coueryng that schuld long to the seyd Bildyng. Also the seyd Ric' Wyllesdon schall wythynne the seyd terme of x ʒer do byld up on the seyd soyle inwarde a chef Dwellyngplace above stag' that ys to wyte a hall of xl fote of lengyth and xxiiij fote of brede a parlour kychyn and boterye as to sych a hall schulde long, and the remen$^a$nt of the soyle accept the Cartway and the seyd wharf of iiij$^{xx}$ fote to do bylde Chambrys and hous' for the merchaundyse sufficienly forseyng that as well undyr the seýd hall parlour and kechyn botery and all the seyd Chambr' be selered undernethe the Grunde vij fote in heygh'. And all the seyd Byldyng to be donn be the seyd Jhon Chirtheseye (*sic*) or hys assign' and ʒyf caas be that the seyd byldyng or eny part therof be not holly performyd in the maner a fore seyd by the ende of the seyd x ʒere then schall hit be lefull unto the seyd John Chircheseye hys executours and hys assignes and to the seyde soyle w$^t$. all portenauntes to reentr' and the seyd Ric' Wyllysdon hys executours and hys assignes holli to put owte for euermor thys Endentur noʒth w$^t$standyng. . . .

---

[1] The feast of St. Erkenwald was 30 April.
[2] *in the themesward*: towards the Thames.         [3] *hosyng*: houses, or buildings.

## 39

*1384 Bamborough Castle*

Although this is not an actual contract with a mason, it contains the materials for such a contract in the details of the work which Sir John Neville is to get done during the next three years, at a total cost of 1300 marks. There is to be a hall, 66 ft. by 34 ft., with three windows on one side and four on the other and a porch; at the upper end of the hall shall be a great chamber, 46 ft. by 20 ft., with two vaulted rooms under it; beyond this the existing tower is to be raised 24 ft., to contain three rooms. At the other end of the hall shall be made pantry and buttery, dresser and dry larder, each 20 feet square (probably in pairs, with a passage between them to the kitchen); over these shall be two chambers, 40 ft. by 20 ft.; and beyond shall be the kitchen, 40 ft. by 28 ft. Turrets, supported by buttresses, are to be built at two points, and the tower at the end of the kitchen is to be raised 24 feet; another tower, near the entrance, is to be raised 16 feet, and a brewhouse and bakehouse to be built near the kitchen.

Exch. K.R. Accts., 458, no. 31.

Ceste endenture faite entre nre. Seignur le Roy dune part et Mons' Johan Sire de Neuill dautre part tesmoigne q' le dit Johan ad empris de faire de nouel deinz le Chastel de Baumburgh dont il est Gardein une Sale de sessante et sys peds en longure et de trente et quatre peds en laeure deinz les murs q' serront de la hautesse de vyngt peds et de quatre peds en espesse ouesque quatre boterasses de lune coste dycelle et de lune partie de la dite Sale serront troys fenestres et quatre de lautre partie de pere [capees]¹ et a la porte de mesme la Sale serra une porche voutee de braces et couert de pere hachee² et serra fait au chief de la dite Sale une grande Chambre de quarante et sys peds en longure et de vyngt peds en laeure de la hautesse de cynquante peds³ et quatre peds espesse et desouz la dite Chambre serront faites bas chambres voutez et iouxt la dite grande chambre est une Tour q' serra enhaucee par vyngt et quatre peds dedeinz en quele serront trois mesons dont deux voutez et la tierce oue une couerture de maerisme et couerte de plumb. Et iouxt mesme la Tour est une autre Tour q' serra nouelmeut couerte de plumb, et au boute de la Sale sont faitz panetrie butillerie dressour⁴ et un larder sek⁵ chescune meson vyngt pedz esquarre et voutez et de la hautesse de dys et sept peds desus quelx serront deux Chambres del hautesse de cynquante pedz de la terre ensus de longure de quarante pedz et de laeure de vyngt pedz deinz les murs et iouxt les ditz dressour et larder serra la Coysyne de la longure de quarante pedz et de la laeure de vyngt et oyt pedz oue trois chymenees deux fournas voutez pour plumbes en quele coisyne serront faitz quatre fenestres oue un fumer⁶ en mylieu q' serra del hautesse de les ditz chambres. Et serra fait au

---

¹ *capees* (interlined): probably, 'gabled'; see above, p. 93.

² *voutee de braces et couvert de pere hachee*: this seems to mean a roof of stone slabs carried on arched beams—as opposed to a groined roof.

³ The height of 50 feet presumably included the rooms below.

⁴ *dressour*: a room for dressing meat.

⁵ *larder sek*: a larder for dry and salted victuals—as opposed to the 'wet larder' for fresh meat.

⁶ *fumer*: a smoke-vent, or louvre.

coigne de lune des ditz chambres iouxt la Sale une boterasse de pere et au coigne de la Coisyne une autre boterasse et desus celx boterasses serront faitz deux Tourettes a bon deuys et a lautre coigne de la Coisyne est une Tour q' serra enhaucee par vyngt et quatre pedz oue trois mesons dont deux voutes et la tierz couerte de maerisme et de plumb et chescune meson de quinze pedz en longure et dys et sept pedz en laeure et pres de la dite coisyne serront faitz la bracyurie et pistrine dont les murs serront de la hautesse de vyngt peds et chescune de vyngt et quatre peds en longure et de vyngt et sys ou trente pedz en laeure; et pres de la bas entree du Chastel est une bas Tour q' serra enhaucee par sesze peds et double voutee et serra couerte de plumb. Et les huys fenestres chymenees priueez vices et touz les murs et boterasses dehors de la dite ouereigne serront de pere hachee et toute louereigne bataille et les Sale Chambres et la Coisyne couerts de double bourde et les Gutters oue plumb quatre pedz et demy de laeure et les couertours aussi et touz autres necessaires serront faitz au poynt et bon deuys; les queles ouereignes il ad fait commencer en partie et les ferra parfaire deinz ces trois anz prochein venauntz. Et prendra de nre. s$^r$ le Roy par celle cause outre les trois cents marcs a li assignez sur mesmes les ouereignes mill marcs dont il auera bons et suffissauntz assignements desquelx il se deuera agreer. En tesmoignance de quele chose a la partie de ceste endenture demorante deuers nre. dit s$^r$ le Roy le dit Johan ad mys son seal. Don a Westmonster le xviij iour de Nouembre lan du regne de nre. dit s$^r$ le Roy oytisme.

## 40

*1387 Edinburgh, St. Giles' Church*

   Three masons undertake to build five chapels in the south aisle, with vaults on the design of the vault of St. Stephen's Chapel, Holyrood. Four chapels shall have a three-light window and the fifth a door like that at the west end of the church. They shall have stone roofs, with gutters between them. They are to have 600 marks Scots—£40 in advance—and are to set 1,200 of ashlar and coigns and to guarantee the work weatherproof.

*St. Giles' Church, Edinburgh* (Bannatyne Club), 24.[1]

   This endentur made at Edynburgh the xxix day of the moneth of Nouember betwene worthy men and nobyl Adam Forster lorde of Nethir Lebertoun Andrew Yutsown prowest of the burgh of Edynburgh and the Communite of that ylke on the ta half and Jonne Prymros Jonne of Scone and Jonne Skuyer masownys on the tothir half berys wytnes in fourme the qwylk eftir folowys, that is for to say, At the forsaidys Jonne Jonne and Jonne al as ane and ane as all sal mak and voute v chapellis on the south syde of the paryce Kyrc of Edynburgh fra the west gavyl lyand in rayndoun[2] est on to the grete pyler of the stepyl, voutyt on the maner and the masonnrys as the voute abovyn Sant Stevinys auter standand on the north syde of the parys auter of the abbay of the Halyrudehous the qwhylk patronne

   [1] I am indebted to the late Dr. G. G. Coulton for calling my attention to this contract.
   [2] *lyand in rayndoun*: ranging.

thay haf sene. Alsua tha ylk men sal mak in ylk chapel of the four a wyndow with thre lychtys in fourme masounelyke the qwilk patron they haf sene and the fyfte chapel woutyt with a durre als gude maner as the durre standand in the west gavyl of the forsaid kyrk. Alsua the chapel and the ylys qwhare the auterys stand sal be voutyt all undir a maner as it is befor spokyn. Alsua the forsayde v chapellys sal be thekyt abovyn with stane and water thycht[1] the buteras fynyt wp als hech as the lave of that werk askys. Alswa betwene the chapellis guteryt with hewyn stane to cast the watir owte and to save the werc for the watir. Alswa the communyte as it is befor spokyn fyndand al coste and al grayth tyle that werk and the forsayde masounys doand thair craft tyl that werk trewly withoutyn fraude as trew men aw to do. Alsua it is accordyt at the forsayde communyte sal gyfe to the forsayde masounys for the forsade werk as it is before spokyne vi[c]. mark of sterlingis of the payment of Scotlande. Alsua it is accordyt at the forsayde communite sal gyf to the forsayd masounys ay xl lib. befor hand for to make thayr awne werk with ay tyl the forsayde werk be brocht tyl ende. Alsua the forsayde masounys sal lay in place on thair cost xij[c]. hewyn stanys astlayr and coynhe[2] swylk as fallys to that werk the qwilke werke the forsaide masounys sal warande watir thicht. And till thise thingis lately to be fulfillit ilke ane of the forsaide masounys is othiris bourcht.[3] Wretyn undir the seillis of the forsaides Adam prouest and the comunite selle anentis tha forsaides masounys to be remaynande. And Join Primros has procurit the selle of James of Fulforde and Join of Scone has procurit the selle of Join of Irwyne in fai . . . thai hade nane of their awyne and Join Squyer has pute to his awyne selle anentis the forsaides Adam prouest and communyteis to be remaynande the yhere of Our Lorde a thousande ccclxxx and vii.

## 41

*1387–8 Southwark, water-mills*

Three carpenters undertake to rebuild two water-mills (apparently both in the same building) belonging to Henry Yevele, the famous master mason, and John Clifford, also a mason. They are to be modelled on the neighbouring mills of the Abbey of Battle. Two adjacent houses are to be pulled down and the timber used for constructing the new mill-house. A wharf is to be made east of the dam of the mill-pool. Yevele and Clifford are to be responsible for clearing and digging the site and the carpenters shall remove the old timbers. The timber is to be brought to the spot, ready for assembling, by 1 August (rather under seven months) and the work completed within a fortnight of Michaelmas. For this they are to be paid £45.

Mr. John Harvey called my attention to this contract, and Mr. K. B. M<sup>c</sup>Farlane, of Magdalen, kindly supplied me with a photostat.

Magdalen Coll. MSS., Southwark, 33.

Ceste endenture faite parentre Henri Yeuele & John Clifford citezeyns & masons de Loundres dune part & Willm. Vynt, Alisaundre Tilsyk, carpenters

---

[1] *water thycht*: water-tight.

[2] *astlayr and coynhe*: ashlar and coigns.

[3] *bourcht*: surety.

de Colcestr' & John Arto<sup>r</sup> carpenter de Kirkeby dautre part tesmoigne q' les auauntditz Willm. Alisaundre & John Arto<sup>r</sup> ount empris de faire de nouell deux molynes eweres dez ditz Henri & John Clifford en la paroche Seint Olaf de Suthwerk les quell iadys furont Symond de Mordon sibien dedeinz la terre come desuys, cest asauer le corps & le Upperbay ioynaunt bien & couenablement a le rerebay ouesque tout la carpentrie qappartient a ceo: dount les nedles¹ serront dune pee dassise de laeur & lespace dune pee parentre checun nedle. Et auxi les ditz carpenters prendront a val les deux veill mesons el partie dest & west dez ditz molyns & ferront de nouell une meson occupant tout la mesme terre & desuys le corps del molyn en la manere come les Batailles molynes en la dite paroche sount faites; et en ycell meson ils mettront del veill merym ceo q' voet seruir & issuit de continuer loeure de carpentrie tanq' ils soient prestes a moler. Et ensement les auauntditz carpenters ferront de nouel les roetz² ouesq' lextrees³ de nouel merym bon & suffisaunt pur tiell ouerayn. Auxi les ditz carpenters ferront la Wharf bon & couenable vers lest del Bay tanq' a un pount de merym illoesqes; et al part de west ilz bayeront⁴ le wharf hors del estank illoesqes come plus profit serra a les molynes; & le wharf serra del longure come il est meyntenant, & retournant le wharf vers le west tanq' a un arbre appell' wilugh⁵ illoesq' esteaunt; et piccheront mettront & seieront⁶ les dites molynes come le conseyll dez ditz Henri & John Clifford voillont ordeigner. A tout le quell ouerayn les ditz Willm. Alisaundre & John Arto<sup>r</sup> troueront tout le merym nouell & tables oue tout manere de cariage & toutz altres choses qappartient a carpentrie & q' loeure & le merym serra accordaunt de auxi gross merym & pluys large come est le merym de les auauntditz Bataillez molyns & q' le merym soit meillour de bon coer de keyne saunz sap⁷ & q' les tables soient de bon & couenable espessur cest assauer ascuns de deux poulces en espesse & ascuns de un poulce & demy dassise come appent a tiel oeure; & q' le test dez ditz molynes soit pluys fort & pluys graunt merym come est le test del dit bataille molyn. Et les ditz Henri & John Clifford ferront voider la terre, et les ditz carpenters voideront le veill merym ouesq' layde dez fossours de la terre, et ceo q' voet servir de ceo pur plates pur la meson les ditz carpenters les aueront & mettront en la dite meson & le remenant serra salue & garde al us & profit dez ditz Henri & John Clifford. Et serra tout le merym & tables prest frames a la dite place des molyns le premier iour daugust procheyn auenir apres la date de cestes, & serra

---

¹ *nedles*: upright supporting posts.

² *roetz*: wheels.

³ *lextrees*: the axles.

⁴ *bayeront*: they shall dam.

⁵ *wilugh*: a willow.

⁶ *piccheront, mettront et seieront*: the exact significance of these terms is obscure. Apparently they are to 'pitch' (i.e. drive in the foundation piles), 'assemble', and ? 'saw', in the sense of arranging the waterworks, but the translation of the last word is not certain.

⁷ *coer de keyne saunz sap*: heart of oak without any sapwood.

le dit ouerayn tout prest & parfait en son droite lieux al quinseyne de Seint Michel Larchangel adunqes procheyn ensuant. Pur le quell ouerayn lez ditz Willm. Alisandre & John Arto$^r$ aueront quaraunt & cynk liuers desterl', dount ils serront paiez de dys liures desterling al fesance de cestes deuaunt la meyn; al feste de Pasq' adunq' procheyn ensuant dys liures; al feste de la Natiuite de Seint John Baptist adunq' procheyn auenir dys liures desterl'; et quaunt le merym est tout venu a la dite place dys liures; et quaunt il est tout parfait & performe ilz aueront cent soutz pour lour pleyn paiement. En tesmoignance de quele chose a y cestes endentures les parties susditz entrechangiablement ount mys lour sealx. Don a Londres le vyntisme septisme iour de Januer lan du regne le Roi Richard seconde unsisme.

<h2 style="text-align:center">42</h2>

*1389 London, Tower Wharf*

The king bargains with three masons to build a wharf, with two side walls. They are to dig out foundations 3 or 4 feet deep, and if necessary the ground shall be firmed with piles at the king's expense. The walls shall be 8 feet thick at their base, diminishing to 5 feet at the top, and $16\frac{1}{2}$ feet in height; the facing to be of ashlar of Kentish stone, the backing of 3 feet of rag and the remainder of chalk; at every 10 feet a long 'end-stone' shall be inserted; and the king shall provide for the filling, of earth and rubble, as the work proceeds. The work shall be under the control of the Treasurer, the Clerk of the Works, and Henry Yevele, and shall be completed within two years, unless payment is interrupted. For this they shall have £9. 13s. 4d. for each perch of $16\frac{1}{2}$ feet square; but if the walls are more or less than $16\frac{1}{2}$ feet in height, payment shall be proportional.

Exch. K.R. Accts. 502, no. 10.

Ceste endenture faite parentre nre. S$^r$ le Roi Richard le second dune part et Johan Westcote de Loundres William Janecok de Maydeston et Thomas Crompe de Otteham masons dautre part tesmoigne q' les ditz masouns ount empris de faire les oueraignes ensuantz cestassauoir un Wharf oue deux reto$^r$nes protendant en longeure del coign de la mure del Estfyn del Tour de Loundres enuers seinte Katerine tanq' al Turret del Watergate del dit Tour et en laeure conteignera cestassauoir lun roto$^r$ne deuers leawe de Thamise de la dit mure en lest fyn trente pees dassise et lautre reto$^r$ne serra suant et accordant a ceo resonablement et couenablement et les ditz masons ferront fower la terre ou le dit Wharf serra fait en profoundesse de troys ou de quatre pees sil enbusoigne et si le foundement ne voet estre sufficeant a quatre pees adonq' nre. S$^r$ le Roi le ferra fosser ou pyler et placer prest tanq' al mayn des ditz masouns pur ouerer desuys. Et serront les mures du dit Wharf dedeinz la terre oet pees en espessure le quell serra de ragg et calx et se leueront en hautesse del primere piere mys en la terre iesq' amont sesze pees et demy dassise et serront en my lieu del espessure de sys pees dassise et paramount en espessure de cynk pees et les ditz mures en la part de hors deuers leawe serront fait de assheler de Kent bon et couenable et bien litez et ioyntez et estuffez pardedeinz de ragg par lespessure de trois pees et le remenant de calx.

Et al fyn de chescun dys pees ferront coucher pieres appellez endestones en longeure bon et couenables en chescun cours. Et tondiz come loueraigne est enfesant nre. S' le Roi a ses custages ferra empler de terre et rubous pur saluacion del ouerage. As queux oueraignes susditz les ditz masouns troueront toute manere piere calx sablon et touz autres choses qappartient a masonrie oue la cariage. Et serront les ditz oueraignes bien et couenablement parfaitz en quaunq' appent as ditz masouns selonc lauys et surueiance del Tresorer nre. S' le Roi S' Johan H'mesthorpe et le clerc des oueraignes nre. dit S' le Roi et Henry Yeuele et serront tout prestes dedeinz deux ans proscheins ensuantz la date de cestes encas qils ne soient mye destorbez par defaute des paiementz. Et prendront les ditz masons pur chescun perche de sesze pees et demy squarre del dit oueraigne noef liures tresze souldz et quatre deniers. Des queux ils serront paiez en mayn al fesance de cestes de cynquante liures et del remenant ils serront paiez par diuerses foitz come le dit oeure esploit et come ils enbusoignent. Et encas q' les ditz mures se extendront en hautesse pluys haut q' xvj pees et demy auaunt specifiez nre. dit S' le Roi paiera pur le surplusage come amountera a ycell selounc lafferant et selonc le pris al perche desuis limite. Et sil soit meyns adonqs serront abatuz resonablement selonc la quantite. Et nre. dit S' le Roi trouera as ditz masons une [   ] durant le temps de lo$^r$ ouerance a oeuerer dedeinz. En tesmoignance de quelle chose a ycest endentures les parties auantditz entrechaungeable[   ] sealz. Don lendemayn de la Nativite seint Johan Baptist lan du regne nre. dit S' le Roi treszisme.

# 43

*1392 St. Asaph's Cathedral*

Agreement with a mason for the completion of the bell tower. He is to build 5 yards of solid wall and 1½ yards of battlement, for 100 marks.

*Royal Com. on Anct. Mons., Wales, 86.*

Hec est convencio facta inter Episcopum Decanum et Capitulum Assavensis ex parte una et Robertum Fagan ex altera videlicet quod idem Robertus sumptibus suis propriis et expensis faciet et perficiet competentem campanilem ecclesie Cathedralis Assavensis tota opera petrosa tam in quarera quam alibi usque ad altitudinem quinque virgarum muri integri et unius virge et dimidie in batall' superius secundum proporcionem competentem fundamenti dicti capanilis meliori modo et forma quibus profici debetur. Et quod predicti Episcopus Decanus et Capitulum solvent prefato Roberto centum marcas secundum quantitatem facture dicti campanilis. Et eciam iidem Episcopus Decanus et Capitulum tenentur ad omnia cariagia lapidum et quod inveniant calcem sumptibus eorundem Episcopi Decani et Capituli. Ita etiam quod totum campanile per prefatum Robertum perficiatur in forma prescripta erga festum Omnium Sanctorum anno millesimo ccclxxxxij.

## 44

*1394/5 Arbroath Abbey*

Agreement with a plumber to cover the roof of the quire with lead and make gutters for it, he providing one assistant and the Abbot a second. He shall have 30 marks, and a further 5 marks for leading the stone alures, when they are finished; and a gown and hood at the end of his work; also, for preparing the lead, 3*d.* for every stone, and one stone in every hundred that he works; and 1*d.* for his 'noon meat' every day that he works.

*Reg. Nigrum Abb. de Aberbrothoc,* 42.[1]

This endentur . . . beris wytnes that the yer of grace mcccxciiij the xvj day of the moneth of Feveryer this cuunande was made betwene . . . Johnne . . . abbot of . . . Abirbrothoc . . . of the ta part and Wilyam Plumer of Tweddale burges of the cite of Andirstoun of the tothir part, that is to say, That . . . Wyllam Plumer sal theke the metail quer . . . wyth lede and guttir yt al abowt sufficiandly with lede, for the quhilkis thekyn and gutteryn the abbot . . . sal pay till hym xxxv marcis at syndry termys as he is wyrkand and of the xxxv marcis v marcis sal dwel style in the abbotis hand . . . quhillys the quer be thekyt and alurryt[2] al abowit with stane, and quhen it is alurryt about with stane he sal dycht it abowt wytht lede suffyciandly as his craft askys, and quhen he has endyt that werk he sal be payt of v marcis and a gown with a hude till his rauarde. Quhilk Wilyam Plumer sal fynd a man on his own cost and the abbot and conuent a man alsua of thar cost quhil the werk be fullyly endyt. The abbot and the conuent sall fynd al maner of gratht[3] that pertenys to that werk quhil is werkande. William sal haf alsua for ilk stane fynyne[4] that he fynys of lede iij[d] and a stane of ilke hyndyr that he fynys til his trauel, and that day that he wyrkis he sal half a penny til his noyn-sankys.[5] In the wytnes of this thyng to the ta part of these endentur to the abbot and the conuent for to dwel the selis of John Brog and of John Prechurrys burges of the burgh of Abirbrothoc ar to put, the tothir part anens Wilyam of Tweddal plummer the comoun sele of the chapyter of Abirbrothoc remanys selyt. Dowyn and gyffyn the yer and the day of the moneth before nemmyt.

[21 May 1396: William Plummer, citizen of St. Andrews, acknowledges receipt of £20 sterling '*pro architectura*[6] *magni chori*', and acquits the Abbot 'de omni condicione et exactione, videlicet pro purificacione plumbi, pro le none-sankys, et de epitogio cum capicio', as specified in the indentures. Ibid. 44.]

---

[1] I am indebted to the late Dr. G. G. Coulton for calling my attention to this contract.
[2] *alurryt*: provided with 'alures', or walks.
[3] *gratht*: equipment.
[4] *fynyne*: refining—melting and working the lead.
[5] *noynsankys*: 'nuncheons', or 'noon meat'.
[6] *architectura*: here used for thacking with lead.

## 45

*1395 Westminster Palace*

Agreement by which two masons are to make the 'tabling', or cornice, at the top of the walls of the Hall; it is to be 2 feet in height and cut to a design supplied by Henry Yevele, at 12d. the foot. They are also to carve, to a pattern supplied, 26 corbels, cutting away the wall for their insertion and subsequently making good the wall, at 20s. apiece. If it prove necessary to take down any pillars (of the Norman arcade), this shall be paid for extra. The king is to supply all materials, and also lodging for the masons and their fellows. The work to be completed in under a year.

Exch. K.R. Accts. 473, no. 21.

Ceste endenture faite parentre nre. seignur le Roy dune parte et Richard Washbourne et Johan Swalwe masons dautre parte tesmoigne q' les ditz masons ont empris de faire bien et loialement toute la table des murs de la grande Sale deinz le Paleys de Westmonster dune part et dautre, la quele table surmontera launcien Mure deux pees dassise parmy le dit Mure ouesq' peres de Reigate sciez, et la ou mestier serra de mettre pere de Marre[1] pur la dite table ens . . . er et le plus haut cours de mesme la table dune part et dautre bien et couenablement enforceront par lyuel,[2] et ferront la dite table selonc le purport dune forme et molde faitz par conseil de Mestre Henri Yeueley et deliuerez as ditz masons par Watkyn Walton son Wardein. Et prendront les ditz masons pur chescun pee dassise en longure du dit mure issuit fait douze deniers. Et ont aussi les ditz masons empris de faire vyngt et sys souses[3] en la dite Sale de pere de Marre et depesseront le mure pur les ditz souses y mettre a lour coustages demesnes et les ditz souses bien et couenablement chescun en son lieu mettront et ferront chescun souse dentaille[4] selonc le purport dun patron a eux monstree par le Tresorer dengleterre et empleront chescun spaunder[5] ouesque pere de Reigate sciez de chescun souse aual tanq' al Arche paramont, preignant pur chescun souse issuit fait par surueue des ditz Mestre Henri et Watkyn son wardein vyngt souldz. Et nre. seignur le Roy trouera touz maneres necessaires et matiere pur les ditz oueraignes cestassauoir pere chalce sabulon scaffold Gynnes et autres matieres queconques, forpris manuele oueraigne et instrumentz pur masons ouerer en lour art. Et si aucune pilere[6] serra abatue, ce serra as coustages de nre. dit seignur le Roy. Et mesme nre. seignur le Roy trouera herbergage pur les ditz masons et lour compaignons par tout le temps quils serront occupiez entour les dites oueraignes.

[1] *pere de Marre*: stone of Marre, near Doncaster—a hard limestone.
[2] The top course had to be levelled to carry the timbers of the roof.
[3] *souses*: an unusual word for corbels; *sources* is sometimes used for image-brackets.
[4] *dentaille*: of carving.
[5] *spaunder*: spandrel; here used, apparently, for the walling between the windows, which would be cut away for the insertion of the corbels.
[6] The walls, before their remodelling at this time, had a Norman arcade supported on little columns, some of which might have to be removed when inserting the corbels. See *Royal Com. on Anct. Mons., London*, ii. 122.

Et les auantditz masons ferront et parformeront la moitee des ditz table et souses en manere come auant est dit parentre cy et la feste de seint Johan le Baptistre prochein venant et lautre moitee parentre la dite feste de seint Johan et la feste de la Chandeleure lors prochein ensuant. En tesmoignance de quele chose a la partie de ceste endenture demorante deuers nre. dit seignur le Roy les auantditz masons ont mis lour sealx. Don a Westm' le xviij io$^r$ de Marz lan du regne de mesme nre. seignur le Roy dys et oytisme.

# 46

*1398 Durham Cathedral Priory*

John de Middelton, mason, undertakes to rebuild the dormitory. The walls are to be 60 feet high, with four off-sets, and 2 ells thick at the base, of smooth ashlar outside and of rubble inside, with parapets. In the west wall, on the ground floor, shall be four or more doors, and nine windows, of which five shall be on the pattern of one in the Communar's room; on the first floor every two cubicles shall have a window like one in the 'study', or cubicle, nearest to the church, and over each cubicle an arch-vault; higher up shall be a range of eight windows; and above these a battlemented parapet with an 'alure'. The east wall, between the minster and the refectory, on the cloister side, shall be blank below, but with similar windows and cubicles above; and in the south gable shall be one great window of such design as the prior decides. A spiral stair to the dormitory shall be put where the mason considers best. The ashlar shall be of at least 1 foot length; and the masonry as good as that of the Constable's Tower in Brauncepeth Castle, which shall be taken as a model. The work is to be finished within three years. The mason shall preserve the existing vaulting intact. He is to provide all materials; but the prior shall assign him quarries of stone and limestone, (growing) timber, and withies for scaffolding and hurdles, within 3 miles of Durham. The convent shall have the old walls pulled down and the foundations grubbed, and he shall have the material, but shall re-work the windows and ashlar. Every year the prior shall give him a tunic of the esquires' livery; and all the time that he is working there, the convent shall provide food and drink for him and his lad. He shall receive 10 marks for each rod, of 6⅔ ells square, of masonry—£40 in advance, and instalments of £40 as each 6 rods is completed. He shall find four persons to join with him in a bond of £40 for each period for the performance of the contract.

*Hist. Dunelm. Scriptores Tres* (Surtees Soc.), clxxx.

Haec Indentura, facta inter Johannem Priorem ecclesiae Dunelmensis et ejusdem loci Conventum ex parte una, et Johannem de Middelton cementarium ex parte altera, testatur, quod praedictus Johannes caementarius promisit et manucepit ac se obligavit ad edificandum et de novo construendum muros Dormitorii infra Abbatiam Dunelmensem situati, modo et forma inferius expressatis. In primis, idem cementarius suis sumptibus et expensis fieri faciet de novo unum murum ex parte occidentali ejusdem Dormitorii, qui quidem murus se extendit in longitudine a Monasterio Dunelmensi usque ad finem australem ejusdem Dormitorii, et in altitudine sexaginta pedum; una cum bretissementis,[1] si necesse fuerit, secundum voluntatem ipsorum Prioris et Conventus; et erit exterius de

[1] *bretissementis*: parapets.

puro lapide vocato achiler,[1] plane inscisso, interius vero de fracto lapide vocato roghwall, et de bono calce bene et sufficienter mixto cemate compositus. Erit etiam planus murus et in fundamento spissitudinis sive latitudinis duarum ulnarum, cum quatuor bonis et securis scarcementis,[2] vel pluribus si oporteat fieri, secundum formam cujusdam exemplaris presentibus indenturis annexi. Erunt etiam in eodem muro quatuor ostia, vel plura si necesse fuerit, bona et conveniencia et de bono et competenti opere, pro introitibus et exitibus oportunis; cum uno bono botras et substantiali inter finem dicti muri et le sowthgavill. Erunt eciam sub volta ejusdem domus in muro praedicto novem fenestrae lapideae; de quibus quinque erunt sculpturae et similitudinis mediae fenestrae in domo Comunarii situatae, vel melioris; quatuor vero aliae fenestrae erunt competentes et de bono opere, pro voluntate dictorum Prioris et Conventus eligendae. Quilibet vero bini lecti monachorum, supra dictam voltam, habebunt unam bonam fenestram pro suis studiis competentem; quae quidem fenestrae erunt ejusdem formae cujus est fenestra studii vicinioris ecclesiae ejusdem partis; et supra quodlibet studium erit unum modicum et securum archewote,[3] supra quod, spacio competenti interposito, erit una historia octo fenestrarum, ejusdem formae cujus est fenestra superior et propinquior parieti Monasterii praedicti in Dormitorio praedicto; et desuper istam historiam fenestrarum erunt honesta alours et bretesmontz batellata et kirnellata; quae quidem alours et bretismentz erunt in puro achiler et plane inciso, tam exterius quam interius. Murus vero orientalis ejusdem Dormitorii, inter Monasterium praedictum et Refectorium dictae Abbathiae, a superficie Claustri erit planus, cum securis scarcementz necessariis de mundissimo lapide achiler plane inciso exterius et roghwall interius; cum studiis et fenestris tam inferioribus quam superioribus ejusdem sectae cujus erit murus alius antedictus. Et erit le beddyng cujuslibet achiler ponendi in isto opere longitudinis unius pedis de assisa vel longioris. Erit eciam le sowtgavill ejusdem Dormitorii a parte inferiori usque ad altitudinem competentem de puro achiler exterius, et inferius de roghwall; cum latitudine, spissitudine, bretismentz et alours, muris antedictis correspondens et conveniens (*sic*): in quo quidem gavill erit una magna fenestra ad voluntatem et arbitrium dicti Prioris facienda. Erit eciam in loco aliquo competenti per discrecionem dicti cementarii eligendo, assensorium vocatum vys,[4] pro ascendendo supra dictum Dormitorium; et opus istud in parietibus adeo decentis formae et fortitudinis, vel melioris, cujus est quaedam turris in castro de Branspett vocata le Constabiltour; quae quidem turris erit exemplar hujus operis. Et erit dictum opus finaliter completum infra tres annos festum Natalis Domini proxime futurum immediate sequentes. Et praedictus cementarius warantizabit et sustentabit woltam infra praedictum Dormitorium nunc existentem

---

[1] *achiler*: ashlar.
[2] *scarcementis*: off-sets.
[3] *archewote*: arch-vault; apparently the scoinson arch of the window.
[4] *vys*: vice, or winding stair.

adeo bono sicut est in die confectionis praesentium, absque aliqua deterioracione ejusdem. Et idem cementarius inveniet omnimoda cariagia dicto operi quomodolibet oportuna; franget quareram; ardebit calcem; ac instrumenta ferrea et lignea alia quoque vasa quaecunque, cum scaffaldes, seyntres[1] et flekes,[2] et aliis omnimodis necessariis oportunis, sumptibus propriis et expensis; exceptis quarera tam pro lapidibus quam pro calce, meremio, ac virgis pro dictis scaffaldes, sentres et flekes, quae dictus Prior assignari faciet eidem cementario infra spacium trium miliarium a Dunelmo distancium. Idem quoque Prior et Conventus, cum consilio et deliberacione dicti cementarii, muros antiquos in eodem Dormitorio nunc existentes prosterni facient; et eorum fundamenta pure mundari, pro novo opere imponendo; quae fundamina erunt incepta et posita per consilium et deliberacionem dicti Prioris et Conventus. Et habebit idem cementarius omnes lapides et cementum de muris antiquis ejusdem Dormitorii prosternendi, et novos lapides pro eodem Dormitorio de novo exscisos et ordinatos ad suplecionem operis supradicti. Ita tamen quod faciet omnes fenestras antiquas et lapides de novo renovari, pro decore et conformitate dicti operis. Praenominati eciam Prior et Conventus dabunt praedicto cementario quolibet anno durantibus tribus annis supradictis, quando praefatum Priorem contigerit liberacionem panni facere generalem, unum garniamentum de secta armigerorum Prioris. Dabunt etiam eidem cementario, durantibus tribus annis supradictis, victum in esculentis et poculentis pro ipso et garcione suo quandocunque pro opere praedicto Dunelmi moram traxerit et ibidem circa opus praedictum fuerit occupatus. Dabunt itaque dictus Prior et Conventus cementario supradicto pro qualibet roda operis praedicti quae continebit sex ulnas et duas partes unius ulnae squar, tam sub terra quam supra terram, decem marcas argenti: unde ad inceptionem operis supradicti idem cementarius percipiet prae manibus quadraginta libras argenti; et postea, cum perfecerit ad valorem sex rodarum operis supradicti, alias quadraginta libras; et sic tociens quadraginta libras quociens perfecerit sex rodas, modo supradicto; donec praedictum opus fuerit plenarie consummatum. Proviso tamen quod ultra praemissa specificata nichil quomodolibet sibi valeat vendicare. Et erit praedictus cementarius et quatuor aliae sufficientes personae obligati dictis Priori et Conventui in una obligacione per concilium dictorum Prioris et Conventus facienda in quadraginta libris singula vice qua quadraginta libras in forma praedicta idem cementarius receperit, solvendis eidem Priori aut ejus successoribus in casu quo idem cementarius defecerit perficere pro singulis decem marcis summae praedictae unam rodam operis antedicti sub forma et condicione superius memoratis. In cujus rei testimonium praesentibus indenturis partes praedictae sigilla sua alternatim apposuerunt. Data die sabbati in festo Sancti Mathei Apostoli et Evangelistae, anno Domini millesimo ccc<sup>mo</sup> nonagesimo octavo.

[1] *seyntres*: centering.
[2] *flekes*: hurdles.

# 47

*1401/2 Durham Cathedral Priory*

Peter Dryng, mason, undertakes the completion of the dormitory,[1] from the new work up to the church. The new work (described in No. 46) is to be taken as a model. In the west wall, on the ground floor, he is to make five windows like one in the Communar's room, and a little window in the wool-house, and certain doors. On the first floor he shall make windows, with arch-vaults, like the first window, at the other end, in the new work; and above, three or more windows in the west and four in the east wall. He shall also make a winding stair in the bell tower adjoining the dormitory. All this is to be finished within about 2¾ years. He is to have the same pay and privileges as his predecessor—the livery of food and drink being defined as a white loaf, a gallon of ale, and a dish from the kitchen.

*Hist. Dunelm. Scriptores Tres* (Surtees Soc.), clxxxvij.

Haec indentura facta inter Johannem Priorem Dunelmensis et ejusdem loci Conventum ex una parte, et Petrum Dryng cementarium ex altera, testatur, quod praedictus Petrus promisit et manucepit et se firmiter obligavit per praesentes ad edificandum et de novo construendum muros Dormitorii infra Abbathiam Dunelmensem situati; incipiendo a muris jam de novo constructis usque ad ecclesiam Dunelmensem antedictam; ita decenter, fortiter et melius sicut sunt praedicti muri jam de novo constructi; videlicet quod murus occidentalis erit in fundamento spissitudinis sive latitudinis duarum ulnarum, cum scarciamentis bonis et sufficientibus prout sunt in muro occidentali jam constructo; et faciet in eodem muro de novo construendo, sub volta, quinque fenestras consimilis formae, vel decencioris vel melioris, sicut est media fenestra in Domo Communi; et unam parvam fenestram in le Wollehouse; secundum avisamentum consilii Prioris; ac etiam tot hostia competencia et honesta quot voluerint dicti Prior et Conventus construi in opere antedicto. Item, pro singulis lectis monachorum faciet idem Petrus in utroque muro fenestras correspondentes, cum securis archevoltis supra se, secundum modum quo prima fenestra in praedicto muro de novo jam facto in altero fine Dormitorii praedicti; supra quas fenestras lectorum monachorum faciet in muro occidentali praedicto tres fenestras, vel plures, si necesse fuerit; et in muro orientali quatuor consimilis formae, sive melioris, cujus sunt fenestrae superiores modo factae in novo opere praedicto. Et supra ipsas fenestras superiores faciet in utroque muro ailours et bretissementa battellata, de puro achiler, secundum exemplar praedictorum murorum iam factorum in novo opere praedicto; quod opus novum erit in omnibus exemplar murorum de novo construendorum. Et erunt dicti muri de puro achiler exterius et de roghwall interius, cum bono calce bene et sufficienter mixto cemate competenti. Item caminum jam in Domo Communi praedicta existens sufficienter et honeste salvabit et perficiet, prout eisdem Priori et Conventui melius visi fuerint expedire. Et erit le beddyng cujuslibet achiler ponendi in isto opere longitudinis

---

[1] John Middleton had evidently failed to carry out his contract and had not built more than the southern half of the dormitory.

unius pedis de assyse ad minus, cum latitudine competenti. Et fiat unum ascensorium, vocatum vys, in campanili propinquiori Dormitorio praedicto secundum avisamentum Prioris et Conventus praedictorum, pro ascendendo supra Dormitorium antedictum. Et erit hoc opus finaliter completum citra festum Omnium Sanctorum quod erit in anno Domini millesimo ccccᵐᵒ quarto. Et praedictus cementarius warantizabit et sustentabit voltam ∴ . . pro decore et conformitate dicti operis [*as in No. 46*]. Habebit eciam dictus Petrus cementarius, durante termino infrascripto, omnia aisiamenta, tam in batello quam in viis et semitis, cum introitibus et exitibus, prout Johannes Mideltoun cementarius habuit pro tempore suo. Dabunt insuper praedicti Prior et Conventus eidem cementario, a die confeccionis praesencium anno Domini Mᵒccccᵐᵒ primo usque ad festum Omnium Sanctorum antedictum, quolibet anno quo praefatos Priorem et Conventum contigerit liberacionem panni facere generalem unum garniamentum de secta armigerorum ejusdem Prioris, ac eciam quolibet die a festo Sancti Cuthberti in Marcio quod erit anno Domini Mᵒccccᵐᵒiiᵒ usque festum Omnium Sanctorum praedictum unum panem album et unam lagenam servisiae ac eciam unum ferculum coquinae, sicut armigeri Prioris praedicti tunc temporis percipiunt. Dabunt itaque praedicti Prior et Conventus cementario supradicto pro qualibet roda . . . plenarie consummatum [*as in No. 46*]. Proviso semper quod nec scaffaldes, seyntres, flekes nec alia feoda quomodolibet valeat vendicare. Et erit praedictus cementarius et aliae sufficientes personae obligati . . . superius memoratis [*as in No. 46*]. Et ad perficiendum opus praedictum in forma praedicta citra festum Omnium Sanctorum praedictum praedictus Petrus se obligat, haeredes et executores suos, per praesentes praedicto Priori et ejus successoribus in centum libris solvendis, si defecerit in perficiendo opus praedictum citra festum Omnium Sanctorum praedictum. In cujus rei testimonium praesentibus indenturis tam dominus Prior quam dictus Petrus cementarius sigilla sua alternatim apposuerunt. Data Dunelmi, in festo purificacionis beatae Mariae anno Domino Mᵒccccᵐᵒ primo.

## 48

*1404 Exeter*

Note, or abstract, of an agreement by which a mason is to build for the Dean and Chapter all the stonework of a house to the north of St. Martin's church. It is to be of the same height as their existing house; to have a gable at each end, fireplaces in the upper rooms, two latrines, and two doors and four windows. For which he shall be paid £6. 6s. 8d.

I am indebted to Mr. D. F. Findlay for a copy of this document.

Exeter, Dean and Chapter MS. 5550, fol. 95.

Convencio Whytten lathomi. Mem. quod in festo Sancte Crucis anno domini millesimo cccciiij . . . Convencio ita conventum est inter Magm. Baldwynum Schill' et dom. Thomam Redman tunc senescallum scaccarii et Johannem Whytten masoun, viz. quod idem Johannes edificabit omnes muros lapideos illius domus juxta ecclesiam Sancti Martini, viz. ex boriali parte ejusdem ecclesie situate; longitudo de murorum (sic) erit a domo dictorum Decani et Capituli ex parte orientali usque ad antiquam fenestram dicte ecclesie Sancti Martini ex parte occidentali. Altitudo de dictis muris erit sicut altitudo domus dictorum Decani et capituli cum duobus competentibus pugnonibus in utraque fine dicte domus, et cum duobus caminis racionabilibus in superioribus cameris ac etiam cum duabus· latrinis ad dictas cameras; et inveniet omnes lapides liberos cum cariagio pro ij hostiis et iiij fenestris ac omnes lapides alios liberos eidem domo necessarios, et faciet fossas competentes pro fundacione dictorum murorum et lath' cum bemefyllyng; et pro istis omnibus faciendis percipiet a Decano et capitulo vj$^{li}$. vj$^s$. viij$^d$.

## 49

### 1405 London, Bucklersbury

   The Dean and Chapter of St. Paul's contract with a carpenter to erect certain buildings on a site where they have had cellars dug and foundations laid. First he is to cover with joists and boards two cellars—one 45 ft. by 10 ft., the other 33 ft. by 16½ ft.—and a latrine pit, 16 ft. by 10 ft. Then he shall build a great shop, 22 ft. 4 in. by 18 ft., with a 'sotelhous', 10 ft. by 18 ft., and a gate and alley leading to the back premises. Over these shall be two stories, the first jutting front and back, the second jutting only towards the street, with a garret above; the first story shall be 11 feet high and have two bay-windows, for a chamber and parlour; the second, 9 feet high, shall have two chambers with handsomely lintelled windows. Behind, over the great cellar, he shall build a warehouse, 9 feet high; and over it a hall, 33 ft. by 20 ft. and 16 feet high to the wallplate, with an open roof, having a bay window and two others. A gallery, full of windows, shall lead from the hall into the first-floor rooms above the shop; above this shall be a small chamber leading into the second floor of the house. Above the west end of the hall and the small chamber shall be a principal chamber, 20 ft. by 11 ft., with a flat battlemented roof. At the east end of the hall he shall make steps and an oriel, giving access to the hall and light to the buttery and pantry, which are to be built, with the kitchen, over a coal-shed, wood-shed, and latrine. Above the buttery and pantry is to be a chamber, with a garret over it; and over the east end of the hall and part of the kitchen is to be another chamber. The dimensions of the various timbers are laid down. He is to cut the necessary timber in the Chapter's wood at Hadleigh, and to work and frame it there; the Chapter will then have it carried to the site, and will provide Eastland boards, nails, and other necessaries. He is to have the whole building completed and ready for tiling and daubing in just under a year. For this he shall have £46. 13s. 4d. and all the chips and bits of wood under a foot in length; the money being paid by instalments of £5 or £10 as the work proceeds. He and another citizen give a bond of 100 marks for performance of the contract.

St. Paul's MS. no. 1717.

   Hec indentura facta inter reuerendos viros Decanum et Capitulum Sancti Pauli London' ex parte una et Johannem Dobson Civem et Carpentarium London' ex parte altera testatur quod predictus Johannes conuenit et manucepit prefatis Decano et Capitulo bene competenter et sufficienter quantum ad carpentriam pertinet quedam domos et edificia subscripta eisdem Decano et Capitulo de nouo facere construere et edificare apud Bokeleresbury in parochia Sancte Sithe Lon-

don' super solum et in solo ubi certa vetera edificia ipsorum Decani et Capituli
per ipsos ad suos custus proprios prosternenda et abinde amovenda modo stant
et existunt quodquidem solum continet in longitudine in parte anteriori prope
viam regiam de Bokeleresbury versus boriam videlicet a tenemento dictorum
Decani et Capituli quod Johannes Permounter tenet ex parte occidentali usque
ad tenementum Johannis Walcote ex parte orientali triginta et octo pedes et
quatuor pollices assise et in parte posteriori iuxta murum Willelmi Walderne
versus austrum continet eciam dictum solum in longitudine a dicto tenemento
quod Johannes Permounter tenet ex parte occidentali usque ad quandam parcellam predicti tenementi dicti Johannis Walcote ex parte orientali quinquaginta
et septem pedes et dimidiam pedem assise in latitudine iuxta dictum tenementum
quod dictus Johannes Permounter tenet ex parte occidentali videlicet a dicto vico
regio versus borialem usque ad dictum murum Willelmi Walderne versus austrum quadraginta et quinque pedes assise et eciam in latitudine iuxta dictum
tenementum predicti Johannis Walcote ex parte orientali mensurando linialiter
a dicto vico regio usque ad dictum murum Willelmi Walderne quinquaginta et
octo pedes assise quodquidem solum sic superius mensuratum cum dicti decanus et
capitulum fundamenta pro edificiis ibidem fiendis competencia prompta fecerint
et parata predictus Johannes Dobson totaliter de nouo edificabit seu edificari
faciet modo et forma subsequentibus videlicet, In primis predictus Johannes cum
gistis et bordis competenter et sufficienter teget et operiet tam quoddam Celarium in dicto solo iuxta dictum tenementum quod Johannes Permounter predictus tenet ex parte occidentali fiendum contenturum in longitudine a dicto
vico regio usque ad fundamenta dicti muri Willelmi Walderne quadraginta
et quinque pedes assise et in latitudine decem pedes assise quam quoddam alium
Celarium in parte posteriori dicti soli contenturum in longitudine per fundamenta dicti muri Willelmi Walderne triginta et tres pedes assise et in latitudine
sexdecim pedes et dimidiam pedem assise. Ac eciam quendam puteum vocatum
Cave ad orientalem finem dicti maioris Celarii fiendum et pro latrina deseruiturum
contenturum in longitudine sexdecim pedes assise et in latitudine decem pedes assise.
Preterea dictus Johannes Dobson faciet construet et edificabit bene competenter
et sufficienter de carpentria super solum et fundamenta predicta iuxta vicum
regium predictum versus boriam unam magnam shopam cum quadam domo
ex parte orientali predicte shope vocanda Sotelhous[1] cum quadam porta et aleia[2]
ex parte orientali dicte shope seruitura pro ingressu et introitu ad quasdam domos
retro dictam Shopam et Sotelhous edificandas, que shopa continebit in largitate
ab oriente usque ad occidentem viginti et duos pedes et quatuor pollices assise,
et continebit dicta Sotelhous in largitate eadem via decem pedes assise, et dicta
porta cum aleia continebit in largitate eadem via sex pedes assise. Et continebunt
dicta Shopa Sotelhous et Aleia in profunditate a dicte vico regio versus boriam
inferius versus austrum decem et octo pedes assise. Super quasquidem Shopam

---

[1] *sotelhous*: possibly a showroom.          [2] *aleia*: an alley, or passage.

Sotelhous et Aleiam predictus Johannes Dobson construet et edificabit duo stages quorum unum videlicet primum gettabit[1] tam supra vicum regium versus boriam quam versus partem australem et aliud gettabit solomodo versus vicum regium cum uno garito supra dicta duo stages. De quibus vero duobus stages primum erit altitudinis ab inferioribus gistis usque ad superiores gistas undecim pedes assise, et secundum stage erit altitudinis nouem pedum assise de inferioribus gistis usque ad superiores gistas, et dictum primum stage habebit duas fenestras versus vicum regium competentes et honestas vocatus Bay Wyndowes unam videlicet pro una camera et alteram pro una parlera ibidem fiendis et equaliter dividendis utraque huiusmodi fenestra continente in claro infra postes sex pedes assise, et in dicto secundo stage fient et equaliter diuidentur dua camera habentes fenestras honeste lintellatas versus vicum regium. Insuper dictus Johannes Dobson super solum predictum retro dictam Shopam et Sotelhous videlicet super magnum celarium construet et faciet unum Warehous altitudinis nouem pedum assise et supra dictum Warehous unam aulam competentem et honestam cum uno Upright roof contenturam in longitudine triginta et tres pedum assise et in latitudine viginti pedes assise, cuius aule postes et muri erunt altitudinis de le Flore usque ad le Reson[2] sexdecim pedum assise; et prope occidentalem finem eiusdem aule versus boriam fient una fenestra honesta vocata Bay Wyndow et ex parte occidentali eiusdem fenestre due alie fenestre honeste lintellate de duobus dayes; et tectum dicte aule fiet competenter et honeste cum soulaces Assheler et Jowpeces cum uno Archecouple[3] in medio eiusdem aule dictum tectum supportante. Et ad occidentalem finem dicte aule iuxta dictam Baywyndow fiet unum Tresaunce[4] plenum fenestrarum ex parte occidentali eiusdem pro introitu in cameram et parleram in dicte primo stage supra dictam Shopam et Sotelhous ut prefertur fiendas. Et supra dictum Tresaunce fiet una parva camera ducens ad cameras superiores supra dictam shopam et Sotelhous in superiori stage ut prefertur edificandas, et eciam ad dictam finem occidentalem aule fiet una principalis camera continens in longitudine viginti pedes assise et in latitudine undecim pedes assise gettans supra illam finem aule inferius simul cum predicta parua camera, quequidem principalis camera habebit unum planum tectum cum uno batilmento circumquaque. Et ad finem orientalem dicte aule fiet unum Oryell[5] cum gradu pro introitu ad eandem aulam quodquidem oryell reddet lumen pro panetria et botilleria ibidem fiendis, quequidem panetria et botilleria sic ad finem orientalem dicte aule fiende se extendent magis versus boriam continentes simul in longitudine deinde versus boriam decem et septem pedes et dimidiam pedem assise et in latitudine duodecim pedes assise, et eciam fiet ad dictam finem orientalem aule predicte una coquina continens in longitudine sexdecim pedes assise et in latitudine quindecim pedes assise simul cum uno stabulo et cum

---

[1] *gettabit*: shall jut.  
[2] *le reson*: the wallplate.  
[3] For these terms see above, p. 211.  
[4] *tresaunce*: a gallery.  
[5] *oryell*: see above, p. 94.

colehous wodehous et latrina communi subtus dicta panetria botilleria et coquina totum remanens soli predicti ibidem perimplentes. Et similiter fiet supra dictam panetriam et botilleriam una camera de uno stage gettante versus occidentem cum garito desuper illud stage. Et insuper fiet ad dictam orientalem finem dicte aule una camera gettans tam supra illam finem aule inferius quam supra parcellam dicte coquine continens in toto viginti pedes in longitudine et decem pedes in latitudine. Et quo ad proporcionem mearemii predictorum edificiorum qualibet principalis postis omnium eorundem edificiorum erit latitudinis decem pollicum assise et spissitudinis sex pollicum assise. Et de principalibus bemes et somers quodlibet erit latitudinis decem et octo pollicum et spissitudinis duodecim pollicum et omnimodum aliud mearemium edificiorum predictorum erit sufficienter proporcionatum quodlibet in sua natura iuxta exigenciam suorum principalium et operum predictorum. Et spacium inter gistas flori dicte aule et flori dictarum camere et parlere in primo stage de dictis duobus stages supra shopam et Sotelhous predictas ac flori dictorum Celariorum non excedet in largitate una gista ab alia sex pollices assise, et spacium inter omnes alias gistas dictorum domorum erit mensuratum iuxta exigenciam suorum principalium, et spacium inter copulas tecti aule predicte non excedet in largitate una copula ab alia decem pollices assise. Et faciet predictus Johannes Dobson ad omnia edificia predicta hostia fenestras et alia luminaria quecumque ac scabella et [      ] in aula et parlera muros interclausuras et gradus pro qualibet domo competentes iuxta formam nature edificiorum predictorum et secundum auisiamentum et discreccionem predictorum Decani et Capituli et consilii sui. Ad que omnia et singula edificia et opera predicta prefatus Decanus et Capitulum inuenient et deliberabunt predicto Johanni Dobson vel suis in hac parte attornatis boscum competentem et sufficientem pro omnimodo mearemio dictis edificiis et operibus pertinente et indigente inde faciendo de et in Bosco ipsorum Decani et Capituli stante et crescente in parochia de Hadlee in comitatu Essex. Et predictus Johannes Dobson boscum predictum sumptibus suis propriis et expensis per visum et deliberacionem predictorum Decani et Capituli vel eorum in hac parte attornatorum prosternet et cecabit[1] seu prosterni et cecari faciet ac boscum illum sic prostratum et cecatum aptabit et in formam mearemii dictis operibus oportuni faciet et ornabit et in unum locum simul tractabit et framabit ac tabulas pro predictis domibus et edificiis necessarias et indigentes excepte Estrichbord inde faciet et sarrabit. Et predictus Decanus et Capitulum totum mearemium illud postquam fiat et frametur ac tabulas predictas deinde usque London' ad locum ubi dicta edificia erunt ut prefertur constructa et edificata cariabunt seu cariari facient sumptibus suis propriis et expensis, et eciam predictus Decanus et Capitulum Estrichbord clauos et omnia alia necessaria tam ferrea quam lignea dictis operibus indigencia ad custus suos proprios prefato Johanni Dobson invenient et deliberabunt. Ita quod idem Johannes nichil aliud inueniet eisdem operibus nisi solomodo

---

[1] *cecabit*: shall cut.

omne opus manuale quantum ad carpentriam et ad prostracionem cecacionem aptaturam facturam et sarraturam mearemii et tabularum predictarum ac edificacionem leuacionem et construccionem domorum et edificiorum predictorum cum suis apparatibus predictis pertinet et incumbit. Que omnia domos et edificia predicta cum omnibus suis operibus et apparatibus predictis iuxta formam predictam predictus Johannes Dobson sumptibus suis propriis leuabit loco predicto et ea plenarie edificabit construet et perficiet in omnibus que ad carpentriam pertinent vigore conuencionum predictarum prompta et parata fore tegulata et daubata citra festum Sancti Petri Aduincula proxime futurum post datum presencium vel per idem festum sine ulteriori dilacione. Pro quibus omnibus operibus supradictis predictus Johannes Dobson habebit et percipiet de prefato Decano et Capitulo quadraginta et sex libras tresdecim solidos et quatuor denarios sterlingorum ac omnimoda chippes et alia proficua cadencia et proueniencia de cecacione et aptatura totius mearemii predicti exceptis talibus remanentibus de mearemio predicto abcecandis que sint longitudinis unius pedis assise et ultra. De quaquidem summa predicta eidem Johanni Dobson soluetur modo subsequente videlicet cum et quociens idem Johannes tantum opus operauerit et fecerit de operibus predictis prout per discreccionem fidedignorum vel per bonam estimacionem ad valentiam decem librarum vel centum solidorum sterlingorum racionabiliter extendi poterit, tunc et tociens dictus Decanus et Capitulum obligant se soluere vel solui facere eidem Johanni vel suo in hac parte attornato decem libras vel centum solidos sterlingorum iuxta exigenciam operis sic operati et hoc de tempore in tempus quousque omnia predicta plenarie sic soluantur. Et insuper testatur presens indentura quod cum predictus Johannes Dobson et Johannes Botiller Ciuis London' teneantur et per scriptum suum obligatorium obligentur prefatis Decano et Capitulo in centum marcis sterlingorum soluendis in festo Natalis Domini proxime futuro post datum presencium [&c.].

Dat' sexto die Septembris Anno regni Regis Henrici quarti post conquestum sexto.

50

### 1409/10 *Hornby Church (Yorks.)*

Agreement with a mason for the building of a south aisle, corresponding to that on the north of the church. It shall have an arcade of two pillars and two responds; four windows; and three buttresses. He shall cover the roof with lead and shall put glass and ironwork in two of the windows. The work shall be done in 8 months; and he shall be paid 51½ marks. Mutual bonds of £40 for performance of contract.

McCall, Richmondshire Churches, 62.

This indenture made betwix John Conyers of Hornby of the ta party and Richard, mason of Newton in the parish of Patrick Brompton, on the tothir party witnesses that the foresaid Richard hase undirtaken for to make the south eill of the parish kirke berand aluis full brede as the north eill of the same kirk beres; the whilk south eill sall be of twa hale pillers and two halfe pillers. And in the end of the same south eill sall be a couenable windowe of thre lightes; and in the syde two couenable windowes of twa lightes; and in the west a couenable windowe of a lighte. And the walles of the same south eill sall be twa fote hegher than the walles of the foresaid north eill, if it like to the foresaid John. And the same south eill sall haue thre boteras, yat is for to say, at eithir end of it a boteras, and a boteras in the syde betwix the tother twa, where it will fall best; and ye fore-said south eill sall be ailled[1] and tabled couenably with stane. And the foresaid Richard sall gar theke[2] the same south eill couenably with lead, savand that the foresaid John sall gif thereto a fothir of lede and the cariage of the same fothir. And alsa the foresaid Richard sall gar glassyn and gryn[3] (*sic*) a windowe in the syde of the same south eill and a windowe in the west end of the same south eill at his own costages. And all this werk beforesaid sall be done weele and couenably in the forme beforesaid at the costages of the foresaid Richard, outaken the gift of the foresaid fothir of leade w$^t$. the cariage of it gifen be the foresaid John, betwix this and the fest of Saynt Mighell next comand after the date of this indenture. For the whilk werke the foresaid John sall gif the foresaid Richard, at times and dayes to the foresaid Richard agreables, li marks and a halfe. To the whilk covenant wele and leelely to be done in the terme before said, the partys before said, aithire party on yair part, bindes thaim till othirs, yair hairis and executors be thes present endenters in xl pound of leele monee of Ingland. In witnes of whilk thinge the partis beforesaid to this endenters entrechaungeably have set yair seles. Gifen the xxviij day of Ianuer the ȝere of o$^r$ lord the kinge Henry fourt eftir the Conquest of England the ellevent.

## 51

*1410 London, Friday Street*

Agreement by which a carpenter and a timber-merchant undertake to joist and floor the cellaring already dug on the site, and to erect thereon three houses. On the ground floor, 10½ feet in height, each shall have a shop with a sale-room and office; on the first floor, 9 feet high and jutting over the street, a hall, larder, and kitchen—the hall provided with suitable windows, benches, and screens; on the second floor, 8 feet high, a principal chamber, a retiring-room, and a privy. Each house shall have a gable on the street front and shall be made throughout according to designs drawn on parchment. The doors and shutters shall be of Eastland boards, the frame timbers of good oak of the size and form of the timbers used in Robert Chichele's buildings in Soper Lane. The whole work shall be completed within a year. For this they shall be paid £45, in instalments as the work progresses. They give a bond for £45 for performance of contract.

St. Paul's MS. no. 1462.

Ceste endenture faite parentre Meistre Waulter Cook et Sir Henri Jolipas clercz dune parte et Johan More Tymbirmongere et Johan Gerard Carpentere

[1] *ailled*: perhaps 'parapeted'.      [2] *sall gar theke*: shall cause to be covered.
[3] *gryn*: presumably a misreading for 'yryn', i.e. 'iron'.

citizeins de Loundres dautre part tesmoigne q' les ditz John et John sount en-
couenauntes ouesque les ditz Meistre Waulter et Sir Henri et ount enpris de lour
faire edifier et suitz mettre bien et couenablement de Carpentrie en Frydaystrete
en la paroche de Seint Mathew en Frydaystrete de Loundres en longeur parentre
les tenementz les ditz Meistre Waulter & Sir Henri et autres iatarde par Will^m
Peuere de nouell faitz et edifies deuers le South et les tenementz de John Frensshe
Orpheour[1] deuers le North et en laieure parentre les tenementz de Waulter
Strete mercer et Richard Craneslee Orpheour deuers le West et le haut Rewe
le Frydaystrete deuers le Est toutz les measons et oueraignes desouth escriptes
Cestassauoir en primes les ditz John & John a lour propres costages et expenses
bien et fortement gisterount et florerount un Celer q' contiendra en longeur et
laieur ataunt come tout le soill et terre parentre les boundes auauntditz se contient
des bones et couenables gistes et somers des keynes[2] chescun giste contenaunt
en laieure xiiij poulces[3] et en espessur viij poulces et les Somers chescun de eaux
serra en laieur xvj poulces et en espessur xij poulces bien et sufficiauntement
oueres et les bordes pardesus serrount bien et ioustement ioynes et assembles
contenauntz en espessur chescun bord par tout un poulce sarrez. Et pardesuis
le dit Flore du dit Celer les ditz John et John a lour propres costages bien
et couenablement ferrount edifierount et suismetterount trois shopes ouesque
trois stalles[4] et trois entrecloos[5] couenables ensemblement ouesque deux Flores
pardesuis et en le primer Flore les ditz John et John ferrount et departerount les
measons apres escriptes Cestassauoir une Sale un Spence[6] et un Cusyne pur
chescun mansion des ditz trois shopes et en chescun Sale ils ferrount Benches et
Speres[7] resonables pur les ditz Sales ouesque fenestres resonables et couenables
pur les measons auauntditz lequele Flore serra gette couenablement et en le
secunde Flore les ditz John et John ferrount et departerount une principal
Chaumbre une Drawyng chaumbre[8] et une Forein[9] et le dit secunde Flore
deuaunt serra fait ouesque une Seylingpece[10] parmye icell et les ditz John et John
ferrount en chescun mansion auauntditz deux esteires[11] bones et sufficiauntz Et
lesqueux trois shopes serrount faitz en hautesse Cestassauoir del terre iesques as
gistes del primer Flore dys pees et demye dassise et les punchouns del primer
Flore serrount en hautesse des gistes dicell tanque as gistes pardesus ix pees dassise
et les punchouns del secund Flore serrount faitz en hautesse Cestassauoir des
gistes dicell iesq' al Reson pece viij pees dassise, les queux measons pardesuis
serrount faitz ouesque trois Roofes gables deuers le haut Rewe deuers le Est par

---

[1] *orpheour*: goldsmith.   [2] *keynes*: oak.
[3] *poulces*: inches.   [4] *stalles*: counters.
[5] *entrecloos*: partitions.   [6] *spence*: larder.   [7] *speres*: screens.
[8] *drawyng chaumbre*: 'withdrawing room', or private room.
[9] *forein*: presumably a privy projecting from the main building.
[10] *seylingpece*: a horizontal beam projecting slightly on the front of the building.
[11] *deux esteires*: two flights of stairs; presumably, one on each floor, not two separate
staircases.

tout a droit bien et couenablement faitz accordauntz a un patron des ditz Shoppes Sales Chaumbres Spences et Cusynes measons et Roofes en parchemyn faites et limites. Et auxi ferrount les ditz John et John a lours propres costages as ditz celer trois Shopes Sales Chaumbres Spences Cusynes et autres measons auauntditz huisses et fenestres de Estricchebord bones et couenables solonc lauis et discrecion du dit Sir Henri Jolypace et Waulter Walton mason et trestoutz les fenestres pardesuis les ditz trois shopes faitz deuers le Haut Rewe serrount lintelles ou ergates[1] en manere come il appiert par le patron suisdit, et serra tout le mereisme des ditz Celer Shopes Sales Chaumbres Spences Cusyns measons et Roofes suisditz fait de bones keynes nettement et sufficiauntement et auxi bien par tout bien fait et proporcione come est le mereisme del Rente de Robt. Chichele ore esteaunt en Soperlane en la paroche de Seint Auntelyn et par tout accordaunt si bien en mereisme et proporcioun dicell come en fesure et oueraigne dicell. As queux oueraigne et measons auauntditz les ditz John et John a lour propres costages et expense troueround tout manere de mereisme borde et latthe as ditz measons et oueraigne besoignables ou escunement spectauntz et regardauntz ouesque le cariage diceux et ouereigne de Carpentrie et serrount les ditz Celer Shopes Sales et trestoutz autres measons auauntditz serrount toutz prestes faitz leuez et parfourmez en manere et fourme auauntditz en quanque appent a Carpentrie par le primer iour daugst proschein venaunt apres la date dicestes sans oultre delaye. Pur les queux measons et oueraignes ency affaire parfourmer et accompleer en manere et fourme come deuaunt est declarre les ditz John et John lour executours ou lour assignes aueround et prendround des ditz Meistre Waulter ou Sir Henri ou de lour executours quaraunt et cynque liueres desterlings dount ils serrount paies en mayn de dys liures al feisaunce dicestes et del remenaunt ils serrount paies en manere et fourme come la dite oueraigne est esploite Et que come les ditz John et John sount tenuz et obliges as ditz Meistre Waulter et Sir Henri en quarant et cynque liures desterlings a paier en le fest de Pasq' proschein venaunt apres la date dicestes sicome en une obligacon ent fait plus plainement est contenuz Nep^rquant les ditz Meistre Waulter et Sir Henri voillent et grauntent pur eaux lour heirs et lour executours paricestes q' si les ditz John et John de lour part bien et loialment teignent et parfourment toutz et chescun couenauntz auaunt specifies qadonq' le dite escript obligator' soit voide et tenuz pur null Autrement estoise en sa force et vertue. En tesmoignaunce de quele chose les parties auauntditz aucestes endentures entrechaungeablement ount mys lour sealx. Don a Loundres le vintisme iour Daugst lan du regne le Roy Henri quart puis le Conquest unszime.

---

[1] *ergates*: meaning obscure.

## 52

*? c. 1412 Hereford Cathedral*

A badly-drawn-up contract, by which a mason undertakes to build part of the cloister, between the chapter house and the chapel of St. Mary Magdalene, with two doors in it. He is to provide stone at 42*d*. (? the ton), and to have 23½ marks for his labour. He is also to make the vaulting, providing the stone and half the chalk (? for the filling, or for lime), and to take what timber the cathedral carpenter considers necessary for the lower roof. For each severey he shall have 4 marks. He shall make one side of the cloister in two years, and finish the whole within six years, provided he is paid regularly. Each year he shall have for himself and his mate two gowns, or 40*s*. Neither party shall have any claim against the other for a loss of 20*s*. or less on the bargain. *Charters and Records of Hereford Cath. 232.*

Hec indentura facta inter venerabiles viros & dominos decanum & capitulum ecclesie cathedralis Hereford' ex parte una & Thomam Denyar mason civitatis Herefordie ex parte altera testatur quod conventum est inter eosdem in hunc modum: ita videlicet quod predictus Thomas faciet fieri vel faciet totum le Uprightwerke[1] unius muri in claustro ecclesie cath' Hereford' juxta domum capitularem extendentis ab ostio dicti claustri usque ad le kuyne[2] juxta capellam beate Marie Magdalene, infra quem murum erunt duo ostia, unum in loco quo processio intrat in claustrum a domo carpentariorum operariorum & aliud ad introitum in palacium, que ostia erunt bene & competenter facta. Et predictus Thomas inveniet ad dictum opus edificandum sufficientes lapides cum toto le cariagio & habebit pro quolibet sothin[3] xlij[d]. Et habebit pro suo labore viginti tres marcas sex solidos octo denarios. Ulterius idem Thomas faciet vel fieri faciet totum le voute ejusdem claustri & inveniet sufficientes lapides ad idem opus & pro dictis lapidibus habebit tantum maremium in bosco dominorum quantum carpentarius ejusdem ecclesie ad inferius tectum ejusdem operis (?)aestimat & proponit quod pertinere deberet.[4] Et idem Thomas inveniet dimidiam partem totius calcis pertinentis dicto le voute. Et pro quolibet cibo,[5] modo dicto le syuere,[6] idem Thomas habebit quatuor marcas. Et dictus Thomas faciet infra spacium duorum annorum unum latus dicti claustri. Et sic a data presentium infra spacium sex annorum finem totius operis antedicti nisi sit in defectu dominorum dictorum de premissis non solutis perimplebit. Et dictus Thomas habebit quolibet anno quousque dictum opus fuerit plene edificatum duas togas de liberata vel xl[s] in festo pasche pro se & socio suo. Et omnia alia dicto operi pertinencia dictus decanus & capitulum invenient sumptibus suis. Insuper conventum est inter eosdem in hunc modum quod si dictus Thomas perdiderit xx[sol] in factura dicti operis aliquam querelam versus decanum & capitulum non habebit, nec dicti domini si ipsi perdant eodam modo versus dictum Thomam querelam aliquam non habebunt.

[1] *uprightwerke*: a term covering plain walling and traceried openings.
[2] *kuyne*: corner.          [3] *sothin*: query a misreading for 'fothir'?
[4] Presumably this timber was really for the scaffolding and centerings of the vaulting.
[5] *cibo*: this should have been *ciborio*: see Willis, *Nomenclature*, 43.
[6] *syuere*: severey, or bay.

## 53

*1412 Catterick Church (Yorks.)*

Agreement by which a mason undertakes to pull down the stonework of the old church and build a new one on another site, supplying such extra stone as is necessary. The quire shall be 55 ft. by 22 ft., with a five-light east window and angle buttresses running up to the parapet; on the south side shall be three windows, of two lights, and a door, and three buttresses; on the north shall be a door for a vestry, for the future building of which he shall leave bonding stones, and a three-light window. The walls shall be 24 feet high with a plain parapet; and he shall make a high altar with three steps, and three sedilia. The nave shall be 70 feet in length, with two aisles, 11 feet broad, and four arches. Each aisle shall have a three-light window at the east end—one from the old church being reset in the north aisle—two-light windows and a door in the sides, and a single light at the west; also an altar and piscina. The aisle walls shall be 16 feet, and the nave, with clerestory, 26 feet in height. At the west end he shall leave bonding stones for a tower. His employers shall provide carriage for all materials, and also scaffolding, which shall revert to them. He shall finish the quire within a year, and the whole building within three years, except the parapets, which he shall complete within the next year. For this he shall have 160 marks, and if he finish within the time, a further 10 marks and a gown. Mutual bonds of £40 for performance of contract.

Raine, *Catterick Church*; MᶜCall, *Richmondshire Churches*, 37–40.

This endentor made atte Burgh the aghtende day of the Moneth of Aprill the yere of Kenge Herry ferth after the conquest of Ingland thrittende betwix dame Katerine of Burgh somtyme the wife of John Burgh William of Burgh the sonne of the forsaide John and dame Katerine of the ta partie. And Richarde of Cracall mason on the tothir partie bereth witnes that the forsaid Richarde takes full charge for to make the kirke of Katrick newe als werkemenschippe and mason-crafte will and that the forsaid Richard sall fynde all the laboreres and servys pertenand to the kirke makynge. And that the forsaide Richarde sall take downe and ridde of the stane werke of the alde kirke of Katrick after the tymber be tane downe. And he sall cary and bere alle the stane warke of the alde kirke to the place where the newe kirke sall be made. And also forsaide Richarde sall take the grounde and ridde the grounde whare the newe kirke sall be made. And the for-saide Richard sall gette or garre gette[1] att the quarell atte his awen coste all the stuff of the stane that misters[2] more of the makyng of the Kirke of Katrik than that stuffe that is founde within the kirke yerde beforsaide. And also the forsaide Richard byndes hym be this endentor that he sall make the kirke and the quere of Katrik newe als werkemanschippe and masoncraft will that is to say the quere sall be of lenght within with the thiknes of both walles fifti fote. And it sall of breede wᵗin that is to say within the walles twa and twenty fote. And the forsaide Richarde sall make a wyndowe in the gauill of fife lightes accordaunt to the hight of the kirke couenably made be werkemenschippe and mason crafte. And he sall make apon the cornere of the southe side of the same windowe a franche botras[1]

---

[1] *garre gette*: cause to be got.
[2] *misters*: is needed.  [3] *franche botras*: see above, p. 96.

rising unto the tabill y^t sall bere the aloring.[1] And he sall make a wyndowe of twa lightes atte the awter ende couenably made be werkmanschippe and mason crafte and a botras risyng unto the tabill als it is before saide. And he sall make a wyndowe on the same side of twa lightes and a botras acordaunt thareto on the same side. And the forsaide Richarde sall make then a quere dore on wheder side of the botras that it will best be and a windowe of twa lightes anense the deskes. And on the cornere of the northest ende of the forsaide quere he sall make a franche botras acordaunt to the hight before saide. And the forsaide Richarde sall putte oute tusses[2] for the makyng of a Reuestery. And he sall make a dore on the same side for a Reuestery and a botras acordaunt to the hight beforesaide. And the forsaide Richarde sall sette a wyndowe of thre lightes anens the deskes the whilk standes nowe in the olde quere on the southe side. The hight of the walles of the quere beforesaide sall be aboue the grounde twenty fote with an aluryng abowne that is to say with a course of aschelere and a course of creste. And also the forsaide Richarde sall make with in the quere a hegh awter ioynand on the wyndowe in the gauill with thre greses[3] acordaunt thare to the largest grese begynnyng atte the Reuestery dore with thre Prismatories[4] couenably made be mason crafte within the same quere. And the forsaide Ric' sall make the body of the kirke acordaunt of widenes betwene the pilers to the quere and the lenght of the body of the Kirke sall be of thre score fote and tenne with the thicknes of the west walle. And at aither side foure arches with twa eles acordaunt to the lenght of the body. And aither ele sall be made of breede of elleuen fot within the walle. And the forsaide Richarde sall make a windowe in the southe ele, that is to say in the este ende of thre lightes acordaunt to the hight of the ele, with a franche botras risand unto the tabill couenably made be mason crafte And a wyndowe of twa lightes atte the awter ende apon the southe side with a botras dyand under the tabil. And then a wyndowe of twa lightes with a botras and a dore. And also the forsaide Richarde sall make a windowe of twa lightes with a franche botras in the southewest cornere acordaunt to the botras beforesaide. And he sall make a windowe of a lighte in the west ende of the same ele. And the ele sall be alourde acordaunt to the quere with an awter and a lauatory[5] acordaunt in the este ende. And also the forsaide Richarde sall take the wyndowe that standes now in the north side of the alde kirke and sette it in the este side of the north ele ouer the awter with a franche botras on the cornere dyand under the tabill. And the for-saide Richarde sall make a window of twa lightes atte the awter ende with a franche botras atte the mydwarde of the elyng and a dore and a botras on the north west cornere. And also the forsaide Richarde sall make a windowe of a

---

[1] *aloring*: parapet.                         [2] *tusses*: projecting stones, for bonding.
[3] *greses*: steps.
[4] *prismatories*: evidently sedilia; Raine suggests that it is meant for 'presbyteries', i.e. the priests' seats.
[5] *lauatory*: piscina.

lighte in the west ende of the same ele and a awter in the same ele and a lauatory acordaunt thareto, the ele alurde acordaunt to the tother. The heght of the walles of aither ele under the tabill abouen the grounde sall be made of sextene fote hight. And the forsaide Richarde sall make the pilers with the arches and the clerestory of the hight of sax and twenty fote abouen erth under the tabill. And also forsaide Richarde sall schote out tusses in the west ende for makyng of a stepill. And also forsaide Richarde sall make tablyng of the endes of the forsaide Kirke of Katrick with seueronne tabill.[1] And also the forsaide Richarde byndes hym and his executors and assingnes be this endentor that the Kirk of Katrik beforsaide ande neunde[2] sall be made suficiauntly and acordaunt to the couenauntez beforsaide fra the fest of seint John of Baptist next folowand after the makyng of the endentors safand the aloryngs vnto the same fest of seint John of Baptist be thre yere next folouande after that and fully fullfilled bot if sodayne were[3] or pestilence make it the whilke may be resonabill excusacon for the forsaide Richarde. And forsaide dame Katerine and William sall cari alle the stane that misters ouer the stuffe more than is fon in the alde kirke and in the kirke yerde atte thare awen coste. And also the forsaide dame Katerine and William sall finde lyme and sande and water and scaffaldyng and Synetres be houely to the same Kirke atte thaire awen coste. And when the Kirke of Katrik beforesaide is fully made and endid the forsaide dame Katerine and William sall hafe alle the scafaldyng and synetres vnto thaire owen vse. And the forsaide dame Katerine and William bindes thame be thes endentors their executoures and assignes for to pay vnto the forsaide Richarde and his assignes for the makyng of the forsaide Kirke of Katrik newe als it is rehersede and beforesaide within the terme of thre yere eght score of markes. And if the Kirke be endid atte the terme before neuende the forsaide dame Katerine and William sall gif unto the forsaide Richarde tenne markes of mone and a gowne of William werings[4] to his reward. And also the forsaide Richarde bynes hym bi this endentourez that the quere of the Kirke of Catrik sall be made newe fre the ffeste of seynt John of baptist next folowande after the makyng of thes endentoures vnto the same ffest of seynt John of Baptist next folowand als be a yere. And also the forsaide Richarde byndes hym be thes endentors that he sall make the aloryng of the Kirke of Katrik newe be mysomer next folowand after the ffest of seynt John of baptist before neuend that the forsaide Kirk of Katrik sall be fully made and endid and that alle thes couenaunte beforesaidez and neuende sall wele and truly be fullfyld and done that forsaide Richarde falles for to do be any mason crafte or any other thyng before neuende the forsaide Richarde byndes hym his heires and his executourez vnto the forsaide dame Katerine and William thaire heires and thaire executoures in fourty poundes of gude and lawfull

---

[1] *seueronne tabill*: eaves table; see above, p. 107.

[2] *neunde*, lower *neuende*: named.

[3] *were*: war.

[4] *William werings*: a slip for 'William's wearing', i.e. an old gown of William's.

mone of Ingland. And that all the couenauntz beforsaide and neuende sall wele and truly be done and fullfilde of the forsaide dame Kateryn and William behalfe that tham falles to do the forsaide dame Katerine and William byndys thame theire heires theire executoures unto the forsaide Richarde in fourty poundez of mone be thes endentoures Writyn atte Burgh the day and the yere beforesaide.

# 54

## *1413 Halstead Church (Essex)*

Agreement with a carpenter for making a new roof for the quire. The roof to be of seasoned oak, containing at least thirty couples of rafters, ceiled throughout with English boards, in the same way as is part of the roof over the high altar in the church of Romford. He is to provide all material and labour, and to have 19 marks for the whole. By a further agreement, he is to have the walls inspected by masons and raised 3 feet or more before setting on the wallplates, and also to have the roof lathed and tiled. For this he shall have all the old roof, 26s. 8d., and a new cloth for a gown.

St. Paul's MS. no. 329.

Hec indentura facta inter dominum Thomam More Decanum ecclesie Cathedralis Sancti Pauli London' et capitulum ejusdem ecclesie ex parte una et Johannem Taverner de Halstede in comitatu Essex ex parte altera testatur quod ita conuenit inter partes predictas videlicet quod predictus Johannes Taverner citra festum Sancti Petri quod dicitur Aduincula proxime futurum post datum presencium faciet seu fieri faciet prefatis Decano et Capitulo unum nouum tectum bonum et sufficiens ac de bono et sufficienti mearemio de corde quercino bene siccato et indurato pro coopertura et tegumine cancelli ecclesie parochialis de Halstede predicte et tectum illud super muros cancelli predicti in bonis et sufficientibus platis ponet et figet seu poni et figi faciet tectumque illud citra festum predictum in omnibus perficiet et perimplebit seu perfici et perimpleri faciet in quanto concernit opus carpentrie forma que subsequitur: quod quidem tectum fiat ad modum unius Chare roof[1] et continebit in se triginta copulas ad minus longitudinem dicti cancelli perimplentes quarum quelibet copula continebit in latitudine per bassum ad pedem octo pollices assise et in surgendo usque ad summum prout racio et conformitas carpentrie exigunt iuxta proporcionem bassi siue pedis cuiuslibet copule predicte, et quodquidem tectum in omnibus suis operibus et in qualibet sui forma et sufficientia concordabit operibus forme et sufficientie tecti cancelli ecclesie parochialis de Rumford in dicto comitatu Essex. Prouiso tamen quod de ampliori et largiori predictus Johannes Taverner per totum subcelabit seu subcelari faciet dictum nouum tectum pro coopertura ecclesie de Halstede predicte ut prefertur faciendum cum bono et sufficienti Englysshbord inter copulas predictas in quanto tectum illud se extendit in longi-

---

[1] *chare roof*: this probably means a 'waggon roof'.

tudine et largitate ad modum et formam prout pars tecti ecclesie de Rumford predicte supra summum altare eiusdem ecclesie subcelatur: Ad quod quidem tectum predictum pro coopertura dicti cancelli ecclesie de Halstede predicte forma predicta faciendum prefatus Johannes Taverner inueniet vel inueniri faciet totum et omnimodum mearemium et bord ac opus manuale et quicquid aliud artem et opus carpentrie concernens iuxta exigenciam operum superius designatorum una cum omnibus et singulis latis[1] quanto pro coopertura eiusdem tecti racionabiliter indigebunt et sufficient. Pro quibus quidem operibus omnibus supradictis forma predicta fiendis et pro omni eo quod predictus Johannes Taverner inueniet vel inueniri faciet ad eadem forma ut predictum est idem Johannes Taverner habebit et percipiet de prefatis Decano et Capitulo decem et novem marcas sterlingorum. Unde dictus Decanus et Capitulum soluere per presentes concedunt et soluent eidem Johanni Taverner executoribus vel attornatis suis ad festum Natalis Domini proxime futurum post datum presencium quadraginta solidos sterlingorum, Ad festum Inuencionis Sancte Crucis extunc proxime sequens quadraginta solidos sterlingorum, et incontinenti super finali complemento omnium predictorum operum totum residuum dicte summe decem et novem marcarum predictarum sine dilacione seu defectu aliquali. Ad quas omnes et singulas conuenciones supradictas ex utraque parte predicta fideliter tenendas et complendas forma supradicta partes predicte mutuo se obligant scilicet altera alteri firmiter per presentes. In cuius rei testimonio partes predicte hiis indenturis sigilla sua alternatim apposuerunt. Dat' London' decimo octavo die Nouembris Anno regni Regis Henrici quinti post conquestum primo.

[*Dorse*] Conventum est ulterius et de nouo inter partes infrascriptas quod infrascriptus Johannes Taverner citra festum infrascriptum omnes muros cancelli de Halstede infrascripti sufficienter scrutabit seu scrutari faciet et ubi necesse fuerit sufficienter emendabit vel emendari faciet iuxta discrecionem lathamorum ac muros illos per quantitatem trium pedum vel amplius si indiguerit in summitate undique augebit et sufficienter exaltabit absque defectu et tectum infrascriptum pro eodem cancello ut infrascribitur de novo faciendum cum sic fiat super muros predictos sufficienter ponet et figet seu poni et figi faciet forma infrascripta tectumque illud cum sic positum et fixum fuerit latthabit et tegulabit seu lathari et tegulari faciet bene et sufficienter ac tectum illud in omnibus suis concernenciis plene et totaliter perficiet, seu perfici faciet sumptibus suis propriis et expensis. Pro qua nova conuencione perficienda infrascripti Decanus et Capitulum concedunt eidem Johanni totum veterem tectum super dictum cancellum iam existens cum omnibus particulis et concernenciis eiusdem. Ac ulterius soluent eidem Johanni super complemento operum predictorum viginti sex solidos et octo denarios sterlingorum et pannum nouum pro una toga precii vj^s. viij^d.

---

[1] *latis*: laths.

## 55

*1415 Hartley Wintney Priory (Hants)*

Agreement with two carpenters to make a flat roof for the church, containing nine beams, with the necessary wallplates, and above it a bell-cote of four posts, with a flat roof; to be finished within about 10 months. The convent shall have the old roof removed, and shall provide timber, ropes, and lifting machines. The carpenters shall have £22, a pig and a wether, and a gown worth 10s.; also lodging and cooking utensils for themselves and their men, and food for six men for a week when they set up the roof. They produce two sureties for performance of the contract.

*Hist. MSS. Com. Rep.* xv (10), 174.

Hec convencio facta inter dominam Johannam Bannebury, Priorissam domus de Wyntenay, et ejusdem loci conventus (*sic*) ex una parte, et Johannem Willam carpenter, de Basyngstoke, & Willelmum Austyn, carpenter, de eadem, ex altera parte, testatur quod predicti Johannes et Willelmus fabricabunt, facient et de novo edificabunt unum tectum supra ecclesiam de Wynteney predicta, quod quidem tectum erit Flatterove et in eodem erunt ix trabes cum platis proporcionatis secundum longitudinem et latitudinem ecclesie Playn werke, et eciam de novo facient & edificabunt ibidem supra tectum unum campanile de quatuor postis cum Flatterove, infra certum tempus ita quod plene perficietur citra festum Sancte Marie Magdalene (22 July) proxime sequentem post datam presencium, et eadem Priorissa serabit omnes tabilos ad idem pertinentes sumptibus suis propriis, et eadem Priorissa inveniet meremium sufficientem et succidet et cariabit ad certum locum ubi fabricabunt, ita quod non impediantur idem Johannes et Willelmus nec illorum servientes, et predicti Johannes et Willelmus percipient pro labore suo xxij libras Anglicane monete et unum porcum et unum multonem et unam gounam precii x^s vel x^s in denariis, et cum levaverint predictum tectum predicta Priorissa inveniet idem (*sic*) Johannem carpenter & sex homines in victualibus per septimanam, & predicta Priorissa inveniet cordas et machinas et propriis expensis vacuabit antiquum tectum, et parietes ad eandem (*sic*) pertinentes patere faciet, et idem Johannes et Willelmus percipient cum ceperint operare x libras et postmodum cum ceperint framare vj libras, deinde cum levaverint predictum tectum vj libras, et idem Johannes et Willelmus habebunt aysiamenta domus pro eis et servientibus suis, una cum diversis utensiliis ad parandum victum sibi et servientibus suis, et ad istas convenciones bene et fideliter observandas et componendas Willelmus Shyrefelde et Rogerus Richard obligant se & quemlibet eorum heredes et executores suos eisdem Priorisse et conventui in xxij libris solvendis eisdem, et ex altera parte predicta Johanna Priorissa et ejusdem loci conventus obligant se & successores suos eisdem Willelmo Shyrefelde & Rogero Richard heredibus & assignatis suis in xxij libris solvendis. In cujus rei testimonium presentibus indenturis partes predicte sigilla sua apposuerunt. Datum apud Wynteney in festo exaltacionis Sancte Crucis (14 Sept.) anno regni regis Henrici Quinti post conquestum Anglie tercio.

## 56

*1418 Alresford (Hants)*

A carpenter undertakes to build, at the inn called The Angel, for the Warden of Winchester College: (*a*) a hall, 18 ft. by 20 ft., with two windows, one above the other; (*b*) a gatehouse, 34 feet long, with gates 9 feet in width, and (over it) a chamber with a bay-window to the street and a flat window to the garden, with a partition and a latrine, and jutting over the street 2½ feet; (*c*) a first-floor room over an existing basement, 34 ft. by 18 ft., with two divisions, one for a parlour, and a room above it, juttied over the street 2½ feet; (*d*) another building, north of the inn, with a shop, a hall, and a kitchen with a chamber over part of it. Scantlings of the timbers are given. He is to provide the timber, set up all the buildings, strengthening them with wooden braces where necessary; the whole to be completed in a little under the year, for £50. For which he gives a bond of 100 marks.

For a transcript of this contract I am indebted to Mr. John Harvey.

Winchester College Muniments, Alresford, 51.

Hec indentura facta sexto die Julii anno regni Regis Henrici quinti post conquestum Anglie sexto inter magistrum Robertum Thurbern Custodem Collegii beate Marie prope Wynton' ex parte una et Thomam Wolfhow carpentarium ex parte altera testatur quod idem Thomas de novo faciet apud Alresford in hospicio dicti Custodis ubi Angelus est signum unam aulam continentem in longitudine xviij pedes et in latitudine xx pedes, in qua quidem aula faciet vj postes unus quilibet cont' in longitudine x pedes in latitudine unum pedem et in spissitudine x pollices, et qualibet grondsull ejusdem aule cont' in latitudine unum pedem et in spissitudine viij pollices, et spacepostes[1] erunt habiles, et lez walplates ejusdem aule quelibet cont' in latitudine ix pollices et in spissitudine viij pollices; et in eadem aula faciet unam trabem[2] que cont' in spissitudine x pollices et in latitudine in medio xiiij pollices et in utraque fine ejusdem x pollices squar'; et in medio ejusdem aule faciet unum wovframe[3] cum uno wynbem.[4] Et quilibet tignus in eadem aula cont' in pede in latitudine vj pollices et in capite ejusdem v pollices et cont' in spissitudine per totum v pollices; et spacium inter tignos dicte aule erit spacium xj pollicum; et in eadem aula faciet duas fenestras versus stratam videlicet unam inferius et aliam superius, et quelibet fenestra erit de quatuor luminibus.[5] Item idem Thomas faciet unum ȝathous in eodem hospicio cont' in longitudine xxxiiij pedes cum duobus grossis ostiis cont' in latitudine ix pedes cum quatuor foliis et duabus wygatis[6] in eisdem ostiis; et onnes postes et grondsulle ejusdem consimiles erunt postibus et grondsullis aule predicte, et lez walplatez ejusdem cont' in latitudine ix pollices et in spissitudine viij pollices; et in eadem domo faciet iiij trabes consimiles aliis trabibus in aula;

---

[1] *spacepostes*: studs between the six main posts (4 corner and 2 central).

[2] *trabem*: a tie-beam.

[3] *wovframe*: a timber-framed wall, apparently above the tie-beam.

[4] *wynbem*: a collar-beam.

[5] The hall, being lit only on the street side, was probably between the gatehouse and the other wing, of which the breadth (18 ft.) was the same as the length of the hall.

[6] *wygatis*: wickets.

et in eadem domo faciet unum baywyndow versus stratam et unam aliam planam fenestram versus gardinum; et in eadem camera[1] faciet unum interclausum[2] et unam latrinam; et lez justez ejusdem camere quelibet cont' in latitudine ix pollices et in spissitudine vij pollices, et spacium inter lez justez erit spacium x pollicum; et subtus eandem cameram faciet ij somerez quarum utraque erit in latitudine xiiij pollices et in spissitudine xviij pollices; et borde arie dicte camere quelibet cont' in spissitudine unum pollicem, et quelibet borda erit sexata[3] ad quantitatem unius pollicis dimidii. Et in eadem camera faciet unum juteye versus stratam cont' in longitudine ij pedes dimidium, et quelibet postis tam in camera interiori quam in camera exteriori erit in longitudine viij pedes ad minus. Item idem Thomas faciet in selario dicti hospicii iiij somerez quarum quelibet cont' in latitudine xiiij pollices et in spissitudine xviij pollices, et in eodem selario faciet iiij postes in medio dicti selarii subtus lez somerez et consimiles ad lez somerez. Super quod quidem selarium dictus Thomas faciet unam mediam cameram cont' in longitudine xxxiiij pedes et in latitudine xviij pedes, in qua quidem camera faciet duo interclausa subtus lez somerez dicte camere, unde unum pro parlour ibidem habendo, cum habilibus et decentibus fenestris per totum latus de le parlour versus stratam. Et lez justez in camera desuper dictum selarium erunt consimiles ad alias justes camere predicte, et ille borde que erunt posite supra dictum selarium quelibet cont' in spissitudine unum pollicem dimidium; et quelibet borda erit sexata ad quantitatem unius pollicis dimidii. Supra quam quidem cameram idem Thomas faciet unam aliam cameram superiorem de eadem longitudine et de eadem latitudine, in qua faciet unum juteye versus stratam de longitudine ij ped' di. Et lez justez et borde necnon omnia alia consimilia erunt ut in la ʒathous preter quod unum walplate erit de latitudine x pollicum et de spissitudine viij pollicum pro uno gutero portando. Et in dicta camera faciet unum interclausum et unum baywyndow versus stratam et unam aliam bonam fenestram versus gardinum. Et faciet in eisdem cameris duas latrinas videlicet unam inferius et aliam superius. Et quilibet postis tam in camera inferiori quam in camera superiori continebit in longitudine viij pedes ad minus. Item idem Thomas faciet unam aliam domum ex parte boriali dicti hospicii in qua faciet unam shopam cont' in longitudine xiiij pedes et in latitudine xj pedes; in qua quidem domo faciet unam cameram cont' in longitudine xviij pedes et in latitudine xiij pedes, in qua quidem camera faciet unam baywyndow; et in eadem domo faciet unam aulam cont' in longitudine xviij pedes et in latitudine xj pedes; et in eadem domo faciet unam coquinam in qua erit camera per medium desuper fundam dicte coquine. Quas quidem aulas et cameras predictas prefatus Thomas faciet apud Alresford predicta de meremio suo proprio cariato usque Alresford ad custus predicti Thome; quod quidem meremium sic cariatum et

---

[1] The chamber was presumably that of the gatehouse.
[2] *interclausum*: a closet, or a partition.
[3] *sexata*: this must mean rebated, so that one board fits over the other to make a tight joint.

ibidem bene framatum dictus Thomas levabit bene et competenter sumptibus suis propriis et expensis. Et ulterius prefatus Thomas faciet in domibus et cameris predictis omnia ostia fenestras scanna sperez[1] guteras wynberges pro tribus cameris et aula predicta competentibus et decentibus secundum formam honestam que decenter in talibus villis solet ordinari et omnia alia qua ad opus carpentrie pertinent ad custus ejusdem Thome per visum dicti Custodis et concilii sui. Et idem Thomas ligabit omnes predictas domos et cameras cum bonis bracez lign' circumquaque prout pertinet tales domos et cameras ligari. Pro quibus quidem operibus modo et forma predictis bene fideliter et competenter citra festum sancti Johannis Baptiste proxime futurum post datam presencium edificandis predictus custos obligat se et successores suos per presentes prefato Thome in quinquaginta libris sterling' solvendis inde eidem ad festum Sancti Petri ad Vincula proxime futurum xij li. x s.; ad festum Natalis Domini proxime sequens xij li. x s.; ad festum Pasche proxime sequens xij li. x s.; et in fine operis predicti xij li. x s. Et ad omnes singulas convenciones prescriptas ex parte dicti Thome tenendas et in omnibus adimplendas idem Thomas obligat se heredes et executores suos per presentes prefato Custodi et successoribus suis in centum marcis sterlingorum. In cujus rei testimonium partes predicte hiis indenturis sigilla sua alternatim apposuerunt. Dat' in Collegio predicto die et anno supradictis.

[Seal, in red wax: a capital R.]

## 57

*1419  Wyburton Church (Lincs.)*

Reference to a contract by a mason to build the church and tower, and details of an informal agreement to insert 12 corbels and to embattle the tower—which extra work has been assessed by four master freemasons as worth 100 marks.

Early Chanc. Proc. 7, no. 104.

Supplie humblement Rog' Denys de Loundres fremason q' come bargaine ceo prist a Wyburton parentre le dit suppliant et Philip Proketo[r] de Wyburton et Roger Robynson de mesme la ville en le fest de Seint Martyn lesuesqz lan de regne le Roy Henry quint pier nre. S' le Roy qorest septisme q' le dit suppliant ferroit lesglise et le steple de la dit ville de Wyburton en manere et forme contenuz en un escript indente entre eux fait preigneunt p[r] le dit bargayne ciiij[xx]x marc . . . come fu apres a la dit ville de Wyburton cestassauoir le lundy proschein apres le fest de Seynt Michell larchangell bargaine ceo prist saunz especialitee[2] parentre le dit suppliant et lez ditz Philip Proketo[r] et Roger Robynson cestassauoir q' le dit suppliant ferroit xij corbellez en le dit esglise et qil ferroit enbatailler le dit esteple ouesqz legementz et tables accordauntz ouesqz franke pere pur quele ils luy paieront a taunt come il expenderoit entre la faisance de le dit

---

[1] *sperez*: screens.

[2] *especialitee*: a formal agreement in writing.

oueraigne outre le primer couenaunt susdit q' amount a cent marz come il a este aiugge par quatre maistres masons de franke pere.

[Philip and Roger now refuse to pay.]

# 58

*1420  Surfleet Church (Lincs.)*

Agreement by a mason and a gentleman (? his surety) to rebuild the chancel on the old foundations, which are to be carefully tested, with a winding stair and parapet walks. They are to provide all materials, including lead for the roof and English glass for a five-light east window and three three-light windows on each side, each light having a figure and inscription. The whole work to be finished within two years.

De Banco R., East. 8 Hen. V, m. 119.

[A suit brought by Mr. Adlard Welby, rector of Surfleet, and John Sutton of the same place, against Roger Dynyce of London, late of Lincolnshire, mason, for £100 alleged to be due on a bond.

The bond, dated All Saints' day, 1418, between the said Adlard Welby and John Sutton of the one part and Roger Dynyce of Lincolnshire, mason, and Richard Bour of Walpole, esquire, of the other, sets forth that:]

predicti Rogerus et Ricardus facerent construerent et de novo edificarent aut fieri construi et edificari facerent unum chorum sive cancellum competentem ad dictam ecclesiam parochialem de Surflet situandum et annexandum ante festum sancti Michaelis archangeli quod esset anno domini millesimo quadringentesimo vicesimo super fundamentum veteris chori sive cancelli ibidem ordinandum. Et si necesse foret et oportunum prefati Rogerus et Ricardus predictum vetus fundamentum scrutarentur vel bene et sufficienter facient scrutari tam pro muris ad altitudinem murorum veteris chori sive cancelli construendis quam pro coopertura predicti chori sive cancelli videlicet tignorum maeremiorum plumbi massarum ad formam similitudinariam ecclesie parochialis predicte ad valorem et quantitatem operis dicti chori sive cancelli ibidem construendi, insuper predicti Rogerus et Ricardus invenirent seu inveniri facerent ad dictum opus omnem materiam competentem et sufficientem prout in lapidibus maeremio cemento plumbo calce repagulis ferreis et vitro anglicano pro septem fenestris ejusdem chori sive cancelli videlicet pro tribus ex parte australi et pro tribus ex parte boreali et quelibet fenestra earundem cum tribus luminaribus et pro una fenestra in fine orientali ejusdem chori sive cancelli cum quinque luminibus ex altitudine et latitudine rationabiliter convenientibus et quod quodlibet luminare fenestrarum predictarum unam ymaginem habeat et scripturam per voluntatem predicti Adlardi in eisdem preparandas, cum aluris in superficie murorum cum quodam introitu et quodam exitu vocato le Vyce. Et iidem Rogerus et Ricardus invenirent seu inveniri facerent omnia alia necessaria ad dictum opus quovismodo pertinentia et oportuna cum omnibus prescriptis et nominatis. Et dicti Rogerus et

Ricardus post primam inceptionem dicti operis illud continuarent vel alter eorum continuaret seu per talescunque vel per talemcumque artifices vel artificem facerent vel alter eorum fieri faceret opus dictum continuari nec ullo modo tardarent prolongarent seu alter eorum tardaret prolongaret seu per talescumque vel talemcumque artifices vel artificem facerent nec fieri facerent opus sepedictum tardari quovismodo seu prolongari nisi esset defectu sue solius solucionis.

[Adlard and John say that Roger and Richard did not complete the choir, in roofing it with lead, before the date fixed. Roger says that they did. The case is adjourned to the Trinity term.]

## 59

*1421/2 Catterick Bridge (Yorks.)*

Three masons undertake to build a bridge over the Swale, like Barnard Castle Bridge, with three arches and two piers, and a parapet of five courses. They shall dig their own sand and limestone & make kilns to burn lime; they shall also hew the stone, and when it has been scappled at the quarries the employers shall have it carried to each end of the bridge. The employers are to provide all necessary timber for scaffolding, &c.; to make the coffer-dams, first for the bridge-ends and then for the piers, and to turn the water from the foundations; and, when the times comes, to set up the centerings for the arches. Also they shall give the masons 3 cwt. of iron and steel. The masons shall complete the whole work in about $3\frac{1}{2}$ years. For this they shall have 260 marks—the dates and amounts of the instalments being named— and each of them every year a gown. A wooden lodge for their use shall be erected near the bridge. Reference is made to a previous contract made with one of the masons for details of the dimensions of the piers.

*Archaeological Journal*, vii. 56.

This indent[r]e made be twene Nicholas de Blakburne Crist' Conyers William de Burgh John de Barton and Rog' de Aske William Franke And Th' Foxhols of ye ta p't and Th' Ampilforde John Garett And Rob't Maunsell masons of ye tothir p't bers witnes: yat ye forsaides Th' John And Rob't schall make a brigg' of stane oure ye wat' of Swalle atte Catrik, be twix ye olde stane brigg' and ye Newbrigg' of tree,[1] quilke forsaide brygge with ye grace of God sall' be mad' Sufficient and workmenly in masoncraft acordand in substance to Barnacastell' brigge Aftir ye ground and ye watyr acordes, of twa pilers two lanstathes[2] And thre Arches And also w[t] v co[r]sees of Egeoves[3] lik And acordande to ye same Thiknes of Egeoves as Barnacastelle brigg' is of. And als ye forsaid brigg' schall have a tabill' of hewyn stane vndir ye Alluryng oure watir mor yan Barnacastell' brigg' has: And ye saides Th' John And Rob't schall gett lymstane And birne itte And care itt And made yair lymkilns of yair own cost, at yair own most ease, Als mekylle will suffis yaim to ye werke abown saide, And all so ye same Th' John And Rob't schall fynde And make cariage of sand als mekyll has yaim nedes to ye warke abownsaid; And ye saides Th' Robt' and John schall haue to yaim and yair men free entree and issue to core frothe and haue a wey to yair most ease

---

[1] *tree*: wood.        [2] *landstathes*: bridge-ends.        [3] *egeoves*: parapets.

and p'fette ye forsaide lymstane and sande; And saides Nich' Will'am John And Rog' schall fynd cariage of all manere of free stane and of fillynge stane to ye forsaide brigg' to be brogth and laide apone yaire cost atte bothen Endes of ye brigg' to ye most p'fette of ye forsaid Th' John And Rob't And ye same Nich' And hys felows schall fynde apon yair own cost Als mykill wode and colles brogth' one ye grounde as will suffys and serryf yaim to ye birnyng of all ye lymkilnes y$^t$ schall be made to ye forsaid werk' And ye forsaid Nich' And his felaws schall get lefe and free entre And issue to ye saides masons And yair men to come to ye wherell$^1$ of Sedbery And to ye qwerell of Rysedalle berk' for to brek ye stane y$^t$ schall go to ye saide brigg' or to any othir qwerell y$^t$ is wyth in ye boundes quilk yt is most p'fitable to ye forsaid werke: And as ye wherreours$^2$ brekes ye saide stones and schapils yaim in ye saides qwerrels y$^t$ yen ye forsaide Nich' and his falaws gare of yair cost void ye stanes fro ye wherreo$^r$s y$^t$ yai be not taride ne Indird' in yair werke be cause of voidyng of ye forsaid stanes And ye same Nich' And his falaws schall fynd mak or gare make apon yair own cost all manere of Tymbirwerke quilke atte schall go or at is nesessar' or nedfull to ye saide brigg' y$^t$ is to say ye branderethes$^3$ of ye pilers and of ye landstathes And ye seentrees$^4$ with all man'e schaffaldyng And othire tre werke$^5$ yt is nedfull to ya saide brigg' to lay And rayse yaim of yair own cost, w$^t$ ye help of ye masons and [    ]rs and yai to haue yaim wene ye werke is p'furnist and don: And ye forsaide Nich' and his felaws schall make ridde ye groundes in ye watir ware ye brigg' schall be of all sydes And in ye mydwarde ware itte is most nedefull; And make ye brandereth of ye ta landestathe be laide befor ye fest of ye Inuencion of ye holy Crosse next comande: And ye tothir brandereth of ye tothire lande-stath' to be laide be ye fest of ye Natiuite of seint John Baptist yen next Eftyr folowand And ye forsaid Nich' and his felaws schall of yair cost kepe ye wat' wer' And defend itte fro ye saides Th' John and Rob't to ye tyme ye branderath be laid and yair werke of masoncraft be passed ye danger And ye noiesance of ye same said water: And all sa ye same Nich' and his felaws schall gar [lay] or mak be layde ye brandereth of a pilere be ye fest of ye Inuenc' of ye hale Crosse yen next efter folowande in ye tothir 3er' And ye tothir brandereth be ye fest of seint John Baptist yen next aftir folowande in ye same 3ere; And ye saides Nich' And his felaws schall raise or make be raised in ye thridde 3ere ye seentrees ye ton p't be ye same fest of ye Inuenc' of ye haly Crosse And ye tothire be ye feste of seint John Baptist next eftir fillovande: And ye saides John Th' and Rob't schall this forsaid brigg' sufficiantly in masoncraft make And fully p'formed in alle p'tie3 And holy endyd be ye fest of seint Michill ye arcangell quilk y$^t$ schall fall in ye 3ere of oure lord gode a M$^1$ccccxxv for ye quilk saide werke ye forsaides Nich' and his felaws schall pay or mak to be payde to ye forsaides Th' John and

---

$^1$ *wherell, qwerell*: quarry.                        $^2$ *wherreours*: quarriers.
$^3$ *branderethes*: coffer-dams.                       $^4$ *seentrees*: centerings.
$^5$ *tre werke*: timber work.

Rob't cclx mᵃrc' of sterlynges And ilkan of yaim ilka ȝere a gounne acordande to ȝare degree atte ye festeȝ And ye ȝeres vndirwrytyn yᵗ is to say in hande xxˡⁱ And thre gouns; And atte ye fest of seint Hillarij in the ȝere of oure lord gode a Mˡccccxxij. xxˡⁱ And atte ye forsaides festes of ye Inuenc' of ye holy Crosse And seint John Baptist next eftir fillowande be even porcions xlˡⁱ quilk saides festes schall fall in ye ȝere of our Lord gode a Mˡccccxxiij. And thre gounns atte ye said fest of Seint John And atte ye fest of seint Hillarij next eftir yat in ye same ȝere of our lord xxˡⁱ. And atte ye said festes of ye Inuenc' of holy Crosse next eftir yᵗ quilk sall fall in ye ȝere of our lord gode a Mˡccccxxiiij. xxˡⁱ. And atte ye saides fest of seint John Baptist next eftir in ye same ȝere of oure lorde xx mᵃrc' And thre gounnes atte ye same fest of seint John swa yᵗ ye brigg' be endede Ande made be yat And if atte be unmade yai sall haue bot x marc. And quen yair werke is finyst And endede x mᵃrc' And all so ye forsaides Nich' And his felaws sall gyft to ye saides Masons atte yair entre ccc yrene and stelle to ye value of vjˢ. viijᵈ. And ye saides Nich' And his felaws schall make a luge of tre¹ ate ye said brigge in ye quilk ye forsaides Masons schall wyrke yᵗ is to say iiij romes of syelles² And two henforkes³ quilk luge sall be made and couerde And closede resonably be fastynenge⁴ next comynge: And if it be fall yᵗ ye forsaides Thomas John And Rob't And yair s'uantz have nogth All yair couᵃntz fulfilde be vj days warnyng eftir ye Indent'e makes mencion yᵗ yane ye saides Nich' and his felaws sall pai yame yair wage daly to ye tyme yᵗ yai haue yair couᵃntz fulfilde. mor our ye saides Thomas John And Rob't sall make ye pilers of ye forsaid briggs Als substanciell in lenth and bred' has te was acorded wyth ye forsaid John Garett be a Indent're trip'tit be twene ye saide Nicholas And hyme made if ye counsell of ye forsaid Nicholas And his felaws acord yaim y'to: To ye wyttnesse of quilk thinge ye p'ties aboven nevend' has sett yair seals Wrytyn atte Catrike in ye fest of seint hillar' ye ȝere of our lord kyng Henri ye fift eftir ye ye (*sic*) conquest ye nyend.

## 60

*1425 Walberswick Church (Suffolk)*

Two masons undertake to build a tower, 12 feet square, with walls 6 feet thick, with four buttresses and a winding stair; the general design to be like that of (?) Tunstall, the west door and windows like those at Halesworth. They shall work yearly from Lady Day to Michaelmas, 'except the first year' (when, presumably, they will be cutting the stone, which could be done at any season). The employers shall provide all materials, and a house for them to

---

¹ *luge of tre*: wooden lodge.

² *iiij romes of syelles*: the space of 4 pair of 'siles', or crucks; see above, p. 197.

³ *henforkes*: gable ends.

⁴ *fastynenge*: Lent.

work and live in, and shall give them 40s. for each yard, in height, built, a barrel of herring yearly, and each of them one gown, if they do their work properly.

B.M. Add. Ch. 17634.

This bille endentyd witnessith that on the tewesday next after the feste of Seynt Mathie Apostle the fourte 3eere of kyng Henry the Sexte A comenaunt was maked by twyn Thomas Bangor Thomas Wolfard William Ambrynghale and Thomas Pellyng of the town of Walbureswyk on the one partye, And Richard Russel of Donewich and Adam Powle of Blythburgh masons on the other partye, that is to sayne that the forsaid Richard and Adam shal make or do to make a Stepel joyned to the Cherche of Walburesyk fornsaid with foure botraes and one vice and tqwelfe foote wyde and sex foote thikke the walles, the wallyng the tabellyng and the orbyng[1] sewtly after the stepil of Dunstale well and trewely and competently, a dore in the west also good as the dore in the Stepel of Halesworth and a wyndowe of two dayes[2] above the dore sewtly after the wyndowe of thre dayes of Halesworth, And thre wyndowes atte nethir Soler and eche wyndowe of two dayes, and foure wyndowes atte ouerer soler the wyndowe of thre dayes sewtly after Halesworth. The fornseid Richard and Adam shal werke or doo werke on the Stepel fornseid two termes[3] in the 3eer saf the ferste 3eer, 3eerly in the tyme of werkyng of settyng and leying that is to say bitwi3en the festes of the Annuncyacion of our Lady and seynt Mychel Archangel but if it be other maner consentyd on bothe partyes. And the fornseid Thomas Bangor Thomas William and Thomas schal fynde alle maner of mateer to the stepel fornsaid, that is to say, freeston, lyme and Calyon,[4] water and Soond, and alle maner thyngge that nedith to stagyng and Wyndyng and Shouellis and alle maner vessel that is nedeful to the stepel fornseid, and an hows to werke Inne to ete and drynke and to lygge[5] Inne and to make mete Inne and that be hadde by the place of workyng. The fornseid Richard and Adam schal take of the fornsaid Thomas Bangor Thomas William and Thomas for the 3arde werkyng xl[ti] scheelyngges of laughfull money of Inglond, and a Cade of full heryng eche 3eer in tyme of werkyng and eche of hem a gowne of leuere ones in the tyme of werkyng, so that they scholden be gode men and trewe to the werke fornsaid.

## 61

*1430/1 Cambridge, Peterhouse*

Agreement with a mason for building the college library. He shall work the stone for all the doors and ten windows (two small counting as one) between 12 February and 30 April; by 1 August he shall have the walls built to a height of 10 feet; the remaining windows shall be worked and ready to set by the following Easter; and by Michaelmas he shall have brought the walls up to the height of the other new buildings. He shall be paid for working the great

---

[1] *orbyng*: panelling.      [2] *dayes*: lights.

[3] *two termes*: two quarters, i.e. six months.

[4] *calyon*: pebbles, or flints.      [5] *lygge*: lie, i.e. to sleep in.

door 5s. 6d; for smaller doors 3s. each; for each large window 5s.; and for a small window 2s. 6d.; and for building at the rate of 3s. 4d. a week. If he works well, he shall also have a gown.

Willis and Clark, *Architectural Hist. of Cambridge*, i. 72.

Hec indentura facta xij die mensis Februarii anno regni Regis Henrici sexti post conquestum nono inter Magistrum Johannem Holbrok magistrum Collegii Sancti Petri Cantebr' et socios ejusdem ex una parte et Johannem Wassyngle de Hynton ex altera testatur quod idem Johannes Wassyngle bene fideliter et sufficienter in fundo et a fundo superius edificabit parietes ostia et fenestras cujusdam bibliothece edificande in Collegio predicto. Sic videlicet quod omnia ostia ad dictum opus necessaria et decem fenestras computando duas minores pro una ex bonis lapidibus et durioribus de inferiori lecto lapidicinii Philippi Grove citra ultimum diem Aprilis proxime futurum post datum presencium dolabit et complete ad posicionem eorundem formabit. Necnon dictos parietes citra eundem diem Aprilis edificare incipiet et citra festum quod dicitur Sancti Petri ad vincula ex tunc proxime sequens ad altitudinem decem pedum supra planam terram eriget. Alias insuper fenestras quotcumque ad opus predictum necessarie fuerint citra festum Pasche secundo futurum post datum presencium dolabit et ad posicionem earundem complete aptabit. Necnon predictas parietes citra festum michaelis Archangeli extunc proxime sequens ad altitudinem aliorum parietum nove fabrice predicti Collegii complete eriget.

Ad quas quidem convenciones bene et fideliter perimplendas idem Johannes Wassyngle se in quadraginta libris obligavit. Et magister Johannes Holbrok et socii superius nominati solvent Johanni Wassyngle predicto pro dolacione et aptura maioris ostii v$^{s.}$ vj$^d$: et pro factura cuiuslibet ostii minoris quotcunque fuerint iij$^{s.}$: pro formacione eciam et aptatione cuiuslibet fenestre maioris v$^{s.}$: et cuiuslibet fenestre minoris ij$^{s.}$ vj$^d$. Necnon omni septimana integra quando ipse Johannes Wassyngle infra dictum Collegium super opere predicto operabitur iij$^{s.}$ iiij$^{d.}$, et in septimana non integra secundum ratum et dierum feriatorum numerum.

Dabunt eciam Johanni Wassyngle unam togam de liberata Collegii predicti si in opere predicto bene se gesserit. In quorum omnium testimonium partes predict' sua sigilla alternatim hiis indenturis apposuerunt.

Dat' Cantebr' predict' Anno et die quibus supra.

## 62

*1432 Norwich, Conesford*

Agreement with a mason to rebuild the city quay. He shall take up the old woodwork and prepare a foundation with piles and planks of oak or poplar; on this he shall build a wall of ashlar, 1¼ yards thick at the base and 1 yard at the top, the ashlars of the uppermost course being of at least the weight of a pipe of wine (i.e. half a ton); the back shall be rammed with marl and gravel; and the work shall be finished in about 9 months. For this, supplying all material, he shall have £53. 6s. 8d., in four instalments, and cloth for a gown. He and another mason give a joint bond of 100 marks for performance of contract.

*Recs. of Norwich*, ii. 389.

This endenture mad betwix Thomas Wetherby, Surveyour of the godys of the comon of the Citee of Norwich, Thomas Balle and Nicholas Stanhowe, Tresorers of the same citee, on the on party and John Marwe, citeseyn of Norwich, Fremason, on the othir party. Witnessith that the seyd John xal make er don make the newe comon kaye of Norwich lying in the paros of Seint Clement of Conesford in Norwich, which kaye extendith hym in lengthe from the mees[1] of John Drewe un to the hous of the comon lying be syde the comon lane in the same paros. Whiche seyd John Marwe xal fynde almaner werkmanship and mater and all othir thyngs that to the seyd kay xal gon, that is to seyne he xal take the ground pile it and plank it with englyssh oke of hert er ebel[2] of a resonable thiknes sufficient for the seyd werk be the seyd length, and therupon be gynne the seyd kaye of freston asshleryd of a conable brede and heythe accordyng to that werk of freston, And the seyd kaye xal halden in brede in the ground upon the plankyng v quarters[3] be the kyngs standard, and the same kaye xal halden in brede under the ouereston iiij quarters by the seyd standard, and yche ston lying in the ouerest party of the sayd kaye xal ben in wyght of a pipe of wyn atte leste asshleryd. And the seyd John Marwe xal rammen and fillen with marl and grauell and make pleyn atte bak of the seyd kaye on hys propir cost, and haue the tymber of the seyd kaye and take it up. And the seyd kaye with al that therto longith the seyd John Marwe xal performen and enden at the ferthest be the first day of Maii nest folwyng after the makyng of this endenture with oute ferther delay. For which seyd kaye wel and sufficiently in al thyngs as it is abouen seyd to ben don the seyd Thomas, Thomas and Nicolas xal paye er don paye to the seyd John Marwe liij[li] vj[s]. viij[d]. þat is to seyne at Lammesse nest comyng aftir the makyng of this endenture xx marc, atte feste of all seints nest folowyng xx marc, atte feste of Candlemesse þan nest folwyng xx marc, and on the first day of Maii than nest folowyng xx marc. And the seyd John Marwe xal frely take up be the watir with help of the crane and brygen in be the lond al maner of mater to the seyd kaye longyng, and to ben had with outen onythyng to ben payed to the comon er to the keper of the seyd kaye. And the seyd Thomas, Thomas and Nicolas xal fynden to the seyd John Marwe and to his werkmen an hous to werkyn in be the seyd tyme. And the seyd Thomas, Thomas and Nicolas xal delyueren to the seyd John Marwe cloth sufficient for a gowne as is convenyent for his degre atte feste of Cristemesse nest after the makyng of this endenture. And if the seyd John Marwe vel and trewly hold and performe on hys partye al maner of couenaunts touchyng the seyd kaye and yche part ther of, that thanne an obligacion of an c. marc in whiche the seyd John Marwe and on Richard Reyner of Thornegge,

---

[1] *mees*: dwelling-house.  [2] *ebel*: poplar.
[3] *quarters*: i.e. of a yard.

fremason, arn bounden to the seyd Thomas, Thomas and Nicolas to payen at Michelmesse nest comyng after the date of this present endenture for nought be had, and ellys that it stande in hys strengthe. In witnesse of all and yche of the premyses the parties befornseyd to thise presents endentures alternatly han set her selys. Wreten at Norwich the x day of Juyll the yeer of the regne of Kyng Henre the sexte after the conquest the x.

## 63

*1433  Chester, St. Mary-on-the-Hill*

A mason undertakes to build a chapel on the south of the chancel, 18 feet wide, with five windows, and an arch (into the aisle) at the west end. The chapel shall be embattled like 'the little closet' in Chester Castle and shall have three handsome finials (at the top and springings of the gables) at each end. All materials shall be supplied, and he shall have £20 and a gown for his work, which shall be done under the supervision of Master John Asser (chief mason of the Duchy).

Earwaker, *Hist. of the Church of St. Mary-on-the-Hill*, 31.

This endenture made bytwene William Troutebek, esquier, on that on partie, and Thomas Betes, mason, on that other partie beres wittenesse that the forsaid Thomas has made covenant and granted to the said William that he shall make a Chapel in the chirche yord of Seynte Marie on the Hill, on the south side of the chauncell of the chirche there, that is to wete the est ende, the south side and the west ende, contenynge the length of the chauncell there and xviij fote wide with-inne the walles, and as high as hit nedes resonably to be: with v faire and clenely wroght wyndowes full of light, that is to say on gable wyndow in the est ende with iiij lightes, and iij wyndowes on the south side, ichone of iij lightes, and on in the weste ende, in the best wise to be deviset; and iiij botras on the south side, with a grete arche in the weste end; and the chapelle to be battellet above, like to the little closet withinne the castell of Chester, with a corbyl table longynge thereto; and at ayther end iij honest fynyals.

And the forsaid William shall pay to the forsaid Thomas xx<sup>li</sup> like as the worke goes forwarde, and also give him a gowne, and also the forsayd William shall fynde fre stone, lyme, sonde, water, wyndelasse and stuff for to scaffolde with, and such manere necessaries as the forsaid Thomas shall, by the oversight of Maester John Asser, make the chappell and all thynges that longen thereto [masoncraft],[1] honestly. In wytnesse of the whech thynge to these presentes endentures the parties forsaid, aither anendes other haven set to their sealx.

Gyven at Chester the Monday next before the feste of the natyvyte of Seint John the Baptist in the yere of kyng Henry the Sixt after the conquest xj.

---

[1] Interlined.

64

*1434  Tilney (Norfolk)*

A carpenter agrees to construct for the Abbot of Bury a landing-place on the sea-shore from material selected from the Abbot's stores, and described in detail. For his work he is to have £13 and a gown. He gives a bond of £40 for performance of the work and a five years' guarantee.

B.M. Add. MS. 14848, f. 74v.

Hec indentura facta inter dominum Willelmum Abbatem monasterii Sancti Edmundi de Bury ex parte una et Thomam Bryd de Tyryngton carpentarium ex parte altera testatur quod idem Thomas faciet dicto Abbati j Shore super ripam maris apud Tylney porcionem dicti Abbatis contingentem cum meremio dicti Abbatis quod idem Thomas certis die et loco inter prefatum Abbatem & ipsum assignatis eleget prout inferius continetur, videlicet iiij$^{xx}$ pecie unde xxx pecie long' xxxiij ped', xx pecie long' cujuslibet xxiiij ped', xviij pecie long' cujuslibet xxvij ped', et xij pecie long' cuiuslibet xviij ped'. Item vij Ouerweys lyne ryght[1] unde vj long' xxiiij ped' et j long' xviij ped', cuiuslibet xij pollic' ex una parte et in thyknes x polic'. Item iiij lodys meremii pro Stage, Tymber et Pylyng, xviij sparrys pro lode. Item iiij stal'[2] quarum ij long' cuiuslibet xxx ped' et ij long' cuiuslibet xviij ped'. Item xv$^c$ de burde long' xij ped' x ped' et viij ped'. Item j pec' meremii de elme pro j Ramme inde faciendo lat' ij ped'. Item vj keyis[3] de elme long' iij xviij ped' cuiuslibet et iij long' cuiuslibet xxiiij ped'. Item iij pecie meremii pro j wyndas long' j pecie viij ped' et ij long' xij ped', in lat' xij pollic' et thyknes x pollic'. Item iij ropys et j cabill pro wyndyng, unde j xx fadom,[4] ij xvj fadom et le cabill xxx fadom. Item iij virall[5] ferr' lat' vj pollic' et thyknes j pollic', lx sokettys ferr' et ij hopys[6] ferr' pro le ramme. Item ccc ped' de thynborde pro shynglyng, ij spyres[7] de elme pro le ramme long' cuiuslibet xxxiiij ped'. Item spikyng ferr' pro le bordedyng de le Shore necessar', ij platys ferr' pro le coler de le ramme, ij stapils et ij rynges. Pro cuius quidem fabrica et labore idem Thomas percipiet de dicto Abbate xiij$^{li}$. et j robam de secta valettorum una cum expensis suis pro eleccione meremii predicti eundo et redeundo et commorando. Et ad huius opus perficiendum et pro tempore quinque annorum absque sumbtibus et expensis dicti Abbatis vel successorum suorum duraturum idem Thomas fatetur se teneri dicto Abbati et successoribus suis in xl$^{li}$ legalis monete prout in quodam scripto obligatorio inde confecto plenius continetur alioquin vult et fatetur quod idem scriptum obligatorium stet in suo robore et effectu. In cuius rei testimonium hiis indenturis partes predicte sigilla sua alterna-

---

[1] *ouerweys lyne ryght*: dead straight 'overweys'—probably the balks that form the upper edge of the wharf.

[2] *stal'*: or possibly *scal'*, i.e. ladders.

[3] *keyis*: pieces that fit into others and hold them in place.

[4] *fadom*: fathom.                    [5] *virall*: circular bands, or rings.

[6] *hopys*: hoops.                     [7] *spyres*: long poles—the shere-legs of the ram.

tim apposuerunt. Dat' in manerio de Redgrave xij die mensis Maii Anno Domini Millesimo cccc$^{mo}$ tricesimo quarto Et regni Regis Henrici Sexti post Conquestum duodecimo.

## 65

### 1434 *Tivetshall (Norfolk)*

A carpenter agrees to build a new windmill. He is to cut the necessary timber and provide boards, and to finish the work in 4 months. For this he shall have the material of the old mill, 9½ marks, in five instalments, and a gown.

B.M. Add. MS. 14848, f. 74v.

Hec indentura facta inter dominum Willelmum Curteys Abbatem monasterii Sancti Edmundi ex parte una et Johannem Hore de Dysse carpentarium ex parte altera testatur quod idem Johannes faciet de nouo molendinum ad ventum dicti Abbatis apud Tyuytishale cum meremio dicti Abbatis sumptibus ipsius Johannis prosternendo. Et ulterius idem Johannes inueniet sumptibus et expensis suis bord siue tabulas necessarias ad opus huius fabricandum. In cuius recompens' idem Abbas concessit predicto Johanni antiquum molendinum, quod quidem molendinum de nouo fabricandum idem Johannes perficiet finaliter citra festum Omnium Sanctorum. Pro cuius factura percipiet de dicto Abbate unam robam ix marcas et vj$^s$. viij$^d$. soluendas ad festa infrascripta, videlicet xxvj$^s$. viij$^d$. ad festa Apostolorum Petri et Pauli proxima, xxvj$^s$. viij$^d$. ad festum Assumpcionis Beate Marie Virginis, xxvj$^s$. viij$^d$. ad festum Sancti Michaelis Archangeli, xxvj$^s$. viij$^d$. ad festum Omnium Sanctorum proxime sequens, et xx$^s$. in plenam solucionem dicte summe quamcitius idem molendinum aptum et sufficiens fuerit ad molendum. In cuius rei testimonium hiis indenturis partes predicte sigilla sua alternatim apposuerunt. Dat' in manerio de Redgrave xx die mensis Junii anno regni regis Henrici sexti post conquestum duodecimo.

## 66

### 1434 *Fotheringay Church (Northants.)*

Agreement by a mason to build the nave of the church, 80 feet long, corresponding to the existing quire. The foundations, up to the plinth, to be of rubble; the outside walls of ashlar, inside of rubble, except for pillars, arches, &c. There shall be two aisles, with windows, buttresses, and battlements as specified, opening into the nave by six arches and into the tower by one arch, on each side. Between the nave and quire shall be a stone screen with fittings for altars. There shall be a porch on either side, and at the west end a tower, 80 feet high, and 20 feet square, the top section being octagonal and finished with ornamental buttresses. All materials shall be provided for him, and he shall have for his work £300, by instalments as specified. Out of this he is to pay his men's wages; the men shall be appointed by those in charge of the work, but if he complains that they are unsatisfactory and they are so found by the judgement of other master masons, they shall be changed. If he does not complete the work within a reasonable time, to be agreed upon, he shall be committed to prison.

Dugdale, *Monasticon*, vi. 1414.

This endenture maad betwix Will. Wolston sqwier, Thomas Pecham clerke, commissaris for the hy and myghty prince, and my right redouthid lord, the duc of Yorke on the too part; and Will. Horwood free-mason, dwellyng in Fodringhey on the tother part: wytnessith, that the same Will. Horwood hath granthid and undretaken, and by thise same has indenthid, graunts, and undertakes to mak up a new body of a kirk joyning to the quire of the college of Fodringhey, of the same hight and brede that the said quire is of; and in lenght iiij$^{xx}$ fete fro the said quere donward wythin the walles, a metyerd[1] of England accounthid alwey for iij fete. And in this cuvenant he the said Will. Horwod shal also wel make all the ground-werk of the said body, and take hit and void hit at his own cost, and latlay hit suffisantly as hit ought to be by oversight of maisters of the same craft, which[2] stuff suffisantly ordeigned for him at my seide lord's cost, as longeth to such a werke. And to the said body he shall make two isles, and take the ground . . . hem in wise aforesaid, both the isles according to heght and brede to the isles of the saide quere, and in height to the body aforesaid; the ground[3] of the same body and isles to be maad within the ende under the ground table stones with rough stone; and fro the ground tableston bo . . . ments;[4] and alle the remanent of the said body and isles unto the full hight of the said quire with clene hewen ashler altogedir in the outer side unto the full hight of the said quire; and all the inner side of roughstone, except the bench-table-stones, the soles of the windows, the pillars and chapetrels that the arches and pendants shall rest upon, which shall be altogedir of freestone wroght trewly and dewly as hit ought to be.

And in eche isle shal be wyndows of freestone, accordyng in all poynts unto the wyndows of the said quire, sawf they shal no bowtels[5] haf at all. And in the west-end of aither of the said isles, he shal mak a wyndow of four lights, according altogedir to the wyndows of the said isles. And til aither isle shall be a sperware[6] enbattailement of free-stoon throwgh out, and both the ends enbattailled butting vpon the stepill. And aither of the said isles shal have six mighty botrasse of free-stone, clen-hewyn; and every botrasse fynisht with a fymal,[7] according in all points to the fymals of the said quere, safe only the botrasse of the body shalbe more large, more strong and mighty than the botrasse of the said qwere.

And the clerstory both withyn and without shal be made of clene asheler growndid upon ten mighty pillars, with four respounds; that ys to say two above

---

[1] *metyerd*: mete-yard, or measuring yard.
[2] *which*: *recte* 'with'.  [3] *ground*: foundations.
[4] *bo . . . ments*: Prof. Willis (*Nomenclature*, 27) suggests 'to [the lege]ments'.
[5] *bowtels*: convex mouldings.  [6] *sperware*: *recte* 'sqware'.
[7] *fymal*: *recte* 'fynial', and so throughout.

joyning to the qwere, and two benethe joyning to the end of the sayd bodye. And to the two respownds of the sayd qwere shall be two perpeyn-walls[1] joyning of freestone, clene wroght: that is to say oon on aither side of the myddel qwere dore; and in either wall three lyghts, and lavatoris[2] in aither side of the wall, which shall serve for four auters, that ys to say oon on aither side of the myddel dore of the said qwere, and oon on either side of the said isles.

And in eche of the said isles shal be five arches abof the stepill, and abof every arche a wyndow, and every wyndow of four lyghts, according in all points to the wyndows of the clerestory of the said qwere. And either of the said isles shall have six mighty arches butting on aither side to the clere-story, and two mighty arches butting on aither side to the said stepull, according to the arches of the said qwere, both yn table-stones and crestis, with a sqware embattailment therupon.

And in the north side of the chirche the said Will. Horwode shall make a porche; the owter side of clene asshaler, the inner side of rough stone, conteining in length xij fete, and in brede as the botrasse of the said body wol soeffre; and in hight according to the isle of the same side, which[3] resonable lights in aither side; and with a sqware embatailment above.

And in the south side to the cloystreward another porche joyning to the dore of the said cloystre, beryng widenesse as the botrasse wol soeffre, and in hight betwixt the chirch and the said . . . dore, with a dore yn in the west side of the said porche to the town-ward; and in either side so many lights as will suffice: and a sqware enbattaillement above, and in hight according to the place where hit is set.

And in the west end of the said body shall be a stepyll standyng . . . the chirche upon three strong and mighty arches vawthid with stoon; the wich steepil shall haf in lenght iiij[xx] fete after the meteyard, three fete to the yard, above the ground table-stones and xx fote square withyn the walls, the walles beryng six fote thicknesse abof the said ground table-stones. And to the hight of the said body hit shall be sqware with two mighty botresses joyning therto, oon in aither side of a large dore, which shall be in the west end of the same stepill.

And when the said stepill cometh to the hight of the said bay[4] . . . then hit shall be chaungid and turnyd in viij panes, and at every schouchon[5] a boutrasse fynysht with fimal according to the fymals of the said qwere and body; the said chapell (*sic*) embattailled with a sqware embattailment large: and abof the dore of the said stepill a wyndow rysing in hight al so high as the gret arche of the stepill, and in brede as the body will issue. And in the said stepill shall be two flores, and abof either flore viij clerestorial windows set yn the myddes of the walle, eche window of three lights, and alle the owter side of the stepill of clen wroght frestone; and the inner side of rough ston. And in the said stepill shall be a ulce[6] (*sic*)

---

[1] *perpeyn-walls*: walls of a single thickness of ashlar.  [2] *lavatoris*: piscinas.
[3] *which*: *recte* 'with'.  [4] *bay*: presumably should be 'body'.
[5] *schouchon*: angle; see above, p. 105.  [6] *ulce*: *recte* 'vice'.

towrnyng, servyng till the said body, isles and qwere, both beneth and abof, with all mannere other werke necessary that longyth to such a body, isles, stepill and porches, also well noght comprehendit in this endenture as comprehendit and expressyd.

And of all the werke that in thise same endenture is devised and rehersyd, my said lord of Yorke shall fynde the carriage and stuffe; that ys to say stone, lyme, sonde, ropes, boltes, ladderis, tymbre, scaffolds, gynnes, and all manere of stuffe that longeth to the said werke, for the which werke, well, truly and duly to be made and fynisht in wyse as it ys afore devised and declaryd, the said Will. Horwode shall haf of my said lord ccc$^{li}$ sterlingues: of the which summe he shall be payd in wise as hit shall be declaryd hereafter: that ys to say when he hath takyn his ground of the sayd kirke, isles, botrasse, porches and stepill, hewyn and set his ground tablestones and his ligements, and the wall thereto withyn and without, as hit ought to be well and duly made, then he shall haf vj$^{li}$ xiij$^s$. iiij$^d$. And when the said Will. Horwode hath set oo$^1$ fote abof the ground-table-stone, also well throughout the outer side as the inner side of all the said werke, then he shall haf payment of an c$^{li}$ Sterling$^2$; and so for every fote of the said werke, aftir that hit be fully wroght and set, as hit ought to be, and as it is afore devysed, till hit come to the full hight of the highest of the fymals and batayllment of the seyd body, hewyng, settyng and reysing . . . of the steple, aftyr hit be passyd the highest of the embattailment of the seyd body, he shall but xxx$^s$. Sterlingues till hit be fully endyd and performyd, in wise as hit is afore devysed.

And when alle the werk abof written, rehersyd and devised is fully fynisht, as hit ought to be, and as hit is above accordyd and devysed betwix the seyd commissaris and the sayd William: then the seyd Will. Horwode shall haf full payment of the sayd ccc$^{li}$ Sterling if any be due or left unpayed untill hym: And during all the sayd werke the said Will. Horwode shall nether set mo nor fewer free masons, rogh setters ne leyers thereupon, but as such as shall be ordeigned to haf the governance and ofersight of the said werke undre my lord of Yorke well ordeign him and assigne him for to haf.

And yf so be that the seyd Will. Horwode mak nought full payment of all or any of his workmen, then the clerke of the werke shall pay him in his presence and stoppe als mykyll in the said Will. Horwode hand as the payment that shall be dewe unto the workemen comyth to.

And duryng all the seyd werke the setters shall be chosyn and takyn by such as shall haf the governance and oversight of the sayd werke by my seid lord; they to be payed by the hand of the said Will. Horwode, in forme and manner abof wrytten and devysed. And yf so be that the sayd Will. Horwode wol complayn and say at any time that the two sayd setters or any of them, be noght profitable ne suffisant workmen for my lordys avayle; then by oversight of master masons of the countre they shall be demyd:$^3$ and yf they be found faulty or unable, then

---

$^1$ *oo*: one.  $^2$ *c$^{li}$*: obviously this should be *c$^s$*.  $^3$ *demyd*: judged.

they shall be chawnghyt, and other takyn and chosen in, by such as shall haf the governance of the sayd werke by my sayd lordys ordenance and commandement.

And yf hit so be that the sayd Will. Horwode make noght full end of the sayd werke withyn therme reasonable, which shall be lymit him in certain by my said lord, or by his counseil, in forme and manere as is afore-written and devysed in these same endentures, then he shall yeilde his body to prison at my lordys wyll and all his movable goods and heritages at my seyd lordys disposition and orden-ance. In wytness, &c., the sayd commissaries as the sayd Will. Horwode to these present endentures haf sett their seales enterchangeably, &c., the xxiv^th day of Septembre, the yere of the reign of our sovereign lord King Henry the Sixt after the conquest of England xiii.

## 67

*1437 Chartham (Kent)*

Agreement by two millwrights to build a fulling-mill. The dimensions of the timbers for the various parts of the mill and watercourse are given, and the timber is to be of beech. The fulling-stocks, i.e. the great beams set in motion by the waterwheel to pound the cloth, to be capable of fulling three 'dozens'—cloths of 12 ells in length. Payment, 22 marks ; the work to be finished in rather less than a year, for the performance of which they give a bond of 50 marks.

I am indebted to Mr. Urry, the Librarian of Canterbury Cathedral, for a photostat of this contract.

Canterbury Cathedral MS.

This endenture made the vj^te day of Nouembre the yere of Kyng Herry the sext aftir the conquest the xvj^th yere bitwix William Priour of Cristyschirch of Caunterbury on that oon partie and Richard Bocho^r and John Bochor of the Parisshe of Plukle in the Shire of Kent Mille Wrightes on that other partie Witnessith that the same Richard and John haue take upon hem and undertake to make a Fullyng mille of the seid Prio^r at Charteham in the same Shire well and sufficiently and profitabely in alle manere werke of Carpentrie belongyng to the same Mille bothe of the bayes, the whelis, the fullyng stokkes, the tayle of the myddel water wey thorugh the melle, and al manere Tymber werke and goyng werke bilongyng therto in eny manere of wise or behovefull therto, Save oonly the hous that is ther now, and to kepe the Scantelons of the water werke of the same Mille in fo^rme as hit folewith that is to say, The brest pece shall be ij fote square, the pece under hym xvj enches of breed and xiiij enches thikke, the nedelis[1] bitwene hem tweyn iiij fote bitwene the joyntes framed up and downe and planked on bothe sides, and bitwene eche nedil x enches, and the scantelon of the same nedilles shall be a fote thikke and xv enches of Brede and planked on either side and rabattid halfe in halfe of ij enche thikke, And under the backe plate bi the sulle[2] of the same frame of the hous a like frame as hit is reherced

---

[1] *nedelis*: supporting beams.　　　　　　　　　　　[2] *sulle*: sill.

bifore, the ij utter [? st]rabfulles[1] on either side must be nedelid and framed lyke the Brest Pece and braced and bounde w[t] sufficiant braces ayens the streme sufficiently and planked and rabattid lyke the other on bothe sides, And the other iiij Frames of the same suyte w[t] braces and plankes in the same wise, and alle this werke shall be of beche, and all the sulles thorugh thorugh [*sic*] alle the werke beying under grounde of beche also. The scantelons of the vj staples and the wynges on either side afore at the brest sufficiently made and imade araswise[2] and also many in the backeside bering the scantelon xx enches of brede and xviij enches of þikknes, Alle the nedilles of all the werke a fote þikke and xv enches of brede and vij enches betwix eche nedill and planked on bothe sides of ij enche thikke, the plankes rabattid halfe in halfe.[3] The Fullyngstokkes eche stocke assised for iij doseyn cloth sufficiently doon and on either side of the whele ij waterwowes[4] of borde covenable þerto imade well and profitably, And also they shall fynde to the same werke alle manere sawyng of tymber þat is nedeful necessarie and profitable þerto. And the seid Prio[r] shall fynde alle manere tymber w[t] the cariage belongyng therto, and the takyng up and makyng ayen the erthe werke of the dammes and bayes bilongyng to the same mille, almanere Iron ware that shall be nedefull and necessarie to the same werke except her axes her sawes and alle oþer tooles bilonging to Carpenters craft. And for alle this werke to be doon and fully to be performed in the manere and forme as hit is rehercid above, the seid Richard and John shall have and receyve of the seid William Prio[r] or of his successours xxij marcs of lawfull money of Inglond to be payed to the seid Richard and John at times suyng, First in the bigynnyng of this werke viij mrc. and whan hit is halfe iframed viij mrc. and whan alle the werks is full made and performed in manere and forme abovesaid and the mille redy for to fulle clooth as it oweþ for to do vj mrc. And alle this werke shall be redy by Michelmasse next comyng aftir the date of this endentur. And therupon they have founde suerte by her obligacon to the seid William Prio[r] and his successours in the somme of l mrc. to be paied to the seid Prio[r] or to his successours if they performe not her covenauntes aboveseid. In witnesse of which þing the parties aboveseid to these present endentures have sette her seales the day and the yere aboveseid.

## 68

*1438 Canterbury*

Five citizens of Canterbury bargain with six persons, of whom three are carpenters and the others substantial householders, to build a Guildhall, 41 ft. 10 in. in length, with a dais and side benches. At the south end of the hall shall be two chambers in a three-storied

[1] A blot makes the reading of this word uncertain.

[2] *araswise*: presumably with their arris, or edge, towards the stream.

[3] *rabattid halfe in halfe*: rebated (so that the adjacent planks overlap and form a tight joint) to half their thickness.

[4] *waterwowes*: literally, 'water-walls', conduits.

building, and at the north end a chamber with a jettied chamber above it. The whole to be finished in about 7 months, for £43. 6s. 8d., of which, apparently, £10 had already been advanced.

For a copy of this contract I am indebted to Mrs. Dorothy Gardiner, F.S.A.

Canterbury city muniments.

The indenture maad the xx^th day of Decembyr the year of King Herry the vi^th of England and France the xvij^th betweene William Benet John Sheldwich Gilbert German William Bryan and John Benet Citesynes of the Cite of Cantyrbury on that on partie and Alayn Echyngham of the paroch of Wodechyrche in the Shyre of Kent yoman John Tuttewyf Pyersys Colyn of the same paroch Rich[ard] Wodeman carpenters William Harlakyndenn of the said paroch yoman and William Tuttwyf of Ivechyrch of the same shyre yoman on that other partie barith witnesse That the said Alayn Ric[hard] John Tuttewyf Pyeris William Harlakyndenn and William Tuttewyf hemself bynden And ech of hem be hymself byndith and grauntith be these present lettres to make and unthertake to make un to the said William Benet John Sheldwich Gilbert William Bryan and John Benet in Cantyrbury aforsaid an halle called an Ildhalle good and sufficiant and well tymberyd of hert ok of xlj foot in length and x enchis well and clenly maad That is to sai iij myddylbemys[1] haldynge in thiknesse xij enchis and xviij enchis in brede in the myddis and ech of hem j-pendantyd with braces as belangith ther to in the beste wise enbowid workmanly forth with walplatis sufficient and fulfyllynge the spandres of the braas with mountantes lyernys braces raftheris with assheleris footlaces or jowe pecis and surlaces,[2] wher of the rafteris shulle contayne in the foot viij enches or better and the top vj enchis and a half in brede and in thicknesse v enchis and iiij enchis; and the hegh deys[3] on the hegh bench of the said halle the tymbyr trymerid[4] of brede of iiij feet; with wyndowis and iiij gapias[5] sufficient for to give lyth into the said halle And the said hegh bench with the ij syde benchis of Okyn tymbyr dwly maad with steiris of sufficient brede of okyn plankis; and too chambrys on the south ende of the said Ildhalle conteynynge in lengthe be the ground of the strete xviij feet with dubble stage geteyyd[6] acordynge to the scantelonys of the newe chambris of the Lyon[7] be the strete or better in the most clenly wyse that hit may ben; and at the North ende of the said halle a chambyr with a stage

---

[1] *myddylbemys*: tie-beams.

[2] For these terms see above, chapters XIII and XIV.  [3] *deys*: dais.

[4] *trymerid*: presumably, trimmed, or finished off. The precise meaning of this passage is elusive.

[5] *gapias*: perhaps dormer windows. A London account of 1450 mentions—'mendyng of dyverse gapyarys wyndewys . . . the wyche wer for weryd w^t y^e wedyr': Mins. Accts. (P.R.O.), 917, no. 23.

[6] *dubble stage geteyyd*: i.e. with two stories, each projecting, above.

[7] The Lion was a large inn belonging to the city, which stood across what is now the south entrance of Guildhall Street.

geteyyd and of the scantelon of the said chambrys be the strete Also that the said Carpenteris shulle fynde all maner of tymber cariage and all other maner thyng that langith to tymber work in the steyris bordis stanchenys latthis and all other thyng langyng to Carpentarie craft for the halle and chambris aforsaid And the forsaid halle and chambris to be maad and performyd be the feste of aduincula of Seynt Petyr next swyng;[1] and to alle these couenants performyd acordynge to the wrytynge abovesaid the said William Benet John Sheldwich Gilbert William Bryan and John Benet shal paie or do paye unto the said Alayn Ric[hard] John Tuttewyf Pyeris William Harlakyndenn and William Tuttewyf xxxiij li. vj s. viij d. acordynge to the obligacions ther of maad in ful payment of xliij li. vj s. viij d. as well as for all maner of tymbyr and cariages for boords and latthe as for his hande workes and workmanship of all the said worke so that hit be wel don and clenly and all redy to Tyle and to dawbe be the said day of Aduincula of Seynt Petyr; and for the swyr and true performynge and fulfyllynge of all and eche of these covenantis above wryten the said Alayn Richard John Tuttewyf Pyeris William Harlakyndenn and William Tutttewyf ben bounden in an obligacion symple to the said William Benet John Sheldwich Gilbert William Bryan and John Benet in lx li. of sterlyng to be paid at the feste of Whitsonday that next comyth afther the date of the present wrytynge. In wytnesse wher of the said parties ech to other han put to here Selys. Wryten at Cantyrbury aforsaid the day and yer above said.

[*Original seals attached.*]

# 69

*1439 Bury St. Edmunds*

Agreement for making a roof, as specified, for the chapel of St. John; also for the enlarging, flooring, and ceiling of a gallery, or upper chamber, in the chapel; and for making a timber porch; for £10. 6s. 8d.

Add. MS. 14848, f. 304; printed in *Journ. of Brit. Arch. Assoc.* xxi. 118.

[Agreement (2 Nov. 17 Henry VI) by John Edwards of Seynt Edmundsbury, mercer, that John Heywod of Ditton (Cambs.), carpenter, before the feast of the Nativity of St. John Baptist,] shal makyn or doo makyn a roof of the hert of ook only competent to the wallys of the Chapel of Seynt John atte Hille in Bury, the whiche roof shal be wrought of vj pryncepal couplys archebounden, wherof eche sparre shal bere the brede of x unches, and the thyknes of viij unches, havyng atwix iche two princepals a purloyne,[2] a iope,[3] and iiij sparrys, havyng a rof tre abovyn suffisaunt, of whiche sparrys ichon shal be brede of vij unche, and thiknesse of iij unchys, and al the seid principal couplys, purloynes and iopes shuln be convenably embowyd, the whiche rof shal be more hight from the leuel of the wallys upwards be a fote than the rof of an hous clepyd Tudenham's Chambr'

---

[1] *swyng*: ensuing.  [2] *purloyne*: purlin.  [3] *iope*: cornice.

in the Abbey of Bury set. The whiche rof on this forme surly, clenly and craftely wrought, the same John Heywod, on his owne coste, shall upreysyn and settyn on the wallys of the seid chapel, be the seid John Edwards in the mene while to be made redy and able to receyve it, and al the same rof reysyd, the seyd John Heywod sufficiauntly shal latthen and dighten redy to be ledyd. Moreover the same John Heywod shal do remove the dormaunt[1] w$^t$ all that is theron of a soler within the seyd chapel now beenge, makyng the same soler more large be vij fete than it is at this tyme, and gysten and plauncheren bothe the nether soler and the over, and the nether soler[2] he shall do selyn with estrich borde wrought with vergys[3] and knottys[4] honestly and wel korven, and to eythir dore of the same chapel he shal do maken a louke[5] of estrich board competent, and to the ton dore there a porche of ij standardys archyd and bownden with a beme couplyd and latthid abyl to be ledyd before the feste of Seynt John before lymyted; and the forseyd John Edwards for the seid rof, soler and porche, and other workys before rehersyd, grauntith and oblesshith hym for to pay unto the seid John Heywod x$^{li.}$ vj$^s.$ viij$^d.$ of lawful mony Englysh [in four instalments. Heywood gives a bond of £20 for performance].

### 70

*1439–40 Oxford, Divinity Schools*

A mason engaged to complete the building, in a less ornate style than it had been begun. He is to have a fee of 1 mark and weekly salary of 4s. in summer and 3s. 4d. in winter, and is to engage good workmen as cheaply as possible.

*Epistolae Academicae* (O.H.S.), i. 192.

Hec indentura facta inter Universitatem Oxoniensem ex parte una et Thomam Elkyn, lathomum, ex parte altera, testatur quod dictus Thomas manucepit edificacionem novarum scolarum sacre theologie in Universitate predicta in quantum pertinet ad lathomiam: et predictus Thomas recipiet septimanatim per estatem quatuor solidos sterlingorum, et per yemem tres solidos et quatuor denarios, quando contigat ipsum ebdomadatim presencialiter sic operari. Eciam dictus Thomas introducet alios lathomos, meliores quos sciverit, et meliori precio quo poterit, ad proficuum dicti operis. Et dictus Thomas recipiet ab eadem Universitate annuatim in dicto opere unam marcam sterlingorum pro annua pensione sua. Et quia plures magnates regni et alii sapientes non approbant, sed reprehendunt, nimiam curiositatem incepti dicti operis, igitur dicta Universitas vult quod dictus Thomas retrahet deinceps, sicut jam retrahere incepit, supervacuam talem curiositatem dicti operis, videlicet in tabernaculis ymaginum, [      6] casimentis

[1] *dormaunt*: the horizontal beam on which the gallery rests.
[2] *the nether soler*: i.e. the ceiling under the floor of the gallery.
[3] *vergys*: the battens of the ceiling.      [4] *knottys*: bosses.
[5] *louke*: according to Halliwell this is a Suffolk term for a lattice.
[6] 'A word here imperfect, apparently *bate et.*' From the context the word is probably some spelling of 'bowtels', convex mouldings. The *casimentis* and *fylettis* are, respectively, hollow mouldings and flat strips.

et fylettis, et in aliis frivolis curiositatibus, que ad rem non pertinent, sed ad nimias et sumptuosas expensas dicte Universitatis et ad nimiam dicti operis tardacionem. Et ad dictas convenciones ex parte dicti Thome fideliter tenendas et observandas idem Thomas obligat se per presentes dicte Universitati in quadraginta libris sterlingorum. In cujus rei testimonium tam sigillum commune dicte Universitatis quam sigillum dicti Thome his scriptis indentatis sunt appensa. Datum Oxonie sexto decimo die Januarii, anno regni regis Henrici sexti post conquestum octodecimo: Magistro Ricardo Riderham, sacre theologie doctore, dicte Universitatis cancellario, Willelmo Orell et Johanne Willey procuratoribus ejusdem ad tunc existentibus.

## 71

*1442 Dunster Church (Somerset)*

A mason contracts with the parishioners to build a tower, with three angle buttresses and stair turret, certain windows designed by another mason, battlements and pinnacles, 100 feet in height. The parish shall bring all materials to the churchyard; shall provide centerings, ropes, winches, &c.; shall help to shift the crane and any stones that are too heavy for two or three men to handle. They shall also provide a place for him to keep his tools, &c., and shall pay him 13s. 4d. for every foot built, and 20s. for the pinnacles. He shall complete the work within three years.

*Archaeological Journal*, xxxviii. 217.

Thys beth the convenants betwyne the paroch of Dunsterr and Jon Marys of Stokgursy in the Schere of Somerset. That is to seyng for the making of a towre in the paroch church of Dunsterr That the sayd Jon Marys schall make suffycyantly the seyde towre with iij french botras[1] and a vice in the fowrtt pyler in stede of a botras fynyng[2] at the Altertabyll [*sic*—i.e. water-table] And in the fyrst flore ij wyndowys On yn the Sowth and another yn the North everych of on day with iiij genelas[3] yn the hedd of every wyndow And iiij wyndowys at the bell bedd of ij days with a trawnson and a moynell according to the patron ymade by the avyce of Rychard Pope Fremason Allso the sayde Jon Maryce schall make suffycyantly the batylment of the sayde towre with iiij pynacles the fowrth pynacle standing upon the vice after reson and gode proportion Acordyng tothe same worke And the sayde schall be embatyle Allso the sayde Jon Maryce schall make iij gargylles in thre corners of the sayde towre And the wall to be iiij fote thykk and a halfe yn to the bell bedd And from the bell bedd ynto the batylment iij fote and a halfe suffycyantly to be made undyr the forme forsayde And the sayde paroch schall bryng all suffycyant materials withyn the palme crosse[4] of the sayde Church And he to have for the workemanchyppe of every fote of the sayde towre xiij[s] iiij[d] And the sayde worke to be full endyd withyn iij ere nexte

---

[1] *french botras*: see above, p. 96.   [3] *fynyng*: decreasing.

[2] *genelas*: cusps; see above, p. 93.

[4] *the palme crosse*: the churchyard cross; here used for the churchyard itself.

folowyng aftyr the date of this present wrytyng And rather[1] yf hit may be by
the power of the sayde paroch And the sayde Jon Maryce schall be redy aftyr the
stuffe of matyr at all tyme by the warnyng of xiiij days and the crane at all tyme
necessary for the same worke with ropys polys wynchchys schall be removyd
at the cost of the paroch forsayd with help of Jon Maryce and his mayny Allso the
sayd paroch schall fynd all syntarnys[2] for the same worke with ropes poleys
winchchys and all other thyngys necessary to the sayd work The towre conteynyng yn heyth from the gras tabyll an hundred fote Allso the sayd Jon Marys schall
be payd for his labour lyk as he doth his work other ellys at the most xx[s]. byfore
as hit aperyth yn work Also the sayd paroch schall fynd an howse for the sayde
Johon Maryce to sett therein his tole and other necessarys Allso if there be any
stone ywroȝyte of such quantyte that ij men or iij at most may not kary hym
the sayde paroch schall helpe hym Allso the sayde Johon Maryce schall receive
of the sayde paroch xx[s]. for the pynaclys of the same towre Into the whych
wytnys y put thereto my seelez I give and y wrytte at Dunsterr in the fest of
Seynt Mychaell the yere of King Herry the vj aftyr the conquest xxi[ti].

72

*1442 Eton College*

An agreement for the supply of stone, worked at the quarries according to patterns
supplied by the clerk of the works. For the technical terms, see above, pp. 105–8, 119.

Willis and Clark, *Architectural Hist. of Cambridge*, i. 385.

The quarrey men of Kent.

Thes endentures made the iiij day of April the yere of Regne of king Henry
the sixte the xx, bytwene William lynde clerke of the werkes of the edificacion
of the kinges college of owre Lady of Eton by syde Wyndesore on the oon
partie. And Thomas Hille Thomas Bridde John Carter John Hook and John
Tyllie on the other partie wittesnesse:

That the same Thomas Thomas John John and John haue made full couenaunts
with the said William that they by Witsontide nex comyng shal at their owne
costes do be made and browght un to London iiij[c]xvj fote of legement table beryng
ful joyntes at ye lest iij ynches or more clene apparailled in the forme that ys
callid casshepeed according to a molde to theym therof deliuered by the said
William. And they shal haue for euery ciiij fote of the same legement whan it
is come to Eton aboue said so clene apparailled xxxiij[s]. iiij[d].

Also the said Tho' Thomas John John and John shal by Mydsomere next comyng do be made and brought at their costes un to London iij[c]xxiiij fote of tweyne
legement tables aftur the forme of certain moldes therof to theym deliuered
beryng ful joyntes iiij ynches or more at the lest. And iiij[c]xvj fote of Seuerant
table scapled with poynts aftur a molde therof to theym also deliuered, with

---

[1] *rather*: earlier.          [2] *syntarnys* : centerings.

xij coynes iiij sconchons-anglers and viij square Anglers to the said first legement table and this seuerant table and vn to the said othere tables asmany as shal nede. And they shal haue of ye said William for euery fote of these thre tables oon with an othere iiij$^d$.

Item the same Thomas Thomas John John and John shal do make and be brought vn to London at their costes xxxij Nowels eueryche of them iiij fote and iij quarter long and of suche brede as the said William shal appoynte. And they shal do the same Nowels to ben apparilled at Eton abouesaid by Mydsomer next comyng. And they shal haue and take of the said William for euery pece of the same Noweles iij$^s$.

Also they shal by Mychelmesse next comyng at their costes to be made and brought vn to London iij$^c$ fote of Crestes and Corbel table aftur the fourme of ij Moldes to theym therof deliuered. And it do be apparilled clene at Eton abouesaid. And they shal haue and take of the said William for euery fote therof oon with an othere vij$^d$.

Also whiche couenaunts wel and truly to ben kept on the parte of the said Thomas Thomas John John and John eueryche of theym by thes presentes bindith seuerally hym self vn to the said William in x li. In wittenesse wherof the said parties to thees endentures entrechaungeably haue put their seelx. Yoven the day and the yere abouesaid.

## 73

### *1444 Salisbury*

Specification for a building to be erected by a carpenter at the sign of 'the Blue Boar'. He shall provide all timber and boards. His employer shall provide all other necessaries, including carriage of the timber, and extra labour at the time of raising the frame, and shall pay him £20 in three instalments. The work to be done in 8 months. Both parties find a surety and give a bond for performance of the contract.

*Wilts. Arch. Mag.* xv. 330.

This Indenture ymade at Newe Salesbury the xvj day of Decembre yn the xxiij$^{ti}$ ȝere of the regnyng of Kyng Harry the vj$^{te}$ bytwene William Ludlowe of the on party and John Fayrebowe carpenter of Busshopestrowe yn the countie of Wiltes of the other party Witnessith that the seyde John shal make to the seyde William an hows with ynne the Boor aȝenst the Market place of Salesbury forseyd conteynyng yn lengthe lxiij fot and with ynne the wallys xx$^{ti}$ fote. And the groundsilles yn brede of xv ynche And yn thiknesse x ynch And xiiij principal postis euery post xvj fote of lengthe and yn brede xiij ynche and yn thiknesse xij ynche And every somer yn brede xvj ynche and yn thiknesse xv ynche And every juyste viij ynche yn thiknesse and ix ynche yn brede And x ynche by twene every juyste And every byndyngbeme yn thiknesse ix ynche and yn brede xv ynche And every walplate of viij ynche in thiknesse and ix ynche in brede And every cours restour$^1$ iiij ynche thikke at the top and at the fote v ynche And of

---

$^1$ *restour*: rafter.

brede vij ynche at the fote and v ynche at the top And with vj wyndowes clenly accordaunt And ij stayers And by twene every restour ix ynche And the Sideresons[1] yn brede of xj ynche and vj ynches of thiknesse with braces wel accordyng. Whiche hows above sayde shal be wel and trewly made of sufficiant tymber and clene without sape or wyndshake reprevable and redy to be set up and arered by the feste of the Nativite of oure Lady next comyng after this present date. To the whiche hows the seyde John shal fynde alle maner tymber bordis for doris and for wyndowes and stodes to alle the walles. And the seyde William shal fynde alle maner naylle yregare[2] breydyng[3] helyng[4] wallyng and masons work thereto langyng Also ij men laboryng with the seyde John vij dayes at the reryng of the forseyde hows with mete and wages and mannys mete and drynke for alle the cariage of the seyde tymber at Salesbury at the seyde William his owen coste And also paye to the seyde John for the seyde hows makyng and tymber therto fyndyng yn alle maner wyse after the forme above seyde ymade and per-formed as workmanship axeth xx$^{li}$ of money at iiij dayes to be payd that ys for to seye at the begynnyng of the seyde hows makyng yn tymber hewyng x markes: at the bryngyng hom of the seyde tymber to Salesbury x markes and whanne the seyde hows ys ful made and doris and wyndowes y set up and hangeth x markes. To alle these covenauntes wel and trewly to be performed the seyde Wylliam yn his party and Robert Warmwell bynden hem to the seyde John yn xx$^{li}$ to paye yn the feste of oure Lady above seyde And also yn the same wyse the seyde John yn his party and Symond Poy bynden hem to the sede William yn xx$^{li}$ to pay yn the feste above seyde. In Witnesse wherof the seylles of the seyd parteys of these yndentures interchaungeably to these present indentures er set the day and ʒer aboveseyde.

[*Dorse*] for byldyng a howse in the blew bore.

## 74

*1444–5 Andover (Hants)*

Contract between the Warden of Winchester College and two carpenters to build an inn according to a detailed drawing, 'or better'. It is to be built round a courtyard, the outside dimensions being 90 feet each way. The east wing to have a chamber, with cellar below, a gateway, hall, and another chamber; south wing stables with chambers over; north wing, kitchen and stables; west wing corresponding to the east. Scantlings of the timbers are given. Timber to be provided by the college but to be cut and hewn by the carpenters, who are to have the loppings and waste wood. They are to be paid £90, and give a bond for that amount to carry out the work.

Transcribed by Mr. John Harvey from Winchester College Muniments, Andover III; inaccurately printed in T. F. Kirby's *Annals of Winchester College*.

This endenture mad bytwene Mr. Robert Thurbern Wardeyn of the college ycallid Seynt Marie College of Winchestr' byside Wynchestr' felaus and scolers

---

[1] *sideresons*: wall-plates.  
[2] *yregare*: iron gear.  
[3] *breydyng*: wattling.  
[4] *helyng*: roofing.

of the same college of that one parte and John Hardyng and Richard Holnerst carpenters of that other parte berith witnesse that the said John and Richard shal wel and counabili' make in so moch as to carpentri bi longeth that is for to sey A inne with inne the towne of Andever the which shal be sette in a voide ground in the north parti' of the land y called Niggeslond conteyning in circuyte xvij$^{xx}$ fete in the Counte of Sutht after a portatur ther of mad or better and a cording to the counantis in this endentur' rehersid Of the which xvij$^{xx}$ fete iiij$^{xx}$x to be billid north and suth a forestrete uppon the same ground wher on shal be sette in the suth parti' of the forseid ground a chamb$^r$ xxiiij fete widnesse north and suth and in lengh xx fete with a joty utward of vj[1] fete est and west under the which chamb$^r$ shal be a seler cont' the same widnesse and brede and the same chambr the forseid John and Richard at here owne coste shal joiste beme and flore. Also northward fro the same chambr a gate conteynyng xij fete bi grounde in widnesse over the which gate shal be a chambr cont' in lengh xxij fete of the which x fete to be trussid over in to the halle. Also a halle north fro the same gate cont' in lengh xxx fete and xx fete in widnesse with a coupel trussid fro the groundsile.[2] Al so a chamb$^r$ in the north parti' of the same halle cont' in widenesse xxiiij fete north and suth in lenth xx fete with a joty utward of ij fote est and west. Al so fro the suthchambr inward al to be billid cont' iiij$^{xx}$ fete in the which shal be stables in widnesse by grond xx fete with chambers above xxij fete in widnesse and v fete jtake owte of the same chambers in widnesse for oriell and every oriel the pryncipal haunsid and ymonellid[3] aboute and ij fote by twyne every monel. Al so fro the north chambr inward iiij$^{xx}$ fete i billid with kechyn and stables in like wyse. Also in the ende of the said Inne that is for to sey in the west party of the same inne al jbillyd cont' iiij$^{xx}$ fete and x like to the north and suth parte savyng a chambr' over a gate in the said parti' with a joti wyndowe a cordyng to the portatur. Also the grondsell of the same inne a fote brode and ix inches thikk. The postes of the same j fote brede and x inches thick. The somers a cordyng to the same werk The joistes aforstret viij inches brede vj thikk and bytwene every joiste vij inches. The joistes inwards vij inches of brede vj thikk and by twyne every joiste viij inches. The walplates viij inches squar thorow al the bildyng. The refters vj inches brode iiij thikk thorow al the bildyng and by twene everi refter ix inches space. Al so the said John and Richard shal make al manner of speris bynches dores wyndows in bordyng of beddys and saw al manner bordes and plankes to the said inne long-yng savyng bord longyng to dores and wyndows and rekkes and mangers. Also the same John and Richard shal make al manner dores and wyndows a cordyng to the portatur a bove rehersid or better. Furthermore to be vounde to the same John and Richard tymbr' with the cariage so moch as hit nedith to the said werk

---

[1] *vj* is probably a slip for *ij*.

[2] *a coupel trussid fro the groundsile* suggests cruck construction.

[3] *ymonellid*: mullioned.

so that the said John and Richard with ther werkmen be nat let in defaute of cariage in dew tyme so that weder fall. Al so the tymbr' to be fillid[1] [*interlined*: and wer[k]manli to be scapulid at wode] at the cost of the said John and Richard and thei to have the offel of the said tymbr' with in kerf for ther labour. Al so of the makyng of this seid werk the forsaid John and Richard hath day fro the feste of the Annunciacion of owre ladi' nexte foluying after the makyng of this present writyng endentid in to the same fest sewyng by tweyne hole yere. Takyng for ther labour iiij^xx pounds and x that is for to sey x pounds at bigyn-nyng and so further to be paid as the werk encrescit in wirchyng. In witnesse of the which thyngs to one parti' of this scrite endentid toward the forsaid John and Richard remaynyng We the forsaid Robt Thurbern Wardeyn of the said College felowes and scolers of the same owre comyn seal we have putte, to that other parti' of this scrite endentid toward us remayning the forsaid John Har-dyng and Richard Holnerst ther sealls thei have putte. J yeve the ferth day of March in the yere of the regnyng of Kyng Harry the sexte after the Conquest thre and twenti'.

[*Endorsed*] (1) Also Robert Thurbern Wardeyn of the College with in wretyn wul and graunt pro hym and his successors by this present writyng that if John Hardyng and Richard Holnerst wel and treuli hold and kepe al and everich of the counantis with in rehersid and by them to be hold and kepte that than a obliga-cion seute of iiij^xx pound and x in the which the same John and Richard to the said Wardeyn and to his successors of the same College wherof the Dat ys the ferth day of March the yere of the regnyng of Kyng Harry the sexte after the conquest thre and twenty for noght be hadd, or ellys stond and a bide both the obligacion and the endentur in ful strength. (2) Indentur' Johannis Hardyng and Ricardi Holnerst Carpentar' [*added*] for buyldinge in Andever.

## 75

*1445 Stamford Priory*

Two agreements with a carpenter. First, for a new floor and roof to the chapter house, made from timber supplied; to be finished in 8 months, for 46*s*. 8*d*. Secondly, for a new roof to the dormitory, 46 yards by 8 yards, using as much of the timber of the old roof as is fit; to be finished within 20 months, for 7 marks.

Exch. K.R. Accts. 504, no. 19.

This is the acorde made the xii^th day of Septembr' the xxiiii^ti ȝere of our souereyn lord Kyng Henry the vj^th betwix John Fox of Wisbeche in y^e counte of Cambridge in that one partie and William Boydell othirwise called Wright of Litill Caisterton in y^e countie of Lincoln on the other partie, that is to sey that y^e seid William shal take downe all the timbre of the chapetre hous atte y^e nonnes of Staunford and make a low flore in y^e same hous contenyng vij someres and lx

---

[1] *fillid*: felled.

trasons,[1] and make a new Rofe for y$^e$ same hous contenyng vj bemes vj wyndbemez[2] vj principals xxvj cople sparres w$^t$ walplates and side trees w$^t$ brasez fro
y$^e$ principals to y$^e$ seid sidetrees, whiche Rofe shall conteyne in lengh xxj ʒerdis
and in brede viij ʒerdes of assise. For whiche werkmanship truly to be made w$^t$
takyng downe of y$^e$ olde Rofe, the seid John shall pey to y$^e$ seid William xlvj$^s$
viij$^d$ acordyng to his werkyng, and agenne and also ordein timbr' to y$^e$ seid
werkes brought in to convenable place w$^t$in y$^e$ ʒerde of ye seid nonnes. This
flore and Rofe to be made and sette up w$^t$in viij monethes next folowyng after
y$^e$ Date herof.

Also the seid John and William acorded y$^t$ y$^e$ seid William shall take downe y$^e$
Rofe of the Dortour of y$^e$ seid Nonnez and make a new Rofe for y$^e$ seid Dortour
contenyng xlvj ʒerdes in lengh and viij ʒerdes of assise in brede, w$^t$ xij grete bemes
xij principals xij wyndbemes lxvj cople sperrez w$^t$ walplates and syde trees according to y$^e$ seid Rofe and xx$^{ti}$ brasez fro y$^e$ principals to y$^e$ side treez. For werkmanship of whiche Rofe and taking doune of the olde Rofe y$^e$ seid John shall pey to
y$^e$ seid William vij marc as y$^e$ seid werk risith and agenne Also y$^e$ seid John shall
ordein timbr' for ye seid Rofe and do bryng h$^t$ to convenable place w$^t$in the ʒerde
of y$^e$ seid Nonnez. And ye seid Willm. shal take asmuche of y$^e$ olde timbre as
wille in any wise serve to y$^e$ seid werkes, and he shal make and sette up the seid
Rofe w$^t$in xx$^{ti}$ monethes next folowyng after y$^e$ date herof.

In Wittenes wherof the seid John and William has putte yeir seles to this Indentures atte Staunford the day and yere forseid.

# 76

*1447–8 Cambridge, King's College*

This is not an actual contract, but is a detailed description of the design approved by
Henry VI for the chapel and other buildings of his new college.

Willis and Clark, *Arch. Hist. of Cambridge*, i. 368.

And as touchyng the demensions of the chirche of my said College of oure
lady and saint Nicholas of Cambridge, I have deuised and appointed that the
same chirch shal conteyne in lengthe ciiij$^{xx}$viij fete of assyse withoute any yles
and alle of the widenesse of xl fete and the lengthe of the same chirch from the
West ende unto the Auters atte the queris dore, shal conteyne cxx fete, And
from the Provostes stalle unto the grece[3] called gradus chori iiij$^{xx}$x fete for
xxxvj stalles on either side of the same quere, answeryng unto lxx felawes and
x prestes conductes which must be de prima forma; and from the said stalles
unto the Est ende of the said chirche lxij fete of assise. Also a reredos beryng the
Rodeloft departyng the quere and the body of the chirch, conteynyng in lengthe
xl fete, and in brede xiiij fete; the walls of the same chirche to be in height

---

[1] *trasons*: the beams between the summers, equivalent to joists.
[2] *wyndbemez*: collar-beams.                                    [3] *grece*: step.

iiij$^{xx}$x fete, embatelled vaute and chare rofed[1] sufficiently boteraced, and every boterace fined with finialx.

And in the Est ende of the said chirch shal be a wyndowe of xj daies, and in the west ende of the same chirch a windowe of ix daies and betwix euery boterace a wyndowe of v daies. And betwix euery of the same boteraces in the body of the chirche, on bothe sides of the same chirche, a closette with an auter therin, conteynyng in lengthe xx fete, and in brede x fete, vauted and finisshed unther the soil of the yle windowes: and the pament[2] of the chirch to be enhaunced iiij fete aboue the groundes without, and the heighte of the pament of the quere j fote di' aboue the pament of the chirche, and the pament at the high auter iij fete aboue that.

Item, on the north side of the quere a vestiarie conteynyng in lengthe l fete, and in brede xxij fete, departed in to ij houses benethe and ij houses aboue, which shal conteyne in height xxij fete in all with an entre fro the quere vauted.

Item, atte the west ende of the chirche a cloistre square, the Est pane conteynyng in lengthe clxxv fete, and the west pane as much; and the north pane cc fete, and the south pane asmuche, of the which the deambulatorie xiij fete wide, and in height xx fete to the corbel table, with clere stories and boteraced with finialx, vauted and embatelled, and the grounde therof iiij fete lower than the chirch grounde; and in the myddel of the west pane of the cloistre a strong toure square, conteynyng xxiiij fete within the walles, and in height cxx fete unto the corbel table, and iiij smale tourettis ouer that, fined with pynacles, and a dore in to the said cloistre ward, and outward noon.

And as touchynge the demensions of the housynge of the said College I haue deuised and appointed in the south side of the said chirche, a quadrant closyng unto bothe endes of the same chirche, the Est pane wherof shal conteyne ccxxx fete in length, and in brede within the walles xxij fete: in the myddes of the same pane a tour for a yatehouse, conteynyng in lengthe xxx fete and in brede xxij fete, and in height lx fete, with iij chambres ouer the yate euery aboue other; And on either side of the same yate iiij chambres, euery conteynyng in lengthe xxv fete, and in brede xxij fete; and ouer euery of thoo chambres ij chambres aboue, of the same mesure or more, with ij toures outward and ij toures inward. The south pane shal conteyne in lengthe ccxxxviij fete and in brede xxij fete within, in which shal be vij chambres, euery conteynyng in lengthe xxix fete, and in brede xxij, with a chambre parcelle of the Provostes loggyng, conteynyng in lengthe xxxv fete, and with a chambre in the Est corner of the same pane, conteynyng in length xxv fete, and in brede xxij fete; and ouer euery of the same chambres ij chambres and with v toures outward, and iij toures inward: the west pane shal conteyne in lengthe ccxxx fete, and in brede withinfurth xxiiij fete, In which atte the ende toward the chirch shal be a librarie, conteynyng in length cx fete, and in brede xxiiij fete, and under hit a large hous for redyng and disputacions, conteynyng in lengthe xl fete, and ij chambres under the same librarie, euery conteynyng xxix fete in

---

[1] *chare rofed*: see above, p. 490.   [2] *pament*: pavement.

lengthe and in brede xxiiij fete, and ouer the said librarie an hous of the same large-
nesse for diuerse stuf of the College: in the other ende of the same pane an halle
conteynyng in lengthe c fete, upon a vawte of xij fete high, ordeigned for the
Celer and Boterie, and the brede of the halle xxxiiij fete on eueri side therof a bay
windowe, and in the nether ende of the same halle, toward the myddel of the said
pane a panetrie and boterie, euery of them in lengthe xx fete and in brede xv, And
ouer that ij chambres for officers, and atte the nether ende of the halle toward the
west a goodly kichen: And the same pane shal haue ij tours inward ordeigned
for the waies in to the halle and librarie: And in euery corner of the said quadrant
shal be ij corner toures, on inward and on outward, mo than the toures aboue
reherced; And atte the ouer ende of the halle the Provostes loggyng that is to
wete moo than the chambres aboue for hym specified a parlour oon the ground
conteynyng xxxiiij fete in lengthe and xxij in brede, ij chambres aboue of the same
quantite. And westward closyng therto a kechen larder hous stable and other
necessarie housyng and groundes; And westward beyond thees housynges and the
said kechen ordeigned for the halle a bak hous and bruehous and other houses
of Offices betwene which ther is left a grownde square of iiij$^{xx}$ fete in euery pane
for wode and such stuffe; And in the myddel of the said large quadrant shalbe a
condute[1] goodly deuised for the ease of the said College.

And I wol that the edificacion of my same College procede in large fourme
clene and substancial, settyng a parte superfluite of too gret curious werkes of
entaille[2] and besy moldyng.

And I haue deuised and appoynted that the precincts of my same College of
oure Lady and saint Nicholas aswel on bothe sides of the gardine from the said
College unto the water, as in alle other places of the same procincte, be enclosed
with a substancial wal of the height of xiiij fete, with a large tour at the principal
entree ageyns the myddel of the Est pane out of the high strete; And in the same
tour a large yate, and an other tour in the myddel of the west ende at the newe
brigge; And the seid wal to be crested and embatelled and fortified with toures,
as many as shal be thought conuenient therto.

# 77 (A)

## 1447–8 Eton College

This is the specification for the building of Eton College, corresponding to the preceding
document concerned with King's College.

Willis and Clark, *Arch. Hist. of Cambridge*, i. 354.

I wol that the Qwere of my saide College of Eton shal conteyne in lengthe
ciij fete of assise; wherof behinde the high auter shal be viij fete, and fro the seide
auter unto the Quere dore iiij$^{xx}$xv fete.

---

[1] *condute*: conduit-house, or fountain.    [2] *entaille*: carving.

Item the same Quere shal conteyne in brede from side to side within the respondes xxxij fete.

Item, the ground[1] of the wallis shal be enhaunced hier than they be nowe on the utter side, or[2] hit come to the leyng of the first stone of the clere wallis iij fete of assise, and in the ynner syde or hit come to the leyng of the first stone of the clere wallis x fete of assise.

Item, the wallis of the seide Quere shal conteyne in height fro the grounde werkes unto the crestis of the batelment iiij[xx] fete of assise.

Item, in the est ende of the seide Quere shal be sette a grete gable windowe of vij daies and ij butterases, and in either side of the same Quere vij windowes, euery windowe of iiij daies, and viij butterases, conteyning in height fro the grounde werkes unto the over parte of the pynnacles c fete of assise.

Item, that the saide groundes be so take, that the first stone lie in the myddel of the high auter, which auter shal conteyne in length xij fete of assise, and in brede v fete. And that the saide first stone be not removed touched nor stered in any wise.

Item, the vestiarie to be sette oon the north syde of the saide Quere, which shal conteyne in lengthe l fete of assise departed into ij houses, and in brede xxiiij fete; and the wallis in height xx fete, with gable wyndowes and side windowes conuenient therto. And the grounde werkes to be sette in height of the grounde of the cloister.

And I wol that the edificacion of my said College of Eton procede in large fourme, clene and substancial, wel replenysshed with goodely wyndowes and vautes leyng a parte superfluite of to grete curiose werkes of entaille and besy moldyng.

Item, in the saide Quere oon either side xxxij stalles and the rode loft there, I wol that they be made in like maner and fourme as be the stalles and rodeloft in the chapell of saint Stephen atte Westminster, and of the lengthe of xxxij fete and in brede clere xij fete of assise.

And as touchyng the demensions of the chirch of my saide College of Eton, I haue deuised and appointed that the body of the same chirch betwȝene the yles shal conteyne in brede within the respondes xxxij fete and in lengthe from the Quere unto the West dore of the said chirch ciiij fete of assise. And soo the seide bodie of the Chirch shal be lenger than is the Quere fro the reredos atte the high auter unto the quere dore by ix fete, which demension is thought to be right or goode, conuenient and due proporcion.

Item, I haue deuised and appointed that the yle oon the either side of the body of the chirch shal conteyne in brede fro respond to respond xv fete, and in lengthe ciiij fete, accordyng to the seide bodye of the chirch.

Item, in the south side of the bodie of the chirch a faire large dore with a porche ouer the same for christenyng of childre and weddynges.

---

[1] *ground*: foundations.  [2] *or*: before.

Item, I haue deuised and appointed vj grecis to be before the high auter, with the grece called gradus chori, eueri of them conteynyng in hight vj ynches, and of conuenient brede, euery of them as due fourme shall require.

Item, in the brede of the chircheyard fro the chirch dore unto the wallis of the chircheyard within the wal atte the west ende, which muste be take of the strete beside the high way, xvj fete of assise.

Item, the groundes of the cloistre to be enhaunced hier than the olde grounde viij fete yer hit come to the pament, soo that hit be sette but ij fete lower than the pavyng of the chirch. Which cloistre shal conteyne in lengthe Est and west cc fete and in brede north and south clx fete of assise. Item, the same cloister shal close unto the chirch on the north side atte the west ende, and oon the north side atte the est ende of the chirch hit shal be close to the College, with a dore into the same College. Item, the same cloister shal conteyne in brede within the walles xv fete and in height xx fete with clere stories rounde aboute ynward, and vawted, and enbatelled on bothe sydes. Item, the space betwen the wal of the chirch and the wal of the cloistre shal conteyne xxxviij fete, which is left for to sette in certain trees and floures, behoueful and conuenient for the seruice of the saide chirch. Item, the cementorie of the chirch shal be lower than the pauyng of the cloistre iiij fete of assise, with as many greces up into the chirch dore as shal be conuenient therto. Item in the myddel of the west pane of the saide cloistre a grete square Tour, with a faire dore in to the cloistre which tour shal conteyne clere within the wal xx fete and in the height with the batelment and the pynacles cxl fete.

Item, from the high way on the south syde unto the wallis of the College a goode high wal with toures conuenient therto. And in like wise from thens by the water side and aboute the gardynes and alle the procincte of the place round a bout by the high way, unto that hit come to the cloisters ende on the west side ageyne.

Item, that the water atte Baldewyne brigge be turned outerthwart in to the Riuer of Thamyse with a dich of xl fete of brede. And the grounde betwene the same diche and the College arreised of a grete height so that hit may atte alle flodes be playn and drie grounde where than wol be in distaunce fro the halle to the water atte alle tymes of drie grounde iiij$^{xx}$ fete.

And as touchyng the demensions of the housyng of my saide College of Eton, I haue deuised and appointed that the south wal of the procincte of the saide College which shal extende from the tenement that Hugh Dier nowe holdeth and occupieth, unto the Est ende of the gardines efterlong the water side, shal conteyne in lengthe M$^{l}$ccccxl fete of assise with a large dore in the same wal to the water side. Item, the Est wal of the saide procincte which shal extende fro the waterside unto the high way atte the newe brigges atte the Este ende of the gardines shal conteyne in lengthe DCC fete of assise. Item the northwal of the said procincte which shal extende fro the Est ende of the gardines afterlong the high way unto the southwest corner of the same procincte shal conteyne in length m$^{l}$xl fete of assise in which wal shal be a faire yate out of the utter court in to the high way. Item the west wal of the saide procincte which shal extende fro the saide west corner of the same procincte unto the saide tenement which the said Hugh Dier nowe occupieth shal conteyn in lengthe DX fete, and so the utter walles of the said procincte shal conteyne in lengthe aboute the same procincte M$^1$M$^1$M$^1$Diiij$^{xx}$x fete of assise.

Item, betwix the seid northwal of the said procincte and the walles of the College in the utter court on the Est parte of the yate and the wey in to the College shal be edified diuerse housyng necessarie for the bakhous bruehous garners stables heyhous with chambres for the stuardes auditours and other lerned counsellis and ministres of the said College and other loggynges necessarie for suche persounes of the said College as shal happen to be diseased with infirmitees. Item in the west partie of the said yate and the way in to the College in the north pane, viij Chambres for the pouer men, And in the west pane vj chambres, and behynde the same a kechene, boterie, panetrie, with gardines and a grounde for fuel for the said pouere men.

Item, the northparte of the College shal conteyne clv fete within the walles in the middel of the which shal be a faire tour and a yatehous with ij chambres on either side and ij chambres aboue, vauted, contaynyng in lengthe xl fete and in brede xxiiij fete. And in the Est side of the said yate iiij chambres ij benethe and ij aboue euery of them in lengthe xxxv fete, and in brede xxiiij fete. And in the west side of the same yate a scolehous benethe of lxx fete in lengthe and in brede xxiiij fete and aboue the same ij chambres either of them in lengthe xxxv fete and in brede xxiiij fete.

Item the Est pane in lengthe within the walles ccxxx fete in the myddel wherof directly agayns the entre of the cloistre a librarie conteynyng in lengthe lij fete and in brede xxiiij fete with iij chambres aboue on the oon side and iiij on the other side and benethe ix chambres euery of them in lengthe xxvj fete and in brede xviij fete with v utter toures and v ynner toures.

Item the west pane of the said College ccxxx fete in lengthe in the which shal be directly agains the librarie a dore in to the cloistre, and aboue viij chambres and benethe other viij with iij utter toures byonde the north side of the cloister and v ynner toures with a way in to the quere for the Ministres of the chirch between the vestiarie and the same quere.

Item the south pane in lengthe clv fete in which shal stande the halle with a vaute unthernethe for the buterie and celer conteynyng in lengthe iiij$^{xx}$ij fete, and in brede xxxij fete, with ij baywyndowes on inward an other outward with a toure ouer the halle dore. And atte the Est ende of the halle a panetrie with a chambre benethe, and atte the west ende of the halle the Provostes loggyng aboue and benethe, conteynyng in lengthe lxx fete with a corner toure inward and an other wythoute. And on the south side of the halle a goodli kichen and in the myddel of the quadrant withynne a condute goodly deuised to the ease and profit of the saide College.

Item the height fro the strete to the enhauncyng of the grounde of the Cementorie vij fete and an half and the same wal in height aboue that v fete di' with grecis out of the high way in to the same pane as many as shal seme conuenient. Item, that the quadrant within the College and the utter court be but a fote lower than the cloister.

Item, alle the walles of the said College of the utter court, and of the walles of the procincte aboute the gardines, and as far as the procincte shal goo, to be made of hard stone of Kent. And the said gardines to be enhaunced with erthe to the height of a fote lower than the cementorie of the said Chirche.

# 77 (B)

*Eton College*

The King's revised scheme for the college chapel.

Willis and Clark, op. cit. i. 366.

The kynges owne avyse as touchyng certayne demensions also [as] well of the Qwere as of the body of the Churche with the yles of h[is] College Royall of oure blessed lady of Eton.

First he is avysed concluded and fully determened that the sayd [Qwere] schall conteyne in lengthe fro the Est ende with Inne the wall u[nto the] Qwere dore cl fote of assise; wher of be hynd the hye A[uter] xij fote. And fro the Reredoce be hynd the hye Auter unto the lowes[t step] called gradus chori xliiij fote. And fro thens for lengthe of the stalles in the Qwere iiij$^{xx}$viij. And be hynde the Provostes stall unto the qwere dore vj fote, for a wey in to the Rodelofte for redyng and syngyng and for the Organs and other manere observance there to be had after the Rewles of the Churche of Salesbury.

Item the same qwere to conteyne in brede fro syde to syde with Inne the walles xl fote of assise.

Item on euery side of the same qwere to be sett viij wyndowes every wyndowe of v dayes clenly and substancially wroght. And in the East ende of the same a grete gable wyndowe of ix dayes.

Itm the hye auter in the seid qwere schall conteyne in lengthe xviij fote and in brede iiij$^{or}$ fote an a half with oute the Reredoce. Whiche schall conteyne in thiknesse ij fote. And on the right syde of the seid hye Auter to be sett an image of oure lady. And on the left syde an ymage of saint Nicholas. And a boue in the seyd Reredoce in the myddes to be sett a grete ymage of our Savyoure with the xij [A]postoles y sett on euery syde of the same ymage with sygnes and [to]kenes of here passion and martirdome.

[Item t]hat in the space be hynd the hye Auter schall be an Auter in [the myd]des under the gable wyndowe conteynyng in lengthe ix [fote and] in brede iij fote with an ymage of oure lady in the [mydd]es holdyng a childe in here armes.

Item that the body of the seyd Churche schall conteyne in lengthe fro the qwere dore unto the west dore of the same Churche with Inne the walles clxviij fote of assyse. And in the west end of the same a grete gable wyndowe of ix dayes.

Item the brede of the same body with Inne the Pylours to conteyne xl fote of assise a cordyng to the wyde of the said qwere.

Item he is avysed and concluded that the yle on eyther syde of the seyd body of the Churche schall conteyne in brede fro respond to respond xx$^{ti}$ fote. And in lengthe clxviij fote a cordyng to the seyd body of the Churche. And in euery ende of the seid yles a wyndowe of vj dayes with a principall moynell in the middes also in euerich of the Este endes of the seid yles to be sett ij Auters with ij Auters in the body of the seid Churche to be sett on euery syde of the qwere dore. And in euery syde of the same yles schall be viij wyndowes euery wyndowe of v dayes to be sett directly a yenst viij Arches of the body of the seid Churche.

Item that the walles of the seid Qwere and Churche schull conteyne in heght from the grownde werke unto the Crest of the batilments of the same iiij$^{xx}$ fote of assise. And fro the Crest unto the fynyng of the pynnacles xx$^{ti}$ fote. And so the heght of alle fro the clere grownde unto the heyest part of the pynnacles to be c fote of assise. And so the seid Qwere schall be lenger than the qwere of the Newe College at Oxford bi xlvij fote brodder bi viij fote. And the walles heyer be xx$^{ti}$ fote. And also heyer than the walles of seynt Stephenes Chapell at Westmonstre.

Item he is avysed and concluded that the first stone which is poynted to lye under the middes of the hye Autere be not stored[1] removed ne towched in any wyse.

Item that the growndes of the Qwere whiche be nowe taken be nott removed ne stored for drede of hurtyng and empeyring of the seid growndes but hitt be in tho places as schall be seen be houffull or necessarye so that the growndes nowe to be takyn be syde the oold growndes for the enlargeyng of the said qwere to take lowe at the bottom of the fundement with ij courses, first j course of platt Yorkschire stone playne and well bedded. After with the secunde Course of Yorkschire and Teynton ston medlyd and couched to gyder. And ther upon the growndes a rysyng to be made with large substanciall fre stone of Teynton w$^{t}$ hethston[2] and flynt y leyd and couched with good and myghty morter made with fyne stone lyme and gravell sonde unto the clere wall. And fro thens upward the walles to be made with Yorkschyre and Teynton ston. The same walles to be filled with the same ston and with hard and durable heth ston and flynt with good morter to be made as hit is before rehersed. So that neyther in the seid growndes ne walles schall in any wise be occupied Chalke Bryke ne Reygate stone otherwyse y called Mestham stone but oonly of the stuffe before rehersed.

Item that the growndes in the sowthe side of the seid qwere be take largeur with owte the clere wall than thei schall be on the North side of the same bi ij fote largely.

[1] *stored*: stirred.     [2] *hethston*: heath stone was a kind of ragstone used for rubble.

## 78

*1448 Cambridge, Queens' College*

A carpenter, jointly with his surety, gives a bond of £100 to carry out all the woodwork —roof, floors, partition walls, and stairs—of a new building, 240 ft. by 20 ft., for £100, payable in three instalments. The scantlings of the timbers are specified.

Willis and Clark, op. cit., ii. 8.

This indenture made the xiiij[th] day of Aprile the yer of the reign of our sovreign lord the King Henry the sixt six and twenty betwen master Andrew Dokett president of the Quene college of seynt Margret and seynt Barnard and the Felowes of the seid college of the one party, and John Veyse of Elesnam in the shire of Essex draper and Thomas Sturgeon of the seides towne and shire carpenter on the other party bereth witeness that—thogh the seides John Veyse and Thomas Sturgeon be holden and strongely by their obligacion bownden to the forseid master Andrew Dokett in an hundred pound of good and lawfull money of Inglond to be paied to hym his heires or to his successours in the fest of the natiuite of seynt John Baptiste next folowyng the forseid,—yat master Andrewe president and of the seid college Felowes wollen, and by thies presentez indentures graunten that—yef the seides John Veyse and Thomas Sturgeon or other of them or elles any other in their name make or do for to be made well and sufficiauntely an house with in the seid college as in werk of carpentre [find]yng also all the tymber that shall nede to the rofe of the seid howse and also lathes and all maner of tymber that shall be ocupyed on the [flore]s and on the Midelwalles and on the steires with all the bord the wich shall be of oke that to the seide flores and steires shall resonable nede of the propre costis and expensez of the seides John and Thomas vndir maner and forme as heer foloweth, that is for to say;

the seid house shall conteyne in lengthe xij[xx] foot of the standard, and in brede xx fote of the standard; and the Someres of the said hows shall be one side xij inch squar and on the other part xiiij inch squar; and all the Gistes shall be on the one part squar vj inches and on the other part viij inches; and the walplates on the one part ix inch and on the other part vij inches; And all the bemes that lyen by hemself they shull be squar on the one side x inch and on the other xv inch; And all the sparres shall conteyne in brede at the netherend squar vij inch and at the overend vj inches and in thiknesse on the other part at the netherend vj inch and at the overend v inches; and all the sowthelases[1] and the asshelers[2] shull accord in brede with the sparres and on the other part thes shull be iiij inches squar; and all the wynbemes shull conteyne in brede squar vj inches and in the other part v inches; And al the stoddes shall be in brede viij inch squar and on the other part v inche squar; and the space betwyn all the sparres all the stoddes and all the gystes shull be but x inch;

[1] *sowthelases*: braces; see above, p. 450.
[2] *asshelers*: upright puncheons between the wallplates and rafters.

and all thies covenauntez beforrehersed be plenerly fulfilled and done by the seides John and Thomas or by any other for theym,—that then the forseid obligacion of an c$^{li}$ stand in non strenketh nor effect, and elles yef hit be not fulfilled that then hit stand in strenketh and virtu. Purveid alwey that the seides John and Thomas shall haue of the forseides master Andrewe his successores and of his felowes of the seid College for the forseid Tymbir bord lath and werkmanship that shall pertene to the seid hows an c$^{li}$ of lawfull money of Inglond to be payed at dayes here expressed, that is for to say, at the fest of seynt George next after the date present liiij$^{li}$. xiij$^s$. iiij$^d$. and at the fest of the natiuite of sent John Baptiste xx$^{li}$ and at the fest of seynt Michaell the archangell then next folowyng xxv$^{li}$. vj$^s$. viij$^d$. in pleyn payment of the c$^{li}$ aforseid.

In witteness whereof bothe partyes to thies presentes indenturez alternatly haue putt to her seales. This wittenesseth Richard Andrewe, John Batisford, Benet Morys and mo other. Yeven at Cambrigge day and yer aboven seid.

## 79

*1448/9 Cambridge, Queens' College*

A contract, similar to the preceding, for the construction of roof, floors, partition walls, steps, and benches for the hall, kitchen, pantry, and buttery, for £80, payable in six instalments.

Willis and Clark, op. cit., ii. 10.

This indenture made the sext day of March the 3ere of the reigne of our souereigne lord the kyng Herry the sext xxvij$^{the}$ between maister Andrew Dokett presidente of the Quenes colage of sente Margrett and sente Barnard of Cambrigge maistere Pers Hirford and maistere Thomas Heywod of the seide colage felowes on the on party, and John Weyse of Elesnam in the shire of Essex draper and Thomas Sturgeon of the seides town and shire carpenter on the other party bereth witteness that—[J. W. and T. S. are bound in an obligation in £80 to the said Master and Fellows]—yef the seid John Weyse and Thomas Sturgeon or otheir of them or elles any othire in their name make or do for to be made well and sufficiauntly the rofe of the hall within the said collage being, fyndyng all tymber that shall perteyn ther to,

the wich hal shalbe and conteyn in lenketh l fete of the standard and in brede xxviij fete and the walplates of the seid hall shalbe viij inches of brede and vij inches of Thiknes with jopees$^1$ from bem to bem and v bemes and euery bem shal be xv inch of brede and x inch thik, and every sparre shalbe in the fote viij inch of brede and vij inch thik and in the topp vij inch of brede and v inch thik, and the principalles shalbe xj inch in breede and x inch thik with a purlyn in the Middes from one principall to a nother with a crown tree$^2$ ix inch of brede viij inch thik,— and all the tymbere with warkmanshipp that shalbe nedfull to the benches in the

---

$^1$ *jopees*: cornices.     $^2$ *crown tree*: ridge-piece.

seid hall, and also thei shull make the Rofes of botry patry and Kechen with the flores to them longyng with all the Midilwalles and greses[1] to the seid howses perteynyng fyndyng tymber to them nedfull, the wich howses extenden in lenketh from the hall in to the hei way with a return of the Chambers ich of hem conteynyng in lenketh xxv foote and in brede xx; and all the sowtlases, asshalers, walplatz and jopees that shull nede to the seides howses shull accord with the other syde the wich is now redy framed next the Freres, fyndyng all tymber and borde of oke to the seid Flores with all lathes tymber for gresynges and Midelwalles to the seides howses parteynyng; and the space between all the stoddes all the sparres and all the Gistes shul be but x inch.

and all thies couauntes beforehesed be planarly fulfilled and doon by the seides John Weyce and Thomas Sturgeon or by any other for them,—that then the forsaid obligacion of iiij$^{xx}$ $^{li}$. stande in no strenketh nor affect, and elles yef hit be not performed that then hit stand in strenketh and vertu. Purveid alvey that the seides John and Thomas shull haue of the forseides master Andrew, master Pers, and master Thomas for the tymber bord lath and warkmanshipp that shall perteyn to the howses aforseid iiij$^{xx}$ $^{li}$. of lawfull money of Inglond to be payed at daies here expressed, that is for to sey: at Estern next comyng xx$^{li}$., at Estern twelmonth after xx$^{li}$., and seynt Thomas day of Caunterbury then next x$^{li}$., at the exaltation of the Holycross then next x$^{li}$., at the reysing of the rofes of the seid howses x$^{li}$., and x$^{li}$. when thei haue plenarly performed all ther couaunentz beforseid; and this to be done in as hasty wise as thei may goodly after the walles of the seid howses be redy.

In witteness wherof bothe partyes to thies present indentures alternatly haue putto her sealles. This wittesnesse Rycherd Andrew, John Batysford and moo other. Yeven at Cambrigge, day and 3ere aboven seid.

## 80

*1452 Cambridge, St. Benet's Church*

Specification for a new roof to be made.

Willis and Clark, op. cit. i. 282.[2]

This indenture made the vj$^{th}$ day of the monyth of Junii the yere of the reygn of kyng herry the sext after the conquest the xxx$^{the}$ bytwene Thomas Byrd and Thomas Wrangyll otherwyse called Thomas Richardesson Cherghe Revys of the Parysshe of seynt Benettys of Cambrigg on the on partye, And Nicholas Toftys of Reche in the shire of Cambrigg Carpentere on the other partye

---

[1] *greses*: steps.

[2] Willis and Clark give three figures reconstructing this roof from the specification. In Fig. 3, however, there appears to be no reason for applying the term 'jowpye' to the spandrel; it must mean 'cornice' here, as elsewhere.

wittenissith that the seyd Nicholas shamake newe a roofe to the cherche of seynt Benettys Aforeseyd.

First iiij principal Bemys with braces and pendaunttes xvj^ne inche in depthe atte the crest and xiiij inche atte the endys And in brede ij of the Bemys shalbe xij inche inbowed with lozinggys And the other ij Bemys the whiche be called end Bemys shalhaue the same depthe and viij inche in brede Also the said Roofe shalhaue a crest tre[1] thorowhe, in depthe xvj^ne inche, conueniently wrowht accordyng to the Bemys.

Item ij sengulere Principalls in werkyng in inbowyng and in Scantlyon accordyng to the Principalls with somere trees conuenient vnto the werk. Also Jowpyes xvj ^ne inche in brede with a Batylment by nethe with a Crest above and a Casement[2] fulfyllyng to the werk.

Also the sparres to same Rooffe shalbe viij inche in brede and vj in thiknesse and viij inche be twene euery sparre.

Also the selyng boord by twene euery sparre shalbe quartere borde an inche thyk clene planed, and the sparres shalbe planed also.

Item atte euery joynt of the Crest tre atte the Principalls and sengulers shalbe halff Angells.

Also atte euery joynt of the somere trees shalhaue a boos.

Item atte euery end of the pendaunt shalbe a angell.

Item atte euery end of the sengulers atte the Jowpye shalbe an Angel.

In witnesse were of the partyes a forseyd to theis present indenturys there selys iche to othere hath putt. Yeuyn the day yere and place before seyd etc.

# 81

## *1457 Cambridge, Corpus Christi College*

Agreement with a mason for building a wall 4½ rods, of 18 feet, in length. He is either to have the same rate per rod that he says he had at Peterhouse, or else 40s. in all, with lodging for 4 men and the right of using the college kitchen to cook their food; he also asks for the help of two of the college workmen in digging the foundations.

Willis and Clark, op. cit. i. 310.

Memorandum quod Johannes Bale mason alias Loose vocat' leyer nuper factor novi muri lapidei apud predicatores dominica proxima ante festum nativitatis beate Marie anno predicto 1457 venit et pepigit cum magistro collegii teste M. Ric. Brochier de factura eciam unius muri lapidei juxta Collegium predictum et terram nuper vicariae sancti Botulphi ad longitudinem 4 rodarum et di' qualibet roda continente xviij pedes de standardo regio. Et habebit in grosso vel xl^s cum decoctione cibariorum in coquina collegii et potagium tantum durante termino facture predicte cum asiamente camere et pistrino ibidem et pro lecto iiij hominum ad prandend' et iacend'. Aut habebit pro qualibet roda et

---

[1] *crest tre*: ridge-piece.   [2] *casement*: a hollow moulding.

iuxta ratam illius di' rodae sicut dicit se habuisse ad domum Petri pro qualibet roda ibidem burs' cum ceteris asiamentis supradictis ad electionem dicti magistri Collegii et erit dictus murus eiusdem latitudinis sicut est latitudo muri latrine hospicii sed altitudo cum crista dict' muri erit tanta quanta est altitudo murorum collegii: petit posterius dictus mason siue layer quod per duos laborarios collegii ad fundamentum adiuvetur: unde in partem solucionis coram magistro Thoma Lane recepit et pro strena[1] totius pacti integri iiij$^d$.

## 82

### 1459 Felmersham

Although this does not give the details of any particular contract, it is of sufficient interest, as showing the number of contracts that might be involved in a single building operation, to merit inclusion here. It contains the record of eight separate contracts (two being with the same carpenter) for the construction of a granary.

King's Hall Accts., vol. 12, f. 241.

Convenciones facte pro granario de Felmersham.

In primis conventum est cum Ricardo Baker pro factura unius tecti granarii apud Felmersham—xiij$^s$ iiij$^d$. Item cum Johanne Ward de Knottyng pro meremio ad fabricam ejusdem tecti—xvj$^s$. Item conventum est cum gardianis ecclesie de Felmersham quod habebunt pro unoquoque quarterio calcis combuste xiiij$^d$. Item conventum est cum Abram pro fodiacione lapidum quod habebit pro c bigatibus xij$^s$ vj$^d$. Item conventum est cum Georgio Latimo pro factura murorum granarii quos de novo faciet propriis suis sumptibus in altitudinem murorum antiqui granarii et habebit pro suo labore xlvj$^s$ viij$^d$ cum toga vel sex solidos et octo denarios. Item conventum est cum Ricardo Baker pro le swarynge[2] duorum som$^a$rs et eorum collocacione in murum [et] pro faccione hostii dorstalys[3] lyntyls ad duas fenestras ejusdem granarii—iij$^s$ iiij$^d$. Item conventum est cum Johanne Ward de Scharnbrok pro una roda mensularum cum cariagio eorundem—x$^s$. Item conventum est cum Johanne Phalet pro tegulacione granarii et inveniet omnia ad idem pertinencia excepta calce et clavis et habebit pro labore xviij$^s$ iiij$^d$.

## 83

### 1459 Cambridge, Corpus Christi College

A confused and obscure contract with a mason for the building of a bakehouse. The walls are to be partly of stone and partly of brick, 4 windows being of brick. The whole to be finished in about 4 months, under penalty of 40s. For his work he shall have 11½ marks— or more, if the college authorities think fit—and a gown worth 6s. 8d.; also he shall have

---

[1] *strena*: earnest-money; probably connected with French *étrennes*.
[2] *swarynge*: squaring.
[3] *dorstalys*: door-posts.

a room and bed in the college and have his food cooked in the kitchen. He produces as sureties the Master of Peterhouse and the rector of St. Benet's.

Willis and Clark, *Arch. Hist. of Cambridge*, i. 308.

This endenture made the iiij[the] day of Decembre the yere of Kyng herry the sixte xxxviii[ti] betwene Maister John Botwright Maister of the college of cor[is] Xri and of our ladi seint Marie en cambrigg and the Felaus of the sayd College on that one partye and John Loose of the same towne or ellis sumtyme of Burston in Norfolk mason on that other partye Witnessith that A Counant is made in maner and fourme folowyng.

That is to say that the seyd John Loose shal make or do make sufficiently the walles of a bakhouse the lenghth acordyng to the ground[1] that also is take by the ouersyght in warkmanship of the sayd John lose with the ground also of a fauce boterace[2] for diuerse considerations to be made in the said counaunt the cause longe bifore know to the said John Loose of the whech Boterace after the grond biforsaid taken therfore: of a foote and half in thikness the heyest of the creste after ij tyles and an half heygh but a foote aboue the wyndows of sent Bernards hostell Notwithstanding the walles of the said Bakhouse beyng of Ragge clunch and Tyle iij fotes of the standard from the gronde leuell to the water tabil round aboute A metyerd in heyght of large mesure and from the said watter tabill the heyght of the walle of the said seynt Bernardis hostell therto adioynant and yet heyer bi a foote of assyse and so rounde aboute leuelled of ston and lyme with ij pyke walles[3] of the same stuffe And a doore in brede iiij foote standard of fre ston from the base soyle also of freston the heyght of iij foote assise large and upwarde in heyght to the thyrd peynt of the Centre[4] v foote more al of breke. Alle the said Freestoon to be hew atte the costis of the said John Loose w[t] iiij Wyndows of breke ych of theym of ij lyghtes and the said water tabell half the house round about alle of freeston hewyn at the costis of the said John Loose that other half tabill of the best endureing breke. Also the said maister and felaus schal fynde al maner of stuffe and mater redy at alle conuenient tyme to werk And alle other ordinaunces that schal parteyne unto the same werk so that this werk forsaid schal be bygonne at the ferrest by sent gregores day in march next comyng And sufficiently be ended by the fest of Lambmess next comyng after the date of this present writeng in peyn of xl[s]. to be payed and content bi the said John Loose, Takeng for his werkmanschip and labour xj marc vj[s]. viij[d]. and a gowne of yomanis leuere of the said college or ellis a noble therefore so alle thyng be thus thorow and content; and more if it can be thought bi conscience of the said Maister and felaus so to doo. And of this xj marc vj[s]. viij[d]. to be payed at theis diuersez tymes that is to say in the bigynneng of the werk liij[s]. viij[d]. and other xl[s]. when the werk is half made. And other xl[s]. when the walles are alle leuelled And

---

[1] *ground*: foundations.  [2] *a fauce boterace*: the meaning is obscure.

[3] *pyke walles*: perhaps 'peaked', or gable, walls.

[4] *the thyrd peynt of the Centre*: meaning obscure.

xxˢ. when the werk is ful complete And more ouer the sayd John schal haue
withinne the sayd College a chambre j bedsteed and a bedde And his mete to be
dyght in the kechyn at there costis as longe as he is werkyng in the said werk
Theis beyng his borows Maister Thomas Lane Maister of Peterhous and Maister
Water Smith parson of sent Benetis in cambregg Witnessis maister Richard
Brochier Maister Thurston and M Rauf Seyton with many other yeuen the day
and yer aboue rehersid.

## 84

### *1464 Coventry*

This is not strictly a contract, being a lease for 60 years of a site in Catesby Lane, Coventry.
The tenant undertakes to build a two-storied house of oak timbering resting on stone
foundations and faced with plaster, the upper story jettied 2 feet towards the lane.

*Ancient Deeds* (P.R.O.), A. 8449.

Hec indentura inter Johannem Stanbury Episcopum Herford (*sic*), Johannem
Barre militem, Willelmum Breteyn clericum, Johannem Norys armigerum,
Thomam Billyng seniorem, Thomam Palmer armigerum, Robertum Tanfeld,
Johannem Catesby armigerum, Johannem Lound clericum, Willelmum Fore-
shaw clericum, Edmundum Newenham, Willelmum Catesby militem, et
Willelmum Catesby armigerum filium ejusdem Willelmi, ex parte una, et
Ricardum Sampson de Couentre deyster ex parte altera, testatur quod predicti
Episcopus [&c.] dimiserunt Ricardo unum mesuagium cum suis pertinentiis in
Couentre continens spacium trium baiarum in longitudine situatum in venella
vocata Catesby Lane ex opposito magnam cameram capitalis mesuagii predictorum Episcopi [&c.] quod predictus Ricardus modo tenet habendum et
tenendum . . . festo Sci. Michaelis Archi. proxime futuro post datum presentium
usque ad finem termini sexaginta annorum . . . reddendo annuatim . . . viginti
denarios. . . . Et predictus Ricardus concedit per presentes quod ipse et assignati
sui de novo edificabunt et construent unam domum et unam cameram continent'
totum spacium mesuagii predicti bene et sufficienter sumptibus suis et expensis
citra festum Nativ. Sci. Johannis Baptiste proxime futurum post datum presentium, videlicet cum sufficiente maeremio quercino cum postibus de altitudine
quindecim pedum situatis super lapides existentes in altitudine unius pedis et
dimidii secundum totam longitudinem mesuagii predicti ex parte venelle predicte et ex altera parte in altitudine super lapides nunc in muro ibidem existentes.
Ita quod maeremium inde sit sufficienter constructum ad plastrandum cum plastr'
de Parys in omnibus muris earundem domus et camere exceptis muris vocatis
lez helow wowes.[1] Et idem Ricardus et assignati sui construent et edificabunt
predictam cameram cum le flore ejusdem de sufficiente maeremio continentem
spacium tocius longitudinis messuagii predicti. Et camera illa erit giteyed per

---

[1] *lez helow wowes*: Halliwell gives 'helwalls—the end outside walls of a gable house':
presumably the actual portion of the wall between the slopes of the 'heling' or roof.

spacium duorum pedum versus venellam predictam; idemque Ricardus et assignati sui facient hostia et fenestras cum uno gryse[1] et cum omnibus aliis ad edificacionem domus et camere predictarum necessariis. Et postquam domus et camera predicte modo et forma predictis edificantur et constructe fuerint idem Ricardus et assignati sui . . . reparabunt et sustentabunt [&c.]. . . . Datum apud Couentre sexto die Augusti anno regni Regis Edwardi quarti post conquestum quarto.

## 85

### 1466 Cambridge, the Schools

Two carpenters undertake to make floors and roof. [For details, see above, pp. 210–15.] Also to make doors and windows, and the roof of the vice. They shall provide and carry all the materials, and shall be paid £23. 6s. 8d., in addition to £10 paid them at the making of the contract.

Willis and Clark, *Arch. Hist. of Cambridge*, iii. 92–4.

This endenture made the xxv day of Juyn the sixt yeere of the Regne of Kyng Edward the fourth betwix Maister William Wylflete nowe being chauncellor of thuniversitie of Cambrigge Maister Nicholas Gay Maister William Smyth Maister Edmond Connesburgh Doctours of the same universite, Maister William Wyche and Maister William Langton nowe being proctours of the said universite, sufficiently and lawfully deputed and ordeyned by the hool congregacion of Regentes and non Regentes of the forsaid unyversite for to purvey rewle surveye and gwyde the werke of the new Scoles in the same universite, of that oon partie, And William Harward of Halsted in the Counte of Essex carpenter and William Bakon of the same Towne and Counte Carpenter of that othir partie, Witnesseth:

That the same Harward and William Bakon haue made feythfull promysse and covenaunt with the forsaid Doctours and proctours in the name of alle thuniversite aforsaid, For alle the tymbre cariage and werkmanship for the Floores and Rofe of the said new scoles, forto be parfitly made of tymbre and werkmanship benethe specified, tofore the Feest of Seynt Petir that is called *Ad vincula sancti Petri* that shalbe in the yeer of oure Lorde M[1]cccclxvii in maner and forme that foloweth.

That is to say: the nethir floore shal have vj Dormauntes in breed of xvj ynches square; the gistes shalbe viij ynches in breede and v ynches thyk with braces and pendauntes and with Angels and enbowed for the dormauntes; And alle the gistes of the same floore shal have an hool casement enbowed; And betwix gist and gist shalbe viij ynches; And the bords that it shalbe plaunched with shalbe ynche thyk; And the bordes shalbe lynyd and leyd on hye on the gistes.

And a Roofe for the said Scole shal have vj right bemes with ioppys purloynes braces pendauntes with angels, and alle shalbe enbowed as longith unto the werke. And the same Roofe shal have a dowble Roofe; that is to say first bemys right, like to the dormauntes of the flore with crosse dormauntes, and the ioppys so that

---

[1] *gryse*: a flight of steps.

alle the gistes of the flore shal rest upon the crosse dormauntes and on the said joppys; which gistes shalbe viij ynches in brede and iiij ynches thyk and borded in lyk wyse as the lougher flore shalbe.

And from every beme a leyrn stood[1] with ij braces into the beme and ij into the crownetree which shal lye upon the said studdes and bere the sparres with a purloyn on both sydes in the middist of the said sparres with punchions fro the bemes to bere the same. And the said sparres shalbe viij ynches in brede at the fote and vj ynches at the toppe and vj ynches thyk at the fote and v in the toppe and shal ryse fro the said beme in the myddist iiij fote and an half. Also the said Roofe shal have sufficient leedlathis of herty ooke sufficiently dried; And alle this tymbir shalbe white oke, not doted nor storvyn nor sappy to hurt the beawty or thynbowyng of the werke.

Also thei shal make alle the dores and wyndowes and the Roofe of the vice of the staire. And the same dores and wyndowes shalbe like of strength and makyng of the dores and wyndowes of the other new scoles there.

And the said carpenters shal semblab[l]y fynde alle the bord and tymbre for the said dores and wyndowes and for the Roof of the vice aforsaid.

And for alle the tymbir and borde above rehersed cariage of the same and werkmanship of Carpentrie in maner and fourme aboveseid, to be done and perfourmed, the forsaid Doctours and proctours shal paie or do to be paid unto the said William Harward and William Bakon whan it shalbe seen unto the said Doctours and proctours expedient and behoveful for the perfourming of the covenauntes aforsaid xxiij$^{li}$. vj$^s$. viij$^d$. of lawfull money of Englond, over x$^{li}$ to the same carpenters paid in hand the day of the makyng of these presentes.

And to alle these covenauntes abovewriten on eyther partie as is abovesaid wel and truly to be holden perfourmed and kept The same parties byndeth theym eche of hem to other alternatly fast by these presentes.

# 86

## 1467 Midhurst (Sussex)

An agreement (badly torn) for the rebuilding of a water-mill. The employer is to provide the materials, but the wright is responsible for sawing up the oaks and working the stone supplied, and for the cost of diverting the water and ramming the banks, &c. The work is to be done, for £11. 13s. 4d., in about six months, the actual setting up of the mill not to take more than 5 weeks from the time of pulling down the old mill. If any defects occur (presumably within a certain time-limit), the wright shall make them good; he, with two sureties, gives a bond for 20 marks for performance of the contract.

Anct. Deeds (P.R.O.), D. 2747.

This endentur made the viij$^{th}$ day of Nouembr' the vij$^{th}$ yere of Kyng Edward the fourth bytwyxt Humfrey Bohun knyght of that[2] on parte and Nicholas Wykford of the other parte Witnesseth that the forseid Humfrey hathe made a

---

[1] *leyrn stood*: king-post.          [2] The initial *th* is written throughout as þ.

couenant w$^t$ the seid Nicholas that the seid Nichs. shall new make well and
sufficiently the Tymbr' brigge of the Northmille of Midhurst and all the North
Mille the Malt Mille and the Corne Mille all of new tymbr' atte his owne costes
and expences Except the whele of the Corne Mille cogwhele Waterwhele and
Rongbeme¹ and except the two mele silles² of the Waterwerke. And the seid S'
Humfrey shall fynde to the seid Nichs. trees of oke redy caryed to the seid Mille
ynow to make the seid werk w$^t$ And the seid Nichs. shall [     ] the seid trees at
his owne costes and expences. And the forseid s' Humfrey shall fynde lyme ston
yrewerke and cley redy [     ] seid Mille. Except the seid Nichs. shall [     ] the
ston and werke it all atte his owne costes and expences, torne the water, ram [     ]
werkes and all other charges for to do att his costes and expences. And the seid
Mille and Brigge to be made redy to go well and sufficiently by Witsonday next
comyng. And [     ] the seide mille shall be new made and sette uppe and be a
settynge uppe redy to go but v wekes after tyme the olde Mille [     ]. And for
the seide werke the forseid S' Humfrey shall pay to the seid Nichs. xvij markes
vj s. viij d. [     ] the fest of Crystemasse next comyng liij s. iiij d. the furst day
of Marche then next [     ] and the residewe of the said xvij s. iiij d. when the
said [     ]. And also if the seid werke fayle in watterwerke or any other thyng
w$^t$ [     ] werke so broken atte his owne costes and charges shall sufficiently make
[     ]. The seid Nich. John atte Rye and Thomas Andrew be bound by ther
obli[     ] S' Humfrey in xx markes to be payed to the seid S' Humfrey atte the
seid [     ] grauntett by these presentes If the seid Nich. well sufficiently make
and kepe [     ] the seid obligacion be voyde. In to Witnesse wherof the forseid
partyes haue putte [     ]. Yeven the day and yere aboueseid.

# 87

*1476 Broxbourne (Herts.)*

Agreement with a mason to lengthen the south aisle of the church eastwards, making a
new pillar and arch between it and the chancel. He is also to make, under this arch, a sunk
tomb and over it the sides of a table-tomb, ornamented with quatrefoils and shields, to carry
a marble slab; also, at the east end of the aisle, a sunk tomb, over which is to be laid a marble
slab. The employer is to provide all material and to pay him £24, in three instalments.

Anct. Deeds (P.R.O.), D. 2638.

This indenture made the xxv$^{th}$ daye of June th xvj$^{th}$ yere of the reigne of Kyng
Edward the iiij$^{th}$ betwen S' John Say Knyght on the oon partye and Robert Stowell
fremazon on the other partye. Wittenessith that the seyd Robert Stowell hath
taken bargaynned w$^t$ the seyd John Saye knyght to performe and make on yle
of Stone Werke and breke in all that belongyth to masonry w$^t$ boterasses convenient and sufficient to the same on the south syde in the parisshe churche of

---

¹ *Rongbeme* = the beam on which are the 'rungs' into which the cogs of the wheels fit.
² *mele silles*: meaning obscure.

Brokesborn in the Countye of Hertford, that is to saye to performe the seid yle to thend of the high awter in lenght after the brede that the seyd Ile is now w$^t$ a wyndow of iij lightes to be set on the same syde. And the wyndow that now standyth in the Este Ende of the seid yle to be taken down and sette up ayen in the Este Ende of the same. Also the seyd Robt. shall make a new pilo$^r$ and an arche on the south syde of the high awter under nethe that arche to make a Cestren[1] and a Tombe of Fre Stone [? vij] fote of lenght at the lest and [ij and *interlined*] an halff of brede and ij fote of height or more as it can be thought good by thadvyce of a marbler w$^t$ moldyng therupon and a range of caters[2] and sco-chyns[3] to be made to ley a stone of marbyll therupon. Also he shall make another Cestren afor the awter of the same the for to leye a marbyl stone upon to be leyd flat upon the ground. It' the seyd Robt. shall do digge Trenches for the Funda-cyons of y$^e$ seyd werk at his costes and expences. And the seyd S' John Say shall fynd at his own coste and expenc' all maner of stuff of stone lyme sond and breke skaffoldes and sentrys[4] w$^t$ the caryage of the same that the seyd Robt. be not lette of his warkemanshipp at noo tyme. And the seyd S' John Say shall geve to the seyd Robt. for warkemanshipp xxiiij li. of lawfull money of Englond that is to say viij li. or that he begynne on the seyd werk, and viij li. whan he begynneth to sette, and the other viij li. at thend of the werk as he shall haue nede therof. In wittenesse wherof the partyes aboue sayd to thise present Indenturez entre-chaungeably haue putte y'e Sealles. Youen the daye and yer aboue seyd.

88

*1477 Bramber Bridge (Sussex)*

William Waynflete, Bishop of Winchester, contracts with a mason to hew and work 100 loads of stone, to be used in the piers of the bridge, of which he shall pull down all that is defective. For this he shall have £19; if more than the hundred loads is used he shall have 3s. 8d. a load for the extra, if less the Bishop shall have 3s. 8d. for each load unused. The Bishop shall have the stone carried and shall provide scaffolding, &c.; and shall also pay 10d. for every load, of 15 feet, of the old stone reused.

Magdalen Coll. deeds, 'Bramber', 16.

This indentur made the xx day of Aprill the xvii yer of the reigne of Kyng Edward the iiij$^{th}$ betwene the Reuerent Fadre in god William Bisshop of Wyn-chestr' on that oon partie and John Cowp[er] of Wynchestr' mason on that othir party Witnessith that the said John shall before the fest of the Assumpčon of our Lady next comyng scapul and hew sufficiantly and warkmanly a c lode of stone euery lode conteynyng xvj fote of stone of a quarr in the Ile of Wight callid Gurnard quarr, and sette sufficiently and warkmanly, and fille the said c lode of stone in dyuers pillers of Bramburue Brigge in the Counte of Sussex in suche places of the said wark as is most nedefull. And also serche trewly and pulle downe

---

[1] *cestren*: a steined grave, like a cistern.      [2] *caters*: quatrefoils.
[3] *scochyns*: shields.      [4] *sentrys*: centerings.

alle that shalbe necessarye of the said pillers. For the whiche c lode of stone so scapuld sette and filled and for the othir couenaunce aforsaid the said Bisshop shall pay unto the said John xix[li] of lawfull money of Engelond. And also the said Bisshop shalmake to be caryed the said c lode of stone fro the said quarre unto the said Brigge, and fynde and make to be caryed, lyme sonde and timbr' for scafoldes as much as shalbe necessarye for the said wark to the said Brigge. Moreouer the said John shall sette and fille sufficiauntly and warkmanly in the said pillers as muche of the olde stone of the said pillers as wille sufficiauntly serue in the said wark. And the said Bisshop shall pay to the said John for euery lode of the said olde stone, conteynyng xv fote, so suffycyanly and werkmanly sette and fillid x[d]. Ferthermor the said John shall scapull and hew and sette and fille sufficiently and werkmanly in the said pillers as much of the said new stone as shalbe nedefull for makyng of the said pillers more than the said c lode. And than the said Bisshop shall pay unto the said John for euery lode stone so scapullid hewid sette and fulfilled as afore said more than the said c lode iij[s]. viij[d]. and for the caryage of the said stone. Moreover it shalbe lawful for the said Bisshop to receyue in his owyn handes iij[s]. viij[d]. for euery lode of the said hundrid lode of stone that is not occupyed in makyng of the said pillers. In witnesse wherof the parties aforesaid to these endentures enterchaungeable haue putt ther sealis, the day and yere aforesaid.

Also the said John hath receyuyd y[e] said day of the said Bisshop in parte payment of the said xix[li]—xl[s]. xx[d].

# 89

*1478/9 Bramber Bridge*

The same mason acknowledges receipt of payment for work already done on the bridge, and undertakes to hew and work as much stone as shall be needed to complete it, and to carry out the necessary repairs, for 20 marks and a gown.

Magdalen Coll. deeds, 'Bramber', 12.

This indentur made the ix day of Januar the xviij[th] yer of Kyng Edward the iiij[th] bitwene the Reuerende fadr' in god William Bisshop of Winchestr' on the oon partie and John Cowp[er] of the Citee of Winchestr' mason on the othir partie. Witnessith that the said John hath receyued of the said Bisshop the day aforsaid iiij[li]. vj[s]. viij[d]. of lawfull money in fulle payment and contentacon for all the labour and crafte of masonry doon before the vj day of Januari laste passid be the said John and his assignes in and uppon a Brigge callid Brambr' brigge in the Counte of Sussex, the peris vautis archis and wallis of the said Brigge or to the said brigge adioynyng and in and upon a chapell and the priory of Seale,[1] xiij[s]. iiij[d] except which remaynethe to be paied to the said John. Moreouer the present indentur barith witnes that the said Bisshop and John hath couenaunted and agreed

---

[1] The chapel on the bridge had belonged to the suppressed Priory of Sele, which the Bishop had acquired for the endowment of Magdalen College.

in the maner and forme after wretyn, that is to say that the said John shalle scapule and hewe sufficiently and warkmanly asmoche stone as is and shalbe nedeful for the sufficiant reparacon and amendyng of the said brigge peris vautez archis and wallis w$^t$ crestis as well at a quarr' in the Counte of Sussex and at a quarr' in the Isle of Wyght ouer xl lode of stone ther paied for for the hewyng and scapulyng by the said Bisshop and xx$^{ti}$ lode tobe paied fore by the said Bisshop, such quarres as be appoynted by the said Bisshop as at and beside the said Brigge. And also serche truly and pulle downe alle that is nedefull of the said Brigge peris vautis archis and wallis aforesaid. And moreouer welle truly sufficiantly and warkemanly hewe sette and fulfill alle stonys that be nedefull to be sett in or uppon the said Brigge peris vautez archis and wallis aforesaid. And also make to repeyr and sufficiently to amende alle that is nedefull to be amended be crafte and labours in and uppon the said Brigge peris vautez archis and walles befor the feste of Seynt Michael the Archaungell next comyng. For the which couenauntes and labour afore rehersid well truly sufficiantly and warkemanly doon and performed by the said John or his assignes, The said Bisshop grauntith to pay to the said John or to his assignes xx$^{ti}$ mrc. of lawfull money of Englond and a gowne. And also the said Bisshop at his coste and charge shalle fynde and make to be caryed alle the said stonne so scapuled and hewed lyme sonde ropis nayles and tymbr' for scafaldes and centrons asmuch as shalbe nedefull for the said warke to the said Brigge. In witnesse wherof the partes aforsaid to these indentures enterchaungeably haue sette to their sealys on Waltham the day and yer aforesaid.

## 90

*1478 Exeter*

Agreement by a mason to build a malt-house, 20 ft. by 14 ft., of two stories, with mud walls on stone sleeper walls, and a roof of 3 crucks; also to make a drain to carry the water from a brewhouse behind into the street. For this he shall have £8, in three instalments. He gives a bond of £10 for performance of contract.

Anct. Deeds (P.R.O.), A. 11545.

This indentur made bytwene Alexander Sedman of the ton party And Willyam Glydon mason of the tother party Wyttenessyth that hit is agreed appoynted and accorded that the said Willyam shall make or do to be made a new hous callid a Malthous wythyn a tenement of the said Alisander sette and billed[1] wyhowt southyate of the Cite of Exceter over ayenst Wynardis almyshous by Mychell-masse next comyng af the date of this present indentur which hous shall conteyng in the lengyth wythyn the wallys xx fote and yn brede xiiij fote whych wallys shal be ij fote aboue grond of lyme and stone and other x fote of mudwalle and uppon the same a sufficiaunt Roffe of iij Coopyll' and euery Copyll to the Stonne-

---

[1] *billed*: built.

werke[1] a Midell Flore with ij new lyren[2] a stare and doris and wendowys to the same competent of the new takyng all maner stuffe beyng wythyn the said hous and all maner New tymber necessary to the same by the deliuerans of the officiars of the said Alexander, and [?ouer this] that said Willyam shal make a Gutter to conuey all Waters from the vttermere part (?) a brewhous there in to the strete takyng for his labur stuff and workemanship of the premiss' viij[li]. at iij payments to be paid that to wete at Selyng of this Indentur iiij marc and myddys of his worke iiij marc and at the ende of his worke marke (*sic*) to the wiche couenauntz well and truly to be kept and performed I the forsaid Willyam bynd me myne heyris and myne executours to the forsaid Alisaunder in x[li]. of lafull mony of England by the presentes In to wittenes where of the partyes abouesaid to these present Indentures interchaunchably haue putt to ther sealez. Yeven the xxvj[th] daye of Aprill yn the xviij[th] yere of the reygn of Kyng Edward the iiij[th].

## 91

*1479 Nottingham*

Two (carpenters) undertake to build a house, on the lines of another recently built, to be finished within a year, under penalty of £10. For this they shall have £6, in three instalments.

*Recs. of Nottingham*, ii. 389.

This indenture made the fest of Scent Marget the Vergyn, in the ʒere and regne of Kyng Edward the iiij[the] the xix[the], betwex William Hurst of Notyngham, on that on' party, and Pers Hydes and Roger Hydes, of Lenton, on that oyer party, wytnesyth, that the said Pers Hydes and Roger hath takun a howse to make of the seid William, whereuppon the seid Pers and Roger schalle fynde alle maner tymber to the seid howse belongyng, with lates[3] to the seid howse, and make ij bay wyndows to the same, with alle other square wyndows belongyng to the seid howse; and the seid howse schalle conteyne of bred within the wallys xviij fote, and in lenght as myche as the grownde wyth in his smythe ʒerd, and in alle maner proporcion accordyng as the new howse of John Tauerner that William Roodes made ys; and yat the seid howse be fenysshit, reryd and made upp betwix this and Whitsonday next foloyng, uppon the payne of forfeture of x[li]. And more ouer, the seid William Hurst schalle pay to the seid Pers and Roger Hydes for makyng of the seid howse vj lb. of lawfulle money of Yngland at serten tymes, that is to say, at the seylyng of this present wrytyng xxx[s]., and when the tymber his hewyn and begon to frame xxx[s]., and when hyt coms whom xxx[s]., and when the work is fenysshit xxx[s].

In wytnes here of eyder party to odur hathe sett yer syels. Yeuen the day and yere abouesaid.

[1] As the 'couples', or principal rafters, were carried down to the stonework they must have been in the nature of crucks.

[2] *lyren*: liernes, or cross-beams.

[3] *lates*: laths.

## 92

*1483  Gloucester*

A carpenter undertakes to build a house, 47 ft. by 15 ft., with two lofts, supplying the necessary oak timber, in 3 months, for £14.

*Hist. MSS. Com. Rep.* xii (9), 416.

This indenture made at Glouc' the xx$^{ti}$ day of Junij in the yere of the reigne of Kyng Edward the Fifte after the Conquest the first, bitwen Richard Russel, John Hartland th'elder, William Cole and Robert Coffe, Stiwardes of the Towne of Gloucester, of the one partie and David Sammesbury carpenter of the other partie, witnessith that bitwix the same parties it is covenaunted in this wise: that is to wete, the said Davy bitwen the date of this present writing and the fest of Seynt Mighell the Archangell then next ensuyng shall worche and of the newe make an house by the Blacke Freris Yate in Glouc' aforseid upon the grounde of the comon rente conteynyng in lengthe xlvij fete in brede xv fete, all the tymber sufficiant and of oke, the sillez of a fote square, the postez in heighte of xviij fete and every post a fote square, the walplates of thiknes ix and x unchis, bitwen every giste x unche, with byndyng bemes and rafters sufficiantly and able behovefull to the same worke, the pynnyons[1] next to the Freris and afore strete of standard werke; and also shall make in the same house ij loftes sufficiantly bordid, the gistis of viij unche in brede and x in thiknes, and also all maner wyndowes, steiris, dores, bulkis[2] with stodes and pentise to the same werke, and all other thynges shall fynde that in any wise is belongyng to carpenters crafte nedefull to the seid werke and to fynde all stuffe and tymber of oke, behovefull to the performyng of the seid werke; for all whiche to be don and performed in maner and forme afore rehercid, the seid stiwardis shall paye or make to be paid xiiij$^{li}$ of laufull money of Englond unto the seid Davy, his executours or assignez.

## 93

*1484  Wainfleet (Lincs.)*

Agreement by a carpenter to make for the chapel and school (founded by Bishop Waynflete) a (combined) roof and floor,[3] 70 ft. by 20 ft., with doors, windows, desks, and other fittings. The floor to be made like one at Esher, and the roof to be of 7 bays. For this he shall have £25. 13s. 4d. and cloth for a gown, or 6s. 8d.

*Chandler, Life of Waynflete,* 369.

This Indenture made the xxv day of Aprill, the yere of the reigne of Kyng Richarde the thirde the furst, betwene the reverend fader in god William Busshop of Winchestre on the oon party, and Henry Alsbroke of Tateshall in the Counte of Lincoln Carpenter on the other party, Witnesseth that the seid Henry hath

---

[1] *pynnyons*: gables.

[2] *bulkis*: balks, or horizontal timbers, as opposed to the 'stodes'—studs, or uprights.

[3] From the particulars, this seems to be a middle floor, the under side being the roof, or ceiling, of the lower room.

covenaunted agreid and bargayned and by these presents graunteth to make for
the seid R. fader at Waynflete in the seid Counte of Lincoln, a flore with a Rofe
of Tymber of good herte of ooke conteyning in lengthe lxx foote, and in brede
within the walles xx<sup>ti</sup> foote with dores windowes steyres hynches[1] reredoses[2]
desks and all other thyngs necessarye that longeth to carpentry werk for a Chapell
and Scolehous to be made within the seid towne of Waynflete and the seid flore
shalbe well and sufficiently made aftur the patron and facyon of the flore of the
chambyr in the Towre on[3] the gate of the manor of Essher in the Counte of
Sotherey and the forseid Rofe to be of vij bayes every bay frome the midds of
the beme shall conteyne x foote in lengthe, and every raffter shalbe xx<sup>ti</sup> foote in
lengthe vj inches in brede and vj inches in thicknes. And the overpurlyon[4] for the
seid flore shalbe of herte of ooke and of inch and quarter thicknes dry and wrought:
for all which tymber stuff and borde necessarye to the same werke beyng of herte
of ooke with the cariage of the same and for all maner of warkmanship nedefull
to be doon by Carpenters in the foreseid werk wele and warkmanly doon set up
and finesshed the seid R. fader shall pay unto the seid Henry by the hand of maister
John Gygur Warden of Tateshall or his assignes xxv<sup>li</sup>. xiij<sup>s</sup>. iiij<sup>d</sup>. and a gown cloth
or ells vj<sup>s</sup>. viij<sup>d</sup>. for a gown cloth. In witnes wherof the parties aboveseid to these
Indentures enterchaungeably have put to ther seales the day and yere aboveseid.

## 94

*1484 Kirklington (Yorks.)*

A vague agreement by two carpenters to build certain rooms.

Whitaker, *Richmondshire*, ii. 146.

This indente, made ye xxviii daye of July ye 2<sup>nd</sup> yere of ye reigne of our
sov'aigne Lorde Richarde ye Thirde, betwixt J. Wandesforde Esquier, on yat
oon p'tye, and John Wryghte and . . . of Richmonde, wryghtes, on yat oth' p'ty,
beryth witness yat ye forseide Jhon Wandesforde hathe agreede w<sup>t</sup> ye forseide
Jhon Wryghte . . . for ye makynge of oon newe place of square,[5] contenynge
xvij yerdes and di' yerde in ye lengthe, and x yerdes in brede, w<sup>t</sup>in ye which place
of sqware shal be conteneyede two p'lores, oon w<sup>t</sup> draghte, oon pantry and butry,
oon larder or two, four chawm'es,[6] two w<sup>t</sup> draghtes, and oon kechyn to bee made
suffyciently and fynyshed in all kynde of wryghte w'ke upon ye costes and charges
of ye seide wryghtes, except oon lawe baye window, ye which shal bee made att
ye charge of ye seide Jhon Wandesforde.

And also it is agreed that ye seid John Wandesford shall paye unto the seide
Jhon Wryghte, &c., vj<sup>li</sup>. xiij<sup>s</sup>. iv<sup>d</sup>.

[1] *hynches*: ? 'bynches', i.e. benches.
[2] *reredoses*: probably panelling behind the benches.
[3] *on*: probably a misreading for 'ou(er)'.
[4] *overpurlyon*: a purlin, running longitudinally over the 'rafters' or crossbeams.
[5] *place of square*: possibly, part of a house built round a courtyard?
[6] *chawm[er]es*: chambers.

## 95

*1485/6 Tattershall College*

A carpenter agrees to construct, out of the timbers of a house pulled down and other new timber supplied, an almshouse, 172 ft. by 19 ft., and 16 ft. in height to the top of the wall-plate. There shall be a gallery on the south side, on pillars, with a porch towards the church-yard and a door at the other end; also, 13 separate chambers, each with two windows; a hall, with a buttery; and two staircases; also a chapel. He shall make the floor of the chambers, which shall be 3 feet higher over the hall and chapel, and other fittings. He shall cut down the timbers of the old roof to fit this new building. For all this he shall have £16, by weekly instalments. Mutual bonds of 40 marks for performance of contract.

Penshurst MS., T. 6.

This indenture made at Tateshale the xiiij[th] day of Januarye the first yere of the reigne of the kinge our souerain lorde Henry the vij[th] betwix Maister John Gigur Wardeyn of the College of Tateshale of that oon partie and Henry Halsebroke of the same town Carpenter of that oyere partie Witnessith y[t] it is couenaunted and aggreed betwix the parties afforsaid y[t] ye said Henry Halsebroke at his own propre costes and charge shall mak or do to be made wele and warkmanly of a grete hous late bought and brought frome Saint Mary Tidde and oyere tymbre necessarye to him to be deliuered all the wright crafte and sawing of tymber and bord of a bedehous[1] by him to be sett up upon a grounde annexed to ye chirchyerde of the parisshe chirche of Tateshale of this half the fest of Pentecost next commyng conteynyng in length clxxij fote by the kynges yerde be the said grete hous more or lesse and in widnesse and brede at the grounde w[t]in the walles xix fote, the poste yereof conteynyng in length xvj fote to the ouerside of the panne. W[t] a galary to be made w[t]in the said hous upon the south side hauyng in euery bay xiiij[th] substanciall pillers of tymbre w[t] a goodly enhaunce[2] clenly and warkmanly wrought and made according to the co[mun]icacion in tyme past hadde. W[t] a conuenient appendice[3] of tymbre and borde rynnyng the length of ye said galary of the brede of a fote and asmuch more as shall seme necessarie and according, also a porche standing iiij fote w[t]out ye said galary toward the chirchyerde w[t] a dore of ij leves to be made in ye same. An oyere dore to be made towarde ye westende of the said galary. Also xiij seuerell chaumbres to be made for xiij bedemen in ye same hous w[t] dornes and walles according. Moreouere an hall w[t] lightes and windous in the same, the chambre flore ouer the same to be risinge and enhaunced higher by iij fote yan ye chambre flore yerunto annexed, euery chamber of the same xiij chambres to haue ij windous, either windowe to be of ij lightes of a competent hight, hauyng a botery ioyned to ye same hall w[t] a thurgh entre[4] upon y[t] oon side going into ye gardeyn. Also two greses where of oon going up to ye Garnere and an oyere chambre beside it and an oyere to the chambre ordeyned and p[r]posed for the parissh preste and an oyere man, the same greses to be keuered

---

[1] *bedehous*: almshouse.   [2] *enhaunce*: rise.
[3] *appendice*: pentice.   [4] *thurgh entre*: way through.

ouere thenn (*sic*) by the said Henry. Also a Chapell to be made in ye estende of the saide bedehous hauyng the chambre rising higher by iij fote than the other chambre flores yerunto adioyned according to ye chambre flore ouere the hall w$^t$ a fair windowe in the estende of iij or v lightes and an other of the north side as shall seme according by Richard Parker Baillif of Tateshale. Also the said Henry shall make or do to be made the wright crafte and sawing of tymbre of the chambre flore rynnyng in length thurghout all the said Bedehous w$^t$ somers and gistes according w$^t$ v pynnyon[1] walles rising up to ye rofe of the same hous, hauyng soles entertaces and stothes[2] necessarie, iij seges[3] to be made of tymbre bynethe and aboue in the said chambres where as shall seme most necessarye and according. And also many mantiltres for chymnes as shalbe expedient for the same. Forthermore ye said Henry shall make and of newe cutt or do to be made and cutted shorter and narrower all the bandes postes balkes and sparres w$^t$ oyere thinges apperteynyng to ye rofe of the same hous whatsoeuer here not named and frame them agayn as shall seme most behouefull and profitable for the same by the aduyse and ouere sight of the said wardeyn and Bailiff of Tateshale, the sparres raised and sett up to haue substanciall fete rynnyng ouere ye panne peces[4] of the same hous and mighty eves borde to be sawen at the costes of the said Henry, the walles of the said hous in lyke case and forme to be splinted[5] by the aforenamed Henry w$^t$ soles entertaces and mighty stothes according, and dores and windows to be made and closed after him w$^t$ euery other thing except yern werke[6] to yem belonging. To haue take and perceyue to the said Henry Halsebroke for the afornamed werke connyngly craftely and warkmanly by him and his in manere and forme aboue writen to be wrought and sett up xvj$^{li}$ sterlinges by the handes of the said Wardeyn and his assignes yereunto by him deputed and assigned, yat is to say at euery wekes ende asmuch money as shall seme according and answeryng to ye same wekes warke, so that by the same warke be perfitely fynysshed and sett up the said xvj$^{li}$. to be paid and fully content. To ye which covenauntes of bothe parties wele and truely firme and stabilly to be kept and holden aswell the said Wardeyn as the said Henry Halsebroke bindes yem yere heires and executo$^r$s either to oyere in xl marcs sterlinges. In witnes wherof the parties afforsaid to yies indentures enterchaungeably haue putt yere seales. The place daye and yere abouesaid.

[1] *pynnyon*: gable. Presumably, three of these walls were carried up (? on each side of the hall, and on the inner side of the chapel) into the roof, inside the house.

[2] *soles, entertaces and stothes*: sills, ties, and studs.

[3] *seges*: 'siege-houses', or privies.

[4] *panne peces*: wallplates.

[5] *splinted*: provided with uprights for wattling.

[6] *yern work*: ironwork.

## 96

*1485/6 Newark Bridge (Notts.)*

A carpenter undertakes to build a new bridge of 12 arches of oak—the scantlings of the various timbers being specified. Also to make posts and rails along it, and to set up a cross in the middle. He shall provide the timber and complete the work within 6 months, for £40. The men of the town undertake to carry the timber, to provide all necessary stone, lime, &c.; and also to build at each end a stone bridgehead for its defence. Mutual bonds of 100 marks.

*Lincoln Diocese Docts.* (E.E.T.S.), 256.

This indenture tripartite, made the [*blank*] day of marche the furst yere of the Reigne of Kyng Henry the vij[th], berith witnesse that wherupon the faileng of the brigge of the town of Newark fast bi the Castell ther in the Countie of Notyngham nowe late happened bi gret rage [of] water flodes, and soe John Philipot, now Alderman, other wise called John Philipot draper, John Calcrofte, Andrew Kelome, William Camme, and William Dawes, in the name of them self and of all other inhabitants of the said towne of Newerk, the ix[th] day of this presente moneth of Marche, [appealed to the Bishop of Lincoln, who promised 100 marks for the rebuilding of the bridge.] Wherupon it hath be aggreed graunted couenaunted accorded and bargayned bi twen the said Alderman and his brethren of the one side and one Edward Downes Carpenter of the parroch of Wyrksop in the Comitie of Notyngham of the other side for the making of the said brigge in maner and fourme as foloweth. The said Edward Downes hath bargayned accorded and couenaunted with the said Alderman and inhabitants of Newerk aforsaid, and they with hym, that the same Edward bi the grace of god hath taken upon hym and graunteth to make, at his owne custes and expenses, of newe tymbre of good and sufficient oke, a brigge of the west side of the Castell of Newerk of xij Arches, euery sele tre[1] under the water wherupon euery post shall stonde to be of square di' a yerd or more and in lenght according to the warke, every post in brede xiiij ynche and in thyknes xij ynche and in height according to the olde brigge, euery somer tre upon the postes heedes in brede di' a yerd and in length a fote longer than the brede of the old brigge. Also euery giste tre of square xij ynche and more, and euery plauncher of thiknes iiij ynche with the bandes accordyng to the same tymber. Also the said Edward shal make of newe tymber, ouer the said Arches, railes upon both sides of the brigge with the postes of ij yerdes of length for the kepyng of the bordres of the said brigge, with a crosse of tymbre to be sot in the myddes of the said brigge. And euery Arche to haue a fense tre[2] a fore it as large as may be caried with any reasonable cariage. For the making of whiche brigge the said Edward shall fynde almaner of coste of tymber and werkmanship at his owne custes and expenses sufficiently

---

[1] *sele tre*: wooden sill.

[2] This presumably means that a massive balk is to be set upstream in front of each pier (not arch) to protect it.

to be made rered and set up of this side the fest of saynt Michell the Archaungell next comyng. For the whiche said werkmanship and tymbre bi the said Edward in fourme abouesaid to be made and finished, the said Edward shall receyue xl li. parcell of the said c marc' bi the handes of the said Alderman and other inhabi-tauntes of Newerk aforsaid. And as toucheng the residue of the same c marc' and the finisheng of the hool werk of the said brigge, the said Alderman and his brethren have taken upon them and couenaunted with the said Reuerend fadre that thei, of their propre goodes, to gedre with the said residue, shall purvey and make to be had cariage of all the said tymbre, and also the costes of stone to be digged and goten upon the ground of the said Reuerend fadre neces-sarie and to be caried to the said brigge, with all maner of other cariages custis and charges whiche shalbe done about the brigge as in cariage of clay lyme and sand grauell and pauyng upon the said brigge, and al maner of other charges to be done to the same brigge in any maner wise necessarie, except that longeth to the Carpenter aforsaid. And also, at the west ende of the said brigge, a myghty stone-werke for the defence and saufgard of the same brigge, with ij displaies goyng out of the same stonewerk,[1] of either side one, for that partie. And in like wise at the Est ende of the same brigge another myghty stonewerk, with ij displaies as is a foresaid. All the premisses, other than suche as the said Edward hath taken upon hym to make in fourme aforsaid, to be done at the custes and expenses of the said Alderman brethren and inhabitauntes afore and bi the fest of saynt An-drewe thapostell next comyng in wynter. [Mutual bonds between the Bishop, the Alderman, &c., and Edward Downes, in 100 marks.] In witnes wherof, aswele the said Reuerend fadre, as the saide Edward, John Philipot Alderman and other iiij of his brethren whiche be bounde in ij of the said obligacions, haue to eche partie of thies tripartite indentures put their seales. At Lincoln the day and yere aboue rehersed.

## 97

### *1487/8 Helmingham Church (Suffolk)*

A mason undertakes to build a tower, 60 feet high, of knapped flint, like that at Framsden, with certain features copied from Brandeston tower. He is to finish it within 10 years, working only between Whitsun and 8 September; and shall be paid 10s. for every foot in height—if the parishioners decide to have it higher than 60 feet, they shall pay accordingly. They shall have all necessary materials ready for him in the churchyard, upon due notice, and shall pay for any delay caused by their failure to do so. They undertake that no bells shall be hung in the tower until 4 years after it is finished. If any defect in the design is found during the next 20 years, he shall make it good. He and three sureties give a joint bond of

---

[1] The masonry blockhouse is to be set opposite the end of the bridge, the road being splayed on either side of it.

£40 for performance of contract. Note, that he and his men shall not damage the materials supplied for their use, and shall be economical with the freestone and knapped flint.

Bodleian Library, Tanner MS. 138, f. 87.[1]

Thys indenture made the xviij[th] day of the monyth of Februarye the iij[de] yer of the reigne of King Herry the vij[th] Betwene Thomas Aldrych of North Lopham in the Counte of Norff' mason of the oon part and John Couper of Helmyngham in the Counte of Suff' thelder, John Coup[er]e the younger, Robt. Coup[er]e theld' and Willm. May of the same town and counte of the other part. Wytnessith that the forseyd Thomas w[th] Goddes Grace shall make or do to be mayd at the west ende of the cherche of Helmyngham aforseyd a sufficient newe stepyll of lx fote of heythe after the brede wydnesse and thicknesse of the stepyll of Framesden w[t] a black wall wroughte of Flynt, and as many tables as the stepyll of Framesden hayth, so that it be mayd after the facion of the stepyll of Bramston, the west dore the lowere west wyndowe and with a place oon eche side of the s[d]. wyndowe for to sette in an ymage, and w[t] alle the other wyndowes and boteracies of the s[d]. stepyll after the facion of the stepyll of Bramston aforseyd. So that the veye[2] of the stepyll of Helmyngham be mayd on the north syde, p[r]vydyth allway that the s[d]. stepyll shall[3] be fynyshyd and endyth wythynne the terme of x yeres next comyng after the date of thes presents. And the said John John Robt. and Willm. shal paye or do to be payd to the forseyd Thomas or hese assigneye for euery fote of the rewle[4] werkyng of heythe of the same stepyll x[s]. of lawfull money of Englond to be payd at euery jorny[5] as he werkyth after the fote. And yf yt plese the said John John Robt. and Willm. for to haue the forseyd stepull of more heythe thanne lx fote, thanne the s[d] Thomas shall make or do to be mayd the s[d] stepyll as many fote heyer as they wole haue yt; taking for euery fote of heythe after the price aforeseyd. And also the s[d] John John Robt. and Willm. shall leye or do to be leyde in the chercheyard of Helmyngham aforsayd alle the freeston cauyon[6] lyme sonde bollys shovelys bokets soys and the staffe[7] bosse[8] rop herdylys stage tymbyr fernetre[9] hamfyr[10] and bords as meche as the s[d] Thomas or hese werkmen shall nede or occupye in tyme of werkyng and makyng of the s[d]. stepyle of Helmyngham, so that the said Thomas or hese assygneye shall yeue warnyng in lefull tyme afore. And yf the s[d] Thomas or hese werkemen be lettyth in ther werkyng or occupacyon be cause or defaulte

---

[1] An eighteenth-century copy. Part of it was printed, inaccurately, in *Building News*, 13 Sept. 1878.  [2] *veye*: *recte* 'vice', or stair-turret.

[3] 'shall' is written throughout 'yhall'; but I think it must be a misreading of an unusual shape of 's'.

[4] *fote of the rewle*: i.e. every foot, level all round.

[5] *jorny*: properly 'a day's work'; here apparently used vaguely for 'a period'.

[6] *cauyon*: flint, or pebbles.

[7] *soys and the staffe*: a soe is a large tub carried, by two men, on a staff.

[8] *bosse*: a mortar-hod.  [9] *fernetre*: a wooden verne, or windlass.

[10] *hamfyr*: *recte* 'haunsyr', i.e. hawser.

of any of these forseyd thinges thro the Faulte of the said John John Robt. and
Willm., thanne the s^d John John Rt. and Willm. shall paye or do to be payd to
the forseyd Thomas or hys assygneys accordyng after the tyme of her lettyng
and losse. And ferthermore the forseyd Thomas grantyth by these presents to
dyscharge the s^d. John John Robt. and Willm. for the summe of ccc^ti lib. the wich
summe the same Thomas is accordyth and agreyd to receyue as he doythe hese
werke, of these personys underwrythyn that ys to seye of John Talmage Esquyer,
Maystres Elizabeth hys wyeff, Edmond Jooce gentylman, John Wyllie thelder,
and Willm. Holm of Helmingham aforseyd,[1] And also the s^d John John Robt. and
Willm. graunten by these presents that ther shall no bellys ne belle be hangyn
in the stepyll of Helmyngham aforseyd wythynne the space of iiij yeres after
the s^d stepyll is fynyshed and endyth. And moreouer the partyes aforseyd are
accordyth that the s^d Thomas Aldrych ne hese werkmen shall not werke upon
the s^d stepyll in no tyme of the yere but betweyn the festes of Pentecoste and the
Natyvyte of our Lady V^rgyn the holle tyme aforeseyd duryng. And also yf any
defaute be found in werkemanshyp of the s^d stepyll of Helmyngham be any
manner of werkemene or werkeman or any other man of kunnyng wythynne
the space of xx^ti yeres next commyng after the date of these presents that the
s^d stepyll be not mayd suffycyently after the patronye and forme aforseyd, That
thanne the seyd Thomas shall make or do to be mayd agen the aforseyd stepyll
of Helmyngham suffycyently in all things after the patronye and forme aforseyd
wythynne as short tyme and as few yeres as the s^d stepyll yn any wyse be any
manner of werkemen may be suffycyently mayd on hys proper costs and expensys.
And moreouer yf the forseyd Thomas Aldrych all and singuler covent' of hys
part before rehersyd welle and truly observe and kepe in manner beforeseyd, That
thanne an obligacon in the whyche the same Thomas, John Wode of Debenham
in the Counte of Suff', John Sewale mason, and Thomas Sherman of the same
towne and counte husbandman, arne bound to the s^d John John Robt. and Willm.
in xl^lib. to wante hys strength and be had for nought, ellwys welyng and grantyng
the forseyd Thomas Aldrych John Wode John Sewale and Thomas Sherman that
the same obligacon abide in all hys strength and virtue. In witnesse hereof to these
present indentures the partyes beforseyd alternately haue putte ther seallys: youen
the day and yer aboueseyd.

[*on dorse* ]

Alwey sakyn that the seyd Thomas and hys werkemen thro here defaute shall
not breke ne spoile no manner of stuffe wythynne rehersyd that shall be to them
delyuyd. And also save all the blacke flint stone and fre ston to be leyd on the
stepyll wythought as ner as they may for the most avayle and best to be savyd
for the profyth of the townshyppe of Helmyngham.

---

[1] I do not understand what this reference to £300 means—unless the mason was being
employed by the persons named to build other parts of the church?

*Appendix B*

# 98 (A)[1]

*1491 Great Chesterford (Essex)*

Contract with a mason for the stonework of 8 chambers, to be 10 feet in height, rough-cast outside and plastered within, with fireplaces, for £20, in three instalments.

Berkeley Castle MS., S.C. 656.

This bill indented made the xxij day of June in the Sixte yere of the Reigne of our soueryn lord Kyng Harry the vij[th] by twene William Marquis Barkeley Erle Marshall and Notyngham and grete Marshall of Englond on the on partie And John Bury of Cambryge Mason on the other partie Witnessith that the seid Marquis hathe let a grete[2] viij chambres to be new made to the seid John w[t] all manere of mason wark, And he to fynde all manere of stuff to the seid chambres bothe stone bryke lyme and sond and all other necessariis perteyning to the seid chambres w[t]in his manere of grete Chesterford And also the foundacon of the seid viij chambres to be made x fote of high thoroughly all the stone walles aboue the ground And the seid John shall make in the seid chambres iiij dubble chymneys[3] conteyning vj fote and an half of brede w[t] viij fyers perteyning to the seid chambres and shall fynde all manere of stuf to the same excepte Mantel Trees the whiche he shall have of the seid Marquis or his assign And also the seid John shall periette the stone walles w[t]in the seid chambres and also rough cast theym w[t]oute as high as the stone walles goith and to make theym euyn for the carpenter to set their wark redely apon hit And for this doing the seid John shall haue of the seid Marquis for his masen wark xx[li] of laufull money that is to sey the seid John shall haue in hande whan he begynnyth his wark x mark' and whan he hathe half done he shall haue other x mark' and whan he hathe fenysshed hole the forseid wark and sufficiently done he shall haue the other x mark' In witnesse wherof as wele the seid Marquis as the seid John ether partie to other haue put their sealis the day and the yeare abouesaid.

# 98 (B)

Contract with a carpenter to make the timberwork of the same chambers—floors, roofs, stairs, doors, and 18 bay-windows; the upper story to project, and to be 9 feet high. To be finished in 7 months; for £43. 6s. 8d., paid in four instalments.

Berkeley Castle MS., S.C. 657.

This indentur made the vij[th] day of Julii in the yere of the Reigne of our soueryn Lord Kyng Harry the vij[th] the vj[th] yere of his Regne by twene William Marquis Barkeley Erle Marshall and Notyngham and grete Marshall of Englond on the on partie and Alewyn Newman of Cambryge carpenter on the other partie

---

[1] I am indebted to the kindness of the Earl of Berkeley for photographs of these three interesting contracts.

[2] *let a grete*: given at contract.

[3] *dubble chymneys*: flues serving two fireplaces, back to back.

Witnessith that the seid Alewyn hathe take a grete[1] and shal make viij chambres
in the manere of grete Chesterford w^t xviij Baywyndowes to be made a boue
and be nethe And by nethe to be made of vj fote of brede and v fote of high And
in the ouere chambres euery Baywyndow to be made viij fote of brede and vij
fote and an half of high and a fote bytwene euery stanchen[2] And he to make xiiij
dores to the seid chambres and to make sufficiently the shyttyng of the wyndowes
and to fynde all manere of tymbr' of carpentriwark to the seid chambres and to
borde wele and sufficiently the flores and the jistes And the seid Alewyn shall jutty
the seid chambres xviij fote[3] thoroughly, and to be made of high fro the flore to
the reysing[4] ix fote And also in all his wark to be made stode and stode rome and
to frame suerly and fayr all the Roffes that shall long to the carpenter is wark
And also all the Steyres Dores and Wyndowes that longith to the carpenter is wark
to be wele and sufficiently done And the seid carpenter shall fynyssh and make an
ende of all the carpentriwark longing to the seid chambres by the First Day of
Marche next commyng And for this done and truly performed he shall haue of
the seid Marquis for his wark and his tymbr' xliij^li. vj^s. viij^d. to be content and paide
at the daies that folowith that is to sey to haue in hand x mark' for his tymbr' and
x mark' for his wark and at Michelmasse next commyng x mark' for his wark
and at Cristemasse then next insuyng x mark' for his wark and when he hath
wele and sufficiently made an ende of his wark he shall haue xvj^li. xiij^s. iiij^d. in
the full payment of the hole somme. In Witnesse whereof as wele the seid Marquis as the seid Alewyn ether to other haue putte their sealys the day and the
yere a boue seid.

## 98 (C)

Contract with the same mason as (A) for the tiling and ceiling of the new buildings.
To be finished within 6 months; for 23 marks, half at the beginning of the work and half
when completed.

Berkeley Castle MS., S.C. 658.

This indentur made the xj day of Decembr' in the vij^th yere of the Reigne of
our soueryn lord Kyng Henry the vij^th by twene William Marquis Barkeley
Erle Marshall and Notyngham and grete Marshall of Englond on the on partie
and John a Bury of Cambryge mason on the other partie Witnessith that the seid
John shall wele and sufficiantly tyle all the newe howses w^tin the manere of grete
Chesterford and sele all the roffes of the seid new chambres fyndyng all manere
of stuff longing therto that is to sey tyle lyme and sond wallyng dawbyng lathing
and pynnyng of all the walles and roffes and all necessariis to the same perteyning
at his own propur costes and charges And whan the seid John begynnith his wark
he shall haue of the seid Markes xj mark' vj^s. viij^d. in hande and whan he hathe
done all the seid wark wele and sufficiently he shall haue other xj mark' vj^s. viij^d.

---

[1] *a grete*: a contract.
[2] *stanchen*: upright, or mullion.
[3] *xviij fote*: presumably a s'. for '18 inches'.
[4] *reysing*: wall-plate.

And this to be truly performed and done by the fest of Sent John Baptist next commyng at the furdist that the seid Markes may enter into the seid manere to dwell w^toute eny defaute in the which premisses the seid John is bounde wele and truly and sufficiently to performe and do hit on his behalf. In witnesse wherof as wele the seid Markes as the seid John ether partie to other haue putte ther sealys the day and the yere aboue seid.

## 99

*1492/3  St. Martin's in the Fields (Middx.—now London)*

This contract is attached to a deed by which the Abbot and Convent of Westminster let to John Noreys for 44 years a messuage and cottage at Charing Cross abutting on the wall of the garden of the 'Mewes' on the north, St. Martin's Lane on the east, the highway on the south, and land belonging to St. Mary of 'Bedelem' outside Bishopsgate on the west. He is to build a messuage as described in the contract and to furnish it with a great copper (*plumbum in fornace*), another, with a brass bottom, called a 'groute lede', a 'taptrough' of lead, a mashtub (*messheton*), two 'yeletonnes', a 'taphose cum le tapstaf', 30 'kymlyns', 32 'kilderkyns', 12 'ferkynes', a quarter measure, and a horse-mill.

By the contract two carpenters undertake to build (*a*) a brewhouse, 31 feet in length, of oak timber of which the scantlings are given; (*b*) a 'cross-house' between the (existing) stable and bakehouse, 27 feet long, adjoining the new brewhouse on the south and standing on a brick wall on the north. Doors, windows, and stairs to be supplied where required. The whole to be completed within 4 months, for £8. 13s. 4d.

Westminster Abbey Muniments, 17178.

This endenture made the ij^de day of Marche in the viij yere of the Reigne of Kyng Herry the vij^th bitwene John Norys of Eybury in the countie of Midd' yoman of the one partie and Richard Wareyn and Nicholas Halywode of the towne of Westm' in the countie of Midd' carpenters of the other partie Witnesseth that the forsaid John hath made a full and fast bargayn w^t the said Richard and Nicholas that is to say that the same Richard and Nicholas by the grace of God shall make or do to be made an new house called A Brewhouse conteyning in length xxxj fete of assise and shalbe set beside Charyngcrosse in the parisshe of Seint Martyn w^tin the ten'te or Inne of the said John called the Rose. And the said Brewhouse shalbe made of good and sufficient tymber of oke and of the heigth of the old house that it shall adioyn unto. And the groundsilles of the same house shalbe viij ynches thikke, and euery principall post therof shalbe x ynches one way and ix ynches another way. And all the resons peces[1] therof shalbe vij ynches one way and vj ynches another way. And all the entertresses[2] of the same shalbe made of sufficient tymber of oke, and in like wise all the punchons that stande on the outeside of the same house to the wetherwardes shalbe made of oke, and the two principall somers of the same house also shalbe made of oke. And all the joystes therof shalbe made of sufficient oke, and the space betwixt euery joyste shalbe xij ynches and made of sufficient tymber of oke, and euery

---

[1] *resons peces*: wall-plates.　　　　　　　　[2] *entertresses*: ties, or braces.

joyste shalbe v ynches thikke and made of good and sufficient tymber of oke. And all the bordes concernyng to the same shalbe made of sufficient borde of oke. And the roof of the same house shalbe purloyned[1] and made all of sufficient tymber of oke and the space bitwixt euery rafter shalbe of xiiij ynches. And the crosse house bitwixt the stable and the bakhouse shal conteyn in lengthe xxvij fete of assise and shalbe made after the scantlon as the other house is made. And the north side of that house shall stonde upon a brekewall, and the southe side therof shall adioyn to the southe[2] side of the other new house w$^t$ a sufficient dormaunde[3] upon the stable. And the rome of the same Crossehouse where the fire (*sic*) shalbe made all of sufficient oke. And in likewise shalbe thorough w$^t$ borde of oke. And the dores and wyndowes of bothe houses necessary shalbe made and steires concernyng to them where need is shalbe wele and competently made. And all the particions of the same howses where as nede is in like wise shalbe sufficiently made. And as for the making of the Ale Joystes[4] the tymber therof shalbe at the charge and fyndyng of the said John Noreys. And ouer this the forsaid Richard and Nicholas shall at theire propre costis fynde almaner of tymber and werkmanship concernyng or belongyng to the forsaid ij houses. And graunten also and bynd them and either of them by these presentes to the same John and his assignes that the same ij houses shalbe fully fynysshed made and set uppon the grounde by the fest of Mydsomer next comyng after the date herof. And the said John Norys and his assignes shalbe (*sic*) pay or do to be paid unto the forsaid Richard and Nicholas or to theire assignes for the making workmanship and settyng up of the said ij howses viij$^{li}$. xiij$^s$. iiij$^d$. sterlinges. Wherof v$^{li}$. xiij$^s$. iiij$^d$. therof is paid in hand at the sealyng of thes endentures. And iij$^{li}$. the residue shalbe paid unto them by the said John whan the said ij houses ar fully fynysshed made and set up. In witnesse whereof the parties abouesaid to these present endentures enterchaungeably haue sett theire seales the day and yere abouesaid.

### IOO

*1495/6 Westminster Abbey*

A blacksmith undertakes to make the ironwork—transom-bars, uprights, and stay-bars—for two windows in the tower of the 'New Work' at the Abbey, under the direction of the warden of the masons. He is to be paid at the rate of 1½$d$. per pound weight of iron used. He finds two sureties in £40 for the due performance of the work.

I am indebted to Mr. John Harvey for calling my attention to this.

Westminster Abbey muniments, 31804.

This endenture made bitwene John by the sufferance of God Abbot of the monasterie of Seint Petir of Westm' on that one partie and Symond Smyth of the towne of Westm' in the countie of Midd' blacksmyth on that other partie

---

[1] *purloyned*: provided with purlins.
[2] 'southe' must be a slip for 'north'.
[3] *dormaunde*: a sleeper, or girder.
[4] *Ale Joystes*: presumably the gantries on which the ale-barrels lie.

Witnesseth that the seid Symond hath made couenaunt and hym byndeth by the endenture for to make or do to be made ij fermentes[1] of iron for the two wyndowes of the steple in the New Werk of the seid monastery wele and werkmanly before the fest of Penticost next comyng after the date herof. And the transumpt barres of the seid wyndowes to be made in lengthe iiij fote iij ynches. And in bignes according to a patron made and deliuered to the seid Symond. And also he shall make standardes and steybarres after suche substance in bignesse as shalbe shewed unto hym by the Wardeyn of the masons with the seid monastery. For the which fermentes wele sufficiently and werkmanly to be made and wrought the seid Abbot shall content and pay or do to be contented and paied unto the seid Symond or to his assignes for euery lb. j d. ob. in suche fourme as foloweth that is to say in hande at the sealing of this endenture v$^{li}$. And when the seid fermentes ben fully made and fynysshed the the seid Symond to be paide of as moche as after the rate can by indifferent weight to hym be founde due. And whereas the seid Symond, John Fanne of the towne of Westm' forsaid cooke, and Alisaunder Liddell of the same towne surgeonbarbour by their obligacion bering date the day of making herof ben bound unto the seid Abbot in xl$^{li}$. of good and lawfull money of Englond paiable at a certeyn day like as in the same obligacion more playnly hit appereth Neuertheless the seid Abbot woll and graunteth for hym and his successours that yf the seid Symond wele and truely hold kepe perfourme and fulfill all and singular couenauntes and grauntes which on his partie ben to be hold and kept and perfourmed that then the seid obligacion shalbe void and hadde for no strengthe Or els it shall abide in all his strengthe and vertue. In witnesse wherof the parties aforseid to thise present endentures entrechaungeably haue sett theire seales. Gyven the xvj day of the moneth of Marche the xj$^{th}$ yere of the Reigne of King Herry the vij$^{th}$.

## IOI

*1497 Canterbury*

Agreement with a carpenter to make a building, 84 ft. by 20 ft., containing four houses. Each house is to contain, on the ground floor, a shop (12 ft. by 8½ ft.) with a buttery (8½ ft. by 4 ft.) at each end on the side facing the street; and on the other side a hall, and a kitchen (12 ft. by 10 ft.). Above, the first floor is to project, and to contain a chamber, reached by a stair from the hall. The employer is to provide all the timber, to carry it to the Friars Austin (where the carpenter's yard was), and thence, after it had been framed up, to the building site, which shall be prepared at his cost. The carpenter is to provide a cart, and is to pay the wages, board, and lodging of the workmen (except those employed in sawing the timber into boards). The work is to be finished in about 7 months, and for it he shall have £20, in three instalments; but if, in the opinion of experts, this is too little, he shall have more.

Anct. Deeds (P.R.O.), B. 5740.

This indenture made the xv day of February the xij$^{th}$ yere of the Reigne of our soueraigne Lord Kyng Henry the vij$^{th}$ between William Haute knyght of thone

[1] *fermentes*: ironwork.

partie and John Browne of Caunterbury carpenter of thother parte Witnesseth that it is bargayned covenaunted and agreed betwene the said parties that the said John his executours or assignes shall make or do to be made wele werkmanly and sufficiantly, iiij newe Tementes to be sette in and vppon the grounde of Freres Augustyns of Caunterbury in the parisshe of Seynt Gorge there Which shall conteyn in length outward adioynyng to the kynges strete lxxxiiij fete of assise, and in brede fro the East vnto the tente. of Jamys White towardis the West, xx fote of assise w$^t$yn the selle.[1] And iiij halles to be devyded and conveniently made w$^t$ their lyghtes on the South syde. And a staire ledyng fro the halle to the chambr' in euery house of the said iiij Tementis. And with iiij seuerall Shoppez next the said strete. And iiij Chambers w$^t$ their Wyndowes ouer. And aboue the same shoppez and halle to be edified euery of the same shoppez to haue ij wyndowes enhaunced[2] And to be made in brede betwene walle and walle of euery of the said shoppez viij fote and a half fote of assise. And in length xij fote. And at euery ende of the said shoppez a Buttery. Which shall conteyne in brede iiij fote of assise and in length viij fote and half a fote of assise. And euery buttery to be made w$^t$ a convenient lygth oute and fro the strete syde. And to euery of the said Tementes a Kechyn to be made conteynyng in brede fro the halle x fote, and in length w$^t$ the halle xij fote, the said kechynnys for to be gabeled in and vppon the halle[3] w$^t$ lyghtes necessary to euery of theym. And the same tementes to be getied[4] in length lxxx[5] fote of assise and in brede the getiez for to rune xxj fote and half fote of assise. And the forsaid William or his assignez shall fynde almaner tymbr' to be ripped bourde and cariage of the same and euery parcell therof asmuch as shall longe and apperteynyng to the full fynysshyng and endyng of and for makyng of the said iiij newe Tementes w$^t$ their appertenaunces as is aforsaid to be layed in and vppon the grounde w$^t$yn the house of the said Freres, and fro thens whan it is framed to be brought and layed in and vppon the said grounde where it shall stand. The said John to fynde a pukweyn.[6] And also the saide grounde where the said newe werke shalbe sette vp shalbe made clene and redyd, and almaner naile and ironwerke asmuche as belongyth to the premissez and euery of theym in forme forsaid to be made shalbe at charge and costes of the said William. And the forsaid John shall fynde hym selfe and all other persons beyng carpenters and sawyers as shalbe occupied in and aboute the full makyng of all the said newe edificacions, bed, borde and wagis at the propr' costes of the

---

[1] *w$^t$yn the selle*: i.e. internal measurement, between the ground-sills.

[2] The wording is rather confused; it is not quite clear whether the '*wyndowes enhaunced*' (i.e. raised up) are in the shops or are dormers above them.

[3] The kitchen was apparently to be built out at right angles to the hall, against the wall of which its gable would come.

[4] *getied*: jutting, or projecting, over the ground floor.

[5] *lxxx*: possibly an error for lxxxx; the upper floor must obviously have been longer than the ground floor.

[6] *pukweyn*: a type of cart; see above, p. 352.

same John, the sawyers that shall sawe bourde for the said werkys oonly to be except, all which said iiij Tents. in maner and forme to be made in all thynges as is afore specified aswell in Durres and wyndowez as in other necessariez apperteynyng to the same And for euery parcell of the same werkys asmuche as belongeth to the said carpenter to do, shalbe fynysshed and ended by the fest of Seynt Michaell Tharchangell next commyng after date herof w$^t$oute any further delay, so that the said Carpenter be not lette by necligence of the said William for lak of such stuf as shall apperteyne to the full makyng therof. For the which werkys and euery parcell of theym as is abouesaid by the said Carpenter to be made fynysshed and ended the said William shal gyf and pay unto the same Carpenter or his assignez xx li. of lawfull mony of Englond at the terms underwritten, that is to say, at thensealyng of thise indenturis ten marc sterlinges, And assone and whan all the premissez is fully framed and redy in forme forsaid to be sette up other ten marc, And whan all the said werkes and euery parcell therof in makyng of the said iiij Tenementes as is abouesaid is fully fynysshed and ended as much as belongeth to the said carpenter to do other ten marc residuez of the said xx li. And if by conscience it can be thought and founde by men havyng good insight of carpentary werk, that the werkes by the said Carpenter in making of the said iiij Tentis. is better worth than the said xx li. Then the said William shall gif and rewarde to the same Carpenter in money ouer and a boue the said xx li. in suche maner and wise as the same Carpenter shall bere ne haue no losse by ouersight of his said bargayne. In Witnesse wherof, the partiez forsaid to thise indenturis entrechaungeably haue sette their seales the day and yere abouesaid.

## 102

### 1506 *Windsor Castle, St. George's Chapel*

Agreement with two masons to make the stone vault of the quire, in 8 bays, and the flying buttresses, parapets, pinnacles, and carved beasts on the roof of the quire and side chapel. The bosses and pendants of the vault, carved with royal badges, to be like those of the nave, but more elaborate. They are to provide all materials, and to finish the whole in 2½ years; for £800, payable in instalments. They give a bond of £400 for performance of the contract.

Sir W. St. J. Hope, *Windsor Castle*, ii. 460.

This indenture made the v day of the moneth of June in the xxi$^{th}$ yeare of the reigne of our Soveraign Lord King Henry the VII$^{th}$, between George Talbott Lorde Steward, Giles Daubeny Lorde Chamberlain, and Sir Thomas Lovell Knight in the name of our said Soverain Lord and all the Lords and Knights of the most honorable order of the Garter of the oon partie, and John Hylmer and William Vertue fremasons onn the other partie, witnesseth that it is covenaunted, bargayned and agreed betwixt the parties above named, that the said John Hylmer and William Vertue at their owne proper costs and charges shall vawlte or doo to be vawlted with free stone the roof of the qwere of the College Roiall of our

Lady and Saint George within the Castell of Wyndesore, according to the roof of the body of the said College ther, which roof conteyneth vij severeyes, as well the vawlte within furth as archebotens,[1] crestys, corses[2] and the king's bestes stondyng on theym to bere the fanes on the outsides of the said quere, and the creasts, corses and beasts above on the outsides of Maister John Shornes Chapell, to bee done and wrought according to the other creastes, and comprised within the same bargayne: provided alway that the principall keyes of the said vawte from the high awter downe to the Kings stall shall bee wrought more pendaunt and holower than the keyes or pendaunts of the body of the said colege, with the Kings armes crowned with lyons, anteloppes, greyhounds and dragons, bering the said armes, and all the other lesser keys to bee wrought more pendaunt and holower than the keyes of the body of the said colege, also with roses, portecolys, floure-de-lyces, or any other devyce that shall please the King's grace to have in them. To all which work the said John and William promysen and by these presents bynden themselves, their heires and executors in cccc$^{li}$. sterlings, to fynde all maner of stone, tymbre of scaffalds, bords, nayles, and all other things necessary, with caryage for the same by water or by land, and to have fully fynished the said vaute with the appurtenances by the Fest of the Nativitye of our Lord, which shall bee in the yeare of our Lord God after the course and accounting of the church of England Mcccccviij: for all which works before named the King's grace and the Lords and Knights of the Garter must paye or doo to be paid to the said John and William, or to their assignes, viij$^c$ li. sterling after this manner and fourme folowing, that is to say at their sealing of this indentures c$^{li}$. At the fest of the nativity of our Lorde, then next folowing c$^{li}$. At the fest of Ester, then next immediately folowing lxxx$^{li}$. At the fest of the Nativity of Seint John Baptist, then next folowing lxxx$^{li}$. At the fest of S$^t$ Michaell the archangell, then next folowing lxxx$^{li}$. At the nativite of our Lorde, then next folowing lx$^{li}$. At the fest of Ester, then next folowing lx$^{li}$. At the nativite of Seint John Baptist, then next folowing lx$^{li}$. And the residue of the somme amounting to fourscore pounds to be payed as the workes goes forward betwixt that and the Fest of the Nativite of Our Lord then next folowing, by which day the said workes must bee fynyshed and ended. To all which bargaynes and covenauntes wele and truly to be kept and performed the parties above named to their present indentures interchaungeably have set to their seales the daye and yere abovesaid.

## 103

### *1508/9 Wycombe Church (Bucks.)*

Agreement by which a mason is to take down the central tower and two of the arches on which it stands, and to make 6 responds, for the chancel arch and side arches; to make over the side arches windows like the nave clerestory, and over the chancel arch a four-light window; to finish off the walls, rough-cast them, and plaster them on the inside; and to

---

[1] *archebotens*: flying buttresses.          [2] *corses*: shafts.

insert such corbels as may be required. For this he shall have £33, paid as the work proceeds. The parishioners are to provide all materials; and if he and his men are delayed through their default, they shall pay them wages during the period that they are held up. If any deficiency is found in the work, by judgement of skilled masons, he shall make it good. He, jointly with two other masons, gives a bond of £100 for performance of contract.

Anct. Deeds (P.R.O.), D. 985; printed in *Recs. of Bucks.* ix. 13.

　　Thys indenture made the xxvj[th] day of Janyver the xxiiij[th] yere of the Reign of King Henry the vij[th] be twene Thomas Pymme Gentilman Richard Byrch Nicholas Devon George Petyfer John Brasebryg and Thomas Baven Wardens and Rulers of the New Workes be longyng to the Chyrche of Wycombe on the oon partie And William Chapman of Chersey in the County of Surr' Fremason on the other partie Wytnesseth that it is covenaunted bargaganed and agreed be twene the seid parties in the forme Folowyng that is to sey that the same William Chapman his executours or assignes shal before the feste of Seynt Laurens the Marter next ensuyng the date herof shall take down or cause to be taken down to the Grownde all the stone and other stuff of an olde Stepull and apperteyning to the seid Stepull nowe stondyng and beyng be twene the quyer and the body of the Chyrche of Wycombe in the County of Bukyngham And also the seid William Covenaunteth graunteth and agreeth to take down or cause to be taken down all the Stones and other stuff of ij Crosse Arches w[t] ther respondes set and nowe stondyng ayenst the seid stepyll w[t]in the seid Chyrch of Wycombe aforeseid and Furthermore the seid William Chapman Covenaunteth graunteth and agreeth to make newe or cause to be made newe sufficiently vj respondes to iiij Arches belongyng whereof ij of the seid arches to raunge in lyke maner as they of the body of the Chyrche doo and the iij[d] arche sufficiently to be made be twene the ij newe hyles[1] over the quyer Dore And also to make ouer euery of the seid arches that raunge w[t] the body of the chyrche ij wyndowes lyke to them that byn in the Clerestory of y[e] body of the Churche aforeseid And ouer the Est wyndowe[2] beforeseid oon wyndow w[t] iiij lyghtes euery lyght genlased[3] And also to Fulfyll all the wallys ouer all the seid newe arches to the heyght of the body of the seid Chyrch. And also to Corbell Tabyll Crest and perpoynt assheler in lyke maner as the body of the Church is And also to Rough Cast all his seid Newe Wallys And to perget them on the in syde And also to Fulfyll up the Cross hyle walle on the North syde to the heygh of the Crosse hyle on the South syde And to Corbell Tabyll perpoynt assheler and Crest as the seid South hyle is And to perget and Rough cast the same And also to make ayen all the wallys that byn brokyn w[t] the havyng a wey of the seid ij Crosse respondes And also to make ij Dores thorough his seid Newe Wark conveying thorough all the iij rode loftes[4] And to make as many Corbell as shalbe thought necessary be

---

[1] *hyles*: aisles. 　　　　　　　　　　　　　　　　　[2] *wyndowe*: this must mean 'arch'.
[3] *genlased*: cusped.
[4] *iij rode loftes*: the rood-loft must have been carried across the aisles as well as the chancel arch.

Carpenters to ber' all the rof[es] longyng and perteynyng to all the seid Newe
Werkes and to the ij Crosse hyles And that he shall make suer and substanciall and
save harmles all the Raunges of the Arches as wele of the seid body of the Churche
as the Newe Werkes And also all the raunge of Arches of the ij Newe Chapellys
of our lady and seynt Kateryn And the seid Wardens and Rulers shal pay or cause
to be payd to the seid William Chapman for his laber and workmanship of the
premisses above wretyn xxxiij$^{li}$. sterling And a hors at the discression of the seid
Wardens and Rulers to be paid in maner and forme folowyng þ$^t$ is to say Accordyng as the seid werk goth forward so the seid Wardens and Rulers to pay hym at
ther discression And also the seid Wardens and Rulers to fynde to the seid William
all maner of stuff þ$^t$ is to sey stone lyme and sond and all maner skaffold tymber
necessary to the seid werkes And also shollys[1] bokettes Trayes with a gynne and all
yern werk as nayles and the Caryage of the same And furthermor the seid William
covenaunteth graunteth and agreyth þ$^t$ if the seid werk be not substancially and
sufficiently wrought and made in euery thing belongyng to Masons work And that
work so adiuged insufficient by sufficient Masons þ$^t$ then he covenaunteth and
graunteth by these presentes by a convenient and resonable tyme after the same
Jugement to make the seid Werk wele and sufficient at his own proper cost and
charge And the [seid Wardens] and Rulers of ye said Werkes graunteth þ$^t$ if the
same William his executoures or assignes observe fulfyll and kepe all covenauntes
grauntes and agrements [ ] in these indentures wich on his parte oweth to be
performed and kept that then a sengle obligacion bering date the day of these[ ]
wherein the same William Chapman by ye name of William Chapman of Chertsey in the County of Surr' Fremason William Billesdon of [ ] in the County of
Berkshir Fremason and Nicholas Benet of Clewer in the County of Berksher
Fremason seuerally be bounden to the above named Wardens and Rulers of the
seid New Werkes in a c$^{li}$. be voide or els to stonde in his full strength and vertue
In wytnes wherof the parties above seid Enterchaungeably have putt ther Seales
the date is the day yere and place above wretyn.

Wliliã (*sic*) Chapman

[*Endorsed*] And also the w$^t$innamed Wardens and Rulers of the seid Werkes
covenaunteth and graunteth by these presentes that if the w$^t$innamed William
Chapman lak or be hyndred of lyme sond stone or eny other thynges or stuff
that be longeth to the Cov$^a$ntes w$^t$in wretyn up on a resonable warnyng moved
and spoken by the seid William Chapman to the seid Wardens and Rulers that
then the seid Wardens and Rulers shal pay to hym and to his servantes duryng
the seid tyme that they shal lak ther wages besyde this Bargyn.

1 *shollys*: shovels.

## 104

*1510 London*

Agreement with a carpenter to build a timber house of two stories, 40 feet long, 22 feet broad, and 24 feet in height to the eaves. The timber to be framed at Kingston and carried to London at the cost of the employer, who shall guarantee the carpenter against interference by the Carpenters' Company. The house to be completed in about two months, for £10, paid in instalments.

Anct. Deeds (P.R.O.), E. 359.

This Indenture made betwene the Prior of the house of the Salutacion of oure lady called the Charter house of London on that one partie And William Dewilde of London Carpenter on that other partie Witnessith that the same William couenauntith and grauntith by these presentes to make and sett up or doo to be made and sett upp for the same prior w^t in the parisshe of seynt Benett beside Baynardes Castell of London where the same prior will name and assigne a house of Newe Tymebre at the costes and charges of the same prior on thisside the Fest of seynt Mighele tharchaungell next for to com after the date of these presentes that is to say the same William couenauntith and grauntith by these presentes that the same house shall haue two loftes and one ouersett[1] w^t ij stayres to the said ij loftes and ij dorres on the strete side and also to make as many playne wyndowis as the same prior shall think most necessary for the said house. And the same hous shall conteyne in length from the one end to the oder xl fote of assise and in bredth xxij fote of assise and betwene the groundsell and the hevesinges[2] xxiiij fote of assise in hight. Whiche said house shalbe in all thinges redy made and fraymed to the setting upp in Kinges Towne upon Thamys, and so from thens to be brought and sett upp in London as it is aforsaid. And for almaner of carriages concernyng the same house during all the tyme that it shalbe in making and settyng upp to be borne and susteyned at the propre costes and expenses of the same prior. And the same prior covenauntith and grauntith by these presentes to save and kepe harmles the same William agaynst the Wardens and occupacion of Carpenters of the Cite of London during all the tyme and space that the forsaid house shalbe in setting upp w^t in the Cite of London as it is abouesaid. For the whiche house so raysed made and fynysshed in the forme abouesaid onthissid the date aforesaid The same prior couenauntith and grauntith by these presentes to content and pay or doo to be contentid and paid unto the same Wylliam his executours or assignes tenne poundes sterlingges in forme folowing that is to wete to be paid alway as the same house goeth forward in making and setting upp. In witnesse wherof the parties aforesaid to these indentures sundrely haue put their sealles. Youen the viij^th day of Julii in the secunde yere of the Reigne of King Henry the viij^th.

[1] *oversett*: a jutty, or projecting upper story.
[2] *hevesinges*: eaves.

## 105

*1511 Great Sherston (Wilts.)*

Contract[1] with a mason to build a church house, 60 ft. by 19 ft. and 16 ft. high; the doorways, windows, plinth, fireplace, and stairs to be of freestone, other walling being of 'rough stone' or rubble; the work is to be completed within 7 months. He is to have £10, by instalments, of which 13s. 4d. is paid in advance.

*Wilts. Notes and Queries*, vi. 448–50.

Thys indenture made the xxv^ti day of marche in the yer' of the Regne of Kyng Herr' the viijth aftur the conquest of ynglonde the seconde yer' by twene John Tomsson gentylman, Welyam Pers, Thomas Bryand, Rycharde Clarke w^t all the wole p'ysch of the towne of Scherstonne w^tin the Count' of Wyltescher' of the onne p'tes and Rycharde Horssale, fre masson, dwellyng in Tettebur' w^tin the Count' of Glowc' of the oder p'te Wyttenusseth that the seyd Rycharde Horssale hath taken graunte to make or lett to be made a churche howse w^tin Scherstonne aforesyd of the lenggethe of iij skore fote w^tin the walls And of heythe xvj fote And of brede xix fote w^tin the walls And ij dores of fre stonne and iij wyndowys of iiij ly3ts apece iiij wyndowys of ij ly3ts apece and iiij oder wyndowys of j ly3te apece Also a grasse[2] tabull afore strete of fre stonne. And the james[3] and the clave[4] of the chymney and the canstycke[5] and the harthe stede of fre stonne And the toppe of the same chemney of fre stonne And the stappes of a styere of fre stonne And to all thys warke of fre stonne afore reherssed the seyd Rycharde Horssale and the seyd p'tes other ther' assignes schall sette att hys quarre the seyde stonne att ther' owne p'p' costs and chargs and thednc to bryng hytt w^tin xx^ti fote of the sayd warke Further more the seyd p'tes other ther' assignes schall ryde[6] the foundacon of the seyde warke att ther owne p'p' costs and chargs And all man' of rowe stonne that therto longgeth yow to fynde bothe lyme and sande and all man' skaffolde tymber and hurdells that therto longeth that ys nedefull yow to fynde And as mech wat'[7] for the lyme and sande that therto longeth And the seyde Rycharde Horssale shall have for hys warkeman-schyppe of the same howse aforseyde x^li. of sterlyngs of good and lawfull mony of ynglonde to be payed att dyverse tymes, of the wyche the seyde Richarde hath recevyd by the handes of Roberte Hewatt in hernyst xiij^s. iiij^d., &c. Further-mor the seyde Rycharde schall receve of us ye p'tes above seyde the xxth day of Marche vij nobyls and as apponne the xviij day of May nexte followyng xl s. And as apponne the morrow aftur trenite sonday nexte to cum xl s. And as

---

[1] I am indebted to Mr. H. M. Colvin for calling my attention to this contract.

[2] Printed 'graffe' but evidently a grass-table or plinth.      [3] *james*: jambs.

[4] *clave*: the keystone, here equivalent, apparently, to the lintel.

[5] *canstycke*: presumably the bracket, often found at the angle of the hood of a fireplace, to carry a candle.

[6] *ryde*: 'rid', or clear, the site.

[7] Mr. W. Symonds, who published this document, points out that water would have to be brought from the River Avon, a quarter of a mile away.

apponne seynte John daye the baptiste calleth myssumm' day nexte folowing xl s.
And att the endyng of the warke aforseyde by seynt Luke hys day at an ende
xxᵗⁱ s. beyng the laste day of payment. And herto whe bynde us the p'tes aboveseyde to Rycharde Horssale aforseyd that these dayes of paymente be well and
truly kepte in the bonnde of xijˡⁱ. Furthermore the seyde Rycharde Horssale
other hys assignes schall well and truly fynnesche the seyde howse as in hys
warkeman schyppe of masson warke as hytt ys above reherssed by seynt luke
hys day nexte to cum. And herto I the seyde Rycharde Horssale byndeth me
wᵗ my suyrtes Hen' Daves, cors', and Rycharde Bode, baker, dwellyng in the
towne of Tettebur' in xijˡⁱ. of sterlyng. In wyttenusse wherof the p'tes above
seyde wyche to oder hath putte ther sealls the day yere and place above seyde.

# 106

### 1511 *Windsor Castle, St. George's Chapel*

Agreement by a mason to make the stone vault of the Lady Chapel, according to a design
drawn for it; also to finish off the stair turret, and the parapets, pinnacles, and carved beasts
on the roof; the bosses and pendants of the vault to be like those of the nave but more
elaborate. He shall also finish and vault the gallery between the chapel and the church. He
is to provide all materials, and to complete the whole within 2¾ years, for £326. 13s. 4d.,
and if at the end of the work he swears that he has not made £20 profit on the contract,
he shall have another £11. 13s. 4d. He, jointly with another mason, gives a bond of £400
for performance of contract.

Hope, *Windsor Castle*, ii. 481.

This indenture made the xxᵗʰ day of December in the iijʳᵈ year of the reign of
our Sovereign Lord King Henry the VIII Betwixt Nicholas West Dean of the
Collegiate church of Windsor and the Chanons of the same on the one part and
William Vertue Freemason on the other part Witnesseth that it is covenanted
granted and agreed betwixt the said parties in manner and forme following that
is to say

The said William Vertue covenanteth and granteth by these presents to vaute
or doo to be vauted with freestone the roof of our Ladie Chapel within the
Collegiate church of Windsor aforesaid according to a platte designed and drawn
for that purpose the counterpaine (*sic*) whereof is and remayneth in the hands of
the said Dean and Channons and also to finish and perform the said Chapell without forth as well in making up the Vise and embatteling the same as also in making
up Crests Corses and the Kings bests standing on theym to beyre fourth on
squychons with armes as by the said Dean and Canons shall be thought most
convenient.

Also the said William covenanteth and granteth by these Presents to make and
perfectly fynish the Galarye betwixt the same Chapell and the Church after the
manner and forme as it is begonnord (*sic*) and to vaute the same accordingly And
to make also a Botrus butting on Master John Schornes Chapell.

Provided always that the principall keyes of the said vaute of our Lady Chapell from the highe Altar down to the coming in of the same Chapell shall be more hollowe than the keyes of the Boddy of the said Colege with the Kings armes crowned with Lyons Antelopes Swanes Dragons and Greyhounds and bearing the said Armes.

Also the said William covenanteth and granteth by these presents to find all manner of stuff as stone lyme sand timber scaffolds boards nails and all other things necessary for the same work with carriage by water and by land and all manner of workmanship necessary and appertaining to the same.

Also the said William Vertue covenanteth and granteth by these Presents the said Vaute Galerye and botrus and all other things herein above specified shall be fully and perfectly made and finished before the feast of Saint Michael the Archangell that shall be in the year of Our Lord God One thousand five hundred and fourteen for which vaute galerye and botrus and all other things above specified made truly sufficiently and workmanly in manner and forme aforesaid to be done the said Dean and Chanons covenant and grant by these Presents to pay or do to be paid to the said William Vertue or to his assignes cccxxvj$^{li}$. xiij$^s$. iiij$^d$. in manner and forme following that is to say the day of sealing hereof c$^{li}$. and at midsummer next following c$^{li}$. and at Christmas after c$^{li}$. in full payment of the said bargain. And if the said William Vertue then say upon his truth that he hath not xx$^{li}$. more in the said bargaine then the said Dean and Channons shall pay or doe to be paid to the said William or to his assignes xj$^{li}$. xiij$^s$. iiij$^d$. over and above the said cccxxvj$^{li}$. xiij$^s$. iiij$^d$.

And where the said William Vertue and Henry Redmayn Freemasons by their several obligation bearing date the day of making of these presents be bounded to the said Dean and Canons in the sum of cccc$^{li}$. payable at a certain day contained in the same obligation as by the same obligation more plainly doth appear, Nevertheless the said Dean and Chanons covenant and grant by these Presents that if the said William Vertue well and truly holde kepe and perform all and singular covenants grants and agreements above specified on his parte to be holden kept and performed Then the said obligation to be void.

In witness whereof to the one part of these Indentures remaining with the said Dean and Chanons the said William Vertue hath put his seale and to the other part remayning with the said William the said Dean and Canons haue put their Chapter Seale the day and year aforesaid.

## 107

*1512 Tempsford Church (Beds.)*

Agreement by which a carpenter is to make in the chancel an enclosed chapel, apparently entered from the rood-loft, with an altar, and a window. He is to undertake no other work till this is finished, and is to provide all the materials. For this he shall have £3. 8s. 4d.

*Hist. MSS. Com. Rep.* viii. 262.

This indenture made the xxij$^{th}$ day of August in the iiij$^{th}$ yere of the reign of our Soverayn lord Kinge Henry the viij[th] betwene Thomas Phelipe, clerk and person of Temesford in the county of Bedford, of that won partye, and William Pond[ur] of the sed Bedford, joyner, carver or carpinder, of that other partye, Witnesseth that this sed William Pond[ur] shall make a floreth from the rodelofft of the chauncell or qwere of the sed Temesford onto the celed worke ouer the hye autour in the sed qwere or chauncell, and shall imbowe, cele and knott and in euery degre shal karve, joyne and make perfitt the sed floreth[1] after the forme and fassion of the ceeled worke ouer the hye autour aforesed, and from the sed floreth shall make after his best maner a kerued and a clene joyned Reredose[2] up to the sed celynge over the sed hye autour, and agayn the middest of the sed reredose shalmake an autour[3] of timberworke, and from the sed reredose vnto the rodelofft aforesed on the sowth side he shall make a clene imbowed kerued windo, and shall make the doores after the forme and fassion of the queredores beneth, and shalfind clene sesonable[4] hart of oke for all and euery aforesed, and ther shall close and shitt in and make perfitt a closse chappell, and shall find all maner stuff and workeman-shipe thereto, and shaltake non other workes in hand to this worke be perfytely ended; So that Thomas Phelipe, the parson aforesed, shalbe at no maner cost nor charge nother of stuff nor of workemanshipp, but the said William Pond[ur], or his assignes shalfind at his costes and charge all maner stuff and workemanshipp other in ston, yron or tymber nedfull to this forsed worke. And the sed Thomas shal pay or cause to be payed to the sed William Pond[ur] or to his assygnes in lawfull money of Yngland iij[li]. viij[s]. iiij[d]. In witnesse that the sed Thomas and William will and shall this bargayne eche to other performe, the sed Thomas and William eche to other to thes indenturs haue put to ther seales the day and tyme aforesed. Suerte for all and euery of the premisses is William Gimber, bocher, of Temesford. Witnesse, William Coper, John Cooper, Henry Tynghey, and the aforesed Gimber and Pond[ur] and more.

## 108

### 1512/13 *Cambridge, King's College Chapel*

Agreement with the mason in charge of the works to make the finials of 21 buttresses, according to a design made, and like one already set up, with the exception of certain details for which templets have been made. He is also to finish off one of the angle towers according to the design. He shall provide Weldon stone, and all other materials, except that the College will lend him some scaffolding and hoisting tackle. The whole to be finished within 3 months. He shall have £6. 13s. 4d. for each buttress—£140 in all, and £100 for the tower; the money being paid as wages and purchases of stone require. He shall keep 60 masons employed, as soon as he can get them, and if any of them misbehave, the surveyor shall deal with them. The College shall provide iron to the value of 5s. for each buttress. Mutual bonds of £300 for performance of contract.

Willis and Clark, *Arch. Hist. of Cambridge*, i. 609.

This Indenture made the iiij[th] day of January in the iiij[th] yere of the Regn of

---

[1] *floreth*: i.e. the under side of the floor, forming the ceiling of the chancel.
[2] *reredose*: partition.      [3] *autour*: altar.      [4] *sesonable*: seasoned.

our sowuerayn lord Kyng Henry the viij^th. Betwene M^r Robert Hacumblen provost of the kynges college Royall in Cambryge and the scolers of the same with the advise and agrement of M^r Thomas Larke Surveyour of the kynges workes there on the oon partye; and John Wastell master Mason of the seid workes on the other partye, Witnesseth,

that hyt is couenaunted, bargayned, and agreed between the partyes aforsaid that the seid John Wastell shall make . . . the fynyalles of all the Buttrasses of the grete churche ther which be xxi in numbre; The seid fynyalles to be wele and workmanly wrought, made and sett upp after the best handelyng and fourme of good workmanship acordyng to the plattes conceyved and made for the same, and acordyng to the fynyall of oon buttrasse which is wrought and sett upp; Except that all thies new fynyalles shalbe made sumwhat larger in certayn places acordyng to the mooldes for the same conceyvid and made.

Also hit is couenaunted . . . that the said John Wastell shall make . . . the fynysshyng and perfourmyng of oon towre at on of the corners of the seid churche, as shalbe assigned vnto hym by the Surveyour of the seid werkes: All the seid fynysshyng . . . with Fynyalles, ryfant[1] gablettes, Batelmentes, orbys,[2] or Crosse quaters,[3] and euery other thyng belongyng to the same to be wele and workmanly wrought, made and sett upp, after the best handelyng and fourme of good workmanshipp, acordyng to a platt therof made, remaynyng in the kepyng of the seid Surveyour.

The seid John Wastell to provide and fynde at his coste and charge asmoche good sufficyent and able ston of Weldon quarryes as shall suffyse [for the finials and tower] . . . Together with lyme, sand, scaffoldyng, mooldes, ordenaunces and euery other thyng concernyng the fynysshyng and perfourmyng of all the buttrasses and towre aforseid, aswele workmen and laborers as all maner stuff and ordenaunces as shalbe required or necessary for perfourmaunce of the same.

Except the seid M^r Provost, Scolers and Surveyour graunten to lende vnto the seid John Wastell sum parte of old scaffoldyng tymbre, and the vse of certayn stuff and necessaryes there; as Gynnes, Wheles, Cables, Robynattes,[4] sawes and suche other as shalbe delyuered vnto hym by Indentures. And the seid John Wastell to delyuere the same agayne vnto the seid Surveyour assone as the seid Buttrasses and towre shalbe perfourmed.

The said John Wastell graunteth also, and byndeth hymself . . . to perfourme and clerely fynyssh all the seid buttrasses and towre on thisside the Feeste of the Annunciacon of our blessed lady next ensuyng after the date herof.

And for the good and sure perfourmyng of all thies premysses as is afore specyfyed the seid provost and scolers couenaunten and graunten to pay vnto the seid John Wastell for the perfourmyng of euery buttrasse vj^li. xiij^s. iiij^d. whiche

---

[1] *ryfant*: Willis (*Nomenclature*, 11) shows that this should be 'rysant' and is equivalent to 'ogee'.    [2] *orbys*: blind panelling.

[3] *crosse quaters*: quatrefoils.    [4] *robynattes*: see above, p. 323.

amouwnteth for all the seid buttrasses cxl$^{li}$.; and for the perfourmyng of the seid towre, c$^{li}$. to be paid in fourme folowyng, That is to say; from tyme to tyme asmoche money as shall suffyse to pay the Masons and other laborers rately after the numbre of workmen, And also for ston at such tymes and in such fourme as the seid John Wastell shall make his provisyon or receyte of the same ston from tyme to tyme as the case shall requyre;

Provided alway that the seid John Wastell shall kepe contynually lx Fremasons werkyng vppon the same werkes assone as shalbe possible for hym to calle them in by vertu of suche Commissyon as the seid surveyour shall delyuer vnto the seid John Wastell for the same entent.

And in case ony Mason or other laborer shalbe founde vnprofytable or of ony suche ylle demeanour wherby the workes shuld be hyndred or the company mysordred not doyng their duties acordyngly as they ought to doo, than the seid Surveyour to indevour hymself to refourme them by such wayes as hath byn ther vsed before this tyme.

And also the fornamed M$^r$ Provost, scolers and Surveyour shall fynde asmoche Iron werke for the fynyalles of the seid buttrasses as shall amownte to v$^s$. for euery buttrasse, that is in all iiij$^{li}$. v$^s$. And what soeuer Iron werke shalbe ocupyed and spent abowte the seid werkes, and for suertie of the same aboue the seid v$^s$. for a buttrasse, the seid John Wastell to bere hyt at his own cost and charge.

And for all and syngle couenaunts afor rehersed of the partie of the seid John Wastell wele and truly to be perfourmed and kepte he byndeth hymself, his heires and executours in ccc$^{li}$. of good and laufull money of Englond to be paid vnto the seid M$^r$ provost, scolers and Surveyour at the Fest of Ester next commyng after the date of thies presentes. And in lyke wise for all and syngler couenaunts afor reherced of the partye of the seid provost, scolers and Surveyour wele and truly to be perfourmed and kepte they bynde them their Successours and executours in ccc$^{li}$. . . . to be paid vnto the seid John Wastell at the seid fest of Ester. In witnesse wherof the partyes aforesaid to thies present indentures entrechaungeably haue sett their Seales the day and yere above wryten.

## 109

*1512/13 Cambridge, King's College Chapel*

Agreement with the mason in charge of the works and his warden for the making of the vaulting of the chapel, according to a design made for it. They are to provide Weldon stone and all other materials, except that the College will lend them certain hoisting tackle, &c. The whole shall be finished within 3 years. They shall have £100 for each bay, paid as the wages and purchases of stone require; and they shall also have the timber of two bays of the great scaffold when it is taken down.

Willis and Clark, *Arch. Hist. of Cambridge*, i. 608.

This indenture made the      day of      in the iiij$^{th}$ yere of the Regn of our souerain lord kyng Herry the viij$^t$ betwyne M$^r$ Robert Hacumblen provost of the Kynges College Royall at Cambryge and the scolers of the same with the advise and agrement of M$^r$ Thomas Larke surveyour of the kynges workes ther on the oon partye, And John Wastell M$^r$ Mason of the said workes and Herry Semerk oon of the wardens of the same on the other partye witnesseth

that hit is couenaunted bargayned and agreed betwyn the partyes aforsaid that the said John Wastell and Herry Semerk shall make and sett upp or cawse to be made and sett upp at ther costes and charges a good suer and sufficient vawte for the grete churche ther to be workmanly wrought made and sett upp after the best handlyng and fourme of good workmanship accordyng to a platt therof made and signed with the handes of the lordes executours unto the kyng of most famous memorye Herry the vij$^{th}$ whos sowle god pardon.

And the said John Wastell and Herry Semerk shall provide and fynde at their costes and charges as moche good sufficyent and able ston of Weldon quarryes as shall suffise for the perfourmyng of all the said vawte together with lyme, sand, scaffoldyng, cynctours, moldes, ordynaunces, and euery other thyng concernyng the same vawtyng, aswell workmen and laborers as all maner stuff and ordenaunces that shalbe required or necessary for the performaunce of the same.

Except the said M$^r$ provost and scolers with thassent of the said surveyour graunten to the said John Wastell and Herry Semerk for the great cost and charge that they shalbe at in remevyng the great scaffold there to haue therfor in recompence at the end and perfourmyng of the said vawte the tymber of ij seuereys of the said grete scaffold by them removed to their own use and profight.

And over that the said provost scolers and Surveyour graunten that the seid John Wastell and Herry Semerk shall haue duryng the tyme of the said vawtyng the use of certeyn stuffes and necessaryes there as Gynnes, wheles, cables, robynettes, sawes and such other as shalbe delyuered unto them by indenture. And they to delyuere the same agayn unto the College there at the end of the said worke.

The said John Wastell and Herry Semerk graunten also and bynde themselff by thies couenauntes that they shall perfourme and clerely fynyssh all the said vawte within the term and space of iij yeres next ensuyng after the tyme of their begynnyng uppon the same.

And for the good and suer perfourming of all the premysses as is afore specyfyed the said provost and scolers couenaunte and graunte to pay unto the said John Wastell and Herry Semerk xij$^c$li. that is to say for euery seuerey in the seid churche c$^{li}$. to be paid in fourme folowyng from tyme to tyme asmoche money as shall suffise to pay the Masons and other rately after the numbre of workmen; And also for ston at suche tymes and in such fourme as the said John Wastell and Herry Semerk shall make their Bargeynes for ston so that they be evyn paid with c$^{li}$. at the perfourmyng of euery seuerey. And yff ther remayn ony parte of the said c$^{li}$. at the fynysshyng of the said seuerey, than the said M$^r$ provost and scolers to pay unto them the surplusage of the said c$^{li}$. for that seuerey. And so from tyme to tyme unto all the said xij seuereys be fully and perfithtly made and perfourmed.

[Agreement, 7 June 1512, by which John Wastell is to bear the costs and have the profits of this bargain, paying yearly 20 marks to Herry Semerk, who is to give daily and hourly attendance to the said work. If John Wastell dies or is incapacitated, then Herry Semerk and John's son Thomas Wastell shall be partners in completing the work.]

## 110

*1512/13 Cambridge, King's College Chapel*

Agreement for building three angle towers similar to one already completed.

Willis and Clark, op. cit. 612.

This Indenture made the iiij$^{th}$ day of Marche in the iiij$^{th}$ yere of the reign of our souuerayn lord king Henry the viij$^{th}$, betwene maister Robert Hacumblen clerk provost of the kinges College Royall in Cambryge . . . and John Wastell maister Mason of the seid werkes on the other parte witnessith: that hit is couuenaunted . . . that the seid John Wastell shall make . . . iij towres at iii Corners of the great new churche there; All the seid fynysshyng and perfourmyng of the seid iij towres with fynyalls, ryfant Gablettes, batelmentes, orbis, crosse quaters, Badges, and euery other thyng belonging to the same to be wele and workmanly wrought, made and set up after the best handelyng and fourme of good workmanship acordyng to oon towre at the iiij$^{th}$ corner that is to say at the North west ende of the seid Church which is now redy wrought.

[The towers, for each of which £100 is to be paid, to be finished before Midsummer; guarantee on both sides, £400.]

## 111

*1513 Cambridge, King's College Chapel*

Agreement for making the vaulting of 2 porches and 16 chapels, with their battlements, according to designs made. The mason is to provide all materials, and to keep 60 masons employed on the work, which is to be finished in 10 months. He shall have for each porch £25; for each of 7 chapels £20; for each of the other 9 chapels £12; and for all the battlements £100. Mutual bonds of £400 for performance of contract.

Willis and Clark, op. cit. 613.

This indenture made the iiij$^{th}$ day of August in the v$^{th}$ yere of the regne of our souuerayn lord kyng Henry the viij$^{th}$, Betwene M$^r$ Robert Hacumblen provost of the kynges College Royall in Cambryge and the scolers of the same with the advise and agreement of M$^r$ Thomas Lark Surveyour of the kynges workes there on the oon partye, and John Wastell M$^r$ Mason of the seid workes on the other party, witnesseth,

that hyt is couenaunted, bargayned and agreed betwene the parties aforsaid, that the seid John Wastell shall make and sett upp, or cause to be made and sett upp, at his propre costes and charges, the vawtyng of ij porches of the new church of the kynges College aforeseid with Yorkshier ston;

And also the vawtes of vij Chapelles in the body of the same Church with Weldon ston, acordyng to a platte made as wele for the same vij Chapelles as for the seid ij porches;

And ix other Chapelles behynd the quere of the seid churche with like Weldon ston to be made of a more course worke, as apperith by a platte for the same made:

And ouer that the seid John Wastell shall make and sett upp or cause to be made and sett upp at his cost and charge the Batelmentes of all the seid porches and chapelles with Weldon ston acordyng to another platte made for the same remaynyng with al the other plattes afore reherced in the kepyng of the seid Surveyour signed with the handes of the lordes the kynges executours:

All the seid vawtes and batelmentes to be wele and workmanly wrought, made and sett up after the best handelyng and fourme of good workmanship, and acordyng to the plattes afore specifyed:

The forsaid John Wastell to provide and fynde at his cost and charge not only as moch good sufficient and hable ston of Hampole quarryes in Yorkshier as shall suffise for the perfourmaunce of the seid ij porches, but also as moch good sufficient and hable ston of Weldon quarryes as shall suffise for the perfourmyng of all the seid chapelles and batelmentes, Together with lyme, sand, scaffoldyng, mooldes, ordinaunces, and euery other thyng concernyng the fynysshyng and perfourmyng of al the seid vawtes and batelmentes, aswele workmen and laborers, as almaner stuff and ordinaunce as shalbe required or necessary for perfourmaunce of the same:

Provided alwey that the seid John Wastell shall kepe contynually lx fremasons workyng vppon the same.

The seid John Wastell graunteth also and byndeth hymself by thies presentes to perfourme and clerely fynysh al the seid vawtes and batelmentes on thisside the feest of the natiuite of Seynt John Baptiste next ensuyng after the date herof;

And for the good and suer perfourmyng of al thies premisses, as is afore speci-fyed the seid provost and scolers graunten to pay vn to the seid John Wastell for ston and workmanship of euery of the seid porches with al other charges as is afore reherced xxv$^{li}$.

And for euery of the seid vij Chapelles in the body of the Church after the platt of the seid porches xx$^{li}$.

And for vawtyng of euery of the other ix Chapelles behynd the quere to be made of more course work xij$^{li}$.

And for ston and workmanship of the batelmentes of al the said Chapelles and porches devided in to xx seuereyes euery seuerey at c$^s$. summa c$^{li}$.

And for al and singler couenauntes afore reherced of the partye of the seid John Wastell wele and truly to be perfourmed and kept, he byndeth hym self, his heires aud executours in cccc^li. of good and lawfull money of England to be paid unto the seid M^r Provost, scolers and Surveyour at the Fest of the Purificacon of our Blessed Lady next commyng after the date of thies presentes; and in lyke wise for all and singler couenauntes afore reherced, of the partye of the seid M^r Provost, scolers and Surveyour wele and truly to be perfourmed and kept, they bynde them self, their successours and executours in cccc^li. of good and laufull money of England to be paid vnto the seid John Wastell at the seid feast of Purificacon of our blessed lady. In witnesse wherof the parties aforeseid to thies present Indentures entre-chaungeably have sett their Seales, the day and yere above wryten.

## 112

### 1516 Holywell (Oxford)

Two masons undertake to build a farmhouse according to a plan; the walls to be 18 feet in height, 3 feet thick on the ground floor, and 2 feet 6 inches on the upper story; doors, windows (all with wooden lintels), and fireplaces are specified. They shall complete the work in 4 months; and shall be paid £29, in five instalments. They give a bond for £10 for performance of contract.

*Reg. Annal. Coll. Merton.* (Oxf. Hist. Soc.), 461.

This indentur made the xi^th daie of Maii the vii^th yere of the reyne of King Henry the viii^th betwene Richard Rawlyns, doctor of divynyte and warden of Marton College in Oxford and the company of the same of the one partie, and Richard Gyles of Winchester and Thomas Phelypp of Oxford fremasons on the other partie witnessith that the seid Warden and company have bargared, con-vented and agreide with the forseid Richard and Thomas for a farme place to be bildid at Holiwell that they shall make werkmanly and sufficiently acording to a plate drawonne for the same, first the walls to be made xviij foote in hyghte and iij foote thicke beneyght the flore, and ij foote and vj ynchis thicke above the flore; and in the walls beneight the flore to be made ij dores of stone, and chemnes one of viij^th foote wide in the hall, another of iiij foote wide in the parlere, and one wyndow of iiij li3ghts in the sowi3the partie of the hall and another of ij li3ghts on the north parte of the hall, every li3ght xv ynche brode, and every wyndow iiij foot of james[1] in hyghte; and five wyndows of ij li3ghts and one wyndow of one li3ght in the nether story; in the story above the flore to be made ij chemnes and ij dores of stone for the widdrawts[2] and vj windows of ij li3ghts and vj win-dows of one li3ght, and all the seide windows above rehersid to have lyntells of tymber and the seid Richard and Thomas shall rovcaste and pargett all the stone walls with beme fillyng of the same howse, and the seid warden and company shall fyne the seid Richard and Thomas all maner of stuft to the same bildyng, and shall also well and trewly content and paye to the forseid Richard and Thomas xxix^li. sterlyng att certayn dais, the xj^th daie of maii v^li., and at mydsomer folow-yng v^li., and the xx^ti daie of Julii x^li., and the xxij^ti of August vij^li., and the xviij

---

[1] *james*: jambs.　　　　　　　　　　　　　　　[2] *widdrawts*: privies.

daie of September xl$^s$.; and the same daie all the walls to be reddy for the roffys to be sett on by the forseyd Richard and Thomas or ther executors, under the peyne of x$^{li}$., if the forseid Richard and Thomas be trewly payd at ther dais above rehersed; or for the lake of ony stuff belongyng to the forseid werks, thene the forseid bound to stand as woyde. Thes covenants to be kept and fulfillyd of every partie alternantly hath puto ther sealls the daie and yere above writtyn.

## 113

*1516 Cambridge, St. John's College*

Agreement with a carpenter to make the quire-stalls and rood-loft on the lines of those in Jesus and Pembroke college chapels; also three gates, and ten doors; a bell-cote on top of the stair-turret of the gateway tower; the floors of all the chambers; and the desks in the library, which are to be like those in Pembroke College. The whole to be finished in one year.

Willis and Clark, *Arch. Hist. of Cambridge*, ii. 243.

This indenture made between M$^r$ Rob. Shorton Clerke, Doctor in Divinity and Maister or Keper of the College of S$^t$ John the Evangelist in Cambridge on the oon parte, and Thomas Loveday of Sudbury in the County of Suffolk Carpenter on the other parte, wytnessyth

that the said Thomas covenaunteth, and also byndeth hym hys Heyres and Executours by thes presents, that he shall make and cause to be made all the Staulls within the Qwier of the said College, that is to say, 24 Staulls on eyther syde of the said Qwyer; the Desks wyth the Bakke halfe, wyth Creests over the Seats and Staulls, as is in the southe parte of the Qwyer in Jhesus College in Cambr', or better in every poynt; and the Seats therof shall be made after and accordyng to the Seats within the Qwyer of Pembroke Hall in Cambr' aforesaid, or larger and better in every poynte; and the oon halfe therof on every syde shall be double staulled, wyth lyke lettours,[1] Staulls, and Seats, accordyng to the said patrone, as is before specyfied, of good substanciall and hable Tymber of Oke, and waynescot;

and a Rodeloft after and accordyng to the Roodelofte and Candell beame in the said Pembroke Hall in Camb', or better in every poynt, wyth Imagery and howsynge,[2] such as shall be mete and convenient for the same werks and such as shall be advised by the discrecion of the said M$^r$ Rob. Shorton:

and also shall make 3 payr of broode Gats, wherof oon shall be mete and convenient for the Tower Gatte, and two goodly Posts byfore the said Gate, which Gate shall be made with a wykket; and the oder Gate shall be mete and convenient for the Gate next unto the Kynges Hall agaynst the Kyngs hygh way; And the thyrde Gate shall be mete and convenient for the gat at the water syde wythin the said College and which gate shall be made also wyth a wykket of good and able Oke and waynescott, better than ony Gats be wythin ony College in Cambr':

and also tene Doors, wherof fyve shall be in the Chyrche wythin the said

---

[1] *lettours*: reading-desks.                    [2] *howsynge*: niches.

College, that is to say two Churche doores, a doore into the Revestry, a doore into the Roodeloft, and a doore into the perclose there; and 5 other doores shall be in the Halle in the same College, that is to say two Halle doores, a Botery doore, a pantere doore, and a doore leadynge towards the Maister's Loggyng ther of lyke oke and wayneskotte with 2 Portalls, wherof one shall be at the parlour doore and the other at the great Chamber doore wythin the said College of lyke oke and waynescotte, mete and convenient wyth the same, also aftur the best workmanship and proportion:

and also a Lantorn over the vice of the Tower wythin the said College of good substanciall and abyll Tymber of oke, mete and convenient for to hange therin the Bell of the said College:

and also shall plancher[1] all the chambers belongyng to the said College wyth goode and abyll boorde of oke which wyll amounte to 51 hundred boorde, when it is plancherd:

and also shall make all the Desks in the Library wythin the said College, of good substanciall and abyll Tymber of Oke mete and convenient for the same Library, aftir and accordyng to the Library within the foresaid Pembroke Hall:

and clerely and holy shall fynishe all the premisses after and accordyng to the best warkmanship and proportion a thys syde the Fest of All Saints next comynge aftir the date herof.

[Dated 1 November 1516. Payment to be, in all, £100. 17s. 8d. N.B. according to an apparently contemporary estimate (p. 245) this work was expected to cost about £210.]

## 114

### 1517 Oxford, Corpus Christi College

Notes of three contracts with carpenters for various woodwork.

C.C.C. MS. 435, ff. 3, 55.

M[d]. couuenawntyd and agreyd w[t] Roger Morwent by Humfrey Cooke for makyng off the benche in the Masteris parlower the which is xviii foot in lengyth to be made suffycyant and clenly: Also for sealyng[2] off the said parlouer wallys rownd abowght the wyndowys by neth and above in the said parlower: and to make too portalles on in the parlower and a nother in the chamber above: and too cobertes[3] on by neth and a nother above off v foot in lengyth a pease and xx[ti] ynchis brood clenly wrowght and hawnsyd:[4] And to seale the flower ouer the said parlower w[t] panys glued and frett w[t] well ynbowyd batons off a yard square:[5] And the said Roger moreouer to make a dore at the stayar foote gluyd: And he to

---

[1] *plancher*: floor.
[2] *sealyng*: panelling.
[3] *cobertes*: cupboards.
[4] *hawnsyd*: raised.
[5] The ceiling of the parlour to be of boards glued together and divided into panels of a yard square by inbowed battens.

have fond hym all maner off stooffe y$^t$ is to say waynscott glew raylis broddes and sawyng: for his workmanshypp to have—v$^{li}$.

M$^d$. comenauntyd and agreid by me M$^r$ John Claymond presydentt of Corpus Xpi college w$^t$ Robert Carow carpenter for to fynd tymber workemanshypp bordes caryage w$^t$ all other maner of necessary thynges belongyng to a carpenter w$^t$ on flower bordid and a rooffe to bere lede w$^t$ lede bord belongyng therto and gisted betwene the bemys to bere sealyng w$^t$ dorys wyndoys partycions and stayars accordyng to a platt made by Humfrey Cooke the which conteyneth a hundred footes xij ync w$^t$in the walles in lengyth and wyde betwyxt the wall above xix footes accordyng att hytt apperyth in the sayd platt. The sayd Robert Carow to receyve and have for the performaco͞n off them xliiij$^{li}$. Att the seallynge hereoff to rec'—x$^{li}$.

M$^d$. comenawntyd and agreid w$^t$ Willm Colyn and Nicholas More for the saw-yng framyng and settyng upp off the rooff off the said cloyster for the workes off Robert Carowys att the Est end towardes the chaple and a long by y$^e$ chaple to the West end of the workes off the seid Robert Carow accordyng to a platt theroff: w$^t$ too clere storys att the rysyng and the fallyng off they rooffys:$^1$ the yoll pease$^2$ to be inboyd and levell geistid$^3$ underneyth at every foote space: M$^r$ president to fynd tymber and all maner off caryage: they to have for the same—viij$^{li}$.

## 115

### *1522 and 1528 Oxford, Balliol College*

Two notes of contracts for work on the college buildings, entered on the last page of the college register; copied by Mr. R. H. C. Davis for Mr. John Harvey.

(A) A Burford mason to make 3 windows in the chapel, and in the vestry a small window and corbels and an offset to carry the joists of the roof; for £8.

(B) Mr. John Lobbens, or Lubyns, and William Jonson undertake to make the heads of three windows, for 21¼ marks.

### (A)

M$^d$ that the iij day of Aprill in the xiij yere of the regne of Kyng Henry the [VIII] that M$^r$ William Eist mason of Burfurth hath promysyde to mak iij great wynd[owes] both the soolls and hedds of the south syde of the new capell with a litill wyndow . . . to y$^e$ vestre with corbell table and iiij corbylls and return the wall at the heght to lay the ioysse$^4$ ouer the litill wyndowe, and sich ston as is w$^t$in the college y$^t$ wyll serue the said Willim to have and all other he to fynd at his own charge *of Burfurth ston*$^5$ cariag *and skaffold* warmanshipe and lyme, and

---

$^1$ Meaning obscure: apparently the roofs were of different levels, and the points of junction were to be left as plain upright partitions.

$^2$ *yoll pease*: 'joppy', a cornice.

$^3$ *levell geisted*: it is not clear how, or why, the cornice was to be 'level joisted'.

$^4$ *ioysse*: joists.          $^5$ Words in italics are interlined.

so the said Willm. hath promosyd to maik it perfit and redy to ly the tymbre worke apon to yᵉ corner of M' Blonston chamber, and for to have for his labor viijˡⁱ of the which he hath resauyd xiˢ and the rest he shall reseve as yᵉ werke goth forwards.

(B)

Mᵈ yᵗ the xx day off Februarye in *the xix yere off the reigne off* Kynge Henry yᵉ viii that it is conventyd and fully agreid betwyx maister and fellows off Ballioll college in Oxforth and M' John Lobbens mʳ *off my lorde wa[rkes]* and William Jonsons fremason to werke or cause to be wroghte iij heddes off wyndos . . . off iiij lyghtes and one off iiij lyghtes off yᵉ northe syde and the heid off yᵉ eiste windoe off v lyghtes, euery wyndow to be wroughte wᵗ wousers and chawmerantes¹ and yᵉ said Mʳ Lobbens to see all maner off stones to be conveid and caryed into oʳ college off Balliol sayff and sownde wᵗowt brekyng or bressing or if so by yᵗ any stone be broke in caryage then the said M' Lobbens to cawse to be mendyd or to be reparyd. And the said maister and fellows to p[ay?] for the caryage off yᵉ stones. And yᵉ said maister and fellows to pay or cawse to be payd to yᵉ Mʳ Lobbens *and William Jonson* for yᵉ performyng of yᵉ premisses xxj markes iijˢ iiijᵈ.

## 116

### ? 1525 Hengrave Hall (Suffolk)

A rather vague contract for the masonry and brickwork of the house. The mason to be paid £200—£10 down and instalments of £20—and he and his workmen to be boarded at 16*d.* a week.

Gage, *Hist. of Hengrave*, 41.

A bargain made betwixt Thomas Kytson, knight, and Jhon Eastawe.—The said Jhon must macke a house at Hengrave of all manor of mason's worck, bricklaying, and all other things concerning yᵉ masondrie and bricklaying, as well as the laborers concerning the same, according to a frame² which the said Jhon has seen at Comby.

Itm, the saide Thomas must clense yᵉ mote as far as yᵉ fondacyon of yᵉ wall, that is to say, ij parts of the house.

Itm, the saide Thomas schall make a baye window in yᵉ hall, of yᵉ south side, of free-stone, and also shal mack yᵉ free-stone work of the gate coming in at the bridge.

Itm, the saide Jhon shall dyck and mack yᵉ residewe of the foundacyons of yᵉ said house within yᵉ motte.

Itm, yᵉ saide Jhon, and all his company yᵗ he setts a worcke for yᵉ said house, shall be bordy'd at Thomas Shethe's for xvjᵈ. a week.

Itm, yᵉ saide Jhon shall at his costs and charges macke all manner of morter belonging to the masondrie.

¹ *wousers and chawmerantes*: voussoirs and jambs.    ² *frame*: model.

Itm, yᵉ saide Jhon must macke all the inder court wᵗ a fyne souvett,[1] and roubed bryck all the schanck of the chymnies,[2] as in the vineyarde; and yᵉ saide Jhon must have for yᵉ saide worke, and finishing thereof ijcˡⁱ. to be payed xˡⁱ. when he begins the foundacyon thereof, and afterward always as xxˡⁱ. worth of worke is wrouhgt by estimacyon.

## 117

### *1529 Orby Church (Lincs.)*

Agreement with a mason to make the battlements of the church like those of Weston Admeals and those of the tower like others at East Keal.

Early Chanc. Proc. 613, no. 10.

[Richard Ballard and John Heryng of Orby in Lincolnshire show that about 10 July 1529 it was agreed between them and William Jacson of Bratofte, freemason, that the said William Jacson, for £12. 13. 4]—

shulde on thysside the feast of [Sᵗ Michael] tharchangell then next ensuyng the sayd bargayne sufficiently batell the churche of Orby wᵗʰ frestone after the forme and fascion of a churche in the seyd countie [called] Westyngadmels wᵗʰ syngall [     ] of either syde and also batell the steple of the seyd churche of Orby with bent croftes[3] fynyalles and all other thynges of freestone [after the] facion and proporcion of the churche steple in the seyd countie callyd Est'erkele, and that the seyd batelment and all other the premisses shuld have ben sufficiently [performed] before the feast of Seynt Michell tharchangell then next ensuyng for the seyd some at the propre costes and charges of the seyd Willm Jacson except all maner of Irnewerke and [cariage of] stone from the pytte to the seyd churche of Orby whiche your seyd oratours shulde fynde at ther proper costes and charges. . . .

[For performance of this contract Robert Pelson of Burgh became surety for William Jacson in £20. At request of Robert Pelson they paid in advance to William Jacson £8. 3s. 4d. for provision of stone, &c., but he has done nothing.

Robert Pelson says that he expressly told them not to advance any money, but only to pay for what was done. Also that William Jacson was taken to work on the king's works and therefore could not finish the job.]

## 118

### *1530 London*

Agreement with a carpenter to make wooden galleries[4] running round three sides of a (walled) garden, with a 'summer house' underneath on one side. There are to be 12 bay windows, and one fireplace; the walls to be rendered in plaster and provided with cornices from which tapestries may be hung. He is to provide two leaden gutters to carry off the

---

[1] *souvett*: soffit, or cornice.

[2] The shafts of the chimneys to be of rubbed brick.

[3] *bent croftes*: meaning obscure.

[4] The galleries must have been something like that which forms part of the President's Lodge at Queens' College, Cambridge.

rainwater. He shall have all the materials of an existing gallery, which is to be pulled down, and supply all other materials required. For all this, which shall be done in about 4 months, he is to receive £110, half in advance and half on the completion of the work.

Ancient Deeds (P.R.O.), D. 10097.

This Endenture made betwene the right noble Lord Henry Marques of Exetour on that one partie and James Nedam one of the Kynges Master Carpenters on that other partie Witnessith that the said James couenauntith and grauntith by this endenture that he his executors or assignes at their owen coste and charge shall wele clenly substancially and workemanly new make of good and substancial oken tymber a gallary at the place of the said lorde Marques in the parisshe of Seint Lawrence Pulteney in London which gallary shall conteyne in length the lenght of the easteside of the garden there next the strete And the same gallary to conteyne in bredth from outeside to outeside xij fote of assise And also the said James to make a gallary at the northende of the said garden to conteyne from the said gallary on the easte side of the garden along the bredth of the said gardeyne on the northende And the said gallary at the northende to conteyne in bredth viij fote. And also to make a gallary on the south end of the said garden And the same to conteyne from the forsaid gallary on the easteside of the garden along close adioynyng to a wyndyng stayre there And the same gallary on the southende to conteyne in bredth xij fote of assise. And all the said iii gallares to conteyne in heithe from the flower to the nether side of the beame ten fote And the outeside of the said gallary towarde the garden to be made w[t] fayre and substancial postes and hawnces[1] betwene the same postes. And also the said Jamys couenauntith and grauntith by this endenture to make a playne flower thrughoute the said gallares wele and substancially bourded And also to make a garret flower[2] along the roffe of the said gallares And all the same roffe to be selid w[t] lyme and here[3] and in likewise the nether flowers[4] of the said gallares And the said gallares to haue xij baie wyndowes wele and clenly as it is now appoynted by the said lorde And the said gallares to haue fayre trymmers[5] w[t]in in the inside w[t] fayre and conuenyent Jowe peces for hangings to hange upon And also the said Jamys couenauntith and grauntith by these presentes to fynde all maner of tymber bourde lathe nayle lyme sande bryk tile and plaster of parrys for all the outeside of the said gallares And all the inside of the said gallares to be seasid[6] clenly with lyme and here and in likewise the roffes And also all glasse ironwerke and all other thinges belongynge to the makinge and fulfynesshinge of the said gallares in all thinges belonginge to the crafte of carpentry masonry smithes wark glasiers werke plastery briklaiers tilars and plommers warke. And also the said Jamys to make

---

[1] *hawnces*: supporting timbers.
[2] There was evidently a garret, or loft, above the galleries.
[3] *here*: hair.                              [4] *nether flowers*, i.e. the under side of the floors.
[5] *trymmers*: both 'trimmers' and 'jowe pieces' were a form of cornice.
[6] *seasid*: ? a slip for 'sealed', i.e. ceiled.

a conuenient chymney[1] in the gallary on the southende of the said garden and to make ij conuenient gutters of lede to conveye the water from the said gallares And to fulfynesshe and make all the forsaid werkes and set up the said gallares and a somerhouse under the gallary on the southende wele plasterid paved and latissed in maner and fourme aforsaid before the Feaste of Pentecoste next comynge after the date hereof. And the said lorde Marques couenauntith and grauntith by these presentes that the said Jamys shall haue and take to his owen use all the olde gallary as it now stondith holie[2] and all the olde brik and stones as well in the fundacion as elles where towarde the newe makynge of the other gallary. For all which werkes so by the said Jamys as is aforsaid to be made and don the said lorde couenauntith and grauntith by these presentes to paye or cause to be paid to the said Jamys to his executors or assignes on hundreth and ten poundes sterlinges in fourme follow-inge that is to saie in hande at thensealinge of this endenture lv li. whereof the said Jamys knowlegith hym selff wele and truly contentid and paide And the lv li. residue of the same cx li. to be paide at the full fynesshinge of the said werkes in fourme aforsaid. In witnesse whereof the parties aforsaid to these endentures entrechaungeably haue set their Seales Youen the xv day of February in the xxj yere of the reigne of kynge Henry the viijth.

## 119

*1532 Ringwood (Hants)*

Agreement with a carpenter for the building of a weir for a water-mill, and the renewal of the mill-wheels.

Ancient Deeds (P.R.O.), B. 11225.

This Indenture made the iiijth day of February in the xxiijth yere of the Reign of our Soueraign lord kyng Harry the viijth bytwyne Nicolas Hardyng gent. Sorveyer unto the noble lady Margaret Countesse of Sar' and Olyuer Frankeleyn gent. Reseyvor generall unto the said Countesse on the one partye and Thomas Everton of Batromsley in the counte of Suth̃ carpenter on the other party Wit-nessith that the said Thomas hath covenauntyd barganyd and agreid to and wythe the said Nicolas Hardyng and Olyuer Frankeleyn to newe make frame and sett a sufficient newe Weyr for the said Countesse at her mylle callyd Ryngwood Mylle in Ryngwood within the said counte of Suth' before the Fest of Seynt Mighell tharchaungell next ensuyng after the date of these presenttes yn the place wheyr the old weyr late stode. The said weyr to be maid with xviij fludyattes euery gate to be bytwen post and post twoo fote and a halff and conteyn yn lengith by twyxt the forsille and the taillsille[3] xxiij fote and all the postes to be sett arreys wyse,[4] And also the sayd Thomas covenaunteth and graunteth to new make the Tumbelyng

---

[1] *chymney*: fireplace.    [2] *holie*: wholly.

[3] *forsille* and *taillsille*: the top and bottom horizontal beams of the gates.

[4] *arreys wyse*: diagonally, presenting their 'arris', or edge, to the stream.

bayes[1] to the sayd weyre That ys to say one before the forsille and the other before the midill sille or under the taillsill as by the officers of the said Countesse shalbe thought most beste, Eyther of the said Tumbelyng bayes to be iiij fote depe, And to enter the plankes of the said weyre with rebates yn to the joystes or tymbars withowt chergyng the said Countesse yn occupying any spykes of Iron or nayles to the same weyre but only for the bordyng of the particions of the same, And yt ys farther agreyd by twen the sayd partyes that the sayd Thomas shall newe make the Whelys of the myll of Ryngewood aforesaid, and also that the fellyng of all maner tymber for the said Weyr and allso squaryng sawyng framyng and settyng of the same with all other thynges that yn any wyse appertenith or belongith to carpenters craft of the sayd weyre and whelys shalbe at the costes and charges of the said Thomas Everton. For the whych couuenauntes bargeyn and agrement and other the premissez on the behalf of the said Thomas yn maner and forme aforesayd to be fulfilled and don the said Nicolas Hardyng and Olyuer grauntten on the behalf of the said Countesse to content and pay unto the sayd Thomas twenty poundes lawfull money of Inglond yn maner and forme folow-yng That ys to say wythin a monethe after the sealyng of these Indentures Fowr powndes to fell and square the Tymber wythall. And when the said Thomas begynithe to frame the said weyre other fowre poundes and yn the Fest of Penticost next after Forty shelynges and the resydewe that ys to say tenne pound to be payd to the said Thomas hys exec' or assign' when the sayd frame ys sett and furnysshyd yn euery thyng accordyng to thys agrement. Providyd allways that yf the sayd Countesse cause hyr Customary Tenauntes of Ryngwood forsaid to make a Skluse before the heed of the old weyre to turne the water to the mylle yn soche wyse as the sayd Thomas shall devyse yt so that the sayd milles may grynd wythin xx[ti] days after the Fest of Ester next comyng Then yt ys agreyd bytwen the sayd partyes that the sayd Thomas shall haue but fyftene pownd lawfull money of Inglond to be payd after the rate aforsaid and the proffitt of all the gryst of the said milles tyll Michilmas next comyng and nomore for makyng fullfyllyng and doyng of all the premyssez. And moreouer yt ys agreyd that a sufficient lease shalbe made by the sayd Countesse unto the sayd Thomas of the sayd millez of Ryngwood for terme of hys lyffe from the sayd fest of Seynt Mihill tharchaungell next comyng, Yeldyng and paying therfor yerly to the sayd Countesse and hyr heyres twenty pownd lawfull money of Inglond at iiij termes of the yere usuall wyth clawsez of distresse and reentre for none payment of the sayd rentt. For whych couenaunttes grauntes and agrementtes on the behalf of the sayd Thomas to be well and truly obseruyd performyd fullfyllyde and done the sayd Thomas byndyth hyme hys exec' and assign' unto the sayd Nicolas and Olyuer yn the somme of twenty pownd sterlyng. In Wytnesse wherof the partyes afforsayd to these Indentures enterchaungeable haue sett theyr sealys the day and yere aforsayd.

[1] *Tumbelyng bayes*: chutes.

## 120

*1532 Tower of London*

Draft of a contract by which a carpenter undertakes to build within St. Thomas's Tower at the Tower of London a timber 'frame', with a double roof, containing a floor composed of exceptionally massive beams and joists and supported by upright posts. He is also to build at the north-west corner of the said tower a house, 20 ft. by 17 ft., and to provide boards and make the necessary doors, windows, &c., for both jobs, for £120; the work to be done, apparently, within 5 months.

S.P. Dom. Henry VIII, vol. 70, fol. 112.

This indenture made the xj daie of June in the xxiiijth yere of the Reigne of our soveraigne Lorde Kynge Henry the viij$^{th}$ Betwene Thomas Crumwell Maister and Thesaurer of o$^r$ soveraigne Lorde the Kynges Juelles on the behalfe of our saide soveraigne lorde the kinge of the oon partie and James Nedeham Maister Carpenter to our saide soveraigne Lorde the Kinge of the other partie Witnessithe that it is covenaunted graunted condiscended and agreed bytwene the saide parties by these presentes to and for the use of o$^r$ saide soveraigne lorde the Kynge in maner and forme folowing that is to say the saide James for him and his executours and administratours covenauntith and grauntith to and with the said Thomas Crumwell by these presentes that he the same James before the xvj$^{th}$ daie of Octobre next comynge after the date hereof att his owne propre costes and charges shall workmanlie and substantiallie make frame bielde and sett up oon frame of good substanciall and seasonable tymbre of woke$^1$ within a certeyne Towre called Seynte Thomas Towre sett and being within our saide soveraigne lorde the kinges Towre of London with oon storie of seasonable Tymbre of Woke to be sett and framed within the saide Frame, which Storie shall conteigne in lenght lxxix fote of assise and in bredith xxxij fote of assise and in height frome the flore to the rofe xiij fote of assise, And uppon which Frame so to be made as is aforesaide shalbe workmanlie and substanciallie sett up and buyelded oon substanciall great doble Rooffe of good substanciall and seasonable tymbre of woke mete and convenyent in every degree and condicion to and for the same Frame. And also the seyde James . . .$^2$ shall sett up and rayse within the same Frame . . . lxxij principall somers and nyne principall storie postes of good and seasonable tymbre of woke, every of the same principall somers conteyninge in thiknes xx inches of assise and in depthe xviij ynches of assise, and every principall storie poste conteinynge in thiknes xij ynches of assise and in breddith xiiij ynches of assise And that every single juiste in the same Frame shall conteine in depthe xvj ynches of assise and in thiknes iiij ynches of assise, every space betwene the same juistes conteignine ix ynches. And furthermore the same James . . . shall workmanlie clenlie and substanciallie make frame buyelde and sett up oon substanciall house of good substanciall and seasonable tymbre of woke att and upon the Northe side at the Weste ende of the sayde Towre called Seynte Thomas

---

$^1$ *woke*: oak.  $^2$ Some repetitive verbiage is omitted.

Towre, whiche howse shall conteigne in length xx fote of assise and in bredith xvij fote of assise and in height according to the proporcion of the forseyde Frame of the seyde Towre. And also the seyde James . . . shall workemanlie and substanciallie borde all the foreseyde Frame and house thrugh oute with clene and seasonable borde of woke, everv borde conteiginge in thikness oon ynche and a halfe. And also . . . shall make as many particions dores and wyndowes yn the seyde Frame and howse as shalbe thought necessarie mete and convenyent for the premysses and every parte therof by the dis[crecion?] of the seyde Thomas Crumwell and suche as he shall therto assigne. [*illegible scrawl*] . . . Tho<sup>s</sup>. Crumwell to paye to the seyde James for the premysses to be [      ] aforeseyde cxx<sup>li</sup> st' yn maner and forme folowyng that is to say [      ] the reste of the [      ] to be payde from tyme to tyme as the [      ] shalbe [      ] yn worke.

## 121

[? *1532*]  *Tower of London*

Draft of a contract by which two carpenters undertake to erect three new houses at the Tower. Scantlings of all the timbers are given. They are to be paid at the rate of 10s. for each foot of length and breadth of the houses.

S.P. Dom. Henry VIII, vol. M, no. 33.

This endenture made betwene the right worshipful Maister Thomas Cromwell Esquyer and treasorer of the Kynges Jewelles on that one partie and Thomas Hall and John Kynge citizens and carpenters of London on that other partie, Witnessith that the said Thomas and John do covenaunt and graunte and bynde them and either of them by this endenture that they their executors and assignes at their owen coste and charge shall well clenly substancially and wirkemanly make frame and set up within the tower of London to and for the use of our said soveraigne Lorde the Kynge thre newe howses adioynyng to the Kynges lodgyng within the said tower; one of which new houses shall conteyn from owtside to outside lij fote off assise and in bredeth from outside to owtside xviij fote and di'; and another of the same iij howses shall conteyn in length from outside to outside xxiij fote, and in bredeth xvj fote; and the iij<sup>de</sup> new howse to conteyn in length from outside to outside xxiij fote, and in bredeth from outside to outside xj fote and di'. And the said Thomas and John do covenaunt and graunte by this endenture that they or their assignes shall make the scantlyns of ij of the first howses in maner and fourme as hereafter is declared: That is to say all the jeystes of the same ij howses beyng of the first flower shall conteyn in thiknes xij ynches one way and x ynches another way; Itm. the reason pece of the first howse to conteyn in thiknes xij ynches one way and x ynches another waye: Itm. the reason pece in the second howse to conteyn in thiknes viij ynches and in bredeth ix ynches. And all the bemes of the same ij first howses to conteyn xij ynches one waye and xiiij ynches another waye. And the sayd Thomas Hall and

John Kynge shall make and frame in the sayd ij houses such and as many good competent and sufficient girders as shalbe mete and convenyent for the same ij howses, And every girder to conteyn a fote one way and x ynches another way; and every joyst of the same ij howses to conteyn iiij ynches one waye and v ynches another way; and pryncipall rafteres for the same ij howses to conteyn vij ynches one way and viij ynches another waye, and every single rafter for the same ij howses to conteyn v ynches one way and vj ynches another way; and every joyst of the thirde howse for the first flower to conteyn vj ynches one way and ix ynches another waye; and the plates for the same iij^de howse to conteyn in thiknes vj ynches and in bredeth x ynches; and the pryncipall postes for the same howse to conteyn xij ynches one way and x ynches another way, with competent sufficient entertaces and punchions for the same; and every reason peces of the same iij^de howse to conteyn ix ynches one way and x ynches another way, and every beme of the same iij^de house to conteyn x ynches one waye and xij ynches another waye, and every joyste for the same to conteyn v ynches one way and iiij ynches another way with good and sufficient rafteres for the same howse according to the proporcion of the same howse. And in the same iij^de howse to be conteyned a greate baye wyndowe with ij clere storys[1] over every side, and also to make in the second howse a greate like baye wyndow without eny storeys. And the said Thomas and John . . . shall bourde the iij flowres belonging to the sayd iij howses and they to fynde at theyr owen coste and charge all substanciall seasonable good oken tymbyr bourde wirkmanship and cariage and to fulffyn-ysshe all the same werkes belongyng to the crafte of carpentry before the Feast of All Seyntes next comyng after the date hereof without contradiccion or further delay. For the doyng and accomplysshing of all which werkes of carpentry to be made and performed in maner and fourme above expressed the said Thomas Cromwell convenauntith and grauntith in the name of our soveraign lorde the Kynge to pay or do to be payed to the said Thomas and John or to one of them their executors or assigneis for every fote of the frame of the said iij howses to be rekened in lengthe and in bredeth at every one ende of the same iij howses x^s. sterlinge. In partie off payment wherof the same Thomas and John have receyved and had the day of making hereof by the handes of [*blank*] Whalley citezen and mercer of London xx^li sterlinges wherof the said Thomas Hall and John do knowledge themselff wele and truly contented and paied, and therof do acquite and discharge the sayd as well the said Mr. Thomas Cromwell as the said [*blank*] Whalley and either of them their heires and executors by these presentes, and the residue of the same money to be paied as the werkes go forthwards. In witnesse whereoff the parties aforsaid to these endentures entrechaungeably have set their seales. Yoven &c.

[1] *ij clere storys*: apparently there were to be two rows of short lights above the main long lights of the window.

## 122

*1537/8 Hengrave Hall (Suffolk)*

Agreement with a carpenter, or joiner, for the panelling of various rooms, and the provision of fittings. He is to have all necessary timber, including some old panelling, and ironwork supplied; and to be paid £116, in instalments as the work progresses, £20 being retained until the whole is complete.

Gage, *Hist. of Hengrave*, 42.

Thys indent^e made y^e xx day of January, y^e yeare of y^e reigne of King Henry y^e viii. xxix, Wytnesse, y^t Sir Thomas Kytson, Knight, and Robert Watson, ruler of his bylding in Hengve. hathe bargeynyd and covenanted with Thomas Neker, of Gret Franshm. in the counte of Norfolke, for the seelyng of his place in Hengve. and also ther doyngs, as hereafter shall be expressed.

In the first, for seelyng of vij chambers benethe, w^t y^e chapel, to be seeled w^t. y^e tremors[1] vj foote on heyghte; and y^e chapel vij foote, w^th iiij stooles on y^e one side and a retorne desk at the ende.

Itm, y^e hall of y^e same lodging to be seelyd, at y^e daysse[2] xv foote of heyghte, w^t a tremor ij foote brode, and all y^e rest of y^e hall to be seelyd, to y^e heyght of y^e windows, w^t a frett on y^e floor[3] w^t hangyng pendants, voute facyon. Itm, y^e said hall to have ij coberds; one benethe at the sper,[4] w^t. a tremor; and another, at the hygher table's inde, w^tout a tremor; and y^e cobards, they be made y^e facyon of livery,[5] y^t is, w^tout doors.

Itm, the same hall to be benched about.

Itm, two parlors to be seelyd, to the heygth of the floor; and eche of them a livery cobard, and benched aboute both parlors, and jopysse[6] above; w^th ij portalls, and eche parlour, a frete on the floor.

Itm, y^e said Thomas Neker shall make y^e gates at y^e cummyng in.

Itm, to seele y^e wardrope ov^r y^e syller; w^tij close pressys,[7] and open pressys round about.

Itm, to be made to y^e vij lodgings, vij portalls.

Itm, y^e said Thomas shall seal y^e ij grett chambers above y^e daysse; eche of them to be seelyed to y^e pendants feet,[8] w^t ij jopysse, and eche of them a portal, and a lyvery cobard.

Itm, y^e saide Thomas shall scele xvj lodgings above; to be seelyd to y^e pendans foote to as many as will serve for y^t, and ij jopysse, and y^e residue to have none:

[1] *tremors*: 'trimmers'—the plain strips of wood separating the panels.
[2] *daysse*: dais.
[3] *a frett on ye floor*: i.e. the ceiling to be divided into panels by battens.
[4] *sper*: screen.
[5] 'livery cupboards', like dressers, on which the day's 'livery' of provisions was set out.
[6] *jopysse*: cornices. (Printed 'ropysse', but subsequently corrected.)
[7] *pressys*: cupboards, or 'wardrobes' in the modern sense.
[8] *to ye pendants feet*: i.e. up to the lower end of the pendants, or corbelled wall-posts of the roof.

and to the same chambers, x portalls, with viij livery cobards, and on the pastry house to make a wardrope, w^t. one close presse, and opyn presses rounde abowte.

Itm, to seel vj drafts[1] iiij foote of heygth.

Itm, y^e ij small towers, whiche shall be stodys,[2] to be seelyd v foot of heyghts.

And I y^e saide Thomas Neker bynd me to make and fulfill all the said work substantially, w^tout decyte, and holly to accomplysse all and singular as ys above written and specified, by y^e day which shall be at Esterne day cum xij mongth after the date above written, w^tout delay.

I y^e said S^r.Thomas Kytson, Knight, bynd me to pay or cause to be payd unto the saide Thomas, or hys assygns, for y^e said premises and covants, truly done and fullfylled, v score and xvj^li of lawful money of Inglond, to be paide as y^e work to be done and got forward, he to receive his money.

Itm, y^e saide S^r Thomas Kytson, Knight, shall fynd all man^r of tymber, hewyn and sawyn, of all manner of skantells, y^t shall be nedeful and redy to y^e worke; and also all manner of iron work, upon hys owne cost and charge.

Itm, ye saide S^r Thomas shall delyv^r, or cause to be delyvered, to y^e saide Thomas Neker, all y^e old seeling and frets of y^e old worke that is in hys keeping, to accomplesse and to fulfill all y^e saide worke.

Itm, y^e seyd S^r Thomas schall find, and have ready sett up, all man^r of stayings[3] as shall be necessary for y^e seyde work.

And y^t those covants. be truly kepte and performed on eyther side, to remayne in y^e hands of y^e seyd Sir Thomas Kytson, Knyth, xx^li untyl y^e time y^t y^e seyd Thomas hath performed and full endyd y^e seyde worke, according to y^e covants. above written.

## 123

*1436  Winchester: a house in St. Pancras Street*

This document, of which Mr. John Harvey kindly sent me a transcript after my manuscript was in the printer's hands, appears to be a crude draft for a contract. It does not seem ever to have been sealed, and it is so lacking in detail that it would not be worth printing if it were not for the reference to a 'trasyng', or plan, on parchment, which evidently contained all that was necessary for carrying out the building of the house.

Winchester College muniments.

This Endenture wytnissyth that this beth the couenaunts bitwyn the Wardeyn of the Newe College of Wynchestir in that on partie and John Berewik of Romesey Carpenter of that othir partie Witnissyng that the sayd John schal make a hous to the forsaid Wardeyn of xxviij fete in lenghe and xxiiij fote of wide bi the grounde with a joteye a boue of xxii inche the hous schal be y sett in the strete of Synt Pankras ther as the boundis of the ground openli schewith. The

---

[1] *drafts*: privies.
[2] *whiche shall be stodys*: i.e. shall be timber-framed, of studs and panels.
[3] *stayings*: staging, or scaffolding.

same John to bigynne the Werk the Monday nexst aftir Pask Wike the yer of Kyng Henri the VIte in the xiiii° yer regnyng. In that the same John have no defaute of tymber nothir of cariage for the same tymber whenne hit is wrought to carye hit to Wynchester to the ground aforesaid.[1] Also the forsaid Wardeyn to paie to the said John for the makyng and workmanchip of the hous that touchith to his craft xi mark and a half that is seye iiii mark the Monday nexst after the Estir wike whenne he bigynnyth his werk Also iiii mark at Whitsond-tide nexst folwyng And whenne this said John hath arerid the house to resseyve of the same Wardeyn for the laste payment that is seye at Lammasse nexst after folwyng iii mark and half Also the forsaid Wardeyn schal do ride[2] the ground that hit be void ther as the hous schal stonde that the said John Carpenter have no lette in reryng of the hous the werk to be y made as the trasyng schewith y drawe in a parchement skyn by twyn hem y made And the same John to do to the hous all that longith to his craft. In wytnesse of thes couenaunts a boue y write eythir partie have y sette to her selis.

[1] Probably a clause by which the Warden was to provide the timber and carriage therefor has been omitted.

[2] *do ride*: cause to be rid, or cleared.

# APPENDIX C

In this Appendix are collected a few examples of contracts made with masons and other craftsmen for the retention of their services, either for a term of years or for life. The earliest, the engagement of a tiler in 1329, is of interest as being made by a private individual, a layman. A somewhat similar appointment, for a period of ten years, of Walter Helyere to keep in repair the roofs of the buildings of Spaxton Manor (Somerset) was made in 1417 by Robert Hulle and Isabel his wife (Anct. Deeds, A. 4136). Probably the latest instance within our period is the agreement made in February 1538 by Robert King, Abbot commendatory (and afterwards Bishop) of Oseney, with two Oxford plumbers, for the term of their lives, to keep in repair the leaden roofs of the monastic buildings (Anct. Deeds, D. 1492); three years later those roofs vanished into the royal melting-pot.

I

*1329 Baycliff (Wilts.)*: engagement of a tiler

Omnibus X$^i$ fidelibus ad quos presens scriptum pervenerit Johannes Basspray de Lullynton salutem in domino sempiterno. Noveritis me tradidisse et concessisse Ade le Helyere de Hornyngesham omnes domos meas apud Baylesclyue ad reparandas et cooperiendas per terminum vite mee quamdiu vixero et terminum vite dicti Ade quamdiu vixerit pro undecim solidis quos sibi dabo pre manibus et omni anno postea tres solid' et quatuor den' reddendis ad festum beati Michaelis Archangeli vel infra octabas ejusdem festi, ita quod dictus Johannes Basspray dicto Ade inveniam lapides et claves et meremium et omnia alia necessaria ad cooperturam dictarum domorum competencia, exceptis clavibus ligneis. Et si ita continget, quod absit, quod dictus Adam deficit in opere suo quin bene faciat et bene dictas domos cooperiat obligat se per scriptum indentatum in quadraginta solidis sterlingorum bene et legalis monete. Et ego Johannes Basspray obligo me in eadem forma dicto Ade si deficiam in solucione dictorum trium sol' et quatuor den' tam per scriptum quam per literam obligatoriam et pariter dictus Adam pro parte sua. In cujus rei testimonio sigilla nostra alternatim apposuimus. Hiis testibus . . . . Dat' apud Lullynton die dominica in festo Sancti Wolfranni episcopi anno regni regis Edwardi filii Regis Edwardi tercii post conquestum tercio. Et [si] ita contingat quod convencio ista bene et fideliter se habeat [ex utraque] parte quod litera obligatoria pro nichilo habetur.

Anct. Deeds (P.R.O.), D. 1971.

2

*1346 York:* appointment of an overseer of the Minster carpentry

Universis sanctae matris ecclesiae filiis ad quos presentes literae pervenerint Capitulum ecclesiae Beati Petri Ebor', Decano ejusdem in remotis agente, salutem in sinceris amplexibus Salvatoris. Noveritis nos concessisse Philippo de Lincoln' supervisionem carpentariae fabricae dictae ecclesiae Beati Petri Ebor' ad terminum vitae suae, pro laudabili servicio suo nobis impenso et imposterum impendendo, dum tamen in dicto servicio bene se habuerit et fideliter laboraverit; capiendo inde annuatim de fabrica per septimanam viginti denarios et omnes alias comoditates, prout predecessores ipsius Philippi in temporibus preteritis melius habuerint et perceperint. Concessimus eciam eidem Philippo, ad terminum vitae suae, modo et forma predictis, officium janitoris clausi dictae ecclesie Sancti Petri Ebor', capiendo inde annuatim de fabrica antedicta decem solidos sterlingorum, ad duos anni terminos, viz. ad festa Pentecostes et Sancti ‧Martini in yeme, per equales porciones. In cujus rei testimonium sigillum nostrum presentibus est appensum. Data Ebor' primo die mensis Augusti anno Domini millesimo ccc^{mo} xlvj^{to}.

*Y.F.R. 165.*

3

*1351 York:* appointment of William de Hoton as chief mason, in succession to his father

Universis . . . . Capitulum Ebor' . . . . Noveritis universitas vestra nos pro artificiosa industria et labore Willelmi de Hoton, cementarii, filii Magistri Willelmi de Hoton cementarii, circa fabricam ecclesiae nostrae Ebor' impensis et imposterum perpetuo fideliter impendendis, decem libras argenti annuae pensionis, una cum habitacione infra clausum ecclesiae Ebor' predictae quam Magister Thomas de Pacenham dum vixit inhabitabat, predicto Willelmo, post decessum Magistri Willelmi patris sui, ad terminum vitae suae in quacumque statu fuerit, dum tamen, cum aliis se intendat operibus, idem nostrum non omittatur, negligatur seu aliqualiter retardetur, dedisse concessisse et assignasse ad duos anni terminos, viz. ad festa Pentecostes et Sancti Martini in yeme, per equales porciones, sibi annuatim per manus custodis ipsius fabricae percipiendas. Qui quidem Willelmus filius predicti Willelmi [      ] et concedit quod si contingat ipsum cecitate, seu aliquo alio morbo incurabili, prepediri quominus laborare potuerit ac dictum opus ut cementarius gubernare, quod extunc solvet annuatim subcementario qui erit magister secundarius cementariorum medietatem salarii predicti subcementarii de sua pensione predicta decem librarum, impedimento hujusmodi perdurante. Et si contingat per negligenciam ipsius Willelmi filii Willelmi laborare et dictam fabricam supervidere valentis, aut omissionem voluntariam, vel circa aliorum operum occupacionem opus ecclesiae nostrae negligi, omitti aut quovis alio modo retardari, extunc omnino cesset predicta pensio, in qua sibi nolumus ultra aliquo modo teneri, et presens scriptum viribus careat totaliter et effectu. In cujus rei testimonium sigillum nostrum parti penes dictum Willelmum remanenti, alteri vero parti sigillum ejusdem Willelmi penes nos remanenti sunt appensa. Data Ebor' primo die mensis Octobris, anno Domini millesimo ccc^{mo} quinquagesimo primo.

*Y.F.R. 166.*

# 4

*1359 Hereford:* appointment of a mason in control of the masonry and carpentry of the cathedral

Hec indentura facta inter decanum et capitulum ecclesie cathedralis Herefordie ex una parte, et Johannem de Evesham, mason, de comitatu Wygornie ex altera, testatur quod idem Johannes convenit commisit et tradidit se ad commorandum in civitate Herefordia, et ad serviendum et operandum cum omni diligencia et facultate sua super fabrica dicte ecclesie cathedralis, et non alibi sine licencia dominorum decani et capituli, in artibus lathomorum et carpentariorum et in omnibus aliis operibus fabricam, refeccionem sive emendacionem concernentibus ecclesie antedicte, sive cancellorum pertinencium ad ecclesiam antedictam, ad terminum vite dicti Johannis, et ad informandum et docendum bene et fideliter alios artifices sub se positos, super fabrica dicte ecclesie operantes, in artibus antedictis quo melius aut utilius poterit aut sciverit expedire; recipiendo Herefordie singulis septimanis durante vita dicti Johannis, tres solidos sterlingorum a dictis decano et capitulo per manus custodis dicte fabrice qui pro tempore fuerit, necnon singulis diebus vite ejusdem Johannis unum album panem communem per manus custodis pistrini canonicorum Herefordie, tam in sanitate quam in infirmitate dicti Johannis. Convenit tamen quod si dictus Johannes propter infirmitatem aut corporis impotenciam vel alium casum fortuitum super fabrica ecclesie antedicte in artibus antedictis non poterit operare per unam septimanam aut per duas septimanas ad majus, quod nichilominus percipiat in septimana illa aut in singulis ipsarum duarum septimanarum tres solidos sterlingorum per manus custodis fabrice, ut prefatum est. Quod si per tres septimanas vel quatuor vel ultra forte tempore vite dicti Johannis in tali infirmitate vel impotencia operandi idem Johannes perstiterit, quod extunc singulis septimanis percipiat duodecim denarios sterlingorum. Et dicti decanus et capitulum concesserunt et tradiderunt dicto Johanni ad terminum vite ejusdem tenementum eorum situatum in vico castri juxta venellam que ducit ad fontem sancti Ethelberti, pro decem solidis sterlingorum eisdem decano et capitulo singulis annis in terminis Annunciacionis Dominice et Sancti Michaelis, durante vita dicti Johannis, per eundem Johannem Herefordie solvendis per equales porciones, termino prime solucionis intrante in festo Annunciacionis Dominice anno Domini millesimo ccc sexagesimo intrante. Et dictus Johannes tactis sacrosanctis evangeliis corporale prestitit juramentum quod bene et fideliter deserviet et operabitur super fabrica ecclesie antedicte ac omnem diligenciam et possibilitatem suam bene et fideliter serviendi et operandi et alios artifices sub se positos informandi et docendi in artibus antedictis super fabrica dicte ecclesie faciet et eciam adhibebit. Ad quas quidem convenciones ex utraque parte hinc inde confectas bene et fideliter tenendas et servandas obligant se dicti decanus et capitulum, ex parte una, et dictus Johannes obligat se, ex altera. In cujus rei, &c. Datum Herefordie nono die mensis Aprilis anno regni regis Edwardi tercii post conquestum tricesimo tercio.

Capes, *Charters and Recs. of Hereford Cathedral*, 230.

## 5

*1367 York:* appointment of a plumber

Hec indentura testatur quod Johannes Plomer, de Blaykestret, operabitur in opere plumbarii, propriis suis manibus, et non per substitutam personam, in coopertura ecclesie B. Petri Ebor' campanilis, berefridi, chori, capituli, et pinniculorum sive turrium ejusdem ecclesie, quocienscumque et quandocumque de cetero necesse fuerit, aut defectus apparuerit in eisdem aut aliqua parte ipsarum, et per magistrum fabricae ejusdem ecclesiae aut alium ex parte sua fuerit requisitus; capiendo, ebdomada qualibet qua in opere predicto laboraverit, a dicto magistro operis duos solidos sex denarios argenti pro stipendio et pro labore suo, sine aliquo amplius exigendo, nisi forsan cum de Capitulo predicto, considerata operis sui quantitate, uberiorem remuneracionem sibi de gratia facere voluerint. Et si dictus Johannes per dietas vel vices in opere predicto laboraverit, recipiet pro dieta secundum ratam sive porcionem summae predictae taliter limitatae, nec amplius idem Johannes quocumque anni tempore poterit vindicare. Sin tamen aliquo tempore anni intermedio fabrica predicta ejus labore vel emendacione non indigeat, petita prius licencia a Capitulo sive magistro operis, et obtenta, licite poterit alibi operari et commodum suum facere, prout sibi videtur expedire: ita tamen quod ad reparacionem et emendacionem dictae fabricae statim et sine difficultate redeat quandocumque opus eo fuerit et per magistrum operis, sicut premittitur, fuerit requisitus. Supradictum eciam opus, quocienscumque necesse fuerit, bene et fideliter et absque omni dolo et fraude faciet diligenter et expediet; et plumbum et stagnum ecclesiae et quicquid ad opus predictum pertinuerit conservabit, & non alibi quam in ipso opere vel circa illud aliquo tempore distrahet et expendet. Si vero aliquo famulo sive serviente ad opus predictum indiguerit, ex consensu et concordia dicti magistri, qui pactum secum faciet pro ebdomada vel dieta, assignabitur sibi famulus hujusmodi in subsidium operis supradicti. Et pro predictis omnibus faciendis et fideliter adimplendis idem Johannes, coram dictis dominis Capitulo, corporale prestitit juramentum. [Bond of 40 marks for his good behaviour. Sealing clause.] Data apud Ebor' die Veneris in festo Sancti Mathiae, anno Domini millesimo ccc$^{mo}$ sexagesimo septimo.

*Y.F.R.* 179.

## 6

*1430 Oxford:* engagement of a mason to control the building of the Schools

Universis Christi fidelibus presentes litteras inspecturis, Cancellarius Universitatis Oxoniensis ac eadem Universitas salutem. Sciatis nos concessisse magistro Ricardo Wynchecombe, lathomo, unam pensionem quadraginta solidorum sterlingorum, annuatim solvendorum ad festa S. Michaelis Archangeli et Pasche per equales porciones, quamdiu ipse steterit et intenderit ad supervidendum opus novarum scolarum theologie in dicta Universitate; et unam togam de liberata generosorum quolibet anno, vel tredecim solidos et quatuor denarios pro eadem; ac pro vadiis suis qualibet septimana cum presens ad opus ibidem fuerit, quatuor solidos: et dictus magister Ricardus habebit unum mansum competens pro se et suis consortibus, sumptibus dicte Universitatis, et habebit eciam racionabiles expensas quociens missus fuerit in negociis dicte Universitatis. In cuius rei testimonium has nostras litteras fieri fecimus patentes. Datum in nostre congregacionis domo, quarto die Augusti, anno regni regis Henrici sexti post conquestum octavo.

*Epist. Acad. Oxon.* (O.H.S.), i. 58.

## 7

*1430 Bury St. Edmunds:* engagement of brickmakers

Hec indentura inter Willelmum Curteys Abbatem monasterii de Sancto Edmundo ex una parte et Johannem Arnold et Hermannum Reinoud brekebrennerys ex parte altera testatur quod predicti Johannes et Hermannus component et bene et sufficienter comburent ad opus dicti domini Abbatis tot lateres vocatos le breke quot bene et seisonabiliter componere et comburere poterint aura eos permittente a festo omnium Sanctorum proxime futuro post datum presentis usque ad finem unius anni ex tunc proxime sequentis. Et dictus dominus Abbas inveniet argillam quam dicti Johannes et Hermannus fodient et sumptibus suis propriis facient cariari excepto quod ad ejusdem argille cariacionem dictus dominus Abbas inveniet unam carectam et ij equos cum hernesiis pro eisdem una cum viij whelbarwys un[de] j holwe ac insuper inveniet zabulum focale stramen sufficiens ac iiij carectas arundinis cum pakthred sufficiente ac dictum zabulum focale stramen et arundinem ad loca opportuna sumptibus suis propriis faciet cariari. Insuperque predictus Abbas inveniet predictis Johanni et Hermanno per tempus antedictum unam cameram ad pernoctandum et salvo custodiendum instrumenta sua equos et alia eorum arti necessaria. Et predicti Johannes et Hermannus habebunt de predicto domino Abbate pro composicione et sufficienti combustione cujuslibet millene bene et sufficienter combuste ij$^s$, et duas togas cum ij capuciis de liberatura valettorum ejusdem domini Abbatis. Et quamdiu placuerit eidem domino Abbati dictos Johannem et Hermannum in suo seruicio retinere ipsi sub conuencionibus antedictis annuatim bene et fideliter eidem domine Abbati deseruient se ab ipsius domini Abbatis seruicio nullatenus distrahendo. Ad que omnia et singula ex parte dictorum Johannis et Hermanni fatentur se et utrumque eorum per se et in solidum teneri et firmiter obligari predicto domino Willelmo Abbati et successoribus suis in quadraginta libris legalis monete Anglie soluendis eidem domino Abbati vel successoribus suis si defecerint vel alter eorum defecerit in premissis vel in aliquo premissorum. In cujus rei testimonium partibus presentis indenture partes predicte sigilla sua alternatim apposuerunt. Datum apud Sanctum Edmundum primo die mensis Aprilis anno regni Regis Henrici sexti post conquestum Anglie decimo octauo.

Ista cedula indentata testatur quod Johannes Arnald et Hermannus Reynold teutonici et tylemakers receperunt . . . ad diversas vices . . . de Willelmo Curteys Abbate . . . xxiij$^{li}$ vj$^s$ viij$^d$. [18 Dec. 20 Hen. VI.]

Add. MS. 7096, f. 150v.

## 8

*1434/5 Canterbury:* appointment of a master mason

This endenture maad be twene Wyllyam Priour of Crystyscherche of Cauntyrbury and the Chapetre of the same place on that oon partye, and Richard Beek, mason, on that othir partye, wytnessid, that hit is acordyd and ful assent of bothe partye in the manere and foorme that folowyth, that is to wete: that the sayd Richard is wytholden and hath put hymself to dwelle and be with the sayd Priour and Chapetre and with here successours, for the terme of the lyef of the said Richard, in the offyce, servyse, and craft of masonrye, and hath grauntyd to the sayd Priour and his successours, and take upon hym to have and to do the governance, disposicion, rewle, and entendaunce sufficiently of alle the werkes of the same chirche, with ynne the chirche aforesayd and wit owte, boothe in the Cytee of Cauntyrbury, in the Cyte of London, and in other places wher the sayd Priour and Chapetre have maners or places to be bylded, renewyd, repayred, or amendyd in the werke of masonrye; takyng wekely of the sayd Pryour and Chapetre and of here successours, for his mete, dryng, and for his labour, and for his othir necessarys duryng the tyme that he schall be ynne the servyce and offyce, iiij$^s$ of sterlyng every weke, and a convenyent hows for the sayd Richard to dwelle ynne, other yerly xx$^s$ for his said hows. Also for his fewell viij$^s$ yerly, and his clothyng yerly, or ellys x$^s$ of money for his clothyng, whan the said Priour yevyth no lyverey. And ij payre hosyng yerly; al so longe as he may stere hym self, see, and walke and have power and bodyly strengthe to have and do the sayd governaunce, ordynaunce, dyposicyon, rewle, and entendaunce in the foorme and manere afore sayd, to the profite of the said Pryor and

Chapetre and of here successourys. And yf the sayd Richard schall see or do any werk of the sayd Pryorys or of his successorys fro the Citee of Cauntyrbury be the space of xx myles or more, than schall he have for his costys resonable as his labour and his costys excedyth hys dayly werk and wages abovesayd. And yf the sayd Richard contynue in suche ocupacyon for the sayd chyrche as hit ys afore-sayd, wyth owte departyng fro his sayd servyce and offyce ayens the foorme of this endenture, and thenne yf hit happe, as God forfende, that the sayd Richard Beek falle in to ympotence of his body, that he schall nat mowe have powere to be stere hymself, but for to lye stylle in hys bedde, or be prived of his bodyly stryngth, and blynde, the whiche All mygythy God defende, than in suche caas, the sayd Pryor and Chapetere wollyng and grawntyng, for hem and for here successours, that the sayd Richard Beek schall have yerely xxˢ or ellys on hows to dwelle and abyde ynne, prys of xxˢ; viijˢ for his fewell; his clothyng yerly, or ellys xˢ for his clothyng; and ijˢ a weke fro hennys forward al so longe as he levyth, for his trewe and profytable labour, bysynesse, and entendaunce which he hath doon here afore and schall doo from hennys forward to the profyte, wele, and worschipe of the sayd Pryour and Chapetre of the same place. And whan hit schall happe at eny tyme the forsayd Richard Beek to be desyryd or prayd be eny worthy or worschipful person or freend of the same craft of masonrye, for to whiche causes he moste absente hym fro his occupacyonys and entendawnce above sayd be a tyme notable, as viij dayes or more, that thenne in suche caas, leve fyrst axed and had of the sayd Pryour and of his successours, the sayd Richard schall mowe absent hym be xv dayes, iij wekes, othir a monethe at the mooste, and be payd of his wagez and for his labour resonably be the partys whiche desyreth hym to suche occupacyon, as they may acoorde; and the sayd Pryour and his successours fully discharged of suche feys, wagez and reward as the foresayd Rychard schoolde receyve of hem for the same tyme of his absence, or ellys agree whyth the Pryour or wyth his successours how he schall be de-mened in suche caas afore his departyng, as for his wagez and for his labour. In to wytnesse whereof to the oon partye of this endenture remaynyng wyth the sayd Rychard the commune seel of the sayd Pryour and Chapetre is put to; and to that othir partye of this endenture remaynyng wyth the sayd Pryour the sayd Rychard hath put to his seel. Yeve at Cauntyrbury in the chapetre hows of the sayd Pryour and Chapetre the fyrste day of Januarie, the yere of the regne of kyng Harry the VIᵗ aftyr the conqueste the xiijᵗʰᵉ.

*Literae Cantuarienses* (Rolls Ser.), iii. 165.

9

*1436 Bury St. Edmunds:* engagement of a mason to rebuild the church
  tower

This bille indentyd maad att Bury the xxv day of Auguste, yn the ₃er of Kyng Herry the vj aftir the conquest the xiiij. between Willyam Abbot of seynt

Edmundys monasterye of Bury aforeseyd, P'our and Couent of the same place on the to partye, and John Wode, masoun, of Colchestr', on the todir partye, bereth wytnesse of certeyn couen'ntys maad betwix the seyd Abbot, P'our and Couent, and the seyd John Wode, that ys to seye, the seyd John Wode schal werke w$^t$ on servant up on the stepil in the seyd monasterye in all maner thynges that longe to fremasounrye fro the feste of seynt Michael next folwyng aftyr the date afore rehersyd yn to the terme of vij ʒeer aftir next folowing, takyng ʒeerly of the seyd Abbot, P'our and Couent, for hys stypend and hys seruauntes x$^{li}$ yn mony at iiij termys in the yeer, that ys to seye, Cristemasse, Esterne, Mydsomer, and Micheelmasse, be the handys of the mayster of the werk assynyd be the Chapetr'. And the seyd John Wode schal haue hys bord in the couentys halle for hym and hys man, for hym self as a gentilman and for hys seruaunt as a yoman; And therto too robys, on for hym self of gentilmannys liuere, and for hys seruaunt anothir of yomannys lyvere of the Sexteyn: And yf no lyuere be youe, he shal haue for the seyd robys xxiij$^s$ iiij$^d$. And for so myche that the seyd John shal haue hys robe, and mete and drynk in the P'ourys name, as on of hys gentilmen, therfore, suche tyme as he ys not ocupyed in hys werk, he shal be tendyng up on the P'our, and not goo out of towne passyng too dayes in a quarter, lesse than he haue a special leue of the P'our and of the mayster of the werk: And yf he or hys man be absent from hys werk passyng ij dayes in a quarter, than the mayster of the werk shal wyth drawe hys stipend aftyr the rate of the forseyd x$^{li}$, that ys to seye, for hys stipend euery day that he ys absent fro hys werk v$^d$. and for hys seruaunt iiij$^d$. And in caas be he or hys seruaunt falle seek, as longe as he ys fro hys werk he schal not take for hys stipend, but alowe the mayster of the werk for euery day as yt ys seyd afore: Neuertheles the seyd Abbot, Priour and Couent grauntyn that althow the seyd John or hys seruaunt be cause of infirmyte may not werke, ʒyt yf they will come to halle to ther mete, they shal haue yt ther frely, and in non othir place, so that the infirmyte be not continually up on them wherthorw they be lyke no more for to werke. In Wytnesse of all that ys seyd to fore, un to the too partye of thys bille indentyd, restyng in the handys of the sayd Abbot, Prio' and Couentys syde, the seyd John Wode hath sett to hys seel: Un to the todir partye of the same bille indentyd, restyng on the seyd John Wodys syde, in the name of the seyd Abbot, P'our and Couent, the Priour hath sette to hys seel. Youyn in the foreseyd monasterye, the yer and day afore rehersyd.

Add. MS. 14848, f. 308; printed in *Archaeologia*, xxiii. 330.

## 10

*1488 Durham:* appointment of a master mason

Thys indenture made bitwix the reverend fadre in God John the Prior of Duresme the cathedral churche of Duresme of that one parte, and John Bell mason of that othre parte, witnesseth, that the said John is reteynd and sworne to serve the said Prior and Chapitre and ther successours wele and trewly in hys science of masonry, during hys lyfe, from the fest of Penticost next commyng after the date of this indenture, in maner and forme folowyng: that is to say, that the said John shall be speciall mason to the said Priore and Chapitre and their successours, and all their works of masonry with ymagre, and other, newe and olde, shall be take on hande at their costes and expenses. And to the goode spede performyng and ending of the said werk shall geve hys due labour and diligens, to hys power, with hys counsell, help and bodyly labour, as far as pertneth to hys crafte; and aftir the witte and cunnyng geveyn to hym of almygty God, with-owte any fraude, decyte or male ingine, to be ministred and gevyn faithfully, as oft as he shall be requiryd therto, be the fore said Priore and Chapitour, or their successours, or ony in their name, except that he have lawfull excuse or impedi-ment. Also he shall concele the secretes and counsell of the said Priour and Chapitre and their successours, and their goodes and catalles and (*sic*) fer as in hym is wele and trewly kepe, nor them to ony person or persons shall delyver or len, withowte their speciall license; hurt he shall not do them, ne knowe to be done of ony other bot he shall therof make them have knawleg and to his power lette it to done; from hys occupacion in dew tyme he shall noght departe withowte their speciall licence; and one yong man their apprentice, to be hyrid for terme of x yeres in the mason crafte, one aftir one other, duryng hys life, well and trewly shall teche and informe, to hys cunnyng and power, without ony fraude concelement malyce or collusion.[1] Also he shall be obedient and buxom to the forsayd Priour and Chapitre and their successours in almaner of thyng lefull and honest: for the which service, wele and trewly to be done and per-formyd, in forme afore rehersyd, the said John shall receyve of the foresaid Prior and Chapitour and their successours, yerly, during all the terme of lyve that he may bodely performe all thes premisses for gret age or sekenes, x marcs at viij tymes of the yere; and every yere, at the fest of Saynt Martyn in wynter x$^s$ in money for hys marte; to be payd be the hands of the sacristane of Duresme for tyme beyng by even porcions; and yerly one garment of the said Priour and Chapitour and their successours competent to hys degre; and one house ferme free, to inhabyte in during hys lyfe, in the which house some tyme inhabit Thomas Barton mason while he levyd. Also it shall be lefull to the said John to have one prentice of his owne for terme of x yeres in the foresaid mason crafte, one after another, during hys lyve, to wirke and labour in the werke of masonry of the said Prior Chapitour and their successours, for the which prentice he shall recyve of the sacristane of Duresme for tym beyng, as is aforesaid, every yere

---

[1] For work on repairing the belfry, which extended over 55 weeks in 1483–4, 'Hugh Wall, the lord Prior's apprentice', received 10*s.*, and 'William Sawnderson, the apprentice of John Bell', £4. 4*s.* 7½*d.* As John Bell himself received 'for his fee' £6. 13*s.* 4*d.* (*Durham Acct. Rolls*, ii. 415), he was presumably already cathedral mason and our document is a confirmation of his appointment for life.

of the iij first yeres of hys prentecehede iiij marcs,[1] and every yere of the iij yeres next folowyng after that vj marcs and the x and last yere vij marcs, at viij tymez of the yere, by equall porcions. And when it shall happyn that the said John have continuall infirmites or gret age, so that he may not wirke ne labour, nor exercise hys crafte and cunnyng, he shall then be content with iiij marcs yerly; to be payd at viij tymes of the yere by even porcions by the handis of the sacristane of Duresme for tyme being. In witnesse herof the foresaid parties to thees indentures entrechangeably hath sett to their seales. Yeven at Duresme, the first day of Aprill, the yere of our Lord MCCCCLXXXVIII[to].

*Hist. Dunelm. Script. Tres* (Surtees Soc.), ccclxxiii.

[1] Presumably—'and every yere of the iij yeres next folowyng after that v marcs'—has been omitted by oversight.

# APPENDIX D

## BUILDING CONTRACTS BROUGHT TO THE AUTHOR'S NOTICE SINCE 1952

*(Not included in index)*

### I

*1341* [*?Brandsby*]

A rather sketchy contract by a carpenter to build the timber framing of a manor-house, with drawbridge over a [? dry] ditch, gatehouse and other buildings, of which, and of the timbers, dimensions are given: those of the roof (to carry stone tiles) to correspond with the roof timbers of Sir Thomas Ughtred's hall in York. The site is probably at Brandsby, adjoining Yearsley.
Printed, with translation, in *Cumb. and Westm. Arch. Soc. Trans.*, xxi. 200.

Cest endenture fait entre Mons. Thomas Ughtred dun part et John del Wod de Rypon dautre part tesmoigne qe le dite John ad empris a edificer le mote en le close le dit Mons. Thomas joust Yeveres le tout entour si pres le fosse tout com le dit Mons. Thomas le wolt edificer a son perille, ove un pount tretise et une chambre a defens de la long de trent pietz ove un garderobe; et tout le meryn sera de cheyn bon et convenable de porter pier. Des quex mesons une sera graunge de la long' de toute le mote, et les postes de la long' le xvj pietz estre les bases de pies, et les balkes de xx pietz, ove deux elynges acordanz, et un sale joust la chambre ove les postes de la long' de xvi piez e les balkes de xx piez; et les postes et les balkes des autres mesons de offices serront de mesme le long' si le dit Mons. Thomas le wolt, et les pannes et les postes au tizon[1] seront de leaese et espesse solonc le scanteloune fait entre les parties. Pour quel overayn lealement fair e perfourmer devant la feste de la purificacion de notre Dame procheyn avenir, le dit Mons. Thomas dorra au dit John oute marcz, dargent ove une robe de soue[2] ove toutz le garrnemetz; a paier en mayn quaraunt souz, et a la fest de Saynt Martyn xl soulz, et quant le overayn sera perfourmy deus marcs et la robe. En testemoignance des quex choses les avauntditz parties entrechaungeablement ount mis lour seales. Done a Brandesby le Mardy procheyn devant la fest del exaltation de la Saynt Croice lan de nostre seig' mcccxli.

[*endorsed*]: le scentelon de leesse et del espessour del meryn demort devers Hen. le Stedman et est merche de purlens[3] de la sale Mons. Thomas Vghtred en Everwyk.

---

[1] *tizon* should probably be *tiron* (= *tirant*, i.e. roof-collar).
[2] *soue*, which Mr. Ragg translates 'silk', should probably be *saie* (i.e. serge).
[3] *purlens* must here stand for the roof timber, generally.

2

*1383  Cockermouth Castle*

Contract with a mason to complete certain work already begun in the castle. Payment to be based on the square rod of walling, taking the rod at 7 statutory ells.
Original in P.R.O. Anct. Deeds D. 5627. Noted by H. M. Colvin and transcribed by John Harvey.

Hec indentura testatur quod ita conuenit inter nobilem virum dominum Henricum de Percy comitem Northumbrie ex parte vna et Rogerum de Barton cymentarium ex parte altera quod idem Rogerus faciet vnum parietem infra Castrum de Cokermouth inter coquinam et murum australem eiusdem Castri tante spissitudinis et altitudinis sicut est idem paries incoatus iuxta coquinam et turres vltra portam introitus erunt tante altitudinis sicut sunt muri coquine capiendo pro qualibet roda quadrata eiusdem parietis exterioris viginti duas marcas sterlingorum computando rodam ad septem vlnas usitatas  Et idem Rogerus faciet duos parietes laterales pro capella erigenda supra eandem portam introitus spissitudinis trium pedum et dimidii et parietes inferiores eiusdem spissitudinis sicut sunt incoati cum gradibus assensibilibus ianujs et fenestris necessariis capiendo pro qualibet roda tam Capelle quam parietis inferioris duodecim marcas sterlyngorum absque mensuracione ostiorum fenestrarum siue caminorum in toto dicto opere nisi tanquam pro integro pariete  Et idem Rogerus inueniet omnia necessaria videlicet lapides calcem sabulum et cariari faciet ad opus predictum suis sumptibus et expensis  Et idem dominus Comes exhibebitur eidem Rogero ferrum sufficiens fabricatum pro ostiis et fenestris et meremium sufficiens pro scarfaldis suis faciendis et octo cariagia bosci pro calce necessaria ad idem opus comburenda prouidebit eciam eidem Rogero de quarrera sufficienti cum libero exitu et reditu pro cariagio ad castrum predictum faciendo  Et idem Rogerus faciet opus predictum finiri infra biennium proxime sequens post datum confeccionis presencium sine vlticereo dilacione  Capiendo quolibet quarterio viginti libras sterlingorum in partem solucionis in quantum se extendit summa pro rodis superius limitata primo termino solucionis incipiet ad festum Michaelis proxime sequens secundo termino ad festum Natalis domini tercio termino ad festum Annunciationis beate Marie et quarto termino ad festum natiuitatis Sancti Johannis Baptiste proxime futurum et eedem summe sibi soluentur in eisdem festis pro anno secundo nisi numerus rodarum ad minus se extendat  Et ad istas conuenciones fideliter perficiendas partes predicte se obligant per presentes sigillis eorum alternatim munitis.  Datum apud Cokermouth die dominica proxime ante festum Natiuitatis beate Marie anno regni Regis Ricardi secundi post conquestum septimo.

[*Endorsed in a contemporary hand*]:

Indentura de opere cementar' infra Castrum de Cokermouth anno etc. vij°

## 3

*1383 London*

A carpenter undertakes to build 5 houses, each with a shop and two jettied floors above, for 58 marks. He gives a bond for 116 marks for due and punctual performance of the contract.

Photograph kindly supplied by Miss Alison Reeve, archivist to the London County Record Office, from Ac. 58.73.

Ceste endenture parentre Thomas Carlton citizein et brouderier de Loundres dune part et John Wolsey citizein et carperntere de mesme la cite dautre part tesmoigne que le dit John ad empris affaire pur le dit Thomas dedeinz sa mesoun propre en Adellane cink mansions ceste assauoir a chescune mansion une shoppe en bas ouesqes ij estages, lune de gette de ij pies et dymy et lautre amounte de ij pies, contignauntz toux en longure l pies de mesure et xij pies de laoure. Item xj pies que serrount deuaunt la aleye et serrount faitz ouesque une hus en mylieu et en chescune coste j petite chambre ouesqes les husses et fenetres et lune ouesqes une degrees pur montier en la sale que serra faite sur les ditz xj pies les queux serount couerez de ij estages de mesme la suite. Item le dit John ferra une bel hus pur la aleye ouesqes une porche desur, Et de perfounde et en hautesse des shoppes parentre les plates et les somers que porterount les gistes ix pies de mesure et en hautesse del primiere etage viij pies de mesure et del estage amount tanque as couples vij pies de mesure. Et serrount les principales pilers de x pouces plat et ix pouces espeisses; et les plates serrount de x pouces plat et vj pouces espeisses, et les somers de x pouces plat et ix pouces espeisses. Et serrount totes les merreynes sufficeaunt at sufficeablement conteignauntz. Et chascune giste del bas estage serra de vij pouces plat at vj pouces espeisses; et del haute estage serrount les gistes vj pouces plat et v pouces espeisses, et les braces et laces suauntz bien apoint. Et le dit John trouera a ses propres costages totes les merreynes plaunchebord estrichebord pur husses et fenestres et plauncheours pur priues et gistes er courtz pipes desout les degrees et seges bien et couenablement faites et totes les apurteignauncez pur entrecloses et pur degres et pues de fenestres. Item le dit John ferra derier les iij shoppes que serrount deuaunt la jardyn j parlour sur iiij pilers en bas et ouesqes ij petit chambres amount en manere dune tofalle de xxviij pies de longe et vij pies et dymy de perfound ouesqes toux les apurtenauncez a ycelles. Pur queles choses bien et couenablement perfourmer en qaunt qa carpentrie appont, horepris estalles er bynches, le dit John prendra del dit Thomas cinquant et eopt marcz en plein paiment de tote le dit oueraigne. Et serra le dit oueraigne prest'en totes degres et mys suis a teigler et argeiller le primiere dysmenge de Quarresime proscheine ensuaunt la date de cestes. A queles couenaunces bien et loialment perfourmer en totes choses auauntescript, le dit John Wolsey se oblige ses heires er ses executours et totes ses biens et chateux en cent et xvj marcs a paier al dit Thomas ses heires et ses assignez al jour de Pasche proschein ensuaunt la date de cestes. En tesmoignaunce de quele chose les parties auauntditz a ces endentures entrechangeablement ount mys lour seals. Dat' a Loundres le jour de Seint Michel lan du regne le Roy Richard secund septisme.

*Seal*: Sigillum: Johannis: Wolsey: *figure of a carpenter's square.*


# 4


*1472  Bristol*

Carpenter undertakes to build a new house in the High Street, with a shop, a hall above it, and chambers over the hall. He to have all the timber of the old house.

Photograph kindly supplied by Bristol City Archivist.

This endenture made betwene Alson Chestre of Brystowe wydowe sumtyme the wyf of Harry Chestre of Brystowe draper on the oon partie and Stephen Morgan of Brystowe carpenter on the other partie witnesseth that the seide Stephen hath covenaunted with the same Alice and hym byndeth by these presentes to make wele werkmanly and surely of good tymbre and bordys a newe hows in the high strete of Brystowe with flores wyndowes dorrys and partesons and all other thyngis of tymbre werk belongyng to the same hows excepte latthes and latyces; whiche seide newe hows shalbe sette betwene the ten[emen]t called The Bull on the oon partie and the ten[emen]t in whiche oon John A Cork corviser nowe dwelleth yn on the other partie, conteynying in length xix fote and v ynches of assise and in wydnes x fote and iiij ynches. And the seide Stephen shall make in the seid hows ə shop and a hall above the same with an oryell, a chambre above the hall with an oryell and another chambre above that, by the feste of Annunciation of oure Lady nexte commyng. For whiche hows soo to be made by the same Stephen the seide Alson graunteth and hir byndeth by this present to paye unto the seide Stephen vj li xiij s. iiij d. sterlinges; that ys to sey atte feste of the Natyvitee of our Lorde next commyng iij li.; atte florying of the seide hows xxxiij s. iiij d., and atte ende of the same werk xl s. Also hit ys accorded that hit shalbe lefull to the same Stephen to have and take as his owne all the oold tymbre of the seide oold hows without any geyneseying of the same Alson or any other for hir or in hir name. In witnes whereof the parties forseid to thise endentures entrechaungeably have sette theire seales. Yoven the xvij daye of the moneth of Novembre in the xij yere of the regne of Kynge Edward the fourthe.

## 5

*1474 Milton (Oxon.)*

Two detailed contracts for building the manor hall and chambers: A. with a mason, and B. with a carpenter.

Transcribed by Mr. John Harvey from Westminster Abbey Muniments 9217.

[A.] Md. that John Sewy of Reding in the County of Berks meyson the xj day of Decembre the xiiijth yer of Kyng E. the iiijth hath take to new make the stonewerke of the hall in the maner of Milton in the County of Oxeford with a chymney in the upper ende of the seyd hall of x fote brede with a mantell bearing and bordures of the hayrth of freyston, two bay wyndowys of frey-stone, ouer euerysyde one at the upper ende of the seyd hall ether of them viij fote wyde comyng round paynwyse withowt the wall with dubyll story cleyr leyghtes and in batellyd uppon the same of freystone. And fro the same wyn-dows thorow the hall the upper story wyndowyed with cleyr leyghtes of freystone ouer both sydes (the maynell vj fote hye—*interlined*); the walles of the seyd hall to be xvj (*altered to*—xviij) fote hye, with two new durrys at the porch of the seyd hall with the stone walles of the chambyrs in the south syde of the courte of the maner sufficiently to be made with two boterres to the seyd hall conuenient. And a squar butteres for a galery to be sett uppon them with all other stone werke to the seide hall or chamburs necessary. And the foreseyde John Sewy to haue for his werkemanship of the same xv marks and a gowne (and if he may not leue on his bargen to be rewardyd ouer the seide som xiij s. iiij d.—*struck out*); and he to hew his stone ate the quarrey and then to be carryed to the seyd maner at the lordes coste; and he to fynysshe the seyd werke in euery thyng by Witsontyde next comyng.

[B]. Md. that Ric. Walshe of Abyndon hath take to newe make sufficiently in euery thyng belongyng to carpenter werke the halle royfe of the maner of Mylton with iiij swepe coupyll arche wyse a beme at euery ende of the same, dowbell wall plate, dowbell syde reysyng, dowbell brases, accordyng to the same with hole raftours of vij ynches brede and x ynches bytwene with asshelers to the same conuenyant a batelment uppon the same abowte the halle with dores wyndowes speres skrenes conuenient to the same; with a newe royf to the chambur ouer the porche and a newe royf to the ij chambers on the sowthe syde of the seyde manor (accordyng to a royf of the lytell chamber within the grete chamber at the hall ende—*interlined*) with a lofte thorowe the same with gystes of vij ynche brede and viij ynches bytwene. And the same to be borded close a long after the gystes; and to amende the royf of the lytell chamber within the kechyn; with dores wyndowes sauyng of tymber and borde and at all other thynges belongyng to carpenter werke conuenient or necessary to the same; and he to haue for the werkemanship of the same xiiij marke and a gowne, to be payed as he werketh, and he to felle and hewe at his charge, and the tymber to be browght to the frame att the lordes charge.

Item the same Ric. shall newe make a galery fro the newe chambur ther with the boteres ouer the stabyll dore conuenient to serue the chambre there: and he to haue for his werkemanshypp x s.

# 6

*1476 Wolverhampton Collegiate Church*

Agreement between the representatives of the parish and a mason for rebuilding the upper part of the church tower in octagonal shape with an octagonal spire. Contingent modifications allowed for.

Transcribed by Mr. D. S. Roper from Sutherland Collection (Staffs. Rec. O.) D. 595.

Thys indenture made at Wolvernehampton. in the feest of Seynt Chadde in the xvth. yere of reynynge Kynge Edward the iiij th. Betwene the Gentilmen Wardens Yomen and Comyns of the town and paryssh of Wolvernehampton on that one parte and John Worseley mason on that oder parte bereth wytnes that the seyd John shall do take adown all the stone warke of the stepull in the Churche there vnto the lower parte of the wyndowes in the seyd stepull and thervppon through the helpe of Almyghty God to sette a Towre of viij square to the highnes of xl fete wth. the boterasses batellynge and fenyals therto belongynge and (? all—*quite illegible*) oder warke acordynge to a pateron lefte wth. the seyd Gentilmen and Wardens and also acordynge in parte to the towre of (*blank—not completed*) and theruppon a spyre of viij square to the highenes of vj score fote, wthjnne the space of iiij yeres nexst folowynge after the date above wreten And the forseyd John to fynde all maner of gabuls and oder cordes of hempe to the seyd warke and all oder toles to hys warke necessary And the seyd Gentilmen yomen and comyns to geve vnto the seyd John to performe and fenyssh the warke as hyt ys above rehersed Cx li. And yf hyt kan be thoughte that the forseyd olde warke necessary to be taken down lower then the neder parte of the forseyd wyndowes in the stepull by the avice of the seyd Gentilmen Wardens and Mason to have a sure fundacion to begynne the warke of the forseyd Towre that the(y) the forseyd Gentilmen Wardens Yomen and comyns to rewarde the forseyd John Worseley for hys labur acordynge to ryght and conciense And yf hyt kan be thoughte by the avice of the seyd gentilmen Wardens and yomen that the forseyd Towre nedeth not to compre-hende the highnes of xl fete as hyt ys above rehersed that then the seyd John Worseley to abate of hys wages acordynge to the rate after the fotes of the seyd Towre. And the forseyd gentilmen Wardens Yomen and comyns shall let brynge in to the Churche yerde there all stone necessary to the forseyd warke and also they shull fynde all yron and lede necessary to the sewre (*sure*) sub-stancialnes of the forseyd warke.

## 7

*1500 Cranbrook*

Exchange of land by which one party agrees to build, in part payment a new house, as detailed, with a smaller thatched house.

Transcribed by Mr. Felix Hull, County Archivist, from Kent, Ch. 9/4.

This endentur berth witnesse that Thomas a Crouch of Cranebroke hath bargeyned & sold & by this presents bargeyneth & sellith unto Gyles Andrews of the same Cranebroke a mesuage a garden & iij peces of londs with pertinences beynge in the seid parissch of Cranebroke & upon the denne of Netherwilfysley. & conteyneth by estimacion vj acres mor or lesse be it hadd as marks & bounds schewyth. Wherfor the seid Thomas a Crouch. schall have of the seid Gyles Andrews. a pece of lond with pertinences called Goldham, lyenge in the seid parissch & denne & conteyneth seven acres of land mor or lesse be it hadd. To have in party of payment for the seid mesuage garden & iij peces of lond with pertinences. Also the seid Gyles or his assign' schall byld upon the seid pece of lond called Goldham. a newe house. which house to be in length. xliiij foot from out [t]o out. & in brede. xviij foot. & in height betwene the joynts. xij foot. & all the seid house to be lofted over. with. iij. particions beneth. & iij. above. Also in the hall for to be wyndows. as is sufficyent & convenyent. & so like wyse of wyndows all the house. with benchys doors locks & other pertinences. also all the seid house to be tyled of Nokholle tyle. & a chymney with. ij fyrs. Also to be a oven in the kechyn. with a rer doyse in the same kechyn. All this seid house to be made & sett upp. with all manner garnesschyngs to the same perteyninge to be made & doon at the charge & cost of the seid Gyles Andrewe. his heirs or assign. & that house to be redy satt up & all garnessched by myghelmesse next comynge after this present date. Also therto be a nother house. & that to be in lenght. xviij foot. & xv foot wyde. with a particion & gysted over with doors & wyndows as belongyth for such an house. & that house to be thacched at the charge of the seid Gyles. & that house to be redy sett up by Cristemesse next after that. all at the charge & cost of the seid Gyles. Also the seid Gyles or his assign schall pale all the stret syde with dobyll rayellys. & that pale to be in height. v. foot & half. In witnesse of all this premysses the parties aboveseid eyther to other ther sealys have sette the. ix day of marche. the xv. yer of the reigne of Kyng Henry the vij[th].

## 8

*1530 Croxton Abbey*

A mason agrees to take down the vaulting lately made (? by him) in the abbey brew-house and build a new vault, subject to the approval of expert workmen.

From Belvoir Castle muniments no. 1 (Croxton formulary), f. 82ᵛ.

Thys indenture mayd the xxiiijᵗⁱ day of February the xxᵗⁱ yer of the Reign of our Souerayn Lorde Kyng Henry the viijᵗʰ betwyxt ye Reuerend father in God Elys th'abbot of Croxton in the Countie of Leicester on the one partye & Thomas Yvenson of Sowstorne fremason in the same Countie of Leicester of the other partie Wytnesseth that it is agreyd couenantyd & barganyd betwyxt the sayd parties that ye seyd Thomas Yvenson shall take dowyn all the vowlte of late mayd in the bruows¹ within the sayd abbey of Croxton of hys coste & charge. and allso the said Thomas promyetes by thies presents to make there of newe a vowlte of frestone with other rogh work longing therto of hys cost and charge substancyally to be done by the seght of workmen of hys occupacion betwyxt this and Whitsonday next commyng after the date herofe. and to make two substancyall pyllors after the sampyll of ye greyte buttre in the common hall with two butments at ether end. And allso it is agreid that yf ther lak any frestone to the said vowte. then ye said Thomas to fynd all suche frestone longynge therto of hys cost & charge. and the said Elys graunts to fynd the said work all centrynge and shaffalyng to the sayd worke belongyng bothe in takyng downe & up-settinge & to be wroght of his cost and charg and also it ys agreyd & couenantyd betwyxt the said parties that ye said abbot shall [fynd] to the sayd workmen to the sayd worke lyme & sand & roughestone & cary it yf any lak to ye said work and allso to cary frestone yf any wante and allso the said Elys to fynde theire mete & drynke & bedding during the said worke and allso the said Elys to gyfe hym for the said worke vjˡ. xiijˢ. iiijᵈ. for his labour. In witness herof the parties aforesaid here sette there seales the day & yere above sayd.

¹ i.e. brew house.

# INDEX OF PERSONS AND PLACES

*(Entries for Appendix D are not included in the Index.)*

*[The letters (m) and (c) after a name indicate respectively 'mason' and 'carpenter'.]*